Gun Digest 2013

Edited by
JERRY LEE

Published by

Gun Digest® Books, an imprint of F+W Media, Inc.
Krause Publications · 700 East State Street · Iola, WI 54990-0001
715-445-2214 · 888-457-2873
www.krausebooks.com

To order books or other products call toll-free 1-800-258-0929
or visit us online at **www.gundigeststore.com**

CAUTION: Technical data presented here, particularly technical data on handloading and on firearms adjustment and alteration, inevitably reflects individual experience with particular equipment and components under specific circumstances the reader cannot duplicate exactly. Such data presentations therefore should be used for guidance only and with caution. Gun Digest Books accepts no responsibility for results obtained using these data.

ISSN 0072-9043

ISBN 13: 978-1-4402-2926-8
ISBN 10: 1-4402-2926-0

Designed by Tom Nelsen
Cover design by Al West

Edited by Jerry Lee & Jennifer L.S. Pearsall

Printed in the United States of America

John T. Amber LITERARY AWARD

We are very pleased to announce that the recipient of the 31st annual John T. Amber Literary Award is Tom Turpin. A long-time contributor to *Gun Digest*, Tom is being recognized for two reasons: first, for his story in the 66th edition, "Fit For A Lady." This story profiled Osa Johnson and a custom Mauser that was made for her more than 80 years ago. Osa and her husband, Martin, were adventurers who traveled the world filming documentaries of their journeys to Africa, Malaysia, and the South Sea islands from 1917 until the mid 1930s.

Tom is also being honored for his many years of devotion to the custom gun trade and his annual report in these pages—always well illustrated with excellent photography—of the finest examples of the gunmaker's art. He was a protégé of the great John Amber himself, editor of *Gun Digest* from 1950 to 1979, and for whom our Literary Award is named. Amber played a major role in promoting the art of the custom gun within these pages as the trade began to grow in the 1950s. We asked Tom to give us his thoughts on John Amber.

"I distinctly remember when I first met John T. Amber. It was in April, 1978, at Alexandria Palace in London, England. I had known who Amber was since the early 1950s, when I first discovered *Gun Digest*. I corresponded with him in the late 1970s about writing an occasional piece for him, which led to our meeting. John and his entourage consisted of a good bit of firearms history. I met John, William B. Ruger, Don and Norma Allen, Al Lind and his wife, and Jim Wilkinson of Rifle Ranch fame, all at the same time. I was truly a kid in the candy store that day.

For some reason, JTA took a liking to me, and took me under his wing, nurturing my budding outdoor writing career along nicely. In addition to publishing some of my early work in *Gun Digest*, he also introduced me around the industry, advising me about who I needed to know, and perhaps more importantly, those I needed to avoid like the plague. His help was invaluable. Over time, he became almost a surrogate father to me."

For this reason particularly, among many others, I am so deeply honored to receive this award carrying his name. I am also honored every year to provide, under my byline, John's favorite part of *Gun Digest*, the custom gun and engraving section."

Tom Turpin was born and raised in Kentucky. After graduating from what is now Eastern Kentucky University in 1959, thanks to the ROTC program, he was commissioned a 2nd Lt. in the United States Army. He entered active duty in the spring of 1960. Early in his army career, he shot competitively on several rifle teams, ending up shooting in the 3rd Army matches at Fort Benning, GA.

Tom's nationally published writing career began in 1972 when Petersen's *Guns & Ammo* published his first article. At the time, he was living in Alaska, during a tour of duty with the US Army. Not long after that, he had a few articles published in *Gun Digest* and *Guns Magazine*. During the seventies and eighties, Tom was very busy balancing a military career, including a couple of tours in Vietnam, an outdoor writing career, and raising a family. He also served as a design consultant to the German firearms manufacturer, F.W. Heym and, from time to time, assisted the German optics company, Schmidt & Bender. Tom's military career ended in retirement as a Lieutenant Colonel after 26 years active duty, at the beginning of 1986.

These days, after more than 40 years in the writing business, several hundred published articles, three books and substantial contributions to several more, he is still at the keyboard. In addition to being a contributing editor to *Gun Digest*, he is a freelance contributor to many other publications in the field. His book, *Artistry in Wood & Metal*, originally published by Safari Club International, was reprinted by Krause Publications in early 2012, and is now on the market.

An avid hunter, he has hunted on four continents. A great fan of the late Jack O'Connor, Tom has found the sage advice contained in O'Connor's writings to be very accurate. As such, his favorite hunting caliber for most situations is the .270 Winchester. Tom and his wife Pauline live and work in the wonderful high desert community of Sierra Vista, Arizona, along with their two Labradors, three German Shorthairs, and 22 Japanese Koi fish. The elk steaks still taste wonderful, the scotch still provides a tranquilizing effect adding to the pleasure of life, and at the ripe old age of 73, Tom is looking forward to his next hunt, and his next story.

WELCOME to the 2013 Edition of *Gun Digest*!

Welcome to the 67th edition of *Gun Digest*. It is a tremendous honor to find myself as the editor of the World's Greatest Gun Book. Like many of you, I feel that *Gun Digest* and I grew up together. When I first developed an interest in guns and hunting around the middle of the last century, *Gun Digest* was one of the few reliable sources to go to for information. There were the writings of Jack O'Connor, Warren Page and Pete Brown in *Outdoor Life*, *Field & Stream*, and *Sports Afield*, respectively, and occasional gun articles in adventure magazines like *True* and *Argosy*. NRA members had *American Rifleman*, and there was Stoeger's *Shooter's Bible*, which was a catalog with no articles or stories.

And there was *Gun Digest*. That was it. No purely "gun magazines" existed until 1955 when George von Rosen started *Guns* and three years later when Bob Petersen launched *Guns & Ammo*. I consider myself fortunate to have worked for both men.

As in all segments of the publishing world, the "shooting press" is highly competitive — some survive and many others do not. One of the icons, *Gun Digest*, is a survivor that has been here year after year. Now into its eighth decade, the publication started during the war years with the first edition coming out in 1944. Many legendary outdoor writers have written for the book and virtually every significant rifle, handgun and shotgun has been profiled within its pages. For many years, the subtitle has been "The World's Greatest Gun Book," and indeed it is. I pledge to do everything within my power to keep it that way.

The 67th Edition

I'm very proud of the content of this edition. Regular readers will see many familiar names along with a few bylines that have not appeared in the book for a while. The popular Reports From the Field section continues with contributor editors who have covered their categories for many years. The only exception is John Malloy who chose to give up the semi-auto pistol report. As he edges into his "golden years," he wants to devote more time to worthwhile projects like teaching shooting skills to Boy Scouts, for which we salute him. John will continue to contribute articles, like his story on "The Last Krag" in this edition. The semi-auto pistol section has been assigned to Gary Paul Johnston, a familiar byline in many books and magazines, and an expert in handguns for law enforcement, competition and personal defense.

I'm especially proud to have a story in this edition on the guns of Robert E. Petersen. Petersen was the founder of a very successful magazine publishing empire that included titles like *Guns & Ammo*, *Petersen's Hunting*, *Motor Trend*, *Hot Rod* and many others. Pete, as he was known to his friends, was an avid hunter and gun enthusiast, and over the years put together one of the finest gun collections in the world. Following his passing in 2007, his widow Margie followed his wishes and donated about 400 items from his collection to the NRA's National Firearms Museum. The Robert E. Petersen Gallery opened in 2011 and has been called the world's best gun room. It is now a permanent exhibit at the museum, which is located at the NRA's headquarters in Fairfax, Virginia. No visit to the Washington, D.C., area is complete without spending a day at the National Firearms Museum. We are pleased to have Senior Curator Phil Schreier take us on a tour of this fabulous firearms collection. Phil's byline and face is familiar to many readers. He is a frequent contributor to NRA publications like *American Rifleman* and is co-host of the television program, *NRA's Guns & Gold*.

Must "mouse gun" be a pejorative term? Or, to filch a phrase, "Is a .25 in your pocket better than a .45 left at home?" Paul Scarlata provides an in-depth comparison of an even dozen small-caliber handguns including drills on the range to test accuracy and reliability. There are many myths associated with shooting and Tom Tabor calls our attention to 10 of them. It's great to have John Taffin's take on Bill Ruger's single actions in this edition, and if you like single actions, you'll like Rick Hacker's "Guns of the Westerns." He gives us an entertaining look at Hollywood guns and tells which ones were practical and those that were not.

How many times have you read a "gun test" and wondered what really was significant information and how it related to whether or not you should by the gun? Jon Sundra is a veteran of hundreds of gun tests, most of them on rifles, and shares his take on the subject in these pages. Wayne van Zwoll takes us behind the scenes at Weatherby, Nick Hahn remembers the great Browning Auto-Five (the original, not the new one) and Massad Ayoob profiles an old favorite, the Broomhandle Mauser.

Few of today's outdoor writers know more about English and European shotguns than Terry Wieland and he provides a detailed look at the history and development of the English double. And guess what was the caliber of Jack O'Connor's last rifle? You're probably wrong. See Tom Turpin's story.

State of the Industry

The SHOT Show (Shooting, Hunting and Outdoor Trade) in February of 2012 set a new attendance record of more than 61,000 people, including industry exhibitors and employees, buyers for wholesalers and distributors, and gun dealers. This was seen as an indication of how well the industry is doing, in spite of the continuing condition of the overall economy. Another positive statistic is that nearly 16.5 million background checks for gun buyers were conducted in 2011. That is about 2 million more than 2010 and is a new record. At this writing, the trend is continuing into 2012. It's an election year, of course, which brings uncertainty about future gun legislation, at both the federal and local level. Most industry observers are predicting that fears about candidates who are not friendly to gun owners will continue to drive increases in sales.

Hot items continue to be concealable handguns, guns for home defense, and tactical rifles, particularly AR-types. Among the product introductions since the last edition we feel are worthy of mention are Ruger's first 1911, and the same company's very moderately priced bolt-action American Rifle. Browning has a new Citori over/under, the Model 725 with a totally new and shallow frame, and there is a new A-5 semi-auto shotgun, which is not anything like the original except for the squared receiver hump-back. Colt has resurrected the Mustang Pocketlite .380, which has improvements over the earlier model, including a thumb safety that can be kept on while retracting the slide. Kimber also has a new .380 that looks somewhat like the Mustang.

Para USA has introduced the Stealth, a compact 1911 DAO .45. Shortly after the SHOT Show it was announced that Para had been purchased by the Freedom Group, parent company of Remington, Bushmaster, DPMS, Marlin, H&R and other industry companies.

Absent from the SHOT Show but shown off at IWA, Europe's big firearms trade show, is what can best be described as a double-barreled, twin-slide 1911 in .45 ACP. What's it for? That is yet to be answered and we mention it only as an oddity because unless U.S. gun laws are changed (highly unlikely), it will never be imported here. That's because both barrels will fire with one pull of the trigger, making it fit the definition of a machine gun. The AF 2011-A1 from Arsenal Firearms — an Italian company with a Russian partner — will no doubt be seen on one or more gun magazine covers, and I would wager it will soon star in a motion picture or TV program. But don't look for it at your local gun shop.

Meet The Editor

I was born and raised on a farm in Texas, and have been interested in guns and hunting as long as I can remember. Some of my earliest memories are of me tagging along with Dad as he hunted doves with his single-shot 20-gauge. My job was to pick up the dead birds and put them in a paper bag or, as we called it in Texas, a paper sack.

I learned to shoot with that Eastern Arms 20-gauge and Dad's Remington 521T bolt-action .22. Soon I got my own .22 (a Winchester Model 67) and did my best to eradicate the jack rabbit population in central Texas, especially from our oat and wheat fields. With those three guns I made frequent contributions to the table with doves, squirrels and quail. I got my first deer with a borrowed .30-30 when I was 16. In the ensuing years I have hunted deer, antelope, upland game and waterfowl in several states but to this day my favorite hunting memories are from those days on our farm.

When I was still in my teens I began my first career, which was in radio broadcasting. From my college years into my 40s, I played the hits, wrote and read the news, interviewed celebrities, and held just about every job there is at a radio station, including general manager. Eventually I grew tired of the rat race and decided to switch to another media. I accepted an offer from the afore-mentioned George von Rosen to be advertising manager for his *American Handgunner* magazine and later was appointed editor of *Guns*, another von Rosen title. A few years later I was hired by Petersen Publishing in Los Angeles where for 16 years I was the editor of various gun titles with the Petersen group and its subsequent owners. These included *Petersen's Handguns*, *Rifle Shooter*, *Wing & Shot* and many *Guns & Ammo* special issues and annuals. I retired from InterMedia, current owner of the former Petersen magazines, in 2009 and now live among the beautiful rolling hills of north central West Virginia.

Meet Ms. Pearsall

Jennifer L.S. Pearsall deserves a lot of the credit for this 67th Edition. She is book editor for several titles in the *Gun Digest* Books Firearms and Knives Group, and has worked in the hunting and firearms industry for more than 20 years. Her career began, one might say, on the front lines of the business with a lengthy stint in firearms retail sales, before being recruited by the NRA where she worked with several of its publications, including *InSights*, *Shooting Sports USA*, and *American Hunter*. Since her time there, Ms. Pearsall has had her essays and photography published in dozens of journals, including *Gun Dog*, *Gun Tests*, *Waterfowl*, and *Petersen's Hunting*, among many others. She has hunted her share of big game, upland birds, and waterfowl in more than a few of the Lower 48, as well as Canada and Mexico, though she confesses her favorite quarries are Wyoming antelope and whatever winged things her bird dogs have fetched up or have in front of their noses. Ms. Pearsall resides in Wisconsin with her retired English pointer, Highway. Her input, editing skills, long hours and positive attitude are greatly appreciated.

Dedication

As reported in last year's edition, the previous editor of Gun Digest, Dan Shideler, passed away in April of 2011. He was at the helm of this book for three editions — numbers 64, 65 and 66 — and made a significant contribution to the continuing success of the world's best-selling firearms book. We dedicate this 67th Edition to his memory.

Sincerely, Jerry Lee

About the covers

FRONT COVER:

There are a mind-numbing array of AR platforms out there, and the demand for these guns and their accessories is nearly insatiable, especially with the advent of cartridges like the .300 AAC Blackout and .300 Whisper. Also of note is a move away from the all-black configurations of yesteryear, as hobbyists and competitors alike are expressing themselves in colors ranging from flat dark earth to snow white and hot pink.

BACK COVER:

On our back cover is one of the over-the-top elegant over/unders from Italian maker Caesar Guerini, shown here in the Magnus Grouse LTD variation, and up top is the Solo CDP (Custom Defense Pacakage) from Kimber, one of the hottest entries in today's concaled carry semi-auto pistol market.

Gun Digest Staff

EDITORS
Jerry Lee
Jennifer L.S. Pearsall

CONTRIBUTING EDITORS
Holt Bodinson: Ammunition, Ballistics & Components; Web Directory
Wm. Hovey Smith: Black Powder
John Haviland: Shotguns
Kevin Muramatsu: Tactical Shotguns
Gary Paul Johnston: Handguns/Autoloaders
Tom Tabor: Rifles
Jeff Quinn: Handguns/Revolvers
Tom Turpin: Custom and Engraved Guns
Wayne van Zwoll: Optics
Larry Sterett: Reloading

FEATURES

REPORTS FROM THE FIELD

ONE GOOD GUN

TESTFIRES

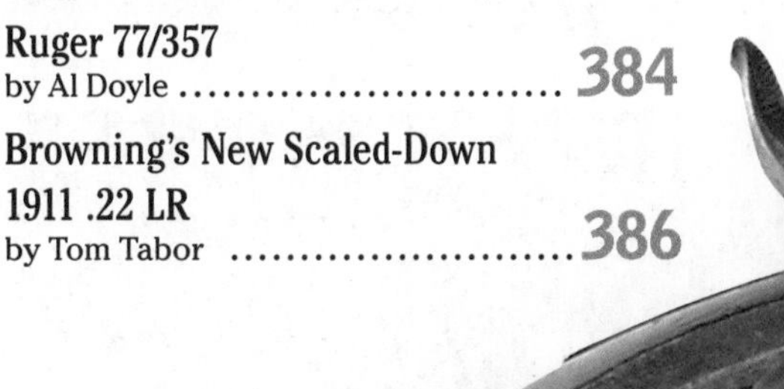

Gun Digest 2013

TABLE OF CONTENTS

BALLISTICS TABLES

HANDGUNS

RIFLES

SHOTGUNS

BLACKPOWDER

AIRGUNS

REFERENCES

Gun Digest Store

Robert E. Petersen's Gift To The

The PETERSEN

A view of Bob Petersen's gun room. Cased sets were located in the drawers below the main display counter.

NRA Museum Sets A New Record COLLECTION

BY **PHILIP SCHREIER**
Senior Curator,
NRA's National Firearms Museum

In 1998, Robert Petersen appeared in a series of NRA membership ads. This second generation of "I'm the NRA" ads were hugely successful.

The NRA's National Firearms Museum, established in 1935, proudly boasts a collection of nearly 6,000 firearms and twice that number of accoutrements and related items. The overwhelming majority of the museum's holdings have come from the more than generous contributions of members, friends, and industry. Recently, a gift from the estate of Robert E. Petersen, of Los Angeles, set a record in philanthropy to the National Rifle Association, with a nearly $20 million gift, the largest in the 140-year history of the NRA.

Through the generosity of Mr. Petersen's widow, Margie Petersen, 425 firearms from his lifelong collection of historic, rare, and extraordinary sporting arms were given to the National Firearms Museum, with the only requirement being that anything gifted

Above: The Gatling Gun exhibit in the Robert E. Petersen Gallery represents the largest collection of Gatling guns on public view in the world.

to the museum must be displayed. The museum staff proudly opened its newest exhibit, The Robert E. Petersen Gallery, to the general public on October 8, 2010. The opening marked the culmination of Petersen's dream of sharing his extraordinary collection of firearms with the world. The collection is on permanent display at the museum, where it will be preserved for the education and enjoyment of future generations.

Husband, father, veteran, publisher, restaurateur, outdoorsman, automobile enthusiast, philanthropist, and friend are all words that partially describe Robert E. Petersen. Born in 1926, in Barstow, California, he proudly served in the U.S. Army Air Corps during World War II. Following his service in the war, he started a hobbyist magazine for car racing enthusiasts entitled Hot Rod. From that initial venture he built the Petersen Publishing empire that included 39 monthly periodicals by the time he sold the company, in 1996. Petersen published a number of iconic American magazines including *Hot Rod, Guns & Ammo, Sports Afield, Petersen's Hunting*, and *Motor Trend*, just to name a few. He hunted on nearly every continent and was credited with being the first person to ever take a polar

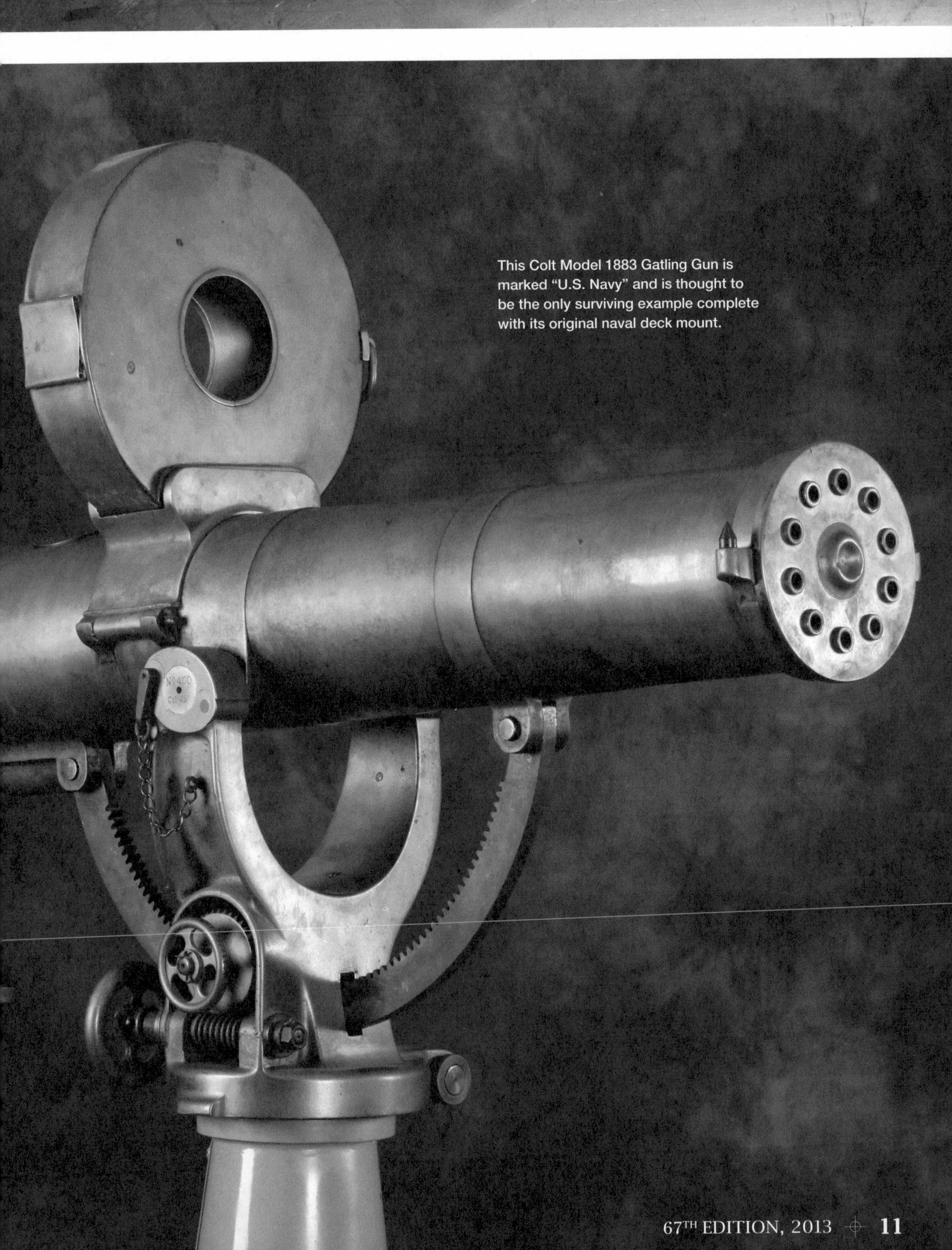

This Colt Model 1883 Gatling Gun is marked "U.S. Navy" and is thought to be the only surviving example complete with its original naval deck mount.

bear with a .44 Magnum handgun. (Both the revolver and the bear are on exhibit in the museum.) He also served as Commissioner of Shooting Sports for the XXIII Olympiad, held in 1984, in Los Angeles.

Pete, as he was called by his friends and his wife, Margie (1936- 2011), first established a relationship with the NRA's National Firearms Museum in the early 1990s, when they loaned a substantial part of his antique Colt's collection for display. Since that time, the museum has always been fortunate to exhibit priceless treasures from Pete's personal collection.

It was through Margie's vision and generosity that the museum's 2,000 square-foot Petersen Gallery was made possible. While every firearm selected for exhibit is exceptional in its own way, notable highlights include:

• Largest collection of fine double rifles on display to the public.

• Exceptional collection of high-end double barrel shotguns.

• Largest Gatling gun collection on public display (10 Gatlings).

• Guns owned and used by noted individuals such as Annie Oakley, John Olin, Robert Stack, Julian Hatcher, John F. Kennedy, Hermann Goering, and Elmer Keith.

This Colt Detective Special "Vampire Hunter" revolver was engraved by Leonard Francolini at the Colt factory. Sterling sliver bullets with carved vampire heads complete the ensemble.

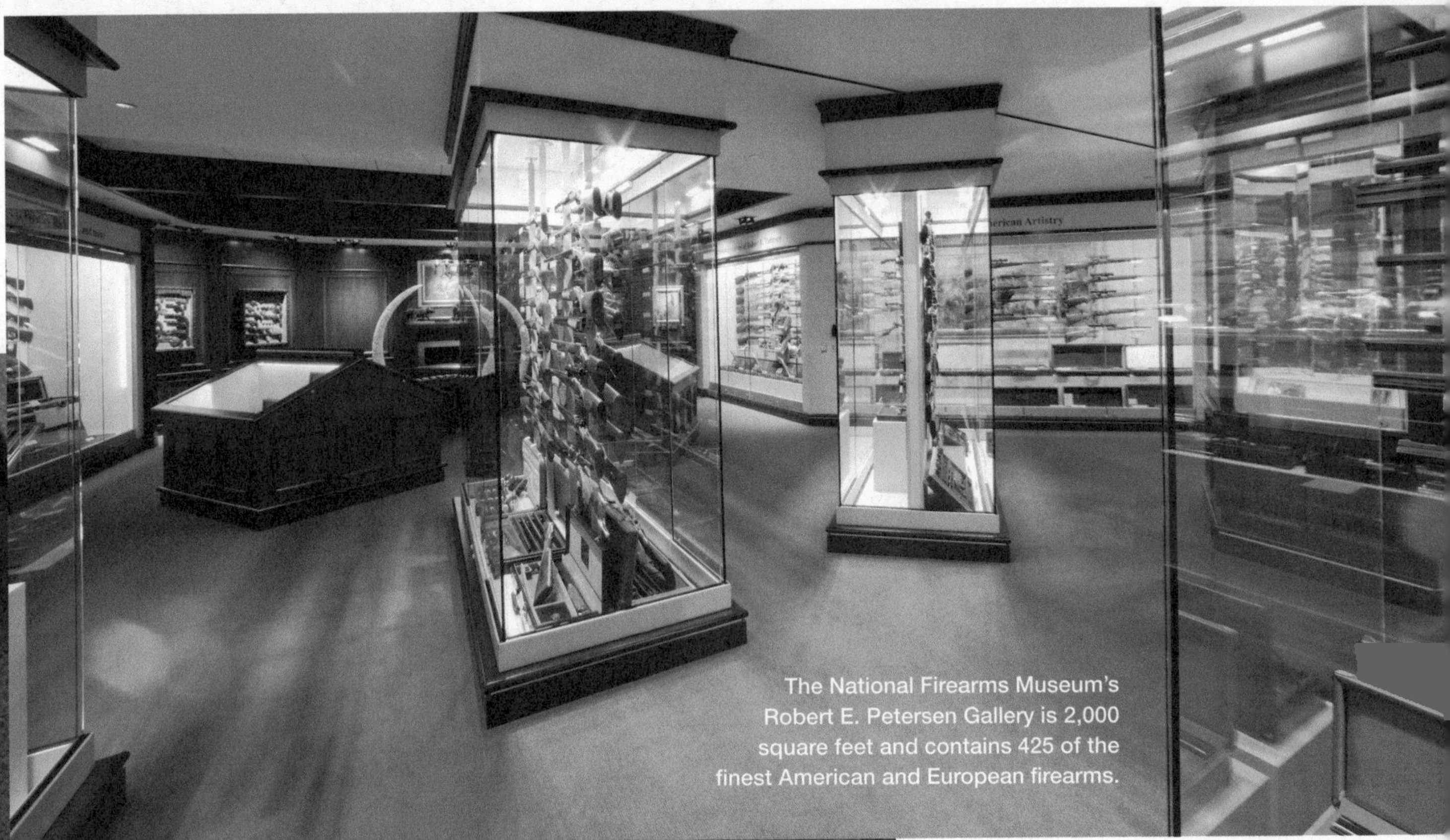

The National Firearms Museum's Robert E. Petersen Gallery is 2,000 square feet and contains 425 of the finest American and European firearms.

While the collection is broad and varied, if there is a pervasive theme, it is that of the finest sporting arms in the world, including those by gun makers such as Beretta, Boss, Holland & Holland, Purdey, Fabbri, Galazan, Westley Richards, Parker, Browning, and Rizzini. Of special inclusion in the Petersen gift are the world-renowned Parker Invincibles—considered by many to be the finest and most valuable set of American-made guns in existence—a "baby" Paterson revolver, and the Grover Cleveland 8-gauge Colt's double-barrel shotgun. The Parkers and the Colt 8-gauge have been on loan to the museum since 2001.

Ken Elliott, a personal friend of the Petersens for over 45 years and an employee for 35 of those years, was Vice President and Executive Publisher of Petersen Publishing's Outdoor Division at the time the company was sold in 1996. After attending the gala opening of the museum gallery, he remarked that, "The Petersen Gallery is indicative of the man. It is what he was all about, from showing the guns he loved to shoot to the finest guns ever created. The gallery is about the man and his passions."

Garry James, another personal family friend and former employee of Petersens, and who now works as the Senior

"The Empire Gun" by Holland & Holland is a 28-gauge Holland Royal, featuring gold inlay by Allan M. Brown. It is thought to be the most exquisite Holland & Holland in the Petersen collection.

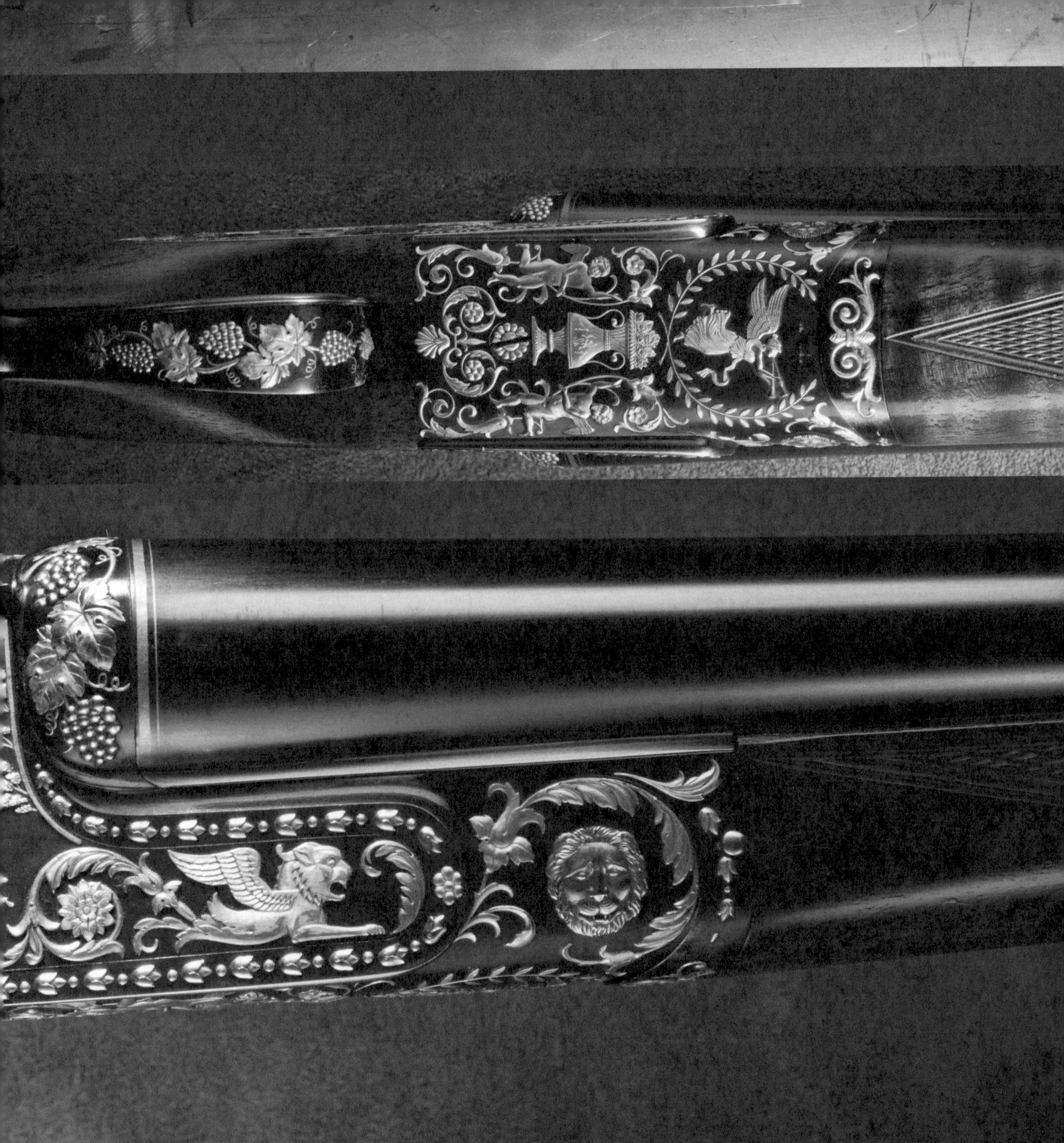

Robert E. Petersen and Margie Petersen, pictured here as hosts of an NRA-sponsored event, were staunch supporters of NRA programs that encouraged the shooting sports.

Below: The Colt New Frontier was named after JFK's 1961 Presidential Inaugural address. This is one of two Colt New Frontiers that were made as presentation pieces to the thirty-fifth President.

The Nock Volley Gun is a .46-caliber seven-barreled English sea service arm used during the age of Admiral Nelson. This original behemoth was used by Richard Widmark in his role as Jim Bowie in the 1960 John Wayne film *The Alamo*.

Editor of *Guns & Ammo* magazine, was a close confidant to Bob Petersen and someone the publisher relied upon for advice and knowledge, when it came to selecting an antique firearm for potential acquisition. Garry recalled recently, "It was a sincere privilege to work for Mr. Petersen and to be able to help him build his extraordinary collection. From 1971 until his unfortunate and untimely passing in 2007, it was always interesting and a great deal of fun to play a role in assembling what, by many accounts, is certainly one of the most historically significant and remarkable private firearms collections ever assembled." He added, "The Petersen Gallery at the National Firearms Museum is a fitting tribute and executed in a manner that would have made both Bob and Margie feel that their legacy is in caring and appreciative hands."

The Robert E. Petersen Gallery replaces the museum's former introduction and orientation space, with a dazzling array of 15 display cases that highlight more than 400 rifles, pistols, and shotguns, as well as his collection of Gatling guns, the famous Colt's display boards from 1918, and the spectacular Harrington & Richardson 1876 Centennial display board. This gallery is now a permanent fixture of the museum and is open to the public daily from 9:30 a.m. to 5 p.m. The National Firearms Museum is located at 11250 Waples Mill Road in Fairfax, Virginia. There is no admission fee. For more information, visit www.NRAmuseum.com.

GUNS OF THE WESTERNS

Just How Practical Were They?

BY RICK HACKER

Although many Model 94s were outfitted with Model 92 .44-40 barrels to take studio blanks for use in TV westerns, the author feels the unaltered saddle carbine makes a superb close-range hunting gun.

Like many of my generation, I was weaned on TV westerns. During the 1950s and '60s, there were shootouts between sheriffs, gunslingers, and outlaws in our living room practically every night of the week, thanks to shows such as *Maverick*, *Tombstone Territory*, and *Cheyenne*. Starting with the *The Lone Ranger* and *Hopalong Cassidy* in 1949 and galloping through the decades to long-running hits like *Bonanza*, which ended in 1973, and *Gunsmoke*, which lasted until 1975 (the longest-running television series in history), the western genre reigned supreme. In fact, the top three shows from 1958 through 1961 were westerns—*Gunsmoke*, *Wagon Train*, and *Have Gun, Will Travel*. However, in many cases, it was not so much the actors we were watching, nor the plot lines we were following, but rather the guns our tall-in-the-saddle heroes were using.

For example, from 1957 until 1963, who could not fail to be transfixed by the opening scene in every episode of *Have Gun, Will Travel*, when Richard Boone, as the character Paladin (no first names, please), smoothly drew and cocked his 7½-inch barreled Colt Single

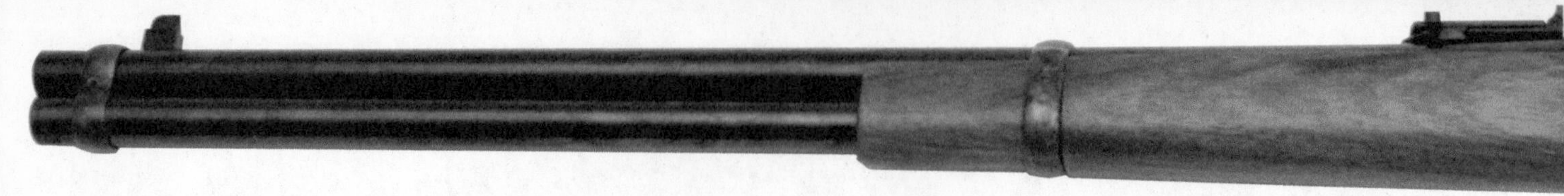

Action Army with its painted black grips (and you thought they were walnut), and aimed it directly at our TV dinners while delivering his soliloquy for that night's adventure. Likewise, the beginning of *Gunsmoke* was a calling out for us to take a stance in front of our television sets, cap guns strapped low on our hips, anxiously waiting for the showdown between Dodge City's Marshal Matt Dillon and the "bad guy" at the end of the street (who happened to be Arvo Ojala, gun coach for *Gunsmoke's* James Arness and fast-draw tutor to countless other Hollywood actors).

Arness was fast, all right (although we never see him draw from the holster during these opening scenes—he just thrusts his ol' hogleg into view and snaps off a fatal shot at Ojala), but many of us thought we were faster. One evening, I was. During the beginning of this memorable episode, my Kilgore Cast Iron "Long Tom" cap gun literally flew from my holster, and then from my hand, and continued on, sailing across the room and through a porcelain family heirloom. The end result was my first exposure to gun confiscation.

Without a doubt, the two most ubiquitous guns of the TV westerns were the Colt Single Action Army and the Winchester Model 1892, usually in .38-40, .44-40 or, in the case of the SAA, .45 Colt calibers, all of which would chamber 5-in-1 blanks used by the studios. (The

The author fired this 50-yard group using one of the late Chuck Connors' rifles, though without employing the trigger screw.

The Rifleman's carbine has been resurrected by Chiappa and Legacy Sports International as a limited-edition commemorative. However, the trigger-tripping screw is non-functional.

With the screw backed out, *The Rifleman's* Model 92 functions like a standard carbine.

With the screw properly adjusted on *The Rifleman's* Model 92, the trigger is tripped every time the lever is closed, enabling the carbine to be rapid fired without endangering the trigger finger by having to place it inside the trigger guard. Connors added the nut to retain the screw during his shooting scenes.

blanks known as 5-in-1s are designed to function in .38-40 and .44-40 rifles, and .38-40, .44-40, and .45 Colt revolvers, thus, five guns in one blank.) Prior to the existence of replicas, the firearms portrayed on screen were original Winchester and Colt's rental guns from prop houses such as Stembridge Gun Room or Ellis Mercantile. But every once in a while there would be an atypical "star" that became as famous as the actor using it.

Interestingly, many of these individualized firearms never existed before the advent of TV westerns, rather, they were created to garner ratings. After all, there was competition among the celluloid cowboys, not just to see who was the fastest gun, but who could also corral the most viewers. It was not enough that Hoppy, Gene, and Roy brought along their loyal posse of fans from the silver screens of movie theaters to the television sets in American homes. Soon there were new hombres in Tinseltown, and new twists on the old west were needed. That's why Guy Madison, starring in *Wild Bill Hickok*, which ran in syndication from 1951 through 1958, wore his Colt's single-actions butt forward, emulating the real Wild Bill Hickok, who carried a pair of 1851 Colt Navies in that same manner. That was also the reason why Don Durant, in the title role of *Johnny Ringo*, which aired on CBS from 1959 to 1960, carried an original LeMat, which had been converted by Stembridge to fire blanks. Indeed, the LeMat's "seventh shot"—a .410 smoothbore under the primary rifled barrel of the revolver—was often employed by screenwriters to get Ringo out of a seemingly hopeless jam in which six shots just weren't enough.

And then there was Nick Adams, who starred in *The Rebel* as an ex-Confederate drifter named Johnny Yuma. Yuma carried an ultra-sawed-off shotgun in the ABC series, which ran from 1959 until 1961 (inexplicably being cancelled right at the start of the Civil War Centennial). That scattergun was a formidable weapon, a mule-eared side-by-side with the barrels cut off just in front of the forearm and a buttstock trimmed at the pistol grip. It's fortunate that Adams only fired blanks in this gun. Using live ammo with those short, open-choked tubes and no stock to help control recoil would have yanked that double hand-cannon right out of the shooter's grip and launched it into the stratosphere.

In reality, it would have been far from practical in the Old West (or any place else, for that matter), but it sure looked good on television.

Did such a gun ever exist? Probably not, no more so than did *The Rifleman's* loop-levered Winchester carbine or the chopped Model 92 on *Wanted: Dead or Alive*. But there was a reason for those guns, which made us suspend reality and believe in them. Perhaps it can best be illustrated by *The Man Who Shot Liberty Valance*, a 1962 movie with one of the most famous lines of any western. (Spoiler Alert: If you have not yet seen this movie, don't read the next two paragraphs.)

Directed by John Ford and starring John Wayne and Jimmy Stewart, this film tells the story of a mild-mannered lawyer, played by Stewart, who shoots down a notorious gunslinger (Lee Marvin), and, based upon this brave act, goes on to become a famous, reform-dealing state senator. Near the end of the film, we learn that Stewart didn't kill Marvin—John Wayne did, after which he faded into obscurity, while Stewart went on to forge a political career based upon something that didn't happen.

After recounting the true version of his story to a local newspaperman, Stewart asks the reporter if he is going to print it. The reporter, played by actor Carleton Young, tears up his notes and utters those now-famous lines, "No sir. This is

Remaining a Hollywood western trademark, the legend of Wyatt Earp is often captured with him carrying a gun sporting a 12-inch barrel. He is often shown using this barrel to subdue prisoners and delinquents in Dodge City and Tombstone. The statue of Wyatt Earp here was created by artist Mary Spurgeon and can be found in Dodge City, Kansas, along the "Trail of Fame." In the photo to the right, is Cimarron Firearms' excellent replica of the 10-inch Buntline used in the movie *Tombstone*, although the TV gun was inspired by Stuart Lake's book, *Wyatt Earp, Frontier Marshall*.

The rudimentary sights of the standard Colt Single Action Army (top) were vastly improved by the introduction of the Colt New Frontier (bottom), which was brought out in 1961, but, of course, never appeared in any TV westerns. It was reintroduced, in 2011, for today's shooters.

the West, sir. When the legend becomes fact, print the legend."

Or, in our case, shoot the legend, thus fulfilling a desire to emulate our TV western heroes by owning and firing the guns we coveted on television. Unfortunately, federal regulations make it impossible for most of us to know what it would be like to fire Johnny Yuma's scattergun, because such a configuration is illegal for the majority of private citizens to own (motion picture production companies and certain prop houses are specially licensed to have such weapons). But we can experience shooting Johnny Ringo's LeMat, albeit as a .44-caliber/20-gauge, Civil War-period cap-and-ball Italian replica, which is available from Dixie Gun Works (www.dixiegunworks.com). Rather cumbersome to be sure, the single-action revolver portion is surprisingly accurate out to 25 yards, when loaded with 30 grains of 3F blackpowder and a lead ball. By flipping down the rotating firing pin on the hammer, the shotgun barrel can be discharged (using a similar blackpowder loading and an ounce of shot), but the results are sporadic, at best. And unless firmly fitting over-powder and over-shot wads are used, there is a possibility of the cap and ball dislodging the shot charge. Johnny Ringo fared far better with his cartridge-firing version.

But what about other guns of the TV westerns? Imagine stepping out onto the Warner Bros. back lot, where many of those weekly episodes were filmed, and experiencing what it might have felt like to shoot these TV guns as if they had actually existed on the real frontier. Well, thanks to the current proliferation of replicas and reissues, it is possible to emulate some of the shooting stars of yesteryear.

Let's start with the Colt Peacemaker, a gun that most certainly did exist in both the real and imagined West. The originals, or first generation, guns were made from 1873 until 1941, with 357,859 Single Action Armies manufactured before production was halted due to the demands of World War II and, quite frankly, a lack of sales. Naturally, a lot of these originals didn't survive the rigors of the frontier. But hundreds of Model Ps (the original factory designation for the Single Action Army) also met their demise on television and movie sets. How many of us have seen these guns, after the hammer had clicked on an empty chamber, being thrown into the sagebrush from a galloping horse by a black-hatted bad guy? Those weren't always rubber prop guns.

In addition, the 5-in-1 blanks fired in these Peacemakers consisted of quarter-, half-, and full-load charges (depending on the effects desired by the director), of highly corrosive blackpowder. After a full day's shooting, these guns were often put away by the studio's armorer without even a cursory cleaning. That, of course, explains why many of these movie guns have bores that resemble an asphalt tunnel.

With the supply of single-actions drying up after World War II, it is ironic that, in 1947—just as the Great Western TV Renaissance was about to saddle up—Colt's announced it would no longer be making this "obsolete" gun. Of course, by 1955, demand for the Peacemaker had grown so strong, thanks to the impact of TV westerns, that Colt's resumed

Chuck Connors, a friend of the author's, made television history with his fast shooting Winchester 92, shown here with the later-styled lever used in The Rifleman series.

Below: For his test, the author fired three types of .44-40 ammo in his original *The Rifleman* carbine (l. to r.): Remington semi-jacketed ammo, Black Hills lead Cowboy loads, and 5-in-1 blanks.

manufacture of what is now known as second generation (1955-1975) and third generation (1976 to the present) versions of the Single Action Army.

Excellent clones of these single-actions are now being made and/or imported by firms such as U.S. Fire Arms, Cimarron, and Taylor's & Company, to name but a few. There has been enough written through the years by this author, as well as others, to warrant no further discussion, other than to say the SAA is one of the most ergonomically designed and "pointable" revolvers in the world, one that balances extremely well and is rugged enough to be fired with many of its parts broken or missing. Its main drawbacks are the rudimentary fixed sights and the fact that most guns shoot low and to the left and require some twisting and filing—Kentucky windage—to get them on target.

It was the Peacemaker's prominence in the real and televised West that inspired a rare variation known as the Buntline Special. This was a standard SAA, except that it featured a 12-inch barrel and was made popular by the TV series, *The Life and Legend of Wyatt Earp*, which ran from 1955 to 1961 and

In the top photo, the author shows the group he rapid fired with the *The Rifleman* carbine. It produced some impressive hits at "gunfighter" range, with four "lethal" shots to the right shoulder of the paper opponent. However, activating the set screw convinced the author this would *not* have been a practical technique in the Old West—note the elevated position of the muzzle as it starts to climb, with two shells already in the air.

The Winchester 92 Mare's Leg used in *Wanted: Dead or Alive* featured a nine-inch barrel and sawed-off stock. The gun was anchored in the special holster by slipping the saddle ring through the steel hook (shown under the receiver) and securing the barrel with a spring clip. Note: Due to BATFE regulations, this non-firing prop gun, originally acquired from a Hollywood studio, features a dummy aluminum barrel.

The Puma Bounty Hunter from Legacy Sports features a 12-inch barrel and a lever patterned after the one used by McQueen in the latter part of the *Wanted: Dead Or Alive* series, in which an octagon-barreled rifle was also made into a Mare's Leg.

Rossi's Ranch Hand is an earlier version of the *Wanted: Dead Or Alive* Mare's Leg, although it sports a 12-inch barrel instead of the nine-inch tube used in the TV series.

starred Hugh O'Brian as Marshal Earp. As legend has it, back in the real West of the 1880s, a flamboyant writer of dime novels, one Edward Zane Carroll Judson, who used the pen name Ned Buntline, presented Earp and four other Dodge City lawmen—Bat Masterson, Bill Tilghman, Charlie Bassett and Neal Brown—with specially ordered Peacemakers fitted with foot-long barrels.

This tale was first brought to light by author Stuart N. Lake in his 1931 biography, *Wyatt Earp: Frontier Marshal.* Unfortunately, the facts don't quite substantiate the story. While it is true that customers could pay a dollar an inch for any Colt Model P barrel length over 7½ inches, and approximately 31 such guns—with barrels ranging from 10 to 16 inches—were produced by the factory from 1876 through 1884, there is no record or evidence otherwise that Earp or any of the other four lawmen were recipients of these "Buntline Specials," as they have come to be called.

In true Hollywood fashion, the legend became fact when, in an early episode of *The Life and Legend of Wyatt Earp*, the marshal is presented with just such a gun by Judson. By the next episode, Earp's

The second-generation Colt Buntline Special, with its 12-inch barrel, was produced as a direct result of the popularity of *The Life and Times of Wyatt Earp*, starring Hugh O'Brian.

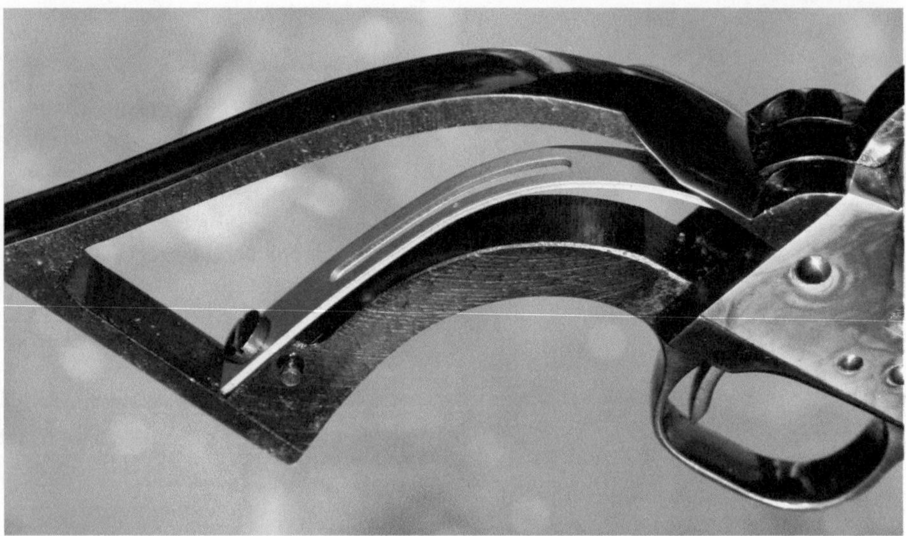

During the heyday of the TV western, many studios filed down the mainsprings of Single Action Armies to enable actors to cock them easier and faster. Today, this same effect can be achieved by the addition of Wolff mainsprings.

double *buscadero* rig, in which O'Brian had previously packed two 4¾-inch Colt .45s, now featured an exaggerated long drop on the right-hand holster to accommodate his Buntline Special, which is seen throughout the rest of the series. Needles to say, just as the TV westerns inspired Colt's to bring back its Model P, this popular show created a demand for Buntline Specials. We all wanted to be like Wyatt Earp—or at least to own the stretch-barreled hogleg Hugh O'Brian was able to draw with amazing dexterity. Thus, in 1957, Colt's introduced the Buntline Special, which remained in the line for an impressive 30 years, being produced in both second- (now highly collectable) and third-generation versions. In addition, in 2010, Colt's came out with a one-year-only reissue, which consisted of a two-gun set of Peacemakers with case hardened frame and hammer. One SAA was a 4¾-inch version, while the other was a Buntline Special. Both guns were engraved "Hugh O'Brian – Wyatt Earp Tribute" on the barrel. Not many of these cased sets were made and it is doubtful, due to their inherent collectibility, any of them are being shot.

For those unable to find, afford, or otherwise acquire a genuine Colt Buntline Special, Cimarron is producing a variation that sports a 10-inch barrel (which some historians feel was more appropriate to the length that the real Wyatt Earp may have used). The gun boasts an inlaid brass plaque copied from the 1990 movie *Tombstone*, rather than the Wyatt Earp TV series. True to the gun that Kurt Russell carried, the shield-shaped inlay on the grip reads, "Wyatt Earp Peacemaker, From the Grateful People of Dodge City, Apr 8th 1878." In addition, U.S. Fire Arms will custom-make Buntlines ranging from 10 to 18 inches, complete with prototypical fold-up rear ladder sights, if desired.

Whether or not the Buntline Special offers a practical advantage over the standard SAA barrel lengths is a matter of opinion. Aside from O'Brian's TV exploits of bashing a desperado over the head with the long barrel (which, in the TV series, was done with a rubber gun), the only other benefits would be a longer sight radius and a slight increase in muzzle velocity. I own two Buntline Specials that I shoot whenever I'm in a "Wyatt Earp" frame of mind. One is a second-generation Colt's, the other is a 10-inch version from U.S. Fire Arms. Both are in .45 Colt.

The first thing one notices with either of these guns is their balance, which obviously has more weight toward the front. In addition, the guns typically shoot lower with Cowboy Action loads, higher with full factory loads such as Winchester Silvertips. The 12-inch Colt's has a bit of whip to the recoil, which, overall, is slightly less than with shorter-barreled single-actions. Although I prefer the 10-inch barrel USFA and Cimarron guns as shooters, the 12-inch Buntline is my favorite—after all, it is a Colt's, and, thus, more historically correct (besides, it's what the "real" Wyatt Earp used on TV!) But, either way, be prepared to order a custom holster with a longer drop or go to a cross-draw configuration, if you want to pack your Buntline Special on the streets of Dodge City or Tombstone.

When it comes to TV western rifles, the Winchester Model 1892 reigned supreme, primarily because there were more of them in shootable condition than Model 1873s (remember, this was the pre-replica era), the actions were smoother, and, unlike the Winchester 94—which was used in a few westerns such as *Sheriff of Cochise*—they were chambered in .38-40 and .44-40, which could take standard studio blanks. (The third Model 92 chambering, .32-20, would not accept 5-in-1s). However, many Model 94s were adapted to take 5-in-1s by retrofitting them with Model 92 barrels.

Most of the Winchester 92s used were regularly configured rifles and carbines. But one of the most famous deviations was the loop-levered "flip special" so expertly welded by Chuck Connors as *The Rifleman*, which aired from 1958 until 1963. I often find myself wondering why no one ever devised such a wide-levered Winchester for use on the real western frontier. Fortunately, as a friend of the late Chuck Connors, I was able to find out, for I spent many a weekend visiting with him at his Tehachapi ranch during the latter years of his life and now own the rifle that hung on his living room wall. I should point out that this was not the rifle used in his TV show—there were actually three of those. This was one of three additional Winchester 92s (that I know of) made for Chuck afterwards, some of which were used by him in personal appearances.

While *The Rifleman's* carbine looked impressive, it is not practical, as the wider lever requires a longer hand movement to work the action. The original lever used during the first years of the show was rounded. Later, a slightly squared-off lever configuration was employed. Both versions had a unique set screw in the trigger guard that could be positioned to trip the trigger every time the lever was slammed home. This was the secret to Chuck's eye-blinking speed in cranking off multiple shots at the beginning of each episode—it was not tricky camera work.

In real life, that set screw feature could be dangerous, as I once demonstrated in a controlled test on the shooting range, using live .44-40 rounds instead of blanks. There is, of course, no recoil with blanks, and so the carbine remains relatively steady while working the lever. But, when rapid firing live ammo, the effect is similar to that of a semi-automatic, and the muzzle rises dramatically. Like fanning a sixshooter (which was never done in the real West) the first shot may go where it is intended, but the rest are scattered, rather than grouped. Still, to prove a point, I cranked off nine rapid-fire shots with Chuck's carbine at a silhouette target set at "gunfighter range," just to see how deadly *The Rifleman's* rifle would have been in a real gunfight. To my surprise, all nine shots hit the target. The total was four lethal body hits in the upper torso, with the remaining five rounds striking in the upper right shoulder area. Of course, the caveat is you have to remember to back out the trigger guard screw when you wish to fire the rifle in a conventional manner. Otherwise, every time you close the lever, it will trip the hammer and fire a round. This can be especially disconcerting when you spin-cock the rifle, as Chuck often did.

Although Chuck's original rifles are in private collections and highly valuable, a few years ago, Chiappa Firearms (www.chiappafirearms.com), and Legacy Sports International (www.legacysports.com), came out with a limited-edition Chuck Connors Commemorative Carbine in .44-40 and featuring the original loop lever configuration (although the non-functioning set screw is strictly for appearance). Chuck's signature is etched on the left side of the receiver and on the right side of the stock, along with an inlaid silver medallion with Chuck's portrait. These commemoratives came with a DVD of two episodes of *The Rifleman*, a certificate of authenticity signed by Jeff Connors, one of Chuck's four sons, and a publicity photo of Chuck in his leading role. Only 1,000 commemoratives were made, but it may still be possible to find some for sale.

Another Hollywood-ized version of the Winchester Model 92 is much more readily available, even though, in my opinion, it is even less practical than Chuck's carbine. That said, it is probably the ultimate TV western "fun gun." From 1958 to 1961, Steve McQueen, as bounty hunter Josh Randall in *Wanted: Dead Or Alive*, brought justice to TV's banditos with a loop-levered Model 92 that featured a dramatically shortened barrel and stock so it could be carried on the hip, like a pistol, in an open-sided holster. McQueen dubbed it the "Mare's Leg," because, as an avid shooter in real life, when he took it to the range to fire with live ammo, he discovered it kicked like a mule.

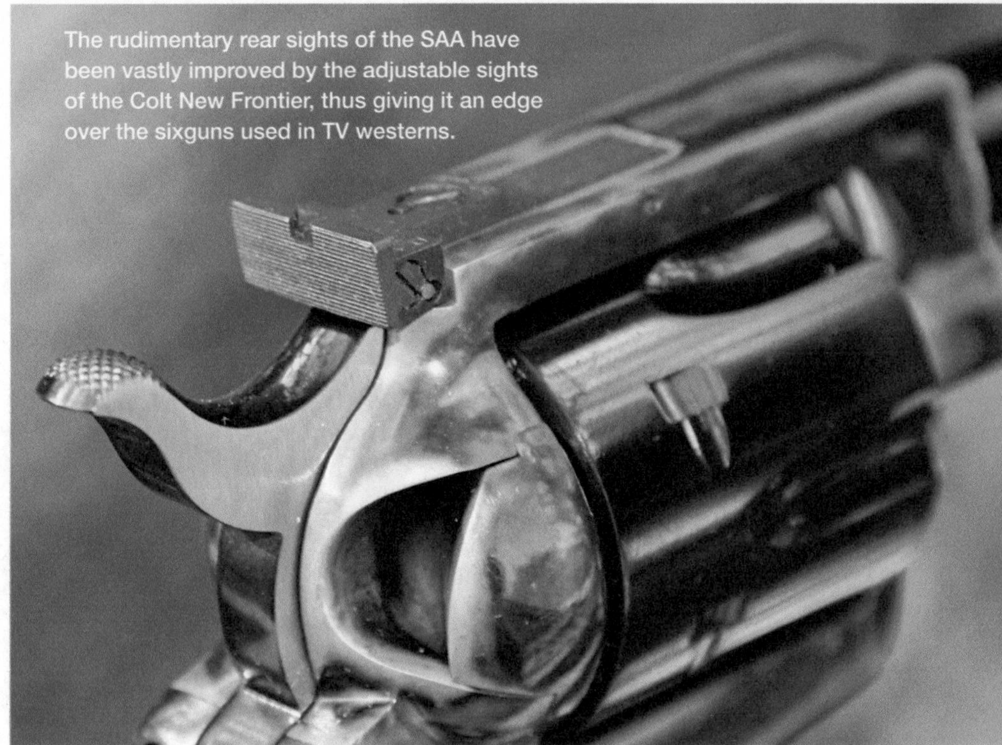
The rudimentary rear sights of the SAA have been vastly improved by the adjustable sights of the Colt New Frontier, thus giving it an edge over the sixguns used in TV westerns.

Needless to say, such a gun had never been seen before in either the real or imagined West. With its nine-inch barrel and no sights, it was a realized figment of imagination born from producer John Robinson, who wanted to outfit his hero with a gun that would garner attention. That it did, causing the U.S. Treasury's Alcohol and Tobacco Tax Division to take notice, when the series premiered on September 6, 1958. The government agency declared the Mare's Leg illegal, as they reasoned it was neither a rifle nor a pistol. After the show's accountants ponied up $11,000 in registration fees (thus making it the most expensive gun of the TV westerns), the Mare's Leg went on to achieve stardom. The Mare's Leg mystique was heightened by the fact that, even though it was a .44-40, Randall carried .45-70 shells in his specially designed gun belt, as Robinson felt the larger cartridges showed up better on camera.

Today, there are no less than four different companies producing the Mare's Leg, all of which have front and rear sights and 12-inch barrels, rather than the original nine-inch tubes. While featuring an earlier-series wider loop lever, unlike the TV gun, the Rossi Ranch Hand is only available in .45 Colt, .44 Magnum, and .357 Magnum. The Puma Bounty Hunter, built by Chiappa and available from Legacy Sports, has McQueen's later-styled triangular loop lever and is available in *Wanted: Dead Or Alive's* prototypical .44-40 as well as .45 Colt and .44 Magnum chamberings. J.B. Custom offers a Mare's Leg built by Armi Sport (Chiappa) in the same three calibers, as well as a take-down version. And Henry Repeating Arms makes two variations, one in .45 Colt and the other in .22 Long Rifle, although neither is built on a Model 92-type action.

Having fired the modern Model 92-style versions of Josh Randall's sidearm, I have to concur with the late Steve McQueen, as it does kick like a mule, especially in .44 Magnum. But, frankly, in .44-40 or .45 Colt, recoil-wise it is no different than shooting a Buntline Special. After all, the barrel lengths are the same. The guns are touted as personal-defense and camp guns. Indeed, I can see packing a .44-40 Mare's Leg in a door-mounted scabbard of a pickup truck or Jeep (it is too short to straddle a cab-mounted gun rack).

As for practicality, I can only relate an incident that occurred years ago, during a promotional fast-draw contest held at the 1960 Pioneer Days celebration in Palm Springs, California. McQueen was able to snap his Mare's Leg from its holster and fan off a shot in a respectable ⅖-second, outdrawing James Arness, John Payne (*Restless Gun*), and Peter Brown (*Lawman*). Thus, once again, the legend became fact.

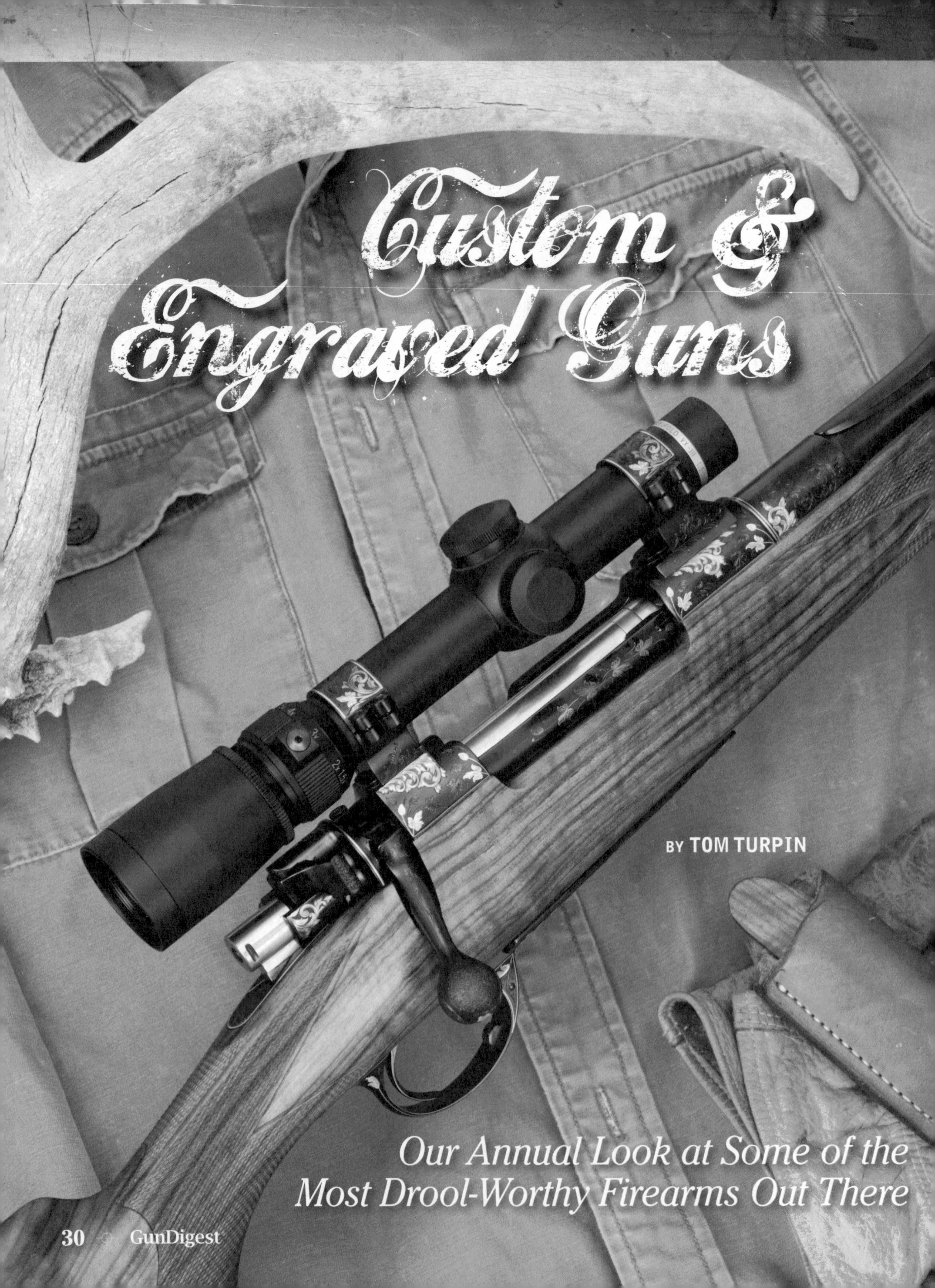

Custom & Engraved Guns

BY TOM TURPIN

Our Annual Look at Some of the Most Drool-Worthy Firearms Out There

Lee Helgeland

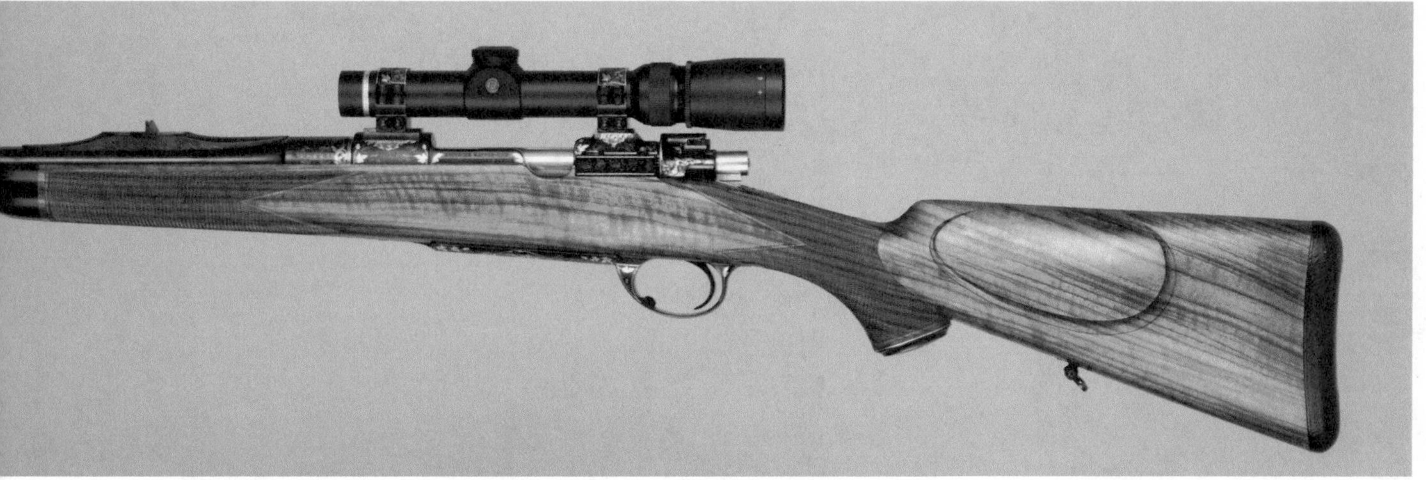

What is the old saying about the cobbler and his kids' shoes? Well, custom rifle maker **Lee Helgeland** decided awhile back to build an elk rifle for himself. He started the project by blueprinting a Mauser 1909 Argentine action. He added a two-position safety kit, which uses the original Mauser shroud, from the late Tom Burgess. He used a Fisher/Blackburn rounded bottom metal unit and a Blackburn trigger. Lee also single-square-bridged the action. To be different, instead of checkering, he stippled the bolt knob, safety lever, bolt release, and floorplate release. He barreled the rifle and chambered it for the 9.3x64 Brenneke, before fashioning a quarter rib with a different shape than is commonly encountered. He also took a barrel-band front sling swivel, cut off the top of the band, and reshaped it.

Lee stocked the rifle with a super, but not flashy, block of California English walnut, fitting a Fisher grip cap and leather-covering the recoil pad. He then checkered the stock in a point pattern at 26 lines per inch.

The finished rifle weighs 7.4 pounds without the scope. Lee tells me that he and the rifle will be headed into the Bob Marshall Wilderness area, in Montana, come elk season.

(Photos by Steven Dodd Hughes)

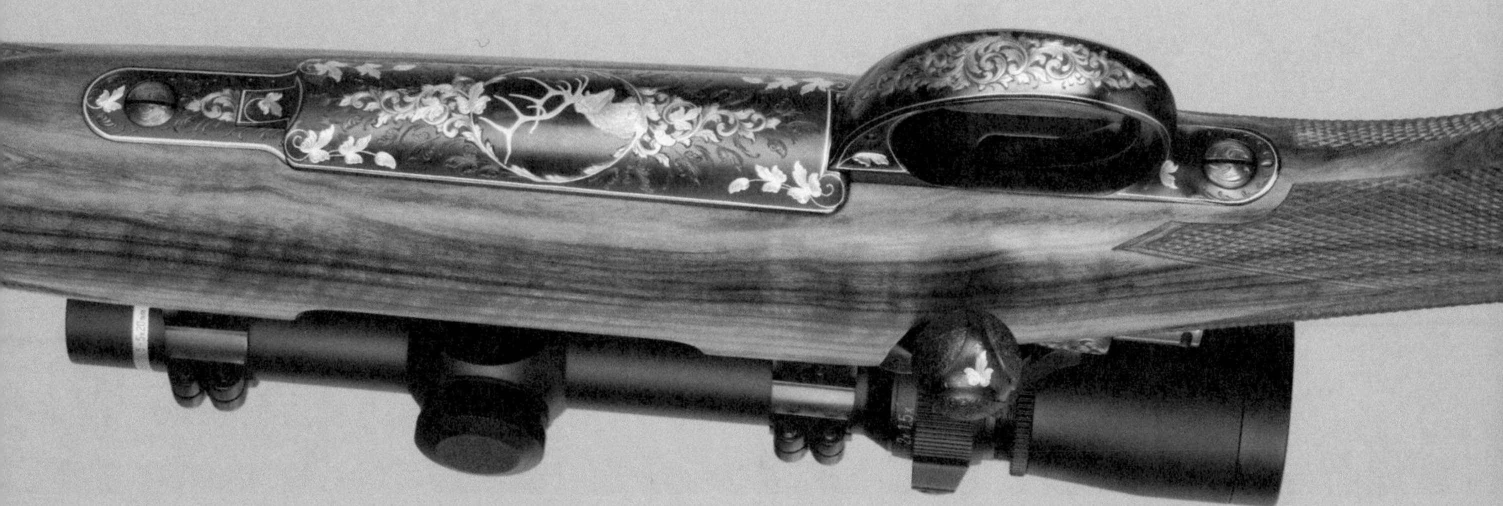

Barry Lee Hands

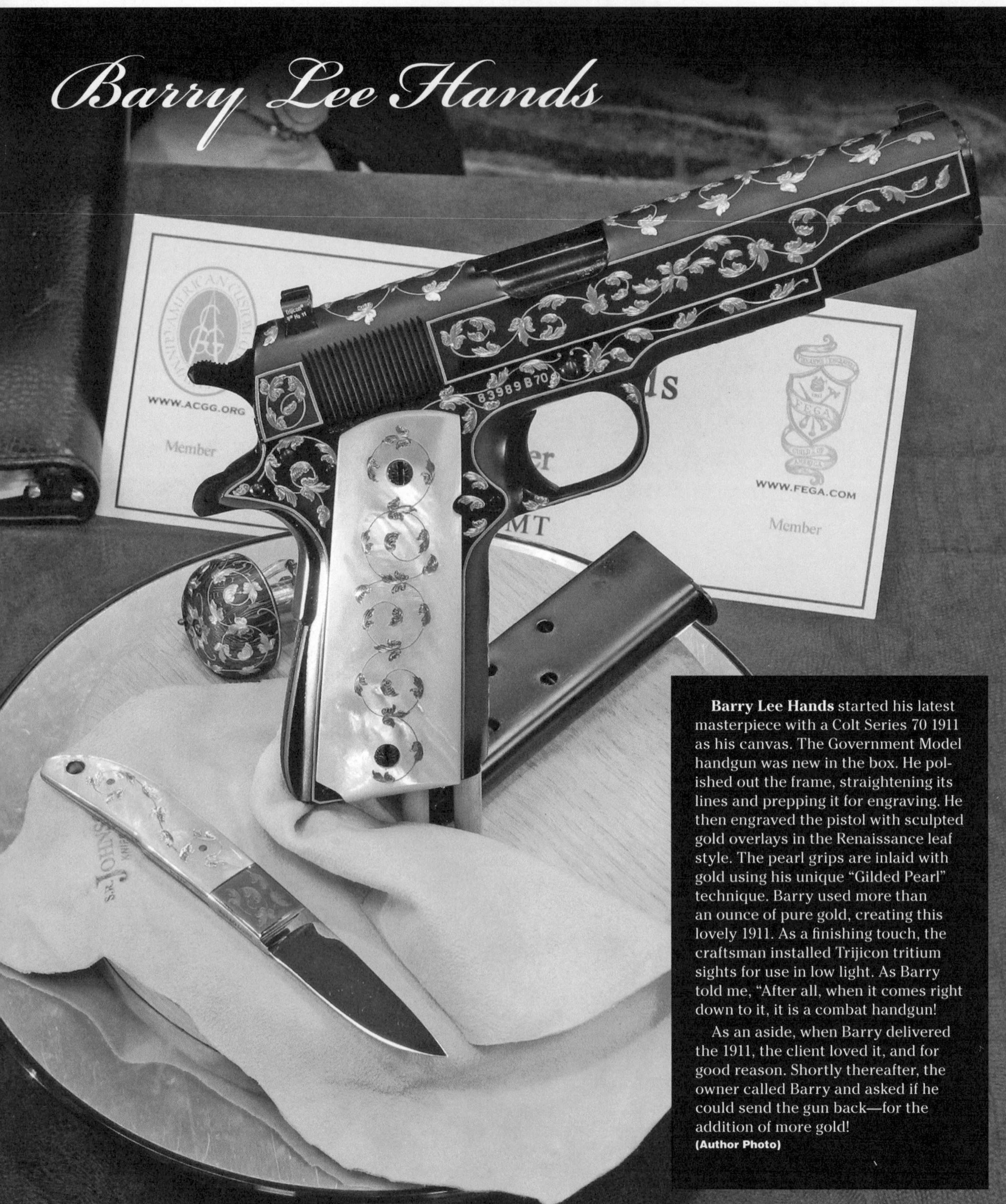

Barry Lee Hands started his latest masterpiece with a Colt Series 70 1911 as his canvas. The Government Model handgun was new in the box. He polished out the frame, straightening its lines and prepping it for engraving. He then engraved the pistol with sculpted gold overlays in the Renaissance leaf style. The pearl grips are inlaid with gold using his unique "Gilded Pearl" technique. Barry used more than an ounce of pure gold, creating this lovely 1911. As a finishing touch, the craftsman installed Trijicon tritium sights for use in low light. As Barry told me, "After all, when it comes right down to it, it is a combat handgun!

As an aside, when Barry delivered the 1911, the client loved it, and for good reason. Shortly thereafter, the owner called Barry and asked if he could send the gun back—for the addition of more gold!

(Author Photo)

Al Lind–Lynn Wright

Gunmaker **Al Lind** began this custom rifle more than 20 years ago. He started with a pre-64 Model 70 barreled action, chambered for, what else, the .270 Winchester cartridge. The rifle shot so well he didn't dare pull the factory barrel for a replacement. Instead, he re-contoured the factory barrel to a more pleasing shape.

In his stash of wood, Al had a blank of genuine French walnut that had been cut in 1936. He decided to use it on this project. He crafted the stock in the classic style, added a Biesen trap buttplate, a skeleton grip cap, Talley sling swivels, and checkered it in a fleur de lis pattern with ribbons, checkered at 24 lines per inch. Since his client had specified that he wanted a very lightweight rifle, Al built the stock with a blind magazine.

Lynn Wright did sparse, but elegant engraving. The finished rifle weighed in at 6¾ pounds. I've not seen a custom rifle using a pre-64 Model 70 action that weighed less.

(Photos by Tom Alexander)

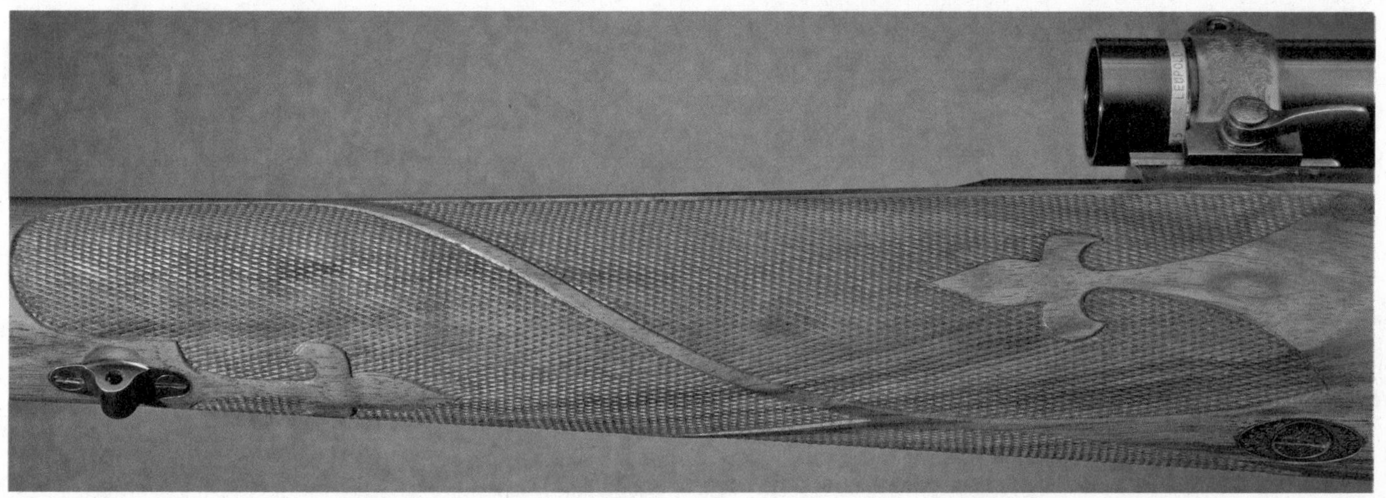

Al Lofgren – Ed LaPour
Brian Hochstrat

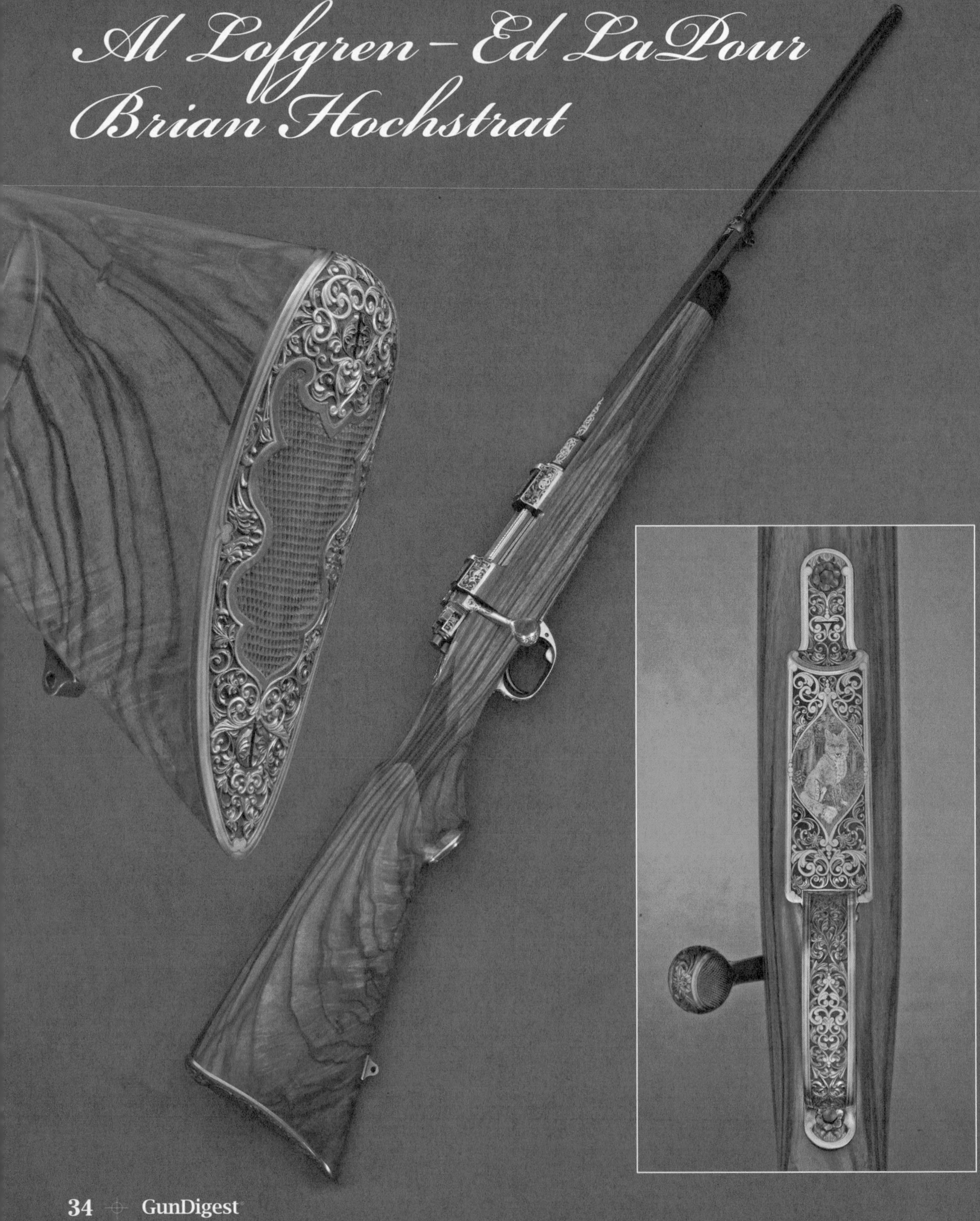

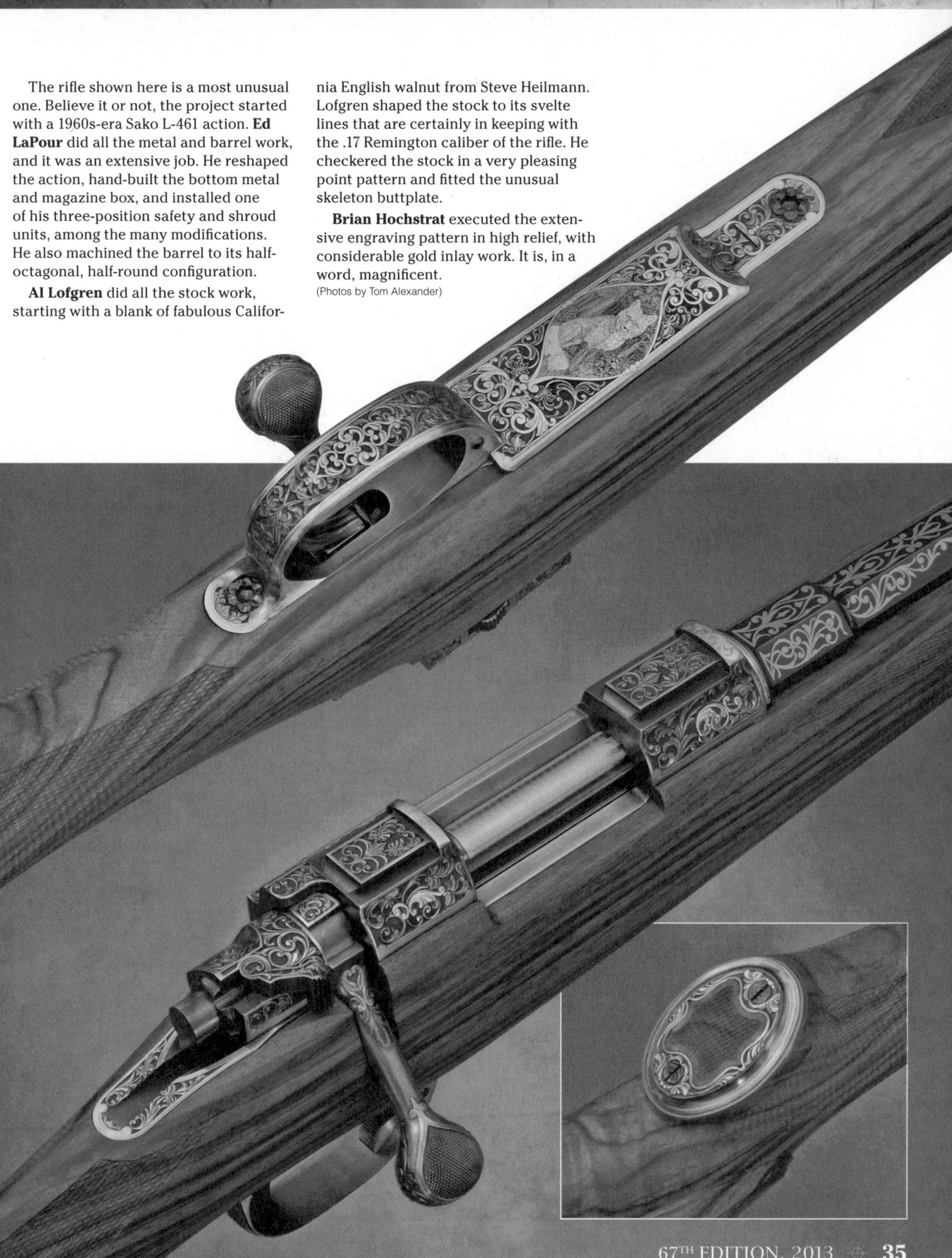

The rifle shown here is a most unusual one. Believe it or not, the project started with a 1960s-era Sako L-461 action. **Ed LaPour** did all the metal and barrel work, and it was an extensive job. He reshaped the action, hand-built the bottom metal and magazine box, and installed one of his three-position safety and shroud units, among the many modifications. He also machined the barrel to its half-octagonal, half-round configuration.

Al Lofgren did all the stock work, starting with a blank of fabulous California English walnut from Steve Heilmann. Lofgren shaped the stock to its svelte lines that are certainly in keeping with the .17 Remington caliber of the rifle. He checkered the stock in a very pleasing point pattern and fitted the unusual skeleton buttplate.

Brian Hochstrat executed the extensive engraving pattern in high relief, with considerable gold inlay work. It is, in a word, magnificent.

(Photos by Tom Alexander)

Len Fewless – Doug Mann Robert Strosin – Turnbull Restoration

In this section of the 2011 *Gun Digest*, I ran a photo and blurb on an unfinished 1870 Gibbs Farquharson that was being worked on by metalsmith **Glen Fewless** and stockmaker **Doug Mann**. I thought that the loyal, year after year readers of *Gun Digest* might appreciate a photo of the finished product. Two additional craftsmen have been added to the mix. **Robert Strosin** added his very talented engraving to the rifle, and **Doug Turnbull** provided the fastidious color case hardening to complete the job.

(Photos by Tom Alexander)

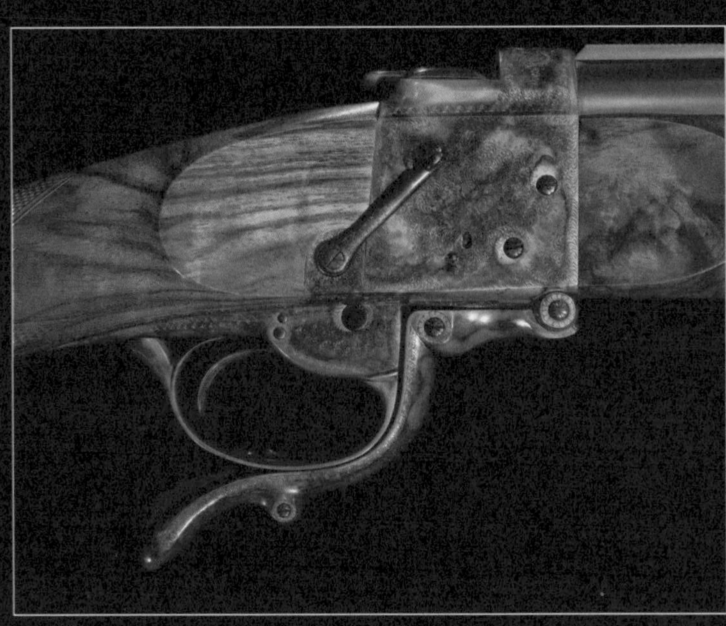

Ed Peugh

A client of California engraver **Ed Peugh** brought him a really nice Second Model Colt Woodsman .22 semi-auto pistol with instructions to "dress it up." Ed executed a combination scroll and oak leaf pattern, complemented with gold inlay work. The old Woodsman is a wonderful pistol. I had one as a teenager that I was very fond of. It is very deserving of the lovely engraving.

(Photo courtesy of Ed Peugh)

D'Arcy Echols – Lisa Tomlin

The gentleman who owns this rifle is preparing to take it to Botswana this year. A couple years back, he commissioned **D'Arcy Echols** to build him a proper tool for the task of taking a big bull elephant. The resulting rifle fits into the category of "It just doesn't get any better than this." Chambered for the massive .505 Gibbs cartridge, it is probably up to the task of slaying a T-Rex, let alone a big tusker.

D'Arcy began his task with a Hartmann & Weiss-made action frame, bolt body, extractor, and firing pin. The rest of the action components were either fabricated in-house or provided by another supplier. For example, the late Tom Burgess machined the three-position safety and shroud unit, and D'Arcy just happened to have one on-hand. The little Mauser bolt stop was replaced by a magnum version made in the Echols shop. The bottom metal and magazine box unit was likewise machined from 4130 steel in the Echols shop. It holds three rounds in the box, plus one in the chamber. D'Arcy fitted the rifle with a shop-made adjustable peep rear sight. He installed a Krieger barrel and chambered it for the .505 Gibbs cartridge.

He fashioned the stock from an exquisite stick of California English walnut, pillar-bedding the action and free-floating the barrel. He added weight to the butt of the stock to achieve a balance point precisely at the front action screw. He fitted one of his own grip caps and a Griffin & Howe recoil pad, then checkered the rifle in his signature point pattern at 26 lines per inch. The rifle then went to **Lisa Tomlin** for one of her superlative engraving jobs. All finished, the rifle weighs 10 pounds 11 ounces.

(Photos by Kevin Dilley)

Mike Roden – Granite Mountain Arms

Mike Roden of **Granite Mountain Arms** produces one of the few newly manufactured 98 Mauser clones available on the market today. Once in a great while, Mike will produce a complete rifle built around one of his actions. This rifle is one such example.

Starting with one of his standard length (.30-06) actions, he had it barreled and chambered for the 9.3x62 cartridge. This old German development has been around since 1905, but, until recently, was seldom seen in the U.S. Lately, however, it has undergone a dramatic increase in popularity, and well it should. It's a hell of a cartridge. I don't know who did the barrel, but I suspect that Danny Pedersen of Classic Barrel & Gun Works did the barrel work for Mike.

Mike then stocked it in a very nice stick of Circassian walnut. I've had the rifle for a while now and have made several trips to the range with it. It consistently delivers between ¼- and ½-inch three-shot groups with about every variety of ammo I've fed it, both factory and handloads. Next up for the rifle is a buffalo in Zimbabwe.

(Author Photo)

Master engraver **Lee Griffiths** was presented with a very unusual canvas on which to lavish his highly talented attention. It was a Model 10 Bergmann-Bayard semi-auto 9mm pistol. (Originally produced in Belgium, production ceased at WWI. It was later produced in Denmark prior to the beginning of the second World War.) I think it is only the second example I've ever seen of one of these guns. Anyway, Lee chose a sea disasters theme for the engraving. He used a sculpted scroll along with gold inlay to embellish the bulino scenes. Lee also made the walnut grips and carved them in relief. The ivory inlay at the top of the grip was not completed when this photo was taken, but has since been carved.

(Author Photo)

Darwin Hensley Steve Nelson

This rifle is the final stocking job in the long career of **Darwin Hensley**. Over the years, Darwin has earned an enviable reputation as one of the very best stockmakers. Alas, he was diagnosed with Parkinson's disease a few years ago, and his stockmaking days are over.

An anonymous and now-retired very talented metalsmith started with an Oberndorf magnum Mauser action. He barreled and chambered it for the .375 H&H cartridge, adding a custom barrel-band front sight ramp, barrel-band front sling swivel base, an exquisitely fitted quarter rib, and custom scope bases and scope rings. He also added a custom three-position Model 70-style safety, and low-scope bolt handle with a checkered knob. He installed a fully adjustable Blackburn single-stage trigger, and a Jerry Fisher-designed/Ted Blackburn-manufactured, trigger guard and floor plate assembly. The Fisher design features a curved floorplate inside and out to fit the curve of the bottom of the stock.

Darwin then stocked the rifle using one of his wonderful Turkish walnut blanks. This stock features the subtle detailing of raised moulding around the loading port, bolt handle, and thumb cut, all identifying features of a Darwin Hensley stock. The stock also features two stock bolts, European style inlet rear sling swivel base, a trap-door grip cap, and leather-covered recoil pad.

Steve Nelson finished the stock by checkering it in a simple, but elegant point-pattern at 24 lines per inch and added mullered borders. Steve also did the slow rust bluing that completed the rifle. (Photos by Tom Alexander)

Jerry Huddleston

This firearm is truly unique in today's world. The planning for it started 20 to 25 years ago in the fertile mind of **Jerry Huddleston**. He told me that he knew everything he wanted to do, but didn't feel his engraving skills were quite up to the task. He delayed starting the project until he had studied and practiced engraving for a number of years. His mentor for the engraving education was fellow Oregonian, Bob Evans.

Jerry chose an 1800s-era French-style fowling piece in the Nicholas-Noël Boutet style to build. Every part in this gun is completely hand-made in the Huddleston shop. Per his research, no one person has ever done a project like this before; even the master Boutet had 20 or so craftsmen working with him. Jerry started the project as a speculation piece, but it was sold during the construction process. He worked on the project for four hours per day, for two and a half years. It is, without question, a masterpiece. (Photos by Tom Alexander)

James Anderson Shane Thompson Roger Kehr

After many years fiddling with custom rifles, it isn't often that I'm overly awed by one—impressed, yes, but rarely awed. This particular rifle though, is one of the nicest I've ever seen, and I've seen more than a few.

The project began with a Charles Daly Mini Mark X action. **Shane Thompson** did the extensive metalwork on the action and Shilen barrel. Shane even milled a thumb cut, a lá the 98 Mauser, into the miniature action to facilitate loading. When Shane finished his work, he sent the rifle to **James Anderson**.

James did some added metalwork, adding a scaled down, Jim Biar-crafted, Oberndorf-style bolt handle, a three-position safety, and shroud. He then made a pattern stock of cherry wood and sent it to the client, who had another Mini Mark X at home, for approval. Once the stock details were worked out, James stocked the rifle in a superb piece of Turkish walnut, using a bit of alkanet root in with the stock finish to add a bit of color to the wood. He checkered the stock at 24 lines per inch with mullered borders, a pattern similar to those used on British stalking rifles.

When the stock was finished, James sent the metalwork to **Roger Kehr** for some modest but exquisite engraving, stippling, and lettering. Some selected small parts were sent to Roger Ferrell for nitre bluing, and James completed the job by rust bluing the remainder of the metalwork. The finished rifle, with scope, weighs just over six pounds.

(Photos by James Anderson)

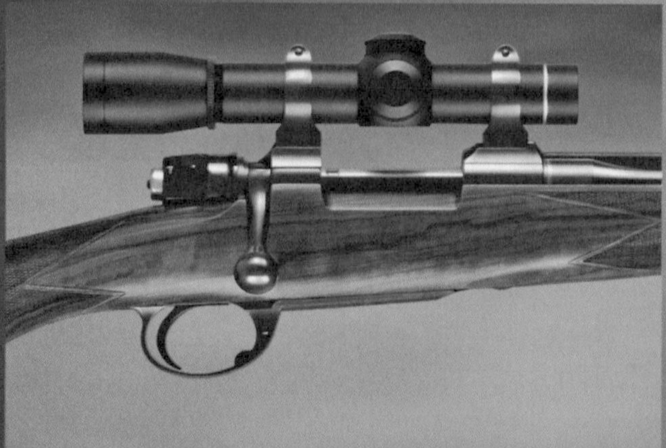

Steve Heilmann – Keith Heppler

Paula Miesen-Malicki

Pete Mazur

This superb Mauser 404 Jeffery rifle is the product of several incredibly talented craftsmen and a craftswoman.

Starting with a Persian 98 Mauser action and a Half Moon 404 barrel, **Steve Heilmann** put the barreled action together, including the addition of a custom quarter-rib, barrel-band front sling swivel, and a front sight ramp with a folding hood. The swivel and ramp were made by Recknagel, in Germany, and purchased through New England Custom Guns. Steve fabricated custom scope ring bases for Talley rings, and also fitted a three-position safety and shroud made by Recknagel. Finally, he fitted a Blackburn drop box magazine unit to the rifle.

Keith Heppler then took over and stocked the metalwork in a really nice stick of European English walnut. He leather-covered the recoil pad and checkered the stock in a fancy multi-point pattern with ribbons at 26 lines per inch. **Paula Biesen-Malicki** then engraved the rifle, and **Pete Mazur** did the final metal finishing.

(Photos by Tom Alexander)

Mike Dubber – Bill Austin Turnbull Restoration

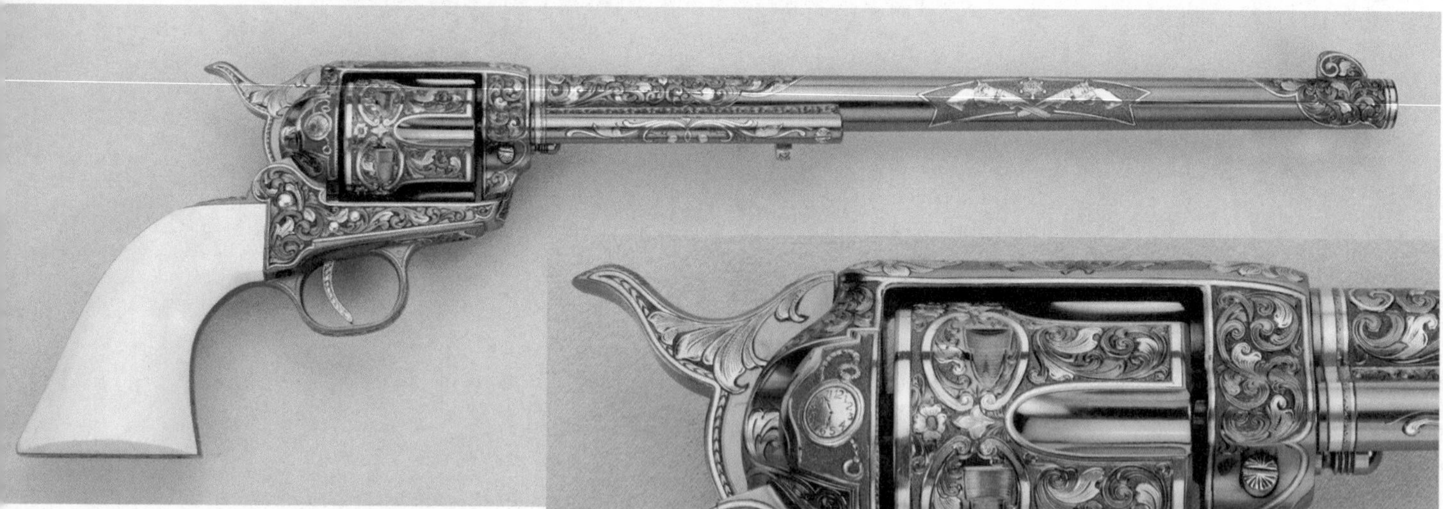

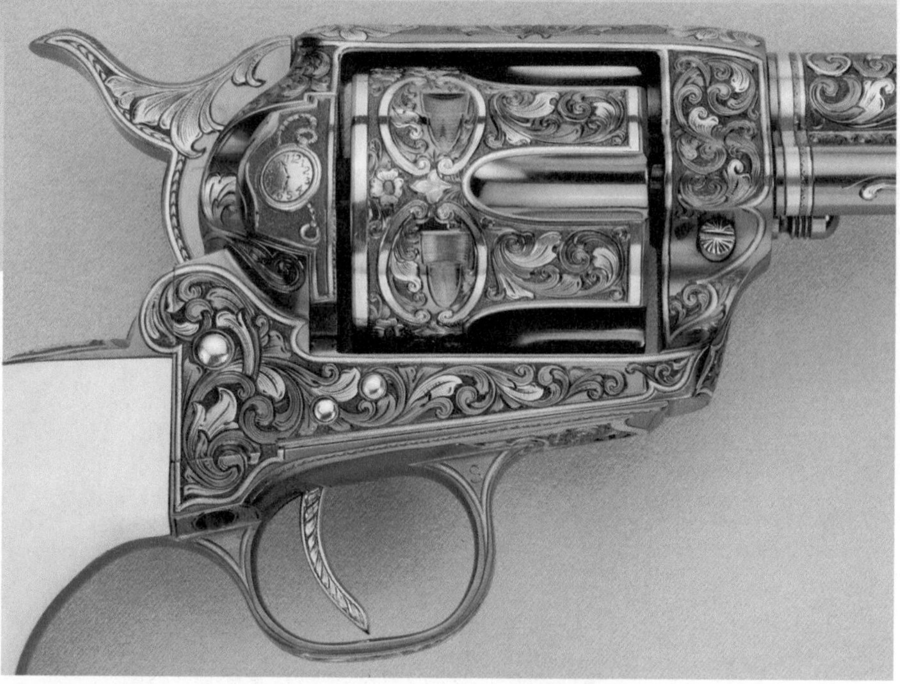

This lovely Colt Buntline received the Howard Dove Award at the 2011 Colt Collectors Association Show. This very competitive award is given to the best-engraved Colt, as judged by the Colt's Custom Shop employees attending the show. Master Engraver **Michael Dubber** engraved the pistol, **Turnbull Restoration** performed the exquisite charcoal bluing, and **Bill Austin** scrimshawed the one-piece ivory grips. This was the third time Mike Dubber has received this prestigious award. Engraver Dubber chose a William Butler "Wild Bill" Hickok theme for his engraving pattern.

(Photos courtesy of Mike Dubber)

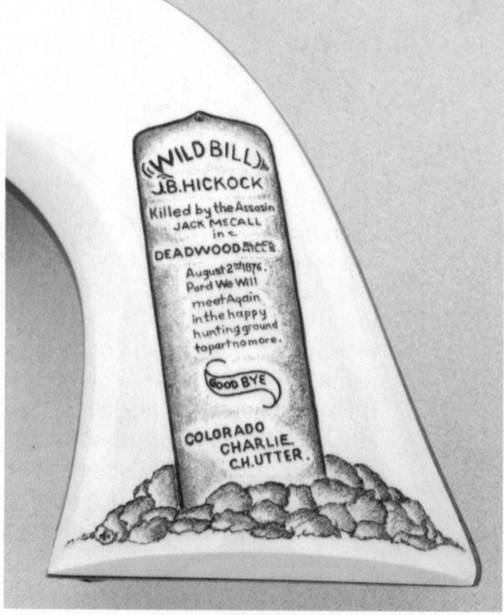

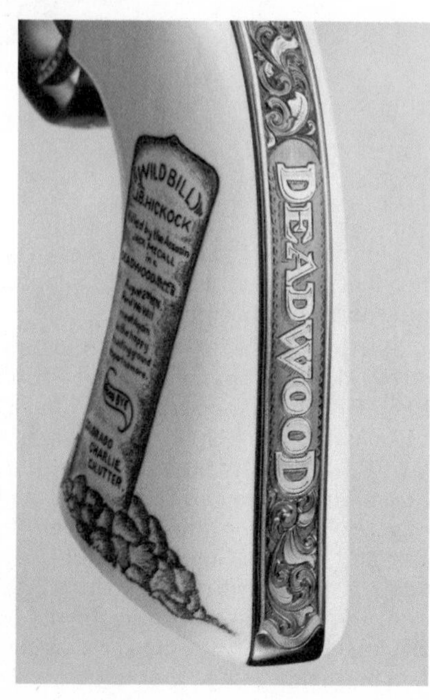

Todd Ramirez

Texas rifle maker **Todd Ramirez** crafted this lovely left-hand rifle for well-known outdoor writer and world hunter Craig Boddington. He started with a Granite Mountain Arms left-hand short action. Craig had specified that the rifle was to be chambered for the 7x57 cartridge, but the short GMA action was too short to accommodate it. Todd fixed that problem by opening up the action top and bottom, milling away excess metal. The GMA factory bottom metal and magazine box was likewise too short, so Todd custom made a bottom metal and magazine box unit in his shop. He also fitted a set of Joe Smithson quick detachable rings to the bridges of the GMA action by milling recesses to accept the rings. Todd then color case hardened the shroud and safety to provide contrast in the action.

Next, Todd selected a stick of Bastogne walnut with exceptional fiddleback figuring for the stock. He shaped and inlet the stock to the metal, crafting his signature cheekpiece shape, and fitted the stock with a skeleton buttplate and grip cap. He added a bit of red stain to the oil finish and applied more than 30 coats to the wood, before hand-polishing it to a deep, lustrous finish. He finished the stock by checkering it in a point pattern of 28 lines per inch.

Todd told me that he was currently working on another rifle for Craig, this time a .338 Win. Mag. on a Model 70 action. In a couple years, perhaps we can feature that rifle on these pages.

(Photos courtesy of Todd Ramirez)

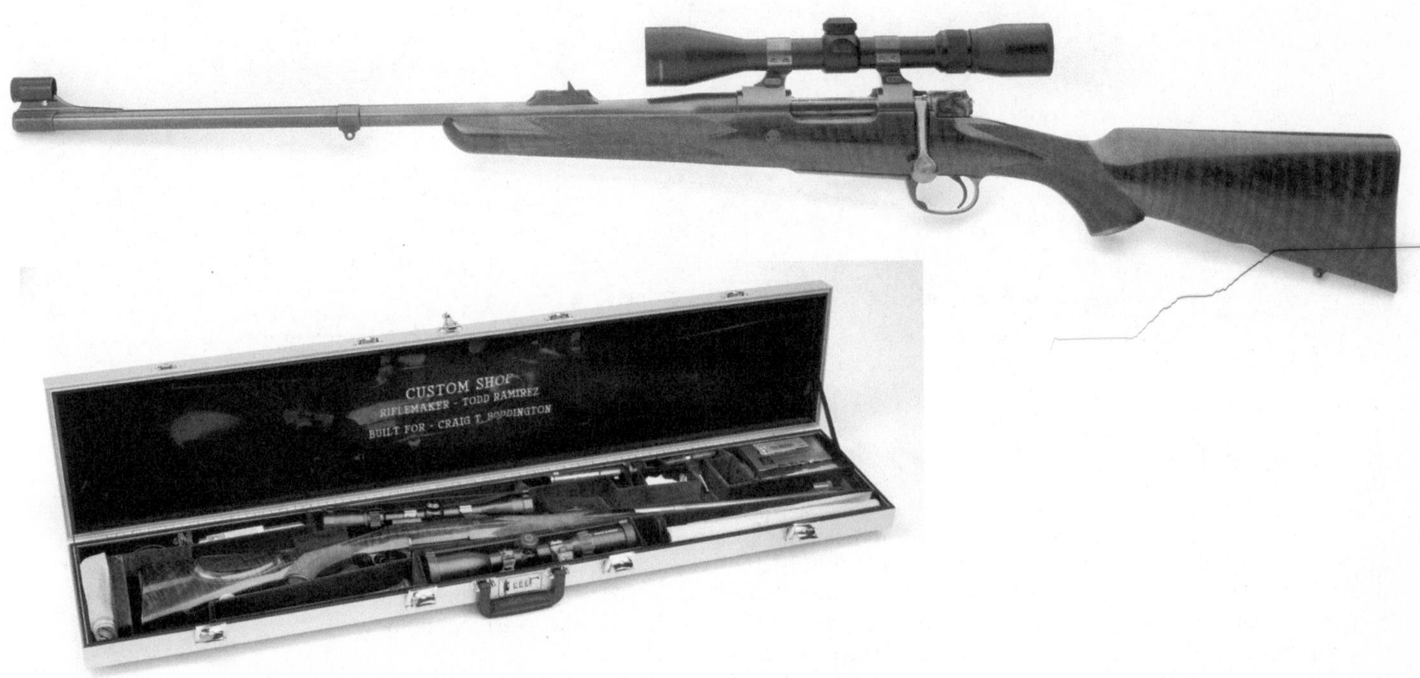

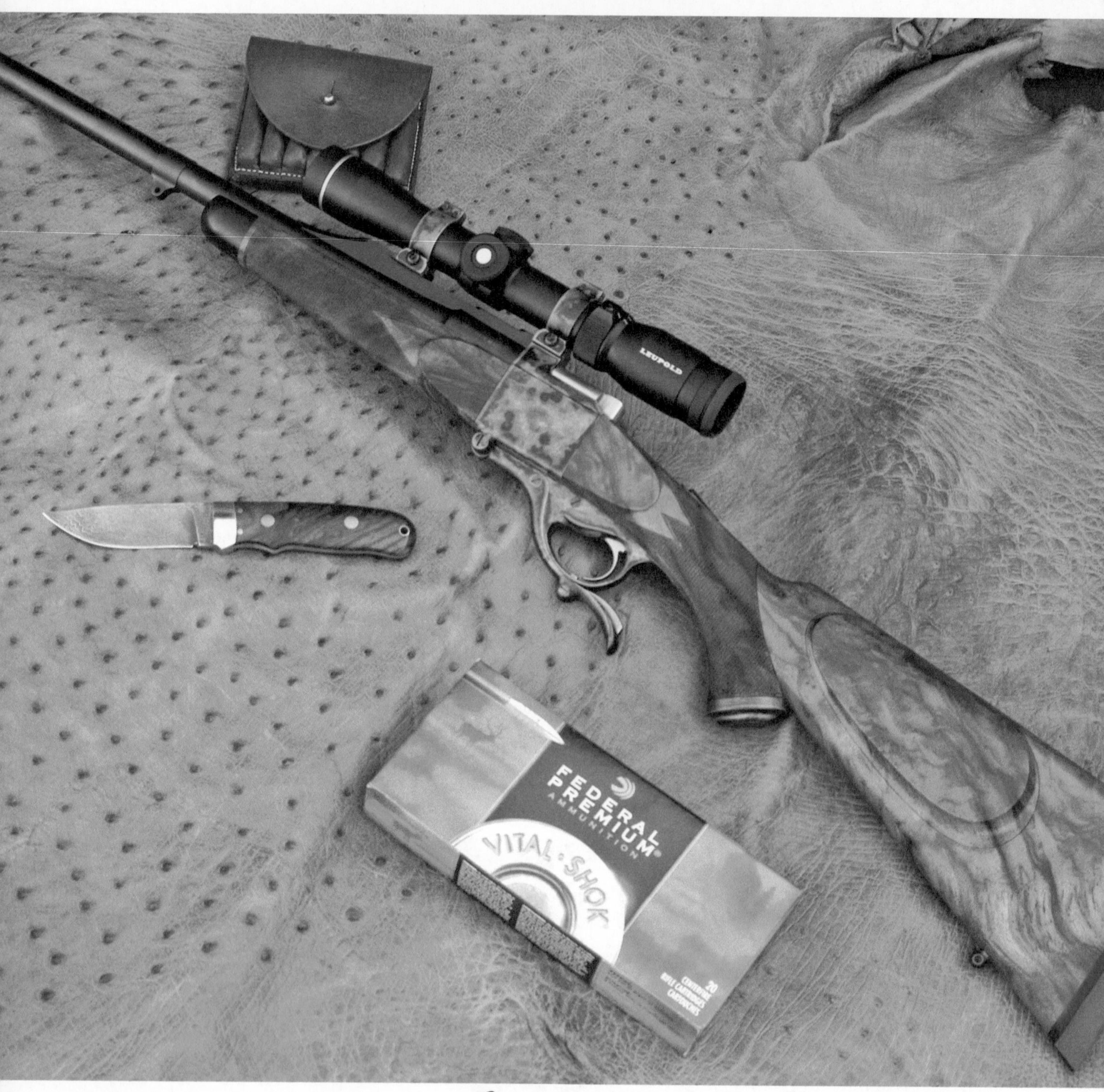

Glenn Soroka

This lovely rifle resulted from one man's vision and determination, along with his willingness and ability to devote the time and investment necessary to bring it to fruition. New Zealander **Glenn Soroka** was that man, and this Farquharson rifle is the result.

Glenn chose the Gibbs Farquharson as his model for styling and aesthetics, and, using modern technology and materials, improved the functional aspects of the rifle substantially. The resultant rifle is a wonderful example of the gunmaker's craft. It exemplifies the term "functional art," combining classic styling with state-of-the-art technology.

(Author Photos)

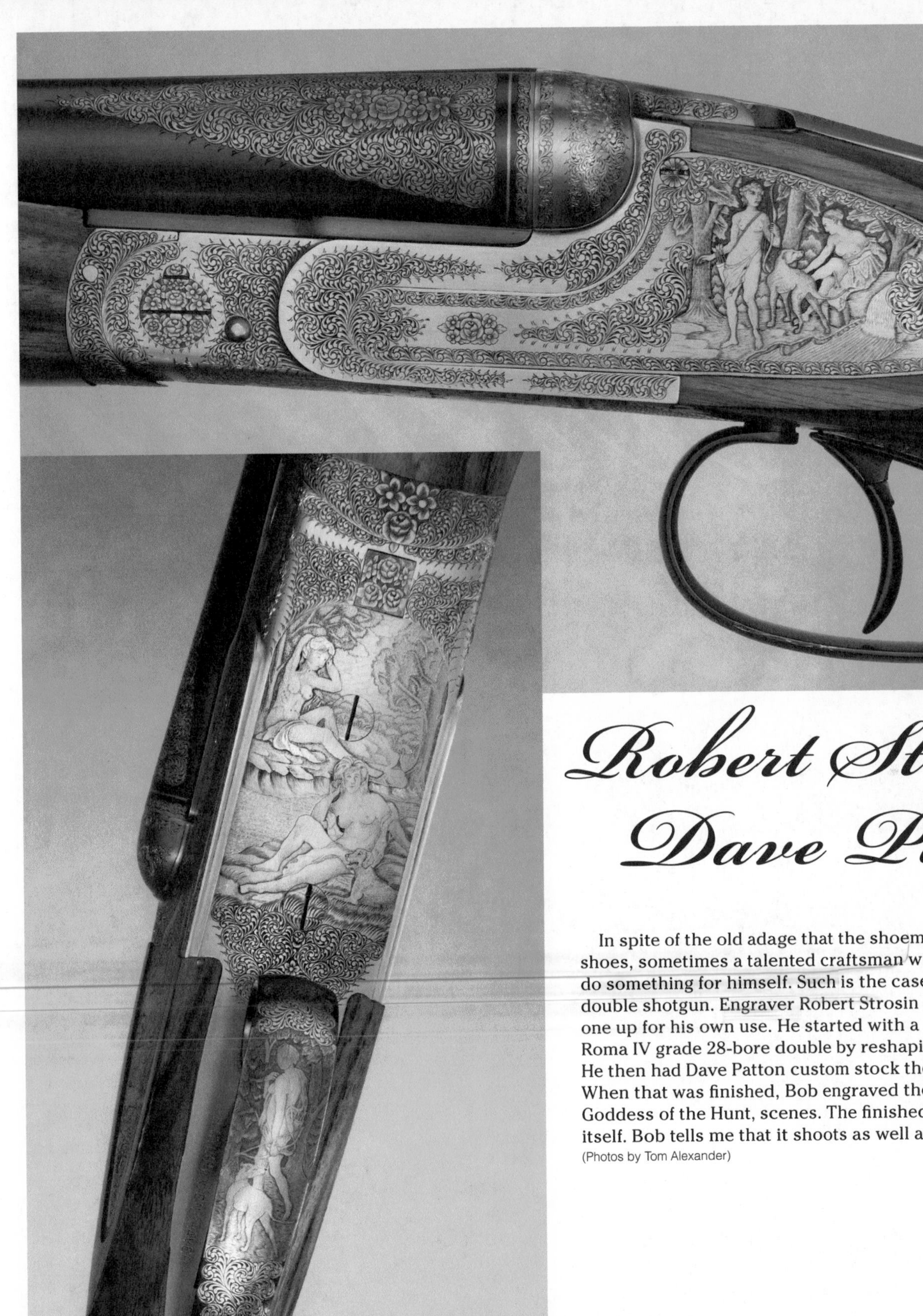

Robert Strosin
Dave Patton

In spite of the old adage that the shoemaker's kids have no shoes, sometimes a talented craftsman will take the time to do something for himself. Such is the case with this lovely double shotgun. Engraver Robert Strosin decided to do this one up for his own use. He started with a stock Bernadelli Roma IV grade 28-bore double by reshaping the action body. He then had Dave Patton custom stock the gun to his specs. When that was finished, Bob engraved the gun using Diana, Goddess of the Hunt, scenes. The finished product speaks for itself. Bob tells me that it shoots as well as it looks.

(Photos by Tom Alexander)

Great, Unsung Guns of England

More than Purdey

BY **TERRY WIELAND**

On January 3, 1880, a young London gun maker named Frederick Beesley left his home at 22 Queen Street, off the Edgware Road, and made his way to Her Majesty's patent office. He was carrying a packet of papers.

At the patent office, Beesley filed the provisional specifications for a mechanism he described as "a self opening hammerless gun." The patent application was assigned No. 31 for that year. Six months later, on July 2, Beesley signed the complete specification, and the next day it was filed in the Great Seal Patent Office.

None of those involved, even Beesley himself, could have had any notion that patent No. 1880/31 would become one of the most famous guns in history—a design so enduring it would still be in production more than 130 years later.

Had Beesley suspected, perhaps he would not have taken his patent to the shop of his old employer, James Purdey, and offered to sell it to him. But he did, and Purdey, searching at the time for a hammerless design worthy of his house, saw the possibilities. On July 29, 1880, he paid Beesley £55 for the rights to his design for 14 years. The first gun was completed later that same year—and to this day, Purdey has never made a "best" side-by-side to any other pattern.

Much has been made of the one-sided nature of this transaction. After all, Purdey made a fortune and, it could be argued, owes its continued survival to the excellence of this design. But Beesley benefited as well, and handsomely. In 1880, £55 was the price of a "best" gun from the finest house—or almost six

The Woodward "Automatic" (left) and the Lancaster "Wrist Breaker" were two of the most famous and widely used English shotgun actions of the late Victorian age.

As yet unrestored, this Gibbs & Pitt's gun, patented in 1873 and proofed with 2½-inch blackpowder cartridges, survived years of shooting with 2¾-inch heavy smokeless waterfowl loads, and was still perfectly tight. The original French walnut stock is gorgeous.

months wages for a skilled craftsman. Many years later, Beesley's granddaughters attested to the fact that the money allowed their grandfather to establish himself in the trade, to move eventually from the Edgware Road to St. James, and to become a significant competitor to his former employer.

In 1880, however, Frederick Beesley was just 33 years old, and both business and life were a struggle. A qualified gun maker who apprenticed with William Moore & Grey and later worked for James Purdey, among others, Beesley had been on his own for barely a year, when he perfected the design that became patent No. 31. He was already known as a skilled, perfectionist workman and a talented innovator, but these traits alone were not enough to get established in the intensely competitive world of London gunmaking.

Beesley was working from the Queen Street house, where he, his wife, and their two children shared the premises with more than a dozen other people. Although he started an order book of his own, in 1871, nine years later he had produced fewer than a hundred guns, and he was not getting rich.

Even at that time, Beesley's interest lay more in invention than production. As he later recounted, the inspiration for patent No. 31 came from studying the workings of John Stanton's rebounding lock, patented in 1867 and employed on the vast majority of hammer guns from that day forward. Stanton had recognized that the two arms of a V-spring had potential for use in more than one function in a mechanism. In his design, the longer arm propels the hammer forward, and the shorter one moves the hammer back from the striker to its half-cock position. In the transfer of tension from one arm to the other and back again, Frederick Beesley saw the basis for a revolutionary design, and so it proved to be. With it, Purdey has set the standard against which every other shotgun action, all over the world, has been measured ever since.

This 10-bore has had a hard century of life, but is still perfectly functional.

Below: W&C Scott guns were beautifully made. Their patented fore-end release, unique to Scott guns, is a work of art.

Significant as Beesley's design was, the history of the London gun neither begins nor ends with patent No. 31. But it did signal the end of a remarkable 30-year period that had revolutionized the world of shooting.

Histories of this period in gunmaking usually begin with the Great Exhibition of 1851, which is reasonable, because it was there that Casimir Lefaucheux displayed his break-action breechloader. That action led to Joseph Lang producing the first such London gun. But there is far more to it than that. Between 1840 and 1880, the planets aligned in an unprecedented way, revolutionizing the world of shooting, gunmaking, and English society itself.

In 1840, Queen Victoria married her cousin, the German Prince Albert. The Prince brought with him to England a passionate love of shooting. Since Waterloo, English aristocrats had been enthusiastic shooters, and many great estates were known for their grouse and partridge. Now, with royal imprimatur, enthusiasm for the pastime engulfed society. Happily, this coincided with the

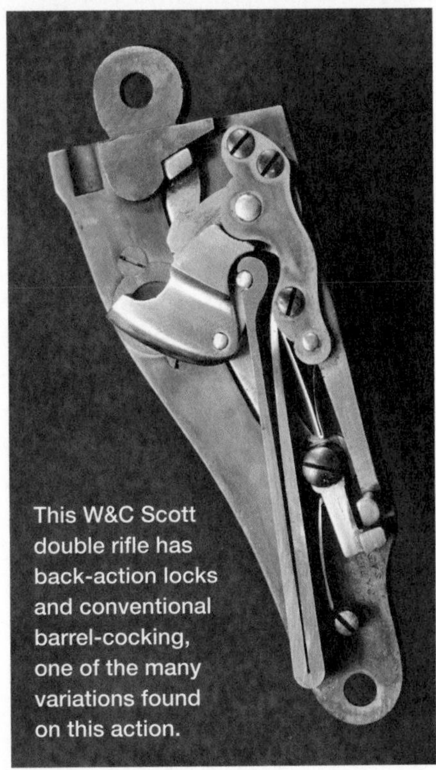

This W&C Scott double rifle has back-action locks and conventional barrel-cocking, one of the many variations found on this action.

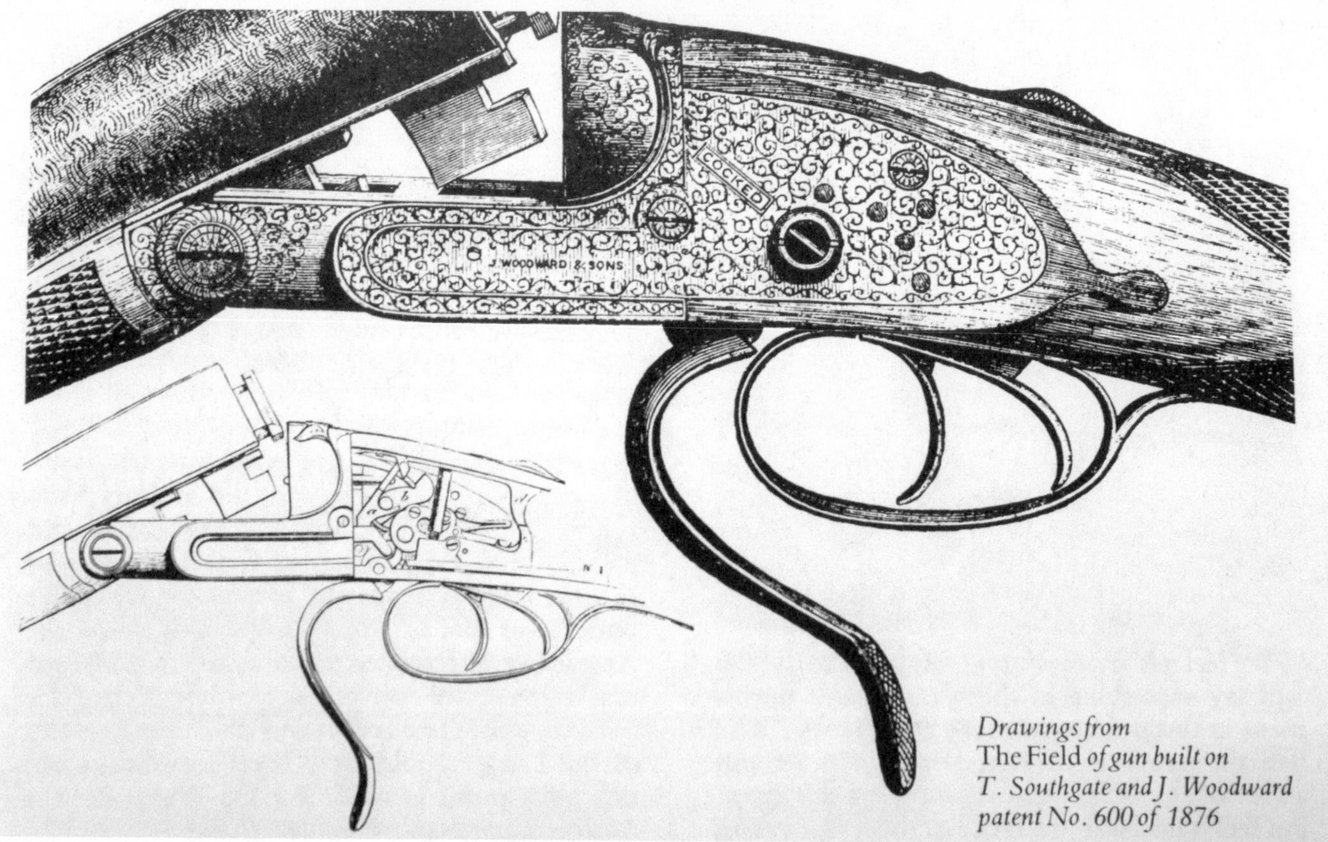

Original drawings of the Woodward "Automatic" from The Field, reproduced in The British Shotgun, (Vol. II, Crudgington & Baker).

expansion of railways, which allowed swift travel to distant points. Combined with the expansion of driven shooting, this made possible that great English institution, the shooting weekend. Even the Great Exhibition itself, where Lang first saw the Lefaucheux gun, can be laid at the feet of Prince Albert. The royal had a strong interest in industry and the arts, and the exhibition was both his idea and his creation.

The wealthy class had developed a lasting passion for shooting and demanded guns that were ever better and more finely made. In London, the Manton brothers had already fostered the principle that a gun should be a fine implement, not a crude tool. So, London attracted the most talented gun makers and inventors in the country, and they set about refining the basic break-action shotgun that Joseph Lang unveiled in 1853.

Between 1850 and 1880, guns evolved from percussion to pinfire to centerfire, from muzzleloader to breechloader, from hammers to hammerless, and from blackpowder to the first smokeless propellants. Never before or since has so much been accomplished in so short a period, and the impetus was competition and serious money.

The rise in driven shooting for grouse, partridge, and pheasant became practical only after the introduction of the self-contained cartridge. Once established, however, it became the driving force behind further improvements, encouraging gun makers to refine their products as they sought speed of use, efficiency of motion, and durability.

This quest for greater speed and convenience began as soon as the centerfire cartridge replaced the pinfire, in the early 1860s, and it was realized the centerfire hammer gun could be improved in a number of ways. One was to find a "snap" action for closing, in which the locking bolts would snap home on their own as the gun was closed, thereby eliminating the need for a separate motion by the shooter, such as pushing a lever back into position. Another was a means of cocking the hammers automatically as the gun was opened. A third was to find a way to eject empty cartridge cases, rather than having the shooter pick out the hulls manually.

Gun makers all over the country tackled these challenges. Through the 1860s, more than 100 patents were filed for different types of snap actions alone. Several makers realized that, with the move to centerfire cartridges, there was no longer any real need for external hammers. The entire mechanism could be moved inside the gun, protecting hammers and strikers from the elements. At the same time, it raised more questions: without a visible hammer, how was the shooter to know the gun was cocked? And, if it was cocked, what kind of safety mechanism would be needed to prevent accidental discharges?

Today, we look at a side-by-side shotgun and see what has become the standard form. The barrels pivot downward on a hinge pin. The movement of the barrels cocks the tumblers. Two underlugs on the barrels fit into a slot in the action and, when the barrels are closed, they are locked in place by a sliding bolt. This bolt is operated by a toplever connected to a spindle down through the frame. A double safety mechanism both blocks the triggers and prevents the tumblers from falling accidentally. Selective ejectors automatically expel fired hulls. All the features just described were invented and patented in England in the 1860s and '70s.

Although many credit William Anson and John Deeley, of Westley Richards in Birmingham, with inventing the first hammerless action (the Anson & Deeley

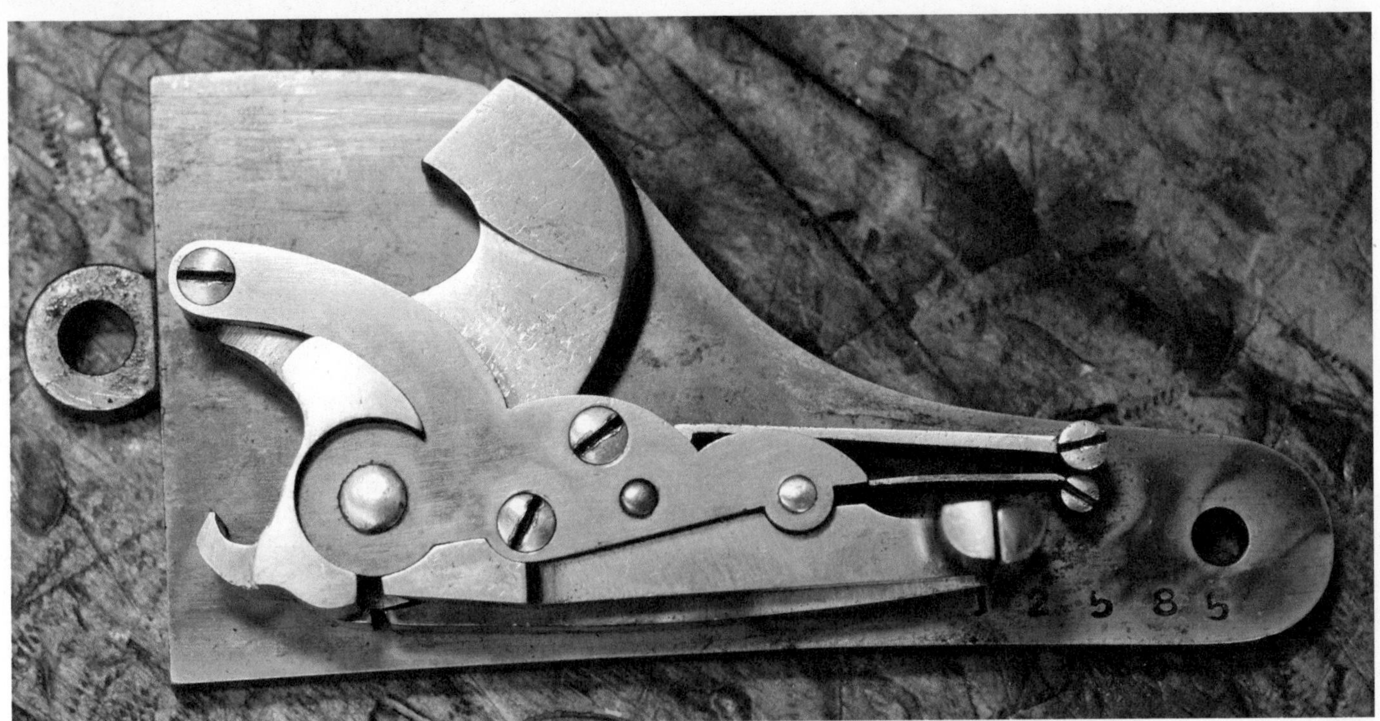

boxlock, in 1875) it was not the first, nor was it even the first really successful one (although, in terms of sheer numbers, it went on to become the dominant double-shotgun design of all time). By the 1870s, several gun makers were trying to create a true hammerless action. The major challenge was not to move the tumblers inside, but to find a means of cocking them.

Out of this period sprang four actions that achieved considerable success at the time and were made in sufficient numbers that we still find them for sale today. One was invented in Bristol, one in Birmingham, and two in London. One is, for lack of a better term, a boxlock, while another is a hybrid via a mechanism that can be married to either a boxlock or sidelock. They all have two common qualities. One, they were so good they were adopted and made, usually under license, by several companies. The second was that the guns themselves were so sound that many are still in use today. These actions are the Gibbs & Pitt's (Bristol, 1873), the W&C Scott (Birmingham, 1878), Woodward's Automatic (London, 1876), and the Lancaster "Wrist Breaker" (London, 1884). Each has a distinct place in the history of the development of the English shotgun, and that significance can best be understood by looking at them chronologically.

The idea of a hammerless (or internal hammer) gun can be traced back to the days of flintlocks, but the first success-

The interior of a Lancaster lock, seen here from the bottom and side, made to the first variation of the Wrist Breaker self-opening design, this one employing a V-spring instead of a straight leaf spring.

ful design for such a gun is generally acknowledged to be Theophilus Murcott's gun of 1871. Murcott was a successful London gun maker, and his design employed internal tumblers with a push-forward underlever to cock them.

Two years later, in Bristol, rifle maker George Gibbs and his partner, Thomas Pitt, designed another lever-operated action, this one with the mechanism on the trigger plate. Gibbs was a well-known gun maker who worked closely with William Metford, and his products were highly respected throughout the country. Other gun makers—including James Purdey—marketed guns and rifles built on the Gibbs & Pitt's patent. (In 1875, Anson and Deeley designed the boxlock that became the world standard for such guns, and though it cut into the Gibbs & Pitt's market, it did not eliminate it.)

We go now to London, where the famous firm of J. Woodward & Sons was also tackling the question of hammerless guns. James Woodward apprenticed with Charles Moore, an established London gun maker of high reputation. Eventually, the company became Moore & Woodward, and then, in 1872, J. Woodward & Sons. The company was known for making the finest of guns, in a class with Purdey and Boss, and was also very inventive.

The Lancaster is distinguished by its leg-of-mutton lock plates and rounded frame. It is an ergonomic delight, in spite of its Wrist Breaker nickname.

In 1876, Woodward filed patent No. 600, in conjunction with Thomas Southgate, for a mechanism employing a push-forward underlever that would both unlock the barrels and automatically cock the external hammers of a conventional gun. They called this the "Automaton" or "Automatic"—probably the first use of that word in connection with firearms.

For Woodward to make a hammerless gun, it was a simple matter to move the tumblers inside the lock plates and use the same mechanism to cock them, which it did. The company launched a major advertising campaign in the periodicals of the day, licensed their design to other gun makers, and made guns on which other makers put their names. The "Automatic" became Woodward's entry in the hammerless race, and was used for both shotguns and rifles.

In Birmingham, W&C Scott, one of the largest, most famous, and certainly among the finest English gun makers, was also looking for a hammerless design. The firm decided to use the fall of the barrels as the cocking mechanism. There was also concern as to how the shooter would know the gun was cocked, and Scott resolved that with its patented "crystal indicator," a small glass porthole through which could be seen the cocked tumbler. This, together with its distinctive lock plate, made the Scott instantly recognizable.

The action became known as the "Classic Scott" and was, again, licensed and marketed under other names. The most famous user was Holland & Holland, which marketed it as the "Climax." So famous did H&H later become that many today think it was that firm that invented it.

By 1881, all of these designs were in production. Some were produced to exclusive patents, others were made under license, or the patentees manufactured guns on which other gun makers put their names. But, the one thing the English gun trade was lacking was a generic design available to all. In 1881, the Rogers brothers of Birmingham solved that problem.

The Rogers brothers were actioners who, in effect, rescued smaller gun makers by patenting an action that eventually became the standard design for members of the trade who lacked one of their own. The Rogers action is the

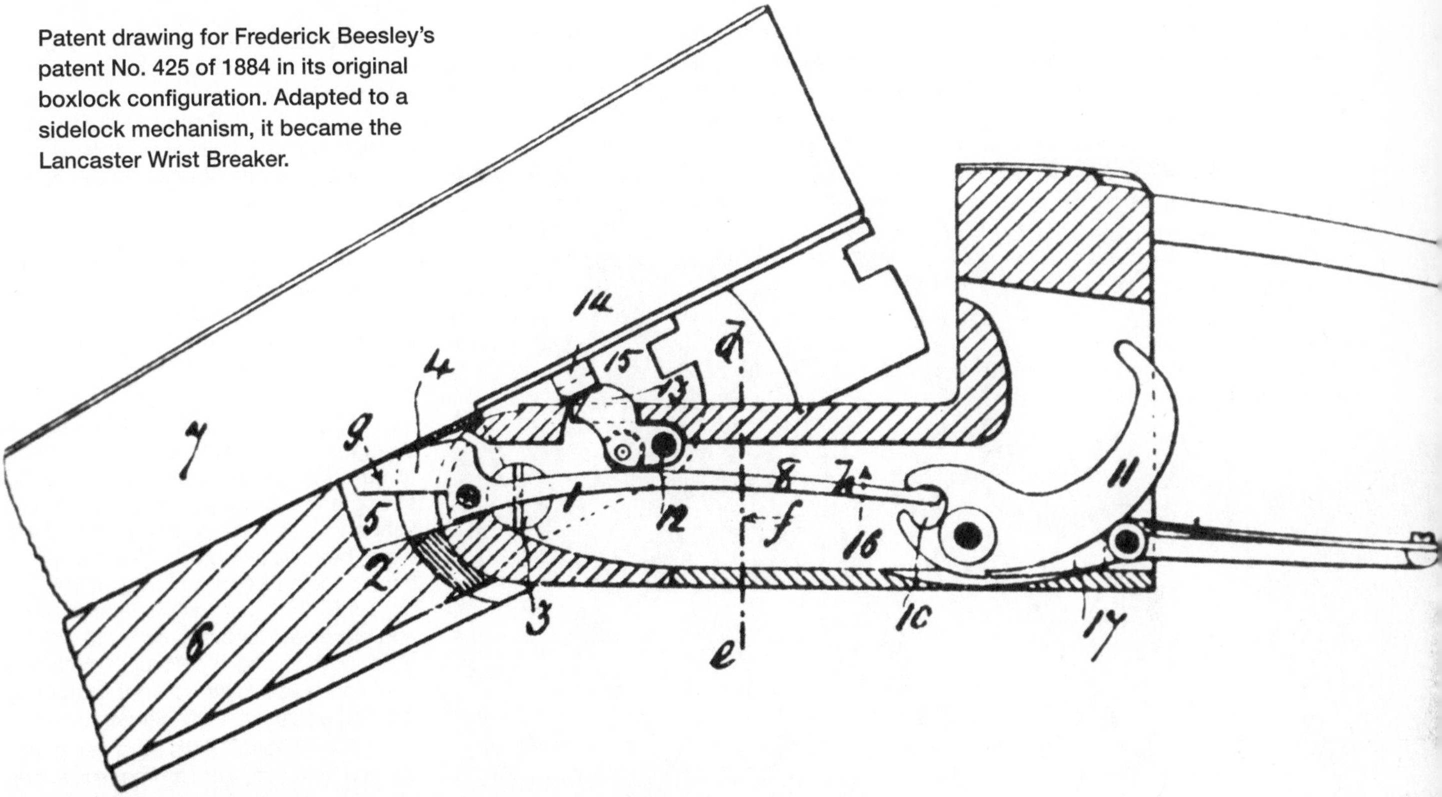

Patent drawing for Frederick Beesley's patent No. 425 of 1884 in its original boxlock configuration. Adapted to a sidelock mechanism, it became the Lancaster Wrist Breaker.

most commonly found, and imitated, of all the English sidelock designs, yet is virtually unknown by its real name. The immediately recognizable characteristic of the Rogers is the cocking levers that protrude from the knuckle of the frame. Frederick Beesley, having sold patent No. 31 to Purdey, was on his way to becoming "inventor to the London trade," as he is now remembered. When he died in 1928, Beesley had 25 patents to his name of which, undoubtedly, the Purdey is the most famous. But it is not the best.

Although Beesley's shop window at 2 St. James's Street proclaimed him "inventor and patentee of Purdey's hammerless gun," he himself believed it could be improved upon, and he set out to do so.

In 1884, Beesley filed another patent, this one No. 425. Like most English patents, the description is deliberately vague, intended that way to put rivals off the scent. But it describes an ingenious mechanism that employs a single leaf spring to perform three distinct and vital functions: cocking the tumbler, powering it forward, and then opening the action.

Beesley considered this a significant refinement of the principle used in the Purdey patent—it was simpler, stronger, and it did more with less. It was a mechanism that could be adapted to either boxlock or sidelock, and, indeed, the initial patent filing describes it as a boxlock. Although Beesley made some guns to the patent, the majority were manufactured by Charles Lancaster, where it became famous as the "Wrist Breaker," so called because of the resistance in closing it against spring pressure. Lancaster was one of London's oldest, largest, and most prestigious firms, and it used the action in thousands of shotguns and rifles.

With the filing of patent No. 425, the only major action yet to appear was the Holland & Holland "Royal," in 1885. In a remarkable 15-year period, between the appearance of "Murcott's Mousetrap," in 1871, and the Lancaster "Wrist Breaker" in 1884, the English shotgun had evolved into the form we know today.

The Gibbs and Pitt's Action

The Gibbs & Pitt's action was invented by George Gibbs and Thomas Pitt of Bristol, and patented in 1873, two years after Murcott's first hammerless design, and two years before the Anson & Deeley. Like the Murcott, it was a lever-cocked design that could be adapted to a variety of lock mechanisms, of which the most commonly seen is a trigger-plate lock that protrudes from the action forward of the trigger guard. The Gibbs & Pitt's is very strong, and it was employed in both rifles and shotguns. Donald Dallas, who has studied the history of the English gun trade and written several books on the subject, estimates 10,000 guns were made to this pattern.

James Purdey is known to have used the Gibbs and Pitt's action, among others, during the brief period between the appearance of the hammerless gun and Purdey's adoption of the Beesley self-opener, in 1880.

Although the Gibbs & Pitt's appears strange to our eyes today, with its unusual frame and under-hung lock, it is both strong and dependable and makes into a light and well balanced gun. Gibbs' guns were beautifully made. The gun shown here is original condition, at least 125 years old, and although it has 2½-inch chambers and blackpowder proof, survived a lifetime of shooting heavy 2¾-inch smokeless duck loads and is still as tight as the day it left Gibbs' shop in Corn Street.

The Gibbs & Pitt's was designed in the very early days of hammerless actions, when gunmakers were experimenting with a variety of approaches for cocking mechanisms and safety catches. The early models used underlevers, but later examples are seen with toplevers.

An early model Gibbs & Pitt's 12-bore shotgun with underlever cocking and trigger plate lock. This is a very strong and durable action that was used on both shotguns and rifles. The T-shaped wooden plug indicates that it was originally built with the very early side safety, then replaced with the more reliable swinging lever.

Gibbs & Pitt's actions were beautifully made. The patent emblem indicates a gun made by Gibbs, not under license by another maker.

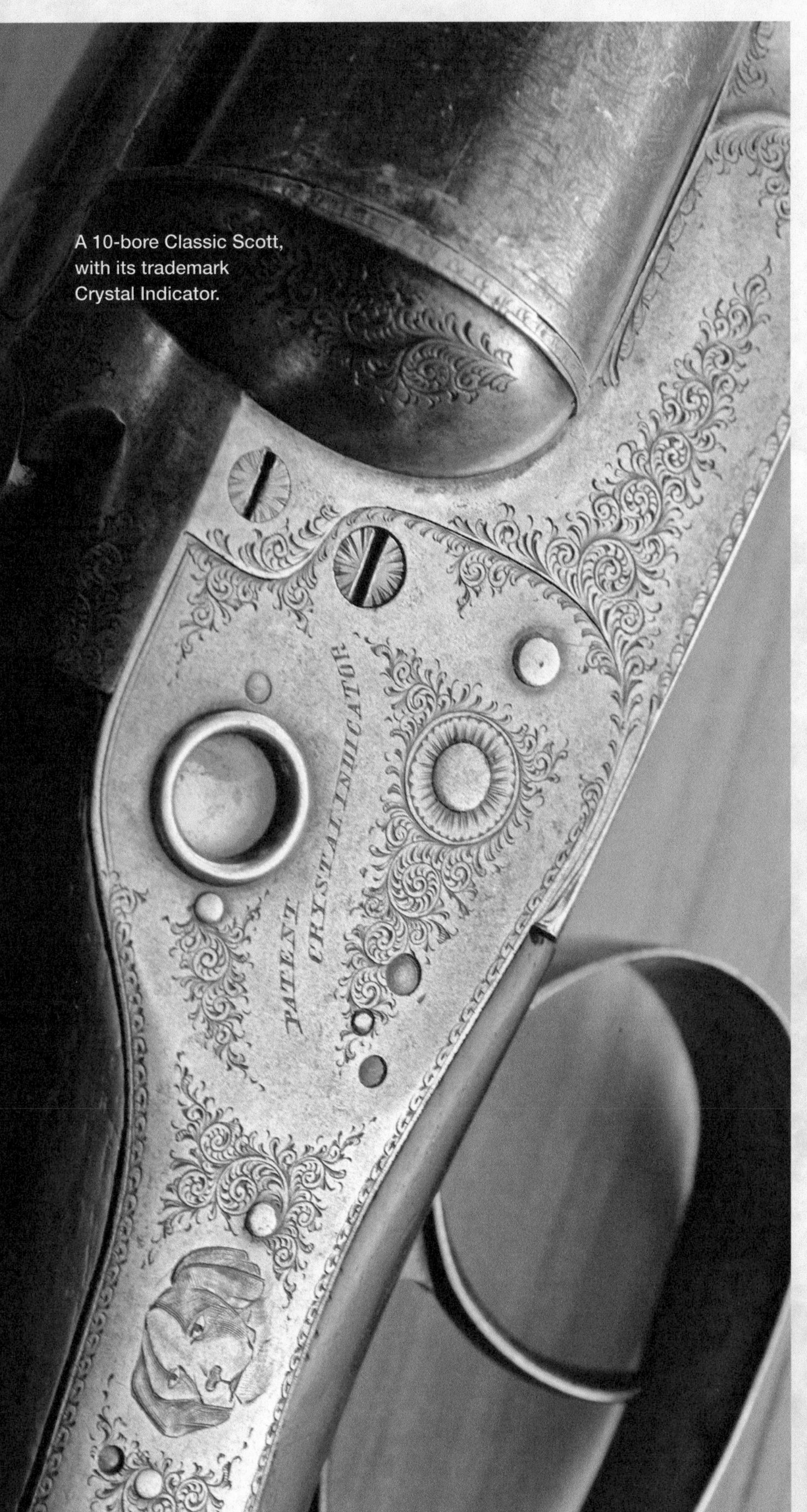

A 10-bore Classic Scott, with its trademark Crystal Indicator.

The Classic Scott

W&C Scott & Sons was one of the largest and best gunmakers in Birmingham. A son, William Middleditch Scott, patented the Scott spindle that, married to Purdey's double underlug, became the standard bolting mechanism for double guns to this day. Purdey held the license for the combination in London, and Scott in Birmingham, profitting both greatly.

In 1878, Scott patented the action that became known as the "Classic Scott," most famous as Holland's "Climax." So well-known did the Climax become, many today think it was H&H's patent.

W&C Scott worked closely with Holland in the years before H&H built its London factory on Harrow Road (1893), and most of Holland's guns and rifles came from Scott's, to be finished in London.The Scott name is better known abroad than in England, where it mainly supplied guns and rifles to the trade for others (like H&H) to engrave with their own name. In the U.S., however, the Scott name became very well known. Captain Adam Bogardus was a particular admirer of Scott guns, and thousands were exported to the U.S.

The Classic Scott is recognizable by a number of features, including the distinctive lock-plate shape and the small glass porthole (crystal indicator) that allows the shooter to see whether the tumbler is cocked. The action is cocked by the falling of the barrels, and Scott tried a number of approaches to this. The best known employs a hook on each side that fit into slots in the action flats. As the barrels drop, the hooks pull the cocking rod forward, pivoting the tumbler back. In one variation, there are coil springs around the rods, which then power the tumbler forward.

Because of the distinctive shape, the Classic Scott is usually described as a "back action" sidelock (meaning the spring is behind the tumbler, rather than in the bar of the action), but this is not necessarily the case.

Donald Dallas describes the Classic Scott as "beautifully made." They are also strong and reliable and are seen on all types of guns, from smallbore double rifles up to massive 8-gauge shotguns.

W&C Scott merged with Philip Webley, in 1897, to become Webley & Scott. In the years that followed, the Scott name was put on the firm's fine doubles. When the company fell on hard times, after 1945, W&C Scott was divested, then later acquired, ironically, by Holland & Holland. The Classic Scott can be found with many different names engraved on the locks, but all were made by Scott'. They are fine and under-appreciated guns.

Woodward's Automatic

James Woodward & Sons was in the absolute top echelon of London gunmakers, mentioned in the same breath as Purdey and Boss. James the elder learned the trade with Charles Moore, brought his sons James and Charles into the business, and became J. Woodward & Sons, in 1872.

Although it remained a small family firm for its 80-year existence (it was absorbed by Purdey in 1948, the only company Purdey ever acquired), the Woodwards were inventors, as well as the finest of gunmakers.

In 1876, James the younger collaborated with the well-known inventor Thomas Southgate to patent an underlever cocking action for hammer guns, called the "Automaton." This mechanism (patent No. 600) was easily adapted to a hammerless sidelock with tumblers and, as such, was called "The Automatic." It was widely advertised, and the name is engraved on the rib near the standing breech. Woodward made a specialty of underlever guns, employing several types from the swiveling Jones underlever to push-forward "snap action" underlevers and the tumbler-cocking snap underlever of the Automatic.

Traditionally, Woodward's main rival in the trade was Boss & Co., which favored sidelevers, until the firm was acquired by John Robertson, in 1892. Robertson not only refined Boss' game guns, he invented the Boss over/under and selective single trigger. Woodward followed suit with an over/under and single trigger of its own and, today, the Woodward over/under is widely considered the finest ever made. Purdey's major motive for buying Woodward, in 1948, was to obtain the over/under design for themselves.

Although the quality of its guns was never questioned, the Woodwards were known for being somewhat iconoclastic. The firm favored 29-inch barrels, while others made theirs 30 inches. Woodwards featured half-pistol hands, when others insisted on straight grips, and their walnut was known for its flair. Among engraving patterns, the Woodward craftsmen preferred tiny scroll, and the arcaded (umbrella-carved) fence became almost a trademark of them, as did protruding tumbler pivots on their lock plates.

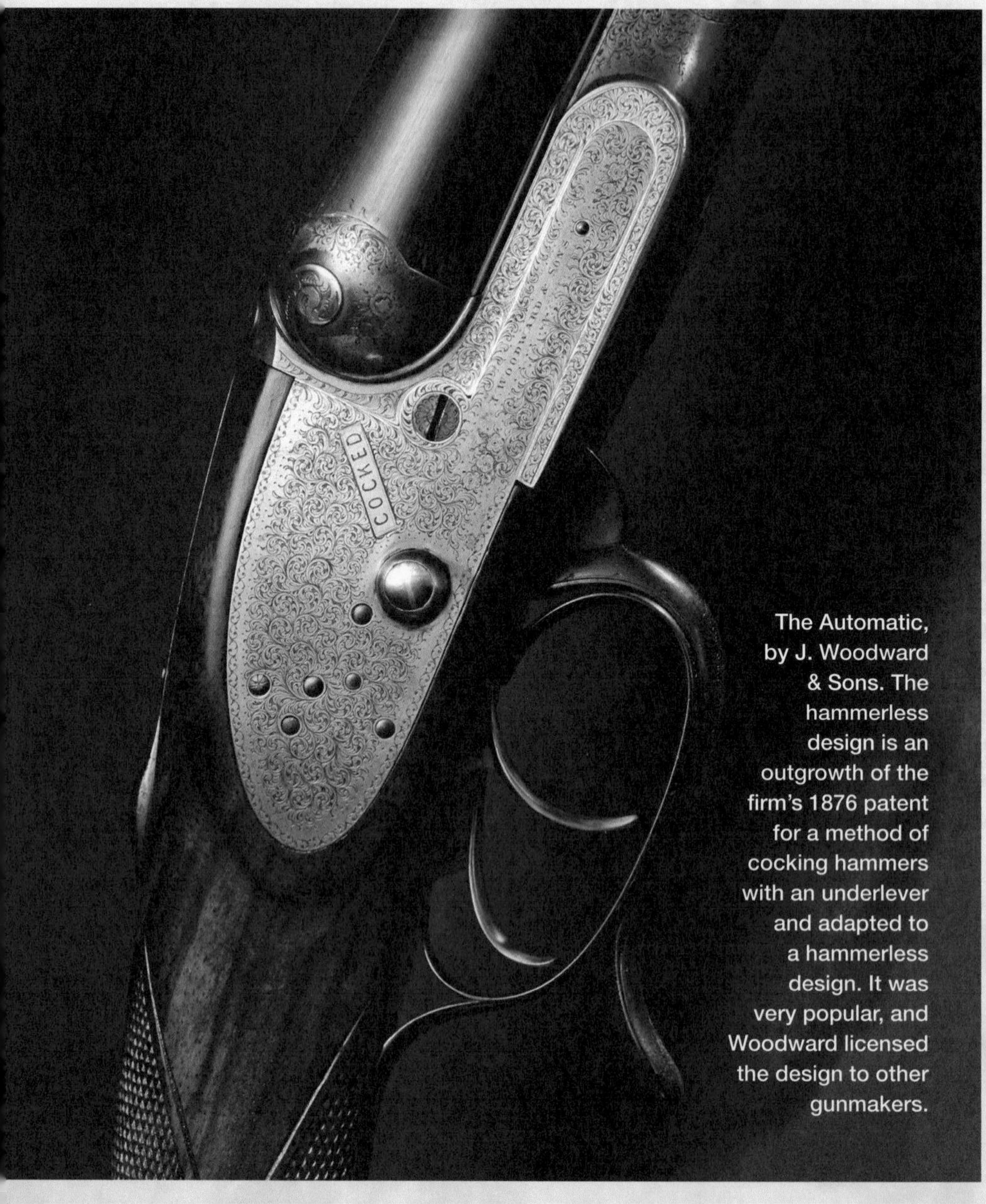

The Automatic became very well known and popular in the 1880s. Woodward's not only used the action for its own guns and rifles, it also made guns for the trade. Donald Dallas states that the action can be found with many different makers' names, and there is at least one that was made for John Dickson & Co. of Edinburgh, the famous Scottish maker, engraved in a typically Scottish pattern.

For many years, Woodward Automatics went begging on the used-gun market, but it is a fine action and extremely well made. Any Automatic, regardless of name, was built by Woodward's and offers an opportunity to own a London best at a price far below those demanded for a Boss or Purdey.

There were other Woodwards in the trade, including two in Birmingham, and one must be careful. As well, J. Woodward's output was not large—only about 5,000 guns and rifles over an 80-year period—and most were purchased by serious shooters who knew guns. As such, they were put to hard use. Steve Denny, a director of Holland & Holland, says he has seen many "tired old Woodwards" over the years, and many have been either rebarreled or sleeved.

Conversely, there are many Purdeys that were purchased for the name, by men who shot relatively little, and are in very fine condition even after many years. Purdey has the Woodward records, offers Woodward guns once again in both over/under and side-by-side configurations (although not the Automatic), and a Woodward owner becomes part of the worldwide Purdey clan. Examining a gun from J. Woodward & Sons shows you what gunmaking can be.

The Automatic, by J. Woodward & Sons. The hammerless design is an outgrowth of the firm's 1876 patent for a method of cocking hammers with an underlever and adapted to a hammerless design. It was very popular, and Woodward licensed the design to other gunmakers.

Lancaster's Wrist Breaker

By 1884, James Purdey was building almost as many hammerless as hammer guns, all of them on Beesley's 1881 patent. And though the Beesley/Purdey design was on its way to immortality, Frederick Beesley wasn't satisfied. Almost immediately, he began work on a further refined self-opening action that he patented in 1884, No. 425 for that year.

In the patent application, the action is described as a boxlock, but in fact it was so versatile that it could be made with various configurations of locks and tumblers. Most that exist today have a sidelock, but not one that can be readily described as either back-action or bar-action.

The heart of the design is a strong leaf mainspring that runs through the action bar and protrudes from the knuckle. This spring performs three functions. In one, the spring propels the tumbler forward to fire the gun. In the second, when the barrels are unbolted, the center of the spring pushes upward on a cam against the barrel flat, pushing the gun open. And, in the third, as the barrels pivot down, they press on the protruding end of the spring, levering the tumbler back into its cocked position. When the gun is closed, the two cams in the barrel flats press down through the action flats, bearing on the spring and increasing its tension to give it maximum power to propel the tumblers forward once again.

This action has several intrinsic advantages. First, when the gun is open or dismantled, the spring is at rest, so there is no need to relieve it. Second, it has the hidden advantage of a self-opener, which only becomes apparent now, after a century of experience. Self-opening guns outlast others that, though they may have been equal quality when built, have not stood up as well. This is because the constant tension applied on the action by the self-opening mechanism keeps the gun from gradually developing play among its moving parts and eventually shooting loose.

Lancaster's Wrist Breaker, built to Frederick Beesley's 1884 patent. Although found with several variations of springs and locks, the lock plates have the distinctive Lancaster "leg of mutton" shape. As a result, they are often erroneously described as back-action locks.

Beesley began licensing his new design to other gunmakers, the most prominent of which was Charles Lancaster. In 1884, Lancaster was one of London's oldest, largest, and finest gunmakers. The first Charles Lancaster had been Joseph Manton's barrelmaker, before going out on his own, in 1826. By 1884, the company was owned by H.A.A. Thorn, himself a talented inventor and gunmaker and a superb businessman. Beesley licensed his design to Thorn, and it became the Lancaster "Wrist Breaker," so called because of the supposed difficulty in closing it.

From 1884 until the early 1920s, Lancaster used Beesley's design for its "best" guns and rifles. That design is mainly known by its distinctive "leg of mutton" lockplate, which often leads to its being (sometimes inaccurately) described as a back-action. Another interesting feature is the shape of the frame. It was the first "rounded action" of the type later made famous by John Robertson on the Boss guns.

There are probably more variations on this gun than any other, with at least five known to exist. One variation, the most common, substitutes a V-spring for the leaf, with one arm cocking the tumbler and opening the gun, and the other arm propelling the tumbler forward. When the craze for detachable locks struck London, in the early 1900s, Lancaster redesigned the lock, turning it into a conventional back-action sidelock with a detachable feature for those who wanted it.

Around 1911, as costs rose, Lancaster began offering a sidelock of more conventional appearance, one built on the Rogers action, as its less expensive, second-quality gun. After the Great War, Beesley's design was discontinued, the Rogers became the "best" gun, and, today, Lancasters with more "modern" lock plates command higher prices than the Beesley.

Frederick Beesley considered patent No. 425 superior to the Purdey and built some guns on it himself, as well as licensing it to Lancaster and others. Lancaster made several thousand, and these are the guns most commonly seen today. A specimen in good condition is a superb example of London gunmaking.

The author's custom-made .280 Ackley Improved was built on the CZ 550 action, fitted with a Montana Rifleman barrel, and decked out with a nice, heavy piece of English walnut. The barrel band swivel was intended to give it a European "safari-style" flair.

My love affair with the custom rifle began like most love affairs do—unexpectedly. The inspiration for the gun came from a lifelong desire to hunt the West, with mule deer being of particular interest. I don't know what triggered this fantasy, but I blame the writings of Jack O' Connor, Elmer Keith, and those crusty old editors from *Gun Digest* editions of old.

At any rate, the project gun was to be a wedding gift from my soon-to-be wife. To seal the deal, I simply had to tell the gunsmith what I wanted, and then face the pastor to mutter the two most dangerous words known to man: "I do."

Sounded simple enough. And it should have been, except for one teensy detail. When you mix together custom guns, a gunsmith of questionable character, and a woman, well, you're bound to end up with something akin to mixing open flame with a barrel of jet fuel. My vision for the gun was to make it of European styling, something that would pass as a "safari" gun. It would be chambered to handle medium-sized big game with authority—from whitetail deer to elk—yet still capable of taking nastier critters like bears and Russian boar.

There's one more thing it had to be, and that was nice. I don't like mean guns. Getting kicked in the shoulder every time the trigger is pulled is not particularly enjoyable. So this rifle and I had a prenuptial agreement of sorts from the get-go. I'd keep her well oiled, fed with good ammo, and shot often enough so as not to leave her feeling neglected. In return, she would be my little Southern belle of guns, sweet and soft spoken, a real lady. That meant that a sharp-recoiling gun was out of the question, and from that moment on, I decided I liked my guns on the heavy side.

Now, no one can complicate the simple like me. I can turn a trivial little matter like choosing a rifle caliber into a federal case like nobody's business. Thus, the gears in my head began to sputter thick black smoke the minute the gunsmith suggested we chamber it in something called the .280 Ackley Improved (AI), which was, allegedly, "one sweet-shooting cartridge." He explained how one would shoot .280 Remingtons in the gun, which would fireform the case to the shape and size of the Ackley chamber. One would then reload the cases, the goal being to squeeze more velocity out of it.

FALLING IN LOVE WITH THE .280 ACKLEY

BY COREY GRAFF

P.O. Ackley gave the world—both wildcatters and average shooters alike—a 7mm to love, with his .280 Ackley Improved. All these years later it's still one of the most versatile big-game hunting cartridges ever conceived.

I was intrigued. But, in hindsight, I was wading in over my suspenders. Heck, I didn't know the name P.O. Ackley from Elmer Fudd. And I sure wasn't inclined to venture into the unknown world of wildcat cartridges. At the time, I figured I simply needed a deer rifle. And, at that stage in my life, I hadn't even begun to handload. To make matters worse, the concept of an Improved cartridge was as foreign to me as the institution of marriage is to a guy living in his mom's basement. Those were the good ol' days, and ignorance was bliss.

As far as gun lovers go, I was a hopeless romantic. Desperately clinging to a dream inspired by 1950s-era gun literature, yours truly was a real true-blue flatlander. I'd read stories about Western hunting guides who would joke about Midwesterners, claiming they all possessed "flat-shooting belted magnums and couldn't hit the broadside of a barn." I was determined, by golly, not to be one of them.

If this .280 Ackley Improved was indeed everything it was cracked up to be, I could sure get used to it. I was schooled as a machinist, so working with precision instruments didn't concern me, and learning how to reload wasn't a problem. Come hell or high water, I was determined to carry the vision into the realm of the absurd, if needed, driven onward by visions of wide-racked mulies prancing through high mountain meadows. My guiding light became the maxim, "Beware the man with one gun, as he surely knows how to use it."

The harsh realities of life had not yet dashed my hopes and dreams to dust, so bring it on, I told the gunsmith. That's how warm and fuzzy things looked through my rose-colored glasses, and the gun project was underway.

The author took this Wisconsin whitetail using his .280 AI custom rifle, shooting Nosler Custom ammunition, the 140-grain Accubond .280 Ackley factory-loaded ammunition. The shot was about 175 yards, which is a long poke for a Wisconsin woodland hunt.

Mr. Ackley and His Wildcats

In the 69-year history of the *Gun Digest*, I find three feature stories published about Mr. Ackley and his wildcats. They include, "The Extraordinary P.O. Ackley ... The Gunsmith Who Showed Them How" (1985 Edition), "P.O. Ackley's Wildcats" (1996 Edition), and "Modernizing the .30-30—The .30-30 Ackley Improved" (2004 Edition). There was also a story in the 1962 edition contributed by the man himself and entitled "Are Wildcats Dead?" And speaking of 1962, it must have been a banner year for the Trinidad, Colorado, gunsmith. That's when

Turning the contour on one of his barrels, P.O. Ackley looks up from his lathe at P.O. Ackley, Inc., in February, 1950. From Gun Digest 1985.

P.O. Ackley looks on, and perhaps kibitzes a bit, while Florence Conti operates a deep-hole drill. She will turn that bar into a famous Ackley rifle barrel, in the Salt Lake City shop, circa 1977. From Gun Digest 1985.

his *Handbook for Shooters & Reloaders, Volume I* was published. (In 1969 he would publish *Volume II*.)

Parker Otto Ackley (1903-1989), originally of Granville, New York, and known simply as "Pee-Oh" to close friends, possessed a spirit of real ingenuity—the kind that made World War II's "Greatest Generation" great. After graduating *magna cum laude* from Syracuse University, in 1927, with a major in agriculture, he gave farming an honest go. He reportedly grew "some of the finest potatoes in the country." But taters weren't going to cut the mustard. Fine as they may have been, the Great Depression was no time to launch a new farming venture. With a young family in tow, it had become apparent a change was needed.

An ad appearing in the classified section of the *American Rifleman* by Ross C. King caught Ackley's eye. King was selling his Roseburg, Oregon, gunsmith shop lock, stock, and barrel for a cool $2,000. It was 1936. Soon the wife and children were packed like sardines into the Oldsmobile and heading west-northwest lickity split.

It was in his newly purchased business that Ackley found his niche and began making ends meet by repairing the locals' guns. But he was a tinkerer at heart. Long believing there was a market for high-end barrel making and admiring a Cincinnati barrel maker by the name of Ben Hawkins, who had been turning gun tubes for nearly 50 years by then, Ackley initiated some correspondence. It wasn't long before Hawkins extended an invite to give Ackley some training. Putting his local business on hold, Ackley raced back east and apprenticed under Hawkins' master barrel maker, a German man who'd learned his trade in the Motherland. During his time in Cincinnati, P.O. fine-tuned his skills, learning how to turn, bore, rifle, and ream from one of the best. It proved to be time well spent.

Ackley would later work a stint at the Ogden Ordnance Department, as part of the war effort. Then, following yet another move, this time to Trinidad, Colorado, he started the P.O. Ackley and Company plant. The shop quickly became known for its high-quality barrels and custom gunsmithing services, where one of P.O.'s trademarks was sharing his knowledge with gun owners. He made a name for himself in the gun industry and, over time, received thousands of letters. He personally responded to most of them.

Ackley must have been a real workhorse, because he also found time

This image appeared in Robert Lucas's 1996 *Gun Digest* article, "P.O. Ackley's Wildcats." The caption read, "These five Ackley's are on RCBS' 'most popular dies' list—.257 Roberts, .22-250, .280, .30-06, and .35 Whelen, all Improved. "

to write on the editorial staff of *Guns & Ammo, Shooting Times* and even, as mentioned above, *Gun Digest*. In addition, from 1946 through 1951, he taught as an instructor at Trinidad State Junior College, where he had a chance to experiment with firearms. This lead to some interesting research into a phenomenon known as "detonation," whereby—as Jack O' Connor and Ackley argued against the protests of the editors at *American Rifleman*—reduced loads were responsible for damaged guns. The pair posited that the reduced load would fail to expel the projectile, and then the powder charge would then get hung up mid-barrel, ignite, and cause one doozy of an explosion, giving the gun and the poor sap who pulled the trigger a very bad day.

This work would largely cater to opinions that put him crossways with the marketing hype of corporate types in the gun industry. It also provided the ultimate excuse to tinker with guns and loads. That experience formed a foundation on which he later developed his many wildcat and Improved cartridges.

P.O. ultimately developed 62 wildcats, his first being the .30-06 Ackley Improved. Of those 62, 19 were true Improved cartridges, by definition made via the fireforming process (explained below). But, there was much controversy as to who developed the first Improved cartridge. During the 1930s, modern gunsmithing underwent a rapid sea change, thanks to a rush of new talent. In fact, Elmer Keith claimed there were gunsmiths fireforming many of these cartridges 20 years before Ackley ever did.

The .280 Ackley Improved—One for All Shooters

In *Are Wildcats Dead?*, Ackley lived up to his reputation as a humble and fiercely objective reporter. He argued that factory ammunition had, by that time, gotten so good that, "This has removed the need for numerous wildcats, including some of the better ones." If Ackley was looking for self-gratification or fame based on his designs—much of which he later credited to wildcatters that had gone before him, such as renowned gunsmith Art Mashburn—this would have been the place to do it. Instead, he informs that, "Since the advent of the .280 Remington, which amounts to little more than a 7mm-06 or .285 OKH, there is no longer much place for 7mm wildcats other than the Imp. 7X57."

This amazing statement is classic Ackley—uninhibited modesty. The truth is, as pointed out by author Rob Lucas in *P.O. Ackley's Wildcats* (1996), the .280 Ackley Improved is indeed a class act unto itself, because it can be loaded nearly into the same ballistic class as the 7mm Remington Magnum. However, the .280 AI burns less powder, recoils less, yields theoretically longer barrel and case life, and is generally much nicer to shoot. Certainly any rational shooter would take these as improvements. Lucas even compares it to one of the hottest 7mm wildcats of the day, the 7mm STW.

"Ask yourself if 3,500 fps (sometimes), with a 140-grain bullet in a necked-down 8mm Remington belted case, is all that much better than 3,300 fps from the '06-sized .280 Remington Improved,'" he wrote. "The .280 Ackley Improved is now No. 10 on RCBS' current list of most popular wildcat dies sold, and it will climb that number because I intend to have one!"

But let's back up. This is not a technical article for wildcatters. I respect them, but I'm not one. In fact, the moment

Here's the .308 family, all with the 40-degree Ackley shoulder. (from left): .243 Winchester, 7mm-08, .308, and .338-08, all Improved. At center, 7mm-08 standard.

From Gun Digest 1996.

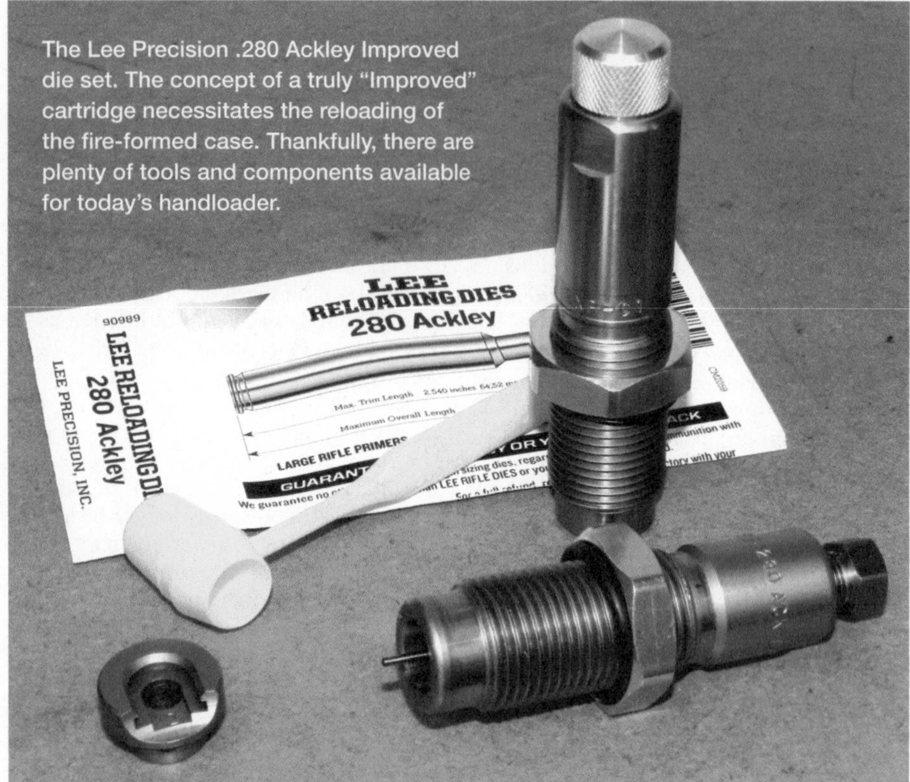

The Lee Precision .280 Ackley Improved die set. The concept of a truly "Improved" cartridge necessitates the reloading of the fire-formed case. Thankfully, there are plenty of tools and components available for today's handloader.

I blasted my Oehler Chronograph to pieces with a magnum-charged muzzleloader, I officially disqualified myself from such prestigious ranks. So, in layman's terms, what exactly is an Improved cartridge and why should it merit your consideration over something more commonly available, such as the .30-06 or .308 Winchester?

First, as stated before, this business of fire-forming simply means that you shoot a standard cartridge in an Improved chamber (the .280 Remington in a .280 AI chamber, for example) and, when you extract the case, you see that the pressure has fire-formed the case to the shape and dimensions of the Improved chamber. You do not need to be a wildcatter or have a degree in machine tool operation to accomplish this. You simply go shooting. And then you do some reloading. It's so simple even a second-rate gun writer living in a propane-heated shanty on the Wolf River can do it.

In *Handbook Vol. I,* Ackley explains that the concept is "… [T]o increase the capacity of any given cartridge through the process of fire-forming, and to perhaps change its shape to what would be considered a more efficient one."

Remember, as Ackley himself noted, the .280 Remington factory cartridge was a real humdinger of a round on its own. Introduced by Remington in 1957, it was, essentially, a .30-06 necked down to .284 (7mm). Based on the 7mm-06 wildcat, some have argued it's a more versatile choice than the .270 Winchester. Of course, for big-game hunting, the 7mm needs no introduction and is well proven in the game fields of the world. But, is shooting, fire-forming, and reloading improved cartridges worth the fuss and bother?

Realize that an Improved cartridge does many things, like giving you the option to load the cartridge hotter than its pre-fire-formed state for increased velocity. But that's not what Ackley viewed as the essence of an Improved cartridge. For him, things like minimizing body taper, creating a sharper 40-degree shoulder angle and pushing case capacity closer to its efficient limit (which is not to be confused with velocity), were of greater concern. In fact, in some of the chronograph results found throughout Ackley's two volumes and other contemporary reloading sources, the Ackley Improved listings, as they stand apples to apples alongside a standard cartridge of given bullet weight, sometimes represents less velocity than the original.

One of the reasons for this is that, as case volume increases, pressure decreases. Ackley gives you a more voluminous case. Loading density, expressed as foot/seconds of velocity per grain of powder, can actually go down. In practical terms, this means that, if you really want to wring out velocity, you'll need to load to the actual maximum powder case of the Improved cartridge.

"[C]hronographing as I go, it happens, " writes Lucas. "Velocity goes over the top and into wildcat country and I'm getting 200, 300 and even 400 fps above factory numbers."

But my rifle must be a defiant old bird. As velocities increase, she starts to throw a temper tantrum and accuracy is thrown to the wind. In fact, the most accurate rounds I've found are among standard

.280 Remington numbers. Some authors have taken this as a good thing, calling attention to the .280 AI's versatility. If the hunter in a pinch can only scrounge .280 Remington and hasn't time to reload, the .280 Remington will shoot just fine in the Improved chamber gun.

Improving a cartridge does other things, too, to wring the maximum efficiency out of the cartridge. As the accompanying photos show, a fire-formed cartridge coming out of an Ackley chamber exhibits less taper and a distinct 40-degree shoulder. Less taper improves the cartridge by reducing the amount of stretch in the brass upon each firing, threby extending case life. It also tends to grab the chamber walls better, lessening the rearward force of the case against the bolt face when fired. The increase in case volume brings benefits already mentioned, and this allows you to load more propellant for a faster, flatter shooting round, but, in some cases, with significantly less (five to 10 percent) powder than in a comparable magnum. Thus, there is less recoil.

Ackley didn't take too kindly to magnums and viewed them as an exercise in the law of diminishing returns. He was keenly aware that there's a point when extra powder in a given bore capacity relative to case capacity negatively impacts case and barrel life. In other words, it didn't really help cartridge efficiency.

I, too, have reasons for not liking magnums. Even worse are lightweight rifles chambered for magnums. I can still feel the pain of that first blow after ticking off a friend's "awesome" 7mm Remington Mag. It was a windy spring day, cold as hell outside (you tend to remember details like that when you get beat up), and my friend had proudly explained how his "flat-shooting" 7mm would surely reach out to take any deer "beyond 400 yards" in the western Wisconsin coulees he hunted. The rifle was a lightweight at just seven pounds one ounce. I remember settling in and looking innocently

The author sights in his custom-made .280, using Nosler Custom 140-grain AccuBond ammo. The recoil is soft, but those .284 bullets are cooking right along at over 3,100 fps. This is just one practical example of the many benefits of Ackley's Improved concept.

Kimber's Model 84L Classic Select Grade, with an MSRP of $1,359, is available in four calibers: .25-06, .270, .30-06, and .280 Ackley Improved.

The Kimber Montana Model (MSRP $1,312.00) is available in .280 Ackley and features a synthetic stock.

through the scope, but all I recall after pulling the trigger is a sharp, stinging pain shooting from my shoulder through my skull, followed immediately by a ringing sound in both ears and a sudden, throbbing headache.

"Awesome," I muttered, limping off to go cry in the corner. I vowed never again to mess with the magnum rifle.

My .280 Ackley, on the other hand, is a pussycat. With its medium-contour Montana Rifleman barrel mated to a CZ-550 action and adorned with a dense piece of English walnut that pushed the gun to nine pounds, shooting it is downright pleasant. Pushing a 140-grain Spitzer around 3,100 fps, it sends a projectile as flat-shooting as you could want in 7mm.

It's versatile, too. For bigger critters, I load up a 175-grain Nosler Partition atop a maximum charge of 51 grains of IMR 4350. That thing leaves the muzzle around 2,700 fps and is a real sledgehammer. I once rained all manner of hell down on a black bear with this combination. Judging by the boar's reaction at the shot, you would have thought a dump truck landed on him.

Come deer season, I fed her with Nosler's excellent 140-grain Accubond, one of the few factory loaded choices out there in .280 Ackley Improved. I used it to put down my best rifle-killed buck at 175 yards, a rather long shot by central Wisconsin woodland standards. Like lightning ripping through a telephone pole, the bullet crashed mid-ship through the buck's shoulder. There wasn't any tracking to do.

My experiences are not alone. The famed custom rifle maker Kenny Jarrett heaps more praise on Ackley's design.

"Several aspects make the .280 AI a wonderful cartridge. First, factory ammo can be used in the Improved chamber. Second, its brass life is good. Third, there's its versatility created by the high degree of accuracy with bullet weights ranging from 120 to 160 grains. One can see there is very little difference, if any, between the magnum 7mms and the .280 Improved," he said.

Jarrett pointed out that lightweight, 120-grain 7mm bullets in the .280 Ackley will outperform any .25-06 on the market. At the other extreme, the 160- and 175-grain offerings edge out the .30-calibers, including the .30-06.

"If you want only one custom rifle, then versatility should be your prime consideration," Jarrett said. "The .280 Improved is totally adequate on small African game or antelope with the 120s. It's perfect for larger deer with the 140s, and a real elk and moose buster with the 160s."

The .280 Ackley Goes Mainstream

In 1962, in talking about the wildcat origins of the .22-250, Ackley made an astonishing, and almost prophetic statement. "It's a mystery why some factory has not seen fit to bring it out commercially," he wrote of the now popular varmint cartridge. Today we can look back on those words with puzzlement, as we buy up case after case of .22-250 from any number of manufacturers.

The .280 Ackley Improved must be too good to ignore, too. Nosler is producing two offerings in its Custom Line of ammunition—the aforementioned 140-grain AccuBond and a 150-grain E-Tip. In testing the Accubond, it was among the most accurate ammunition I have ever shot in my custom rifle—better than reloads. (And it better be, when it's about $3 a crack, or $60 retail for a box of 20.) But, if time is money and you haven't much of the first to spare reloading, it's worth every penny. Nosler also produces both a 140-grain and 160-grain cartridge in .280 AI from its Trophy Grade line, using the Accubond and Partition bullets, respectively.

For the reloading side of the Ackley experience, Hornady, Lee Precision, Redding, and RCBS all offer dies for the cartridge. L.E. Wilson, makers of case trimmers and the like, sells a case holder and neck trimming die specifically designed to accommodate the .280 Ackley's 40-degree shoulder. Brass is available from Norma in .280 AI, eliminating the need for initial fire-forming. There are no shortages of recipes, either, with both Sierra and Nosler publishing reloading data in their current manuals. Additionally, the *Cartridges of the World 12th Edition* book features dimensions and data on the .280 Ackley Improved and is another fine reference (see sidebar).

Then there are the rifles. Certainly, any gunsmith worth his salt these days can cook you up a fine little rifle in .280 Ackley. Among the very best are turned out by the Jarrett Rifle Company.

"If I had to lay my finger on one thing that really brought Jarrett Rifles to the dance, it would be the .280 Improved," said Jarrett. "We have made over 700 rifles in this caliber and probably rebarreled at least that many."

In 2007, Nosler showed up with a fine new number so chambered. It says a lot about a cartridge, when a notable gun like the Nosler Custom Rifle is available in only three calibers and one of them is the .280 Ackley Improved. For the more budget-minded, Kimber's Model 84L Classic Select Grade and Montana are both available in .280 AI. As more people discover the advantages and versatility of the Improved cartridge, I wouldn't be surprised to see this list grow. Who knows? Perhaps in some future edition of *Gun Digest*, someone will look back on my quaint little list in awe that more companies didn't jump on the Ackley bandwagon sooner.

We get a sense of how far ahead of his time Ackley truly was, when we ponder an interesting question posed by Lucas to the readers of *Gun Digest* in 1996. "What, fifty years from now for the 100th Anniversary of *Gun Digest* will be written about Parker O. Ackley and his place in the 'Wildcatter's Hall of Fame?'" he wrote. Lucas even suggested that, someday, Ackley's cartridges might become obsolete and forgotten. I don't see that happening. In fact, I think it's fair to say that, with Ackley's designs standing on the shoulders of names like Nosler, Kimber, Jarrett, Lee Precision, Hornady, Redding, and others, his Improved cartridges are a legacy here to stay.

Nosler is one company producing .280 Ackley ammo. The 140-grain AccuBond ammunition from Nosler Custom is not cheap, but, if you don't have time to reload, it is a superb performer.

REFERENCES RECOGNIZE THE .280 ACKLEY

When I first picked up the *11th Edition* of our *Cartridges of the World* book, I was sorely disappointed to see just about every one of the Ackley cartridges listed existed in the Wildcats chapter, save for one—the .280 Ackley. Thankfully, the editors and publisher corrected this injustice in the *12th Edition*. The .280 AI was, of course, still included, but with a surprise. It appeared in the "Current American Sporting Cartridges (Centerfire Rifle)" chapter, rather than under "Wildcats." It was more evidence that Ackley's .280 at least (the other Ackleys, such as the .30-06 AI and 7X57 Mauser AI remain in the Wildcats chapter), had gained mainstream acceptance.

"The criterion used to determine which cartridges should be included in Chapter 2 [*Current American Sporting Cartridges* – CG] is the requirement that the cartridge be currently manufactured and available to the American sportsman through local dealers either on an over-the-counter basis, or by special order," wrote the editor at the time, Frank C. Barnes. "One thing that can be said about many cartridges in Chapter 2 is that they have stood the test of time and include among their number the best and most useful designs available to the American shooter."

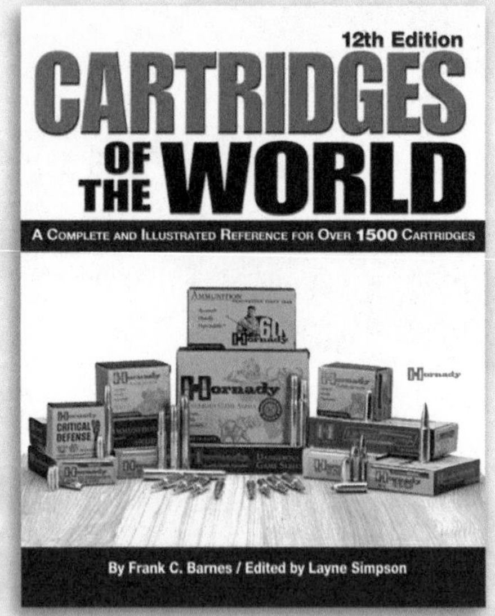

From *Cartridges of the World, 12th Edition*

Historical Notes: In addition to being a famous gunsmith, a barrel maker, and a college professor, P.O. Ackley ruled the roost, when it came to creating wildcat and Improved cartridges. One of his earliest was the 7mm-06 Improved, which was formed by necking down the .30-06 case and fire-forming it to less body taper and a 40-degree shoulder angle. Years later, and not long after the .280 Remington was introduced, reloading equipment maker Fred Huntington reformed its case to the Improved configuration with minimum body taper and a 35-degree shoulder angle and called it the .280 RCBS. Since cases for Huntington's cartridge could be formed by firing .280 Remington ammo in a rifle chambered for it, Ackley abandoned his 7mm-06 Improved and started chambering rifles for the .280 RCBS. But rather than staying with its 35-degree shoulder angle, he changed it to 40 degrees. So was born a cartridge we know today as the 280 Ackley Improved.

After close to a half-century of being something only handloaders could love, the .280 Ackley Improved became a factory number, when Nosler registered it with SAAMI, started loading the ammunition, and began chambering rifles for it, in 2007.

General Comments: I am tempted to say the .280 Ackley Improved is more accurate than the .280 Remington. But doing so would be unfair, since all the rifles I've tried it in have been rather expensive custom jobs, while all chambered for the standard .280 have been off-the-shelf factory rifles. It is a fine old cartridge. When loaded with the right bullet, it is big enough medicine for game up to moose.

Even so, the .280 Ackley Improved is not as fast as the 7mm Remington Magnum, as several of its avid supporters would have us believe. All things being equal, including barrel length and the chamber pressure to which the two are loaded, the .280 Ackley Improved is about 100 fps faster with all bullet weights than the standard .280 Remington. Cases are easily formed by firing .280 Remington factory ammo in a rifle properly chambered for the .280 Ackley Improved.

–Editor Frank C. Barnes

To see more of Ackley's designs and thousands of other cartridges, visit www.gundigeststore.com to get your own copy of Cartridges of the World. *Our newest and best ever* 13th Edition, *with more than 50 new cartridges, should be available shortly after this annual edition of* Gun Digest *is in your hands.*

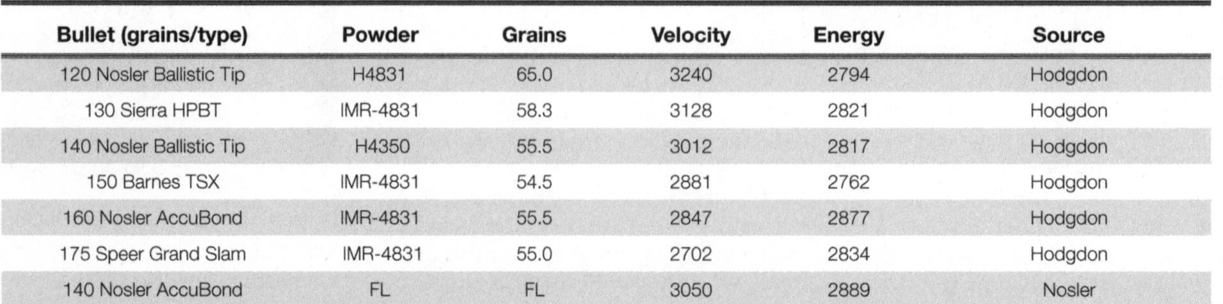

280 Ackley Improved Loading Data and Factory Ballistics

Bullet (grains/type)	Powder	Grains	Velocity	Energy	Source
120 Nosler Ballistic Tip	H4831	65.0	3240	2794	Hodgdon
130 Sierra HPBT	IMR-4831	58.3	3128	2821	Hodgdon
140 Nosler Ballistic Tip	H4350	55.5	3012	2817	Hodgdon
150 Barnes TSX	IMR-4831	54.5	2881	2762	Hodgdon
160 Nosler AccuBond	IMR-4831	55.5	2847	2877	Hodgdon
175 Speer Grand Slam	IMR-4831	55.0	2702	2834	Hodgdon
140 Nosler AccuBond	FL	FL	3050	2889	Nosler

To fire-form cases in the Ackley chamber, you simply shoot standard .280 Remington ammunition. The cartridge on the left is the CorBon Hunter .280 Remington 140-grain T-DPX. The case on the right is what it looks like after you shoot. Note the straighter case walls, 40-degree shoulder, and approximately an extra eighth-inch in case length before the shoulder.

Conclusion

The more I shoot my .280 Ackley, the fonder I become of the Improved cartridge concept. Can I say for certain that it is the perfect big-game cartridge? That'd be a tall order for sure. I can say it's indeed an improvement over a standard .280 Remington, and that's not easy to do. It's also a far cry better than a hard-kicking, over-bored, max-capacity magnum, in my opinion.

What I really like about it is that a corporate marketing department didn't conceive it for the sake of advertising hype. Instead, it represented the confluence of a man's life work in wildcat experimentation and hunting. It was born in a machine shop, probably at that West Bend lathe, by a gunsmith and avid shooter who toiled away into the wee hours of the night making metal chips and blowing up barrels. Ackley doesn't seem to have been out to strike it rich on mass production, and he wasn't one to puff himself up as the eminent wildcatter. Instead, this modest man chiefly concerned himself with bettering the guns and cartridges that his customers shot in the game fields.

When someone asks me what I recommend for the best all-around big-game rifle, I answer without any hesitation at all. It's the .280 Ackley Improved. As for my rifle and me, we get along just fine. Love affairs are a somewhat different matter. Some last forever, and some come crashing to a bitter end the same way they start—unexpectedly. Thus, I've since gotten rid of the wife, but I'll be damned if I ever part with this pretty little rifle. What's not to love? She's a true sweetheart and a real beauty. There's no other like her. In fact, I plan to keep my .280 Ackley until she can be passed onto someone who will appreciate her like I have or, as they say, until death do us part.

— To download a FREE P.O. Ackley Compilation of the four Gun Digest *articles mentioned in this story, visit gundigest.com/Ackley*

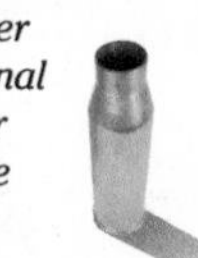

Corey Graff is the online editor for our popular www.gundigest.com site, as well as its sister site, www.tacticalgearmag.com. His personal interests in firearms includes handguns for hunting and self-defense and guns from the World War II-era.

Bibliography

Ackley, P.O., *Handbook for Shooters and Reloaders Volume I*, Plaza Publishing, 1848 West 2300 South, Salt Lake City, Utah, 1962.

Ackley, P.O., *Handbook for Shooters and Reloaders Volume II*, Plaza Publishing, 1848 West 2300 South, Salt Lake City, Utah, 1969.

Amber, John T., *Gun Digest 1962 16th Edition*, The Gun Digest Company, Chicago 24, Illinois, 1962.

Ramage, Ken, *Gun Digest 2004 58th Edition*, Krause Publications, Gun Digest Books, F+W Publications, Inc., Iola, Wisconsin, 2004.

Warner, Ken, *Gun Digest 1996 50th Edition*, DBI Books, Inc. Northfield IL., 1985.

Warner, Ken. *Gun Digest 1985 39th Edition*, DBI Books, Inc. Northfield IL., 1985.

Barnes, Frank C., *Cartridges of the World, 12th Edition*, Krause Publications, Gun Digest Books, F+W Media, Inc., Iola, Wisconsin, 2009.

Barnes, Frank C., *Cartridges of the World, 11th Edition*, Krause Publications, Gun Digest Books, F+W Publications, Inc., Iola, Wisconsin, 2006.

Starting in 2005 and manufactured through 2007, Smith & Wesson produced a .41 Magnum revolver with a super-lightweight scandium/alloy frame. The gun featured a six-round titanium cylinder and weighs only 27.5 ounces. It came with Hogue synthetic grips and a Hi-Viz sighting system.

WHATEVER HAPPENED TO THE .41 MAGNUM?

BY **FRANK W. JAMES**

Introduced in 1964, the .41 Magnum cartridge, housed in a heavy, service style, double-action Smith & Wesson revolver, was supposed to be the definitive answer to the law officer's need for stopping power in a duty sidearm. That it didn't work out quite the way many of its proponents visualized became the stuff of gunshop arguments and fodder for gun writers in the decades since, but the failure was due to a combination of unforeseen factors. The fact remains that the .41 Magnum round was and remains an extremely good revolver cartridge, in terms of its inherent accuracy and terminal ballistics.

Early Problems

One of the first problems affecting the usefulness of the round in law enforcement applications was the fact that the three firms involved early in its introduction—Smith & Wesson, Ruger, and the Remington ammunition company—were never truly on the same page, when it came to commercial production of their affiliated .41 Magnum product lines. Sturm, Ruger & Co. first introduced the .41 Magnum in its single-action Blackhawk line of revolvers, very soon after Smith & Wesson and Remington introduced the round itself. While these single-actions have always worked exceedingly well for sport applications like hunting and plinking, they seldom received serious consideration as a law-enforcement sidearm, even in the mid-1960s.

Smith & Wesson initially built two specific N-frame revolvers for the round. The first was a fixed-sight, service-style, double-action with a four-inch straight barrel on the N-frame platform. It was called the Model 58. The adjustable-sight, ejector rod-underlugged barrel model was offered in two barrel lengths—four and six inches. It was called the Model 57.

The Smith & Wesson Model 57 Mountain Gun was yet another .41 Magnum that was offered with the thin, lightweight barrel. It was a limited run and offered only for a few years by the factory.

Since 2001, all N-frame Smith & Wesson revolvers have, as an added feature, the internal, key-operated trigger lock. This lock can be seen here, located just above the cylinder release. Otherwise, this gun differs little from the guns seen previously to the introduction of this feature.

In the first years of its production, the Model 57 came in a fitted wood box, had a red plastic insert in the middle of the serrated front sight blade, and offered a deep blue finish along with a wide target trigger and hammer. The very early models came equipped with the much-heralded and still sought after "coke-bottle" grips or target stocks that featured an extremely short wrist dimension that easily and comfortably fit a wide variety of hand sizes. In short, those early Model 57s were exquisite firearms, and they immediately gave their possessors the feeling of owning an exclusive and high-quality handgun.

The Round's Initial Goal

The reasoning behind this cartridge's creation was to develop a round that was less powerful than the previously introduced .44 Magnum, but one that would be more effective than the smaller .357 Magnum. It was a situation of compromise that relied upon bore diameter, bullet weight, and muzzle velocity. But, at the time, and unlike today, the construction of the projectile was seldom given any serious thought, regarding the elusive problem of trying to achieve "one-shot-stops" in law enforcement shootings. Later, advancements in bullet manufacturing technology would rewrite the rules in this regard and, in the process, turn the .357 Magnum 125-grain jacketed hollowpoint into one of the most effective law enforcement handgun caliber and cartridge combinations police officers world-wide would ever see. Prior to the advancements in bullet construction however, the emphasis in ammunition for self-defense handguns focused on three primary design characteristics: bore diameter, bullet weight, and muzzle velocity. The .44 Magnum exemplified the ultimate, but it was actually too much, in that it had too much recoil, too much muzzle blast, and way too much projectile penetration when human beings were shot. And, if the .357 Magnum was considered too little, there had to be a compromise somewhere between the two. That's where the .41 Magnum came into the picture.

Unfortunately, the message was distorted in the delivery.

Remington was the only ammunition company manufacturing the round in its early stages and made it in two flavors. One was a 210-grain jacketed soft-point round that supposedly clocked right at 1,500 fps out of an 8⅜-inch barrel. The

The author picked up this gun after he learned it was one of 12 such revolvers made by the S&W Performance Center from left-over parts found in the factory. As such, it features the short, three-inch barrel, a Patridge front sight with a McGivern gold bead, and a tuned trigger. He considers it to be an excellent revolver in .41 Magnum.

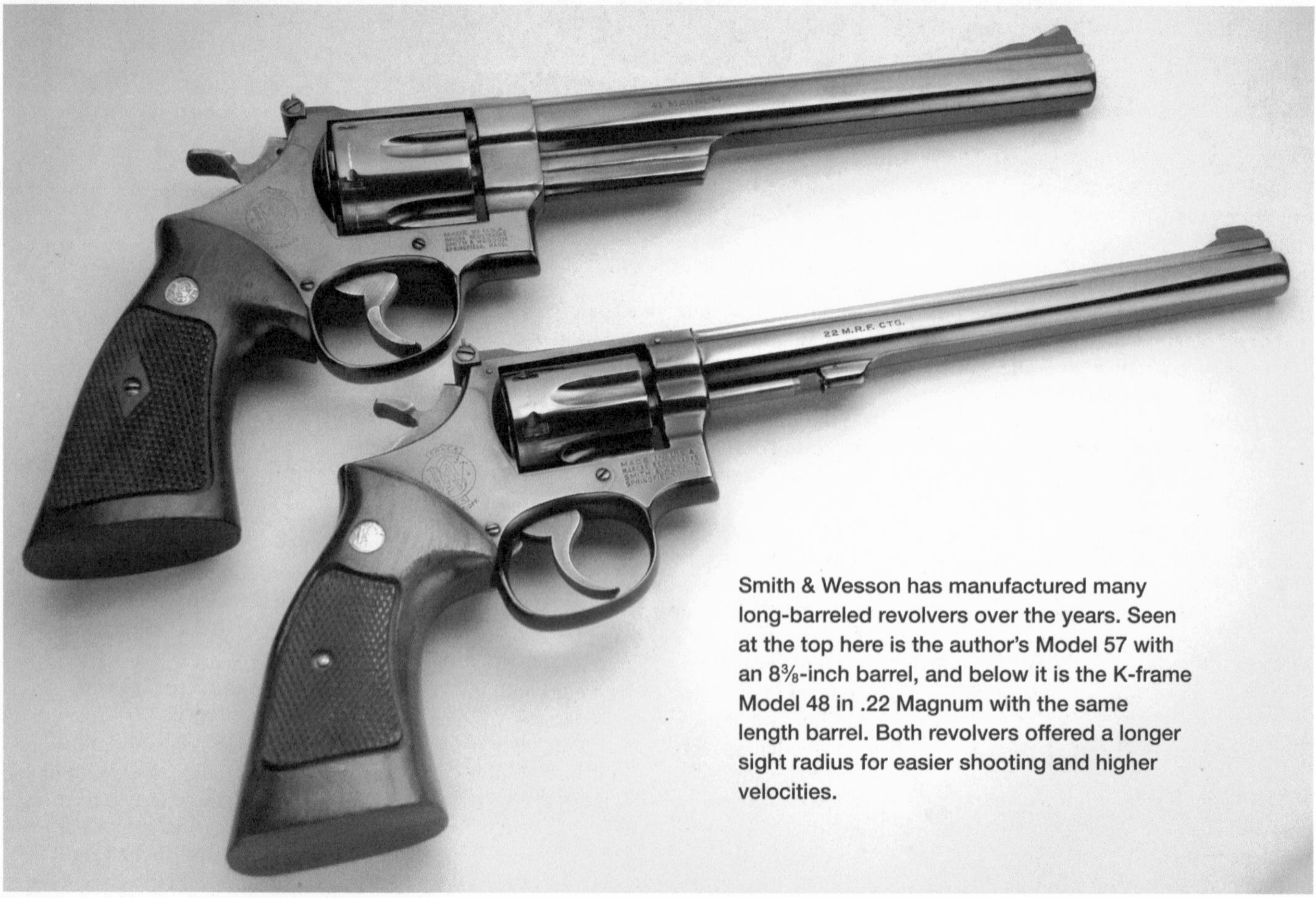

Smith & Wesson has manufactured many long-barreled revolvers over the years. Seen at the top here is the author's Model 57 with an 8⅜-inch barrel, and below it is the K-frame Model 48 in .22 Magnum with the same length barrel. Both revolvers offered a longer sight radius for easier shooting and higher velocities.

This .41 Magnum revolver from Smith & Wesson is another member of the Classic line of revolvers. It is the Model 58-1 and, as such, it pays tribute to the original Military & Police .41 Magnum. The Model 58-1, unlike the original, has a four-screw sideplate, a lanyard ring, the internal key-operated trigger lock, and stocks whose style was originally seen on the Triple Lock Hand Ejectors.

The newer .41 Magnum Model 58-1 Smith & Wesson sports a four-screw sideplate, which was never seen on the original Model 58 Military & Police .41 Magnum.

difference between this load and most any .44 Magnum load at the time was small and hard to discern, in terms of felt recoil. The alternate load that was meant for police duty employed a 210-grain lead semi-wadcutter bullet with a published muzzle velocity of 1,050 fps out of the same 8⅜-inch barrel, but out of the more common four-inch barrel it dropped down to something much less. This made the recoil acceptable.

The problem was that just about every police agency getting these new "mid-Magnum" revolvers got the high-velocity ammunition instead of the load intended for police duty. Additionally, when an agency *did* get the correct ammunition, they soon discovered the lead semi-wadcutter ammo leaded the barrels something awful, because of the soft lead used to swage the bullets. In short, things were fouled up from the beginning.

By the early 1970s, the ammunition companies were creating new and advanced bullets for the .357 Magnum cartridge and, in many ways, this rang the death knell for the .41 Magnum in law enforcement. But the round actually found wide acceptance in an unexpected area, with those who used handguns for hunting or long-range shooting.

I've seen training videos from police departments that actually issued the .41 Magnum, and they are not pretty. The truth is it took a dedicated individual to master the heavy revolver chambering this round, and if he was unfortunate enough to get the wrong ammunition, you could literally see his marksmanship disintegrate with each successive shot.

As much as I love this round and its assorted revolvers, I'm convinced it really does take a dedicated individual to realize the true potential the round offers. It is not for the faint of heart, nor is it a round for those who are casual shooters. I know that may sound elitist, but it's a reflection of what has troubled this cartridge from the start.

Smith & Wesson now offers the Model 57 as part of its Classic line of historic revolvers. The difference now is the newer gun has a four-screw sideplate, when the originals never did. Still, the gun harkens back to the style and look when this cartridge and revolver were first introduced. At the upper right is the author's original S-prefix armalloyed Model 57 with a four-inch barrel. At the upper left is another S-prefix, ivory stocked, highly-engraved Model 57 that commemorates his deceased daughter.

The Guns

Selection of a favorite firearm is always an extremely personal choice, but I've always had a fondness for four- and five-inch barreled Smith & Wesson N-frame revolvers in .41 Magnum. As a farmer, my primary concern is downrange ballistics, not how badly the gun printed under a covering garment or how heavy the gun was to carry. The Model 57 with the four-inch barrel weighs approximately 44 ounces, while the six-inch version weighs 48 ounces and the 8⅜-inch model comes in at 52.5 ounces. The Model 58 in turn weighs "only" 41 ounces.

I own three Smith & Wesson .41 Magnum revolvers with five-inch barrels, and each is a custom-made revolver. Naked six-inch barrels were used to create these guns, as the big problem has always been the front sight base. Getting something that approximates the factory original is difficult. Still , the result, in my view, is worth it.

A number of lawmen did carry guns in .41 Magnum caliber. Probably one of the more famous was Buford Pusser. I was told once, by a man who claimed to know who actually owns Pusser's nickel-plated .41 Magnum, that its serial number was S29482. If that serial number series had another digit I would have believed him, because all the early Smith & Wesson S-prefix .41 Magnums I've seen had six digits after the "S," but not five. Jim Supica and Richard Nahas, in their book *Standard Catalog of Smith & Wesson*, claim the first gun made in .41 Magnum was serial number S236941, while a serious collector says he has one with serial number S236908. Roy Jinks, in his book *History of Smith & Wesson*, says the first Model 57 made had the serial number S256481.

In any case, the Model 57 was made from 1963 to 1993. The Model 58 was made from 1964 to 1977, and then, two years ago, a new version, named the Model 58-1, was reintroduced in the S&W Classic line that features the internal trigger lock/key-activated safety. The stainless steel version of the Model 57 was the Model 657, and it was made from 1986 to the present in various forms and formats, but the four-inch Model 657 was only available for two years and discontinued in 1988. A four-inch, thin-barreled Mountain Gun was introduced in 1998 as a stocking dealer special-run product.

Some years ago it became apparent that heavy use of full-charge .44 Magnum loads in the Model 29 was creating some serious durability problems. "Skipping," whereby the cylinder would rotate backwards, was one symptom, and the Model 29 and all subsequent Smith & Wesson .44 Magnums were redesigned for greater durability and reliability. At a press conference where Smith & Wesson was explaining these design improvements, fellow gun writer John Taffin asked me if I had ever seen these problems develop in a Model 57 or Model 58. My answer was that I hadn't. Neither had he, so, despite the fact that many look down

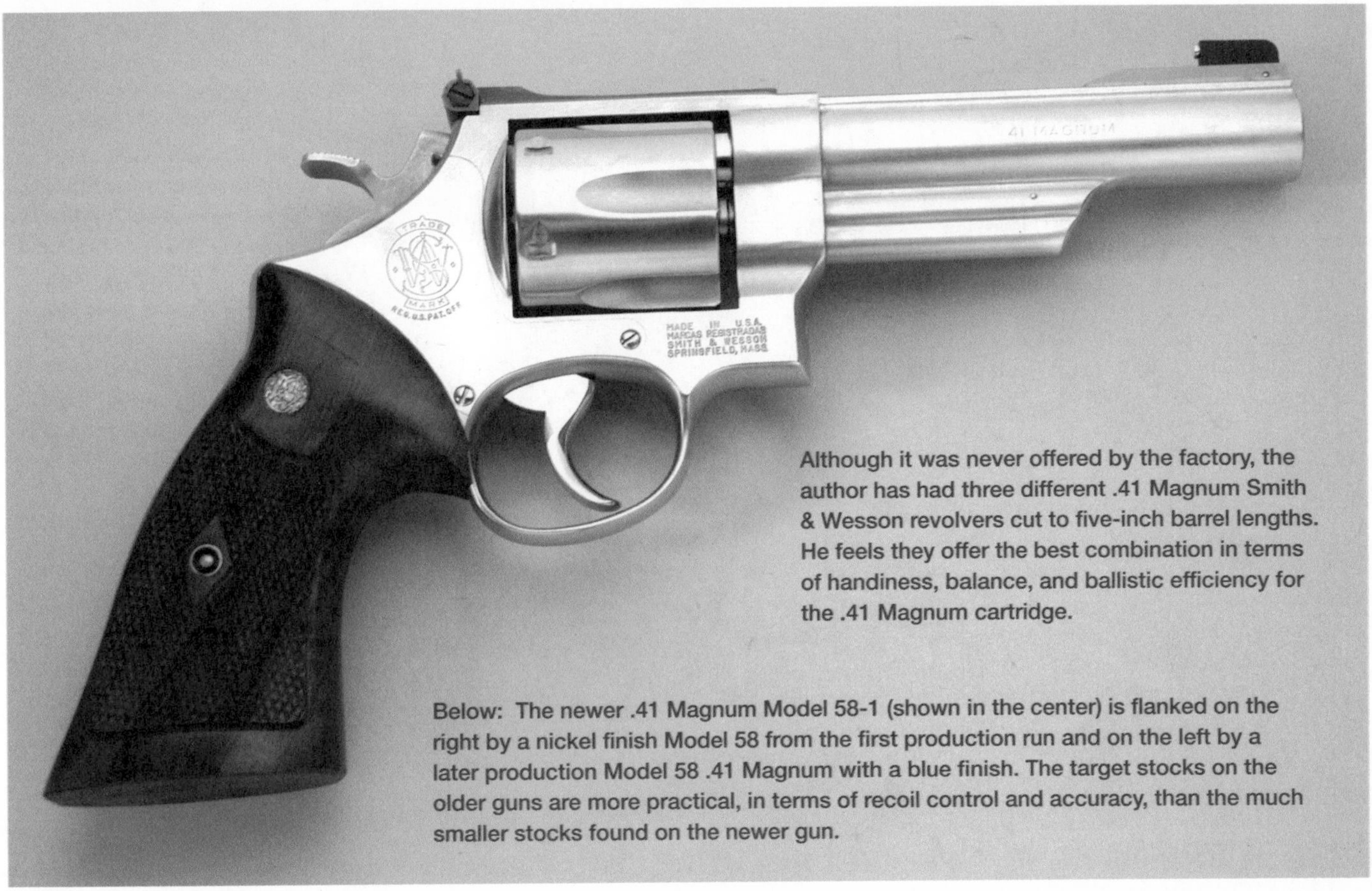

Although it was never offered by the factory, the author has had three different .41 Magnum Smith & Wesson revolvers cut to five-inch barrel lengths. He feels they offer the best combination in terms of handiness, balance, and ballistic efficiency for the .41 Magnum cartridge.

Below: The newer .41 Magnum Model 58-1 (shown in the center) is flanked on the right by a nickel finish Model 58 from the first production run and on the left by a later production Model 58 .41 Magnum with a blue finish. The target stocks on the older guns are more practical, in terms of recoil control and accuracy, than the much smaller stocks found on the newer gun.

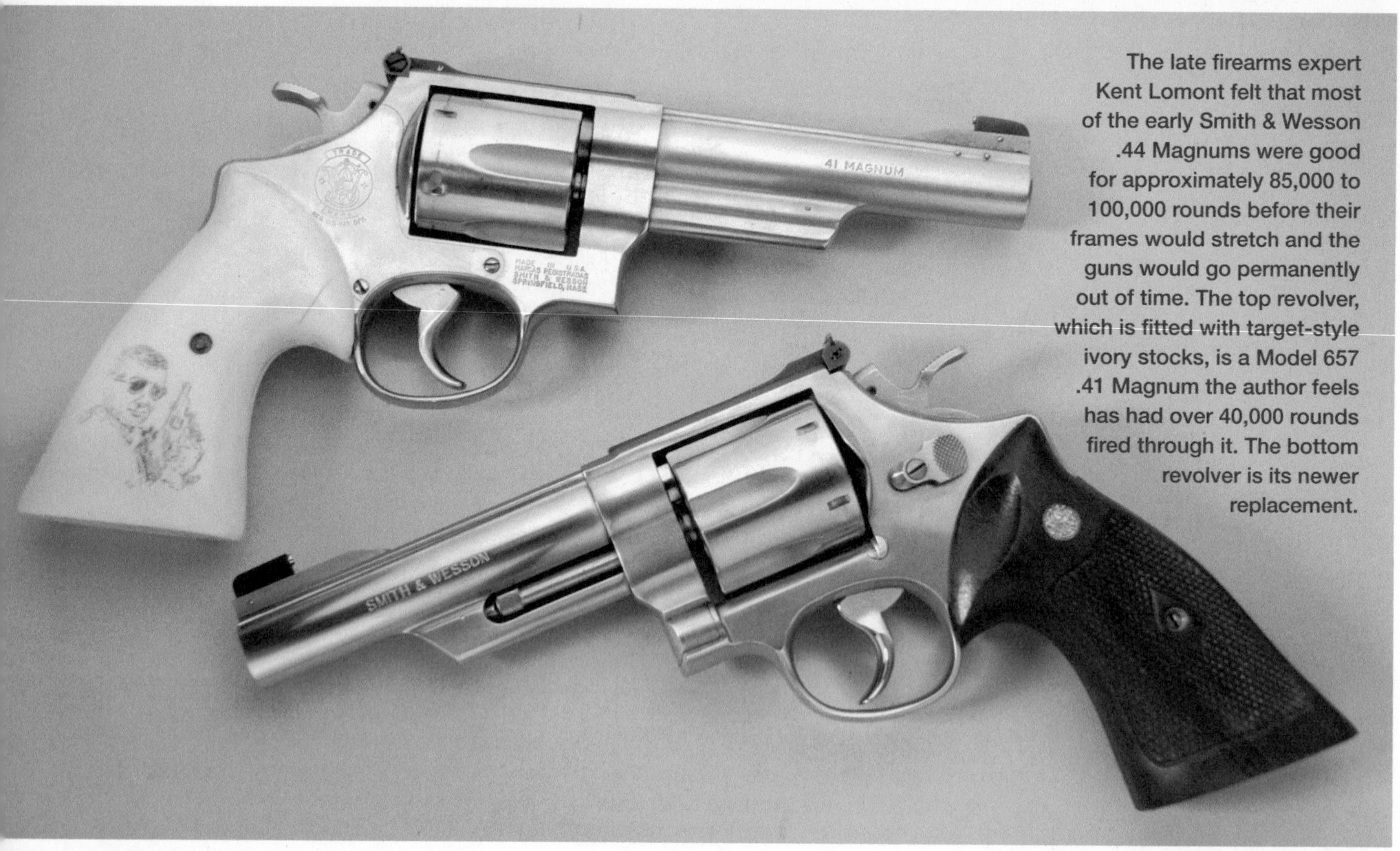

The late firearms expert Kent Lomont felt that most of the early Smith & Wesson .44 Magnums were good for approximately 85,000 to 100,000 rounds before their frames would stretch and the guns would go permanently out of time. The top revolver, which is fitted with target-style ivory stocks, is a Model 657 .41 Magnum the author feels has had over 40,000 rounds fired through it. The bottom revolver is its newer replacement.

their noses at the Model 57 and Model 58 Smith & Wesson revolvers, the truth is those heavy N-frame revolvers may have been better suited to the .41 Magnum round than they were its .44 Magnum big brother.

Elmer Keith lamented the lack of a square-cut grease groove on the Lyman #410459 cast bullet that mimicked much of his design. It weighed 220 grains, while the RCBS bullet (shown on the right) did have the square-cut grease groove and weighed 210 grains. Both featured a semi-wadcutter bullet shape.

In discussions with the late Kent Lomont, and from my own experiences, I've always felt the average Model 57 or Model 58 revolver could last for at least 80,000 rounds before the frame would suffer from stretching (usually around the frame window) or warped and bent sideplates, which would essentially end their lives as usable firearms.

Pros and Cons

I started working with the .41 Magnum in 1970 and immediately realized that I had discovered a round that was flat shooting, hard hitting and, in my view, offered manageable recoil. Yes, there was significant recoil, but to me there was a noticeable difference between it and a Smith & Wesson Model 29 in the same barrel length, when both were shot with the available factory loads, i.e., the .41's 210-grain JSP load versus the 240-grain JSP .44 Magnum load.

The far narrower selection of both bullet styles and loaded ammunition for the .41 Magnum, when compared to either the .357 Magnum or .44 Magnum, is the Achilles heel of the round and, over all the years since its introduction, this really hasn't changed. This has forced those, like myself, who appreciate this round to thoroughly investigate handloading and bullet casting. If you're willing to venture into these areas, there really is no shortage of ammo or bullet options available for the .41 Magnum.

Elmer Keith consistently wrote about reloads employing 2400 smokeless powder, but, since Elmer's day, there have been a number of other powders developed that meter every bit as easily and accurately as 2400, only without the resounding muzzle flash and immediate recoil impulse. IMR-4224, H-4227, Winchester's 296, and Vihtavuori N-110 are all excellent smokeless powders for full-power loads in the .41 Magnum. I've used Lil' Gun from Hodgdon, as well, but the truth is I've never been able to duplicate the muzzle velocities reported with the early factory ammo, so I question some of those reports from years ago with a healthy grain of salt. Just about all the reloading manuals offer a number of good loads utilizing these propellants with any of the commonly available commercially available projectiles.

Where there is a real deficiency in .41 Magnum loading data is in the lack of moderate-velocity loads that many would use for practice, target shooting, or even home defense. I've found that Winchester's Super-Target (WST) is an excellent propellant for this usage, and I use 6.5 grains of WST under a wide variety of bullets for both target practice and even to take coyotes on the farm. I especially like using a 180-grain Speer Gold Dot that was originally sold to reload the .41 AE round over this powder charge, as it is extremely soft recoiling, flat shooting, and will stay within a coyote when they are shot through the thorax.

Among the cast bullets I've used over the years are the Lyman #410459, which is a 220-grain cast lead bullet that mimics the Keith-style. Elmer didn't design it, nor is it a true copy of his original design, because it doesn't have square-cut grease grooves, but it is a good bullet and, when cast properly, it shoots extremely well.

Another Lyman bullet had proven elusive, but I found a mould for it on an Internet auction site recently. It is the Lyman #410426, which is a 240-grain cast lead round-nose bullet. It's a big heavy bullet for the .41 bore diameter and it increases the felt recoil even with moderate powder charges. I'm researching it, because I feel it offers potential for use against feral hogs, where there is a great need for penetration to vital areas in an emergency situation.

RCBS makes a mould that throws a good overall cast bullet of a 210-grain semi-wadcutter design, and this slug works well with both moderate and heavy loads. I think Elmer would approve of it, as well, as its grease grooves are square-cut, so they should hold more grease for bullet lubrication.

The author feels his .41 Magnum Mountain Gun saved him from some time in the hospital, while working feral hog control a couple of years ago, in Texas. He was out of rifle ammo, and the feral hog took exception to the fact he had ventilated him twice with the semi-auto .308. The action was close and quick, but the .41 Magnum literally saved the day.

The Future

There will always be those like myself who will continue to use revolvers chambered for this round simply because it is accurate, hard hitting, and flat shooting. No, it was never the round its proponents said it would be, but the truth is it hasn't disappeared, either, when so many over the years continually predicted its demise.

It's hard to argue against such an accurate shooting cartridge that relies more on power than it does high-tech bullet designs. It will always be a *great* revolver/handgun cartridge, no matter how popular or unpopular it may prove to be.

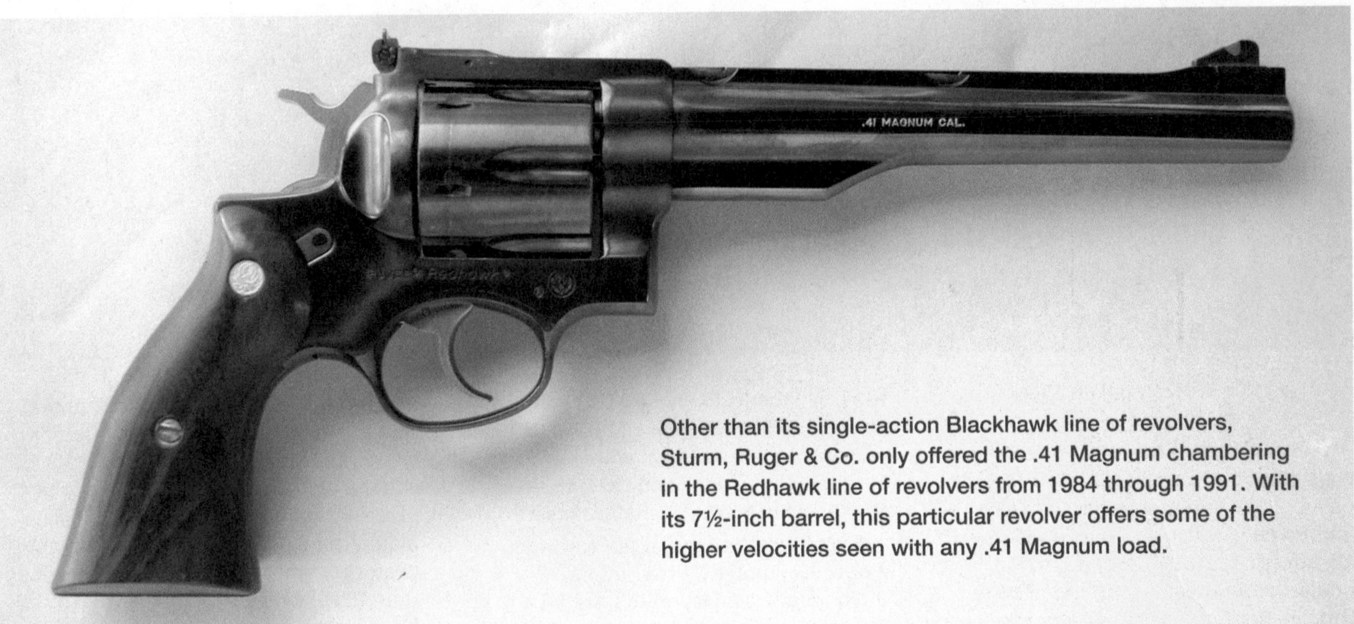

Other than its single-action Blackhawk line of revolvers, Sturm, Ruger & Co. only offered the .41 Magnum chambering in the Redhawk line of revolvers from 1984 through 1991. With its 7½-inch barrel, this particular revolver offers some of the higher velocities seen with any .41 Magnum load.

THE TRUTH ABOUT "GUN TESTS"

BY JON R. SUNDRA

The first thing author Jon Sundra does is weigh the test gun, as that's the one spec that is often optimistic.

A significant percentage of hunters and shooters who read gun magazines and annuals like *Gun Digest* on a regular basis do so because they're interested in rifle tests. Why? Well, there are several reasons, all of which fall under the umbrella of curiosity, but the three major ones are: 1) you already own the basic model in question; 2) you're shopping for a new rifle and want to make an enlightened decision; and 3) it truly is a new design, in which case we're all interested in learning what makes it so.

Expanding on reason No. 1, when a new variation of "your" gun is introduced, it's natural to have an interest in reading what writers have to say about it; it's looking for affirmation that you made a good choice. But let's face it, the vast majority of gun tests consist of reviewing minor variations of existing models. Think about it. The major, domestically produced bolt-action centerfire rifles have been around a long time. The Savage 110 and Weatherby Mark V, for example, have been with us

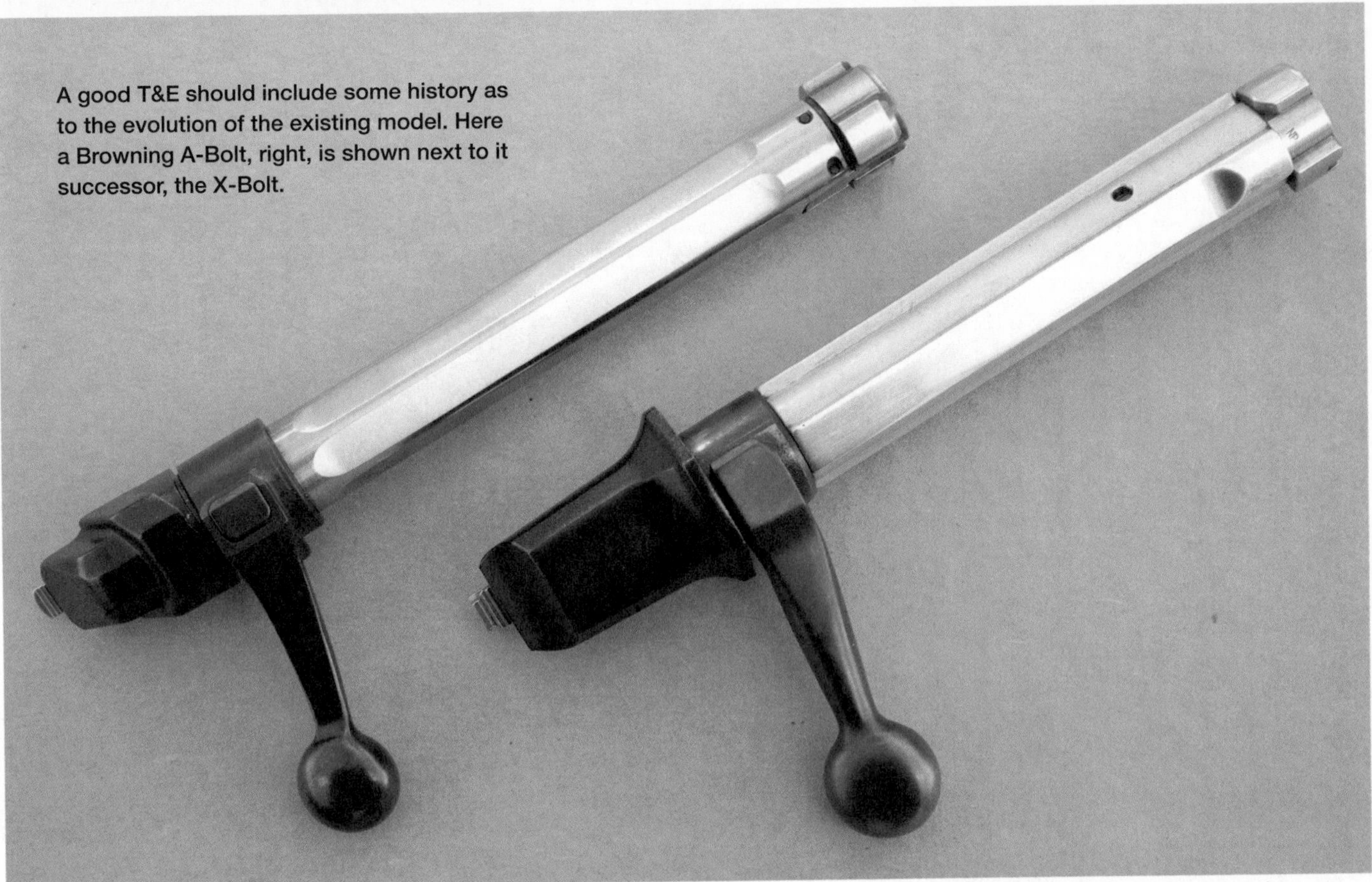

A good T&E should include some history as to the evolution of the existing model. Here a Browning A-Bolt, right, is shown next to it successor, the X-Bolt.

since the late 1950s, and the Weatherby Vanguard/Howa for almost as long. The Remington 700 just celebrated its fiftieth anniversary (though, in reality, the basic action goes back to 1948). As for the Winchester Model 70 Classic and Ruger 77 MK II, they both surfaced in the early '90s. The bottom line is that what are touted as new models differ from others in their respective product lineups in only minor details.

As for reason No. 2, it needs little further comment, other than to say that most of us want to make our buying decision knowing what the alternatives are. Unless we've already made up our mind, comparison shopping simply makes good sense. And, finally, reason No. 3 should be self-explanatory.

So, then, just what is it that readers expect to learn from the typical rifle test and evaluation (T&E)? Well, if you're not familiar with the gun in question, you really can learn a great deal about it by reading an article or two (presumably written by a credible authority). But there are some things you cannot learn, and those things just may be the most important of all.

Gun tests, if not unique, are quite different from reviews of most other consumer products, because each is a law unto itself, when it comes to performance. Take, for example, a toaster, a camera, or a television. If we were to buy the same product that we'd read about, we know that it will perform exactly as described by the reviewer. The toaster will toast, the camera will operate exactly as described and render pictures of the same color and sharpness, and the TV will have the same picture quality as the one reviewed.

A rifle, on the other hand, is a different story, because there are so many variables involved that affect its performance, not the least of which is the person shooting it. But more about that factor later. Let's start by looking at those things we *can* learn about a rifle from a typical gun test.

I'm not sure how many rifle evaluations I've done over the past 42 years, but it has to be at least 600, so I've long since developed a somewhat formulaic system, as I'm sure most of my colleagues have. The first thing I check, the moment I pick up the gun, is its weight. I've never encountered a rifle that didn't conform to its printed specs except in the weight department. I've reviewed rifles that were as much as a pound off spec, and it's always been on the optimistic side—in other words, I've never seen a gun that was lighter than the maker said it was!

Among the many things that can be checked before going to the range are cartridge feeding and extraction. Sometimes I'll use dummy rounds—no powder or primer—to check functioning, but it can also be done at the range with live ammo. If a rifle has a tendency for its bolt to bind, it will manifest itself when the action is cycled from the shoulder. That's because the pressure on the bolt handle tends to come from a different direction when the action is operated in a port arms position, compared to when the gun is shouldered. In the port arms position, the bolt handle can easily be pushed in the direction parallel to the bore, which induces very little torque to the bolt. But, when operated from the shoulder, there is a tendency to push upward on the handle, which applies torque that has a tendency to bind all but the smoothest of bolts. Generally speaking, if the bolt on the test rifle has a tendency to bind, so, too, will all other examples.

Other functions that can be assessed prior to a visit to the range are trigger

The more a rifle departs from convention, like this Blaser R8, the more a writer has to both show and describe the differences.

tension, smoothness, and creep, as well as the effort required to cock the action (upward pressure to achieve handle lift). I've encountered many rifles that required so much effort to cock, they could not be cycled with the rifle shouldered. All the aforementioned functions can vary among rifles of the same make, model, and caliber, though it's usually within fairly narrow parameters.

Whether a barrel is free-floated or pressure-bedded is a fact not usually found among the manufacturer's specs, but it can easily be verified. If you can't slip a piece of paper between the barrel and fore-end tip and slide it all the way back to the receiver, you know the barrel is pressure-bedded—or not. I've encountered some test guns that had large gaps along the sides of the barrel and no pressure band at the fore-end tip, indicating they were supposed to be floated, yet they wouldn't pass the paper test.

If the gun in question is really new, we want to see what makes it tick, so taking it apart to see its innards is mandatory. Lifting the barreled action from the stock reveals all kinds of things a reader would want to know. Is the receiver pillar-bedded, partially glass-bedded in the receiver ring/recoil lug area, or sitting on a metal bedding block? What about

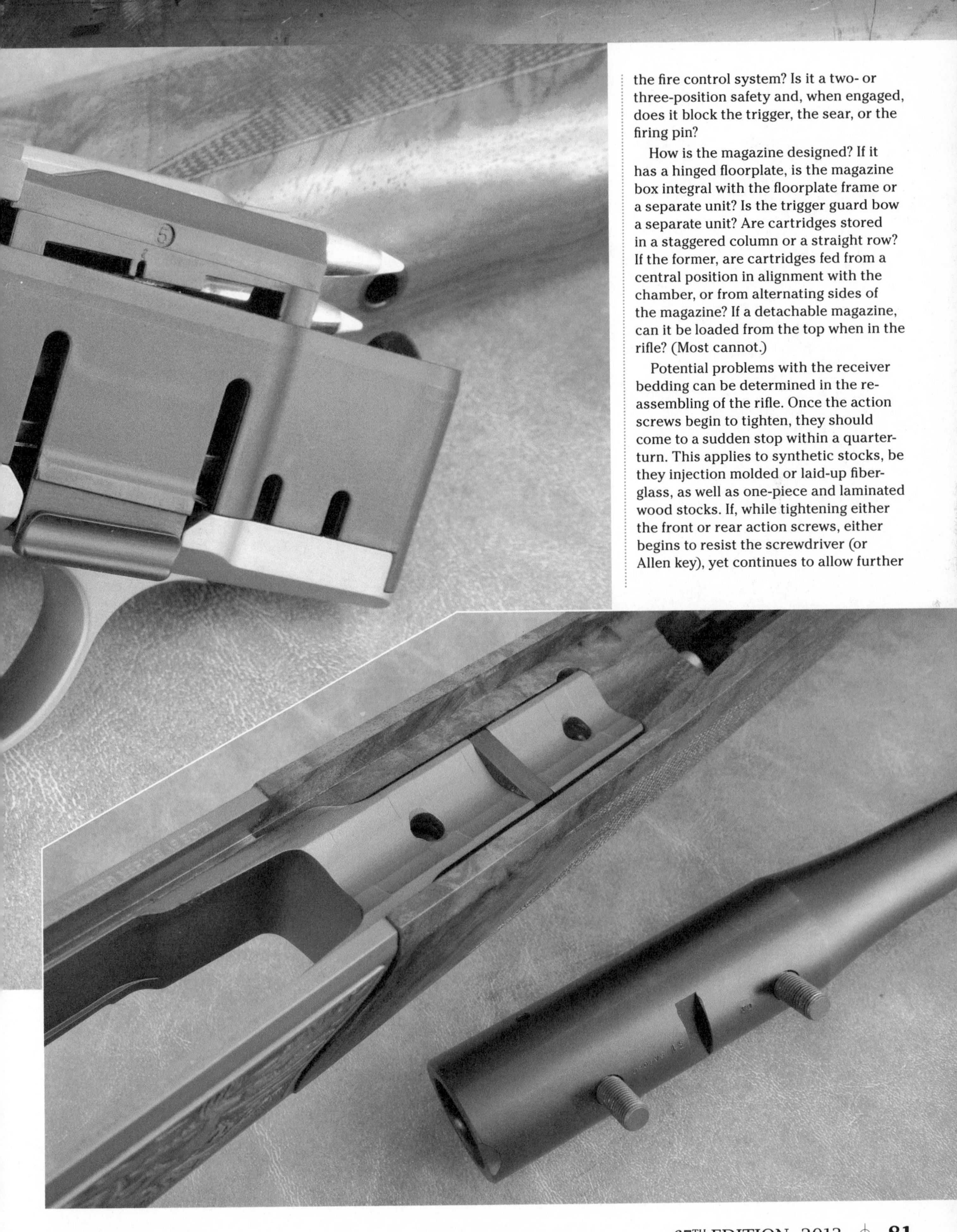

the fire control system? Is it a two- or three-position safety and, when engaged, does it block the trigger, the sear, or the firing pin?

How is the magazine designed? If it has a hinged floorplate, is the magazine box integral with the floorplate frame or a separate unit? Is the trigger guard bow a separate unit? Are cartridges stored in a staggered column or a straight row? If the former, are cartridges fed from a central position in alignment with the chamber, or from alternating sides of the magazine? If a detachable magazine, can it be loaded from the top when in the rifle? (Most cannot.)

Potential problems with the receiver bedding can be determined in the re-assembling of the rifle. Once the action screws begin to tighten, they should come to a sudden stop within a quarter-turn. This applies to synthetic stocks, be they injection molded or laid-up fiber-glass, as well as one-piece and laminated wood stocks. If, while tightening either the front or rear action screws, either begins to resist the screwdriver (or Allen key), yet continues to allow further

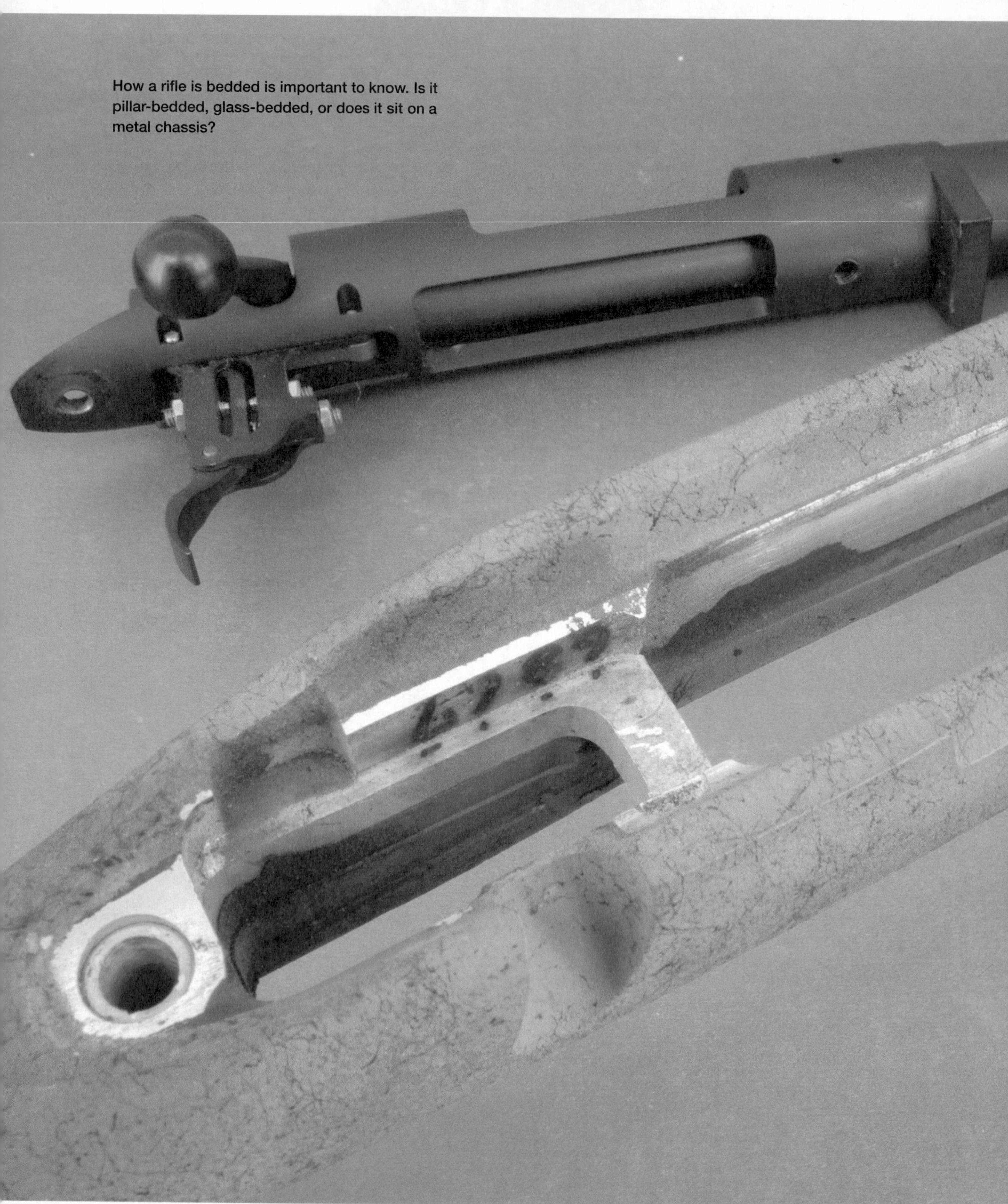

How a rifle is bedded is important to know. Is it pillar-bedded, glass-bedded, or does it sit on a metal chassis?

tightening with increased torque on the screwdriver, something is wrong with the bedding. In other words, if it feels like the screw is almost snug, yet continues to tighten with a mushy feel, that means the stock or receiver tang is bending. In either case, there are serious strains being induced to the bedding dynamics between these two critical components, and that can (and usually does) affect group size and consistency.

If there are obvious bedding problems with a test rifle, should they be addressed by the writer before going to the range? That's a tough call, but if the writer does fiddle with the bedding, is that rifle still representative of that make and model? One thing is sure, if I do any tuning of the rifle, I always mention it. It has to be minor stuff, however, the kind that any owner can address, like shimming the receiver ring to float what was not but should have been a free-floating barrel, or shimming it at the fore-end tip to apply dampening pressure where there was none. That's really about the limit of what tinkering I'll do.

It's almost a given that, if we were to take two identical rifles of the same make, model, and caliber, the best-shooting load in one will not be

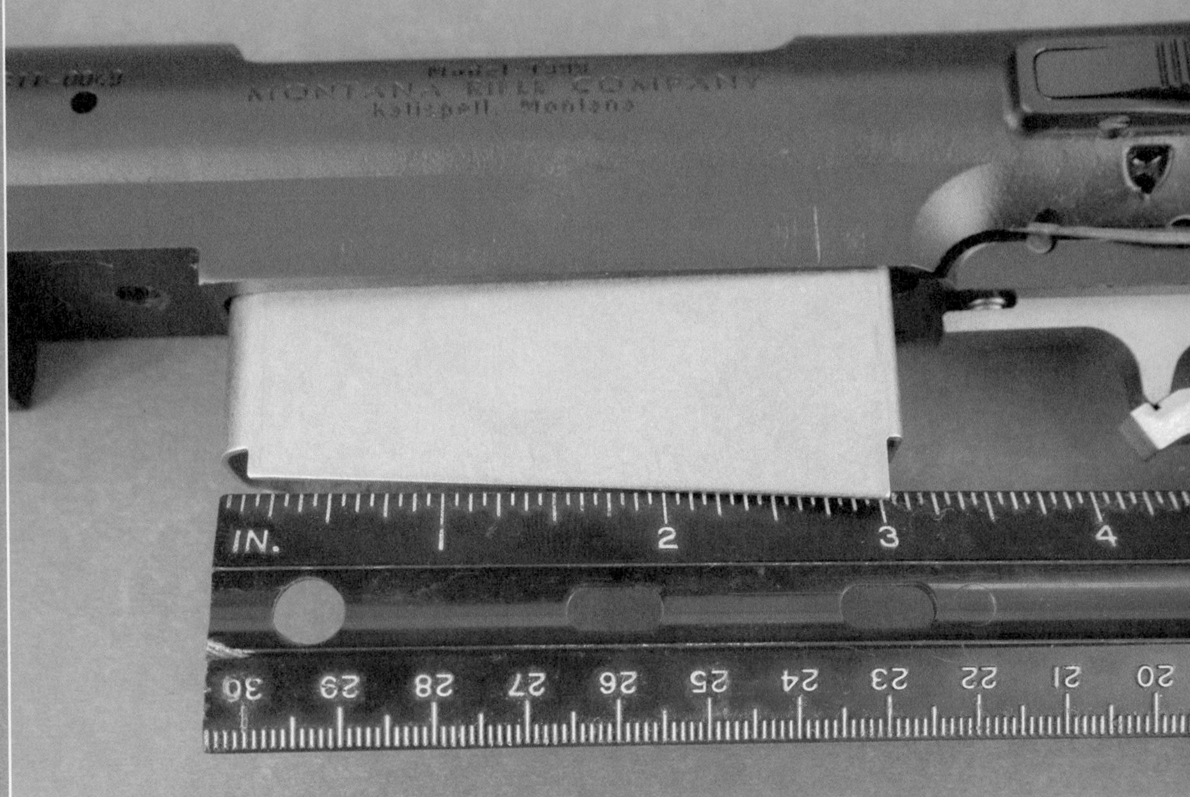

The maximum cartridge length that can be accommodated by the magazine is another spec that is often lacking in the factory owner's manual.

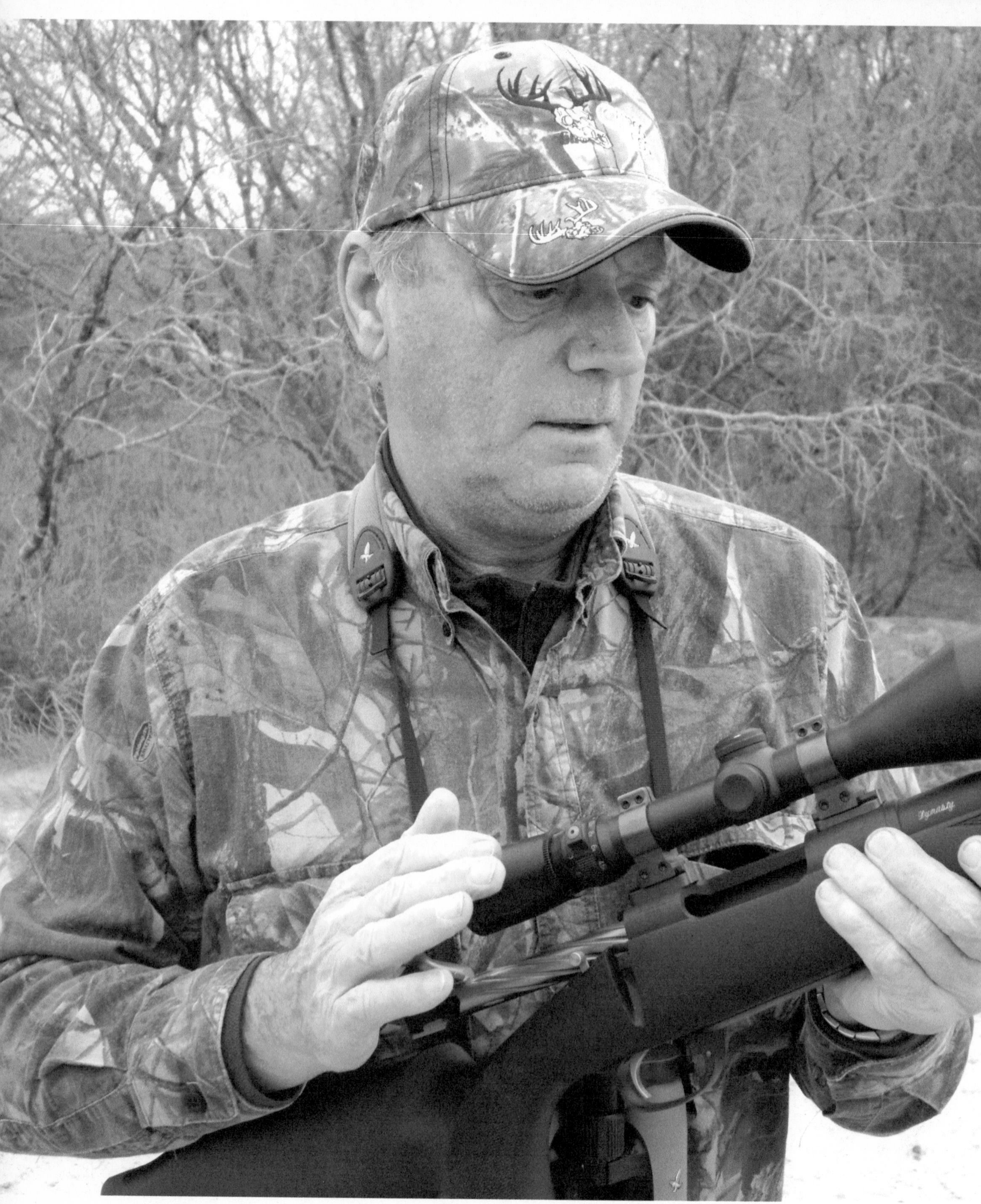

There are many criteria used in evaluating a rifle, two of which are overall quality and features relative to price.

It's easy to check and see if the barrel is free-floated. Sometime it isn't but is supposed to be, and other times vice-versa.

the best-shooting load in the other. As already stated, that's due to many factors, the barrel being the starting point. Though both barrels are ostensibly identical, each of the various operations of drilling, reaming, rifling, turning to contour, hubbing, and threading is done to within certain dimensional tolerances. So long as each operation is within those tolerances, it's acceptable.

As close to exactly the same as two barrels appear to be, they are not. Neither is the granular structure of the steel, nor the harmonics of the barrel as a bullet accelerates down the bore. Harmonics can be changed by altering the bedding or shortening the barrel slightly and re-crowning the muzzle, but these certainly are not things that should be done to a test rifle.

Other factors that can vary from rifle to rifle but cannot be checked by anyone other than a machinist are the concentricity of the bolt and the "squareness" of its face relative to the bore line. Receivers can warp in the heat-treating process and, as a result, the bolt and bolt face will not be square. When such is the case, there can be uneven contact between the locking lugs and their abutment surfaces. I've seen twin-lug actions where one lug was barely contacting its bearing surface, even after several boxes of ammo were put through the gun. Again, these conditions can be present in a rifle that passes its manufacturer's tolerances. Rectifying these conditions is part of what they call "blueprinting" an action.

Another condition that can occur in one rifle but not the next one off the assembly line is uneven bearing of the recoil lug. Generally speaking, if it's a wood stock, recoil forces of the first few boxes of ammo will compress and seat the lug so that it is bearing across its entire surface. However, with a synthetic stock or one with a metal abutment surface, the condition does not rectify itself.

There was a time when I worked up handloads, if a test rifle didn't perform as well as I thought it should, but I no longer do that. The only thread of commonality between the rifle I test and the rifle you buy is factory ammunition. Even though you may get better or worse accuracy than I got, we at least can try the same loads. Even then, chances are you'll be using a different lot (manufacturing run) of ammo, even though it's the same load. It's not much, but that's about as close as we can get to duplicating conditions.

With handloads, there's a near infinite number of possible combinations of bullets and seating depths, powder type and charge weight, primers, and differences in case preparation, any one of which can make a rifle a stellar performer—but only that particular rifle, because, remember, every one is a law unto itself.

Now we come to that variable alluded to at the outset: the man behind the gun. Say we have a genuine half-minute rifle. How many of us can shoot it up to its potential, especially if we're talking a big-game rifle in the .300 Magnum class or more? Having fired a couple hundred thousand rounds from the bench, I'm a fair to middlin' shot, but I'll be the first to admit that I can't match what an accomplished benchrest shooter could probably wring out of that same rifle if it's

The quality and features of these numerous Dakota Model 76s, which are virtual clones of the Winchester Model 70 Classic, cost roughly triple what a production Winchester does. Each must be evaluated in those terms.

chambered for a mild-recoiling benchrest cartridge. I might have an edge with larger and more heavy-recoiling calibers because I test all of them, from .17s to .470s, but it wouldn't be much of an edge.

There are a few rifle companies that guarantee accuracy, mostly expressed

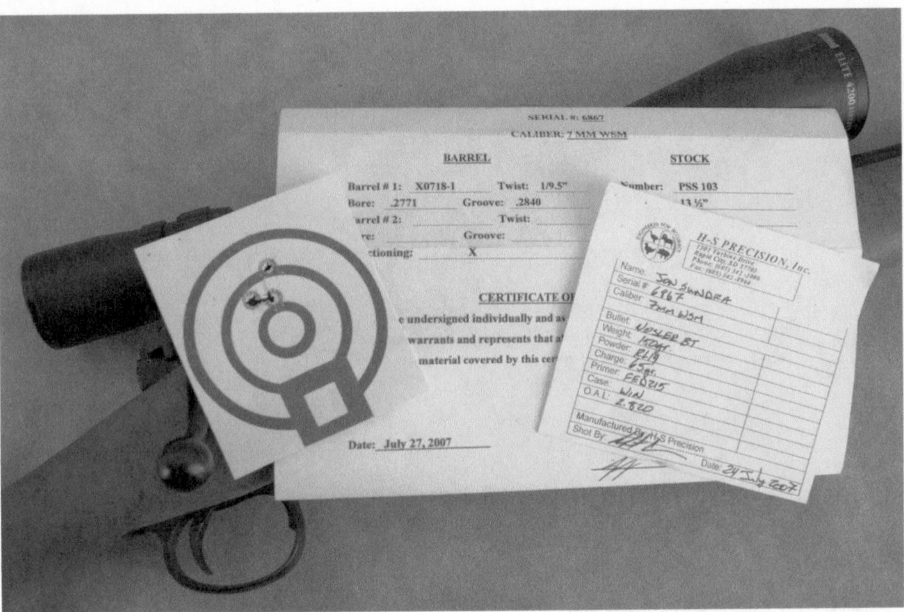

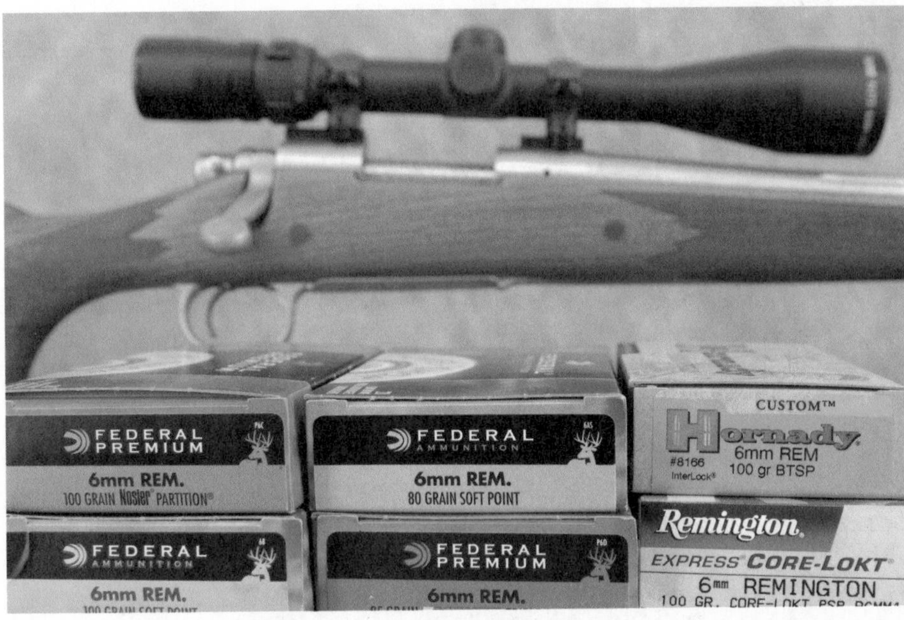

Top: Some manufacturers guarantee accuracy, if the same factory load or handload used in testing the gun at the factory is used by the customer. Just remember that range conditions, equipment, and shooting skills also come into the equation.

Middle: Given the quality of today's rifles and ammunition, the consumer should expect his rifle to shoot three-shot groups of 1¼ inches at 100 yards, with at least one factory load out of five tried.

Bottom: In his gun reviews, author Jon Sundra likes to note the worst groups fired, along with the same load that fired the best groups.

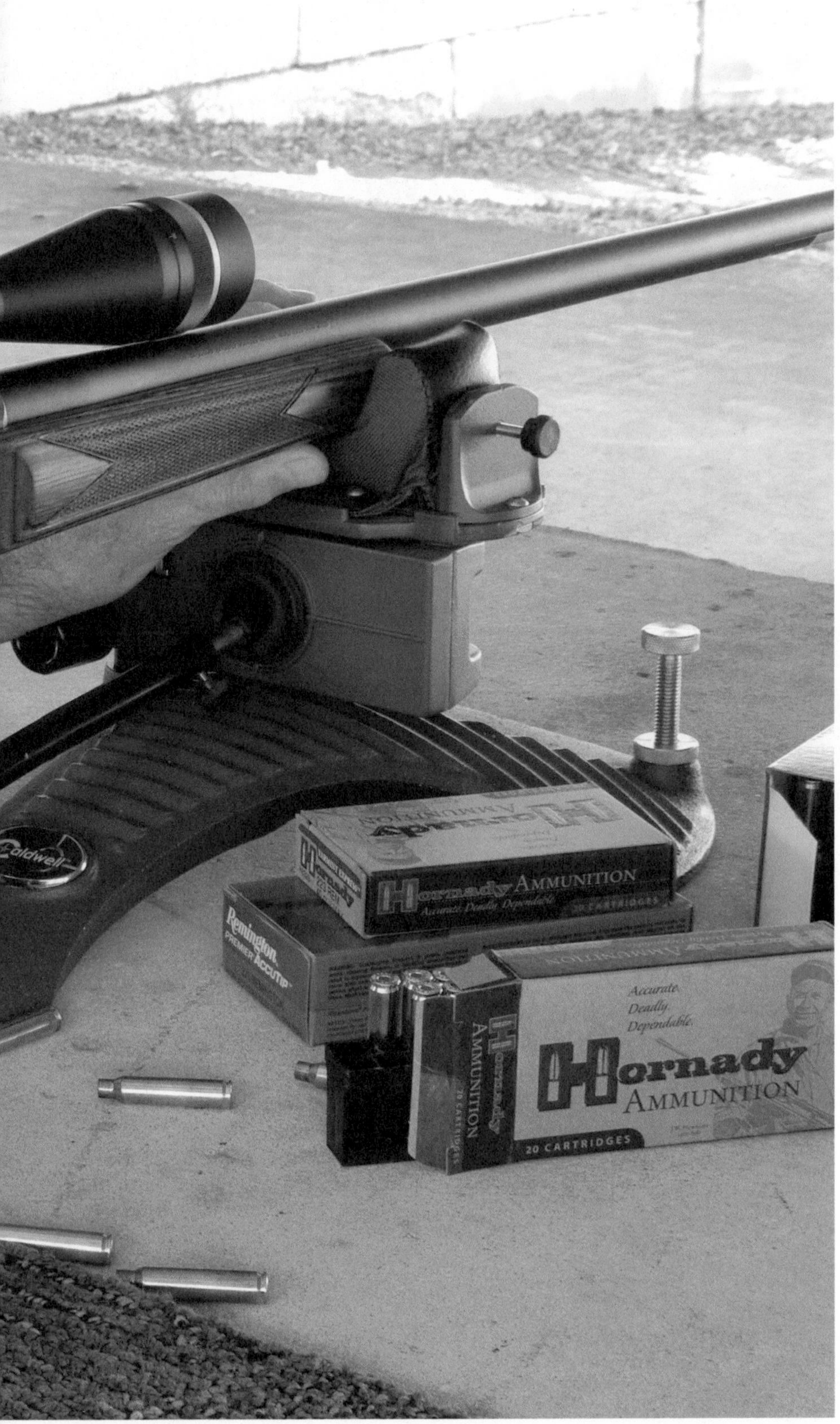

Shooting atop sandbags from a rock-steady bench should take the shooter's abilities out of the equation to a great extent, but not altogether. Some shooters are simply not capable of shooting half-inch groups with a half-minute rifle.

as minute of angle (MOA, or 1 inch at 100 yards), but some even guarantee ½-MOA. If the consumer gets reasonably close to what the maker claims, he's usually satisfied, because he knows the sample target sent with the rifle was probably fired in an underground test tunnel where there was no wind and mirage to contend with, that the scope used was probably of a much higher magnification than the one he's using, and the guy doing the shooting was a pro.

Still, there's always a few who will send the rifle back to the maker because they can't duplicate the accuracy that was guaranteed. In some cases, it was because the buyer didn't use the same control factory load or handload. In other cases, it was due to a change in the bedding dynamics of the rifle, be it the result of tinkering or simply climatic changes. And, in still other cases, it could be due to the fact that the customer simply couldn't shoot well enough. In the latter case, if a returned rifle is checked out and it does indeed pass the maker's guarantee, it brings about the awkward situation where the buyer has to be told, as diplomatically as possible, that he can't shoot.

What it all boils down to is there are many things one can learn about a rifle by reading a T&E, but, when it comes to accuracy, it only applies to the rifle in the test. I've shot groups with test guns that were so small I hesitated to report them, for fear some reader would buy that same gun and not get the same results. Such is the nature of this gun-writing business. With today's rifles and premium ammunition, a buyer can expect the sporter-weight rifle he buys to shoot— and I'm sticking my neck out here—1¼-inch three-shot groups at 100 yards, with fair consistency and with at least one in five factory loads tried. Many will do better, much better, especially if it's a heavy-barreled varmint or target rifle.

Last but not least, the writer has an obligation to express his subjective analysis of the gun's design, what he sees as its good and bad features and how the gun's overall quality and mechanical performance relate to its price. The latter is important, because you can't expect a $500 rifle to be of the same quality as one that is $1,500. As for all the other elements— the fit, finish, mechanical performance, etc.—the consumer has every right to expect the same, should he purchase that same gun.

FAMED AS THE "BROOMHANDLE"

The Mauser C96

BY MASSAD AYOOB

This landmark design changed things in a dimension far beyond the world of the pistol.

Here's the distinctive grip shape that gave the "broomhandle" its name, inlaid with the "red 9" denoting 9mm Luger chambering.

The C96 pistol is one of the most recognizable handguns ever made. Its integral magazine, loaded via stripper clips, sat ahead of the trigger guard, and its rather awkward grip-shape gave it the nickname "broomhandle." The C96 was the first military semiautomatic pistol to prove itself both rugged enough and reliable enough for field use, though its substantial size and a shape not conducive to concealment would limit its appeal as a "personal gun." Its stripper clip loading mechanism would never be as fast to reload as a semiautomatic with removable box magazines, particularly if the design encompassed the thumb button magazine release popularized by the Luger of 1902.

Many of these Mauser pistols left the factory with tangent sights that could supposedly be adjusted for accurate fire at hundreds of meters. That proved to be rather over-optimistic.

However, the Mauser was a far-reaching weapon in a much more important way. It was a harbinger of things to come, of the profound changes in battle tactics and technology that would take place in the 20th century. It was also very much a catalyst in the mind of one great leader who would be hugely influential in that enormous change in the face of modern warfare.

A brief history

Completed in prototype in the year 1895, patented in 1896, and coming off the production line in 1897, this pistol would be produced by Mauser until the late 1930s. It was the first truly successful semiautomatic pistol. The design is credited to three brothers: Fidel, Friedrich, and Josef Feederle.

Patented with a spur-shaped hammer, the gun would be produced primarily with a ring-shaped hammer, and for a time early in its epoch with a "coned" hammer. This had extensions that tapered out to the sides, intended to give better traction to the shooter's thumb, rather like the hammer spur attachments found on modern lever action rifles that have been mounted with telescopic sights.

Built with a short-recoil, locked breech mechanism, the C96 loads with stripper clips through the top of the mechanism's ejection port. The rectangular bolt enclosed in its receiver or frame is locked back during this procedure. A rearward tug on the bolt then chambers the topmost cartridge. While awkward and cumbersome by today's standards, the Mauser C96 design represented a quantum leap forward in handgun reloading speed in the late 19th century.

Its integral magazine machined into the gun forward of the trigger guard, the magazine's housing normally extended down level with the bottom of the trigger guard. It rode higher, almost to the top edge of the trigger guard, on the rare and short-lived compact model that did not survive into the 20th century; this model held only six cartridges. Still rare, though not as much so, were the later machine pistol variations with detachable, extended magazines that reached down almost parallel with the butt of the gun.

There were long gun versions, notably the *Kavallerie Karabiner* (cavalry carbine, complete with a wooden fore-end that extended from the magazine to well out under the barrel). Far more popular, however, was the detachable buttstock fitted to a C96 pistol with standard length barrel. This was made of wood, of course, and was cleverly hollowed out to also be a combination holster and storage box for the pistol itself, attaching to the rear of the grip frame and turning the pistol into a light, handy, short-barreled carbine. An ad for the gun, circa 1900, promised: "The Pistol is provided with a Walnut Butt Stock instantly attachable by a sliding tennon and spring catch to the back of the Grip.(sic) When not in use as a stock this Butt serves as a Holster its interior being hollowed out to the shape of the Pistol whose Grip projects about half its length outside to facilitate quick drawing."

C96 9mm in wooden holster/case/shoulder stock.

Over a span of some 40 years, Mauser produced approximately a million of these pistols. A very significant quantity of Mauser C96 copies were produced in Spain, mostly under the Astra and Royal marques, the latter produced by Beistegui Hermanos. In China, this pistol was adopted by military and police alike, and became hugely popular when the 1919 Arms Embargo Agreement stopped the import of battle rifles into that country. A loophole left shoulder-stocked pistols exempt, and Chinese warlords bought them in vast numbers. It was this market that led to the rise of the Spanish clones, and of China's own indigenous copies, the best generally recognized to be those from the Shanxi Arsenal and Hanyang Munitions Works.

The original caliber would be the most popular: 7.63X25mm Mauser, known at the time as simply 7.63mm Mauser. It sent a full metal jacket bullet weighing 86 grains downrange at a then-awesome velocity of 1450 feet per second, generating 402 foot-pounds of energy at the muzzle.

They would also be produced in significant numbers in 9mm Parabellum, and in small quantities for a proprietary cartridge called the 9mm Mauser Export. This was simply the bottlenecked 7.63mm Mauser case blown out to straight-wall dimensions to take a 9mm bullet. The People's Republic of China would eventually manufacture a clone chambered for the 7.62X25 Tokarev round. In China, the Shanxi Arsenal made oversize Mauser C96 clones chambered for the American .45 ACP cartridge, for commonality with the Thompson submachine guns that were then extremely popular in that land. Finally, Mauser briefly tried a proprietary cartridge, designated 8.15 mm, but it never got past the experimental stage.

The experimental cartridge was part of a fascinating chapter in the history of the broomhandle Mauser. After the Treaty of Versailles, ownership of firearms in military calibers was banned by the Weimar Republic. Oddly enough, 7.63mm Mauser was not considered a prohibited caliber, but 9mm Luger was. Mausers in 9mm Parabellum had to be altered to use an approved caliber, and stamped with the legend "1920," thus creating a collectible category of C96 pistols that became known as M1920 Reworks. Most were re-barreled to 7.63mm Mauser, and some to .30 Luger, but at least one specimen – pictured here – received the "1920" stamp but remained chambered for 9mm Parabellum. (It also retained its standard 5.5-inch barrel length, despite the fact that the rule permitted nothing longer than a 4-inch barrel, which was coincidental with the introduction of the 3.9-inch Bolo Mauser.)

One of the most famous variations of this pistol is the *Schnellfeuer* (fast-fire), a machine pistol with fully automatic capability. Ironically, this was a case of "imitating the imitator." It is widely believed among firearms historians that it was the Spanish clone-makers who first came up with selective-fire copies of the C96 for the Chinese market, and that Mauser introduced their version in response, even though Mauser had earlier developed full-auto models but not put them on the market. These were the Mausers with extended and removable magazines, the release button being ergonomically placed just above and ahead of the trigger guard for easy access by the shooter's (right) trigger finger. The selector switch also seems to

Closeup of Mauser in its wooden case which functions also as shoulder stock.

The "red 9" on stock panels distinguished 9mm Luger caliber from Mausers chambered for their usual 7.63mm Mauser cartridge.

Sight gradations on rear sight denoted distance settings in meters. Yes, they were optimistic...

have been more ergonomically placed on the Mauser *Schnellfeuer* than on the Spanish machine pistols.

Within the scope of this book, there simply isn't room to touch on all the vast number of Mauser C96 variations within a forty-year production run of a million pistols. For a short overview, the Wikipedia entry on the Mauser C96 seems complete and correct at this writing. For a deeper perspective, the reader is referred to *The Broomhandle Mauser Pistol 1896-1936* by Erickson and Pate, *The Mauser Self-Loading Pistol* by Belford and Dunlap, and *System Mauser* by Breathed and Shroeder.

Shooting the C96

I know of no shooting championship ever won with the Model 96, but that was never part of its design parameters. My old and much mourned friend, the late Dean Grennell, once wrote of his personal C96, "Neither impressively accurate nor reliable in comparison to several other auto pistols, it had a most disconcerting habit of letting off two or three (shots) together, now and then."[1] The great handgun historian Geoffrey Boothroyd would write, "To modern eyes, the Mauser pistol is rather clumsy, complicated, and by no means easy to shoot without the shoulder stock attachment. On the other hand, it is beautifully made to an extremely high standard, and a delightful pistol to own even if only for the pleasure of dismantling and the subsequent feeling of astonishment at the ingenuity with which it has been

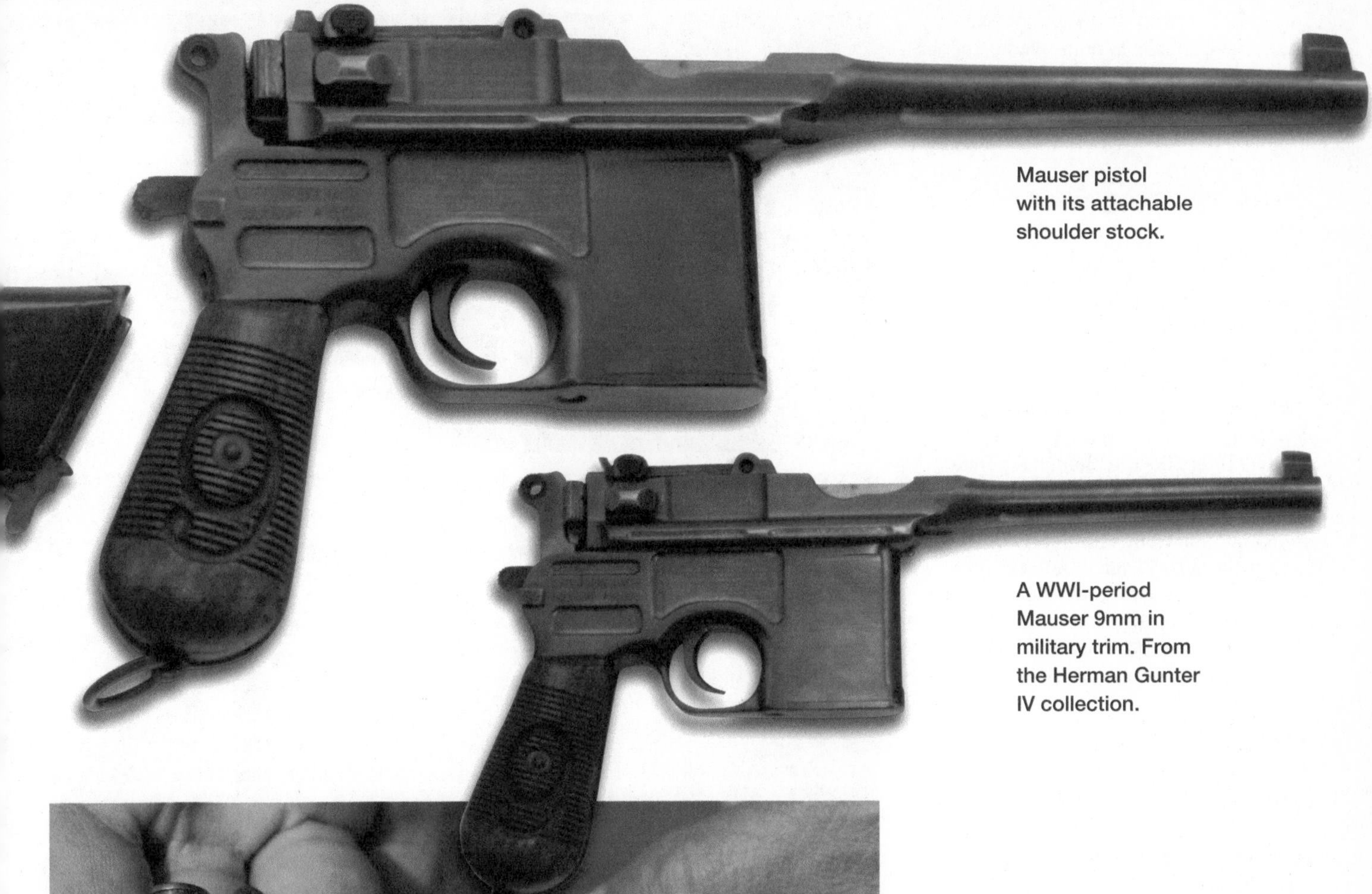

Mauser pistol with its attachable shoulder stock.

A WWI-period Mauser 9mm in military trim. From the Herman Gunter IV collection.

7.63mm Mauser ammo. Its relatively high velocity caused significant "secondary fragment" wound damage when the bullet hit bone.

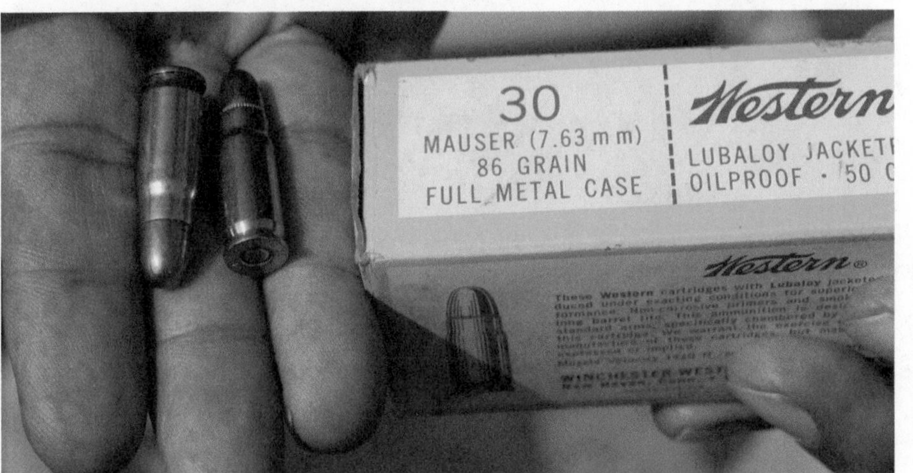

constructed. It was also the first pistol to incorporate a feature now considered essential, a hold-open device to ensure that the breech remains open after the last cartridge has been fired."[2]

Pedigree

For most, the C96 is a pistol of history and of fiction. Its ungainly shape and slow-to-reload mechanism had rendered it obsolete as a service handgun long before Mauser discontinued it. Movie directors loved it for its exotic, sinister looks. Frank Sinatra wielded a shoulder-stocked version in the movie "The Naked Runner," and George Lucas and his prop

This "1920" stamp was supposed to show that gun was in non-military caliber and sported shortened barrel, per post-WWI military weapons restrictions on German arms industry...

crew kitted out Harrison Ford's Han Solo character with a broomhandle Mauser reshaped into his space gun "blaster" in the *Star Wars* movies. This pistol is the one which fans of Sax Rohmer novels would expect the evil genius Dr. Fu Manchu to draw from beneath his silken robes.

Yet, the gun was very real. Fairbairn and Sykes, the revolutionary combat pistol trainers for the Shanghai police in the 1920s, noted that the C96 was popular with the Chinese underworld and much feared by law enforcement. Its high velocity 7.63mm bullet tended to cause hideous wounds when it struck bone and shattered it into secondary missiles coursing out of the wound path in the victim's body.

...but as camera draws back we can see it still has military length barrel, and examination shows it is still chambered for "forbidden" 9mm Parabellum. An early warning that Germany was not entirely complying... Pistol is from the Herman Gunter IV collection.

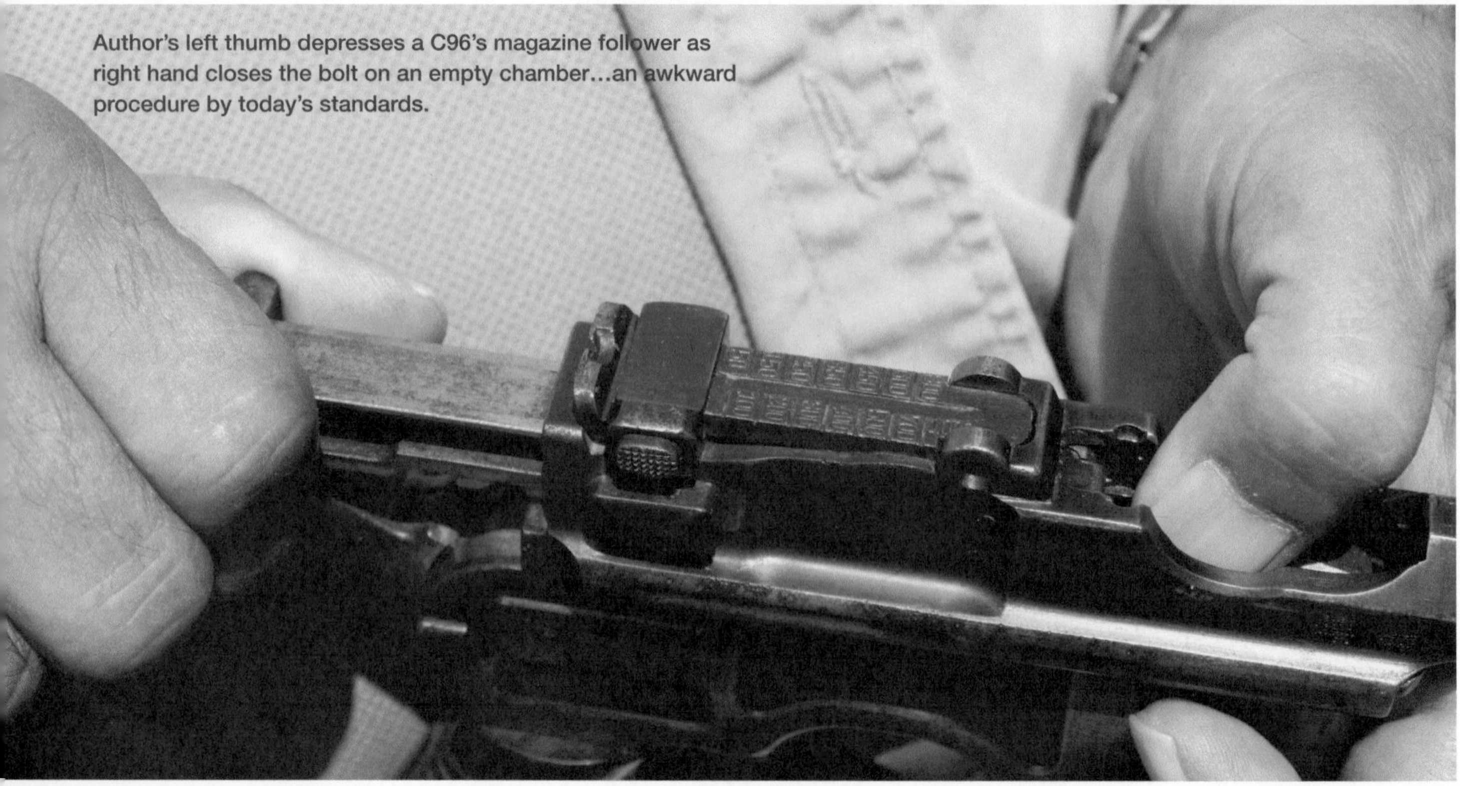

Author's left thumb depresses a C96's magazine follower as right hand closes the bolt on an empty chamber...an awkward procedure by today's standards.

A 7.63mm Mauser C96 at "bolt-lock." This Mauser was the first pistol to lock its mechanism open automatically when it ran dry of cartridges, the better to facilitate reloading. Mauser set a standard for auto pistol design with this feature.

In WWI, 150,000 Mauser 96s were ordered by the Imperial German Army to supplement the Luger pistol. It had become abundantly clear that, in trench warfare, a handgun was a vital tool of close-quarter survival. These guns were chambered for the 9mm Luger cartridge. To help assure that they wouldn't be mistakenly loaded with the original 7.63 mm. Mauser ammunition, these particular C96s were produced with a huge, crimson-color numeral "9" on each side of the wooden grips. They would become known as "Red Nine Mausers," and dubbed by some collectors the 1916 Prussian model. The German contract for the supplemental Mausers was a stark parallel to United States orders for heavy frame Colt and Smith & Wesson Model 1917 revolvers during the same period to augment the Colt 1911 semi-automatic pistol, which also couldn't be manufactured in enough volume to outfit every combat soldier on the line.

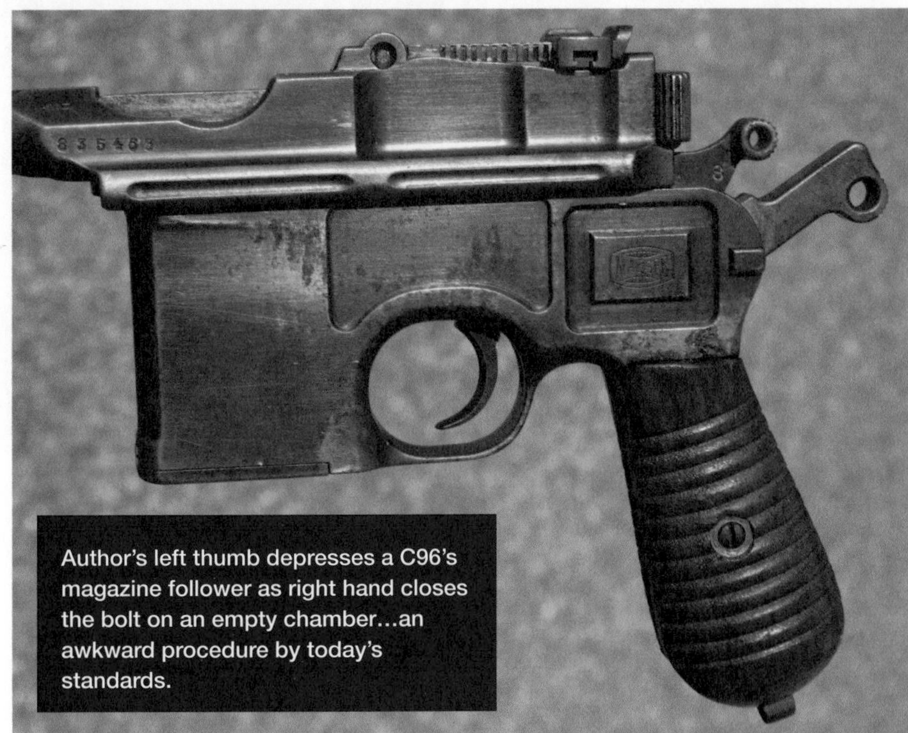

Author's left thumb depresses a C96's magazine follower as right hand closes the bolt on an empty chamber…an awkward procedure by today's standards.

Indeed, the German military used these guns through WWII. Almost 8,000 C96s, the M30 commercial grade, were reportedly furnished to the Luftwaffe and proofmarked by the Wehrmacht. These were produced from the early 1930s to no later than 1940.

The C96 saw extensive use in the Spanish Civil War, and was a favorite of Chinese warlords. China was so taken with these guns that they couldn't get enough Mausers, giving rise to Spanish-made and eventually Chinese-made copies.

Many refer to the C96 as the "Bolo Mauser" as if this was as generic a nickname for it as "broomhandle." Not so; the term "Bolo" was short for Bolshevik. After the Bolsheviks took over Russia, they ordered large quantities of a C96 variant produced from 1920 to 1921, which featured smaller grips and a handy 3.9-inch barrel. This was the true Bolo Mauser.

However, when we think of famous people who used this gun in real life, one name stands out conspicuously above all others…Sir Winston Churchill.

Left: This 19th Century single action auto was actually surprisingly ergonomic when taken from "cocked and locked" carry to "Fire" mode. Here it's on safe. Note that BALL of author's thumb is on the safety lever, now in "on safe" position...

Far Left: ...and has ample leverage to bring it down into "Fire" position, as shown.

The Churchill Connection

On September 2, 1898, the man some would later call the greatest statesman of the 20th century was a 23-year-old cavalry Lieutenant, sent forward at the Battle of Omdurman. British army officers were expected to provide their own handguns, and cavalry officers were expected to use them only as backups for their traditional sabers. Wielded one-handed, as it must be from horseback, the long sword grows heavy in extended encounters, and in the battle some of Churchill's counterparts came to grief when their sword-arms fatigued faster than the enemy fell.

Churchill was armed with a Mauser C96, carried in the wooden holster that doubled as a shoulder stock. Historians say his doting mother, the beautiful and powerful Jennie Churchill, used her substantial influence to get him to the front. He had desperately wanted to be there, but some senior officers just as desperately didn't want him. They called him a "medal-hunter," a glory hound. There was some truth to this. Churchill himself frankly admitted that he sought to test himself in combat and win honors. However, what may not have been known to all of his superiors was the fact that he had also made a deal with publishers in England to send back accounts of battle, "dispatches from the front." He had already realized that writing was one of his natural talents, and he wanted the writing fees not only to augment his relatively meager pay from his military service, but to become independent of his mother, who managed his late father's estate and was quickly depleting it with her lavish lifestyle.

Jennie Churchill figured into the matter in another way: many of those historians believe she gave him the pistol. One, however, states that young Winston Churchill got to Egypt and realized he had forgotten to pack his revolver, and acquired the Mauser there.

A third version of the acquisition, to which I have to assign the most credibility, comes from Churchill himself in a quote discovered by the great British firearms expert Geoffrey Boothroyd. He quotes Churchill as follows: "On account of my shoulder (which had been dislocated in India) I had always decided that if I were involved in hand-to-hand fighting, I must use a pistol and not a sword. I had purchased in London a Mauser automatic pistol, then the newest and latest design. I had practiced carefully with this during our march and journey up the river."[3]

Trigger reach wasn't bad at all on the Mauser C96, shown in author's hand.

It was "the latest and newest," just the sort of thing to appeal to a modern young man as the turn of the 20th century approached. Whether it was he or his mother who bought it, the price would have been about five English pounds at the time, according to Boothroyd in his classic book, *The Handgun*. Churchill was certainly not the only Brit who acquired one and took it to war. Thomas Edward Lawrence, the legendary "Lawrence of Arabia," also carried a Mauser C96. He would have been ten years old when Churchill wielded his Mauser at the Battle of Omdurman.

Wherever he had acquired the pistol, Winston Churchill was inarguably grateful to have it. He had suffered an arm/shoulder injury earlier, and knew he was in no shape to swing a heavy cavalry saber. The Mauser was his weapon throughout the historic fight.

I've seen no more detailed account of the incident than the one from the great historian and biographer William Manchester, in *The Last Lion: Winston Spencer Churchill*. Weaving other accounts of the conflict in with Churchill's own remembrances, Manchester reconstructs those two minutes of hell as follows:

Scrambling into their saddles, the massed lancers walked forward at a deliberate pace, stepping over the crisp desert toward the city, stirred by what Churchill called "a high state of excitement." Presently they noticed, three hundred yards away and parallel to their course, a long row of blue-black objects, two or three yards apart. At that moment the bugles sounded Trot, and the regiment began to jingle and clatter across the front of these crouching dervishes. It was a lull in the battle. Except for the sound of the harnesses, silence was near perfect. Abruptly the Arabs broke it, firing a volley; three horses and several lancers toppled to the ground. Until then the colonel had intended to swing around the flank of the enemy riflemen, but now he decided to attack them head-on. The bugles sounded Right Wheel into Line. There was no further order. As Winston wrote Hamilton: "Gallop & Charge were understood." In a solid line, the regiment lunged toward what appeared to be 150 dervish riflemen.

At this critical moment, Winston became preoccupied with a personal problem. He had every confidence in his gray polo pony, but until the regiment wheeled he, like the other officers, had been carrying a drawn sword. Because of his bad shoulder, he had decided early in the campaign that if hand-to-hand combat loomed, he would rely on his pistol. At full gallop, he had to return his sword to its scabbard and fumble for his wooden holster. He explained to Hamilton: "I drew my Mauser pistol – a ripper – and cocked it. Then I looked to my front. Instead of the 150 riflemen who were still blazing I saw a line nearly (in the middle) – 12 deep … of closely jammed spearmen – all in a nullah with steep sloping sides 6 foot deep & 20 foot broad." The lancers found themselves heading into a mob of nearly three thousand dervishes led by mounted emirs waving bright flags. What had happened? The Khalifa's black flag, which had moved to within five hundred yards of this dry watercourse, should have told them. He had anticipated the flanking movement and reinforced the khor. Thus, the 310 shouting lancers, plunging furiously ahead in crescent formation, their overlapping flanks curving inward like the horns of a moon, their helmets bowed against the enemy musketry like the cuirassiers at Waterloo, were hurtling toward a wall of human flesh.

The collision was tremendous. Nearly thirty lancers and their horses, Churchill wrote, "fell knocked A.O.T. (arse over tip)." Some two hundred dervishes were down. Winston himself had passed between two riflemen; both had fired at him, missed, and hit the trooper just behind him, who was immediately stabbed to death as he slid from his mount. But most of the dervishes – and the British – were too stunned to fight. "For perhaps ten wonderful seconds no man heeded his enemy." Terrified horses were wedged in the mob. Bruised men lay in heaps, dazed and astonished. Several lancers, unhorsed but alert, had time to remount. Then the Arabs began to come to their senses. They threw spears at their enemies, swung heavy swords, cut reins and stirrup leathers, and tried to hamstring horses. Troopers jabbed back with their lances, officers with their sabers. Churchill saw his men being "dragged from their horses and cut to pieces by the infuriated foe."

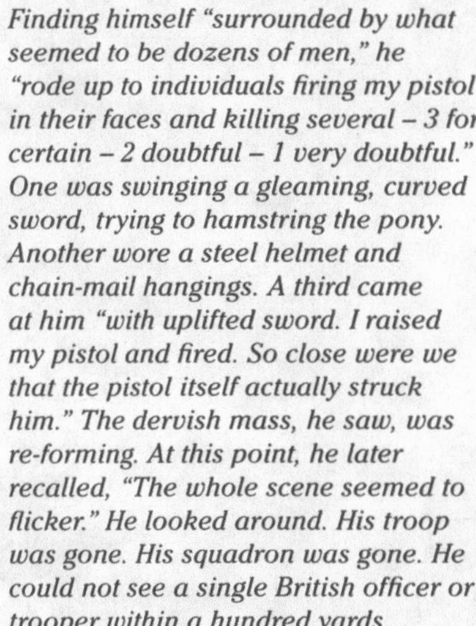

Finding himself "surrounded by what seemed to be dozens of men," he "rode up to individuals firing my pistol in their faces and killing several – 3 for certain – 2 doubtful – 1 very doubtful." One was swinging a gleaming, curved sword, trying to hamstring the pony. Another wore a steel helmet and chain-mail hangings. A third came at him "with uplifted sword. I raised my pistol and fired. So close were we that the pistol itself actually struck him." The dervish mass, he saw, was re-forming. At this point, he later recalled, "The whole scene seemed to flicker." He looked around. His troop was gone. His squadron was gone. He could not see a single British officer or trooper within a hundred yards…

…Hunching down over his pommel, he spurred his pony free and found his squadron two hundred yards away, faced about and already forming up. His own troop had just finished sorting itself out, but as he joined it a dervish sprang out of a hole in the ground and into the midst of his men, lunging about with a spear. They thrust at him with their lances; he dodged, wheeled, and charged Churchill. "I shot him at less than a yard. He fell on the sand, and lay there dead. How easy to kill a man! But I did not worry about it. I found I had fired the whole magazine of my Mauser pistol, so I put in a new clip of ten cartridges before thinking of anything else." It occurred to him that if he hadn't injured his shoulder in Bombay, he would have had to defend himself with a sword and might now be dead. Afterward he reflected, "One must never forget when misfortunes come that it is quite possible they are saving one from something much worse." He wrote Jennie: "The pistol was the best thing in the world."[4]

Young Winston Churchill's use of a C96 in combat would have far reaching consequences.

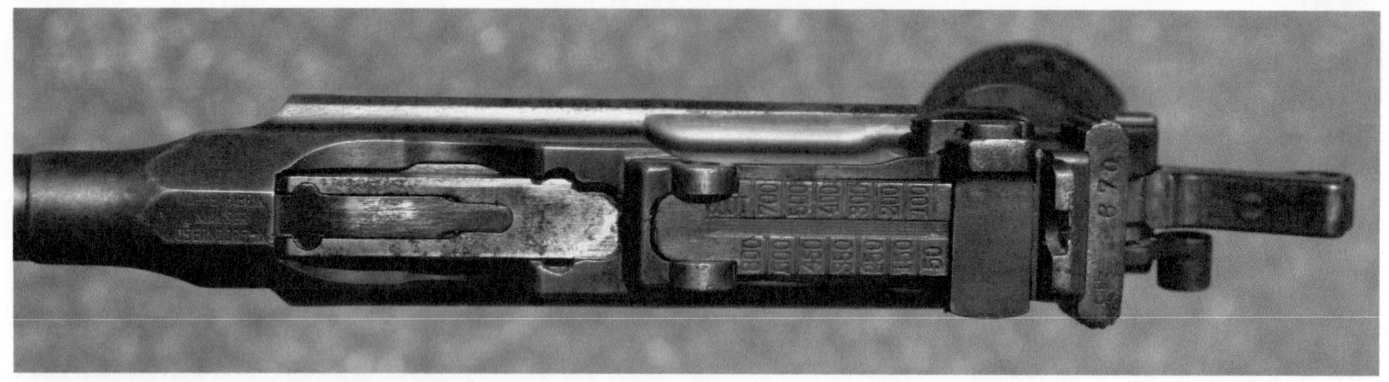

Above: Seen from above, the C96 Mauser was a "Flat" pistol... "the shape of things to come" in semiautomatic pistol design.

The front sight of a Mauser C96. It didn't give much to line up, from a shooter's eye view.

View from the shooter's side of the gun before the trigger is pulled...

...and after the hammer has fallen. Note the relatively tiny rear sight notch.

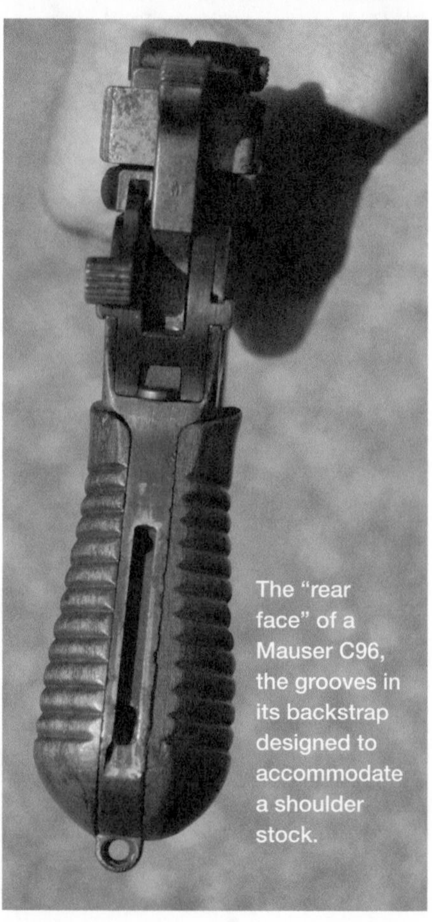

The "rear face" of a Mauser C96, the grooves in its backstrap designed to accommodate a shoulder stock.

Churchill and his biographer were not the only ones to conclude that the ten-shot Mauser had saved his life, and that neither the saber nor a revolver with five or six shots might have sufficed. There had been little time in the melee for a young officer who needed one hand to control the reins of his horse to eject spent casings and insert live cartridges into a wheel gun. Notes another biographer, Martin Gilbert in Churchill: A Life, "The cavalry charge was over and the troop dispersed. 'It was, I suppose, the most dangerous two minutes I shall live to see,' Churchill told Hamilton. Of the 310 officers and men in the charge, one officer and twenty men had been killed, and four officers and forty-five men wounded. 'All this in 120 seconds!' Churchill commented. He had fired 'exactly 10 shots' and had emptied his pistol, 'but without a hair of my horse or a stitch of my clothing being touched. Very few can say the same.'"5

An electronic publication from London's Churchill Centre and Museum puts it even more succinctly: "The 21st Lancers came close upon the enemy, only to find that they had ridden into a trap—for behind the original force of Dervishes the enemy was arrayed twelve men deep in a shallow ravine. There followed hand-to-hand combat of the fiercest and most deadly kind. In 1955 Churchill recalled for Anthony Montague Browne: "...it was most exhilarating. But I did reflect, 'suppose there is some spoil sport in a hole with a machine gun?"' Churchill was lucky in that he was on the far right of the line where the enemy was not so thick. He owed his survival to his position, and the fact that he was armed not with a sword but with a Mauser automatic pistol, 'a ripper,' which saved his life. He used a pistol instead of a sword because of an old shoulder injury."[6]

Some have speculated that Churchill's two minutes with the Mauser C96 constituted the first documented use of the semiautomatic pistol in actual combat. I can't confirm that with absolute certainty, but it's certainly the first such usage that I've been able to find.

It definitely made Churchill himself a believer in the Mauser C96. He kept it to the end of his days. It is said to now repose in a museum in England, and the story goes that this actual gun was used in the filming of the movie, "Young Winston."

Winston Churchill was always a man who appreciated a good handgun. My old friend Richard Law, one of the foremost firearms authorities and researchers in the British Isles, documented that in World War II, Sir Winston off-handedly asked his lead bodyguard what he was carrying for a pistol. It was a legitimate concern, since the threat of assassination by Nazis and their agents was very real. That worthy replied that he carried a small caliber Webley. Churchill immediately requisitioned a Colt .45 automatic for the man most likely to have to protect him. Not long after, Churchill asked the same question, and discovered that his bodyguard was still carrying the smaller gun. In a huff, the Prime Minister demanded the Colt .45 back, loaded it, and shoved it into the pocket of his own heavy overcoat. Law would later find WWII era photographs of Churchill where he was in positions where his suit coat was drawn tightly against his body, revealing the unmistakable "print" of a 1911 pistol stuffed into the great man's waistband. It is known that in the early 1950s, Colt presented Sir Winston Churchill with one of the very first lightweight Colt Commander pistols. I have little doubt that the pugnacious bulldog of Britain kept it loaded and close to hand.

Master combat handgun instructor Tom Givens shows how to bring the holster/stock and the C96 together...

There we have, in microcosm, the single most famous actual use of the Mauser Model 96 pistol in action, and perhaps the very first.

But let's look at what it led to in macrocosm.

Reading the voluminous legacy of written wisdom that Sir Winston Churchill left behind – particularly *The River War*, his own account of Omdurman and the campaign in the Sudan – it is clear that he went into it as a young soldier seeking honor and revering the old ways of martial Britain. In his very early work, we see if we look for it his wistful sadness that he had witnessed the passing of traditional "gentlemen's warfare" and the nobility that concept had conjured in him before he faced the

foe in Omdurman, outnumbered some ten to one.

The battle created a marked change in the way he thought. Omdurman would mark, not the last cavalry charge, but what many military historians considered the last great cavalry charge. Though Churchill had been in the thick of it, had fought and killed hand to hand, he also saw the big picture once it was over. Before he and the 21st Lancers moved forward toward the enemy, the opposing force had been greatly softened by a massive artillery barrage, and by the judicious application of Maxim machine guns. Martini-Henry rifles, fired in volleys by British soldiers trained for deadly accuracy, had had some effect, too, before the historic cavalry advance.

From the electronic research source "Suite 101: Winston Churchill and the Last Cavalry Charge," comes this very telling insight: "For Winston Churchill significance of the battle of Omdurman was never lost on him. He came to understand that technology, discipline and firepower could overwhelm any enemy, a belief he espoused in his later years when describing the fight in World War II against Nazi Germany, and which he put into words shortly after the battle when he wrote, 'Thus ended the Battle of Omdurman—the most signal triumph ever gained by the arms of science over barbarians. Within the space of five hours the strongest and best-armed savage army yet arrayed against a modern European Power had been destroyed and dispersed, with hardly any difficulty, comparatively small risk, and insignificant loss to the victors.' For Churchill, it was also just one more remarkable personal event in a life that would in ensuing years overflow with them."[6]

Winston Churchill had gone to Egypt a young idealist, and remained so in many respects. The campaign there under Lord Kitchener was something of a crusade for revenge. The British public thirsted for justice against the forces that had slaughtered their beloved general "Chinese" Gordon, mercilessly putting his entire garrison to death, at the Siege of Khartoum almost a decade and a half earlier. Sir Herbert Kitchener, who led the great victory at Omdurman, ordered a reciprocal slaughter of the many wounded enemy combatants. Churchill was forever sickened and angered by this. Sir Winston would write later, "The stern and unpitying spirit of the commander was communicated to his troops, and the victories which marked the progress of the River War were accompanied by acts of barbarity not always justified even by the harsh customs of savage conflicts or the fierce and treacherous nature of the Dervish." Said Churchill,"It may be that the Gods forbad vengeance to man because they reserved for themselves so intoxicating a drink. But the cup should not be drained to the bottom. The dregs are often filthy-tasting."7

If his ideals remained staunch insofar as honor and humanity after his time in the Sudan, Churchill's idealism in regard to old-fashioned warfare did not. Saved by a ten-shot semiautomatic pistol when friends and brothers armed with more primitive weapons died around him, fully aware that in the larger scope it had been modern heavy weapons that crushed a vastly outnumbering foe with a gratifyingly low casualty count on his own side, he left any delusions of the honor of traditional 19th century warfare behind him in the blood-soaked sands of Omdurman. He would, thereafter, be an advocate for the most modern killing machines for the side of Right when killing had to be done.

Lost to the general world public in the scope of this great man's achievements in the second World War was a Churchill

Master self-defense instructor Tom Givens demonstrates what may be the most efficient two-handed firing hold of the shoulder-stocked Mauser pistol.

achievement from the first: the man was a visionary of armored warfare. Historian William W. Lace called Winston Churchill "The Father of the Tank." Writes Lace, "In 1915, Churchill, searching for a way to break the stalemate brought on by trench warfare in Europe, urged that several current ideas be merged to create a new weapon, the tank."

Here, Lace quotes the letter Churchill wrote to then-Prime Minister Herbert Asquith: "It would be quite easy in a short time to fit up a number of steam tractors with small armoured shelters, in which men and machine guns could be placed, which would be bullet-proof. Used at night they would not be affected by artillery fire to any extent. The caterpillar system would enable trenches to be crossed quite easily, and the weight of the machine would destroy all wire entanglements. Forty or fifty of these engines prepared secretly and brought into position at nightfall could advance quite certainly into the enemy's trenches with their machine-gun fire and with grenades thrown out of the top. They would then make so many points d'appui (points of support) for the British supporting infantry to rush forward and rally on them. They can then move forward to attack the second line of trenches. The cost would be small. If the experiment did not answer (work), what harm would be done? An obvious measure of prudence would have been to have started something like this two months ago. It should certainly be done now."8

Lace wrote, "Armored tanks, Churchill's idea, helped break the stalemate resulting from trench warfare in World War I."

Like Isaac Newton's inspiration of understanding gravity when an apple fell on his head, Winston Churchill's two minutes of desert combat with a Mauser C96 pistol in his hand had far-reaching consequences. It was there that he learned the value of modern machinery when men had to fight to the death for the causes in which they believed, the better to protect one's own and destroy in self-defense those whom they fought.

In summary

Seen merely in the light of handgun history, the Mauser Pistol of 1896 stands on its own as a classic. It was the first semiautomatic pistol to prove itself reliable and effective enough for combat, setting the stage for the Luger, the Colt/Browning 1911, and all the others that followed to this day. It was apparently the first auto pistol to lock itself open when shot dry, signaling to the shooter that it was time to reload, and mechanically facilitating that process. It was sufficiently popular to sell a seven-figure production count, and engender numerous clones in numerous countries.

Seen in the bigger picture, though, there is a direct continuum not often found in the history of specific makes and models of firearms. First, this particular gun appears promising enough for a young soldier to take into battle. Then, its unique features save his life, and teach him at an inescapable gut level the importance of deliverable, practical firepower in combat. That young man becomes a member of Parliament in a position to influence major decisions in the biggest war thus far in the history of mankind. His idea turns mechanized warfare into highly mobile mechanized warfare. During the peak years of his life he will see a similar dynamic occur when Albert Einstein inspires Franklin D. Roosevelt to fund the development of the nuclear bomb… and the rest, of course, is history.

By those lights, the Mauser C96 is not merely worthy of "classic status," but is a front-runner for the title of Most Influential Handgun of All Time.

Notes

[1] Grennell, Dean, *The Gun Digest Book of Autoloading Pistols*, DBI Books, Northfield, IL, 1983, Page 31

[2] Boothroyd, Geoffrey, *The Handgun*, 1970, Bonanza Books, NYC, Pages 393-394.

[3] Boothroyd, ibid., Page 397.

[4] Manchester, William, *The Last Lion: Winston Spencer Churchill*, Little, Brown, 1983, pages 277-279.

[5] Gilbert, Martin, *Churchill: A Life*, 1991, Henry Holt & Co., NYC, Page 96.

[6] Lt. Churchill: 4th Queens Own Hussars, Churchill Centre and Museum, London

(Suite 101 Cite) Winston Churchill and the Last Cavalry Charge | Suite101.com http://www.suite101.com/content/winston-churchill-and-the-last-cavalry-charge-a276217#ixzz1U0QDrDq6

[7] Churchill, Winston, *The River War: An Historical Account of the Reconquest of the Soudan*, 1899, via Martin Gilbert.

[8] Lace, William W., *The Importance of Winston Churchill*, 1995, Lucent Books, San Diego, CA, Page 54.

The History Behind The Popularity Of Today's Smallest Handguns

THE TRUTH ABOUT MOUSE GUNS

BY PAUL SCARLATA

PHOTOS BY Michael Hughes & Dick Cole

According to Wikipedia, a mouse gun is "... a category of small revolver, or semi-automatic handgun intended for self-defense. Typically, such small pistols are of .380 ACP (9mm Short) caliber or less, with .32 ACP and .22 Long Rifle calibers also being common." The on-line encyclopedia goes on to explain, "Among mouse gun users, the term itself is not usually considered to be pejorative, but is instead affectionately used ... . Those who favor larger, heavier handguns do often use the term mousegun for any small caliber firearm in a disparaging way ... . Among those who prefer larger, heavier guns, the term mousegun is sometimes applied to junk guns, especially those in .22 Long Rifle or .25 ACP."

So, there you have what looks like grounds for a good argument among shooters. And while it might not be one that generates the same level of heated debate as those perennially favorite discussions—the 9mm versus .45, or the .270 versus the .30-06—I believe the subject deserves examination.

By the way, despite what Wikipedia says, I don't believe the .380 is truly a mouse gun cartridge. It is generally agreed that the .380 is the minimum pistol caliber considered adequate for personal protection and, with some of the modern loadings now available, its performance comes close to that of lower-end 9mms. In addition, most of the pistols chambered for it are larger than their .22-, .25-, and .32-caliber brethren.

Let me begin by stating that, even before the introduction of cartridge-firing handguns, so-called mouse guns were extremely popular. In its day, Henry Deringer's tiny, muzzleloading percussion pistol was carried by gamblers, lawmen, ladies-of-the-night, and even presidential assassins. In fact, its popularity was such that, to the present day, the term "derringer" is synonymous with any small single- or multi-barrel pistol.

I believe it's germane to the discussion to state that the first American-made, metallic cartridge revolver was a mouse gun. Introduced in 1857, the Smith & Wesson Model 1 was chambered for the first successful rimfire cartridge, the .22 Short. Loaded with a mere four grains of blackpowder, this miniscule cartridge propelled a 28- to 30-grain lead bullet to approximately 800 fps, creating barely 44 ft-lbs of energy. (One might have had trouble stopping a really determined mouse with it.) But, despite its lack of knockdown power, the No. 1's small size and rapid (for the time) reloading made it an instant favorite with the same people who had carried derringers, and it was widely used as a backup gun by Union army officers during the Civil War.

With developments in both rimfire and centerfire ammunition, the post-Civil War era saw dozens of manufacturers offering cartridge-firing revolvers. While the popular image of that time is of a cowboy wearing a holstered .45-caliber Colt Peacemaker, the fact is the most popular handguns on the civilian market were small, solid-frame and top-break revolvers firing .22- and .32-caliber rimfire and centerfire cartridges. In other words, mouse guns.

The early 1870s saw the introduction of the .32 Colt, followed a few years later by the .32 S&W cartridge. Both launched 80- to 85-grain bullets to approximately 700 fps, creating 90 to 100 ft-lbs of energy. While unacceptable by today's standards, at the time, both were considered suitable for personal/home-defense and police service. Both rounds—along with the improved .22 Long—were also chambered in a plethora of small, inexpensive revolvers, the quality of some being so suspect that the breed was dubbed "Suicide Specials."

Beginning in the 1880s, military revolvers in calibers ranging from 7.5mm to 8mm were fielded by the armies of France, Austria-Hungary, Sweden, Norway, Belgium, Russia, and Switzerland, and several of these firearms would remain in service until the 1950s. In 1896, Smith & Wesson introduced its .32 S&W Long cartridge, which propelled a 98-grain lead bullet to 780 fps for 132 ft-lbs of energy. But the year after the introduction of the .32 S&W Long, the development of mouse guns took a totally different direction, thanks to a Mormon genius from Utah, named John Moses Browning.

By the end of the nineteenth century, Browning was already recognized as one of the world's premier firearm designers. In the 1890s, his mechanical genius turned towards the design of self-loading firearms, and his first U.S. patents for a semi-auto pistol were granted in April of 1897. That year, Browning offered the Belgian firm of Fabrique Nationale d'Armes (FN) the design for a .32-caliber pistol, and the shrewd Belgians quickly saw its commercial possibilities. A contract was signed and, two years later, FN began production of the Pistolet Automatique Browning Mle. 1900, which quickly became the hottest item on the world firearms market—so much so, in fact, that, in many parts of the world, "Browning" became synonymous with "semi-auto pistol."

The Model 1900 was a blowback design in which the weight of the slide and tension of the recoil spring held the breech closed until the bullet had left the barrel. The slide then moved to the rear, extracting and ejecting the spent case before being pulled forward again by the recoil spring, stripping a new cartridge out of the magazine and chambering it as it did.

Where it all began. The Smith & Wesson Model No. 1 was the first cartridge-firing revolver made in the U.S. and introduced the .22 Short rimfire round before the Civil War.

The Model 1900's cartridge, the 7.65mm Browning—or, as it's known in the USA, the .32 ACP—became even more famous than the pistol itself. It utilized a semi-rimmed case 17.3 millimeters long and was loaded with a seven-grain full-metal-jacketed (FMJ) bullet that achieved a velocity of approximately 900 fps. It was well suited to blowback-operated pistols and was immediately embraced by European military and police forces. Both President Theodore Roosevelt, as well as John Browning himself, carried Model 1900 pistols for personal protection.

The FN firm next asked Browning to design a small pistol that could be carried handily in a pocket, and, in 1905, John Moses presented the Belgians with a 6.35mm (.25 ACP) pistol. Released on the market the following year as the Pistolet Automatique Browning Mle. 1905, it was the smallest semi-auto pistol made at the time and was another instant hit. In the U.S., Colt's produced the same pistol as the Model 1908.

Browning had also designed the

Designed by John Browning, FN's Model 1905 was the first .25 caliber autoloading pistol on the world market.

new cartridge. The 6.35mm Browning consisted of a semi-rimmed case 15.6 millimeters long, topped with a 50-grain FMJ bullet propelled to 760 fps. While woefully underpowered by American standards, Europeans felt it was perfectly adequate for close-range defensive purposes, and 6.35mm pistols proved very popular with civilians, police detectives, and high-ranking military officers. Because they could be readily carried in a coat pocket, the 7.65mm pistols became known as "pocket pistols" (*taschenpistoleni*, in German), while their smaller 6.35mm brethren were baptized "vest pocket pistols" (or *westentaschenpistolen*).

To meet what became an insatiable demand for these semi-auto mouse guns, manufacturers in Germany, Spain, Belgium, Austria, France, England, and Italy were soon producing a plethora of 6.35mm and 7.65mm pistols. These guns saw wide use during both World Wars. Many armies—including the U.S. Army—issued 7.65mm pistols as service sidearms, while the smaller 6.35mm pistols were often carried by European and Japanese officers. By the 1920s, the vast majority of European police agencies issued 7.65mm pistols, and production of these pistols by manufacturers such as Walther, Beretta, FN, Astra, CZ, and Mauser continued into the 1990s. (An interesting note: one reason for the continuing popularity of 6.35mm and 7.65mm pistols and .32 revolvers outside of the U.S. is that a number of foreign countries forbid civilian ownership of handguns chambered for larger cartridges.)

Available in 7.65mm and 9mm Browning Short (.32 ACP & .380 Auto), the FN Pistolet Automatique Browning Mle. 1910 was one of the slimmest and sleekest of all pocket pistols. It was used by many European military and police forces.

On this side of the Big Pond, before WWII, Colt's, Savage, Harrington & Richardson, S&W, and Remington all produced pocket and vest pocket pistols in .25 ACP and .32 ACP. While they were moderately popular, they never replaced the small-frame, snub-nosed revolvers as the preferred concealed carry handgun of American police and civilians. The primary reason for their lack of acceptance in this country was the lackluster cartridges for which they were chambered. The .25 ACP and .32 ACP were traditionally loaded with FMJ bullets that produced only modest levels of energy, not even close to that of .38 Special revolvers. So, the only real advantage that .25- and .32-caliber pistols provided was concealability. Their short lengths and flat profiles made them much more convenient to carry and conceal in a pocket or under light clothing than did a revolver. Their low levels of recoil also made them suitable for people with small hands or who had trouble handling recoil, which is why many manufacturers marketed them as "ladies guns."

Except for Colt's, U.S. production of .25 and .32 ACP pistols ceased prior to WWII; Colt's stopped manufacturing its M1903 .32 (and M1908 .380) pistol in 1945, while that of the .25 ACP M1908 ended two years later. Smith & Wesson's introduction of the small-frame Chiefs Special revolver in .38 Special, in 1950, effectively sealed the fate of the semi-auto mouse gun on the U.S. market for the next four decades. During this period, there were attempts to reinvigorate American shooters' interest in such .22- and .25-caliber pistols in guns such as the Colt Junior (made by Astra), the S&W Model 61 Escort, and Beretta's 950 Jetfire. Several American companies also offered inexpensive .22- and .25-caliber pistols, while Harrington & Richardson continued to produce small-frame revolvers chambered for the .22 LR and .32 S&W Long, which had retained a degree of popularity because of their economical prices. Too, while they saw limited acceptance with police as backup handguns, and with civilians who needed a deep-cover handgun or could not afford a more expensive product, none of them put a discernible dent in the sale of .38 snubbies.

The 1990s saw many U.S. states adopt "shall-issue" concealed carry laws, and this caused a dramatic increase in demand for small, concealable handguns. While most manufacturers raced to reduce the size and weight of their .38-, .357-, .40-, and .45-caliber and 9mm handguns, others decided to market a new breed of mouse guns. These new-age small pistols took advantage of advances in materials, and many of them utilized stainless steel, high tech alloys, and polymers in their construction. While the majority of pre-WWII mouse guns were single-action designs, many of the new breed utilized double-action-only triggers, while others had a traditional

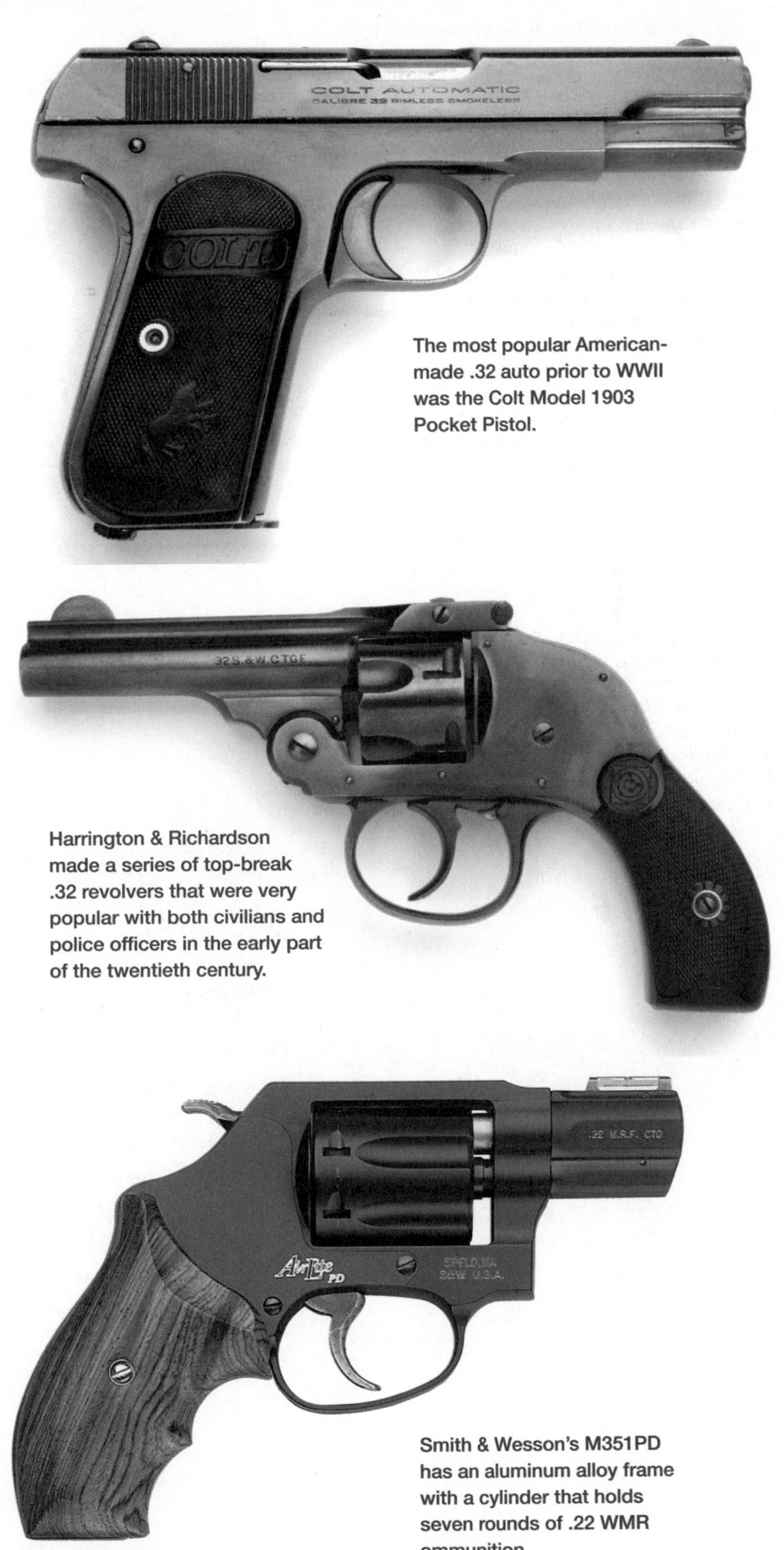

The most popular American-made .32 auto prior to WWII was the Colt Model 1903 Pocket Pistol.

Harrington & Richardson made a series of top-break .32 revolvers that were very popular with both civilians and police officers in the early part of the twentieth century.

Smith & Wesson's M351PD has an aluminum alloy frame with a cylinder that holds seven rounds of .22 WMR ammunition.

DA/SA trigger mechanism. It should be noted that the latter was pioneered by Walther, in 1929, on its PP pistol.

While alloy-framed revolvers have been around since the 1950s, they were usually chambered in .38 Special. More recently, Smith & Wesson began offering several rimfire models with alloy frames and high-capacity alloy cylinders. The Model 351PD revolver holds seven .22 WMR, while the Model 317 boasts eight .22 LR rounds of ammunition. Taurus offers its small-frame 940 series Ultra-Lite revolvers in .22 LR (9 rounds) and .22 WMR (8 rounds). The newest kid on the revolver block is Ruger's LCR-22. It utilizes a stainless steel barrel and eight-round cylinder, an aerospace-grade aluminum frame, and a fire-control housing molded from glass-filled nylon.

Another development that renewed interest in the mouse gun was improved

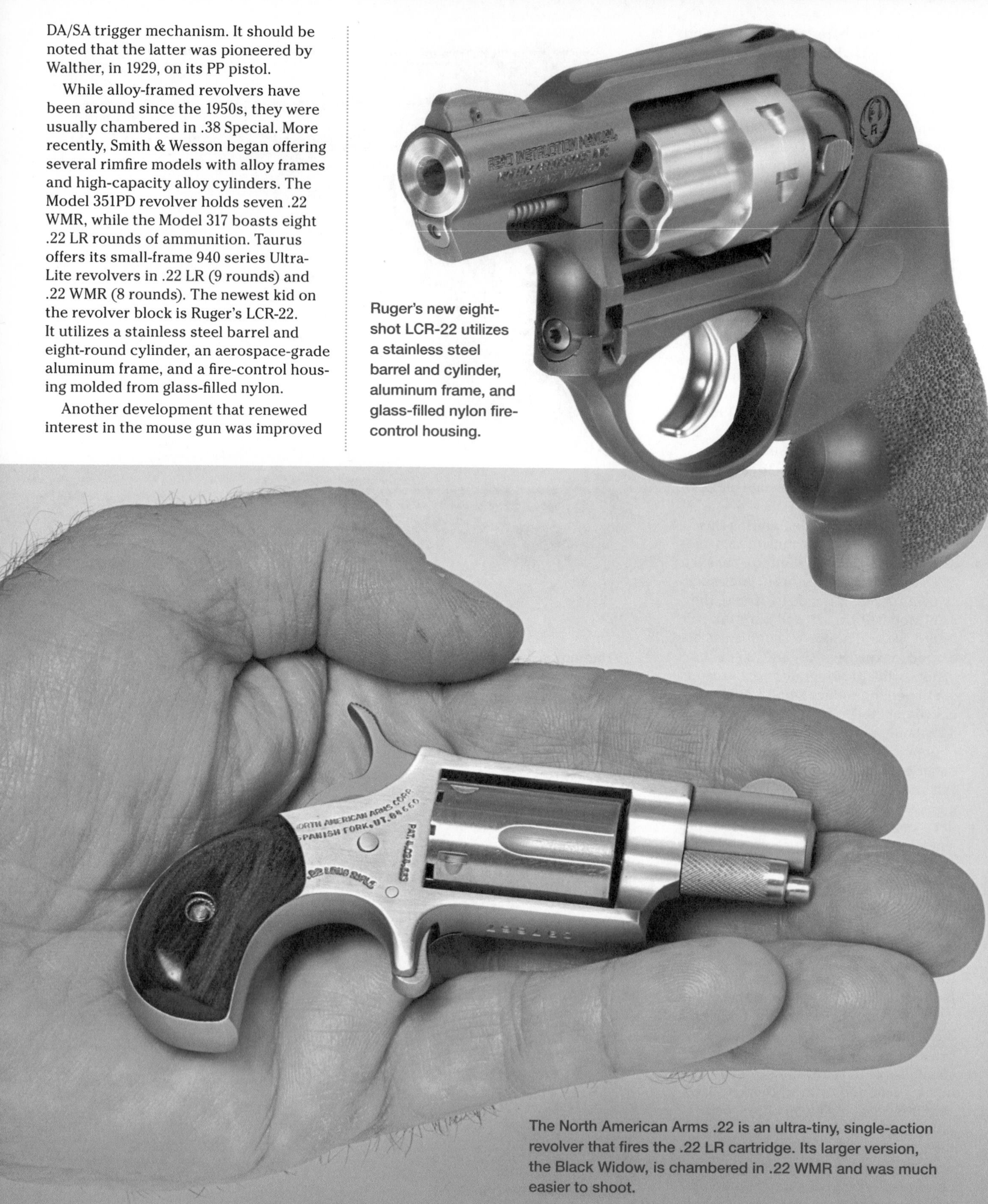

Ruger's new eight-shot LCR-22 utilizes a stainless steel barrel and cylinder, aluminum frame, and glass-filled nylon fire-control housing.

The North American Arms .22 is an ultra-tiny, single-action revolver that fires the .22 LR cartridge. Its larger version, the Black Widow, is chambered in .22 WMR and was much easier to shoot.

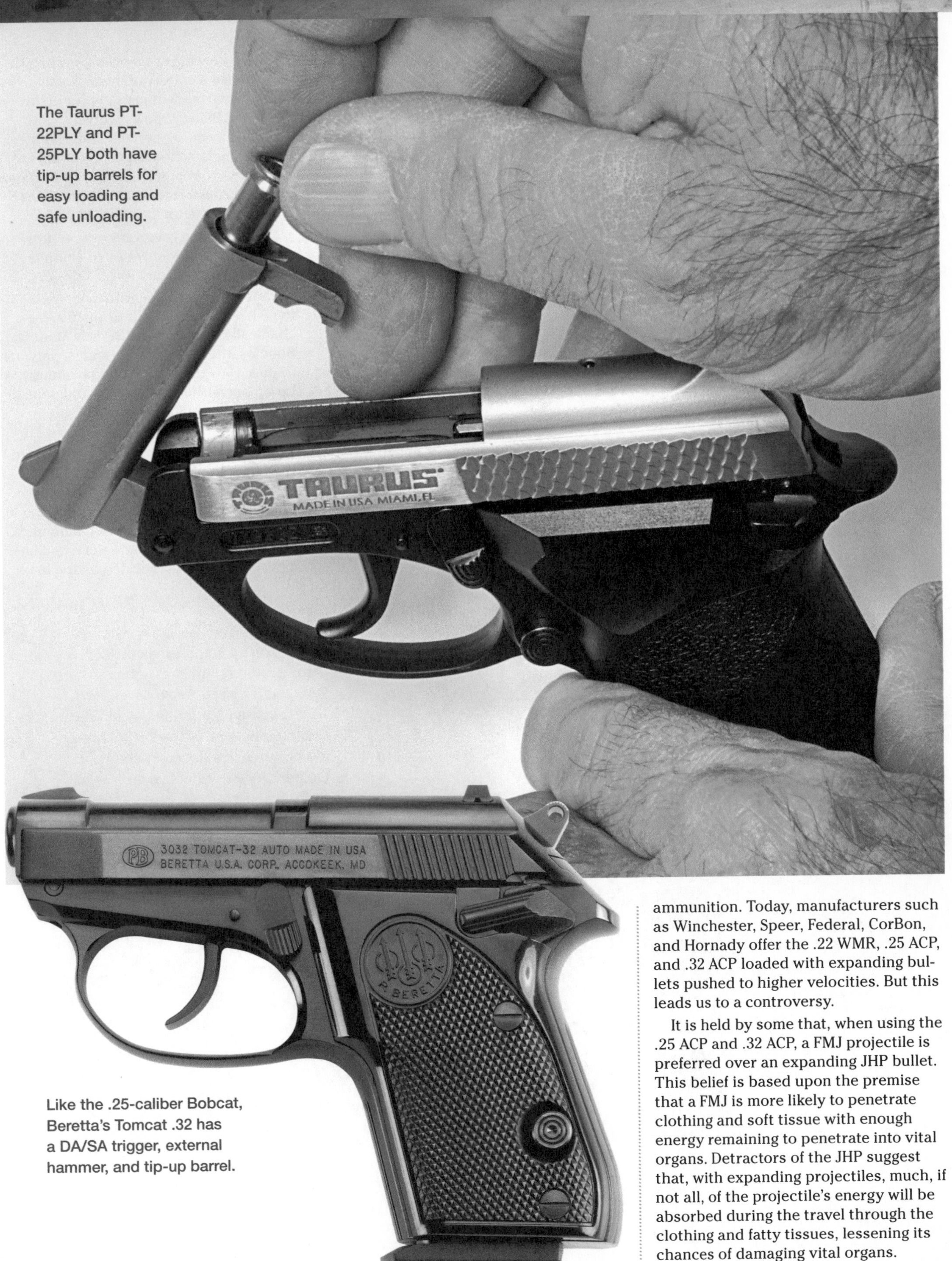

The Taurus PT-22PLY and PT-25PLY both have tip-up barrels for easy loading and safe unloading.

Like the .25-caliber Bobcat, Beretta's Tomcat .32 has a DA/SA trigger, external hammer, and tip-up barrel.

ammunition. Today, manufacturers such as Winchester, Speer, Federal, CorBon, and Hornady offer the .22 WMR, .25 ACP, and .32 ACP loaded with expanding bullets pushed to higher velocities. But this leads us to a controversy.

It is held by some that, when using the .25 ACP and .32 ACP, a FMJ projectile is preferred over an expanding JHP bullet. This belief is based upon the premise that a FMJ is more likely to penetrate clothing and soft tissue with enough energy remaining to penetrate into vital organs. Detractors of the JHP suggest that, with expanding projectiles, much, if not all, of the projectile's energy will be absorbed during the travel through the clothing and fatty tissues, lessening its chances of damaging vital organs.

The North American Arms .32 Guardian features 100-percent stainless steel construction, a DAO trigger, rubber grips, snag-free exterior, and is only 4⁵⁄₁₆ inches long.

To see how today's mouse guns handle, I assembled a variety of them. North American Arms sent me samples of the 22 LR and Black Widow revolvers. Both are made from 100-percent stainless steel, feature single-action trigger mechanisms, and have five-round cylinders. As its name indicates, the former is chambered in .22 LR, while the latter fires the .22 WMR.

Double-action revolvers were represented by the aforementioned Smith & Wesson Model 317 and Ruger LCR-22.

Taurus provided me with samples of the PT-22PLY and PT-25PLY pistols. Mechanically similar to the Beretta Model 21 Bobcats, they feature steel slides, polymer frames, DAO triggers, bobbed hammers, tip-up barrels for fast loading and unloading, and a manual safety.

I was supplied with a Beretta 3023 Tomcat by Davidson's Supply. An upsized version of the Model 21 Bobcat in .22 LR or .25 that was introduced in 1984, the .32-caliber Tomcat features an alloy frame and forged steel slide, external hammer, tip-up barrel, and manual safety, and has its magazine release located on the lower

The Seecamp is the smallest .32 pistol on today's market. It has a DAO trigger, snag-free exterior, and heel-mounted magazine catch. The California Edition of the LWS-32 has a trigger block safety to meet the Golden State's restrictive gun laws.

part of the left grip panel. Like the Taurus pistols, the Bobcat lacks an extractor, relying upon the expanding powder gases to force the spent casing rearward. This means that racking the slide will not remove either unspent or defective cartridges. Also, while it has a DA/SA trigger, there is no hammer drop system, so the hammer must be lowered on a loaded chamber manually.

Larry Seecamp sent me sample of his LWS-32 pistol, the smallest .32 ACP pistol on the market today. The LWS-32 is made from stainless steel. It has a recessed ring in the chamber into which the case expands on firing. This delays the opening of the breech, making it a retarded-blowback pistol. I received one of the new Seecamp "California Edition" pistols, which feature a push-button trigger-block safety. The LWS-32 was the only one of our test pistols that did not have some sort of sighting equipment, but, considering the distances at which these pistols are likely to be used, the manufacturer does not see this as a shortcoming.

Besides its extensive line of rimfire mini-revolvers, North American Arms offers the Guardian line of centerfire pistols. The stainless-steel Guardian 32 is chambered for the .32 ACP and has a DAO trigger. It can be had with an Integral Locking System that uses a key to immobilize the hammer to prevent unauthorized firing of the pistol. It is available with a 10-round magazine and a grip adaptor for a full three-finger purchase.

Kel-Tec is well known for its line of polymer-frame mini-pistols and sent along a sample of the popular P-32 for me to evaluate. Weighing a mere 6.6 ounces, it was the lightest of our .32 test pistols and the only one besides the Taurus Millennium Pro to use a locked breech. The P-32 is available with an extended magazine that provides 10 rounds of ammunition and a full-size grip. I should mention that the Kel-Tec P-32 is the standard-issue backup pistol of my local sheriffs department.

Cobra Firearms produces a number of economically priced handguns, and I requested one of its CZ-32 pistols to include in my evaluation. A blowback-operated, single-action design, it features a steel slide atop an alloy frame, a manual safety, and six-round detachable magazine and weighs 22 ounces.

From the 1920s through the 1990s, Walther's 7.65mm PPK was the favored pistol of European police, Wehrmacht officers, and secret agents ("Bond, James Bond"). Walther pioneered the DA/SA trigger with a hammer-drop lever, a design that

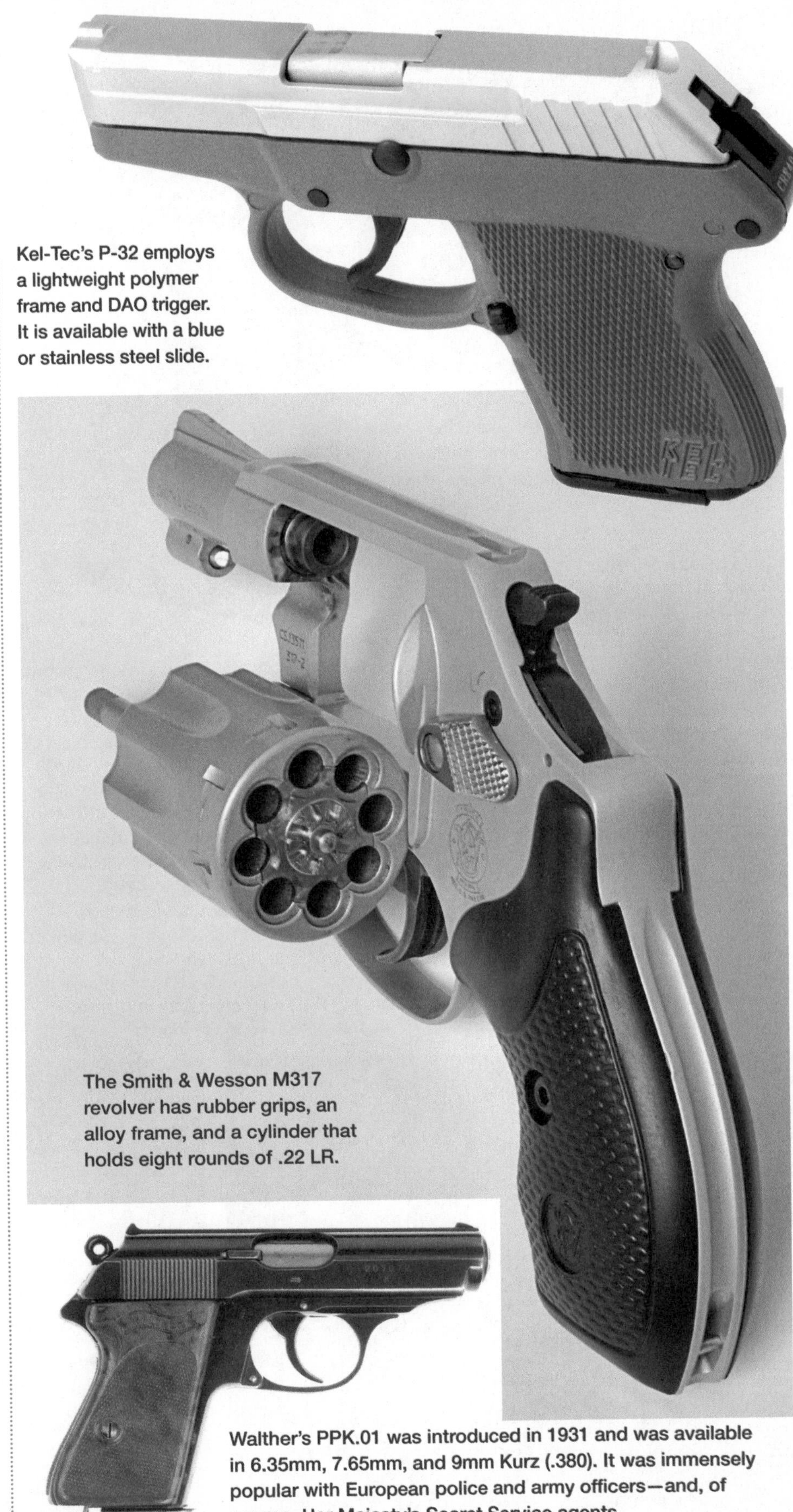

Kel-Tec's P-32 employs a lightweight polymer frame and DAO trigger. It is available with a blue or stainless steel slide.

The Smith & Wesson M317 revolver has rubber grips, an alloy frame, and a cylinder that holds eight rounds of .22 LR.

Walther's PPK.01 was introduced in 1931 and was available in 6.35mm, 7.65mm, and 9mm Kurz (.380). It was immensely popular with European police and army officers—and, of course, Her Majesty's Secret Service agents.

The Taurus Millenium Pro-132 is one of the larger .32 ACP pistols on the market. It uses a polymer frame and DA/SA trigger mechanism.

with a hammer-drop lever, a design that is used on the majority of service pistols today. The PPK's popularity remains such that it is currently manufactured under license in this country by Smith & Wesson.

Because of Brazilian laws restricting the caliber of civilian-owned handguns, the firm of Taurus offers its Millennium Pro 132 pistol in .32 ACP. The largest of our .32 mouse guns, it is a locked-breech design and employs a polymer frame, DA/SA trigger, manual safety, and a 10-round magazine.

After loading this wide selection of handguns and ammunition into my truck, I met my friend Dick Cole at our gun club to see if these mouse guns could do what was needed to be done. As Dick and I felt it would be an exercise in futility to try and shoot serious groups on bull's-eye targets with most of our sample guns, we ran them through the following series of offhand drills on combat targets positioned at "real life" distances. A mixture of Winchester, Hornady, Speer, and Remington FMJ and JHP ammunition was utilized. Because of the varying magazine capacities, all drills were limited to five rounds.

Because we did not have holsters suitable for all of the test guns, we began each drill holding the handgun at the low-ready position. With those pistols having DA/SA triggers, the first round was always fired in DA mode.

Mouse Gun Test Drills

Drill No. 1 at Three Yards

Raise gun and fire five shots rapid-fire on the target, with an unsupported one-handed grip. Reload and fire five rounds on the target's "head" using a supported (two-handed) grip.

Drill No. 2 at Five Yards

Raise gun and fire five rounds on the target, with a supported grip. Reload and repeat.

Drill No. 3 at Seven Yards

Raise gun and fire five rounds on target, slow, aimed fire, with supported grip.

Once the smoke had cleared, Dick and I discussed each pistol's positive and negative points and came up with the following analyses.

NAA 22LR: This tiny revolver was quite difficult to shoot at anything other than "reach out and touch someone" distances. As can be seen in the photos, all but four of the 50 rounds we fired found their way onto the target. In fact they were all over the target!

NAA Black Widow: Shot much better then its smaller cousin. The sights were easy to see and dead-on, but recoil with .22 WMR ammo was a bit snappy. I had one misfire with it. Besides being a "powerful" .22 for defensive purposes, it would make a great mini trail gun.

Ruger LCR-22: This one had a rather decent DAO trigger, excellent sights, shot to point of aim every time, and functioned 100 percent. What else can

Ruger's LCR proved to be one of the best shooting handguns of the day in the author's testing.

While it tended to string its groups vertically, the S&W Model 317 proved to be 100-percent reliable.

we say? Dick and I both felt it was the best of the .22 revolvers we tested.

S&W 317: Excellent ergonomics, but the DA trigger was rather stiff. In addition, the alloy front sight tended to disappear from view, if the light hit it a certain way. It needs a colored insert or fiber optic. While it tended to string groups vertically, functioning was 100 percent.

Taurus PT-22PLY & PT-25PLY: These were the Cinderella stories of the day. Both displayed above-average ergonomics, had smooth DAO trigger pulls, shot to point of aim, and functioned 100 percent. Dick didn't want to give up either of them.

NAA Arms 32 Guardian: This one had a heavy trigger pull that caused groups to open up. Recoil was snappy. While using the extended 10-round magazine with grip adapter improved things considerably, it reduced concealability. I had two failures to feed, both with JHP ammo and each time with the last round in the magazine.

Taurus Millennium Pro 132: This was the largest of our test guns, so ergonomics and recoil control were first rate, as were the sights. It loved both FMJ and JHP ammo, and accuracy was excellent. On the downside, we found it impossible to load the magazines to capacity and could only get eight rounds in them. Other than that, we were very pleased with its performance.

Cobra CA-32: It surprised both of us by providing a very decent performance, along with low recoil. Despite the front sight's propensity for disappearing in bright sunlight, it proved quite accurate. On the downside, the safety was difficult to manipulate and it took quite a bit of effort to remove empty magazines and rack the slide. While it would not feed JHPs, with FMJ ammo, it ran like gangbusters.

Seecamp LWS-32: The smallest of the .32 pistols tested was also the biggest surprise. As instructed by the owner's manual, we fired it exclusively with Winchester Silvertip ammo. Despite the fact that it had no sights at all, we were able to put rounds just where we wanted, simply by using the top of the slide as an "aiming device." Recoil was a bit stiff, and we both agreed that handling would benefit from a finger-rest magazine base pad. Dick had a single smokestack jam.

Beretta Tomcat: A fine-handling and -shooting little pistol. The optional Trijicon front sight's tritium insert is surrounded by a highly visible white "doughnut" for use in normal light. The rear is a shallow V "express sight" with a white bar, a combination that provided fast sight acquisition and alignment for close-range shooting. The DA trigger was on the stiff side, but the SA was light and crisp, allowing us to produce some very impressive groups. Dick had a single smokestack jam. Our only complaint was that the short tang and burr hammer resulted in a bit of hammer bite.

Walther PPK: A truly classic handgun. Other than one smokestack jam I had with the first magazine fired, we could not find a single derogatory thing to say about James Bond's "favourite" pistol. It ate up FMJ and JHP ammo with equal aplomb, had rather decent DA and SA trigger pulls, good recoil control, and decent sights, all of which combined to produce a well perforated target.

Kel-Tec P-32: We fired the Kel-Tec last and, to put it honestly, we were both surprised. Despite being the lightest of our .32s, its recoil—no doubt thanks to its polymer frame—was amazingly soft and controllable. While the sights were tiny, the pistol shot dead on, and with the extended magazine/grip adapter it could be fired fast and accurately. Functioning was 100 percent with both FMJ and JHP ammo.

Other than the tiny NAA 22LR, Dick and I agreed that the rest of the dozen handguns could all serve well for concealed carry, deep-cover concealment by police officers, and home-defense. The one caveat is that their rather lackluster cartridges would require a great deal of practice and careful shot placement to be effective.

I believe it would be germane to end this discussion by relating what happened one day at a local gun shop. A group of us were sitting around discussing concealed carry guns. As is usual in these give and take sessions, we each had our favorites and were quick to denigrate the choices of the others. One of the attendees—a member of the local police force with many years experience—had remained quiet during the discussion, and so I inquired if he carried a backup gun, whereupon he pulled up the cuff of his uniform trousers to expose a snub-nosed .22-caliber revolver in an ankle holster. When one of our company asked why he carried a mouse gun for backup, he responded, "I don't know anyone who *wants* to be shot with a .22. Do you?"

The silence that followed was deafening.

The oldest design tested was the Walther PPK, and it lived up to its reputation as a reliable, accurate pistol.

The little Kel-Tec P32 showed it could perform just as well as its larger and more expensive .32 Auto cousins.

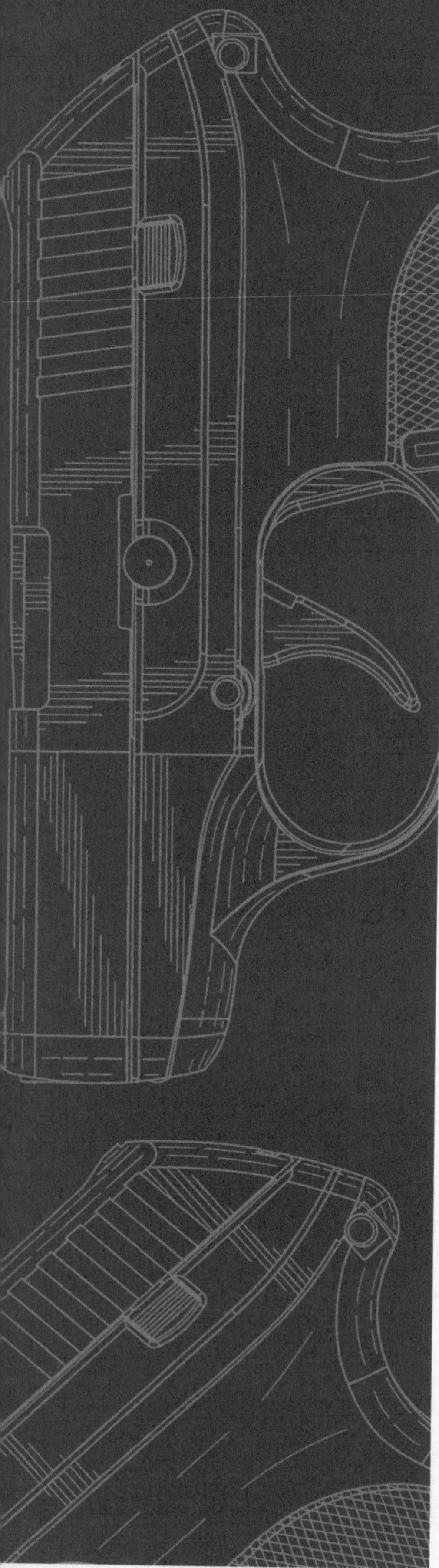

Specifications:

North American Arms 22LR

Type: Single-action Revolver
Caliber: .22 Lr
Overall Length: 4 Inches
Barrel Length: 1.125 Inches
Weight (Unloaded): 4.5 Ounces
Height: 2.25 Inches
Width: 0.875 Inches
Capacity: Five
Construction: Steel
Sights: Front Blade;Rear N/A
Grips: Smooth Wood
Extras: Padded Gun Rug, Lock, Manual
MSRP: $199

North American Arms Black Widow

Type: Single-action Revolver
Caliber: .22 Wmr
Overall Length: 5.875 Inches
Barrel Length: 2 Inches
Weight (Unloaded): 8.8 Ounces
Height: 3.675 Inches
Width: 0.875 Inches
Capacity: Five
Construction: Stainless Steel
Sights: Front Serrated Blade; Rear Square Notch
Grips: Rubber Finger Groove
Extras: Carrying Box, Lock, Manual
MSRP: $269

S&W Model 317

Type: Double-action Revolver
Caliber: .22 Lr
Overall Length: 6.25 Inches
Barrel Length: 1.875 Inches
Weight (Unloaded): 10.8 Ounces
Height: 4.375 Inches
Width: 1.38 Inches
Capacity: Eight
Construction: Aluminum Alloy
Sights: Front Blade; Rear Groove In Topstrap
Grips: Synthetic
Extras: Padded Gun Rug, Internal Lock, Manual
MSRP: $699

Ruger LCR-22

Type: Double-action-only Revolver
Caliber: .22 Lr
Overall Length: 6.5 Inches
Barrel Length: 1.875 Inches
Weight (Unloaded): 14.9 Ounces
Height: 4.5 Inches
Width: 1.38 Inches
Capacity: Eight
Construction: Stainless Steel Barrel/ Cylinder; Aluminum Alloy Frame; Glass-filled Nylon Fire-control Housing
Sights: Front Blade; Rear Groove In Topstrap
Grips: Hogue Tamer
Extras: Padded Gun Rug, Lock, Manual
MSRP: $525

Taurus PT-22PLY/PT-25PLY

Type: Double-action-only Blowback-Operated Semi-auto
Calibers: .22 Lr/.25 Acp
Overall Length: 4.875 Inches
Barrel Length: 2.3 Inches
Height: 4.25 Inches
Width: 1.105 Inches
Weight (Unloaded): 11.3 Ounces
Capacity: Eight
Construction: Polymer Frame; Steel Slide (Stainless Optional)
Sights: Front Blade; Rear Square Notch
Grips: Polymer
Extras: Tip-up Barrel, Manual Safety, Carrying Box, Internal Safety Lock, Manual
MSRP: $273 (Blue), $289 (Stainless)

North American Arms Guardian 32

Type: Double-action-only Blowback-operated Semi-auto

Caliber: .32 Acp

Overall Length: 4.3 Inches

Barrel Length: 2.3 Inches

Weight (Unloaded): 13.6 Ounces

Height: 3.3 Inches

Width: 0.8 Inch

Capacity: Six

Construction: Stainless Steel Frame And Slide

Sights: Front Blade; Rear Square Notch

Grips: Plastic

Extras: Carrying Box, 10 Rd. Magazine (Optional), Lock, Manual

MSRP: $402

Walther PPK

Type: Double-action/single-action Blow Back-operated Semi-auto

Caliber: .32 Acp

Overall Length: 6.1 Inches

Barrel Length: 3.35 Inches

Height: 3.8 Inches

Width: 0.98 Inches

Weight (Unloaded): 22 Ounces

Capacity: Seven

Construction: Stainless Steel Frame And Slide

Sights: Front Blade With Red Dot; Rear Square Notch With White Bar

Grips:plastic

Extras: Carrying Box, Spare Magazine, Lock, Manual

MSRP: $626

Beretta 3032 Tomcat

Type: Double-action/single-action Blowback-operated Semi-auto

Caliber: .32 Acp

Overall Length: 4.9 Inches

Barrel Length: 2.4 Inches

Height: 3.7 Inches

Width: 1.1 Inches

Weight (Unloaded): 14.5 Ounces

Capacity: Seven

Construction: Aluminum Alloy Frame; Blued Steel Slide

Sights: Front Blade; Rear Square Notch

Grips: Plastic

Extras: Tip-up Barrel, Manual Safety, Stainless Steel Construction (Optional) Night Sights (Optional)

MSRP: $435 (Blued), $555 (Stainless Steel)

Kel-Tec P-32

Type: Double-action-only Locked-breech Semi-auto

Caliber: .32 Acp

Overall Length: 5.07 Inches

Barrel Length: 2.7 Inches

Height: 3.5 Inches

Width: 0.75 Inches

Weight (Unloaded): 6.6 Ounces

Construction: Polymer Frame, Steel Slide

Capacity: Seven

Sights: Front Blade; Rear Fixed Notch

Grips: Polymer

Extras: Carrying Box, Lock, 10-round Magazine (Optional), Manual

MSRP: $318

Cobra Firearms CA-32

Type: Single-action Blowback-operated Semi-auto

Caliber: .32 Acp

Overall Length: 5.4 Inches

Barrel Length: 2.9 Inches

Height: 4.75 Inches

Width: 1.35 Inches

Weight (Unloaded): 22 Ounces

Construction: Alloy Frame, Steel Slide

Capacity: Six

Sights: Front Blade; Rear Notch

Grips: Polymer

Extras: Padded Carrying Case, Lock, Manual

MSRP: $318

Seecamp LWS32 California Edition

Type: Double-action-only, Retarded-Blowback Operated Semi-auto

Caliber: .32 Acp

Overall Length: 4.25 Inches

Barrel Length: 2.06 Inches

Height: 3.25 Inches

Width: 0.725 Inches

Weight (Unloaded): 11.5 Ounces

Construction: Stainless Steel Frame/slide

Capacity: Six

Sights: None

Grips: Plastic

Extras: Push-button Trigger Safety, Carrying Box, Lock, Manual

MSRP: $525

Taurus Millennium Pro 132

Type: Double-action/single-action Locked-breech Semi-auto

Caliber: .32 Acp

Overall Length: 6.125 Inches

Barrel Length: 3.25 Inches

Height: 4.5 Inches

Width: 1.3 Inches

Weight (Unloaded): 19.9 Ounces

Capacity: 10

Construction: Polymer Frame, Blue Steel Slide

Sights: Front Blade With White Dot; Rear Heinie Straight-8

Grips: Polymer

Extras: Carrying Box, Manual Safety, Internal Safety Lock, Manual

MSRP: $441

When a box or factory round is marked 5.56, it is a round that really needs a 5.56 chamber. A .223 chamber may get you in trouble.

.223 vs 5.56: What's the Problem?

BY PATRICK SWEENEY

If you are testing accuracy and pressure, you need a setup like this. Lacking this, your efforts will be a bit less precise.

To a whole lot of shooters, ammo is ammo—if it fits, it shoots. These shooters tend to be the guys with seriously tired, worn, or even busted firearms. They also tend to focus on the wrong thing; you know, the guy who scrubs the brass marks off his ejector lump, at least until one day his rifle stops working or breaks into many pieces.

Ammo is not ammo. And the .223 and the 5.56, while almost identical, are not the same. To know why, we have to go back to the beginning.

The early 1960s were an interesting time. The returning GIs from WWII and Korea had a decade to get things the way they liked. Two tastes they acquired during that time were varmint shooting and benchrest. Varmint shooting was simple. Various members of the rodentia clan, going about their usual business in a field or pasture, served as animate targets. They were prolific breeders, there was no limit, no season, no quitting. You could shoot all day if you wished. Well, as much as shooters then and now like to shoot, shooting varmints with a .30-06 was just silly. The recoil would beat you up, the noise was alarming, barrels got really hot really fast, and the cost of ammo, even back then, was just off the charts.

So they went down in caliber until they found that various rifle cartridges using .224-inch bullets did the job nicely.

Benchrest shooting was a refinement and variant of target shooting. Instead of trying to coax all the shots into a 10-ring, the group was the score. The smaller the group, the better the score. Again, smaller was better, and the common .224-inch diameter bullet served well.

The premier cartridge in the early 1950s, when varminting and benchrest got started and began revving up, was the .222 Remington. Introduced, in 1950, in the Remington 722, it was superbly accurate, and the rifle was also a brilliant out-of-the-box shooter. The mild recoil would not cause a benchrest shooter to have aiming problems, and the mild report, efficient powder charges and low bore erosion made it a useful varmint cartridge.

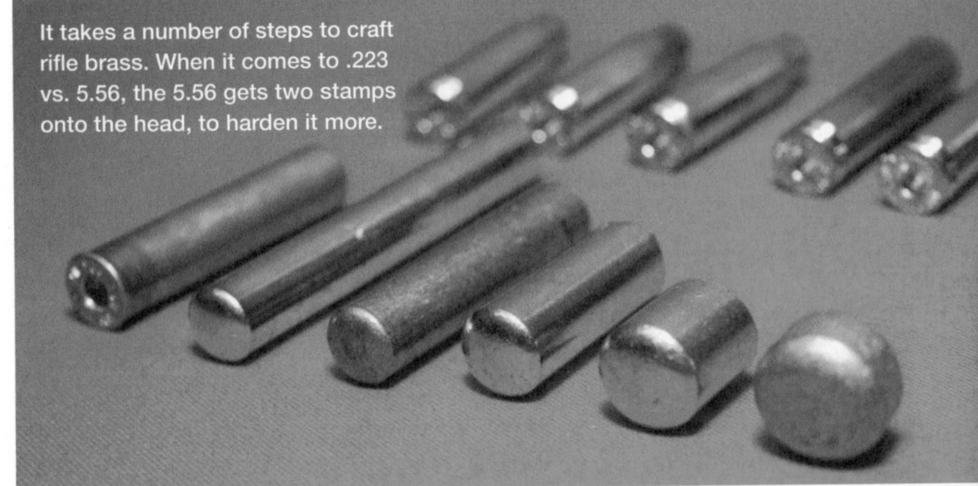

It takes a number of steps to craft rifle brass. When it comes to .223 vs. 5.56, the 5.56 gets two stamps onto the head, to harden it more.

While it is comforting to read what is marked on the barrel, you can't always believe the chamber designation. You have to do as Reagan advised—trust, but verify.

For those who needed more reach in the varmint fields, Remington came out with the .222 Magnum in 1958, offering 2-300 fps more velocity than the little .222.

Now we shift gears from varminting to the on-going soap opera of the U.S. Army rifle situation. Having spent a decade and millions of taxpayers dollars, the U.S. Army Ordnance bureau has brought forth ... an improved M1 Garand. And so screwed up is the process that they can't even produce rifles quickly enough to arm the U.S. Army in any reasonable time frame. I once looked into the numbers and came to the conclusion that, at the rate the Army was buying and building (the U.S. arsenal at Springfield was still open then), the entire U.S. Army would not have been switched over to the M14 before the bicentennial. For those who don't remember that occasion, the year was 1976.

So, the Army finds, in the mid-1960s, that the Armalite rifle is one that could actually be forced upon them. They pull out all the stops and do everything they can to prevent this. "Real men shoot .30 rifles" was the prevailing ethos of the day (and in some circles, still is).

The cartridge the Armalite rifle was chambered for was the ".222 Special," a case halfway between the .22 Rem. and the .222 Rem. Mag. It also split the difference between them in velocity. The Army, recognizing an opportunity, first accepted the velocity as sufficient. Then they upped the stakes and insisted on better and better down-range performance. Basically, they kept asking until they had exceeded the pressure limits of the .222 Special. But the problem is that pressure is not simply velocity-dependant. Still, the designers had managed to meet the velocity specs, and the rifle was adopted.

I have now, in less than 700 words, summarized years of work, 100,000 man-hours of engineering, manufacturing and range testing, and we've only begun.

Now, remember the beginning? Accuracy was king. To shoot small groups, or shoot small vermin in the middle of a field, you need accuracy. Part of accuracy is the shape and dimensions of the entry of the bullet into the barrel. In order to make the .222 and .222 Rem. Mag. as accurate as possible, the Remington designers made the leade short and the onset steep. With that in mind, we'll back off, tack around, and come at this from a different direction.

Each pressure barrel is clearly marked as to what it is, and its use is meticulously tracked and recorded.

The Bullet's Flight

The primer goes off and the powder is ignited. Except that, in the time frame of a sub-millisecond we're about to enter, it doesn't. What happens is, the primer goes off and ignites the powder at the back of the case. The powder burns forward, but, as it does, it expands—it *has* to, the gases generated by combustion are the whole reason we're doing this, right?—and pushes the yet-unburned powder ahead of it. Now, in a handgun, the powder combustion happens, at least in some calibers, so quickly that the bullet does not have time to move before the powder is consumed. In others, the bullet begins to move, but has not left the case before combustion of the handgun powder charge is completed. In rifles, that is not so much the case. In fact, in some rifles, the bullet has moved a *lot* before the full powder charge has been consumed.

So, like a champagne cork popping out of the bottle, the bullet pops out of the case, with the expanding gases and unburned powder behind it. It travels forward of the case, in a section specially reamed for it. That section is some small amount larger than the bullet, but smaller than the case neck.

At some point forward of where the case neck ends, the rifling begins. The distance between those two points is called the "freebore," as in, free of rifling and at bore diameter.

The bullet pops out of the case and slides forward until it comes to the rifling, where it stalls. That's right, the bullet *slows down.* Hey, it got popped out of the case and was sliding forward with little friction, but then the rifling intruded upon its course, and, in order to move forward, the bullet has to be impressed by the rifling and begin to spin. What it does then is slow down and skid a bit as it begins to spin.

The pressure builds up until it is great enough to push the bullet forward. But, when the bullet stops, what happens? Since the powder is still burning and the bullet has slowed down, the various gas laws (Boyle's, Charles, and Gay-Lussac, mostly), tell us one thing must happen: *pressure must increase*. Obviously, if you start at a lower pressure you will have a lower peak on the spike, but the increase will be the same, regardless.

Two dimensions control the pressure spike in this scenario, the length of the freebore and the steepness of the onset angle of the rifling. We can decrease the height of the pressure spike if we move the onset of the rifling forward and make the ramp that guides the bullet shallower. And that is exactly what the designers did back then, to meet the Army requirements for velocity and range. So far, so good.

Then the ammo makers, in search of more performance, went looking for extra fps. I was shooting .223 and 5.56 three decades ago, and the difference wasn't so great back then. I don't know if it was because the ammo we laid hands on was rejected for low velocities, poor storage, or there just wasn't as much difference then, but now there is.

If, in the early 1980s, you had told me that a 16-inch carbine could deliver 3200 fps from a 55-grain bullet, I'd have looked at you as if you had grown horns. That was what a 20-inch barreled rifle did, on a good day. But ammunition these days does deliver that. I've seen 20-inch rifles do over 3300 fps with XM193 Federal ammo.

Now the problems begin.

There is a recognized situation in engineering, where designers put more safety, more margin, into a system. And

A close-up of a pressure barrel in place, ready to start recording the events of the day.

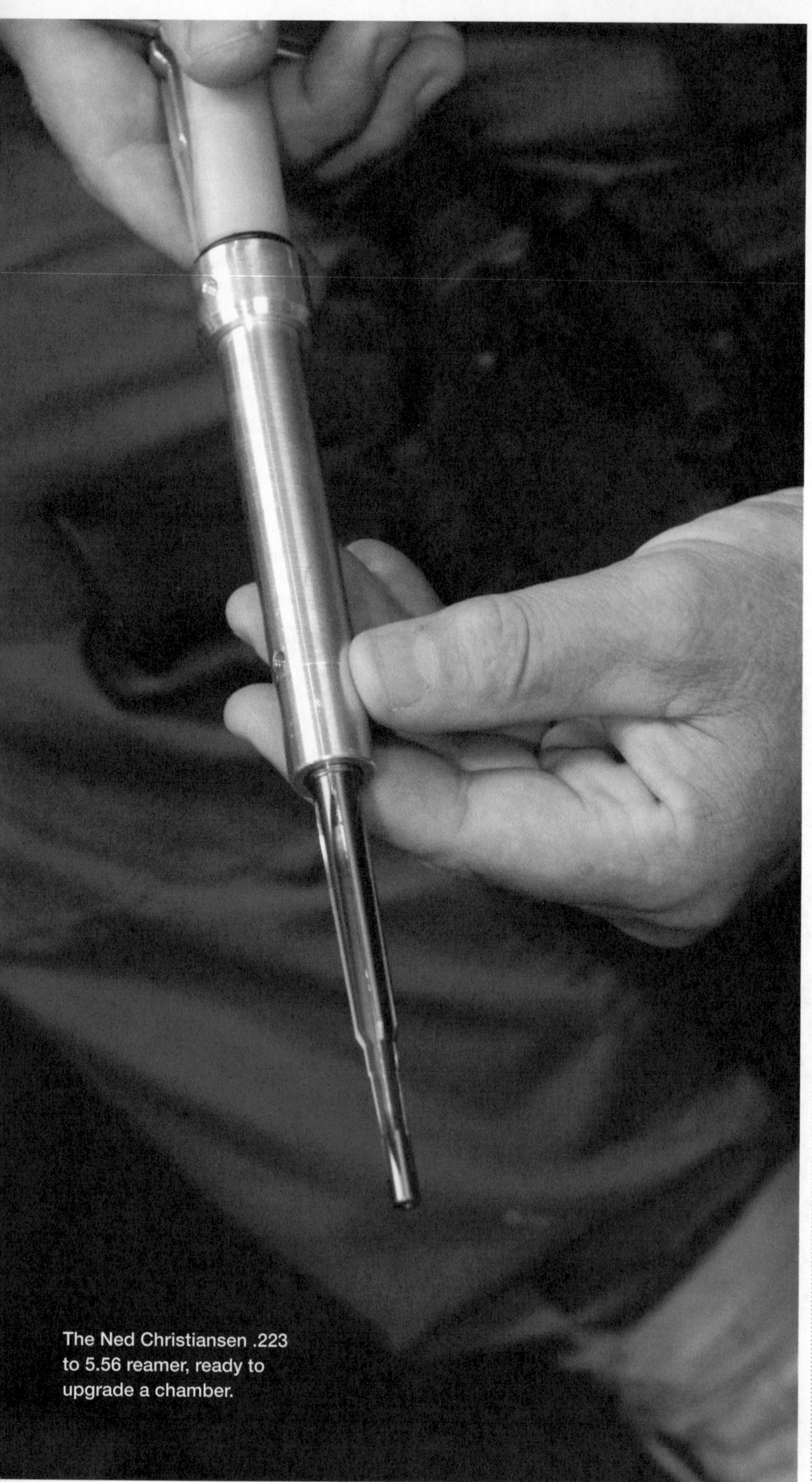

The Ned Christiansen .223 to 5.56 reamer, ready to upgrade a chamber.

the end users then burn up the extra margin to bring themselves back to the level of risk/use they were accustomed to. A good comparison is anti-lock brakes. Back when brakes were just brakes, people kept a certain distance between themselves and other cars. After all, you needed it in case you had to stop. Add anti-lock brakes into the mix and, after a while, people drive with shorter intervals between them and the next car. They can, because the car will stop faster/sooner and they don't need as much margin.

But, what happens if you put them back driving a car without anti-lock brakes? (If any exist any more.) If they add margin back, they're fine. If they don't, and something happens, they are crunched.

And exactly that has happened with the ammo and chambers. The extra velocity comes as a result of the lowered spike from the longer leade and, when you suddenly "take out the anti-lock brakes," you get not just the old spike, but an *enhanced* one.

The Details

Before we get too deep into this, you also have to be aware of a change that happened in our lifetimes (well, the lifetimes of the old farts among us), and that is the change in pressure measuring. If you have an older reloading manual, you'll see the measuring units denoted in C.U.P., and in some older manuals "CUP" and "PSI" are used interchangeably.

The old way of measuring pressure was known as the copper crusher method. In it, a test barrel would have a hole drilled through it to a specified set of dimensions. Then, a little copper cylinder was clamped in place over the hole. When the round was fired, the copper cylinder got hit with the pressure and was compressed. By measuring the length of the cylinder before and after, ballisticians could determine the peak pressure. This was known as "copper units of pressure," or CUP, but was often expressed in pounds per square inch, or PSI. The copper (and lead cylinders, used for lower-pressure calibers) could only tell us what the peak pressure was, however, not how fast its onset was, how long it lasted, etc.

Today, transducers, or strain gauges, are used to measure pressure. Here, the gauge, which is essentially a transistor (it is more complicated than that, but we're discussing firearms, not electrical

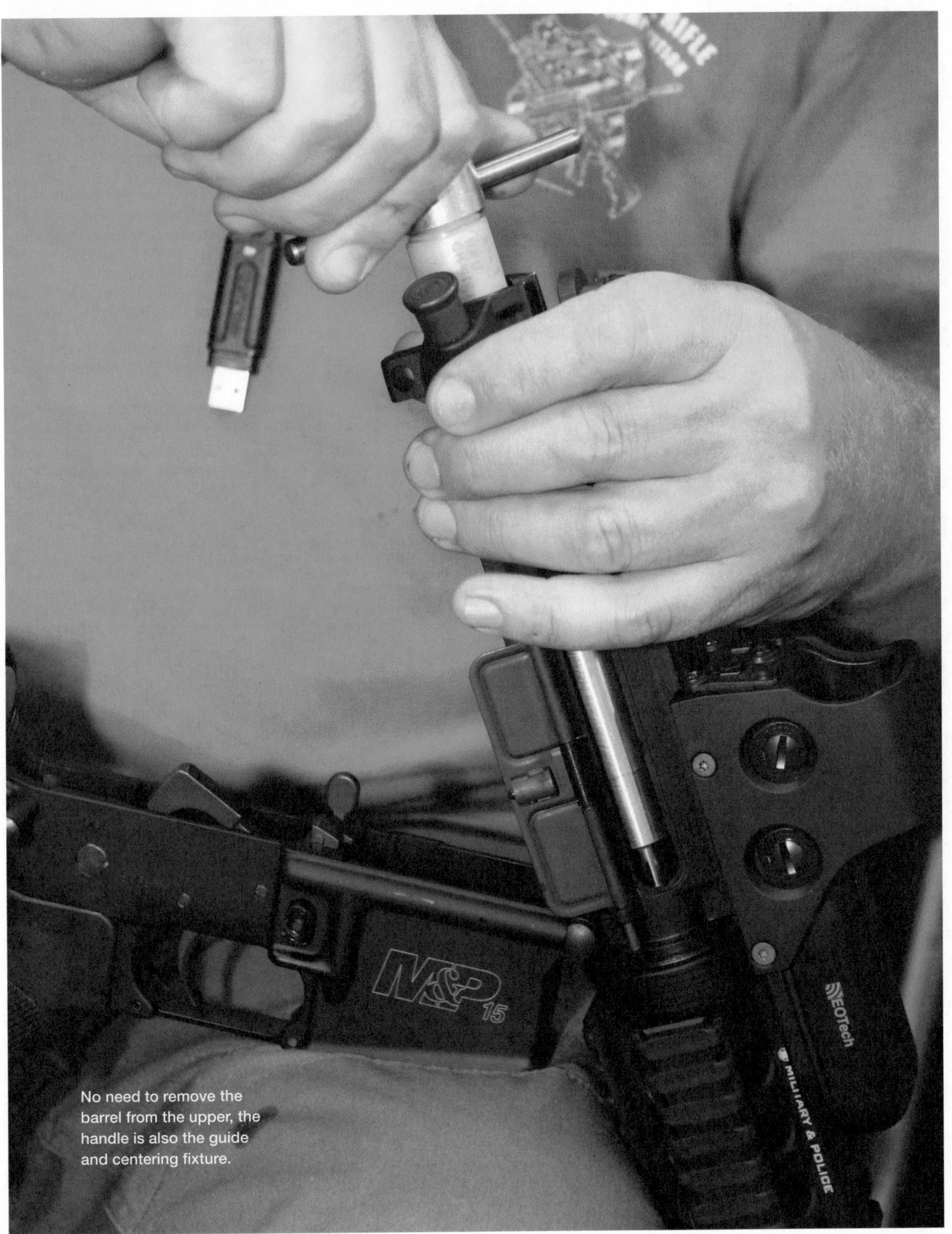

No need to remove the barrel from the upper, the handle is also the guide and centering fixture.

As with .223/5.56, there is a difference between 308 and 7.62. The manufacturers are being as clear as they can when they mark their brass.

engineering) is fastened to the barrel. When the gauge is stressed, the electrical resistance of the gauge changes. The beauty—and the problem—with this method is that it is dependant on a computer or other recording device. Depending on how much you spend, you can record the pressure of the event hundreds, thousands, or more times per second. This caused problems in published loading data.

Let's construct our own cartridge, just so we can remain theoretical for the moment. The ".30 Zoomer Magnum" has a maximum average pressure (MAP, or the allowed peak) of 50,000 CUP. We use the newfangled transducer to measure the standard reference load (in this case, 42 grains of "XYZ" powder under a

The military, police, and you all require ammunition to perform exactly as expected.

183-grain soft-point) and come up with 57,000 PSI. The "new" MAP for the .30ZM is now 57,000 PSI, where before it had been 50,000 CUP. But the actual pressure has not changed, we are simply using a new yardstick to measure it with.

Then we run into problems. In checking loading data, we find that some of the data wasn't as "clean" as we thought. An example: using "123" powder under the same 183-grain soft-point, we had found that we could get 100 fps more and still only see 50,000 CUP pressure. With the new transducer and seeing things in thousandth of a second slices, we see that, yes, the main pressure peak is only 57,000 PSI, the allowed max by the new yardstick, but we also see a second, higher, spike from the bullet hitting and stalling in the rifling. That spike comes in at 63,500 PSI, well over the maximum allowed. So, we have to throttle back the load data, and all of a sudden "123" powder loses its 100 fps advantage.

The problem came from the copper cylinder not being sensitive enough to register the second, over-max pressure spike, so, no, we have not "slowed down the load data to satisfy the lawyers." We didn't know we were going over-max before. We do now, and we have to adjust the data. (Oh, and just to add to the confusion, where you place the transducer can also have an effect on the pressure you measure.)

The SAAMI-spec pressure ceiling, the MAP allowed for the .223, is 55,000 PSI. No, there is no handy-dandy formula that lets you convert old copper-crusher pressures to PSI. The ballisticians tried, and they tried *really* hard, to come up with a conversion factor. The trouble they ran into was that every cartridge seemed to have its own factor. It was bad enough converting from CUP to PSI, but trying to tell people (and this is just an estimate, don't use these as numbers to go by) that where they could use a plus-12 percent CUP-to-PSI factor for the .293, the .34-06 used a plus-15 percent, and the .305 used a plus-nine percent. (And, yes, I deliberately used nonsense calibers. Don't try to decipher them, there is no pattern, nor any useful info beyond what I just told you.)

Above: Three sectioned chambers show the differences between the types.

The location of the transducer is precisely defined and meticulously placed. Barrels are carefully stored and their service life recorded.

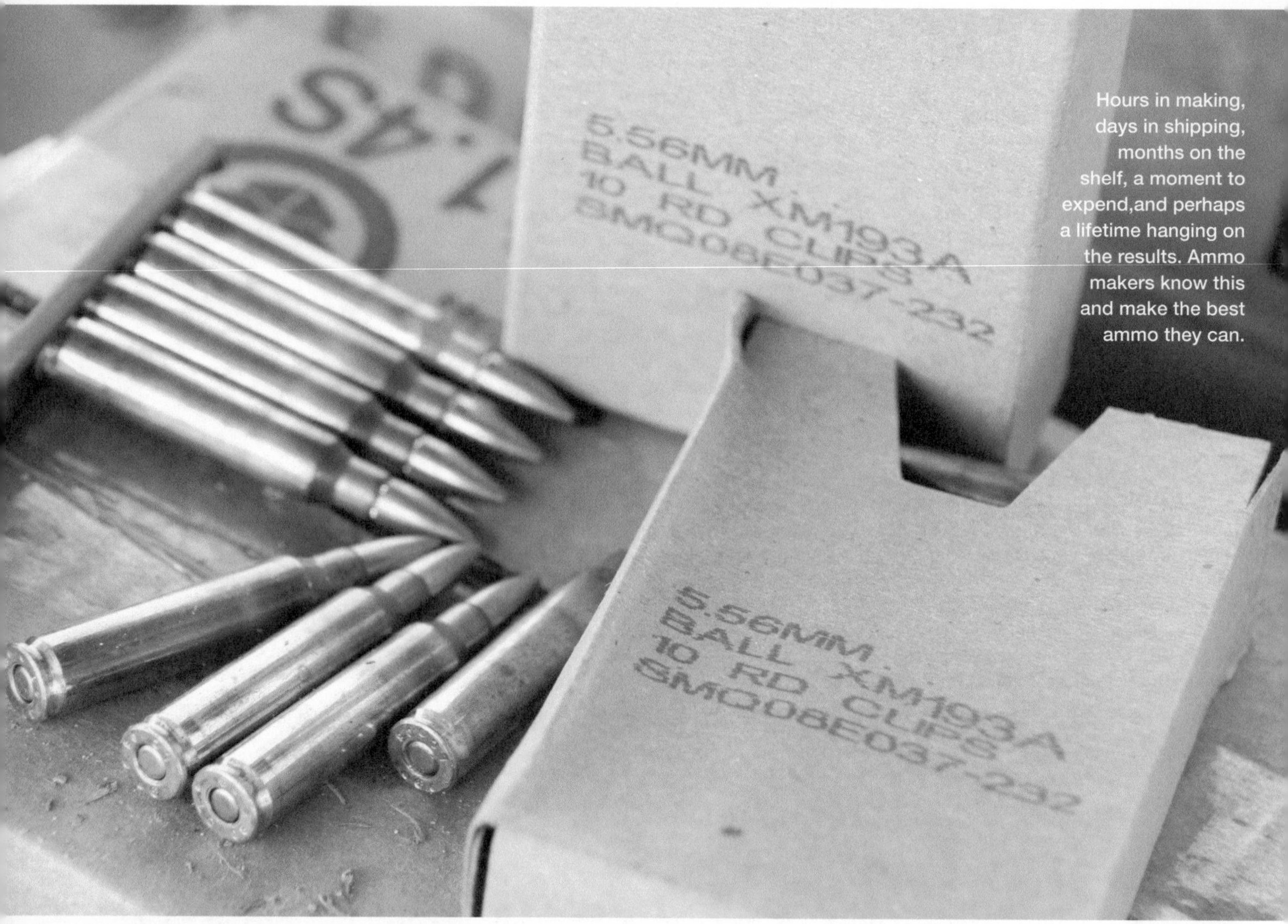

Hours in making, days in shipping, months on the shelf, a moment to expend,and perhaps a lifetime hanging on the results. Ammo makers know this and make the best ammo they can.

Here we see the chips from a 5.56-marked barrel that obviously wasn't.

On a good .223 barrel, the reamer will only remove steel in the neck and throat area. It stops when it is done.

There was no way to formulate an equation for a "universal translator" of CUP to PSI. Give it up, forget the conspiracy theories your gun club buddy tells you, just accept the new info for what it is.

The NATO spec for 5.56 has a higher "ceiling," but it's also measured slightly differently, and, again, there is no handy-dandy conversion. The SAAMI method measures pressure at the middle of the case. NATO (the European measuring group is known as C.I.P.) measures at the case mouth. A CIP-spec 5.56X45, measured at the case mouth, shows a pressure of 62,000. Measured at the case middle, as SAAMI does, it shows 60,000 units of pressure.

But the problem isn't just pressure. That CIP pressure of 62,000 PSI? It is measured in a 5.56 chamber. If we take the same round, which shows 60,000 PSI/SAAMI (still 5,000 PSI over the .223 max) and put it into a .223 chamber, things get ugly. *Really* ugly, and *really* quickly. The pressure spike piles onto an already over-pressure round. I've talked to professional ballisticians, guys who use million-dollar labs to measure ammo for their ammo manufacturing bosses. (You know, those guys with the computers and transducers than can measure pressure by the thousandth of a second or finer.) They have reported some instances of 5.56 ammo in .223-chambered pressure barrels demonstrating peak pressures at or above 75,000 PSI. That is the pressure of the *proof* load each rifle gets tested with at the rifle maker's, before shipping.

Proof loads, for those who aren't remembering, are the deliberate, plus-30 percent loads that each rifle maker fires, once per gun, in their rifles before they ship them. They do so in the full expectation that the rifle will do just fine. Once. More is abusive, stupid and asking for trouble.

At this point, many an advocate of "there is no difference" will say "I've shot thousands of rounds through my AR and it hasn't given me any problems." I've worked in gun shops for too many years to accept round-counts mentioned across the counter at face value. Nothing personal guys, but the true number of rounds fired is typically a quarter to a tenth of the asserted number. I teach law enforcement patrol rifle classes in the summer, and I see how much work

From Left to Right: The end of the leade on a 5.56-spec chamber. You can see, at the tip of the knife blade in the center photo, where the .223 leade ends. Pretty short, eh? On the right is a .223 chamber reamed to the 5.56 NEMRT, as done by the Ned reamer.

(and have done it myself) it takes to run 1,000 rounds through a rifle. If your buddy says "Yea, we went to the range this weekend and put a thousand rounds through each rifle," he's exaggerating. And if he isn't, you do not want to borrow any of his rifles, as a thousand rounds in two days is enough to smoke the barrel.

Also, most shooters haven't fired enough real 5.56 ammunition to actually test their rifle. Almost all the "generic" ammo you shoot is not 5.56. Oh, it says ".223 Remington/5.56" on it, but it isn't really 5.56. The high-volume, low-cost bulk ammunition that most of us use is not loaded right to the red line. I've chrono'd enough of it to know that much of it falls 100 to 200 fps short of full-book 5.56 spec. That right there is enough to make it no big deal chamber pressure-wise, because the peak pressure of the .223 load is sufficiently less than that of the 5.56 that the artificially-induced spike still falls below the pressure ceiling.

The extra pressure produces faster wear on your rifle. Since most shooters don't shoot enough to wear out their rifles in any reasonable time frame, the extra wear is hardly noticed. But you can have a serious problem if the variables stack up against you in a range session. Rifles get hot when you shoot them. They also get hot in the summer, in the heat and the sun.

So there you are on a hot summer day, shooting your supply of real-deal 5.56-spec ammo through your .223-chambered rifle. The summer sun beats down and pressures rise. Black rifles left in the sun can easily reach 140 degrees even before they're fired. Add to that the temperature increases from shooting, and you have some real heat problems coming on. Let's make it worse: the particular lot of your 5.56 ammo is at the top of the allowed pressure and at the bottom of the allowed brass hardness. The ammo maker tested it in a 5.56-chambered test barrel and, while it was in the top end of the allowed specs, it is within the safety margin.

You're having a blast, when all of a sudden your rifle stops working. What happened? Well, the heat increased the already maximum-made-excessive pressure and, on extracting a fired case, the pressure had expanded the case enough for a primer to fall out of the primer pocket and into your rifle. Actually, it probably has been losing primers for the last couple of magazines—pick up and inspect all your brass. You'll see you've been losing ne or two primers per magazine. But it wasn't until one fell into your action and tied things up that you noticed.

How bad can this get? In a patrol rifle class last year, a police officer was pushing his safety back to Safe (and the selector was resisting), when the rifle suddenly spat out a three-shot burst, then stopped working entirely. He'd blown a primer, and the anvil of the primer had wedged under the trigger in just such a way as to create the burst. Typically, the primer wedges under the trigger in such a way as to keep the rifle from shooting at all. Either way, not good.

Solving the Problem

One solution would be to only use .223-spec ammo. That can be okay, but, if you find a deal on 5.56 ammo, it kind of makes no sense to buy a "deal" you can't use. Also, some of the best ammo for some applications is 5.56-only. Plus, you can't control the outside temperature and probably not how much ammo you may need to fire. It would be nice to have a rifle that handled 5.56 with aplomb. But how? To begin with, you have to be able to measure what is there.

The first thing you have to know is this isn't about headspace. A headspace gauge only tells you the dimensions of the shoulder and case body, not the neck and leade. You need a leade/throat gauge, and for that you need to get a .223/5.56? Gage (yes, the "?" and misspelled "Gage" are the part of the correctly named product), from Michiguns (www.m-guns.com). I have to be up front and tell you that I have known Ned, the inventor, for nearly

30 years. I don't get anything but thanks from him for recommending his great gizmo, and I think it is useful enough that I'd recommend it if I didn't know or even like him.

The Gage is simple and ground to just under the maximum specs of a 5.56 leade/throat. Drop it in and, if it drops free, you have a 5.56 leade. If it sticks (it is hardened steel, don't pound it in), you have a .223 leade. If you're curious and want to know just where exactly it is catching, you can mark it up with a felt-tip pen and, with a little careful turning (clockwise), you can see where it rubs. If you are *really* curious, browse through your Brownells catalog—you do have a Brownells catalog, don't you? You don't? Get one, before you get severe deductions from your man-card—and order Cerrosafe. Cerrosafe is a special metal alloy with a low melting point. You push a cleaning patch until it is in front of your chamber, heat the Cerrosafe, pour it in the chamber and let it cool. Once cool, you push it out of the chamber, and now you have a cast of the chamber, throat, and leade. You can inspect and measure to your heart's content.

So, with the Gage or Cerrosafe you find that you have a .223 chamber and you wanted a 5.56. If the rifle is still brand-new, you can send it back. However, the maker probably only has more barrels of the same kind from the same maker, and you may not get a 5.56 no matter how many times you ask. So, you need a specialized reamer. One that cuts the leade and the leade only. (You don't want your headspace changed.) Ned makes that, also. Now, I can hear some of you saying, "But, I have a chromed barrel, I don't want to cut the chrome!" Okay, stick with a chromed .223, that's fine. But, if you want a 5.56 leade, yes, the reamer will remove chrome. But guess what? The area being cut is the area where the chrome is blasted off first, so if you've put more than a few hundred rounds down your barrel, there's probably not much chrome left there anyway, especially if you did rapid-fire shooting or heated the barrel up to the point where you had to wait for it to cool.

In all fairness, you don't *have* to have Ned's reamer. Other various reamer makers will be happy to supply you with a 5.56-spec finish reamer. You just have to be aware that a finish reamer will also ream the shoulder, if you aren't careful. So, you may go in attempting solely to make a 5.56 throat and end up creating excessive headspace along the way. Ned's reamer does not cut on the chamber shoulder at all, therefore, when you feel it stop cutting, you are safely done. It also makes a leade longer even than that of 5.56, though by a small margin.

What's that, another protest? "But my barrel is marked 5.56, I can't have a problem." Alas, that is not the case.

At my latest LEO patrol rifle class, I chamber-gauged the two dozen rifles the officers had brought. All but two were marked "5.56." One of those was an M16A1 and the other had a completely unmarked barrel. Of the 24 rifles, six failed the .223/5.56? Gage test. Two of those were not just .223-chambered, but clearly on the small side of the dimensions, as I had to use force to remove the Gage.

How can this be? Remember how barrels are made. The manufacturer uses a chambering reamer to turn the chamber out of the back and of the barrel blank. As reamers dull, they are re-sharpened. Each sharpening makes them fractionally smaller. Reamers start at the maximum size and, as they "shrink" from repeated sharpening, the chamber they cut also changes. Once they get to the minimum, they are discarded and a new reamer is employed. Well, some use reamers for a bit too long, and the chamber cut can be at minimum or smaller dimension.

Of those six that failed the Gage, three ended up showing pressure signs later in the class, so we reamed them with the Michiguns reamer and those problems went away. Two of them were the markedly undersized barrels. The other barrels/rifles continued to work, but for how long? They may have been getting fed .223-pressure ammunition, and thus would not show pressure signs.

Having a .223 chamber in your AR is a greater concern than just the social ostracism of having a rifle that is "not Mil-Spec." However, it is something you can test and fix, if needed. Me, I've long-since checked all my rifles, and those that didn't pass the test have been corrected.

A LUST FOR LEVERS

BY WAYNE VAN ZWOLL

Battlefield, scabbard, safari – lever-gun venues all. Grab a handful of power, Pilgrim, and saddle up!

The Savage action is designed so lever resistance on opening and closing occurs close to the grip.

The bear-busting .450 Alaskan, a necked-up .348, came from Harold Johnson's bench.

Oliver Fisher Winchester may have seen them queuing up—people and patents that would come to define the most remarkable period in firearms history. After the Mexican War, inventors raced to bring metallic cartridges, breech-loading rifles, and repeating mechanisms to market. In 1847, Stephen Taylor patented a hollow-based bullet with a powder charge secured by a perforated cap. An external primer sent fire through the cap. New York inventor Walter Hunt followed a year later with a similar bullet; sparks drove through its paper-covered cork cap to ignite the charge. What made Hunt's Rocket Ball significant was his Volitional Repeater, a tube-fed rifle with a pillbox device that advanced metallic primers. Alas, the lever-action mechanism was prone to malfunction. Short of the money to promote or improve his rifle, Hunt sold patent rights to fellow New Yorker George Arrowsmith, who hired a talented young engineer, Lewis Jennings, to fix the Volitional Repeater.

In 1849, shortly after he received patents for Jennings' work, Arrowsmith sold the Hunt rifle, for $100,000, to Courtland Palmer. Well funded from his hardware business and railroad investments, Palmer engaged Horace Smith and Daniel Wesson to develop a metallic cartridge like that patented in 1846 and 1849 by the Frenchman Flobert. Smith and Wesson then modified a Rocket Ball to include a copper base that held the fulminate priming. In 1854, Palmer put $10,000 toward a partnership with his employees, forming a firm that would become known as Smith & Wesson.

A year later, 40 investors bought out Smith, Wesson, and Palmer to form the Volcanic Repeating Arms Company. The group, some of which were from New Haven, Connecticut, included Oliver Winchester, who was named company director. Winchester moved Volcanic from Norwich to New Haven. When sluggish sales sent the firm into receivership, in 1857, Winchester bought all the company's assets for $40,000. A reorganized Volcanic Repeating Arms became the New Haven Arms Company, and Benjamin Tyler Henry hired on as chief mechanic. In 1860, Henry received a patent for a 15-shot repeating rifle in .44 rimfire.

In an appeal to the U.S. Government, Oliver Winchester described his Henry rifle thusly: "... Where is the military genius [to] modify the science of war as to best develop the capacities of this terrible engine—the exclusive use of which would enable any government ... to rule the world?" In another age, the same might as easily been written about the bow. Or the atomic bomb. Wielded by Union troops, the Henry was to Confederates a "rifle you loaded on Sunday and fired all week." It could spew a stream of 15 bullets with barely a blink between shots.

The brass-framed Henry would spawn Winchester's Models 1866, 1873, and 1876. The 1866 had a receiver loading gate and a wooden fore-end, both features lacking in the Henry. But it still fired the Henry's anemic .44 rimfire round, whose 28 grains of blackpowder pushed a 216-grain bullet 1,025 fps. The Model 1873 chambered the .44-40 (.44 WCF), Winchester's first centerfire cartridge. Its 40-grain charge drove a 200-grain bullet at almost 1,200 fps. When .44-40 rifles sold to the walls, Colt's began chambering the round in its single-action revolver. That 1878 decision drew cheers. Now shooters on the frontier could stock one load for both rifle and pistol. The .44-40 had enough punch for big game and more than enough for bandits.

Wayne heart-shot this Alaskan black bear at 90 yards, with a Marlin rifle in .30-30.

This Montana bull fell to Wayne's .30-30 Marlin, with Hornady LEVERevolution ammo.

The Model 1876 Winchester, introduced at the 1876 Philadelphia Centennial Exposition, shared features of the 1873, but its bigger action took the .45-75 WCF round. It lasted just a decade. That iron-framed repeater might have been Winchester's last, had not one of its salesmen stumbled upon a second-hand rifle during his travels west. Of obscure manufacture, the dropping-block single-shot showed clever thinking. The salesman showed it to Thomas Bennett, company president and Winchester's son-in-law. Bennett hied it off to Ogden, to the "biggest gun shop between Omaha and the Pacific." There he found a small factory staffed by four brothers. The oldest was still in his twenties.

A Touch of Genius

All rights to the rifle? "Ten thousand dollars," said John Browning. It was a fortune, in 1883. Bennett countered, without blinking, at eight. John consented. It was the start of a 17-year relationship that would give Winchester more than 40 firearm designs, 11 between 1884 and 1886 alone! When Bennett offered $50,000 for a stronger lever-action to replace the Model 1876, Browning delivered one with the vertically sliding lugs that gave his single-shot (Winchester's Model 1885) such strength. It became the Model 1886. Soon after it appeared, Bennett requested a short-action version. He offered John $10,000 "if you deliver in three months, $15,000 if you can finish in two." John is said to have replied, "The price is $20,000. I'll get it to you in 30 days. If I'm late, it's free." He delivered early. Bennett was buying everything John drew up, even designs Winchester would not produce, just to keep Browning's genius from the competition.

The compact Model 1892 became an instant hit. Chambered in .44-40, .38-40, .32-20, and .25-20, it earned a worldwide following. The magazine held up to 17 rounds; lightweight versions of the rifle scaled as little as 5½ pounds. The 92 lasted in carbine form until 1941. Counting half-magazine variants Models 53 and 65 (circa 1924 and 1933, respectively), more than 1,034,000 shipped. Meanwhile, the Model 1886 became the repeating rifle for hunters hurling heavy bullets at the biggest game.

The Model 1894 followed. "Saddle gun" in the West and "deer rifle" in the East, it vaulted to the top of sales charts. The Browning-designed 94 chambered several mid-length cartridges, notably the .30 WCF, or .30-30, the first successful smokeless cartridge for sporting rifles. Loaded then with a 160-grain bullet at 1,970 fps, it now has more horsepower. In 1924, a half-magazine version of the 94, the Model 55, appeared. It gave way, in 1933, to the Model 64. The 94 in various versions lasted 112 years, before falling from Winchester's book in March, 2006, upon the closing of the New Haven plant. It remains the most popular lever rifle of all, with more than *six million* produced!

While Winchester scrambled to maintain its dominance, John Marlin and Arthur Savage were earning patents. By the 1890s, both had come up with fine rifles. Marlin's had solid-top receivers and side ejection. Savage's hammerless Model 1895 had a rotary magazine that permitted use of pointed bullets. These rifles owed some of their success to Winchester chamberings, but Savage soon trotted out its own .303, with a

The author killed this pronghorn with a Browning/Winchester reproduction M71 in .348 Improved.

.45-70
Browning 1886
Rem. 300 SJHP

An open-sighted Browning/Winchester 1886 Extra Light in .45-70 printed this 50-yard group.

190-grain bullet moving as fast as the .30 WCF's 160-grain.

Winchester next upped the ante, with a more potent lever rifle from its Utah gun wizard. Announced in June 1896, the Model 1895 was a bow to smokeless powders and cartridges with pointed bullets and high breech pressures. It was the first successful lever rifle with a vertical magazine. The single-column, fixed box design was charged from the top, and capacity depended on the cartridge. The Model 1895 was initially offered in .30-40 Krag, .38-72-275 and .40-72-330. The .236 U.S. Navy round also made the charter list, but rifles for it were never manufactured. In 1898, the .303 British joined the roster, followed, in 1903, by the .35 Winchester, and the next year by the .405. Then came the .30 Government 03 (in 1905) and .30 Government 06 (in 1908). Teddy Roosevelt liked his 1895 in .405, claiming the rifle "did admirably with lions, giraffes, elands, and smaller game" on safari. The U.S. Army bought 10,000 Model 95s in .30-40

Marlin has built some of the best centerfire lever rifles, and arguably the best rimfire, its M39.

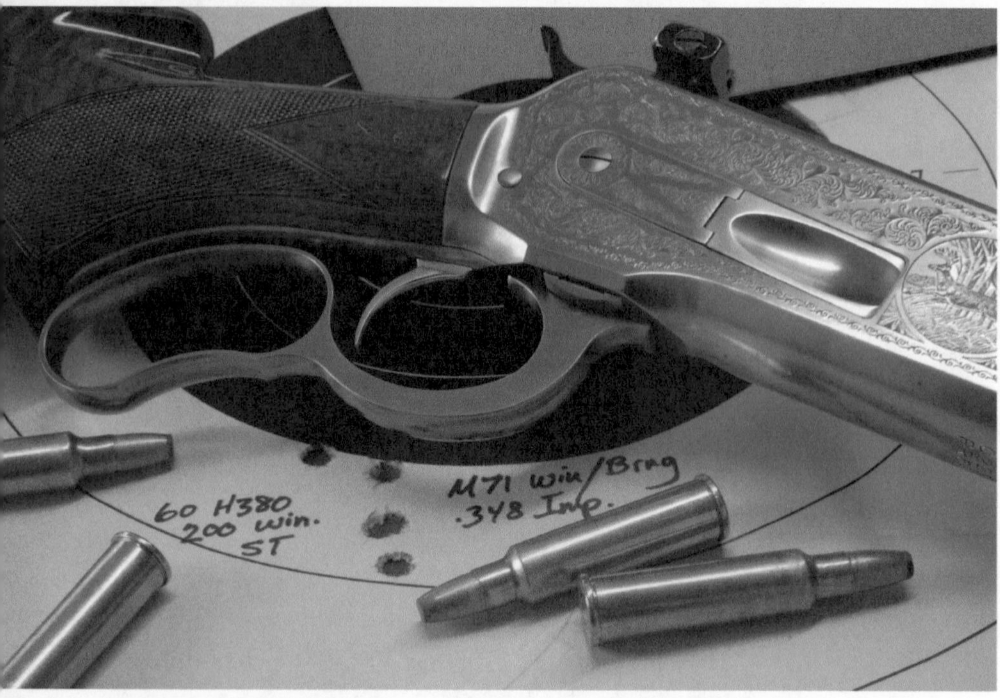

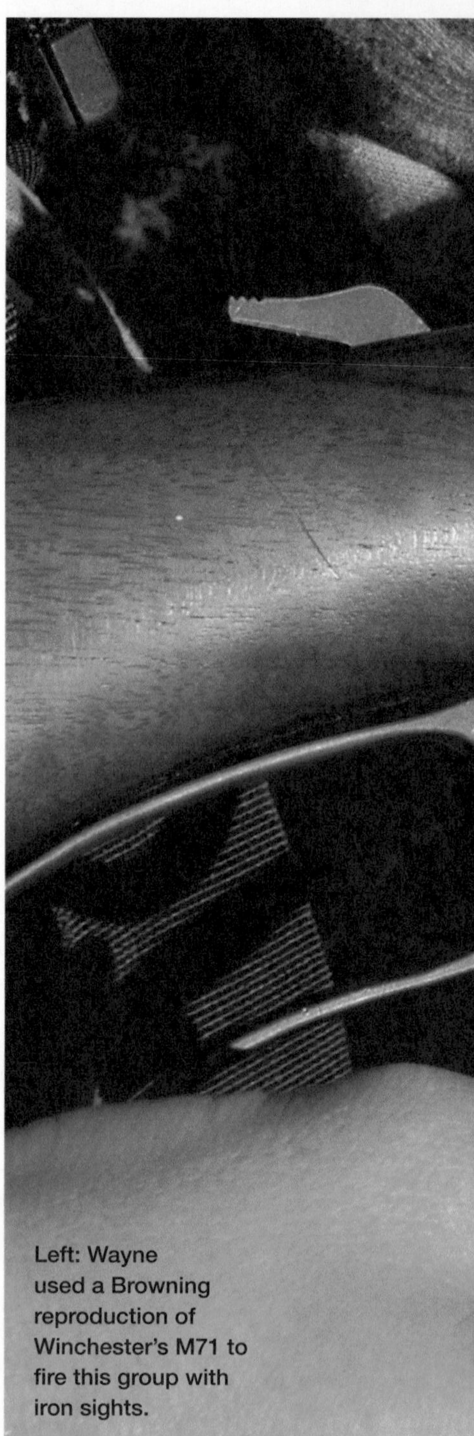

Left: Wayne used a Browning reproduction of Winchester's M71 to fire this group with iron sights.

Krag for the Spanish-American War, and Russia secured nearly 300,000 in 7.62mm Russian before our troops entered WWI. The 1895's military tenure was truncated by the 1898 Mauser and 1903 Springfield bolt-actions.

I'm no fan of the 95, though it does exhibit the fine machining and finish common to firearms of its day. Its vertical stack lets you load pointed bullets that fly flat, and it is strong, though also heavy. In

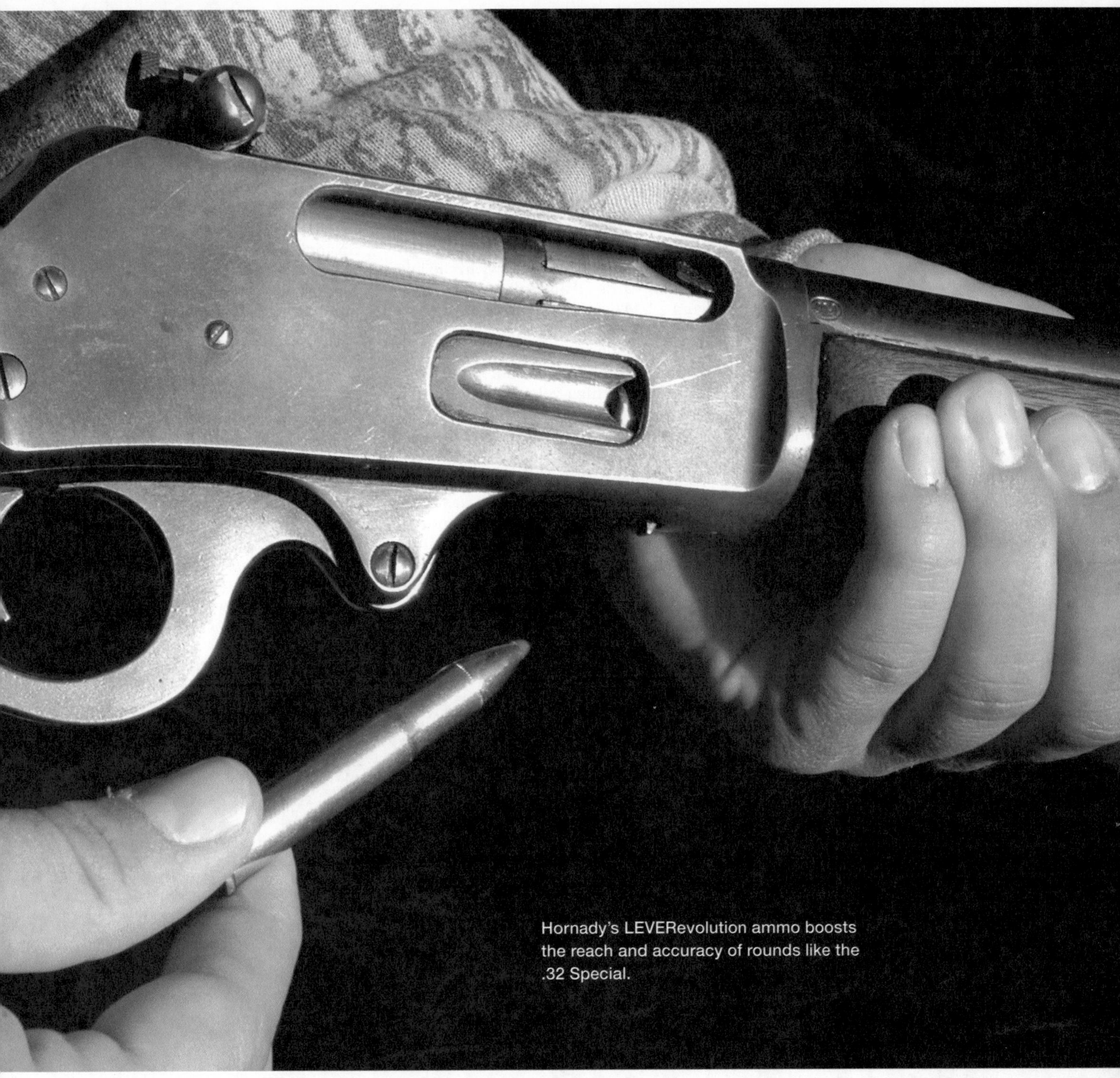
Hornady's LEVERevolution ammo boosts the reach and accuracy of rounds like the .32 Special.

spite of the weight, the 1895 is a vengeful rifle. The stock comb is sharp and has lots of drop. It jabs you viciously in the chops. And cycling an 1895 is like operating a corn-picker—the machinery is massive and noisy and wants to snare your fingers.

By 1900, three of every four guns used by American sportsmen were of Browning design, and they were all Winchesters. That year, Thomas Bennett and John Browning had a falling out over a self-loading shotgun. The firm's line of lever-actions had few empty slots, so few, in fact, that Winchester would wait 35 years before introducing another lever gun, when the Model 71 descended and replaced the 1886. Chambered for the big, rimmed .348 Winchester, the 71 came in rifle and carbine lengths and both standard and deluxe versions. Alas, steep production costs and the trend to bolt-action rifles strangled this elegant rifle in just two decades. It dropped from the line in 1958, after a run of about 47,000.

Savage Changes the Rules

By this time, optical sights were drawing converts, their need hastened by high-speed bullets. In 1913, Charles Newton developed the fast-stepping .250-3000 for Savage, which chambered it in the Model 1899 rifle. In 1920, the .300 Savage appeared, bridging the ballistic gap between the .30-30 and .30-06. Like the side-ejecting Marlins, the Model 99 was scope friendly. Also, its rotary magazine was better protected and easier and faster to load than were gated tubes—and, as it emptied, it did not affect rifle balance. Nor did it affect accuracy, like the bands securing the tube magazine to the barrel.

Arthur Savage was an able inventor. His hammerless repeating rifle earned him patents in 1892, when he was just 35. The first lever-action with a coiled mainspring, it also featured a buttstock held by a through-bolt. Savage submitted his 29-inch barreled No. 1 rifle for U.S. Ordnance trials, but it was upstaged by the Krag-Jorgensen .30-40 bolt-action. Savage refined his lever gun for hunters, trimming its lines by paring magazine capacity from eight to five. He formed the Savage Arms Company in Utica, New York, in 1894. The following year he unveiled his Model 1895 rifle in .303 Savage.

Launching a 190-grain bullet at just over 2,000 fps, this .303 was a lethal cartridge. Bullet arc was flatter than the .45-70's, and the higher sectional density of the .303 meant deeper penetration. A British Columbia hunter claimed 18 kills (including two grizzlies) with a single box of cartridges! Harry Caldwell, who worked as a missionary, in China, used a Savage lever gun in .303 to kill tigers. W.T. Hornaday, author of *Campfires in the Canadian Rockies,* wrote, "I have just [shot] one bull moose and two bull caribou, all ... stone dead in their tracks with one of your incomparable .303 rifles. I shot the moose at a distance of 350 yards ... [my guide] killed a very fine large mountain sheep [with] the first shot 237 yards off and in a very strong wind ... . [There's] no long magazine to catch the wind ... ." The .303 survived early challenges from the .30-06 and .300 Savage, before succumbing to the trend toward high-velocity rounds after WWII.

In 1899, Arthur Savage rightly divined that the future lay in lightweight, fast-stepping bullets. The only big-bore chambering in the Model 1899 was the .38-55. Though Charles Newton reportedly urged a .250 load with a 100-grain bullet at 2,800 fps, Savage instead pushed an 87-grain bullet at 3,000, reaching an elusive bar and giving Newton's round a catchy name. The .22 Hi-Power came from the Newton bench about this time. By 1920, when the Model 1899 became the Model 99, and flat-shooting rifles held sway.

Some famous outdoorsmen carried Savages—Roy Chapman Andrews, for instance. Unabashedly a Winchester fan, T.R. declared his Savage 99 one of the best-built rifles he'd owned. The Krag-Jorgensen that had trounced it in ordnance trials quickly gave way to the Springfield, while Savage's lever-action would steam on for a full century, before high costs for fitting and timing actions would sink it from Savage's line, in 1998.

In mid-life, Arthur W. Savage sold his interest in the Savage Arms Company to a group of Utica, New York, businessmen and moved to San Diego, where he indulged a spirit of adventure evident years earlier. He had explored Australia in a covered wagon, married there, and fathered eight children while building a cattle empire. He'd sold out to manage a Jamaica coffee plantation. One of his most celebrated inventions was the Savage-Halpine torpedo, adopted by the Brazilian navy. Retiring, he and his son, Arthur John, formed the Savage

During the '40s, the .348 (left) gave muscle to lever guns. The .500 S&W powers the Bighorn 89.

A young hunter fires a Marlin 336, one of the great lever-actions of all time. It's a .32 Special.

Tire Company. Then, the elder Savage bought citrus groves and drilled two oil wells. As the wells gave out, a gold mine he and his son had developed was lost to flooding. Arthur Savage died in 1941.

I carried a Savage Model 99 last season, because the rifle feels so good in hand. On a Wyoming plain some years ago, I bellied through sage to kill a pronghorn and a mule deer with another 99, an iron-sighted rifle in .300 Savage. Yet another, a .250 with irons, downed an elk. A 99 Featherweight wearing a 3X Leupold slipped with me through a Northwoods thicket to circle a whitetail buck. The shot came fast, and the deer spun, sprinted, and collapsed—thrilling! Long pokes with scoped bolt-actions can't compare!

In 1955, Winchester brought out its own hammerless rifle, the Model 88. Fed by a detachable box, the 88 had a front-locking rotating bolt and a trigger that stayed with the lever in its sweep. It chambered the new, frisky .308, with the .243 and .358 to follow in a year. All generated pressures exceeding 50,000 psi, more than exposed-hammer rifles of earlier days could safely bottle. Sako's Finnwolf, introduced in 1962, had many features of the Winchester 88, including a one-piece stock. Neither

In rough, steep country, the Model 94 Winchester carries like a wish and points like a wand!

Fast repeat shots endear lever-actions to whitetail hunters. Side ejection gave Marlin a boost.

rifle lasted into 1975—or unseated the Savage 99.

Modern, with Hammers

Not long before these sleek rifles expired, Browning introduced its BLR. Like them, it boasted a front-locking bolt and a trigger pinned to the lever. Unlike them, however, it had an external hammer and its stock was of a traditional two-piece design. Browning had originally scheduled the rifle for manufacture by TRW in Cleveland, Ohio. But prototypes built in 1966 did not result in a commercial run. As many as 250 of these earliest BLRs may exist, though some records show they were slated for destruction. BLR manufacture began in Belgium, in 1969. Five years later, it moved to Miroku, Japan. In 1977, Winchester's .358 joined the original .308 and .243 chamberings. Renamed the BLR 81, in 1981, this rifle appeared with a longer action 10 years later. Browning changed little but the label, in 1995, when long- and short-action rifles became the New Model Lightning BLRs. In 2003, they were christened BLR Lightweights.

Currently, Browning lists a BLR Lightweight with pistol grip and schnabel fore-end, plus a BLR Lightweight 81 with straight grip and barrel-band fore-end. Chamberings include 11 for the short-action (.223 to .325 WSM) and four in the long-action (.270, .30-06, 7mm Remington, and .300 Winchester Magnums).

I wish I had snared one of the early carbines with a steel receiver. While today's alloy receivers are lighter and as strong (the bolt locks into the barrel), I prefer the profile of the original BLRs. Not long ago, I carried a BLR Lightweight in .450 Marlin to Africa. A take-down rifle equipped with XS sights, it excelled at the bench, firing Hornady LEVERevolution ammo into minute-of-angle groups. Take-down and reassembly were as easy as flipping the recessed tab in the fore-end, and did not affect the zero of this .450.

If, in the wake of the Great War, you owned a lever-action that wasn't a Winchester, it was likely a Marlin. John Mahlon Marlin began his career at age 18, in 1853, when he apprenticed as a machinist. He agreed to work for no wages for six months, after which he'd earn $1.50 a week! The Connecticut shop that employed him first produced derringer-style pistols, then Ballard rifles. The first successful Marlin lever-action was the top-ejecting Model 1881 in .40-60 and .45-70. It sold for $32. The subsequent 1889 had side ejection and a more reliable carrier. It followed the Model 1888, designed by L.L. Hepburn for the .32-20, .38-40, and .44-40. Hepburn's 1893 accepted longer cartridges, including the .32-40 and .38-55, then the .25-36, .30-30, and .32 Special. By the 1920s, Marlin's 93 was competing vigorously with the Winchester 94.

In 1937, Marlin introduced its Model 1936 as "a new gun especially for American big game." It had a "solid frame, 20-inch round tapered special smokeless barrel [and] Ballard-type rifling, visible hammer, case-hardened receiver … full pistol grip buttstock of genuine American black walnut … ." All variations, in .30-30 and .32 Special, cost $32. A year later, the Model 336 replaced this rifle. The obvious difference was a new round bolt "encased … by a solid bridge of steel in the receiver." The extractor was new, and the 36's flat mainspring gave way to a coil spring.

The 336 and 1895 (same receiver, but equipped for .45-70 size rounds) have changed little since WWII. Current rifles exhibit pre-war quality in fit and finish. The Model 1895 got a hike in horsepower, with the introduction of the .450 Marlin. Short-barreled Guide Guns now wear stainless steel, laminated wood, XS sights, and big levers. Cowboy Action competitors adore Model 1894s in .357, .44 Magnum, and .45 Colt. Then, Dave Emary at Hornady devised a cartridge that challenges the .308 Winchester ballistically, but feeds through a 336 and hews to a pressure limit of 47,000 psi. New ball powders gave Dave more latitude in designing the hull—at 1.92 inches, it is a tad shorter than its parent, the .307 Winchester. The .308 Marlin hurls 160-grain FTX bullets at 2,600 fps. They still clock 2,000 fps at 300 yards and pack 1,200 ft-lbs of punch at 400.

I shot a New Mexico elk with the .308 Marlin Express, in October lodgepoles. Dave Emary was pleased, but still he thought the Model 1895 had more to give. The following year he fashioned an even more powerful round, based loosely on the .376 Steyr. The .338 Marlin Express hits as hard with its 200-grain bullet as does a 180-grain .30-06. At 2,565 fps, the .338 ME bullet scribes an arc all but identical to that of the '06 out to 300 yards. It reaches farther and with more precision than Winchester's .348 or the .450 Marlin. Aided by a GreyBull scope, I once fired a Model 1895 in .338 ME at a 12-inch disk from 100, 200, 300, 400, 500, and 600 yards. Prone, from a sling, loosing just one shot at each distance (no sighters!), I hit the mark with every bullet!

Bullets Big as Your Thumb

Interest in .45- and even .50-caliber lever rifles has returned. Actually, the resurrection began a half-century ago at the bench of Harold Johnson, in Cooper's Landing, Alaska. Brown bears had muscle and momentum that made even the .35 Whelen seem anemic, so Johnson necked up the .348 Winchester hull to accept .458 bullets. The .450 Alaskan is still a fine choice for hunters who want more punch from their Model 71s. Its rimmed case, sharp-shouldered and straighter than its parent, holds fuel enough to jar your molars. Loaded stiff, the .450 Alaskan beats even the British .450/400 that, in another time, proved a match for Africa's heavy game. Even my case-forming loads drive 400-grain bullets 2,000 fps. Tossing the lever, that huge hull arcing above iron sights, I imagine bush-bred hunters in shin-high boots, probing willow jungles for bears the size of chest freezers, and moose as tall as draft horses.

Among the best-looking big-bore reproduction rifles of late is a slim version of John Browning's Model 1886 Winchester, our first repeater with vertically sliding lugs. The 1886 chambered the .38-56, .40-65, .40-70, .40-82, .45-70, .45-90, and also the .50-100-450 and .50-110. The .33 Winchester arrived in 1902.

The Miroku-built Winchester 1886 Extra Light in .45-70 is mostly true to the original. Two visible deviations are its rebounding hammer (the first 1886 had a half-cock notch), and a safety inletted into the tang. The safety is neat and small and moves like an expensive switch. The straight-grip stock and capped fore-end are of plain, oil-finished American walnut, well fitted

The .303 Savage was a charter chambering in the 1899 rifle with its superb rotary magazine.

Test-Fire: Browning/Winchester 1886 Extra Light, .45-70 (averages, five shots)			
Round	Velocity (fps)	std. dev.	50-yd. group (inches)
Remington 300-grain semi-jacketed hollowpoint	1,632	32	1.8
Federal 300-grain hollowpoint	1,772	18	2.3
Winchester 405-grain soft-point	1,360	4	2.1
Black Hills 405-grain lead (Cowboy Action)	1,244	6	1.8

to the polished, deeply blued metal. Wood and steel have flat, even surfaces. The action feeds even square-nosed bullets smoothly. Remington 300-grain hollowpoints and Black Hills 405-grain lead bullets print tight groups. Neither the stock comb nor the steel shotgun butt-plate punish me. At six pounds, the trigger breaks reluctantly, but with snap. An elegant rifle made stronger by use of modern steels, the Winchester 1886 Extra Light shows uncommon care in fit and finish.

Another firm trading on the romance of big-bore lever rifles is Bighorn Armory, with its Model 89 in .500 Smith & Wesson. Combining elements of the Winchester 1886, 1892, and 71, the action cycles with an easy grace, thanks to twin lugs rising in machined races to wed bolt with receiver. The long, smooth arc of the hammer feels good, as I rock a steel plate with a stream of 400-grain bullets at a pre-production shoot.

"I'll loan you one," offers Frank Ehrenford, who builds the Bighorn 89 in Cody, Wyoming. And he does, sending me a rifle with 22-inch barrel. Both it and the 18-inch barreled carbine are handsome, but the rifle starts bullets faster, and its extra muzzle heft tames recoil.

Frank describes the Model 89 stock as "specially treated walnut." Honey and black hues enrich a dull gloss finish. The un-checkered wood marries up well with the satin stainless barrel and receiver. Long tangs, top and bottom, show close fit. The ⅔-length magazine is dovetailed to the barrel just forward of the cap, which features an integral swivel stud. An XS front sight tops a short ramp, while the bolt wears a neat aperture sight. Lever and trigger guard are bigger than on Winchesters—not sleek, but practical for gloved hands.

Hornady's FTX bullets chamber easily. So do 350-grain hollowpoints, 400-grain

A tang sight close to your eye helps you shoot better with rifles like this Winchester Model 94.

Marlin builds fine lever rifles, this one in the potent, Hornady-developed .308 Marlin Express.

flat-points and Winchester 400-grain Platinum Tips. No cycling glitches with any. A plunger ejector tosses hulls smartly.

Reporting on the accuracy of rifles with iron sights is a challenge. Almost anyone can quarter a bull's-eye with a high-power scope, but shooting well with irons requires keen vision and experience. Still, rifles like the Bighorn 89 just aren't meant to be scoped! So I benched this boomer with irons. It shoots as well as I can see and hold—three minutes of angle that day. While the .500 S&W cartridge brings more than 1,500 ft-lbs to 150 yards (from a rifle barrel), I limit game shooting with irons to 100. A rifle that prints into *four* minutes will center the vitals of deer-size game 100 yards off and kill predictably twice as far.

Custom makers also hawk powerful lever-actions. Wild West Guns, of Anchorage, bases its line (including take-downs) on Marlin's 1895 action. Cartridges include the company's .457 Magnum, with a 350-grain bullet at 2,200 fps (and a chamber that accepts .45-70 ammo). The .50 Alaskan kicks 450- and 500-grain bullets downrange with two tons of energy.

Doug Turnbull, known for his skillful restoration of lever rifles, has designed a round for shooters who want more smash from 1886 Winchesters. The .475 Turnbull began as an alternative to the .45-70, .45-90, and .50-110 (.50 Express), classic buffalo rifle cartridges in the 1886. Based on the .50-110 hull trimmed from 2.4 to 2.2 inches, the .475 Turnbull was also tended to by Hornady engineers and Dave Manson of Manson Reamers. "We necked it down to boost sectional density," Doug said. In other words, to add reach and boost penetration. The .475's long (.465) neck clamps bullets firmly, so they don't pound loose in tube magazines.

Commercial .475 Turnbull ammo has been available for three years, and Doug's work with it dates back six. He fired "at least 500 of each bullet weight" refining loads—hardly a task for the recoil-shy! Grizzly and CorBon now supply ammunition. After SAAMI approved the cartridge, CorBon loaded 400-grain TSX and solid bullets at an advertised 2,150 fps. Muzzle energy exceeds 4,100 ft-lbs, matching the punch of the .404 Jeffery and .450/400 Nitro Express. The .50-110's original 300-grain loads managed 1,605 fps for 1,720 ft-lbs. Cartridges supplied to me by Turnbull clocked 1,940 fps over Oehler sky-screens.

In 2007, Doug began adapting Winchester 1886 rifles to his .475 round. He still offers the service. No stack of '86s behind the Christmas ornaments in the closet? You can order a Turnbull 1886 in .475. It costs a tad more than an 1886 in .45-70, but if you're visiting this shop, you're not looking for the ordinary!

Test-Fire: Bighorn 89, .500 S&W, 22-inch barrel (averages, five shots)

Round	Velocity (fps)	std. dev.	50-yd. group (inches)
Hornady, 350-grain hollowpoint	2,105	19	2.5
Winchester, 400-grain Platinum Tip	1,957	23	2
41.5 H110, 400-grain Hornady flat-point	1,955	30	1.8

BR WN

John Browning posing with his FN/Browning Auto 5 shotgun

NG A-5:

A Gun With Soul

BY **NICK HAHN**

In America, if you mention the name Browning to someone of the Vietnam generation or older who served in the Army or Marines, especially in the infantry, more than likely they will think of the BAR (Browning Automatic Rifle) or possibly even the .30-caliber machine gun. On the other hand, if you reference Browning to a shotgunner, it is likely that the person will immediately think of the old hump-backed autoloader popularly known as the Automatic Five, Auto Five, or A-5.

Although the more expensive Superposed over/under was Browning's premier shotgun, to many Americans, if you wanted a Browning—the best of the best—it meant the gun commonly known for the first half of the last century as the "Browning Automatic." Americans were not alone in this. Much of the world's population of shooters identified the name Browning with this venerable old autoloader. The popularity of the Browning Automatic was such that it was not confined just to average people, but also to those who could afford much more expensive guns. Everyone, from members of European nobility to Bedouin tribesmen, owned or wanted a Browning Automatic.

There have been hundreds of articles written about the Browning A-5. The history and the mechanics of this re-

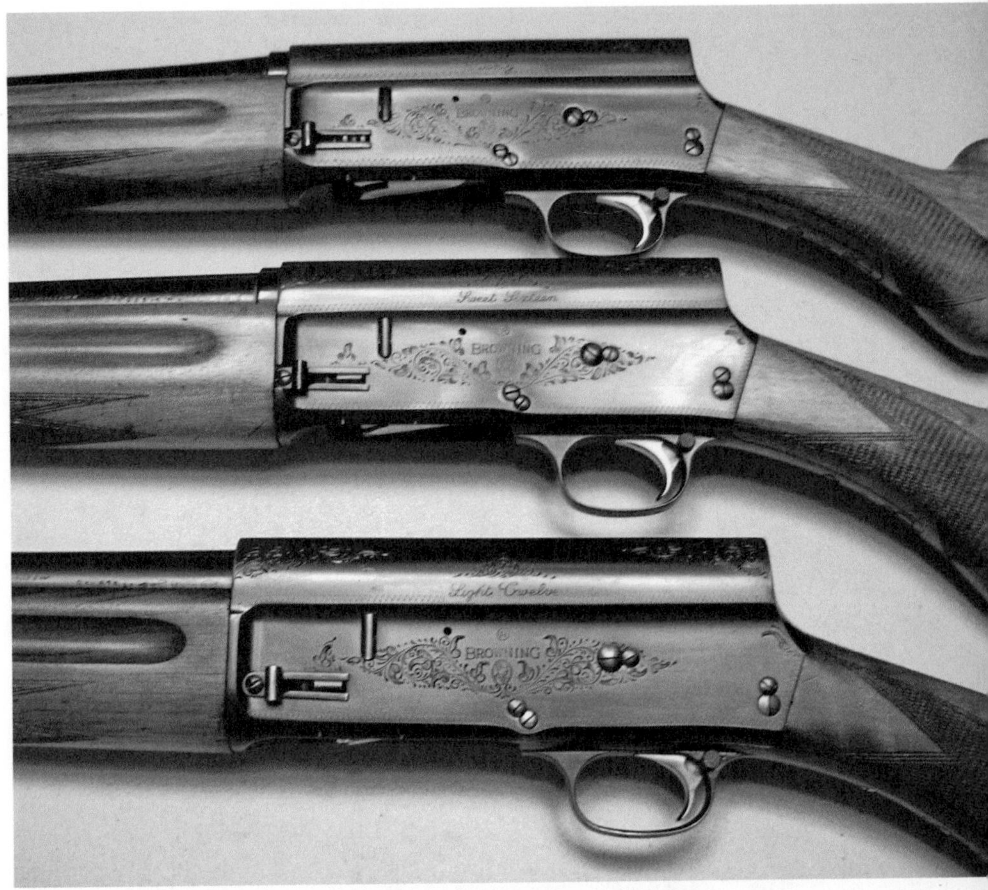

Comparative receiver sizes of the Light Twelve on the bottom, Sweet Sixteen in the middle, and the Twenty, popularly called "Light Twenty," at the top.

markable design have been covered very well over the years by many writers, so my intention is to simply provide some lesser known information—no technical descriptions, just small bits and pieces and anecdotal accounts of John Browning's classic shotgun.

In 1954, Japan's Crown Prince Akihito (the Emperor of Japan today) went on a tour of Europe. During his visit to Belgium, he was taken to Liege to visit the country's pride and joy, the arms factory of Fabrique Nationale, the makers of Browning guns. During the tour of the factory, the Crown Prince was asked if he was a shooter and familiar with Browning arms. The Crown Prince responded that he had shot duck and pheasant and was indeed familiar with the Browning brand.

Before the Crown Prince's arrival, FN factory officials had arranged to present him with a high-grade 20-gauge Superposed; the Crown Prince being a man of small physical stature, the officials thought a lighter gun was the appropriate choice. However, before the presentation could be made, the Crown Prince remarked that he had always been fond of the Browning Automatic, but unfortunately did not own one. Asked what he was currently shooting and informed that the Crown Prince carried an English Best 16-gauge double, there was a flurry of commotion by FN officials as they scurried about to correct their choice of a presentation shotgun. Their efforts prevailed, and the Crown Prince left the factory with a Browning Automatic Sweet Sixteen (the lighter 20-gauge autoloader wasn't available until 1958). Upon returning to Japan, the Crown Prince proudly posed with his new Browning Automatic and told the reporters he was anxious to try out the gun on pheasant. The resulting picture appeared on the front page of every newspaper in Japan.

How times change. Today, such a display would bring down the wrath of an indignant public who no doubt would bombard the offending newspapers via e-mail, text messaging, and Twitter, criticizing the Crown Prince for his politically incorrect behavior and the newspapers for publishing such an "offensive" photograph.

Three 1950s-vintage A-5s, the Light Twelve on the left (made in 1953), Sweet Sixteen in the middle (made in 1953), and the Twenty on the right (made in 1958, first year of production for the Twenty).

What's in a Name?

Today just about everyone reading *Gun Digest* knows that the proper term for a gun such as the Browning "Automatic" is "semi-automatic" or "autoloading." But, from its very beginning, in 1903 until 1953—half a century—it was simply called an "automatic." It wasn't until the appearance of the new Browning Double Automatic that the name Automatic Five (Auto Five or A-5) was applied to the old humpback to differentiate it from the newer Double Automatic.

If you look at the butt-plate of the older A-5s, the name "Browning" appears on the right and "Automatic" on the left, both surrounding the letters "FN" in the center. The Double Automatic has "Browning" on top and "Double Automatic" on the bottom, with a portrait of John M. Browning in the middle. All Browning advertising simply referred to the old autoloader as the Automatic. But, after the appearance on American gun dealers' shelves of the Double Automatic, in 1953, the old humpback got a new nickname, the "Automatic Five," which then became shortened to "Auto Five" or to "A-5." It's this last name that stuck the hardest.

A Long History

The Browning A-5 was in production from 1903 until it was discontinued in 1998—95 years. At one time or another, it was made in three different countries, and while there were changes here and there through the years, none were really major. The A-5 was produced mostly in Belgium, but it was also made in America for a short period. These latter guns are known as American Brownings, produced from 1946 until 1952 to help fill the demand for sporting arms. FN did produce some A-5s during this period, but in much smaller numbers, because they were heavily involved in making military arms for the newly created NATO.

To relieve the demand for sporting arms in the U.S., Browning had Remington tool up for the A-5. These guns were essentially the same as the old Remington Model 11, except they had the magazine cut-off and some superficial changes to make them more like the FN version. Although very well made, they were not as beautifully finished as the FN versions. The Remingtons featured rolled-on engraving, rather than hand-cut, and the polishing of parts both

The Twenty A-5, weighing somewhere south of 6½ pounds, an excellent and very popular upland autoloader.

internal and external was not up to the level of FN-made guns. Still, since the Remington Model 11 was made in 12-, 16-, and 20-gauges, the American Browning was available in all three gauges, as well.

Some 73 years after its start, production of the Belgian-made A-5 ceased in 1976, at least for the American market. Japan's Miroku factory picked up production next and continued to make the model for the next 22 years. A little-known bit of history: the very early Japanese-made A-5s were actually made by SKB. Miroku wasn't set up to make the autoloader at first, although they had marketed the so-called "Auto Pointer," an A-5 lookalike that was actually made by Daiwa and sold under the Miroku label. So, the initial run of the Japanese made A-5s were subcontracted to SKB, a practice common in the Japanese gun-making industry in the 1970s. Once the factory was set up, all A-5s were made at the Miroku plant. The Miroku A-5s continued until 1998, when, to the dismay of die-hard fans, Browning decided to stop production of this classic shotgun.

According to Glen Jensen, who has been a Browning employee since shortly after the end of World War II, the A-5 was the most popular Browning firearm ever made. Even now, almost 15 years after its discontinuance, Browning still receives queries from those wanting to know if the old gun will ever be produced again. Jensen, who is Browning's official historian, believes that the A-5 was the best shotgun the company ever produced. (Editor's note: A new Browning Auto-5 was introduced in late 2011. Except for the "humpback" shape of the receiver, it is a totally different design than the original subject of this article.)

Superficially, at least the unmistakable profile has stayed the same throughout its 98 years of life, and what changes there have been along the way have been small. For instance, the very early guns of first couple years in production were absent the lock/set screws on the receiver. But that lasted only a short period before FN started to supply all receivers with lock/set screws. In 1951-'52, the cross-bolt safety replaced the front safety that had been used for half a century. And, starting somewhere in 1953 or '54, Browning began to provide the speed-load feature on the A-5s, which was initially developed for the Double Automatic. Aside from these, the other changes, however slight, were mostly cosmetic.

A Hundred Variants

No one, not even avid fans of the A-5, will call the old humpback graceful looking. The receiver's angular profile, with its abrupt, squared back, may not be aesthetically pleasing, but it did help many shotgunners connect with their target, a sort of a built-in rear sight alignment. Yes, I know, shotguns are supposed to be pointed, not aimed, and the "rear sight" on a shotgun is the shooter's eye. But try telling that to millions of those who shot and still shoot the A-5. They'll swear that the rear hump helps them align the barrel with the target. And although it may not have the flowing lines of a side-by-side double or even a modern repeater,

The Sweet Sixteen, considered by many in the 1950s, '60s, and '70s as the ultimate autoloader for pheasant.

it definitely has its own charm and charisma.

Initially, the A-5 was imported from Belgium in a plain, un-engraved version. Soon the Grade I appeared with some engraving, and then others with more. At one time or another, there were 11 different grades offered, but, after World War II, Browning dropped all the other grades and upgraded the Grade I. Only on special order could other grades be purchased. In Europe, FN continued to market the plain version as Grade I, while the American customer got an upgrade; the Grade I sold in America was actually a "Special" Grade, a Grade II with a slightly modified engraving pattern. The higher grade A-5s are rarely seen in America, as very few were imported.

The receivers of the A-5 were originally rust blued, but were switched to hot blue, in 1961. Some claim that the rust blue was better but, in reality, there is very little difference, if any. The wood was oil finished on pre-war guns. Post-war guns were lacquer finished until the mid-1960s, when a glossy polyurethane finish was applied to all Browning long guns. In the case of wood finish, the old oil finish and lacquer finish were definitely better than the glossy synthetic finish (but then, some do like the glossy stuff!). The buttplates were mostly horn, while some guns came with hard rubber until the mid-1960s, when all became plastic, with the exception of the 12-gauge Magnum model, which came with a recoil pad.

The buttstock of the A-5 could be ordered as a straight grip or with the rounded semi-pistol grip popularly called a "round knob." The straight grip option was available for a long time, from 1903 until 1966. In 1968, the iconic round knob was replaced by the so-called "flat knob," a design Browning called a "modern" full pistol grip in its advertising. Apparently, "moderniza-tion" wasn't all that successful; in 1987, Browning resorted back to the old round knob grip, albeit with a slightly different checkering pattern.

All Light Twelve, Sweet Sixteen, and Twenty A-5s had gold-plated triggers. The Standard Models and the Magnums had blued triggers. However the Standard Models were dropped in 1970 and, beginning in 1979, the Magnum models also had gold-plated triggers. If you find a Standard Model on the used gun market with a gold-plated trigger, it was plated after market, not at the factory.

Barrels were available as plain, plain with a matte surface, hollow matte rib (solid rib), and, of course, a ventilated rib. The solid or hollow matte rib was discontinued in 1962, and Belgian plain barrels were discontinued in 1975, a year before Belgian-made guns were discontinued altogether. There are some Japanese made A-5s with plain barrels, but, for all practical purposes, Miroku made only ventilated rib barrels (with the exception of their slug barrels bearing rifle sights). The few Japanese plain barrels that are around are from the early Japanese production run that were mostly made by SKB.

A number of barrel lengths were available, starting with a 24-inch (actually 23½ inches, or 60cm), and running in two-inch increments up to 30 inches. A 32-inch barrel was also made for the Standard and the Magnum Twelve, though not the Light Twelve. All barrels were cut to metric measurements, so exact inches are a bit off, generally a half-inch shorter than indicated. One note of interest regarding the barrels is that the 24-inch barrels didn't appear until 1963 and were correctly listed at the time as being 23½ inches. However, a few years later they were listed as being 24 inches, although the length hadn't changed at all. Also, these short barrels were all made as rib-less barrels with rifle sights. Later, some of these short barrels were special ordered with ventilated or even plain without a rib and Cylinder or Improved Cylinder choking for bird shooting. These options were never cataloged, but available on special order.

All degrees of choking were available in the A-5s and, unlike most gun makers, Browning offered the A-5 barrels in whatever choke the customer desired, regardless of the barrel length. The barrels could also be had with either a Poly Choke or Cutts Compensator device, until 1970. The Japanese-made barrels, of course, were available with the Invector choke system.

Pre-war and early 1950s guns had the same serial number on the receiver and the barrel. The A-5 barrels were always interchangeable within gauge and chamber length, and, until 1953, guns left the factory with matching numbers. Collectors will note that quite often guns with different serial numbers are found. That is because different barrels were substituted for the original. By the time the Magnum Twelve and the Twenty came out, in 1958, matching numbers were a thing of the past, extremely rare, except for special models that were heavily engraved or on the higher grades that were available on special order only.

For its first six years, the A-5s were made in 12-gauge only. A 16-gauge version first appeared in 1909, but, in 1936, owing to the demands of upland hunters for a less hefty gun, a lightened version of the 16-gauge appeared and dubbed the "Sweet Sixteen," although the name was not inscribed anywhere on the gun. At the end of World War II, in 1946, a lightened version of the 12-gauge was introduced and simply called the "Lightweight." Like the 16-gauge, this model branding wasn't identifiable by inscription or other marking. However, both the Sweet Sixteen and the Lightweight 12-gauge could be identified by their actual lighter weight and gold-plated triggers. Starting in 1952-'53, they could also be identified by their serial numbers, which had letter prefixes, the Light Twelve with an "L" and the Sweet Sixteen an "S." At the same time the letter designations started, Browning began to engrave the name "Sweet Sixteen" on the left side of that gun's receiver, while the 12-gauge version got a name change to "Light Twelve" with that name so inscribed. At this point, Browning had both a 12-gauge and 16-gauge in standard weights and lightened versions.

All Browning A-5s were extremely popular and sold better than any other gun in their line. They were never popular on the trap and skeet fields, instead finding their niche with hunters. It was due to this following that, in 1958, the 3-inch Magnum 12-gauge and the 20-gauge versions were introduced, becoming immediate hits. The 20-gauge was available only in one version, so the single word "Twenty" was engraved on the receiver. (Ironically, though only one weight version was available, it was commonly referred to as "Light Twenty.") The 12-gauge 3-inch Magnum version bore the word "Magnum" on the side of the receiver. In 1968, Browning introduced the 20-gauge 3-inch Magnum with "Magnum Twenty" on the side of the receiver, which saw the 12-gauge magnum changing its wording to "Magnum Twelve."

The standard Model A-5 was a substantial gun, weighing something in the neighborhood of 8¼ pounds for the 12-gauge and 7½ pounds for the 16-gauge. The Light Twelve and Sweet Sixteen, with their lightened receivers, shaved off about a half pound. On the average, a "Light Twelve" with a 28-inch ventilated rib barrel will weigh around 7¾ pounds and, with a 28-inch plain barrel, closer to 7½ pounds—not exactly a lightweight, despite its moniker. The Twenty was advertised as being "below 6½ pounds," and some of the very early ads claimed 6¼ pounds—a bit optimistic, I think. A Twenty with a 28-inch vent rib barrel will weigh over 6½ pounds, and some of the commemorative Japanese-made guns with dense, fancy wood will tip the scales over seven pounds. On the heaviest side, the Magnum Twelve averaged 8½ pounds and the Magnum Twenty about 7¼ pounds.

All in all, the A-5 was never a light gun except in the Sweet Sixteen and the Twenty models, and even then only with plain, short barrels. In general, a ventilated rib added about a quarter-pound to the weight of the barrel, depending on length. That is why many field shooters prefer plain barrels, especially for upland gunning.

All A-5s were built on their own dedicated gauge-specific frames. The Magnum Twelve frame may look the same as the Standard 12 frame, but it is larger, and the same applies for the Magnum Twenty and Twenty frames. Likewise, the Sweet Sixteen frame is not the same as a Magnum Twenty's though it is hard to tell at first glance. Naturally, the smallest A-5 frame is the one on the Twenty, which is, of course, the lightest of all A-5s sold in America. At one time there were rumors that Browning was going to come out with scaled 28-gauge and 410-bore A-5s to compete with Remington, which at one point was the only manufacturer making autoloaders in those two gauges on scaled receivers. But, apparently, they were just rumors, and no A-5s in these sub-gauges were ever produced.

At one point, FN attempted to market alloy-framed A-5s. These models were called "Superlight" and were similar to the lightweight version of the Superposed over/under. Some of these alloy-framed guns were marked as "Superlight" on the left side of the receivers, while others were unmarked. I have seen both an unmarked 20-gauge version and a Superlight-marked 12-gauge that belonged to a friend. These guns were made in the 1970s, when the manufacture of marked

A Light Twelve, the most popular of all A-5s.

A-5s was switched to Japan. They all had flat knob pistol grips and looked exactly like the steel-framed A-5s. The ones I saw were unengraved models, or the European Grade I versions, and they were definitely lighter than the steel-framed models. One thing I did notice in handling those alloy-framed A-5s was that they lacked that solid between-the-hands feel that steel-framed A-5s have. That, of course, is understandable, since at least a half-pound is shaved from the receiver area by the use of alloy. The alloy-framed versions were never imported by Browning.

The Big Hits

When all is said and done, it appears that the most desirable versions of the A-5 are those that were made during the decade between about 1951 and 1962. Cross-bolt safeties replaced the old front safeties around 1951, and the speed load feature was introduced between 1953 and '54. Of course, there are other things that die-hards look for, such as the use of screws throughout instead of the rolled pins Browning used in some places on later guns. Vent rib barrels are preferred by collectors, although, as mentioned earlier, many field gunners prefer the plain barrel. Even in the older guns, the speed load feature is preferred. This feature first appeared in 1952, with the introduction of the new Double Automatic. It became very popular, leading to subsequent A-5s being provided with the feature. Indeed, many older guns were retrofitted with it, either by Browning or private gunsmiths. The old Browning A-5 manual even had instructions on how to convert older guns to speed load.

If you are not a collector and just want a good autoloader for hunting, then any of the A-5s will do. They will all function reliably if they were and are properly maintained and not abused, even those that were made in the early years of the twentieth century. Many people don't realize that, at the FN factory, as much care and attention was given to making the A-5 as it took to make the more expensive Superposed. No assembly line semi-auto shotgun in the world was made with as much care and attention to detail as the FN Browning A-5. They were built to last.

The A-5 has had many copies and clones, with many licensed copies made before World War II, most notably by Remington and Savage. In Europe, there were outright pirated copies, especially coming out of Germany. Post-war, the Italian Franchi and the Breda with modified receivers and mechanism are basically Brownings, while in Japan, SKB produced Browning-type shotguns with a streamlined receiver, and Daiwa made an almost exact copy once the Browning patents ran out. Daiwa guns, incidentally, were available with all-steel receivers or with alloy. In America, the Remington 11-48 and the new Savage autoloaders were nothing but slightly modified Brownings, mainly with streamlined receivers. (Savage's attempt to streamline the receiver in the 1950s wasn't very successful, and they actually went back to the old humpback design in the early1960s and stayed that way until they were discontinued altogether in 1967.)

All A-5s produced under the Browning name are worthy of the gun's lofty reputation. The only exceptions are the guns of the last year of Belgian production (1976), which were sloppily put together with less engraving and were overall below Browning's standard finishing. Also, in 1986 and '87, some Belgian A-5s appeared, put together with leftover parts. They were not of the quality one expected from Browning shotguns. The short-lived "American Brownings" were also not as well finished as the FN versions, The Miroku-made A-5s, on the other hand, are equal to the mid-1960s-'70s Belgian-production A-5s, though just not quite up to the level of those made 1950s to the early 1960s, which are considered to be the best to come out of the FN factory and even better than the pre-war versions.

The Japanese versions were excellent, but they did have some variations, the most obvious being that the barrel hangers were brazed on and not integral, as on the Belgian barrels. However, the Japanese barrels were much harder and could be used with steel shot. Also, with the exception of the very early 1970s versions, the Japanese barrels came with Browning's Invector choke tubes. There were other differences. The magazine caps on Belgian guns had two knurled bands, while the Japanese version had three. The buttplate on the Japanese A-5s naturally discontinued using the letters "FN" surrounded by the words "Browning Automatic," as on the Belgian guns, and, instead, the buttplate was like those on the Superposed and the Citori, bearing just the name "Browning" on it. But, aside from some of these minor differences, cosmetically, the Japanese Brownings were very well finished, beautifully polished and blued.

Today, there is a plethora of auto-loading shotguns on the market. Only one is of the long-recoil, A-5-type gun, that being the Franchi 48AL. Most guns today are either gas operated or inertia driven, like the Benelli. In a way, the auto-loading shotgun market is much like the auto-loading pistol market! The auto pistol field is flooded with double actions and, in fact, there are more double-action high-capacity pistols out there than there are any other kind. Yet, the old 1911 keeps chugging along. Unfortunately, the Browning A-5 has not enjoyed the same fate, a hurt to those who have shot this gun in the field and firmly believe there is no other auto-loading shotgun quite like it.

United the A-5 Stands

The Browning A-5 has not only a long, distinguished, and storied background in hunting, it has served in combat with distinction. Our military never used the A-5 in combat, at least not that I am aware of, although the A-5 clone, the Remington Model 11, was used extensively by Navy and Army Air Corps to train aerial gunners. But other countries, like Great Britain, did use the Browning A-5s in combat. I remember back in the early 1960s, when I was in the Army, my unit, the 7th Special Forces Group, had an exchange program with the British 22nd SAS. Two members of our unit trained with the 22nd SAS in England, and they in turn sent two of their members to train with us. I spent six months with one of the members of the SAS assigned to my detachment, a veteran of the so-called "Malayan Emergency" that took place from 1949 until 1960. The SAS member lavished heavy praise on the FN Browning A-5, which was their standard-issue along with the Browning Hi Power pistol. The SAS patrols were armed with A-5s wearing 28-inch Full-choke barrels—not short riot guns—and loaded with buckshot. He said the guns never failed them.

I have been a fan of the Browning A-5 ever since I became interested in guns and hunting as a kid. I remember being mesmerized by the full-page ads in the outdoor magazines of the 1950s that spelled out phrases such as "The Aristocrat of Automatic Shotguns" and "Rugged as the Rockies and Smooth as Silk." I also remember reading and gazing at wonderful color photographs in a *National Geographic* magazine that had a story about wild and free Bedouins in the Arabian Desert. They were all armed with long-barreled Browning A-5s. Yes, to me the A-5 was the best gun in the world, bar none!

I did some of my most memorable hunting with my A-5s. I shot my first California limit of geese, three snows and three specs, with my Light Twelve, on a foggy, Thanksgiving Day morning, and my first limit of seven bull sprigs with a Sweet Sixteen, back in the 1970s. More recently, I had perhaps the best pigeon shoot of my life with an A-5. I shot up a case of ammunition on a hot, dusty, afternoon in the Mexican desert, with a Sweet Sixteen that chugged along without a hiccup.

Perhaps the most significant reason for my fondness and attachment to the A-5 is that the man who took me hunting when I was a kid and taught me just about everything that I know about hunting shot an old pre-war Browning A-5. His was the heavy, unengraved version with the safety in front of the trigger guard, a gun that was made before the appearance of the Light Twelve. I witnessed some of the most remarkable shooting I've ever seen a man do, when he picked up that gun. That's an impression that stays.

Yes, the Browning A-5 is very special to me. When I hold it in my hands and feel that wonderful heft, I conjure up old memories of long-ago hunts and adventures. It doesn't matter whether it is a 12-, 16-, or a 20-gauge, the A-5 has the same between-the-hands feel. If you haven't owned an A-5, with its careful, old-world workmanship and the wonderful handling, then you have really missed out. Today's modern autoloaders may be technologically superior, made of all sorts of modern wonder materials, but they lack soul and have no history. Don't get me wrong, I think the modern autoloaders are excellent shooting implements—I own several and like to shoot them—but, they are not made like the old Browning, have none of that careful hand-polishing and fitting. And, so, it's the A-5 I turn to time and again, a classic with character.

RUGER®

SIXTY YEARS OF SINGLE-ACTION SIXGUNS

BY JOHN TAFFIN

"Many an eye was dampened when the startling news was broadcast that Colt's would discontinue manufacture of the grand Old Peacemaker." So said Colonel Charles Askins of the 1940 announcement that the Colt Single Action Army, after being produced continuously since 1873, would be no more. The country had been locked in the Great Depression for a decade; this certainly did not help sales of the Single Action Army and, since the ending of WWI, in 1918, shooters had more and more discovered not only the double-action revolver, but the semi-automatic pistol, as well. The Colt Single Action was dead, never to be seen again.

In 1940, anyone paying attention knew we would be at war once again. Actually, WWII had already started in Europe, our involvement was just a matter of time, and it was obvious manufacturing facilities would be needed for wartime firearms, not Single Action Armies. War came, was fought successfully, and ended the Great Depression. By 1945, the country was ready to switch over to peacetime production and prosperity once again, and history was about to take one of its many twists and turns.

In 1949, with financial backing from his partner Alexander Sturm, an unknown firearms manufacturer by the name of William Ruger was about to challenge the big boys. Sturm, Ruger & Co. brought out a .22 semi-automatic pistol that cost a lot less than those produced by Colt's or High Standard and, in many cases, actually shot better. The Ruger Standard Model .22 was an instant success.

That might've been the extent of Ruger production, except for something else that was happening in America. By the late 1940s, a major change was sweeping across the country. Suddenly, living rooms were darkened all over the

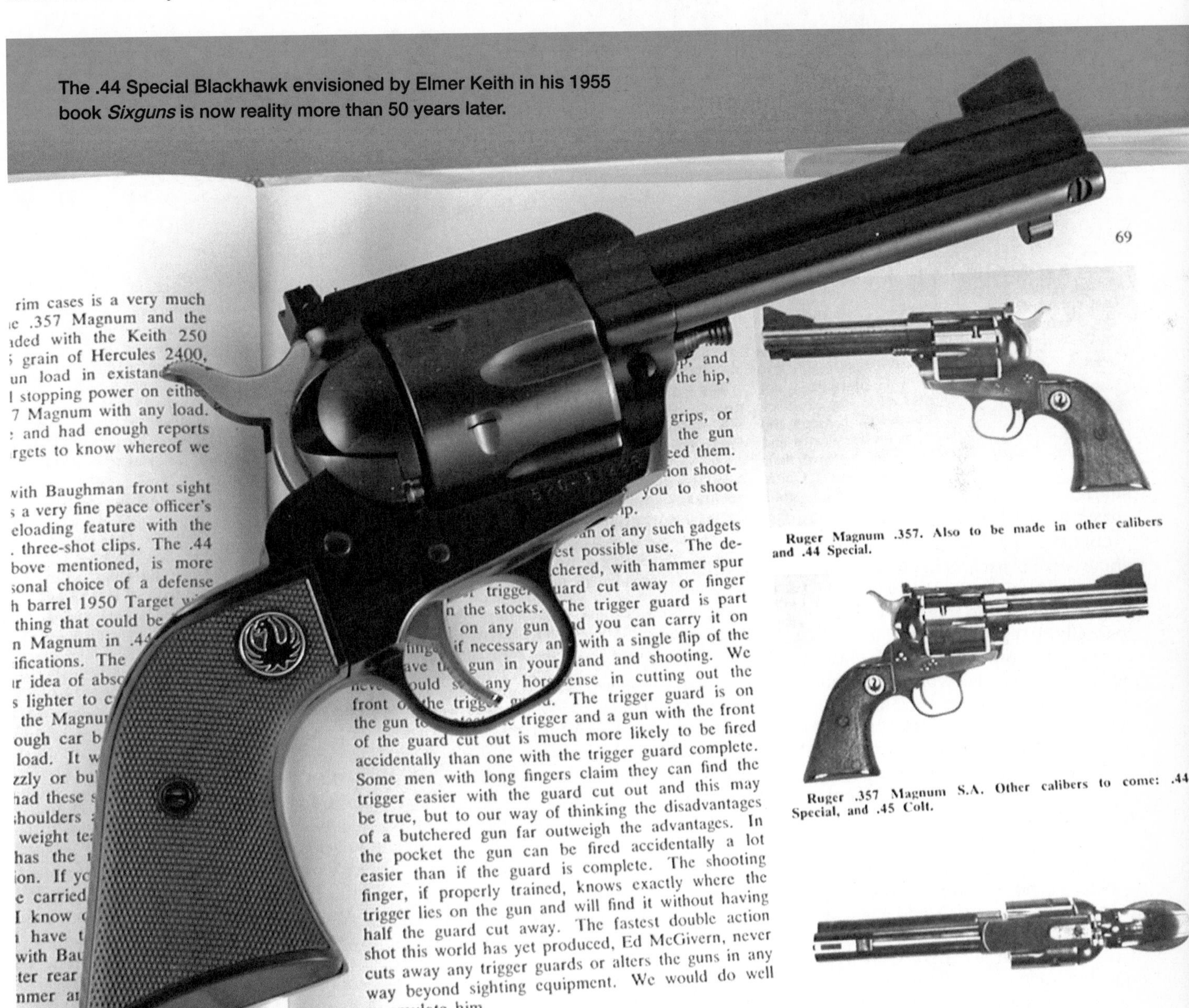

The .44 Special Blackhawk envisioned by Elmer Keith in his 1955 book *Sixguns* is now reality more than 50 years later.

The author shooting one of his New Model Ruger .44 Magnums, first introduced 40 years ago.

land, except for a glow coming out of one corner of each. That glow was television.

Compared to today, most early TV programs were of exceptionally poor quality and transmission was spotty at best. However, television was not only about to totally change our society, it was also to have an affect on firearms manufacturing. Much of television broadcast time was taken up with wrestling matches and old western movies from the 1930s and 1940s. Those old westerns had both good guys and bad guys using Colt Single Actions, and suddenly a demand arose for what was no longer available. Bill Ruger stepped into the void.

Used Colt Single Actions in excellent shooting condition were selling for $90 or more, at the time. Colt's had no plans to bring its famed revolver back and would have had to charge $125 or more if they had. Bill Ruger decided the time was ripe for a quality single-action sixgun, and his answer to the demand was the Single-Six. Ruger didn't just copy the Colt. He downsized it slightly, replaced all the flat springs with virtually unbreakable coil springs, and chambered it in a cartridge everyone could afford to shoot, the .22 rimfire. To maintain the feel of the original Colt, Ruger's Single-Six had a grip frame identical to the Single Action Army. It was 1953, and a firearms manufacturing dynasty had begun.

When the Single-Six arrived, I was a freshman in high school. It would be three years before I would graduate, go to work, and be able to buy my own Single-Six. When I did, I was in sixgun heaven. I wish I could capture today some of the great feelings I had shooting my first single-action sixgun, along with the smell of gunpowder and Hoppe's No. 9.

The .22 Ruger single-action was not meant to take the place of the Colt, which had been available in such chamberings as .45 Colt, .44-40, .38-40, and even .357 Magnum before production ceased. The Ruger, instead, was designed for the average shooter, providing a totally dependable, relatively inexpensive sixgun for outdoor use. The original price was $63.25. When I purchased mine, in 1956, I was making 90 cents an hour, and .22 shells were about a penny apiece. Like thousands of other young men, I could afford to purchase and shoot the Ruger Single-Six.

Two years after the arrival of the Single-Six, Bill Ruger went big-bore with his first Blackhawk. Using the grip frame and relatively indestructible coil-spring action of the little .22, Ruger increased the size of the frame and cylinder to that of the Colt Single Action, then flat-topped the frame and added excellent adjustable sights, and the .357 Blackhawk was born. Now shooters had the choice of two excellent, modernized single-actions in either the economical .22 chambering or the most powerful chambering of the time, the .357 Magnum. I'd learned to shoot with the .22 Single-Six, and now I added the .357 Blackhawk. What more could any sixgunner need, or even want?

We were about to find out.

While Ruger was working on bringing out the magnificent .357 Blackhawk,

Above: Sixty years of Ruger .22 Single-Sixes, the original Flat-gate, Super Single-Six, and Hunter Model.

In 1959, the Ruger Super Blackhawk was as fine a single-action sixgun as could be found.

Smith & Wesson and Remington were working secretly on another project. In the closing days of December 1955, Smith & Wesson unveiled the .44 Remington Magnum. This big-bore sixgun and cartridge combination delivered a 240-grain bullet at the same muzzle velocity of the 158-grain bullet out of a .357 Magnum. It was nearly unbelievable power in a revolver, and its debut meant it was time for Ruger to go really big-bore.

Here is one of those stories that, if not true, should be. Actually, there are two versions as to how Bill Ruger found out about the .44 Magnum project. One version says someone went dumpster diving at Remington and found some cartridge cases. The other, which is more plausible, says a friend of Bill Ruger's working for Remington dropped a sack of cartridges on his desk. Whatever the case, Ruger was soon at work chambering the .357 Blackhawk to the new .44 Magnum.

This proved to be a mistake. The frame and cylinder were simply not large enough. When one of three prototypes blew, Ruger then had the frame and cylinder enlarged to come up with its first .44 Magnum Blackhawk. I purchased mine in 1957. I still have it, I still shoot it, and it remains one of my favorite all-time single-action sixguns. The original barrel length was 6½ inches, a length I have never particularly cared for, and the barrel was soon cut even with the ejector rod housing to match my .357 Blackhawk. Forty-five years ago I sent it back to Ruger to be re-barreled to 7½ inches.

The .22 Single-Six started as a 5½-inch, no-frills revolver, with a windage adjustable rear sight set in a dovetail, and a flat loading gate instead of the nice contour found on Colts and subsequently produced Rugers. Other barrel lengths—4⅝, 6½, and 9½ inches—were soon added, along with an extra cylinder for the .22 Winchester Magnum Rimfire. These were followed in the early 1960s with the Super Single-Six wearing fully adjustable sights. To this day, nearly all Ruger .22 Single-Sixes are dual-cylinder Convertible Models with fully adjustable sights.

The .357 Magnum Blackhawk was offered originally with a 4⅝-inch barrel, with the 6½- and rare 10-inch soon to follow. The .44 Magnum version started with the 6½-inch barrel length and was joined by two rare versions wearing 7½- and 10-inch barrels. All three of the original Ruger single-actions had alloy grip frames, which basically duplicated the size and shape of the original Colt Single Action, a grip well known for reducing felt recoil. However, when it came to the .44 Magnum and its recoil far and above anything previously known, Ruger started to get complaints about the punishing aspect of shooting the .44 Blackhawk. So, in 1959, the original .44 Flat-Top Blackhawk was "improved." To add weight, the barrel was lengthened to a standardized 7½ inches, the cylinder was left un-fluted, and, most importantly, the grip frame was totally changed. Not only did Ruger drop the lightweight alloy composition in favor of steel, he also totally changed the size and shape of the gun. Reaching all the way back to before the Civil War, Bill Ruger equipped his new Super Blackhawk with a square-backed trigger guard from that long ago era, as well as a longer grip frame as had been found on the early Colt Dragoons. Most shooters heartily welcomed the new, heavier .44 Magnum and this new grip frame. I found the original more to my liking.

What budding young sixgunner could resist the early advertising for the Single-Six?

The early Ruger single-actions, those from 1953 to 1972, are now known as "Old Models." Actually, there are two

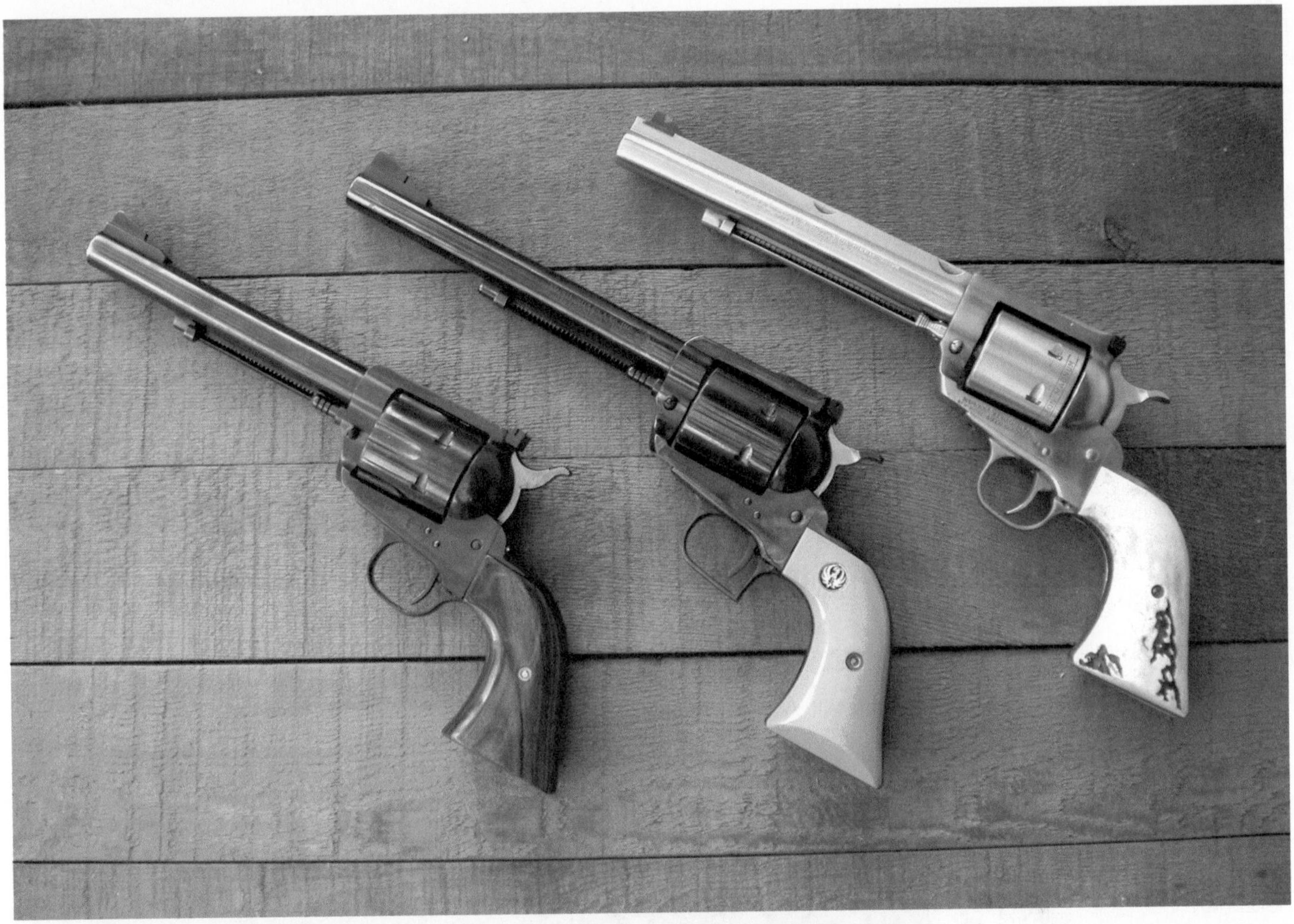

Above: Evolution of the Ruger .44 Magnum: Flat-Top Blackhawk, Super Blackhawk, and Hunter Model.

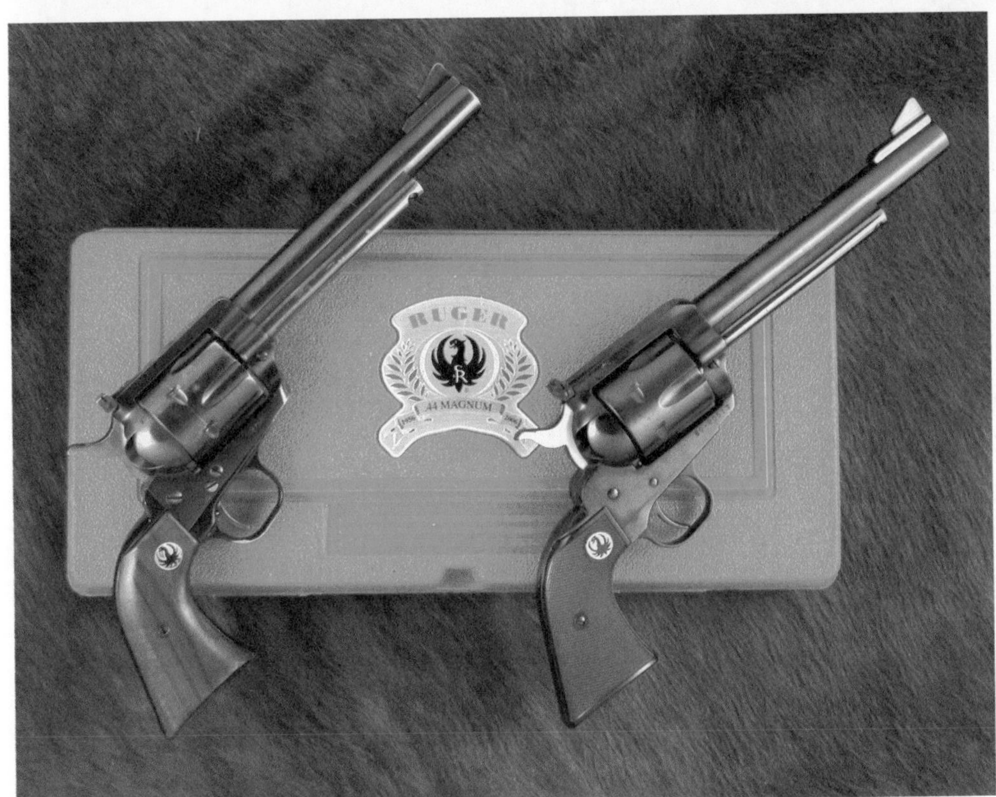

Fifty years separate this original .44 Magnum Blackhawk from the 50th Anniversary Model.

Ruger's original .44 Super Blackhawk and the 50th Anniversary Model. Leather is by the author.

groupings. The first Blackhawks from 1955 to 1962 are called Flat-Tops, as their frames were flat-topped and in distinction from the models produced from 1963 to 1972, which had protective ears on both sides of the rear sight (these first appeared on the 1959 Super Blackhawk). The second grouping of Blackhawks saw the addition of three new chamberings, namely the .41 Magnum, .45 Colt, and .30 Carbine. All three of these were built on the .44 Magnum-sized frame.

With the introduction of the .45 Colt Blackhawk, shooters had an exceptionally strong .45-caliber single-action and were soon shooting 300-grain bullets at 1,200 fps, something that simply wasn't possible with the old Colt Single Action. Ruger had turned the .45 Colt into a modern hunting handgun.

Every Ruger mentioned thus far had the same three screws on the side of the mainframe as found on the original Colts, although the screw heads were on different sides. This was about to change. In 1972, the New Model Rugers emerged. Gone were the three screws, which were replaced by two pins. The

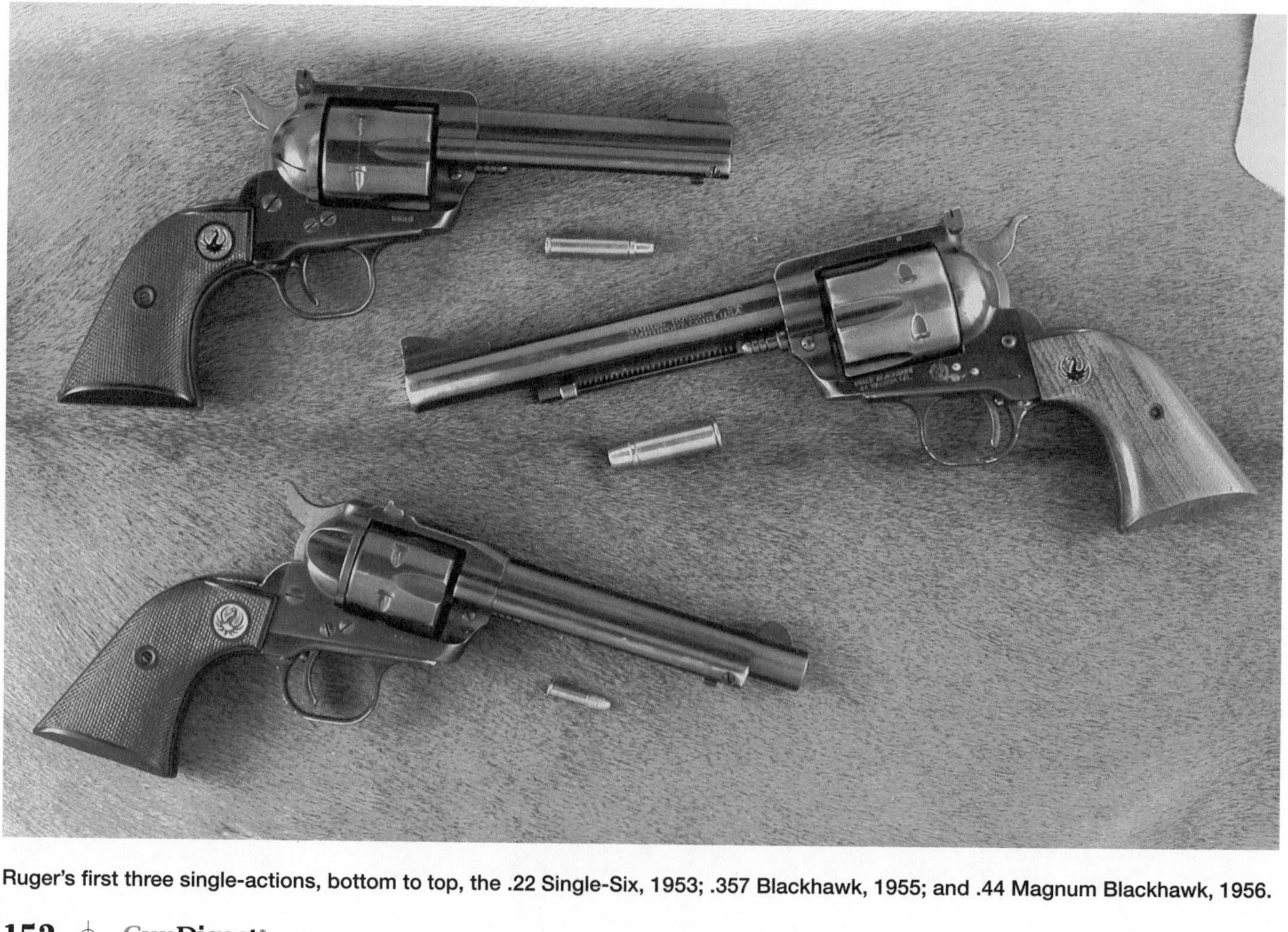

Ruger's first three single-actions, bottom to top, the .22 Single-Six, 1953; .357 Blackhawk, 1955; and .44 Magnum Blackhawk, 1956.

A pair of the author's custom .44 Special Rugers, with current production .44 Special Flat-Tops.

The latest .22 single-action revolver from Ruger is a 10-shot, stainless steel model known as the Single-Ten.

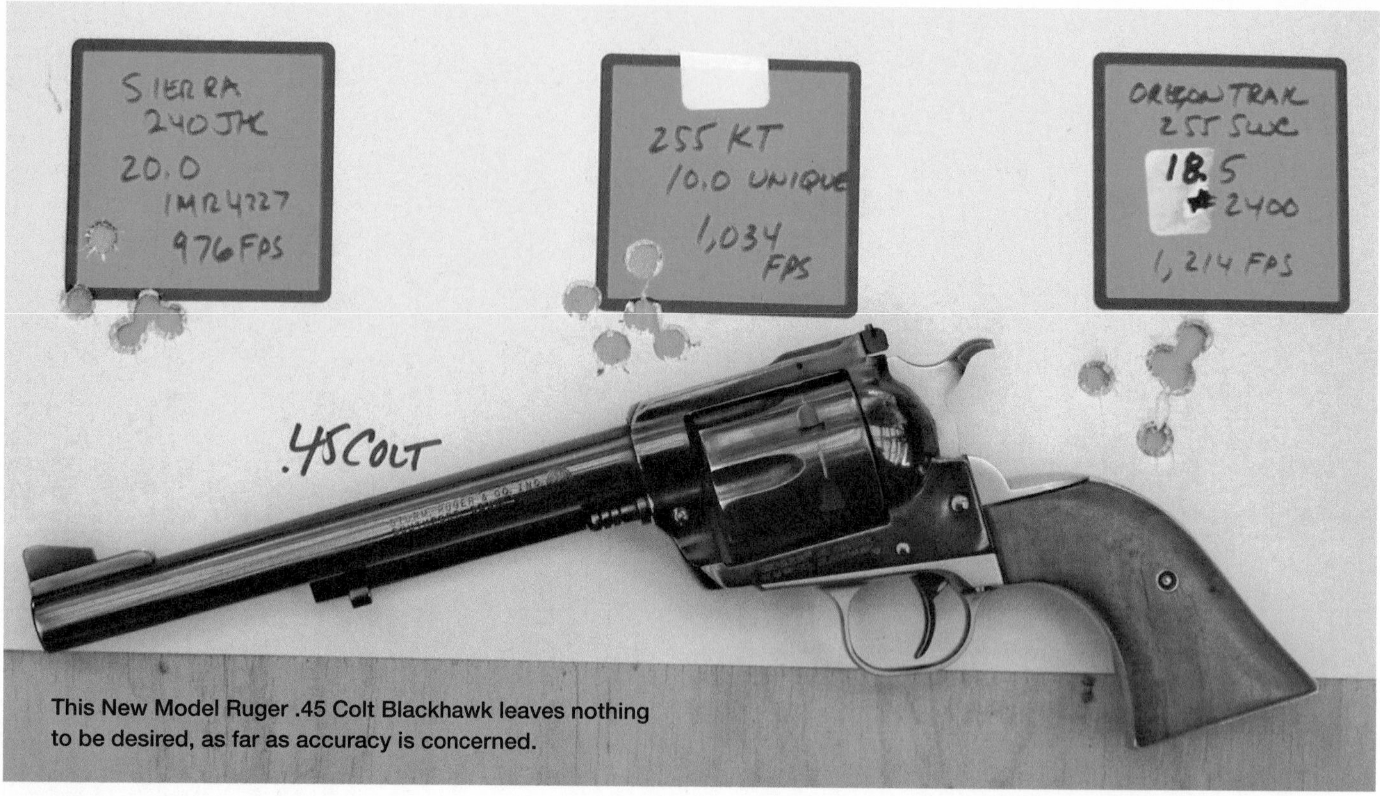

This New Model Ruger .45 Colt Blackhawk leaves nothing to be desired, as far as accuracy is concerned.

action was also changed to incorporate a transfer bar safety.

There was a very important reason for this change. From the original Colt Single Action Army of 1873 through the original Single-Six and the Blackhawks, all single-action revolvers were only safe when carried with the hammer down on an empty chamber. They all did have so-called safety notches on the hammer, but these could fail with a sharp blow and set off any cartridge under the hammer. Every knowledgeable, responsible sixgunner knew the drill when loading a single-action: open the loading gate, place the hammer on half-cock, load one, skip one, load four, close the gate, carefully cock the hammer, and let

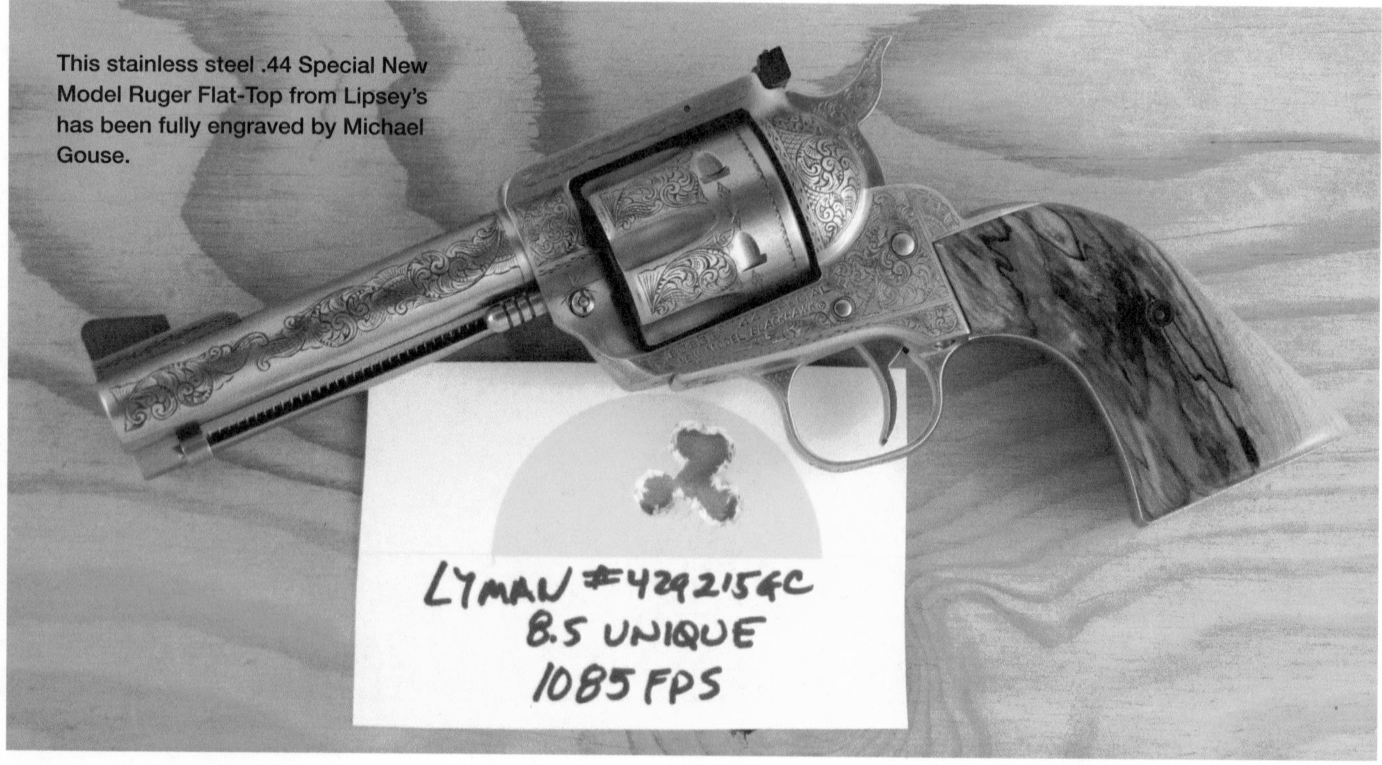

This stainless steel .44 Special New Model Ruger Flat-Top from Lipsey's has been fully engraved by Michael Gouse.

The Anniversary Model .44 Magnum Blackhawk is safe to carry fully loaded with six rounds. The original .44 Blackhawk is for five rounds only, and should be carried only with the hammer down on an empty chamber.

it down on an empty chamber. The traditional single-action was now safely carried or holstered. However, by the 1960s, a new generation of shooters had arrived without basic knowledge of handling a single-action sixgun, resulting in negligent discharges. Ruger's New Model action, incorporated in both the Blackhawk and Super Blackhawk models, came to the rescue, making it safe to carry a single-action sixgun fully loaded with six rounds.

Until the arrival of the New Model Rugers, centerfire Blackhawks used two frame sizes, namely one for the .357 Magnum, which was the same size as the Colt Single Action, and the larger .44 Magnum frame for all the other chamberings. But, with the New Model born, all Ruger centerfires now used the larger frame. This, of course, made the .357 Blackhawk exceptionally sturdy and heavy. Ruger also soon offered its New Models in stainless steel versions in .357 Magnum and .45 Colt, as well as the .44 Magnum Super Blackhawk. The .22 Single-Six was also changed over to the New Model action in 1972, though it maintained the same small frame size. It, too, is available in both blue and stainless steel models.

In the late 1920s, Elmer Keith put together what he called the "last word in a single-action sixgun." There is no doubt in my mind that Bill Ruger looked at pictures of Keith's No. 5 SAA before he came out with the .357 Blackhawk. Elmer's custom .44 Special used a flat-topped frame and fully adjustable sights. There was something else also found on Elmer's .44, namely a custom grip frame made by incorporating the back strap of the Bisley Model Colt with the trigger guard of a Single Action Army. In the 1980s, Bill Ruger took the next step and offered his version of Elmer Keith's single-action, which is simply known as the Bisley Model. Basically a Super Blackhawk, the Bisley Model Ruger has a wide, target-style Bisley hammer and trigger and a modified grip frame. Elmer had very small hands, something his grip frame attests to. So, Bill Ruger enlarged the frame to make it fit most sixgunners' hands. The Ruger Bisley Model grip frame aptly handles felt recoil, *very* heavy felt recoil, for most sixgunners better than anything ever offered. Originally, the Bisley Model Ruger was offered in .357 Magnum, .41 Magnum, .44 Magnum, and .45 Colt. Today, only the latter two chamberings are currently cataloged and only in blue with a 7½-inch barrel.

In the early days of long-range silhouetting, Ruger offered shooters

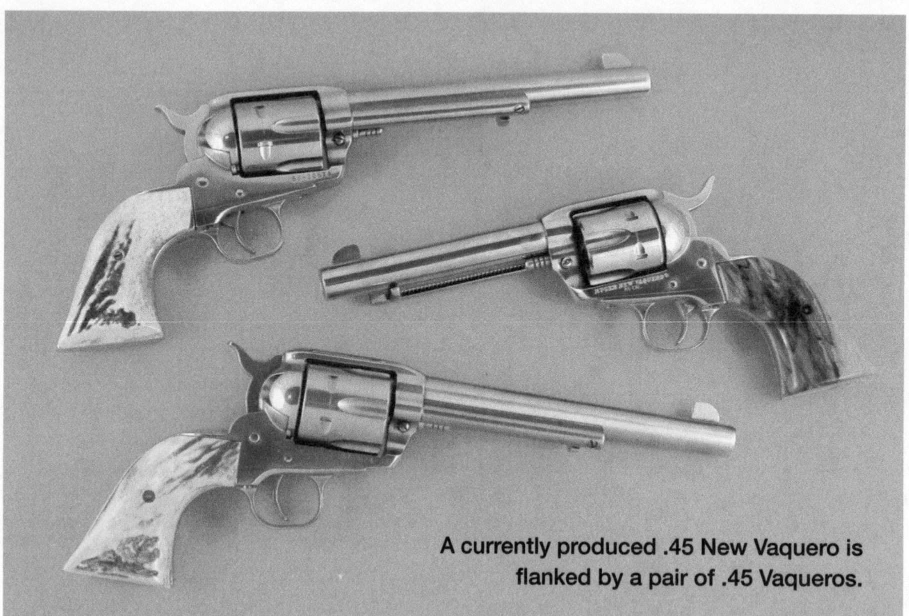
A currently produced .45 New Vaquero is flanked by a pair of .45 Vaqueros.

a 10½-inch .44 Magnum New Model Super Blackhawk. Both my wife and I competed with the long-barreled Ruger, but since we saw the sights differently and held the guns differently, we each needed our own sixgun. Ruger soon offered a 10½-inch stainless steel version, and this became one of my favorite hunting handguns. However, Ruger didn't stop there, next bringing forth the Hunter Models, one of the greatest bargains ever offered to handgun hunters. The Hunter Model is basically a stainless steel Super Blackhawk with a heavy barrel, as well as a longer ejector rod for positive removal of fired cartridges. Most importantly, the barrel is scalloped to accept Ruger scope rings for the easy mounting of a long eye relief optic. There are still many who maintain scopes do not belong on sixguns, but, as eyes become older, and when precision shooting for hunting is necessary, a scope is invaluable.

Ruger's Hunter Model Super Blackhawk does not have the square-back trigger guard, this feature instead being rounded off. Currently, Ruger also offers the Bisley Model Hunter with all the accoutrements found on the Bisley Model, as well as the heavy barrel and scope mounting capability. For the smallbore shooter, Ruger even offers a .22 Hunter Model, with the same easy scope mounting qualities.

More than 20 years ago, I sat in Bill Ruger's office, as he showed me a new revolver the company was about to offer. From 1955 forward, all centerfire Rugers had adjustable sights. But the sport of Cowboy Action Shooting had recently become very popular, and Bill Ruger wanted to offer a traditionally styled single-action for those competitors. The result was a giant step *backwards*, one that resulted in a rounding off of the top of the frame, removal of the adjustable rear sight, and the cutting of a traditional "hog wallow trough" sight through the top of the frame, in total, a traditionally styled Vaquero. These were immediately and extremely popular with Cowboy Action Shooters, and more than 750,000 were produced.

Around the middle of the first decade of our newest century, Ruger dropped the Vaquero and replaced it with the New Vaquero. The original Vaqueros were built on the .44 Magnum frame, but some shooters wanted a smaller, easier to handle sixgun. The New Vaquero arrived with the same frame size as the Colt Single Action Army. I like the Vaquero—and I like the New Vaquero even more. It fits any of my holsters that were made for the Colt Single Action, handles much more easily, for me at least, and it has the grip frame that's the same size and shape as the original .357 Blackhawk. The New Vaquero is available in both blued and stainless steel finishes and chambered in .45 Colt or .357 Magnum.

The years 2005, 2006, and 2009 marked the fiftieth anniversary of the .357 Blackhawk, .44 Blackhawk, and .44 Super Blackhawk, respectively. In each one of these years, Ruger brought out anniversary models that closely followed the originals (except for the New Model action). Both the original Blackhawks have flat-topped frames without protective ears around the rear sight, and the original Colt Single Action size and shape of the grip frame has been maintained. In addition to this, the .357 Blackhawk Anniversary Model is the same size as the original of 1955. When it was introduced, I talked to the then-president of Ruger about bringing out a version in .44 Special, such as we had expected 50 years earlier. He didn't say yes ... but he also didn't say no. However, thanks to Lipsey's, one of our premier firearms distributors, the 50th Anniversary Model .357 Magnum Blackhawk was used as the basic platform for a .44 Special Flat-Top. Lipsey's offered these with both 4⅝ and 5½-inch barrels in blued versions, and the next year Ruger put them in the standard catalog.

Lipsey's didn't stop there. Today, the firm still offers the two the original .44 Special versions, as well as stainless steel counterparts, a Bisley Model, and a New Vaquero, all in .44 Special. These are some of the finest single-actions ever offered by Ruger. Just recently, Lipsey's expanded its offerings to include both blue and stainless steel .45 Flat-Tops complete with an auxiliary .45 ACP cylinder. These are exceptionally good shooting sixguns, and it is my hope they eventually become standard offerings from Ruger.

The original single-action from Ruger 60 years ago was the .22 Single-Six. It is appropriate the latest single-action offering from Ruger is the Single-Ten. This latest "Single-Six," as the name suggests, is actually a 10-shooter, that is, the cylinder is chambered for 10 rounds. It is offered in stainless steel only, with a 5½-inch barrel, fiber optic sights, and in .22 Long Rifle only. The sights take some getting used to, at least for me, but this could very well be the ultimate outdoorsman's .22-caliber sixgun.

Bill Ruger saw the future, with the introduction of his .22 single-action six decades ago. I have no idea how many millions of Ruger single-actions have been produced and are still in service. I do know, thanks mainly to Bill Ruger, that the single-action was resurrected and is alive and well today. With all our modern polymer pistols and double-action revolvers of every size, shape, and chambering, the single-action is still a most viable choice, especially so for the handgun hunter and outdoorsman. Thank you, Bill Ruger.

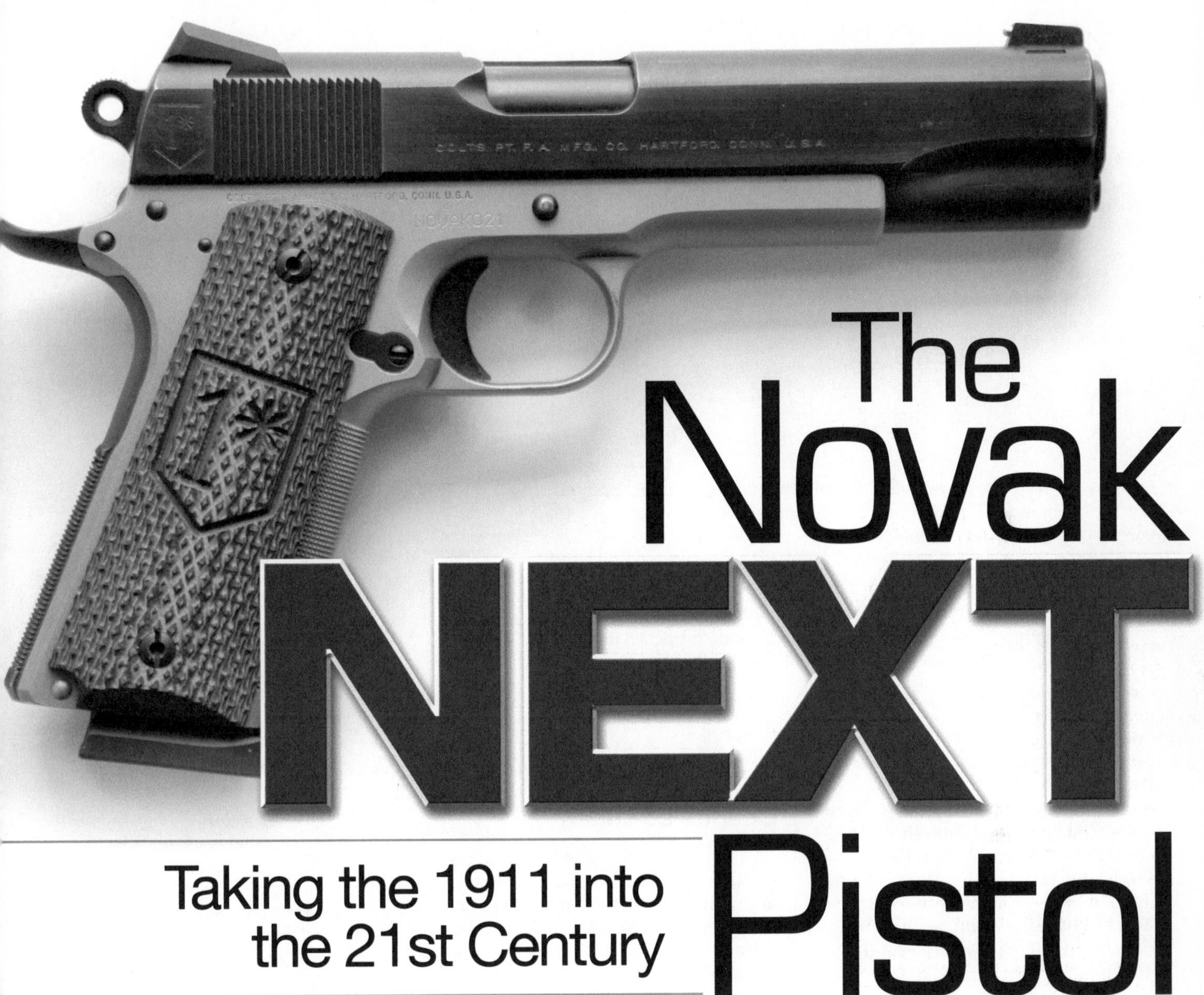

The Novak NEXT Pistol

Taking the 1911 into the 21st Century

BY GARY PAUL JOHNSTON

A little more than a century ago, John Moses Browning created what most firearms historians believe to be the perfect pistol, the gun that came to be adopted as the caliber .45 ACP Model of 1911. That statement about "perfection" was arguably as true 50 years or more after Browning's masterpiece was debuted, but things were bound to change if ever so subtly.

Actually, there were earlier changes. Following a few very minor changes during the first year of production, the Model of 1911 was produced not only by Colt's, during World War I, but also Springfield Arsenal and Remington-UMC. After The Great War, there were a number of improvements made to the Colt Model of 1911, enough that it was redesignated the Model of 1911A1. These changes included better sights, a shorter trigger, relief cuts on the frame behind the trigger, an arched mainspring housing, a shorter, narrower hammer spur, a Parkerized finish, and plastic grips.

During WWII, the pistol was made by Colt's, Remington Rand, Ithaca, Union Switch and Signal, and Singer Mfg. Co., and went on to serve uninterrupted with all branches of the U.S. military for 74 years, until 1985, when, for political reasons, it was replaced. Well, mostly replaced, except for the Marine Corps MAR-SOC element, which retained the 1911A1, upgrading it with various improvements desired for special operations.

It was no surprise that the Model of 1911, like virtually all other firearms adopted by the U.S. military, enjoyed equal if not greater reception by the civilian sector. Called the "Government Model" by Colt's, this version was more refined in fit and finish than its military counterpart, and it also became popular with law enforcement agencies such as

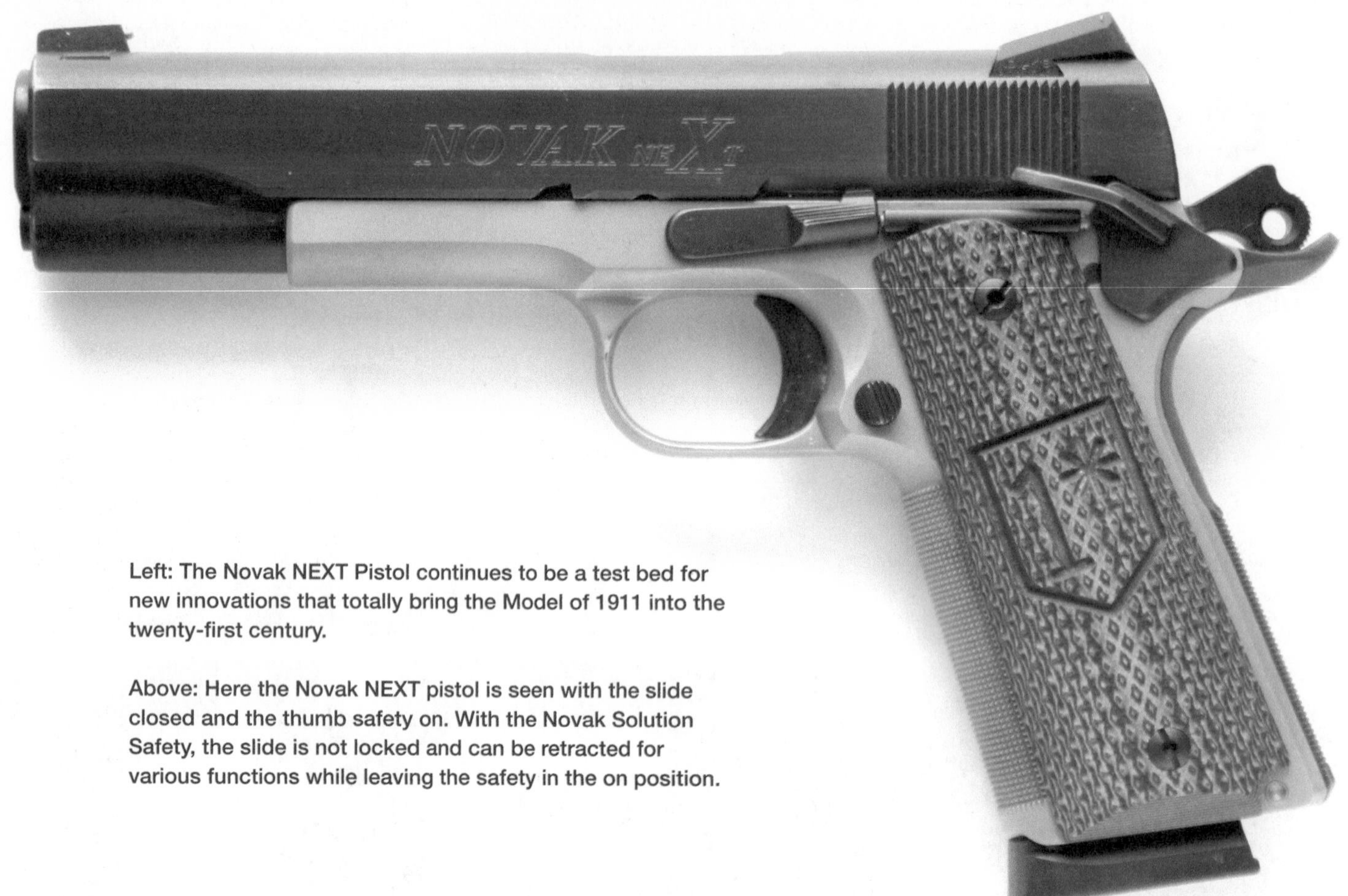

Left: The Novak NEXT Pistol continues to be a test bed for new innovations that totally bring the Model of 1911 into the twenty-first century.

Above: Here the Novak NEXT pistol is seen with the slide closed and the thumb safety on. With the Novak Solution Safety, the slide is not locked and can be retracted for various functions while leaving the safety in the on position.

the FBI, where it was adopted in the .38 Super caliber. In the standard .45 ACP caliber, the Government Model was offered in a Match competition version and that enjoyed modifications such as target sights, grips, and much more.

During the mid-twentieth century, a good number of custom pistolsmiths specialized in customizing the Model of 1911 and Government Model pistols. One of the best known was Armand Swenson, of Gardena, California. In the 1970s, when Swenson's reputation grew to national recognition, he hired a young apprentice who had recently graduated as a gunsmith from the Colorado School of Trades. His name was Wayne Novak.

Working for Swenson, Wayne learned quickly, and Armand taught him many of his own customizing techniques, secrets that remain closely guarded this day. Not one to accept what was the norm, Novak began developing techniques and ideas of his own and, in 1981, designed a rear sight for the Model 1911 pistol that Armand adopted and marketed as the Swensight.

Charles C. Kelsey

In 1982, Wayne Novak decided to start his own gunsmithing business and, at the urging of friends, relocated to Parkersburg, West Virginia, where he opened the Novak .45 Shop, specializing in custom Model 1911 and Browning Hi-Power pistols. Novak also became acquainted with other gunsmiths, one of whom was the late Charles C. Kelsey, the founder of Devel Corporation, located a few hours north, in Cleveland, Ohio.

I was a police officer in a suburb of Cleveland, at the time and was a good friend of Kelsey's. My wife, Nancy, worked for Devel for some time. Having been a 1911 enthusiast since my first one at the age of 14, I spent much time at the Devel shop, following the progress there that was nothing short of groundbreaking. A number of the improvements in the Model of 1911 and Browning Hi-Power pistols we take for granted today were first seen on pistols from Devel. These include the conical bushing-less barrel, beavertail grip safety, the Hi-Power firing pin safety, and many that were eventually showcased in a book on Charles Kelsey and his achievements.

In 1982, I also sought to remedy what I had considered, for many years, to be a problem with the Model of 1911. The issue I had was having to take the pistol's thumb safety off "safe" in order to retract the slide and perform administrative functions. Admittedly, many other pistols, including what I consider Browning's other timeless pistol, the Hi-Power, also have this feature, but I always considered it obsolete and a detriment to safety. Thus, I painstakingly modified one of my 1911s to allow the slide to be retracted for loading and unloading while the thumb safe remained on.

When I showed my invention to Charles Kelsey, it was love at first sight, but he said he could never afford to spend the time it took with Swiss files to complete it. Still, he borrowed my converted 1911 to study. A few days later, Kelsey called and asked me to stop by his shop. There he showed me his improved method of converting the pistol so the slide could be operated with the safety on. In the couple of years that followed, Devel converted and sold about 25 custom 1911 pistols with this feature.

In the meantime, Novak's reputation was growing as one of America's great pistolsmiths, a reputation that was highlighted with the invention of his renowned Novak LoMount Sight. Now standard with several of the largest firearms companies in America, Novak Sights are offered for a great number of pistols and, more recently, revolvers.

Although Wayne Novak and I knew many of the same people and I followed his progress closely, I did not meet him until 1985, when I was writing an article about a pistol and wanted to feature his sight. Devel had closed its doors by then, and Wayne had assembled quite a collection of Devel custom Smith & Wesson, 1911, and Hi-Power pistols. I mentioned to him the thumb safety conversion I had done, and that Charles Kelsey had refined and produced a number of custom 1911 pistols with the modification. Novak told me that none of the Devel custom 1911 pistols in his large collection had it. But it turned out the modification is so subtle that Wayne never noticed that three of his Devel 1911s actually *did* have it.

The Novak Ghost Sight

As time went by, Novak continued to develop and implement new improvements to his custom pistols, one of which was a sight I designed for law enforcement. Consisting of the bottom half of a ghost ring, this sight is used in exactly the manner as a standard sight, but with a huge half-round notch instead of a tight square one. In designing the sight, my premise was that, 99 percent of the time, law enforcement officers draw their pistols and give orders, but almost never have to fire their weapons. The wide rounded notch allowed me to focus on the front sight and still see more of what a suspect was doing. Most importantly, though, was that this rear sight would help prevent losing sight of the front sight when much movement was taking place, along with recoil from multiple shots. After having the Ghost Sight tested by a law enforcement agency and gaining more than 90-percent approval, Novak put the first production Ghost Sight on a 1911 for me in 1994. I still have it, along with several more on 1911 and Hi Power pistols.

The Novak "Answer"

Long a sore point with Novak and many others (this author included) was the so-called "grip safety" John Browning had first been forced to include on the Model 1905/Pattern 1907 .45 ACP pistol tested by the U.S. Cavalry, and later the Model of 1911. Without a doubt the most useless feature of the 1911 (in my opinion), is the grip safety. It is not a true safety, but one that rather only blocks the trigger from moving if the pistol is not in the hand. Even the U.S. Marine Corps referred to this part only as a safety "device."

One of the key improvements to the Model of 1911 is the Novak Answer, a high-precision, one-piece backstrap.

Even if the hammer is cocked with the thumb safety in the off position, the sear locks the hammer with a half-cock notch serving as backup, and the trigger is completely out of the picture. Thus, the grip safety serves no useful purpose—but it does get in the way.

With virtually all training academies teaching the high thumb hold, with the right thumb on top of the thumb safety, the hand is therefore cocked upward. This prevents some hands from adequately depressing the grip safety and firing the pistol, especially when the gun is drawn quickly under stress. If the pistol can't be fired during a gunfight, the grip safety is rendered unsafe for the user and safe for the assailant. To further illustrate how needless a grip safety is, simply count the number of modern self-loading pistols that use it.

Wayne Novak's solution to the grip safety was what he simply calls, the "Answer." Designed to mate perfectly into the rear of the frame of any Mil-Spec Model 1911 with professional fitting, the Novak Answer Backstrap comes with a gracefully and ergonomically designed integral beavertail tang and can be had with either a flat or arched mainspring housing machine-checkered at 25 lines per inch. It is available in lightweight aircraft alloy or steel. You may see it become standard with a special new 1911 type pistol by late 2012. In the meantime, it is available on custom Model 1911 pistols from Novak. In my opinion, it truly takes the Model 1911 pistol into the twenty-first century.

The Novak "Solution" Thumb Safety

In 1985, when Novak realized that he had three pistols with Kelsey's take on my thumb safety modification in his collection of Devel 1911s, he called me to report this and described one of them as Charles Kelsey's personal and highly modified pistol. I knew that gun well, having watched Kelsey build it years before. Being interested in the ability to manipulate the slide with the thumb safety on, Novak designed an improved version of Kelsey's design, calling it the "Solution." He has furnished it as an option for several years, now.

In 2003, Novak took on a part-time apprentice named Charles Pulit. A U.S. Army veteran, Pulit was a true gun guy, who had a good job with a chemical company but wanted to be in the firearms industry. Working part time, Pulit quickly learned gunsmithing and began designing innovations of his own. Soon, he went to work for Novak full time. In 2008, Pulit designed and patented a three-position variation of the Novak Solution Thumb Safety. As this is written, the new safety is being evaluated by a major manufacturer but is not available. However, you may see some form of it hit the market in the near future. In the meantime, the original Solution Thumb Safety is an option from Novak.

The features of the Novak Ghost Sight are seen here. The author designed it especially with law enforcement officers in mind.

The Novak NEXT Pistol

The above new and unique features have been incorporated into a family of Series 70 Government Model .45 ACP pistols and others, with one group made especially for Novak by Colt's with serial

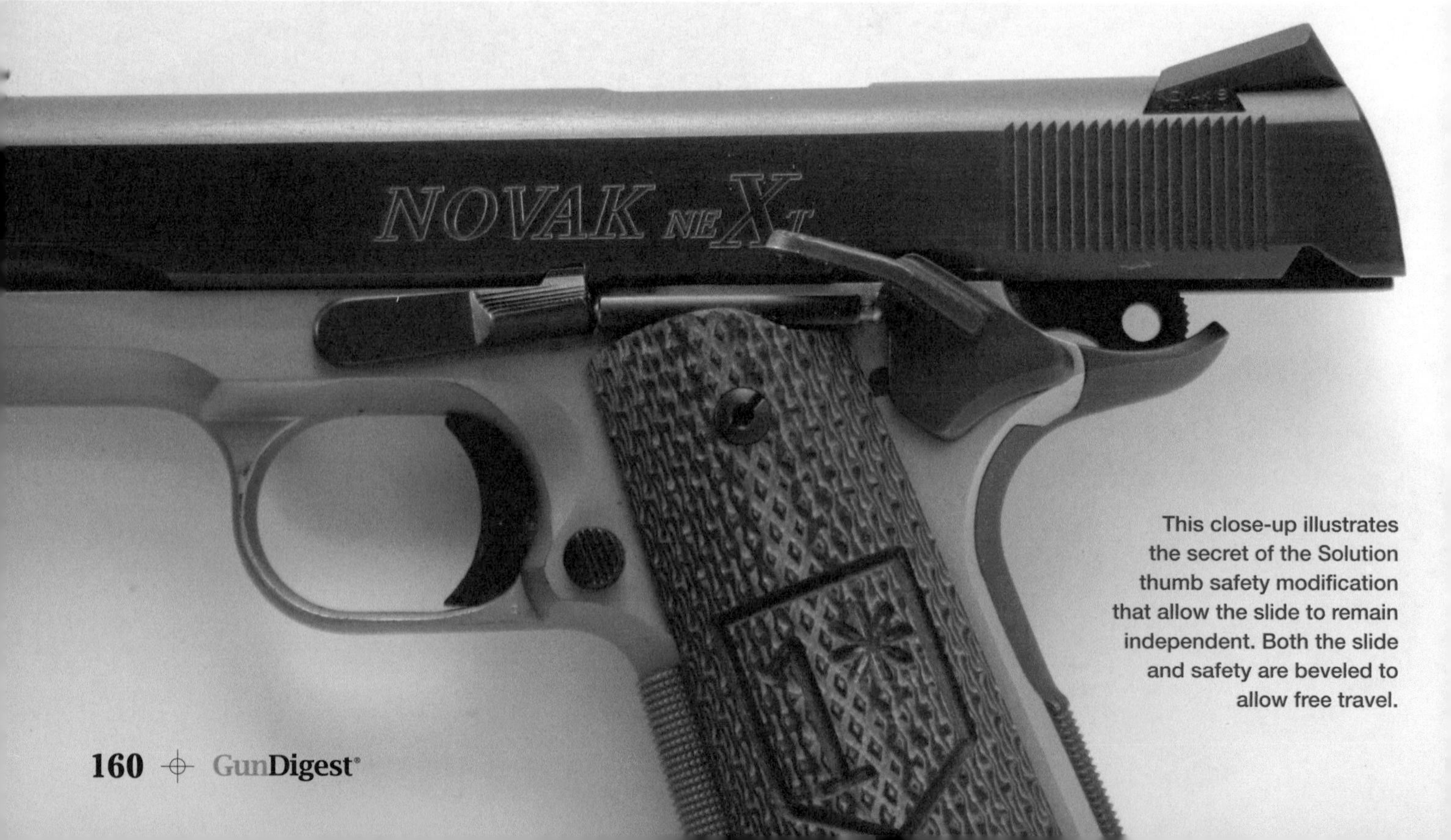

This close-up illustrates the secret of the Solution thumb safety modification that allow the slide to remain independent. Both the slide and safety are beveled to allow free travel.

One of Johnston's favorite Novak NEXT pistols is this Series 70 Colt, the serial number of which is 911. The custom grips are by Rio Grande Grips of Denver, Colorado.

numbers from NOVAK 001 to NOVAK 100. The even-numbered pistols are in blue steel, the stainless bear odd numbers. Negating any questionable need for a firing pin block, the NEXT Pistols are equipped with a weapon-grade titanium firing pin and a Wolff extra-power firing pin spring.

Coming standard with a Kart Match Grade barrel, speed hammer, and sear, the Novak Answer, and a host of other full-house custom features, the NEXT Pistol amounts to an evolutionary pistol in progress. The gun can be had with many options, such as trigger type, undercut trigger guard, checkering, grips, and sights. As this is written, sight choices consist of the Novak LoMount sight with standard square notch and choice of plain, white dots, tritium dots, 18 karat gold bead, or fiber optic front, as well as the Novak Ghost Sight. But, as this reaches you, that's not all. Designed by Charles Pulit is the new Novak NEXT Adjustable Sight. Shown to a select few at the 2012 SHOT Show, at first glance this sight looks exactly like the Novak LoMount fixed sight, yet it is uniquely adjustable for both windage and elevation. What's more, it is extremely robust and totally protected. The new sight fits in the standard Novak slide cut and will likely be available on 1911 pistols from several firearms manufactures, as well as from Novak. While it is too soon to detail, Novak is also working with a totally new night sight technology.

And there's more. Although it as yet has no official name, a revolutionary new magazine improvement was designed by Charles Pulit, in 2009. So unique is this invention that Novak locked it in a safe, showing it to no one while it was being patented. No details of this development will be provided here, but I can tell you that it solves a problem that has plagued most box magazines for more than a century, and a problem Charles Kelsey went to great lengths and expense trying to solve. Look for it soon.

With all of its groundbreaking features and improvements, while the Novak NEXT Pistol is beautiful, it has little or no pin striping, no lizard scales or scallops, but real machine checkering. Investment quality? You bet, but first and foremost it is what the Model of 1911 was always meant to be, a fighting pistol. For more information, visit Novak's at www.novaksights.com.

This Leupold magnetic boresight is a great way to get your bullets initially on paper and for verifying that your sight settings haven't changed.

Below: Boresights take various forms. This Simmons tool comes with a built-in screen for easy viewing and comes with arbors to fit most firearm bores.

One of the problems we all face in life is trying to ferret out truth from fiction. We've all heard, at one time or another, that drinking coffee could be injurious to our health, but, as is often the case, that claim was followed up with a study purporting coffee as being good for our health. For decades, we've been told that occasionally partaking of an adult beverage would likely kill our livers and turn us all into alcoholics, but now we know (or at least we *might* know) that an occasional indulgence could be beneficial to most individuals. Such bogus and confusing pretenses aren't limited to our health issues. We seem to have an equal amount of confusion within the shooting community. Following are a scant 10 of those misleading claims and my attempt to separate fact from fiction.

Damaged Bullet Points Hinder Accuracy

Down through the years, many gun writers have warned shooters that flattened and damaged bullet points can severely affect shooting accuracy. The issue is one primarily a product of cartridges having been stored inside the magazine of a heavy-recoiling rifle. In such a case, when the rifle is fired, the cartridges sometimes are forced forward, causing the bullet points to impact the front of the magazine, thereby resulting in the flattening of the soft lead points. Over the years, it seems that many shooters have accepted the pretense that such imperfections can cause a bullet to go astray in flight. Until a few years back, I had no way of either validating or discrediting those claims, so, I decided to find out for myself how large a problem this really was.

I began by severely damaging the bullet points of a diverse variety of cartridges.

Those cartridges were then shot along with an equal number of pristine, undamaged cartridges at 100 yards. Test rifles were sandbagged front and back to ensure the maximum degree of steadiness. Without getting into a great deal of detail, I will only say that, at 100 yards, the amount of accuracy deterioration was so slight that I don't believe any shooter under normal field conditions would notice the slightest degree of difference between the damaged and undamaged bullets.

Of course, whenever the aerodynamic lines are disrupted, a decrease in the bullet's ballistic coefficient would result, and *that* would translate into slightly poorer trajectories and a reduction in the bullet's ability to resist the effects of the wind. But, in most cases, and with the exception of shooting at extremely long range, I feel the consequences would be minimal. What I believe to be a larger potential problem is the fact that the same heavy recoil could result in driving the bullets deeper into their cases. If this should occur, it could result in elevating chamber pressures. The best way to prevent this from occurring would be to tightly crimp the case mouths around the bullets.

My Bullet Hit a Twig!

I've often heard hunters attempt to justify a missed shot because the bullet clipped a small limb or twig on its way to the target. Even the legendary Jack O'Connor occasionally used this as an excuse for a failed shot. It's certainly logical that a bullet encountering an obstacle could be disrupted, but I was at a loss to as to how serious a problem this could be.

In an effort to find out, I constructed a type of wooden manifold, wherein I inserted a series of hardwood dowels to simulate limbs. The dowels were

In order to determine what effect damaged bullet points would have on shooting accuracy, the author purposely battered the soft lead tips, possibly deforming them more than would occur naturally inside a magazine under heavy recoil.

positioned close enough together to ensure that a bullet traveling to a paper target on the other side would be sure to contact at least one. Three calibers were selected for testing, the .300 Win. Mag., .30-30 Winchester, and .22-250 Remington. Because of the current variety of .308-caliber bullets, three different bullet weights and styles were shot in the .300, with one style for each of the .30-30 and .22-250. I began with doweling measuring 3⁄16-inch and placed the obstruction 10 feet in front of the target. In my first rounds of testing, and in all calibers, the amount of deflection was nearly indistinguishable. So, next, I increased the dowels to ¼-inch and moved the obstruction 30 feet from the target. This increased group sizes, but still not substantially. Of course, as the size of the object struck increases or the distance between the obstruction and the target is increased, you should expect a

If you are recoil-sensitive, it is always a temptation to let someone else sight-in your rifle, but it is much better if you do it yourself.

Some shooters mistakenly believe that the firearms marketed as stainless are impervious to rusting. This assumption is wrong. What the factories call stainless is not true stainless steel, and, like a blued firearm, they will rust if not properly cared for.

greater degree of deviation. The important thing here is that shooting through grasses and fairly light vegetation should not be problematic for a hunter, as long as the game is a reasonable distance behind the interfering obstacle.

Round-Nose Bullets Penetrate Deeper and are Better in Brush

My previously mentioned bullet deflection tests included both pointed and blunt-nosed bullets. After seeing no noticeable difference in the amount of deflection between the two, I decided to take the tests one step further and see if blunt-nosed projectiles had either or both a tendency to penetrate deeper or retain a higher level of retained weight when shot into a bank of old magazines.

You have to be a bit careful, when drawing a conclusion like this, because both these traits are closely related to the quality and construction of the bullets. Nevertheless, as long as the bullets were

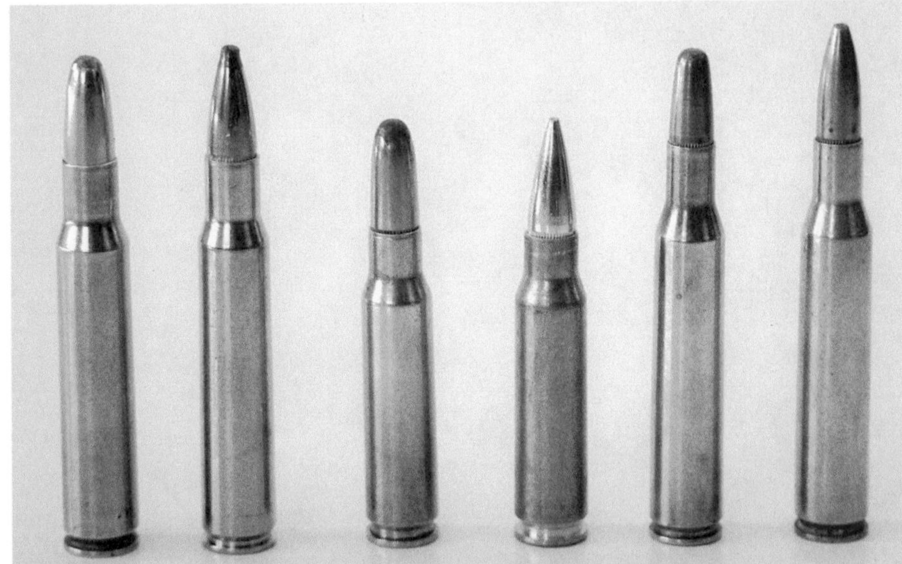

It is believed by many shooters that blunt-nosed bullets are the better choice when hunting in dense brush, but the author found no substantial difference between the performance of those bullets and pointed styles, the latter of which typically possess considerably higher ballistic coefficient values.

of the same high-quality construction, I saw nothing in these tests to indicate that a round- or flat-nosed bullet would perform any better. Pointed bullets routinely carry a higher ballistic coefficient and, for that reason, will buck the wind better and shoot flatter at long range. That makes it an easy choice in my own mind, regarding which bullet style to shoot. As long as you aren't shooting a rifle with a tubular magazine that requires the use of blunt-nosed bullets for safety reasons, my choice will always be pointed projectiles.

Stainless Guns Require Less Maintenance

The trend in firearms clearly seems to be away from the classic blued ones and in favor of those being marketed as stainless. But, a big misconception comes into play, when a person thinks these *stainless in appearance* firearms are impervious to rust. In reality, they are every bit as susceptible to rusting as a blued gun—it may take a little longer for the rust to take hold, but rust they will, if proper precautions aren't taken. The reason this happens is based on the fact that, while the gun metal may *look* like stainless steel, it really isn't stainless at all. Because of this, it is advisable to take the same precautions to prevent rust on both blue and these so-called "stainless" guns. The best protection comes from thorough cleanings and frequently wiping down the metal surfaces with an oil-soaked rag.

To simulate a bullet clipping a limb or brush, the author developed a manifold, which held ¼-inch hardwood dowels. This obstruction was placed in the direct line of fire, where the bullets would have to make contact prior impacting the target.

Bore-Sighting is a Good Way to Get Your Rifle Zeroed

Bore-sighting a firearm should *never* be considered an alternative to actual live-fire zeroing on the range. Just because the center axis of the barrel may be perfectly aligned to the crosshairs of your scope does not necessarily mean that your bullet will follow that same line of flight. In fact, it rarely does. Bore-sighting should be used only as an intermediary step, after which actual live-fire shooting should follow to fine-tune the adjustments. But the usefulness of a boresight is not limited to only getting your initial shots on paper. Once you have completed the sighting-in process, you should take another reading, followed by recording that relationship on paper. That way, if your gun gets bumped hard or dropped, you have an easy way to confirm that no ill effects have occurred.

I Always Let Someone Else Sight-In My Rifle

Some shooters who have a tendency to be recoil-sensitive may be inclined to let someone else sight in their rifle for them. This should, however, never occur. There are several advantages to sighting-in your own rifle. First, it gets the shooter used to the recoil of the rifle, and, second, it familiarizes them with the gun. But aside from those very valuable advantages, it is important to recognize that differences in how people actually see things can effect where the bullets will impact on a target. Different shooters shooting the same rifle and ammunition will quite often have their bullets impact at a different point on a target.

A Clean Firearm is a Better Firearm

How could anyone make an argument against firearm cleanliness? Well, I can think of only a single instance when a little dirt might be a good thing, and that is inside your gun barrel when it comes to heading out for a hunt. One of the factors necessary for consistent shot placement has to do with the consistency of the firearm bore. Simply put, a round fired through a clean bore will almost always impact at a different point that those shots that follow—and that first shot is often the most important you will take in a hunting situation. I have frequently found the amount of variation can be from about an inch all the way up to three or four inches at 100 yards. If you never shoot past 50 yards, this might not be an issue of concern, but, if you find yourself trying to pull off a shot at a record-book bighorn ram on that once in a lifetime hunt at 400 or 500 yards, it could easily become a substantial problem to overcome. I like to remove

It's always good to clean your gun and keep it in top-notch shape. For shooting consistency, though, it's best to foul the bore by sending a shot down the barrel prior to heading out on a hunt. Why? Typically the first shot from a clean bore will impact in a different spot than the follow-up shots. This was the case in the photo below, with the clean bore round printing high and to the left.

all the variables I can and, in so doing, I always send a round down the barrel and foul the bore before heading out to hunt.

I Always Carry my Rifle Muzzle Down in the Vehicle

When traveling, it has become a common practice for many shooters to position their rifle with the muzzle down against the floorboards. I suppose most believe that placing their rifle in this position provides a degree of safety, but there is a problem in doing so.

The condition of the barrel crown is crucial to good accuracy. Floorboards, particularly in hunting rigs, are frequently dirty, and this dirt can easily result in a marring of the crown. A better way to carry a rifle in a vehicle is in a carrying case, but, sometimes a hunter likes to have their rifle more accessible (for obvious reason). If you fall into this category, and as long as the rifle is unloaded with the action open and the muzzle is pointed in a safe direction and away from people, carrying it upright, muzzle towards the truck roof, simply makes good sense and can go a long way towards preventing damage to your rifle that can affect its accuracy.

My Rifle Shoots Better at Long Range

I have occasionally heard shooters purport that their rifle shoots more accurately at long range than at close range. This is simply untrue and cannot be.

One of the major factors in accuracy has to do with the yawing of the bullet. Yawing is when the back of the bullet begins to wobble in flight. This eventually results in the entire bullet moving about in a circular manner, as it makes its way to the target. The theory is that the yawing eventually begins to settles down, resulting in a lessening of the size of the bullet's circular movement. Nevertheless, whether the yawing is lessened in flight or not, when the bullet initially starts to oscillate, its

Below: Some shooters are under the mistaken impression that their rifles shoot better at long range than they do at closer range. This simply is not, *can* not be true.

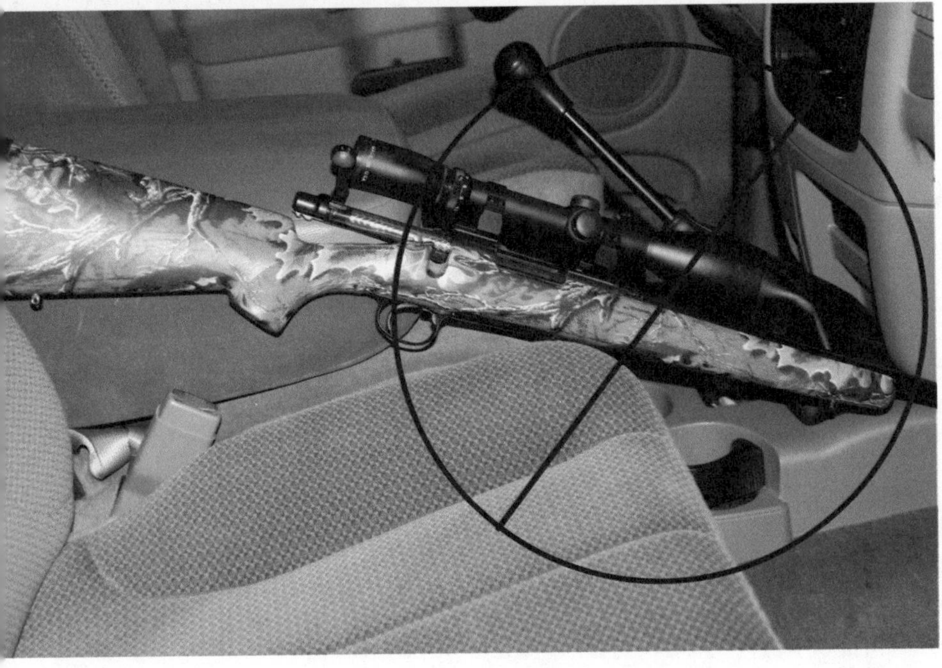

Some shooters prefer to transport their rifles with the muzzle down against the floor of the vehicle. Doing so, however, could easily damage the crown of the barrel and adversely affecting your shooting accuracy. A much better way is to keep the firearm pointed in a safe upward position, with the butt against the floor. Of course, the gunt should always be unloaded and the action in the open position.

destiny is then cast. Having begun these movements, it is impossible for the bullet to lessen the size of its rotation and get itself back on a straight-line track. In reality, if your rifle is capable of shooting, say, a two-inch group at 100 yards, it won't be capable of one-inch at 300 yards—in fact, under the best conditions, that same rifle will most likely shoot a *six-inch* group at that range.

You Can't Beat Factory Ammo with Handloads

Without a doubt, factory loaded ammunition has never been better than it is today. A shooter has more choices in bullets styles and weights than were ever available in the past. But mass production can never equal attention to detail—and that is why factory loaded ammunition virtually always falls short in the area of accuracy and performance, when compared to handloads.

For years, it puzzled me why that was the case. The factory frequently loads the same bullets that handloaders use, using the same primers and cartridge cases, and, while the factory seldom divulges what types of powders they're loading, I feel their choices are of equal quality to what handloaders use. I eventually decided to investigate the situation a little closer and began pulling the bullets from a wide variety of factory-loaded cartridges to check the weight of the powder charges.

I took five cartridges from each manufacturer and each load type, weighed the charges, and what I found shocked me. While most handloaders attempt to hold their charges to within plus or minus 0.1-grain or less, apparently the ammo factories aren't so critical. To my surprise, the factory-load charge weights varied from a low of 0.5-grains all the way up to a whopping 1.7-grains! In most cases, I found the cartridges containing the heavier powder charges usually possessed the largest amount of deviation in their charge weights. Also, it was the larger cartridges that typically contained the coarsest grained powders, which can pose a problems when it comes to metering accuracy. I wondered how such a slack standard could take place, so I followed up by contacting several mainstream ammo manufacturers and was told by each one that their powder charges are metered out in volumetric form, rather than being measured by weight. Of course, the factories usually run their own in-house checks to make sure they fall within their own preset standards. But my issue is with what those standards are, when it comes to fluctuations in powder charge weight. I am quite sure that, if my own handloads contained powder charges that varied that much, my loads would be shooting on par with those of the factories.

A close-up of the engraving and gold inlay work. Note the reinforced action at the standing breech and the watertable junction.

The .450-400 JEFFERY DOUBLE RETURNS

BY **JIM DICKSON**

PHOTOS BY **Marc Newton, J. Roberts & Co.**

For the first time since WWII, the .450-400 Jeffery cartridge is being offered in a Jeffery double rifle. This cartridge is the .450 Nitro necked down to .400-caliber and firing a 400-grain bullet at 2,150 fps. This was the minimum legal caliber for dangerous game for years in many places, due to hunters who used smaller calibers like the .375 H&H getting killed with predictable regularity.

In a 10-pound double, you have a sweet-shooting rifle with less felt recoil than a 12-gauge shotgun. If the gun is stocked to fit you correctly, you should not feel very much recoil at all. The doubles were often made heavier for steadiness, because holding a light gun on target after running after game in the tropical heat can be an exercise in futility.

The .450-400 Jeffery was always one of the most popular cartridges of British hunters pursuing game in Africa and India. It was truly an all-purpose cartridge for shooting camp meat and deer and antelope, as well as dangerous game. (Because so much camp meat of all sizes was shot with the .450-400, some of the old soft-point bullets were made with so much lead showing that they caused leading in the barrel.) In the old days, when you hunted alone, anyone hunting with a lesser cartridge for smaller game in proximity to dangerous game could be considered to have a death wish. You never knew when that trophy antelope hunt might turn into a charging elephant hunt, whether you had an elephant license or not.

They were widely admired for shooting Cape buffalo, because the bullet will stop under the hide on the far side instead of exiting and wounding another in the herd. Faced with a charging buffalo, they were somewhat lacking, but generally got the job done. Bigger calibers, of

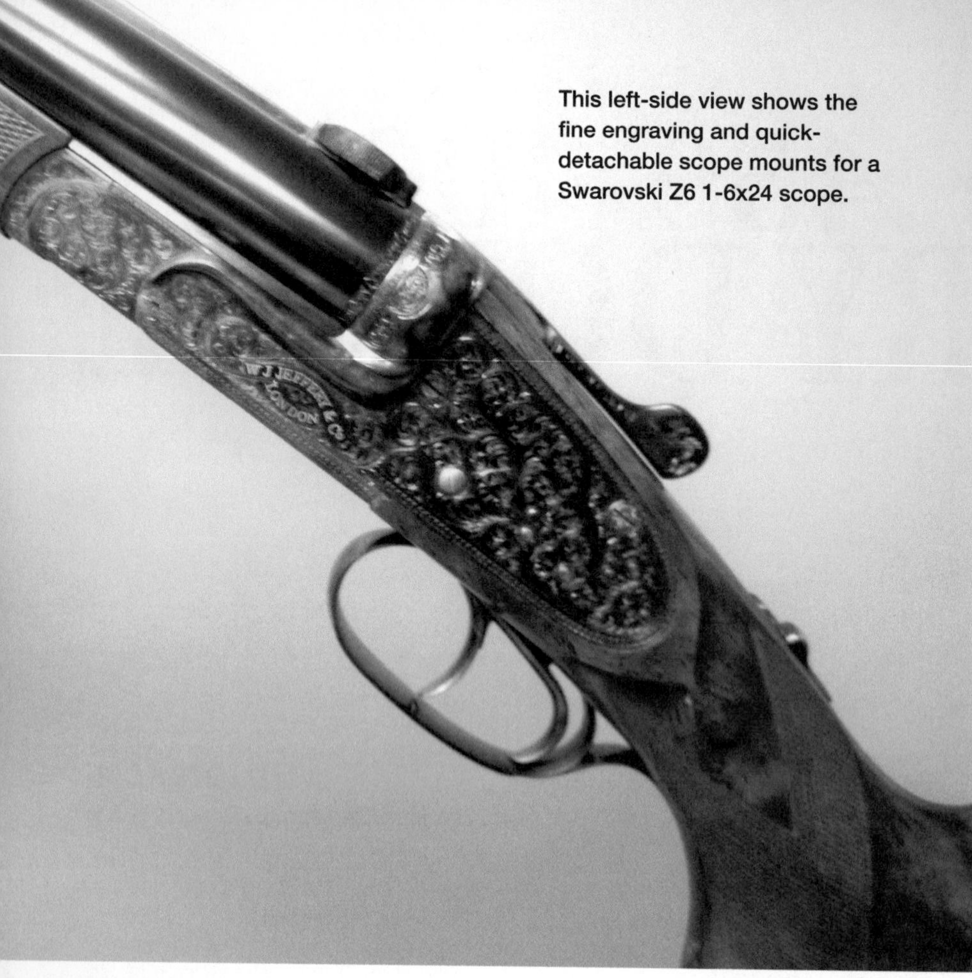

This left-side view shows the fine engraving and quick-detachable scope mounts for a Swarovski Z6 1-6x24 scope.

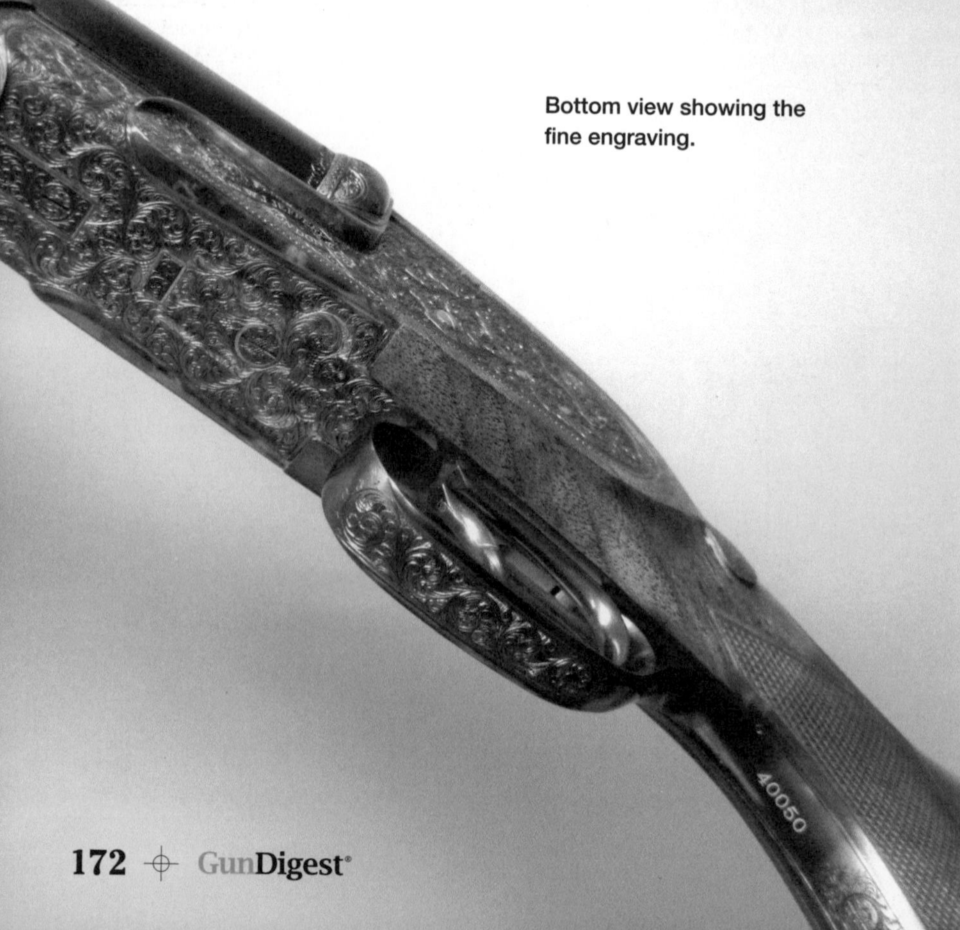

Bottom view showing the fine engraving.

course, had and have an extra margin of safety, so most dangerous game hunters moved up to a .465 or .500 for the greater room for error these bigger bores provided. Still, that doesn't change the fact that the largest elephant on record (elephant, not tusks) was killed with a .450-400. The first shot was deflected on the elephant's temple bone, but the second went true to the brain—another good reason to carry a double. That being said, it's not the recommended cartridge for elephants. (As can be seen by that tale, funny things can happen to bullets in the real world, and that's another reason for using the biggest caliber you can handle. The .465, 500, and my favorite, the mighty .577 3-inch, will knock down an elephant for longer with a near miss on the brain and are much quicker and more humane when taking the shoulder shot on elephants. This is why some men preferred to carry a .500 or .577 for the big stuff in thick cover, while using the .450-400 the rest of the time.)

In North America, the .450-400 is probably the ultimate double-rifle caliber. American game is much easier to kill than African game, and the .450-400 is more than adequate for any situation you can get into in the New World. Whitetail deer are famous for making a 100-yard dash after being heart shot with a .30-caliber rifle—they don't do that when hit with a .450-400. They drop on the spot, and you don't have to track them in the briar patch and swamp or worry about another hunter claiming them. That's reason enough right there to invest in one.

If you hunt moose, bison, or bear, you have plenty of power for a humane one-shot kill (though I always advocate putting an extra round in to prevent unnecessary suffering and speed a mortally wounded animal's demise). British hunter and Best Quality gunmaker Giles Whittome once stunned his hunting companions, in Canada, by flattening a bear with one shot from a .450-400 double in a more dramatic and decisive manner than anything that they had ever seen before.

If you are charged by anything in the Americas, you will find nothing lacking in the stopping power of the .450-400, and the speed of a stocked-to-fit double can save your life when a factory stocked bolt-action can get you killed. You can hit with a double that has been stocked to fit you by simply pointing it like a shotgun and ignoring the sights. In the dense bush of the Alaskan interior, the

The .450-400 rifle with its case and all accessories.

range of grizzly encounters sometimes is measured in feet instead of yards, and the unsurpassed speed, accuracy, and stopping power of a fitted double can save you when nothing else can.

A double will also give you a chance for a fast second shot that you won't have time for with a bolt-action. If a firing pin or anything else breaks on a bolt-action or a cartridge is a dud, you get to wrestle with a bear. Good luck. Since a double is really two single-shots in one receiver, you will always be able to get a shot off no matter what goes wrong—this is something to appreciate, when you have to meet a bear at a few feet.

Some people will say that a double is a short-range affair. Personally, I don't like to shoot game past 200 yards. I don't get the thrill of seeing the game when it's a tiny spot in the distance, and I don't want to take a chance on wounding anything. A double rifle firing a round-nose bullet at 2,150 fps (which describes most all of the Nitro double-rifle cartridges) will easily kill out to 200 yards and beyond. That's good enough for me, since most dangerous game is not normally fired upon past 50 yards. You get as close as you can get, and then get 10 yards closer, so there is no chance of your first shot not being perfect. That also separates the true hunters from the long-range snipers.

One of the greatest joys of hunting is the pride of having the best firearm money can buy made to fit your individual measurements so that it handles like an extension of your own body instead of a piece of machinery. Nothing fulfills this better than a fitted double. Nothing is more efficient as a hunting weapon or easier to hit with, and nothing lasts as long in hard use. Every shooter owes it to themselves to get a Best Quality side-by-side double shotgun or rifle that is fitted to their measurements.

Handling qualities are one of the things you pay for and stake your life on when you buy a double rifle. A gun that lacks the all-important qualities of liveliness in the hand and steadiness on target results in missed game in a tight spot. At best, you lose a fine trophy, and at worst, the trophy kills you. A good example of this is when you blunder into dangerous game that has been wounded by another hunter. You don't know the animal is there and has lain in ambush for you. When the beast boils out of thick cover a few feet away, there is no time to set up the shooting sticks, adjust the power on your scope, and take a careful aimed shot. That fitted double suddenly becomes the best life insurance you ever bought.

The ability to carry a soft-nose bullet in one barrel and a solid in the other with instant selection at your fingertip can be another lifesaver in these spots. If you have a soft-nose for hunting antelope in a bolt-action and suddenly must have a solid, it's too late to get a double then.

The firm of W.J. Jeffery was established, in London, in 1888. In 1902, it developed a short-necked version of the old .450-400 3¼-inch cartridge and called it the .450-400 3-inch Jeffery. This was intended to eliminate extraction problems in rusted or pitted chambers. The wonderful attributes of this cartridge made it a favorite in India and Africa, and the Jeffery double rifles chambered for it became a staple in the hunting trade. The W.J. Jeffery company ceased production, in 1955, and Westley Richards purchased the firm, in 1957.

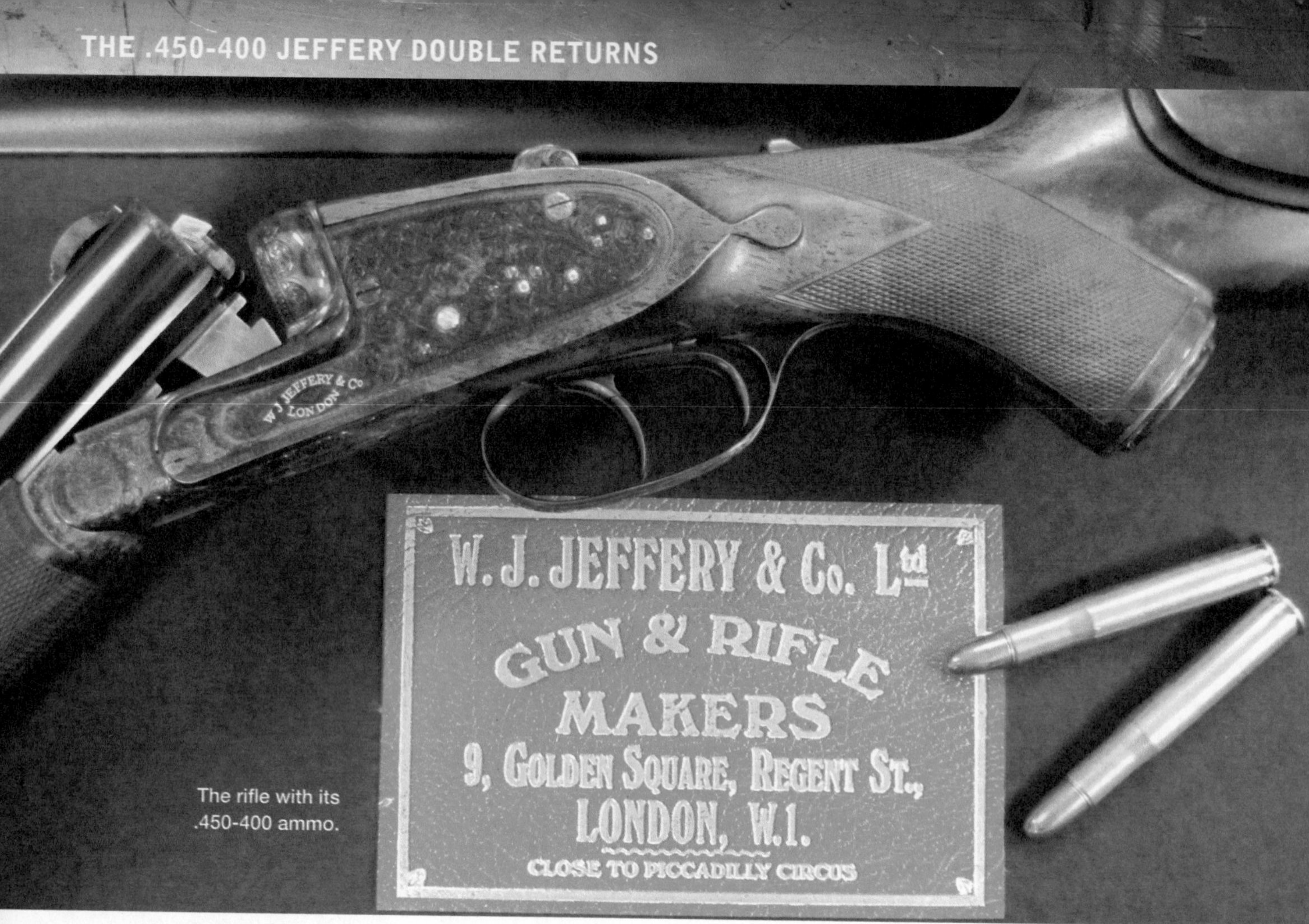

The rifle with its .450-400 ammo.

Westley Richards then sold it to Holland & Holland, in 1959, and, about 12 years ago, the company was purchased by the current owner, Thomas Friedkin.

Like many in the British gun trade, W.J. Jeffery jobbed a lot of his work out to John Wilkes and other gun makers, including piece work assigned to individual workmen in the trade. The new owners carried on the tradition of jobbing out the work, contracting the firm of J. Roberts and Son to build the first .450-400 double. J. Roberts was founded by Joseph Roberts, in 1950. His son Paul, the current owner, joined the firm, in 1959, and is considered one of the most experienced British big-game hunters. Once, when I was complimenting him on the wonderful handling qualities of a .500 double made by his firm, he replied that he knew how a double rifle should handle after all the safaris that he had been on.

In 1984, J. Roberts & Co. acquired John Rigby and made guns under that name until 1997, when the name was sold to an American company. The J. Roberts firm continued making guns under the J. Roberts name. I have been in the workshop where the guns are made, and it is a first-class operation. This is further proven by the fact that they have been able to sell every rifle made to British shooters, the world's most discriminating gun buyers. J. Roberts & Co. is well accepted as a member of the elite group of London Best Quality gun makers. The location is 22 Wyvil Road, London SW8 2TG, England; telephone 011-44-207-622-1131.

J. Roberts & Co.'s assistant manager Marc Newton oversaw the .450-400 double rifle project, including the regulation of the barrels at the range. Paul Willis did the metal work and Andy Miles the engraving, with Mark Renant doing the woodwork, checkering, and stock finishing. The crew is justifiably proud of this masterpiece.

The new .450-400 is a beautifully engraved classic sidelock, with bases for quick-detachable scope mounts and an exhibition grade walnut stock. It is an outstanding example of the gunmaker's art. I have the highest respect for the kind of art that finds expression in hand building a useful tool or weapon via skills that took years to master. Art as mere decoration pales in comparison to something produced by a skilled workman expressing his artwork as something useful. This fine rifle is a work of art that you can admire and enjoy while fulfilling one of man's most basic and primordial needs, the hunt. It is also a valuable heirloom that will be passed down and used through the generations.

The first thing you notice about this fine rifle, even from across the room, is the exhibition grade piece of Turkish walnut, chosen for the maximum figuring possible, while still being able to handle the recoil; highly figured wood isn't as strong as straight-grained wood, so the pretty part has to be confined to areas where less strength is required. The proper balance of strength and beauty has been perfectly achieved in this stock.

Beauty is as beauty does, and this gun delivers in the accuracy department. An accompanying photo shows a one-inch group at 65 yards. You will be hard pressed to duplicate that accuracy level firing offhand in a hunting situation. This gun has plenty of accuracy to spare.

The rifle is fully engraved in the traditional Best Quality English fashion. The idea behind engraving is such that, when the finish is rubbed off in hard use afield, the gun still looks good. In the old days of African and Indian hunting, a professional hunter commonly wore off the finish, but sending the gun back to England for re-blacking was not an option.

The barrel length is the classic 24 inches that has prove best for handling in thick brush. The stock length of pull is 14 ⅝ inches and the weight is 10½ pounds. The iron sights have an inlaid gold triangle and are sighted in at 65 yards. There is a quick-detachable claw mount for a Swarovski Z6 1-6x24 scope.

The .450-400 3-inch cartridge is currently experiencing a revival. As more double rifles are made, the world is once again embracing the finest all-around cartridge ever made. In this writer's opinion, today's best .450-400 ammunition is made by Wolfgang Romey, of Petershagen, Germany. Wolfgang uses the Woodleigh bullets made by Jeff MacDonald of Australia, in both soft-nose and full metal jacket loads. I believe Romey loads the highest quality ammunition in the world, bar none. Hornady is also loading some excellent .450-400 ammo, and I have never heard of any complaints.

The new W.J. Jeffery Company is based in Boulder, Colorado. It is owned by Tom Friedkin and is run by Charles Williams, men who are determined to build the best hunting guns possible. The normal yearly output is only 10 guns, on average about eight Mauser bolt-actions and two doubles.

These men are serious hunters who know guns. Williams was born in Rhodesia and attended Capetown University. He worked as a game warden with the Department of National Parks and Wildlife, in Rhodesia, for 13 years, where he did a lot of culling work, killing hundreds of elephants, buffalo, and hippos. That's serious old-time professional hunting experience.

In 1975, Williams met Tom Friedkin, who wanted him to manage his Botswana safari company Safari South. Friedkin accepted and became a licensed professional hunter. Today, the two men operate Tanzania Game Trackers Safaris, in Tanzania. They currently lease 6.5 million acres from the government for safaris, where they offer 41 different species of game.

Tom Friedkin is a highly successful Texas businessman and entrepreneur. His Friedkin Conservation Fund spends $1.5 million a year for anti-poaching work and employs more than 100 rangers who make in excess of 1,000 arrests and prosecutions every year. The rangers also do community development projects drilling wells, teaching animal husbandry, and showing the natives the importance of game management and how poaching prevents them from getting their share of the game that is killed. This is a very effective anti-poaching and conservation approach for underdeveloped lands.

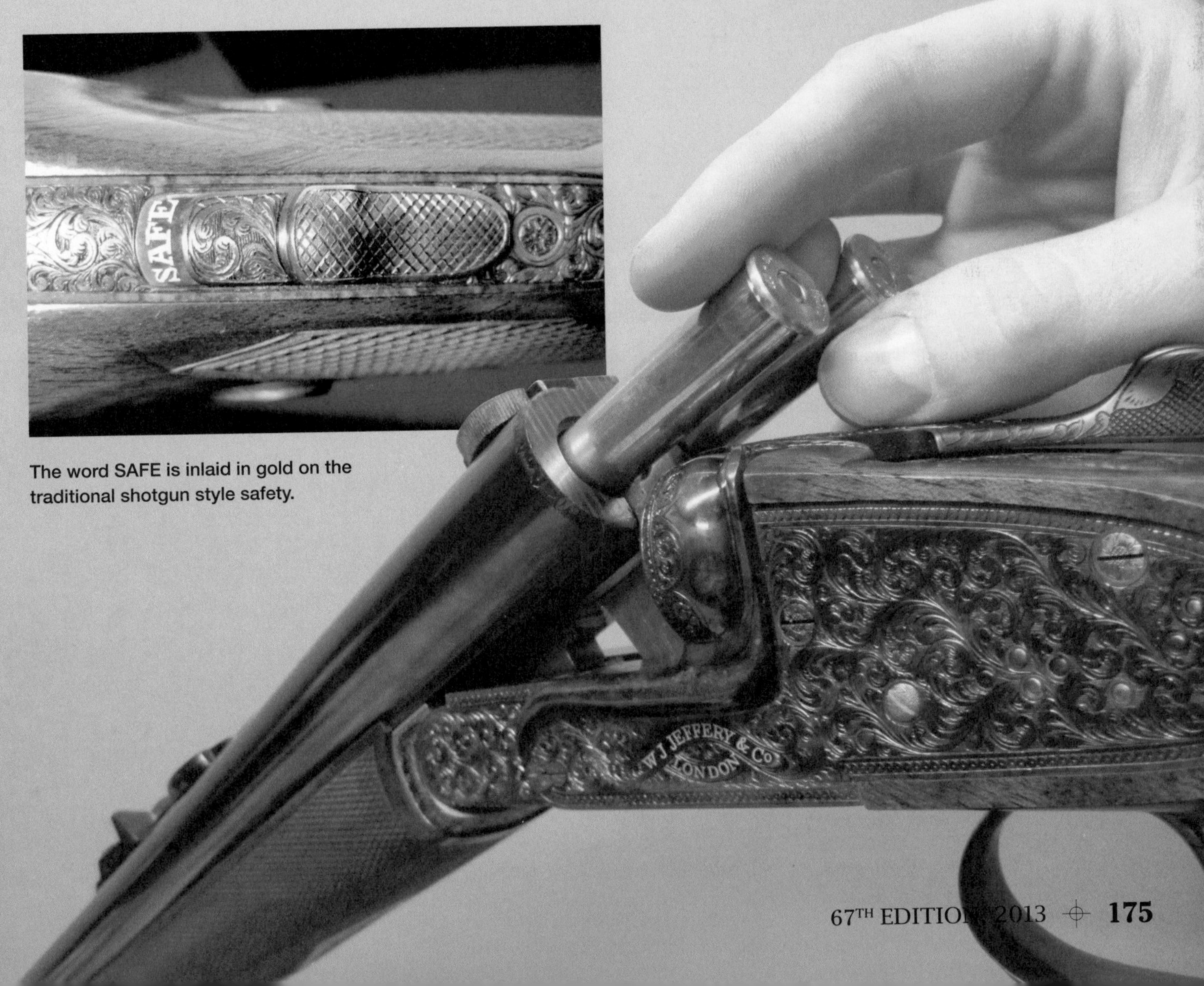

The word SAFE is inlaid in gold on the traditional shotgun style safety.

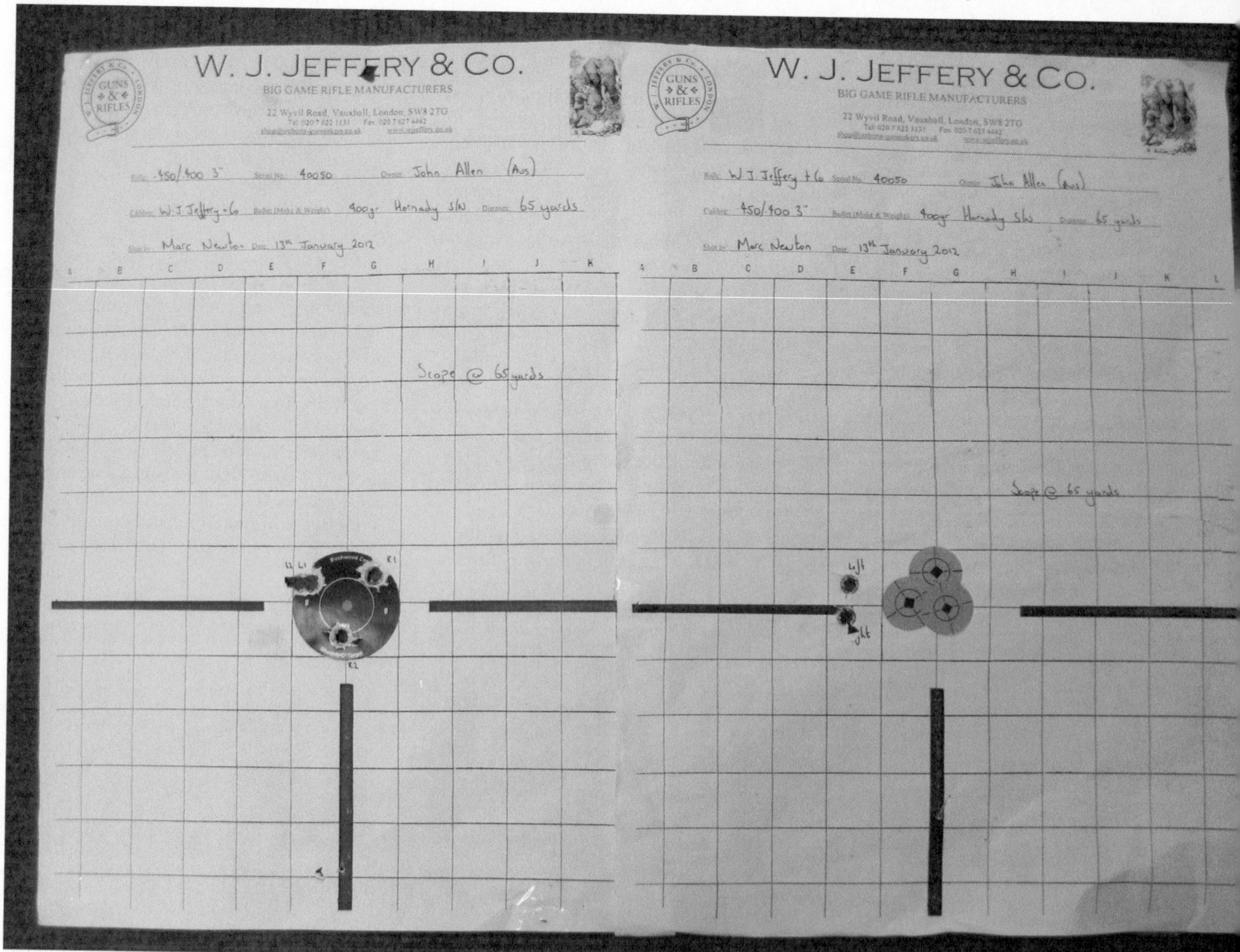

W. J. JEFFERY & Co.
BIG GAME RIFLE MANUFACTURERS
22 Wyvil Road, Vauxhall, London, SW8 2TG

Rifle: 450/400 3" Serial No: 40050 Owner: John Allen (Aus)
Calibre: W.J. Jeffery + Co Bullet (Make & Weight): 400gr Hornady S/N Distance: 65 yards
Shot by: Marc Newton Date: 13th January 2012

Scope @ 65 yards

W. J. JEFFERY & Co.
BIG GAME RIFLE MANUFACTURERS
22 Wyvil Road, Vauxhall, London, SW8 2TG

Rifle: W.J. Jeffery + Co Serial No: 40050 Owner: John Allen (Aus)
Calibre: 450/400 3" Bullet (Make & Weight): 400gr Hornady S/N Distance: 65 yards
Shot by: Marc Newton Date: 13th January 2012

Scope @ 65 yards

Targets showing the one-inch group at 65 yards. This is the range the gun is sighted in for. You don't shoot dangerous game at long range.

The rear sight is the classic shallow V, but with a gold inlaid center post, a very classy touch not normally found on today's rifles.

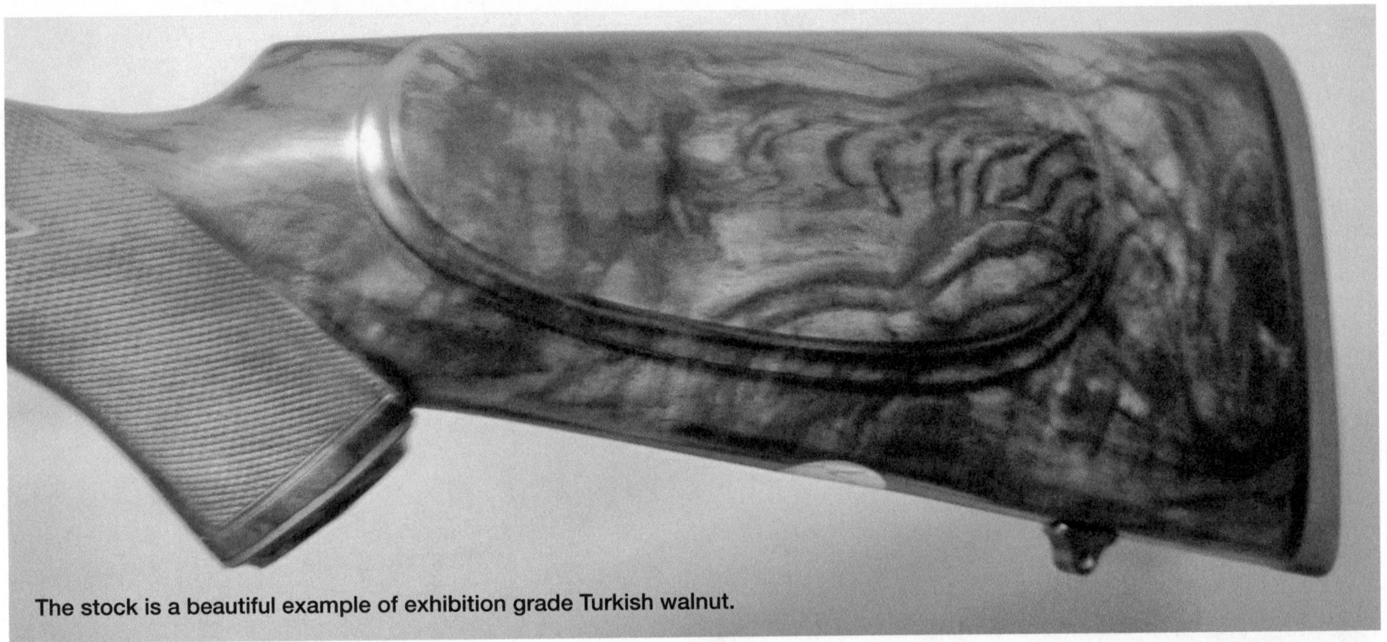
The stock is a beautiful example of exhibition grade Turkish walnut.

The company name and caliber are inlaid in gold.

The new W.J. Jeffery Company has engaged Jack Rowe, of Enid, Oklahoma, as a consultant to handle their dealings with the gun trade. Jack is one of the grand old men of the British gun trade and one of its most respected workmen. He can build a Best Quality double entirely by hand by himself and is one of the last men working who has done so on a regular basis. I have never heard his name spoken except in the most complimentary and reverent terms among his peers. The men who run the big gun companies talk the same way. Malcolm Lyle, the old director of Holland & Holland, praised Jack's work, and he was not known for issuing idle compliments. Now that Jack is on board, I expect the W.J. Jeffery Co. to produce true Best Quality guns made in America in the coming years.

Jack is making plans to produce the Webley Screw Grip boxlock in the United States, with proper forgings finished up by transplanted English Best Quality gun makers who have moved to this country for the increased freedom it offers. The Webley Screw Grip boxlock is universally regarded in the gun trade as the most rugged and long-lived boxlock action design. Unlike most modern gun makers, who tend not to care about the quality you can't see, Jack is going to make these guns from forgings. A forging is much stronger than a part that is simply cast to shape or milled out of bar stock. I believe Jack Rowe will take the reputation of W.J. Jeffery far beyond what it enjoyed in England.

The .450-400 Jeffery rifle in this article is a fitting example of things to come in W.J. Jeffery's third century of operation. It has a most distinguished pedigree, being the product of some of the most experienced English gun makers and African hunters living today. Everyone connected with this gun is a top professional hunter or an English Best Quality workman. This is a gun to treasure throughout a lifetime of hunting and for generations to come, and it is chambered for the most versatile, all-round double-rifle caliber ever made. It doesn't get any better than this.

Jack O'Connor's LAST RIFLE

BY TOM TURPIN

O'Connor's last custom rifle is rather unique for several reasons. First, it is truly his last rifle, as he passed away before it was finished. Second, it is a Ruger M77 and is believed to be the only custom rifle using that action that O'Connor ever ordered. Third, instead of being chambered for the cartridge he is most known for, the .270 Winchester, this final rifle is a .280 Remington.

The two outdoor writers who made the greatest and most lasting contributions to the custom gun genre in general and the custom rifle trade specifically, are Jack O'Connor and John T. Amber. A third, Jim Carmichel, O'Connor's successor at *Outdoor Life*, picked up nicely where his predecessor had left off. O'Connor, though, commenced touting custom rifles when Carmichel was still in diapers (or, perhaps, still a gleam in Papa Carmichel's eye), and well before Amber.

To those of you who have followed my ramblings over the years, it will come as no huge surprise that I am a great O'Connor fan and have been since I learned to read. As a youngster, I devoured every copy of *Outdoor Life* magazine I could find. In my old hometown in rural Kentucky, copies of *Outdoor Life* were hard to come by, but I managed to find one now and again. While I did read an occasional yarn by other writers, it was the prose of Jack O'Connor I lusted for.

I don't think his writing influenced me to become the avid hunter that I am—that basic instinct was apparently already embedded in my genes. He did, however, influence my preferences in rifles and their stock designs. Through his writings, O'Connor also motivated me to try the .270 Winchester cartridge, which became my favorite hunting round. Even today, so many years later, it still is—and for good reason.

I learned about custom rifles and the work of many of the old master gun makers from reading his material. From his writings, I eventually came to favor pre-'64 Winchester Model 70 actions, classic-styled stocks crafted from European walnut, and fleur-de-lis checkering patterns. And it was from O'Connor that I first heard the name Al Biesen.

Alas, by the time I arrived on the outdoor writing scene, in the early '70s, Cactus Jack was no longer traveling to attend trade shows and, much to my great regret, I never met him. Yet, I did meet and converse with many of his friends and acquaintances. I learned a lot about the man from those conversations.

Bill Steigers was one of those friends and, like Jack, he lived in Lewiston, Idaho. It was Bill Steigers and his Bitterroot Bullet Co. that started the now popular trend toward using premium bonded-core bullets for hunting. Bill told me much about his experiences with O'Connor. So did my mentor in the outdoor writing trade, John T. Amber,

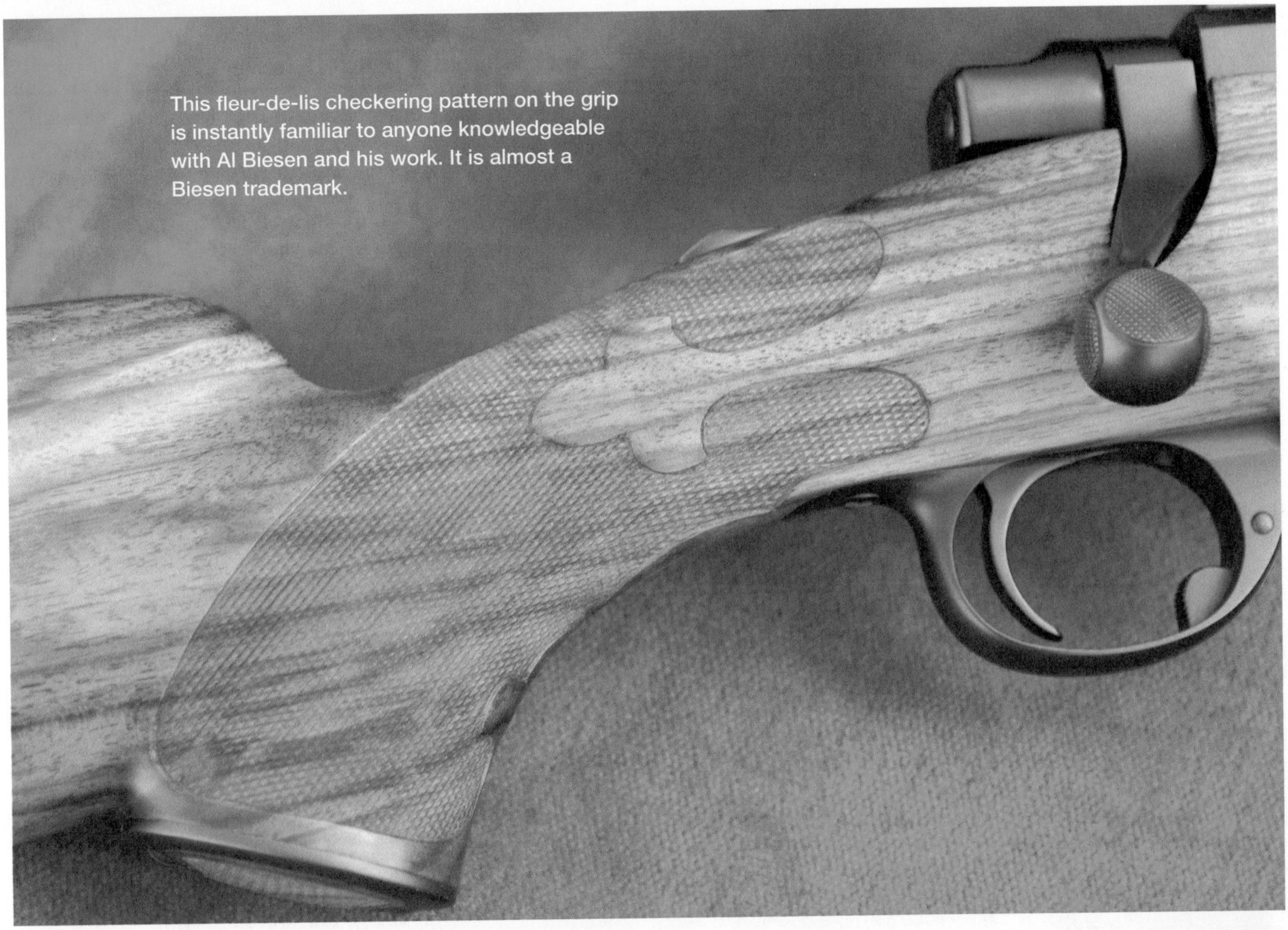

This fleur-de-lis checkering pattern on the grip is instantly familiar to anyone knowledgeable with Al Biesen and his work. It is almost a Biesen trademark.

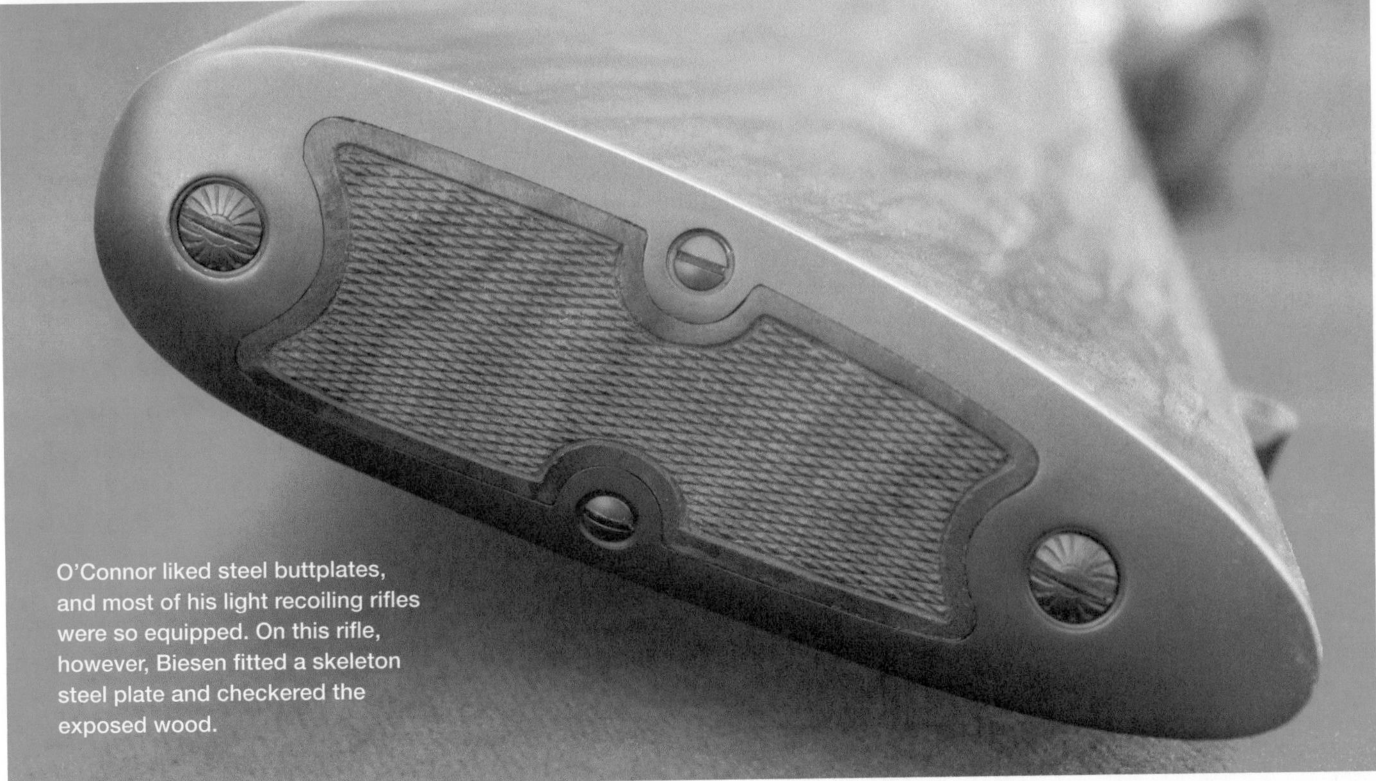

O'Connor liked steel buttplates, and most of his light recoiling rifles were so equipped. On this rifle, however, Biesen fitted a skeleton steel plate and checkered the exposed wood.

THE JACK O'CONNOR HUNTING HERITAGE & EDUCATION

Some will argue the point, but I believe our greatest outdoor writer was the late Jack O'Connor. O'Connor was a trained journalist, a college journalism professor, a successful novelist and nonfiction book author, a freelance writer for some of the best-known magazines of his era, a worldwide hunter, a gun nut supreme, and, the shooting editor for *Outdoor Life* magazine for some 34 years. He was writing for *Petersen's Hunting* magazine, when he died in January of 1978, two days shy of his seventy-sixth birthday.

O'Connor was articulate, witty, and even charming, when the occasion was appropriate. He was also loud, sometimes profane, and, particularly later in life, could be aloof and bordering on arrogant—or, at least, he came across that way to many. He even alluded to such himself in his Last Book. I won't quote it here, but it deals with one fan shooting a hole in his roof, another breaking a piece of porcelain that he had bought in London, and an expository on a group who spent a few days camped out at his homestead, eating his grub and, worst of all, drinking his Passport Scotch! O'Connor ended the little dissertation by stating, "If I am sometimes a little gun-shy in the presence of my readers, I must be forgiven."

Born in Nogales, Arizona Territory, on January 22, 1902, the writer's teaching career began at Sul Ross State Teachers College, in Alpine, Texas, in 1927. He taught there until 1931, when he next accepted a position at Arizona State Teachers College (now Northern Arizona University), in Flagstaff. In August 1934, he accepted the position as Associate Professor of Journalism at the University of Arizona, in Tucson.

In June of 1941, he was chosen to replace Major Charles Askins (father of Colonel Charles Askins) as Arms and Ammunition Editor of *Outdoor Life* magazine. In March 1945, he resigned from the faculty of the University to become a full-time gun editor with that magazine. He remained in Tucson, until July 1948, when he and his family moved to Lewiston, Idaho. He'd felt that Tucson was getting too big to suit him, and he wasn't a big fan of the Tucson summers. He remained in Lewiston until his passing.

I had long wanted to visit Lewiston, but didn't make it until a couple years ago. For an O'Connor fan like me, it was somewhat akin to a believer visiting Mecca! As I stood in front of the neat white house at 725 Prospect Avenue, I had similar feelings to those I had experienced as a teenager visiting Mt. Vernon, Monticello, the Lincoln birthplace—well, you get the idea.

When O'Connor passed, he bequeathed his hunting trophies to the University of Idaho in Moscow, Idaho, and his papers to Washington State University in Pullman. Neither knew quite what to do with their new acquisitions. The UI displayed the hunting trophies for a few years, but eventually they ended up in storage. I am told that WSU is helpful in freely granting access to O'Connor's papers, and the collection is catalogued. A listing of what they have in

The Jack O'Connor Hunting Heritage & Education Center, in Lewiston, Idaho, is housed in this neat and rather small building, located on a high hilltop overlooking the Snake River. It offers much the same view as from the O'Connor's front yard, not far, perhaps a couple miles or so, from the Center.

Another display of hunting trophies in the Center. This wall shows more of O'Connor's sheep trophies, along with an excellent caribou and numerous photographs.

the collection is also contained on the WSU website. Presumably, anyone interested can show up at the WSU library and request to see the collection of O'Connor papers. Until recently, however, the hunting trophies were stored away in Moscow, Idaho, and not available for viewing.

In recent years, a group of O'Connor's devoted friends and admirers managed to get a small museum started in Lewiston. Located on a bluff high above the Snake River, it offers the same view as from the O'Connor front yard, some two miles down the river. First opened on June 3, 2006, and called the Jack O'Connor Hunting Heritage & Education Center, it is a must-visit place for any O'Connor fan.

While in Lewiston, my wife and I also had the opportunity to visit with Henry and Mary Kaufman, Jack and Eleanor's best friends in Lewiston. Henry owns quite a few of Jack's rifles, and I thoroughly enjoyed drooling over them. My wife and I also met up with Eldon "Buck" Buckner, another O'Connor family friend and also an owner of considerable O'Connor memorabilia, including guns. Buck is the unofficial O'Connor biographer, as he knows more about Jack than Jack did. Buck and Henry, among others, had a great deal to do with the founding of the Center.

The Center now contains the O'Connor hunting trophies previously stored at the UI, on permanent loan from the University to the Center. Perhaps, some day, a similar arrangement can be negotiated with WSU and the O'Connor papers can be brought to the Center, as well. In addition, there are a few of O'Connor's firearms on display, plus personal memorabilia from the family. His desk and typewriter are prominently showcased, as are many photographs and copies of books and magazines. Even his old Borsolino hunting hat that he bought in Florence, Italy, in 1967, is on display.

—Tom Turpin

One of the first trophies seen in the O'Connor Center is this Bengal tiger rug, from a very nice tiger taken by Jack O'Connor in India, in 1955.

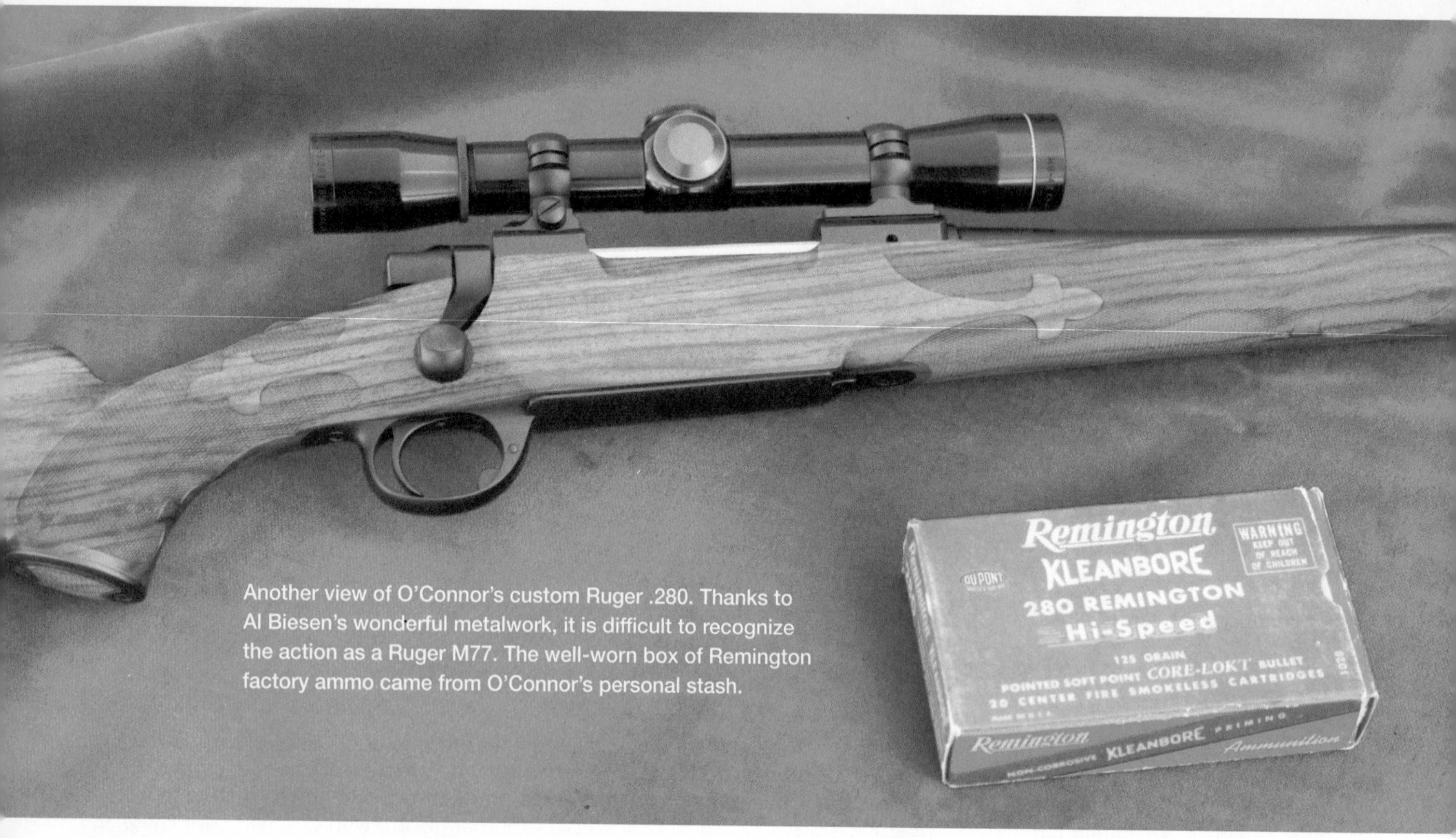

Another view of O'Connor's custom Ruger .280. Thanks to Al Biesen's wonderful metalwork, it is difficult to recognize the action as a Ruger M77. The well-worn box of Remington factory ammo came from O'Connor's personal stash.

the editor of *Gun Digest* for almost three decades. I spent a great deal of time with Jack's old friend Jim Wilkinson and his former neighbor in Tucson, Roy Dunlap. In recent years, I've met Jack's friend and unofficial biographer, Eldon "Buck" Buckner. Buck introduced me to the O'Connor's best friends in their final few years, Henry and Mary Kaufman. All regaled me with tales about him. Also through Buck, I met Jack and Eleanor's son, Bradford O'Connor, and his delightful wife, Anne.

When I finally met one of Jack's other steadfast friends, Al Biesen, he bent my ear for hours relating his experiences with Jack, and it was from him that I first learned of the existence of Jack's final custom rifle. When I heard about it, I knew that I simply had to do a story on it. I knew where it was—Henry Kaufman owned it. I called and spoke with Henry on the phone, and he was more than willing to allow me to photograph the rifle, but I'd have to travel to Lewiston to do so. It took me only about 15 years to make that trip!

Biesen told me the details about the last rifle in a letter from March of 1992. He related that he had received a phone call from O'Connor, asking which he thought was the best off-the-shelf rifle. Biesen told him that he thought the Ruger Model 77 was the best bolt-action rifle for the money. O'Connor heartily agreed, saying, "That's what I was thinking, as well," according to Biesen.

O'Connor then told Al that he'd ask Bill Ruger to send him a .280 Remington barreled action, and that Al should get the lead out and finish it up. That call took place on November 23, 1977, and the barreled action arrived in Biesen's Spokane shop just before Christmas. A little more than a month after that, O'Connor succumbed to his first and last coronary.

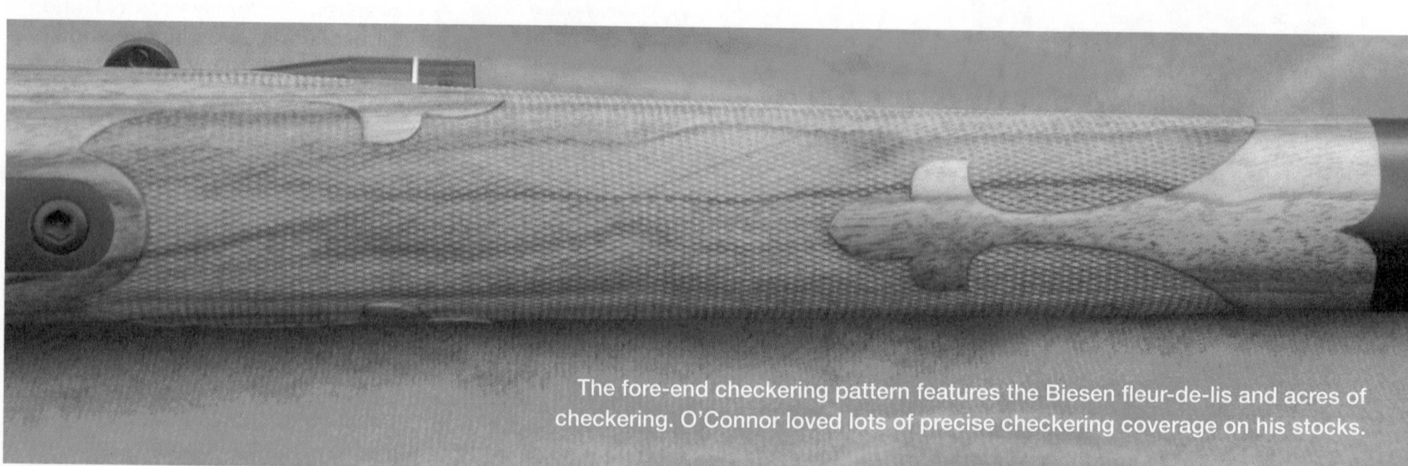

The fore-end checkering pattern features the Biesen fleur-de-lis and acres of checkering. O'Connor loved lots of precise checkering coverage on his stocks.

Factory bottom metal just wouldn't do for this rifle. Biesen had ordered the bottom metal work from a specialist, but, after a long wait, decided to make it himself. The author believes this is the only example Biesen every made.

Brad O'Connor asked Biesen to complete the rifle, which he did. When notified that it was finished, Brad asked Henry Kaufman if he'd like to have it, and Hank picked it up. It has not been fired since. According to Biesen's notification letter to Brad that the rifle was finished, here's what he did to the rifle:

Stock French walnut in a nice grained contrasty piece not so elaborate with Deluxe Fleur-de-lis checkering, ebony forend tip, skeleton grip cap and skeleton butt plate. Old Win. Style swivel studs. Metal work Barrel was recontoured to light weight dimensions. Trigger guard hand made Blackburn style one piece model etc. Bolt handle knob hand checkered in four panel design, trimmed for style and shape. Trigger reworked and tightened with a nice let off. Action trued and hand polished, hand finished inside and polished for smooth working etc. Bolt jeweled. Special scope rings and mounts hand made to lighten them. Leupold 4 power scope. All metal parts blued with a Black Velvet non glare finish. Front swivel stud on barrel. Safety reworked and a Silver letter "S" ahead of safety showing safe position. Al Biesen Gunmaker Spokane Wn And Rem. 280 in Silver on the barrel." [Sic]

That description is typical of the Biesen/O'Connor-style rifles that evolved over a long period of time. Biesen said that, in all, he made O'Connor between 20 and 25 rifle stocks with metal work, and some seven or eight shotgun stocks. What really distinguishes his final rifle for Jack from the others is that it was made on a Ruger M77 action and not

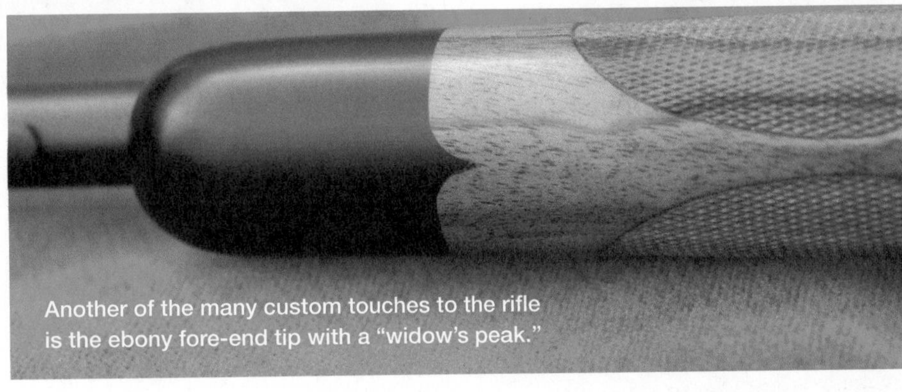

Another of the many custom touches to the rifle is the ebony fore-end tip with a "widow's peak."

his preferred Mauser or Model 70 Winchester actions. (The fact that he chose a Model 77 action speaks volumes for his appreciation of the quality of that rifle, and of his dissatisfaction with the Winchester produced Model 70 produced in 1977.) It is also seemingly peculiar that the rifle is chambered for the .280 Remington, and not Jack's beloved .270 Winchester.

Though O'Connor did have other rifles made in that chambering, I believe the Ruger was the third or fourth custom rifle he had crafted in .280. I've not read, or if I have, I've forgotten about it, that he ever used any of them on game, though. I've seen one other rifle of his chambered for the .280, a lovely Mauser with a Bliss Titus barrel and a stock by Earl Milliron, but it, too, is unfired.

Biesen also told me that just after the barreled action arrived from Ruger, he had a call from O'Connor, telling him that he was leaving on a cruise with his wife and would get in touch to discuss the details when he returned. That was the last time the two men ever spoke. It was during that cruise, aboard the *U.S.S. Mariposa*, on January 26, 1978, that O'Connor suffered his fatal heart attack.

Biesen related to me that, at the funeral, he intended to drop a couple of .270 cartridges in O'Connor's casket so that, whichever direction he went, he'd have some ammunition. Thankfully, shortly before he did so, he learned that O'Connor was to be cremated! "Not wanting to send the old boy out with a bang, I didn't follow through," Biesen told me.

Jack O'Connor wrote about many, if not all, of his custom rifles. One that he did not have the opportunity to describe in his ingenious prose was his last one. Alas, he never saw it, a particular shame, as it is one of Al Biesen's finest pieces.

Wayne killed this Montana elk with a Mark V in .270 Weatherby Magnum at 300 yards.

Weatherby 50 YEARS INSIDE

Dean Rumbaugh recalls working with Roy in his first shop. No one is better qualified to tell the inside story. **BY WAYNE VAN ZWOLL**

Had Dean Rumbaugh entered military service right after high school, he could have retired after 20 years, in 1980 or '81. Then he could have taught in public school for 30 years—or worked elsewhere—for another full retirement. Instead, he has been employed by the same company for 50 years now, and he's not really wanting to leave.

"Weatherby is a great place to work. Always has been. It's an American story!" An unassuming man, and soft-spoken, Dean is of modest height and ordinary build. His hair has whitened over time, but his eyes smile. He treads with measured steps, as he shows me around the Weatherby headquarters, in Paso Robles, close by the central California coast. It's been the company's home for four years now, after a 12-year tenure in Atascadero, a few miles to the south.

"We moved to Atascadero in two stages, in late 1994, early 1995," Dean remembers. "We were all ready to leave Los Angeles."

The City of Angels. That's where Roy Weatherby opened his first retail store, in 1945, confirms Dean. "It was on Long Beach Boulevard, with a big neon sign. Roy moved to a better facility five years later."

That second shop, on Firestone Boulevard, in Southgate, remained Weatherby's home base for more than four decades. Roy put down roots there, established his name and branded his business there. Southgate handed Weatherby its corporate image. Big, glossy, full-color catalogs showing Weatherby rifles also pictured Roy in his office there, the man nattily dressed, courting war heroes, business tycoons, and entertainment celebrities. His enormous mural of the East African plain became a trademark Weatherby background.

"We still have that mural," smiles Dean.

Weatherby eventually outgrew the Firestone/Southgate digs.

"In 1964, not long after I joined the company, we added 10,000 square feet for rifle production, warehousing, and shipping," Dean explained. It wasn't

Roy (right) and Fred Huntington of RCBS were among California's pioneers in the shooting industry.

A self-promoter, Roy knew the value of photos and sat patiently for portraits. Well, maybe not patiently.

Above: Early on, Roy and his crew made Weatherby barrels with Timken steel, deep-hole-drilling the bores.

Below: The first Weatherby store in Southgate had neon signs, many marketing strategies still practiced today.

nearly enough. Two years later, the company leased a skating rink close by and converted it. "That was a great boon," he continued. "We soon realized Weatherby couldn't keep growing without that building, so, in 1971, Roy bought it."

But Los Angeles was changing. When Roy's son, Ed, moved up the coast to find a rural home site, and Brad Ruddell came aboard as Vice President of Sales and Marketing, commuting from his home even farther north, Dean figured a relocation was imminent.

"Judy and I had moved out of the city to Orange County, in 1973. When Ed took the headquarters to Atascadero, we weren't surprised." The Rumbaughs followed. "We both adore the Central Coast. Still, we all felt a bit hollow for a time. Roy had died in 1988. The Firestone Boulevard store held a lot of history, for those of us who'd worked with him. It represented a great pioneering effort. Roy incorporated many of the sales strategies and displays used by successful gun stores today. He was far ahead of his time."

Anyone who knows anything about the high-octane salesman from Oklahoma,

Left: This 1950 Ford was Roy's sales vehicle. He believed in an active, mobile sales force. And he liked cars.

The showroom at Weatherby's Paso Robles office has new and historical rifles and hunting trophies.

and his enormous contributions to rifle and cartridge design, would agree.

Born in 1910 to a Kansas sharecropper, Roy Weatherby spent most of his childhood working in the fields. He earned his first BB gun by peddling garden seeds on foot to neighboring farms. College was just a dream, for most country boys in the 1930s, but Roy worked to make it come true. While employed at Southwestern Bell, he took night classes at the University of Wichita. As restless as he was ambitious, Roy left the Midwest in 1937. He and his wife, Camilla, headed for California and its fabled fortunes. Roy started an insurance business and prospered. In his spare time, he equipped his basement shop with a lathe and a drill press from Sears, wildcatting cartridges and building rifles on surplus military actions.

Roy Weatherby (left) and Elmer Keith take a pipe break on a sedan's grille. Roy courted gun writers.

World War II-vintage machinery was snapped up by Roy Weatherby and other gun makers of the day. This is the Old Southgate barrel lathe machine at work.

Even Hollywood stars felt comfortable in Roy's plush Firestone Boulevard office. Note teh wall mural behind him. It survives today.

By 1945, Roy had developed several of the cartridges that would later bring him fame. Based on the .300 Holland & Holland Magnum, they had minimal body taper, which hiked powder capacity and velocity. And radiused shoulders may have been less functional than cosmetic, but they became Weatherby's signature.

Roy eventually dropped his insurance job and began hiring people to help him build and promote his new line of semi-custom rifles. Cash was scarce; he had to borrow from friends to stay afloat. In 1946, he sold half his business to Bill Wittman, his attorney and friend, to secure $10,000 in additional venture capital. But about this time, Roy's wife, Camilla, inherited $21,000 from the sale of her family's 160-acre Kansas farm, and Roy used that money to buy back the stake he'd sold. Still, the company struggled, and an auto accident just before Christmas, in 1946, put Roy on crutches for three months; he took comfort in the image of the Weatherby rifle on the cover of the *American Rifleman* that month. Sheldon Coleman had become a customer. So, too, had Gary Cooper. Roy courted Elmer Keith and Jack O'Connor, Jimmy Doolittle and Joe Foss, showing a talent for hobnobbing with people of high station—he knew how valuable they could be in promoting his business. Photos of Hollywood stars, from Roy Rogers to John Wayne and Robert Stack, appeared in photos with Weatherby rifles. Yet Roy didn't neglect flint-eyed shooters who paid more attention to ballistics and group sizes than to the silver screen, and, so, when writer like firearms guru Phil Sharpe gave Weatherby rifles and cartridges prominent exposure in his 1948 revised edition of *Complete Guide To Handloading*, the results were even more dramatic.

Despite a growing inventory in the Long Beach store and the reflected glow of Hollywood, Roy craved faster growth. To raise more money, he decided to offer stock. Weatherby's (later Weatherby), Inc. was formed in May 1949. It drew $70,000 from investors. One of the most important was Herb Klein, a wealthy Texas oil man who had bought a Weath-

Weatherby's scope appeared in 1954, before variables were perfected or popular. The Lee Dot, by T.K. Lee, was a common reticle in those days.

"Tomorrow's Rifles Today" was a perfect slogan for Weatherby. This ad predated the Mark V rifle and shows a Mauser action in a signature Weatherby stock.

This 1963 magazine ad shows a Hertel & Reuse "Imperial" scope built briefly for Weatherby. The image shows how Roy wanted people to think of his rifle—and to whom he directed his marketing.

Light recoil, flat trajectory: the lightning-fast .257 Weatherby in a Mark V rifle is deadly on deer far away. It drives an 87-grain bullet at over 3,800 fps!

erby rifle in 1946. He committed $10,000 for stock in the new company and, with Phil Sharpe, became a vice president.

"Herb was crucial to Roy's survival, in those early years," says Dean Rumbaugh. "But those two men didn't always see eye to eye. The relationship was strained, when Roy was compelled to approve a comptroller, Bill Hansen, who'd been hired to oversee Weatherby's finances by Herb's business manager, Ralph Maddox. After many employee complaints, Klein dismissed Hansen, in 1957."

But that wasn't the end of friction between Klein and Weatherby, and sadly, Hansen's replacement didn't work out, either. After a decade of calm under a subsequent comptroller, Herb Klein suggested that Weatherby hire John Coapman as sales manager. Coapman worked for Coca Cola, but had guided Klein on a hunting trip. He eventually put all his time into outfitting big-game hunters overseas.

"He [Coapman] wanted Weatherby to provide him an office in Europe and give him three months off to attend his hunting business. Roy figured Coapman was going to benefit more than Weatherby from this arrangement," explains Dean.

Roy's friend Elgin Gates agreed. He was hunting all over the world and knew the shooting industry, too. But Herb insisted on hiring John Coapman. Put on the payroll in August of 1961, Coapman was fired that November. Roy had to explain the sales manager's dismissal to Herb, when he returned from a hunting trip. To his credit, Herb understood, and the two agreed that Klein would take a more active role in the company. The Weatherby-Klein team worked well enough for a time. Both were bright and energetic and had vision. But their views on how to direct operations differed, and when Herb's nephew Lloyd Klein, a young attorney, was brought into the company as Roy's legal assistant, the union faltered again.

"By this time," Dean remembers, "Klein owned half interest."

Weatherby rifles—"Tomorrow's Rifles Today" as Roy said—have logged 70 years afield.

Resolving problems with his long-time associate and benefactor, Roy had to face a fundamental change. He proposed a buyout. Herb agreed—but stipulated a minimum $125,000 profit over what he had invested. Immediately Roy sought another partner, this time in Udo van Meeteren, who owned J.P. Sauer Company. One roadblock? "Roy found J.P. Sauer had just been acquired by

Dynamit-Nobel, so he had to negotiate as well with Manfred Holzach, the parent company's managing director," Dean told me. After much consultation, an agreement was forged in October 1962, with the two German firms each getting 25 percent of Weatherby."

They remained partners for only four years. In 1966, the German companies sold their interest in Weatherby to Roy's friend and NASCO Industries owner Leo Roethe, for $500,000—$187,000 less than they'd paid for it!

Herb Klein and Roy Weatherby remained good friends until Herb's death, in 1974. "By that time, the corporate aspects of Weatherby were getting hard to follow, and I wasn't in that loop," says Dean Rumbaugh. "I was more interested in the rifles and cartridges."

Roy's first rifles were built on the most available bolt-action mechanisms: the 1898 Mauser, 1903 Springfield, and 1917 Enfield. He also used Model 70 Winchesters and other actions supplied by customers, and he rebarreled and rechambered for his cartridges.

"The first commercial Weatherbys—those not custom built—were on FN Mauser actions." They're still sharp in Dean's mind. "Roy imported these, beginning in 1949." Charter chamberings included the .220 Rocket, a blown-out .220 Swift; it did not become a commercial offering. Neither did the .228 Weatherby Magnum. But the .270 Weatherby Magnum that followed, a high-velocity big-game round trimmed to fit .30-06-length actions, endured. It became a favorite of Roy and, later, his son, Ed. The .270, along with the .257 and 7mm Weatherby Magnums that appeared about the same time, set the stage for a spate of short belted rounds from other makers. The .300 Weatherby, with its 2.85-inch case, arrived in 1945. It drove a bullet nearly 300 fps faster than the .300 H&H Magnum from which it was formed. Roy hawked his .300 in print and demonstrated its power in films, severing a thick tree branch with a single shot and a straight face.

Roy barreled Schultz & Larsen actions (left) and Mausers to build early Weatherby rifles.

"Sako also provided Mauser actions to our specifications," Dean says. "Late 1950s until 1961, if I'm right." (I get the impression he's usually right.) "Weatherby assembled Mauser-based rifles long after the Mark V was in production. Roy deep-hole-drilled his own barrels and contoured them. He shaped his own stocks. He installed Jaeger triggers, Buehler safeties, and scope mounts. Roy and Maynard Buehler were good friends."

In 1954, Weatherby introduced its Imperial scope, with two adjustments on top of the tube. One was a focusing knob, while the other incorporated both windage and elevation dials. The scope was made by Hertel and Reuse.

In 1955, Weatherby contracted with Timken for its barrel steel "after failed experiments with chromed bores. Look closely, and you'll see a 'T' stamped on the right-hand side of these barrels. Roy favored Douglas barrels as replacements in custom work." My host smiled. "He was pretty shrewd. He rebarreled completed rifles to keep his warehouse stock in synch with demand."

In 1957, Roy and company engineer Fred Jennie developed a rifle action of their own. The Mark V rifle came to define "Weatherby Magnum." It replaced the Danish Shultz & Larsen action, one of few in common use that was big enough to accommodate Weatherby's .378 Magnum cartridge. Introduced in 1953, the .378 was not only longer than the .300 H&H Magnum (case lengths: 2.908 and 2.850, respectively), it was also larger in diameter (.603 and .532, respectively, at the belt). The subsequent .460 and .416 Weatherby Magnums, announced in 1958 and 1989, are based on the .378's hull—essentially a belted .416 Rigby. The figured claro walnut that was to become a hallmark of Weatherby rifles would sometimes yield to the pounding of these potent rounds, so Roy substituted dense-grained European walnut and tough, heavy mesquite from our Southwest.

"You'll notice what we call football

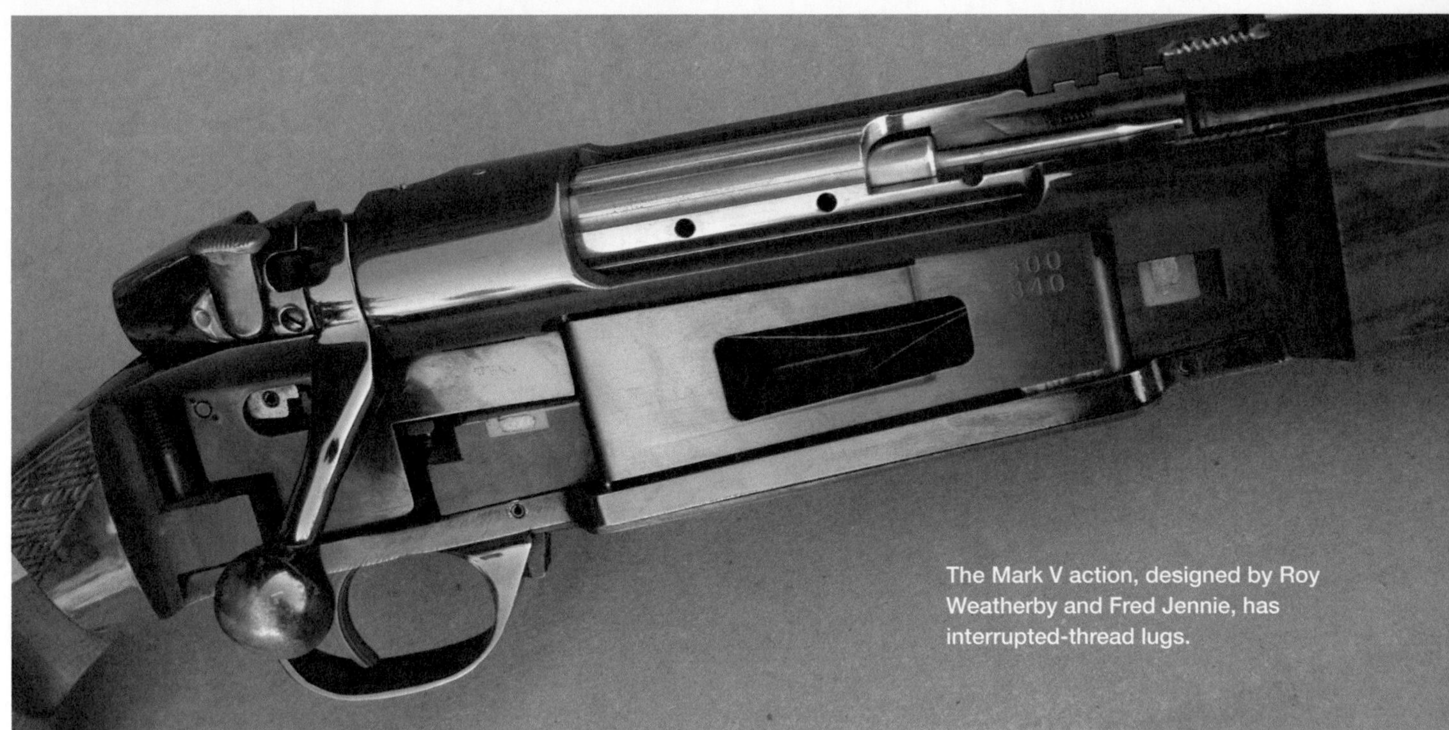

The Mark V action, designed by Roy Weatherby and Fred Jennie, has interrupted-thread lugs.

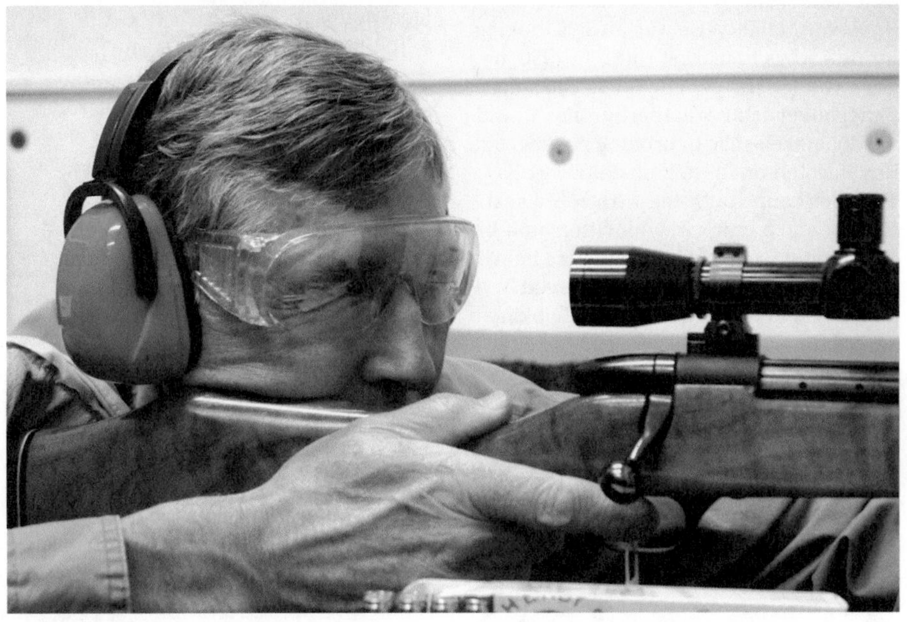

The author fires an original Mark V test rifles, a .300 Magnum. It shot very tight groups!

patches on the mesquite." Dean points to a rifle in the showroom. It wears a beautiful honey-and-black stock. But there is a small knot expertly filled with a carefully matched and seamlessly mated patch—in the shape of a football. "It's almost impossible to find clear mesquite."

Dean Rumbaugh came to work at Weatherby just four years after the Mark V debuted. In many ways, his early years mirrored Roy's.

"I was born in Los Angeles," he tells me. "But shortly thereafter, in 1939, my father moved back to Kansas, to farm. That didn't pan out, so we moved to Colorado, in 1946. He rode fence there until 1950, when our family returned to California. Dad snared a job in El Segundo, with McDonnell-Douglas. The company trained him as a pattern maker. With a partner, he also started his own aluminum heat-treating business. That service later earned him lucrative aircraft contracts." Dean pauses. "I'm proud of my dad. He was a hard-working man, with sound ideas and the discipline to make them profitable. He retired at 50 and lived until he was almost 90."

Dean has held just about every position at Weatherby, "Except president," he laughs. "I started as part-time help, working in retail sales evenings and weekends at the Firestone Boulevard store. Roy was always just a little short-handed—by design. He had to chase efficiency, in those early days. So, it was easy for me to get more hours.

"In 1963, I moved to the shipping department. That's what we called the two-car garage where we stacked boxed rifles and ammo. The next year I worked in the tool crib. We had all the tools for building rifles. By that time, the Lawrence Warehouse was buying and storing Weatherby rifles. It was essentially a loan arrangement. Roy got up-front money to operate. To fill orders, he bought rifles back from Lawrence. Roy sold barrels and loading equipment, as well as rifles and ammunition, from his retail outlets. He and Fred Huntington of RCBS were friends. Roy pursued commercial ammo suppliers in the 1940s and was stocking loaded Weatherby cartridges by 1948. Norma has loaded for the company since the early 1950s."

According to Dean, the first Weatherby Mark V receivers were manufactured by Pacific Foundry International, in California, from sand castings. "The high failure rate quickly sent Roy to J.P. Sauer, where receivers were forged. That was in 1959, just before I started at Weatherby. German Weatherbys, and the Japanese- and U.S.-made rifles since, are of extremely high quality and incredibly stout. By the way, you probably won't find any Mark Vs with single-digit serial numbers. If memory serves, the PFI rifles were numbered from 15,000 into the 16,000s. Sauer-built actions began at 20,000.

"Fred Jennie was a veteran of the cavalry in World War II," recalls Dean, who dredges up people, products, and events of that by-gone era in remarkable detail. "Fred had great talent and applied it to many projects, not just the Mark V. He re-engineered the box magazine on a Beretta .22 rifle, in the mid-'60s, to give Weatherby its first rimfire. A tube-fed version followed, built in Japan, but with C&K of southern California supplying stamped trigger groups. In the early 1970s, we sold .22s with very fancy walnut, but also pepperwood, which gave our stock makers a rash." Fred Jennie retired when Roy died, in 1988. Fred passed away in 2007.

Turnover at Weatherby has always been low, Dean points out, to explain his impressive grasp of the past. "We all got to know each other well, because we shared so many years." Dean recalls that Ed Lishka was born in 1928, "as was Chuck Murray, company shop superintendent during the 1980s, now retired in Roseburg, Oregon." He says Al Schameria came from Sears to run the retail store on Firestone Boulevard. "Stock maker Leonard Mews worked for us for a time."

Ed Lishka was one of Fred's contemporaries. He checkered bolts for Weatherby. "When I started working on custom rifles," says Dean, "Ed taught me to checker. But I could never keep up with him. Ed could cut three knobs in the time it took me to finish one. He'd checker a Mark V bolt in 15 minutes. And it always looked good!"

Marty Noonan also contributed, during those early days. An L.A. policeman in the 1940s, he stopped at the store on Long Beach Boulevard and soon became a regular. Eventually, Weatherby employed him as a sales representative. "Marty's wife, Betty, was even more valuable," Dean tells me. "She climbed the short employee ladder in record time and became Roy's assistant, remained there for decades."

Those decades brought many changes to the company. "Roy worked as hard as anyone while we ran the Firestone Boulevard facility. He was always looking for new ways to market rifles. In 1950, he got a van for travel to dealers. The side-panel advertising Weatherby rifles would hardly make sense in urban L.A. now, but Roy insisted on it. He took delivery of a Chrysler coupe outfitted with zebra seat covers, and a Buick wagon with a built-in walnut gun vault. Pull-out drawers held scoped rifles for display. He believed in a mobile and active sales force. Looking back, it's easy to see why. He was a super salesman; personal contacts earned him a lot of business. For years long after postage costs made it a questionable business practice, Roy sent Christmas cards to everyone who bought a Weatherby rifle. He cared about the rifles and the people who used them."

A hunter and shooter, Roy enjoyed taking his rifles afield. "But, if you pinned me down," Dean concedes, "I'd have to say he relished the promotion above the sport. He made two safaris, in 1948 and 1952, expressly to evaluate and generate publicity for his rifles."

Roy groomed his son, Ed, to take the helm. "Like Roy, Ed was—and is—tech savvy," says Dean. "Both have kept the company up to speed with the latest electronic equipment. Ed was active in the firm until the mid-1970s. He spent three years in Applegate, Oregon, then returned to run Weatherby." Roy had two daughters as well. The youngest, Connie, is married to Paul Shepherd, an attorney who has also served as the company's legal counsel.

By the late 1970s, Weatherby had established a good working relationship with Calico, a walnut supplier in California.

"Calico still furnishes most of our wood," says Dean.

By the time the Mark V had been in production 20 years, Weatherby had introduced most of its current line of cartridges—at least most that were of

Dean Rumbaugh has been with Weatherby for 50 years. Here he shelves a rifle in the warehouse.

Cubicles, cubicle The Paso Robl office looks muc like any. Turnover exceptionally lo

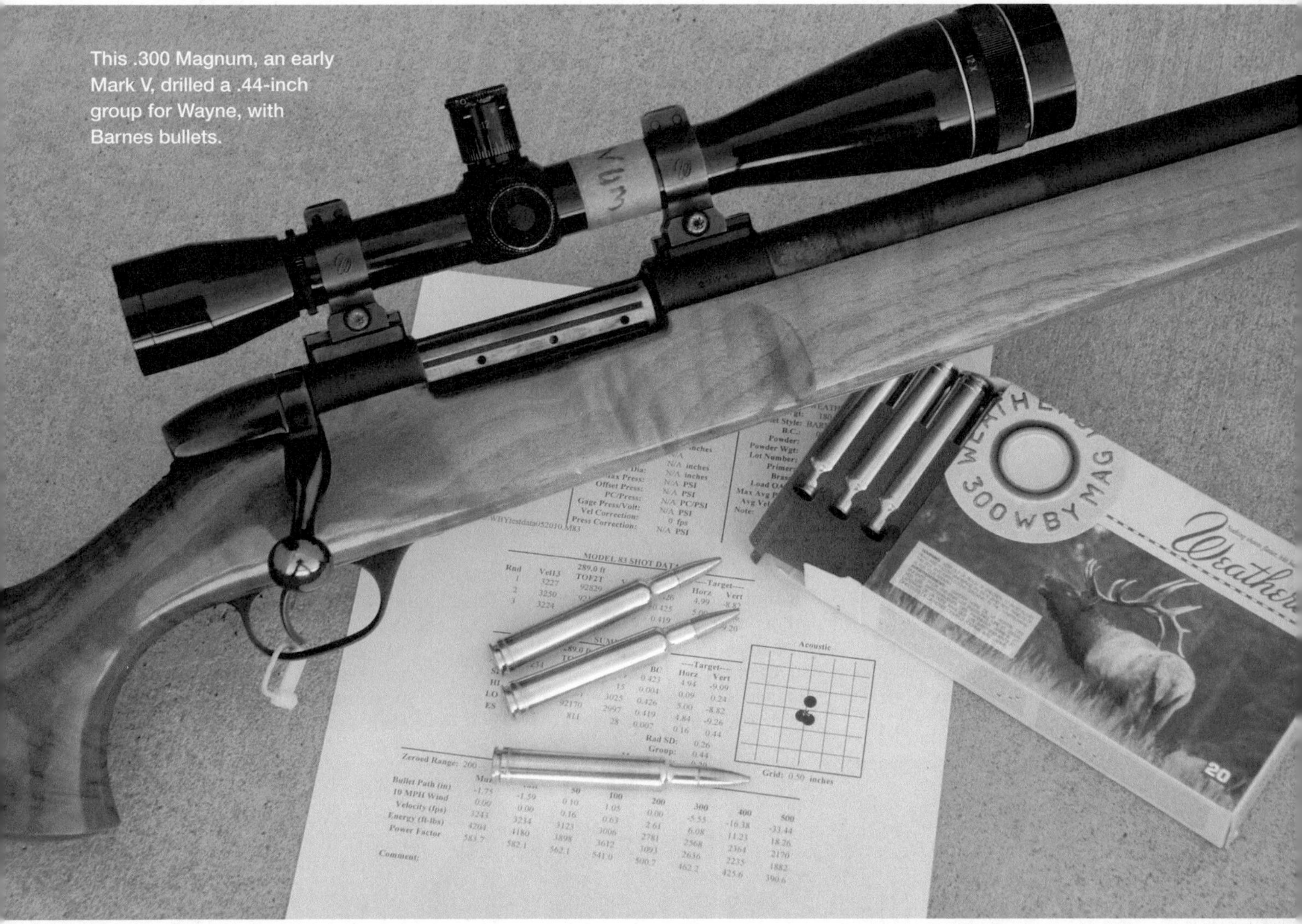

This .300 Magnum, an early Mark V, drilled a .44-inch group for Wayne, with Barnes bullets.

Left: Roy Weatherby was a Midwest farm boy whose ambition, dedication and energy brought success.

"This is Roy's original table," says Dean. It's still used in the Paso Robles conference room.

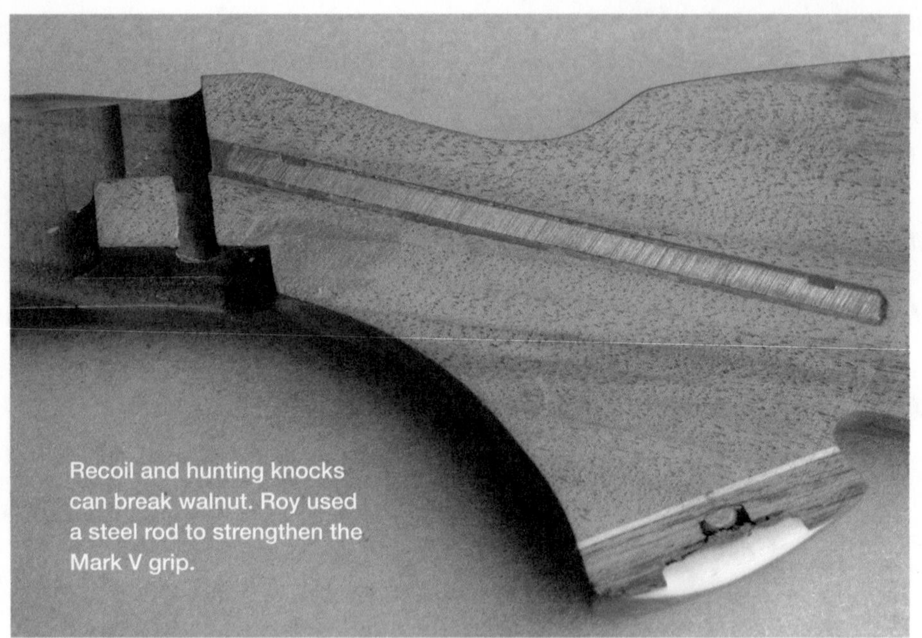

Recoil and hunting knocks can break walnut. Roy used a steel rod to strengthen the Mark V grip.

practical use in the big-game field.

"In 1962, we brought out the .340, a necked-up .300. In 1968, we announced the .240, a belted round, but not on the Holland case. It's essentially a 6mm on a 30-06-size hull. Very pleasant to shoot. The .30-378 came much later, in 1998. It was not so easy on the ears or shoulder, but shooters loved it. Still do. It's at the top of our popularity chart."

Dean goes on to explain that the .30-378 resulted from a request from Alabama's Redstone Arsenal for a round that would launch a bullet at over 6,000 fps—in 1959! "We actually clocked a very light bullet at over 5,000," he explained.

In 1981, Elgin Gates, who'd been shooting special handguns at long range, urged Roy to build a pistol on the petite .224 action.

"Incidentally," says Dean, "that cartridge was 10 years in the making. We didn't catalog it until 1963, when we had the mechanism to match. I'll admit Elgin had a good idea. The bolt-action pistol we came up with shot tiny groups. Of course, you could barrel it to just about any small rifle cartridge. The Japanese produced it for us. Everything was just fine, until they declared they couldn't in good conscience ship a rifle whose barrel was going to be lopped on arrival to produce a pistol." Dean shakes his head. "I'd like to have had one of those pistols. Earlier, Roy had agreed to keep serial No. 5 of every new Weatherby for me to add to my collection. Elgin took the first 25 handguns. I didn't think it my place to suggest he make it 26 so I could have No. 5!"

In 1977, Mark V production was moved from Germany to Japan, a cost-saving measure that didn't affect rifle quality. Weatherby brought its Mark V stateside

Mike Schweibert, who has returned to the company, zeroes a rifle at the indoor range.

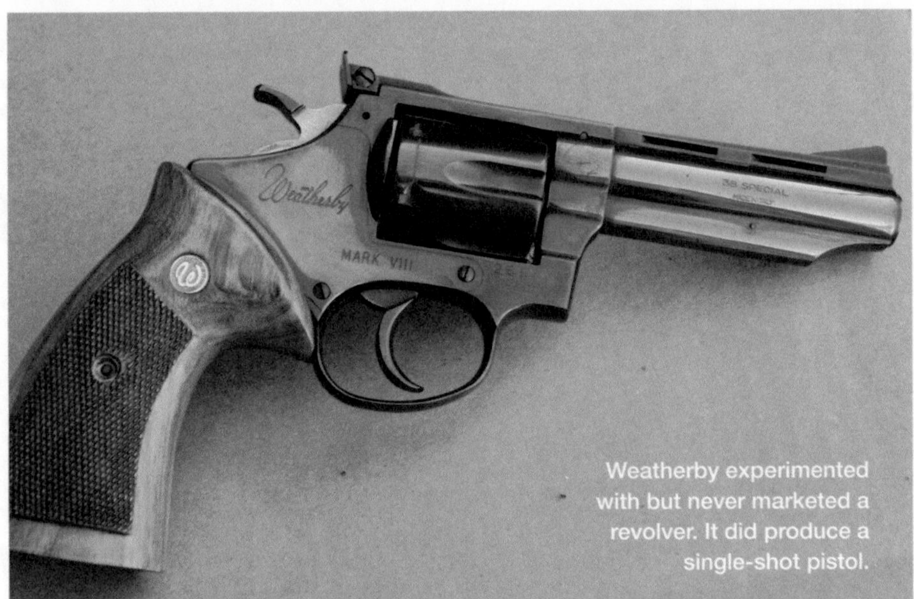

Weatherby experimented with but never marketed a revolver. It did produce a single-shot pistol.

again, in 1996, when it contracted with Saco Defense in Saco, Maine, to build the nine-lug magnum version. Assembly of six-lug rifles for the likes of the .30-06 and other rounds then on the production list went to Acrometal, in Brainerd, Minnesota. The 150-year-old Saco complex had been updated during World War II for production of M2 .50-caliber and M60 .30-caliber machine guns. It later produced its own Mk 19 40mm automatic grenade launcher. Belt-fed and having a cyclic rate of up to 385 rpm, the $25,000 Mk 19 weighs 80 pounds, with a 14-pound bolt machined from a 28-pound block of steel. An "ISO9001" company with top ratings for holding tolerances, Saco had hammer-forging machines able to produce the barrels Weatherby wanted. Calico supplied walnut blanks to Lone Tree Manufacturing in South Dakota, which shaped the stocks.

"Acrometal's plant was smaller, but it's still one of the cleanest, most modern around," Dean tells me. "The Criterion division of John Krieger's company provided button-rifled barrels. Bell & Carlson got the stock contract. Adjustable triggers on the six-lug action gave us consistent sear engagement of .012 to .015. Barrels for the Super Varmint Master rifles were cryogenically treated and hand-lapped."

Excellent results from the Brainerd facility, along with an ownership change at Saco, shifted all Mark V rifle production to Acrometal, in 2001. By this time, the Beuhler scope mounts, once standard on Weatherby rifles, had been replaced by those from Talley. Operated first by Dave Talley, then by his son Gary Turner, this firm has grown with Weatherby. Talley's finely sculpted rings, included with Mark V rifles, bear the signature "W."

The Custom Shop was Dean's first love. "Building rifles one at a time gave Roy his start. One-of-a-kind projects also stave off the boredom that creeps in when you stamp out rifles like cookies. Custom work, suspended for a time but revived in 1998, now produces about 10 percent of Weatherby revenues. That segment includes "banquet rifles," marked for conservation groups like the Wild Turkey Federation and the Rocky Mountain Elk Foundation.

Dean and Roy shared another passion: antique cars.

"Roy owned a 1930 Franklin, when I came to work in 1961," Dean recalls. "He loved classics and always dreamed of picking up a Deusenberg. That didn't happen. But Roy collected Lincolns and Packards. He owned a Clipper and a Patrician. The pump shotgun we introduced as the Patrician probably owes its name to the car. He liked to buy and sell, too. I remember once, at an Orange County auction, he bought a '48 Lincoln coupe, then sold it before he left to the second bidder!"

Dean still has some impressive automobiles, according to Mike Schweibert, who has returned to work for Weatherby after a short hiatus that took him to southern Arizona. "I'm not surprised he came back," Dean grins. "This place is hard to leave."

Is retirement on the horizon for Dean Rumbaugh?

"It'll have to happen, I suppose," he says, as if he were a youngster on second base in an evening softball game, hearing his mother's call to dinner. Dean might chuckle if he reads that. We both remember such childhoods, in gentler neighborhoods than salt the news today. Dean had left L.A., before Weatherby's 1994-'95 move to Atascadero, "to get out of the city." It had grown gritty, since the '40s.

"The Firestone store was too often the target of burglars. Though relocating up the coast uprooted us, Judy is as happy as I that we made the move." Dean has been married to Judy 46 years now, almost as long as he's been working at Weatherby! They have four grown children.

"Eventually you must give way to another generation," Dean says philosophically. "We have, as usual, an excellent crew growing with Weatherby. Ed has taken the company up a notch, during his tenure. Brad Ruddell, who joined the company in 1991 and left only recently, was very capable. Ed and now Mike Schweibert again are still actively engaged in Roy's mission—to make Weatherby ever more prosperous. Under their leadership, Weatherby has grown its rifle line to include the profitable Vanguard series, with Howa actions."

Shotguns, introduced early in Dean's career, have included models from many sources built to Weatherby standards.

"Antonio Zoli delivered the first Regency over/under; Nikko, the Olympian. In the late '70s, we contracted with SKB, which has a fine reputation, for a series of doubles and over/unders. Not all our shotguns have shown the market muscle of our rifles. I imagine that's largely because Roy branded Weatherby as a rifle company. But years ago, we learned how to sift out all the mediocre smoothbores to catalog the best. The side-by-sides and over/unders, by Fausti, of Italy, were top-rung. So, too, are our current PA-08 and SA-08 pump and autoloader models. We've acceded to market demand, with the addition of tactical-style repeaters like the PA-459 Threat Response shotgun." Dean smiles. "It's probably not what Roy envisioned for the company's future, but I believe he would sell that gun." A pause. "Yes, you can bet he'd sell it!"

Selection • Service • Sa

BROWNE

A Family Legacy

The name Brownells is known worldwide for its comprehensive line of tools, parts, and supplies for gunsmiths, shooters, and hobbyists, and its business model is described by its famous motto "Selection, Service, Satisfaction."

sfaction

LS

BY **STEVE GASH**

"Thank goodness for Brownells!"

How many times have you said that? If you have anything at all to do with guns or shooting, I'll bet more times than you can count. If you just have to have a part, tool, or maybe just some coaching on how to do some gun project, a phone call to Brownells is the answer. The words "Selection, Service, Satisfaction" are more than just a motto, at Brownells. It's a way of doing business.

Selection—The breadth of gun-related activities that rely on Brownells products is comprehensive and complete, as the firm stocks more than 30,000 products from more than 1,400 suppliers, with more being added all the time. For example, over 1,000 new products were added in 2011 alone. It is no exaggeration to say that, "If Brownells doesn't have it, you probably don't need it."

Service—The person who answers the phone at Brownells is not just an order taker. Each phone representative is a knowledgeable gun person who can electronically zip through the catalog labyrinth in a flash and lead you right to the item you need. Brownells also offers help to shooters with its Tech Support team. If you have a problem, they probably have the solution. The tech guys even have a library of test guns close by, and they can grab the model you're asking about and check it out. Sometimes they do this while you're on the phone with them. More than once I've had a gunsmithing dilemma I couldn't resolve, so I called the Tech Line and explained my problem. In a jiffy, the appropriate tool, fixture, or whatever, was identified and on its way to me.

Satisfaction—Brownells has a simple and iron-clad guarantee: "The Customer is Always Number One." If you're not 100-percent satisfied with any Brownells purchase, for any reason, just return it for a full refund or exchange. No time limit, no paperwork, no hassles, no restocking fees, no arguments, period.

This straightforward motto is utterly simple, but its implementation is truly complex and sophisticated, with an organization of dedicated and gun-savvy people and a gigantic integrated computer system to make it happen. Brownells even has a complete back-up system of huge UPS units powered by three large diesel engines that kick in should there be a power failure.

The large, ultra-modern company of today is hard to reconcile with its humble roots. Bob Brownell started what he called the Gunman's Mart in a Shell gasoline station in Montezuma, Iowa, in 1939. This was a traditional retail operation. In those days, Bob figured no one would send money through the mail to a place in Iowa they'd never heard of. But the type of antifreeze used in gas stations at the time seriously affected Bob's health, and, in 1951, he had to close the walk-in store and go to a strictly mail-order operation. Thus, Brownells as we know it today was born.

The "Uniquely Brownells" horizontal catalog is a staple in virtually every gunny household. Counting flyers and specialty catalogs, over a million hard-copy catalogs are published. There's also a comprehensive website that has even more products than are in the catalog. As a sign of the times,

Right: Bob Brownell started his business in his hometown of Montezuma, Iowa, in 1939. It is still a family business and is a major corporate citizen in the local community.

Brownells Public Relations Manager Larry Weeks (left), CEO Frank Brownell (center), and the author discuss the company's operations and get ready to tour the huge warehouse.

Brownells' Internet sales recently surpassed those from traditional mail and phone orders.

The quaint hamlet of Montezuma, Iowa, was Bob Brownell's hometown, and the company that bears his name has always been located there. The current building was built in the mid-1970s and is located right on Front Street. Due to steady growth, the building has been enlarged several times and today encompasses more than 120,000 square feet.

Director of Operations Matt Buckingham and Public Relations Manager Larry Weeks recently gave me a guided tour through the plant, and I got to see first hand what makes the company tick. CEO Frank Brownell took time out of his busy day to tell me about the company's roots

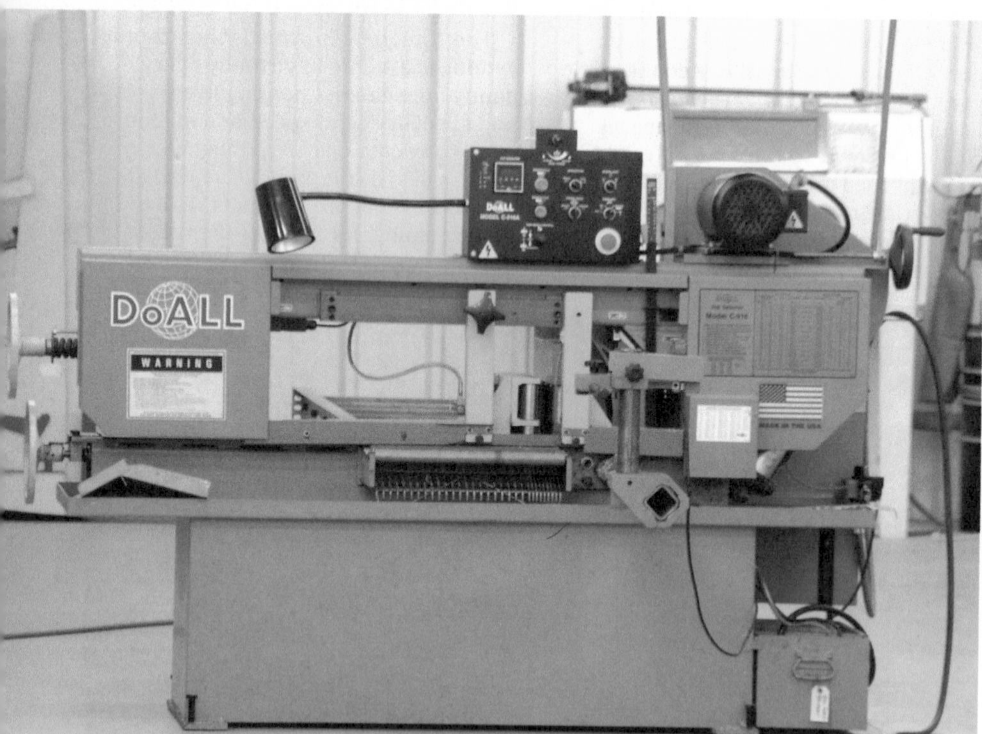

Numerous sophisticated machines dot a corner of the facility that is used to make specialized equipment for the operation, as well as for Research & Development projects.

and its future. "We're always looking for better ways to serve our customers," Frank said. "They're why we're here."

In a nutshell, dedicated people and ultra-modern electronics make it happen, but the details were mind-boggling. It was fascinating to follow an order through the entire process, from receipt (by mail, phone, or internet), to packaging and shipping. Along the way, we veered off to other specialized sub-units, such as product development and the tech support area.

When the phone rings at Brownells, the goal is to answer it within 20 seconds, and the company has proprietary computer software that "recognizes" the caller, so no time is wasted duplicating information. When an order is placed, it is immediately entered into a computer and assigned an order number that follows it until it is on the truck for shipment. This initial order information goes—electronically, of course—to members of the "Pick And Pack Team," multi-tasking individuals who gather order items or box them up. The order pickers carry hand-held scanners and push carts through the warehouse, collecting order items. The computer has pre-analyzed the order and selected the shortest route to accomplish the task of gathering, so that the pickers can retrieve products with as little time and effort as possible.

The carts themselves are sturdy steel units that are barcoded and assigned to individual pickers. Even the plastic bins on the carts are barcoded, to maintain order integrity and efficiency. There is total order control at all times.

As I watched, people moved efficiently through the labyrinth of shelves, picking items, filling orders, and *zip!*—it's on its way to packaging and shipping. Everywhere I went, smiling workers graciously let us interrupt their highly regimented duties to help explain exactly what was going on and why.

The Brownells warehouse is two stories and, if an order includes items from the second floor, the bins move inexorably along a conveyor through the warehouse. At a "Y" junction, the barcode is read just before the bin gets to an automatic gate, where the bin is then directed to the next appropriate loca-

Over 31,000 products are organized in row after row of shelves in the Brownells warehouse. Note how neat and tidy this industrial facility is.

tion in the second floor. Remember, all along an order's route, the omnipresent computer tracks it to make sure it's what and where it's supposed to be and that it goes where it's supposed to go. When an order bin arrives at packaging, it is once again scanned and then boxed.

Order packaging at Brownells is an art form. Flattened boxes are brought to the packer on huge pallets, where they are then folded into boxes at lightning speed, filled with the merchandise, padded with "air pillows," checked against the computer order, sealed, and scanned again as a final check. Then it's off to the loading dock, where a fleet of UPS trucks awaits its cargo.

Brownells' goal is to have all orders out the door by five p.m. the same day it's received, and that's how it's done. Considering the huge volume of orders and products handled, you'd think there would be all sorts of mix-ups, but the error rate for orders is—get this—only .03 percent.

The Research & Development group monitors Internet blogs, customer suggestions, and thinks up ways to aid various shooting situations. These brainstorming sessions frequently lead to innovative new products. On my visit, I met Marc D'Aguanno, who was busily refining an F-Class bipod design for the long-range crowd. It was a funny looking contraption, but Mark enthusiastically assured me it was the red-hot set-up for these long-range

Below Left: A rack in the Brownells office lobby displays a small fraction of the gun literature available, including the four *Gunsmith Kinks* books and this very tome, the *Gun Digest*.

shooters. This specialized item is now in the Sinclair catalog.

Brownells isn't just about gunsmithing tools, parts, and shooter support. The company has branched out into peripheral areas that complement the core business and serve even more shooters. These include reloading and law enforcement supplies.

Brownells carried a full line of reloading supplies from the early 1970s to the mid-1980s. The motto was "carry it all," but soon, "all" became too much and the line was dropped. Still, reloading continued to be an important part of the shooting sports, so, in 2007, Brownells purchased Sinclair International, a premier supplier of all manner of specialized and arcane tools and gadgets used by benchrest shooters (and we all know how persnickety those shooters are). Sinclair's operation and inventory were soon moved from Fort Wayne, Indiana, to Montezuma and integrated into Brownells, though Sinclair President Bill Gravatte remains in Fort Wayne, as do several other employees that take phone orders. Goeff Esterline moved from Fort Wayne and now manages this brand from Montezuma. All Sinclair products can be ordered through Brownells, too, of course.

Brownells has always been a staunch supporter of law enforcement and, to that end, has developed a new branch

Automated conveyors move the order bins from one area of the warehouse to another as needed to pick up more items to fill an order.

A recent expansion of services for law enforcement is the new "Policestore" division that supplies all manner of unique products for police departments.

One of Brownells' most popular products is the "Gunsmith Kinks" series, made up of tips and suggestions sent in by practicing gunsmiths and hobbyists everywhere. Here a pallet of Kinks III, with several already gone to orders. They're up to Volume 4, with number five in the works.

Technical support is a big part of Brownells, and the Tech Team is available to answer questions and solve problems. These highly experienced gun guys even have a library of popular guns that they can quickly access and talk the caller through a problem on the spot.

R&D Engineer Marc D'Aguanno describes the highly specialized features of the new F-Class bipod for long-range shooters to the author and Larry Weeks.

At Brownells' Big Spring shooting facility, Ryan Deveraux, Goeff Esterline, and the author watch as Larry Weeks prepares to crush a clay at Station 1 High House on one of the skeet ranges.

called "Policestore," which is under the direction of Steve Denny. This business unit addresses the specialized needs of law enforcement personnel, with a wide array of specialized gear.

The company's latest foray is ammunition and, today, Brownells stocks an impressive inventory from most of the major manufacturers. The most popular calibers and loads are shown in the main catalog, but the full lines are shown on the website. During my visit, I saw pallet after pallet of ammo of all brands neatly arranged, ready to go into orders, with flat-rate shipping and with no minimum order.

Brownells also has a registered shooting preserve, eight miles from the warehouse, called Big Springs. The area has skeet, trap, rifle, and pistol ranges and is actively managed as wildlife habitat by Kelly Bryan. It offers guided pheasant hunts with dogs, from September through April. The Linden House, a quaint bed and breakfast also owned by Brownells, is close by Big Springs for overnight stays.

After our tour, Brownells' Promotions Planner, Ryan Deveraux, joined Goeff, Larry, and me for a few rounds of skeet on one of the Big Springs ranges. Conditions were, shall we say, challenging (Larry suggested renaming the facility the "Big Windy"), but we managed to bust a few birds and, in general, had a fine time. These ranges are available to hunters who want to sharpen their swings before going after pheasants.

Brownells never forgets its roots and, to that end, generously supports a number of shooting and law enforcement organizations. In addition, the 4H Club, the Scholastic Clay Target Program, Scholastic Steel Challenge, and many other charitable shooting organizations, as well as local police and sheriff departments and other pro-gun groups, use the range facilities at Big Springs.

Brownells had a circuitous start, in 1939, and, over the ensuing decades of steady growth, developed into the American icon it is today. While large and complex, it is really still the family-owned business started by Bob Brownell so long ago. Bob passed away in 1991, and, today, his son Frank and Frank's son Pete, continue the family tradition. "Selection, Service, Satisfaction? is still the Brownells credo.

Above: Bob Brownell started a business in 1939 that has grown into the major force in the gun and shooting industry it is today.

Left: Brownells is still a family run business, and CEO Frank (right) and his son Pete (left), president, keep the tradition alive.

"Gentlemen, I

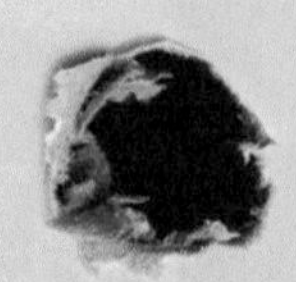

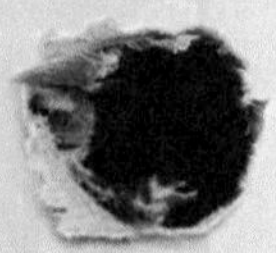

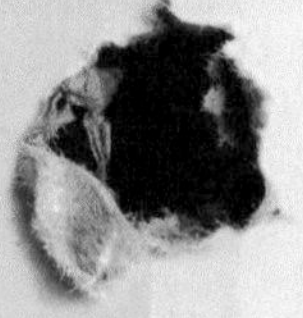

"The exact sequence of events, who fired the first shot and who actually shot whom, is still a matter of dispute a century later."

March 14, 1912, was a cold and dreary day, the sort of day typical of early spring in southwestern Virginia. At 8:30 that morning, in the courthouse at Hillsville, the seat of Carroll County, the trial of one Floyd Allen was entering its final day. The jury had heard arguments from both sides and was prepared to pronounce sentence on Floyd for "unlawfully rescuing prisoners," a relatively minor offense in that era. As uneventful as that proceeding should have been, though, within minutes of the opening of this third day of the trial, four people would be killed and several grievously wounded in a hail of bullets.

Floyd Allen was a prosperous and well-known farmer and landowner, the head of the area's Allen clan. All the Allens were contemptuous of the law, made no secret of their contempt, and did whatever they pleased. They were involved, allegedly, in counterfeiting, illicit whiskey manufacture, and other offenses. Whatever the truth of these accusations may be, there is no question that many in the community lived in fear of them; the family was generally regarded as a dangerous bunch to mess with.

Floyd Allen was universally considered to be the most dangerous member of his family. He terrified the people of Carroll County, with his uncontrol-

Photograph of Floyd Allen, #47, Records of the Virginia Penitentiary, Series II.
Photographs State Records Collection, Library of Virginia.

Ain't A-Goin'!"

— Guns of the Hillsville Courthouse Tragedy

BY THOMAS CACECCI

lable temper and his willingness to use violence and intimidation to get what he wanted. Many felt that putting him on trial for any offense was taking a serious risk and that the authorities should just let well enough alone. In essence—and with considerable reason—the Allens believed they were beyond the reach of the law.

Even as a child, Floyd had a reputation for violent behavior (his mother was known to have had to tied him up from time to time in an attempt to subdue him), and, as he grew to manhood, incidents grew more frequent and nastier. At one point, he and his brother Jack shot each other in a dispute over whiskey. Floyd was badly wounded and, as he lay "dying," asked for Jack to come and reconcile with him. When Jack was foolish enough to do so, Floyd drew a gun from under his pillow and tried to kill him as he approached the "deathbed."

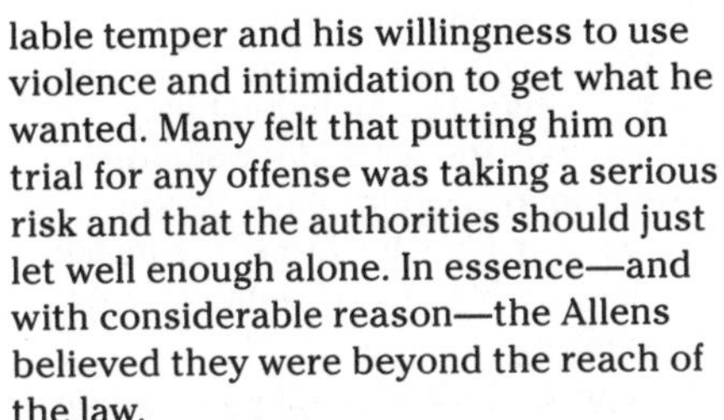

Other occurrences of violence ensued. In 1904, another man bought a piece of land Floyd wanted, thus earning a bullet from the enraged Floyd's revolver.

Floyd was charged with and tried for assault. He wasn't pleased and let it be known that, if convicted, he would kill the judge and jurors, the probable reason for an extraordinarily lenient sentence of a $100 fine and a symbolic single hour in jail. Yet even that was too much for Floyd, who had a morbid fear of imprisonment. Floyd swore he would "die and go to Hell" before he'd serve even a minute in a jail cell, and not only did he flatly refuse to serve the nominal sentence, he managed to get it dismissed and forced the man he'd shot to pay the $100 fine!

SMITH & WESSON HAMMERLESS.

Made by Smith & Wesson, Springfield, Mass. Latest type new model hammerless, automatic shell ejector, patent safety catch, self cocking rebounding hammer, double action, blued steel or nickel plated finish, fitted with rubber handle. This is positively the best hammerless revolver made.

Catalogue No.	Caliber	Length Barrel	Finish	No. of Shots	Shoots Cart'ge	Weight	Price
6H1756	32 c.f.	3½ in.	Nickel	5-shot	6H2377	15 oz.	$13.80
6H1757	32 c.f.	3½ in.	Blued	5-shot	6H2377	15 oz.	
6H1762	38 c.f.	4 in.	Nickel	5-shot	6H2388	18 oz.	14.90
6H1763	38 c.f.	4 in.	Blued	5-shot	6H2388	18 oz.	
6H1764	38 c.f.	5 in.	Nickel	5-shot	6H2388	19 oz.	14.91
6H1765	38 c.f.	5 in.	Blued	5-shot	6H2388	19 oz.	
6H1766	38 c.f.	6 in.	Nickel	5-shot	6H2388	19 oz.	14.92
6H1767	38 c.f.	6 in.	Blued	5-shot	6H2388	19 oz.	

...T QUALITY PEARL HANDLE, EXTRA.....$1.00
...istered mail, postage extra, 32-caliber, 45 cents; ... cents. See our prices on cartridges.
...acked for shipment, about 3 to 4 pounds.

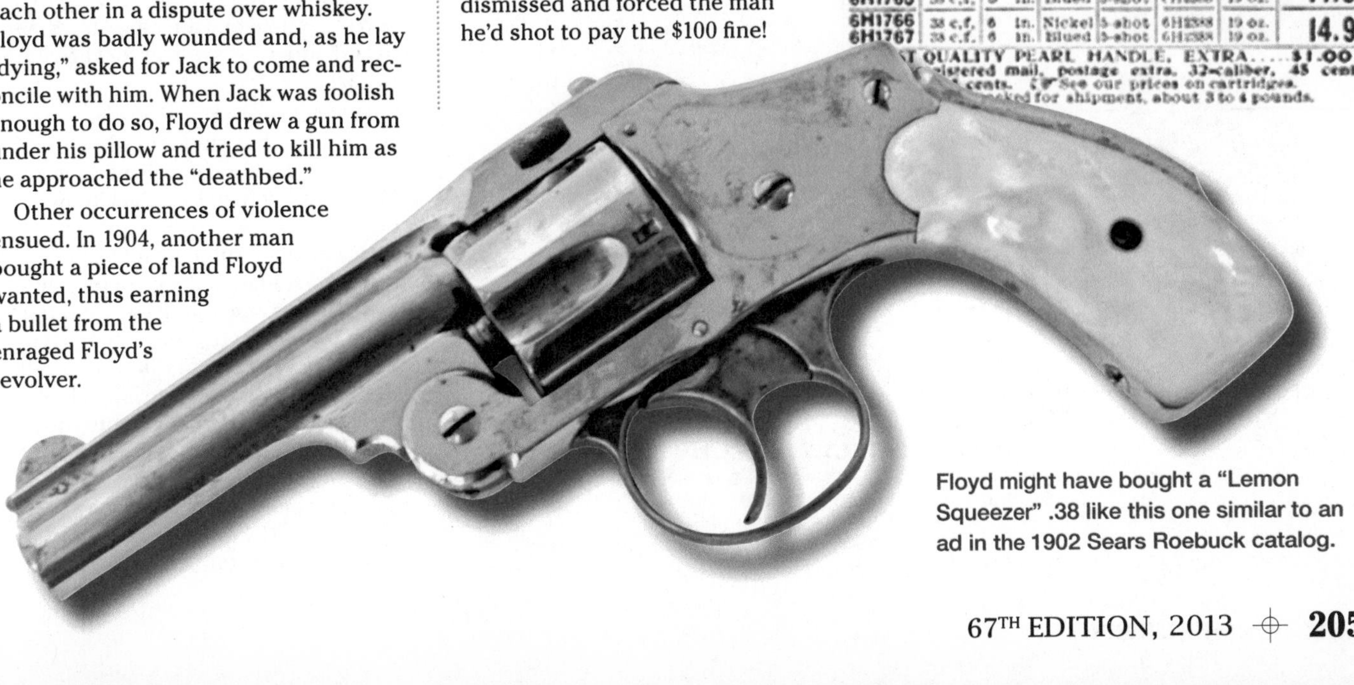

Floyd might have bought a "Lemon Squeezer" .38 like this one similar to an ad in the 1902 Sears Roebuck catalog.

One authority on the tragedy believes Floyd's successful evasion of punishment created a background of enmity between him and the court officers that boiled into the violence that erupted at his 1912 trial.

It was a trivial incident that prompted that 1912 trial. Floyd's nephews Wesley and Sidna Allen had had a fight with a third young man outside a church during worship services, the favors of a young woman being at the center of their disagreement. Wesley and Sidna were arrested, charged with disturbing a church service, tied up by Sheriff's deputies, and put in a wagon to be brought back to Hillsville to stand trial for this quite minor crime. But the road to Hillsville passed the home of their Uncle Floyd, who, outraged at the disrespectful treatment of his nephews, enlisted some family help to free the boys from their bonds. Floyd then transported them himself, in a somewhat more dignified manner, to Hillsville, where they were sentenced to short jail terms.

$2,800.00 REWARD

ONE THOUSAND DOLLARS ($1000) REWARD—DEAD OR ALIVE.

SIDNA ALLEN—Age 46. Height 5 feet 9 or 10 inches. Weight 145 to 155 pounds, light brown hair, mixed with grey. Blue eyes. Long hatchet face, long nose. Complexion rather sallow. Smooth shaven. Very large-mouth, left handed, and reported shot through the muscle of left arm, and also slight wound in left side, rather in front. Two gold bridges in the upper part of his mouth, one with four teeth, and the other with five, and both running back from the two eye-teeth and anchored by hoods and crowns.

Allen is not as heavy now as when photograph was taken; he is very resourceful, has traveled some, and may try to make his way out of the country horse back or in a wagon. He may undertake to make his way west, where he has relatives, or may possibly go to some seaport town with the view of sailing to some foreign country.

Sidna Allen was the leader of the gang, consisting of Sidna Allen, Claude Allen, Freel Allen, Wesley Edwards, and Sidney Edwards, who murdered Judge Thornton L. Massie, Commonwealth's Attorney W. M. Foster and Sheriff L. S. Webb, and others at Hillsville, Carroll County, Virginia, on March 14th, 1912. This was the most brutal murder ever committed in the United States, and we appeal to all officers and citizens to assist us in apprehending these murderers. These men may undertake to leave together or may separate.

EIGHT HUNDRED DOLLARS ($800) REWARD—DEAD OR ALIVE.

CLAUDE ALLEN, son of Floyd Allen, age 22 years; weight 190 to 200 pounds; height 6 feet; black hair, ends slightly curly; smooth face; dark complexion; gray bluish eyes; good teeth; long, black eyebrows that connect; large, round face; very prominent cheek bones; rather good looking, but features a little bit rough.

This man has traveled very little and may undertake to make his way west or out of the country via some of the seaport cities.

He was a member of the gang consisting of Sidna Allen, Claude Allen, Freel Allen, Wesley Edwards, and Sidney Edwards, who murdered Judge Thornton L. Massie, Commonwealth's Attorney W. M. Foster, Sheriff L. S. Webb, and others at Hillsville, Carroll County, Virginia, on March 14th, 1912. This was the most brutal murder ever committed in the United States, and we appeal to all officers and citizens to assist us in apprehending these murderers. These men may undertake to leave together or may separate and may be traveling on horseback or in wagons through the country.

FIVE HUNDRED DOLLARS ($500) REWARD.

FREEL ALLEN, son of Jack Allen and nephew of Sidna Allen. Age 18 years; height about 5 feet 7 or 7½ inches; weight 130 to 135 pounds; slender build, light hair, blue eyes; complexion fair; features about regular.

This boy was a member of the gang consisting of Sidna Allen, Claude Allen, Freel Allen, Wesley Edwards, and Sidney Edwards, who murdered Judge Thornton L. Massie, Commonwealth's Attorney W. M. Foster, Sheriff L. S. Webb, and others at Hillsville, Carroll County, Virginia, on March 14th, 1912. This was the most brutal murder ever committed in the United States, and we appeal to all officers and citizens to assist us in apprehending these murderers. These men may undertake to leave together or may separate and may be traveling on horseback or in wagons through the country.

FIVE HUNDRED DOLLARS ($500) REWARD.

WESLEY EDWARDS, nephew of Floyd and Sidna Allen, age 20 years, height 5 feet 7 or 8 inches; weight 160 to 170 pounds; stock built; dark hair, slightly curled on ends; gray eyes; features regular; face always flushed; complexion dark; smooth shaven. Bad and dangerous man.

This man is illiterate and has spent most of his life operating illicit distilleries in the mountains of Virginia and North Carolina. He was a member of the gang, consisting of Sidna Allen, Claude Allen, Freel Allen, Wesley Edwards, and Sidney Edwards, who murdered Judge Thornton L. Massie, Commonwealth's Attorney W. M. Foster, Sheriff L. S. Webb, and others at Hillsville, Carroll County, Virginia, on March 14th, 1912. This was the most brutal murder ever committed in the United States, and we appeal to all officers and citizens to assist us in apprehending these murderers. These men may undertake to leave together or may separate and may be traveling on horseback or in wagons through the country.

These rewards are offered by us upon authority of His Excellency William Hodges Mann, Governor of the State of Virginia. The rewards are offered for the arrest and conviction of these men, but there is no question about them being convicted if arrested, as the murders were committed in broad open day-light in the presence of fifty or more witnesses.

WIRE ALL INFORMATION TO

BALDWIN-FELTS DETECTIVES, Inc.

Roanoke, Va., or Bluefield, W. Va.

WATCH ALL TRAINS, ESPECIALLY WEST AND SOUTH
WATCH OUTGOING VESSELS AT ALL SEAPORT CITIES

March 23, 1912. Sidney Edwards was arrested March 22.

Whether or not violence and threats were part of the "rescue" is still a matter of debate, but Floyd's offense against the laws of the Commonwealth of Virginia was great enough to earn him an indictment of his own and a subsequent trial. The Commonwealth felt it was time the Allens were brought to heel, finding this incident the perfect opportunity to do so. After some delay, court proceedings began on March 12, 1912.

Local historians agree that, a couple weeks before this trial began, the Commonwealth's Attorney, William Foster, received a death threat from Floyd. Foster showed the letter to the Judge, Thornton Massie, and asked for extra deputies in the court, a request the Judge denied, as it would "show cowardice." There is evidence the judge also received a threat, but not only did he refuse the request for deputies, he refused to arm himself or to ban spectators from being armed, as he felt the "majesty of the law" would protect everyone.

The jury returned a guilty verdict on Floyd and recommended a sentence of imprisonment for a year and a $1,000 fine. A motion to set the verdict aside and free Floyd on bail was denied. The jail cell seemed inevitable, and Sheriff Lew Webb started to take the prisoner in hand, but, as he did, Floyd stood up and announced to the world, "Gentlemen, I ain't a-goin'," then reached under his sweater for the gun he was carrying.

The exact sequence of events, who fired the first shot and who actually shot whom, is still a matter of dispute a century later. It is known for certain that at least 57 shots were fired in the courtroom by numerous participants, including Floyd, his son Claude Allen, Court Clerk Dexter Goad, Commonwealth's Attorney Foster, and the law officers present. The gun battle lasted only about a minute and a half, moving from the courtroom into the street outside before it ended. When the smoke cleared, Judge Massie, Sheriff Webb, Commonwealth's Attorney Foster, and a juror, C.C. Fowler, lay dead in the Courtroom. A bystander, Betty Ayers,

Judge T. L. Massie

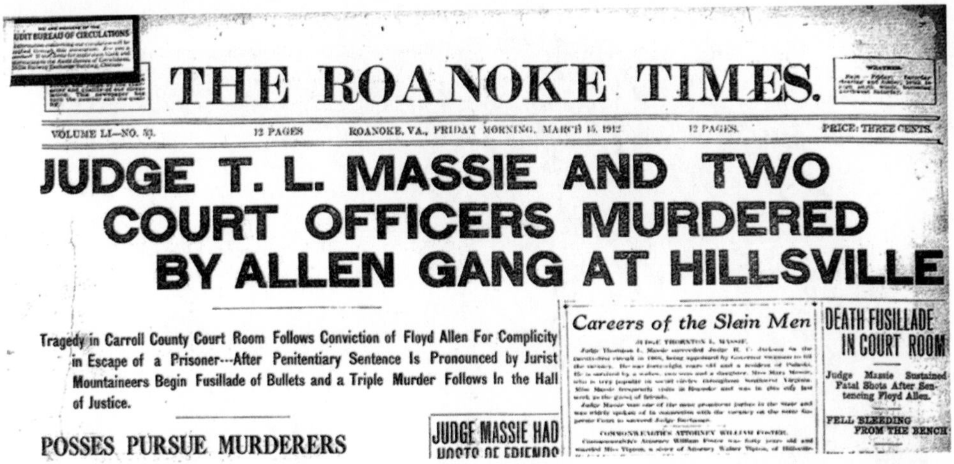

was mortally wounded and died the next day. The Clerk, Dexter Goad, was badly wounded. Floyd was shot in the leg and injured seriously enough that he was unable to escape. And the two young men, the nephews whose fight had really started everything, escaped with Claude Allen from the immediate vicinity and managed to evade capture until after a massive manhunt had been launched.

The incident caused a sensation and was headline news all over the country, until it was crowded off the front pages by the sinking of the *Titanic* a month later. Eventually, all the fugitives were apprehended and brought to trial. Floyd and Claude Allen were executed and the others all served prison terms. To this day, many feel that Floyd and his family were the subjects of political persecution and that the executions amounted to judicial murder. It is beyond the scope of this article to go into the details of the cases for and against the Allens or the echoes of the incident that reverberate still in Carroll County a century later. Numerous books have been written about the subject (I've provided a short bibliography at the end of this piece). All curious to more than a few, but for me, it was the guns of that Floyd Allen trail that interested me and really what this essay is about. Now, to give fair credit, much of the information given below is taken from Ronald Hall's book, *The Hillsville Courthouse Tragedy.* Many details are missing, but it's possible to make educated guesses as to who was armed with what based on this book and surviving pictures of the participants.

In 1912, Virginia—even the rugged and isolated southwestern region—was hardly a frontier society. Nevertheless, many frontier attitudes and traditions persisted; a sense of complete and absolute personal independence, reliance for success solely on self and kin, and contempt for the very concept of government (many residents had fought for the Confederacy or were the children of those who had), were still strong. Too, and far more common then than today, was the tradition of going

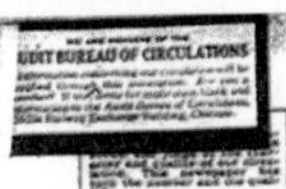

THE ROANOKE TIMES.

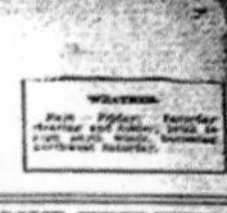

VOLUME LI—NO. 53. 12 PAGES ROANOKE, VA., FRIDAY MORNING, MARCH 15, 1912 12 PAGES. PRICE: THREE CENTS.

JUDGE T. L. MASSIE AND TWO COURT OFFICERS MURDERED BY ALLEN GANG AT HILLSVILLE

Tragedy in Carroll County Court Room Follows Conviction of Floyd Allen For Complicity in Escape of a Prisoner---After Penitentiary Sentence Is Pronounced by Jurist Mountaineers Begin Fusillade of Bullets and a Triple Murder Follows In the Hall of Justice.

POSSES PURSUE MURDERERS

JUDGE MASSIE HAD

Careers of the Slain Men

DEATH FUSILLADE IN COURT ROOM

Judge Massie Sustained Fatal Shots After Sentencing Floyd Allen.

FELL BLEEDING FROM THE BENCH

The Times Dispatch

RICHMOND, VA., TUESDAY, MARCH 19, 1912. PRICE TWO CENTS.

Repentant and Prayerful, Outlaw Leader Floyd Allen Wants Fellow-Murderers to Surrender and Stand Trial

NEW BISHOP GLAD HE IS HOME AGAIN

Cardinal, Too, Is Gratified That Good Man Will Rule Here.

INSTALLATION SERVICE TO-DAY

BANDITS KILLED IN RUNNING FIGHT

Two Escaped Convicts Shot Down and Third Surrenders.

FUGITIVE CAUGHT AFTER HARD CHASE

FORMER TERROR OF MOUNTAINSIDE IS OLD AND BROKEN

Trembling in His Cell, He Talks to The Times-Dispatch of His Troubles Following Fatal Battle in Courtroom

HE COULD HAVE ESCAPED, BUT REMAINED IN HILLSVILLE TO PROTECT FLEEING RELATIVES

SIDNA ALLEN AND GANG PENNED IN SQUIRREL'S SPUR FORTRESS, AND DAYBREAK MAY SEE BATTLE

SEARCH OF DETECTIVES IS FUTILE, AND ALLEN GANG STILL AT LARGE

about one's daily business armed. In the society of 1912, it was a given that any male adult could and would carry a gun. While it is today a felony to enter a courthouse armed, in that time it wasn't. Judge Massie's refusal to issue an order disarming everyone in the place is today regarded as hopelessly naïve, but his logic was completely consistent with the spirit of the time and place and with his regard for the Constitutional rights of citizens. So it was that not only spectators, but even the *defendant*, who came to the court ready to use force against force, and, thus, it was unfortunate for all present that day that Floyd Allen and his relatives were people prepared to do exactly that.

Floyd was armed with what is described as a "5 shot hammerless .38 Special," but this is probably a mistake, at least in regard to the caliber. No one in 1912 was manufacturing a hammerless .38 Special, though several companies did produce hammerless revolvers in the common .38 S&W caliber. The .38 Special had been introduced only a decade before, so, at the time of the courthouse shooting, the older .38 S&W round, dating from 1887 and far more common, was well suited to small and concealable revolvers.

Most likely Floyd carried a top-break S&W New Departure .38, colloquially referred to as "The Lemon Squeezer," an acknowledgement to the grip safety in the rear strap. This five-shot revolver would not fire unless firmly gripped and the safety depressed, a somewhat unusual feature in revolvers of that era. Top-break revolvers had come into widespread use by the 1870s and found great favor as personal-defense weapons. At one time, nearly every household in the Commonwealth probably had some sort of top-break revolver in a bedside drawer. The New Departure "Lemon Squeezer" was one of the best of these, a cash cow for S&W that sold steadily from its introduction, in 1889, until production ceased, in 1941. This revolver was an ideal concealed carry weapon of the age, being compact, reliable, easily reloaded, and respectably powerful by the standards of the day. According to contemporary accounts, Floyd had only four of the five chambers loaded. Leaving an empty chamber under the hammer was a common practice dating from the era of single-action revolvers, though the "New Departure" was safe to carry fully loaded.

Claude Allen has been described as having carried a "Colt .38 Special revolver," too, and, in this case, the serial

number is known: #63855. This firearm though, was not, in fact, a .38 Special. The only contemporaneous Colt that carried that serial number was a Model 1892 New Army, chambered in .38 Long Colt, the one-time official issue caliber of the United States Army. It's very possible, however, that Claude did in fact use .38 Special ammunition in it. Most 1892 New Armies will accept the .38 Special cartridge. Despite its case being a bit longer than the .38 Long Colt's, in all other dimensions the two cases are identical, and the Armies lack the "step" in the chamber that would have prevented the longer case from entering. At the same time, the .38 Special ammunition of 1912 was probably not powerful enough to create a serious hazard, even if Claude was aware of the difference between the two calibers, which he likely wasn't—he'd have used what was easiest to get.

According to Hall's account, Claude had left his gun at home, as he traveled on his way to his father's trial, but it was brought to him at the courthouse by Victor Allen, Floyd's other son. Victor was armed too. He was carrying a .32-caliber of unspecified make, most probably another top break and possibly what is sometimes called an "Owl Head." This would have been an Iver Johnson, the gun's nickname derived from the company logo of an owl's head molded into the gutta-percha grips. These Iver Johnsons were also immensely popular, in large measure because they sold for less than the S&W guns and still gave good service. There is dispute about whether Victor actually fired any shots himself, but there's no doubt he brought Claude the .38 he'd left home.

Others in the Court were armed with .38s, including Deputy Elihu Gillaspie, who probably also had a .38 Lemon Squeezer, and Deputy Frank Fowler, who was armed with a .38 Special with "a six inch barrel." Fowler's gun was either a Colt or S&W. A barrel that long would have been very awkward to conceal, and the gun would have been carried openly in a holster, especially if Fowler was on duty. Both Colt and S&W had contracts with police agencies, so, if this was Fowler's issue weapon, it would have been either the S&W Model of 1905 (later renamed the Military & Police) or Colt's competing product, the Police Positive Special. Both of these were high-quality guns, the best available in their time. In fact, the M&P is one of the most successful revolver designs ever introduced and is still made today.

Although .38-caliber guns were highly favored, not everyone who was armed that day was carrying one. Wesley Edwards—one of the boys who'd been in the fight that sparked the whole sequence of events—was carrying a .32-caliber revolver described as a Colt, so it wasn't a top-break action, because Colt didn't make those. The most likely candidate is the Colt New Police .32, more or less the same as the Police Positive, but in a lighter caliber. Later, while on the run with his uncle Sidna Allen, the latter described Wesley as armed with an "automatic pistol," not otherwise specified. Sidna was carrying a .32-caliber revolver and a "repeating shotgun" while on the lam.

Not everyone actually used a revolver. Some of the people in the court were using the "newfangled" semi-automatic pistols, including Sheriff Lew Webb. His choice of weapon may have got him killed: Webb had borrowed a Colt semi-automatic pistol from a relative before going to the courthouse and didn't know how to use it. That gun was a Colt Model 1903, designed by John Browning.

The Model 1903 was a slick and easily concealed gun in the .32 ACP caliber, one with a grip safety and a safety catch on the left side that also served as a slide lock. The Model 1903 was accurate, despite its rudimentary sights, but Webb's unfamiliarity with it may have had fatal consequences. Far more familiar with revolvers, which rarely have any sort of safety catch, the lawman might have fumbled trying to put the safety off. This could easily have taken long enough that one of the Allens had a window in which they could finish him off first. Oddly enough, Commonwealth's Attorney William Foster also carried a Colt .32 Automatic. Presumably he knew how to use it, as the gun belonged to him, but, in the end, he, too, was cut down.

Dexter Goad, Clerk of the Court, was also armed with an automatic pistol, this one described as a ".38 Automatic." There are two contemporaneous products that meet this description, Colt's Model of 1902 Military pistol and its smaller Model 1903 Pocket version, a gun essentially identical to the Military version except for barrel length. Both were chambered for the then-revolutionary .38 ACP caliber. Presumably, Goad was armed with the shorter and more easily concealed Model 1903. The "parallel ruler" locking mechanism used in that gun is the direct predecessor of the one used in the Model of 1911 .45 ACP, yet another result of the genius of John Browning. In fact, the Model 1903 was rather state-of-the-art, in 1912. Goad was very grievously wounded in the shootout, but survived.

Goad's Assistant Clerk, Woodson Quesenberry, also carried a Colt's autoloading pistol. It seems that Quesenberry was more interested in concealment than power, because he was toting a Model 1908 Vest Pocket in .25 ACP. This little "popgun," earning its name due to its tiny size, was one of Browning's most successful designs and widely imitated after its introduction. Browning had sold the design to FN, in Belgium, but Colt's had an exclusive license to manufacture and sell it in the Americas. Many, many thousands of Model 1908s were made by both firms up to the beginning of World War II, and they're still commonly encountered in shops today. The Model 1908 was a sleek seven-shooter, with no sharp edges or protruding parts. Though a decidedly minor contributor to the carnage, Quesenberry fired his little gun at least once in the course of events.

In the aftermath of the shooting, Floyd was captured almost immediately, but Claude Allen, Sidna Allen, Wesley Edwards, and Friel Allen fled the scene, triggering a manhunt. The Governor of the Commonwealth, William H. Mann, enlisted the services of the Baldwin-Felts Detective Agency of Roanoke, and also sent some National Guardsmen to the scene.

The Baldwin-Felts men were primarily armed with long guns, which were shown in the many dramatic photos for which they posed. The agency equipped most of its men with a frontier-era firearm, the Winchester Model 1873 rifle, better known as the "Gun that won the West." The Model 1873 was issued in several calibers, and it's not known

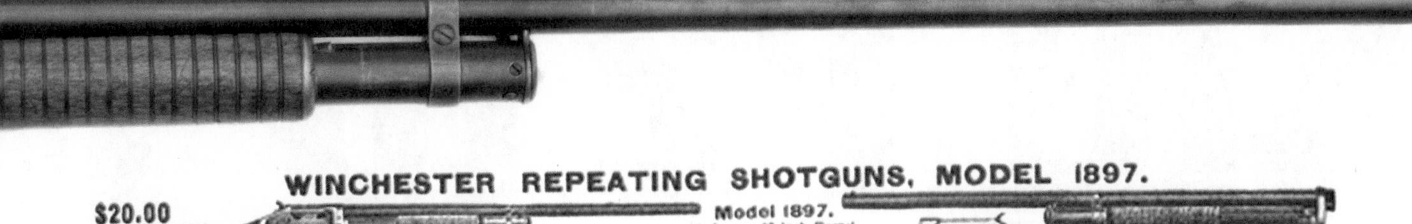

WINCHESTER REPEATING SHOTGUNS, MODEL 1897.

$20.00 — No. 6H550

Model 1897.
12-Gauge, 30-inch Barrel.

No. 6H560 — $21.60

THE PRICES on these goods are fixed by the manufacturers, and we are compelled to sell them at these prices. Every Winchester Gun is doubly guaranteed, both by the factory and ourselves, and in addition to the rigid examination given them by the factory, they are furthermore carefully inspected by our inspectors, and every Winchester Gun we sell is guaranteed to be perfect in material, workmanship and mechanical construction.

THIS IS THE IMPROVED MODEL WITH DOUBLE EXTRACTORS, constructed so that accidental discharge is impossible. The gun is operated by the sliding forearm, which, when pushed back, unlocks the breech box, ejects the empty shell, places another shell in the carrier, and cocks the hammer. To open gun when full cocked, press button at right side of frame. The stock is 13¼ inches long, 2¼-inch drop. The gun is fitted with blued steel barrel, chambered for 2⅝-inch and 2¾-inch shells. The take down gun can be taken apart in a moment's time, and as quickly assembled. There are no screws to lose, as when taken apart, the gun is in two parts, namely, the barrel and magazine, and stock and frame.

Catalogue No.	GRADE	Length of Barrel	Number of Shots	Weight	Price
6H550	Model 1897, Solid Frame	30 inches	6	7[illegible] pounds	$20.00
6H560	Model 1897, Take Down	30 inches	6	7[illegible] pounds	21.60

what the agency chose, but it most likely was the .44-40, the most powerful round chambered in this rifle. The .44-40 is said to have "... killed more game, large and small, and more men, good and bad, than any other caliber ever made." This certainly would have been a fine caliber for a manhunt in the brush-covered hills of laurels and dogwoods prevalent in Virginia. Also useful there would have been the detectives' handsome Winchester Model 1897 shotguns.

All in all, the detective force was ideally armed for a gunfight at short range—if they had ever managed to get within range of their quarry, which they didn't. Friel surrendered quickly, as did Sidna Edwards, saving the Baldwin-Felts Detective Agency some trouble. Claude Allen had been captured fairly soon after the manhunt began, but Wesley Edwards and Sidna Allen led the detectives a merry chase for five weeks through the hills and hollows they knew so well. As the Baldwin-Felts men hunted them in cold and wearisome March weather, often sleeping in the rain while staking out an alleged hiding place, the two fugitives received assistance from friends and relatives that enabled them to easily elude the bumbling agents of the law for as long as they did. After more than a month a on the run, the hue and cry died down a bit, and Sidna and Wesley simply went to a train station and rode away to work as carpenters in Des Moines, Iowa. They were captured six months later, when Wesley wrote to his sweetheart and revealed their location—to this day she is accused by Allen partisans to have "sold" them to the detectives.

Justice moved swiftly in those times. In September of 1912, Floyd and Claude Allen were tried for murder in the circuit court of nearby Wythe County (it was felt that they couldn't get a fair trial in Hillsville). Both were duly convicted and sentenced to death, though efforts were made to spare them that fate.
In the intervening year, the pair had actually become objects of sympathy in the eyes of the public. Allegations had been made that they had, in fact, acted in self-defense—to this day it's disputed who fired the first shots—and were being railroaded, victims of a conspiracy by their political enemies in Carroll County. Petitions to the Governor carrying thousands of signatures were circulated, but ultimately rejected. With Virginia's Governor Mann out of the state at the time, the Commonwealth's Lieutenant Governor attempted to finesse the situation with a last-minute commutation. But Governor Mann, on hearing of this, immediately returned to Commonwealth soil and issued an order to carry out the sentences. Floyd and Claude died in Virginia's electric chair, on March 28, 1913.

Modern forensic methods that might have helped sort out the actual sequence of shots and other crucial details were unknown in 1912, so the complete truth of exactly what happened in Hillsville will never be understood. But echoes of those long-ago shots still reverberate: a century after the fact, debate still rages in Carroll County and other parts of southwestern Virginia as to what *really* occurred, including whether the Allens were guilty as charged, as well as if they were "judicially murdered" for reasons of political and personal rivalry. The family names of the participants are still common in that part of the world, and descendants on both sides of the divide still argue the case for and against the Allen clan.

Was justice served? That will always be the question, but some answers to that puzzle are likely somewhere in a dusty evidence vault or private collection in the form of the actual guns used, they having long outlived those who fired them in anger, despair, or self-defense. They remain—wherever they may be a century later—as mute, inanimate, and perhaps even immortal artifacts forever linked to a tragedy that could perhaps have been avoided, had the living, thinking, flesh-and-blood men involved chosen to try.

Bibliography

Hall, Ronald W. *The Carroll County Courthouse Tragedy: A True Account of the Gun battle that Shocked the Nation; Its Causes and the Aftermath.* 1998. Carroll County Historical Society (Hillsville).

Lord, W. G. *The Red Ear of Corn.* 1999. Blue Ridge Institute & Museum (Ferrum).

Virginia Law Register 18 (11):840-842. *Claude S. Allen v. Commonwealth and Floyd Allen v. Commonwealth. Richmond, January 15, 1913. [7 Va. App. 271.]* 1913.

Credit & Acknowledgements

The Honorable Michael Valentine, Fairfax County Court (Retired)

Mr William G. Lord

Mr Ronald W. Hall

The Roanoke Times Archives

Roanoke Public Library

Woodcuts, Engravings, & Photos

1902 Sears Roebuck Catalog, reprinted by *Gun Digest*

1889 Great Western Gun Works Catalog, reprinted by *Gun Digest*

Mr. K. Nasser

The New York Times Archives

SIG P210-9

—A Classic for the Ages, Made New

BY PATRICK SWEENEY

Okay, so it's "only" a single-stack magazine. How many rounds of superbly accurate 9mm are you going to need? Besides, the P210 is brilliantly accurate and a joy to shoot, and that's excuse enough.

If you hear the phrase "classic IPSC," your thoughts will probably drift to a single-stack 1911, most likely a Colt, chambered in .45 ACP. It will not have a red dot sight, it won't have a compensator, and, if you were active back then, it probably has some funky, hand-cut checkering.

The first IPSC World Shoot was held in 1975, in Zurich. The second and third were each a year later, then the three after that at two-year intervals, until, beginning in 1983, the schedule was changed to every three years. The inaugural World Shoot was won by Ray Chapman, using a 1911 in .45. However, the championships were not won with a .45 again until 1979. In between, in Salzburg, Austria, and Salisbury, Rhodesia, they were won with a 9mm. Heresy. Worse yet were the pistols that were used. In 1977, Dave Westerhout used a Browning Hi-Power, and, in 1976, Jan Foss had used a SIG P210. The IPSC world in the late 1970s was all abuzz, and people were fairly concerned. Not only had 9mms been used to win, but one of them had even been a single-stack!

The P210 began life before WWII, when the Swiss determined that the M-1900 Lugers they had been using were perhaps not the best military sidearm to be had. In 1900, the Luger was cutting edge, and the .30 Luger cartridge it was chambered in was a real hot number. But, by the late 1920s, it was clearly not up to snuff. So, the Swiss Army embarked on a replacement plan. They liked the technical designs of Charles Petter and licensed the principles of his M1935, which had been adopted by the French. The Swiss wisely adopted the idea, but not the actual French pistol, itself an under-powered little beast. The irony of a Swiss designer developing a French pistol that the Swiss then had to pay to license is a head-scratching one. But I guess Charles wasn't the first one to find a warmer reception away from home.

Advancing plans for the new gun was slowed with the start of WWII, since the Swiss had bigger problems than replacing useable, albeit less than optimum, sidearms. But the advancement didn't entirely stop, and, once the war was over, the Swiss proceeded to finish testing and adopting their new pistol. In Swiss service it was known as the Pistole 49, in 9mm Parabellum, .30 Luger, and .22LR. The first and last are obvious choices; the Swiss wanted the 9mm for its greater performance and common

Specifications

Type:	Hammer-fired semiauto
Caliber:	9mm Parabellum
Capacity:	8+1
Barrel:	4.7"
Overall length:	8.5"
Width:	1.3"
Height:	5.6"
Weight:	37.4 oz
Finish:	Nitron
Grips:	hardwood wrap-around
Sights:	steel patridge
Trigger:	single action
Price:	$2,199
Manufacturer:	Sig Sauer

availability, while the rimfire made for an inexpensive practice pistol. But 7.65X21? Remember, in the Swiss defense system, every citizen is a member of the defense. Once through basic training, everyone goes home with a rifle and ammo and, when they retire, they generally retain the individual weapons. A family may have four or five generations of smallarms locked in the home armory. When adopted in 1949, the Swiss had a half-century of the .30 Luger ammunition existing as the established standard, and there was probably a large amount of it on hand. Since the difference was a new barrel and recoil spring, why not make it in 7.65?

The P210 is a single-stack, all-steel 9mm, and the aspects of the Petter design that the Swiss adopted were worth it. The military pistols were clearly products of their time and place. The grips were wood or plastic, and there was a half-rectangle steel bracket on the left side of the frame, with the grip on that side cut away for clearance. Given that the lanyard loop, safety, and slide stop were all on the left side, convenient for right-handed shooters, I have to conclude that no one in the Swiss Confederation is born left-handed. If there was ever a lanyard clipped to the loop, I'm not sure you could comfortably shoot the P210 left-handed.

Below the lanyard loop was the heel clip, the typical European method of retaining magazines. I have long wondered what the horror or fear of magazines falling free is, such that it grips European firearms designers (or buyers) with the need for such a three-handed design. It also had a magazine disconnector, so, when the magazine was out, it was a steel club. The Swiss Army replaced the P210 with the SIG P220, in 1975, but production of the P210 continued until 2005. I can easily imagine that the P210/Pistole 49 continued to be made because people still wanted it.

One big reason for this is the gun's accuracy. However, used P210s couldn't satisfy the market for highly accurate, beautifully machined pistols, so, SIG Sauer undertook a slight redesign and began making them again. The one we have here is the P210-9, the modern version of the P210, and the improvements have all been for the good.

First up, one aspect of the original that was not all that satisfactory was the shape of the tang. Designed back when handguns were still being fired one-handed, the tang worked fine for a

Here you can see the trigger package retention screw (no need to remove it) and the hammer strut and spring.

The magazine well is now beveled, for faster magazine changes. Back in 1949, no one cared about fast mag changes. Now we do, so the P210 has been updated.

The extractor is external, but set into the slide and protected from just about everything.

low-thumb, one-handed hold. But the moment you tried to fire it with anything like a modern grip, you would pay the price. I am particularly disadvantaged in this regard, and the original P210, along with a select few other pistols, is one I simply cannot shoot without assistance, as in I have to wear gloves or prepare my hand with duct tape before shooting. If I do not, I will bleed. Not an exaggeration, shooting a P210 can have me bleeding like a stuck pig, in less than a box of ammo. With a pristine P210 going for more than two grand, you can imagine the looks of horror that would create from the owner who so rashly loaned me one. The -9 variant, imported by the SIG Sauer folks in New Hampshire, has a re-designed tang. It is now in the same league as a beavertail safety on a custom 1911 and protects the hand from the hammer. I was able to spend a full day shooting the new 210 without fear of bleeding.

The new 210 has a proper, American-style magazine catch. Nestled right behind the trigger guard, it allows the magazine to drop free when pushed. And, yes, the magazine does drop free, there being no magazine disconnector in the new pistol.

The grips, since they do not have to accommodate a lanyard loop, are symmetrical, but not interchangeable. They are made of oiled hardwood, and the fit is such that you can remove the grip screw (a torx-headed screw, by the way) and still have little or no fear of losing the grips. In fact, if you aren't careful, you risk damaging the grips, trying to take them off the frame.

The grip shape, under the grips, makes no concession to hand shape. The front strap is proportioned for your hand, but the rest of the frame is simply a place to hold the magazine. The grips are expected to make the grip fit your hand. That's a proper bit of engineering.

The thumb safety is not what people will expect. Instead of being a lever at the back of the frame, like the 1911, it is a lever in front of the grip. Your thumb can reach it, but, if you haven't practiced with it, it will be a bit awkward. On the -9, the safety is fitted so as to be easy to move back and forth (or up and down, if you will), and it is only the thickness of the grip panel that makes it a bit of a reach. If you really wanted to use the 210-9 as a competition gun and had to have ready access to the safety, you could carve on the grip to make that possible. You might want to consider doing so to a spare grip set, so you will have the original grips un-molested for the future.

The slide stop is big, hard to miss, and, for me, a bit in the way. My thumb is long enough to reach it in my firing grip, and the slide stop is big enough to bump, if I'm not careful. Of course, on reloads, being big and hard to miss is good, because dropping the slide via the "slingshot" method isn't easy.

The slide on the -9 has fixed sights, with both the front and rear held in transverse dovetails. An interesting detail, laid out in the owner's manual, is that both the front and rear come in a variety of sizes (denoted with numerical markings), so that, if a particular pistol is off the sights, the blades can be swapped, mixed, and matched until it is dead on. The brother P210 that SIG is importing is the P210 Legend Target, which has an adjustable rear sight.

The 210-9 lacks a barrel bushing; the Swiss are clearly comfortable with the idea of precision machining and keeping the tolerances close enough so that they can produce an accurate pistol without the need of a bushing. Disassembly is easy. Unload and then ease the slide back a quarter-inch or so. Press the slide stop out to the left and, once it's clear, you can slide the upper assembly off the frame. The recoil spring is a captured unit, and it has an interesting attention to detail—the head of the recoil spring assembly has stamped on it the torque limits of the rod assembly. The "5 Nm" is newton-metres, a measure of torque, which translates to just over 44 pound-inches. In other words, it's tightened down about the same as a scope mount screw and meant to stay there.

The recoil spring guide rod has a hole in the end, and it is part of what the slide stop shaft passes through. The barrel lugs are like the cam slot of other pistols that you may be more familiar with (no

The grip screw is a torx type (as is the trigger package screw), so make sure you have one of these (a No.15, specifically), when it comes time to work on your P210.

link here), but with a twist. The lugs are made as a pair and widely-spaced (as handgun parts go), so they provide a wide base for the barrel on the slide stop. I have to think that has something to do with the accuracy. The barrel locks into the slide the same way as every other Browning-derived pistol does, with lugs on the barrel engaging slots in the slide.

One aspect of the P210 is obviously contrary to the way things are now done. The rails on the frame are on the inside, while the rails on the slide are on its outside. The idea was to reduce wear and retain accuracy. It also increased potential accuracy, but not due to the inside-outside design. A secondary aspect of the design is that the contact between the slide and rails extends a lot further on the 210 than it does on other pistol designs. Think of it like sight radius: the further apart the sights are, the easier it is to notice aiming errors. On rail contact, the further apart the front and back contact points are, the more aligned the slide and frame will be. I love the 1911, but the P210 has twice the rail

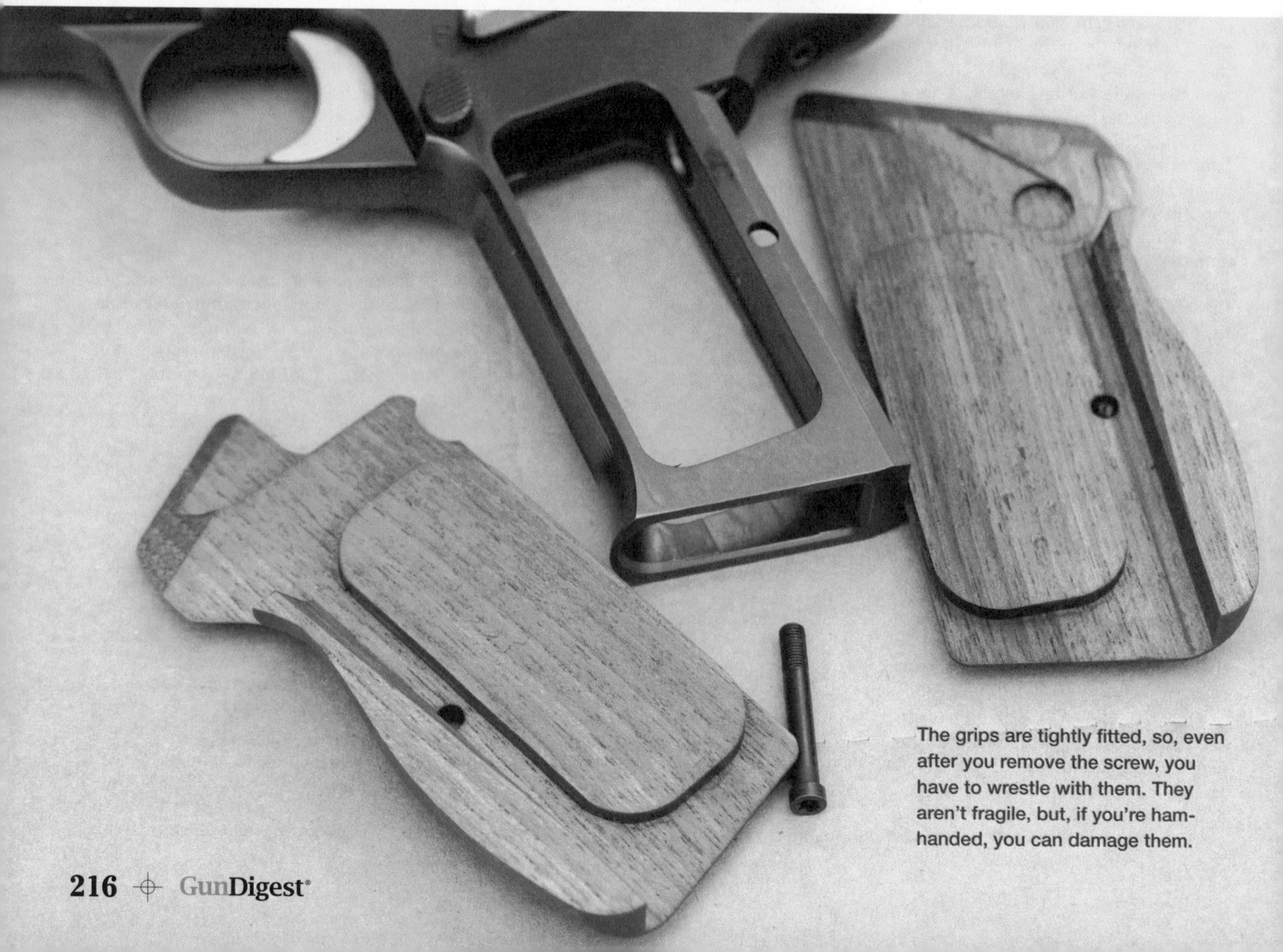

The grips are tightly fitted, so, even after you remove the screw, you have to wrestle with them. They aren't fragile, but, if you're ham-handed, you can damage them.

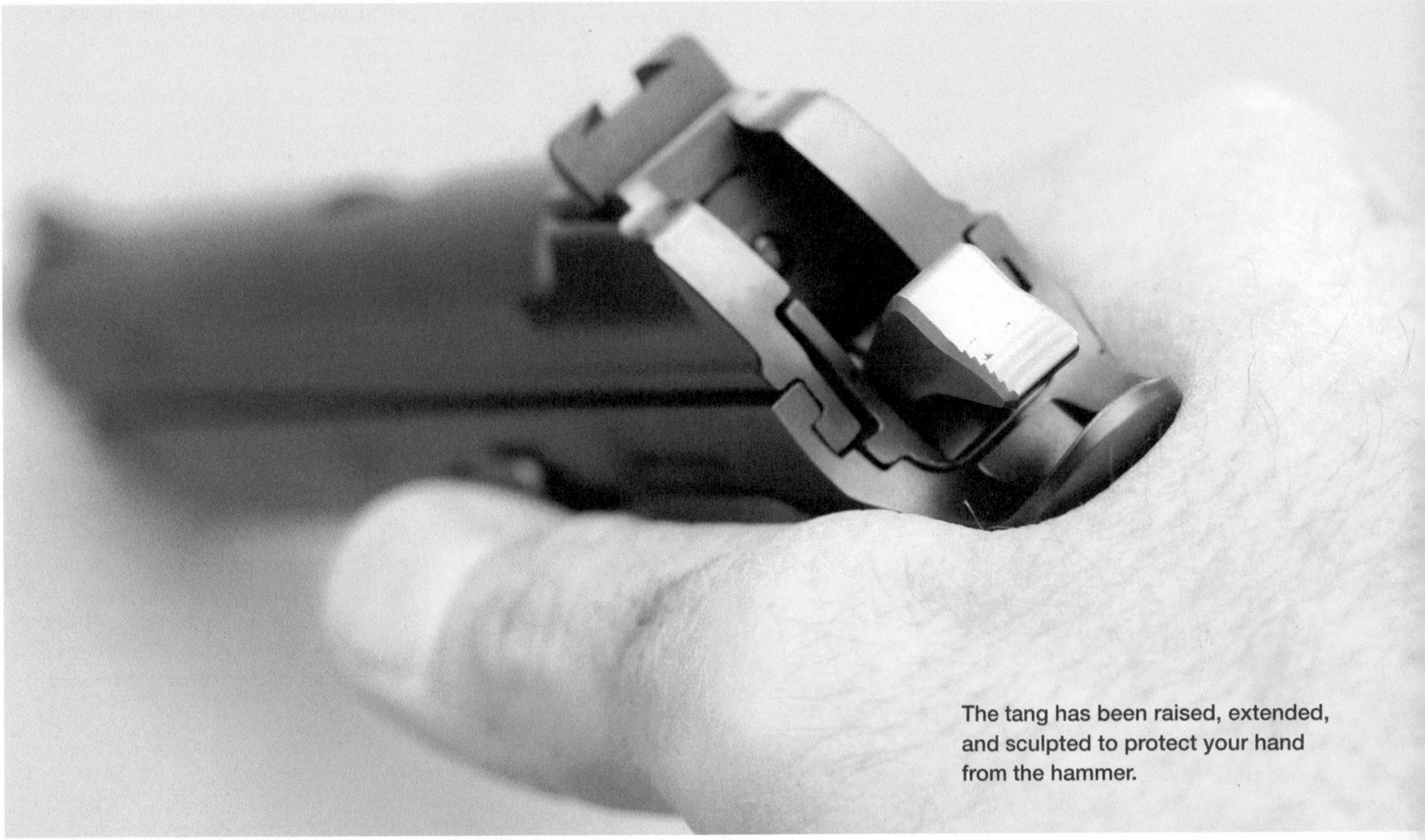

The tang has been raised, extended, and sculpted to protect your hand from the hammer.

length as the Browning. That increases repeatability, which improves accuracy.

One of the Petter details included was a hammer/sear assembly that went into or came out of the frame as one piece. No separate hammers, sears, etc. Now, I see this mostly as an organizational advantage. If you are the armorer of a police force or military unit, you can have a set of pistols that are issued to the troops, and you can have, in the armory, a selection of assembled, tested, and sealed units. If someone has a problem or a pistol shows wear, it is perhaps a minute to swap out the old, install a new, and send the owner on their way. No down-time for the officer or pistol, and now you, the armorer, can work on the recalcitrant assembly without someone hanging over your shoulder or having to deal with the paperwork of checking in the busted

The magazine catch is now in the normal place, behind the trigger guard.

The P210 safety pivots under the grip, pushed by the tip of your thumb. It is there so the hammer/sear assembly can be removed as a single unit. Actually, very clever, even if it only blocks the trigger bar.

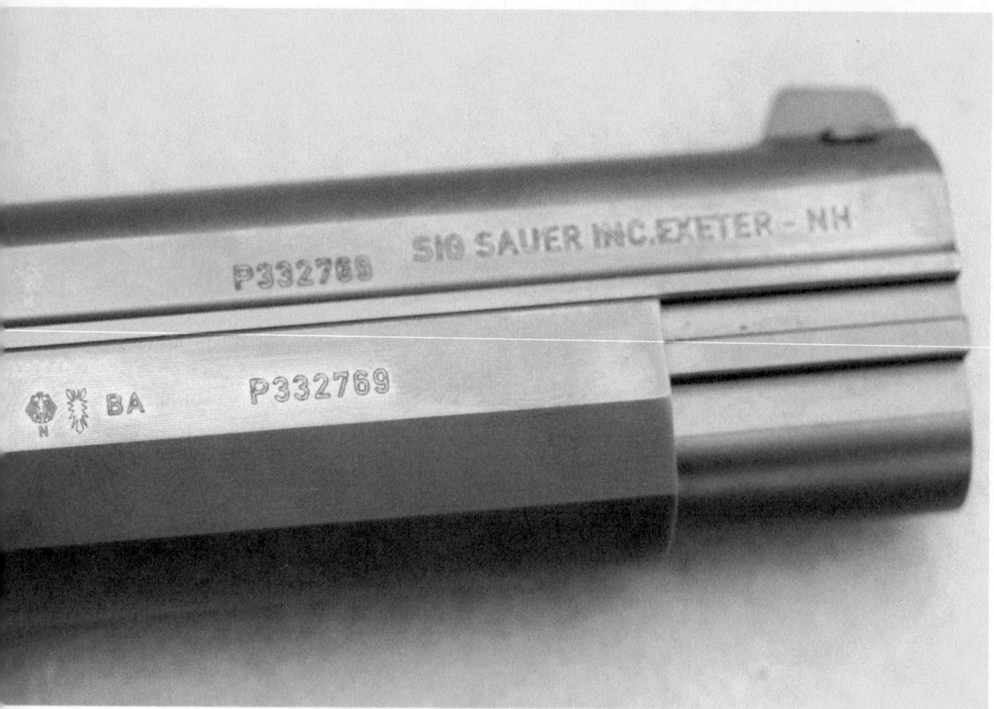

pistol, issuing a new one, and repeating all that when the repair is done.

But for that, it is a cracking good idea, and, had I a hat, off it would be to the Swiss for having adopted it. For us, however, it doesn't matter much. The trigger assembly and its removal isn't mentioned in the owner's manual (SIG would be very happy if you just left it alone), and unlike the old design, where the assembly was held in with a pin, the -9 has the assembly locked in place by means of a screw up through the tang. Again, it's a torx, and there's no need to remove it. If you do, you're on your own.

The slide and frame are machined from steel billets, given a satin matte surface, and then treated to the SIG Nitron finish. The trigger, safety, hammer, and slide stop are left bright, but not polished to a mirror finish.

The interesting thing—as if all the above was of no interest—is the trigger. We are used to light and crisp, or "combat" and crisp, and the Swiss

Made in Germany, and so stamped by the Proof House.

Here you can see the torque spec on the recoil spring assembly, as well as the wide cam lugs of the barrel feet.

clearly have a different idea about these things. The trigger is light, but it has take-up, and then it has travel, which, if you aren't slowly pressing, feeling as you go, feels the same. It's almost as if it were the world's shortest double-action PPC trigger. I first felt a trigger like this when test-firing an Stg90, the Swiss military rifle in 5.56. That trigger was light, but with enough travel that you know you're pulling the trigger. On the -9, this took a bit of dry-firing to get used to, as I found transitioning from "regular" triggers to the P210 trigger to be too much in one range session. When I tried, I ended up nearly perforating my chronograph a few times, as I, too, up the slack on the P210 trigger and shot sooner than anticipated.

But, I'm glad I persisted. I've been mentioning accuracy all along, and the P210 is a scary-accurate kind of handgun, a one-inch-groups-at-25-yards kind of handgun. And, unlike some pistols, the P210 did not get picky about what it liked to shoot. Yes, it shot better with

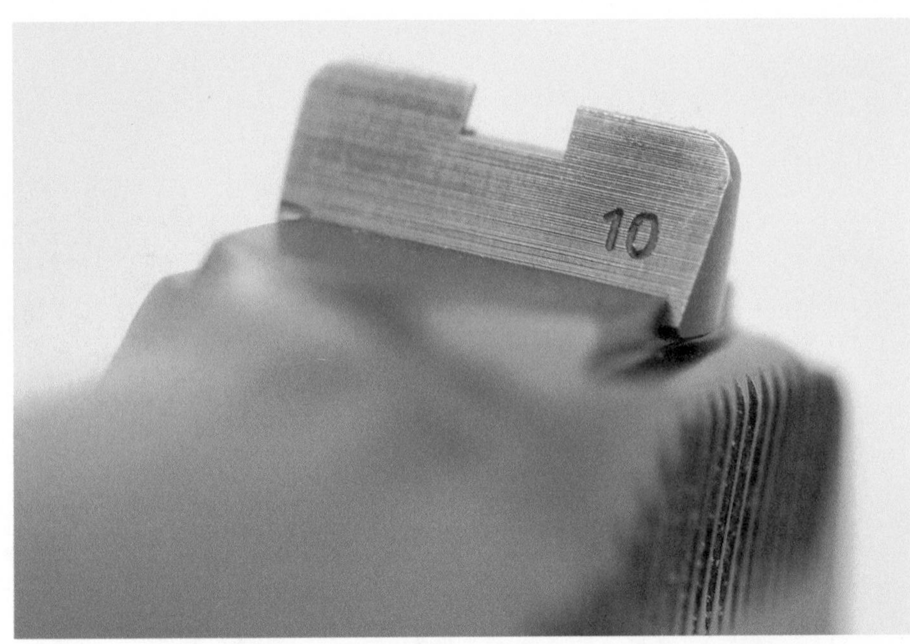

Sights are marked, so they can be changed to adjust the zero. Very Swiss and German.

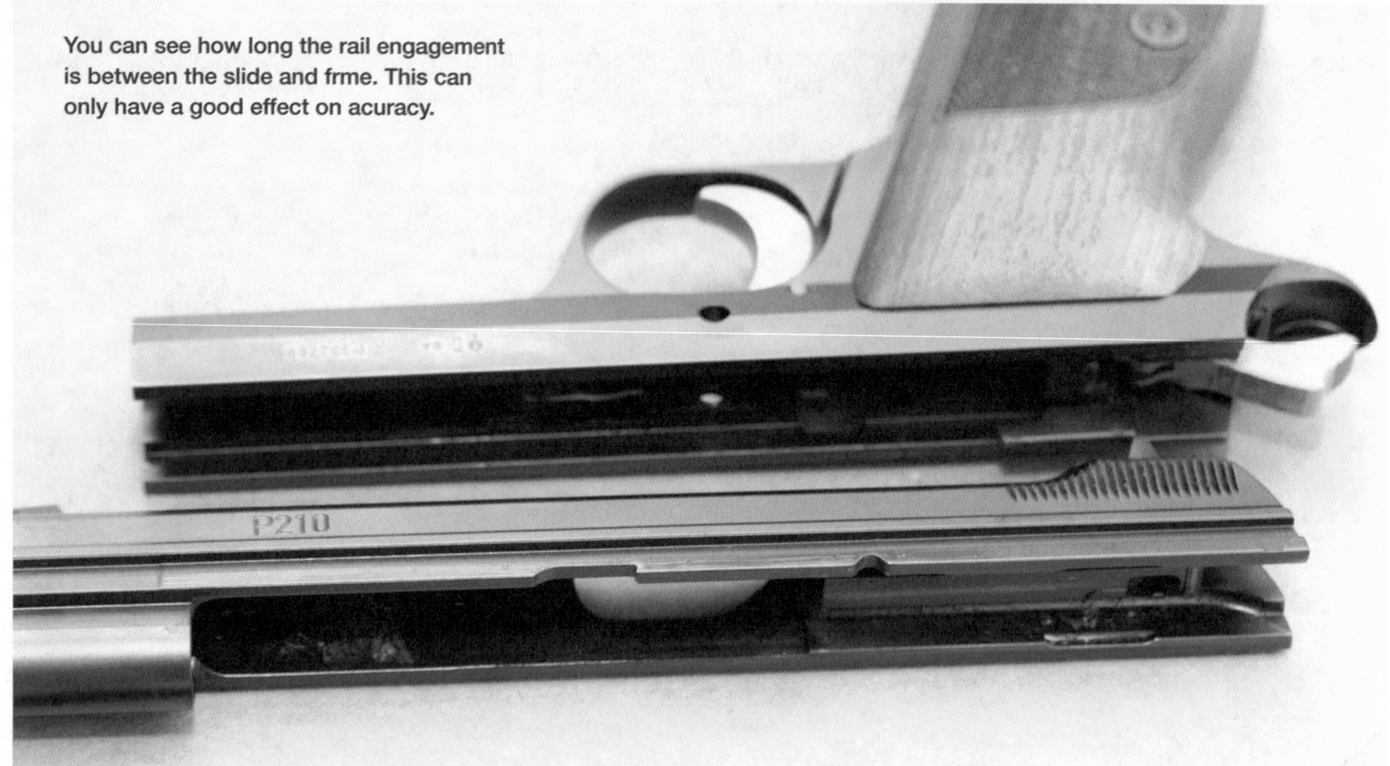

You can see how long the rail engagement is between the slide and frme. This can only have a good effect on acuracy.

some, but the differences were almost immeasurable. I mean, if one ammo groups a quarter-inch larger or smaller than another, can we really say the pistol "prefers" it? That level of accuracy, and that small of a difference, requires several things. First, a Ransom rest, of which mine is on loan and for which I do not have a set of P210 holders. Second, you need a pile of ammo, all of it with the potential for gilt-edged accuracy. And you need the the time to shoot groups, and I mean statistically significant groups, not your basic five-shot groups and not even four consecutive five-shot groups, but real number-crunching efforts like five ten-shot groups with each brand and bullet-weight ammo. This is the kind of shooting that's a full-time job by itself.

So, once I had done the usual group-testing, I amused myself by plinking—on the 100-yard range. Pick an object, something safe to shoot at. Aim, press. OK, it got hit, now what? Pick something smaller. Same results. This handgun is almost scary to shoot,

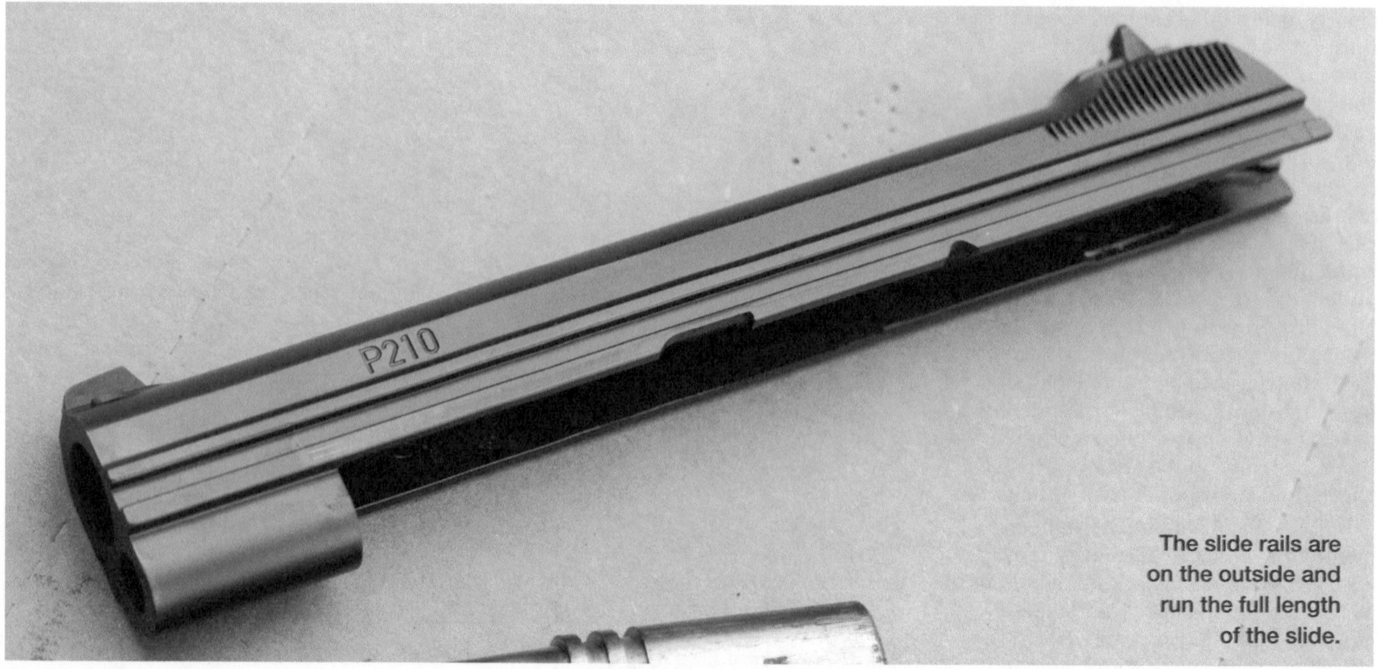

The slide rails are on the outside and run the full length of the slide.

SIG P210 CHRONOGRAPH AND ACCURACY DATA

Bullet make/type	Bullet Weight (grains)	Velocity (fps)	Standard Deviation	Accuracy (group inches)
Hornady FTX	115	1,131	14.2	1.0
Hornady XTP	115	N/A	33.7	1.0
Hornady XTP	147	N/A	15.3	1.5
Winchester PDX1	147	999	32.0	1.5
Winchester Ranger JHP+P+	115	1,389	10.3	1.75
Federal Guard Dog	105	1,235	21.3	1.00
Speer Lawman TMJ	115	1,256	34.8	1.5
Wilson Combat XTP+P	115	1,285	19.2	1.5
Black Hills (Red) JHP	115	1,272	7.6	1.0
CorBon JHP+P	125	1,249	10.5	1.5
Asym Action Match JHP	125	1,149	15.1	0.75

NOTES: Accuracy results are averages of 4, 5-shot groups at 25 yards off an MTM K-Zone shooting rest. Velocities are averages of 10 shots measured on a PACT MKIV chronograph set 15 feet from the muzzle.

This is a normal target for the P210, as long as the shooter pays attention and does their part.

and a little intimidating to own. Imagine owning a handgun and knowing that, if you shoot it at the gun club, everyone knows that any miss, any shot that drops a point is your fault and not the gun's. A P210 would be brilliant for shooting in a PPC league. Do some experimental reloading, find a load that shoots small groups (won't be too difficult), hits to the sights, and prepare to have your average rise.

One small obstacle might be magazines. With an MSRP of $72 each, you will want to take really good care of them and not let them get stepped on during the winter indoor leagues and tight range spaces. You certainly don't want to drop them on concrete with the same abandon you'd jettison a $15 1911 magazine. But, if you can see your way to four or five of them, you'll have a tack-driving 9mm to shoot.

Oh, and those early days of IPSC? After Ross Seyfried won the World Shoot in 1981 with a very plain, by today's standards, .45 1911, the world changed. Starting with Robbie Leatham, in 1983, the .38 Super was king of the hill. Then, in 1990, the 9X21 gained glory, and that's the way it has been. There will not be another World Shoot champion using a .45 ACP pistol until 2014. Maybe. Then, the new Single-Stack/Cassic Division will be contested, and the .45 has a chance again—unless someone wants to give it a try with a P210. This one is certainly up to it.

BAT MASTERSON'S POCKET P

"A tenderfoot with a Savage Automatic and the nerve to stand his ground could have run the worst six-shooter man the West ever knew right off the range." So is quoted W. B. "Bat" Masterson of the 1907 Savage Pocket Pistol.

I was not aware of this glowing tribute by Bat Masterson to this model Savage Arms gun, when I found and purchased one at a gun show. Mine was a Savage Arms automatic pistol in .32 Auto caliber, and what struck me, while examining the small gun, was that there was not a single screw showing on the outside of it. The gun displays a deep blue finish, with slight wear, and the trigger shows the bluish swirled designs of color case hardening. The hard rubber grips wear the familiar

Dodge City Peace Commissioners, from left to right: Chas. Bassett, W.H. Harris, Wyatt Earp, Luke Short, L. McLean, Bat Masterson, Neal Brown.

Savage Arms Pocket Automatic Model 1907

Caliber:	.32 ACP
Magazine Capacity:	10 Rounds (Double Stack)
Barrel Length:	3½ inches
Material:	Blued Carbon Steel
Length:	6⅝ inches
Height:	4¼ inches
Thickness:	1 inch
Weight (w/empty mag.):	20 ounces
Weight (w/full Mag.):	23 ounces

BY DUANE FREEMAN

STOL

Indian head symbol of the Savage Arms Company of Utica, New York. There was the slight scent of Hoppe's No. 9 powder solvent, and the bore of the gun showed a bright mirror reflection upon using a bore light. The little pistol contains a 10-shot magazine, and with a barrel of 3¾ inches and an overall length of 6½ inches, it is a handy pocket gun and a fine example of quality workmanship of the gun maker's art.

The 1907 Savage Pocket Pistol was designed by Major Elbert H. Searle, previously an ordnance officer at the Springfield Armory. According to John T. Callahan, a Savage Arms researcher, this particular gun was sent from the factory to the Savage Arms warehouse on July 13, 1913. The gun was originally sold to the Dentz Company, that business' address unknown. For some reason, the gun was returned to the factory and then shipped to the Dyas-Cline Company of Los Angeles, California. The price of the gun about that time was $15.

In 1909, the Savage Arms Company published a small booklet by W.B. "Bat" Masterson entitled, *The Tenderfoot's Turn*. The booklet, reprinted by Packbasket Publications of Tumwater, Washington, described the author as the "… Famous dead shot of palmy days of the old Southwest Trail" and the "Whilom Sheriff of Dodge City."

W.B. "Bat" Masterson joined the other Peace Commisioners in 1876, serving as a sheriff's deputy alongside Wyatt Earp, in Dodge City. Shortly after Masterson had arrived, he was criticized for his treatment of a man while arresting him. The local marshal jailed and fined Bat for this, but his fine was returned by the city council upon review and, within a few months, he was elected sheriff of Ford County, Kansas.

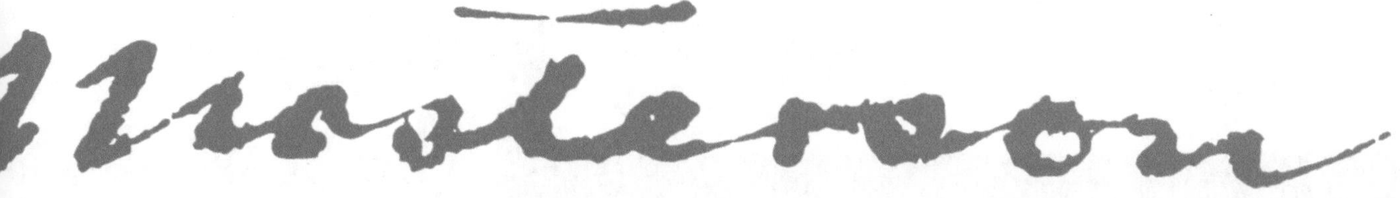

DODGE CITY

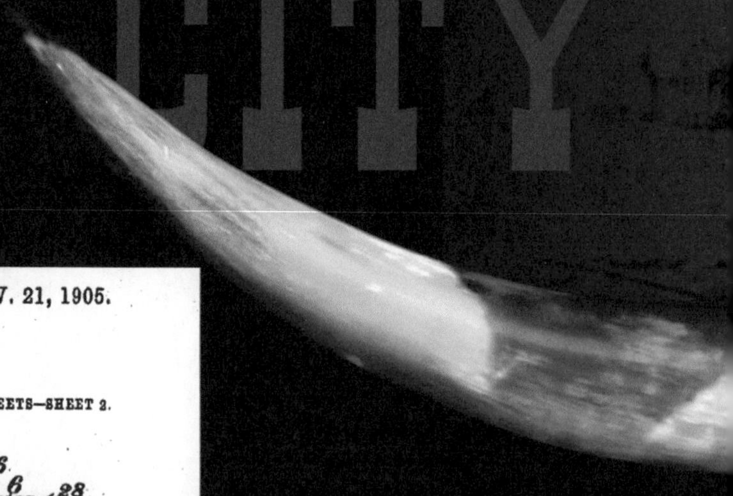

No. 804,985. PATENTED NOV. 21, 1905.

E. H. SEARLE.

FIREARM.

APPLICATION FILED OCT. 1, 1904.

4 SHEETS—SHEET 2.

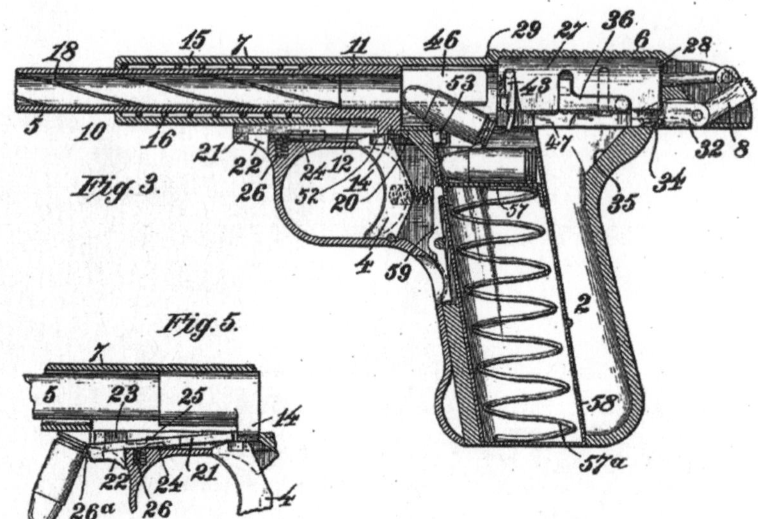

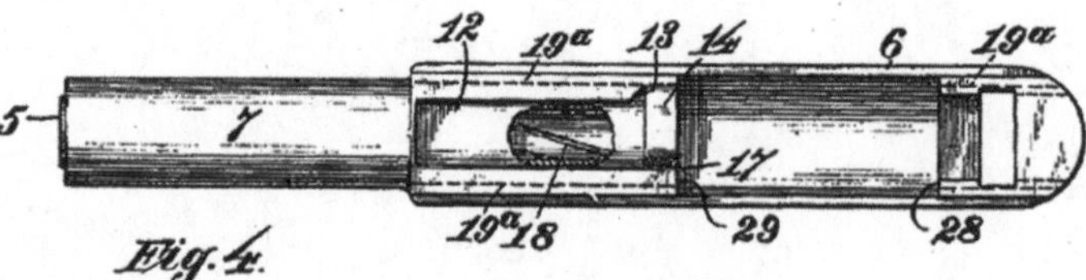

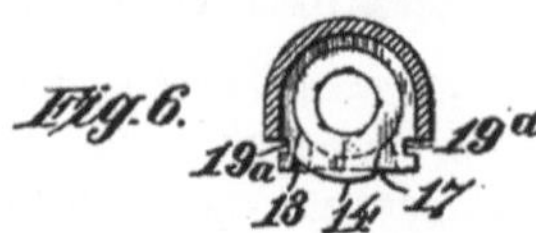

Witnesses:
H. S. Austin
Edwin S. Clarkson

Inventor
Elbert H. Searle
By Knight Bros
Attorneys.

In glowing terms, the booklet claimed the Savage Automatic was said to have been able to "... put the James Boys out of business before they got started." Also, that same booklet noted, "No woman who has a Savage Automatic need be afraid. Shoots straight without aiming and every crook fears it." Pretty impressive, but here's how Masterson, or at least the booklet, described the gun more fully:

The Savage Automatic Pistol is something entirely new and different in pocket

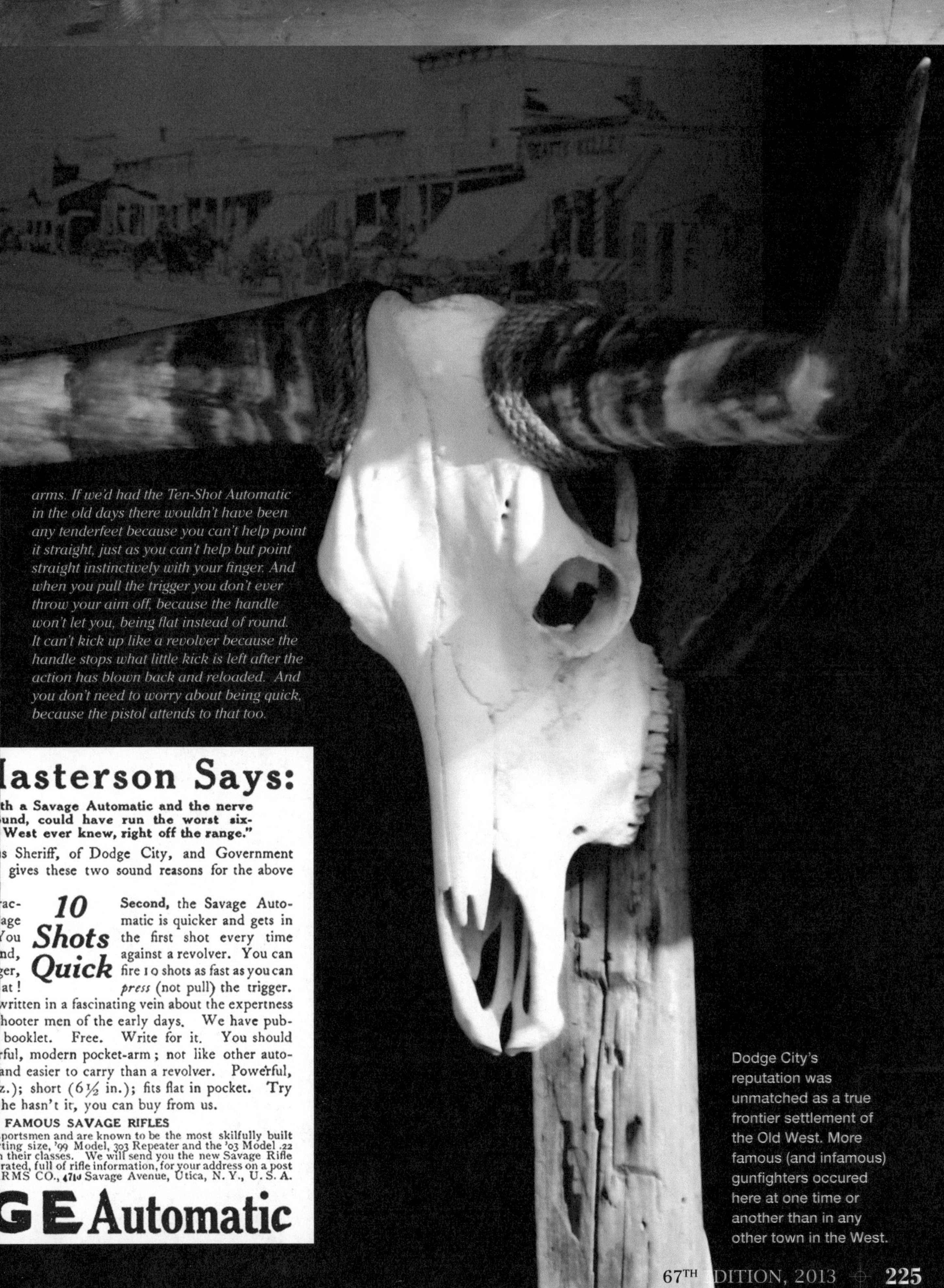

arms. If we'd had the Ten-Shot Automatic in the old days there wouldn't have been any tenderfeet because you can't help point it straight, just as you can't help but point straight instinctively with your finger. And when you pull the trigger you don't ever throw your aim off, because the handle won't let you, being flat instead of round. It can't kick up like a revolver because the handle stops what little kick is left after the action has blown back and reloaded. And you don't need to worry about being quick, because the pistol attends to that too.

Dodge City's reputation was unmatched as a true frontier settlement of the Old West. More famous (and infamous) gunfighters occured here at one time or another than in any other town in the West.

Savage comissioned Bat Masterson to write a promotion of Savage Pistols. It was originally copyrighted in 1909.

By 1886, the cowboys, saloon keepers, gamblers, and brothel owners moved west to greener pastures, and Dodge City became a sleepy little town much like other communities in western Kansas.

This statement from a man such as Masterson, a shooter familiar with firearms and a working knowledge of ballistics, is a bit hard to believe. Masterson had been a buffalo hunter, sheriff of Ford County, Kansas, a deputy U.S. Marshal, and marshal of Trinidad, Colorado. And Bat Masterson truly preferred the Colt Single Action Army in .45 Colt. He personally ordered nine guns from the Colt's factory. Why he had an affinity for the little Savage is a bit of a mystery—there are no surviving Savage Arms Company records indicating Masterson's endorsement of the Savage Pocket Pistol.

The .32 Auto was a popular pistol cartridge world-wide at the beginning of the twentieth century. Savage claimed the Model 1907 chambered in .32 Auto was so effective that it was adopted as the standard arm for commissioned officers of the Portuguese Army. The .32 Auto round was and is, however, a rather mild, insipid cartridge. One writer said it was very likely that anyone being hit with the .32 Auto would make that person angry—quite angry. Modern .32 Auto cartridges are a bit more potent, but even these are unlikely to run off "the worst six-shooter man of the West." Nor would this pocket pistol make an ideal woman's defense gun, as the slide is not easily moved to chamber a round.

As I said at the beginning, what I found fascinating is that no screws appear on the outside of the gun. However, take down is fairly simple without tools. After the magazine is removed and the chamber cleared, the safety catch is put on and the slide is pulled back by grasping the hammer and slide extension. The hammer is then pressed down tightly and rotated a quarter turn. The slide will then come off the gun.

The grips are retained by dovetail slots in the frame. They are removed by placing the first finger of each hand in the magazine well and pushing at the center of the grip. The resiliency of the hard rubber grips allows them to be snapped out with out breaking.

There are strict safety precautions in handling this little pocket pistol. If this gun is not kept thoroughly—and I do mean *thoroughly*—clean, the gun is prone to go fully automatic! Dirt, fouling, and buildup between the sear and the breechblock may cause the gun to fire as the slide slams foreword, resulting in multiple and unintentional repeat firing. My advice? If you find one of these interesting old pistols, think fondly of Bat Masterson and keep the gun clean!

MODEL 1907 SERIAL NUMBERS BY YEAR (APPROXIMATE)

Year	Serial Number Range	Number Produced*
1908	115	2,000
1909	115	13,000
1910	147	15,500
1911	147	20,000
1912	115	30,000
1913	105	19,500
1914	115	15,750
1915	115	14,250
1916	115	16,752
1917	125	17,748
1918	125	1,346
1919	125	38,004
1920	125	5,951
	Total Number of Model 1907 Pistols Made	209,791

* The disparity between the actual serial numbers and the number of pistols produced is caused by several unexplained gaps in the serial number sequence, along with the fact that Savage used some serial numbers for the Model 1915 and Model 1917 pistols.

Sources

Graham, Kopec, and Moore. *A Study of the Colt Single Action Revolver.* Taylor Publishing Company, Dallas, Texas, 1992.

National Rifle Association, *Illustrated Firearms Assembly Handbook.* National Rifle Association of America, Washington, D.C., Vol. 1, Page 48.

Research of original factory serial ledgers in Savage Arms Company files by J. T. Callahan, Arms Historian, Westfield, Massachusetts.

Savage Arms Company Catalogue No. 60, Utica, New York, Undated. Reprint by Packbasket Publications, Tumwater, Washington.

W. B. "Bat" Masterson. *The Tenderfoot's Turn.* Savage Arms Co., Utica, New York. 1909. Reprint by Packbasket Publications, Tumwater, Washington.

TIGHTENING UP THE M1 .30 CARBINE

—This little rifle is often dismal as issued, but it can be accurized

BY ROBERT K. CAMPBELL

The U.S. M1 .30 Carbine's sights are simple enough, but they are brilliantly quick on target at moderate range.

Among the most popular of all World War II firearms is the U.S. MI Carbine. In my opinion, there is no more enjoyable recreational shooter. Light, handy, light kicking, and very reliable, the Carbine has much to recommend.

The Carbine was not designed as a battle weapon, but rather as a PDW, or personal defense weapon. Of course, in 1940, that term hadn't yet been coined, but it was the gun's purpose, intended to give soldiers behind the lines a weapon light enough to be with them at all times. Tank crewmen, truck drivers, ammo bearers, and officers had previously been armed with a handgun. The idea was to give the troops a service weapon superior to the handgun, but not as heavy and difficult to manage as the M1 Garand. Winchester succeeded admirably, with the introduction of its .30 Carbine.

The M1 Carbine was a traditionally designed rifle in some ways. It featured the typical short stock, with much of the barrel exposed, same as the Springfield and Krag carbines. But the M1 Carbine featured a modern gas-operated action, and, as it featured a 15-round magazine, soldiers were provided a considerable reserve.

The cartridge was often the subject of discussion. The new round was not

The commercial Plainfield, above, is shown with a 30-round magazine. The WWII Inland, below, is shown with ammunition and accessories.

a full-power rifle round, but a unique, straight-walled cartridge that has sometimes been compared to magnum-class handgun rounds; it jolts a 110-grain jacketed bullet to a little over 1900 feet per second. The view of this by some was that it did not generate sufficient velocity for effective use past 200 yards—and some say the limit is just 100. Too, the bullet did not break at the cannelure as some bullets will, which means it basically pushed a .30 hole through the target. While criticisms as to the knockdown power of the Carbine are valid and it proved to be a somewhat ineffective battle rifle, in the end, the Carbine, was a wonderful PDW weapon.

The M1 .30 Carbine has remained popular. The little gun is very easy to use well and, by all accounts, has a reputation for sterling reliability. It is a

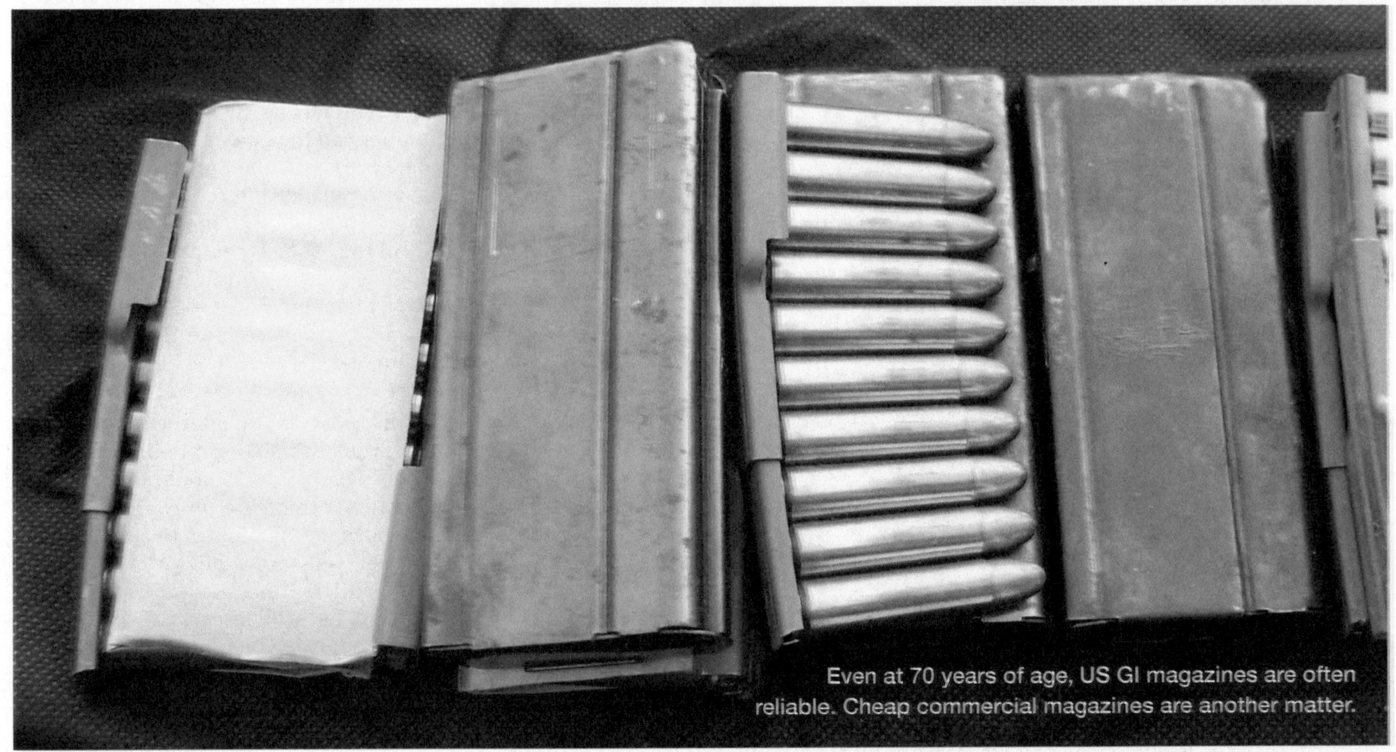
Even at 70 years of age, US GI magazines are often reliable. Cheap commercial magazines are another matter.

The Inland is shown with 15- and 30-round magazines and a supply of South Korean military ammunition.

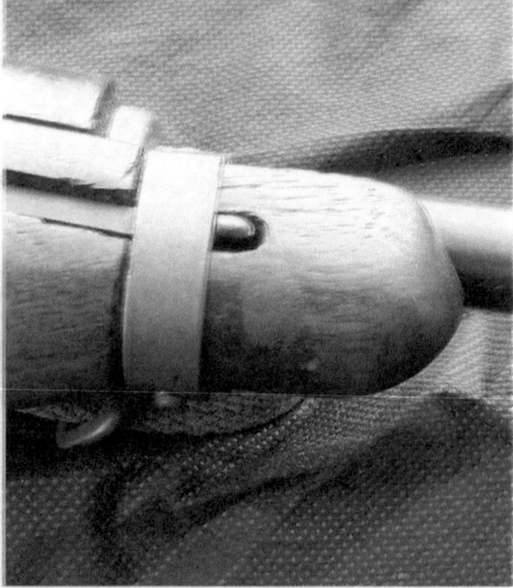

This is the narrower band for the M1 Carbine—it just doesn't look right.

great plinker and recreational shooter, and perfect for introducing youngsters to center fire rifles. Quite a number of police departments have availed themselves of the readily available and inexpensive .30 Carbine, employing the rifle for carry in police cruisers and for use in stake-out squads. In short-range work, when loaded with soft-point or hollowpoint ammunition, the rifle has also proven effective in the personal defense role. When I first became a peace officer, shootings with the Carbine were about as common as shooting with the .223 rifle these days. The Carbine is to be respected.

I own several Carbines, including an original World War II Inland Carbine. There is really no such thing as matching numbers on the guns you're likely to come across, as the Carbines had to have completely interchangeable parts. Just the same, my Inland is as tight as any of the other six million-plus Carbines produced during World War II. I also own a Plainfield commercial Carbine. The action seems tighter than that of the Inland, but the magazine catch and other controls are not as crisp.

This brings me to another shortcoming of the Carbine, right behind the power deficit of its ammunition. Truthfully, the Carbine is a bit rough around the edges when it comes to accuracy. Another well-known military rifle, the AK 47, suffers from much the same problem, but while the AK is what it is, the Carbine may be helped, and the advantage gained is often worth the effort.

I have fired my Carbines with South Korean military ammunition, jacketed

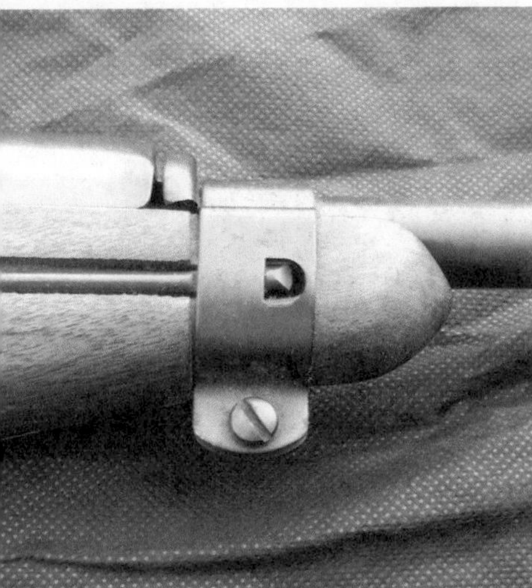

This is the wider, more desirable barrel band for the M1 Carbine.

This is the carbine receiver and the tang that butts into the recoil plate.

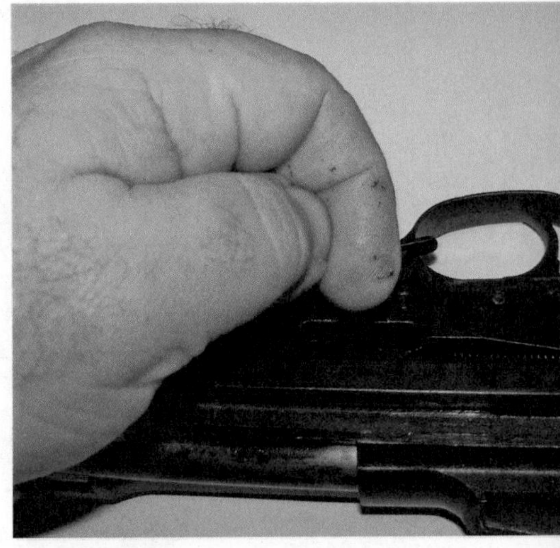

Clean the trigger group, and you may improve the action. The author ran his finger across the action of this carbine and came up with considerable congealed oil.

loads from the major makers, and the newer CorBon DPX loading. While the custom-grade CorBon loading is the most accurate, it is so only by a small margin. A pretty decent Carbine will give you a five-shot group measuring about five inches at 100 yards. An exceptional rifle will go three inches or a little more. For hitting a coyote at 35 yards, the Carbine excels. For long-range work, well, let's hope your aspirations are recreational. As for ammunition, I am certain there are handloaded combinations that must be more accurate than factory ammunition, but I handload primarily for economy, not for precision. I have tried the proven combinations, and while they are often more accurate than factory loads, it is not by any great margin.

Recently, I elected to tighten up my Carbines as best I could. I have become interested in the Carbines, due to the introduction of the exceptional new CorBon DPX load. Locating the Plainfield at a fair price at a pawn shop was a prompting to me, too, so there we go. The work was straightforward and produced good results, all we can ask.

First things first, you need to know what you're looking at to begin with. The rifle fieldstrips easily; the locking rat-tail tang at the rear of the receiver and the barrel band are all that hold the rifle together. (Such straightforward assembly works without complaint, but this system isn't a solid base for accuracy.) Take a look at the rear receiver tang, which engages the recoil plate that is in the stock. If the fit is good when assembled and there is a need to depress the barrel into the stock when fitting the barrel band, then you may have a more accurate rifle. If, on the other hand, the recoil plate fit is loose, the rifle is likely inaccurate.

The are several means of tightening up the Carbine that are worth a look. First and simplest is to simply tighten the screw holding the recoil plate to the stock. Admittedly, if this is loose, poor

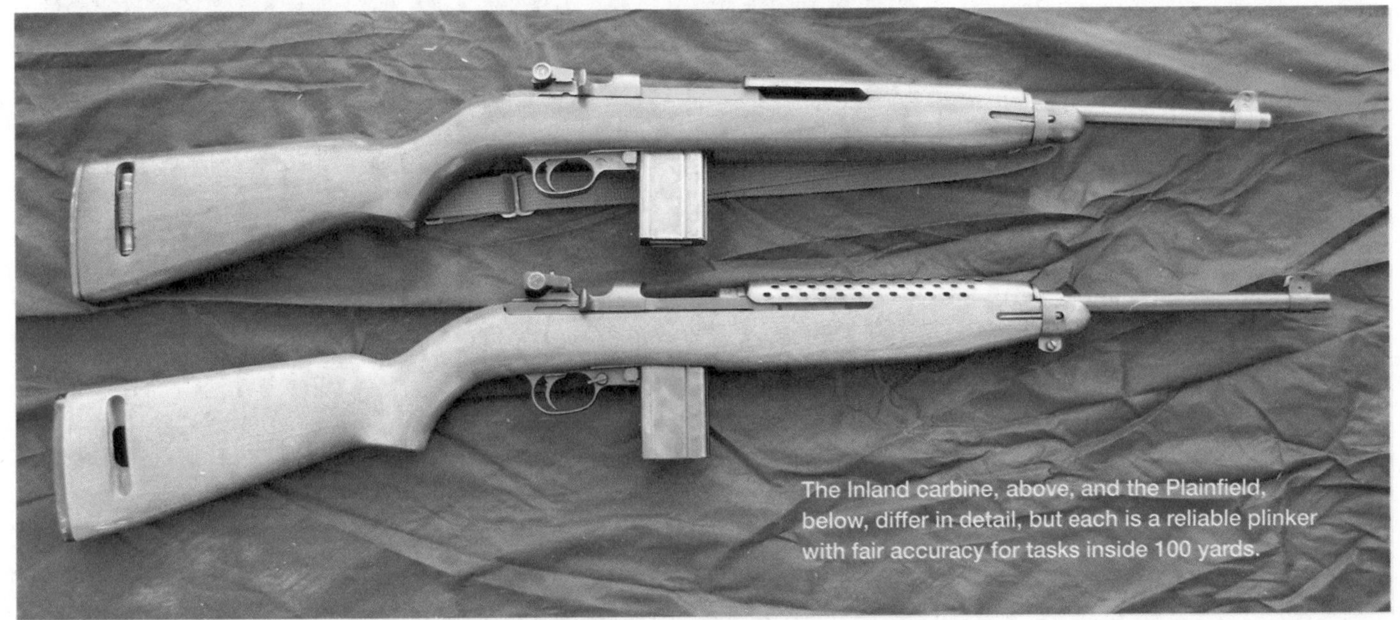

The Inland carbine, above, and the Plainfield, below, differ in detail, but each is a reliable plinker with fair accuracy for tasks inside 100 yards.

Right: Note the detail difference in these two carbine stocks. The stock on the right is in the more accurate rifle, one that is inletted ideally for a free-floating barrel.

Below: The Plainfield, left, compared to the Inland stock inletting configuration. The Inland is the more accurate rifle.

accuracy may not be noticeable at close range, but the looser groupings will be noticeable at 100 yards. It is easier to tighten the recoil plate effectively if the recoil plate is fully fitted into the stock. A method I am familiar with from the by-God-and-by-gosh school is to take the recoil plate out and peen it, a tooling maneuver that involves hitting the part until it is longer and therefore produces a tighter friction fit.

Next, you should examine the stock itself. Remember, the M1 Carbine is primarily a triumph of mass production. It has been produced by the millions and always works, but accuracy was always second to its reliability. (Yeah, the more we look at it, the M1 can almost be called the "American AK!") Take a look at the stock and be certain it fits the Carbine well. Route out the mortise in the stock that holds the recoil plate if necessary until the barrel, with the rifle assembled, floats about a half inch above the channel in the stock. A few shavings off the back of the stock usually results in a greater effect at the barrel end. Take care and frequently drop the barreled action back into the stock to check your progress.

Barrel bands are a fertile field for accuracy experiments. There are several

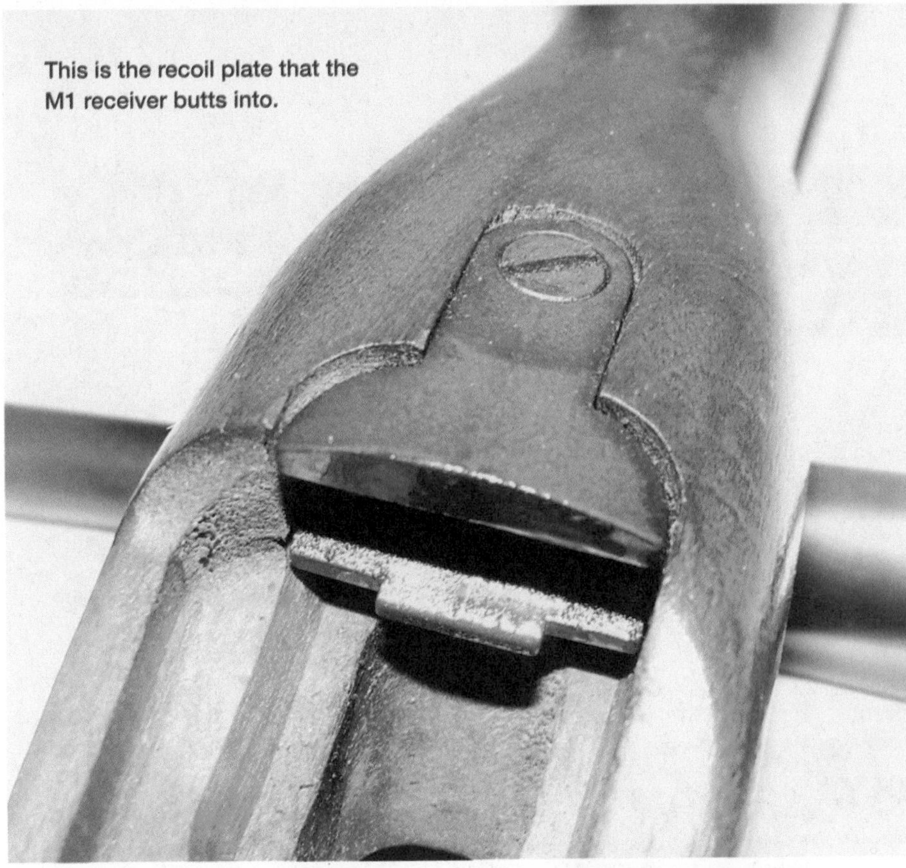

This is the recoil plate that the M1 receiver butts into.

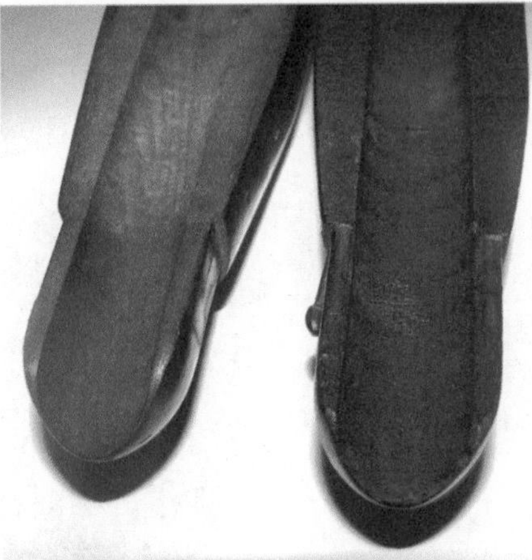

The carbine stock is pretty fat for such a little rifle. The stock lip seems to make little difference. These are typical stocks.

These recoil plates differ in detail, the significant difference being that the one on the left is of cast construction.

This inletted stock is typical of commercial "knock off" productions from the 1960s to 1970s.

The U.S. M1 Carbine is not powerhouse—the .30 Carbine cartridge, left, is compared to the .30-30 WCF, center, and 12-gauge shotgun shell, right.

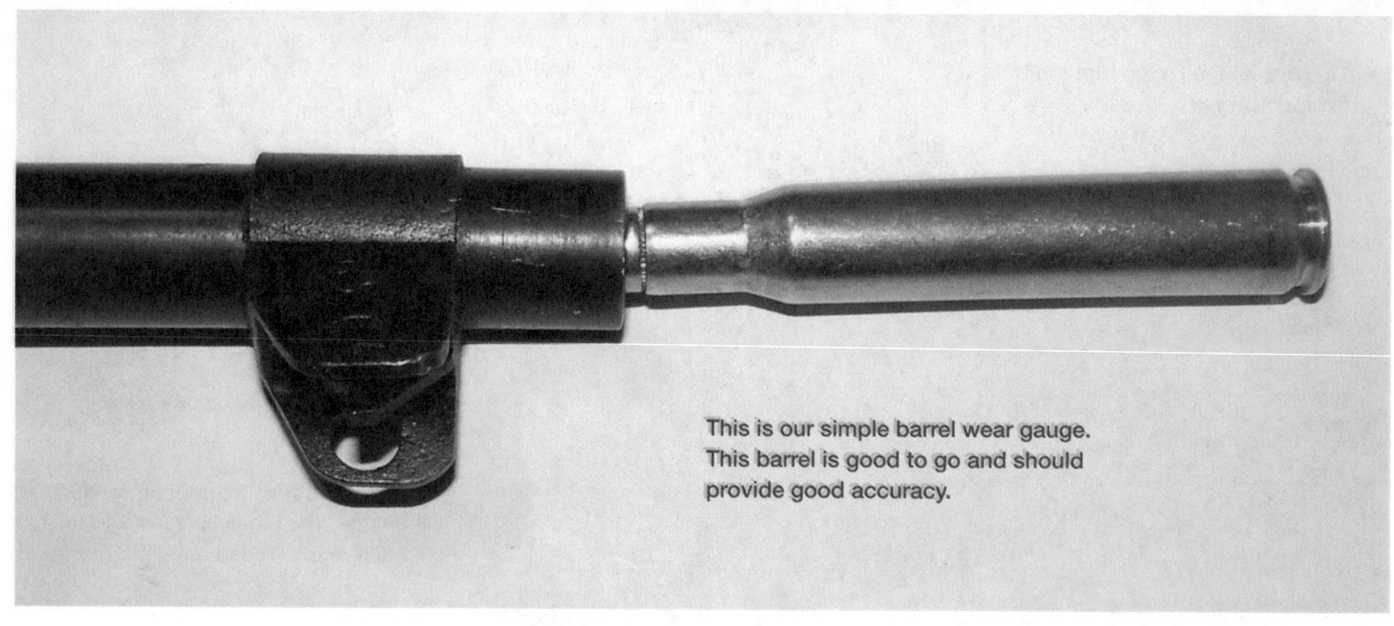

This is our simple barrel wear gauge. This barrel is good to go and should provide good accuracy.

This is the receiver setting in the stock, showing the relationship to the recoil plate. The recoil plate has been removed for this illustration.

ACCURACY RESULTS WITH THE AUTHOR'S INLAND .30 CARBINE

Ammo	Powder (grains)	Velocity (fps)	Accuracy (group inches)
Speer 110-gr. JSP	14.0 H110	1,943	4.5
	14.5 H110	1,998	3.9
Winchester 110-gr. FMJ	N/A	1,960	4.5
Winchester 110-gr. JSP	N/A	1,976	2.95
Corbon 100-gr. DPX	N/A	2,011	3.5

types, and I will not pretend to be an expert, but the narrow half-inch bands seem to be the worst for accuracy. They often mismatch the stock and simply do not get the job done. The alternate types that are an inch thick are much betting at snugging up. The best type of barrel band by all reports seems to be the bayonet lug type, but this design is a bit difficult to find. If this band design interests you, check with Fulton Armory first, then the pages of *Shotgun News*. You will probably be able to obtain decent accuracy with the standard barrel band if you check the recoil plate mortise, but the superior wide bands do help. So, after working with the recoil plate and the recoil plate mortise, then making certain the barrel is flee floating as much as possible, you should be able to observe a difference in accuracy.

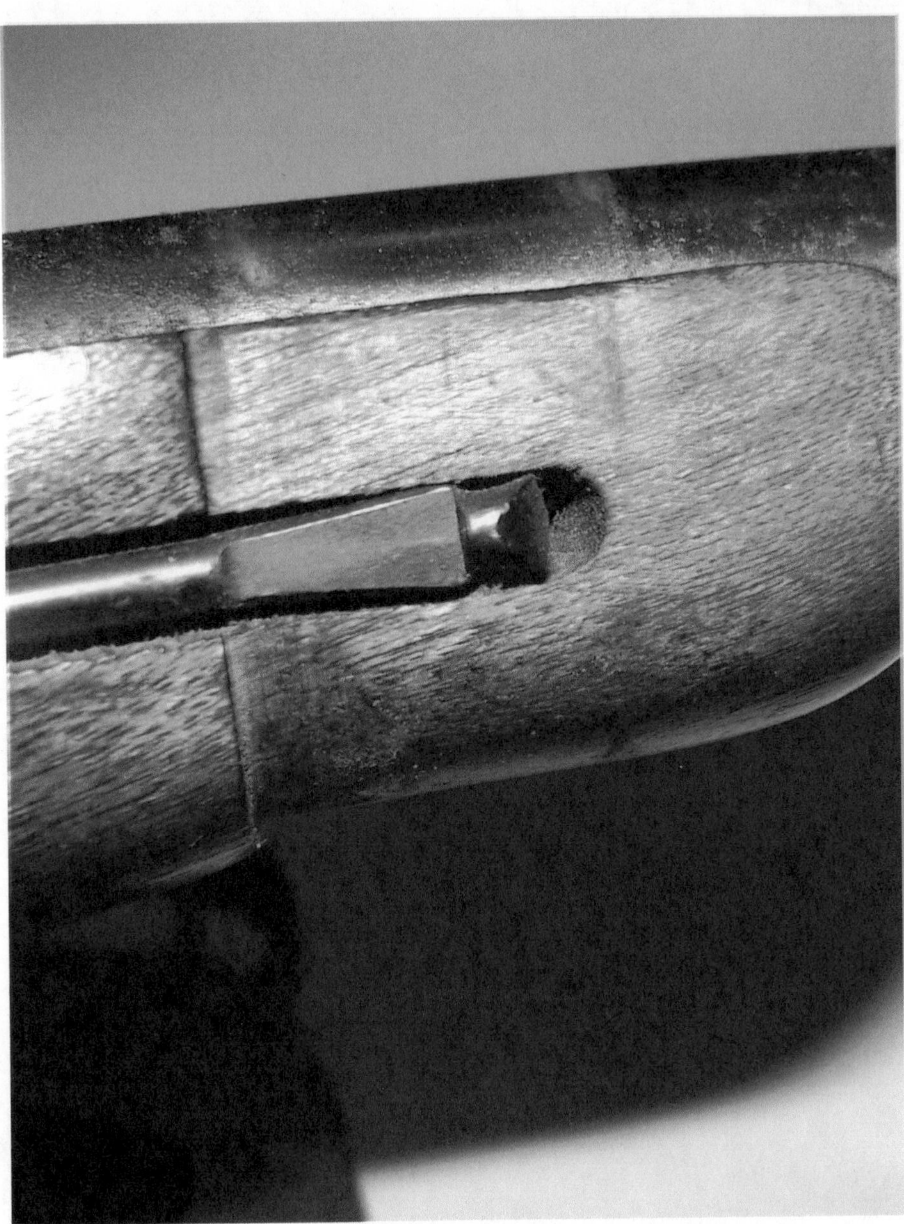

This barrel band has been on the rifle a long time. But the barrel has some upward spring when the band is removed, usually a good sign for potential accuracy.

At this point, barrel wear is a question. The use of noncorrosive ammunition in the Carbine is a great aid in barrel life. In fact, few Carbines will be found with rusty bores. But overaggressive cleaning has shortened the life of many Carbine bores. There are gauges available to test the muzzle to see just how much damage the GI bore cleaner has done, but a more simple test with a centerfire rifle cartridge is adequate for evaluation. Now, the .30 Carbine cartridge is too short to use as a gauge, so use a .308 Winchester or, better still, a .30-06 Springfield cartridge. With the Carbine checked to be certain it is unloaded and with the action locked back, attempt to fit the ball portion of the cartridge into the Carbine muzzle. If the bullet goes in up to the cartridge case mouth, your muzzle is pretty much shot out. If the bullet stops at insertion at about an eighth of an inch, you have a shooter—and in between these two will probably exhibit in-between accuracy. I admit the mechanical gauge is more scientific, but this simple test works well enough to get a preliminary grip on the potential your M1 Carbine might have.

There is little point in addressing the trigger action. The military two-stage trigger usually breaks at 4.5 to 6 pounds. I would never attempt to file hardened parts to produce a clean break. In any case, those few competitions that specify the M1 Carbine also demand a 4.5 pound or heavier trigger action. What is beneficial is to carefully clean and lubricate the trigger action.

The .30-caliber M1 Carbine is a versatile little rifle. It is usually completely reliable, accurate enough for personal defense and pest popping, and, above all, it is user friendly. While not as inexpensive as it once was, the Carbine still remains an excellent addition to anyone's tactical repertoire. This is a design with no flies on it.

The 10-gauge is still a world apart from all the other gauge offerings, especially when it comes to its effectiveness on waterfowl.

The 10-GAUGE MAGNUM

Still the Super Gun in the Hunter's Arsenal

BY L.P. BREZNY

If there is one gun that has been resurrected from the dead more times then a lucky cat, it is the 10-gauge magnum. Developed as a hunting shotgun back in 1870, the big gun was found to be a first-class piece of equipment with stagecoach guards, lawmen who worked to maintain order in the American West, and hunters alike. The chamber of the big gun at first was not the 3½-inch length of today, but rather a short 2⅞ inches. Aside from that difference, the big .775-inch bore size has always been the standard and, being the largest bore diameter of all American shotguns, it has long been known for its massive firepower.

My affair with the 10-gauge started way back in the early 1960s or, as they say, "back in the day." At that time, the three-inch 12-gauge was pushing the big 10-bore out of its rightful place among hunters, and it looked like it was a dying round. However, it was still the very best show in town, when it came to gunning large Canada geese over passing points,

The author checking the wind before a day's 10-gauge gunning over small water.

or, once in a great while, over handmade plywood decoys.

With steel shot on the doorstep a bit later down the line, the 10-gauge got a real boost in the area of load development. Federal, Winchester, and Remington were all on board with their new 3½-inch 10-gauge loads. The big case could hold massive amounts of large steel shot and was able to maintain good velocity downrange, while doing so with a pile of shot in the pellet count department. This was the answer to the problem of keeping energy per pellet up by way of larger shot, while still maintaining good pattern density at game-taking ranges.

For my part, being involved with my load testing-based company, Ballistics Research & Development, I found I was spending vast amounts of free time with Dave Fackler, companies like his Ballistics Products, Inc., and also an old-timer and good friend Don Vizecky, owner at the time of Minnesota Steel Shot Reloaders. We were all working on better loads

Some of the new load offerings in 10-gauge based on nontoxic applications.

The author chronographing new loads in 10-gauge for the fall of 2011. The 10-gauge has picked up a good deal of velocity over the years, thanks to advanced components.

The author at the bench with the SP-10. Pounding work, but it needs to be done, when evaluating new loads.

in steel shot, and again the 10-gauge was king in the development department, largely because of that big working area in the 3½-inch hull.

Pet loads of the day included DuPont 4756 and a Remington S.P. 10 wad, which was then lined with roofing aluminum to protect the bore from the 54 No. F steel shot "ball bearings" that were installed in the wad column. When that mess went off and a goose came down stone dead at 60-plus yards, every game warden in the county came running; most steel at that time couldn't knock down a sick rice hen at 40 yards. In effect, every hard-nose goose hunter I spent time with in those days shot a 10-gauge.

When the next plague came rolling in against the big gun, it was in the form of much better 12-gauge iron shot loads that had surfaced over the years, loads that were in line with the development of the 3½-inch 12-gauge super magnum. Now the 10 was dead for sure, right? The new 3½-inch 12-gauge could hold as much steel shot as a 10 and almost stay with the big gun in terms of muzzle velocity (today it does so with ease). Best of all, it was housed in a standard 12-gauge receiver and stock system. Buying a 3½-inch 12-gauge and getting a super magnum for the price of a three-inch gun became the new big deal in hunting camps around the country.

There is no question about it, the 3½-inch 12-gauge has taken a real bit out of the massive 10-gauge, but, rest assured, for those of us who have stayed with the super gun in smooth bores, the 10 still retains some very major bragging rights. Hunters in the far north, when required to fend off bears, often turn to the big 10-gauge and its heavyweight 1¾-ounce Foster slug as offered by Federal Cartridge. At the muzzle, the big chunk of lead generates 1,280 ft-lbs of energy and, at 50 yards, it's still turning out 1,085 ft-lbs of force.

With a 40-year background in smoothbore ballistics, I have shot my share of 3½-inch 12-gauge guns right alongside my current pair of 10-gauge waterfowl pieces. When your head is about rattled off your shoulders due to massive recoil from the lightweight 12-bore and field accuracy starts to suffer, the big, heavyweight, static-position 10-gauge starts to look darn good to even this experienced waterfowl hunter. Tack on a good turkey woodland or a call location for coyotes, and, again, the 10-gauge rules supreme over any and everything else out there in the shooting world.

Currently, we are seeing a gradual elimination of many of the so called "designer" tungsten iron loads on the shotshell market. Tungsten, due to its extreme price per pound, is just about gone as of this date, and more options in the advanced smoothbore ballistics department will be reduced during the year ahead. But because it has volume to work with and those heavy loads of very large shot, the 10-gauge could well see a resurgence. I am not about to tell you that the 10-gauge can outgun the 3½-inch 12-gauge, when it comes to advanced types of nontoxic shot, but in the standard steel/iron shot (which is about to become the new standard once again among waterfowl hunters), the big gun will indeed outshoot the new, skinny-barreled 3½-inch 12-gauge kid on the block.

As a general assessment of the two gauges, I use the 3½-inch 12-gauge because it is the only gun that can come close to the big-bore 10-gauge sky master, and I have elected to shoot my old Richland fixed super-choked 10 against a Benelli Super Black Eagle and the outstanding Winchester Super X3 in the 3½-inch 12-bore. Chokes used are the Hevi-Shot Super Full, as applied to the X3, and the Benelli SBE Waterfowl Full. In terms of loads, three of the latest loads in steel and combined tungsten/steel were selected from Winchester, Federal, and Hevi-Shot in both gauges. No lead loads were tested, as the massive 10-gauge two-ounce loads and the huge 1½-ounce slug loads by Federal have cut long paths shotgunning history and require no further review. All tests were conducted on 30-inch patterning targets set at 40 yards. Note the table "A" in terms of pattern percentage points.

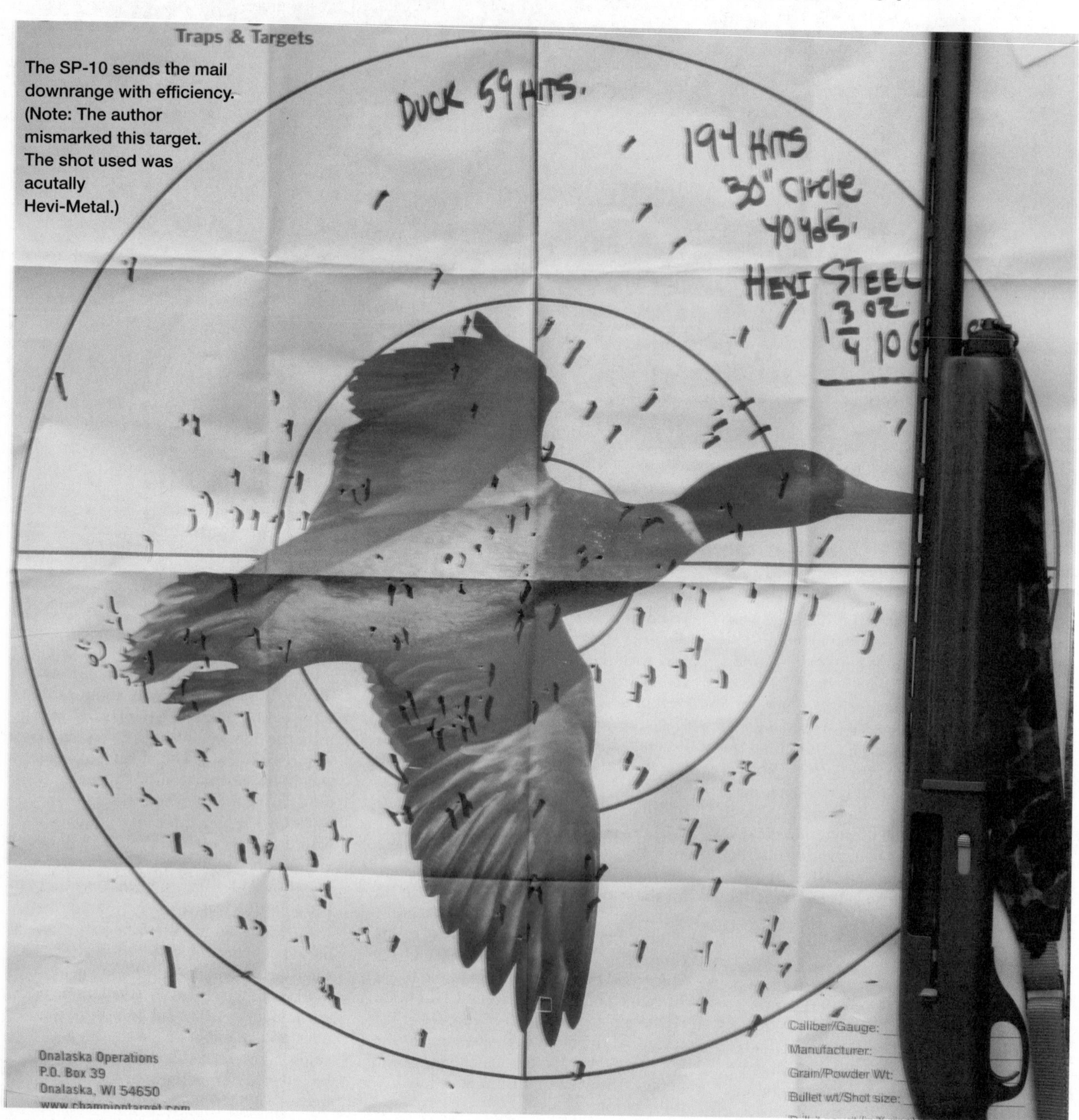

The SP-10 sends the mail downrange with efficiency. (Note: The author mismarked this target. The shot used was acutally Hevi-Metal.)

As you can see, patterns with both the 10- and 12-gauges from high-quality ammunition were found to be excellent across the board. The 10-gauge has a very slight edge, as it should, given the bore size and effective payload systems. At one time, British waterfowl shooters stated that the American overloading of the 12-gauge was ridiculous. Across the pond, the 10-bore was average, regarding its use for waterfowling, and the 12 was considered a sub-gauge. Today, many American 10-gauge shooters feel exactly the same way. Spend some time with the big stick and you will understand the total concept of using the 10-bore in the field.

Shooting the 10-gauge in the field is very different from pattern work. When hunting, you can see the difference in knockdown punch and, at times, multiple kills with a single round down range.

10-Gauge Pattern Results, Richland Side-By-Side "A Battery" Super Waterfowl Full Choke
Load: Black Cloud Flite Control 1⅝-ounce, BB steel.
Muzzle Velocity: 1,375 fps
Pattern: 90 percent, average two rounds.
Load: Winchester Supreme 1⅜-ounce, No. 2 steel
Muzzle Velocity: 1,450 fps
Pattern: 83 percent, average three rounds.
Load: Hevi-Shot /Hevi-Metal 1¾-ounce, No. 2 steel/tungsten.
Muzzle Velocity: 1,350 fps
Pattern: 81 percent, average three rounds.

12-Gauge 3½-inch Pattern Results
Load: Black Cloud Flite Control 3½-inch Magnum, 1½-ounce, BB steel
Muzzle Velocity: 1,500 fps
Gun: Winchester Super X3 Hevi-Shot Extra-Full "Extreme Range" choke.
Pattern: 81 percent, average three rounds.
Load: Winchester Supreme 3½-inch Magnum , 1⅜-ounce, BBB steel
Muzzle Velocity: 1,475 fps
No. 1 Gun: Benelli SBE, Full choke
Pattern: 76 percent, average three rounds.
No. 2 Gun: Winchester X-3, Hevi-Shot "Extreme Range" Extra-Full choke
Pattern: 83 percent, average three rounds.
Load: DryLok 3½-inch Magnum, 1 9/16-ounce, T steel
Muzzle Velocity: 1,400 fps
Gun: Winchester X-3, Hevi-Shot "extreme Range" Extra-Full choke.
Pattern: 84 percent, average two rounds

Why? I believe it is a combination of large bore size and the shot string control provided. This is not technical data, but rather gut feeling stuff after shooting the large-bore gun for most of a lifetime.

Nothing but Performance

As you can see, patterns by way of the 10-bore and that old-school Richland side-by-side are always outstanding. Add the developments surrounding the new types of ammunition (listed in this review), and total payload control is nothing but positive. Traveling from 1,350 to 1,700 fps (Remington's new Hypersonic), today's steel pellets move like lightning. On the pass-shooting range, the big gun is still king. Its performance combination is very hard to beat, regardless of what you're taking afield in a 12-bore of any chamber length. About the only gun I have ever fired that flat-out supersedes the 10- is an English market hunter's 4-bore—in a five-inch chambered gun, it was beyond description in terms of shock effect, when touched off.

An Example of Efficiency

Mass terminal effect can best be described by the following example. On a recent goose hunt, 11 birds descended quickly into the decoy spread, but slipped to the left and landed a full 55 yards out and to my far side of the spread. As I was the only shooter in position to safely take a shot, I came out of my blind, yelling at the flock to get up and leave. As the whole flock lifted and cleared the decoys, I pulled on a single bird and, with my first round, killed two geese outright. My second and third rounds each killed birds cleanly, for a complete quad-count kill (bird limit, was eight per hunter per day), as administered by the Remington SP-10 and the very effective Hevi-Metal 10-gauge loads. I was doubly impressed, when the last bird dropped a full 70 yards out. These loads, consisting of No. 2s in the iron shot pellets and about a No. 4 size in the second layer of tungsten shot, were hitting very hard. This was, without question, some very solid work for smaller shot at ultra-long range over decoys.

Today the Remington SP-10, at least at the time this review was being written, is still being manufactured, but word has it that The Freedom Group is about to drop the big gun from the lineup. That's a mistake overall, with tungsten falling by the wayside. Browning's BPS pump-action

and Auto Gold 10-gauges are nearly all that are being built currently by the industry in the American marketplace. Even if Remington isn't going to make the SP-10 any longer, they are still going to offer the Hypersonic ammunition in 10-gauge—excuse me, but what's all *that* about?

Left: The author's 10-gauge Richland side-by-side and below his Remington SP-10, two very solid game-getting systems.

The old Richlands and varied other side-by-sides or stack-barrels in a wide range of hard-hitting Spanish guns are drying up fast, as well. If you are in the market for a 10-gauge and find a clean double gun at a good price, my advice is to buy it fast.

When writing this review, my son-in-law Scott went to work back in Minnesota, where he located two 10-bore guns in metro-area gun shops. He sent one to me and kept one for himself. He never had any idea of the possibilities associated with the big 10, until he took his to the range and touched off a few rounds on pattern boards at 60 yards. He was sold, and now there are two more Spanish long forcing cone-designed super guns in the family.

I will freely admit that, for many years, my 10-gauge guns didn't see much, if

Right: The author on a stock dam hunt for puddle ducks with his Richland 10-bore. Some range extension is a big help on these small, western state waterholes.

Author L.P. Brezny with an SP-10 during an early season goose hunt. On this hunt, the big gun took four geese with three shots.

ODE TO THE PASS-SHOOTER

So often we writers spend countless hours screen processing rough drafts on the subject of decoy gunning all types of waterfowl. But left out all too often from these discussions are the pass-shooters that hunt from government blinds set up by state and federal game and fish. And beyond that method of hunting comes the freelance hunter who rolls across the goose range, spotting, stalking, and then gunning birds going to and coming from feeding areas. The bottom line is that even well into the very ultra-modern age of American waterfowling with all its bells and whistles, the pass-shooter is still alive and well and their 10-gauges still fully entrenched as a strong part of the total equation. While 200 decoys of the full body types are very nice, as are off-road rigs to haul gear, quality layout blinds, and owning open road units in 4X4 configurations, the fact is simply that not everyone can afford hunting waterfowling that way. Now, add the fact that a major part of advanced ballistics in smoothbore firearm is about to go away, and the 10-gauge could well again fill the much-needed notch in the field ballistics picture regarding nontoxic shot. Therefore, covering some of the guns and loads needed by this brand of hunter seems to make a whole lot of common sense to me.

Guns in 10-gauge New & Used

Remington SP-10-gauge semiautos. New, three-shot waterfowl and turkey models available.
Richland over/unders and side-by-sides.
Armsport Model 2700 over/unders: used
American Arms WT over/unders: used
Ithaca Mag 10: used
Browning Gold semi-auto: new
Browning BPS pump-action: new
Other assorted off-brand Spanish double guns: used

Current 10-gauge 3½-inch Magnum Factory Loads

Winchester 10-gauge Supreme: 1⅜-ounce, No. 2/BB/BBB
Winchester Super X: 1⅝-ounce, No. 4/BBB/T
Remington Hypersonic Steel: 1½-ounce, BB/BBB (1,700 fps) New for 2012!
Remington Nitro Steel: 1¾-ounce, No. 2/BB/BBB/T
Remington Sportsmen: 1⅜-ounce, No. 2/BB
Remington HD: 1¾-ounce, No. 2/No. 4/BB
Federal Cartridge Wing-Shok Magnum: 2 ¼-ounce, BB
Federal Cartridge Speed-Shok Waterfowl: 1½-ounce No. 2/BB/BBB/T
Federal Cartridge Black Cloud FS Steel: 1⅝-ounce, No.2/BB
Enviornmetal Inc. Hevi-Shot (Hevi Metal): 1¾-ounce, No. 2/No. 3/No. 4/BB/BBB

The author with a goose taken with his favorite Remington SP-10.

The 10-gauge in action over decoys in late winter.

any, work afield. The industry race for advanced nontoxic loads was running at full speed, and there was little time to dwell on those old super-gauge guns that were just about being out-shot at every turn by advance shot types in the 3½-inch 12-gauge guns. Well, that was then and this is now and, if you look closely, the 10-bore never went away for the pass-shooters. Currently, with steel shot back as the main-line nontoxic shot type for 2012, I believe the bigger gun is going to find a new home among many gunners that want more range and energy on target.

Rolling with some of my friends in the outdoor business last year across the winter landscape of eastern South Dakota, we came across seven-foot snow drifts covering miles of open ditches and blocking the airborne entry and exit points of Canada geese that were feeding on blown-out sections of cut grain crops or, in some cases, standing corn that was now barely sticking out of the drifts. Goose hunters on roads along the Missouri river were packing some very heavy ordnance in their 10-bore doubles, pumps, and autoloaders, due to the fact that these pass gunners needed all the ballistics assistance they could get. While a decoying Canada can be taken with ease by a 20-gauge loaded with a heavy charge of powder and No. 2 iron shot over decoys, the passing goose in an open country environment is a completely different story.

In their snow forts and hollowed out foxholes among the drifts, the white-clad hunters clad in white coverups just blended into the landscape, and the hungry, phone line-high and higher Canadas never had any idea of what lay in wait below them. This was absolutely the place for the big 10-bore.

"Weath

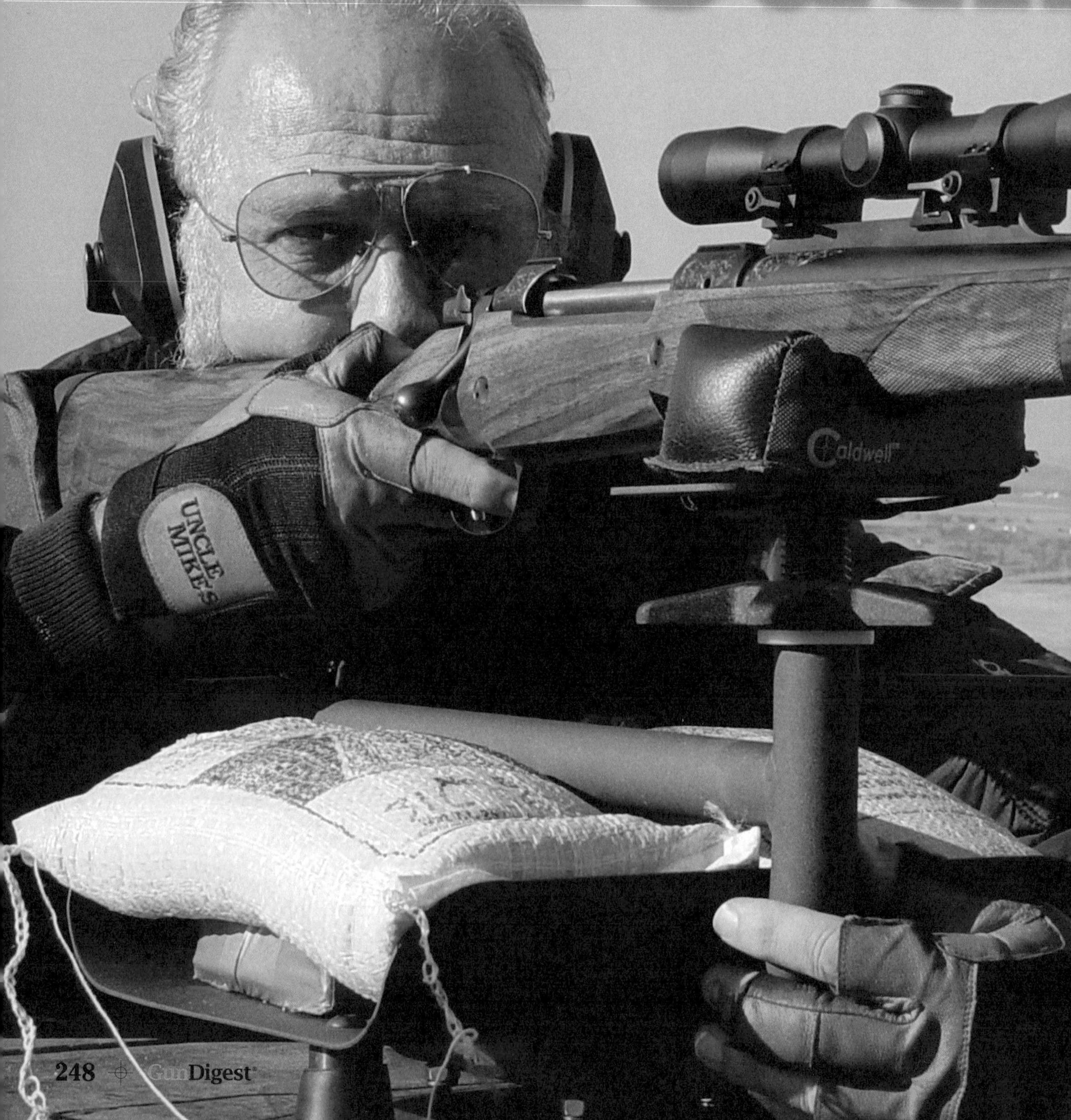

erby Eye" BE GONE

Shooting with both eyes open comes naturally with the use of an extended eye relief scope.

BY **TOM TABOR**

Ever had the rim of your rifle scope slam into your face? I know such a thing is human caused, nevertheless, it does happen and, when it does, personal injury is sure to result. Possibly the most common scenario when this occurs is when a high overhead shot is being attempted from the prone position. In this case, the shooter struggles to get low enough in relation to the rifle to make the shot. As the trigger is squeezed, the recoil of the rifle causes the rifle butt to slip off the shoulder and under the shooter's armpit, driving the scope directly into the shooter's face.

I have to admit to making this error on a couple occasions and can attest to the fact that it really doesn't feel all that good. On one such occasion, I was hunting deer with my 12-year-old daughter in tow. I was shooting a .300 Winchester Magnum rifle with ammo loaded to the hilt, when the butt slipped free from my shoulder, driving the scope back into the bridge of my nose. As is often the case with a head wound, the blood started to gush, and soon the snow around me looked as if a sadistic massacre had occurred. I quickly struck a course for the truck, in order to get the first aid kit to slow the bleeding, leaving a trail in the snow-covered ground that certainly wouldn't have required an experienced bushman tracker to follow. That occurred a couple of decades ago, but the resulting stigma on my daughter lingers on to this day; fearing that a similar thing could happen to her, she is still wary of shooting any rifle more powerful than a .22-caliber.

Whether you call this problem scope-bite, "Weatherby eye," or any of a number of other terms unsuitable for mixed company, the effects are the same, and it certainly is something to be avoided. One way to eliminate the possibility of such an accident involves moving the scope further out on the rifle barrel, but doing so requires the use of a scope with longer than normal eye relief. Some refer to this type of mounting system as a "scout mount."

I suppose that term has its roots in the early days of scopes and Winchester lever-action rifles. Because rifles like the Model 1894 and a variety of other lever-actions commonly eject out the top of the action, their design prohibits the use of a traditionally mounted scope. In these cases, the choices are to simply be satisfied with using the iron sights, mount your scope along the side of the action, or use an extended eye relief scope and mount it in front of the action. Still, eliminating the possibility of scope bite is only one of several benefits associated with the use of an extended eye relief scope.

Most traditionally styled rifle scopes come with an optimum eye relief of somewhere around three inches. In some cases, this can be stretched out to around four, and even five inches, in a few instances, but seldom much further than that. So, if you intend to mount a scope in front of the rifle action, it will be necessary for you to use either a rifle scope specifically designed as an extended eye relief model or, in some cases, the possibility of a handgun scope. Many scope manufacturers offer these models, but your selection will be considerably limited, when compared to the traditional eye relief models.

A person I greatly respect, Carl Laburschagne, now a retired South African Professional Hunter, first introduced me to the benefits associated with extended eye relief mountings. Carl and I have been friends for many years, and I look at him as being an expert in areas like this. He has guided and hunted throughout southern Africa for virtually every type of game the Dark Continent has to offer, and that includes the dangerous Big Five. As such, he is a devout believer that, if you shoot a scoped rifle for dangerous game, the scope should be mounted out on the barrel for a host of reasons, including eliminating the possibility of getting punched in the nose with the scope. Eventually, I put his recommendation to use and built a pair of rifles that both wear extended eye relief scopes.

Selecting a Scope

One thing to keep in mind, when selecting and mounting any scope, is

The finished scope mounting system, shown here from above the rifle, included an N.E.C.G. Classic safari-styled folding leaf sight that was mounted between the two Leupold QRW scope bases.

Even with the low-magnification 2.5X scope, the author's custom-built .500 Jeffery Rimless produced some excellent three-shot groups at 100 yards.

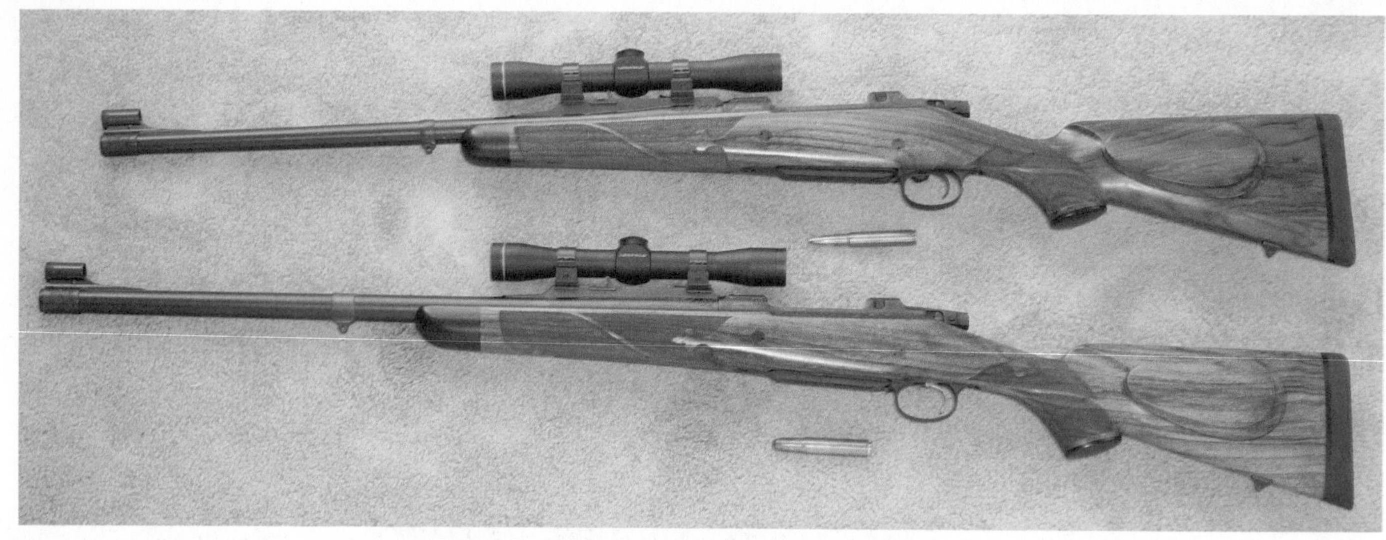

Tom Tabor's two extended eye relief rifles consist of a .416 Rigby and .500 Jeffery Rimless. Both rifles were built on CZ 550 actions and were close to identical, with the primary exceptions of size and weight. Note, below, how far his face is from the scope when the gun is mounted in actual use on Tom's shoulder. No chance for the dreaded "Weatherby Eye" here!

the fact that the lower the magnification, generally the more flexibility you will have when it comes to eye relief. In other words, a low-powered scope possessing possibly only 2X magnification will usually be much more tolerant and forgiving when it comes to how far your eye can be from the scope than, say, with a 20X scope. All rifles are built a little differently and, when you start to deviate from a standard scope mount, you can expect to encounter variations in where you can mount the scope. For this reason, it is to your advantage to have a little built-in flexibility, when it comes to eye relief distance.

Possibly the best way to demonstrate how this flexibility is helpful can be seen in my own rifles. I mounted a Leupold FX-II 2.5X28mm IER (Intermediate Eye Relief) Scout scope on both the rifles I built. This particular low-magnification scope was designed to have an optimum eye relief of 9.3 inches, but the design of the rifle prevented me from mounting it that close. Using the mounting system we developed, I could not get the scope any closer than 11.5 inches, but the amount of eye relief variation built into this scope allowed me that extra two-plus inches I needed. I'm quite sure that, if I were mounting some of the other available higher magnification scopes, that positioning would not have been possible.

This was just one of the many Asian buffalo that fell to Tom's extended eye relief scope mounted on the .500 Jeffrey, used during the Australian culling operation.

Other Advantages

Aside from never having to worry about Weatherby Eye, there are other important advantages inherent in the use of an extended eye relief scope mounting. One of the things to consider is the increased speed with which it allows you to get on your target. There are advantages associated by shooting with both eyes open with any scope (closing a shooter's non-shooting eye only reduces depth perception and narrows the field of view), but the ability to do so seems to come much more naturally with an extended eye relief mounting. For quick, close-quarters shooting, it is imperative the target be acquired quickly. In some cases, the speed at which the shooter is able to get on their target and squeeze off the shot can mean the difference between a trophy and simply a story to be told around the campfire. In my mind, shooting with both eyes wide open, using a rifle that possesses a low- or moderate-powered scope mounted out on the barrel, is the best possible scenario for success in this type of situation—and, when it comes to encounters at close quarters with dangerous game, the stakes are usually much higher. In this case, being able to get on the game and to pull off a fatal shot can mean the difference between life and death for the hunter.

How Do You Get There?

Now, assuming you accept the fact that an extended eye relief scope could be a beneficial thing for your particular type of shooting, you are probably wondering how to go about achieving that objective. Unfortunately, there will be some fairly significant hurdles that must be overcome. In most cases, you won't be able to simply jump in your car, head down to your local sporting goods store, and purchase everything you need to do the job. Because rifles and barrel contours are not universal and mounting of an extended eye-relief scope isn't what I would call mainstream, it's likely you will have to utilize the services of a qualified gunsmith to fabricate or modify a mounting system for your rifle. For the two custom rifles I had built, I started by purchasing a Dakota Arms quarter rib blank and had it fitted to the rifle barrel, then machined it to accept the type of scope rings I wanted to use. Dakota quarter rib blanks can be purchased through Brownells, which also carries ribs contoured to match Douglas or Shilen barrels. In my case, it became necessary to custom fit the ribs. Another approach is

Tom's .416 Rigby took this excellent bull elk at a stellar 320 yards, helping to demonstrate how a low-power extended eye relief scope isn't limited to only short-range shooting situations.

to start with a set of Leupold gunmaker bases. These are specifically designed for custom firearms work and come equipped to handle the traditional style of scope rings. The bases are considerably oversized, with plenty of metal for manipulating into whatever shape is necessary to fit the situation.

My Own Extended Eye-Relief Custom Rifles

I had always dreamed of building a custom big-bore rifle and, after years of trying to decide on the perfect cartridge, I finally settled on the historical .500 Jeffrey Rimless. Once that decision was out of the way, my gunsmith Dan Coffin and I turned our attention to designing the scope base system. For a dangerous-game rifle like the .500, I didn't want to be tied solely to the use of a scope, so I purchased an N.E.C.G. Classic Express Sight from Brownells and dovetailed it into the center of the quarter rib. But, in order to use the express sights, it became necessary to install a set of quick-release scope bases. I've had exceptionally good luck in the past with Leupold's QRW rings and have always found that my bullet point of impact never changes when using them, even after repeated removals and remounts of the scope. So, that choice was an easy decision to make. The QRW bases took a little modifying in order to get them to fit properly on the quarter rib, but soon they were positioned with the express sight in the center.

By mounting the express sights on the quarter rib, it made the distance between the front and rear sights only 18.5 inches on the Jeffrey and, because of the shorter barrel of my second rifle, this span was shortened even further to 16.5 inches.

That's not a bad thing. It is the belief of many shooters that a shortened sighting plane actually enables a shooter to get on their target quicker. But, no matter where the iron sights are placed on the rifle, an important consideration to be made whenever dual sights are used is the height of the stock comb. It doesn't really matter whether you are modifying a pre-built rifle or building a custom rifle, you need to make sure that, once the rifle is finished, you will be satisfied with how your eye aligns with the sights. In my case, there would be a variation of about ⅝-inch between the center of the scope and the "V" notch of the express sight, and I had to decide which sighting plane would take priority. Did I want my eye perfectly aligned to the iron sights or the scope, when the rifle was brought up to my shoulder? I decided to give priority to the iron sights, thinking that, when I would be using the open sights, it might be under very close quarters and tight time constraints. When using the scope, I thought I might have a little more time to precisely align it. I know, no matter what type of sight you're using, they're supposed to be perfectly aligned with the shooter's eye, but, with two sighting systems, you simply can't have it both ways.

At the onset of building the .500 Jeffrey, I didn't envision constructing a second rifle having an extended eye relief scope. I'd always dreamed of building a custom big-bore primarily for hunting Cape buffalo, but, once I had worked all the kinks out of the design and had the finished rifle in hand, I simply couldn't resist building another one. This time it would be chambered in a little smaller caliber, but it would still be classed in most circles as a dangerous-game rifle. The .416 Rigby seemed to fit perfectly with my wishes, and, so, the rifles were built as a matching set, very close to identical, but the .416 was scaled back a few pounds from the heavy 12.5 pounds of the .500, and rather than having a Cape buffalo engraved in the floor plate as the .500 had, the .416 was more appropriately engraved with the head of a lion.

Getting used to shooting a rifle possessing extended eye relief scope comes quite naturally and, when the shooter keeps both eyes open, such technique provides both depth of field and a phenomenally wide view.

Leupold gunmaker bases could be the perfect answer to fabricating a custom set of scope bases for an extended eye relief scope mounting system.

Use in the Field

After building my .500 Jeffrey, I had intentions of heading to Africa on safari for Cape buffalo. Well, that hasn't yet materialized, but I did manage a trip to Australia, where I went after the Cape's cousin, the Asian water buffalo. My Northern Territory outback safari involved hunting two different areas, one for trophy buffs, where I took a pair of fine bulls, and then I was off to help out a game ranger on a buffalo culling operation in the Aborigine Territory. The Jeffrey worked splendidly well and resulted in something around a dozen buffalo succumbing to its charms. I was amazed at how naturally the 2.5X extended eye relief scope performed. The rifle and scope came up cleanly; I shot with both eyes open, and I could pick up my targets with amazing speed. I also found I was easily able to stay on the buffalo, as they wove their way through the bush.

The .416 Rigby hasn't seen quite so much action yet, but this past hunting season, in Montana, a really great six-point bull elk fell to its report at a whopping 320 yards. This was considerably longer-range shooting than you'd normally expect with the big, 400-grain .416 Barnes Triple Shock bullet and a 2.5X scope, but the rifle and the scope pulled it off just fine. The extended positioning of the scope didn't hinder the long shot in any way and actually helped me in the placement of my shot, as the bull wandered in and out of the 90 or so animals in the herd.

Have I had any regrets with the extended eye relief mountings? I would answer that question with a resounding, "Nope!" For potential dangerous game hunting, I don't think there's any better way to go. My answer would be the same for other types of shooting and hunting that sometimes involve close-quarters action. I just don't think you could go wrong with a scope mounting like this. I continue to worry a bit about those hunters shooting extremely heavy recoiling rifles with their scopes mounted a mere three inches from their faces. A rifle like my .500 Jeffrey, which sends a huge, 570-grain bullet out the muzzle at nearly 2400 fps, would surely do a lot of damage to the face of a shooter if the gun and scope should fly back and make contact. In that instance, the old cliché that a rifle kills on both ends would certainly apply.

Another example of the shooting technique of keeping both eyes open, a practice that provides both depth of field and a wide view while focusing on a downrange target.

THE LAST KRAG

BY **John Malloy**

The last Krag was an unusual variation of the bolt-action Krag-Jorgensen rifle. It was made at a United States arsenal, but was never issued as a standard military arm. It was, instead, a special carbine made for members of the National Rifle Association (NRA), provided to them only through the Director of Civilian Marksmanship (DCM). It was the last official variation made of our country's first smokeless powder rifle.

Going Smokeless

The Krag-Jorgensen rifle, often simply called the "Krag," had an interesting place in our nation's history. It was the first U.S. high-velocity smallbore rifle. It was also the first American smokeless powder military magazine rifle, and the first official U. S. rifle to use a knife bayonet. The Krag rifle was adopted as our official military rifle in 1892, though it did not go into production until a couple years later, in 1894. From that time until its replacement in 1904, it was in a decade of almost continuous use. The Krag rifle, adopted in 1892, was America's first smokeless powder rifle. European countries had been rapidly converting from blackpowder big-bores to smallbore smokeless powder military rifles, since 1886. In that year, the introduction of the 8mm French Lebel was shaking the military world.

The Lebel was the first smallbore, high-velocity smokeless powder rifle to be used by any nation, and its use as a military rifle gave French forces a decided advantage. In short order, in 1888, Germany also adopted a smokeless 8mm. Russia went to a "three-line" (.30-caliber, or 7.62mm) rifle in 1891, and Italy went even smaller, to 6.5mm, in that same year. During this era, America was still using the blackpowder .45-70 single-shot Trapdoor Springfield as its standard rifle. U.S. military planners realized they must modernize the issued rifle of the soldier, and so they did, adopting a new, high-velocity .30-caliber cartridge and a fast-operating repeating rifle.

The cartridge was an American design. The rimmed, bottleneck cartridge case was a bit over 2¼ inches long. It used a .30-caliber 220-grain round-nose jacketed bullet in its ½-inch-long case neck. Forty grains of a new smokeless powder pushed the bullet to a velocity of about 2,000 fps. It was known variously as the .30 Government, .30 Army, .30 USA, or, more commonly later, as the .30-40 Krag. It was a good cartridge, one that would stand the test of time. It proved effective in military use and became a favorite of American big-game hunters. Winchester and other companies made sporting rifles for the .30-40 cartridge, as it was considered adequate for any game on the North American continent. (As a side note, rifles for that caliber have been made for a long time, and ammunition companies still load cartridges for this effective round).

Although the cartridge was American, the design of the rifle was not, rather being the product of two Norwegian firearms specialists. Ole Krag, director of the Kongsberg Arsenal, in Norway, worked with Erik Jorgensen, the chief armorer of the same facility, in developing the rifle. A patent was issued to the two men for their unique new rifle, soon to be known as the Krag-Jorgensen.

This new bolt-action rifle had a unique magazine. The cartridges were fed in from the right, passed horizontally in a passageway under the bolt, and came up on the left side of the receiver. At that point, the bolt could push a cartridge forward into the chamber.

To insert the cartridges into the magazine, a special hinged mechanism on the right side was opened, and cartridges could be dropped into the cavity of the magazine. When the mechanism was closed, a spring-loaded follower arrangement pushed the cartridges into line and fed them across to the left, then up into the path of the bolt. An

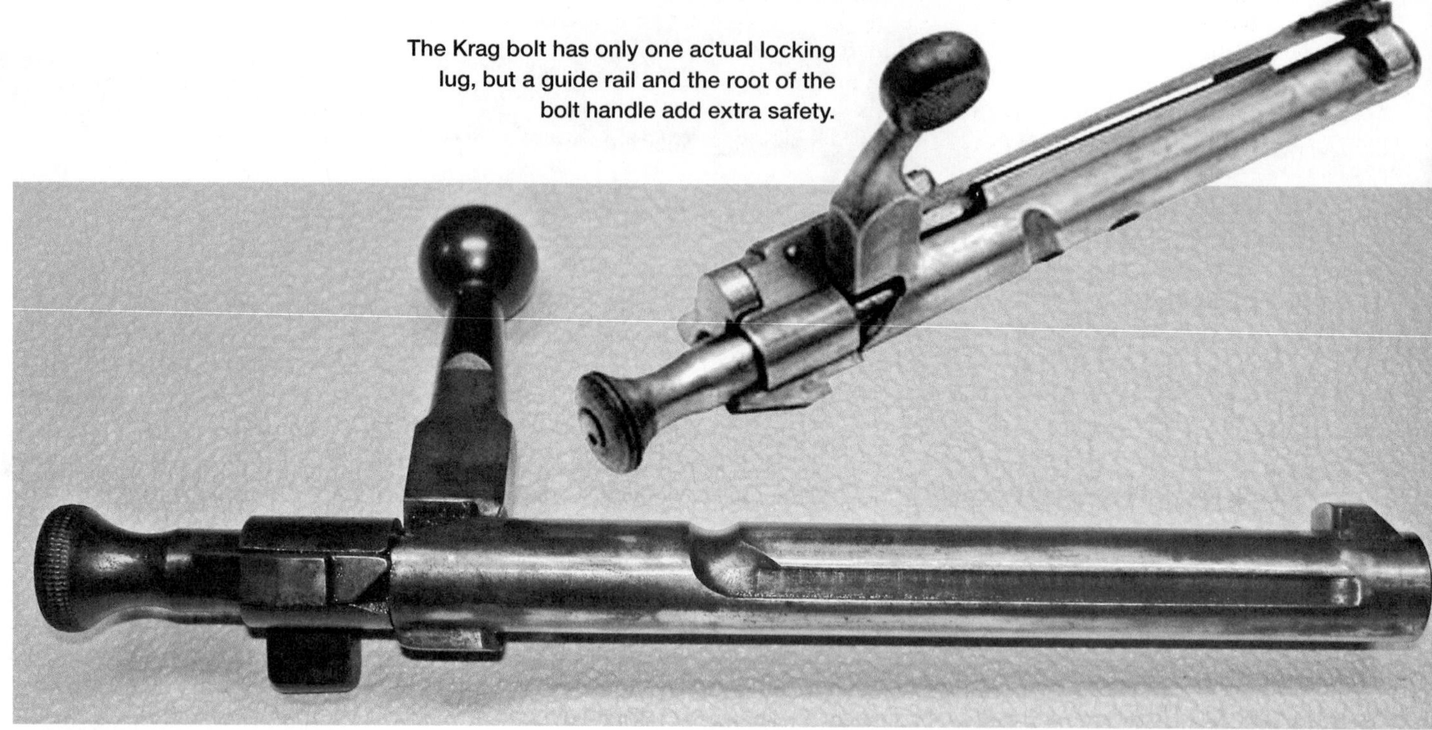

The Krag bolt has only one actual locking lug, but a guide rail and the root of the bolt handle add extra safety.

advantage of this arrangement was that the magazine could be "topped off" with extra rounds at any time, as the bolt could be either open or closed during reloading.

The design of the bolt and its locking system, while not the strongest, made the Krag one of the smoothest bolt-action rifles ever produced—some would say the smoothest. The Krag bolt has only one actual locking lug, but it has a long guide bar on the bolt that contributes to its glass-smooth operation. This guide bar also adds strength, as it turns to face the receiver bridge, when the bolt is closed. In addition, the root of the bolt handle turns into a recess at the rear of the receiver and acts as a safety lug.

The good points of the Krag-Jorgensen rifle were soon recognized. Denmark adopted the Krag in 1889, the U.S. in 1892. The inventors' native Norway, for some reason, waited until 1894 to embrace the Krag as its official rifle.

The Krag made a timely appearance, for the American military. Beginning in 1878, the U.S. Army had been thinking about a replacement for the .45-70 Springfield. The defeat of General Custer and his command at the Battle of the Little Big Horn, in 1876, had shocked military planners. It had shown, among other things, the obsolescence of the single-shot Trapdoor Springfield design. The .45-70 cartridge itself was still, at that time, considered adequate, so repeating rifles chambered for that round were tested. Tests were made of the Remington-Lee, the Winchester-manufactured Hotchkiss, and other repeating rifles, but still there seemed to be no particular urgency. Then, in 1886, the smokeless powder French Lebel, with its high-velocity smallbore jacketed bullet, caused a flurry of activity among European armies, and the attention of the U.S. Army was forced to take a different direction.

New tests were called for. In 1890, the U.S. held its first competition for a smokeless powder smallbore magazine rifle. It was an extensive test. Fifty-three rifles, a variety of American and foreign designs, were submitted and tested, including six different variations of the Krag-Jorgensen. (Interestingly, modified trapdoor rifles chambered for the new .30-caliber cartridge were also tested.) The tests concluded in August 1892, and the fifth variant of the Krag was chosen to be the new U. S. Army rifle. It was officially adopted on September 15, 1892, but production did not begin as planned. A number of Americans were distressed that a foreign offering had been selected, and a campaign began against the Krag. Appeals were made to the United States Congress to call for more tests. Then as now, it seems, politics played a role in things that should have been above political interference. Congress passed a bill requiring additional tests of the Krag and encouraging the testing of more rifles designed by Americans. Yet, when the tests were conducted, the results were the same. By the end of 1893, the previously adopted Krag had outperformed all the other entries—again! Production began, belatedly, in January 1894.

The first Krag produced was the Model 1892, a designation reflecting its original adoption date. With its 30-inch barrel, the long, slim Krag stood about 49 inches long and weighed about 9½ pounds.

As the Krag was phased into service, small design changes were implemented, among them a change in the sights, and the original long cleaning rod being replaced by a jointed rod housed in the butt cavity. Within a few years, more than 40 changes had been suggested and, so, a new variant, the Model 1896, was made to incorporate such improvements. The rifles looked about the same and had the same general specifications, but the weight went down about a half pound, due primarily to the wood removed from the butt in order to store the cleaning rod. Older 1892 rifles were soon modified to 1896 specifications, and the first official Krag carbines were made in the 1896 series. The carbines had 22-inch barrels, were 41 inches in overall length, and weighed about 7½ pounds.

As the Krag saw service, even more improvements were suggested. A modified rifle, the Model 1898, was approved in March of that year, and, as before, earlier rifles were modified to meet the new design standards. (It is very difficult for collectors to find an original and unmodified 1892 or 1896 rifle today.)

A corresponding 1898 carbine was also manufactured, with the action characteristics of the 1898 rifle, but its production was short-lived; the very short forearm of the 1898 carbine was thought to be too short for comfortable holding or accurate shooting. In the following year, the final military Krag production model—the Model 1899 Carbine—was approved and put into production. It had a stock that had the butt dimensions of the Krag rifle, while the forearm had been lengthened.

The Krag's first duty was to gradually replace the single-shot Trapdoor Springfields on the frontier. Soldiers were glad to get the long, slim new rifles, with their slick actions and powerful long-range smokeless powder cartridges. With the first model 1892s in hand, the old trapdoors and their blackpowder cartridges were sent back and used to equip Home Guard units.

Mounted soldiers wanted a carbine, and the new Model 1896 Krags came in both rifle (62,000 made) and carbine (about 20,000 made) variants. These 1896 guns, and the updated Model 1892 rifles, were soon to serve in a full-fledged war.

Battle Abroad

In 1895, Cuba revolted against Spanish occupation. The revolt had been brutally suppressed by the Kingdom of Spain, but American sympathies were with Cuba. On February 15, 1898, the U.S. battleship Maine was blown up, under mysterious circumstances, in Havana harbor. On April 25, the United States declared war on Spain, and, by July 1, about 16,000 United States troops were in Cuba, ready for battle.

Other battles in other places were involved, but, to most Americans of the time, the Spanish-American War was a war waged over Cuba. Cuba meant San Juan Hill, and San Juan Hill meant the Rough Riders and their Krags; of course, it was not that simple, but the Krags, both the carbines in the hands of Roosevelt's Rough Riders and the long rifles in the hands of the regular Army, performed well.

In this famed battle, the American forces moved to take the fortified military center at Santiago, Cuba. Between the Americans and Santiago stood a series of low prominences, known collectively as the San Juan Ridge. Fortifications along the ridge consisted of masonry forts, wood blockhouses, and deep trenches. The fortifications at a village called El Caney were the first to be attacked by the Americans, and during that battle, roughly 600 Spanish defenders were subjected to a barrage of rapid fire from the more than 7,000 smooth-working Krags in the hands of the Americans.

Taking place almost simultaneously, the next areas of engagement included Kettle Hill and San Juan Hill. The same situation was repeated, with some 7,000 or so additional Krags firing as rapidly as possible. It was probably the greatest single concentration of individual hand-held small arms fire the world had ever seen at the time (and possibly since). A historian noted that, "It surpassed anything of a like nature in the history of small arms." The battle ended with an American charge up both Kettle and

The author operates the bolt of a Krag NRA Carbine. The Krag action has a reputation for unsurpassed smoothness of operation.

The original Krag front sights were machined with the barrels. Shortening the barrel to make the NRA Carbine required a new front sight system. Fortunately, the band front sight of the 1903 Springfield provided an easy solution.

San Juan Hills. American casualties were high, but the defenders fell back to Santiago. On July 17, Santiago formally surrendered. On December 10, 1898, the Treaty of Paris was signed causing Spain to relinquish its authority over Cuba and granting the United States control of the Philippine Islands, Guam, and Puerto Rico. America, almost overnight—and, in part, because of the Krag, which had shown the world that the age of firepower had arrived—had become a world power.

Getting control of the Philippines proved to be a mixed blessing. A revolt against Spain was already in progress, and the fledgling Philippine Republic did not want American rule any more than they had liked Spanish domination. The resulting Philippine Insurrection went on for two years, until 1901. The war was officially over, but only officially. Fighting in some parts of the Philippines, especially in the southern islands, went on for another decade, as fierce Moro (Muslim) tribesmen fought to the death for a chance to kill infidels and achieve heavenly rewards. It was our first experience with such fanatical adversaries.

It's interesting to note that, during the trouble with the Philippines, some soldiers modified the jacketed Krag bullets for better close-range stopping power. The simplest method seemed to involve reversing the bullet in the cartridge case, so that the blunt base, with its exposed lead core, went first. Too, though it was officially replaced before the end of fighting, the Krag-Jorgensen was the one rifle truly associated with the Philippine conflicts. In fact, a favorite marching song contained the lines, "Underneath the starry flag, Civilize them with a Krag."

Krag-armed troops were also called into amphibious campaigns against pirates who preyed on shipping lanes in the South China and Sulu seas. The area was between the Philippines

The author poses with a Krag NRA Carbine, the last official Krag variant. It is a nice-handling rifle, easy to use and chambered for a cartridge capable of taking North American big game.

The unique Krag magazine, shown here with the right-side cover open, held five cartridges. The American Krag used the .30-40 Krag cartridge, and five original military cartridges are shown near the rifle. The Krag magazine could be loaded with the bolt either open or closed.

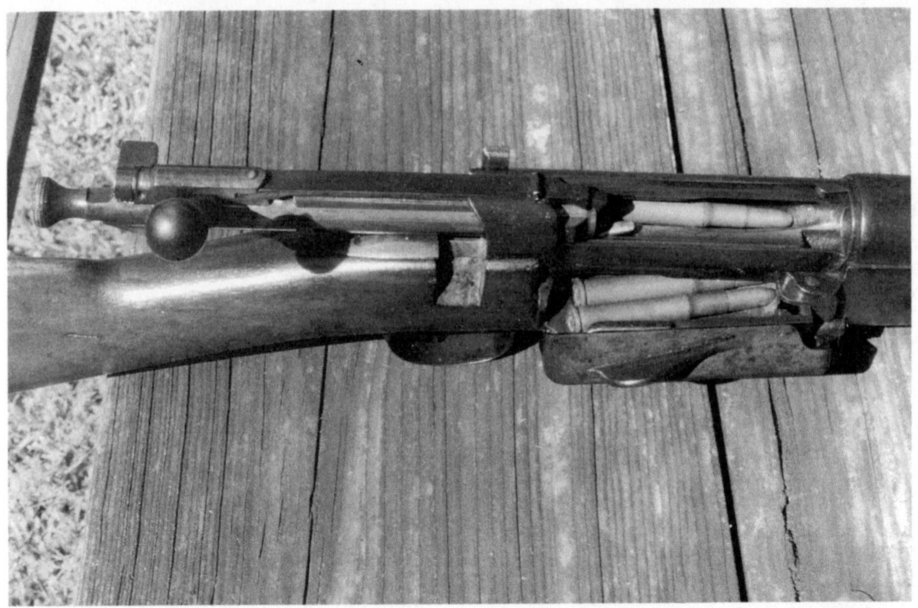

To load the Krag, the five cartridges were placed into the magazine from the right. They moved horizontally underneath the boltway, and the first cartridge traveled to the far left, to be pushed into the chamber by the closing bolt. With the magazine side cover closed, all cartridges would be fed to the left under spring pressure.

and Borneo, which was then a British protectorate. So, it wasn't until groups of American soldiers and their Krags were withdrawn from the Philippines and sent to China in 1900, that the rifle experienced a change of location, with a mission to rescue western citizens trapped by the Boxer Rebellion.

At the turn of that century, Chinese resentment against foreigners had broken out into open rebellion. A secret society, roughly translated as "The League of the Righteous Fists of Harmony" gained power. The group used a clenched fist as their symbol, and its members came to be known as the Boxers. They declared death to all foreigners, especially Christian missionaries. Hundreds of foreigners were trapped in Peking, most in the walled compound of the British delegation. Beside U.S. military, seven other major powers sent troops, but the Americans were the only ones with any recent combat experience. American soldiers, with their long Krags, did most of the fighting, and American casualties were highest. In the end, they cleared the way for a British column (which had not seen combat) to march in and rescue the trapped Occidentals.

The Last Indian War

While all this was going on overseas, the Indian Wars in America had phased down to more-or-less peaceful coexistence. But, there was to be one last officially recorded Indian battle. This would become known as The Battle of Sugar Point, and it took place near the Indian Reservation in Minnesota, close to the Canadian border, in the Leech Lake area.

In Minnesota, the Pillager Indians, a small Chippewa tribe of about 200 or so individuals, had been poorly treated; timber on the Reservation had been harvested without proper compensation. In September 1898, one of the tribe's chiefs was to be arrested on rather vague grounds. This indignity was prevented, when about two dozen Pillager braves rescued the chief. The group escaped to Bear Island on Leech Lake.

Twenty soldiers of the 3rd U.S. Infantry were sent to meet with the Indians. When

the tribe refused to retreat, the solders, increased in number to 100 and armed with Krags, moved against them. On October 5, 1898, the troops steamed to Bear Island, found it deserted, and so moved on to Sugar Point. Conditions required the soldiers to pole their vessel to shore. The landing was difficult and was not accomplished until after nightfall.

As the Americans arranged their new camp, the Indians began quietly circling. A report from the battle stated that the tired troops "were ordered to Stack Arms" as the encampment was established, "but one recruit failed to engage the safety on his weapon." We can only imagine that the new recruits may have been originally trained with the trapdoor and may not have been really familiar with their Krags. At any rate, a rifle reportedly fell and discharged a shot into the night.

The shot apparently indicated to the circling Indians that they had been discovered. They opened fire, reportedly with "Winchester rifles." The commanding officer and several soldiers of the U.S. troops were killed and the others were pinned down. The next day, several hundred Home Guard troops headed to Leech Lake to help. But the Indians allowed the soldiers to leave and, apparently, then simply disappeared into the woods without casualties. Seven soldiers had been killed and 16 wounded. The last recorded battle of the Indian Wars period was over. The Krag, through no fault of its own, had not gained any distinction from this incident.

End of an Era

For a short time, the Krag-Jorgensen was distinguished on the target range. Though it had not been designed as a target rifle, with good sights it turned out to be capable of excellent target accuracy. It was also the first American military rifle with sling swivel placement that allowed use of the sling as a shooting aid. At the 1901 Creedmoor target matches, the Wimbledon Cup was won by a regular Army team using Krags. In 1902, another Army team with Krags won the match again. The year 1903 marked the beginning of the National Matches,

The Krag NRA Carbine, with its 22-inch barrel and sling swivels, which allowed use of a 1907 leather sling as a carrying strap or shooting aid, turned out to be the Krag variant most suitable as a hunting rifle.

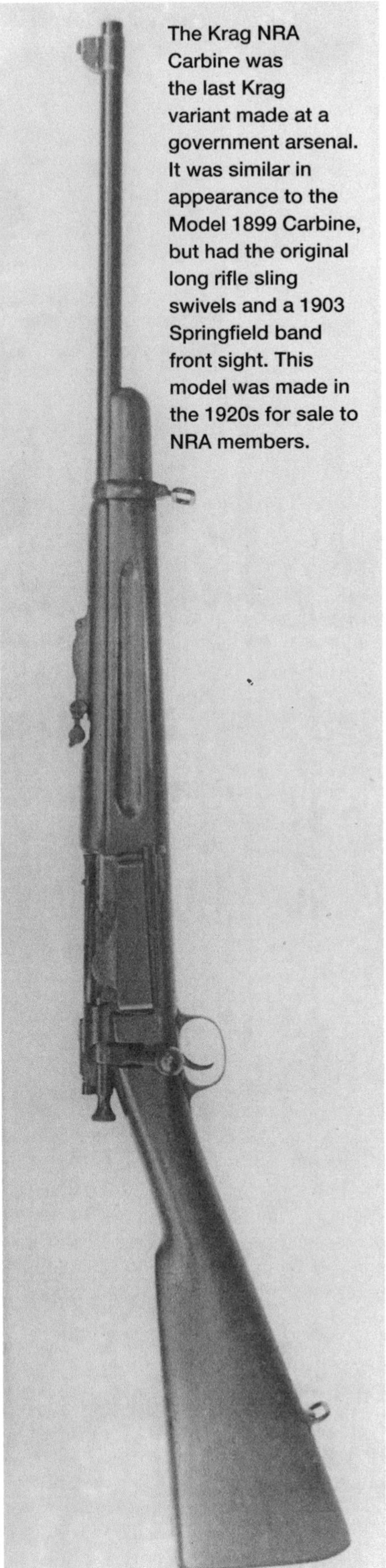
The Krag NRA Carbine was the last Krag variant made at a government arsenal. It was similar in appearance to the Model 1899 Carbine, but had the original long rifle sling swivels and a 1903 Springfield band front sight. This model was made in the 1920s for sale to NRA members.

and also the official beginning of the National Guard. A New York National Guard team, armed with Krags, was the winner of that first National Match.

The war with Spain had shown some of the advantages of the Krag over the 7mm Mauser rifles used against U.S. forces, but clip loading and higher velocities were seen as superior features of the Mausers. In this era of rapid change, the U.S. military designed a new clip-loading rifle, one patterned after the improved Mauser '98 action. It used a higher-velocity, rimless .30-caliber round. It was adopted as the Model 1903 rifle (almost always thereafter called the "Springfield"), and the production of the Krag was discontinued in 1904. The Krag had served for only 10 years, but it had seen enough action to solidly reserve its place in history.

As the 1903 Springfield replaced the Krag as the standard rifle, the Krags were sent to Home Guard units. Many were stored at government arsenals and eventually offered for sale to individual NRA members through the Director of Civilian Marksmanship (DCM). Although the .30-40 cartridge had been the long-range powerhouse of pre-.30-06 cartridges, Americans still preferred lever-action rifles for hunting. As a result, there was only moderate interest in the surplus Krags over the next several years.

Then, on April 6, 1917, the United States entered World War I. When it did, production of the 1903 Springfield was insufficient to supply the troops, and so the 1917 Enfield, a .30-06 rifle modified from the British Pattern 1914 rifle, was adopted as a substitute standard rifle. (Ordnance officer General John T. Thompson, later to be noted for his sub machine gun, was in charge of the modification).

Now, up until that time, the traditional hunting rifle used in America had been a lever-action. The new war in Europe would be the first time large numbers of American men would be introduced to, and have the chance to use, bolt-action rifles. In the life-and-death circumstances of battle, the bolt-action proved its worth to Americans.

At the end of the war, American doughboys returned home with a respect for the bolt-action and a desire to use similar rifles in the hunting field. It was a natural step that the surplus .30-40 Krags proved to be popular and excellent hunting arms. (Indeed, Krags, while serving as military rifles, had been used successfully for shooting game that supplied food for far-flung outposts.)

Krag sales to NRA members picked up steadily, during the 1920s. Many hunters preferred the shorter Krag carbine, with its handy 22-inch barrel, over the full-length rifles, and soon the carbines (which had always been made in smaller numbers) were gone. Still, the demand for carbines remained.

To accommodate this demand, the government's Benicia Arsenal, in California, created what came to be known as the NRA Carbine. Benicia Arsenal, which had been established in 1851, was the primary U.S. Ordnance facility on the West Coast. It had been a garrisoned post during the Spanish-American War and was a major storage and repair facility for Krags after the adoption of the 1903 Springfield. With surplus supplies of the original Krag Carbines gone and demand still high, the arsenal staff began converting their supply of full-length rifles into carbines for sale to NRA members. This would be the last Krag variation made under official government authorization.

The 30-inch rifle barrels were cut to the carbine length of 22 inches. The original Krag front sight had been machined with the barrel, however, and could not be used. The problem was easily solved, as the new 1903 Springfield had a separate band-type front sight. Springfield front sights were fitted to the shortened Krag barrels. The forearms of the stocks were cut to carbine length, extending to a few inches forward of the barrel band. None of the original carbines had been equipped with sling swivels, but the rifles had been, so these swivels remained with the newly shortened arms.

An extra fee was charged for the machine work and assembly required to create the new carbines. An *American Rifleman* item in the August 1926 issue stated that the price for the regular Krag rifle was $1.50, but the rifle "cut to carbine length" was more than twice as much, at $3.50. But, even at this "exorbitant" price, the NRA Carbines were desirable hunting rifles and sold well. Within a year, they were no longer available, and the September 1927 *American Rifleman* announced that the supply of Krag rifles at Benicia Arsenal had been exhausted. NRA members were notified that some regular Krag rifles were still available for $1.50, but had to be shipped from the only remaining source, the Rock Island Arsenal in Illinois. And, so, the Krag story ended.

BY **TOM TABOR**

RIFLES

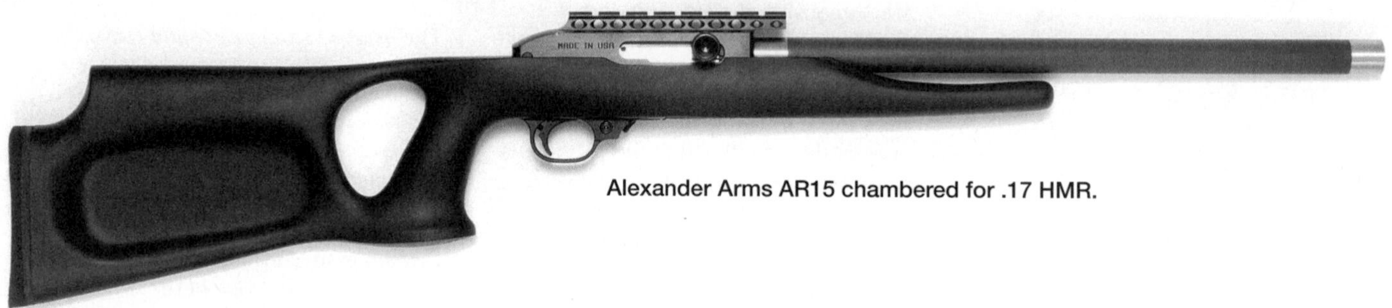

Alexander Arms AR15 chambered for .17 HMR.

The New Year is always an exciting time for shooting enthusiasts. Whether your preferred shooting activity consists of punching holes in a paper target, tipping over metal silhouettes at long range, or hiking to the top of a mountain in search of an ancient old mossback muley buck, the new firearms ushered in each year always seems to get the shooter's blood pumping. These new additions frequently come with innovative features and enhancements and, in some cases, even an added bit of eye-catching beauty. I find it extremely exciting to hold in my hands the latest gunsmithing art and give a lot of credit to those individuals hidden away in the dark recesses of the world's manufacturing facilities, diligently working their magic and helping me to become a better shooter.

It would be an impossible task to cover all the great new models, combinations, and cartridges that have recently been introduced, so, due to space limitations, I can only highlight a meager few. Still, the ones I've picked will hopefully provide the connoisseur of fine firearms a tantalizing look into what the world's great gunsmithing artisans have to share.

ALEXANDER ARMS

A decade ago, Bill Alexander, a top weapons designer in the U.K., packed up his imagination and expertise and brought it to the U.S. Those hopes and dreams eventually resulted in a line of U.S. built AR-style rifles that perform their duties equally well, whether being used for fighting terrorists, hunting, or for competition. Operating out of the Radford Arsenal, in southwestern Virginia, Alexander recently joined forces with the folks at Hornady to construct an AR chambered for .17 HMR. The initial production run will be 500 units, all of which will come standard with a straight-fluted 18-inch stainless barrel, A1 flash-hider, free-floating solid G-10 composite handguard, and two 10-round magazines. Available options include a spiral-fluted barrel and MK3-railed upper receiver. MSRP for the complete basic rifle is $1,1750.

CHIAPPA

For those shooters who like a bit of tradition mixed into their sport, one of Chiappa's new .45-70 carbines might be just the ticket. Two new models are now offered, the 1886 Traditional Trapper and the 1886 Kodiak Trapper. Features in both models mirror many of those in the

Chiappa .45-70 1886 Kodiak Trapper.

Chiappa .45-70 1886 Traditional Trapper.

original Winchester 1886, but Chiappa's designs have benefited from the use of modern manufacturing techniques and materials, which have added strength and improved accuracy. The Traditional Trapper comes with a fully octagonal, 4140-alloy blued steel barrel, with a receiver, lever, and crescent butt plate that have been beautifully case colored. The 1886 Kodiak Trapper is the same basic rifle, but with twenty-first century ergonomics and design elements blended in. The barrel is half round and half octagonal, but, rather than being case colored, the barrel, action, hammer, and lever come with a weather-resistant brushed nickel finish. To further add to the rifle's ability to resist the effects of inclement weather and save it from knocks and abuse, the walnut stock has been encased in a tough, armor-like rubberized finish. MSRP for the Chiappa 1886 Traditional Trapper runs $1,249, $1,395 for the 1886 Kodiak Trapper.

The author shooting the Savage Model 25 Lightweight Varminter in .17 Hornet at Wyoming prairie dogs.

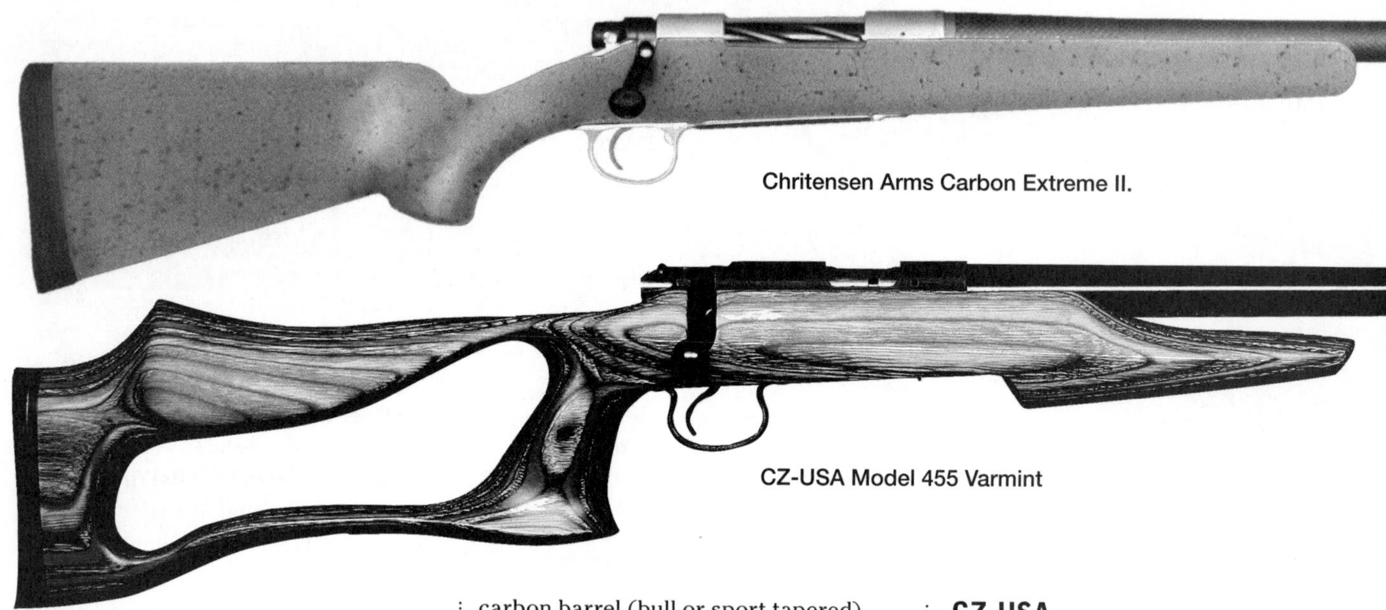

Chritensen Arms Carbon Extreme II.

CZ-USA Model 455 Varmint

CHRISTENSEN ARMS

Doctor Roland Christensen established Christensen Arms, in 1995, and since that time, the company has established itself as a leader in the manufacturing of graphite stocks (said to be the lightest and strongest stocks made anywhere), disruptor barrels, titanium muzzle brakes, and many other cutting edge products. One of the most recent additions to the company's line of fine sporting rifles is the Carbon Extreme II. This is a mid-level rifle that delivers high-end performance through the use of carbon fiber technology. It features a match-grade, spiral-fluted, stainless steel carbon barrel (bull or sport tapered), a trigger set to a crisp three pounds, a Teflon-coated bolt, and a choice of a Carbon Classic or Carbon Thumbhole stocks. Various upgrades are also available, including Weatherby, Sako, or Browning actions, titanium muzzle brakes, adjustable custom triggers, Teflon actions, 20-minute Picatinny rails, and camouflage dipping. Total weight runs between 5½ to seven pounds, depending upon the options.

CZ-USA

Over the last few years, CZ has become a major player in the world's firearms industry. I personally believe this success is simply a matter of selling high-quality products at moderate prices. One of CZ's major successes is its extensive line of rimfire rifles, especially its diverse selection among the CZ-455 series. One of the most eye-catching

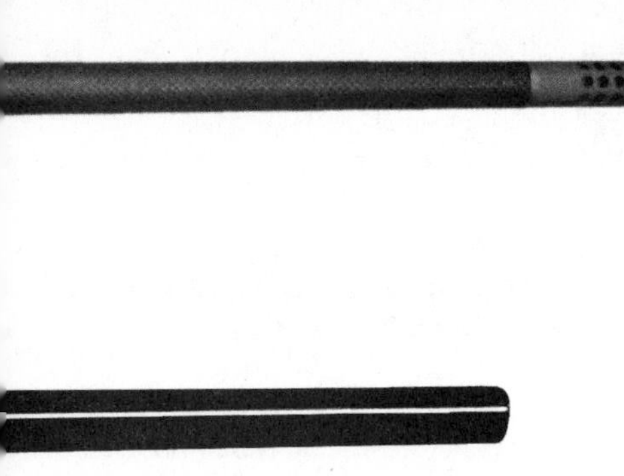

of those is the CZ-455 Varmint, which comes equipped with the company's SS Evolution Stock. This is a bolt-action rifle that comes with a radical "Sky" blue/gray laminated hardwood stock. Even though it is currently available only as a right-hand model, the rifle is ambidextrously designed in its cheekpiece, teardrop pistol grip, and palm swell. The action of the 455 Varmint and stock will accept any of the accessory barrels available within the 455 platform. The CZ-455 series rifles begin at an MSRP of $456 for the basic Varmint Model and run up to $899 for the Precision Trainer Model. The CZ-455 Varmint with the SS Evolution stock, chambered for .22 LR, carries an MSRP of 522.

HENRY REPEATING ARMS

Henry Repeating Arms is an age-old company, one that dates back to 1860 and the Civil War, when Benjamin Tyler Henry invented and patented the first practical repeating rifle. Quickly, the Henry rifle became known as "The gun you could load on Sunday and shoot all week long." But possibly above all else, Henry Repeating Arms today has established itself as a symbol of patriotism and a company extremely loyal to the U.S.A. As the company slogan proudly puts it, "Henry rifles will be made in America, or they won't be made at all."

Furthering that mantra, Henry is now offering a special edition, all American-made, Henry Golden Boy .22 LR rifle, as a tribute to all those dedicated individuals who have worn a badge in the service to their community and country. The Golden Boy's receiver is elegantly engraved in 24-karat gold-plated artwork patterned by the world-famous engraver Heidi Roos. On the right side of the nickel-plated receiver is an ornate sculpted roll, a police officer's badge, and a gold banner that's been inscribed with, "In Tribute to Those in the Line of Duty." The front panel has been engraved with a police officer's hat and a set of handcuffs. The left side showcases an engraving of Michael the Archangel, the patron of police, with a sword in one hand and the scales of justice in the other. There is also a banner bearing the motto "To Protect and Serve," and on the front panel is an American flag.

This Law Enforcement Tribute edition comes with a hand-selected American walnut stock that has been laser etched with the image of the American bald eagle set in a hand-painted royal blue circle inscribed with "God Bless America's Finest." The rifle comes equipped with a 20-inch octagon barrel, which has been topped with classic buckhorn sights. This lever-action rifle is capable of shooting .22 Short, Long, or Long Rifle cartridges.

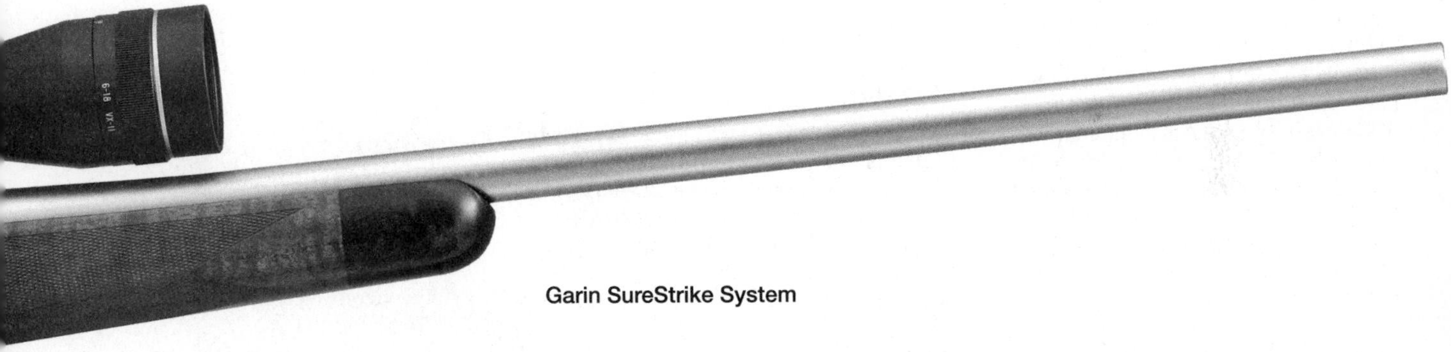

Garin SureStrike System

Henry Golden Boy Law Enforcement Tribute Edition .22 LR rifle.

Loki Weapons Systems model Loki Hunter in .300 Blackout.

LOKI WEAPONS SYSTEMS

Loki Weapons Systems, Inc., of Atoka, Oklahoma, builds a plethora of neat, high-quality, semi-custom ARs, in a variety of calibers and configurations. The company's latest offering is the Hunter Model, in the equally new .300 Blackout. Seasoned shooters will recognize the Blackout as a reincarnation of SSK Industries' .300 Whisper, a .221 Remington Fireball case necked up to .30-caliber.

The Loki Hunter we tested fits the definition of a modern sporting rifle pattern to a "T." It has an A2 stock, flattop receiver, and a free-floating tubular handguard. While the barrel muzzle is threaded to accept a flash hider or muzzle break, the test gun wore an inconspicuous thread protector. The 16-inch hand lead-lapped barrel is from Saturn Custom Machining of Estherville, Iowa, a company well known for producing high-quality match barrels. The rifle also has an adjustable gas block that allows the user to fine-tune gas bleed to the recoil impulse of the ammo being used, based on that ammo's velocity and bullet weight. To top it off, Loki had the rifle finished in a pleasing, light tan "flat earth" color, although you can have just about any finish you want. Also of note, shooters no longer have to neck up .221 Fireball cases, as both Hornady and Remington are now making factory-loaded ammunition for the .300 Blackout.

The Loki Hunter functioned flawlessly and was superbly accurate with a variety of loads. Shooters looking for an efficient, low-cost, and accurate rifle-cartridge combo should give this little gem a close look.

LYMAN

The Sharps rifle was made famous by its long-range accuracy and it buffalo-killing potential in the early years of our country. Lyman's Ideal Mode Sharps is a unique variation on this popular design. Scaled down in both weight and size, the design is a superior single-shot hunting rifle that is now available in either .38-55 or .22 Hornet. Its streamlined profile and vintage-styled laser engraving makes this rifle a Lyman exclusive. It comes with a Lyman tang rear sight and target and hunting apertures, and a globe front sight with inserts. The bore has been optimized to shoot both cast and jacketed bullets, and the double set triggers encourage a full measure of shooting accuracy. Unlike the original Sharps, the Lyman Ideal Model weighs only six pounds and has an overall length of 42 inches. MSRP for the Ideal is $1,595 in either cartridge offering.

MERKEL

A pair of Merkel engineers recently decided it was time to create the next generation of the company's firearms. The straight-pull design of the new RX Helix encourages fast cycling, and its

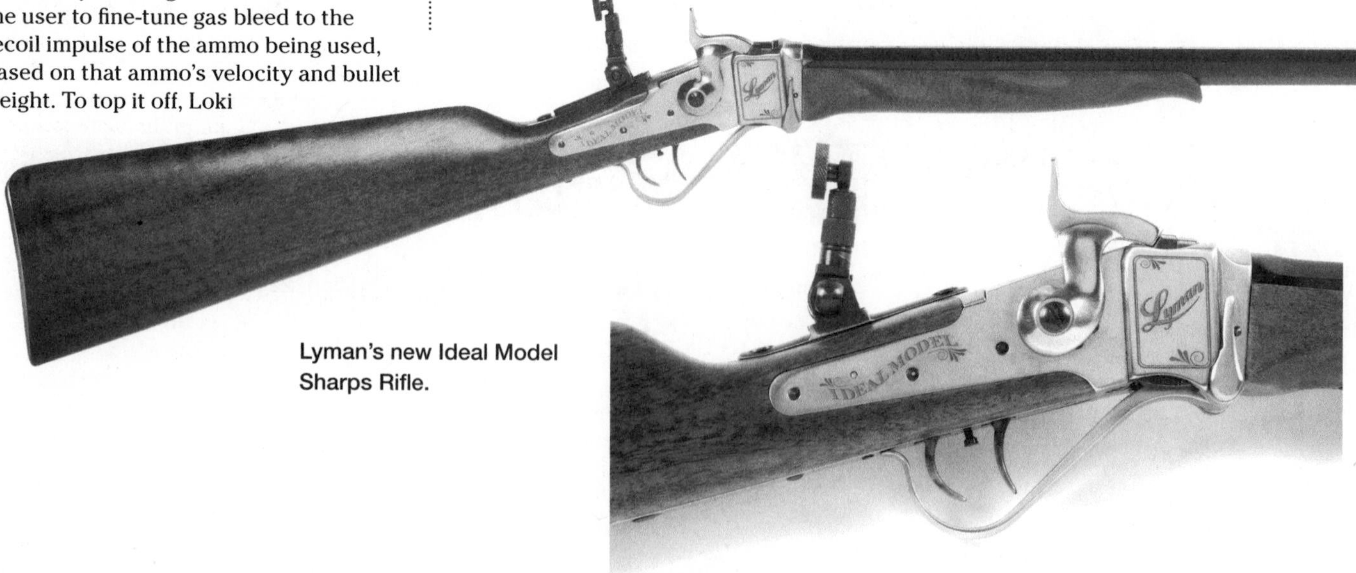

Lyman's new Ideal Model Sharps Rifle.

Merkel RX Helix.

Mossberg MMR Hunter chambered for 5.56mm NATO (.223 Remington).

Mossberg MMR Tactical chambered for 5.56mm NATO (.223 Remington).

unique, seven locking lug rotary bolt head helps ensure a strong and secure lockup. The linear motion of the bolt handle is transmitted to the bolt head at a ratio of one-to-two by way of a transmission "gearing" system that can be easily manipulated by either left- or right-handed shooters. The RX Helix features a manual cocking lever on the tang, and the fast take-down design allows the shooter to change calibers in less than a minute. Currently, the RX Helix is available in a standard black configuration and four levels of upgraded design—Arabesque, Wild Boar, Spirit, and Deluxe. A wide selection of caliber

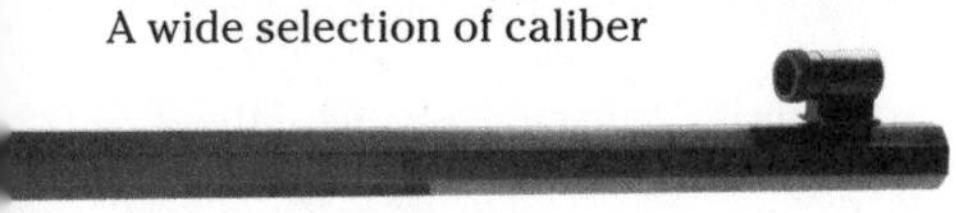

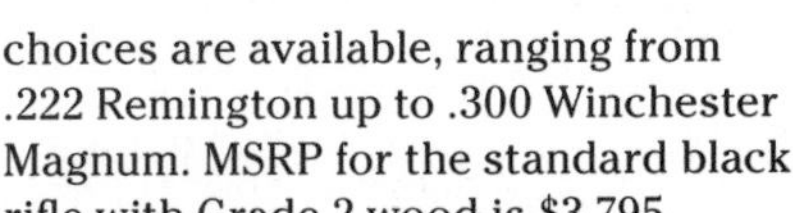

choices are available, ranging from .222 Remington up to .300 Winchester Magnum. MSRP for the standard black rifle with Grade 2 wood is $3,795.

MOSSBERG

Referred sometimes as the "modern rifle," the AR-15 was originally conceived for use by the military and law enforcement agencies. Today, those applications have since been expanded to include much more diverse usage. Mossberg has tapped into that growing interest, with two new rifle models the company calls its MMR (Mossberg Modern Rifle). These models are the MMR Hunter and MMR Tactical.

Dedicated to predator, varmint, and small-game hunting, the new MMR Hunter includes three variations, all chambered for 5.56mm NATO (.223 Remington). These include a black phosphate/anodized version and two fully camoed models (either Mossy Oak Treestand or Mossy Oak Brush 2). All three come equipped with a slender, checkered, aluminum tubular fore-end and A2-style buttstock. The 20-inch barrels come with a 1:9 twist rate and possess a recessed hunting crown, while the machined aluminum receiver has been integrated with a Picatinny rail. The MMR Hunter comes standard with a five-shot magazine, but any AR-15 style magazine can be used. The MMR Hunter carries an MSRP ranging from $921 to $1,010.

The MMR Tactical is designed for both sporting and tactical applications. Like the MMR Hunter, it is available with a black phosphate/anodized finish and two stock styles, a six-position adjustable or a fixed stock allowing up to four inches of length of pull adjustment. It comes with or without the removable Picatinny-mounted front and rear sights and includes a 16¼-inch free-floating barrel, a removable A2-style muzzle brake, a Picatinny aluminum quad-rail fore-end, receiver-mounted integral Picatinny rail, and standard dust cover. A choice of a 10- or 30-round magazine is supplied. Depending upon the options selected, the MSRP runs from $885 to $921.

OLYMPIC ARMS

Olympic Arms continues to turn out top-quality ARs, and its latest offering is chambered for the inexpensive 5.4x39 Russian ammunition. It is available in different barrel lengths and weights, as well as a multitude of handguard, receiver, and gas-block options. The design of the magazine is unique to the ammunition, but they are readily available from Olympic. The upper we tested snapped easily into the lower unit, functioned 100 percent, and was very accurate. Complete rifles are available, or you can purchase an upper ready to pop on to one of your current ARs. Either way, it's the red-hot set-up for super-cheap shooting fun.

PROOF RESEARCH

Proof Research specializes in the construction of lightweight bolt-action and AR-style firearms. Proof's unique,

Proof Researach's Monte Carlo Rifle equipped with the company's patented carbon fiber-wrapped barrel.

Proof Research's AR.

patented, carbon fiber-wrap barrel process works to shed extreme barrel heat, thereby increasing longevity and durability and encouraging a higher degree of accuracy. Proof Research's Monte Carlo bolt-action rifles are available chambered for cartridges from .204 Ruger up to and including the .338 Lapua and have a weight of only seven pounds. They come with a myriad of very favorable features, like a choice of standard or bull barrels, optional Cerakote finish, Picatinny rail bases, Mag-Pul magazines, and cut-rifled, five-groove barrels. The company's AR also comes with a Proof carbon fiber-wrapped barrel and is available in these calibers: .204 Ruger, .223 Remington, .223 Wylde, 6.5 Grendel, 6.8 SPC, and .300 Blackout. Barrel contours can be standard or bull and lengths vary from 10 ½ inches up to 24 inches. The company utilizes Mega Machine actions, Mag-Pul stocks, and Geissele triggers and are available in Type 3 anodized or Cerakote finishes. Other finishes are available on a custom basis.

ROCK RIVER ARMS

As interest grows in the use of AR-style firearms for hunting, Rock River Arms (RRA) has risen to the occasion with its new Fred Eichler Series Predator .223 Rifle. Designed to be lightweight and fast handling, the Fred Eichler Series Rifle comes with a 1:8 twist rate, 16-inch, stainless steel barrel that has been cryogenically treated to relieve stress and improve accuracy. The free-floated handguard has a full-length Picatinny top rail and a 2½-inch rail positioned at three, six, and nine o'clock, angles that are commonly used for mounting lights, lasers, and/or bipod attachments. This rifle comes stock with a chromed RRA National Match two-stage trigger, a low-profile hidden gas block, and a custom muzzle brake with directional porting intended to reduce muzzle jump and recoil. Two styles of stocks are available, an RRA Operator Stock or the RRA 6-position Operator CAR Stock, and the gun comes with a 21-round magazine (10-round, where restricted by law), and its own hard case.

ROSSI

Rossi continues to add new cartridge choices to its popular Rio Grande Lever Action Series. The most recent of these include the history-rich .45-70 Government and even the .410-bore shotshell.

Rossi Rio Grande Lever Action Rifle Series available chambered in .45-70 Government or even for .410-bore shotshells.

Both firearms offer fast side loading, closed tubular magazines, buckhorn sights, and a Brazilian hardwood stock. The .45-70 Rio Grande comes with a cartridge magazine capacity of six, with the ability to house an additional round fed directly into the chamber. The .410 holds five rounds and is available in either a blued or stainless finish. The side ejection port allows for normal scope mounting over the top of the receiver, and the gun comes with a recoil pad, cross-bolt safety, lever-actuated safety, and the unique, onboard Taurus Security System. The barrels are 20 inches long and the guns have an overall length of 38.8 inches. Weight is 5.8 pounds. MSRPs for these two new choices run from $536 to $583.

SAVAGE ARMS

Working in conjunction with Hornady, Savage is now offering its Model 25 chambered for the Hornady-designed .17 Hornet cartridge. There are three sub-models within the line to select from, including the Lightweight Varminter, Lightweight Varminter T (thumb-hole stock), and Walking Varminter. The .17 Hornet round propels the 20-grain V-Max bullet out the barrel at 3,650 fps, which is intended to mirror the trajectory of a 55-grain bullet from a .223 Remington load, but with the benefit of the felt recoil similar to that of a .22 WMR. I had the pleasure of testing one of the first of these rifles on a Wyoming prairie dog shoot and found it to be excellent out to somewhere between 250 and 300 yards. Factory ammunition and reloading dies are available from Hornady.

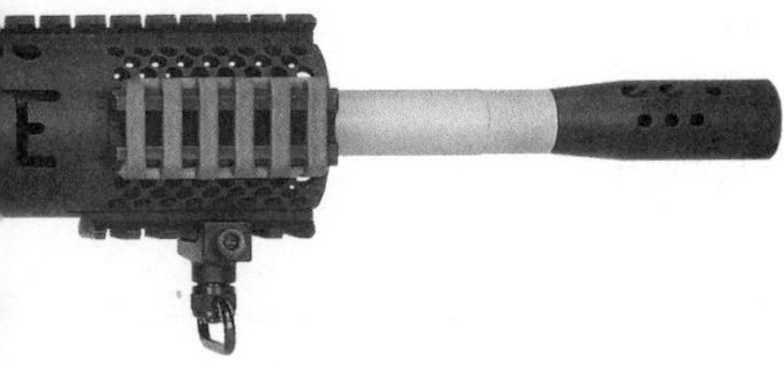

Rock River Arms Fred Eichler Series Predator .223 rifle.

STURM, RUGER & COMPANY

Ruger has expanded its very popular line of Model 77 rifles to include a new sub-model called the 77/357. This is a lightweight bolt-action rifle chambered in the versatile .357 Magnum and fed by a rotary five-shot magazine. It features a Ruger All-Weather configuration, which includes a brushed stainless steel finished barrel and receiver and a rugged black composite stock, and it comes equipped with both iron sights and Ruger scope rings. The front sight is a gold bead design and the rear sight is fully adjustable. Barrel length is 18½ inches with a 1:16 right-hand twist. Total rifle weight is a mere 5½ pounds.

Also new is the Ruger American Rifle. This moderately priced centerfire rifle is 100-percent American made and available in .30-06, .308, .270, and 243. It includes such favorable features as Ruger's new Marksman Adjustable Trigger, integral stainless steel bedding blocks as part of the company's Power Bedding System, flush-fit four-round rotary magazine, and a three-lug bolt with a 70-degree bolt throw. The 22-inch hammer-forged barrel is free floated, and the receiver is drilled and tapped for mounting a scope. Scope bases are included. Depending upon the caliber, the total weight of the rifle runs 6¼ pounds or less. MSRP for the Ruger American Rifle runs only $449.

SURESTRIKE SYSTEM

Wildcat cartridges come and go, but when Paul Garin formed SureStrike System, he took a different marketing approach to his project. Once the necessary research and testing had been completed and he was happy with the performance, Garin began offering virtually everything that a shooter would need in order to own and shoot one of his cartridges. That includes complete rifles based on a variety of actions and designs, even including a switch-barrel model. He is now supplying reloading dies for each of his five SureStrike System cartridges, as well as bullets, pre-formed brass, chamber reamers, loaded ammunition, various reloading tools, and reloading data (the reloading data can be found in a book he has published called *Taming the Tiny Terrors*). The Garin SureStrike System of cartridges are all based on the .30 Carbine case, which is necked down to form his .17 Garin, .20 Garin, .22 Garin, .243 Garin, and 6mm Garin calibers. The results are phenomenal velocities and performance, up to and including pushing a 15-grain bullet out of the muzzle of his .17 Garin at speeds of over 4,300 fps.

I was fortunate to have done some of the initial testing and load development work for the Garin SureStrike cartridges and came away very impressed. Their light recoil, high velocities, exceptional accuracy, and the availability of reloading components all make these cartridges worth a closer look. For more information on the complete products offered by Paul Garin, call 800-232-8205; www.SureStrikeSystem.com.

VOLQUARTSEN CUSTOM

Volquartsen Custom is a leader in .17-caliber rimfire rifles and pistols of semi-automatic design. I've tested one of the company's rifles on the range and in the field and found it to be very well built, functionally flawless, very accurate, and exceptionally pleasing to the eye. Currently, Volquartsen offers far too many choices to adequately be covered here, but of note, there is a

Volquartsen Custom semi-auto rifle chambered in .17 HMR.
(Author Photo)

The author shooting the Volquartsen Custom semi-auto rifle chambered in .17 HMR.
(Author Photo)

diverse selection of stocks to choose from, including a McMillan thumb-hole composite and laminated wood stocks in a wide variety of colors and designs, including a completely radical one the company calls its "Inferno." The barrels can be non-fluted or fluted in a variety of designs and patterns, and metal finishes vary from blue/black to brushed stainless and even camo. The general specifications for all Volquartsen rimfire rifles include such features as a stainless steel CNC-machined receiver with a threaded 0.925-inch diameter barrel. The bolt is also CNC machined and features a round titanium firing pin and heavy-duty extractor. The trigger group is a TG2000, which is capable of very light pull weights. The magazine is a Ruger JMX-1 rotary type, in this case capable of holding up to nine .17 HMR cartridges. The built-in receiver scope base on the test rifle was a Picatinny rail style, which accepts Weaver-style scope rings. If the .17 HMR doesn't meet your fancy, the company also produces rifles and pistols chambered for .22 LR, .22 WMR, and one of my personal favorites, the .17 Mach 2. Prices vary dramatically based on models and the optical choices.

WEATHERBY

With the ever-increasing popularity of the .338 Lapua Magnum cartridge, Weatherby is now offering this chambering in the company's Mark V, Accumark, and TRR (Threat Response Rifle). Originally designed as a long-range sniper cartridge for military use, many shooters are now finding other applications for it be-

Weatherby Mark V Accumark TRR (Threat Response Rifle) RC (Range Certified) rifle.

Weatherby Mark V Accumark TRR (Threat Response Rifle) Custom Magnum chambered for .338 Lapua.

Winchester Repeating Arms Model 70 Featherweight Compact bolt-action rifle.

Winchester Repeating Arms Model 94 Sporter.

Winchester Repeating Arms Model 94 Short rifle.

yond punching holes in unsuspecting terrorists.

The Accumark features a hand-laminated, raised-comb Monte Carlo composite stock and a 26-inch, No. 3 contour, button-rifled, chrome moly, free-floated fluted barrel (0.705-inch muzzle diameter). The barrel comes with a recessed target crown and, for reduced felt recoil, it is equipped with a Weatherby Accubrake. Other features include a CNC-machined 6061 T-6 aluminum bedding plate and a factory tuned, fully adjustable trigger.

The Weatherby TTR Custom Magnum also comes with a composite stock and free-floated 26-inch No. 3 contour barrel, and it possesses a recessed target crown and Accubrake. The buttstock is fully adjustable, allowing a shooter to match the stock specifically to their size and shape. The hand-tuned, fully adjustable trigger comes from the factory set at three pounds pull weight with the sear engagement set at .008 to .014. The Mark V TTR RC (Range Certified) rifles are tested and guaranteed to shoot sub-MOA (a three-shot group of 0.99-inch or less), with Weatherby-specified factory or premium ammunition.

The .338 Lapua Magnum Mark V Accumark carries an MSRP of $2,300, the Mark V TRR runs $2,900, and the Mark V TRR RC is at $4,100.

WINCHESTER REPEATING ARMS

Virtually no other firearms manufacturer has a more colorful historic past than that of Winchester. After all, it was the rifle that won the West. But, it's not a secret that Winchester has experienced some financial problems in the past. Thankfully, those difficulties now seem to be behind it. Once again the company has established itself as a vibrant and valued member of our shooting community. As part of that reorganization, the company has introduced a new Model 70 Featherweight Compact rifle that would be perfect for a wide variety of hunting and shooting applications. It comes with a 20-inch barrel, a 13-inch length of pull, an overall length of 39½ inches, and it weighs only 6½ pounds, making it a perfect choice for ladies, young shooters, and those looking for a lightweight mountain rifle.

The Compact Model 70 action has the pre-'64 controlled-round feeding, a three-position safety, a jeweled bolt body, and knurled bolt handle. It includes the M.O.A. Trigger System that is easily adjustable, and a satin-finished checkered walnut stock. The action is bedded and the barrel has been free floated for enhanced accuracy. Currently, the Compact Model 70 is available in, .22-250 Remington, .243 Winchester, 7m-08 Remington, and .308 Winchester and carries a MSRP of $899.99.

Also available from Winchester are two lever-action versions of the Model 94. The new Sporter 94 features a blued, 24-inch, half round/half octagon barrel and comes with semi-buckhorn rear sight and a fine gold bead on the front. The straight-grip walnut stock is checkered and equipped with a traditionally styled, crescent-shaped blued steel buttplate. The receiver is drilled and tapped for scope mounts and the hammer is drilled and tapped for a spur extension. The Sporter 94 is chambered for either .30-30 or .38-55 and carries an MSRP of $1,299.99.

The new Model 94 Short Rifle comes with a 20-inch round blued barrel and has a semi-buckhorn rear sight and a Marble gold bead front sight. Overall length is only 38 inches and the gun weighs a mere 6¾ pounds. Like the Sporter, it is drilled and tapped for scope mounts, but this model is chambered only for .30-30 Winchester. MSRP for the 94 Sport Rifle is $1,199.99.

BY **JOHN HAVILAND**
With a Special Section by **Kevin Muramatsu**

Sales have dramatically increased for most segments of firearms and ammunition over the last few years. However, shotguns sales have suffered some, due to a continuing depressed economy and, as the financial folks phrase, it "a lack of discretionary income." The National Shooting Sports Foundation stated that, in 2010, imports of handguns into the United States increased 22.2 percent, 124.6 percent for rifles, and 71.1 percent for muzzleloaders. But, shotgun imports *declined* 26.8 percent, from 50,980 to 37,341 guns. The NSSF also reported imports of rifle and handgun cartridges increased 27.4 percent, while imported shotgun cartridges declined 24.1 percent, from 9.8 to 7.4 million shells, in 2010

This year, the usually prolific Beretta, Browning, and Remington companies are introducing only a couple new guns and refinements of established models. Also, Ruger dropped its Red Label over/under shotguns, although it says it is developing a replacement. Let's see what these companies and others have to offer.

Benelli

A 12-gauge waterfowl gun and an ultra-light autoloading 28-gauge highlight Benelli's new guns.

The Super Black Eagle II Performance Shop Waterfowl Edition features an Inertia Driven operating system that has been honed and polished, and a tuned trigger group that provides a crisp pull. The Waterfowl Edition has a 28-inch barrel with a lengthened and polished forcing cone, along with Rob Roberts Custom Triple Threat choke tubes for short-, medium-, and long-range shooting. Each gun is test fired with Federal Premium Black Cloud steel shotshells, to ensure it produces consistent, even patterns.

A 28-gauge that weighs 4.9 pounds is the newest addition to Benelli's Ultra Light family. The Ultra Light 28 uses the Inertia Driven operating system with a two-shell capacity magazine. The 26-inch barrel is topped with a raised, carbon fiber ventilated rib with a midbead and a red bar front sight. Cylinder (C), Improved Cylinder (IC), and Modified (M) choke tubes are included. The stock and forearm are walnut with a WeatherCoat finish and an AirCell recoil pad.

Beretta

A field version of Beretta's A400 XPLOR has a bronze-colored receiver. The autoloader weighs around 6¾ pounds and is chambered for 12-gauge 2¾ and three-inch loads. The walnut stock and forearm are enhanced Xtra wood grain with an oil finish. The new Gun Pod delivers a digital readout of the air temperature, pressure of the round fired, and the overall number of rounds fired through the shotgun.

The SV10 Perennia I over/under has a redesigned receiver with reinforced hinge pins and deeper breech shoulders that reinforce the lockup between the receiver and barrels. The Nano-Ceramic coated receiver interior reduces iron wear, and the adjustable ejection/extraction allows the shooter to select between automatic ejection and mechanical extraction.

Browning

The Browning A-5 12-gauge autoloader is back, if in name only, because the humpback receiver is about the only thing shared between the new and old A-5. The original A-5 was made of steel, and it was heavy. Its recoil-operated action was as reliable as time. But the mechanism contained so many parts it would baffle even a gifted gunsmith. The new A-5's receiver is aluminum, and the gun weighs six pounds 13 ounces, which is nearly two pounds lighter than the old three-inch A-5. The new A-5 also has a much simpler, recoil-operated Kinematic Drive System. Browning states "it will work, come hell or high water" and backs it with a 100,000-round or five-year guarantee.

OTGUNS

Beretta SV10

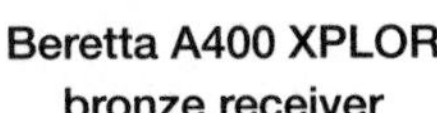

Beretta A400 XPLOR bronze receiver

The new A-5 comes with a three-inch chamber, 26-, 28-, or 30-inch barrel with a Vector Pro lengthened forcing cone and IC, M, and F Invector-Double Seal (DS) choke tubes. The Invector-DS choke tubes have a brass alloy ring around the outside base of the tube that seals out grit from gas and powder fouling from working its way between the bore and tube, allowing easy unscrewing after extended shooting. An Inflex II recoil pad is included on the Hunter model that comes with a walnut stock and forearm, and the Stalker model with a Mossy Oak Duck Blind, Infinity camo patterns, or all black with a Dura-Touch Armor Coating synthetic stock and forearm.

The A-5 includes features from other Browning shotguns, such as a Turnkey magazine plug that allows quick removal and insertion of the magazine plug, quarter- and half-inch stock spacers to adjust length of pull, and Browning's Speed Load Plus technology that cycles the first shell fed into the magazine directly into the chamber. I shot one of the new A-5s at clay targets, and it was much quicker to point and swing than my 40-year-old A-5.

Gail Haviland shooting a Browning Hunter A-5 12-gauge at clay targets.

Browning 725-Field

Browning 725-Sporting

Browning A-5 Hunter

Browning A-5 Mossy Oak-Break-Up-Infinity

Browning A-5 Mossy-Oak-Duck-Blind

Browning A-5 Stalker

A lower-profile receiver adds a bit more grace to the Browning Citori 725 over/under, yet the gun retains the same full-width hinge pin and tapered locking bolt as other Citoris. The 725 has the all-new FireLite Mechanical Trigger that offers a clean trigger pull and short overtravel; Sporting models have a pull weight of three to 3½ pounds, and Field guns four to 4½ pounds. Vector Pro lengthened forcing cones are included, along with the Invector-DS Choke System in IC, M, and F tubes. An Inflex II recoil pad directs the pad down slightly during recoil, to pull the comb down away from the cheek.

The Citori 725 Field features high-relief engraving on its silver nitrate-coated receiver. A gloss oil finish Grade II/III walnut stock is shaped with a tightly radiused grip, and its trim forearm has cut checkering. Lightweight 26- or 28-inch barrels and a ventilated rib put gun weights at seven pounds four ounces to seven pounds six ounces.

The Citori 725 Sporting model has 28-, 30-, or 32-inch barrels with a HIVIZ Pro-Comp fiber-optic front sight and ivory mid-bead. Gloss oil finish Grade III/IV walnut is used for the close radius-gripped stock and trim fore-end. Browning's Triple Trigger System allows fine tuning of the length of pull and switching between a wide checkered, a narrow smooth, or a wide smooth trigger shoe. HIVIZ Pro-Comp fiber-optic front sight and ivory mid-bead are supplied. Skeet (SK), IC, M, Improved Modified (IM), and F extended Invector-DS choke tubes are supplied. Gun weights vary between seven pounds six ounces and seven pounds 10 ounces.

CZ USA

CZ has added five variations to existing models.

The 712 Target 12-gauge gas-operated autoloader is built for the price-conscious shooter. It has a 30-inch barrel with a 10mm stepped rib topped with a fiber optic bead for rising trap targets. Interchangeable F, M, and IC choke tubes are included. The 712 Adjustable Length Stock is fitted with an ATI synthetic stock that adjusts from a 12- to 14-inch length of pull. Interchangeable F, M, and IC chokes are included.

The Redhead Target is CZ USA's first gun designed for target shooters. The Target is based on the Redhead over/under model, with a boxlock frame, single selective trigger, auto ejectors, and a 12-gauge three-inch chamber. New features include a Monte Carlo stock, a 30-inch barrel with a stepped rib, and F, IM, M, IC, and C choke tubers. The Turkish walnut stock and forearm contrast nicely with the silver receiver.

The Ringneck side-by-side comes in two new models. Each Ringneck frame is based on its gauge, so there are four different action sizes for the model. The straight grip 20-gauge has a Turkish walnut stock, 26-inch barrels with three-inch chambers, and C, IC, M, IM, and F flush-fitting choke tubes. The receiver is case hardened and includes a single selective trigger and extractors, instead of ejectors. The Ringneck Target 12-gauge has many of the same features, but with a full-size target grip and 30-inch barrels.

Franchi

The Affinity 12- and 20-gauge autoloaders are constructed with aluminum receivers having steel inserts that ensure solid steel-to-steel lock-up. That lightweight metal brings the 12-gauge in at 6.4 pounds, and the 20-gauge at 5.6 pounds. The Inertia Driven action 12-gauge cycles 1⅛-ounce target loads through to heavy, three-inch magnums, and the 20-gauge functions with ⅞-ounce loads through to three-inch magnums.

The Affinity's synthetic stock and forearm are available in black, Realtree

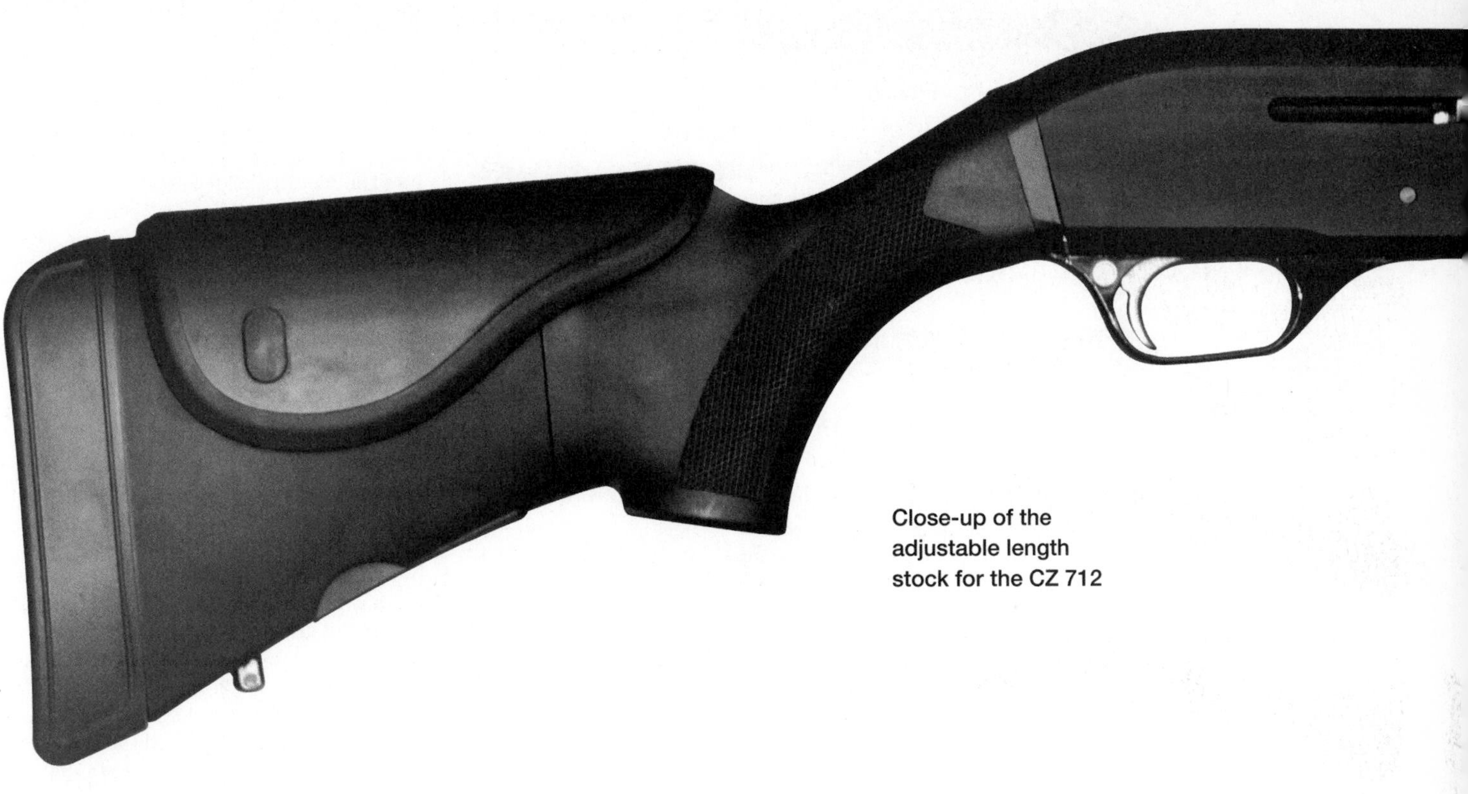

Close-up of the adjustable length stock for the CZ 712

Max-4, or APG camouflage. Stock drop at heel is adjustable from two to 2½ inches in four increments, and comb height can be changed 1½ inches with an included shim kit. A new recoil pad compresses to spread recoil energy over a wide area of the shooter's shoulder.

The Franchi Instinct L over/under has an all-steel case colored receiver with an automatic tang-mounted safety that also acts as a barrel selector. Barrels are 26 or 28 inches in 12-gauge and 28 inches in 20-gauge, and are chrome-lined, have a fiber-optic front sight, and include IC, M, and F choke tubes. The oil-finish walnut stock has a Prince of Wales grip. It and the slim forearm sport cut checkering. The 12-gauge weighs 6.4 pounds, and the 20-gauge is 6.1 pounds. Everything stores in a hard case.

An aluminum receiver reduces the Instinct SL over/under 12 and 20-gauge weight .7-pound, compared to the Instinct L. The Instinct SL weighs 5.7 pounds in 12-gauge and slightly more than five pounds in the 20-gauge. The SL has the same features as the L, but its receiver is finished with a combination of polish and brushing with nominal engraving that contrasts nicely with its Turkish walnut stock and forearm.

The Franchi 48 AL autoloader has been shooting targets and game for

CZ 712 Adjustable Length Stock

CZ 712 Target

CZ Redhead Target

CZ Ringneck StraightStock

CZ Ringneck Target

Franchi 48AL Deluxe 20-gauge

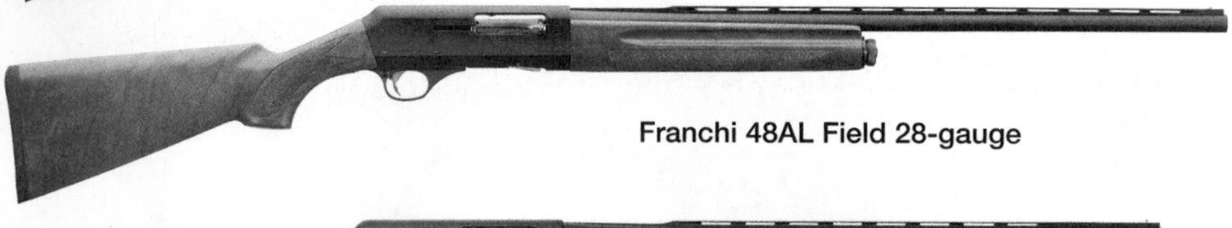

Franchi 48AL Field 28-gauge

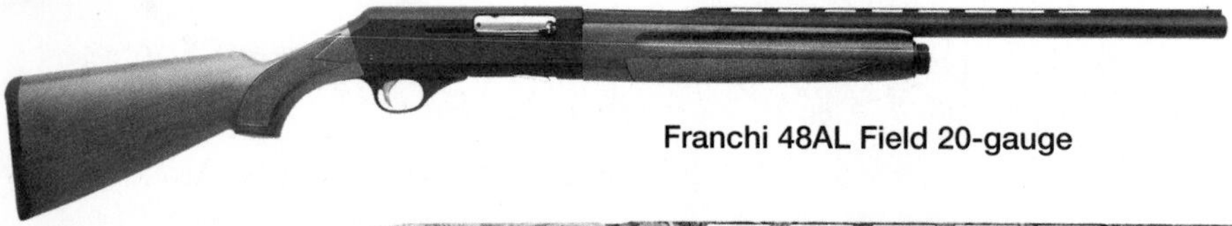

Franchi 48AL Field 20-gauge

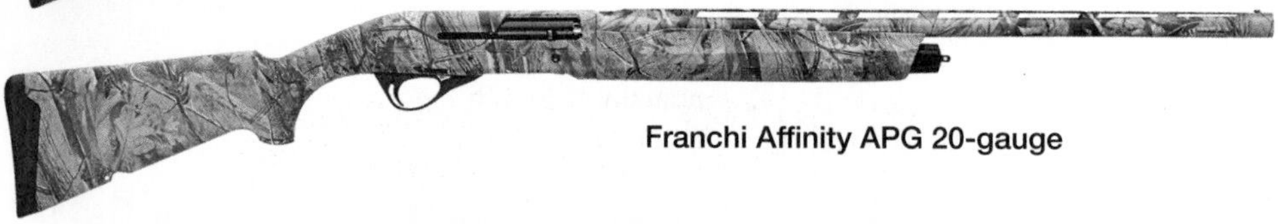

Franchi Affinity APG 20-gauge

Franchi Affinity-BlackSynth 12ga-silo

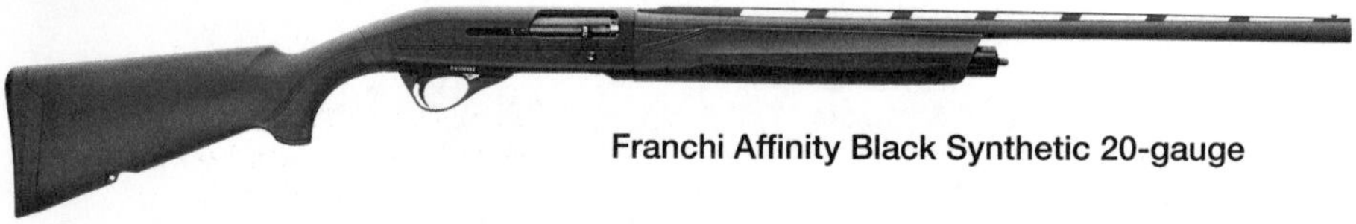

Franchi Affinity Black Synthetic 20-gauge

Franchi Affinity MAX4 12-gauge

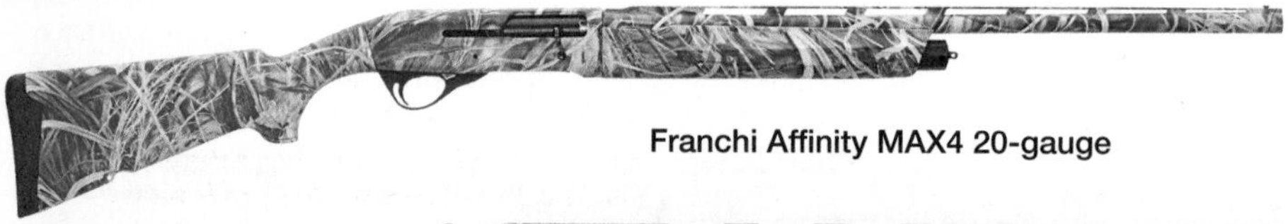

Franchi Affinity MAX4 20-gauge

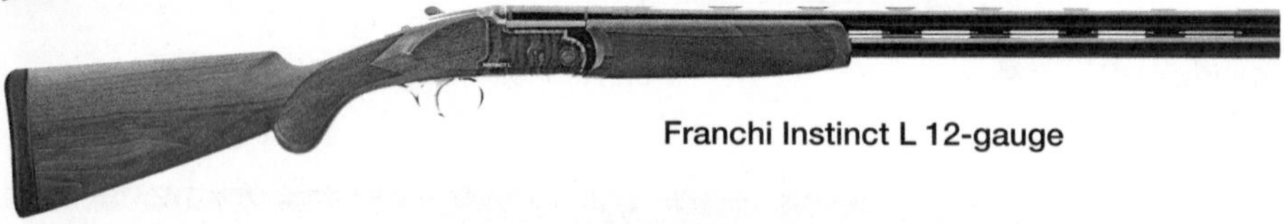

Franchi Instinct L 12-gauge

Franchi Instinct SL 20-gauge

years. The 48 AL Deluxe Prince of Wales version provides a bit more class to that shooting. The walnut stock with a Prince-of-Wales style grip goes together with polished and deep blued metal and a gold trigger. The 20-gauge gun weighs just 5.6 pounds, and its chrome-lined bore accepts IC, M, and F choke tubes. Franchi includes a seven-year warranty.

Mossberg

Mossberg's FLEX system allows quick modification of a 500 or 590 pump-action FLEX-fitted receiver with a variety of stocks, forearms, and recoil pads. Add into the mix 18½-, 20-, 24-, 26-, or 28-inch smoothbore barrels and a 24-inch rifled barrel, and the options are nearly limitless. The FLEX system is based on a Tool-less Locking System (TLS) that allow stocks, fore-ends, and recoil pads to be switched out for a variety of shooting. The T-shaped TLS lifts from the connector, and a twist disengages it. That allows installation of 16 FLEX accessory components. They include a stock with 12½-, 13½-, and 14¼-inch lengths of pull, a six-position adjustable tactical stock, a four-position adjustable, dual-comb hunting stock, a six-position adjustable tactical stock, dual-comb hunting stock, or a pistol grip stock. Three different recoil pads of ¾-, 1¼-, and 1½-inch thicknesses can be switched out to create a gun that grows with the shooter. Push the forearm release button, and the handle can be fitted with one of three standard or a tactical tri-rail synthetic forearms.

Mossberg FLEX Recoil Pad Comparisons

Mossberg FLEX Recoil Pad Release Button

Buyers can choose a basic FLEX shotgun from three 500 All-Purpose, four 500/590 Tactical, and four 500 Hunting options, each with 12-gauge three-inch chambers. FLEX All-Purpose models have either a 26- or 28-inch ventilated rib, ACCU-CHOKE ported barrel with matte metal finish or optional all-weather Marinecote finish, full-length synthetic stock with a medium recoil pad, and a standard synthetic fore-end. FLEX 500/590 Tactical models are available with matte, OD Green, or Coyote Tan finishes on receivers, and cylinder-bore 18½- or 20-inch barrels. FLEX Hunting models are available with 24- or 28-inch ventilated rib barrels and choice of OD Green, Coyote Tan, Mossy Oak Break-Up Infinity, or Realtree MAX-4 camo receiver finishes. Standard full-length stocks and fore-ends also feature Infinity or MAX-4 finishes.

Nearly 10 million Mossberg 500 pumps have been sold since it came out in 1961. Now you can own a 500 Classic All-Purpose Field 12-gauge with a three-inch chamber, much like the original, with high-gloss walnut stock and forearm. Checkering on the stock grip and wrap-around checkering on the forearm go nicely with the Pachmayr red recoil pad and a white line spacer. The 28-inch ventilated rib barrel is ported and comes with interchangeable ACCU-CHOKE IC, M, and F tubes.

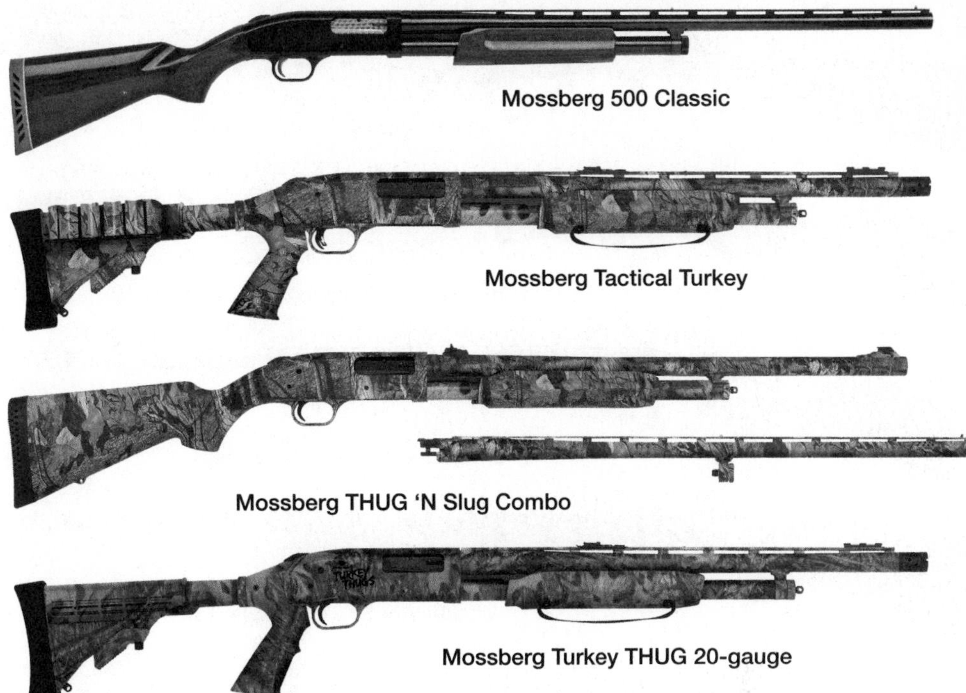
Mossberg 500 Classic

Mossberg Tactical Turkey

Mossberg THUG 'N Slug Combo

Mossberg Turkey THUG 20-gauge

The 500 Turkey THUG Tactical is available in 12- and 20-gauge, either with three-inch chambers, and features tactical-style adjustable length of pull from 10¾ to 14⅝ inches that's modifiable via a click of the adjustment latch. The stock also has a molded holder that stores five extra rounds. The stock, forearm, and exposed metalwork are camouflaged in Mossy Oak Obsession. A short 20-inch ventilated rib barrel has an X-FACTOR ported choke tube and is topped with adjustable fiber optic sights. A padded sling allows easy carrying.

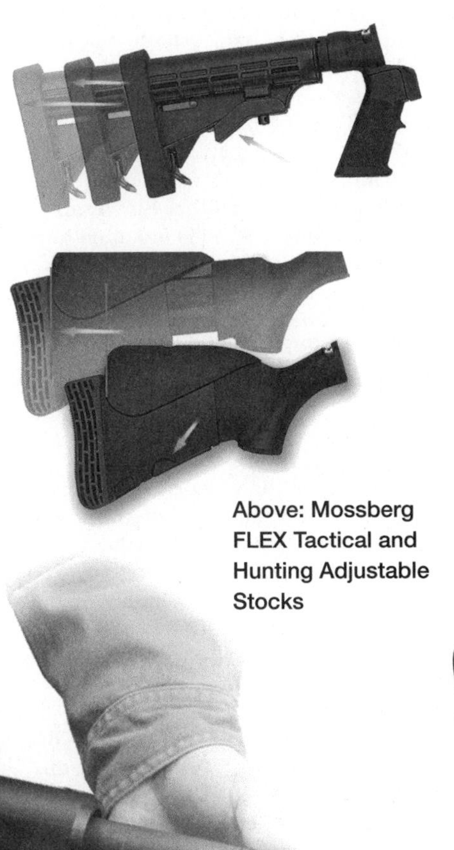
Above: Mossberg FLEX Tactical and Hunting Adjustable Stocks

The 500 THUG 'N Slug Combo has two barrels. The 24-inch ported barrel with adjustable fiber optic sights and XX-Full Turkey choke tube is for the turkey woods. The 24-inch fluted, fully-rifled barrel with adjustable rifle sights is for chasing deer. The 500 Combo's LPA trigger is adjustable from three to eight pounds of pull. Mossy Oak Break-Up Infinity camo pattern covers the synthetic stock, forearm, exposed metalwork, and two barrels. A matching sling attaches to the gun's sling studs.

Remington

Previously, Remington had dressed up and tricked out its Model 870 pump every which way until it had 28 models in the current lineup. This year it introduced the 870 Express Tactical BLACKHAWK! The 870 BLACKHAWK! has

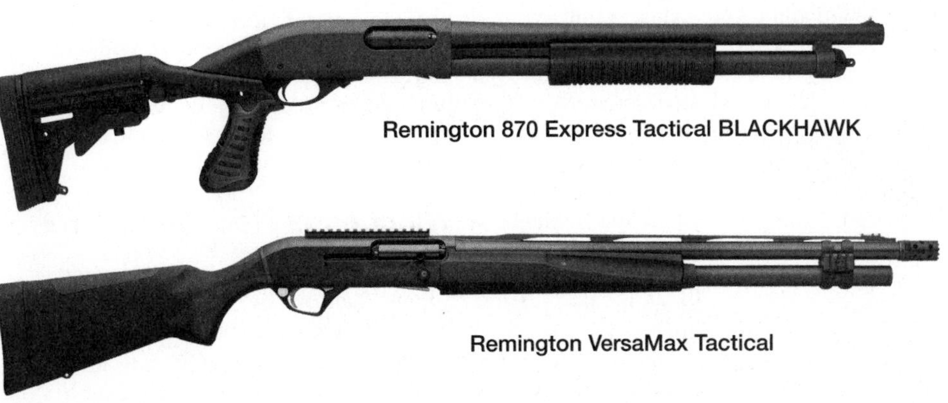
Remington 870 Express Tactical BLACKHAWK

Remington VersaMax Tactical

Winchester SXP Turkey Hunter

Winchester SX3 Black Field Compact

Winchester SX3 Black Field

Winchester SX3 Black Shadow

Winchester SX3 Cantilever Buck

Winchester SX3 NWTF Cantilever Turkey

Winchester SX3 Waterfowl Hunter

a factory-installed two-round magazine extension that increases overall capacity to seven rounds beneath the 12-gauge 18½-inch barrel. The shotgun features a synthetic BLACKHAWK! SpecOps II Adjustable Stock with seven positions in the length of pull. Remington's SuperCell recoil pad and a Knoxx dual recoil-compensation spring system in the stock and grip reduce felt recoil. Other features include a vertical grip with interchangeable rubber grip inserts, and quick-detachable sling swivels.

Remington wasted no time decking out its VERSA MAX autoloader in black dress. The VERSA MAX Tactical wears a 22-inch barrel with a ventilated rib that tapers from 10 millimeters at the receiver down to seven at the muzzle. Improved Cylinder and Tactical ProBore choke tubes are included. A Picatinny rail on the receiver and barrel hold sights, lights, and other options. The cross-bolt safety, bolt-release button, and bolt handle are over-sized. A magazine extension raises shell capacity to nine. A synthetic stock with rubber panels on the grip and forearm provide a sure hold. The stock has a thick SuperCell recoil pad and Adjustable Length of Pull Spacer Kit to extend pull one inch. An interchangeable padded cheek comb insert raises comb height for better sight alignment.

Winchester Repeating Arms

Advances to the Super X pump and Super X3 autoloader are the focus of Winchester's new shotguns.

The Super X pump (SXP) now has three versions in a 12-gauge 3½-inch configuration. All have a hard-chrome chamber and bore with Invector Plus IC, M, and F choke tubes in a 26- or 28- inch barrel. The SXP Waterfowl Hunter has a choice of a 26- or 28-inch barrel with a TRUGLO Long Bead fiber optic front sight. Its synthetic stock has textured gripping surfaces and is covered in Mossy Oak Duck Blind camo pattern. The SXP Black Shadow wears a brass front bead. Its black synthetic stock and forearm match the black chrome finish on the bolt and other metal. The SXP Turkey Hunter's synthetic stock, forearm, and barrel are covered with Mossy Oak Break-Up Infinity camouflage. An Invector-Plus Extra-Full turkey choke tube is standard. An Inflex Technology recoil pad cushions some of the sting from shooting 3½-inch magnum shells out of the 6⅝-pound gun.

The Super X3 line of 12- and 20-gauge autoloaders has seven new models. The Black Field has an oil-finished and checkered walnut stock and forearm with a matte black receiver and barrel. A Pachmayr Decelerator recoil pad softens recoil. The Black Field Compact is the same gun, but with a shorter, 13-inch length of pull. A matte black synthetic stock and forearm with textured gripping surfaces defines the Super X3 Black Shadow. The Cantilever Buck also wears a matte black synthetic stock and forearm, but its rifled 22-inch barrel shoots 2¾- and three-inch sabots. A Weaver-style rail is mounted on this version's barrel and extends back over the receiver to support a variety of optics, while an adjustable rear sight brings the TRUGLO fiber optic front sight into alignment. The Waterfowl Hunter is covered in Mossy Oak Duck Blind camo. A TRUGLO Long Bead fiber optic front sight provides a precise relationship of the muzzle to the target. Cast and drop shims and length-of-pull spacers provide perfect stock fit. The Universal Hunter is similar, but covered with Mossy Oak Break-Up Infinity camo. The NWTF Cantilever Turkey also has an adjustable rear sight with a TRUGLO fiber optic front sight. A Weaver-style rail extends over the receiver on the NWTF version to provide the option of mounting optics. The Turkey's 24-inch barrel is cut with Quadra-Vent ports to vent excess powder gas in order to keep the system cleaner. An Invector-Plus Extra-Full Turkey choke tube provides tight patterns with three-inch 20-gauge or 3½-inch 12-gauge shells.

The short and handy Kel-Tec KSG.

TACTICAL SHOTGUNS

BY KEVIN MURAMATSU

While the tactical market has been driven mostly by the Modern Sporting Rifle craze, that trend has been closely tailgated by the loads of advances in the tactical shotgun realms. Let's just call them the Modern Sporting Shotguns, for now.

These models tend to follow some generic guidelines. First, most of them are black, though some might be in earth tone of some sort or camouflaged. Second, most have an extension on the magazine tube to maximize the ammo capacity. Six, seven, or eight rounds are not atypical. Third, the barrel will usually stay below 22 inches in length, in order to keep the door jam interactions down. Fourth, pistol grips are common, though not universally present. Fifth, the guns usually incorporate some sort of close-quarters sight, often with the assistance of tritium inserts. Finally, the vast majority are chambered for 12-gauge shells. Let's take a look at some of the newer models to come down the turnpike

Shotties for Defense

Possibly the most exciting, and certainly the most unique, is the Kel Tec KSG. This is a bullpup-style pump shotgun, and you load it through a large port behind the pistol grip. You also load it 14 times, seven times each in each of two side-by-side magazine tubes. Besides the higher than normal capacity, this duality allows the user to utilize two different loads at the same time, say buckshot

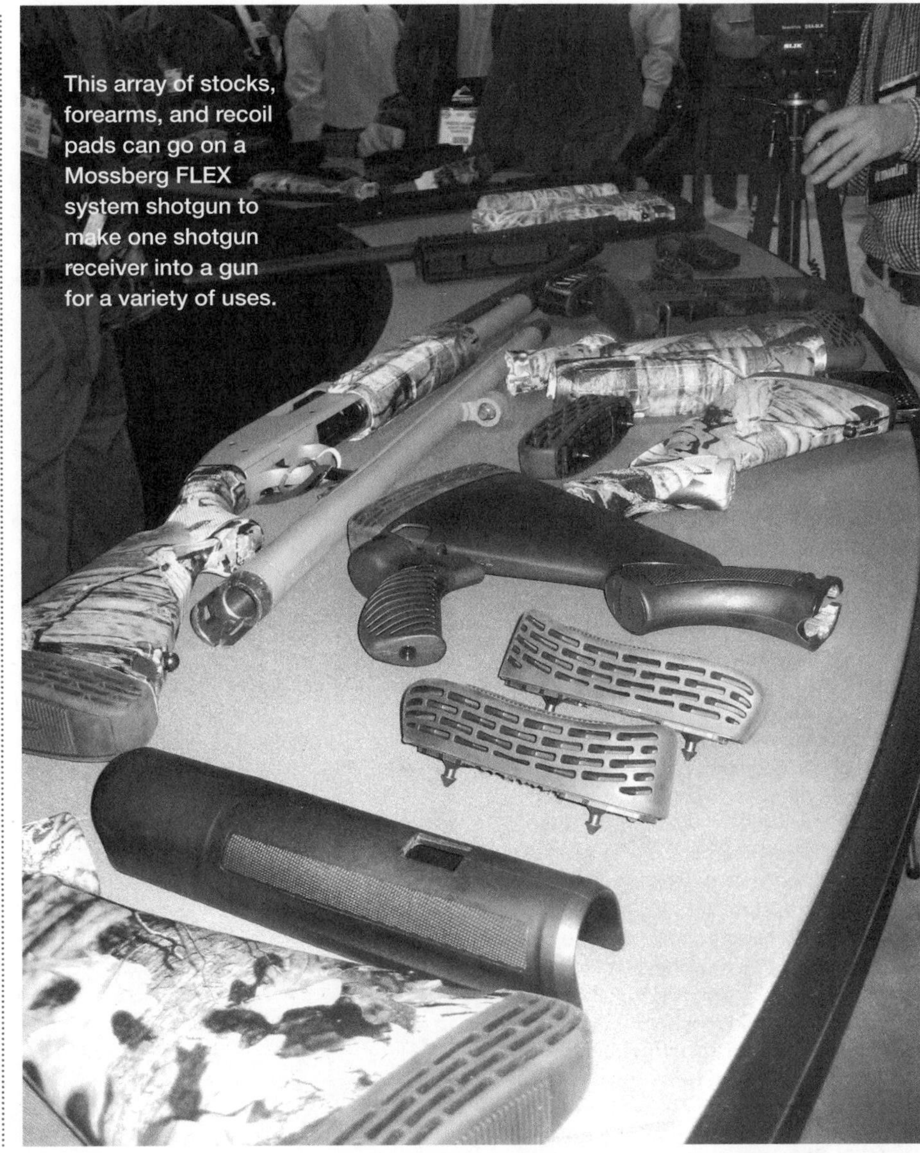
This array of stocks, forearms, and recoil pads can go on a Mossberg FLEX system shotgun to make one shotgun receiver into a gun for a variety of uses.

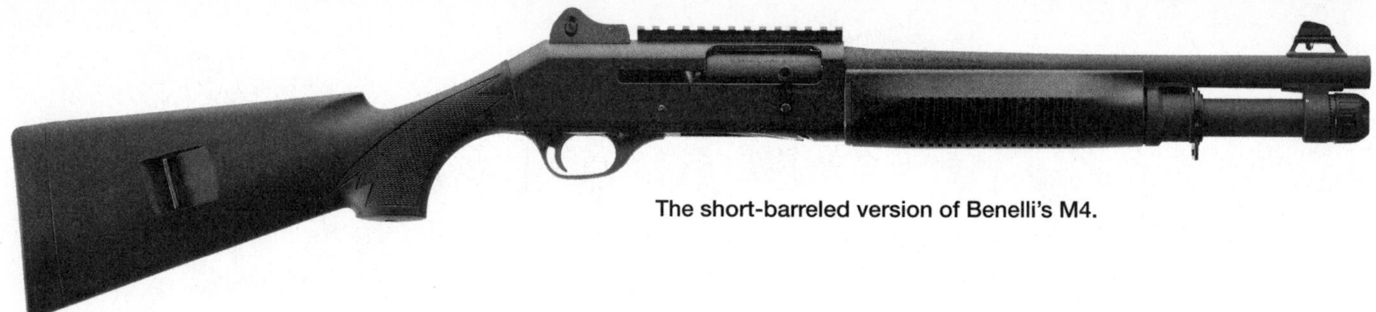
The short-barreled version of Benelli's M4.

and slugs. Merely flipping a switch in the loading gate allows the shooter to access either mag tube, or to eject a shell to empty the chamber without another round feeding up. Ejected hulls are thrown down out of the loading area. Even with an 18-inch barrel, the overall length is still quite short at a hair more than 26 inches. The KSG was brought into full-scale production just at the end of 2010 and is available in several colors.

Mossberg continues to expand its line of tactical shotguns with the SA-20. This is a semi-auto designed for the home-defense market, and it's in 20-gauge, rather than 12. Manufactured overseas by one of Mossberg's partners, it is available in several tactical and hunting configurations, including a youth model. Distinguishing points on the tactical models are protected ghost ring sights and a Picatinny rail on the receiver.

One interesting nod to the modular gun concept is Mossberg's FLEX 500 line of shotguns, some of which John Haviland already talked about in the previous section. Several are set up to be used for home-defense or tactical purposes. Different combinations of extended magazine tubes, pistol grips, and collapsible stocks are the ticket here. The really interesting thing with these shotguns is the FLEX technology built into them. With the press of a button under the handguard, the fore-end can be pulled right off and replaced with another. The stock, likewise, can be quickly removed by lifting a key of sorts and rotating it 90 degrees. Then the stock is rapped with the hand and can be pulled right off its fixture point on the back of the receiver. Not guarding the fort? You can put on a more appropriate set of furniture and a longer barrel and you are out the door in about one minute for a round of sporting clays. Different sizes of recoil pads can be quickly switched in and out, as well, allowing rapid adjustment of the length of pull. These three quick-change mechanisms form the Tool-less Locking System.

Benelli has finally made available to the American public the M4 shotgun with the collapsible stock and extended magazine tube that it was always supposed to have. Previously only available in this setup to law enforcement and military, it will likely be a welcome item to the many shooters who have had the M4 on their wish lists. As well as the standard version in the ubiquitous black, Benelli has also released a limited production model with the NP3 coating for superior corrosion protection. This H2O model is quite snappy looking, and the high lubricity inherent in the coating makes this shotgun much easier to maintain. Fouling can be easily wiped off with a simple rag. Benelli is also selling NFA versions of the M4 with short barrels for those with the right paperwork.

Remington has, of course, been around for many a year, as has its 870 shotgun. Still available is the current line of tactical and police models, but a twist has been added to the newest example. Teaming up with MagPul Industries, the

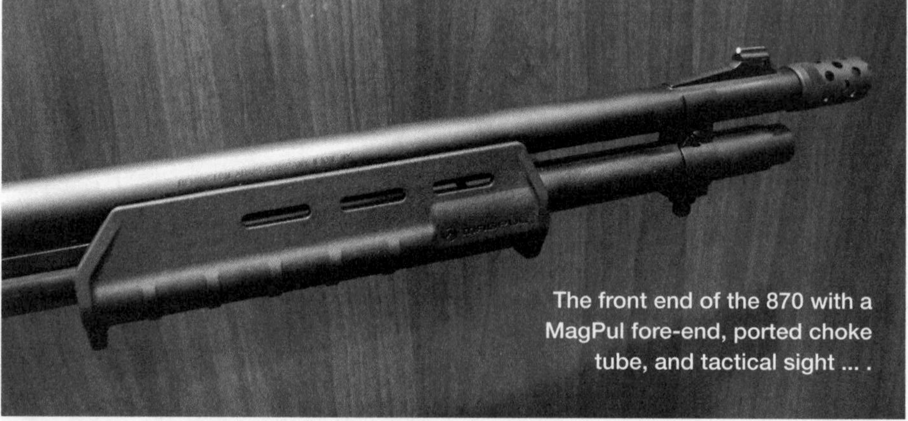
The front end of the 870 with a MagPul fore-end, ported choke tube, and tactical sight ... .

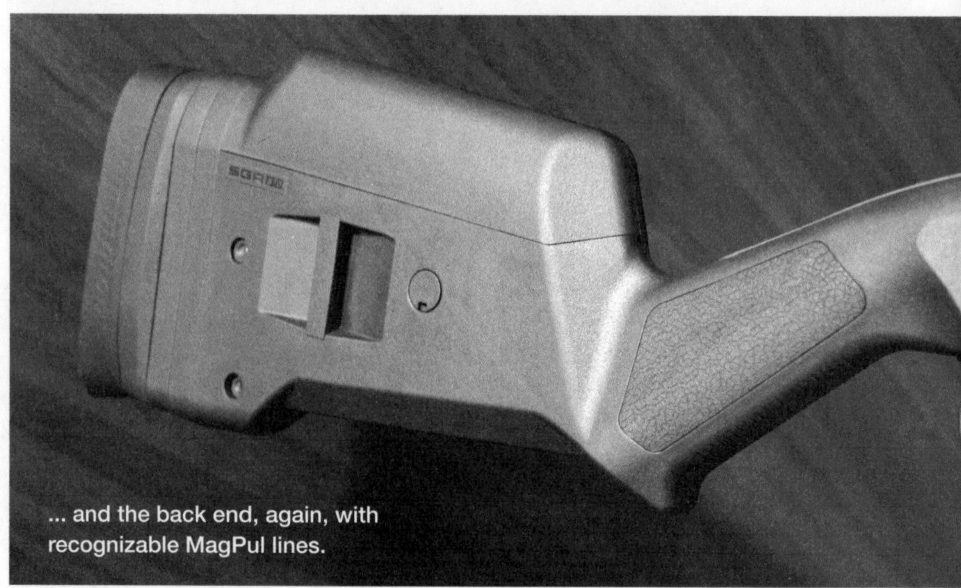
... and the back end, again, with recognizable MagPul lines.

The new semi-auto tac gun from Weatherby. The SA-459 is above, and below is a camo-stocked PA-459 pump gun. Both were new in 2012.

870 now has its own set of the excellent MagPul furniture. A synthetic forearm and buttstock replace the standard wooden set, both with recognizable MagPul lines and feel. The stock forms a relatively long and down-turned pistol grip that happens to result in a quite natural feel, despite it's rather radical appearance. The gun also is equipped with ghost ring sights, as well as Picatinny rails for the mounting of accessories such as lights or lasers.

Ithaca Gun Company has a new sister, Ithaca Tactical. Besides ARs, this division will handle the tactical and defensive lineup of shotguns. Like many others, Ithaca has made its pump gun more suitable for home-defense purposes by adding extended magazine tubes and ghost ring sights. Ghost rings are essentially a standard aperture, or peep sight, but with a much larger hole to look through, a design created for high visibility and fast target acquisition. One of the rather unusual things is that at least one model in the lineup has a fully rifled slug barrel, on the rationale of using slugs as home-defense projectiles, rather than shot. This barrel is rigidly held in the receiver to preserve the best accuracy and is fitted with rifle sights, rather than a bead or ghost ring set up.

Weatherby has entered the tactical shotgun market. The entry level option, the PA-08 PR, is a pump gun without frills and comes in any color you like, as long as it's black. The PA-459 TR is the next level up, with a pistol grip stock and available in any color you like, as long as it is black or digital camouflage. The SA-459 TR is the final entry and is the semi-automatic of the bunch. With the same features as the PA-459 it is also available in 20-gauge to back up the 12-gauge models and its less-fancy brothers. It is also available in any color as long as it's black. The PA-08 has a white dot blade front sight, while the PA-459 and the SA-459 have protected ghost ring sights, the rear of the latter mounted to a Picatinny rail on the top of the receiver and paired with a tall-winged front sight. All three models wear 18½-inch barrels with cylinder bores, though the SA-459 and the PA-459 have removable, ported, extended choke tubes.

Savage has expanded its selection of inexpensive, imported shotguns, with the Stevens Model 320. Like many other brands, the 320 can be found with various combinations of tactical-style equipment, such as extended magazine tubes and pistol grip stocks. Combo sets are also available and, with a starting MSRP of under $250, it's almost impossible to argue over the value in this deal.

A very fun new submission in the tactical shotgun field is the Akdal MKA 1919. This series is manufactured in Turkey and imported by RAAC. AR-15 owners should love this shotgun, since it looks, feels, and pretty much functions like an AR. The safety, magazine catch, and all the rest, including the detachable box magazine, are all straight AR. Training is thus minimized. The barrel is retained (and easily removed for cleaning) in an aluminum upper receiver attached to a polymer lower receiver/buttstock unit. An internal choke tube system is installed, and differing finishes are available. MSRP is a reasonable $700, and the gun comes with two five-round magazines. So far it is 12-gauge only. Of

RAAC's Akdal MKA1919 AR-type 12-gauge shotgun in camo.

Ithaca's new tactical model, based on the Model 37. Note the racy barrel shroud, sights, and rails.

particular note, Firebird Precision is taking these guns and making three-gun competition versions of them, any of which are eminently suitable for tactical/ defense purposes. While the price tag will jump significantly, the usability and versatility of the gun will commensurately improve.

Shotgun Accessories

We also want to take a look at some new tactical shotgun accessories. If a shooter doesn't want or cannot afford to purchase a tactical gun outright, but still would like some of the features, then the aftermarket accessory world is the place to go. As with the ARs and 10/22s, there is a burgeoning selection of items to make the wing or upland gun stand in for a ready-made home-defense gun. Of course there has for some time been

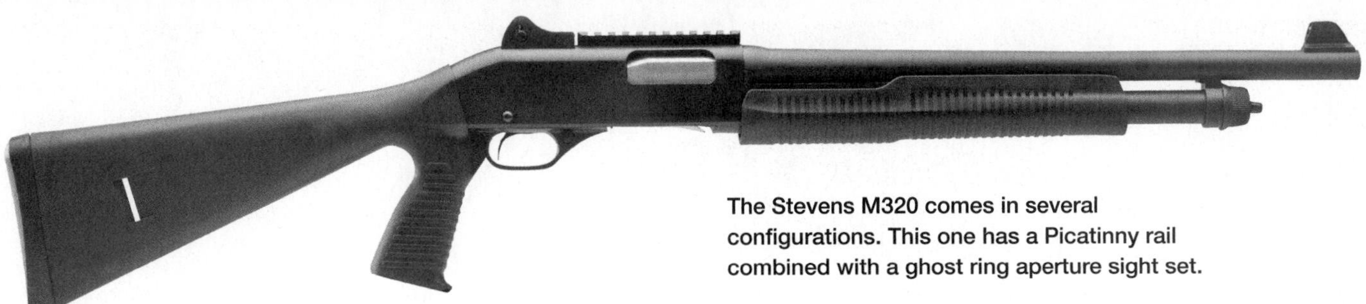

The Stevens M320 comes in several configurations. This one has a Picatinny rail combined with a ghost ring aperture sight set.

the ability to swap out field barrels for shorter more handy-dandy barrels, but we are talking other things here.

Known more for its translucent AR magazines, Lancer Systems has also begun to produce other accessories for the shooter. Applicable in this instance is its new extended magazine tubes. These tubes, except for the nut to affix them to the shotgun's original tube, are entirely carbon fiber. There is no liner of aluminum inside the tube, rather the carbon fiber layer on the inside is quite smooth. There is no separate end cap on this tube, nor can the nut be removed from the tube, though a separate barrel clamp is available. This keeps the unit simple and strong. This tube is well-nigh weightless, very rigid in strength, and has the usual attractive appearance associated with carbon fiber anything, the fiber weave being quite visible on the exterior of the tube. As of this writing, it is available in capacities of plus-two all the way through plus-nine rounds, and models are available for Remington 11-87s, 1100s, 870s, VERSA MAX guns, and the Benelli M1/M2 series of shotguns.

Mesa Tactical has developed a great accessory for the Kel Tec KSG. Side-saddle ammo mounts for seven on the left, seven on the right, and a combo of fourteen to fully reload the KSG are available. These saddles attach to a railed aluminum rail system that replaces the top rail originally on the KSG. Mesa also makes a full-length rail system/saddle shell carrier for the Mossberg 500 series. You can mount a serious amount of stuff on this rail, and it looks mega-cool besides. It's a drop-in fit, using the receiver scope mount holes and a barrel/mag tube clamp, which allows the mounting of folding back-up sights along with an optic, just like on a tactical rifle.

GG&G, another company well known for its line of AR stuff, also has introduced some new shotgun goodies. For Remingon shotguns comes a new sidesaddle shell carrier. What makes this one unique is that the shells are held at a 15-degree angle, ostensibly to make withdrawal and subsequent feeding into the magazine tube or ejection port a little bit less cumbersome.

Also new are a series of enhanced charging handles—quite enhanced actually, rather huge to be precise—for Remington 1100s/11-87s, Benelli M2s, and Mossberg 930s. Knurled and large enough to grasp by your pinkie toe, these things *should* have no finger slippage issues. And last, GG&G has introduced a series of shotgun sling attachments, both quick- and non-quick-detach. They are placed in between the receiver and butt stock, and between the magazine nut or extension and the magazine tube itself. The quick-detach models use the standard push-button QD loop commonly available. These units are also available for the Benelli M2, the Remington series of tactical guns, and the Mossberg 930.

Conclusion

The new 2012 lineup was very impressive, in the tactical and defense realms. Particularly welcoming to this author was the decision to finally make the M4 available with the original extended mag tube and collapsible stock, an event that has been long overdue. While the KSG actually was new in 2011, no one was able to get one until the very end of 2011 or the beginning of 2012, and thus it might as well have been brand new again—the demand certainly never degraded. Of particular note was the increasing availability of low-cost imported models designed expressly for the American home-defense market. While the argument is always made against foreign-made stuff, it is very difficult to argue with a low price point on an otherwise well-made gun. Even poor folks have a right to self-defense, and these models allow the less affluent the ability to purchase a nice, accessories-laden shotgun for a price they can afford. At least four different companies (I won't say which ones) are importing the exact same series of shotguns manufactured in Turkey and privately branding them with their own labels. Functionality is the same, general appearance is quite clearly related, and, hopefully, time will also say the same of their reliability.

There is no denying the usefulness of the tactical/defense shotgun for those purposes over the simple and plain field shotgun. Shorter, handier barrels, additional magazine capacities, and close-in sighting systems are perfect for the tactical/defense environment. Look for these guns and accessories in a store near you or find them online if you don't want to step out the front door.

A look into the chamber of Firebird Precision's conversion of the Akdal MKA1919.

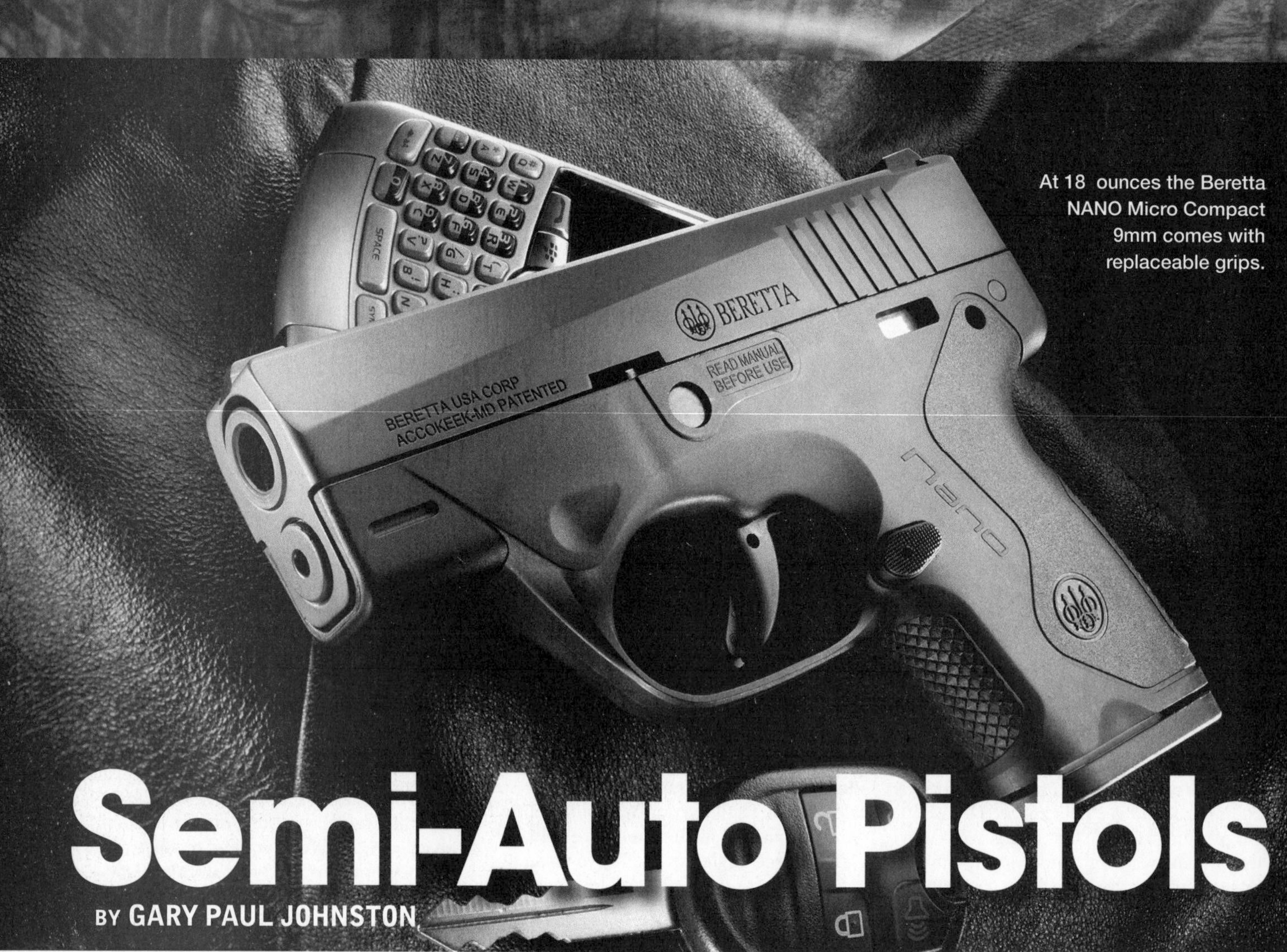

At 18 ounces the Beretta NANO Micro Compact 9mm comes with replaceable grips.

Semi-Auto Pistols

BY GARY PAUL JOHNSTON

To many of today's shooters, it probably seems that the self-loading or semi-automatic pistol has been around as long as the revolver. For its 50 years, the semi-auto handgun fought the belief that this family of handguns was prone to "jamming." In reality, with good quality factory ammunition, the semi-auto was and still is as reliable as the revolver. I believe the difference was that, when a revolver malfunctioned, few shooters talked about it, but, when the "new-fangled" self-loader didn't work, the word spread rapidly.

Eventually, the semi-auto's strong points—ease of handling, slim profile, larger ammo capacity and quick reload capability—began to catch on. Semi-auto pistol designs have steadily improved over the years and have now virtually taken over as the duty sidearm of law enforcement and military personnel throughout the world. They are also extremely popular with the civilian sector, a fact very apparent at the 2012 SHOT Show. From entry-level plinkers to high-end competition models and personal protection pistols of all sizes, there was plenty to see in the way of new products. Most readers of this book would agree you can't own just one, so sit back and enjoy looking over a few of what's new in auto-pistols.

ARMSCOR

New from Armscor is a Commander-size high-capacity variant of the .22 TCM 1911-type pistol shown at the 2010 SHOT Show in prototype form. Made from shortened, resized .223 cases, the .22 TCM (Tuason Craig Magnum) reaches muzzle velocities in the high teens. A 9x19mm barrel will interchange, allowing the pistol to also use that caliber. Armscor also offers its MAP-1 Series, a 9x19mm pistol that's a copy of the CZ design.

BERETTA

Brand new from Beretta is the Nano, a micro-compact carry pistol in 9mm. Using a modular, serial-numbered sub-chassis, the Nano can be easily modified with replaceable polymer grip frames and is simple to disassemble and maintain. Its low-profile, snag-free design makes for easy carry, and its magazine release can be changed to either side. The pistol's adjustable sights are equally user friendly. With its three-inch barrel, the Nano weighs in at less than 18 ounces and has a capacity of six-plus-one.

BROWNING ARMS

Browning continues to offer versions of its 9mm and .40-caliber Hi Power, 1911-22, and .22 LR Buckmark pistols. Word of a new Hi Power model has been circulating for some time, but Browning's lips are sealed. While Browning representatives were asked about another new 1911, the answer was "no comment." We'll be watching.

CABOT GUN COMPANY

First seen at the 2011 NRA Convention, in Pittsburgh, the Cabot Gun

Company is located just north of that city, in Cabot, Pennsylvania. Relatively new to the gun business, Cabot hit the ground flying with several Model 1911 variations manufactured using technology new to producing this pistol, such as high-precision EDM—electro discharge material—machining. Included in Cabot's lineup are the Jones 1911 (the flagship model); Range Master, a model especially designed for competition; GI Classic, essentially a copy of the pistol used by the U.S. Military from 1924 until 1985; the C/GI Classic, a more civilianized version of the GI Classic; the National Standard, a 440 stainless 1911 with optional Lexan see-through grips; the National Standard Deluxe; and, last but not least, the brand new Southpaw. Machined from a solid billet of 4140 stainless steel, the Southpaw is a totally left-handed version of the Model 1911, the first of its kind ever.

Cabot 1911 pistols remind me of the designer shirt I saw on a beautiful woman at the 2012 SHOT Show, the front of which read, "Expensive." When she passed by, the back of her shirt read, "But worth it."

CHRISTENSEN ARMS

Pioneers in super-light, carbon fiber-barreled rifles, Christensen Arms offers four high-grade Model 1911 pistols, all with full-house custom features. They include the five-inch barreled Classic, the four-inch Commander, the three-inch Officer's Model, and the Tactical, a five-inch version with an integral frame rail. The difference between these and other 1911s is that the Christensen models all come with stainless steel slides and lightweight, aircraft-quality alloy frames. The Tactical Model is the only aluminum-framed 1911 with an integral light rail, which will go a long way towards lightening the load of a duty or SWAT office or military operator. All four models are offered in either .45 ACP or .40 S&W, with magazine capacities of eight or nine rounds, respectively.

COLT'S MFG. CO.

Colt's continues to make a huge comeback in the commercial market, not only in rifles, but in handguns, especially the self-loading variety. Making its debut at the 2012 SHOT Show was the return of the Mustang Pocketlite pistol. Once again in .380 ACP, the new Mustang comes with a stainless steel slide and a lightweight

Cabot's National Standard .45 1911 is a stainless steel masterpiece that can be had with deluxe walnut or see-through Lexan grips.

A truly unique 1911 pistol is Cabot's .45 ACP Southpaw, made totally and exclusively for those left-handed.

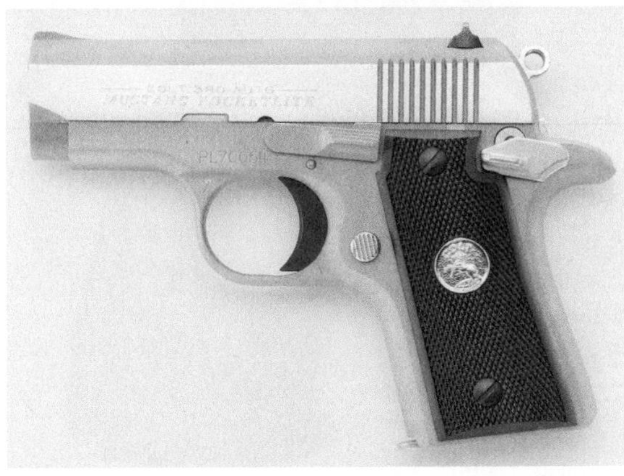

Colt's has reintroduced an improved .380 Mustang Pocketlite, a stainless steel over silver anodized alloy frame single-action.

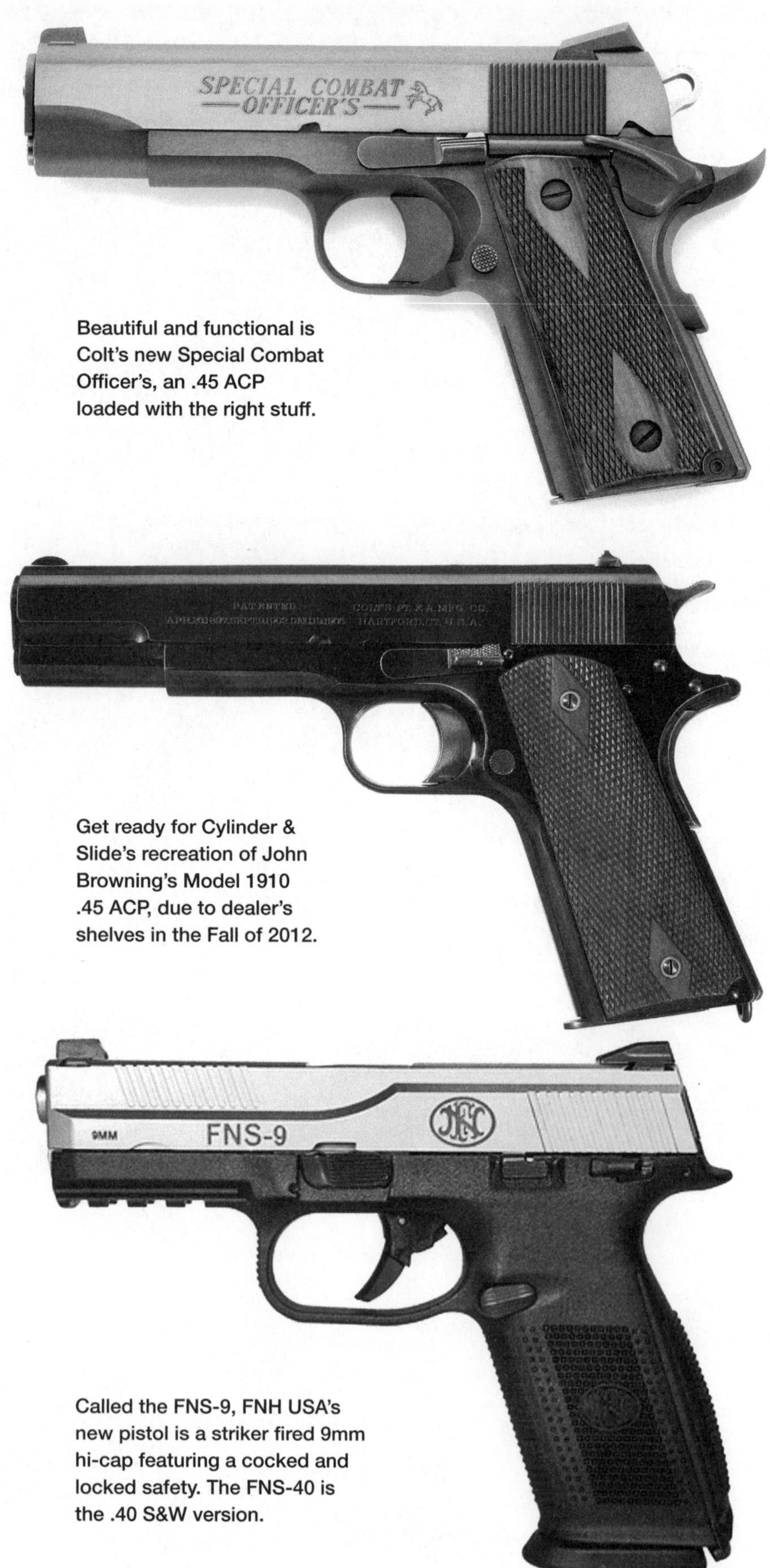

Beautiful and functional is Colt's new Special Combat Officer's, an .45 ACP loaded with the right stuff.

Get ready for Cylinder & Slide's recreation of John Browning's Model 1910 .45 ACP, due to dealer's shelves in the Fall of 2012.

Called the FNS-9, FNH USA's new pistol is a striker fired 9mm hi-cap featuring a cocked and locked safety. The FNS-40 is the .40 S&W version.

frame. It also has a thumb safety that can be kept on while retracting the slide, an excellent safety feature. Newer loadings of the .380 ACP cartridge make this caliber more viable than ever for close-up self-defense. Colt's also displayed several new 1911 variations available from the Colt's Custom Shop.

CYLINDER & SLIDE

Better sit down for this one, especially when you view the accompanying photo. Now famous for his historical reproduction 1911 pistol, Cylinder & Slide's Bill Laughridge is still catching up on orders for this gun while planning the next. When I asked Bill about his new plans, he reluctantly told me he would be making an exact reproduction of the Browning Model 1910 .45 ACP, the predecessor to the Model of 1911. When I pursued, Bill told me he had gone into Browning's inner sanctum and studied John Browning's personal "in-the-white" 1909 and 1910 prototypes, along with the first pre-production Model of 1910! When he also told me he had beautiful images of the guns, I refused to leave until he promised to send them to me for *Gun Digest*. However, Bill made me promise to stress that this project will not begin until the last quarter of 2012, so give him time to catch up. No drooling.

FNH USA

FNH USA came to the 2012 SHOT Show with its newest pistol, the FNS-9 and FNS-40. A striker-fired double-action-only pistol, the FNS can be had in 9mm with a 17-round magazine or in .40-caliber with a 14-round capacity. Being fully ambidextrous, the FNS has a thumb safety, Mil Spec frame rail and slide-cocking grooves front and back. A deep V-notch rear sight, ergonomic yet aggressive grip frame, and undercut trigger guard complete the package.

GLOCK

This year Glock added three more pistols to its 4th Generation line. They are the .45 ACP G21, the long slide 9mm G34, and the G32 in .357 SIG caliber. Like all Gen 4 Glocks, the latest additions come with three interchangeable back straps that enable the pistol to point higher or lower in the natural grip. The G34 also comes with an adjustable rear sight.

H&K

H&K's newest pistol is the .45 ACP Combat Tactical, a pistol designed especially for the U.S. Navy SEALS. Featuring a threaded muzzle, dual retraction grooves, polymer frame, a DA/SA action, and a rear sight that can be used to retract the slide, the Combat Tactical has interchangeable backstraps and a huge removable magazine well funnel. A frame rail is also standard, as are eight- and 10-shot magazines.

KAHR ARMS

Introducing what could be the smallest .40-caliber auto pistol of all time, Kahr Arms showed off its new CM40 micro-compact pistol. A sibling to Kahr's DAO CM9, it has a stainless steel slide over a black polymer frame and a barrel of a hair over three inches. It weighs right under a pound, but holds five-plus-one rounds. Overall length is 5½ inches and the slide width is .94-inch. Like all other Kahr pistols, the CM40 has one of the smoothest double-action triggers going.

KIMBER

Surprising everyone, Kimber introduced a brand new .380 ACP pistol at the 2012 SHOT Show. Called the Micro CDP II, the pistol looks almost exactly like the Colt Mustang, except that its alloy frame is hard anodized in black and the entire surface of the pistol is devoid of any sharp edges. The gun is a single-action with an outside hammer and can be safely carried with the hammer cocked and the safety on. Another good feature is that the little pistol's thumb safety can be put into the on position while allowing the slide to be retracted to load or unload, or while being inspected. The Micro CDP II is expected to ship in September 2012.

Another new Kimber is the Classic Carry Pro, with an all-steel 4¼-inch barrel and an all Royal Blue finish by Doug Turnbull, along with gorgeous bone grips and a round butt.

Last, but not least, is Kimber's new 1911 Sapphire. Based on the Ultra Aegis II, it's a beautiful 9mm pistol that has a super sapphire blue finish and Aegis blue grips. There's never been another Kimber quite like this one.

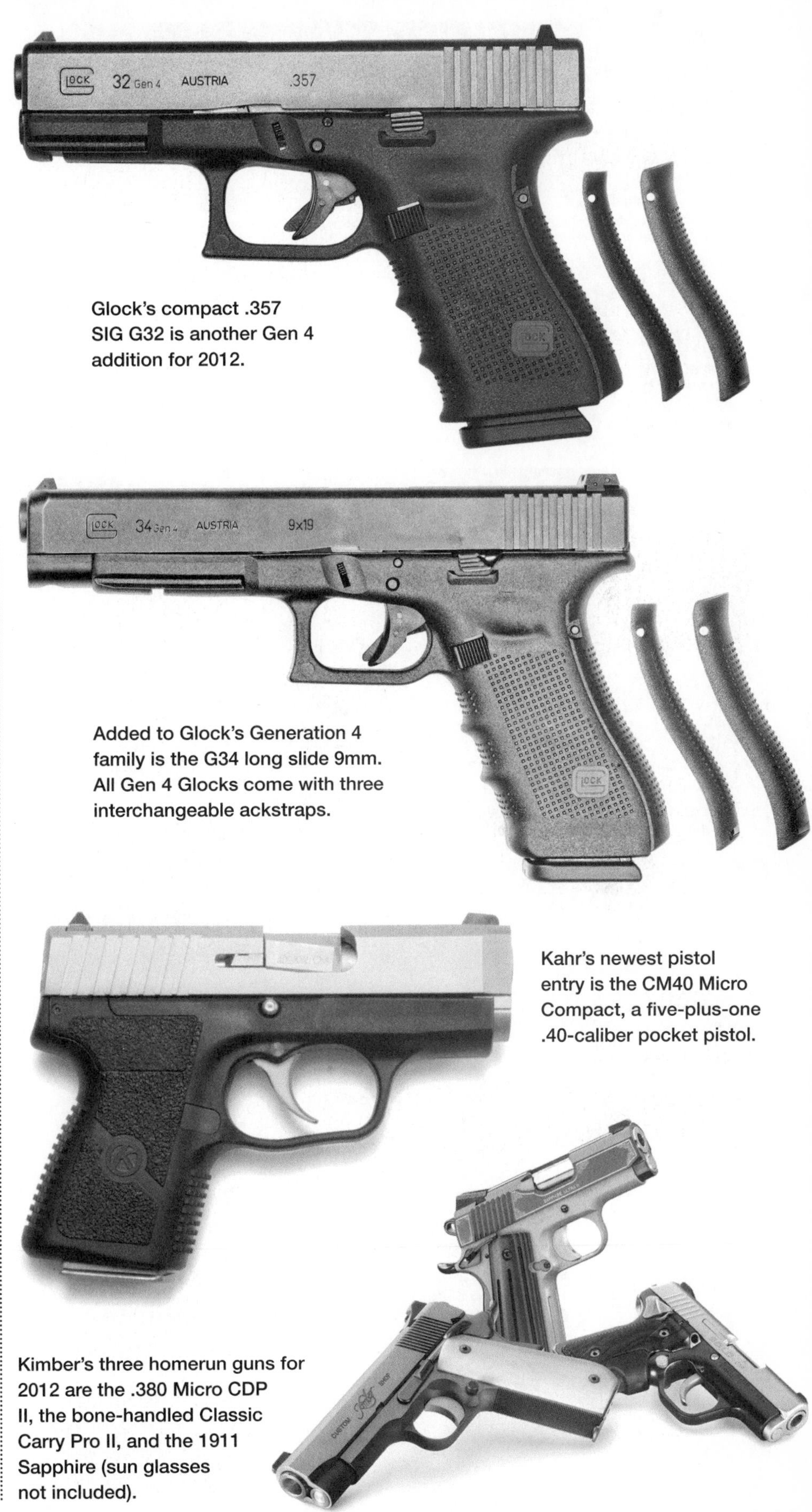

Glock's compact .357 SIG G32 is another Gen 4 addition for 2012.

Added to Glock's Generation 4 family is the G34 long slide 9mm. All Gen 4 Glocks come with three interchangeable ackstraps.

Kahr's newest pistol entry is the CM40 Micro Compact, a five-plus-one .40-caliber pocket pistol.

Kimber's three homerun guns for 2012 are the .380 Micro CDP II, the bone-handled Classic Carry Pro II, and the 1911 Sapphire (sun glasses not included).

Les Baer's new BOSS is a no-nonsense .45 1911 with all the right stuff.

Just one of Nighthawk's new 2012 1911 pistols is the full-house Chris Costa Recon .45.

Possibly the fanciest Recon 1911 going is this Heine Signature version designed for Nighthawk.

LEGACY SPORTS

Adding to Legacy's extensive line of firearms is the Model 1911 centerfire line with the M1911 .22 G.I. and .22 Tactical 10-shot .22 LR pistols. Looking like a 1911A1, the .22 G.I. has a matte finish and wood grips, while the .22 Tactical comes with adjustable sights. Also new is the ISSC M-22, a 10-shot .22 LR polymer pistol made in Austria.

LES BAER

Brand new from Les Baer is the BOSS, a high-end Model 1911 pistol featuring a very attractive blued slide on a stainless steel frame. Totally match grade and full-house throughout, the BOSS comes with a fully adjustable Bo-Mar type rear sight and a dovetailed fiber optic front sight, making it suitable for any serious role.

NIGHTHAWK

Nighthawk Custom has taken a giant step this year, with no less than seven full-house PLUS Model 1911 .45 ACP pistols. They include three designed by noted pistolsmith Dick Heine, to include the Heine Signature Series, Competition Model, Compact Model (ACP) type frame, and the Recon, a highly adorned presentation and investment grade 1911 that most recon operators would keep in a glass case. Chris Costa also designed two custom 1911 pistols for Nighthawk. One is the Costa Compact, with an ACP-type frame, and then there's Chris's own Recon Model, which, while not as fancy as Heine's Recon pistol, would again be one I'd keep in the safe. Also competing in Nighthawk's 2012 Model1911 beauty contest are its T3 TIN Compact and Bob Marvel's Custom 1911. If these seven beauties aren't as good as gold, they've got to be the next best thing.

PARA USA

Coming in a close second behind Nighthawk, Para USA launched six new 1911 pistols, five of them full size with match barrels (three hi-caps included), and one highly concealable compact. They are the 14-45 Black Ops Hi Cap with fixed sights and frame rail; 1911 Black Ops with adjustable sight, fiber optic front sight and frame rail; 1911 Black Ops with fixed sights and frame rail; P-1445 with fixed sight and frame rail; P-1445 Stainless with fixed rear sight and fiber optic front sight; and the Stealth, an LDA six-plus-one .45 with fixed sights and a three-inch match barrel. All the Black Ops models and the Stealth have G-10 grips.

REMINGTON

Remington's 1911R1 is now enhanced with a fiber optic front sight, dual slide retraction grooves, target hammer, and trigger, beavertail, extended safety, and G10 grips. Also new is a stainless steel R1 with an integral frame rail and a threaded muzzle.

ROCK RIVER

Unveiled at the 2012 SHOT Show was a prototype of Rock River's new RRA 1911 poly, a .45 ACP high-capacity pistol built on a polymer frame with rubber over-molded grips and a host of other modern features. Set at a retail of about $800, the RRA 1911 Poly will offer various colors of the polymer frame.

RUGER

Sturm, Ruger & Co. is now offering a new rimfire, the SR22P, an SA/DA pistol with a polymer frame, integral rail, and adjustable sights. Other features normally not seen on rimfire pistols are a combination safety/decocking lever, interchangeable grips, floorplate extensions, and an extra magazine. The very popular LCP (.380) and LC9 (9mm) pocket pistols are now offered with built-in LaserMax laser sights.

SIG SAUER

SIG takes the 2012 cake for introducing new pistols. I count 53—yes, *fifty-three*—including all varieties. From centerfire and rimfire 1911s to compacts, micro-compacts, and camouflaged, threaded-muzzle operator types, SIG has something for everyone. Just one of these is the Rainbow Model, a P239 with a seven-plus-one round .40-caliber capacity and a "rainbow" titanium slide on a black hard anodized frame. According to my count, this brings the models of the SIG auto-pistol family to the following tally:

P220, .45 ACP: 16
P224, 9mm & .40: 4
P226, 9x19mm: 18
P229, 9mm & .40: 12

New this year from Para USA is the 1445 Black Ops, a tactical 1911 with adjustable sights.

Also introduced at the 2012 SHOT Show was Para USA's Stealth R, a three-inch barreled LDA compact.

Remington's 1911R1 is now enhanced with your favorite features.

Seen for the first time is Remington's stainless 1911R1 with a frame rail, this one with a suppressor mounted.

Seen in prototype for the first time is Rock River's RRA 1911 Poly, a hi-cap .45 with a polymer frame, which will be offered in several colors.

The latest in Ruger's auto-pistol lineup is the LC9 (seen here) and LCP, both with a LaserMax laser module trigger guard.

Another addition from Ruger is its polymer framed SR 40 pistol with a stainless steel slide.

Ruger's surprise came in its brand new SR22 DA pistol with ambidextrous safety and adjustable sights.

One of a boatload of new pistols from SIG is the P239 Rainbow, a .40-caliber compact with a rainbow titanium slide.

P290, 9mm: 5
SP2022, 9mm & .40: 6
1911 .45 (three in .22): 32
1911 Traditional .45: 3
Mosquito, .22: 14

I get a total of 136 different SIG auto pistols. There may be more by the time you read this.

SPRINGFIELD

In the wake of the big success of its improved XDM family of pistols, Springfield Armory introduced the .45 ACP compact XDS at the 2012 SHOT Show. With the same aggressive grip surface as its larger siblings, the XDS also comes with a fiber optic front sight and a frame rail for Springfield's tactical pistol light. This little "big gun" holds five-plus-one rounds of your favorite brand of .45 ACP ammunition and weighs just 29 ounces.

STEYR USA

Steyr's M-A1 and S-A1 9mm and .40-caliber pistols are now offered with an improved trigger and other features, including conventional sights in addition to the triangular sights first furnished with the gun. American shooters will appreciate these new sights. I know I do.

TAURUS

The only auto-pistols "new" from Taurus as this is written are its 22/25 PLY micro-pistols and the 24/7 G2 Compact. Being double-action-only, the tiny PLY pistols weigh just 10.8 ounces and hold eight- and nine-plus-one, respectively. Loaded with fire control choices like its larger sibling, the 24/7 G2 Compact can now be had in 9mm, .40, and .45 ACP calibers with capacities of 17-plus-one, 15-plus-one, and 12-plus-one, respectively, or a flush 10-shot magazine. All three variants weigh just 27 ounces.

UMAREX

The latest from Umarex is the R350CR. A Commander-size pistol, this .45 ACP sports an integral frame rail, beavertail grip safety, extended thumb safety, Hogue Grips, and a checkered front strap. A Commander-type hammer and dovetailed front sight are also standard.

The Umarex Regent R350CR is a new .45 ACP Commander-size pistol with full-house features at an affordable price.

A new addition to Springfield's XDM family is the XDS, a compact single-stack .45 weighing just 29 ounces.

Offered in stainless steel over polymer, the .22-caliber Taurus 22 PLY is a micro-compact weighing a hair over 10 ounces.

New this year on Steyr's M40 Series 9mm and .40-caliber pistols are optional square "U" notch sights.

The Ms. Sentinel pistol was specifically designed to be carried equally well in a purse or in a holster. The configurations of some of the controls are subdued to avoid snagging. A round butt frame was used, and a shortened trigger, better suited to smaller hands, was installed. To reduce weight, an aluminum frame and a fluted 3½-inch barrel were used. The result, Wilson feels, is a 9mm pistol that will be a very good choice for a woman's protection pistol.

Uberti Dragoon

Revolvers

BY **JEFF QUINN**

The revolver handgun design has been popular ever since Sam Colt introduced his Paterson revolver in 1836, and it shows no signs of becoming obsolete. The revolver, as well as the derringer, has a place in the world of armament that has yet to be supplanted by any other design. The design can handle cartridges small enough to cleanly take a bird for the camp pot or large enough to take down any animal that walks the earth. For defense and personal protection, the revolver is now better than it ever was, and it can also offer hours of shooting pleasure. The semi-auto has its place, but when it comes to versatility and power, the revolver is still king.

While sales of new revolvers, single-shots, and derringers pale in comparison to the numbers of semi-auto pistols sold, each year we see the number and variation of these reliable old designs increasing. Sales are fast-paced these days, but brisk guns sales bring both good and bad news. The good news is that arms makers are producing guns as quickly as they can. The bad news is that many popular firearms are very difficult to find. Speaking with executives of the major gun manufacturers, as well as those running some of the smaller ventures, they tell me they're adding machines and machine operators, but still cannot meet the demand for new firearms.

With firearms being among the most durable of durable goods, this is amazing. Firearms are *not* disposable, unlike clothing, shoes, and even automobiles, which must periodically be replaced. The guns our grandfathers owned are still in use, and unless they have been abused, are still as capable today as when they were originally made. I have a firearm or two that each exceed 100 years in age, and they still shoot like new. The point is that the millions of firearms added annually to the supply are not replacing anything, but are instead *adding* to the number of firearms available for use.

Besides the extensive number of manufacturers making revolvers, single-shots, and derringers, there is another industry within our industry that specializes in transforming production sixguns into specialized weapons for those who desire the best of the best. Custom gunsmiths such as Hamilton Bowen, David Clements, Gary Reeder, Ben Forkin, Andy Horvath, Jim Stroh, John Gallagher, and Alan Harton, along with a few others, can take a very good sixgun and make it into something that

Jeff Quinn with a .45 Schofield.

Rossi Ranch Hand

and Others

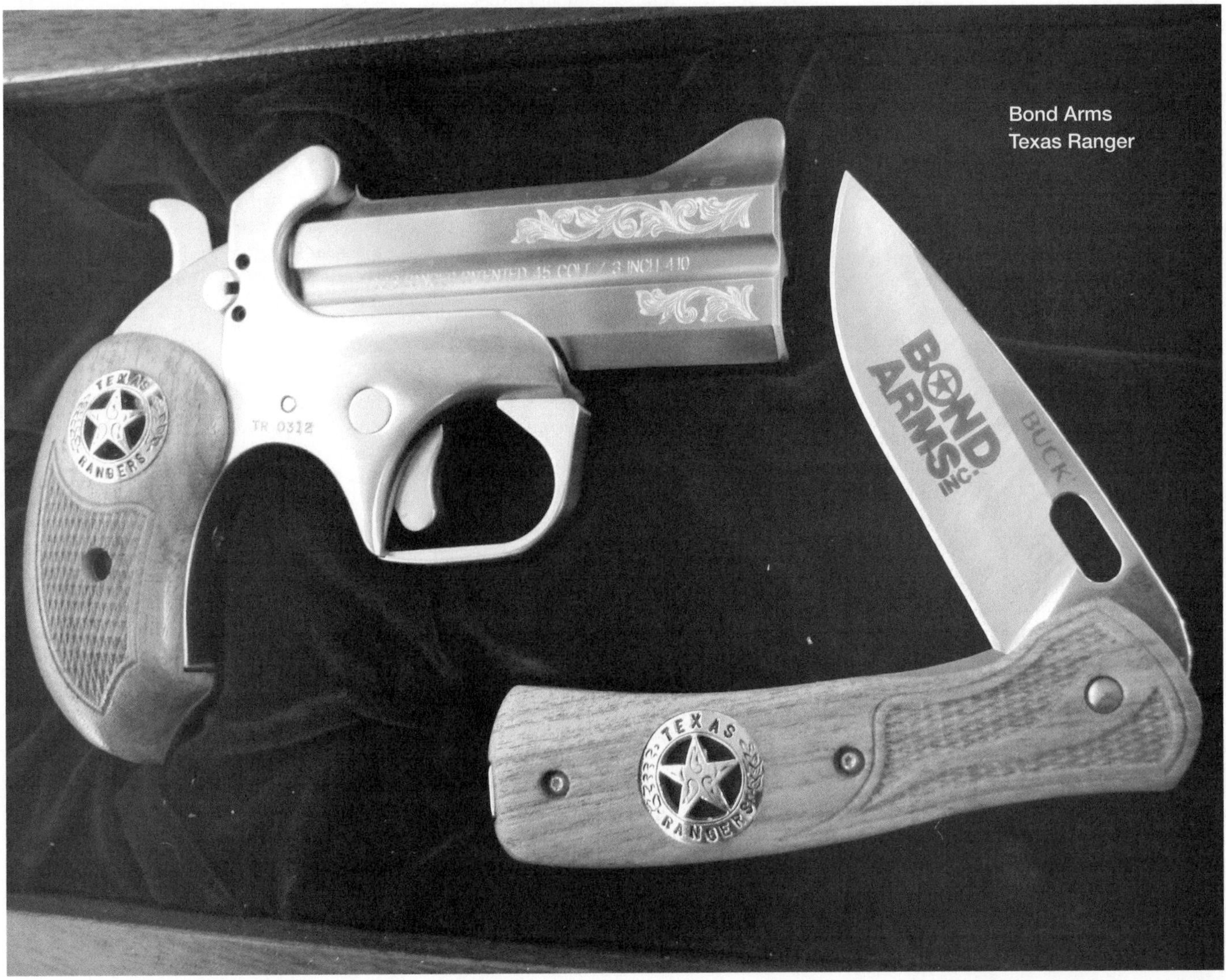

Bond Arms Texas Ranger

bridges the gap between craftsmanship and fine art. These skilled craftsmen have the talent and patience to push the revolver design to its limits, chambering it for powerful cartridges that are capable of killing any game animal on earth, while at the same time making that piece of machinery suitable for display in the finest museums. Others, like Doug Turnbull, specialize in restoring a firearm to perfection, with classic case hardening and polished bluing that exhibit the look of a masterpiece.

Besides upgrading the sights, springs, and bolting something to the rail, a modern, plastic, semi-auto pistol is pretty much as good as it's going to be right out of the box. Revolvers on the other hand, lend themselves to customization much more so than do modern semi-automatic pistol designs. Other, simpler modifications really enhance a revolver's usefulness, such as the moon clip conversions done by TK Custom. (I recently had a Smith & Wesson Schofield modified by TK, and popping in a moon clip loaded with six .45 ACP cartridges is much quicker than thumbing in six separate .45 S&W cartridges.) Black polymer does not show off intricate engraving as blued steel does, and a gold-inlaid, case hardened Glock slide does nothing for me—but that level of skill and art on a single-action Colt's, when properly executed by one of the masters, stirs the soul as can no other class of art can.

The custom handgun is *functional* art. Case hardening the finish and fitting a set of stag grips does not make a sixgun shoot any straighter, nor does it make its bullet hit any harder, but it adds something to the level of satisfaction of the owner that cannot be quantified. For this reason, while we will, of course, look at the firearms offered by the various manufacturers and importers, I have included a few pictures of custom sixguns in this section, as the craftsmen of such firearms are becoming a larger part of the industry each year. While most revolvers are perfectly suited to their intended purposes just as delivered, there are those who desire something a bit different and more personalized, and for those who have the money and the patience, the rewards of owning such a custom revolver are well worth it. My only advice to those who desire a custom handgun be built is to place your order and try to forget about it; with several of the better craftsmen, the wait is measured in months and years.

AMERICAN WESTERN ARMS

Differing a bit from other popular mare's leg-style pistols, AWA has a pump-action version of that famous lever-action design. Chambered for the .45 Colt cartridge, the AWA Lightningbolt wears a 12-inch barrel and is offered in a variety of finishes. AWA still catalogs the Mateba upside-down revolver chambered for the .357 and .44 Magnum cartridges, as well as the .454 Casull. There are also its Classic and Ultimate replicas of the Colt Single Action Army, the most replicated revolver in the world. The AWA sixguns exhibit very smooth actions.

BERETTA

When Beretta acquired Uberti Firearms several years ago, it added its own line of single-action revolvers patterned after the Colt Single Action Army, but utilizing a transfer bar safety system. The Beretta Stampede line includes those with the classic plow handle grip design that was first used on the Colt 1851 Navy cap-and-ball revolvers. This grip points naturally for most shooters and handles recoil pretty well. Beretta has dropped the Bisley-gripped sixgun from its lineup, but still has the bird's-head Stampede Marshall. In addition to nickel plating or polished bluing, Beretta has a worn and weathered looking Old West finish that has the appearance of a sixgun made in the eighteenth century and used every day since. Beretta also has cap-and-ball replicas of the most popular Remington and Colt's sixguns that predated the cartridge revolvers, and these also offer the look and feel of era originals.

BOND ARMS

Bond Arms has made a name for itself by making the best two-shot derringers in the industry. The fit, finish, and workmanship are second to none. Bond offers a wide variety of chamberings, from .22 Long Rifle on up, with the most popular being the .45 Colt/.410 shotshell combination. Bond offers various grip styles and sizes, and one Bond frame can accommodate any or all of the Bond barrel sets in any chambering. Switching barrels is quick and easy, and extra sets of barrels can be ordered without the need to send in the frame of the derringer.

I have a few of the Bond derringers, with my favorite being the .45 Colt/.410 Snake Slayer II. This pistol rides well in the hip pocket or in the Bond Driving Holster. Being made primarily of stainless steel, it has enough corrosion resistance to make it suitable for wear while working and sweating in the woods or field. Loaded with No. 8 birdshot, the Bond can shred a venomous snake, if necessary, at close range, and is also very effective for close-range social work.

Bond has several variations of its derringer in addition to the wide array of chamberings. A very special one that Bond introduced recently is the cased set with a knife, commemorating the two-hundredth anniversary of the Texas Rangers. The Rangers were formed in 1823, so the anniversary is a bit early, but it's a fine tribute to that group of lawmen, and the glass-topped case with the Buck knife makes for a great-looking display. The gun, of course, can also be used for more practical purposes, as the pistol is chambered for the .45 Colt/.410 shotshell combo. The pistol grips and the knife scales are made of Texas mesquite wood. The set will be available in a very limited run.

CHARTER ARMS

Charter Arms has built its business upon making compact, reliable, and affordable revolvers. The .44 Bulldog stands pretty much alone in filling the need for a lightweight, compact, big-bore belly gun. It packs a lot of power into its compact five-shot cylinder. I have a few of the "vintage," original Charter Bulldog revolvers, as well as the newer Bulldog Pug, but I prefer the three-inch tapered barrel of the original design. Charter is now producing the Bulldog once again in a limited production revolver. These are made of blued steel and wear synthetic rubber grips and, like the original Bulldogs, they are all chambered for the dandy .44 Special cartridge.

The .44 Special has, for many decades, been an effective and manageable revolver cartridge. It's better today than it ever was, with plenty of modern hollowpoint loads available. I particularly like the full-wadcutter Anti-Personnel ammo from Buffalo Bore. This load throws a flat-faced 200-grain lead slug at somewhere around 1,000 fps and is packed with a low-flash powder. It's an excellent choice for stoking the Bulldog.

Charter Arms still has its extensive line of affordable .38 Special revolvers available, with either exposed or concealed hammers. The rimfire Pathfinder line in .22 LR and .22 Magnum, along with revolvers chambered for the .32 H&R Magnum, .327 Federal Magnum, and the highly-respected .357 Magnum cartridge, fill out the revolver chamberings from Charter, with the exception of its newest revolver, which is chambered for the popular .40 S&W auto-pistol cartridge.

For many years, firearms manufacturers have looked for ways to successfully chamber rimless cartridges in a swing-out cylinder double-action revolver. The most successful attempts have used moon clips, thin pieces of stamped spring steel that hold the rims of the cartridges in sets. Usually, the moon clips will hold two, three, five, or six cartridges, but there are clips made to hold seven and eight shots, as well. The moon clip method works satisfactorily, but there have also been designs that use wire springs or other methods to retain and eject the cartridges. Most of these came and went without much commercial success.

As a solution to the moon clip, Charter Arms of has been developing a rimless double-action revolver. I fired a prototype in January of this year, and the revolvers are now in production. The Pit Bull uses a patented spring-loaded rim engagement assembly. As the cartridges are loaded into the chambers, they push the extractor out of the way. As the cartridge is fully chambered, the extractor, a sliding piece of stainless steel about 3/16-inch wide snaps solidly into the rim. Upon ejection, when the ejector rod is operated as is normal with a double-action revolver, the extractor rod system ejects all five rounds at once, positively and quickly.

The execution of the system is a very good design, but why build a revolver for a rimless cartridge, when plenty of rimmed cartridges exist? The answer to that lies in the performance, availability, and popularity of the .40 S&W cartridge. It is one of the most popular handgun cartridges in the United States. As such, .40 S&W ammo is available almost anywhere. So, too, the cost of the ammo is reasonable, especially compared to many popular revolver cartridges. Most importantly, the .40 S&W is a good, efficient cartridge for a medium-bore belly gun.

Charter is now making a true left-handed snubnose revolver called the Southpaw. Chambered for the .38 Special cartridge, this revolver is a mirror image of its standard revolver design, only with the cylinder latch on the right side. The cylinder swings out to the right, as well. Charter is also still producing the dandy little Charter Dixie Derringer. The Dixie is a five-shot .22 LR or Magnum mini-revolver, with a cross-bolt safety and built of stainless steel. Weighing in at just six ounces, the Dixie Derringer slips easily into a pocket. The gun is now available as a combo Dixie,

Charter Arms .40 S&W

Colt New Frontier

which comes with both .22 Long Rifle and .22 Magnum cylinders.

CHIAPPA

Chiappa Firearms now has the Rhino revolver in production. Built upside-down, compared to other revolvers, the Rhino fires from the lowest chamber in the cylinder, instead of the uppermost. This design lowers the axis of recoil, greatly reducing muzzle flip upon firing and lessening felt recoil. This enables the Rhino quickly get back onto target between shots. I've had the opportunity on several occasions to briefly fire a Rhino revolver, but have not yet had the chance to do a full review on one. I do like the concept.

Chiappa also has a line of muzzle-loading single-shot pistols, including the .36-caliber and .45-caliber Rochatte design, and both percussion and flintlock Kentucky style pistols. Also, the Napoleon LePage pistols are offered individually or in cased sets with accessories. In the single-action revolver line, Chiappa has a very affordable Colt Single Action Army replica chambered for the .22 LR cartridge.

CIMARRON

For many years, shooters have looked to Cimarron Firearms of Fredericksburg, Texas, for quality firearms that replicate the guns of the late eighteenth century. Cimarron has an extensive line of Pietta and Uberti cartridge revolvers, such as the 1875 and 1890 Remingtons, along with the Colt Single Action Army and various cartridge conversion firearms of the transition period out of cap-and-ball to self-contained cartridge revolvers. Cimarron continues to offer some of the most authentic cap-and-ball replica revolvers available, as well as a line of two-shot derringers. The company can provide engraved revolvers, as well as various finishes, including nickel, blued, case hardened, and antiqued.

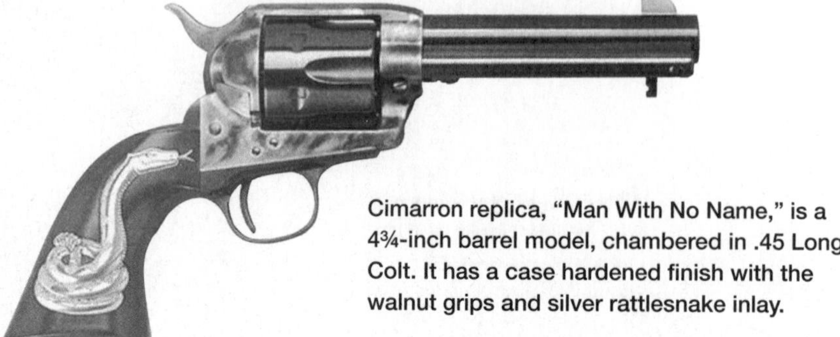
Cimarron replica, "Man With No Name," is a 4¾-inch barrel model, chambered in .45 Long Colt. It has a case hardened finish with the walnut grips and silver rattlesnake inlay.

COBRA

Cobra manufactures some very affordable small and reliable two-shot single-action derringers marketed under the Cobra name, as well as making those derringers for other firearms brands. These are made in .22 LR, .22 Magnum, .25 ACP, .38 Special, 9mm Luger, .32 Auto, .380 Auto, and .32 H&R Magnum. The larger Titan model is built of stainless steel and is offered in 9mm or .45 Colt/.410. The Cobra derringers are available in a variety of finishes. Cobra also has a line of compact double-action revolvers, offered in a multitude of finishes.

COLT'S

After many decades of production, with a few marked periods of none being built, Colt's still has the legendary Single Action Army revolver. It is the most copied sixgun in history, probably the most recognized revolver ever built, and the ones made today are as good as any to ever leave the Colt's factory. It is still available in the three classic barrel lengths, 4¾, 5½, and 7½ inches, and comes chambered in a choice of .357 Magnum, .44 Special, and .45 Colt. The .38 Special, .32 WCF, and .38 WCF chamberings have been dropped from the current Colt's catalog. The SAA is available in blued/case-hardened or nickel finishes. Through the Colt's Custom Shop, many options are available, such as non-standard barrel lengths and hand engraving.

The newest revolver from Colt's is a reintroduction of the beautiful New Frontier. Introduced by Colt's in 1961, it was a very special sixgun. Colt's flat-topped the frame to install a fully adjustable rear sight. To match up with the rear, the front sight was a long ramp, beautifully and gracefully perched atop the barrel. The combo made for a sight picture that was much improved over the traditional Single Action Army sights. With its deep bluing on the barrel, trigger guard, cylinder, and grip frame contrasting nicely with the case hardened cylinder frame, the New Frontier was the classiest, most elegant and useful single-action that Colt's had ever produced.

The New Frontier production was stopped in 1974, but resumed again in 1978, with the production of the third generation single-action Colt's revolvers. The New Frontier ceased production again around 1982, with a very few trickling out of the factory for the next year or two. The newest New Frontier revolvers are every bit as beautiful as the originals and better built than the older ones, in my opinion. Like the originals, the grips are pretty plain, but bolting on a set of stags really does wonders for this gun! I have one of the new-production New Frontier sixguns, and it is timed perfectly, fitted just right, and is very accurate. They are offered chambered in either .44 Special or .45 Colt and in the same barrel lengths as the SAA.

EUROPEAN AMERICAN ARMORY

EAA Corp has a line of imported Single Action Army replica revolvers called the Bounty Hunter, as well as a double-action revolver called the Windicator. The single-action sixguns are available chambered for the .22 LR and .22 Magnum cartridges, with an alloy frame and a choice of six- or eight-shot cylinders. The larger Bounty Hunter revolvers are chambered for the .357 and .44 Magnums and the .45 Colt cartridges. These centerfire sixguns are built with all-steel frames in a choice of nickeled, blued, or case hardened finishes. These replica Colt's-style revolvers have the traditional half-cock loading feature, but have a modern transfer bar safety action that permits carrying with a live round under the hammer without fear of firing if accidentally dropped.

The double-action Windicator revolvers that are chambered for the .38 Special cartridge are built on an alloy frame, but the .357 Magnum version is built upon an all-steel frame. Both revolvers have synthetic rubber grips and a business-like matte blue finish in a choice of two- or four-inch barrel lengths.

FREEDOM ARMS

The Freedom Arms Model 2008 Single Shot pistol is a high-quality single-shot handgun made for hunting and long-range target shooting. Current chamberings offered are the .223 Remington, 6.5 Swede, 7mm BR, 7mm-08, .308 Winchester, .357

Freedom Arms .500 Wyoming Express

Magnum, .357 Maximum, .338 Federal, and .375 Winchester. Standard barrel length options are 10, 15, or 16 inches, depending upon the caliber chosen, but non-standard lengths are also available for a nominal extra cost. The barrels are interchangeable, allowing the shooter to switch among any of the available barrel and caliber options all on one frame.

The Model 2008 weighs in around four pounds, depending upon the barrel and caliber chosen. The barrel is drilled for a Freedom Arms scope mount, and the scope stays with the barrel, allowing barrel swap-outs without affecting the sight adjustment. The Model 2008 wears beautiful, expertly fitted laminated wood grips and fore-ends; the grips are the best-feeling, most comfortable single-shot handgun grips I have ever handled. There also is a new fore-end available that's contoured better for a smoother hold, yet still has enough of a flat on the bottom for use on a sandbag or machine rest. It looks better, to my eyes, than the original style.

This year, one of the most interesting things shown to me was some new sights for the Freedom Arms revolvers. A couple months ago, Bob Baker handed to me an FA revolver that wore a set of his new aperture rear and fiber optic front sights. Also, I got to try one with an aperture rear and brass bead front. Both are amazingly fast for getting on target. I had seen aperture sights for handguns before, but none quite as nice as the ones on these Freedom Arms revolvers. They are very well crafted, fully adjustable and, as mentioned, very quick to the target. Used like an aperture on a rifle, the eye naturally centers the front sight within the rear aperture, looking more through the rear sight instead of at it. Anyway, this is a very good option for a hunting handgun.

Heading up the Freedom Arms revolver line is the large-frame Model 83. It is chambered for the .454 Casull and .475 Linebaugh cartridges, in addition to the .357 Magnum and .500 Wyoming Express and .41 an .44 Magnum cartridges. They are available with fixed or adjustable sights. The adjustable sight guns will also accept a variety of scope mounts. The fixed-sight models have an available dovetailed front sight that can be changed out to easily regulate bullet impact, while still retaining a low profile.

The Model 97 is Freedom's compact-frame single-action revolver. Built to the same tight tolerances as the Model 83 revolvers, the Model 97 is a bit handier to carry all day and is chambered for the .17 HMR and .22 LR/Magnum rimfire cartridges, as well as the .327 Federal, .357 Magnum, .41 Magnum, .44 Special, and .45 Colt centerfire cartridges. Also available in this revolver is Freedom Arms' own .224-32 cartridge, a fast-stepping .22 centerfire based on the .327 Federal cartridge case.

HEIZER DEFENSE

Heizer Defense has introduced its Double Tap two-shot pistol, and it should be on the market by the time this *Gun Digest* goes to print. I've handled a couple of the prototypes, and they are very thin and lightweight for a pistol that fires the .45 ACP cartridge. Also available chambered for the 9mm Luger cartridge, the Heizer has two superposed barrels, and the grip carries two spare rounds for a quick reload. The barrels are ported to reduce muzzle jump and are interchangeable.

HENRY FIREARMS

Henry Firearms now has both rimfire and centerfire mare's leg lever-action pistols available. These pistols are based upon the comparable and popular rifle design, are made in the U.S.A., and are available with black or brass receivers.

LEGACY SPORTS

The Legacy Sports Puma lever-action pistol, replicating the sawed-off lever gun made famous by the old television western series, *Wanted: Dead or Alive*, has been a big success. Nostalgia aside, the Puma Bounty Hunter is a fun, handy lever gun and scratches the itch of those who have always longed for a mare's leg rifle without the legal hassle of cutting down a lever-action carbine. The Bounty Hunter is legally a pistol and can be purchased just as easily as any other handgun in most states.

Legacy Sports also has an 1873 Colt SAA replica sixgun called the Puma Westerner. It is a reliable and well-built sixgun chambered for the .357 Magnum, .44 WCF, and .45 Colt cartridges, with 4¾, 5½, and 7½-inch barrels. These replica sixguns are offered with a blued and case hardened finish and walnut grips, nickel finish and walnut grips, or with a stainless finish and white synthetic ivory grips. The Puma line also includes a very affordable single-action replica chambered for the .22 LR or .22 Magnum cartridge that would make a good trainer for the larger bores, but will be a lot less costly to shoot.

MAGNUM RESEARCH

Magnum Research is now part of the Kahr family of firearms. The company is well-known for its Desert Eagle line of semi-auto pistols, but it also has some very powerful, rugged, and accurate revolvers. The revolver offered by Magnum Research is called the BFR. These robust single-actions are built for hunting the largest, most dangerous game on the planet, as well as for recreational shooting. The BFR is available in high-performance calibers like the .460 and .500 Smith & Wesson Magnums, the .44 Magnum,.454 Casull, .50 Action Express, .475 Linebaugh, and .480 Ruger revolver cartridges, as well as the .30-30 Winchester, .444 Marlin, and .45-70 rifle cartridges and the ever-popular .45 Colt/.410 shotshell combination. The BFR is made primarily of stainless steel and is built in the U.S.A.

NORTH AMERICAN ARMS

North American Arms still offers its excellent line of high-quality mini-revolvers. Unfortunately, the NAA break-top Ranger introduced last year was a limited run revolver and is now out of production, with the ones that do show up for sale now bringing three times their original price. Of the little five-shot revolvers still in the lineup, they are more often than not bought as deep-concealment handguns. These lightweight firearms are small enough to fit into most any pocket and are handy enough to always be with you, no matter what the attire or climate. Chambered for the .22 Short, .22 LR, or .22 Magnum, as well as a cap-and-ball version, these little jewels surprisingly accurate within their intended range. There are several grip options available, as well as a couple of sight choices. The dandy little Earl, in particular, is a fine mini-revolver and reminds me of the old Remington revolvers of the late nineteenth century, modernized and miniaturized.

ROSSI

Rossi has been producing reliable and affordable revolvers for many years. These double-action sixguns are available chambered for the .38 Special and .357 Magnum cartridges, in either blued steel or stainless finishes. Available with short barrels and fixed sights for concealment, or longer barrels and adjustable sights for precision shooting, the Rossi name still means a quality product at a reasonable price.

The new Rossi Ranch Hand is a version of the mare's leg lever-action design, which is basically a shortened Model 92 Winchester replica in pistol form. It has a polished blued steel finish and wears a walnut-stained hardwood stock. The abbreviated buttstock includes a blued steel buttplate. The lever loop is large, with ample room for the largest gloved hand and just right for twirling the lever gun to work the action—yeah, I tried it, while no one was watching. The left side of the receiver wears a traditional saddle ring and has a short leather thong attached. The magazine holds six cartridges, plus one up the spout for a total loaded capacity of seven. Currently, the Ranch Hand is available chambered for the .357 Magnum, .44 WCF (44-40), and the .45 Colt cartridges.

The Ranch Hand weighs in at four pounds nine ounces unloaded on my scale. It wears a 12-inch tapered round barrel that measures .640-inch at the muzzle. The overall length measures 24 inches. The rear sight is of the buckhorn style and is ladder adjustable for elevation and drift adjustable for windage. The front sight is a brass bead on a blued steel blade and is adjustable for windage correction in its dovetail. The blued steel magazine tube is attached to the barrel by both a screw near the muzzle and a barrel band about a ½-inch aft of that.

Cartridges are loaded into the magazine tube through the loading gate on the right side of the receiver. Working the lever fully chambers a round from the magazine tube, and the magazine can be topped off any time the bolt is closed. The locking bolts are of the traditional '92 Winchester style and securely keep the bolt from movement during firing. It is a very strong and reliable system, designed by John Browning originally for the larger Model 1886 Winchester.

RUGER

Sturm, Ruger, & Company's single-action Single-Six, Bearcat, Blackhawk, Super Blackhawk, and New Vaquero revolvers are relied upon by hunters, plinkers, and competitive shooters to deliver reliable performance without fail. The Blackhawk line includes the Bisley and Blackhawk Flattop variations, some of the slickest Ruger single-actions ever built. The Ruger double-action revolvers include the GP100, Redhawk, Super Redhawk, SP101, and the newer LCR polymer revolvers. The LCR .38 and .357 revolvers have proven to be very popular.

The newest gun is the LCR22, chambered for .22 LR. Besides serving for defensive purposes when the limitations of the user preclude the use of something more powerful, the LCR22 is also a good pocket gun to carry for use against unwanted animals around the camp or to dispatch venomous snakes around the homestead. The CCI .22 shotshell loads pattern better than they do in any of the centerfire calibers, tightly enough to dispatch at any distance a snake might pose

Ruger .45 Convertible

Ruger LCR .22

a threat. The gun also slips easily into a pants pocket to be within reach when needed, and it has sufficient accuracy at close range for defensive purposes. However, the short sight radius makes it difficult to make clean head shots on small game, at least for me, at distances greater than about 15 yards. One remedy is the Crimson Trace Lasergrip that fits the centerfire LCR, since it will also fit the LCR22. This greatly adds to the usefulness of this revolver in low-light situations. The XS Big Dot tritium front sight will also fit the LCR22 and is also useful for making quick hits on targets in low-light situations.

Ruger has also been busy with other .22 rimfire revolvers, the Single-Ten and the four-inch "Kit Gun" version of the SP101. The Single-Ten is available in either stainless steel or a blued steel finish and, as the name implies, the cylinder capacity is 10 rounds. The sights are a matte black, with the rear being fully adjustable, but different than those on other Ruger single-action revolvers.

Ruger Single-Ten

Ruger SP101 .357

The rear face of the blade on this model is slightly angled, serrated, and wears a square notch with two green fiber-optic dots set into an aluminum base. It matches the square post, and its single fiber optic rod is good for accurate target work. The aluminum front sight blade and base are a one-piece unit, attached to the barrel with a single screw. This new sight arrangement gives the shooter the best of both worlds, a good square sight picture for paper-punching, and the fiber optics for hunting and field use.

Another advantage the new 10-shot single-action has over the six-shot is in ease of loading. Opening the loading gate releases the cylinder to rotate, just as it does on the New Model Single-Six revolvers, but upon each "click' of the rotation, the chambers align perfectly with the ejector rod, making unloading faster, easier, and more natural. Loading cartridges into the chambers is also very easy, and two can be loaded at a time, if desired, before the cylinder is rotated to load more. This is a real advantage.

When Ruger first introduced the .38 Special SP101 double-action revolver, back in 1989, I immediately had high hopes for a .22 Long Rifle version for use as a trail gun and plinker. Basically a scaled-down GP100, the SP101 was rugged, reliable, and compact. When Ruger finally did introduce the .22 LR version, though, I was disappointed. A .22 Kit Gun (generic term for a handy little trail, backpacking, woods-bumming gun), it needed good sights. I like mine fully adjustable, to set the sight perfectly for a particular load, as sometimes the Kit Gun is called upon to make an accurate shot to put meat in the camp pot or for other precision shooting chores. The rear sight on the original .22 LR SP101 was an afterthought. It was a thin blade set into the top of the frame, adjustable for windage correction only. The gun deserved a better rear sight, and with the reintroduction of the .22 Long Rifle SP101, it has one.

The new four-inch Ruger SP101 .22 has a sturdy, fully adjustable rear sight. The sight is matte black, as it should be, and the blade is large and easy to see. The sight notch has ample width (.14-inch), allowing plenty of light on either side of the front sight, which is a squared-profile matte black post with a green fiber optic insert. Both front and rear sights are, thankfully, made of steel. The balance of the SP101 is made primarily of stainless steel finished to a satin sheen, and the gun now has an eight-shot cylinder. Also new is a "Kit Gun" version of the .357 Magnum SP101, which makes a dandy little trail gun for times when more power is needed.

SMITH & WESSON

Smith & Wesson still probably has the most extensive line of revolvers ever offered by a gun manufacturer. With models of all sizes chambered in cartridges such as the .22 LR, .22 WMR, .38 Special, .357 Magnum, .44 Special, .44 Magnum, .45 Colt, and the big .460 and .500 Magnums, S&W has you covered.

Handguns that shoot shotshells have been around for decades, starting with single-shot and two-pipe break-opens from over a century ago. These were pretty popular until legislated out of

S&W .500 Magnum

production decades ago. Later, there were some cheap one- and two-shot pistols made of low-quality materials and sloppy workmanship, but they never gained much popularity. Now there are some very high-quality derringers on the market that shoot the .45 Colt/.410 shotshell combination, such as the Bond Arms derringers. It wasn't until the Taurus Judge handguns hit the market about six years ago that the popularity of the versatile .45 Colt/.410 shotshell revolver idea took off. To that end, the new Governor from S&W, following the trend, is now getting a lot of attention.

Firing the .45 Colt, .45 ACP, and .410 shotshells, the Governor's ability to quick-load the .45 ACP cartridges and fire good defensive ammunition, along with the gun's six-shot capacity, makes the it an excellent choice for such a revolver. It's built with a scandium alloy aluminum frame; scandium is a Smith & Wesson proprietary alloy for lightweight frames and has proven itself well in other S&W fighting handguns. It offers a real weight savings over steel, while still being strong, tough, and durable. The Governor has a stainless steel cylinder, and the revolver is finished in a business-like matte black. The barrel is also stainless and is finished in its natural color.

TAURUS

Taurus USA continues to introduce new revolvers every year. It makes quality revolvers suitable for concealed carry, hunting, or target shooting. From

S&W Schofield TK Custom Conversion

Taurus 992 Tracker

its small, lightweight pocket revolvers up through the .454 Raging Bull, Taurus has a wide selection.

Taurus small-frame snubnose revolvers are available chambered for the .22 LR, .22 Magnum, .32 H&R, .327 Federal, .38 Special, and .357 Magnum calibers. They are available in blued, nickel, or stainless finishes, mostly with fixed sights, though a couple models have fully adjustable rear sights. Duty-size four- and six-inch .357 Magnum revolvers are still in production, with a wide variety of models available. The Raging series of hunting handguns chamber powerful cartridges like the .44 Magnum and .454 Casull and are good choices for hunting dangerous game. Taurus still has more .45 Colt/.410 Shotshell revolvers on the market than anyone else, and the demand for such revolvers, as has been noted, keeps growing.

Rimfire revolvers with interchangeable cylinders have been popular for decades. Most of these are, and historically have been, single-action revolvers of the Colt Single Action Army lineage. Double-action switch-cylinder revolvers are pretty scarce, with only a few manufactured since the introduction of the .22 Magnum cartridge, in 1959. Switching the cylinders in a double-action design usually requires the use of a screwdriver, though the operation still only takes a couple of minutes. It would be nice if more switch-cylinder rimfire double-action revolvers were available, and just as I wished that, enter the new Taurus Tracker Model 992, which comes with both .22 LR and .22 Magnum cylinders. The LR cylinder can also fire .22 Short and Long ammo, as well as .22 shotshell ammunition. Built on the medium-frame Taurus double-action, it wears a heavy-profile barrel and carries nine cartridges in either of its cylinders. Taurus has designed a push-button release for the cylinder crane, eliminating the need for any tools to switch out the cylinders.

USFA Turnbull

TAYLOR'S & COMPANY

Taylor's has a very good line of Colt SAA sixgun replicas, with a couple models having some very tasteful engraving coverage at very affordable prices. The Taylor guns have smooth, reliable actions and represent good value for a quality Colt's replica.

UBERTI

Uberti Firearms is the premier Italian producer of quality replica revolver designs, marketing handguns under its own banner, as well as for several importers. It offers many different caliber options and finishes and replicates some of the less popular, but historically accurate, designs such as the cartridge conversions, transition model Colt's, and the Remington 1875 and 1890 cartridge revolvers. Uberti is the leading manufacturer of classic revolver reproductions, allowing shooters hands-on access to designs that would otherwise only be available looking through glass at a museum.

US FIRE ARMS

US Fire Arms has a line of very high-quality U.S.-built Colt Single Action Army-style revolvers. Also, the USFA sixguns are the basis for the beautiful Turnbull Open Range revolvers.

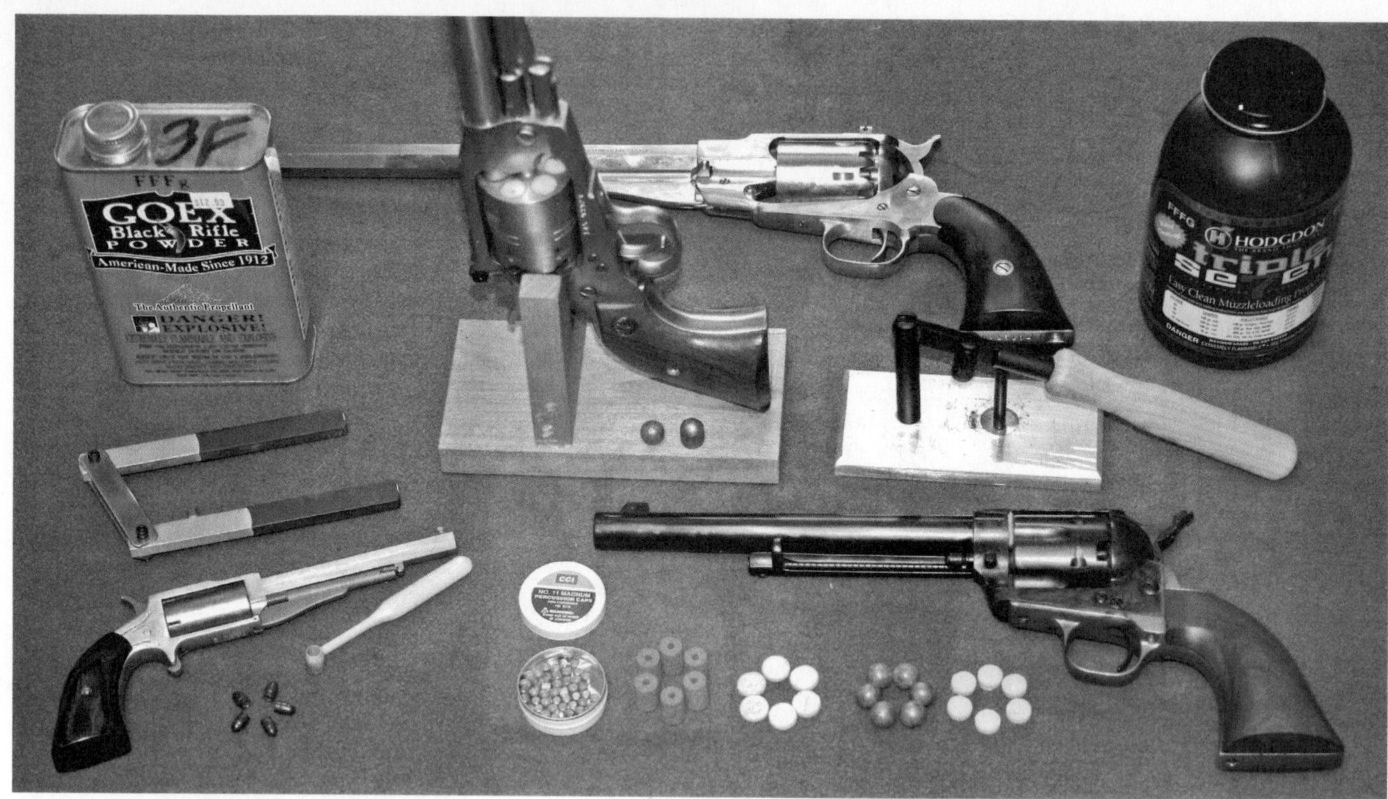

MUZZLE LOADERS

Loading options for modern percussion revolvers may require the use of external tools for those guns without attached ramrods.

BY WM. HOVEY SMITH

Each year brings challenges, but producers of muzzleloading firearms have hung in there and introduced some new guns in 2012, many of which were redesigned to reduce retail prices. Companies using this tactic were Thompson/Center Arms, Davide Pedersoli, and Knight Rifles. Before we get to these new guns, though, let's take a look at my year afield with several percussion revolvers.

The Percussion Revolver

A revolving cylinder was the most successful of many approaches that were developed to enable muzzleloaders to discharge more than two shots prior to reloading. Other attempts included hand-rotated chambers and the mechanically operated cylinder on Elisha Collier's flintlock revolver, which was patented in 1818.

Some sea captains purchased Collier's revolver, and it may have been that the young seaman Samuel Colt saw or heard of such guns. He used his idle time at sea to whittle a model of what was to become his successful pistol. This led to a patent, in 1832, and production of a folding trigger revolver in Patterson, New Jersey.

In mechanical design, the first models of anything tend to be overly complex and more delicate than those that follow. After experiences with the Paterson revolver, while fighting Comanche Indians in Texas, Col. Samuel Walker, of the U.S. Mounted Rifles, wanted Colt to make a more robust version of his revolving pistol.

The resulting .44-caliber Walker revolver was a "horse pistol," in that the revolver was designed to be issued in pairs and carried in holsters suspended from the saddle, and shoot a charge capable of disabling a horse. With its cylinder capacity of 60 grains of blackpowder and a round-ball load, it was the most powerful revolver made until the advent of Remington's .44 Magnum a century later.

Three deficiencies plagued the Colt open-top revolvers. The sights—a notch in the rear hammer and a small pin on the front of the barrel—were non-adjustable, and very often the pistols shot high. And, though the open-top design was advantageous in that it made it somewhat less likely that the copper cap fragments would tie-up the gun, persistent use of heavy loads resulted in the barrel wedge having to be periodically reshaped to insure tight lock-up between the frame and the barrel on less well-made guns.

Having an attached and strongly built loading lever made it possible to reload the gun with combustible cartridges reasonably easy, but the Walker's lever was weakly retained by a spring-hook, and the lever often fell when the gun was fired, pushing the steel ram into a chamber and tying up the gun. This was corrected with a more positive latch design, which improved the reliability of the Dragoon and subsequent Colt's.

The Remington, Spencer, Savage, Starr, and Adams revolvers, as well as the Root model Colt's and revolving Colt's rifles, used a stronger top-strap design. The French Le Mat, despite having nine-shot .36- or .40-caliber cylinders and a combination cylinder-pin shotgun barrel, also retained the open-top feature. Modern Le Mat replicas are now made in the more popular .44-caliber.

Percussion revolving pistols included guns chambered for .22-, .28-, .31-, .36-, .38-, .40-, .44-, .45-, .50-, and .54-caliber bullets. Because of Colt's dominance in the U.S., the "standard" U.S. calibers became the .31-, .36-, and .44-caliber. Modern replicas are available in these calibers and the .22 from North American Arms, and a nominal .45 (.457 versus a .454 ball) for the Ruger Old Army.

Modern Percussion Revolvers

Although interested in the history and artistry of muzzleloading guns, I am passionate about hunting with them. My first attempt was in the late 1950s, with a .36-caliber Colt 1851 Navy replica. This gun was imported by Navy Arms, to take advantage of the renewed interest in percussion guns sparked by the Civil War Centennial.

This gun shot impossibly high for small-game hunting, my home-cast balls of salvaged lead were too hard, and the hammer notch rear and low front sight compounded the difficulty of shooting accurately (to say nothing of my lack of skill). The gun was also time-consuming to clean, difficult to keep shooting because of blackpowder fouling, and I gave up on the gun in favor of a .22-caliber Harrington & Richardson revolver with adjustable sights. A succession of cartridge pistols followed, and it was decades before I revisited the percussion revolver.

Because I was more interested in performance than historical authenticity, Bill Ruger's Old Army immediately attracted my attention. Here, finally, was a cap-and-ball revolver gun with high-quality adjustable sights.

Although it was the most advanced percussion revolver ever made and loved by competitors, the Old Army struggled to be a big-game hunting handgun, because insufficient amounts of blackpowder could be put into the revolver's chambers to reach the 500 ft-lbs of muzzle energy that most writers consider the minimum for taking deer-sized game. Production of the Old Army was discontinued three years ago, and the gun is no longer in the Ruger catalog.

There were and are a small group of people who have taken big game with this gun and even with the older revolver designs. But I thought that such guns were best employed for small-game hunting and making point-blank shots for finishing off wounded animals. My principal use of the Ruger was for squirrel hunting and making brain shots on alligators drug up beside the boat.

For me the game changer was Hodgdon's Triple Seven powder, which developed 10-percent more muzzle energy than equivalent volumes of blackpowder. In the Old Army, this load offered the promise of breaking the 500 ft-lb threshold, which it ultimately proved to do. I was sufficiently encouraged to do a seven-part video series on "The Modern Percussion Revolver," which is available on YouTube and may be seen on the wmhoveysmith channel and blog entries at www.hoveysmith.wordpress.com.

These videos featured North American Arms' .22-caliber revolvers, CVA's .44-caliber brass-framed Confederate Revolver, Traditions' 1873 Peacemaker look-alike, and Cabela's stainless steel Buffalo with its 12-inch barrel. These guns, with the addition of the "Old Army," provided a reasonable sampling of modern designs. None were exact replicas of period revolvers—true in spirit, but not in detail.

North American Arms .22

These percussion adaptations of North American Arms' .22-caliber cartridge revolvers are fully functional percussion revolvers. Although the four-inch Earl has a cylinder-retaining assembly that resembles a loading lever, both the two- and four-inch guns are reloaded using external tools. They employ four grains of FFFFg blackpowder and a 30-grain bullet. They are, in a word, puny. Even the longer-barreled version generates only about 30 ft-lbs. For comparison, the .22 short fired from a 22-inch rifle has about 80 ft-lbs.

Lightweight pistols of any sort are difficult to shoot. The Earl would benefit from a better trigger and adjustable

Two .22-caliber stainless revolvers by North American Arms, CVA's .44-caliber Confederate revolver, .44-caliber Ruger Old Army, Cabela's Pietta-made Buffalo Revolver and (right) Traditions' 1873.

sights. As is, I use it for finishing shots on squirrels that I have taken with my muzzleloading shotguns. It would be interesting to have a percussion version of the firm's .22 Mini-Master, which has larger grips, a heavier barrel, and adjustable sights.

CVA's Confederate Revolver .44

As sold by CVA and others, these brass-framed pistols are likely the most common "replica" percussion revolvers in the country, because of their relatively low cost. Those wanting to own a cap-and-ball will find these guns to be functional and attractive. The original brass-frame Confederates were made in .36-caliber, and this is why I consider these "modern revolvers," rather than replicas.

While fine for occasional shooting and plinking, the brass-framed guns are weak and will shoot loose in time. Steel-framed guns are preferred for those who are going to put a lot of rounds through their pistols or use hunting loads.

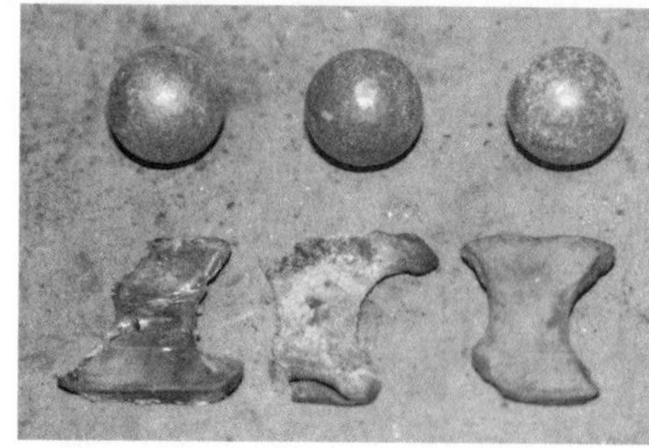

Bullets flattened against the frame of Traditions 1873 Peacemaker percussion-revolver look-alike during chain-fire events.

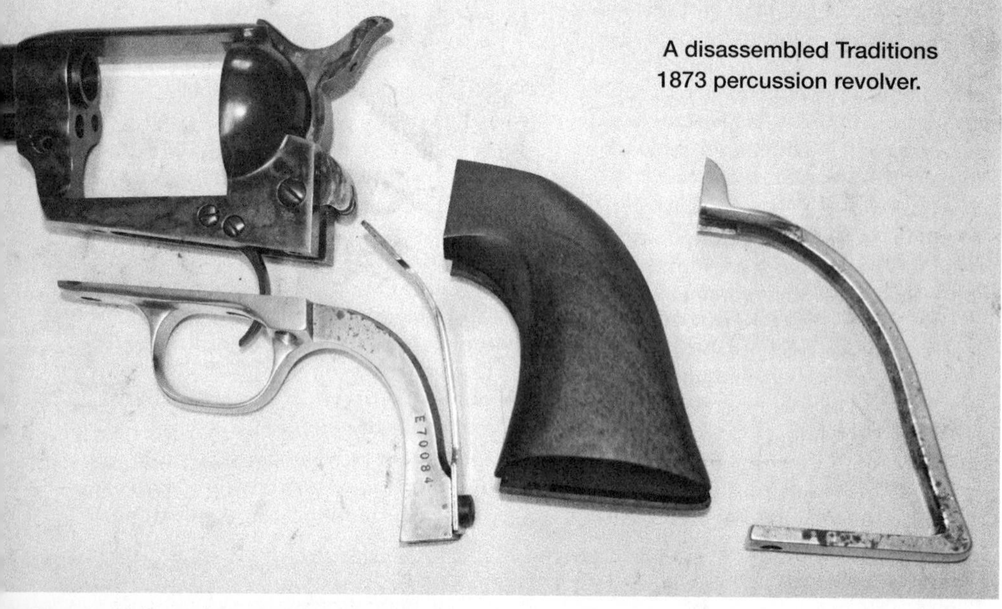

A disassembled Traditions 1873 percussion revolver.

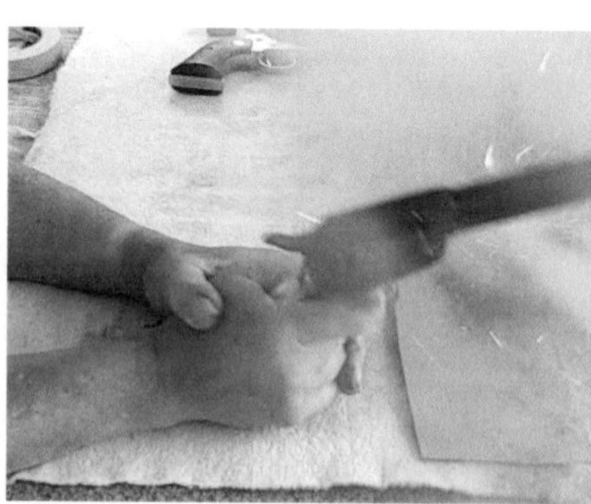

Loading the Traditions to maximum levels resulted in chain fires, as seen in these photos. Loads in this gun should be restricted to 25 grains of FFg blackpowder and round-ball loads for best results.

CVA's Optima Pistol was one of the few new guns introduced in 2012. This .50-caliber pistol is available with either iron sights or a scope base for mounting optical or red dot sights. The CVA Optima pistol has a 15-inch barrel and Quick Release breech plug and comes with either a scope base or iron sights.

Traditions' 1873 .44

This gun is attractive because it is a percussion revolver, yet has the look of the Colt Peacemaker. Previously, I shot the gun with 30-grain loads of FFg GOEX blackpowder and a round ball. In these loads I used a felt Ox-Yoke Wonder Wad under the ball and a daub of grease over it. This gun, like the Peacemaker, did not have adjustable sights, but I managed to take close-range squirrels and backyard rattlesnakes with it.

Attempting to get more energy, I tried loads of Hodgdon's Triple Seven and 30 grains of GOEX FFFg behind a round ball. The results were double and triple fires—the added recoil generated by the individual loads caused the nipples to slam back into the fixed breech of the gun with sufficient force to detonate the caps in other chambers simultaneously.

Such events were prevented in the original Colt's and Remingtons by having strong metal fences between the nipples, keeping the caps from striking the

The loading stand for the Colt's Peacemaker-style Traditions 1873 percussion revolver.

breech should "slam-backs" occur. Use only low-pressure loads of FFg or FFFg in this revolver with round balls in the Traditions' 1873s and similar guns.

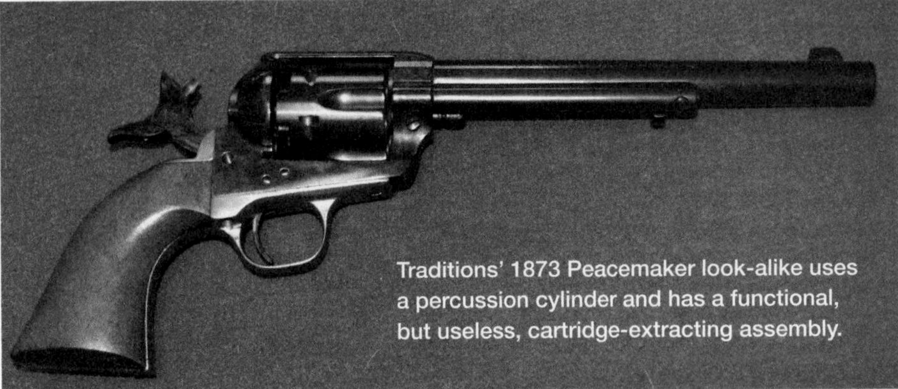

Traditions' 1873 Peacemaker look-alike uses a percussion cylinder and has a functional, but useless, cartridge-extracting assembly.

Cabela's Stainless Steel Buffalo Revolver

I had been interested for some years in Cabela's 12-inch-barreled, stainless steel version of the 1858 Remington "Buffalo" revolver that is made by Pietta, in Italy. Not only did this gun's longer barrel offer the promise of increased velocity, it also had adjustable sights.

When I decided that I was going to feature percussion revolvers, this was obviously a gun I needed to consider. I found that this gun was not quite up to the quality my Ruger Old Army. I ended up polishing some sharp edges on the trigger guard and removing some metal from the hammer nose, where it was scrubbing against the frame.

My Pietta shot much better with round-ball loads than with bullets designed by Lee, Buffalo Bullets, or two new designs by Kaido Ojamaa. I finalized my load for this gun as 42.5 grains of Hodgdon's FFFg Triple Seven, an Ox-Yoke Wonder Wad under the .454 round ball, and Ox-Yoke's wax Wonder Seals over the top of the ball. The particular jug of Triple Seven used in my testing was older and weaker than more recent production and, for the best combination of accuracy and power, 40 grains of Triple Seven is the better choice using fresh powder. This load will produce over 475 ft-lbs from the long-barreled revolver.

Ruger Old Army

Mechanically, the Ruger Old Army is the best factory percussion revolver made to date. This gun used a modified version of the Blackhawk cartridge revolver's frame, lock work, and adjustable sights, along with a 7½ -inch barrel. This Ruger also used a new loading lever with a strong retaining system. As long as Bill Ruger lived, the company made this gun to fill the limited demand from cap-and-ball revolver shooters who wanted pistols of advanced design.

As I wrote about these guns, others, including Florida hunter Rudy Betancourt and Kaido Ojamaa, contributed their experiences. The former is a fan of the stainless-steel Buffalo, and the latter designed a Keith-style 240-grain bullet for percussion revolvers and a 255-grain bullet that is particularly suitable for the Old Army. Ojamaa reported that both bullets would also work in the .45 Long Colt cartridge.

The heavier bullets did not reach me in time for me to hunt with them.

Cabelas' Buffalo revolver, top, made in Italy by Pietta, and the North American Arms' .22 provide a visual lesson in size contrast for modern percussion revolvers.

Of the pistols I had, the Ruger shot the 240-grain bullet best and developed 519 ft-lbs of energy when the bullet was loaded directly over 35 grains of Hodgdon's Triple Seven powder and sealed with a smear from Ox-Yoke's wax wads. This load completely filled the chamber. Although they arrived late, the 255-grain version (566 ft-lbs) had two slightly oversized driving bands, was made of harder lead, and used a stiff lube. These factors prevented bullet creep, which sometimes occurred with the lighter weight bullets and softer lube.

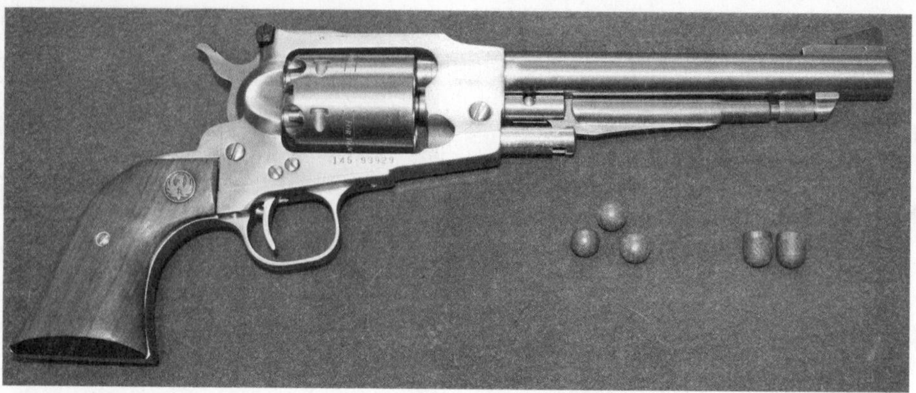

Ruger's now discontinued Old Army percussion revolver with adjustable sights and all stainless construction is based on the company's Blackhawk single-action cartridge gun and is the best percussion revolver produced by a commercial firm to date.

Hunting Load Development for Blackpowder Revolvers

Pietta. Cabela's Stainless "Buffalo" with 12-in barrel and adjustable sights.					
Bullet Weight (grains)	Powder Charge (grains)	Low Velocity (fps)	High Velocity (fps)	Average Velocity (fps)	Muzzle Energy (ft/lbs)
.454 RB.	141* Triple Seven** 40/30.7	1037	1123	1074	361
.454 RB.	141* Triple Seven** 42.5/33.0	1092	1294	1139	406
.454 RB	141* FFFg 35/36.5	847	876	864	234
Buffalo	180 Triple Seven** 42.5/33.0	981	1087	1031	425
Kaido***	240 Triple Seven** 32/26.1	832	1020	952	483
Kaido***	240 Triple Seven** 30/22.6	801	867	823	361
Kaido***	240 FFFg 25/28	609	666	638	217

Ruger Old Army Stainless with 7½-inch barrel and adjustable sights.					
Bullet Weight (grains)	Powder Charge (grains)	Low Velocity (fps)	High Velocity (fps)	Average Velocity (fps)	Muzzle Energy (ft/lbs)
.457 RB.	145* Triple Seven** 40/30.7	916	1008	963	299
.457 RB.	145* Triple Seven 35/28	1000	1011	1004	325
.457 RB.	145* Triple Seven 35/Hodgdon published data	987	314		
.457 RB.	145* Pyrodex P 40/31.3	977	1061	1019	334
Buffalo	180 Pyrodex P 40/31.3	1127	1176	1156	534
Lee Real	250 Pyrodex P 30/23	NA	NA	866	416
Lee Real	250 Triple Seven 30/22.6	894	912	904	454
Kaido***	240 Triple Seven 35/28	961	999	987	519
Kaido	255 Triple Seven 35/28	955	1040	1000	566

* A felt lubricated Wonder Wad was used under the round balls. When velocities increased to the point where these wads were destroyed accuracy suffered.

** This was a three- to four-year-old old jar of Triple Seven that had apparently somewhat deteriorated. With fresher powder, the velocities increased a significant amount.

*** This was the first shooting of Kaido's C&B Revolver Hunter, which is designed to be a universal bullet for percussion and cartridge revolvers and intended to provide improved long-range performance. This first lot of bullets was both lighter weight—240 vs. 255 grains—than designed and slightly undersized.

Bullet creep can sometimes tie up a revolver. This was solved in the Ruger Old Army by using a larger-diameter 255-grain bullet made by Kaido Ojamaa.

Hunting with the Guns

When I have a new round-ball muzzleloading rifle or shotgun, I squirrel hunt with it before I take on larger game. I had taken many squirrels with the Ruger, and it was time for the Buffalo pistol to prove itself with the round-ball load.

My hunts often produce only one or two squirrels per outing. Out of a dozen squirrels seen, I can only shoot at the five or so that have safe backstops, and out of those I kill two. Ultimately, I took five squirrels to make squirrel dumplings, as deer season was approaching.

My nearly 20 trips afield with this gun highlighted the problems of hunting with this pistol. I spooked deer because of the gun's shiny finish and the noise

Reloading Cabela's Pietta Buffalo revolver in the field is not usually necessary, but might be as when multiple shots are taken on a squirrel hunt.

of the cocking the gun. Because I was shooting at close range, I was tempted to commit the extremely dangerous act of pre-cocking the pistol. This is a fine way to shoot one's self in the foot or elsewhere should the gun fall from a tree-stand. I cannot recommend this method of hunting. I mention it because this pre-cocking is such an obvious means of solving the problem of revolver noise that I know people will do it, whether I mention it or not. This problem is not limited to percussion pistols, but also all revolvers. Regardless, I never place my finger inside the trigger guard until I am ready to shoot. If you are going to pre-cock your revolver, despite my admonition that you should not, adopt this practice and lay your finger alongside the trigger guard until you are ready to shoot.

Cabela's Buffalo Revolver's Deer

I was hunting on the ground, in an area overlooking a small valley. On previous sits I had seen deer, but they were too far away or moving too fast to shoot. This time, though, a small doe appeared to my left, and it looked like she would walk through an opening to my front. I raised the gun and sighted at the opening as the doe moved into it. When the deer filled the sights, I squeezed off a shot. The ball struck high, clipping the top of the spine, and the deer fell. As she struggled to rise, I re-cocked the gun and fired again. This shot passed through the heart and the deer quickly expired. Both shots penetrated the deer. This doe weighed about 60 pounds.

One deer down, one to go.

Old Army's Deer

My hunting setup with this gun was also on the ground, but this time at the edge of cut-over timber and more mature hardwoods. Deer liked to walk this edge. Not long after daylight, a buck approached from my right. I raised the gun when he stepped behind some cover, but the deer saw me, stopped, and took three steps towards me. As he started to turn away, I shot him through the point of the shoulder. Ojamaa's 240-grain cast bullet penetrated the shoulder joint and raked the 110-pound deer, exiting behind the off-side leg.

After a stumbling run of 30 yards, the buck expired. The bullet had penetrated 12 inches of deer and appeared to give similar damage as the .44-Remington Magnum, but without quite so large a wound channel. This was impressive performance for a lead pistol bullet fired from a 7½ -inch barreled gun.

Cabela's Pietta Buffalo revolver with the 60-pound doe taken with the pistol. The first shot (above the hammer) knocked the deer down. The second one (below the trigger guard), penetrated the heart and killed the animal. This quick second-shot capability is one of the desirable features of using a percussion revolver for hunting.

Three sizes of cylinders indicate different capacities for the .44-caliber revolvers that were tested. From left to right are the cylinders of the Traditions, Cabela's Buffalo (Pietta) and Ruger Old Army revolvers.

Conclusions

What do I think of these revolvers as hunting guns? Even with round-ball loads, and particularly with heavier bullets designed for them, these stainless steel revolvers loaded with Hodgdon's Triple Seven powder will take average-sized deer and hogs at close range. With Ojamaa's bullet and the Old Army, these would be as efficient as the hot .44 Special cast-bullet loads Elmer Keith used on many big-game animals.

My aging eyes no longer permit me to shoot while wearing my prescription glasses, and I am likely going to have to go to scope-sighted guns. Scopes are more easily mounted on single-shot muzzleloading pistols that can take more powerful loads. Given the choice of more precise sighting and a more powerful load versus having repeat shots, I will stick to my longer barreled, single-shot muzzleloading pistols for deer hunting. The revolvers are more attractive for small-game and hog hunting, because of the potential for multiple targets and/or the need for rapid repeat shots to down a game.

Percussion revolvers are more time-consuming to clean than single-shots. With these stainless guns and Triple Seven powder, I found that I could shoot one or more chambers and then clean them and the barrel with soapy water while leaving the other chambers loaded (but uncapped), thereby forgoing having to completely clean the gun for a next-day hunt. For longer times between hunts, I strip the gun to component parts and wash, dry, and lubricate them all.

A 12-minute video "Modern Percussion Revolvers. Part 7B. Hunting Big Game" is available on YouTube at http://youtube.com/watch?v=LWNh24pbpZs. The other six parts of the series covers the guns, cleaning, loading and small-game hunting.

New Products

Here's a look at the new and improved products that will greet muzzloader and blackpowder fans in the coming year.

Colt's

Colt's new gun at the SHOT Show was actually one of its old ones, an 1877 Colt Bulldog Gatling gun in .45-70 that was

Shooting a replica Colt 1877 Bull Dog Gatling gun in .45-70 caliber was certainly a hit with gun writers who attended the Range Day prior to the 2012 SHOT Show.

the undisputed hit among writers at the Media Range Day that preceded the actual show. This gun was shown last year at the Navy Arms booth, but U.S. Armament Co., of Ephrata, Pennsylvania, sold the distribution rights to Colt's. If interested, the price is about $39,000.

Chiappa

Chiappa's new muzzleloaders are exacting replicas of the 1853 three-band and 1858 two-band British Enfield rifles that were used in large numbers by both sides in the Civil War. The Italian proof marks are located on the bottom of the barrel, and all markings and engravings are as they were on the originals.

CVA (BPI Industries)

CVA captured my attention with its new Optima .50-caliber drop-barrel muzzleloading pistol. The gun's 15-inch barrel comes with either a scope base or fiber-optic sights. The 3.7-pound pistol has polymer grips and fore-end to help ease the recoil from 100-grain charges. Powder charges in these types of guns may be varied according to the game being taken. In similar guns, I have found that a 100-grain powder charge (FFFg equivalent) with a 370-grain T/C MaxiBall to be an effective load on U.S. and small-ish African game. About 85 grains does better for me with 240-grain bullets in these short-barreled guns. Short barrels require the added resistance from heavier bullets or saboted projectiles to more completely combust the powder.

Also new from CVA is the Accura Mountain Rifle with a WeatherGuard Coating and a Dead-On one-piece scope mount. With the 25-inch barrel, the gun comes in at 6.3 pounds, one pound less than the standard model with a 27-inch barrel. All Accura guns are provided with a QuakeClaw Sling, new all-steel fittings, reversible cocking spurs, and Bergara barrels with Bullet Guiding Muzzles.

CVA has continued the industry trend of continuously upgrading guns, and all of CVA's lineup, including the Optima Pistol, now have hand-detachable breech plugs, which aids gun cleaning considerably.

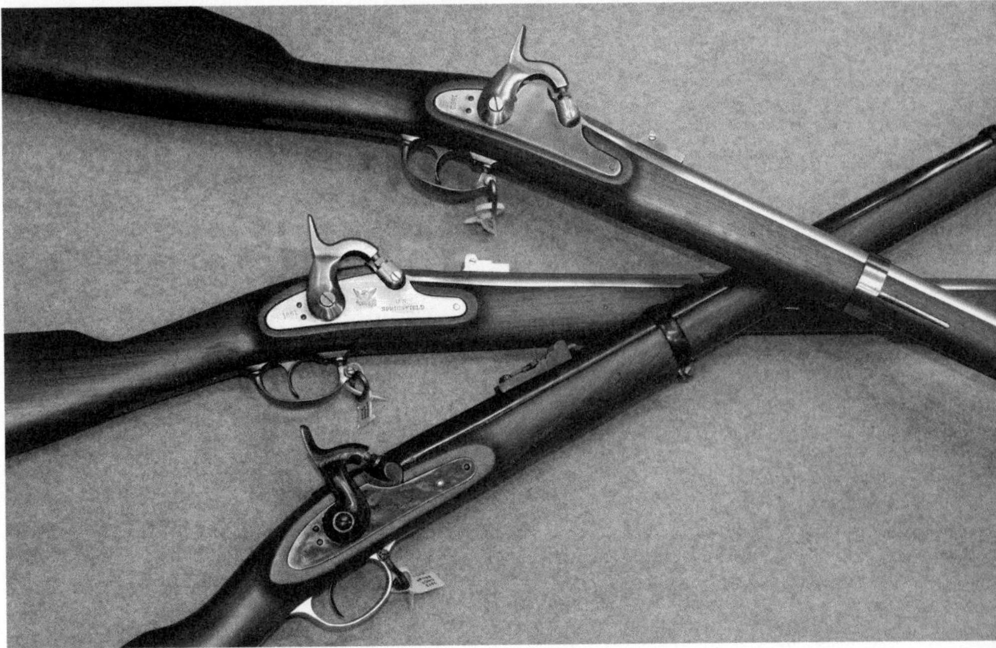

Three of Davide Pedersoli's new Civil War rifles for 2012. From the top is the CSA Richmond rifle, three-band Enfield Rifle and Springfield rifle. All are done with original markings and line engravings.

Davide Pedersoli

This Italian maker has the most extensive line of replica blackpowder military and civilian arms, including target guns that win international competitions. This year's new muzzle-loaders include a CSA Richmond Rifle, three- and two-band Enfield rifles, a Springfield rifle, and a Mississippi (Zouave) rifle with its brass patchbox. According to Stefano Pedersoli, these guns are not only the most exacting replica guns to date, but good perform-ers on the range.

On the civilian side, a non-selective single-trigger 12-gauge shotgun is of-fered with 11-inch, 20-inch, and 28-inch barrels. This gun features back-action locks and has either Cylinder/Cylinder barrels in the shorter lengths or Improved Cylinder/Modified chokes in the longer gun. This should make a fine upland game gun.

Dixie Gun Works

Dixie remains to be the one-stop supplier for muzzleloading parts and accessories and often has hard-to-find items available nowhere else. The com-pany's selection of guns was modestly expanded this year, with the addition of Davide Pedersoli's Philadelphia Der-ringer and a full magazine-tube version of the 1886 Winchester rifle in .45-70.

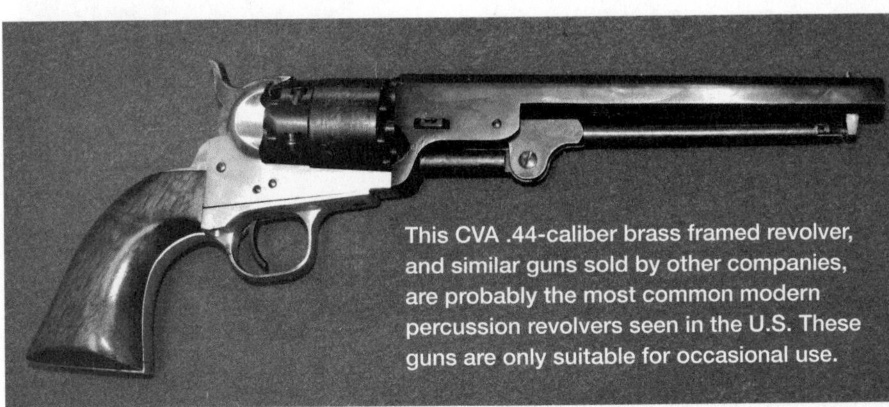

This CVA .44-caliber brass framed revolver, and similar guns sold by other companies, are probably the most common modern percussion revolvers seen in the U.S. These guns are only suitable for occasional use.

Knight Rifles

After purchasing the company and relocating its operations to Tennessee, Knight has resumed production. In striker-fired guns, Knight is offering the TK-2000 12-gauge muzzleloading shotgun and its base-line model, the Bighorn. Among its bolt-action guns, both .50- and .52-caliber versions of the Disc Extreme are being produced

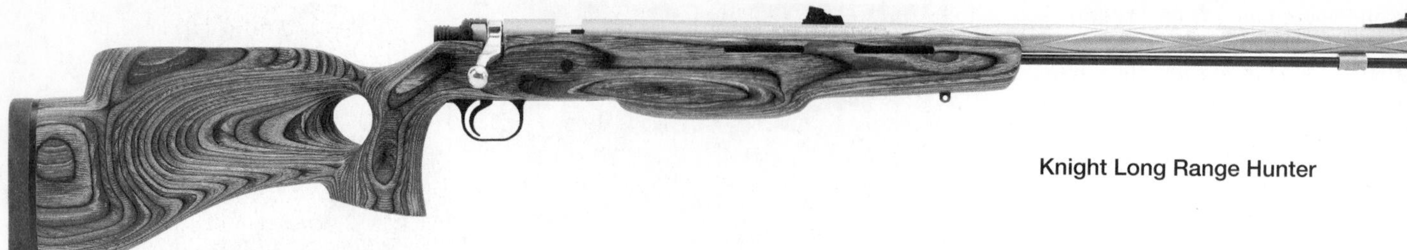

Knight Long Range Hunter

with the option of breech plugs to use the plastic No. 209 primer holders or the option to load naked primers. The Hot Shot primer holders are also available pre-loaded with Winchester No. 209s. The drop-barreled KP 1 will be returned to Knight's lineup, but only as a muzzleloading gun. The company has no immediate intention to make the Revolution or Rolling Block styles or offer any cartridge guns, according to spokesman Sam Brocato.

Knight rifles is bucking the trend towards alloy receivers and ultra-light components. Its steel receiver guns are simple and rugged.

Traditions

While CVA and Thompson/Center Arms have eliminated or significantly reduced their offerings of side-hammer flint and percussion guns, Traditions continues a full line and has improved its drop-barrel .50-caliber hunting rifles. Customer demand is pushing makers to offer lighter weight rifles and, in response, Traditions has introduced chromium-molybdenum barrels in two of its rifles, a change that allowed these already lightweight guns to shed an additional pound.

The Vortex Ultra Light and Northwest Magnum guns combine an alloy frame with the lighter barrels to bring the gun's weight down to 6¼ pounds. The Northwest gun has its barrel cut to expose the primer, as required in several states. Both guns feature Accelerator Breech Plugs, Cerakote protective finishes, drop-out trigger mechanisms, and over-molded stocks with rubberized panels. Additional features include an attached bipod on the 30-inch barreled Vortex UL LDR.

The revamped Pursuit Ultra Light weighs only 5.15 pounds, with most of the exterior options as the Vortex. This gun does not have the drop-out trigger group of the Vortex, but comes with a shorter 26-inch barrel (compared to the 28- and 30-inch barrels of the Vortex UL and Vortex UL LDR).

Thompson/Center Arms

Although Thompson/Center has only its Hawken and Firestorm rifles remaining in its side-hammer muzzleloading guns and has mostly concentrated expansion in the cartridge gun line, the company continues to improve its modern muzzleloading rifles. New for 2012 is the ProHunter FX (Fixed Barrel), which features the stocks, action, and accessories available for the Encore, but without the interchangeable barrel feature. This allows the gun to be sold at a reduced costs, compared to the popular Encore Pro Hunter series that does have interchangeable rifle, shotgun, and muzzleloader barrels.

Taylor's & Co./Cimarron Arms

Although Dixie picks up some of the cowboy action, the firms that most often supply guns of the Civil War/1890s periods are Taylor's & Company and Cimarron Arms. Between the two are offered an amazing selection of replica guns that are often re-chambered for readily available cartridges instead of the now-obscure original rounds. Made in Italy on CNC machines, these guns are often better than the originals, and all are subjected to Italian proofing. These replicas are sometimes "modernized" to feature adjustable sights, stainless steel, and barrel lengths or stock configurations not found on the originals. For example, Taylor's 1887 Winchester lever-action 12-gauge has a higher comb to fit modern shooters and is chambered for 2¼-inch shells. These are fun guns and are as useful for hunting as they ever were.

Taylor's has, for the past several years, offered convertible cylinders that enable owners of percussion .44- and .36-caliber revolvers to load cylinders full of .45 Long Colts or .38 Specials. These are not inexpensive, at about $200 each, and provide increased versatility to the owners of these guns.

Cimarron's owner, Mike Harvey, is a hunter, and his method of turning a conventional Sharps rifle into a muzzleloader was to use a No. 209 primer in a new breech plug. The user doesn't have to make combustible paper cartridges or re-

Author with a young swan taken in 1912 with a Thompson/Center Arms Mountain Magnum 12-gauge shotgun and a load of 1¼ ounces by volume of HeviShot 4s.

load .50-caliber brass cases to shoot this rifle. The Hybrid is a double set triggered, double keyed, side-hammer, drop-block Gimmer Sharps, except that it loads from the muzzle. Not only will the Hybrid throw 400- to 500-grain bullets at the heaviest game, the Gimmer-style Sharps looks very good on the wall. Cimarron also sells Pedersoli's Santa Fe Hawken, a .50-caliber half-stocked side-hammer muzzleloading rifle with a 30-inch barrel and a premium maple stock. Finish is rust-brown.

Components

There were several updated offerings in powders and bullets, and even a neat new accessory this year.

Powders

Alliant introduced BlackMZ, a new blackpowder substitute the company states is clean burning, has dependable ignition, and is virtually non-corrosive. The sample I received appears to be about Fg granulation. This powder may be used as a volume-for-volume substitute for blackpowder. As with any new component, work up your loads slowly until you reach your desired result or accuracy starts to suffer.

American Pioneer Powder has introduced a new version of Jim Shockey's Gold with about 10-percent more energy, to compete with Hodgdon's Triple Seven. Neither the Alliant nor Pioneer powders contain sulfur, and guns can be cleaned with water (although I still use a splash of dishwashing soap). Shockey's Gold is offered in both FFg and FFFg grades, as well as in pre-measured charges and 100-grain-equivalent rectangular sticks.

Bullets

Machined-turned brass bullets for muzzleloading guns are being sold as saboted bullets by Knight Rifles. Cutting Edge Bullets of Drifting, Pennsylvania, also introduced brass bullets in a variety of sizes for cartridge guns, and these bullets may also be used with sabots and shot from muzzleloaders. Cutting Edge Bullet products are designed to fragment their front ends after penetrating two inches, thus scattering secondary projectiles through the animal while the base continues to penetrate.

Harvester bullets makes a Crushed Ribbed sabot that the company sells with its copper-electroplated lead Scorpion hollowpoint and polymer-tipped bullets. This sabot takes only half the force to load and is available as a separate component for .40-caliber bullets shot from .45-caliber guns, and for .40-, .44-, and .45-caliber bullets in .50-caliber guns. Harvester's

Alliant BlackMZ is a new blackpowder substitute powder that is much less corrosive than blackpowder and permits guns to be cleaned with only water.

Saber Tooth has an attached polymer base, similar to PowerBelt Bullets, but is full-diameter and has a star-shaped cavity to promote rapid expansion. In addition, the company makes the Winchester/Olin-discontinued Red Winchester 12-gauge shotgun wad for 1¼ ounces of shot. I often use this wad in my muzzleloading shotgun charges of HeviShot.

Accessories

Items that I found useful included CVA's new palm saver, which attaches to a gun's ramrod, and that company's combination 5-in-1 Field Loading Tool. This tool combines the functions of a speed loader, short starter, 209 primer extractor, palm saver, and primer dispenser in one device.

Taylor's convertible cylinders allow many varieties of percussion revolvers to use .45 Long Colts and .38 Specials by swapping out percussion cylinders with pre-loaded cartridge cylinders. For hunters, this is an interesting option for all-weather hunting.

The Cimarron Gimmer-Sharps Hybrid is a .50-caliber muzzleloader that uses a No. 209 primer, making either the paper cartridges for the original percussion Sharps rifles or loading .50-caliber brass cases obsolete. This gun allows powerful loads of blackpowder to be used along with 400- to 500-grain bullets than can take down anything that walks, so long as you can do it with a single shot.

AMMUNITION, BALLISTICS AND COMPONENTS

BY HOLT BODINSON

Zombie ammunition! Razorback boar ammunition! Ted Nugent ammunition? Varmin-A-Tor bullets at Barnes and Varmageddon ammunition at Nosler! This is the year of the catchy name and the specialized load. Meanwhile, Hornady has cooked up a dandy new varmint load, the .17 Hornet. On the other end of the caliber spectrum, Wild West Guns is introducing its .457 Wild West Magnum cartridge for the Marlin lever-action and reviving the powerful .50 Alaskan. Then there are the exciting new propellants this year. Alliant has developed an excellent blackpowder substitute, Black MZ, which is as friendly in a flintlock as it is in a percussion gun. Hodgdon is introducing its radical Copper Fouling Eraser powder, which is proving highly accurate in addition to significantly reducing copper fouling.

All-around, it's proving to be an exciting year in the ammunition, ballistics, and components business.

ALLIANT POWDER

Alliant's first blackpowder substitute, Black MZ, is finally getting into the hands of shooters. The new formula is a volume-for-volume replacement for actual blackpowder in muzzleloaders and cartridges. It's described as being "virtually non-corrosive" and highly resistant to humidity and moisture. I've shot a lot of it in traditional muzzleloading rifles. It's an extremely accurate powder that leaves so little fouling in the barrel that one can clean a barrel with four patches dampened with any handy powder solvent. In my experience, velocities generated by Black MZ

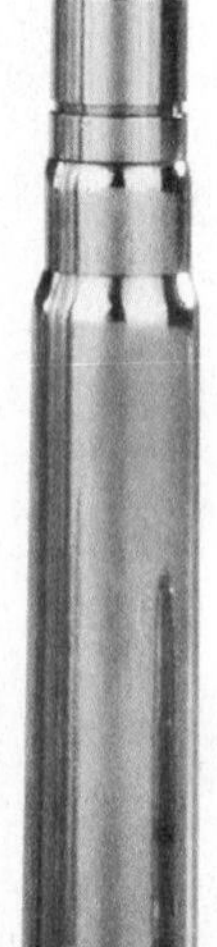

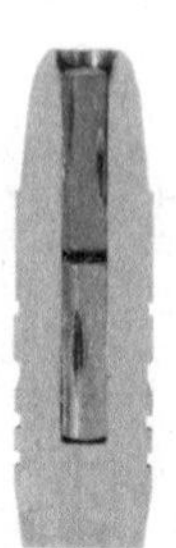

Century International Arms is the source for the Sauvestre's high-tech ammunition.

are slightly less than those reached by equivalent loads of actual blackpowder, but there's no sulfur smell and there's lots of white smoke.

On the smokeless side of the powder business, there's a new temperature insensitive, easy metering powder designed specifically for AR-15 rifles utilizing heavy .223 or .308 match bullets. It's called "AR-Comp" and is being imported from Sweden. www.alliantpowder.com

BALLISTIC PRODUCTS

Ballistic Products is the unchallenged champ, the universal mart, for anything relating to shotshell reloading components, tooling, and thoroughly original and entertaining handloading guides. Added to the component line this year are some long-sought-after .410-bore and 28-gauge wads designed to protect fine little bores from the vicissitudes of tungsten-based, non-toxic shot. Being the exclusive dealer for ITX tungsten-iron shot, Ballistic Products is now also able to supply the muzzleloading world with ITX-formed round-balls and sabot-driven .50-caliber conical slugs. With the most entertaining catalog in the component business, see them at www.ballisticproducts.com.

BARNES BULLETS

Look out zombies and varmints! Barnes is bringing back its highly explosive line of lead-core varmint bullets, the Varmin-A-Tor. The new lineup includes a 32-grain .20-caliber, 40- and 50-grain .22-calibers, and 58- and 72-grain 6mms. All the Barnes bullet families seem to be growing. There's a new 180-grain .35-caliber in the Tipped Triple-Shock X line; a 171-grain 7mm in the Match Burner line; a 127-grain 6.5mm, 168-grain 7mm, and a 280-grain .338-caliber in the Long-Range X line. There is also a new

Barnes is introducing a 110-grain tactical bullet for the .300 AAC Blakout and Whisper cartridges.

Barnes is bringing back the highly popular and explosive Varmin-A-Tor line.

The .300 AAC Blackout/Whisper and the .35 Whelen are being added to the VOR-TX line of ammunition.

110-grain .308-caliber TAC-TX bullet designed specifically for the .300 AAC Blackout and .300 Whisper cartridges. If you don't have time to handload, Barnes can fix you up with two new cartridges in its VOR-TX ammunition line—a 110-grain TAC-TX loading for the .300 AAC Blackout and .300 Whisper, and a 180-grain Tipped Triple-Shock X bullet in the good old .35 Whelen cartridge. See it all at www.barnesbullets.com.

BERGER BULLETS

Tactical is in at Berger Bullets, which has five new "tactical," match-quality offerings: a 77-grain .22-caliber, 175-grain .30-caliber, and 185-, 230- and 300-grain picks in .338-caliber. Berger's "Hybrid" bullet, which incorporates many of the benefits of its famous Very Low Drag bullet while being less sensitive to seating depth, is increasingly popular with shooters. See them all at www.bergerbullets.com.

BERRY'S

The home of the most refined copper-plated lead bullet, Berry's has mastered the art of incorporating a hollowpoint in an economical design. Pictures of the new HP after expansion are dramatic. Performance looks excellent in .44- and .45-caliber. See Berry's extensive line-up at www.berrymfg.com.

BLACK HILLS AMMUNITION

Whether it's the company's Factory New or Factory Remanufactured ammunition, Black Hills has the well-earned reputation of producing some of the most consistently accurate ammunition ever offered. The military thinks so, too. The most recent contract from the U.S. Navy is for 50 million rounds of Black Hills proprietary long-range 5.56 rounds, featuring a specially produced Sierra 77-grain MatchKing loaded to a velocity of 2,750 fps from a 20-inch barrel. The .300 Whisper and .300 AAC Blackout cartridges are coming on strong in the marketplace, and Black Hills is right on top of it with loads carrying 125- or 220-grain open-tip match bullets, the latter being subsonic for use with a suppressor. Being right in the middle of fabulous South Dakota prairie dog country, Black Hills has now

Black Hills .204 Ruger ammunition is the highest velocity round available for the AR-15.

Black Hills .300 Whisper loads are available as a 125-grain HP or subsonic 220-grain HP.

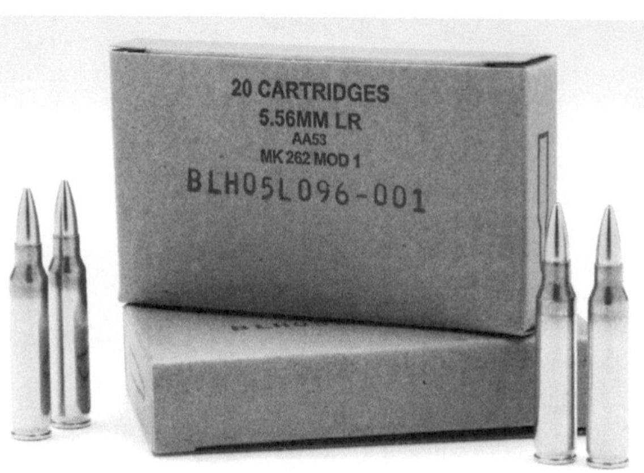

Black Hills has been awarded a Navy contract for 50 million rounds of its 5.56 long-range ammo.

added the .204 Ruger to its line. Loaded with a 32-grain Hornady VMAX bullet, the .204 Ruger is the highest velocity round available for the AR-15 platform. Customers also asked for a target-quality 5.56 loading that would be stable in their ARs having a 1:9 twist. Black Hills has responded with a 69-grain Sierra MatchKing loading generating 2,875 fps from a 20-inch barrel. Finally, by packaging its personal-defense ammunition in 20-round boxes this year, Black Hills is offering premium ammunition to the public at a very affordable price point. See it all at www.black-hills.com.

BRENNEKE USA

Brenneke invented the shotgun slug, in 1898. Since then, it's never stopped refining the original. New this year is the 12-gauge Magnum Crush slug for rifled bores. It's big, weighing 1½ounces, and powerful, with a muzzle velocity of 1,604 fps and muzzle energy of 3,752 ft-lbs Brenneke claims an accuracy level of three inches at 100 yards for five-shot groups. See the company's excellent catalog at www.brennekeusa.com.

Brenneke's latest slug weighs a whopping 1½ ounces and is loaded to a muzzle velocity of 1,604 fps.

CCI

"Quiet" is in the name. Offering a 40-grain .22 LR round that's no louder than a pellet gun, CCI has cooked up the Quiet-22 cartridge with a velocity of only 710 fps. CCI claims that, at that velocity, the decibel level of the Quiet-22 round is only 25 percent of that of a standard velocity .22 LR. It looks like the ideal plinking and training rimfire. Get the entire scoop on the world's largest offering of rimfire ammunition in the world at www.cci-ammunition.com.

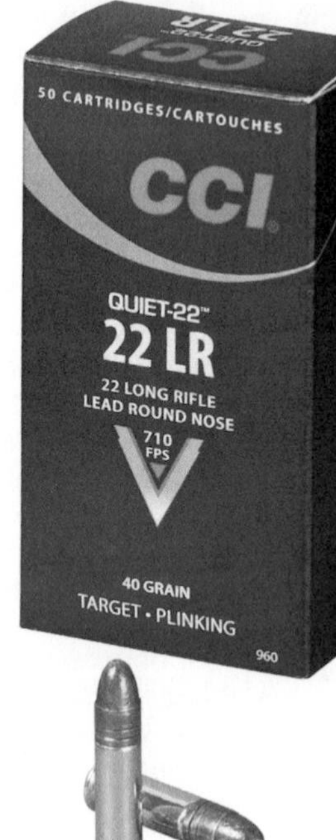

With a velocity of only 710 fps, CCI's new Long Rifle is as quiet as an airgun.

CENTURY INTERNATIONAL ARMS

Century is importing the rifle and shotgun slug lines of the finest French sporting ammunition produced by Sauvestre. The Sauvestre products are known for their high-tech designs and outstanding performance on game. The Sauvestre shotgun slug—available in 12- and 20-gauge in either 2¾-inch or three-inch cases and for smooth or rifled bores of any choke restriction—is a unique projectile in the world of slugs. It looks exactly like a small, finned torpedo and comes encased in a two-piece, breakaway sabot. The central core of the torpedo is hard and surrounded by a lead or non-lead alloy sheath that expands upon impact. The Sauvestre rifle ammunition line is loaded with a distinct-looking, machined, non-toxic hollowpoint bullet, grooved to reduce pressure and fouling. The Sauvestre rifle ammunition line currently being imported by Century consists of a 126-grain .270 WSM, a 132-grain 7mm Rem. Mag., and a 164-grain .300 WSM loadings. See the details of these and other arms and ammunition at www.centuryarms.com.

CLAYBUSTER WADS

The Claybuster brand of shotshell wads covers the waterfront, when handloaders go looking for a less expensive wad, yet a wad of equal quality, to replace factory components that can often be scarce. New this year is a ¾-ounce wad for putting together light loads in the 20-gauge. There's a wad for every purpose at www.claybusterwads.com.

CorBon is loading Wild West Guns' new big-game cartridge, the crushing .457 WWG.

CORBON

It's news! CorBon will be loading Wild West Guns' big, proprietary boomer, the .457 WWG Magnum, which Wild West barrels in the Marlin lever-action platform. Ballistics are impressive: a 350-grain Swift A-Frame with a muzzle velocity of 2,150 fps. CorBon is also unveiling a completely machined, magnum-length bolt-action that combines the best features of the Winchester Model 70 and the '98 Mauser. See them at www.corbon.com.

DOUBLE TAP

A relatively new firm, Double Tap offers an impressive selection of premium handgun and rifle ammunition. This year it's greatly expanded its Safari Grade ammunition line to include the 9.3x62, .375 Ruger, .416 Ruger, .416 Rigby, .404 Jeffery, .425 Westley Richards, .470 and .500 Nitro Express, .500 Jeffery, and .505 Gibbs. See this company's extensive catalog at www.doubletapammo.com.

D DUPLEKS

Always on the side of high-tech shotgun slug designs, D Dupleks has developed a new and intriguing, frangible 12-gauge shotgun slug. Suitable for rifled or smooth bores, the 400-grain slug is designed for training, door breeching, and other law enforcement applications. With a muzzle velocity of 1,340 fps, the Kaviar 26L slug is said to be capable of three-inch groups at 55 yards. See the company's radical hunting slugs, as well, at www.ddupleks.com.

FEDERAL

Copper is king at Federal this year, with a new copper shotgun slug and a complete line of Vital Shok Trophy Copper rifle bullets promising improved accuracy, high weight retention, and lethality. The new, polymer-tipped Trophy Copper Sabot Slug will be offered in 20- and 12-gauge for both the 2¾- and three-inch shells and is said to be capable of minute-of-angle groups at 100 yards from a rifled barrel. The polymer-tipped, Trophy Copper rifle bullets will be introduced across the whole caliber spectrum from .243 Win. through .338 Federal under the successful Federal Premium label. Finally, there are two new loadings of the effective Trophy Bonded Bear Claw bullet this year. The .30-06 gets a 200-grain Bear Claw at 2,540 fps, and the never-say-die .45-70 is upgraded to a 300-grain Bonded Bear Claw at 1,850 fps.

Federal's Trophy Copper bullets will be introduced across the whole rifle caliber spectrum.

Federal is introducing copper projectiles in both its slug and rifle bullet lines.

New Heavyweight shot turkey loads are long on range and light on recoil.

A new Black Cloud Flitestopper steel load has been fine-tuned for 20- to 30-yard waterfowling.

For shooting over decoys or in flooded timber, Federal is introducing a Black Cloud Flitestopper Steel Close Range loading in the 20- and 12-gauge three-inch magnums. The patterning characteristics of the Close Range loads simply concentrate more pellets on target at 20 to 30 yard ranges than conventional shells.

Want a mild-recoiling 12-gauge turkey load that will outperform a three-inch load of lead No. 5s? Federal has it, and it's new this year. Carrying 1¼ ounces of No. 6 or No. 7 Heavyweight shot in a 2¾-inch case, the new loading is said to extend effective shot range by 20 yards while cutting felt recoil in half; it's the Heavyweight shot that gets the job done. www.federalpremium.com.

FIOCCHI USA

"Tundra" is the cool name Fiocchi has given its heavier-than-steel and heavier-than-lead non-toxic shot. The outstanding quality of Tundra shot is that it deforms like lead. It's safe for chokes and expands upon impact. In short, Tundra non-toxic shotshells are a sensational new product for waterfowlers. Great stuff at www.fiocchiusa.com.

GRIZZLY CARTRIDGE COMPANY

Grizzly loads some of those can't-ever-find-'em calibers. It's the place to go shopping for the .475 Linebaugh, .500 JRH, .500 Wyoming Express, .500 Linebaugh, .348 Win., .50 Alaskan, and .50-110 Win+P. Check this maker out at www.grizzlycartrtidge.com.

HEVI-SHOT

If you shoot the big 10-gauge, you're going to love the new recipes cooked-up by Hevi-Shot this year. Available with 1½ ounces of BB or Nos. 2, 3, or 4 of Hevi-Metal shot, this new "High Speed" load is zinging out at a scorching 1,500 fps—that's a *fast* 10! For shooting over decoys, there's a new 10-gauge "Magnum Blend" load mixing Nos. 5, 6, and 7 of Hevi-Shot for super dense patterns. Combining steel shot with Hevi-Shot, there are three new No. 4 turkey loads for the three-inch 20-gauge and three- and 3½-inch 12 gauge. See these and Hevi-Shot's new line of choke tubes at www.hevishot.com.

HODGDON

Taking on a special composition, 5.56mm military powder and bringing it into the civilian realm, Hodgdon is introducing its new Copper Fouling Eraser (CFE) powder. This revolutionary, easy metering ball powder not only significantly reduces copper fouling, but is proving to be highly accurate while delivering exceptional velocities in the cartridges it's loaded in. See the CFE loading data in the *Hodgdon 2012 Reloading Manual* that covers more than 5,000 loads for all the powders in the line. Great material at www.hodgdon.com.

HORNADY

Hornady seems like a kitchen for new cartridges. One of this year's top creations is the revival and commercialization of an old wildcat, the .17 Hornet—and it's a dilly. With a muzzle velocity of 3,650 fps with Hornady's 20-grain V-MAX and a trajectory that tracks that of the outstanding 55-grain .223 Rem. load, the .17 Hornet will be an attention grabber in the varminting world. Apparently,

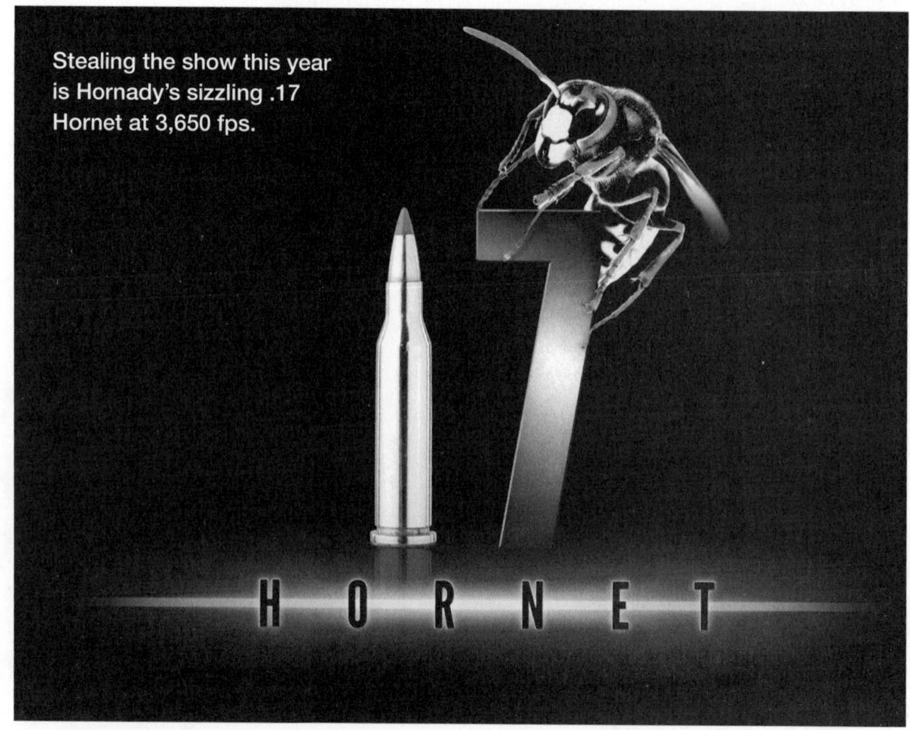

Stealing the show this year is Hornady's sizzling .17 Hornet at 3,650 fps.

Hodgdon's Copper Fouling Eraser powder cuts fouling and is proving to be very accurate.

Hornady is also highly concerned about a potential zombie uprising, so why not some factory-loaded Zombie MAX ammunition and Z-MAX component bullets—just in case! Then, to counter barriers like heavy clothing, sheet metal, plywood, and auto glass, Hornady also designed a new hollow point bullet with a polymer insert it named "Flexlock" and claims will penetrate those barriers, maintain an open hollowpoint, and get the terminal job done. Offered in 9mm, 9mm+P, and .40 S&W, it carries the Critical Duty label at your local gunshop.

There are always lots of new component offerings at Hornady, but one that caught my attention in particular was a 200-grain spitzer Flex Tip bullet for the old, but effective, .348 Win. Another intriguing addition to a conventional line is the introduction of match ammunition for the 6.5x55, .303 British, 7.62x54 Russian, and 8x57. Unlimber those old war horses and go at it! See the complete line-up at www.hornady.com.

HUNTINGTON

If you are fortunate enough to own a .275 Rigby, but don't have any properly marked ammunition, you're in luck. Huntington has located a cache of cases made by Norma that were headstamped, simply, ".275 Rigby." Huntington also has a new run of high-quality .280 Ross brass and lots of other cool finds at www.huntingtons.com.

INTERNATIONAL CARTRIDGE COMPANY

Green is the thing at International Cartridge, which provides probably the most extensive offerings of totally non-toxic, military, police, home-defense and hunting ammunition available today. Go green at www.iccammo.com.

JAGEMANN TECHNOLOGIES

With an industrial background in deep-drawing technology and products, Jagemann is entering the component brass field. Holding its brass cases to match/military specifications, Jagemann already produces a variety of handgun

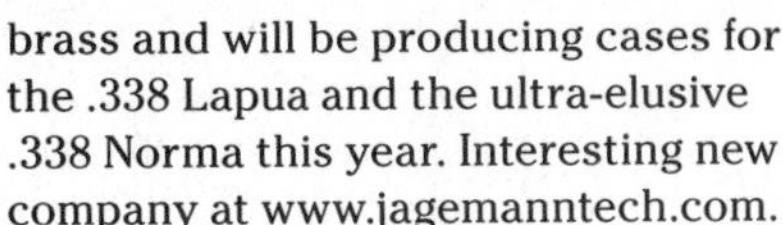

brass and will be producing cases for the .338 Lapua and the ultra-elusive .338 Norma this year. Interesting new company at www.jagemanntech.com.

KENT CARTRIDGE

Turkeys are going to have a hard time this year. Kent has developed a 50/50 blend of No. 5 Tungsten Matrix and No. 5 lead Diamond Shot loaded in the 3½-inch 12-gauge at 1,326 fps and the three-inch 12-gauge at 1,200. The shot loads are 2¼ ounces and 1⅞ ounces, respectively. Respectfully speaking, that's a heck of a turkey tamer. See all the Kent quality ammunition at www.kentgamebore.com.

LAPUA

Lapua has developed a powder for the .308 Win. that absolutely minimizes zero changes from minus-65 Fahrenheit to plus-145. It will be loaded in a new HPS-Ti cartridge featuring the legendary 170-grain Lock Base FMJBT bullet and become the ultimate sniper round. The match-quality Scenar bullet line has been expanded with the addition of 69- and 77-grain .224-caliber and 90- and 105-grain 6mm.

Finland has long been known for being hotwired, so this year you can download a complete Lapua ballistics program on your mobile phone supporting basic Java or Android. It may prove to be the most tested and sophisticated program available, and it's free. See Lapua at www.lapua.com.

LIGHTFIELD

It's the formidable Zombie invasion possibility again. Lightfield has the answer for this "problem" with a full line of Zombie Blaster ammunition for .410-bore through 12-gauge. The Blaster projectile is composed of crushed walnut shells and said to be highly effective against Zombies, door locks, and other animate and undead objects. Zombies aside, Lightfield is a serious, specialized shotshell company. See the full product line at www.litfld.com.

MAGTECH

Taking its existing line of solid copper hollowpoint (SCHP) handgun ammunition to a new performance

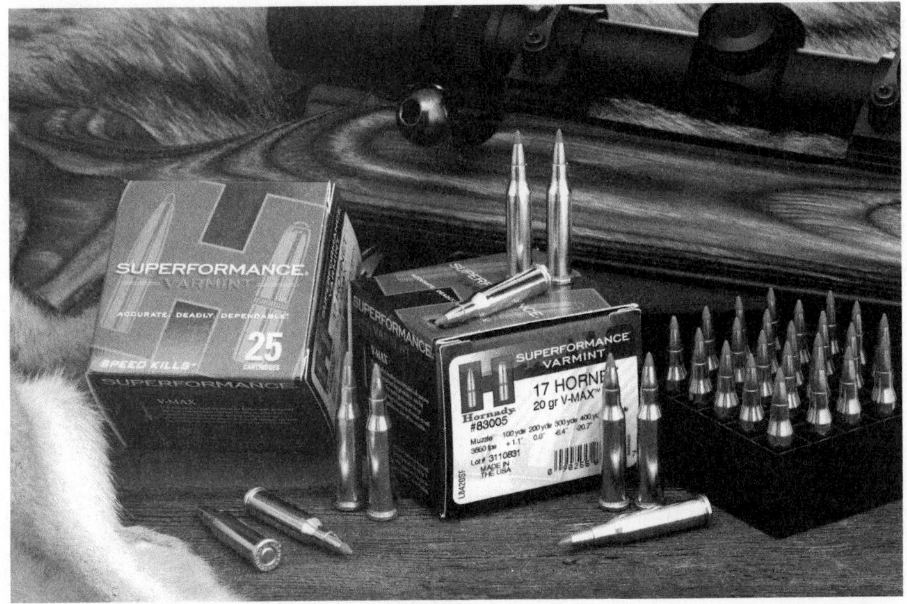

level, Magtech is adding a thin coating of tin, resulting in less barrel wear and higher energy levels. See the SCHP line at www.magtechammunition.com.

NORMA USA

It's official! After a number of difficult starts in the American market, Norma has decided to anchor the company here with its own subsidiary, Norma USA. Heading up the new organization is Ron Petty, a seasoned marketing veteran formerly with Federal Cartridge and Hevi-Shot.

This year, Norma continues to expand its extensive dangerous-game and African lines with the addition of a new brass-alloy solid loading in all the popular dangerous-game calibers from 9.3x62 through .505 Gibbs. For longer range shots at light to medium-size game, Norma is introducing its Kalahari line of ammunition, which includes the .270 Win., .270 WSM, 7x64, .280 Rem., 7mm Rem. Mag., .308 Win., .30-06, .300 Win. Mag., and .300 WSM. The Kalahari bullet is an anti-fouling coated, copper-based, monolithic hollowpoint. Loaded to maximum pressures to ensure the flattest possible trajectory, the bullet sheds the front hollowpoint section upon impact, while the solid shank continues to deliver deep penetration. Learn all about them at www.norma-usa.com.

NOSLER

"Varmageddon!" It's a catchy description of Nosler's new lines of highly frangible varmint bullets and loaded ammunition in .17 Rem., .204 Ruger, .221 Rem. Fireball, .222 Rem., .223 Rem., .22-250 Rem., and .243 Win. For the varmint hunter who reloads, Nosler is offering fully prepped brass in .17 Rem., .222 Rem., .221 Rem. Fireball, and .223 Rem.

Right & Lower Left: Varmints beware! It's Nosler's destructive "Varmageddon" ammunition and bullets.

With the increasing interest in big-game hunting, Nosler is also introducing a new Safari Ammunition line of soft-points and solids in all the popular dangerous-game calibers, ranging from the .375 Flanged to the .458 Lott. Lots of new Nosler bullets this year, including a 300-grain .338 and 200-grain .358 AccuBonds, a 140-grain 6.5mm Ballistic Tip, and three new Custom Competition bullets: a 123-grain 6.5mm, 168-grain 7mm, and a 140-grain .308. See the extensive Nosler lineup at www.nosler.com.

PMC

This popular and competitively priced brand is expanding its soft-point, "Precision Rifle Ammunition" line, intended for hunting and featuring Hornady bullets and PMC brass. The new calibers being introduced this year are a 150-grain .270 Win., 162-grain 7mm Rem. Mag., 165-grain .300 Win. Mag., 165-grain .308 Win., 165-grain .30-06, and a 170-grain .30-30. Interesting lineup at www.pmcammo.com.

PRVI PARTIZAN

This famous Serbian ammunition company continues to introduce some of the hardest to find calibers and loads. This year you'll find the following: 6.5x54 Mannlicher Schoenauer, 6.5x55 Swedish Match, 7.62x54 Russian Match, 8x57 Mauser Match, and the .338 Lapua loaded with a HPBT. There's a new line of Thunder hunting ammunition loaded with a proprietary partition bullet in calibers .308 Win., .30-06, .300 Win. Mag., 7mm Mauser, 7mm Rem. Mag., and 8mm Mauser. www.ppu-usa.com.

REMINGTON

Waterfowl hunters thought they'd gone to Heaven, when Remington released its HyperSonic Steel 12-gauge loads clocking right at 1,700 fps. They were fast, and they put a lot of energy behind steel shot. This year the 10- and 20-gauge get the HyperSonic treatment, with 1½ ounces of BBB, BB, or No. 2 shot in the 10-gauge, and one ounce of Nos. 2, 3, or 4 shot in the 20-gauge.

The 10-gauge and the 20-gauge get the Remington HyperSonic treatment this year. Waterfowlers should be happy.

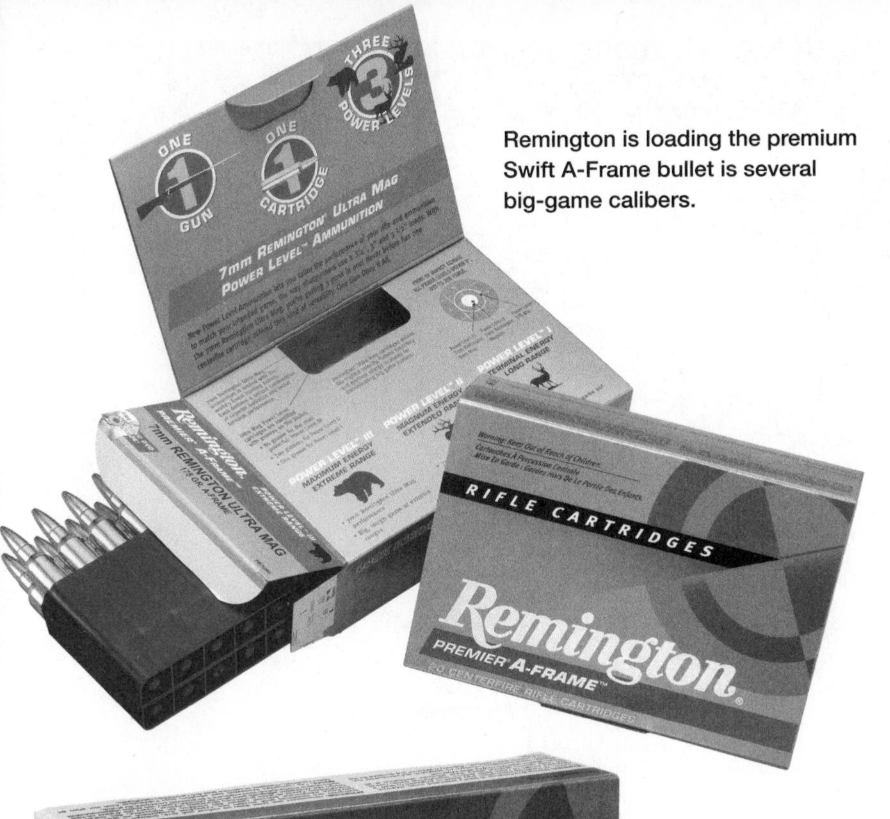

Remington is loading the premium Swift A-Frame bullet is several big-game calibers.

The Core-Lokt line (above) is now available in 7x64 Brenneke and 9.3x62, both with pointed soft-points.

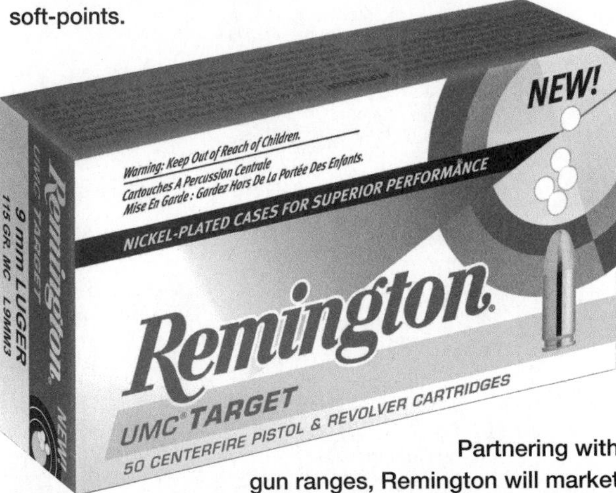

Partnering with gun ranges, Remington will market an affordable line of UMC target ammo.

Remington's answer to the perfect AR round is the 6.8 Remington SPC, which fills in the gap between the 5.56 and the 7.62 NATO rounds. A new load makes its appearance this year. It's a 115-grain FMC in the UMC line with a muzzle velocity of 2,625 fps.

Remington likes metrics, as indicated by its introduction of sporting cartridges in 5mm, 6mm, 7mm, and 8mm. It comes as no surprise that this year it will be loading the company's excellent Core-Lokt pointed soft-point bullets in two European favorites, the 7x64 Brenneke and the 9.3x62. The 7x64 will be offered with either a 140-grain (muzzle velocity 2,950 fps) or a 175-grain (muzzle velocity 2,600 fps) Core-Lokt, while the 9.3x62 will carry a 286-grain Core-Lokt loaded to a muzzle velocity of 2,360 fps.

Offering a slightly more premium bullet for the world's toughest game, Remington will be loading the Swift A-Frame in the 7mm Rem. Mag. (a 160-grain at 2,900 fps), the .300 Win. Mag. (a 180-grain at 2,960 fps), and the .300 Rem. Ultra Mag. (a 180-grain at 3,250 fps). Also, partnering with active gun ranges, Remington will begin offering through range-based shops 50- and 250-round boxes of moderately priced target ammunition featuring nickel-plated cases in 9mm, .380 Auto, .38 Special, .40 S&W, and .45 Auto. See the full Big Green line-up at www.remington.com.

RIO AMMUNITION

Bismuth is back! Rio will be loading Evo 111 Bismuth shot with fiber wads in the 2¾- and three-inch 12 gauge and 2¾-inch 20-gauge. Based on Rio's testing, the new Bismuth/tin shot shows no signs of fracturing upon impact and delivers deep penetration. The new Bismuth line will be marketed under the Venatum Bi label. Read all about it at www.rioammo.com.

RUAG AMMOTEC USA

RUAG is planning on better American market penetration with its RWS rifle and handgun ammunition lines and the Rottweil shotgun slug brand. Among the current offerings will be a complete line of frangible, micro-pulverizing Copper Matrix ammunition in .223 Rem., .308 Win., 9mm Luger, .38 Special, .357 SIG, .40 S&W, and .45 Auto. The Copper Matrix line, which also includes buckshot and slugs, is environmentally friendly and simply disintegrates when impacting on a steel target or backstop. There's also a complete line of budget-priced rifle and pistol ammunition under the MFS label and, of course, the well-known lines of Rottweil smooth- and rifle-bored shotgun slugs. Check them out at www.ruag-usa.com.

SIERRA BULLETS

With the success of the .300 Whisper and .300 AAC Blackout, Sierra has developed a finely tuned, 125-grain HP MatchKing for these efficient AR and bolt-action cartridges. Read all about them at www.sierrabullets.com.

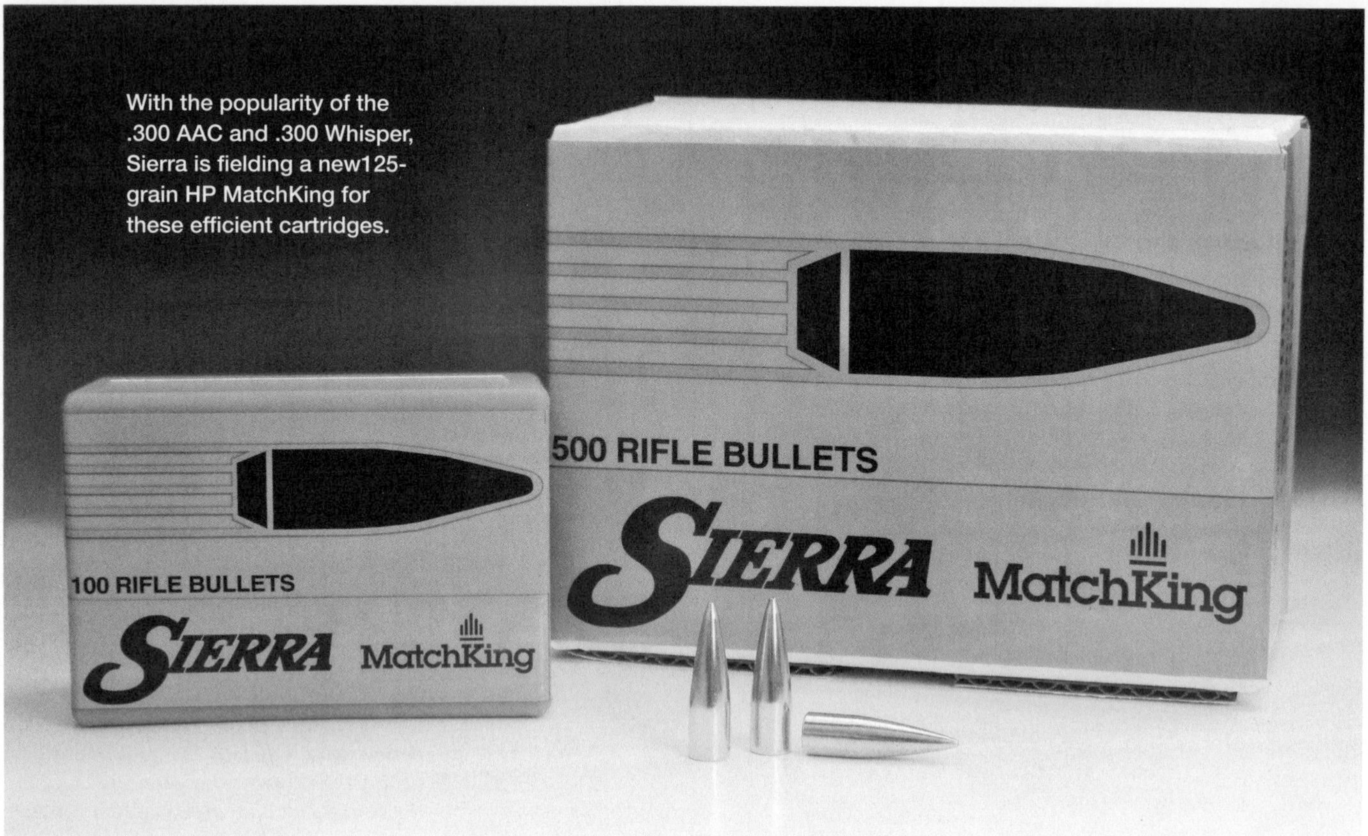

With the popularity of the .300 AAC and .300 Whisper, Sierra is fielding a new125-grain HP MatchKing for these efficient cartridges.

SILVER STATE ARMORY

SSA specializes in offering the widest selection of ammunition for the 6.8 SPC cartridge. Its newest loadings are an 85-grain Nosler E-Tip at 2,900 fps, a 95-grain Barnes TTSX BT at 2,750 fps, and a 140-grain Berger VLD at a velocity that's yet to be announced. The company website offers an excellent overview of the advantages of the 6.8 SPC over the 5.56 NATO. See it at www.ssarmory.com.

SPECTRA SHOT

Colored shot? Spectra Shot has developed a non-toxic, color-coded shot for waterfowling. Offered in blue, green, orange, and yellow and loaded in Spectra shotshells, the new "marker" shot will forever end any disagreements in the blind as to who took the duck or goose with a band on its leg. Spectra is also working on a plated target shot that becomes luminescent when fired on a range in the presence of ultraviolet lighting. See the full story at www.spectrashot.com.

SWIFT BULLET COMPANY

The most exciting news from Swift is about its new line of A-Frame bullets for the classic lever-action cartridges. Called, appropriately, the Lever Action Series, the new line features a reconfigured A-Frame design that will expand readily at the lower velocities generated by the .30-30 Win., .348 Win., .45-70 Govt, .457 Wild West Magnum, and the .50 Alaskan. See the new offerings at www.swiftbullets.com.

TED NUGENT AMMUNITION

It's official. There's a new brand of ammunition on the market carrying the Ted Nugent name. It will be marketed by American Tactical in a variety of rifle and handgun calibers and feature premium

It's official! American Tactical is marketing a full line of Ted Nugent brand ammunition.

Winchester's HEX shot will be offered in Nos. 1, 3, and 5 sizes this year.

The SuperX lead-free Power Core bullet is made from a 95/5 alloy of gilding metal.

New to the PDX1 Defender line is a 45-grain JHP .22 WRM load that hits 1,200 fps from a two-inch barrel.

bullets by Barnes and Speer. See it at www.americantactical.us.

TOP BRASS

Here's a company that takes once-fired, DOD spec brass in 9mm, .40 S&W, .45 ACP, .223 Rem., and .308 Win., completely reconditions it, and wholesales it out to dealers at approximately 50-percent of the cost of new brass. See this company's quality products at www.topbrass-inc.com.

WILD WEST GUNS

Best known for putting big-bore cartridges in lever-action rifles, Wild West is introducing its own new cartridge, the .457 Wild West Magnum, and reviving a great big thumper from the past, the .50 Alaskan, which was designed by Harold Johnson. The .457 WWM is offered with a 350-grain Swift A-Frame bullet loaded to a muzzle velocity of 2,150 fps. The .50 Alaskan gets a 450-grain Swift A-Frame loaded to a muzzle velocity of 2,000 fps. Bullets, brass, loaded ammunition, and lever-action rifle conversions for these calibers can be ordered from Wild West at www.wildwestguns.com.

Added to Winchester's PDX1 Defender line is a segmenting 12-gauge slug.

WINCHESTER AMMUNITION

Look out wild boars! Winchester has designed a unique, lead-free bullet featuring beveled flats on its ogive that compress and delay the expansion of the hollowpoint bullet as it passes through a boar's thick hide, bone, and muscle. Under the Razorback XT label, it will be offered as a 64-grain in the .223 Rem. and as a 150-grain in the .308 Win.

Split Core Technology is changing the face of the PDX1 Defender rifle ammunition line. The Split Core Technology bullet features a soft, non-bonded front core that ensures rapid expansion, while the rear core is bonded and ensures penetration. The SCT is available this year as a 77-grain .223 Rem. and a 120-grain .308 Win. Also being added to the PDX1 Defender line is a 12-gauge slug that breaks into three segments upon impact, and a new .22 WRM load featuring a 40-grain hollowpoint bullet at 1,200 fps. New lead-free offerings include a 32-grain Ballistic Silvertip tearing out at 4,000 fps in the .204 Ruger, and the Super-X Power-Core 95/5 line featuring hollowpoint, solid, gilding-metal bullets for the .243 Win., .300 WSM, .308 Win., .270 WSM, and 7mm-08 Rem.

In the Winchester shotshells, there's a new, lowered recoil AA target load for the 2¾-inch 20-gauge, featuring 7/8-ounce of No. 8 at 980 fps. Shot size Nos. 1, 3, and 5 are being added to the Blind Side HEX waterfowl loads. See all of Big Red's new recipes at www.winchester.com.

Winchester's gone hog wild with a new "Razor Back" line of hog ammunition.

The new PDX1 .223 Rem. load features a split-core technology bullet for rapid expansion and penetration.

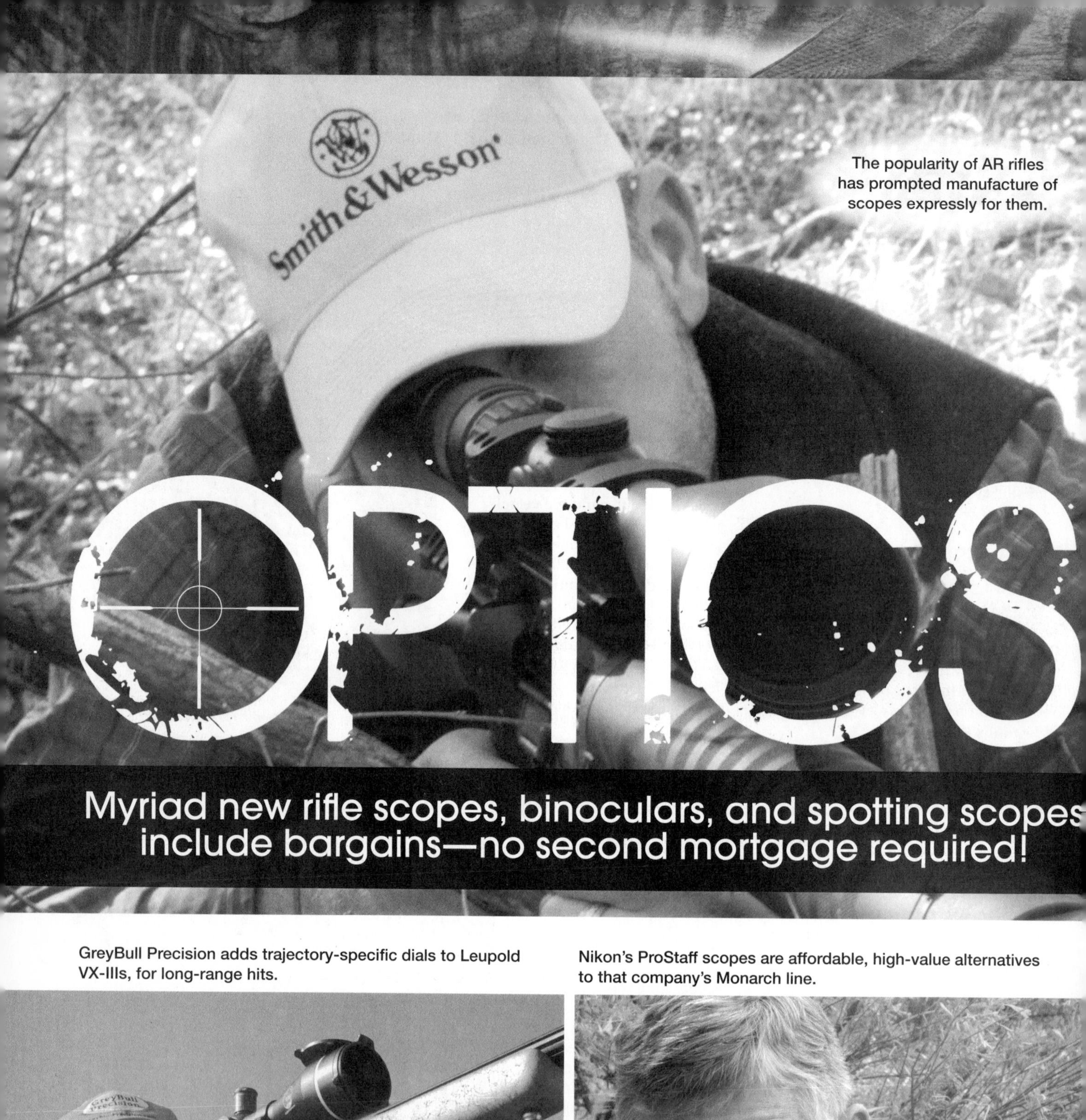

The popularity of AR rifles has prompted manufacture of scopes expressly for them.

OPTICS

Myriad new rifle scopes, binoculars, and spotting scopes include bargains—no second mortgage required!

GreyBull Precision adds trajectory-specific dials to Leupold VX-IIIs, for long-range hits.

Nikon's ProStaff scopes are affordable, high-value alternatives to that company's Monarch line.

BY **WAYNE VAN ZWOLL**

The Shooting, Hunting and Outdoor Trade (SHOT) show, held this past January in Las Vegas, loaded me up with boxes of catalogs, discs, and thumb-drives. Over the decades I've attended SHOT, print has given way to electronic media. The dream books I ogled in my youth, late in the Miocene, are slipping away. Something is lost there. You might argue that all you need to know about any optic can be mined from a visit to Google. Still, hard copy has substance. It's the substance we came to expect from Bausch & Lomb binoculars, and Kollmorgen rifle sights we clamped to Remington 721s and Savage 99s and Model 70s built before the debacle of 1964.

I may get used to specifications on-screen. Someday.

Meantime, the electronics that matter are those in the optics. They're proliferating. From laser rangefinders in scopes and binoculars to illuminated, range-compensating reticles and night-vision gear, we've added bounce to the staid science of lenses and light. Traditionalists are yet blessed with glass that works without batteries. The best of the ordinary is, in fact, getting better. Discernible differences between top-end and value-priced optics have diminished. Unless you've very sharp eyes, those disparities will likely elude you in blind tests. The daunting news? There are so many fresh items that picking one at any price point can be a chore. This *Gun Digest* roundup should help with your sifting.

I'll try to stay even-handed, forgiving manufacturers who follow the market when it leads them astray. What's popular, alas, is not always most useful. Scopes the size of sewer pipe sell to shooters who value bulk over utility; reticles as busy as Sanskrit evidently add value to fields disturbingly blank behind crosswires. The practical may later supplant the bizarre in optics; it is making slow progress displacing the audacity of hope in politics.

Another point. I'm obliged to report on glass that's absurdly expensive. As a youth, I settled on a Weaver K4, because, at $59.50, a Leupold 4X seemed an indulgence. These days, a top-end scope can cost more than my first three automobiles combined. Granted, the scope will last longer, and you needn't change the oil. But, on the value scale, it may, arguably, rank as low as the cheapest optic—which also merits print. A modern scope that costs less than a tank of gasoline is unlikely to fail you—but it's still an odd match for a $7,500 elk hunt.

Pricing of outdoors optics is a shadowy business. Few products trade at MSRP (manufacturer's suggested retail price). Indeed, MSRP is equivalent to the opening plea of an optimistic auctioneer. "Street price" used to be the more useful figure, but even that is now clouded by sales that cut deeply into profits. It was not always so. In by-gone days, companies selling optics also made them. That tradition changed, in the 1960s, when Dave Bushnell began importing scopes from the Orient to compete with Lyman, Redfield, and Bausch & Lomb. Those latter brands have since capitulated. Lyman is now a loading-tool company, and while Redfield's name was resurrected recently by Leupold, B&L vanished into the Bushnell line. Japan, China, and the Philippines now produce more optics than the Germans and Austrians, whose glass once defined the state of the art. The best scopes from the Orient are very, very good. At all quality levels, many come from the same production lines that make scopes for the competition.

A crowded field brings forth bargains. Witness the 3-9X rifle scope. All major optics firms offer 3-9Xs, and high sales volumes allow them to keep prices close to the bone. These companies are also acutely aware that a beginning shooter satisfied with an inexpensive 3-9X will likely show brand loyalty when they upgrade to a costlier scope. Anyone buying a 3-9X gets the benefit of the brisk trade and fierce competition in these scopes.

Enough preamble. On with the show.

Author van Zwoll thinks the Weaver K series a great value. This Ruger No. 1 wears a sleek K6 (6X38).

This Savage tactical rifle wears a Sightron scope. An affordable package with great reach!

AIMPOINT

In 1974, Gunnar Sandberg developed a "single-point sight" that didn't allow you to see through it. You looked into the sight with one eye while your other saw a dot on the target. Sandberg refined the device and founded Aimpoint to build it. Still considered the leader in red dot sights, Aimpoint catalogs models for both tactical and sporting rifles. The new PRO (Patrol Rifle Optic) is a 1X sight with a 2-minute dot and night-vision compatibility. Designed for AR-style rifles, it fits a Picatinny rail and so suits any rifle or shotgun so equipped.

All 1X Aimpoints give you unlimited eye relief. The smallest are the Micro sights. Each weighs less than four ounces, including mount, and features a 4-minute dot with 12 brightness settings.

The Comp Series is Aimpoint's flagship. The M4 wears an integral clamp for a rail. One AA battery can power an M4 for up to eight *years*—without shut-off!

Aimpoint front lenses are achromats (doublets) that correct for parallax—unlike lenses in many competitive sights, which have reflective paths that move with eye position. An Aimpoint's dot comes to your eye in a line parallel with the sight's optical axis. You hit where you see the dot, even if your eye is off-axis. Windage/elevation adjustments move point of impact a ½-inch at 100 yards. One CR-2032 battery (standard power for all but the M4) lasts 50,000 hours with a mid-level setting. Aimpoints have been adopted by armed forces and sportsmen in 40 countries. I've killed moose with these sights in Europe. They're ideal for close, fast shooting, but they are also more precise than many hunters think. It's no trick to maintain 2-minute accuracy at 100 yards. www.Aimpoint.com.

ALPEN

Demand for highly rated Alpen optics has limited supply and throttled new-product introductions.

But the pipeline is now spewing the Apex XP one-inch rifle scopes, introduced last year. They feature turret-mounted parallax knobs and fast-focus eyepieces. Pick 1.5-6X42, 3-9X40, 2-10X44, 4-16X44 or 6-24X50. A new 30mm IR line has lighted reticles: 1.5-6X42, 2.5-10X50, and 4-16X56.

New XP binoculars headline the 2012 stable. They boast top-quality glass and coatings, and very sturdy construction. Alpen's Wings ED binocular, in 8X42 or 10X42, is lightweight. I've found the images extraordinarily bright and sharp. You'll pay much less than for European optics of similar design. A new 8X30 IPD Porro prism binocular also gets my attention. Though almost all roads these days lead to roof-prism binoculars, I like the Porro prism design (with offset rather than straight barrels; it's named after an Italian who long ago fashioned an early bino of that configuration). Many Porro prism glasses weigh less than corresponding roof-prism models, even if their wide stance makes them appear heavy. Where weight matters less than reach, Alpen's Apex 12X50 excels as a mid-range alternative to a spotting scope. It's reasonably priced and easier to use for extended glassing. www.Alpenoptics.com.

BRUNTON

The new Icon, in 8X44 and 11X44, ranks as the best of four series of Brunton binoculars. The Epoch, in 8X5X43 and 10.5X43, follows, with a couple of pocket binoculars, as well. There are four Eterna models. The Echo anchors the Brunton stable, at a lower price. My Brunton Epochs deliver excellent images, and bird-watching colleagues have told me Eternas perform right alongside costlier glasses.

This year, Brunton lists five rifle scopes under the Eterna banner, six as Echoes. Eternas, 1.5-5X20 to 6.5-20X50, climb in street price to nearly $1,000. Echo scopes list at $165 to $295. This Wyoming-based company has been around long enough to know what hunters value in optics, and it offers those features at prices cowhands can afford. And it stands behind its products. www.Brunton.com.

BURRIS

Additions to the value-priced Fullfield E1 family caught my eye at SHOT. Fullfields have proven themselves to be exceptional values—I have several! The Fullfield E1 series has new 3-9X40 and 4.5-14X42 scopes with 30mm tubes, and a 6.5-20X50 on a one-inch pipe.

The Burris Fullfield scope on this CZ affords the author quick aim at big animals in cover.

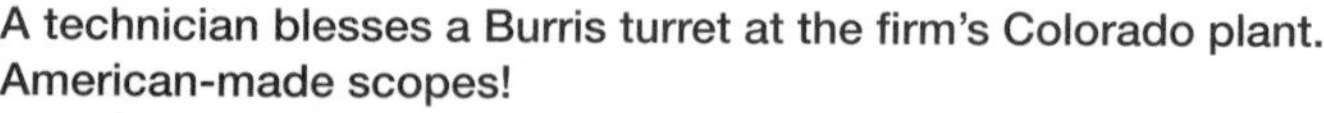
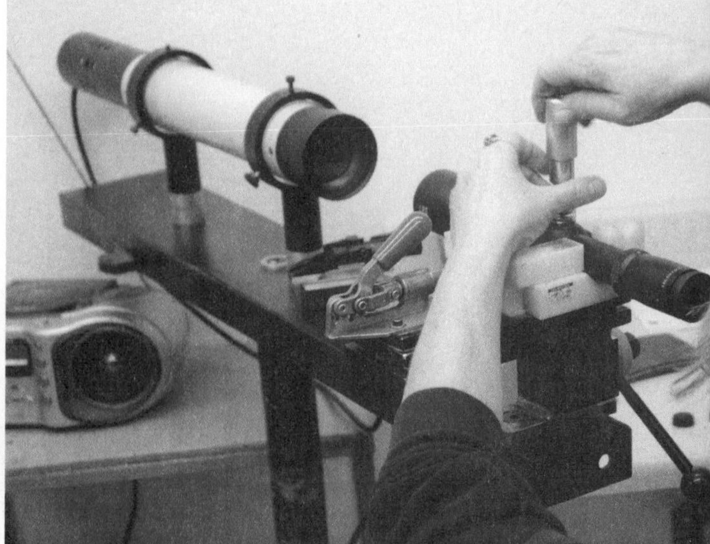

A technician blesses a Burris turret at the firm's Colorado plant. American-made scopes!

The Ballistic Plex E1 reticle assists with drop and drift. Choose illumination on the 3-9X. Also new is a fresh line of tactical scopes and an updated 4-12X42 Eliminator. This programmable scope is heavier than the first model, introduced a couple years ago, but lean, sleek lines make it more attractive, and it delivers more with the ballistic data you provide. As with its predecessor, Eliminator's laser rangefinder gives instant reads. A dot that lights up on the reticle serves as your aiming point, automatically compensating for bullet drop. I managed a sub-minute group at 400 yards, while testing this scope. It was just a vertical inch from center—Eliminator knows what its job is.

New Burris MTAC scopes, in 1-4X24 to 6.5-20X50, have 30mm tubes and Mil Dot reticles (Ballistic CQ on the 1-4X). The FastFire III is an upgrade of the FastFire II. I've used this red dot sight on shotguns and handguns. Its compact profile and light weight make it ideal for both. Put the dot where you want it and press the trigger—no alignment necessary! I tried a FastFire-equipped pump-gun from the left shoulder at skeet targets. Impossibly awkward as a lefty, I shattered several clays with that unerring dot. www.Burrisoptics.com.

BUSHNELL

In rifle scopes, Bushnell's recent 30mm Elite 6500 series still defines the top end. But the 4200s and 3200s have been merged into a single Elite category. I've used both and find them among the best of mid-priced sights. Legend Ultra HD rifle scopes are a 2012 highlight. Check the resolution beside traditional Elite scopes.

Bushnell pioneered laser rangefinders for outdoorsmen and still dominates that market. The new 6X G-Force 1300 stores your rifle's zero data to deliver accurate angle-compensated reads at the press of a button.

In binoculars, I'm impressed by Bushnell's new 10X36 Legend Ultra HD. Compared to a bright 8X32, it transmits very nearly as much light, with 25 percent more power and no more weight or bulk. In fact, I found the *outside* front diameter of a popular 8X32 was bigger! The Legend's magnesium frame keeps its weight to just 20.6 ounces, so you can carry it as I prefer, on a single strap. Bushnell provides a quick-release strap, as well as a harness. The Ultra HD's rubber armor is easy to grip when wet and cushions the binocular against knocks. The center focus wheel has enough drag to prevent accidental movement, but raised ribs make it easy to turn with gloved fingers. The right-hand adjustment locks when shoved forward. Twist-up eyecups have three stops.

With a retail price of $250, the 10X36 (or 8X36) Legend Ultra HD performs above its class. The fluorite component of its ED front lenses all but eliminate chromatic aberration by bringing waves of red, blue, and green light to a common point. Bushnell describes the 60 coatings on its BaK-4 prisms as "Ultra Wide Band." BaK-4, by the way, is a high-end barium-silicate glass used in many binoculars. It's appropriate in some but not all lenses. In advertising, BaK-4 enjoys more status than it merits. Naturally, the Bushnell Legend Ultra HD has RainGuard coating to bead and shed water. www.Bushnell.com.

CABELA'S

Renowned as a one-stop sportsman's shopper, the Cabela's catalog lists many optics from top-ranked companies. But this company also markets glass under its own label. You might dismiss Cabela's Alaskan Guide scopes as inexpensive surrogates, items built under contract in big, nameless factories in the Far East. Truth is, many scopes sold under other recognized brands originate in the same places. Techniques and materials used in building sturdy, reliable, optically excellent rifle scopes and binoculars are widely shared. A CNC machine doesn't know if the tube in its oil spray is being threaded for Cabela's or another company known only for its optics.

Weaver, once a Texas firm, now gets its scopes from the Orient. They're good values. So are Cabela's Alaskan Guide scopes. Starting about $200, they're also affordable. I've used them on expensive and demanding hunts. A 4X44 on a hard-kicking 9.3X62-chambered rifle dropped a moose and a goat for me in British Columbia's backcountry. I took another Alaskan Guide scope on a wilderness hunt for elk. All AG's feature one-inch tubes, 3½ inches of eye relief, fast-focus eyepieces, and plenty of free tube to space the rings as you prefer. The 3-9X40

The author likes this Bushnell Legend 10X36, a new binocular that performs above its price.

Bushnell's big stable boasts extended eye relief scopes, like this variable on the author's BL-81.

A Cabela's Alaskan Guide 4X on a CZ 9.3X62 put this moose down in thick cover.

scales 13 ounces, the 4-12X40 AO and 6-20X40 AO just a couple ounces more.

Cabela's Pine Ridge Lever Action line comprises 3-9X40s, each with a reticle specific to a single Hornady LEVERevolution load. Reticle hash marks correspond to specific points of impact for each load. A generous 5½ inches of eye relief lets you to place these scopes well forward to clear exposed hammers. www.cabelas.com.

LEICA

A short list of the most versatile hunting scopes must include Leica's marvelous 3.5-14X42, with its turret-mounted parallax dial. Cosmetically and optically, this 30mm scope is top drawer. Choose from five reticles. Weight is 16.5 ounces. The 2.5-10X42 is an ounce lighter and comes with a fixed parallax setting. Both have tough, slippery, AquaDura lens coatings to shed water.

This year, Leica announced a new Ultravid binocular, which it claims is optically superior to the older Ultravids—binoculars that strike me as peerless! At this writing, I've yet to field-test the new model, but a look through those lenses shows the unit to be absolutely brilliant—just like its predecessor.

I *have* used Leica's laser rangefinders, the CRF 1000 and CRF 1600. Both feature 7X magnification and AquaDura lens coatings. Carbon-reinforced bodies are lightweight and waterproof. The LED display adjusts for brightness. You also get readings for temperature, barometric pressure, and holdover. Leica's ballistics calculator will chart the bullet path of your load and compensate for shot angle. www.leica-camera.com.

LEUPOLD

This spring, VX-1 and VX-2 riflescopes have been upgraded. The VX-2s go to lead-free Quantum lenses with Index Matched and DiamondCoat 2 coatings, while the VX-1 gets the Quantum lenses with Multicoat 4 coatings. VX-2s come in magnification ranges from 1-4X to 6-18X, with AO and target-knob versions. I've a 3-9X40 ready for a new Ruger American rifle in .30-06. Though higher power seems a trend, big-game hunters may still be best served by the 3-9X40, a winning combination of light weight and slim profile, with enough field for the fastest shooting, and magnification to reach the most distant targets. I've just finished a long-range training course at FTW ranch, using a 3-9X to hit 12-inch targets out to 700 yards—that's twice as far as I normally consider shooting at game.

Leupold's VX-1 and Rifleman scopes offer value in popular 2-7X, 3-9X and 4-12X magnifications. FX fixed-power scopes remain among my favorite sights. They're very lightweight and complement any svelte hunting rifle. So do the new variables in Leupold's Ultralight line. The company has added to its air rifle, AR-15, competition, and Mark 8 combat series. The VX-6 rifle scope, with its 6X power range, was new last spring. Now you can get the 1-6X24 and 2-12X42 with FireDot illumination and 12-position brightness dial. A big eye-box means generous eye relief, even at high magnification. Blackened lens edges keep light where it belongs.

In South Africa, Dave Emary bears down with Bushnell's 6500 Elite and a T/C Icon.

Dialing with target knobs helps this rifleman hit far away with a Blaser R8 in .300 magnum.

Muzzleloading enthusiasts find optics useful too! A Leupold helped down this Illinois buck.

DiamondCoat 2 lens coatings resist scratching. Twin beryllium/copper leaf springs secure the erector assembly against knocks afield. The VX-6's CDS (Custom Dial System) option comes on selected VX-3, VX-R, and VX-2 scopes, too, so you can program bullet trajectory into the elevation dial. Then you simply dial the yardage, hold center, and fire. The scope compensates for bullet drop. www.Leupold.com.

MEOPTA

The 3-9X42 MeoPro debuted two years ago as a "killer value" (so reported by *Outdoor Life*). It still ranks high. Like the companion 4-12X50 and 6-18X50 scopes, it has a one-inch tube and first-cabin lens coatings. I like its relatively short, fast-focus eyepiece and the snappy windage and elevation adjustments. The MeoPro series features second-plane reticles and transferable lifetime warranties.

Meopta's 30mm line, the R1, starts with a 1-4X22. Its illuminated dot excels for quick shots in cover. The R1 4-12X50 is a dandy long-range rifle scope, with a sleek profile and an etched second-plane reticle. MeoStar scopes come in other sizes, too, including a 3-10X50, 3-12X56, 4-14X44, and even a 7X56 for European boar shooting under the stars.

MeoStar B1 binoculars, 7X to 12X, include an 8X32 that strikes me as ideal for all-around hunting. The MeoPro series features a 6.5X32, a very bright glass. It also has more reach than most hunters realize. Meopta lists a top-drawer S175mm spotting scope with a 30X wide-angle or a 20-60X standard eyepiece, angled or straight. www.Meopticsportsoptics.com.

MINOX

Known mainly for binoculars, Minox (MINN-ox) recently cataloged 3-9X40, 2-10X40, 3-15X42, and 4-20X50 riflescopes. The line has grown this year, with models in 1.5-8X32, 3-9X50, 2-10X50, 3-15X50, and 6-30X56. The 3-15X and 6-30X feature parallax knobs. The 6-30X has a 30mm tube, while the others are one-inch scopes. All feature fully multi-coated Schott glass, resettable windage/elevation dials, and generous four-inch eye relief. Choose from five reticles. Weights range from 12 to 24 ounces. Minox scopes come with no-questions-asked lifetime warranties.

New APO-HG and HG (High Grade) binoculars, built in Wetzlar, boast wider fields of view, phase-corrected prisms, a quick-close-focus dial that brings you from infinity to spitting distance with one spin. Magnesium frames keep weight to a minimum. MinoBright and M* lens coatings enhance images; argon gas purging prevents fogging. Choose an 8X33, or an 8X or 10X with 43mm or 52mm front lenses. There's also an 8X56 for hunters looking into the night. www.Minox.com.

NIGHTFORCE

Big, powerful scopes with illuminated reticles and high price tags define Nightforce. But the line now includes two versatile hunting sights, a 2.5-10X32 and a 1-4X24. Both these NXS models, each under 20 ounces, feature ZeroStop resettable windage/elevation adjust-

Top-quality binoculars keep your eye to the glass, a requisite for spotting game in big country.

Leupold VX lines are getting upgrades. The 2.5-8X36, here on a Tikka, is the author's favorite.

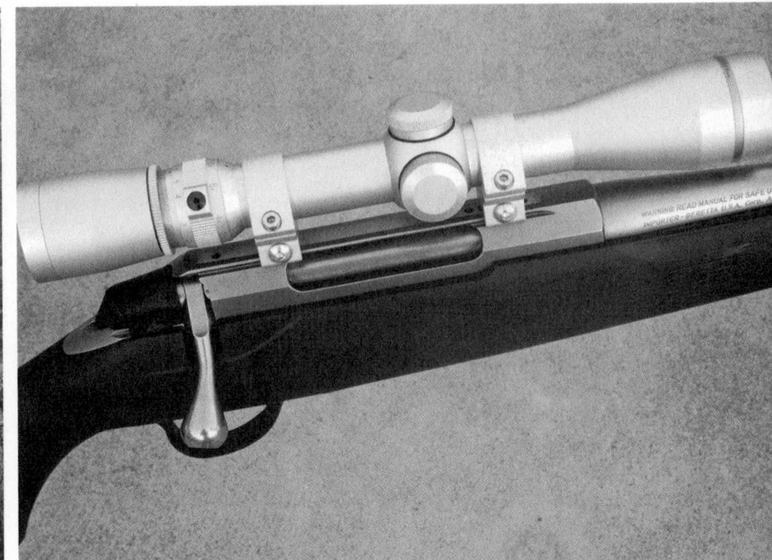

ments, illuminated reticles, and 30mm tubes. Need more magnification? The 5.5-22X50 makes sense for long shots. Other, absurdly powerful scopes, plus a 5.5-22X56, serve long-range target shooters. (Mirage and wind can play havoc with sight pictures when you crank that dial much above 20X).

Nightforce counts many top marksmen among its customers, including Matthew Kline, whose 2.815-inch 10-shot group broke the three-inch barrier at 1,000 yards! He did it with a custom-built .300 WSM (Heavy Gun class) and an NSX 8-32X56. On the 8-32X56, incidentally, you can specify windage/elevation clicks of ¼-minute, ⅛-minute or .1 mil (10 mils per revolution). The current Nightforce stable of a dozen scopes includes a 3.5-15X50 F1, with a first-plane reticle for military application. The firm offers ballistic software and custom turrets to track bullet arcs of standard loads. I'm partial to the design of Nightforce reticles, which are fine, sharp, and limited to the center of the field, for an open, uncluttered view. www.Nightforceoptics.com.

NIKON

The 2012 emphasis at Nikon is tactical. I like the compact 3X32 scope with resettable dials, a 12-ounce sight ideal for compact AR-style rifles. The P-22 2-7X32 has a military bearing, but the BDC-150 reticle is calibrated for .22 LR loads. A target version has sleeker lines and an AO sleeve on the objective bell. The P-223 AR riflescope has a BDC-600 reticle. M-308 and M-223 4-16X42 rifle scopes feature resettable dials, a parallax knob, and your choice of a BDC-800 or Nikoplex reticle.

In specialized hunting optics, the Inline XR muzzleloading scope, a 3-9X40, has the BDC-300 reticle. Force XR 2X20 and 2.5-8X28 handgun scopes have the innards to take the sharp recoil of that Casull round. Value-priced Buckmaster scopes include new 3-9X50 and 4-12X50 models. Building on the huge success of its on-line ballistics program, Nikon now offers Spot-On custom scope turrets you can order engraved with the ballistic data of your pet load.

In binoculars, the Monarch 5 ATB includes a 12X42, as well as 10X42 and 8X42 models. New ProStaff laser rangefinders with 6X magnification read to 550 and 600 yards. ProStaff 5 Fieldscopes (60mm and 82mm) complement Nikon's new EDG Fieldscope, an 85mm 20-60X with vibration damping (a pair of miniature motors minimizes the blur caused by scope movement). Seven bayonet-lock eyepieces range from 20X to 70X, including the popular 20X-60X. www.NikonHunting.com.

REDFIELD

Resurrected by Leupold three years ago, the Redfield name again stands as a worthy American brand. Those of us who remember John Redfield's earlier scopes, and who've shot competitively with Redfield target sights, are delighted to see the new line expand. This year, there are two series of Redfield scopes, the Revolution (2-7X33, 3-9X40, 3-9X50, and 4-12X40), and the Revenge (2-7X34, 3-9X42, 3-9X52, 4-12X42, and 6-18X44 AO). The Revenge, just cataloged, features a range-compensating ABS reticle—actually, your choice of four, from one configured for crossbows to those suitable for long shooting at big game and prairie dogs. An Accu-Range reticle helps you hit at distance with the Revolution scope. Finger-friendly Accu-Trac windage/elevation adjustments are much easier to use than the dials of the past. These Redfields *look* good too, on new rifles and old. They all feature one-inch tubes and are much better optics than their predecessors. The Redfield name also appears on spotting scopes and binoculars, and the Raider 550 laser rangefinder. www.Redfield.com.

SCHMIDT & BENDER

Among thoroughbred optics, Schmidt & Bender stands out. A relatively small firm, it occupies a rural factory that, on my first visit, reminded me of a veterinary clinic. But the white-frocked staff and sterile environment also lend themselves to producing rifle scopes. S&B's star has risen mostly on the reputation of its P/M (Police/Marksman) series, but the company's hunting scopes are just as fetching. Newest is a 30mm illuminated 1-8X Zenith sight. The 1-8X24 features both a black reticle and S&B's brightness-adjustable Flash Dot in the rear focal plane. The 1-8X24 follows a scope

Nightforce scopes, favorites of long-range shooters, feature resettable dials with clutches!

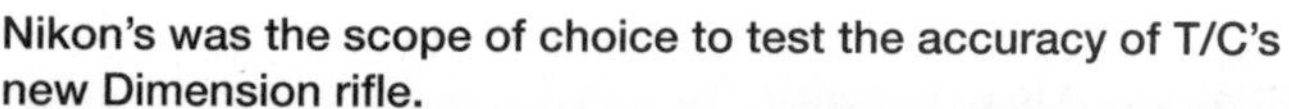

Nikon's was the scope of choice to test the accuracy of T/C's new Dimension rifle.

built specifically for American sportsmen, S&B's 2.5-10X40, with a one-inch tube and ¼-minute clicks. S&B is also fielding a new 3-20X50 P/M II, with a 34mm tube, turret-side parallax knob, and an illuminated reticle in your choice of first or second plane. As on other P/Ms, this variable has lockable, resettable windage/elevation adjustments. My favorite Schmidt & Bender scopes take a more traditional form, in 6X42 and 10X42 and the 3-12X42 Classics, all with 30mm tubes and dial rotation indicators that show where the erector tube lies in its adjustment range. www.Schmidt-Bender.de.

STEINER

Predator Xtreme binoculars and rifles wear Steiner "sixth generation" contrast-enhancing optics. They filter out light wavelengths near 550 nanometers, so you can quickly distinguish color differences between game and cover. Three PX riflescopes—2.5-10X42, 3-12X56, and 4-16X50—feature 30mm tubes and Steiner's Plex S1 ballistic reticle. The 4-16X has a parallax-correction knob. A quartet of center-focus binoculars share roof-prism design, high-contrast lens coatings, and twist-up eyepieces. The rubber armor is new. Upgrades of the popular Merlin binoculars, these four models weigh from 21 to 26 ounces. Pick a 10X32, an 8X42, a 10X42, or a 10X50. They focus as close as 6½ feet. All come with a padded travel case. www.Steiner-binoculars.com.

SWAROVSKI

Big news for 2012 is the EL Range binocular, laser-equipped with HD Swarovision glass. Fast-pitch focusing brings you from near to far in two spins. The range-finding button on the left hinge is easy to reach, but unobtrusive. Both the 8X42 and 10X42 EL Range read in yards or meters, with compensation for vertical angles. One CR2 battery powers this sleek, relatively lightweight binocular. Choose from five levels of screen brightness.

Equally fetching from this Austrian firm is its modestly priced CL Companion 30mm binocular in 8X and 10X. It features a black, green, or tan exterior, center focus, and twist-out eyecups. A street price of less than $1,000 belies the images you'll get with the CL. At just 18 ounces, it's a great hunting binocular. An honest 91-percent light transmission rating puts it in distinguished company! If you hunt from a stand or must glass far in dim light, consider the Swarvovski EL 10X50 or 12X50, the modern version of the SLC 10X50 I carried for years as a hunting guide.

In rifle scopes, the Z-6 continues to lead in sales. The 1.7-10X42 on my Remington .30-06 is as versatile a hunting scope as I can imagine, with needle-sharp resolution and superior light transmission. At 17 ounces, this 30mm sight is no burden. Z-5 and Z-3 lines have narrow but still useful magnification ranges. I'm quite satisfied with 3X power range, like that of the AV 3-9X36. I chose one for my latest custom rifle, a fine .25-06 by ace gunmaker Patrick Holehan. www.Swarovskioptik.com.

TRIJICON

The illuminated ACOG (Advanced Combat Optical Gunsight) gave Trijicon a high profile in the shooting community. The company uses fiber optics and tritium to light reticles in its AccuPoint hunting rifle scopes, too. I've used the AccuPoint to take elk and find it a great aid for quick aiming in cover. Choose a delta or a standard dot, now in amber and green, as well as red. Mil dot, plex, and No. 4 reticles are options. From 1-4X24 to 5-20X50, AccuPoints feature adjustable fiber optic windows. The 1.25-4X24 and 3-9X40 are lightest, at 12 and 13 ounces; thank their one-inch tubes. The other three (including a 2.5-10X56) have 30mm tubes.

For 2012, Trijicon is offering a companion to the RMR (Ruggedized Miniature Reflex) red dot sight. Called the SRS (Sealed Reflex Sight), it has an LED-lit, 1.75-MOA dot. A solar panel boosts illumination, prolonging the life of the single AA battery. Built to tough ACOG standards of forged 7075-T6 aircraft alloy, the SRS is parallax-free and waterproof. It has 10 brightness settings and an auto-locking mount. A natural for AR-type rifles and shotguns, it does not magnify the target; you get a 70-foot field of view at 100 yards. The SRS is less than four inches long and weighs just 14 ounces with the supplied lithium battery. Also from the Wixom,

Steadying a Remington 700ti, the author aims with a Swarovski Z6 1.7-10X42. Superb glass!

This Swarovski-equipped Remington in .300 Ultra Mag is handsome, accurate, and versatile.

Michigan, firm is the TriPower, the first triple-illuminated sight. It boasts fiber optic, tritium, and battery-powered illumination. Its short 30mm tube, of forged 7075-T6, is waterproof to 100 feet! The red chevron reticle is parallax-free. www.Trijicon.com.

TRUGLO

While it offers scopes and scope mounts, shotgun chokes, and binoculars, TruGlo is best known for its red dot sights and illuminated open sights. The new Triton 20mm Tri-Color affords an instant choice of red, green, or blue 5-minute dot. It includes the 3V-CR2032 battery and a mounting clamp, high or low, for a Weaver scope base. The new 30mm Tri-Color shares all the 20mm's features—unlimited eye relief, finger-friendly windage/elevation adjustments, and rheostat brightness control. The larger diameter speeds aim. A remote on/off pressure switch helps in turkey blinds, where movement is anathema. Reticle choices are either a dot or circle dot.

Perhaps most remarkable is the new 28mm Tri-Color Triton. It gives you 12 reticle choices, three colors each in 2½- and 5-minute dots, and 2½-minute and 5-minute circle dots. Like the 30mm, it accepts a detachable sunshade. It's worth a look; I've been impressed by other TruGlo reflex-style sights with multiple reticles. The firm has now applied that technology to crossbow sights, as well. Magnification? TruGlo lists 2X tube-style dual-color sights.

You get color choices in its Xtreme illuminated variable rifle scopes, too. Optional is a bullet drop-compensating reticle in the Xtreme line and in the Maxus 3.5-10X50. TruGlo's fiber optic open sights, including dual-color beads, catch your eye for quick aim. www.Truglo.com.

WEAVER

Like many firms, Weaver has harkened to the demand for tactical sights. Its new 3-15X50 comes in illuminated and standard versions. Or choose a 1-5X24 with close-range reticle, or a 4-20X50 with Mil dot. In hunting optics, Weaver SuperSlam scopes with one-inch tubes and 5X magnification ranges complement the 30mm Euro series. The Grand Slam stable incorporates all important features. From 1.5-5X32 to 6-20X40 AO, they're a notch above the Classic V-Series in Weaver's catalog. Alas, the K-Series fixed-power line has diminished, retaining just 4X and 6X models. For target rifles and varminters, there's the Classic T line, and the firm still offers Classic Rimfire scopes. The Buck Commander 2-9X36 scopes, new in 2011, are still great bargains. This year, Weaver adds the economical Kaspa series of rifle scopes. Four reticles are available in five models, from 1X20 to 4-16X44. Prices run $121 to $325. Also under the Kaspa label is an open-hinge binocular in either 8X42 or 10X50, at $119 and $131, respectively. www.Weaveroptics.com.

VORTEX

For short-range shooting, Vortex announces the Razor reflex red dot sight, powered by one CR 2032 battery. Ideal for carbines and handguns, it's parallax-free and weighs just 1.4 ounces. Choose a 3-minute or 6-minute dot. Crossfire variables now include three scopes with illuminated reticles. Two new 30mm Vipers, a 4-16X44 and a 6-20X50, have ED glass and your choice of a front- or rear-plane reticle. A Viper tactical riflescope series offers a trio of glass-etched ranging reticles. Vortex's Razor label also now goes on a new HD binocular, 25 ounces in 8X42 and 10X42. It's Argon purged, with ArmorTek glass protection and an open-hinge, magnesium chassis. The new 6X Ranger 1000 laser rangefinder runs on a CR2 battery, has coated optics, and delivers angle-corrected reads to 1,000 yards. It weighs 7.7 ounces. To help you shoot far, Vortex also has an on-line ballistics calculator, from which you can order a TMT (Trajectory Matched Turret) for your Vortex scope. www.Vortexoptics.com.

ZEISS

I got an advance look at the new Zeiss Duralyt rifle scope last fall, when I took a 2-8X42 to Idaho, for elk. My only shot came at 290 yards. The bull collapsed to one 140-grain Nosler Partition from my E.R. Shaw rifle, a 6.5-284—the Duralyt has my vote! Actually, this new member of the Con-

Wayne used a GreyBull-equipped Leupold to take this pronghorn with a .243 at 290 yards.

Fully multi-coated optics are now standard even on mid-priced glass, a boon in dim light.

quest clan is a fine optic. An affordable alternative to Zeiss's Victory stable, it shares the Victory's 30mm tube and has an upsized erector *assembly*, not, as is common, an erector tube designed for one-inch scopes. Choose illuminated or non-illuminated reticles in 1.2-5X36, 2-8X42, and 3-12X50. Like the one-inch Conquests, Duralyts have rear-plane reticles, which stay one apparent size through the power range. The open "three-post" No. 6 plex reticle with fine center wire is currently the only style and, in my view, is an appealing one! The No. 60 Zeiss illuminated reticle for Duralyts is identical to the No. 6, except for a crystal-sharp .3-minute (at 12X) fiber-optic dot. You control brightness with on/off buttons. There's also an auto shut-off. The Duralyt's 3½ inches of eye relief stays almost constant, as I dial magnification up on my 2-8X42. Parallax-corrected at 110 yards, the 1.2-5X, 2-8X, and 3-12X deliver 110, 63, and 43 inches of "square adjustment," respectively, in crisp 1/3-minute clicks. The 1.2-5X and 2-8X Duralyts weigh just under 17 ounces; an unilluminated 3-12X50 scales 19. Duralyt scopes have a classy look, with a dark-grey earth-tone finish and black highlights. The scopes list from $950 to $1,350.

Zeiss has also added Conquest HD binoculars to its catalog. In 8X42 and 10X42, with Schmidt-Pecan prisms and dielectric mirror coatings, they focus down to eight feet and weigh roughly 25 ounces. LotuTec coatings on the HD lenses shed water. www.Zeiss.com.

There's not room here to feature all optics displayed at SHOT 2012 or its European equivalent, the IWA show. Pentax has a limited line, but its Gameseeker 3-9X40 and 4-12X40 are best buys in rifle scopes. Premier, long revered for its reticles, produces a brilliant, if heavy, 30mm scope, the Heritage 3-15X50 Hunter, with turret-mounted AO. Tight times have nudged hunters to modestly priced scopes from the likes of Sightron, as well. I've used Sightron scopes on dangerous-game rifles and on varminters. All have performed very well and qualify as overlooked bargains! GreyBull Precision is not a scope maker, but modifies Leupold VX-3s with custom turrets. Built to match your specific load, a GreyBull elevation dial delivers 1/3-minute clicks, to give you great reach with dead-on holds. I've used these scopes on steel targets as far as a mile distant. They've proven very accurate, truly extending my effective range.

Increasingly, sights from the Far East are coming ashore under home country banners—or names the makers hope will stir the souls of American consumers. Some are worth a peek. Konus, for example, is so confident that its products will stand up to hard service that, if one ever fails, the company will ship a replacement overnight—*even to your hunting camp!* Should that option prove untenable, you can buy a new scope locally to finish your hunt, then bill Konus the cost of a replacement! "We don't expect many hunters will need this guarantee," a company representative told me, "but the gesture should tell shooters they've nothing to fear buying a Konus!"

Wayne killed this prairie whitetail with a Ruger rifle in .303 British and wearing a Zeiss Conquest.

Famous for superior binoculars, Zeiss has added 8X42 and 10X42 Conquest HDs to its line.

Turret-side parallax correction sharpens target focus. Knobs are handier than front sleeves.

BY LARRY STERETT

Handloading of metallic and shotshell cartridges is alive and well. In fact, with the continually increasing retail prices of ammunition of all kinds, many shooters are discovering it can pay to reload. Yes, component prices have also increased, but if you can reload a metallic case five to 10 times, and a shotshell hull between 15 and 25 times for some brands (there are many variables, of course, that affect brass and hull life), you've saved the cost of this component big time. True, you do have to offset the price of your loading equipment before the real savings show, but it doesn't take long if one shoots a good many rounds per year. Of course, an added plus is the ability to tailor your loads for a particular gun and shooting purpose. Let's take a look at what's out there for handloaders in 2012.

THE .303 SAVAGE

In the early part of the last century, the .303 Savage cartridge was a favorite among Savage Model 99 users. (This shooter had an uncle who swore the .303 Savage was the ideal cartridge for Utah mule deer.) Gradually, as time passed and new chamberings were added to the Model 99, the popularity of the .303 decreased and, eventually, it was discontinued, both as a chambering in the Model 99 and as a loaded cartridge by the ammunition manufacturers.

There are a good many rifles around chambered for this round. Loading dies are available from Huntington Die Specialties, as is unprimed brass, with bullets of the correct size available from several sources, including dealers handling Speer components. Other possible sources for the cases include Quality Cartridges (www.qual-cart.com) and TR & USA Trading Corporation in Connecticut. (Quality Cartridges produces unprimed brass cases for many obsolete and wildcat cartridges, and, while not all calibers are always in stock, it is worth checking.) A source for complete .303 Savage cartridges is Wisconsin Cartridge, LLC (www.wisconsincartridge.com). This firm produces loaded ammunition using new brass cases and has a few other old-timer loads in the works. Woodleigh Bullets, available through Huntington Die Specialties, has a new 150-grain soft-point bullet suitable for the .303 Savage.

BRASS AND BULLETS

In addition to its contribution to the .303 Savage loads, Huntington Die in also producing new Hydrostatically Stabilized Bullets in 7mm, 8mm, and 9.3mm sizes. These complement the line of these bullets currently available in the larger calibers.

Lehigh Defense LLC (www.lehigh-defense.com) produces some of the most specialized ammunition and components available, including multiple projectiles for handgun cartridges. The non-lead bullets are individually machined from solid material on CNC lathes and are designed to produce maximum expansion and shock. The firm produces eight 6:1 segmenting expansion bullets for Knight Rifles (www.knightrifles.com). Four of these bullets are .50-caliber in weights from 220- to 300-grain; three are .52-caliber in weights from 220- to 300-grain; and there's one 325-grain .54-caliber bullet.

Another firm producing solid copper and brass bullets, in calibers from .22 to .62, is Cutting Edge Bullets (www.cuttingedgebullets.com). A number of designs are currently available, including the ESP Raptor, the Dangerous Game Brass, and the Solid Copper. The Raptor is designed to be shot as a solid, hollowpoint, or hollowpoint with Talon tip installed. The Dangerous Game bullets are available in solid (DGBR) or hollowpoint (DGBR-HP) designs, while the solid copper bullets are available in Match Tactical Hunting (MTH), Match Tactical (MTAC), or Flat Base Hunting Hollow Point (FBH HP) designs, these last intended for long-range shooting.

Handloaders looking for new brass cases might check out Starline (www.starlinebrass.com). This Missouri firm produces nearly six-dozen different caliber cases from the .32 S&W Long to the .500 S&W Magnum. Most are handgun calibers, but a few, such as the .458 SOCOM, .50 Alaskan, .50-110, and others, are for rifles. Starline also has a fair number of blackpowder rifle cases, from the .40-65 to the .50-90 Sharps, .50-70 Gov't., and the .56-50 Spencer. Other new calibers are on the drawing board.

Quality Cartridge, mentioned above as a resource for reloading the .303 Savage, has unprimed brass cases for the .256, .30, .35, and .400 Newton cartridges. If anyone has a Newton rifle chambered for the .280 or .33 Newton cartridges, the .30 Newton case can be necked down or expanded to produce cases for either of these cartridges, and dies can probably be obtained from Huntington Die Specialties.

LOADING EQUIPMENT

MEC

One of the best-known manufacturers of shotshell reloading equipment is the Mayville Engineering Company (better known as the MEC people) of Wisconsin, in business now for over 50 years. (www.mecreloaders.com). From single-stage to progressive, the firm currently produces eight different models from the 600 Jr. Mark V to the 9000E. All but the Steelmaster model are available to load 10-, 12-, 16-, 20-, and 28-gauge shells, plus the .410-bore. The Steelmaster is designed specifically for loading the 3½-inch 10- or 12-gauge shells, but a kit is available for the 12-gauge model to also permit loading of standard length shells. Sizemaster die sets can also be used on the Steelmaster to convert to other gauges.

Since charge bars throw different volumes of powder, depending on the bushing, MEC's powder bushing chart is a must for shotshell loaders using a MEC press. Powder brands for which data is provided include Accurate, Alliant, Ramshot, IMR, Hodgdon, and Winchester, with nearly 40 different powders listed, and the MEC bushing chart provides ample brand data for each bushing. Bushing No. 27, for example, will throw 17 grains of Alliant Red Dot, 21.7 grains of Accurate No. 2, 16.2 grains of IMR 700-X, 15 grains of Hodgdon's Clays, 33.3 grains of Hodgdon's Lil'Gun, or 18.6 grains of Winchester WAA Lite.

CORBIN

Considering swaging your own bullets or shotgun slugs? How about reloading for the .50 BMG cartridge? Corbin, in White City, Oregon (www.Corbins.com), has the equipment. Jacketed .224 and .243 bullets can be produced from fired .22 LR rimfire cases and scrap lead or lead wire, while other sizes can also be produced with lead wire. Corbin also has the necessary supplies and presses. Its S-Press will swage bullets up to .458-inch size. The Mega-Mite can handle shells up to 25mm, plus it can be set up to load the .50 BMG cartridge. For the really serious who have, perhaps, a small business in mind, the Hydro-Press takes all the manual effort out of the process. You design the bullet or slug—rebated base, fin-tail, hollowpoint, semi-wadcutter, soft-point, spitzers, aluminum tip, whatever—Corbin can set you up for production.

LYMAN

Lyman Products Corporation (www.Lymanproducts.com) has a number of new products, from a new .50 BMG Multi-Tool to ultrasonic cartridge case cleaners. New die sets, an E-Zee case gauge, load data booklets, and more are also newly available.

The Lyman TS-700 cleaner has a capacity of 700 ml and will hold 100 9mm cases or the equivalent of other cases or small parts, including jewelry, etc. It doesn't have a drain valve or a heater, but it does have five timed cleaning cycles, push-button digital controls, and a stainless steel tank with plastic parts basket. The larger TS-6000 has a 6,000 ml capacity and will hold up to 1,300 9mm cases, four handgun frames, or the equivalent. It features a heated stainless steel tank and a basket with handles. Powered by two industrial-grade transducers, the TS-6000 has a drain valve to make emptying the tank easier, push-button digital controls, and five timed cleaning cycles. Lyman also stocks the proper Turbo Sonic solutions for most jobs, whether brass, steel, or jewelry. Available in sizes from four to 32 ounces, the solutions should be matched to the material being cleaned.

The new Lyman .50 BMG Case Prep Multi-Tool is double ended, permitting inside and outside case mouth deburring. Other components stored inside the hollow handle include tools for reaming, cleaning, and uniforming the primer pocket (the case mouth deburring heads are detachable). Lyman also has a one-piece deburring tool that will handle case mouths up to .60-caliber, but the handle isn't hollow, the reamers are not removable, and there is no primer pocket tool with it.

The Micro-Touch 1500 electronic scale is new to the Lyman line. Powered by bat-

The Lyman .50 BMG Case Prep Multi-Tool will handle all case mouth deburring on the big cases, plus reaming, cleaning, and uniforming of the primer pocket. The primer pocket tools are stored in the handle of the Multi-Tool, which unscrews in the middle.

The Lyman Turbo Sonic 700 Cleaner will hold up to 100 9mm cases and features a stainless steel tank with a plastic basket.

The Lyman Turbo Sonic 2500 Cleaner has a capacity of up to 900 9mm cases and features a heated stainless steel tank with a stainless steel basket.

The ultimate Lyman Turbo Sonic Cleaner, the TS-6000, has a capacity of 1,300 9mm cases or four handgun frames. All Lyman Turbo Sonic Cleaners feature digital displays.

teries or an AC adapter, the Micro-Touch has a 1,500-grain capacity and comes with its own powder pan, calibration weight, and dust cover.

The latest E-Zee case gauge in the Lyman line is for handgun cases. The previous model could handle 70 of the most popular handgun and rifle cases, but the new E-Zee gauge is smaller and designed to handle most cases originally designed for handgun use, including up to the .460 S&W Magnum. Just slip the empty case into the appropriate space and, if it fits, the length is satisfactory. If not, the case is beyond the maximum length and needs to be trimmed.

Handloaders having a Lyman Case Prep Xpress unit and loading for the .50 BMG cartridge can now get an upgrade kit for the Xpress. This kit provides the same deburring and primer pocket tools for use on the .50 BMG Case Prep Multi-Tool.

In the loading die line, Lyman has new three-die sets advertised as "Two Die Sets in One." Featuring a deluxe carbide expander assembly containing a free-floating carbide expander button, a neck-sizing die, full-length sizing die, and a regular bullet seating die, the new sets are available for a dozen different cartridges from the .204 Ruger to the .338 Lapua Magnum. The expander button assembly and the neck-sizing die with the carbide button assembly are available separately, if a handloader already has a full length sizing die for that particular cartridge.

REDDING RELOADING EQUIPMENT

Redding Reloading Equipment (www.redding-reloading.com) has reloading

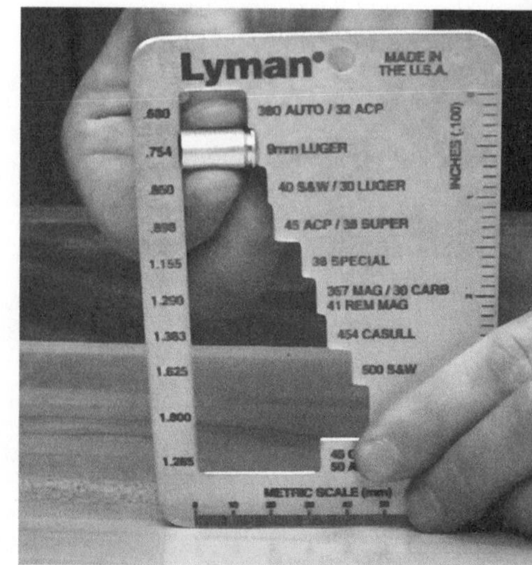

The new Lyman E-Zee pistol case gauge is easy to use. If the case doesn't fit in the correct slot or gap, it needs trimming. The case shown is satisfactory.

dies for the .300 Blackout in Series C and National Match grades. The 3-die Match set contains a full-length sizing die, competition bullet seating die, and a taper crimp die. The two-die Series C set contains a full-length or neck sizing die and a bullet seating die, with the Deluxe Series C set containing both the full-length and neck sizing dies. A form and trim die is also available separately for this cartridge, but is not included in either die set.

Other new products in the Redding line include Dual Ring Carbide Sizing Dies for seven popular handgun cartridges, and Bullet Seating Micrometers for seating dies having ½x20 threads. The Micrometers replace the original seating plugs and can be changed from one die to another. They're available for standard or VLD bullet shapes.

Handloaders who own a Redding powder measure and wanting to load for some of the smallbores can now do so without the need for a separate funnel, thanks to the new Drop Tube Adapter to fit .17- and .20-caliber cases.

Imperial lubricants are among the best on the market, and Redding is now producing the line. The newest items are a Bio-Green Case Lube, which is biodegradable and water soluble. A Convenience Pak for dry lubing case necks is another addition.

SINCLAIR INTERNATIONAL

Sinclair (www.sinclairintl.com) not only carries the handloading supplies of other manufacturers, such as RCBS, Hornady, Forster, and others, it also manufactures a specialized line of its own design. Such items include the Stainless Ultimate Trimmer, various primer pocket uniformers, flash hole deburring tools, and its own stainless steel priming tool for those handloaders who like to feel the primer set. This last is a precision tool that takes Sinclair shell holders, with some 20 different sizes available to handle most cartridges from the .17 Remington Fireball to the .505 Gibbs. (As a side note, Sinclair is also a good source for Lapua brass cases from the .220 Russian to the .338 Lapua Magnum.)

For those handloaders devoted to 1,000-yard shooting or other serious competition, Sinclair has a concentricity gauge to measure runout of loaded round. Said to be the most accurate device of its type on the market, the gauge is available in two models, with dial indicator or digital indicator. It will handle cartridges up to the .50 BMG in size.

DILLON PRECISION PRODUCTS

Dillon Precision Products, the "Blue Press People" (www.dillonprecision.com), has a line of four loading presses for loading metallic cartridges in volume, plus a progressive shotshell reloader. A specialty item, the massive "Big Fifty Reloader," handles the .50 BMG cartridge, where users, with some practice, can crank out 300 rounds per hour.

The auto-indexing progressive Dillon Square Deal 'B' press is designed for loading moderate quantities—350 rounds per hour—of handgun cartridges in the .32 Smith & Wesson to .45 Colt range. It comes factory set to load one caliber, and caliber conversion units are in the $85 to $95 range.

Next up is the manual-indexing RL 550B press, capable of loading over 160 calibers, for both handgun and rifle, at a rate of approximately 500 rounds per hour. Caliber change time takes about five minutes, and an automatic case feeder is available for handgun calibers. Caliber conversion kits for the RL 550B, from the .22 Remington Jet to .460 Weatherby Magnum, are in the $46 to $56 range.

One more step up, and the XL 650 features automatic indexing and is available for most handgun and rifle cartridges (caliber change takes about 10 minutes). With an optional automatic case feeder, the XL 650 can produce about 800 loaded rounds per hour. Caliber conversion kits for the XL 650, from .32 ACP to .458 Winchester Magnum, are in the $80 to $90 range.

Handloaders interested in commercial production might find the Super 1050, with an output of approximately 1,000 rounds per hour, to their liking. It's available in all handgun calibers and rifle calibers form the .223 to the .30-06. Conversion time is about 20 minutes, and the conversion kits are in the $118 to $198 range.

The SL 9000 is Dillon's auto-indexing shotshell reloader. Available in 12-, 20-, or 28-gauge, the 9000 can be converted from one gauge to another for less than $350, and accessories, such as a hull feeder, low powder sensor, and an aluminum roller handle, are options.

Dillon has a large inventory of handgun and rifle caliber die sets, plus other accessories, powder measures, case trimmers, and a primer pocket swager that really handles military brass cases. Its Reloader Toolholder helps organize the needed hex wrenches.

RCBS

RCBS (www.rcbs.com) has some great new trimmers, the Trim Pro-2 Manual and the Trim Pro-2 Power, along with a Trim Pro-2 Shell Holder Conversion Unit. Handloaders using a progressive press of handgun cartridge reloading should find the new RCBS pistol bullet feeder handy. It will fit any press having ⅞x14 threaded die stations and is available to handle bullets from .380/9mm/.38/.357 to .45 ACP. This unit places the bullet into the case

The new RCBS Trim Pro-2 power trimmer, set up and ready to trim. This Pro-2 has the new spring-loaded universal shell holder installed.

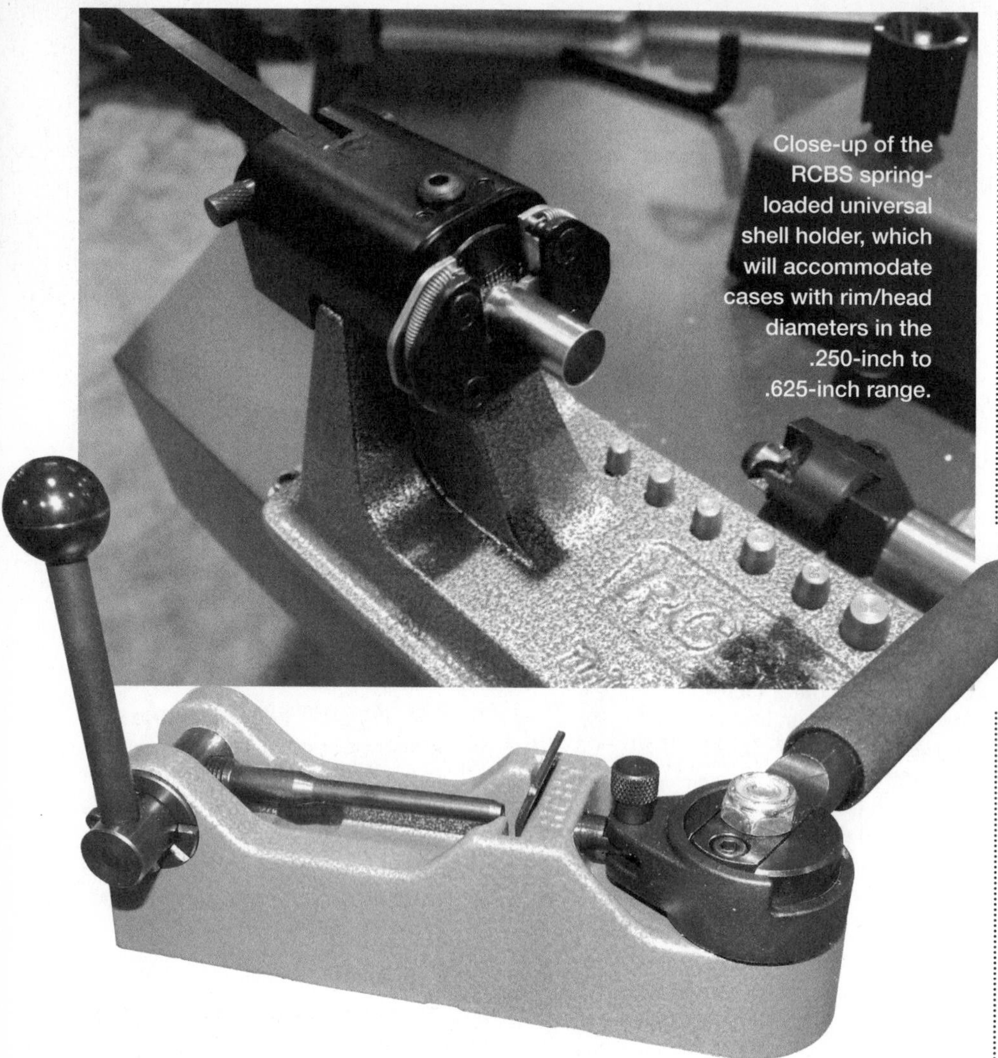

Close-up of the RCBS spring-loaded universal shell holder, which will accommodate cases with rim/head diameters in the .250-inch to .625-inch range.

The RCBS primer pocket swager makes removal of the primer pocket crimp on military and some commercial cases easy and fast.

mouth in proper alignment for seating at the next station and can be used with cast, swaged, plated, and jacketed bullets. RCBS also has a new rifle bullet feeder adaptor to allow the use of the RCBS rifle bullet feeder on Dillon's RL 550 and XL 650 progressive presses that use the Dillon Powder Measure.

Progressive press users having more than a single die plate can now keep them organized with an RCBS die plate/shell plate rack. This steel rack is designed to be mounted horizontally on a bench or vertically on the wall.

Surplus military brass in 5.56mm and 7.62mm calibers is being used more and more frequently, and the staked or crimped primer pockets can be a problem. The new RCBS bench size primer pocket swager solves this problem. Featuring an aluminum base and hardened steel swaging head, this swager comes with small and large swaging heads and rods to handle most cases .22-caliber and larger. (Note: some commercial cases also have crimped primer pockets.)

The new Case Trimmer Pro-2s have a spring-loaded universal shell holder that locks the case into alignment with the cutter. It will accommodate case head diameters from .250- to .625-inch, or from the 5.7x28mm to the .338 Lapua Magnum. (Cases with head/rim diameters greater than .625-inch require trimming on the No. 90352 high-capacity trimmer.) The power trimmer features a high-torque, low-RPM motor, an integral power switch, and a manual on/off switch to aid in setting case trim length.

In the loading die line, RCBS has added the .280 Ackley Improved to its Group D series. It's available as a complete set or as a neck or full-length sizing die only.

For handloaders just getting started, all RCBS Reloading Kits have been updated. They now include a universal case loading block, .17- to .60-caliber deburring tool, and accessory handle.

HORNADY

Handloaders wanting to get into the business big time should check out Hornady's new 3-in-1 Lock-N-Load Ammo Plant. It comes complete with a Lock-N-Load AP press, bullet feeder, case feeder, small and large primer tubes, pistol and rifle metering inserts, die wrench, and more—there's even a vintage tin sign for fun! Best of all, for less than the price of most used cars, you can be in business. (Die sets, shell plates, case feeder plates, and bullet feeder dies are extra.)

There are a couple of do-all kits in the Hornady line now, including the Lock-N-Load Classic Deluxe and the Precision Reloaders Kit. The Classic Deluxe includes the Classic Kit with the Lock-N-Load single stage press and accessories that help speed up the loading process.

Every handloader needs a powder trickler, and Hornady has a new Lock-

Close-up of the dispensing knobs on the Hornady Quick Trickler, showing the three-to-one gear ratio arrangement.

The Hornady Lock-N-Load Quick-Trickler, ready to dispense powder into the pan of the Lock-N-Load Bench Scale.

N-Load Quick Trickler that stands high enough to trickle powder right into the pan atop a digital scale. Hand operated, this new high-volume trickler features high and low speeds with a three-to-one gear ratio.

Hornady has now added another sonic cleaner to its line, the Lock-N-Load 2L, featuring a two-liter stainless steel tank. Capable of holding 150 .308 cases or 300 .223 cases, the 2L has an 80-watt ceramic heater and a timer that runs up to 30 minutes. Coupled with One Shot Sonic Clean solution, the 2L can make your old brass cases look like new. It's available in 110- or 220-volt models.)

Another new Hornady item for handloaders is the Lock-N-Load Case Prep Trio. Compatible with 110- or 220-volt power, the Trio has a three-tool capacity and will handle both case mouth and primer pocket operations. It comes with both inside and outside chamfer and deburring tools, and large and small primer pocket cleaner and reamer heads are available as options, in addition to case neck brushes in seven calibers form .17 to .45.

Handloaders currently using loading presses of other manufacture and that have 1¼x12 threads can now convert to Hornady Lock-N-Load die use. Hornady has the necessary conversion kit and die bushings. The kit comes with three Lock-N-Load bushings and one conversion bushing, and separate bushings are available in packs of two, three, and 10.

Note that loading dies for the new .300 AAC Blackout round are now available from Hornady, as well as Forster Products.

LITTLE CROW GUNWORKS

To provide easy chambering and avoid undue high pressures, keeping cases trimmed to the correct length is a must. Little Crow Gunworks, LLC (www.littlecrowgunworks.com), offers up its W.F.T.—World's Finest Trimmer—to handle trimming of any bottleneck case up to the .338 Lapua; since this trimmer references on the case shoulder, straight-walled cases are out. Little Crow advertises the tool can trim up to 500 cases per hour and is self-cleaning, thanks to a sealed bearing construction. Keep your eyes open, a larger model capable of handling cases up to the .50 BMG may be available by the time you read this.

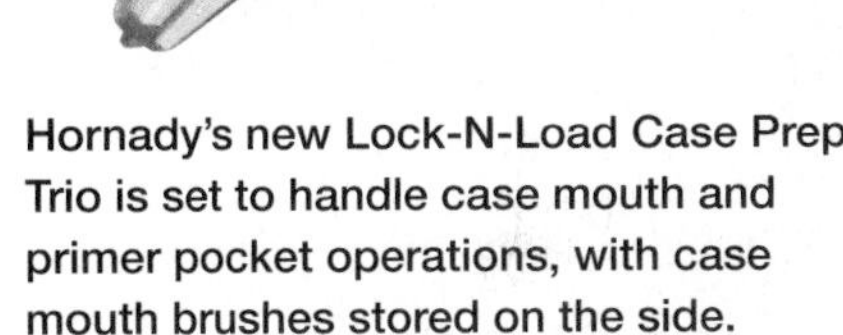

Hornady's new Lock-N-Load Case Prep Trio is set to handle case mouth and primer pocket operations, with case mouth brushes stored on the side.

JOHNSON DESIGN SPECIALTIES

Johnson Design Specialties (www.quick-measure.com) has an adapter to permit the use of its Quick Powder Measure on progressive type loading presses. It can be moved to another tool head in a minute or less time. Capable of handling long extruded powders such as 4831, it provides 0.1-grain accuracy and can be used to load even the small .17- and .20-caliber rounds.

PMA TOOL

Need to turn your case necks? PMA Tool (www.pmatool.com) has a small tool to do just that. It comes with the mandrel installed and the cutter preset to the purchaser's specifications.

Handloaders using a Dillon Powder Measure can increase the capacity of the hopper with a new 14-inch polycarbonate tube that replaces the Dillon tube. Available from UniqueTek, Inc. (www.unique.com), the 14-inch tube comes with a powder baffle, but requires the original Dillon metal power measure lid.

LEE PRECISION

Lee Precision (www.leeprecision.com) has several new products for handloaders. Among them is a three-legged reloading stand ideal for shooters having limited space for reloading. Constructed of powder-coated steel, it features a 10-inch triangular steel top with the Lee Patented Quick-Change Bench Plate system, one storage bin, a pre-drilled wood bench block, and two steel hangers for holding stabilizing concrete blocks.

Lee now has a large number of aluminum block moulds for those handloaders who like to cast their own bullets. A wide variety of designs for handgun and rifle bullets is available, plus designs for muzzleloading rifles. Shotgunners get tools, too, for Lee has moulds for casting either 7/8- or one-ounce 12-gauge slugs. For those shooters with a preference for buckshot, Lee has an 18-cavity mould to produce a choice of No. 4, 00, or 000 buckshot.

CAMDEX

Camdex (www.camdexloader.com) produces loading presses for mass production. The Rifle Case Processor is just what the name states. It takes cleaned fired cases, removes the military crimp via swaging, automatically ejects Berdan-primed cases, as well as split or cracked cases, and stops if a foreign object in a case is located or a loaded round is encountered. The final stop is the processing, which consists of full-length resizing in a tungsten carbide sizing die. The processor is available in most rifle calibers from .223 up to .308 (7.62mm NATO).

The Camdex 2100 Series Loading Machine operates on 110 or 220 volts and is speed-adjustable to 4400 cycles with 11 in-line stations. Available to load most commercial or NATO handgun cartridges, the 2100 comes set up to load one caliber, with conversion packages available. This press monitors 10 different functions: case level (low level in feed tube); case probe (foreign object in case or loaded round); primer pocket probe; primer slide (shuts machine off if a primer jam occurs); primer feed (shuts machine off if it runs out of primers); primer level (maintains some 60 primers in the feed system); powder probe (checks for both low and high powder charges); bullet fault (shuts machine off if a bullet fails to feed or it runs out of bullets); vacuum system (checks vacuum pressure to assure primer feeding); and currant sensor (shuts machine off if pre-set amperage changes.)

The Camdex 2200 Series loader is similar to the 2100, except it's capable of loading most popular rifle cartridges, while the 2300 Series is similar to the 2200 Series loader, but designed to handle cartridges from the .300 Winchester Magnum to the .50 BMG. The 2300 comes with large-capacity case, powder, and bullet feeders and has a pulsating powder slide bar to ensure an accurate powder charge. As with the 2100 and 2200 Series loaders, the 2300 is computer controlled.

PRINT MATERIALS

Handloaders can never have enough up-to-date loading data, and the new 72-page *Reloading Guide Edition 10* from VihtaVuori provides data for more than five-dozen rifle cartridges and nearly two-dozen handgun cartridges, plus five popular cowboy action cartridges. Handloaders will also find data for some cartridges not always featured in other manuals, such as the 9x23 Winchester, 6.5x47 Lapua, 9.3x66 Sako, and 7MM GJW. Data includes case brand used, bullet type and brand, starting and maximum VihtaVuori powder charges listed, and velocities in both metric and English units. Maximum loads are highlighted with gray shading to be more obvious. There is also a burning rate chart provided for 11 different brands of powders, including VihtaVuori, Ramshot, Norma, IMR, W-W, RWS, and Vectan.

Lyman has always had an excellent line of handbooks and manuals on reloading metallics and shotshells, casting bullets, and even a 50-page *Reloading Data Log* for keeping a record of pet loads. Now there's a *Load Data Series* consisting of a dozen booklets for various calibers and categories. One booklet is devoted to the 12-gauge shells, while another is devoted to the other gauges—16-, 20-, and 28-, plus the .410-bore—but not the 10-gauge. The other 10 booklets are devoted to loads for metallic cartridges—pistol, revolver, .30-calibers, popular varmint calibers, old military calibers, classic American rifle calibers of the late nineteenth and early twentieth centuries, and big-bore calibers up to the .460 Weatherby Magnum. Data for most popular bullet and powder brands are provided, along with data for bullets cast using Lee, Lyman, RCBS, and Saeco moulds.

Hodgdon, the "Powder People," have, in recent years, put out an annual reloading manual with the most up-to-date loading data available. The latest edition, available for less than a sawbuck, contains info for more than nine-dozen rifle cartridges from the .17 Ackley Hornet to the .50 BMG and including the .300 AAC Blackout, .416 Ruger, and .50-110 Sharps. Data is also provided for six-dozen handgun cartridges from the .22 Remington Jet to the .500 S & W Magnum and includes the .30 Herrett, .375 JDJ, and the .500 Wyoming Express. Other features of this 2012 edition include seven feature articles covering such topics as Eraser, Hodgdon's new copper fighting powder for the .223, the story of Hodgdon's H110 powder, and an essay on loading for the .300 Blackout. With new cartridges and components seemingly being introduced on a regular basis, it pays to keep the reloading data up-to-date also, and the *Hodgdon Annual Manual* is one way to do so.

Hodgdon also puts out a *Basic Reloading Manual* without feature articles and with fewer loads, but with some shotshell reloading data incorporated. Additional information, such as a

One of the new Lyman load data booklets. This one for big-bore rifle cartridges provides data for cartridges from the .375 H & H Magnum to the .460 Weatherby Magnum.

The *Basic Reloading Manual* from Hodgdon provides loading data for popular metallic rifle and handgun cartridges.

relative burn rate chart, description of various powders, loading data for some three-dozen rifle cartridges from the .17 Remington Fireball to the .50 BMG, plus handgun cartridge loads to cowboy action loads, are features of this manual. The shotshell loading data is mainly devoted to 12-gauge shells, but the 16-, 20-, and 28-gauge are not forgotten, and loads for the two common .410-bore lengths are provided. Powder bushing charts are provided for Lee, Hornady, Spolar, MEC, and Ponsness/Warren loading presses.

The *Hodgdon 2012 Annual Manual Reloading* provides up-to-date data for most popular cartridges, including a few wildcats and the new Eraser powder.

The VihtaVuori *Reloading Guide Edition 10* and those from Western Powders provide loading data for metallic cartridges and shotshells, depending on the guide. Every handloader needs up-to-date information.

Most powder manufacturers provide brochures or manuals listing loads using their particular powder brands and grades. Western Powders (www.accuratepowder.com) has manuals for Accurate, Ramshot, and Buckhorn 209 powders. Buckhorn is designed for use with blackpowder arms and is intended to be loaded in volumetric equivalents to actual blackpowder. Data is provided for .50-caliber muzzleloaders and cartridges from the .32 H&R Magnum to the .50-90. Ramshot data is provided for handgun cartridges from the 5.7x28mm to the .500 Maximum, and rifle cartridges from the .17 Remington Fireball to the .550 Magnum. Load data for Accurate powders is basically for the same cartridges as that provided for Ramshot powders. A separate guide, *Edition 2.1*, lists loads for shotshells using Ramshsot and Accurate powders. Hull type and brand, primer type and brand, wad column type and brand, powder brand and charge, and shot charge weights are listed, along with pressures and velocities for each load.

RIMFIRE AMMUNITION

BY C. RODNEY JAMES

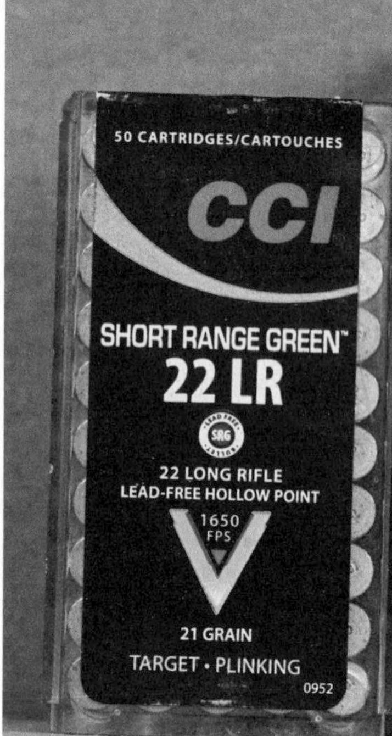

Recent developments in this most popular cartridge can best be summarized in one word—specialization. Loadings are being tailored for special purposes and individual types of guns. This trend began around 2007-'08, with the introduction of Long Rifle ammunition crafted especially for autoloaders, including top-end loadings for competition use.

AGUILA

After introducing its hot (1,470 fps) Interceptor in a 40-grain solid, Industrias Tecnos (Aguila) now offers the Interceptor as a high-velocity hollowpoint (HVHP). In our Winchester Model 52C bull-barrel target rifle, the new version offers better accuracy, with .8-inch, .7-inch, and .7-inch five-shot groups at 50 yards. A .73-inch average for a hunting round isn't bad.

CCI

Following the introduction of CCI Select, a Long Rifle for autoloaders, CCI offered its "tactical" LR for .22 autoloaders of the AR-15/M-16 pattern. For 2011, CCI has added an additional wrinkle, with what might be described as a long rifle CB Cap. The Quiet-22, or Q-22, features a 40-grain bullet at 710 fps. In a rifle barrel, it makes a pop about like a soft hand-clap. The Q-22 is a short-range proposition, grouping 1.2 inches, 2.1

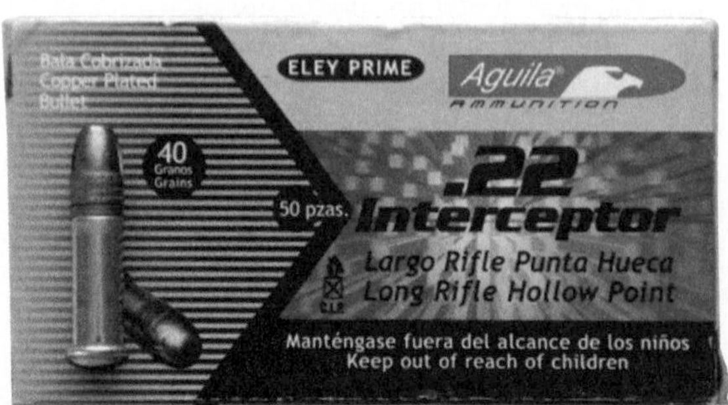

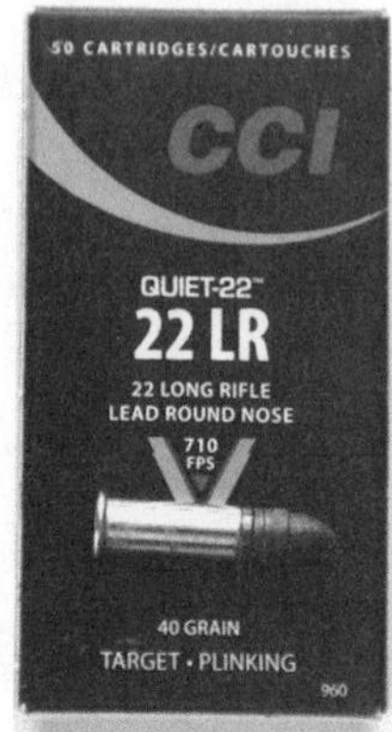

Left: Aguila's Interceptor HP, a hard-htting varmint round. Right: CCI's Quiet-22, a low-noise option for short-range shooting.

CCI's Gold Dot .22 Magnum for self-defense use functions well in both handguns and rifles.

inches, and .9-inch at 50 yards in our 52C Winchester. For giggles, we tried it in a Gévarm E-1 autoloader with the removable counterweight in the bolt removed. Amazingly, it functioned, delivering .9-inch, .9-inch, and 1.3 inches for an average 1.03 inches at 25 yards. At about 35 yards, it was possible to get three in the air without any of the reports overlapping hits on a sheet-metal target. This receives my "Neat-O!" commendation for the year.

In the .22 Magnum department, from CCI comes the Gold Dot Short Barrel, a 40-grain hollowpoint (HP) for personal protection. This performed well in a Kel-Tec PMR-30 semi-auto pistol with fiber optic sights and 4¼-inch barrel. This round produced significant muzzle flash, but just an average muzzle velocity of 1,257 fps. Groups averaged 3.2 inches at 25 yards. Figuring there might be varmint potential, three five-shot groups were run through an Anschütz 1720 heavy barrel rifle at 100 yards, grouping .7-inch, 1 inch, and 1.4 inches, averaging 1.03 inches. Good for varmints on two or four legs.

GEMTECH

Gemtech is known for making firearm suppressors and is now marketing a Long Rifle cartridge designed for optimized suppressor use. The 42-grain bullet at 1,050 fps is designed for penetration. At 50 yards, in the Winchester Model 52C, groups were .3-inch, .7-inch, and .6-inch, averaging .53-inch. Through this 28-inch rifle barrel the report was mild, and accuracy was well within target-grade specs.

Gemtech's 42-grain solid .22 LR is engineered for suppressor use. Accuracy was near target quality.

HORNADY

Hornady has fielded a .22 WMR called the Critical Defense. The FTX bullet weighs 45 grains. I'm not sure what "FTX" stands for, but the bullet is a hollowpoint filled with a red, latex-type substance. The purpose of this filler is to ensure controlled expansion, i.e., an ability to penetrate heavy cloth without expanding, but then expanding in tissue behind it.

As we had no way of testing the cloth aspect, when fired through the Anschütz 24-inch barrel, this bullet penetrated 20 inches of water-filled half-gallon paper cartons at 100 yards. Divided by 1.5, this equals 13.33 inches worth of gelatin penetration. The bullet expanded to .303-inch. Muzzle velocities for this round through the Anschütz were 1,700 fps, and an amazing 1,000 fps in a $1^{7}/_{8}$-inch handgun barrel. Five-shot groups at 100 yards were 1.7 inches, 1.6 inches, and 2.2 inches, with an average of 1.83 inches. The day was breezy, with a crosswind of around 10 mph. Under calm conditions, accuracy would likely be better.

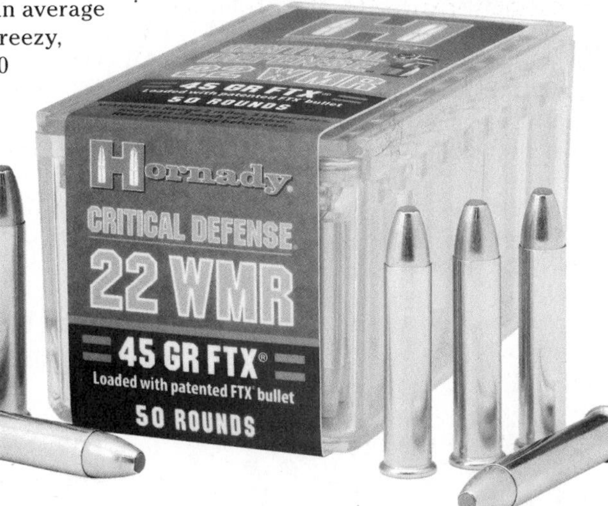

Hornady's .22 WMR is a heavyweight with a hollowpoint featuring controlled expansion.

PINEY MOUNTAIN AMMUNITION

Piney Mountain appears to be the only domestic manufacturer of .22 LR tracer ammunition. These are used primarily for training purposes—and fun. The product is non-corrosive and now available in both standard and high velocity, as well as both red and green tracer colors. The bullets produce a surprisingly brilliant flare. They burn for a good 200 yards, substantiating the 100-plus-yard range printed on the box. The 40-grain bullets are dabbed with a paint dot on the nose that indicates the color of the trace.

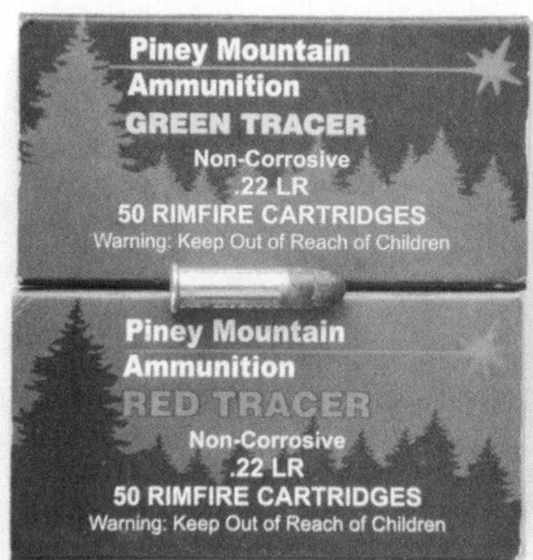

Piney Mountain now offers its LR tracer rounds in both red and green and at standard and high velocities.

These functioned well in a T/C R55 autoloading rifle, but, true to form, reflected my experience in that accuracy has never been a strong point of any tracer I've ever encountered. Five-shot groups were 1.8 inches, 3.2 inches, and 2.9 inches, for an average of 2.63 inches at 50 yards. This ammunition is sold mainly by mail through Cheaper Than Dirt! and Cabela's. Needless to say, these can start fires and should be used with care around areas where flammable ground clutter may be present.

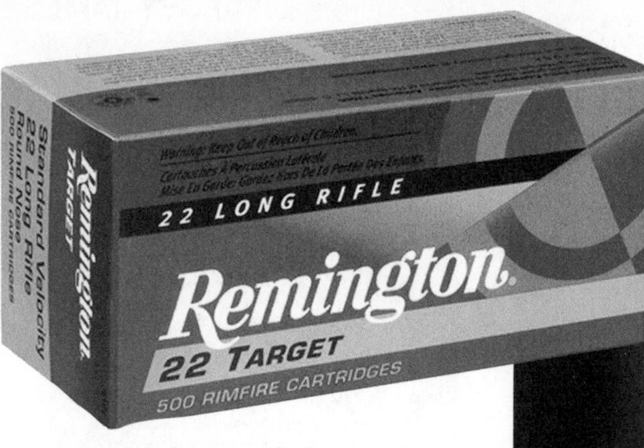

Remington has brought back its Target .22 LR that should be good for practice and precision hunting shots.

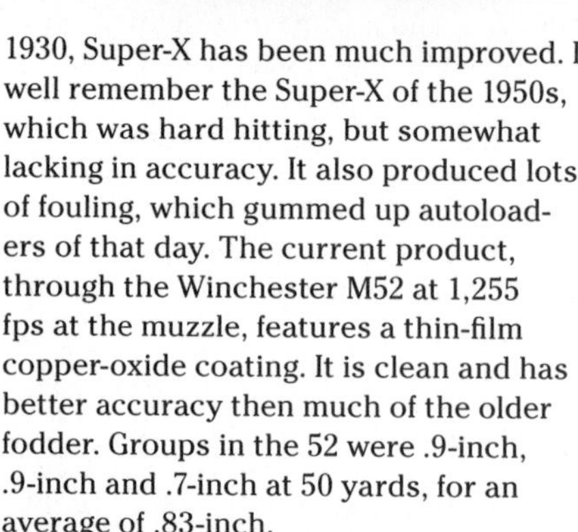

REMINGTON

Remington has reintroduced its .22 Target Long Rifle. The 40-grain solid at 1,150 fps has long been a favorite for practice in pet M-37s and 513Ts. As a precision squirrel cartridge, its accuracy and quiet report have made it a favorite for woods use. In the Model 52, five-shot groups ran .6-inch, .5-inch, and .9-inch, averaging .67-inch at 50 yards.

WINCHESTER

In .22 LR, Winchester's newest offering is the Varmint HE, a 37-grain HP round that offers segmenting expansion; to wit, the bullet separates into three segments. At 50 yards, it did exactly that in our water-filled paper carton test. At 100 yards the bullet stayed together, but expanded nicely, with the equivalent of nine-plus inches of gelatin penetration. Expansion was to .35-inch. Five-shot groups were 1.3 inches, 1.3 inches, and 1 inch at 50 yards, for an average of 1.23 inches. A single 100-yard group was 2 inches.

Winchester is again offering its Super-X in a bulk pack. Since its introduction in 1930, Super-X has been much improved. I well remember the Super-X of the 1950s, which was hard hitting, but somewhat lacking in accuracy. It also produced lots of fouling, which gummed up autoloaders of that day. The current product, through the Winchester M52 at 1,255 fps at the muzzle, features a thin-film copper-oxide coating. It is clean and has better accuracy then much of the older fodder. Groups in the 52 were .9-inch, .9-inch and .7-inch at 50 yards, for an average of .83-inch.

In .22 WMR, Winchester has joined Remington, CCI, and Hornady in offering a 30-grain V-Max. This bullet, with its sharp polymer point and a muzzle velocity of 2,200 fps, offers flat shooting and long-range varmint potential. The Winchester V-Max product grouped 1.4 inches, 1.4 inches, and 2.1 inches, with an average of 1.63 inches in the Anschütz at 100 yards. In the Kel-Tec PMR-30, the V-Max did groups of 2.5 inches, 2.5 inches, and 2.6 inches, averaging 2.53 inches at 25 yards. Recoil was low and there was no visible muzzle flash. Handgun velocities averaged 1,523 fps.

Winchester also entered the .17 HMR field this year, with the lightest rimfire bullet to date, a 15.5-grain, lead-free poly-tip bullet at a muzzle velocity of 2,500 fps. All of the .17 HMR bullets I have shot are incredibly accurate. An additional advantage of the .17 HMR is the ability of this small bullet to buck wind. Groups at 100 yards through a Marlin 17V heavy barrel were .7-inch, .7-inch, and .9-inch, for an average .73-inch. The problem with the .17 in taking varmints is that, for those much above prairie dog size, these small, light bullets tend to lose velocity rather quickly. On woodchucks and varmints of similar size, they fail to penetrate deep enough to hit vital organs—you must make head shots.

Winchester now offers a WMR 30-grain V-Max poly-tip bullet for varmint use.

Winchester is now in the .17 HMR business, with the introduction of a 15.5-grain poly-tip bullet at 2,500 fps.

BY C. RODNEY JAMES

GREEN RIMFIRE AMMUNNITON HOW GOOD IS IT?

With the growing concern over lead contamination and selective banning of lead ammunition by states such as California, Arizona, and New Mexico, ammunition companies are looking to come up with viable alternatives to lead. These lead-free products are about double the cost of conventional lead rimfire ammunition. But whether you're required to use it, have gone green and feel compelled to use it, or just have curiosity getting the better of you, the primal question here is, just how good is it? The current crop of non-lead offerings include two .22 Long Rifle and two .22 WMR loadings.

CALIBER .22 LR

As of this writing, Winchester and CCI are the companies offering non-lead rimfire ammunition. CCI/Speer introduced the Short Range Green Long Rifle in Spring 2010. The bullet is made of compressed copper powder under a polymer binder. Like the sintered iron bullets from the 1950s (if you remember the Remington Rocket), this one is designed to disintegrate on striking a hard surface, thus avoiding ricochets. The Short Range Green is listed as weighing 21 grains. The bullet has a dimple in the nose and is therefore dubbed a hollowpoint. Velocity is advertised as 1,650 fps. An unusual feature is that this bullet is of a bore-riding design. There is a short drive band (about .055-inch wide) extending forward from the case mouth. This is the only portion of the bullet that is in hard contact with the lands of the barrel. The comparatively long heel of the bullet (about .11-inch) does not expand. The base of the bullet contains a small sprue bump in the center.

Bullets fired into snow and water-filled paper juice cartons evidenced no expansion. When fired at a range of 30 feet at a piece of 1.5-inch hard-pine plank, the bullet passed through. The recovered bullet evidenced no measurable expansion. The exit hole was similar to that of a full metal jacket bullet. Angled shots at a concrete walk produced a spall on the surface, but disintegrated.

Shortly after CCI entered the field, Winchester introduced the Tin Hollow Point .22 LR cartridge. This Winchester product has the appearance of a conventional LR bullet, with a small cavity in the nose. Weight is 26 grains at a claimed velocity of 1,650 fps.

There is evidence of melting and gas cutting in the heel portion of fired bullets, as this bullet's heel does not expand. Nor does this tin bullet expand in the nose portion, even when fired through a 1.5-inch hard-pine plank. Since tin is harder than lead, these are more prone to ricochet than a lead bullet.

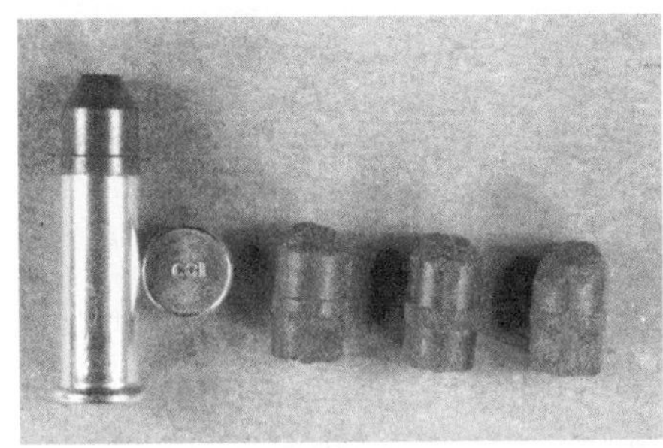

Both cartridges are intended for indoor/outdoor target use, with the purpose of reducing lead contamination at shooting ranges. Both are intended for short-range (50-yard/50-meter) target shooting.

The warning on the CCI box includes the directive *not* to use in match-chambered rifles. Tests were therefore

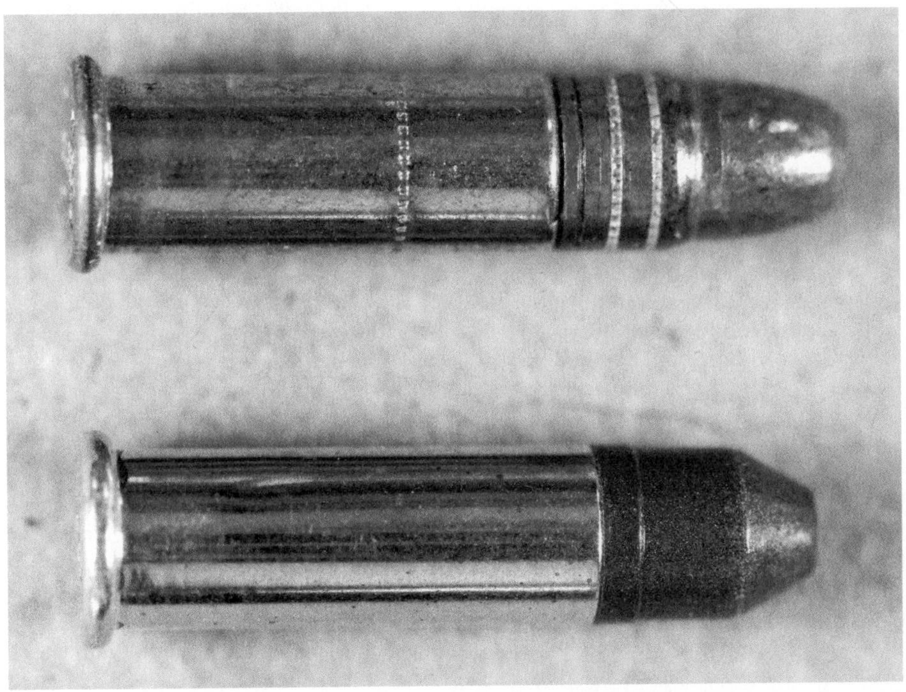

limited to one of the more accurate LR autoloaders, the T/C R55 Classic rifle. A second reason for this choice was that the CCI box also advised that the Short Range Green might not function in all autoloaders. This particular test rifle would shoot a few good lots of LR into .5-inch at 50 yards. At 75 yards, with selected ammunition, it averages about 1.3-inch groups.

All testing for this project was done outdoors from a two-point bag rest on a heavy shooting bench. Wind conditions were three to eight mph on partly cloudy days. For both round types, we fired four five-shot groups at 50 yards. The CCI groups were 1.5 inches, 1.3 inches, 1.35 inches, and 1.45 inches for an average of 1.4 inches. With the Winchester ammo, groups were 1.5 inches, 1.2 inches, .8-inch, and 1.2 inches, for an average of 1.18 inches.

Both ammunitions functioned through this rifle without problems. In further function testing, both the CCI and Winchester rounds would work in the actions of Ruger's 10/22 and the Gévarm semi-auto rifles. They would not function in a S&W M41 pistol. Run through two different Ruger Mark II semi-auto pistols, one pistol ran fine, but not another.

While the accuracy tests would seem to favor the Winchester, there is insufficient data to establish a statistical advantage. For giggles, the Winchester Tin was tried at 75 yards. One group was 2.4 inches, the other 3 inches. This confirms the "short-range" notion.

CALIBER .22 WMR

These two rounds are of a more conventional design in that both have copper jackets.

The CCI TNT Green .22 WMR (introduced in 2009) features a 30-grain HP bullet and a core of powdered copper. This round has an advertised velocity of 2,050 fps. The TNT Green, however, is not identical to the TNT lead varmint round, which has a nose cavity (according to CCI engineers) about seven times the diameter of the TNT Green.

For penetration testing, a round was fired from an H&K M-300 .22 WMR autoloading carbine at 50 yards into water-filled half-gallon paper juice cartons. Penetration was a nominal 4 inches, with only two fragments of the jacket retained in the second carton. At 100 yards, the bullet penetrated 19 inches, exiting carton No. 5 and retained by the

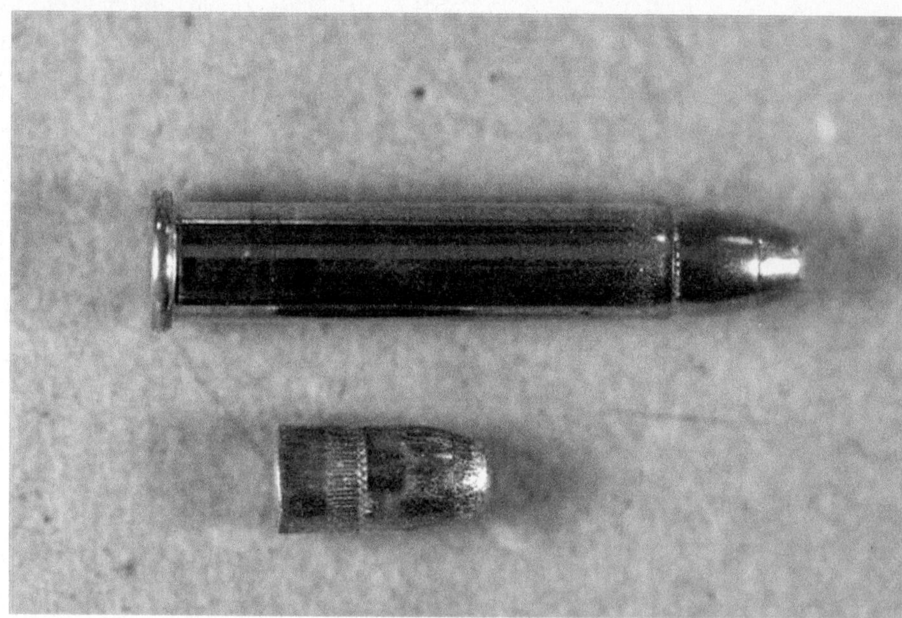

cardboard "capture carton" at the rear. (For gelatin penetration comparisons, as we did with our regular .22 ammo, divide the water carton penetration by 1.5.) This bullet showed no sign of expansion beyond a negligible enlargement of the nose cavity at 100 yards.

For comparison, the 31-grain *lead*-core TNT at 100 yards yielded a penetration of 7.5 inches, with an expansion to .325-inch and 100-percent weight retention. The TNT Green jacket fragments (all that remained) weighed 8.2 grains, a retention of a little over 27 percent at 50 yards.

The Winchester Jacketed Tin Hollow Point is listed at 28 grains with a muzzle velocity of 2,200 fps. It contains a tin core swaged in a copper jacket. In a 100-yard water carton test, the bullet penetrated 20 inches. There was no expansion, though the hollowpoint was marginally opened.

For accuracy testing, we fired four five-shot groups of each at 100 yards through the H&K semi-auto, and three five-shot groups through the Anschütz 1720.

In the H&K, the CCI produced groups of 1.8 inches, 1.25 inches, 1.7 inches, and 1.2 inches, for an average of 1.49 inches. The Winchester grouped 1.9 inches, 1.3 inches, 2.8 inches, and 1.7 inches, for an average of 1.93 inches. Both these brands functioned perfectly in this autoloader with one exception, a CCI failure to fully eject.

In the Anschütz, the CCI grouped 1.3 inches, 2 inches, and 1.4 inches, for an average of 1.57 inches. The Winchester tin round grouped 1.4 inches, 1.1 inches, and 1.4 inches, for an average of 1.3 inches.

Both bullets were tested in water-filled half-gallon juice cartons. At 50 yards, the CCI bullet disintegrated, and neither expanded at 100 yards. Since the .22 WMR is specified as a 100- to 150-yard varmint cartridge, the lack of any expansion pretty well damns both for varminting.

Though Winchester may seem to have the accuracy edge in this rifle, the difference is not statistically significant. Overall average is 1.43 inches. This isn't bad and certainly more than adequate accuracy for chuck hunting. The average for a dozen similarly tested WMR loadings in this rifle was 1.32 inches, so the above, which contained 100-yard groups between .93-inch and 1.6 inches, fall within this range. The problem is the lack of expansion! As a control for accuracy to monitor shooting conditions, a four-shot group (max capacity for the Anschütz magazine) of CCI V-Max was fired. This is the best-shooting ammo in this rifle. It went in .7-inch.

In the final analysis, you can't beat lead bullets. Since the best science does not conclude that lead bullets are a significant hazard in the environment, it is to be hoped that legislators will see the light and keep bans to a minimum and base their decisions on solid scientific information, rather than the shrill warnings of would-be environmentalists operating on hunches and gut feelings. In that vein, it is also to be hoped that these non-lead cartridges will soon become curiosities for cartridge collectors.

Acquiring that ideal handgun can be a journey, sometimes a long one. One vintage Colt revolver took 33 years and four handguns to find. It was worth the wait.

The 33-Year Itch COLT®

BY ANDY EWERT

At age 16, with a little help from my dad, I bought my first handgun, a 6-1/2-inch-barrelled Smith & Wesson Highway Patrolman .357 Magnum. Almost four decades, dozens of handguns, and thousands of handloads later, I'm looking at the sidearm from a vastly difference perspective. Having crossed the half-century mark and then some in age, logic tells me I own too many handguns. It's time to start thinning their ranks or leave the task to someone less discriminating when I pass on – not that I'm planning on departing this earth soon.

Mae West reportedly said that too much of a good thing is "simply marvel-

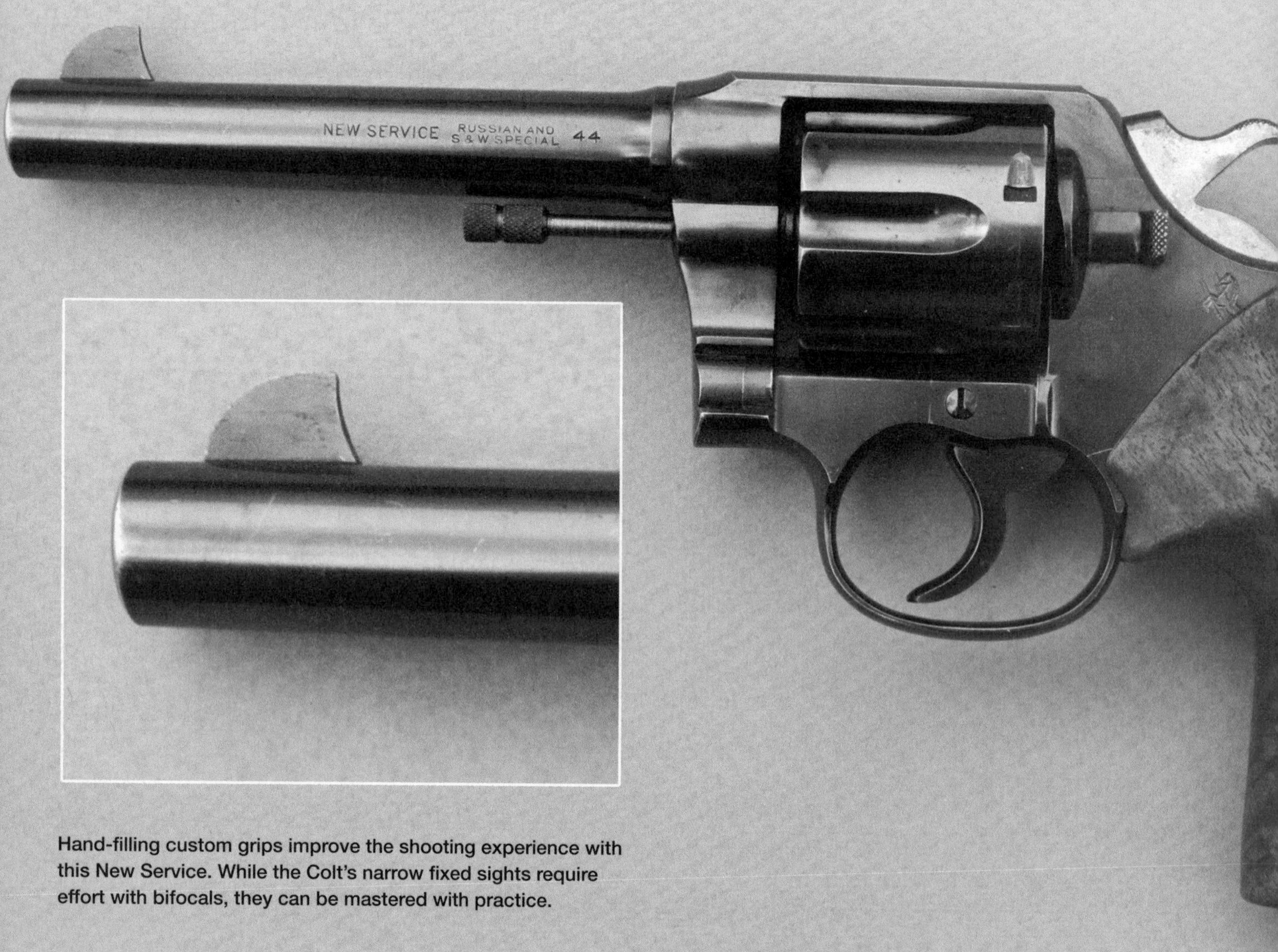

Hand-filling custom grips improve the shooting experience with this New Service. While the Colt's narrow fixed sights require effort with bifocals, they can be mastered with practice.

ous." I wholly agree. However, my reality now is more pragmatic. Thoreau's appeal to "simplify, simplify, simplify" better reflects my current state of mind. OK, but how to decide what stays and what goes out of the 25 handguns I currently own? The solution: Find that ideal pistol in my menagerie and, over time, dispose of the rest.

Understand that I'm a shooter, not a collector. My handguns, an eclectic mix of revolvers, semi-automatics, an old, inherited single shot, and a handsome pair of cap and ball sixshooters, were acquired for the pleasure of use. I've shot them all and reload for most of them. Each occupies a specific niche, however obscure and redundant it might be. Calibers range from .22 Long Rifle, .32 ACP, 9mm Parabellum, 9mm Makarov, .38 Special, .357 Magnum, .44 Special, and .44 Magnum to .45 ACP. Almost all these handguns are at least 25 years old. They include specimens by Colt, Smith & Wesson, Ruger, Mauser, Astra, Browning, Walther, and Hopkins & Allen, among others.

What I've learned about handguns in over four decades of burning powder can be summed up thus:

Once you've mastered your handgun, practical accuracy is less dependent on the firearm itself than on the fitness of the shooter. Take all the handguns I own and fire, say, six rounds offhand at 25 yards. Group sizes on a good day will vary from the size of a plum (a 1933 vintage Colt Woodsman) to the spread of your hand, fingers extended (a second generation Colt 1860 Army cap and ball).

With practice, a good trigger pull, and – if necessary – optically corrected vision (in my case bifocals), even the most rudimentary sights are usually adequate for shot placement up to 25 yards. This assumes good ammunition, a clean bore, and a steady hold and release. The squared rear- and front-sight configuration seems to work best for me, but others are satisfactory. Because I reload, it isn't vital that handgun sights be adjustable, assuming correct lateral alignment. If necessary, I can load up or down to a 25-yard zero. In my experience, nothing thwarts consistent shot placement more than a bad trigger.

Assuming a Weaver grip, some pistols fit in my hand better than others. Those that fit best usually shoot best. Custom grips can improve shot placement and make

The 1920s-era Colt New Service .44 Special that took the author's father more than three decades to find and acquire. Reliable, powerful, and accurate, the New Service served U.S. and foreign militaries, law enforcement, outdoorsmen, and target shooters with distinction for more than half a century. This specimen continues to provide shooting pleasure more than 80 years after it came off the assembly line.

shooting a more pleasant experience, especially with hard-kicking magnums.

When striving for shot placement, handgun size and weight matter. Too little or too much stymies practical accuracy. Balance affects placement too.

OK, enough wisdom. Let's get down to business and make those first cuts. My initial battery must include one .22. That's a no-brainer. They're easy to hit with, economical, and fun. Of my four .22s, the keeper is that 60-plus-year-old Woodsman. Even with a six-inch barrel, it's compact, dead accurate, and reliable. The bull-barrel Ruger Target, Smith & Wesson K22 and .22 Combat Masterpiece in my possession all fit this bill, but the Woodsman does it best.

My 2-inch barrel, fixed-sight S&W .38 Chiefs Special is a highly specialized pocket pistol for personal defense where concealment is a priority. But the Smith 696 three-inch barrel, adjustable-sight .44 Special is a real seducer. Stuffed with 300-grain lead flat points and Bullseye powder, it's a manstopper par excellance and surprisingly accurate at 25 yards. But at two-pounds-plus it's no pocket pistol. My S&W 2-inch-barrelled, adjustable sight .22 snubby is compact, but its fixed-sight .38 Special rival packs more punch in a comparable size/weight package. If I needed a hide-out pistol – I really don't – it probably would be my '60's vintage East German Makarov. Accordingly, all the shorties go.

My initial battery must include one .22. That's a no-brainer. They're easy to hit with, economical, and fun.

I'm comfortable parting with two treasured 9mms: a vintage Belgium Browning Hi Power and a Spanish Astra 600. Both are beautifully crafted, accurate sidearms. Their problem is caliber. For defending the hearth and paper punching, the .45 ACP gets the nod, hands down.

With deep regret, I can bid adieu to a fine trio of .357 Magnum revolvers, based solely on my preference for big bores. The 1930s-vintage, five-inch barrel Colt New Service is a classic example of American manufacturing excellence, as is an equally classic six-inch Colt Python, the most elegant, out-of-the-box-perfect handgun I own. The S&W four-inch, fixed-sight, heavy barrel Model 13 fits my mitt and balances best of all my sidearms (with the Colt Single Action Army and Hi Power very close seconds), but in the end the medium bores lose out to their big brothers.

My Mauser 1914 .32 automatic, purchased on a whim after reading about its effective use in the Elliot Tokson thriller *Desert Captive*, is wonderfully crafted and sports excellent fixed sights and a very good trigger. It would be a pocket pistol *par excellence* if it didn't reliably jam. This is too bad because – 3-1/2-inch barrel and all – it's amazingly precise at 25 paces. Still, it never would make the cut.

Likewise for a nickeled, single-shot, 7-inch barrel .22 Hopkins and Allen target pistol my grandparents potted tin cans with in the 1930s. With minicaps and CB and BB caps it excels in friendly basement shootouts, but if I'm going to achieve my goal there's no place for sentimentality or this peculiar, hair-triggered relic.

My second-generation Colt 1851 and 1860 cap and balls are sleek, straight shooting, and a lot of fun. In their day, either one could have been my ideal handgun. With easy-to-clean black powder substitute, I enjoy their company as much as any six-shooter I own. And no handgun points like the 1851 Navy. But in the end, if one is to choose their ideal sidearm for the 21st century, both of them silently slip to the sidelines.

It's a combat revolver extraordinaire, points like a charm, and perforates paper admirably, all in a most agreeable size/weight package.

My most recent acquisition, a 1942 vintage Walther P38, was purchased solely on impulse. It's a prime specimen of German technology and craftsmanship. It fits my hand like a glove. I take great pleasure in holding it and imagining the past life this stylish warhorse must have led. Sadly, the time for letting it go is at hand.

Now we're getting somewhere.

Somehow I own five 45 ACP semi-automatics: a 1930s vintage Colt, an Argentine Model 1927, its successor the Ballaster Molina, and two 1970 Series Colts. My nickeled, stag-gripped 70 Series with a Bar-Sto match barrel outperforms 'em all in accuracy and reliability with lead SWC handloads. It's the keeper of the lot.

Another prize is my 1916-vintage, naval-issue Webley Mark IV .45 ACP convert. It's a combat revolver extraordinaire, points like a charm, and perforates paper admirably, all in a most agreeable size/weight package. Still, it goes, only because I have other revolvers that do even better. This Brit is a sentimental favorite. I'd hate to part with it. Likewise, I must say goodbye to a 1930s-vintage Colt New Service .44 Special. It's accurate, superb in fit and finish, and does everything a handgun is called upon to do very nicely. It's

Standard Colt New Service chamberings in the United States include (left to right): 38 Special, .357 Magnum, .38-40 WCF, .44 S&W Special, .44-40 WCF, .45 ACP, and .45 Colt. Over its lifetime, the big revolver was chambered in 18 calibers, ranging from .38 Long and Short Colt to to .476 Eley.

a classic American revolver by every measure.

One sixgun that does everything with a little more authority than its peers is my 35-year-old S&W Model 29 .44 Magnum. Two decades ago I had its 6-1/2-inch tube docked to 5 inches, slapped on a set of smooth Herrett Jordan Trooper grips, and never looked back. It has power to spare, is more accurate than I can hold, and parked in a shoulder holster is my absolute field carry limit. With the Model 29, one has extreme flexibility in load selection to accommodate anything from perforating paper to discouraging large, hostile beasts. (Note: If I'm expecting a life-threatening experience, you can bet I won't intentionally make my stand with a handgun.) The .44 Smith makes the first cut.

The final handgun in my battery is a third generation, 4-1/2-inch-barrel Colt Single Action Army. This American classic does its brand proud in looks and performance. Whatever issues Colt purists have with Third Generation SAAs do not apply to this example. Its fit and finish are impeccable. With 255-grain flatpoint handloads at standard velocity, it shoots dead center and point-of-aim at 25 yards. Its trigger pull is just right and the fixed sights work very well for me. This Peacemaker has more than earned its set of genuine ivory grips.

Now we're down to the final four of this exercise: the Colt Woodsman, the Colt 1911A1, the S&W Model 29, and Colt SAA. At this point, each cut is just downright painful.

The first to go is the Woodsman. My personnel preference for big bores prevails. For many, particularly the casual handgunner, this pony is a perfect one and only.

As we're down to the final three, let's refocus our selection criteria from caliber to size, weight, and balance.

Now we're down to the final four of this exercise: the Colt Woodsman, the Colt 1911A1, the S&W Model 29, and Colt SAA. At this point, each cut is just downright painful.

The only knocks I have against the Model 29 are its size and 2 lb. 14 oz. heft. Still, if a magnum is on the agenda, who wants a lightweight .44? Not me. But then, are the .44 Magnum's power and bulk necessary for my regimen of informal paper punching, small game potting, and self defense? No. For that reason, in the most agonizing decision of this exercise, the Model 29 is expendable. If I lived in some wilderness outback where pistol power might carry the day in a pinch, or entertain the possibility of hunting Wisconsin whitetails, it would without debate be my one and only handgun. It's that good.

Now we're down to two Colts: powerful, accurate, and joys to hold and behold. In deciding which one to keep, the focus shifts back to caliber, not capacity or speed of reloading. If I had to rely on one caliber, now that I've eliminated the .44 Magnum/.44 Special tandem, would it be the .45 ACP or .45 Colt? It's a tough call.

After considerable soul-searching, the one handgun I'll carry until the last roundup will be the Colt Peacemaker. Surprised? So am I. Despite my deep affection for Old Hogleg, until this exercise I never considered it as a choice for my final compadre. Since its introduction more than 130 years ago and to this day, the SAA's combination of power, size, weight, and balance make it a solid, all-round contender for the one-gun pistolero. At this point in my life I really don't need magazine loading. If I can't rely on six big, fat .45 caliber slugs to accomplish the task, it's time to grab a 12 gauge or run like hell.

At my self-proclaimed handgun range limit of 35 yards (no disrespect to Elmer Keith), 255 grains of .45 diameter lead at 800-plus fps is all I need. The Single Action Army balances better than any big bore handgun I've ever curled fingers around. It's easy on the hand and hip, and consistently places slugs where I want them to go.

This very subjective exercise is based on personal needs and preferences. Twenty years ago, I suspect the final three probably would have been the same, had I owned a Peacemaker then. However, I'm almost certain my final selection would have been different.

I expect some readers will have issues with my selection methodology and final choice. So be it. Perhaps a good number of you are in a similar position and facing the same hard choices. Set your criteria, conduct your selection process, and let the cards fall as they may.

COLT'S PT. F. A. MFG CO HARTFORD CT U.S.A.
PAT'D AUG. 5, 1884 JUNE 5, 1900 JULY 4, 1905

Patent dates on the New Service's barrel indicate its nineteenth century origin.

REMINGTON Model 514 Routledge

BY STEVE GASH

My pal Bob French continually comes up with delectable guns that represent the concept of "One Good Gun" to a "T." A good example is a Remington Model 514 he recently acquired and then graciously loaned to me for this report.

The M514 is a single-shot .22 rimfire, but this one is unique because it is a two-diameter smoothbore designed especially for .22 shotshells. It is a specialized tool from a bygone era that merits our respect and attention.

To place the utility of the M514 in its proper historical context, think back to the days before the Federal Government took control over virtually every aspect of American life. Back then, individuals were responsible for their actions and free to solve their own problems. This was especially true with firearm ownership and use, and many neat firearms designed for specific purposes were developed. If the then-free citizen encountered a problem that could best be solved by a firearm, he just went down to the hardware store, bought one, and took it home.

This is the story of one of them.

Gun companies then, as now, were loath to spend more money than necessary on research and development, and, if a basic design could be used for several models, so much the better. In the late 1930s, Remington embarked on the development of a new line of bolt-action .22s, and the Model 500 series was born. The receivers were made from seamless drawn steel tubing instead of the more expensive forged steel, plus many parts were interchangeable. The 500 series continued through the 1950s and '60s, and eventually encompassed single-shots (M510) as well as repeaters, with box (M511) and tubular (M512) magazines. These rifles were dainty, but well made.

Citizens who had rats or other vermin to eradicate needed a close-range tool. In response, Remington introduced variants of the popular 500 series in smoothbore configurations for .22 shotshells, designated as the Models 510SB, 511SB, and 512SB. The Model 510 was even offered in the "Skeetrap" version.

The Model 514, as I've said, was a single-shot, bolt-action .22. It was a handy 41 inches long and weighed a svelte 4¼ pounds. The bolt handle was the locking lug, and pulling the trigger back with the bolt handle up allowed removal of the bolt. A rotating safety was situated at the back of the bolt, and the walnut stocks had no checkering.

he Remington Model 514 Routledge Bore
 a specialized version of the firm's popular
950s-era single-shot rifle and was designed
 shoot .22 shotshells for pest control.

Bore

Shotshells for the .22 have been around since at least 1892, when the ".22 Long Shot" cartridge was listed by Remintgon. Unfortunately, patterns of such shells from rifled bores were abysmal, and not much better from guns with full-length smoothbores.

Enter Fred Routledge. He decided it would be fun to shoot trap and skeet indoors, and designed small clay targets for that purpose. He experimented with various designs to see if patterns could be improved and eventually came up with a two-diameter bore in a

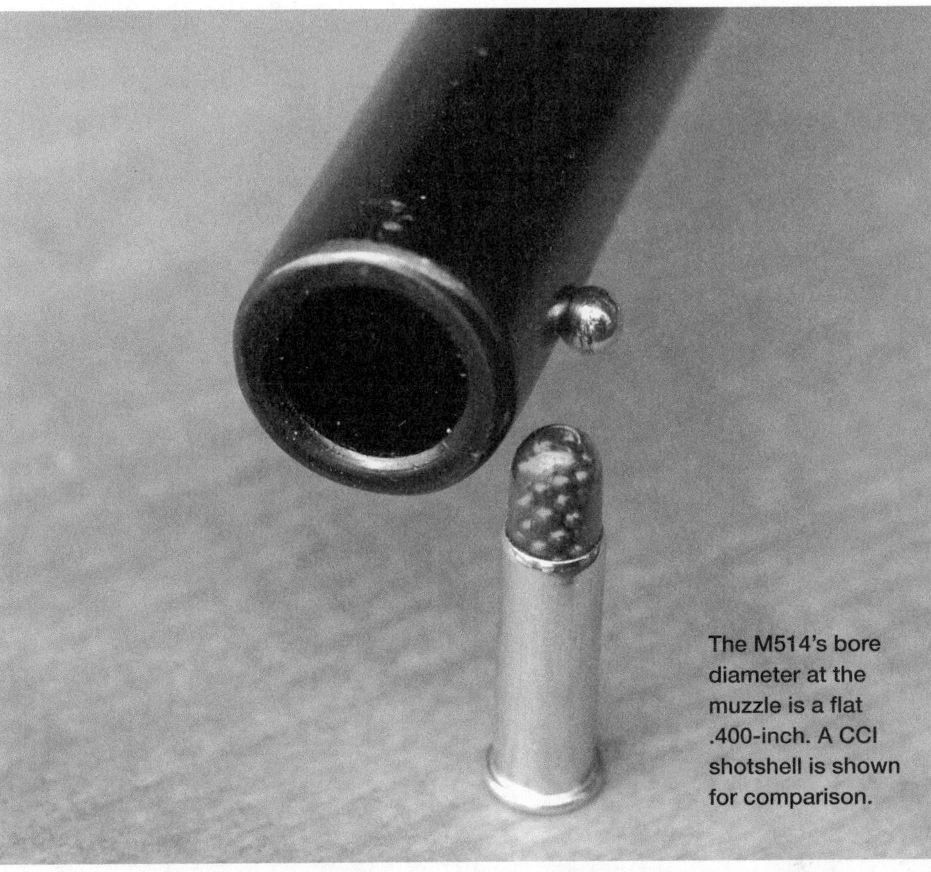

The M514's bore diameter at the muzzle is a flat .400-inch. A CCI shotshell is shown for comparison.

The Remington's Routledge Bore barrel barrel was clearly marked for use with .22 shotshells.

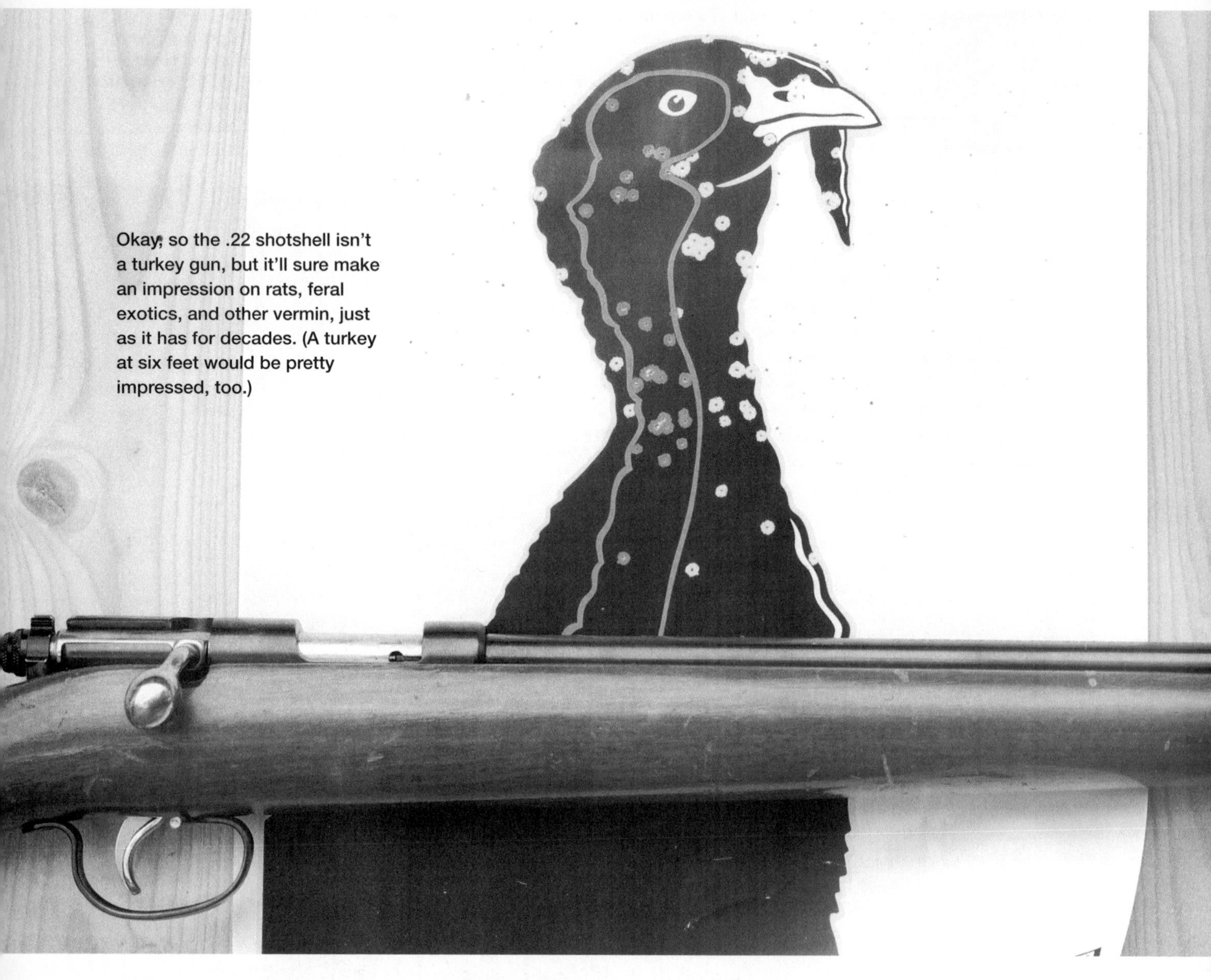

Okay, so the .22 shotshell isn't a turkey gun, but it'll sure make an impression on rats, feral exotics, and other vermin, just as it has for decades. (A turkey at six feet would be pretty impressed, too.)

24-inch barrel that featured a .223-inch section that opened up after 12 inches to .400 inches. The shell's fast-burning powder was spent by then, and this limited the scrubbing of the tiny pellets in the smaller portion of the barrel. Patterns were considerably improved, as much as 30 percent by some reports. In July, 1938, Remington engineers began evaluating Routledge's design, and shipments of the Model 121 (14-round tubular magazine) with the new Routledge Bore began in February 1939.

The single-shot Model 514 came later. Official company records show that, while 776,549 M-514s were produced from 1947 through 1971, the specialized Routledge Bore model was made from 1951 to 1969, with only 5,557 produced. The M514 Routledge Bore model had no rear sight, but sported a .147-inch bead front sight.

The .22 Long Rifle shot cartridge remains in production today by Winchester, Federal, and CCI. All use the tiny No. 12 (.050 inch) shot. Winchester's version is housed in a full-length brass case that is crimped at the end to hold in the shot. These shells also have an over-powder wad. The Winchester catalog lists neither a charge weight nor a velocity, but points out that it is "awesome pest control." The Federal shot charge is listed at 25 grains.

CCI's ammo contains the shot charge in a blue plastic capsule, much like the company's shot cartridges that have been so successful for centerfire handguns. CCI says that the load propels 31 grains of pellets at a velocity around 950 fps. I'll take their word for it, as chronographing such miniscule pellets is problematic.

Bob's M514 is in used, but not abused, condition. We surmise that it was some sort of a gallery gun, as it has odd letters stamped on the end of the pistol grip that are not of Remington origin. It has no serial number, but the Remington date code is PM, which translates to June 1965.

The patent number on the M514's barrel is 2,490,922, issued on December 13, 1949, to Peter B. Rutherford and Kenneth J. Lowe (then deceased) and assigned to Remington Arms. The patent was for a "safety mechanism for a firearm," and had nothing to do with the Routledge Bore. The M514's barrel is marked as follows, in two lines:

MODEL 514 ROUTLEDGE BORE FOR
.22 LONG RIFLE SHOT CARTRIDGE

This is exactly the way the M510 Routledge Bore models were marked. Since the M510 was discontinued in 1962, it is possible that the M514s were actually made with leftover M510 barrels that otherwise would have been scrapped (the latter of which the accounting department wouldn't have liked).

Guns are made to be shot, so I had to see for myself if this unique combination of gun and ammo indeed came together as a functional "problem solver" of the past—and, potentially, for the present. I had a good supply of Federal Champion Turkey Targets and some CCI shotshells, so I gave it a go. Every round went bang, and, at all ranges, the patterns were extremely uniform—but, after about 12 feet, they were thin enough to allow a small critter to slip through. A six to 10 feet, though, snakes, rats, and other pests would be in real jeopardy. Heck, at that range, I think it would kill a turkey.

The only hiccup was that, after several shots, the tip of the extractor broke off. Remington no longer supplies this part, but the Jack First Company, in Rapid City, South Dakota, mills precise replicas of this extractor. I had the replacement part in a jiffy, and eventually got it installed (I'm not good with mechanical things). After that, everything went swimmingly.

As I fired the M514, I pondered where this fine old gun had been, what it had seen, what problems it had solved for its owner. Vivid visions of its past uses in rural and urban life sprang forth at each report. Those days may be gone forever, but that doesn't diminish the nostalgic impact of the Model 514—nor the universal usefulness of One Good Gun.

Acknowledgements: Special thanks to Bob French for graciously loaning me the M-514 (yes, I returned it), and to Fred Supry, formerly of Remington, and Tom Nagle of Remington for supplying much historical, production, and other pertinent technical information.

INSTRUCTIONS FOR
OPERATION AND CARE

of the

Remington

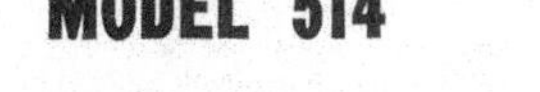

MODEL 514

BOLT ACTION RIFLE

IMPORTANT: *REMOVE GREASE FROM BORE OF BARREL BEFORE FIRING*

REMINGTON ARMS COMPANY, INC. Ilion, N.Y., U.S.A.

Form RD-5642 10-1-53

The owner's manual that came with the Model 514 was for the single-shot rifle, but served for the smoothbore version, as well. This original manual is dated "10-1-53."

.22 shot cartridges are virtually the same length and shape as regular .22 Long Rifle bulleted cartridges and function through pump- and bolt-action repeaters, as well as in single shots.

The Miniature WELLS EXPRESS

BY **HOLT BODINSON**

What's a classy rifle look like? It may be all in the eyes of the beholder, but I think rifles like the Mannlicher Schoenauer carbine, the Model 52 Winchester, the Rigby stalking rifle, and the Oberndorf Type A Mauser are all classy rifles that stand out from the pack because of their great lines and styling, balance, and handling qualities. These are rifles that are more than "form follows function." They're inspired designs, and I often wonder who it was that first put their hands to wood and metal and shaped and crafted the original prototypes. He had to be a craftsman whose taste and artistic abilities would be on the level of the most gifted custom gunsmith working today.

Having been a hunter all my life and having owned and used a number of those classy production rifles, I reached a

The author (right) and friend Gerald Stewart christened the new rifle on its first coyote hunt.

The small Sako action and Leupold Compact scope are perfectly scaled to the .223 Rem. cartridge.

It's a custom creation that any gunsmith would be proud to put his name on.

Tagging a Hill Country buck with the little rifle was a thrill.

The elegance and fine lines of the miniature Wells express rifle speak for themselves.

point in life where I realized I was doing a lot more small-game hunting than big-game hunting and enjoying it more because there was more of it to enjoy. Successful draws for in-state big-game tags were getting fewer and further in between. Out-of-state, non-resident tags had become financially crushing, as had trophy fees and guiding services throughout the world. No, it was to be coyote, fox, bobcat, and jack rabbit hunting around the old homestead or nothing.

All that was missing was a classy varmint/small game rifle.

Living in Tucson, Arizona, spoils you, when it comes to fine rifles built by leading custom gunsmiths. Years ago, names like Roy Dunlap and Harry Lawson dominated the trade. Today, it's artisans

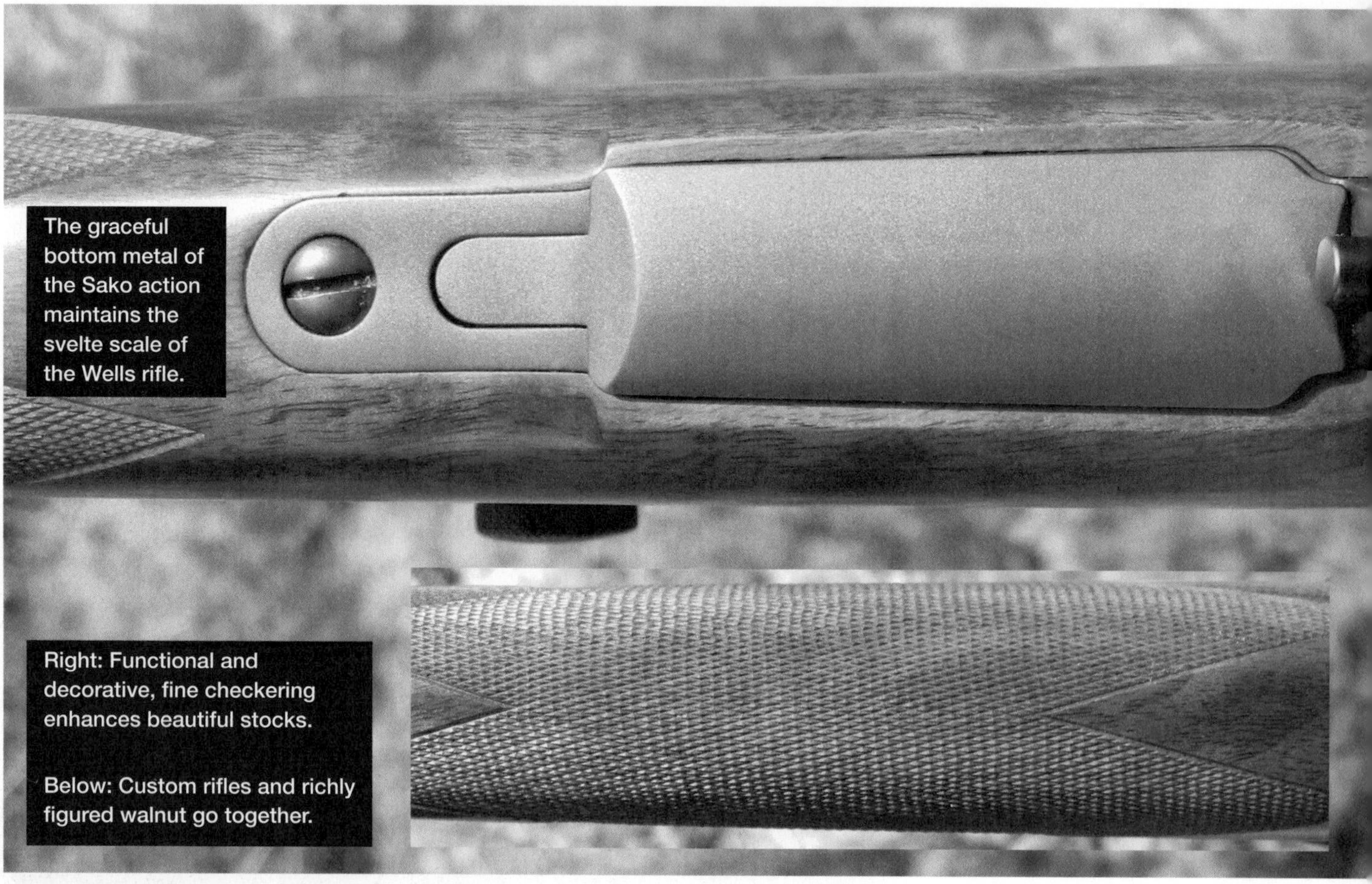

The graceful bottom metal of the Sako action maintains the svelte scale of the Wells rifle.

Right: Functional and decorative, fine checkering enhances beautiful stocks.

Below: Custom rifles and richly figured walnut go together.

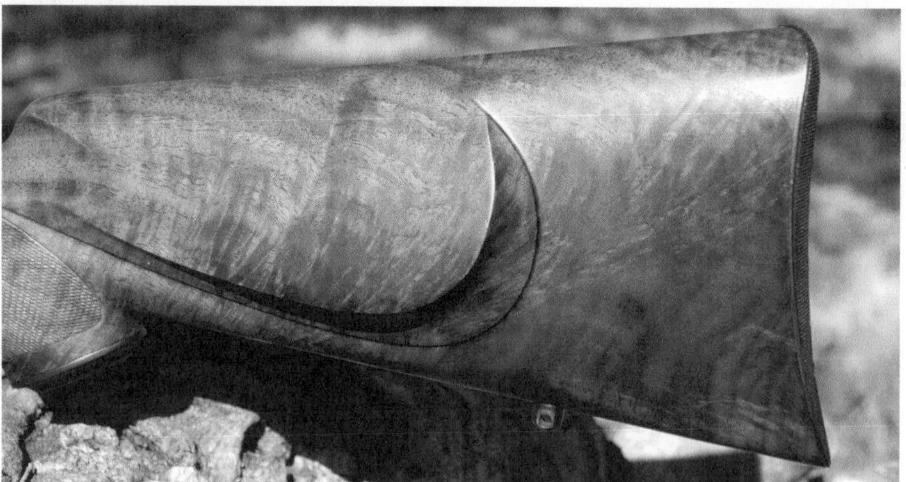

like Frank Wells, Patrick Holehan, and David Miller who command an international following. Every custom gunsmith has a certain style he brings to the final product. Frank Wells' guns have always struck me as being unusually sleek and nicely proportioned without any evidence of excess wood or metal, plus he's been a versatile gunsmith, building everything from refined target rifles to the largest caliber, dangerous game guns. I knew that I wanted Wells to build that special small-game rifle, but I didn't know exactly what I wanted.

Sitting down together, Wells and I began the task of translating my general thoughts and his specific recommendations into a custom design. The rifle would be chambered for the universally popular .223 Remington. To keep the rifle scaled to the size of that petite cartridge, it was agreed we would use the beautiful, miniature Sako action. The rifle would be stocked and checkered in the classic style, with a subtle "express rifle" appearance, using a highly figured blank of American walnut that I had been hauling around for 30 years. The fore-end would be finished off with an ebony tip.

Sights? The little Sako action was already dovetailed to accept Sako scope rings, but we decided you never know when those varmints might try to make a meal of you or if your scope might suddenly became inoperable, so we added a banded, hooded, ramped front sight, and a rear quarter rib carrying a two-leaf express sight. For a scope, we selected the scaled-down, Leupold 4X Compact.

Since we weren't concerned with recoil, we decided to use an elegant Neidner steel butt plate and a complementary Lenard Brownell steel grip cap. But, as a serious hunting rifle, it needed sling swivel bases, so to maintain its express rifle lines, it was decided to fit it with a barrel band swivel base. Wells also recommended a matte blue overall metal finish to eliminate any possible glare or flashing highlights in the field.

Upper Right: Simple and clean, the steel grip cap was designed by stockmaker Lenard Brownell.

Lower Right: A quarter rib, two-leaf sight, and banded front sight add to the "express" lines of the Wells rifle.

Gun artisans Frank Wells (left) and Patrick Holehan are two of Tucson's leading custom gunsmiths.

Having covered the essential details, Frank headed to his shop. What emerged a month later is the most treasured rifle I own. Its elegance and fine lines speak for themselves, and it has proved to be a sensational game getter in the field.

On its first hunt, I was joined by friend Gerald Stewart, at the time the president of Johnny Stewart Wildlife Calls. We were hunting coyotes in the foothills of the Rincon Mountains, just outside Tucson. I was shooting a handload in my new Wells rifle that consisted of 26.2 grains of Winchester 748 and a 52-grain Sierra hollowpoint. At 100 yards, the little rifle would slip that handload into a half-inch for five shots. We did a number on those prime coyotes, which were proving to be a real threat to the local Coues white-tailed deer population.

The next most memorable hunt came a few months later, in Texas, where the .223 Rem. is legal for deer hunting. It was an early, wet, misty morning, and I was sitting with my back against a tree overlooking a weedy field stretching between two woodlots. The little express rifle in my lap was loaded with Winchester's new, .223 Rem. deer load—a heavy jacketed 64-grain soft-point. I was getting wet, the rifle was getting wet, and I was just about to break off the hunt, when a beautiful little Texas Hill Country buck came charging across the opening. It was a classic, broadside running shot. The little buck somersaulted at the shot and lay still.

There have been many more memorable hunts with the little Wells rifle over the last 25 years, and it still is a guaranteed head-turner every time I uncase it. Hopefully, every serious hunter will have at least one opportunity in a lifetime to have a rifle built to fit them and to see their concept of the perfect rifle expressed in wood and steel. The result and the accompanying pride-of-ownership are worth every penny put into the effort.

The Ansc

hütz 1720
Heavy Barrel .22 Magnum

BY C. RODNEY JAMES

As the 22 WMR became more popular and ammunition companies began producing a greater variety of loadings while steadily improving WMR accuracy, this cartridge became more attractive to shooters. The first WMR rifle I owned was an HK M-300 autoloader, which I picked up used at a gun show in 1989. The gun proved to be an excellent shooter (for an autoloader) delivering 1½-inch groups at 100 yards with some of the best shooting ammunition. Additionally, hollowpoints and other expanding bullets proved very effective on chucks to this range.

This got me thinking about finding a true "tack driver" in this caliber. For my writings about ammunition analysis, I try to bracket things, in terms of performance, by testing in a bolt-action target rifle and an accurate and reliable, out-of-the-box autoloader. This provides data on function, as well as accuracy for both. I have taken to referring to these as "benchmark" rifles to add to my personal collection. By benchmark, I mean the best out-of-the-box rifles capable of drawing the best potential accuracy of all the currently available ammunition and that to come. To go to a custom rifle of some sort, I feel, isn't quite fair to the reader, nearly all of whom are going to acquire factory rifles of one sort or another. But my problem with the WMR round was finding a target-grade rifle chambered for it. Remington offered their M-40X rimfire in WMR. This would have filled the bill, but I already owned a M-40X centerfire rifle. With scope and sling, it weighed something over 14 pounds. After a few trips to the field, this one became a permanent bench gun. Plus, the rimfire version was a drop-in single-loader. I needed magazines I could load, and I wanted a rifle that could be comfortably carried into the field.

I tried a CZ with fair results, but the accuracy I sought simply wasn't there. Ruger made a varmint WMR, the M77, with a medium-weight barrel. It turned in a few excellent groups (the best one .9-inch at 150 yards), with one type of ammunition, and close to that with one other. Unfortunately, several other types of ammunition shot very poorly. I replaced the barrel and got excellent results with two types of WMR that, oddly enough, were not the same rounds I'd gotten the best groups with through the original barrel. And everything else was mediocre to poor. This rifle would have been fine if all I needed was a good varmint gun and could simply stick to the best-shooting loadings.

For a while, I had hoped Kimber would produce a WMR rifle, but so far it hasn't. With an eye to accuracy, but also to finding a light enough rifle for field use, I investigated Anschütz. Its target rifles were winning competitions over the world, so it was apparent the company knew about making rifles for accurate shooting. In sorting through catalog materials, I found the rifle I was looking for—the 1720 Heavy Barrel. It featured the M-54 action and a target trigger. It came with a European Walnut stock and a 23½-inch barrel that measures .8-inch in diameter at the muzzle.

I don't know about the experiences of others, but getting the exact gun I want always seems to involve stress, complications and difficulties. The 1720 HB was no exception. None of my local gun stores carried rifles of this sort, so I called the distributor . The distributor informed me the rifle was no longer in production in .22 WMR, but, if I wanted a .17 HMR, no problem. There was an M-1516 DKL in .22 WMR, but it had a shorter, lighter barrel, making it a sporting rifle.

This was in 2004. At the NRA convention that year, I approached Dieter Anschütz to plead my case. Dieter looked a bit stern, as he listened. Perhaps the tear that ran down my cheek helped. He informed me that there were, exactly, four 1720 HB rifles in the warehouse in Hamburg. Our discussion was overheard by Carl Joose, owner of Champion's Shooter Supply in New Albany, Ohio, and a mere 50 miles from my home. Champion's catered to the target shooting trade, and it turned out Carl was an old buddy of Dieter's. It took about six weeks, but at last I held the object of my desire.

I have tried about every WMR loading (except shot cartridges) in the 1750 and have no regrets. In terms of accuracy, I feel this rifle is capable of delivering the best from all the ammunition I have put through it. Comparatively speaking, its accuracy equals my M-52C bull-barrel Winchester .22 LR match rifle using hunting ammunition.

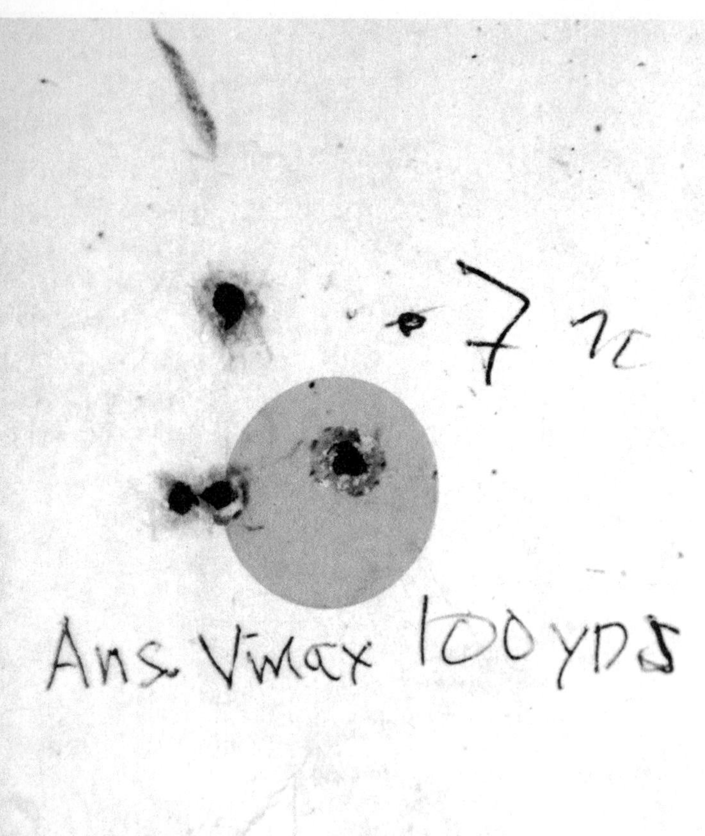

At nine pounds, 11 ounces with sling and a Burris 12X scope, it's a comfortable rifle to carry afield. I've taken chucks at more than 130 yards. The most accurate ammunition through it is the 30-grain V-max made by CCI. The Winchester 45-grain copper-plated lead bullet, the Dynapoint, in three, five-shot groups, averaged under an inch at 100 yards. With these two loadings, five-shot groups average around two inches at 150 yards (under good conditions). I expect to take some more chucks at that range, which I consider about the limit for a rimfire gun. Maybe, one of these days, someone will produce a 22 WMR round capable of match-target accuracy. If so I'll be at the head of the line to get some.

My Anschütz 1720 is the ideal balance between a sporter and a target rifle. The weight is toward the muzzle, which I like. The hold is solid, the trigger is smooth, and the magazines feed flawlessly. What's not to like? I guess my only complaint (more of a whine) is that the magazines hold only four rounds—a bit of a pain, when I want to focus on five-shot groups. Maybe a good—emphasis on "good"— after-market magazine will come along with greater capacity. There was one once produced. I tried it, and it was a dud, failing to feed a single cartridge. The elusive five-shot magazine being all that I wish for, in summation, the Anschütz 1720 HB is the most reliable, comfortable, best-shooting 22 WMR I have yet to encounter. It is indeed my "benchmark" WMR.

By my count, this Czech/German/Yugoslav/American battle rifle/plinker/hunting rifle is on its fourth life. I'd love to be around if my one good gun ever reaches number five, but that seems unlikely. It's a burden someone else down the line will have to bear.

MARLIN'S MODEL 62 LEVERMATIC AND THE .256 WINCHESTER MAGNUM

Too Late or Too Soon?

The Marlin Model 62 Levermatic. About 8,000 rifles were produced in its original chambering of .256 Winchester Magnum.

BY **TERRY WIELAND**

In late March, 1961, Winchester and Remington took a step that was strange, to say the least. The two companies each announced a new cartridge, billed as a combination rifle/handgun round and based on the .357 Magnum case, necked down.

The cartridges were .22 Jet, from Remington, and the .256 Winchester Magnum. But, though both companies had firearm divisions, neither one adopted its new round in a rifle. The cartridges were unveiled, shown the door, and left to make their way in the world. They were orphans virtually from birth.

For a year, they wandered the roads of Gun Valley until Smith & Wesson, Ruger, and Marlin all decided they had possibilities. S&W produced a new double-action revolver, the Model 53, chambered for the .22 Jet, while Ruger designed the single-shot Hawkeye for the .256 Winchester. Marlin liked both cartridges and had just the rifle for them. Modifying a version of its .22 caliber Model 57M, the new Marlin centerfire rifle was dubbed the Model 62 Levermatic.

These announcements were greeted with considerable fanfare. The S&W Model 53 "Dual Caliber Magnum" graced the cover of the 1962 Gun Digest and was billed as "The most exciting handgun news of the year," with a report inside by Kent Bellah. Bob Wallack and Ken Waters received rifles from Marlin for testing, and articles appeared in back-to-back issues of Gun Digest (1963 and 1964), discussing rifles, cartridges, and handloads.

That was the high-water mark for all concerned.

Ruger produced only 3,300 Hawkeyes from 1963 to '64 and called it a day. S&W kept the Model 53 in production until 1974, but it was nagged by problems. Ironically, the Model 53 was also slated for production in .256 Winchester, but it never came to pass.

The Marlin Mode 62 Levermatic and Ruger Hawkeye single-shot handgun were the only firearms produced in .256 Winchester Magnum, a fine small-game cartridge that deserved a better fate.

The short-throw Levermatic is a solid, well-made rifle. C-H still makes forming dies for .256 Winchester Magnum, which is easily fashioned from readily available and inexpensive .357 Magnum brass.

At Marlin, the reverse occurred. Although the Levermatic was formally announced in .22 Jet, only one is known for certain to exist—the one Wallack and Waters tested. The combination was never produced commercially. The Levermatic did go into production in .256 Winchester, however, and between 1963 and 1969, Marlin made about 8,000. In 1966, it added a .30 Carbine version and produced 8,000 more in that caliber before the Levermatic was dropped completely in 1971. Overall, it was not a triumph for Marlin. Nor for Ruger, Remington, Winchester, or Smith & Wesson.

In retrospect, it's easy to pick holes in both the concept and the execution. Up against high flyers like the .222, the .22 Jet was both a failure as a varmint round and a nagging problem as a revolver cartridge. No rifle was ever chambered for it.

The .256 Winchester had potential as a small-game cartridge along the lines of the .25-20, but such cartridges were heavily out of favor in the velocity-mad '60s. Who wanted a flat-nosed, 60-grain bullet strolling along at 2800 fps when a .220 Swift delivered 4010 fps with a 48-grain spitzer?

The .256 fared no better in the Ruger Hawkeye. The gun itself was an oddball, and firing a shot was ear-splitting. The Hawkeye was built on the Blackhawk frame and resembled a long-barreled single-action revolver, but, instead of a cylinder, it had a hinged breechblock. Ruger's limited production run had one notable result: the Hawkeye eventually became the most highly prized collector's item in the Ruger line.

In retrospect, the two cartridges—and certainly the Levermatic rifle—deserved better.

The Model 62 was the last iteration of an innovative design that began in 1956, with the .22 LR Model 56 Levermatic. The Levermatic principle was based on a patent that originally belonged to the Kessler firearms company and used for that company's "Lever-Matic" shotgun. After Kessler's demise, Marlin made a deal with the patent holders to develop a line of small rifles.

The "short-stroke lever" used a cam-and-roller accelerator system that reduced overall lever movement to just 25 degrees (two inches at its farthest point), compared to six inches or more for a conventional lever rifle. According to the catalog, the lever could be operated simply by flexing one's fingers.

Outwardly, it resembled not the western-style lever-actions for which Marlin was famous, but the more modern Savage 99 or Winchester 88. It was stocked in American walnut, with round, graceful lines and none of the garish features that make many rifles from the 1960s look as dated as Beatle boots.

With its internal hammer and side ejection, the Levermatic allowed low scope mounting. The stock was a rigid one-piece walnut, promoting greater ac-

Stages of production of .256 Winchester Magnum brass from its parent cartridge, the .357 Magnum.

The .256 Winchester Magnum was originally offered with a 60-grain flat-nosed bullet, but later it was variously produced in spitzer, hollowpoint, and round-nosed configurations.

curacy than a two-piece. When the lever was closed, the rear of the breechblock tipped up, locking into position in the frame, like the Savage 99. And, as on the early Savage, the safety was a sliding latch behind the trigger.

Marlin envisioned the Levermatic pioneering a new style of lever rifle and produced five distinct variations—the 56, 56DL, 57, 57M, and 62—each named for the year of introduction. The Levermatic progressed through the .22 rimfires to include the .22 WMR. Some had clip magazines, others tubular; some were aluminum receivers, others steel; in some, the receiver was rounded, others it was squared off. Over a 15-year period, Marlin produced a total of about 150,000 Levermatics of all types.

When the .22 Jet and .256 Winchester arrived on the scene, Marlin saw an opportunity to expand into centerfires. The first announcement said the Model 62 would be offered in .357 Magnum, as well as its two offspring, but only the .256 ever materialized.

In operation, the Levermatic is fun to use and certainly accurate enough for its cartridge out to 200 yards. Wallack, testing the rifle in its final form with 1:14 twist, achieved five-shot groups of one to two inches at 100 yards with factory ammunition. Ed Yard and C.H. Helbig, writing in Gun Digest a year later, reported handload groups under an inch, and Winchester engineers obtained three-inch 10-shot groups at 200 yards from a standard Levermatic and factory ammunition.

So what went wrong?

Marlin certainly made an effort to produce a good rifle, fine-tuning the mechanics such as barrel length, rate of twist, and magazine and stock design. Marlin's Micro-Groove rifling was noted for its accuracy, and the 24-inch barrel utilized all the cartridge's potential. The result felt like a real rifle, not something for the kids' market.

The writers who reviewed the Levermatic and its cartridges were serious, knowledgeable riflemen, highly respected and not given to gushing over new products. All of them were enthusiastic about the cartridges and, particularly, the rifle.

The problem was, the Levermatic was neither fish nor fowl. It was too much money for a teenager's small-game rifle, yet had neither the pinpoint accuracy nor the blazing velocity demanded by varmint hunters, who were in love with the .222 Remington, the .22-250, and the .220 Swift. And a rimmed cartridge in a lever rifle? Please. This was 1962.

Having said all that, however, the .256 Winchester Magnum is a neat little cartridge with serious possibilities. The only factory loading was a 60-grain flat-nose, and, later, a round-nose, but there was always a wide variety of .257 bullets available for handloading. There were jacketed 60-, 75-, and 87-grain .257s, all of which worked well. Unfortunately, there were limitations on overall cartridge length, so anything heavier ran out the powder capacity. In cast bullets, there was a wide variety of moulds available. The possibilities were almost endless. For small game at lower velocities, one could hardly have asked for better. It was gentle, quiet, and accurate enough for squirrels, possums, and the whole range of small game, both edible and pestilential.

Today, both rifle and cartridge are almost forgotten. In 1990, Winchester stopped making .256 brass, so not only is it now strictly a handloading proposition, Levermatic owners even have to make their own brass by necking down .357 Magnum, if they can't find ready-made .256 metal from custom brass makers. Fortunately, C-H still makes sizing dies, and the resizing operation is painless.

A few rifles trickle onto the market, usually offered by shooters who don't handload. They don't command a high price. For rifle lovers who do handload, however, the .256 Winchester Magnum can be loaded to a level where it's a nice medium-game round for those who like to stalk in close and place their bullets precisely. At least one western Levermatic lover uses his for pronghorns.

In some ways, the Model 62 Levermatic came along a few years too late. The era of the lever rifle was passing, as was interest in traditional small-game hunting. But, in view of the popularity later achieved by rifles like Ruger's Mini-14 in 7.62x39 and various rifles in .30 Carbine, the Levermatic may have just been a few years too early.

For those lucky enough to find one, it still offers all the pleasures of a nice rifle and a friendly cartridge, made the way Americans used to make them.

TEST FIRE CZ Ringneck 16-gauge

BY Steve Gash

The Anson & Deeley action opens easily for the insertion or removal of shells. Note the cross-bolt, which is also engraved on its end.

The grand old 16-gauge and the shotguns that shoot it represent one of those classic combinations that just refuse to die. The 16 seems to stage a periodic resurgence every few years, and we seem to be experiencing one these days. This is good, as the old has much to offer in the new.

The 16-gauge has been produced in numerous pump and semi-auto shotguns over the years, as well as the occasional over/under. But the classically configured 16 continues to be the side-by-side. While there are a host of fine old 16-gauge guns out there begging for attention, every now and again an innovative new model with classic lines appears. A great example is the Ringneck from CZ-USA, and it's a doozy.

The Ringneck is but one of a slew of shotguns made for CZ in Huglu, Turkey, a city of about 3,500 on the slopes of the Taurus Mountains, at the southern edge of the Anatolian Plateau. Huglu, the company, is no flash-in-the-pan operation. Two master gunsmiths started their first workshop there, in 1914, and later organized a cooperative right after World War I. Today, the firm employs more than 600 craftsmen and another 500 workers. This modern factory, with over 107,000 square feet, turns out about 65,000 high-quality guns a year of all action types, and about 15 percent are side-by-sides.

We've all seen Turkish guns that were nothing short of dreadful. The Ringneck is not one of them. While Huglu has much modern CNC machinery, the majority of the work on these premium firearms is still done by hand, and it shows. The metal work is top drawer, as is the fit and finishing of the wood.

The Ringneck is available in five bore sizes, 12, 16, 20, and 28-gauges, and the .410-bore. Significantly, each is made on its own proportionally sized frame. This is particularly important for the in-between gauges, the 16 and 28. There is none of that sticking a pair of 16-gauge barrels on a 12-gauge frame or 28-gauge barrels on a 20 and calling it good.

Overall, the Ringneck simply exudes restrained elegance. The action is a sleek boxlock, with nicely done false sideplates that are tastefully color case hardened to shimmering purple, bronze, and blue hues. The sideplates are adorned with hand engraving that really highlights the colors, and the screws are perfectly aligned. The action is based on the time-honored Anson & Deeley, and it locks up with double Purdey underlugs and a cross-bolt at the top.

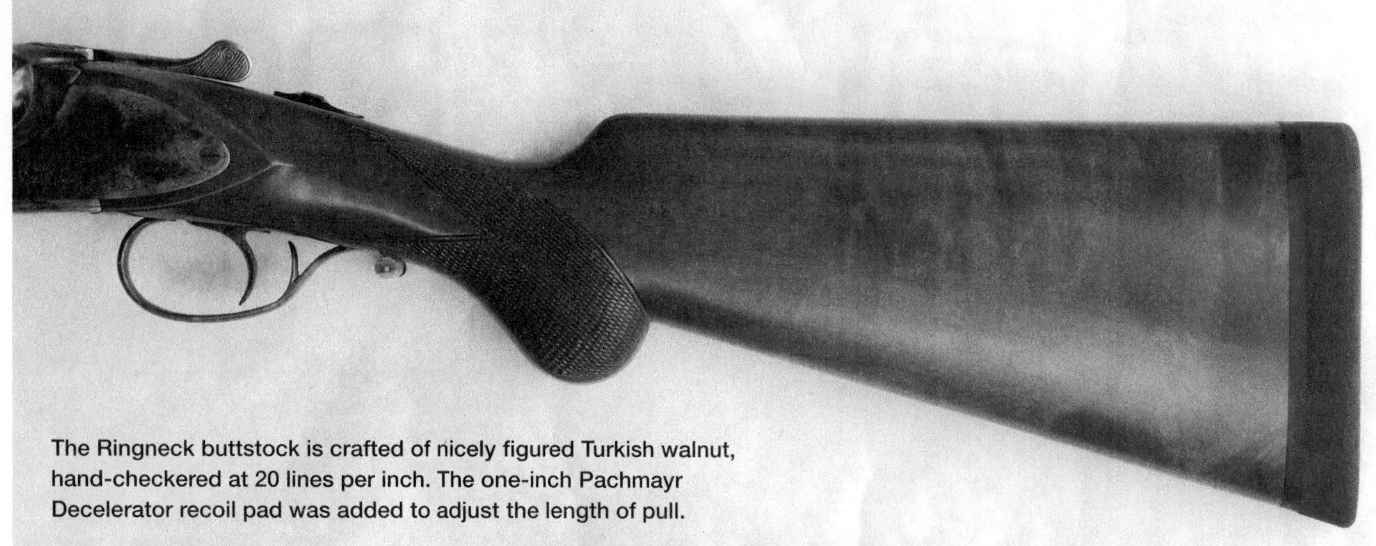

The Ringneck buttstock is crafted of nicely figured Turkish walnut, hand-checkered at 20 lines per inch. The one-inch Pachmayr Decelerator recoil pad was added to adjust the length of pull.

The single trigger fires either barrel, and the selector is on the non-automatic tang safety. The trigger is mechanical, so if the first barrel is empty or there's a dud shell, just pull the trigger again. If the other barrel is loaded, it'll go bang. There are no ejectors, just a robust extractor that lifts both shells, fired or not, for inspection or removal. Thus, we handloaders do not have to look for our empties in the weeds.

The barrels are assembled in a monoblock, but where the barrels and block meet is cleverly camouflaged by a series of little engraved rings that encircle the joint. The Ringneck's barrels are chrome lined, which makes them resistant to wear and easier to clean. Even after firing a heap of shells, these slick bores were a snap to scrub.

Ringnecks in 12, 20, and 28-gauge come with five choke tubes, but the 16-gauge and .410-bore models have fixed improved cylinder (right) and modified (left) chokes. If this is any great disadvantage, I have so far not discovered it. Plus, it's hard to lose or misplace choke.

The stock and forearm are made of nicely figured Turkish walnut, are hand checkered at 20 lines per inch, and beautifully finished to an ultra-smooth satin. The semi-beavertail fore-end sports a very slight schnabel at its end and attaches to the barrels with the elegant Deeley latch. The buttstock has a very nice Prince of Wales pistol grip and terminates in an attractive, but thin and relatively ineffective, recoil pad that has a slick, hard heel.

That leads me to one of only two small nits to pick on the entire gun. The

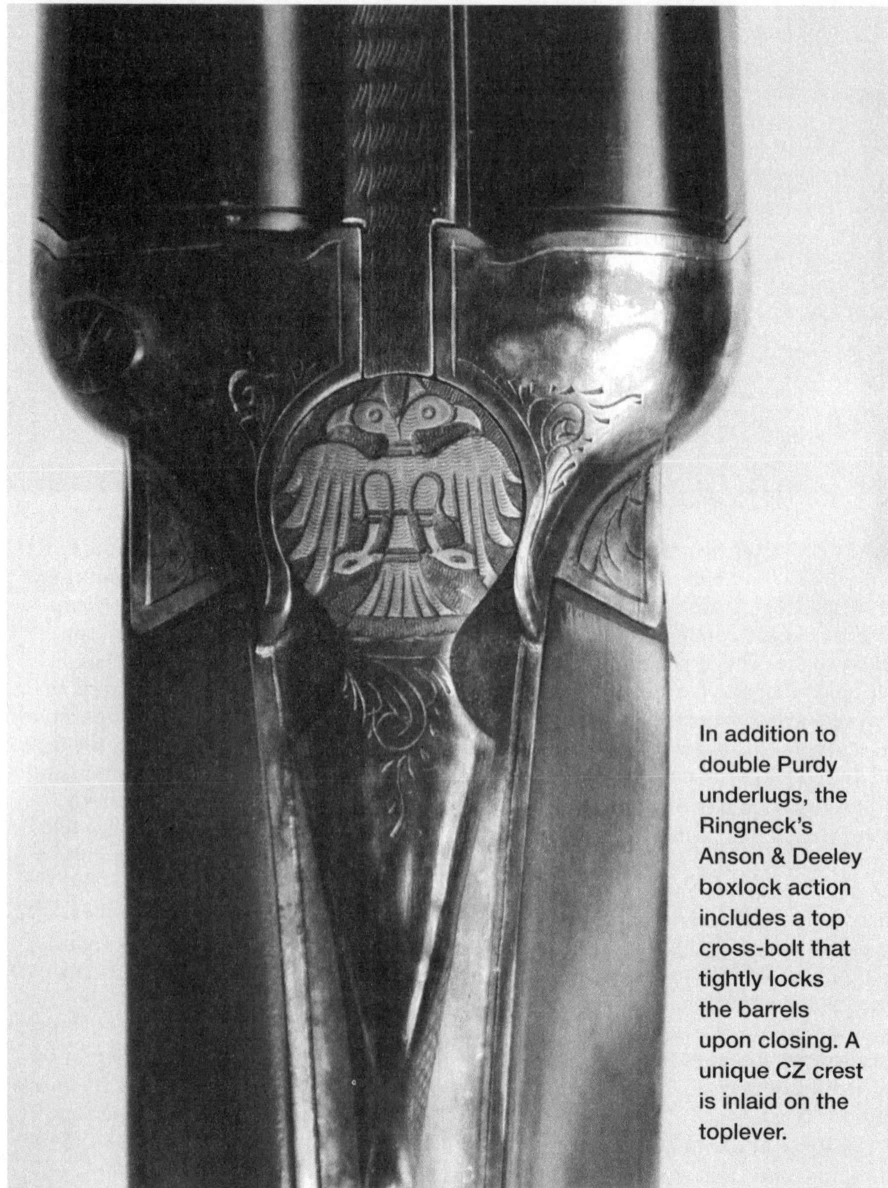

In addition to double Purdy underlugs, the Ringneck's Anson & Deeley boxlock action includes a top cross-bolt that tightly locks the barrels upon closing. A unique CZ crest is inlaid on the toplever.

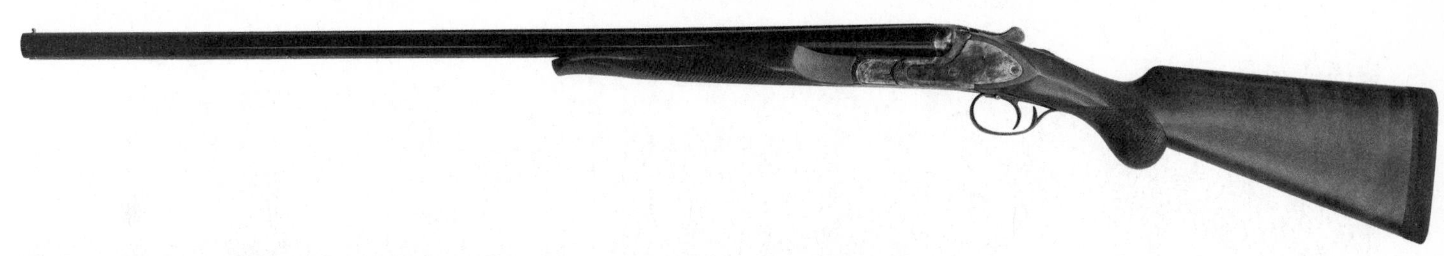

Above: The CZ Ringneck recreates the classic configuration of side-by-side doubles and offers the shooter elegant beauty and performance at a moderate price.

Left: The tang safety is not automatic and contains the barrel selector.

Below: CZ's logo, name, and its headquarters location in Kansas City, Kansas, adorn the right barrel.

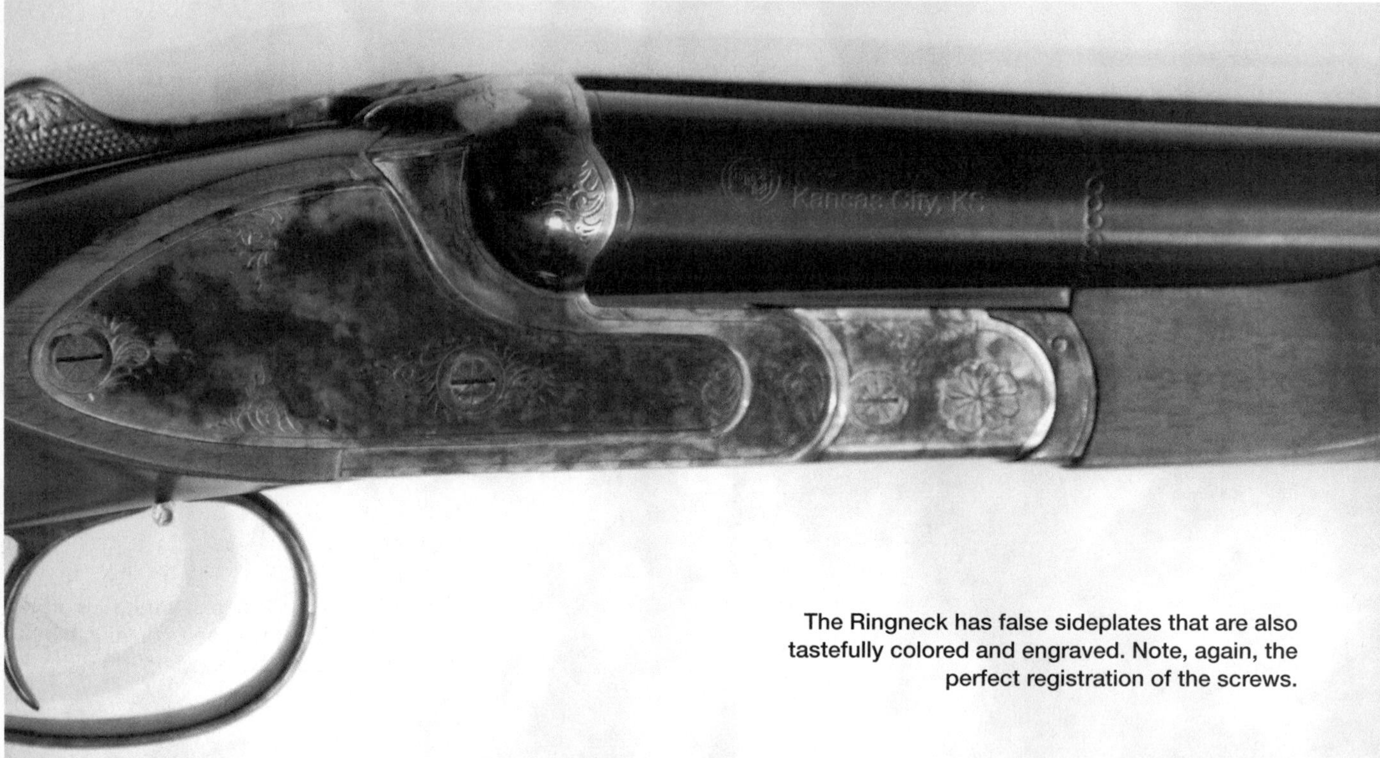

The Ringneck has false sideplates that are also tastefully colored and engraved. Note, again, the perfect registration of the screws.

Specifications: CZ Ringneck	
Gauge:	16 (tested), 12, 20, and 28-gauges and .410-bore.
Action type	Break-action, side-by-side double barrel boxlock, with false sideplates
Barrel length	28 inches, raised solid rib, brass bead front sight, 2¾-inch chambers
Chokes	Fixed, Improved Cylinder (right barrel) and Modified (left barrel)
Overall length	45¼ inches
Weight	7 pounds 13 ounces
Trigger	Single selective, pull weights 5 pounds
Safety	Tang-mounted, non-automatic, with barrel selector
Stock	Turkish walnut, hand-checkered 20 lines per inch
Stock dimensions	Length of pull 14½ inches; drop at comb 1½ inches; drop at heel 2¼ inches
Finish	Barrels blue-black chrome; receiver color case hardened with scroll engraving; stock semi-gloss polyurethane
MSRP	$1,179
Manufacturer	Huglu, located in Huglu, Turkey
Importer	CZ-USA, www.cz-usa.com

length of pull was a bit long for me at a hair over 14½ inches, so I took this opportunity to install a cushy Pachmayr Decelerator recoil pad and reduce the LOP to 14¼ inches to better fit me. Also, the extractor was very hard to move in and out, and this in turn made the gun a little difficult to open and close. The extractor is held in by one screw, so I removed it and filed and stoned the extractor here and there until it moved freely in its recess, and now all's right with the world.

The 16-gauge cartridge dates from at least the 1880s, and was extremely popular back in the day. Many considered it the perfect all around gun, as its bore diameter of .662-inch and frame size was smack dab between the 12 and 20 gauges. Many 16-gauge shotguns were used in the uplands, and the ammo produced reflected that popularity.

The 16 was originally loaded in cases that were $2\frac{9}{16}$ inches in length, both in the U.S. and on the Continent, and, while this length is still loaded in Europe, in 1929, S.A.A.M.I. standardized the U.S. length at 2¾ inches. Today, all 16-gauge ammo is that length, the same as most 12 and 20-gauge and all 28-gauge loads.

The 16-gauge soldiers on, and, today, virtually every U.S. manufacturer pro-

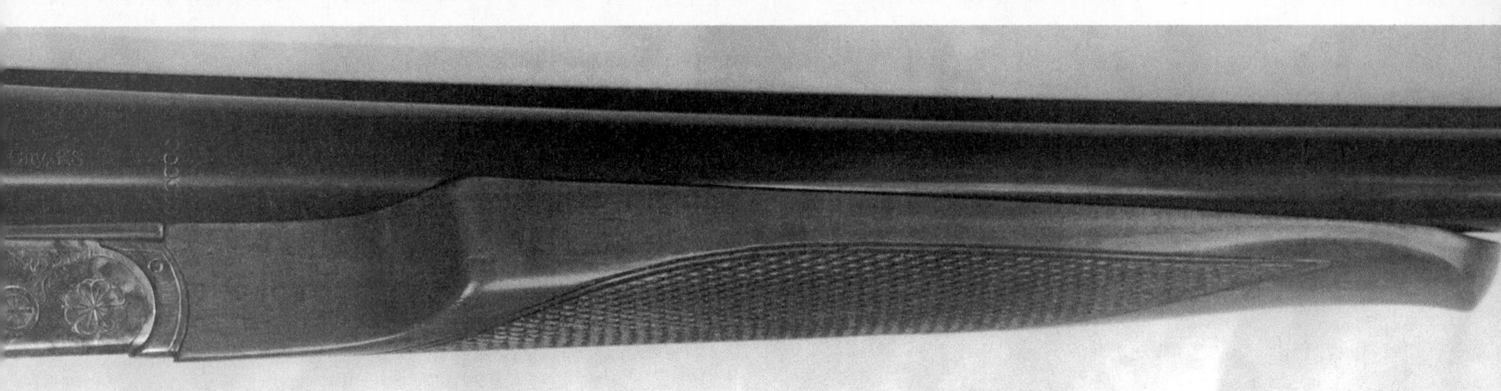

The trim, semi-beavertail fore-end carries an ample amount of 20 lines-per-inch checkering. Its shape is hand filling and comfortable to use without being bulky.

The entire receiver is beautifully case color hardened and embellished with light scroll engraving. Note the perfect timing of the screws.

The Ringneck's semi-beavertail fore-end is also nicely checkered, is attached with a Deeley latch, and terminates with a tasteful schnabel.

duces a terrific array of 16-gauge factory loads, including steel shot and other non-toxic varieties. Never mind that there are 20-gauge loads that duplicate virtually anything available in the 16-gauge, from one to 1¼-ounce shot charges, plus the 20's ¾ and ⅞-ounce loads.

Since I happen to own two other 16s, I had a representative cross-section of ammo on hand for testing in the CZ Ringneck, so I ran seven factory loads and five of my favorite handloads over the chronograph (the results are shown in the accompanying chart).

You will note that the "listed" and measured velocities are sometimes considerably different. This is a very common in shotshells, not only because the chronograph systems we use are vastly different than those used by the ammo factories, but also due to inherent variations in the ammo, as evidenced by the large differences in standard deviations of these factory loads. Nonetheless, chronographing allows us to compare shells and pick the handload that duplicates our favorite factory load. It's an apples-to-apples thing.

Use and gun weight will, in large part, determine what load should be used in one's 16-gauge. The one-ounce loads offer a good balance between pattern density and low recoil. The 1⅛-ounce

A day afield with a classic 16-gauge side-by-side is a refreshing step back to a less complicated age.

loads are the traditional field load for the gauge and are offered in a wide variety of shot sizes and velocities, most of which are easy to duplicate with handloads. While a "magnum" load with 1¼ ounces of shot is offered, and I had some, I saw no reason to ruin a perfectly good day by shooting them, as their recoil takes the 16-gauge out of the fun-to-shoot category in a hurry.

I generally avoid traditional pattern testing like root canals and lutefisk, so a pal and I took turns shooting at clay targets thrown from a hand trap. For ammo, we used factory one-ounce and 1⅛-ounce loads from Winchester and Remington, and some of my special ultra-light loads with ¾ and ⅞-ounce of No. 8s. The 16-gauge is not fastidious as to diet, and the ¾-ounce loads were pure delight. They were mild of voice, had little flinch-inducing recoil, and broke targets convincingly. The ⅞-ounce is almost as mild and is a great dove or skeet load.

On clay birds, the improved cylinder barrel was downright deadly at just about any range within 35 yards. With the tighter modified barrel, you had to center a clay pigeon at 25 yards to hit it, but, when you did, it really powdered 'em, and it broke birds out to about as far as I could lead them. All in all, the Ringneck was a delight to use.

The CZ Ringneck offers a lot of class and fine features for the money. Anyone looking for an elegant European side-by-side that doesn't break the bank would do well to give the CZ Ringneck a close look. Best of all, this high-quality double is available in all bore sizes, so the fine-gun aficionado can pick and choose to suit his needs. It's a win-win situation for all.

TEST FIRE

BY C. Rodney James

NEW LOADS for the .410

Back in 1987, I wrote a piece for the *11th Edition of Handloader's Digest* called "Handloading the .410 for Defense." At that time, the .410 was considered little more than a close-range squirrel and pest gun. The available ammunition consisted of shot loads no larger than No. 4s and "deer" slugs weighing 93 to 97 grains. Not so good. Experimental buckshot loads, six 00 Buck pellets in the three-inch shell, produced some rather remarkable (at least to me) results, grouping within a 12-inch circle at 20 yards and having penetration virtually equal (in pine boards) to 00 buck police loads from a 12-gauge riot gun.

About that time, Mossberg was marketing its Model 500 in a security version that wore an 18½-inch barrel and had a magazine holding six to eight shells. In Italy, Luigi Franchi was developing special-purpose automatic shotguns (SPAS) for police and military use. The Uzi-size SPAS 410 featured a 10- to 12-round box magazine capable of semi- and full-automatic fire, with a five-pellet discarding sabot.

Jump ahead 25 years, and we have an influx of revolvers and a revolver rifle capable of handling the .45 Long Colt and the .410 shotshell. Suddenly, ammunition companies are producing all sorts of "improved" loads for self-defense or pest and varmint control. Shotshell ballistics in short-barreled .410 handguns are in the handgun range for velocities, but, as expected, these perform far better in longer barrels, holding tighter patterns for longer distances.

BUCKSHOT LOADS

A decade ago, a three-ball load was produced for the American Derringer Company for its .45 LC/.410 pistol, and that was it. Currently, multi-ball loads are available from Winchester, Remington, Federal, Barnaul in Russia (Golden Bear, Silver Bear), and Sellier & Bellot in the Czech Republic. Remington and Federal offer 000 Buck (five pellets) and No. 4 Buck (nine pellets) loads, while the remainder feature five-pellet 00 Buck in a three-inch shell. These in a cylinder barrel all group in or very near to a 12-inch pattern at 20 yards, which makes them an excellent choice for defensive use. The Federal and Remington No. 4 group easily inside 12 inches, with an occasional flier out to about 17 inches.

Winchester's product is by far the most interesting and innovative. The Winchester defense load is a new wrinkle on the old Buck and ball loadings that predate the Civil War. The Supreme Elite is a 2½-inch shell with three, .427-inch in diameter by .217-inch in thickness copper-plated cylinders, each weighing about 70 grains, the same as a 000 Buck pellet. Behind these are a dozen copper-plated lead BB shot pellets. The three-inch PDX1 Defender contains four cylinders and 16 BBs. Winchester's Brad Criner told me these would group close enough for woodchuck shooting at ranges to about 30 feet. Skepticism turned to astonishment, when I shot these.

The cylinder-bore Model 42 Winchester shot pretty much like a rifle. At seven yards, everything was contained in a spread of 3½ inches There were two distinct holes, one with a scalloped edge and a separation of 1.6 inches. The latter was made by the shotcup holding a number of BBs still in it. At 20 yards, the BBs had spread to 18½ inches, but the load was still together and punching one hole. At 25 yards, the BB spread stayed in a roughly eight-inch group, while the cylinder spread was only a half-inch—that's a half-inch with the holes overlapping! At 30 yards, the cylinders had separated to ¾-inch, with the same two-hole pattern. At 40 yards, the two- hole spread was 6¾ inches. A second 40-yard shot yielded a two-hole spread of 3½ inches, but one of the cylinder holes was irregular and wore a faint dark streaking indicative of a shot cup, one undoubtedly with some shot still in it. At 50 yards, the spread was vertical at 9½ inches between two holes. Finally, at 75 yards, the three-cylinder load produced a triangular group 7¼ inches by 5½ inches. By this time, the cylinders had begun to tip. One of these was thought to be a possible shot cup hole, but was in fact an excellent fit for a cylinder on edge. Frankly, I can see little use for adding the BB shot. Why not simply put in another cylinder? With this type of tight grouping, this is an excellent solution for problem woodchucks.

Why the two entry holes? This was fairly consistent. No idea. It must be remembered that these loadings are designed for use in rifled-barrel revolvers. Spinning these cylinders might cause them to drift apart, as is the case of firing Buck and similar shot loads in rifled deer slug barrels. With no rotation, they tend to remain in a compact mass, behaving much like slug loads to a range of 50-plus yards. When fired at close range into soft targets, however, the cylinders quickly lose stability and separate to produce individual wound channels.

LETHALITY

For those who think of the .410 as a weak sister to heavier gauges, this is not the case. Penetration tests in plywood sheets and water cartons yielded travel equal to buckshot from a 20-inch 12-gauge riot gun barrel at the same distance. The main difference between the 00 Buckshot and No. 4 is that the 00 penetrates more deeply. Wound ballistician Dr. Martin Fackler ran close-range (10-foot) tests into gelatin with both 00 and No. 4, with the result that the 00 penetrated about two inches deeper and was effective for self-defense use. The No. 4 may be suitable for some pest shooting, but penetration is lacking for self-defense purposes.

SLUGS

What practical use is a .410 slug? In Ohio, where I live, .410 slugs have been alternately illegal and (currently) legal for deer hunting. Since our major ammunition companies produce them, somebody must be buying them. The late Frank Barnes, in his *Cartridges of the World*, made contradictory observations about .410 slugs. On page 386 of the *7th Edition* is the statement, "The .410 slug is not good for anything but small game at short range." On page 393, however, he states that, while inadequate for deer, the slugs are quite effective in guns such as the Savage M-24 combination gun (with rifle sights) and that it is possible to hit rabbit-size targets at 80 yards and claim clean kills on bobcats and coyotes at this range.

ACCURACY

The most extensive development of smoothbore shotgun slug barrels was done by the Ithaca Gun Company a couple decades ago. Its conclusion was that best accuracy was obtained from Cylinder-bore barrels with highly polished bores. But few .410s have Cylinder

The test guns were a Winchester 9410 and a vintage Model 42 with a Cylinder barrel. A good variety of buckshot loads are now available for the .410. As expected the three-inch shells give the most effective performance. Best of all, you can even load your own.

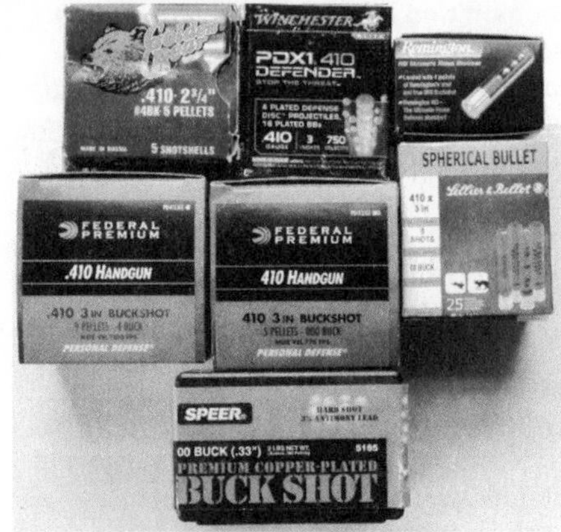

barrels. For this article, a Winchester 9410 and a Winchester Model 42, both with Cylinder barrels, were used. The 9410 came with adjustable open sights and was set up for scope mounting. The 42 was equipped with a scope mount.

Both guns shared a Burris 4X Mini. It soon became evident that 50 yards was about the limit for both these guns, when it came to reasonably precise shot placement. As a not-recommended-but-legal deer round, careful shot placement is the only means of taking a deer with this cartridge.

All three U.S. makes of slug loads were tested, and the 2¾-inch RWS Rottweil Brenneke and Barnaul (Russian) slugs were fired in the 42. (The 9410 is chambered for 2½-inch shells only.) The results are in Table 1. Within the limits of the test, the Remington slugs were the best U.S.-made performers, while Winchester was the worst and Federal landed in the middle. Since the slugs were all of the Foster type and appeared much the same, what was the cause of these considerable differences in these groups?

Most obvious was that the hollowpoint dimple on the Federal and Winchester slugs appeared off center in many of the shells I examined, as though the slug was slightly tipped in the shell, while the flat points on the Remington appeared properly centered. Seems that was part of the problem, but dissection of the shells revealed that the slugs were not the same diameter! The Remington measured .402-inch, the Federal was .394-inch, and the Winchester came in at .389-inch. The RWS Rottweil was .409-inch. The ammunition companies confirmed these findings. The Remington slugs are made for true Cylinder-bore barrels, while the slightly smaller Federals and Winchesters are intended for modestly choked Improved Cylinder and Modified barrels. The polymer "tail" on the Brenneke also added guidance and, possibly, some protection against the scuffing that wiped out the helical grooves on the American Foster slugs. Additionally, the Russian Barnaul had several unusual features. Inside the zinc- or brass-plated steel shell is a long cushion wad to reduce distortion, and the 97-grain Foster slug is protected by a two-piece discarding sabot. Entry holes in the target evidenced toothed edges, indicating that the grooves were not ironed out in firing.

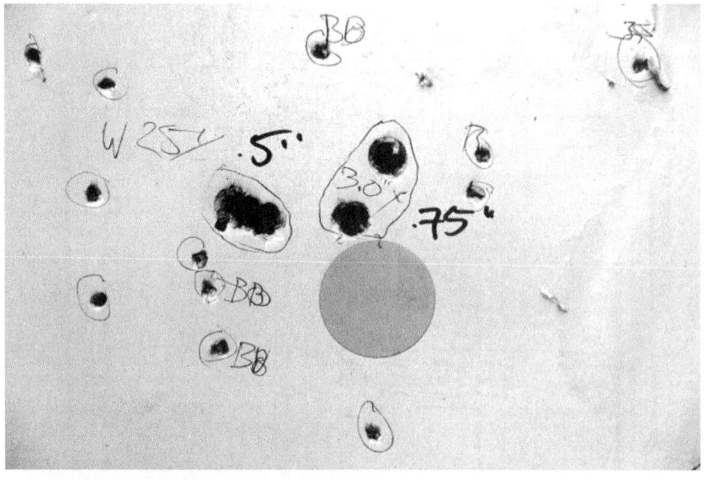

Left Top: At 25 yards the three-inch load from the M-42 put everything within five inches. The long hole on the left is the shot cup, possibly with a cylinder or two still in it. Separation between two separated cylinders is ¾-inch.

Whether rifled slugs actually rotate in flight is a matter of conjecture. Foster slugs have their grooves ironed out in firing, as they obturate in the barrel. A source at Federal told me that, in the firm's high-speed motion picture studies, these slugs do *not* rotate. Additionally, slugs moving at supersonic velocities push a shock wave and, thus, there is a vacuum along the exterior until the slug reaches subsonic speed. At such time (theoretically), they should rotate. I once balanced an unfired Foster slug (12-gauge) on a needle and stuck it in the flow from a sink tap. It spun like a top. Water, of course, is much denser than air, but the idea is the same.

Interestingly enough, a couple of the .410 Breakneck slugs in the test hit the 50-yard target sideways, indicating that neither the guide wad nor the helical vanes were having the proper effect at that range.

Anyone planning to do any serious slug shooting in their .410 should have it equipped with sights and target all available makes of ammunition to determine which will work best in their gun.

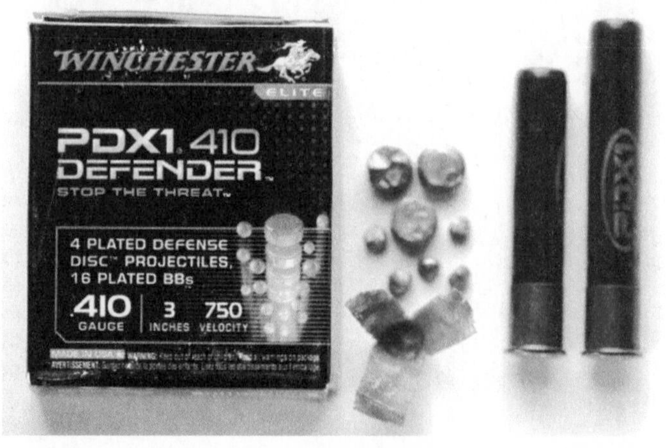

The most interesting innovation in Winchester's .410 offerings is the Winchester Supreme Elite Defender, featuring cylindrical shot plus BBs.

SLUG LETHALITY

The best method of bullet testing for effect on living bodies is ballistic gelatin. A reliable and cheap substitute for this medium is water-filled, half-gallon, coated-paper juice or milk cartons placed standing in a row and touching one another. Penetration in water-filled cartons divided by 1.5 yields a penetration roughly approximate to that in ballistic gelatin.

Table 1

Group accuracy (in inches) with .410 slugs, 50-yard five-shot groups unless otherwise indicated by number in parentheses. Sandbag rest.

Slug	Remington	Federal	Winchester	RWS	Barnaul
Winchester Model 42	3.8	4.7	6.6	2.6	5.5
Winchester Model 42	4.0 (20	3.0 (4)	3.0 (4)	4.0	
Winchester Model 9410	4.5"	4.7"	8.3	---	2.6 (4)

Table 2

Chronographed Velocity, .410 slugs, Winchester Model 42 five-shot groups. Results were obtained with an Oehler 35P chronograph set four feet from the muzzle. (+) = highest; (-) = lowest; E =extreme spread; M = mean; S = standard deviation.

Remington	Federal	Winchester	RWS	Barnaul
+1930	+1676	+1930	+1547	+1535
-1789	-1599	-1896	-1448	-1450
E/141	E/0077	E/0034	E/0099	E/0085
M/1860	M/1645	M/1916	M/1503	M/1481
S/0060	S/0028	S/0013	S/0043	S/0041

For police combat use, the FBI recommends 12 inches of gelatin penetration. Assuming that an adult male person and a deer are of about the same weight class, this figure seems a valid standard. Penetration tests were made with the Winchester 42 into water-filled cartons at a range of 50 yards. The Barnaul, Remington, Federal, and Winchester slugs all penetrated 11¼ inches. Divided by 1.5, that converts to 7½ inches of penetration through gelatin. The RWS was the only one that stood out, penetrating the cartons to 26 inches, which equates to 17.33 inches of gelatin penetration.

In terms of performance, there is really no comparison. The flat-point and hollowpoint Foster slugs, with Winchester at 93 grains and Remington, Federal, and Barnaul at 97, are completely outclassed by the 114-grain Brenneke. The Fosters tended to shatter into flat slivers, while the Brenneke maintained its integrity, expanding to .455-inch. The Brenneke's performance is roughly comparable to a hot, light-bullet load in a .40 S&W pistol. The performance of the Foster slugs is somewhere around the .32 S&W Long to .32 H&R Magnum level. The greatest fault with the Foster design is that the slugs come apart after relatively short penetration.

The Brenneke could be considered an adequate deer load at close range. The Fosters are strictly for small game. Having said this, it must be admitted that a lot of deer have been taken with the .22 LR cartridge, and my local gun shop owner told me of one of his customers who claimed a deer a year for eight years with Foster .410s. Unfortunately, that customer is no longer living, so no insights are available.

The Silver Bear slugs are from the Russian company Barnaul. Like the Remington, Federal, and Winchester slugs, it penetrated 11¼ inches into the water-filled milk cartons at 50 yards, at best a close-range small-game load.

The .410 must ultimately be classed as an expert's gun for hunting and used much like a rifle—sights are mandatory and careful aim must be taken. If you have one, it might be worth your while to explore its potential. For the security minded, the Mossberg M-500 .410 pump with its 18½-inch barrel offers harder hits than a handgun, a better grip with less muzzle blast (about like a .38 handgun), and more manageable recoil. The three-inch loads will fit few revolvers and, while the kick is noticeable in a long gun, in a handgun recoil it runs towards the .357/.44 Magnum class.

Super X3

BY Brad Fitzpatrick
PHOTOS BY Mark & Cretia Hayes

White Sulphur Springs, West Virginia, is the home of the Greenbrier, a sprawling resort situated at the foot of the Allegheny Mountains. The Greenbrier has been called "America's Resort," and the 6,500-acre property offers just about any outdoor activity you can imagine, including multiple golf courses, an off-road driving course, fly fishing, horseback riding, and tennis.

Despite all its outward beauty, the Greenbrier is home to a very big secret. Since the 1960s, the Greenbrier has been the site of an underground fallout shelter designed to house U.S. government leaders in the event of nuclear war. In fact, the entire West Virginia wing of this magnificent resort was built in an effort to disguise the enormous amount of concrete and steel being trucked in at a steady pace to build the massive shelter.

There are other bunkers at the Greenbrier, but these are situated across the road from the main resort at the Kate's Mountain Shooting Club, a

Above: Rapid choke tube changes are snap, thanks to the Super X3's five extended tubes. Even in black and white, you can see also see how well the fiber optic front sight captures the light.

Right: The Super X3 is right at home at the Greenbrier's historic Kate's Mountain Shooting Course. Will the Super X3 be the next legendary Winchester gun? That remains to be seen.

Adjustable Sporting

Waiting on a clay. The Super X3 Sporting is one of the softest recoiling semi-autos available today and it is comfortable to shoot even at the end of a long day on course.

favorite destination of resort guests who want to test their shooting skills on the British Shooting School-designed clays course. Unlike the massive fallout bunker underneath the West Virginia Wing of the hotel (the top of which you can just barely see between the hardwoods atop Kate's Mountain), which was designed to hold the members of Congress and enough staff to support them through the months after a nuclear explosion, the bunkers on Kate's Mountain only hold a few hundred clays. And the only war going on in the scenic setting is the battle between visiting shooters and clay targets.

On my battlefield of the sporting clays, I was losing the fight. It wasn't the fault of my gun, the new Winchester Super X3 Sporting. Nor was it the fault of my coach, Curtis Kincaid, the Greenbrier's shotgunning instructor. Mark Hayes, who'd shot clays with me at Northern Kentucky University, took the Super X3 and tried the same shot I had been failing on.

"High overhead," Curtis said. "Lean back and let the bead pass the clay. Then shoot." Mark nodded, called for the bird, and I heard the mechanical clap of the machine on the hill above us. The clay appeared high above, somehow passing through outstretched branches, as it flew into a narrow window between the trees directly above us. Mark pressed the trigger and the Super X3 barked, turning the clay into a shower of dust. I congratulated Mark and took back the Super X3, happy to head on to the next station.

Winchester firearms, like the Greenbrier, are part of the fabric of America. No gun company can match Winchester's status for producing guns that earn legendary status. From the Models 1873 and 1894 to the Model 12 pump and the "Rifleman's Rifle" Model 70, Winchester has produced guns that leave firearms enthusiasts drooling. Unlike other companies that are well known for producing either famous rifles or shotguns, it can be debated whether one or the other of Winchester's long gun types have had a bigger impact on the American shooting public. Many Winchester rifles are well known and loved by American sportsmen. Still, the Winchester 1897 and Model 12 pump shotguns arguably set the standard for American pump guns and are, without question, largely responsible for the popularity of pump shotguns throughout the last century. Too, despite being out of production for years, the Model 21 side-by-sides are perhaps more popular today than at any time in history and fetching very impressive prices, while the Model 101 over/under was always popular among hunters and competition shooters, enough so that the company recently resurrected the model.

Notably *absent* from the discussion are semi-auto shotguns. Winchester has produced several autoloaders over the years, including the model 50, 59, 1400, 1500, and the Super X. The problem was that none of these ever reached the status of the Model 12 and Model 70, nor achieved legions of followers like the Browning Auto 5 and the Remington 1100. The Winchester shotguns had their share of fans, but never competed for the top spot among American shooters.

In 2006, Winchester announced the release of its current semi-auto model, the Super X3—and it had the technology and quality to make it a contender with anything on the market. The company had set out to build a semi-auto shotgun that would be extremely reliable under even the worst conditions. The Super X3 was a gas-operated gun that entered onto the shooting landscape when Benelli's Inertia Driven guns were all the rage, due to the fact that they continued to shoot almost no matter what and didn't require the rigorous cleaning regimen necessary to keep traditional gas guns running. The Super X3's claim to fame was that it had the advantage of softening recoil by lengthening the transfer of recoil from the gun to the shooter.

If it was ever going to win fans, though, it had better be extremely reliable. It did that, proving it would continue to work under the worst conditions, and quickly gained a reputation as one of the most dependable semi-autos on the market. One of the first examples of this was when Dr. Scott Breeze, also known as the "Dovenator," took over 15,000 doves *in a single day of shooting* in Argentina with a pair of 20-gauge SX3s, setting a new world record. The Super X3's design had shown itself to be fail-safe, even under such brutal shooting conditions.

Such utter reliability gives thanks to the Winchester/Browning Active Valve system, which uses vented gases to work the action. The gas piston and the Active Valve system work independently to ensure prolonged piston life, though I have never heard of any gas piston going bad on any Active Valve gun despite torturous tests like Scott Breeze's 15,000-bird day. The Active Valve system on the Super X3 Sporting is designed to handle 2¾-inch ammunition only, but it handles all target ammo effectively, from the lightest training loads to the hottest sporting loads.

The Sporting version of the Super X3 comes with five Signature Invector Plus choke tubes (Light Modified, Improved Modified, Modified, Improved, and Skeet) and a .742-inch back-bored barrel. Both the barrel and the chamber are chrome plated for durability and ease of cleaning. The receiver is made of an aluminum alloy that is both durable and lightweight. With 28-inch barrels, my test Sporter still weighed under 7½ pounds, very good for a dedicated sporting-clays gun.

Despite its relatively light weight, the Super X3 Sporting produces very manageable recoil levels. Shooters accustomed to carrying an over/under on the clays course will be amazed at how little pain the Winchester inflicts. This is due in large part to the Pachmayr Decelerator recoil pad the Super X3 is fitted with, as well as the ported barrel and excellent design of the shotgun stock. If you are a serious sporting clays shooter, you know that recoil fatigue can quickly mount, particularly

Mark Hayes breaking a clay on the Kate's Mountain course at the Greenbrier resort in West Virginia. Notice the action of the Super X3 cycling. Thanks to the Active Valve system, the Super X3 has one of the fastest, smoothest actions of any semi-auto on the market.

The Super X3 Sporting comes with a molded hard case for easy transport.

The Super X3's aluminum receiver is light, durable, and attractive. The bolt and shell carrier are nickel coated and the action is chrome-lined for durability.

The Super X3 Sporting's barrel is treated with Winchester's Perma-Coat UT and the receiver is polished aluminum. It is a most distinctive and attractive sporting semi-auto.

after days of extended shooting in tournaments. Between a gas system that reduces felt recoil, ported barrels, and an excellent recoil pad, the Super X3 is a pleasure to shoot. I can't say that about all the inertia-operated sporting semi autos I've shot, and I certainly wouldn't claim to enjoy shooting a light over/under all day long. The Super X3 Sporting is a great gun for the recoil-sensitive shooter and, in truth, anyone who wants to break a lot of clays should be shooting a comfortable gun. The Super X3 simply fits that bill.

Besides a heavily recoiling gun, another score-killer on the clays course is a bad trigger. Although most conversation about good triggers revolves around rifles, a shotgun trigger should break cleanly and smoothly when pressed. The concept seems simple enough, but many competition guns have all the bells and whistles of a first-rate clays gun, except for the fact they have lousy triggers that are mushy or heavy. Sporting clays is more than a game of inches, it's a game of millimeters and milliseconds. A really good gun has to have a good trigger, and the Super X3 has one of the best of any semi-auto on the market. Crisp, clean, and smooth, it makes it easier to hit tough birds, because you aren't fighting to make your gun shoot.

The satin walnut stock of the Super X3 has a fully adjustable comb that allows the shooter to manipulate the

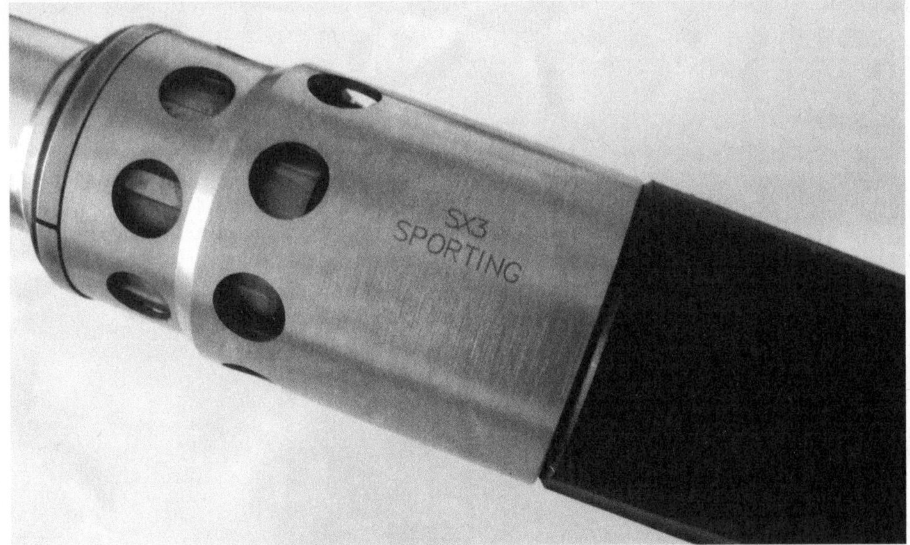

The Super X3 Sporting's Active Valve is specifically designed to handle the full range of 2¾-inch shells.

The Super X3 Sporting comes standard with five extended Signature Invector Plus chokes in Light Modified, Modified, Improved Modified, Improved Cylinder, and Skeet.

point of impact, something essential to good shooting. Most good gunsmiths can add an adjustable comb to a fixed-stock shotgun, but the cost is going to be at least a couple hundred dollars. The standard adjustable comb on the Super X3 means the shooter can, with a little time on the range, ensure the shotgun is shooting exactly where they need it when the pad hits their shoulder.

There are many other special touches that make the Super X3 stand out as a top choice for anyone considering a semi-auto for shooting sporting clays. The barrel of the Super X3 Sporting has been treated with Winchester's Perma-Cote UT, which is virtually scratch-, dent-, and rustproof. Both the bolt and the shell carrier are nickel plated for durability. The mid-bead and interchangeable fiber optic front beads are a nice touch, and the oversized safety, located just aft of the trigger guard, is easy to locate and positive. The walnut forearm is wide for added stability, with a finger groove for added grip and security. Magazine capacity when unplugged is five rounds of 2¾-inch ammo.

It's easy to like the Super X3, and it should be on the short list of anyone considering a semi-auto competition gun. This year marked 100 years since the introduction of Winchester's game-changing Model 12 shotgun. Could it be possible that the Super X3 will be the next classic Winchester? It's hard to say. What is for certain is that the Super X3 has been given all the equipment and engineering necessary to make it one of the best semi-autos ever.

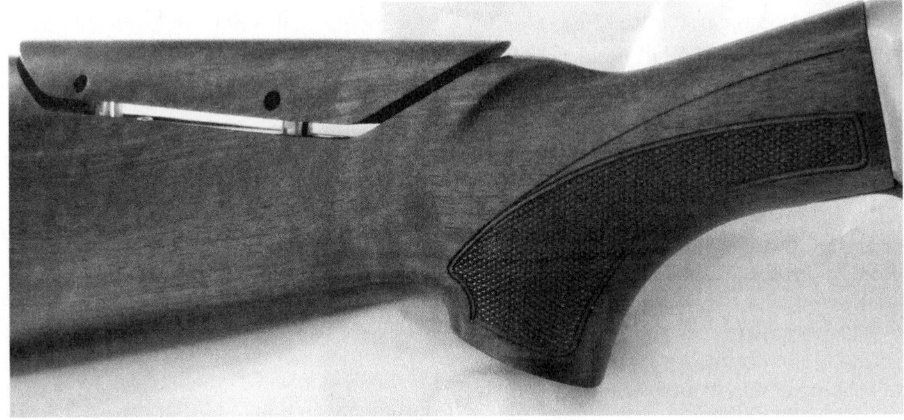

The adjustable comb allows the shooter to manipulate the point of impact, a valuable feature on any target gun.

Specifications
Winchester Super X3 Adjustable Sporting

Action Type: Semi-Auto Shotgun; 2¾-inch
Weight: 7 pounds 6 ounces
Overall length: 49¼ inches
Barrel length: 28 inches
Finish: Aluminum receiver; Perma-Cote UT barrel
Stock: Satin walnut; adjustable comb
Capacity: Five
MSRP: $1,699.99

RUGER 77/357

BY Al Doyle

Just when it seems there are no new concepts or ideas left, something very different appears on the firearms market. But, in this instance, what's so unusual about a bolt-action carbine?

Lever-actions by Marlin, Rossi, and Henry Arms, the Harrington & Richardson break-action single-shot, and the short-lived Timber Wolf pump-action have all been chambered in the very popular .357 Magnum cartridge, but the caliber was never built as a mass-market bolt-action rifle—that is until Ruger recently came out with the stainless 77/357. With an 18½-inch stainless steel barrel and synthetic stock, this gun is ideal for use in wet and sloppy places.

So what's the purpose for a .357 carbine, when there are numerous other choices in more potent calibers? For one, many gun owners like the idea of owning both a pistol and rifle in the same round. Plus, there's no shortage of potential customers who prefer bolt-actions to other types of long guns.

A .44 Magnum version (the 77/44) preceded the 77/357, so perhaps it was time to satisfy another niche of the revolver-buying market. After all, a .357 rifle goes nicely with the single-action Ruger Blackhawk or Vaquero, or the double-action GP-100 and SP-101. Ruger is a company with a long history of successfully anticipating what customers want, and the 77/357 has been a very brisk seller, since it first became available in June 2011.

Taking the carbine to the range and describing what it was to onlookers quickly drew unsolicited reactions, all positive. Some people commented on how a bolt-action .357 should have been available years ago, while several declared, "Looks like an ideal truck gun" after glancing at the 5½-pound carbine. No one had to be asked twice if they wanted to handle it and fire a few rounds.

As appealing as the concept of a .357 Magnum bolt-action proved to be, performance and accuracy are always the real tests, when deciding if a gun is worth buying. Any rifle chambered in a handgun caliber and tested with iron sights isn't going to shoot minute of angle, but the results from this gun were satisfactory. Two-inch off-hand groups at 50 yards were common with various name brands of ammo in the 125- to 142-grain range. That kind of accuracy was also achieved with Remington 130-grain full metal jacket .38 Specials. Naturally, the less powerful caliber shot to a lower point of aim than the .357s. The 77/357 doesn't feed .38 Special wadcutters, but they can be loaded singly in the chamber for those who want quiet shooting and nothing more than a hint of recoil.

If you can shoot from a kneeling position, the 77/357 is capable of impressive

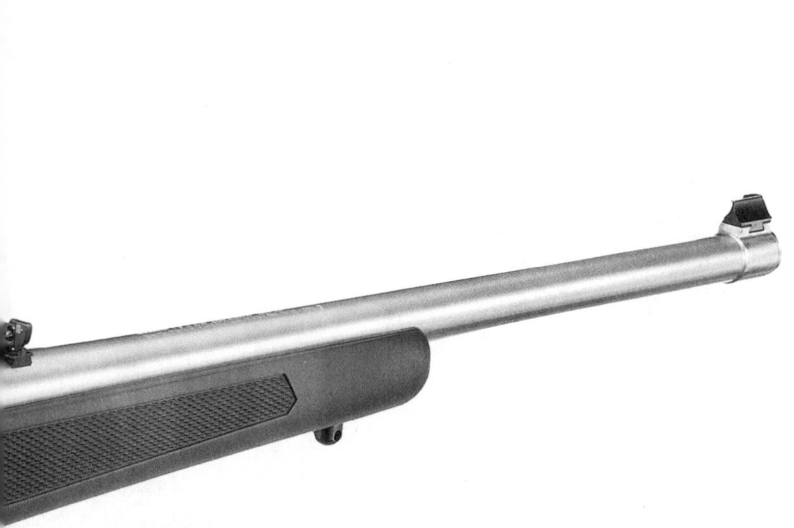

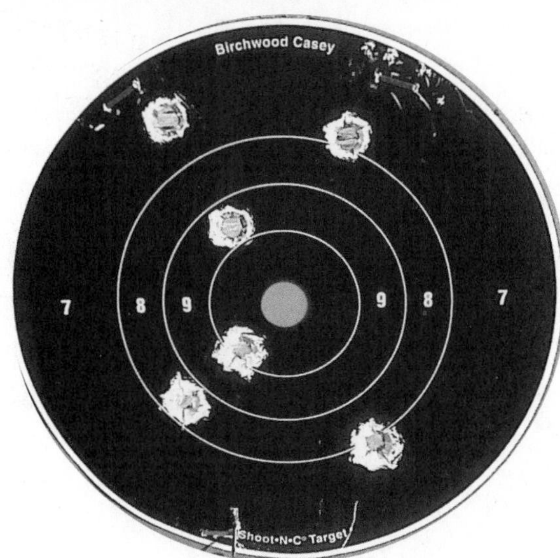

results. I was able to produce a pair of ¾-inch three-shot groups at 50 yards—once with 125-grain CorBon hollow-points and again with 142-grain Fiocchi truncated-cone solids. The only ammo that proved to be inconsistent in accuracy were the light (100- to 110-grain) rounds designed for self-defense.

Those tendencies weren't surprising, as the 77/357 is marketed at least in part as a short-range deer rifle, so next it was time to try out some 140- and 158-grain handloads. Predictably, the heavier bullets tightened the average groups a bit and shot to a higher point of aim than factory ammo. Take that combination of rifle and homemade ammo to the woodlots of Pennsylvania or the upper Midwest, and you have a good chance of coming home with venison.

The test rifle had one interesting quirk. Group sizes were fairly similar among those who shot the 77/357, but the rounds were dispersed vertically in every instance.

In addition to the 150 rounds I fired through the carbine, I have never had a gun tested by so many different shooters. In a rare unanimous vote, recoil was deemed to be minimal, even with the hotter handloads. A light fleece jacket or sweatshirt is all the "protection" needed to take this carbine to the range. That makes the 77/357 an ideal centerfire training gun for young shooters or a logical option for those who may have physical conditions aggravated by excessive recoil.

There was one drawback to this otherwise nifty rifle. It came equipped with only a single five-round magazine, and that one balked when more than three rounds were loaded. Ruger quickly sent a pair of replacements, when they were alerted to the problem. One of the new magazines functioned flawlessly, while the other one also couldn't handle a full loading. Make sure to check the magazine(s) immediately, when purchasing this otherwise trouble-free carbine. The magazines are based on the rotary 10-rounders used on the venerable Ruger 10/22 .22 rimfire, and they are flush to the bottom of the rifle.

It took just a few rounds after the gun came out of the box before the bolt worked with delightful smoothness. The three-position safety will be a familiar feature to anyone who has experience with the Ruger Model 77 rifle series.

The 77/357 comes with a pair of stainless rings for mounting a scope, and this is an ideal rifle for a fixed-power optic in the 2X to 3X range. I have been searching for a reasonably priced vintage Weaver K2.5 for months; that old classic scope would have been just right for the carbine. Once I locate the right K2.5, I'll place it on the 77/357 and shrink the groups achieved with the open sights.

Speaking of sights, that's one area that could use some improvement. The 77/357 carries the adjustable rear sight found on the 10/22, but the .357 rifle could benefit from a good peep sight. This shortcoming will likely be dealt with by an enterprising mind in the secondary market.

In addition to being a truck gun, versatile plinker, and woodland deer rifle, the 77/357 could fill other niches. This is an ideal choice for hunting medium-sized hogs. Take it to the desert southwest, and the carbine would be a good choice for pursuing javelina.

With an MSRP of $829, the Ruger 77/357 isn't the least expensive bolt rifle on the market, but it fills several niches and elicits smiles from those who get a chance to handle this nicely balanced piece. It's safe to say that it is going to be another successful and profitable item in the Ruger product line.

Ruger 77/357 Specifications

Action: bolt
Caliber: .357 Magnum/.38 Special
Overall length: 38½ inches
Barrel length: 18½ inches
Weight: 5½ pounds
Capacity: five-round magazine
Sights: Adjustable rear; gold bead front
Construction and finish: Stainless steel, brushed
Stock: Black synthetic
Length of pull: 13½ inches
MSRP: $829.00

BROWNING'S NEW SCALED-DOWN 1911 .22 LR

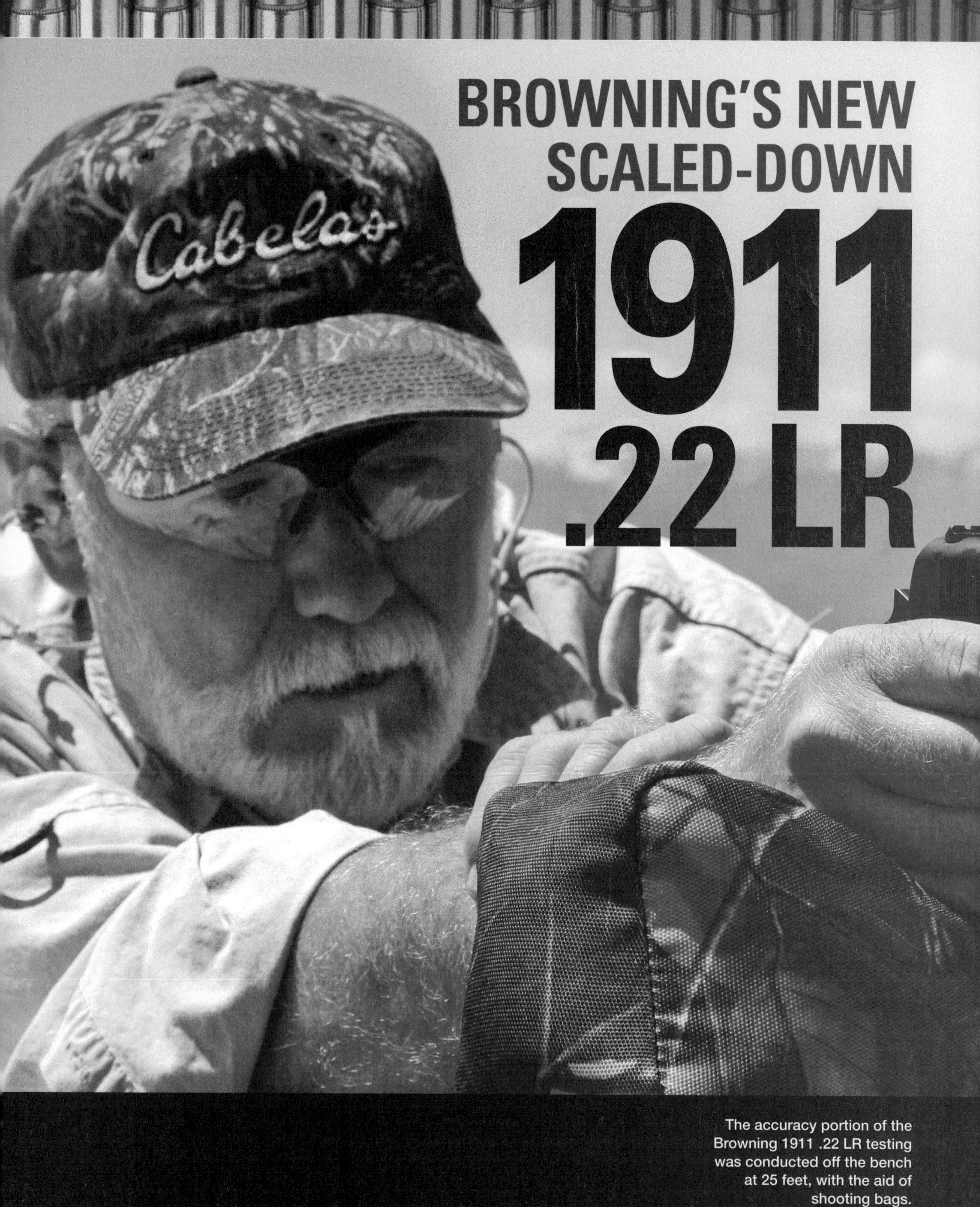

The accuracy portion of the Browning 1911 .22 LR testing was conducted off the bench at 25 feet, with the aid of shooting bags.

TEST FIRE

BY **Tom Tabor**

No other handgun can boast of having a more distinguished military service record than the Model 1911. Chambered for .45 ACP, it became the preferred sidearm of the U.S. troops during World War I, World War II, the Korean Conflict, and Vietnam. More recently it was selected by some of our U.S. Army Special Forces and Marine Corp units operating in the Persian Gulf. This impressive and unprecedented long-running track record only became possible as a result of the 1911's well-established reputation for dependability. As is often said, one of these stalwart companions could be pulled from a mud hole, be dripping with all type of goo and debris and, as long as the bore was clear, it would continue to cycle, function, and shoot as if new out of the box.

Admirable, but in order to achieve that reliability objective, close tolerances of the parts had to be reduced. The military needed a handgun that could be quickly repaired in the field by simply swapping out the parts. Still, while this lack of precision seemingly solved the dependability problem under battlefield conditions, there were sacrifices. Possibly the most severe of those came in the form of shooting accuracy or, rather, the *lack* of shooting accuracy. That is not to say all 1911s were so inhibited. While the GI-issued military versions generally suffered in this area, many of the newer civilian Model 1911s have proved to be tack-driving weapons, fully capable of winning many competitive shooting matches.

Like so many of our favorite firearms today, the 1911 was the design brainchild of world-renowned gun designer, John M. Browning. Even though some shooters relate the 1911 with Colt's, Colt's was only one of many manufacturers that contracted with the U.S. government to build them for our troops. And, by 2011, when the 1911's 100-year anniversary rolled around, it seemed that every company that ever had the faintest inkling of producing a semi-auto handgun were showcasing their own version. Many of those commemorative pistols were highly pleasing to the eye and clearly worthy of ownership. But among the masses, one manufacturer took a starkly different approach—Browning Arms. Rather than producing a fancy, engraved, limited-edition model that, in most cases, would simply wind up collecting dust on a shelf or taking up space in a gun safe, Browning decided to go a different direction and build a handgun that was intended to be used and frequently shot. To that end, this new Browning is nearly an exact replica of the original model, but scaled back to about 85 percent of the original model's size, and rather than being chambered to shoot the often expensive .45 ACP ammo, the Browning 1911 comes with the benefit of firing the economical and fun to shoot .22 LR.

In order to keep weight to a minimum, the frame and slide of the Browning 1911 22 LR are machined from aluminum-alloy stock. The barrel comes with a stainless steel barrel block and target-style crown. Some of the other features include a single action trigger and a straight blow-back action for enhanced simplicity and reliability. Like the original G.I. model, Browning's new .22 version comes with fixed sights, and, for enhanced safety, it has a typical manual thumb safety, a grip safety, and a half-cock hammer position. Due to the smaller size of the .22 LR cartridges, the magazine holds 10 cartridges, rather than the seven of the full-size .45 model. To round all this out, with the exception of the rear most portion of the barrel, which remains the color of silver polished metal, the entire handgun is finished in a nice matte bluing, and the brown composite grips are checkered with the same pattern as used on the original GI model.

There are two versions of the Browning 1911 .22 LR currently available. The

Right: At 85 percent the size of the original 1911, the Browning .22 LR (right) is perfectly sized for carrying.

When Browning's new 1911 .22 LR (below) is compared to a GI issue (Colt manufactured) 1911 .45 ACP, the similarities are remarkable.

A1 Model possesses a 4¼-inch barrel, a 5½-inch sight radius, and overall length of 7⅛ inches, and a weight of 15½ ounces. The Compact 1911 .22 LR model is equipped with a 3⅝-inch barrel, a sight radius of 4⅞ inches, an overall length of 6½ inches, and a weight of 15 ounces. In both cases, the controls and functions are the same as original John M. Browning-designed Model 1911.

25-FOOT SHOOTING PERFORMANCE

While some shooters might recognize the obvious differences between standard velocity cartridges and the new era of high velocity .22 LR ammunition, I think many shooters tend to group all .22 cartridges together, when it comes to performance. In reality, however, nothing could be further from the truth. While I don't believe there is such a thing as "bad" .22 ammo, some currently manufactured cartridges clearly perform better in some firearms than others. For this reason, whenever I am testing and evaluating any .22 firearm, be it rifle or pistol, I feel it is extremely important to shoot as wide of a variety of ammo as possible, across the spectrum of different manufacturers and different bullet styles. In this case, I put the Browning 1911 A1 .22 LR through its paces, using a diverse selection of

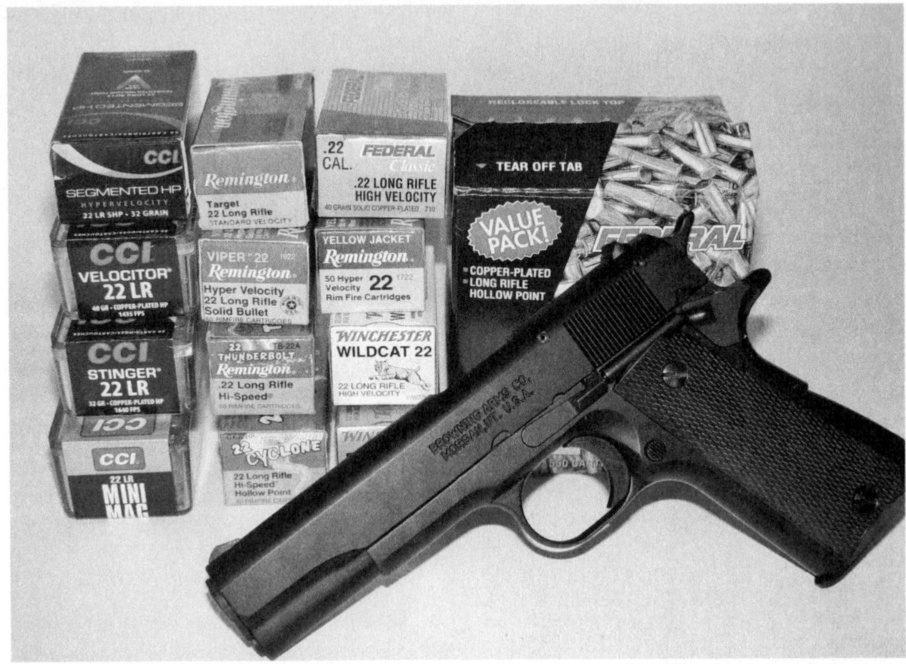

Shooting a variety of .22 LR ammunition helps to provide a more diverse set of data with which to judge the potential accuracy potential of the Browning 1911 .22 LR

14 different cartridges spread over four different major manufacturers.

While I have never professed to being a highly proficient handgun shot, when properly equipped, I can usually get my holes somewhere in the vicinity of one another when shooting at paper at a moderate distance (I will admit there is no shortage of shooters who would likely produce much smaller groups than I am capable of). But even with this personal disclaimer of my generally mediocre handgun shooting performance, I was quite pleased by the accuracy I was able to achieve with this Browning. What came of particular note was that, in some cases, as can be seen in accompanying chart entitled "Browning

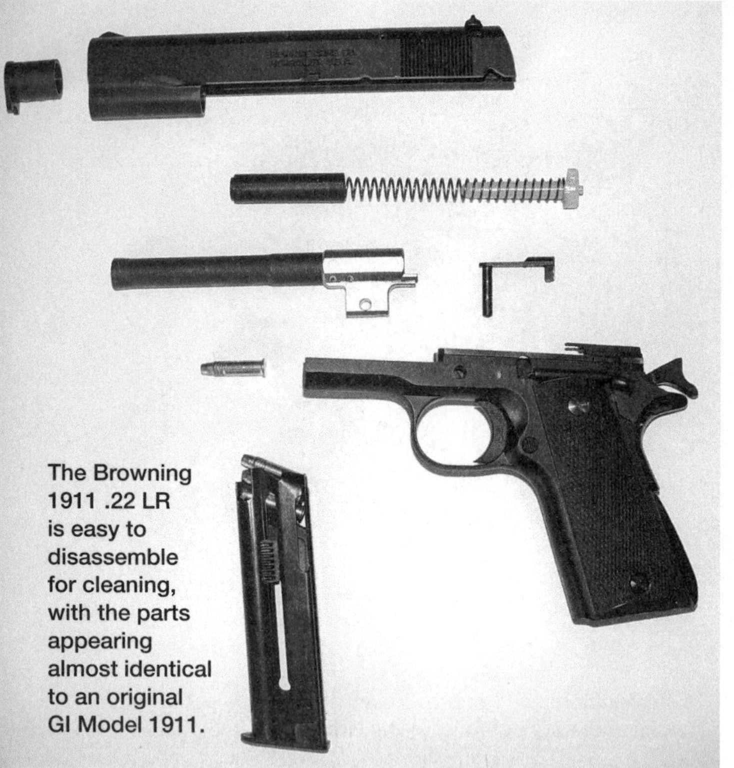

The Browning 1911 .22 LR is easy to disassemble for cleaning, with the parts appearing almost identical to an original GI Model 1911.

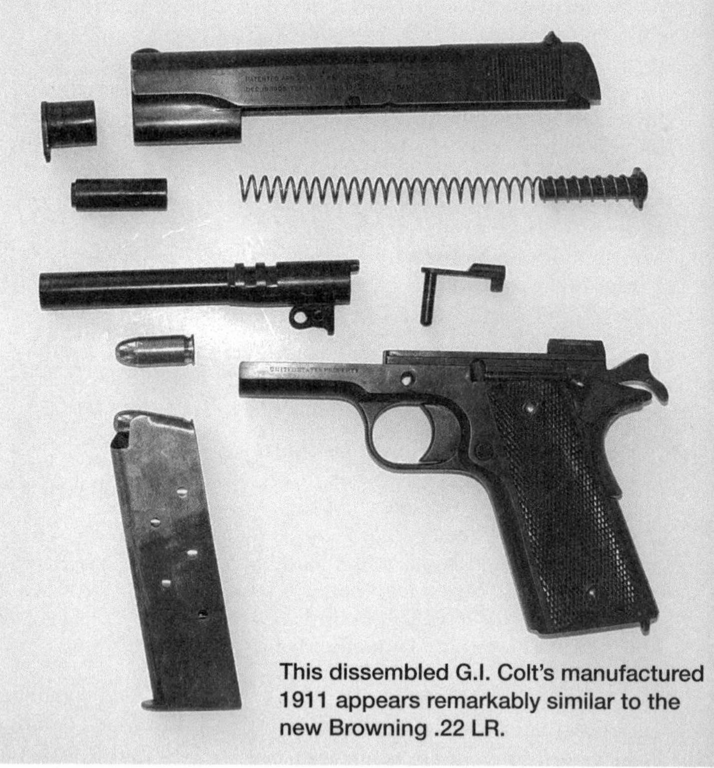

This dissembled G.I. Colt's manufactured 1911 appears remarkably similar to the new Browning .22 LR.

1911 .22 LR 25-foot Five-Shot Groups", as the velocities were increased, frequently the accuracy seemed to erode. This is not unique to this particular firearm however. I have often encountered this to be the case with a wide variety of .22 chambered handguns and rifles. In my testing, I found the best accuracy was produced with the Winchester Super X H.P. ammo, which produced velocity a little faster than the traditional standard of 1,200 fps, but did not generate the hyper velocities of other rounds. The second-best group was produced by the Remington Thunderbolt ammo and taped two inches.

I have often found that the manufacture's touted muzzle velocities are higher than those I achieve in the field with my own firearms. This is largely due to the factory using different testing gear, including longer barrels and bolt-action rifles. When I was able to locate the factory muzzle velocity data, I listed

BROWNING 1911 22 LR—25-FOOT FIVE-SHOT GROUP TESTING

MANUFACTURER/CARTRIDGE	BULLET STYLE & WEIGHT	MUZZLE VELOCITY (FPS)	BEST GROUP
CCI Stinger	Hollowpoint - 32 grains	1,640 fps*	2¾"
CCI Quick Shok	Hollowpoint - 32 grains	Unknown **	2¼"
CCI Velocitor	Hollowpoint - 40 grains	1,435 fps*	3½"
CCI Mini-Mag	Round-nose - 40 grains	Unknown **	3¼"
Federal High Velocity Classic	Solid Copper-plated - 40 grains	Unknown **	3¾"
Federal Value Pack	Hollowpoint Copper-plated - 36 grains	1,280 fps*	2¾"
Remington Thunderbolt	Lead - 40-grains	1,255 fps*	2"
Remington Viper	Truncated Cone Solid Copper Jacketed - 36 grains	1,410 fps*	4⅛"
Remington Yellow Jacket	Truncated Cone Hollowpoint - 33-grains	1,500 fps*	3⅜"
Remington Cyclone	Hollowpoint - 36 grains	1,280 fps*	2⅝"
Remington Target	Lead - 40 grains	Standard Velocity*	3"
Winchester Super X High Velocity	Hollowpoint Lead Lubaloy® Coated - 37 grains	1,280 fps*	1⅜"
Winchester Wildcat	Lead Round-nose - 40 grains	1,255 fps*	3⅞"

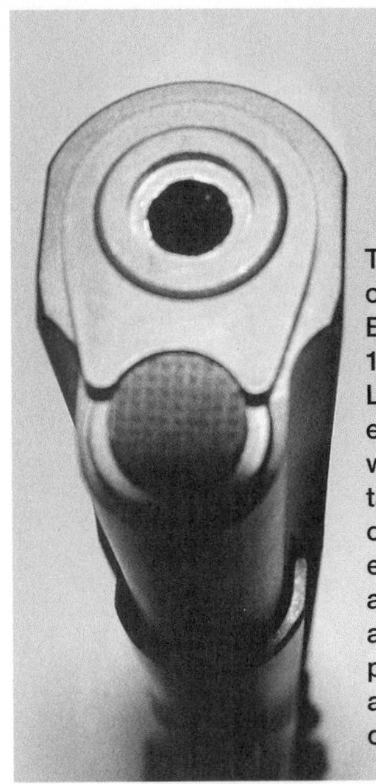
The barrel of the Browning 1911 .22 LR comes equipped with a target-style crown for enhanced accuracy and protection against damage.

The only "issue" the author had with the gun was with its low-profile sights whose finish matches the rest of the gun. This can be hard on aging eyes.

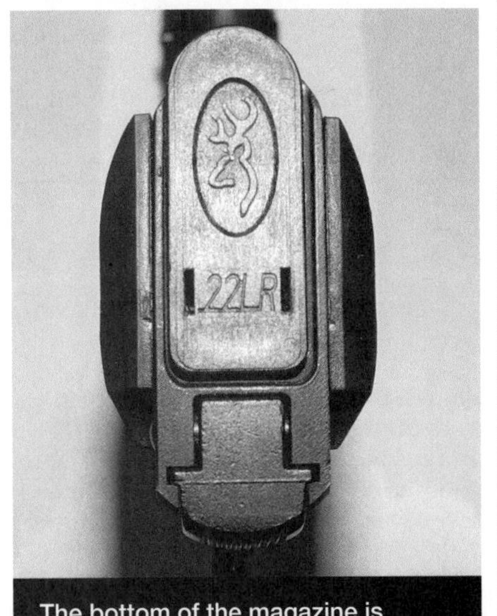

The bottom of the magazine is engraved with the Browning logo, as well as with the cartridge size of .22 LR.

The slide lock and thumb safety on the Browning 1911 .22 LR is, for all practical purposes, identical with the original Model 1911's.

it in the chart, primarily for comparison purposes. In all likelihood, however, it would be logical to expect the velocities from this relatively short-barreled semi-auto to be up to a couple hundred feet per second less than those values.

GENERAL FUNCTIONALITY AND PERFORMANCE

I became quite an admirer of this little Browning. Certainly, being chambered to shoot low-cost .22 ammo is a real advantage. But it was also comfortable and fun to shoot and performed its duties very well. It cycled extremely well, which is certainly not always the case with many semi-auto .22 handguns. The "Z"-stacked clip provided consistent and reliable feeding of the cartridges no matter what cartridge I put through it, as long as I kept the action relatively clean. Ejection was flawless. And, while many shooters find the huge and heavy frame of the standard Model 1911 a bit too cumbersome to pack, the reduced size of the Browning, coupled with its light weight, made it the absolutely perfect sidearm strapped to my hip. When holstered in my Uncle Mike's hip holster, it was almost like it wasn't even there.

The single-action design is essentially identical to that of the full-sized G.I. .45 ACP, which requires the hammer to be cocked for the first firing. Typically, this is accomplished by bringing the slide rearward, then allowing it to drop and close, which moves a cartridge up from the clip and into the chamber. As the trigger is pulled and the first shot is fired, the slide automatically moves rearward, ejecting the empty shell casing, then moving the next cartridge from the magazine up and into the chamber. When the last shot has been fired and the magazine is empty, the slide locks in the open position.

The little Browning was exceptionally comfortable to carry in an Uncle Mike Side Kick size 15 holster.

I found the trigger to be relatively smooth and creep-free, but, as is typical with many production semi-auto handguns, a small amount of slack must be taken up before the trigger and sear becomes fully engaged. Using my Lyman trigger pull gauge, I found the trigger pull was set at 7¼ pounds over a five-pull average.

Breaking down the little Browning was relatively easy and similar in procedure to the typical full size 1911. This simplicity of disassembly makes cleaning quick and effortless. When broken down, the similarities between the Browning .22 and a G.I. .45 model is remarkable, as can be seen in the comparison photos.

Overall, the finish on the Browning 1911 .22 LR was flawless. While I usually prefer a nice gloss or semi-gloss blue job on a handgun, the matte finish of the Browning 1911 .22 LR just seemed to fit this particular handgun. This was further enhanced by the brown composite grips, which also possessed a flat or matte look. The grips were nicely checkered over their entire surface, with sharp, well-pronounced diamonds in the pattern and a defining ridge around the perimeter of the checkering pattern.

About the only negative remark I have to say about the Browning 1911 .22 LR is one closely tied to my birthday. My aging eyes simply aren't what they once were and, for that reason, I found it a little difficult at times to precisely align the front and rear sights. Both sights were matte blue, matching the finish of the gun. This equated to a lack of contrast, making it especially difficult to shoot at a dark colored target. Understandably, Browning wanted to mirror the characteristics of the original Browning specs as closely as possible, but, for me, the lines were blurred, as it were. An easy fix to this problem was to simply use a little fingernail polish to help differentiate the sight surfaces. I often do this on many, if not most, of my handguns. It just makes precise shooting a little easier.

I once heard a military general say that few enemies were ever killed with a G.I.-issued Model 1911, that, rather, they were primarily issued to give the soldier an extra degree of confidence when in battle. By having an ol' reliable 1911 strapped to the hip, the G.I. was assured that, if all else failed, he could pull it from the holster and have seven shots quick at hand. I suppose there's some validity to those comments.

While the G.I. 1911 lacked a little in the way of outward appeal and looks, I found Browning 1911 .22 LR, to the contrary, to be quite appealing. While certainly not meant for military combat usage, it is a remarkably nice handgun.

Browning is understandably proud that this handgun is made in the U.S. The pistol comes in a free, limited-edition commemorative canvas and leather zippered pistol case. The MSRP for either the A1 or Compact Model is $599.99, which seems to be a bargain, when compared to many of its full-sized counterparts carrying price tags frequently running over $1,000. A nice package overall, one I'm quite sure that John M. Browning, if he was still walking among us and smelling of burnt gunpowder, would be quite pleased at having his name associated with.

AVERAGE CENTERFIRE RIFLE CARTRIDGE BALLISTICS & PRICES

Many manufacturers do not supply suggested retail prices. Others did not get their pricing to us before press time. All pricing can vary dependent on the exact brand and style of ammo selected and/or the retail outlet from which you make your purchase. Pricing has been rounded to the nearest dollar and represents our best estimate of average pricing. An * after the cartridge means these loads are available with Nosler Partition or Swift A-Frame bullets. Listed pricing may or may not reflect this bullet type. ** = these are packed 50 to box, all others are 20 to box. Wea. Mag.= Weatherby Magnum. Spfd. = Springfield. A-Sq. = A-Square. N.E.=Nitro Express.

Cartridge	Bullet Wgt. Grs.	VELOCITY (fps)					ENERGY (ft. lbs.)					TRAJ. (in.)				Est. Price/box
		Muzzle	100 yds.	200 yds.	300 yds.	400 yds.	Muzzle	100 yds.	200 yds.	300 yds.	400 yds.	100 yds.	200 yds.	300 yds.	400 yds.	
17, 22																
17 Hornet	20	3650	3078	2574	2122	1721	592	421	294	200	131	1.10	0.0	-6.4	-20.6	NA
17 Remington Fireball	20	4000	3380	2840	2360	1930	710	507	358	247	165	1.6	1.5	-2.8	-13.5	NA
17 Remington Fireball	25	3850	3280	2780	2330	1925	823	597	429	301	206	0.9	0.0	-5.4	NA	NA
17 Remington	25	4040	3284	2644	2086	1606	906	599	388	242	143	+2.0	+1.7	-4.0	-17.0	$17
204 Ruger (Fed)	32 Green	4030	3320	2710	2170	1710	1155	780	520	335	205	0.9	0.0	-5.7	-19.1	NA
204 Ruger	32	4225	3632	3114	2652	2234	1268	937	689	500	355	.6	0.0	-4.2	-13.4	NA
204 Ruger	40	3900	3451	3046	2677	2336	1351	1058	824	636	485	.7	0.0	-4.5	-13.9	NA
204 Ruger	45	3625	3188	2792	2428	2093	1313	1015	778	589	438	1.0	0.0	-5.5	-16.9	NA
5.45x39mm	60	2810	2495	2201	1927	1677	1052	829	645	445	374	1.0	0.0	-9.2	-27.7	NA
221 Fireball	50	2800	2137	1580	1180	988	870	507	277	155	109	+0.0	-7.0	-28.0	0.0	$14
22 Hornet (Fed)	30 Green	3150	2150	1390	990	830	660	310	130	65	45	0.0	-6.6	-32.7	NA	NA
22 Hornet	34	3050	2132	1415	1017	852	700	343	151	78	55	+0.0	-6.6	-15.5	-29.9	NA
22 Hornet	35	3100	2278	1601	1135	929	747	403	199	100	67	+2.75	0.0	-16.9	-60.4	NA
22 Hornet	45	2690	2042	1502	1128	948	723	417	225	127	90	+0.0	-7.7	-31.0	0.0	$27**
218 Bee	46	2760	2102	1550	1155	961	788	451	245	136	94	+0.0	-7.2	-29.0	0.0	$46**
222 REM	35	3760	3125	2574	2085	1656	1099	759	515	338	213	1.0	0.0	-6.3	-20.8	NA
222 Remington	40	3600	3117	2673	2269	1911	1151	863	634	457	324	+1.07	0.0	-6.13	-18.9	NA
222 Remington	50	3140	2602	2123	1700	1350	1094	752	500	321	202	+2.0	-0.4	-11.0	-33.0	$11
222 Remington	55	3020	2562	2147	1773	1451	1114	801	563	384	257	+2.0	-0.4	-11.0	-33.0	$12
22 PPC	52	3400	2930	2510	2130	NA	1335	990	730	525	NA	+2.0	1.4	-5.0	0.0	NA
223 Remington	40	3650	3010	2450	1950	1530	1185	805	535	340	265	+2.0	+1.0	-6.0	-22.0	$14
223 Remington	40	3800	3305	2845	2424	2044	1282	970	719	522	371	0.84	0.0	-5.34	-16.6	NA
223 Remington (Rem)	45 Green	3550	2911	2355	1865	1451	1259	847	554	347	210	2.5	2.3	-4.3	-21.1	NA
223 Remington	50	3300	2874	2484	2130	1809	1209	917	685	504	363	1.37	0.0	-7.05	-21.8	NA
223 Remington	52/53	3330	2882	2477	2106	1770	1305	978	722	522	369	+2.0	+0.6	-6.5	-21.5	$14
223 Remington (Win)	55 Green	3240	2747	2304	1905	1554	1282	921	648	443	295	1.9	0.0	-8.5	-26.7	NA
223 Remington	55	3240	2748	2305	1906	1556	1282	922	649	444	296	+2.0	-0.2	-9.0	-27.0	$12
223 Remington	60	3100	2712	2355	2026	1726	1280	979	739	547	397	+2.0	+0.2	-8.0	-24.7	$16
223 Remington	64	3020	2621	2256	1920	1619	1296	977	723	524	373	+2.0	-0.2	-9.3	-23.0	$14
223 Remington	69	3000	2720	2460	2210	1980	1380	1135	925	750	600	+2.0	+0.8	-5.8	-17.5	$15
223 Remington	75	2790	2554	2330	2119	1926	1296	1086	904	747	617	2.37	0.0	-8.75	-25.1	NA
223 Rem. Super Match	75	2930	2694	2470	2257	2055	1429	1209	1016	848	703	1.20	0.0	-6.9	-20.7	NA
223 Remington	77	2750	2584	2354	2169	1992	1293	1110	948	804	679	1.93	0.0	-8.2	-23.8	NA
223 WSSM	55	3850	3438	3064	2721	2402	1810	1444	1147	904	704	0.7	0.0	-4.4	-13.6	NA
223 WSSM	64	3600	3144	2732	2356	2011	1841	1404	1061	789	574	1.0	0.0	-5.7	-17.7	NA
222 Rem. Mag.	55	3240	2748	2305	1906	1556	1282	922	649	444	296	+2.0	-0.2	-9.0	-27.0	$14
225 Winchester	55	3570	3066	2616	2208	1838	1556	1148	836	595	412	+2.0	+1.0	-5.0	-20.0	$19
224 Wea. Mag.	55	3650	3192	2780	2403	2057	1627	1244	943	705	516	+2.0	+1.2	-4.0	-17.0	$32
22-250 Rem.	40	4000	3320	2720	2200	1740	1420	980	660	430	265	+2.0	+1.8	-3.0	-16.0	$14
22-250 Rem.	45 Green	4000	3293	2690	2159	1696	1598	1084	723	466	287	1.7	1.7	-3.2	-15.7	NA
22-250 Rem.	50	3725	3264	2641	2455	2103	1540	1183	896	669	491	0.89	0.0	-5.23	-16.3	NA
22-250 Rem.	52/55	3680	3137	2656	2222	1832	1654	1201	861	603	410	+2.0	+1.3	-4.0	-17.0	$13
22-250 Rem.	60	3600	3195	2826	2485	2169	1727	1360	1064	823	627	+2.0	+2.0	-2.4	-12.3	$19
220 Swift	40	4200	3678	3190	2739	2329	1566	1201	904	666	482	+0.51	0.0	-4.0	-12.9	NA
220 Swift	50	3780	3158	2617	2135	1710	1586	1107	760	506	325	+2.0	+1.4	-4.4	-17.9	$20
220 Swift	50	3850	3396	2970	2576	2215	1645	1280	979	736	545	0.74	0.0	-4.84	-15.1	NA
220 Swift	55	3800	3370	2990	2630	2310	1765	1390	1090	850	650	0.8	0.0	-4.7	-14.4	NA
220 Swift	55	3650	3194	2772	2384	2035	1627	1246	939	694	506	+2.0	+2.0	-2.6	-13.4	$19
220 Swift	60	3600	3199	2824	2475	2156	1727	1364	1063	816	619	+2.0	+1.6	-4.1	-13.1	$19
22 Savage H.P.	71	2790	2340	1930	1570	1280	1225	860	585	390	190	+2.0	-1.0	-10.4	-35.7	NA
6mm (24)																
6mm BR Rem.	100	2550	2310	2083	1870	1671	1444	1185	963	776	620	+2.5	-0.6	-11.8	0.0	$22
6mm Norma BR	107	2822	2667	2517	2372	2229	1893	1690	1506	1337	1181	+1.73	0.0	-7.24	-20.6	NA
6mm PPC	70	3140	2750	2400	2070	NA	1535	1175	895	665	NA	+2.0	+1.4	-5.0	0.0	NA
243 Winchester	55	4025	3597	3209	2853	2525	1978	1579	1257	994	779	+0.6	0.0	-4.0	-12.2	NA
243 Winchester	60	3600	3110	2660	2260	1890	1725	1285	945	680	475	+2.0	+1.8	-3.3	-15.5	$17
243 Winchester	70	3400	3040	2700	2390	2100	1795	1435	1135	890	685	1.1	0.0	-5.9	-18.0	NA
243 Winchester	75/80	3350	2955	2593	2259	1951	1993	1551	1194	906	676	+2.0	+0.9	-5.0	-19.0	$16
243 W. Superformance	80	3425	3080	2760	2463	2184	2083	1684	1353	1077	847	1.1	0.0	-5.7	-17.1	NA
243 Winchester	85	3320	3070	2830	2600	2380	2080	1770	1510	1280	1070	+2.0	+1.2	-4.0	-14.0	$18
243 Winchester	90	3120	2871	2635	2411	2199	1946	1647	1388	1162	966	1.4	0.0	-6.4	-18.8	NA
243 Winchester*	100	2960	2697	2449	2215	1993	1945	1615	1332	1089	882	+2.5	+1.2	-6.0	-20.0	$16
243 Winchester	105	2920	2689	2470	2261	2062	1988	1686	1422	1192	992	+2.5	+1.6	-5.0	-18.4	$21
243 Light Mag.	100	3100	2839	2592	2358	2138	2133	1790	1491	1235	1014	+1.5	0.0	-6.8	-19.8	NA
243 WSSM	55	4060	3628	3237	2880	2550	2013	1607	1280	1013	794	0.6	0.0	-3.9	-12.0	NA
243 WSSM	95	3250	3000	2763	2538	2325	2258	1898	1610	1359	1140	1.2	0.0	-5.7	-16.9	NA
243 WSSM	100	3110	2838	2583	2341	2112	2147	1789	1481	1217	991	1.4	0.0	-6.6	-19.7	NA
6mm Remington	80	3470	3064	2694	2352	2036	2139	1667	1289	982	736	+2.0	+1.1	-5.0	-17.0	$16
6mm R. Superformance	95	3235	2955	2692	2443	3309	2207	1841	1528	1259	1028	1.2	0.0	-6.1	-18.0	NA
6mm Remington	100	3100	2829	2573	2332	2104	2133	1777	1470	1207	983	+2.5	+1.6	-5.0	-17.0	$16
6mm Remington	105	3060	2822	2596	2381	2177	2105	1788	1512	1270	1059	+2.5	+1.1	-3.3	-15.0	$21

Cartridge	Bullet Wgt. Grs.	VELOCITY (fps)					ENERGY (ft. lbs.)					TRAJ. (in.)				Est. Price/box
		Muzzle	100 yds.	200 yds.	300 yds.	400 yds.	Muzzle	100 yds.	200 yds.	300 yds.	400 yds.	100 yds.	200 yds.	300 yds.	400 yds.	
240 Wea. Mag.	87	3500	3202	2924	2663	2416	2366	1980	1651	1370	1127	+2.0	+2.0	-2.0	-12.0	**$32**
240 Wea. Mag.	100	3395	3106	2835	2581	2339	2559	2142	1785	1478	1215	+2.5	+2.8	-2.0	-11.0	**$43**
25-20 Win.	86	1460	1194	1030	931	858	407	272	203	165	141	0.0	-23.5	0.0	0.0	**$32****
25-35 Win.	117	2230	1866	1545	1282	1097	1292	904	620	427	313	+2.5	-4.2	-26.0	0.0	**$24**
250 Savage	100	2820	2504	2210	1936	1684	1765	1392	1084	832	630	+2.5	+0.4	-9.0	-28.0	**$17**
257 Roberts	100	2980	2661	2363	2085	1827	1972	1572	1240	965	741	+2.5	-0.8	-5.2	-21.6	**$20**
257 Roberts+P	117	2780	2411	2071	1761	1488	2009	1511	1115	806	576	+2.5	-0.2	-10.2	-32.6	**$18**
257 R. Superformance	117	2946	2705	2478	2265	2057	2253	1901	1595	1329	1099	1.1	0.0	-5.7	-17.1	**NA**
257 Roberts+P	120	2780	2560	2360	2160	1970	2060	1750	1480	1240	1030	+2.5	+1.2	-6.4	-23.6	**$22**
257 Roberts	122	2600	2331	2078	1842	1625	1831	1472	1169	919	715	+2.5	0.0	-10.6	-31.4	**$21**
25-06 Rem.	87	3440	2995	2591	2222	1884	2286	1733	1297	954	686	+2.0	+1.1	-2.5	-14.4	**$17**
25-06 Rem.	90	3440	3043	2680	2344	2034	2364	1850	1435	1098	827	+2.0	+1.8	-3.3	-15.6	**$17**
25-06 Rem.	100	3230	2893	2580	2287	2014	2316	1858	1478	1161	901	+2.0	+0.8	-5.7	-18.9	**$17**
25-06 Rem.	117	2990	2770	2570	2370	2190	2320	2000	1715	1465	1246	+2.5	+1.0	-7.9	-26.6	**$19**
25-06 R. Superformance	117	3110	2861	2626	2403	2191	2512	2127	1792	1500	1246	1.4	0.0	-6.4	-18.9	**NA**
25-06 Rem.*	120	2990	2730	2484	2252	2032	2382	1985	1644	1351	1100	+2.5	+1.2	-5.3	-19.6	**$17**
25-06 Rem.	122	2930	2706	2492	2289	2095	2325	1983	1683	1419	1189	+2.5	+1.8	-4.5	-17.5	**$23**
25 WSSM	85	3470	3156	2863	2589	2331	2273	1880	1548	1266	1026	1.0	0.0	-5.2	-15.7	**NA**
25 WSSM	115	3060	2844	2639	2442	2254	2392	2066	1778	1523	1398	1.4	0.0	-6.4	-18.6	**NA**
25 WSSM	120	2990	2717	2459	2216	1987	2383	1967	1612	1309	1053	1.6	0.0	-7.4	-21.8	**NA**
257 Wea. Mag.	87	3825	3456	3118	2805	2513	2826	2308	1870	1520	1220	+2.0	+2.7	-0.3	-7.6	**$32**
257 Wea. Mag.	100	3555	3237	2941	2665	2404	2806	2326	1920	1576	1283	+2.5	+3.2	0.0	-8.0	**$32**
257 Scramjet	100	3745	3450	3173	2912	2666	3114	2643	2235	1883	1578	+2.1	+2.77	0.0	-6.93	**NA**
6.5																
6.5x47 Lapua	123	2887	NA	2554	NA	2244	2285	NA	1788	NA	1380	NA	4.53	0.0	-10.7	**NA**
6.5x50mm Jap.	139	2360	2160	1970	1790	1620	1720	1440	1195	985	810	+2.5	-1.0	-13.5	0.0	**NA**
6.5x50mm Jap.	156	2070	1830	1610	1430	1260	1475	1155	900	695	550	+2.5	-4.0	-23.8	0.0	**NA**
6.5x52mm Car.	139	2580	2360	2160	1970	1790	2045	1725	1440	1195	985	+2.5	0.0	-9.9	-29.0	**NA**
6.5x52mm Car.	156	2430	2170	1930	1700	1500	2045	1630	1285	1005	780	+2.5	-1.0	-13.9	0.0	**NA**
6.5x52mm Carcano	160	2250	1963	1700	1467	1271	1798	1369	1027	764	574	+3.8	0.0	-15.9	-48.1	**NA**
6.5x55mm Swe.	93	2625	2350	2090	1850	1630	1425	1140	905	705	550	2.4	0.0	-10.3	-31.1	**NA**
6.5x55mm Swe.	123	2750	2570	2400	2240	2080	2065	1810	1580	1370	1185	1.9	0.0	-7.9	-22.9	**NA**
6.5x55mm Swe.	140	2550	NA	NA	NA	NA	2020	NA	NA	NA	NA	0.0	0.0	0.0	0.0	**$18**
6.5x55mm Swe.*	139/140	2850	2640	2440	2250	2070	2525	2170	1855	1575	1330	+2.5	+1.6	-5.4	-18.9	**$18**
6.5x55mm Swe.	156	2650	2370	2110	1870	1650	2425	1950	1550	1215	945	+2.5	0.0	-10.3	-30.6	**NA**
260 Remington	125	2875	2669	2473	2285	2105	2294	1977	1697	1449	1230	1.71	0.0	-7.4	-21.4	**NA**
260 Remington	140	2750	2544	2347	2158	1979	2351	2011	1712	1448	1217	+2.2	0.0	-8.6	-24.6	**NA**
6.5 Creedmoor	120	3020	2815	2619	2430	2251	2430	2111	1827	1574	1350	1.4	0.0	-6.5	-18.9	**NA**
6.5 C. Superformance	129	2950	2756	2570	2392	2221	2492	2175	1892	1639	1417	1.5	0.0	-6.8	-19.7	**NA**
6.5 Creedmoor	140	2820	2654	2494	2339	2190	2472	2179	1915	1679	1467	1.7	0.0	-7.2	-20.6	**NA**
6.5-284 Norma	142	3025	2890	2758	2631	2507	2886	2634	2400	2183	1982	1.13	0.0	-5.7	-16.4	**NA**
6.71 (264) Phantom	120	3150	2929	2718	2517	2325	2645	2286	1969	1698	1440	+1.3	0.0	-6.0	-17.5	**NA**
6.5 Rem. Mag.	120	3210	2905	2621	2353	2102	2745	2248	1830	1475	1177	+2.5	+1.7	-4.1	-16.3	**Disc.**
264 Win. Mag.	140	3030	2782	2548	2326	2114	2854	2406	2018	1682	1389	+2.5	+1.4	-5.1	-18.0	**$24**
6.71 (264) Blackbird	140	3480	3261	3053	2855	2665	3766	3307	2899	2534	2208	+2.4	+3.1	0.0	-7.4	**NA**
6.8 REM SPC	110	2570	2338	2118	1910	1716	1613	1335	1095	891	719	2.4	0.0	-6.3	-20.8	**NA**
6.8mm Rem.	115	2775	2472	2190	1926	1683	1966	1561	1224	947	723	+2.1	0.0	-3.7	-9.4	**NA**
27																
270 Winchester	100	3430	3021	2649	2305	1988	2612	2027	1557	1179	877	+2.0	+1.0	-4.9	-17.5	**$17**
270 Win. (Rem.)	115	2710	2482	2265	2059	NA	1875	1485	1161	896	NA	0.0	4.8	-17.3	0.0	**NA**
270 Winchester	130	3060	2776	2510	2259	2022	2702	2225	1818	1472	1180	+2.5	+1.4	-5.3	-18.2	**$17**
270 Win. Supreme	130	3150	2881	2628	2388	2161	2865	2396	1993	1646	1348	1.3	0.0	-6.4	-18.9	**NA**
270 W. Superformance	130	3200	2984	2788	2582	2393	2955	2570	2228	1924	1653	1.2	0.0	-5.7	-16.7	**NA**
270 Winchester	135	3000	2780	2570	2369	2178	2697	2315	1979	1682	1421	+2.5	+1.4	-6.0	-17.6	**$23**
270 Winchester*	140	2940	2700	2480	2260	2060	2685	2270	1905	1590	1315	+2.5	+1.8	-4.6	-17.9	**$20**
270 Winchester*	150	2850	2585	2336	2100	1879	2705	2226	1817	1468	1175	+2.5	+1.2	-6.5	-22.0	**$17**
270 Win. Supreme	150	2930	2693	2468	2254	2051	2860	2416	2030	1693	1402	1.7	0.0	-7.4	-21.6	**NA**
270 WSM	130	3275	3041	2820	2609	2408	3096	2669	2295	1564	1673	1.1	0.0	-5.5	-16.1	**NA**
270 WSM	140	3125	2865	2619	2386	2165	3035	2559	2132	1769	1457	1.4	0.0	-6.5	-19.0	**NA**
270 WSM	150	3120	2923	2734	2554	2380	3242	2845	2490	2172	1886	1.3	0.0	-5.9	-17.2	**NA**
270 Wea. Mag.	100	3760	3380	3033	2712	2412	3139	2537	2042	1633	1292	+2.0	+2.4	-1.2	-10.1	**$32**
270 Wea. Mag.	130	3375	3119	2878	2649	2432	3287	2808	2390	2026	1707	+2.5	-2.9	-0.9	-9.9	**$32**
270 Wea. Mag.*	150	3245	3036	2837	2647	2465	3507	3070	2681	2334	2023	+2.5	+2.6	-1.8	-11.4	**$47**
7mm																
7mm BR	140	2216	2012	1821	1643	1481	1525	1259	1031	839	681	+2.0	-3.7	-20.0	0.0	**$23**
7mm Mauser*	139/140	2660	2435	2221	2018	1827	2199	1843	1533	1266	1037	+2.5	0.0	-9.6	-27.7	**$17**

Cartridge	Bullet Wgt. Grs.	VELOCITY (fps)					ENERGY (ft. lbs.)					TRAJ. (in.)				Est. Price/box
		Muzzle	100 yds.	200 yds.	300 yds.	400 yds.	Muzzle	100 yds.	200 yds.	300 yds.	400 yds.	100 yds.	200 yds.	300 yds.	400 yds.	
7mm Mauser	154	2690	2490	2300	2120	1940	2475	2120	1810	1530	1285	+2.5	+0.8	-7.5	-23.5	**$17**
7mm Mauser	175	2440	2137	1857	1603	1382	2313	1774	1340	998	742	+2.5	-1.7	-16.1	0.0	**$17**
7x30 Waters	120	2700	2300	1930	1600	1330	1940	1405	990	685	470	+2.5	-0.2	-12.3	0.0	**$18**
7mm-08 Rem.	120	3000	2725	2467	2223	1992	2398	1979	1621	1316	1058	+2.0	0.0	-7.6	-22.3	**$18**
7mm-08 Rem.*	140	2860	2625	2402	2189	1988	2542	2142	1793	1490	1228	+2.5	+0.8	-6.9	-21.9	**$18**
7mm-08 Rem.	154	2715	2510	2315	2128	1950	2520	2155	1832	1548	1300	+2.5	+1.0	-7.0	-22.7	**$23**
7-08 R. Superformance	139	2950	2857	2571	2393	2222	2686	2345	2040	1768	1524	1.5	0.0	-6.8	-19.7	**NA**
7x64mm Bren.	140	Not Yet Announced														**$17**
7x64mm Bren.	154	2820	2610	2420	2230	2050	2720	2335	1995	1695	1430	+2.5	+1.4	-5.7	-19.9	**NA**
7x64mm Bren.*	160	2850	2669	2495	2327	2166	2885	2530	2211	1924	1667	+2.5	+1.6	-4.8	-17.8	**$24**
7x64mm Bren.	175	Not Yet Announced														**$17**
284 Winchester	150	2860	2595	2344	2108	1886	2724	2243	1830	1480	1185	+2.5	+0.8	-7.3	-23.2	**$24**
280 R. Superformance	139	3090	2890	2699	2516	2341	2946	2578	2249	1954	1691	1.3	0.0	-6.1	-17.7	**NA**
280 Remington	140	3000	2758	2528	2309	2102	2797	2363	1986	1657	1373	+2.5	+1.4	-5.2	-18.3	**$17**
280 Remington*	150	2890	2624	2373	2135	1912	2781	2293	1875	1518	1217	+2.5	+0.8	-7.1	-22.6	**$17**
280 Remington	160	2840	2637	2442	2556	2078	2866	2471	2120	1809	1535	+2.5	+0.8	-6.7	-21.0	**$20**
280 Remington	165	2820	2510	2220	1950	1701	2913	2308	1805	1393	1060	+2.5	+0.4	-8.8	-26.5	**$17**
7x61mm S&H Sup.	154	3060	2720	2400	2100	1820	3200	2520	1965	1505	1135	+2.5	+1.8	-5.0	-19.8	**NA**
7mm Dakota	160	3200	3001	2811	2630	2455	3637	3200	2808	2456	2140	+2.1	+1.9	-2.8	-12.5	**NA**
7mm Rem. Mag. (Rem.)	140	2710	2482	2265	2059	NA	2283	1915	1595	1318	NA	0.0	-4.5	-1.57	0.0	**NA**
7mm Rem. Mag.*	139/140	3150	2930	2710	2510	2320	3085	2660	2290	1960	1670	+2.5	+2.4	-2.4	-12.7	**$21**
7 R.M. Superformance	139	3240	3033	2836	2648	2467	3239	2839	2482	2163	1877	1.1	0.0	-5.5	-15.9	**NA**
7mm Rem. Mag.	150/154	3110	2830	2568	2320	2085	3221	2667	2196	1792	1448	+2.5	+1.6	-4.6	-16.5	**$21**
7mm Rem. Mag.*	160/162	2950	2730	2520	2320	2120	3090	2650	2250	1910	1600	+2.5	+1.8	-4.4	-17.8	**$34**
7 R.M. Superformance	154	3100	2914	2736	2565	2401	3286	2904	2560	2250	1970	1.3	0.0	-5.9	-17.2	**NA**
7mm Rem. Mag.	165	2900	2699	2507	2324	2147	3081	2669	2303	1978	1689	+2.5	+1.2	-5.9	-19.0	**$28**
7mm Rem Mag.	175	2860	2645	2440	2244	2057	3178	2718	2313	1956	1644	+2.5	+1.0	-6.5	-20.7	**$21**
7mm Rem. SA ULTRA MAG	140	3175	2934	2707	2490	2283	3033	2676	2277	1927	1620	1.3	0.0	-6	-17.7	**NA**
7mm Rem. SA ULTRA MAG	150	3110	2828	2563	2313	2077	3221	2663	2188	1782	1437	2.5	2.1	-3.6	-15.8	**NA**
7mm Rem. SA ULTRA MAG	160	2960	2762	2572	2390	2215	3112	2709	2350	2029	1743	2.6	2.2	-3.6	-15.4	**NA**
7mm Rem. WSM	140	3225	3008	2801	2603	2414	3233	2812	2438	2106	1812	1.2	0.0	-5.6	-16.4	**NA**
7mm Rem. WSM	160	2990	2744	2512	2081	1883	3176	2675	2241	1864	1538	1.6	0.0	-7.1	-20.8	**NA**
7mm Wea. Mag.	140	3225	2970	2729	2501	2283	3233	2741	2315	1943	1621	+2.5	+2.0	-3.2	-14.0	**$35**
7mm Wea. Mag.	154	3260	3023	2799	2586	2382	3539	3044	2609	2227	1890	+2.5	+2.8	-1.5	-10.8	**$32**
7mm Wea. Mag.*	160	3200	3004	2816	2637	2464	3637	3205	2817	2469	2156	+2.5	+2.7	-1.5	-10.6	**$47**
7mm Wea. Mag.	165	2950	2747	2553	2367	2189	3188	2765	2388	2053	1756	+2.5	+1.8	-4.2	-16.4	**$43**
7mm Wea. Mag.	175	2910	2693	2486	2288	2098	3293	2818	2401	2033	1711	+2.5	+1.2	-5.9	-19.4	**$35**
7.21(.284) Tomahawk	140	3300	3118	2943	2774	2612	3386	3022	2693	2393	2122	2.3	3.2	0.0	-7.7	**NA**
7mm STW	140	3325	3064	2818	2585	2364	3436	2918	2468	2077	1737	+2.3	+1.8	-3.0	-13.1	**NA**
7mm STW Supreme	160	3150	2894	2652	2422	2204	3526	2976	2499	2085	1727	1.3	0.0	-6.3	-18.5	**NA**
7mm Rem. Ultra Mag.	140	3425	3184	2956	2740	2534	3646	3151	2715	2333	1995	1.7	1.6	-2.6	-11.4	**NA**
7mm Firehawk	140	3625	3373	3135	2909	2695	4084	3536	3054	2631	2258	+2.2	+2.9	0.0	-7.03	**NA**
7.21 (.284) Firebird	140	3750	3522	3306	3101	2905	4372	3857	3399	2990	2625	1.6	2.4	0.0	-6.0	**NA**
30																
30 Carbine	110	1990	1567	1236	1035	923	977	600	373	262	208	0.0	-13.5	0.0	0.0	**$28****
300 Whisper	110	2375	2094	1834	1597	NA	1378	1071	822	623	NA	3.2	0.0	-13.6	NA	**NA**
300 Whisper	208	1020	988	959	NA	NA	480	451	422	NA	NA	0.0	-34.10	NA	NA	**NA**
303 Savage	190	1890	1612	1327	1183	1055	1507	1096	794	591	469	+2.5	-7.6	0.0	0.0	**$24**
30 Remington	170	2120	1822	1555	1328	1153	1696	1253	913	666	502	+2.5	-4.7	-26.3	0.0	**$20**
7.62x39mm Rus.	123/125	2300	2030	1780	1550	1350	1445	1125	860	655	500	+2.5	-2.0	-17.5	0.0	**$13**
30-30 Win.	55	3400	2693	2085	1570	1187	1412	886	521	301	172	+2.0	0.0	-10.2	-35.0	**$18**
30-30 Win.	125	2570	2090	1660	1320	1080	1830	1210	770	480	320	-2.0	-2.6	-19.9	0.0	**$13**
30-30 Win.	150	2390	2040	1723	1447	1225	1902	1386	989	697	499	0.0	-7.5	-27.0	-63.0	**NA**
30-30 Win. Supreme	150	2480	2095	1747	1446	1209	2049	1462	1017	697	487	0.0	-6.5	-24.5	0.0	**NA**
30-30 Win.	160	2300	1997	1719	1473	1268	1879	1416	1050	771	571	+2.5	-2.9	-20.2	0.0	**$18**
30-30 Win. Lever Evolution	160	2400	2150	1916	1699	NA	2046	1643	1304	1025	NA	3.0	0.2	-12.1	NA	**NA**
30-30 PMC Cowboy	170	1300	1198	1121			638	474				0.0	-27.0	0.0	0.0	**NA**
30-30 Win.*	170	2200	1895	1619	1381	1191	1827	1355	989	720	535	+2.5	-5.8	-23.6	0.0	**$13**
300 Savage	150	2630	2354	2094	1853	1631	2303	1845	1462	1143	886	+2.5	-0.4	-10.1	-30.7	**$17**
300 Savage	180	2350	2137	1935	1754	1570	2207	1825	1496	1217	985	+2.5	-1.6	-15.2	0.0	**$17**
30-40 Krag	180	2430	2213	2007	1813	1632	2360	1957	1610	1314	1064	+2.5	-1.4	-13.8	0.0	**$18**
7.65x53mm Arg.	180	2590	2390	2200	2010	1830	2685	2280	1925	1615	1345	+2.5	0.0	-27.6	0.0	**NA**
7.5x53mm Argentine	150	2785	2519	2269	2032	1814	2583	2113	1714	1376	1096	+2.0	0.0	-8.8	-25.5	**NA**
308 Marlin Express	160	2660	2430	2226	2026	1836	2513	2111	1761	1457	1197	3.0	1.7	-6.7	-23.5	**NA**
307 Winchester	150	2760	2321	1924	1575	1289	2530	1795	1233	826	554	+2.5	-1.5	-13.6	0.0	**Disc.**

Cartridge	Bullet Wgt. Grs.	VELOCITY (fps)					ENERGY (ft. lbs.)					TRAJ. (in.)				Est. Price/box
		Muzzle	100 yds.	200 yds.	300 yds.	400 yds.	Muzzle	100 yds.	200 yds.	300 yds.	400 yds.	100 yds.	200 yds.	300 yds.	400 yds.	
7.5x55 Swiss	180	2650	2450	2250	2060	1880	2805	2390	2020	1700	1415	+2.5	+0.6	-8.1	-24.9	NA
7.5x55mm Swiss	165	2720	2515	2319	2132	1954	2710	2317	1970	1665	1398	+2.0	0.0	-8.5	-24.6	NA
30 Remington AR	123/125	2800	2465	2154	1867	1606	2176	1686	1288	967	716	2.1	0.0	-9.7	-29.4	NA
308 Winchester	55	3770	3215	2726	2286	1888	1735	1262	907	638	435	-2.0	+1.4	-3.8	-15.8	$22
308 Win. PDX1	120	2850	2497	2171	NA	NA	2164	1662	1256	NA	NA	0.0	-2.8	NA	NA	NA
308 Winchester	150	2820	2533	2263	2009	1774	2648	2137	1705	1344	1048	+2.5	+0.4	-8.5	-26.1	$17
308 W. Superformance	150	3000	2772	2555	2348	1962	2997	2558	2173	1836	1540	1.5	0.0	-6.9	-20.0	NA
308 Winchester	165	2700	2440	2194	1963	1748	2670	2180	1763	1411	1199	+2.5	0.0	-9.7	-28.5	$20
308 Winchester	168	2680	2493	2314	2143	1979	2678	2318	1998	1713	1460	+2.5	0.0	-8.9	-25.3	$18
308 Win. Super Match	168	2870	2647	2462	2284	2114	3008	2613	2261	1946	1667	1.7	0.0	-7.5	-21.6	NA
308 Win. (Fed.)	170	2000	1740	1510	NA	NA	1510	1145	860	NA	NA	0.0	0.0	0.0	0.0	NA
308 Winchester	178	2620	2415	2220	2034	1857	2713	2306	1948	1635	1363	+2.5	0.0	-9.6	-27.6	$23
308 Win. Super Match	178	2780	2609	2444	2285	2132	3054	2690	2361	2064	1797	1.8	0.0	-7.6	-21.9	NA
308 Winchester*	180	2620	2393	2178	1974	1782	2743	2288	1896	1557	1269	+2.5	-0.2	-10.2	-28.5	$17
30-06 Spfd.	55	4080	3485	2965	2502	2083	2033	1483	1074	764	530	+2.0	+1.9	-2.1	-11.7	$22
30-06 Spfd. (Rem.)	125	2660	2335	2034	1757	NA	1964	1513	1148	856	NA	0.0	-5.2	-18.9	0.0	NA
30-06 Spfd.	125	3140	2780	2447	2138	1853	2736	2145	1662	1279	953	+2.0	+1.0	-6.2	-21.0	$17
30-06 Spfd.	150	2910	2617	2342	2083	1853	2820	2281	1827	1445	1135	+2.5	+0.8	-7.2	-23.4	$17
30-06 Superformance	150	3080	2848	2617	2417	2216	3159	2700	2298	1945	1636	1.4	0.0	-6.4	-18.9	NA
30-06 Spfd.	152	2910	2654	2413	2184	1968	2858	2378	1965	1610	1307	+2.5	+1.0	-6.6	-21.3	$23
30-06 Spfd.*	165	2800	2534	2283	2047	1825	2872	2352	1909	1534	1220	+2.5	+0.4	-8.4	-25.5	$17
30-06 Spfd.	168	2710	2522	2346	2169	2003	2739	2372	2045	1754	1497	+2.5	+0.4	-8.0	-23.5	$18
30-06 Spfd. (Fed.)	170	2000	1740	1510	NA	NA	1510	1145	860	NA	NA	0.0	0.0	0.0	0.0	NA
30-06 Spfd.	178	2720	2511	2311	2121	1939	2924	2491	2111	1777	1486	+2.5	+0.4	-8.2	-24.6	$23
30-06 Spfd.*	180	2700	2469	2250	2042	1846	2913	2436	2023	1666	1362	-2.5	0.0	-9.3	-27.0	$17
30-06 Superformance	180	2820	2630	2447	2272	2104	3178	2764	2393	2063	1769	1.8	0.0	-7.6	-21.9	NA
30-06 Spfd.	220	2410	2130	1870	1632	1422	2837	2216	1708	1301	988	+2.5	-1.7	-18.0	0.0	$17
30-06 High Energy	180	2880	2690	2500	2320	2150	3315	2880	2495	2150	1845	+1.7	0.0	-7.2	-21.0	NA
30 T/C Superformance	150	3000	2772	2555	2348	2151	2997	2558	2173	1836	1540	1.5	0.0	-6.9	-20.0	NA
30 T/C Superformance	165	2850	2644	2447	2258	2078	2975	2560	2193	1868	1582	1.7	0.0	-7.6	-22.0	NA
300 Rem SA Ultra Mag	150	3200	2901	2622	2359	2112	3410	2803	2290	1854	1485	1.3	0.0	-6.4	-19.1	NA
300 Rem SA Ultra Mag	165	3075	2792	2527	2276	2040	3464	2856	2339	1898	1525	1.5	0.0	-7	-20.7	NA
300 Rem SA Ultra Mag	180	2960	2761	2571	2389	2214	3501	3047	2642	2280	1959	2.6	2.2	-3.6	-15.4	NA
7.82 (308) Patriot	150	3250	2999	2762	2537	2323	3519	2997	2542	2145	1798	+1.2	0.0	-5.8	-16.9	NA
300 RCM Superformance	150	3310	3065	2833	2613	2404	3648	3128	2673	2274	1924	1.1	0.0	-5.4	-16.0	NA
300 RCM Superformance	165	3185	2964	2753	2552	2360	3716	3217	2776	2386	2040	1.2	0.0	-5.8	-17.0	NA
300 RCM Superformance	180	3040	2840	2649	2466	2290	3693	3223	2804	2430	2096	1.4	0.0	-6.4	-18.5	NA
300 WSM	150	3300	3061	2834	2619	2414	3628	3121	2676	2285	1941	1.1	0.0	-5.4	-15.9	NA
300 WSM	180	2970	2741	2524	2317	2120	3526	3005	2547	2147	1797	1.6	0.0	-7.0	-20.5	NA
300 WSM	180	3010	2923	2734	2554	2380	3242	2845	2490	2172	1886	1.3	0	-5.9	-17.2	NA
308 Norma Mag.	180	3020	2820	2630	2440	2270	3645	3175	2755	2385	2050	+2.5	+2.0	-3.5	-14.8	NA
300 Dakota	200	3000	2824	2656	2493	2336	3996	3542	3131	2760	2423	+2.2	+1.5	-4.0	-15.2	NA
300 H&H Magnum*	180	2880	2640	2412	2196	1990	3315	2785	2325	1927	1583	+2.5	+0.8	-6.8	-21.7	$24
300 H&H Magnum	220	2550	2267	2002	1757	NA	3167	2510	1958	1508	NA	-2.5	-0.4	-12.0	0.0	NA
300 Win. Mag.	150	3290	2951	2636	2342	2068	3605	2900	2314	1827	1424	+2.5	+1.9	-3.8	-15.8	$22
300 WM Superformance	150	3400	3150	2914	2690	2477	3850	3304	2817	2409	2043	1.0	0.0	-5.1	-15.0	NA
300 Win. Mag.	165	3100	2877	2665	2462	2269	3522	3033	2603	2221	1897	+2.5	+2.4	-3.0	-16.9	$24
300 Win. Mag.	178	2900	2760	2568	2375	2191	3509	3030	2606	2230	1897	+2.5	+1.4	-5.0	-17.6	$29
300 WM Super Match	178	2960	2770	2587	2412	2243	3462	3031	2645	2298	1988	1.5	0.0	-6.7	-19.4	NA
300 Win. Mag.*	180	2960	2745	2540	2344	2157	3501	3011	2578	2196	1859	+2.5	+1.2	-5.5	-18.5	$22
300 WM Superformance	180	3130	2927	2732	2546	2366	3917	3424	2983	2589	2238	1.3	0.0	-5.9	-17.3	NA
300 Win. Mag.	190	2885	1691	2506	2327	2156	3511	3055	2648	2285	1961	+2.5	+1.2	-5.7	-19.0	$26
300 Win. Mag.*	200	2825	2595	2376	2167	1970	3545	2991	2508	2086	1742	-2.5	+1.6	-4.7	-17.2	$36
300 Win. Mag.	220	2680	2448	2228	2020	1823	3508	2927	2424	1993	1623	+2.5	0.0	-9.5	-27.5	$23
300 Rem. Ultra Mag.	150	3450	3208	2980	2762	2556	3964	3427	2956	2541	2175	1.7	1.5	-2.6	-11.2	NA
300 Rem. Ultra Mag.	150	2910	2686	2473	2279	2077	2820	2403	2037	1716	1436	1.7	0.0	-7.4	-21.5	NA
300 Rem. Ultra Mag.	180	3250	3037	2834	2640	2454	4221	3686	3201	2786	2407	2.4	0.0	-3.0	-12.7	NA
300 Rem. Ultra Mag.	180	2960	2774	2505	2294	2093	3501	2971	2508	2103	1751	2.7	2.2	-3.8	-16.4	NA
300 Rem. Ultra Mag.	200	3032	2791	2562	2345	2138	4083	3459	2916	2442	2030	1.5	0.0	-6.8	-19.9	NA
300 Wea. Mag.	100	3900	3441	3038	2652	2305	3714	2891	2239	1717	1297	+2.0	+2.6	-0.6	-8.7	$32
300 Wea. Mag.	150	3600	3307	3033	2776	2533	4316	3642	3064	2566	2137	+2.5	+3.2	0.0	-8.1	$32
300 Wea. Mag.	165	3450	3210	3000	2792	2593	4360	3796	3297	2855	2464	+2.5	+3.2	0.0	-7.8	NA
300 Wea. Mag.	178	3120	2902	2695	2497	2308	3847	3329	2870	2464	2104	+2.5	-1.7	-3.6	-14.7	$43
300 Wea. Mag.	180	3330	3110	2910	2710	2520	4430	3875	3375	2935	2540	+1.0	0.0	-5.2	-15.1	NA
300 Wea. Mag.	190	3030	2830	2638	2455	2279	3873	3378	2936	2542	2190	+2.5	+1.6	-4.3	-16.0	$38
300 Wea. Mag.	220	2850	2541	2283	1964	1736	3967	3155	2480	1922	1471	+2.5	+0.4	-8.5	-26.4	$35

Cartridge	Bullet Wgt. Grs.	VELOCITY (fps)					ENERGY (ft. lbs.)					TRAJ. (in.)				Est. Price/box
		Muzzle	100 yds.	200 yds.	300 yds.	400 yds.	Muzzle	100 yds.	200 yds.	300 yds.	400 yds.	100 yds.	200 yds.	300 yds.	400 yds.	
300 Pegasus	180	3500	3319	3145	2978	2817	4896	4401	3953	3544	3172	+2.28	+2.89	0.0	-6.79	NA
31																
32-20 Win.	100	1210	1021	913	834	769	325	231	185	154	131	0.0	-32.3	0.0	0.0	$23**
303 British	180	2460	2124	1817	1542	1311	2418	1803	1319	950	687	+2.5	-1.8	-16.8	0.0	$18
303 Light Mag.	150	2830	2570	2325	2094	1884	2667	2199	1800	1461	1185	+2.0	0.0	-8.4	-24.6	NA
7.62x54mm Rus.	146	2950	2730	2520	2320	NA	2820	2415	2055	1740	NA	+2.5	+2.0	-4.4	-17.7	NA
7.62x54mm Rus.	180	2580	2370	2180	2000	1820	2650	2250	1900	1590	1100	+2.5	0.0	-9.8	-28.5	NA
7.7x58mm Jap.	150	2640	2399	2170	1954	1752	2321	1916	1568	1271	1022	+2.3	0.0	-9.7	-28.5	NA
7.7x58mm Jap.	180	2500	2300	2100	1920	1750	2490	2105	1770	1475	1225	+2.5	0.0	-10.4	-30.2	NA
8mm																
8x56 R	205	2400	2188	1987	1797	1621	2621	2178	1796	1470	1196	+2.9	0.0	-11.7	-34.3	NA
8x57mm JS Mau.	165	2850	2520	2210	1930	1670	2965	2330	1795	1360	1015	+2.5	+1.0	-7.7	0.0	NA
32 Win. Special	165	2410	2145	1897	1669	NA	2128	1685	1318	1020	NA	2.0	0.0	-13.0	-19.9	NA
32 Win. Special	170	2250	1921	1626	1372	1175	1911	1393	998	710	521	+2.5	-3.5	-22.9	0.0	$14
8mm Mauser	170	2360	1969	1622	1333	1123	2102	1464	993	671	476	+2.5	-3.1	-22.2	0.0	$18
325 WSM	180	3060	2841	2632	2432	2242	3743	3226	2769	2365	2009	+1.4	0.0	-6.4	-18.7	NA
325 WSM	200	2950	2753	2565	2384	2210	3866	3367	2922	2524	2170	+1.5	0.0	-6.8	-19.8	NA
325 WSM	220	2840	2605	2382	2169	1968	3941	3316	2772	2300	1893	+1.8	0.0	-8.0	-23.3	NA
8mm Rem. Mag.	185	3080	2761	2464	2186	1927	3896	3131	2494	1963	1525	+2.5	+1.4	-5.5	-19.7	$30
8mm Rem. Mag.	220	2830	2581	2346	2123	1913	3912	3254	2688	2201	1787	+2.5	+0.6	-7.6	-23.5	Disc.
33																
338 Federal	180	2830	2590	2350	2130	1930	3200	2670	2215	1820	1480	1.8	0.0	-8.2	-23.9	NA
338 Marlin Express	200	2565	2365	2174	1992	1820	2922	2484	2099	1762	1471	3.0	1.2	-7.9	-25.9	NA
338 Federal	185	2750	2550	2350	2160	1980	3105	2660	2265	1920	1615	1.9	0.0	-8.3	-24.1	NA
338 Federal	210	2630	2410	2200	2010	1820	3225	2710	2265	1880	1545	2.3	0.0	-9.4	-27.3	NA
338-06	200	2750	2553	2364	2184	2011	3358	2894	2482	2118	1796	+1.9	0.0	-8.22	-23.6	NA
330 Dakota	250	2900	2719	2545	2378	2217	4668	4103	3595	3138	2727	+2.3	+1.3	-5.0	-17.5	NA
338 Lapua	250	2963	2795	2640	2493	NA	4842	4341	3881	3458	NA	+1.9	0.0	-7.9	0.0	NA
338 RCM Superformance	185	2980	2755	2542	2338	2143	3647	3118	2653	2242	1887	1.5	0.0	-6.9	-20.3	NA
338 RCM Superformance	200	2950	2744	2547	2358	2177	3846	3342	2879	2468	2104	1.6	0.0	-6.9	-20.1	NA
338 RCM Superformance	225	2750	2575	2407	2245	2089	3778	3313	2894	2518	2180	1.9	0.0	-7.9	-22.7	NA
338 WM Superformance	185	3080	2850	2632	2424	2226	3896	3337	2845	2413	2034	1.4	0.0	-6.4	-18.8	NA
338 Win. Mag.*	210	2830	2590	2370	2150	1940	3735	3130	2610	2155	1760	+2.5	+1.4	-6.0	-20.9	$33
338 Win. Mag.*	225	2785	2517	2266	2029	1808	3871	3165	2565	2057	1633	+2.5	+0.4	-8.5	-25.9	$27
338 WM Superformance	225	2840	2758	2582	2414	2252	4318	3798	3331	2911	2533	1.5	0.0	-6.8	-19.5	NA
338 Win. Mag.	230	2780	2573	2375	2186	2005	3948	3382	2881	2441	2054	+2.5	+1.2	-6.3	-21.0	$40
338 Win. Mag.*	250	2660	2456	2261	2075	1898	3927	3348	2837	2389	1999	+2.5	+0.2	-9.0	-26.2	$27
338 Ultra Mag.	250	2860	2645	2440	2244	2057	4540	3882	3303	2794	2347	1.7	0.0	-7.6	-22.1	NA
338 Lapua Match	250	2900	2760	2625	2494	2366	4668	4229	3825	3452	3108	1.5	0.0	-6.6	-18.8	NA
338 Lapua Match	285	2745	2623	2504	2388	2275	4768	4352	3966	3608	3275	1.8	0.0	-7.3	-20.8	NA
8.59(.338) Galaxy	200	3100	2899	2707	2524	2347	4269	3734	3256	2829	2446	3	3.8	0.0	-9.3	NA
340 Wea. Mag.*	210	3250	2991	2746	2515	2295	4924	4170	3516	2948	2455	+2.5	+1.9	-1.8	-11.8	$56
340 Wea. Mag.*	250	3000	2806	2621	2443	2272	4995	4371	3812	3311	2864	+2.5	+2.0	-3.5	-14.8	$56
338 A-Square	250	3120	2799	2500	2220	1958	5403	4348	3469	2736	2128	+2.5	+2.7	-1.5	-10.5	NA
338-378 Wea. Mag.	225	3180	2974	2778	2591	2410	5052	4420	3856	3353	2902	3.1	3.8	0.0	-8.9	NA
338 Titan	225	3230	3010	2800	2600	2409	5211	4524	3916	3377	2898	+3.07	+3.8	0.0	-8.95	NA
338 Excalibur	200	3600	3361	3134	2920	2715	5755	5015	4363	3785	3274	+2.23	+2.87	0.0	-6.99	NA
338 Excalibur	250	3250	2922	2618	2333	2066	5863	4740	3804	3021	2370	+1.3	0.0	-6.35	-19.2	NA
34, 35																
348 Winchester	200	2520	2215	1931	1672	1443	2820	2178	1656	1241	925	+2.5	-1.4	-14.7	0.0	$42
357 Magnum	158	1830	1427	1138	980	883	1175	715	454	337	274	0.0	-16.2	-33.1	0.0	$25**
35 Remington	150	2300	1874	1506	1218	1039	1762	1169	755	494	359	+2.5	-4.1	-26.3	0.0	$16
35 Remington	200	2080	1698	1376	1140	1001	1921	1280	841	577	445	+2.5	-6.3	-17.1	-33.6	$16
35 Rem. Lever Evolution	200	2225	1963	1721	1503	NA	2198	1711	1315	1003	NA	3.0	-1.3	-17.5	NA	NA
356 Winchester	200	2460	2114	1797	1517	1284	2688	1985	1434	1022	732	+2.5	-1.8	-15.1	0.0	$31
356 Winchester	250	2160	1911	1682	1476	1299	2591	2028	1571	1210	937	+2.5	-3.7	-22.2	0.0	$31
358 Winchester	200	2490	2171	1876	1619	1379	2753	2093	1563	1151	844	+2.5	-1.6	-15.6	0.0	$31
358 STA	275	2850	2562	2292	2039	NA	4958	4009	3208	2539	NA	+1.9	0.0	-8.6	0.0	NA
350 Rem. Mag.	200	2710	2410	2130	1870	1631	3261	2579	2014	1553	1181	+2.5	-0.2	-10.0	-30.1	$33
35 Whelen	200	2675	2378	2100	1842	1606	3177	2510	1958	1506	1145	+2.5	-0.2	-10.3	-31.1	$20
35 Whelen	225	2500	2300	2110	1930	1770	3120	2650	2235	1870	1560	+2.6	0.0	-10.2	-29.9	NA
35 Whelen	250	2400	2197	2005	1823	1652	3197	2680	2230	1844	1515	+2.5	-1.2	-13.7	0.0	$20
358 Norma Mag.	250	2800	2510	2230	1970	1730	4350	3480	2750	2145	1655	+2.5	+1.0	-7.6	-25.2	NA
358 STA	275	2850	2562	229*2	2039	1764	4959	4009	3208	2539	1899	+1.9	0.0	-8.58	-26.1	NA
9.3mm																
9.3x57mm Mau.	286	2070	1810	1590	1390	1110	2710	2090	1600	1220	955	+2.5	-2.6	-22.5	0.0	NA

Cartridge	Bullet Wgt. Grs.	VELOCITY (fps)					ENERGY (ft. lbs.)					TRAJ. (in.)				Est. Price/box
		Muzzle	100 yds.	200 yds.	300 yds.	400 yds.	Muzzle	100 yds.	200 yds.	300 yds.	400 yds.	100 yds.	200 yds.	300 yds.	400 yds.	
370 Sako Mag.	286	3550	2370	2200	2040	2880	4130	3570	3075	2630	2240	2.4	0.0	-9.5	-27.2	NA
9.3x64mm	286	2700	2505	2318	2139	1968	4629	3984	3411	2906	2460	+2.5	+2.7	-4.5	-19.2	NA
9.3x74Rmm	286	2360	2136	1924	1727	1545	3536	2896	2351	1893	1516	0.0	-6.1	-21.7	-49.0	NA
375																
375 Winchester	200	2200	1841	1526	1268	1089	2150	1506	1034	714	527	+2.5	-4.0	-26.2	0.0	$27
375 Winchester	250	1900	1647	1424	1239	1103	2005	1506	1126	852	676	+2.5	-6.9	-33.3	0.0	$27
376 Steyr	225	2600	2331	2078	1842	1625	3377	2714	2157	1694	1319	2.5	0.0	-10.6	-31.4	NA
376 Steyr	270	2600	2372	2156	1951	1759	4052	3373	2787	2283	1855	2.3	0.0	-9.9	-28.9	NA
375 Dakota	300	2600	2316	2051	1804	1579	4502	3573	2800	2167	1661	+2.4	0.0	-11.0	-32.7	NA
375 N.E. 2-1/2"	270	2000	1740	1507	1310	NA	2398	1815	1362	1026	NA	+2.5	-6.0	-30.0	0.0	NA
375 Flanged	300	2450	2150	1886	1640	NA	3998	3102	2369	1790	NA	+2.5	-2.4	-17.0	0.0	NA
375 Ruger	270	2840	2600	2372	2156	1951	4835	4052	3373	2786	2283	1.8	0.0	-8.0	-23.6	NA
375 Ruger	300	2660	2344	2050	1780	1536	4713	3660	2800	2110	1572	2.4	0.0	-10.8	-32.6	NA
375 H&H Magnum	250	2670	2450	2240	2040	1850	3955	3335	2790	2315	1905	+2.5	-0.4	-10.2	-28.4	NA
375 H&H Magnum	270	2690	2420	2166	1928	1707	4337	3510	2812	2228	1747	+2.5	0.0	-10.0	-29.4	$28
375 H&H Magnum*	300	2530	2245	1979	1733	1512	4263	3357	2608	2001	1523	+2.5	-1.0	-10.5	-33.6	$28
375 H&H Hvy. Mag.	270	2870	2628	2399	2182	1976	4937	4141	3451	2150	1845	+1.7	0.0	-7.2	-21.0	NA
375 H&H Hvy. Mag.	300	2705	2386	2090	1816	1568	4873	3793	2908	2195	1637	+2.3	0.0	-10.4	-31.4	NA
375 Rem. Ultra Mag.	270	2900	2558	2241	1947	1678	5041	3922	3010	2272	1689	1.9	2.7	-8.9	-27.0	NA
375 Rem. Ultra Mag.	300	2760	2505	2263	2035	1822	5073	4178	3412	2759	2210	2.0	0.0	-8.8	-26.1	NA
375 Wea. Mag.	300	2700	2420	2157	1911	1685	4856	3901	3100	2432	1891	+2.5	-.04	-10.7	0.0	NA
378 Wea. Mag.	270	3180	2976	2781	2594	2415	6062	5308	4635	4034	3495	+2.5	+2.6	-1.8	-11.3	$71
378 Wea. Mag.	300	2929	2576	2252	1952	1680	5698	4419	3379	2538	1881	+2.5	+1.2	-7.0	-24.5	$77
375 A-Square	300	2920	2626	2351	2093	1850	5679	4594	3681	2917	2281	+2.5	+1.4	-6.0	-21.0	NA
38-40 Win.	180	1160	999	901	827	764	538	399	324	273	233	0.0	-33.9	0.0	0.0	$42**
40, 41																
400 A-Square DPM	400	2400	2146	1909	1689	NA	5116	2092	3236	2533	NA	2.98	0.0	-10.0	NA	NA
400 A-Square DPM	170	2980	2463	2001	1598	NA	3352	2289	1512	964	NA	2.16	0.0	-11.1	NA	NA
408 CheyTac	419	2850	2752	2657	2562	2470	7551	7048	6565	6108	5675	-1.02	0.0	1.9	4.2	NA
405 Win.	300	2200	1851	1545	1296		3224	2282	1589	1119		4.6	0.0	-19.5	0.0	NA
450/400-3"	400	2050	1815	1595	1402	NA	3732	2924	2259	1746	NA	0.0	NA	-33.4	NA	NA
416 Ruger	400	2400	2151	1917	1700	NA	5116	4109	3264	2568	NA	0.0	-6.0	-21.6	0.0	NA
416 Dakota	400	2450	2294	2143	1998	1859	5330	4671	4077	3544	3068	+2.5	-0.2	-10.5	-29.4	NA
416 Taylor	400	2350	2117	1896	1693	NA	4905	3980	3194	2547	NA	+2.5	-1.2	15.0	0.0	NA
416 Hoffman	400	2380	2145	1923	1718	1529	5031	4087	3285	2620	2077	+2.5	-1.0	-14.1	0.0	NA
416 Rigby	350	2600	2449	2303	2162	2026	5253	4661	4122	3632	3189	+2.5	-1.8	-10.2	-26.0	NA
416 Rigby	400	2370	2210	2050	1900	NA	4990	4315	3720	3185	NA	+2.5	-0.7	-12.1	0.0	NA
416 Rigby	410	2370	2110	1870	1640	NA	5115	4050	3165	2455	NA	+2.5	-2.4	-17.3	0.0	$110
416 Rem. Mag.*	350	2520	2270	2034	1814	1611	4935	4004	3216	2557	2017	+2.5	-0.8	-12.6	-35.0	$82
416 Wea. Mag.*	400	2700	2397	2115	1852	1613	6474	5104	3971	3047	2310	+2.5	0.0	-10.1	-30.4	$96
10.57 (416) Meteor	400	2730	2532	2342	2161	1987	6621	5695	4874	4147	3508	+1.9	0.0	-8.3	-24.0	NA
404 Jeffrey	400	2150	1924	1716	1525	NA	4105	3289	2614	2064	NA	+2.5	-4.0	-22.1	0.0	NA
425, 44																
425 Express	400	2400	2160	1934	1725	NA	5115	4145	3322	2641	NA	+2.5	-1.0	-14.0	0.0	NA
44-40 Win.	200	1190	1006	900	822	756	629	449	360	300	254	0.0	-33.3	0.0	0.0	$36**
44 Rem. Mag.	210	1920	1477	1155	982	880	1719	1017	622	450	361	0.0	-17.6	0.0	0.0	$14
44 Rem. Mag.	240	1760	1380	1114	970	878	1650	1015	661	501	411	0.0	-17.6	0.0	0.0	$14
444 Marlin	240	2350	1815	1377	1087	941	2942	1753	1001	630	472	+2.5	-15.1	-31.0	0.0	$13
444 Marlin	265	2120	1733	1405	1160	1012	2644	1768	1162	791	603	+2.5	-6.0	-32.2	0.0	$22
444 Mar. Lever Evolution	265	2325	1971	1652	1380	NA	3180	2285	1606	1120	NA	3.0	-1.4	-18.6	NA	Disc.
444 Mar. Superformance	265	2400	1976	1603	1298	NA	3389	2298	1512	991	NA	4.1	0.0	-17.8	NA	NA
45																
45-70 Govt.	300	1810	1497	1244	1073	969	2182	1492	1031	767	625	0.0	-14.8	0.0	0.0	$21
45-70 Govt. Supreme	300	1880	1558	1292	1103	988	2355	1616	1112	811	651	0.0	-12.9	-46.0	-105.0	NA
45-70 Lever Evolution	325	2050	1729	1450	1225	NA	3032	2158	1516	1083	NA	3.0	-4.1	-27.8	NA	NA
45-70 Govt. CorBon	350	1800	1526	1296			2519	1810	1307			0.0	-14.6	0.0	0.0	NA
45-70 Govt.	405	1330	1168	1055	977	918	1590	1227	1001	858	758	0.0	-24.6	0.0	0.0	$21
45-70 Govt. PMC Cowboy	405	1550	1193				1639	1280				0.0	-23.9	0.0	0.0	NA
45-70 Govt. Garrett	415	1850					3150					3.0	-7.0	0.0	0.0	NA
45-70 Govt. Garrett	530	1550	1343	1178	1062	982	2828	2123	1633	1327	1135	0.0	-17.8	0.0	0.0	NA
450 Bushmaster	250	2200	1831	1508	1480	1073	2686	1860	1262	864	639	0.0	-9.0	-33.5	0.0	NA
450 Marlin	350	2100	1774	1488	1254	1089	3427	2446	1720	1222	922	0.0	-9.7	-35.2	0.0	NA
450 Mar. Lever Evolution	325	2225	1887	1585	1331	NA	3572	2569	1813	1278	NA	3.0	-2.2	-21.3	NA	NA
457 Wild West Magnum	350	2150	1718	1348	NA	NA	3645	2293	1413	NA	NA	0.0	-10.5	NA	NA	NA

Cartridge	Bullet Wgt. Grs.	VELOCITY (fps) Muzzle	100 yds.	200 yds.	300 yds.	400 yds.	ENERGY (ft. lbs.) Muzzle	100 yds.	200 yds.	300 yds.	400 yds.	TRAJ. (in.) 100 yds.	200 yds.	300 yds.	400 yds.	Est. Price/box
458 Win. Magnum	400	2380	2170	1960	1770	NA	5030	4165	3415	2785	NA	+2.5	-0.4	-13.4	0.0	**$73**
458 Win. Magnum	465	2220	1999	1791	1601	NA	5088	4127	3312	2646	NA	+2.5	-2.0	-17.7	0.0	**NA**
458 Win. Magnum	500	2040	1823	1623	1442	1237	4620	3689	2924	2308	1839	+2.5	-3.5	-22.0	0.0	**$61**
458 Win. Magnum	510	2040	1770	1527	1319	1157	4712	3547	2640	1970	1516	+2.5	-4.1	-25.0	0.0	**$41**
450 N.E. 3-1/4"	465	2190	1970	1765	1577	NA	4952	4009	3216	2567	NA	+2.5	-3.0	-20.0	0.0	**NA**
450 N.E. 3-1/4"	500	2150	1920	1708	1514	NA	5132	4093	3238	2544	NA	+2.5	-4.0	-22.9	0.0	**NA**
450 No. 2	465	2190	1970	1765	1577	NA	4952	4009	3216	2567	NA	+2.5	-3.0	-20.0	0.0	**NA**
450 No. 2	500	2150	1920	1708	1514	NA	5132	4093	3238	2544	NA	+2.5	-4.0	-22.9	0.0	**NA**
458 Lott	465	2380	2150	1932	1730	NA	5848	4773	3855	3091	NA	+2.5	-1.0	-14.0	0.0	**NA**
458 Lott	500	2300	2062	1838	1633	NA	5873	4719	3748	2960	NA	+2.5	-1.6	-16.4	0.0	**NA**
450 Ackley Mag.	465	2400	2169	1950	1747	NA	5947	4857	3927	3150	NA	+2.5	-1.0	-13.7	0.0	**NA**
450 Ackley Mag.	500	2320	2081	1855	1649	NA	5975	4085	3820	3018	NA	+2.5	-1.2	-15.0	0.0	**NA**
460 Short A-Sq.	500	2420	2175	1943	1729	NA	6501	5250	4193	3319	NA	+2.5	-0.8	-12.8	0.0	**NA**
460 Wea. Mag.	500	2700	2404	2128	1869	1635	8092	6416	5026	3878	2969	+2.5	+0.6	-8.9	-28.0	**$72**
475																
500/465 N.E.	480	2150	1917	1703	1507	NA	4926	3917	3089	2419	NA	+2.5	-4.0	-22.2	0.0	**NA**
470 Rigby	500	2150	1940	1740	1560	NA	5130	4170	3360	2695	NA	+2.5	-2.8	-19.4	0.0	**NA**
470 Nitro Ex.	480	2190	1954	1735	1536	NA	5111	4070	3210	2515	NA	+2.5	-3.5	-20.8	0.0	**NA**
470 Nitro Ex.	500	2150	1890	1650	1440	1270	5130	3965	3040	2310	1790	+2.5	-4.3	-24.0	0.0	**$177**
475 No. 2	500	2200	1955	1728	1522	NA	5375	4243	3316	2573	NA	+2.5	-3.2	-20.9	0.0	**NA**
50, 58																
50 Alaskan	450	2000	1729	1492	NA	NA	3997	2987	2224	NA	NA	0.0	-11.25	NA	NA	**NA**
505 Gibbs	525	2300	2063	1840	1637	NA	6166	4922	3948	3122	NA	+2.5	-3.0	-18.0	0.0	**NA**
500 N.E.-3"	570	2150	1928	1722	1533	NA	5850	4703	3752	2975	NA	+2.5	-3.7	-22.0	0.0	**NA**
500 N.E.-3"	600	2150	1927	1721	1531	NA	6158	4947	3944	3124	NA	+2.5	-4.0	-22.0	0.0	**NA**
495 A-Square	570	2350	2117	1896	1693	NA	5850	4703	3752	2975	NA	+2.5	-1.0	-14.5	0.0	**NA**
495 A-Square	600	2280	2050	1833	1635	NA	6925	5598	4478	3562	NA	+2.5	-2.0	-17.0	0.0	**NA**
500 A-Square	600	2380	2144	1922	1766	NA	7546	6126	4920	3922	NA	+2.5	-3.0	-17.0	0.0	**NA**
500 A-Square	707	2250	2040	1841	1567	NA	7947	6530	5318	4311	NA	+2.5	-2.0	-17.0	0.0	**NA**
500 BMG PMC	660	3080	2854	2639	2444	2248	13688	500 yd. zero				+3.1	+3.9	+4.7	+2.8	**NA**
577 Nitro Ex.	750	2050	1793	1562	1360	NA	6990	5356	4065	3079	NA	+2.5	-5.0	-26.0	0.0	**NA**
577 Tyrannosaur	750	2400	2141	1898	1675	NA	9591	7633	5996	4671	NA	+3.0	0.0	-12.9	0.0	**NA**
600, 700																
600 N.E.	900	1950	1680	1452	NA	NA	7596	5634	4212	NA	NA	+5.6	0.0	0.0	0.0	**NA**
700 N.E.	1200	1900	1676	1472	NA	NA	9618	7480	5774	NA	NA	+5.7	0.0	0.0	0.0	**NA**
50 BMG																
50 BMG Match	750	2820	2728	2637	2549	2462	13241	12388	11580	10815	10090	1.5	0.0	-6.5	-18.3	**NA**

Notes: Blanks are available in 32 S&W, 38 S&W and 38 Special. "V" after barrel length indicates test barrel was vented to produce ballistics similar to a revolver with a normal barrel-to-cylinder gap. Ammo prices are per 50 rounds except when marked with an ** which signifies a 20 round box; *** signifies a 25-round box. Not all loads are available from all ammo manufacturers. Listed loads are those made by Remington, Winchester, Federal, and others. DISC. is a discontinued load. Prices are rounded to the nearest whole dollar and will vary with brand and retail outlet. † = new bullet weight this year; "c" indicates a change in data.

Cartridge	Bullet Wgt. Grs.	VELOCITY (fps)			ENERGY (ft. lbs.)			Mid-Range Traj. (in.)		Bbl. Lgth. (in).	Est. Price/ box
		Muzzle	50 yds.	100 yds.	Muzzle	50 yds.	100 yds.	50 yds.	100 yds.		
22, 25											
221 Rem. Fireball	50	2650	2380	2130	780	630	505	0.2	0.8	10.5"	$15
25 Automatic	35	900	813	742	63	51	43	NA	NA	2"	$18
25 Automatic	45	815	730	655	65	55	40	1.8	7.7	2"	$21
25 Automatic	50	760	705	660	65	55	50	2.0	8.7	2"	$17
30											
7.5mm Swiss	107	1010	NA	NA	240	NA	NA	NA	NA	NA	NEW
7.62mmTokarev	87	1390	NA	NA	365	NA	NA	0.6	NA	4.5"	NA
7.62 Nagant	97	790	NA	NA	134	NA	NA	NA	NA	NA	NEW
7.63 Mauser	88	1440	NA	NA	405	NA	NA	NA	NA	NA	NEW
30 Luger	93†	1220	1110	1040	305	255	225	0.9	3.5	4.5"	$34
30 Carbine	110	1790	1600	1430	785	625	500	0.4	1.7	10"	$28
30-357 AeT	123	1992	NA	NA	1084	NA	NA	NA	NA	10"	NA
32											
32 S&W	88	680	645	610	90	80	75	2.5	10.5	3"	$17
32 S&W Long	98	705	670	635	115	100	90	2.3	10.5	4"	$17
32 Short Colt	80	745	665	590	100	80	60	2.2	9.9	4"	$19
32 H&R Magnum	85	1100	1020	930	230	195	165	1.0	4.3	4.5"	$21
32 H&R Magnum	95	1030	940	900	225	190	170	1.1	4.7	4.5"	$19
327 Federal Magnum	85	1400	1220	1090	370	280	225	NA	NA	4-V	NA
327 Federal Magnum	100	1500	1320	1180	500	390	310	-0.2	-4.50	4-V	NA
32 Automatic	60	970	895	835	125	105	95	1.3	5.4	4"	$22
32 Automatic	60	1000	917	849	133	112	96			4"	NA
32 Automatic	65	950	890	830	130	115	100	1.3	5.6	NA	NA
32 Automatic	71	905	855	810	130	115	95	1.4	5.8	4"	$19
8mm Lebel Pistol	111	850	NA	NA	180	NA	NA	NA	NA	NA	NEW
8mm Steyr	112	1080	NA	NA	290	NA	NA	NA	NA	NA	NEW
8mm Gasser	126	850	NA	NA	200	NA	NA	NA	NA	NA	NEW
9mm, 38											
380 Automatic	60	1130	960	NA	170	120	NA	1.0	NA	NA	NA
380 Automatic	85/88	990	920	870	190	165	145	1.2	5.1	4"	$20
380 Automatic	90	1000	890	800	200	160	130	1.2	5.5	3.75"	$10
380 Automatic	95/100	955	865	785	190	160	130	1.4	5.9	4"	$20
38 Super Auto +P	115	1300	1145	1040	430	335	275	0.7	3.3	5"	$26
38 Super Auto +P	125/130	1215	1100	1015	425	350	300	0.8	3.6	5"	$26
38 Super Auto +P	147	1100	1050	1000	395	355	325	0.9	4.0	5"	NA
9x18mm Makarov	95	1000	930	874	211	182	161	NA	NA	4"	NEW
9x18mm Ultra	100	1050	NA	NA	240	NA	NA	NA	NA	NA	NEW
9x21	124	1150	1050	980	365	305	265	NA	NA	4"	NA
9x23mm Largo	124	1190	1055	966	390	306	257	0.7	3.7	4"	NA
9x23mm Win.	125	1450	1249	1103	583	433	338	0.6	2.8	NA	NA
9mm Steyr	115	1180	NA	NA	350	NA	NA	NA	NA	NA	NEW
9mm Luger	88	1500	1190	1010	440	275	200	0.6	3.1	4"	$24
9mm Luger	90	1360	1112	978	370	247	191	NA	NA	4"	$26
9mm Luger	95	1300	1140	1010	350	275	215	0.8	3.4	4"	NA
9mm Luger	100	1180	1080	NA	305	255	NA	0.9	NA	4"	NA
9mm Luger Guard Dog	105	1230	1070	970	355	265	220	NA	NA	4"	NA
9mm Luger	115	1155	1045	970	340	280	240	0.9	3.9	4"	$21
9mm Luger	123/125	1110	1030	970	340	290	260	1.0	4.0	4"	$23
9mm Luger	140	935	890	850	270	245	225	1.3	5.5	4"	$23
9mm Luger	147	990	940	900	320	290	265	1.1	4.9	4"	$26
9mm Luger +P	90	1475	NA	NA	437	NA	NA	NA	NA	NA	NA
9mm Luger +P	115	1250	1113	1019	399	316	265	0.8	3.5	4"	$27
9mm Federal	115	1280	1130	1040	420	330	280	0.7	3.3	4"V	$24
9mm Luger Vector	115	1155	1047	971	341	280	241	NA	NA	4"	NA
9mm Luger +P	124	1180	1089	1021	384	327	287	0.8	3.8	4"	NA
38											
38 S&W	146	685	650	620	150	135	125	2.4	10.0	4"	$19
38 Short Colt	125	730	685	645	150	130	115	2.2	9.4	6"	$19
39 Special	100	950	900	NA	200	180	NA	1.3	NA	4"V	NA
38 Special	110	945	895	850	220	195	175	1.3	5.4	4"V	$23
38 Special	110	945	895	850	220	195	175	1.3	5.4	4"V	$23

Notes: Blanks are available in 32 S&W, 38 S&W and 38 Special. "V" after barrel length indicates test barrel was vented to produce ballistics similar to a revolver with a normal barrel-to-cylinder gap. Ammo prices are per 50 rounds except when marked with an ** which signifies a 20 round box; *** signifies a 25-round box. Not all loads are available from all ammo manufacturers. Listed loads are those made by Remington, Winchester, Federal, and others. DISC. is a discontinued load. Prices are rounded to the nearest whole dollar and will vary with brand and retail outlet. † = new bullet weight this year; "c" indicates a change in data.

Cartridge	Bullet Wgt. Grs.	VELOCITY (fps)			ENERGY (ft. lbs.)			Mid-Range Traj. (in.)		Bbl. Lgth. (in).	Est. Price/ box
		Muzzle	50 yds.	100 yds.	Muzzle	50 yds.	100 yds.	50 yds.	100 yds.		
38 Special	130	775	745	710	175	160	120	1.9	7.9	4"V	**$22**
38 Special Cowboy	140	800	767	735	199	183	168			7.5" V	**NA**
38 (Multi-Ball)	140	830	730	505	215	130	80	2.0	10.6	4"V	**$10****
38 Special	148	710	635	565	165	130	105	2.4	10.6	4"V	**$17**
38 Special	158	755	725	690	200	185	170	2.0	8.3	4"V	**$18**
38 Special +P	95	1175	1045	960	290	230	195	0.9	3.9	4"V	**$23**
38 Special +P	110	995	925	870	240	210	185	1.2	5.1	4"V	**$23**
38 Special +P	125	975	929	885	264	238	218	1	5.2	4"	**NA**
38 Special +P	125	945	900	860	250	225	205	1.3	5.4	4"V	**#23**
38 Special +P	129	945	910	870	255	235	215	1.3	5.3	4"V	**$11**
38 Special +P	130	925	887	852	247	227	210	1.3	5.50	4"V	**NA**
38 Special +P	147/150(c)	884	NA	NA	264	NA	NA	NA	NA	4"V	**$27**
38 Special +P	158	890	855	825	280	255	240	1.4	6.0	4"V	**$20**
357											
357 SIG	115	1520	NA	NA	593	NA	NA	NA	NA	NA	**NA**
357 SIG	124	1450	NA	NA	578	NA	NA	NA	NA	NA	**NA**
357 SIG	125	1350	1190	1080	510	395	325	0.7	3.1	4"	**NA**
357 SIG	150	1130	1030	970	420	355	310	0.9	4.0	NA	**NA**
356 TSW	115	1520	NA	NA	593	NA	NA	NA	NA	NA	**NA**
356 TSW	124	1450	NA	NA	578	NA	NA	NA	NA	NA	**NA**
356 TSW	135	1280	1120	1010	490	375	310	0.8	3.5	NA	**NA**
356 TSW	147	1220	1120	1040	485	410	355	0.8	3.5	5"	**NA**
357 Mag., Super Clean	105	1650									**NA**
357 Magnum	110	1295	1095	975	410	290	230	0.8	3.5	4"V	**$25**
357 (Med.Vel.)	125	1220	1075	985	415	315	270	0.8	3.7	4"V	**$25**
357 Magnum	125	1450	1240	1090	585	425	330	0.6	2.8	4"V	**$25**
357 (Multi-Ball)	140	1155	830	665	420	215	135	1.2	6.4	4"V	**$11****
357 Magnum	140	1360	1195	1075	575	445	360	0.7	3.0	4"V	**$25**
357 Magnum FlexTip	140	1440	1274	1143	644	504	406	NA	NA	NA	**NA**
357 Magnum	145	1290	1155	1060	535	430	360	0.8	3.5	4"V	**$26**
357 Magnum	150/158	1235	1105	1015	535	430	360	0.8	3.5	4"V	**$25**
357 Mag. Cowboy	158	800	761	725	225	203	185				**NA**
357 Magnum	165	1290	1189	1108	610	518	450	0.7	3.1	8-3/8"	**NA**
357 Magnum	180	1145	1055	985	525	445	390	0.9	3.9	4"V	**$25**
357 Magnum	180	1180	1088	1020	557	473	416	0.8	3.6	8"V	**NA**
357 Mag. CorBon F.A.	180	1650	1512	1386	1088	913	767	1.66	0.0		**NA**
357 Mag. CorBon	200	1200	1123	1061	640	560	500	3.19	0.0		**NA**
357 Rem. Maximum	158	1825	1590	1380	1170	885	670	0.4	1.7	10.5"	**$14****
40, 10mm											
40 S&W	135	1140	1070	NA	390	345	NA	0.9	NA	4"	**NA**
40 S&W Guard Dog	135	1200	1040	940	430	325	265	NA	NA	4"	**NA**
40 S&W	155	1140	1026	958	447	362	309	0.9	4.1	4"	**$14*****
40 S&W	165	1150	NA	NA	485	NA	NA	NA	NA	4"	**$18*****
40 S&W	180	985	936	893	388	350	319	1.4	5.0	4"	**$14*****
40 S&W	180	1015	960	914	412	368	334	1.3	4.5	4"	**NA**
400 Cor-Bon	135	1450	NA	NA	630	NA	NA	NA	NA	5"	**NA**
10mm Automatic	155	1125	1046	986	436	377	335	0.9	3.9	5"	**$26**
10mm Automatic	170	1340	1165	1145	680	510	415	0.7	3.2	5"	**$31**
10mm Automatic	175	1290	1140	1035	650	505	420	0.7	3.3	5.5"	**$11****
10mm Auto. (FBI)	180	950	905	865	361	327	299	1.5	5.4	4"	**$16****
10mm Automatic	180	1030	970	920	425	375	340	1.1	4.7	5"	**$16****
10mm Auto H.V.	180†	1240	1124	1037	618	504	430	0.8	3.4	5"	**$27**
10mm Automatic	200	1160	1070	1010	495	510	430	0.9	3.8	5"	**$14****
10.4mm Italian	177	950	NA	NA	360	NA	NA	NA	NA	NA	**NEW**
41 Action Exp.	180	1000	947	903	400	359	326	0.5	4.2	5"	**$13****
41 Rem. Magnum	170	1420	1165	1015	760	515	390	0.7	3.2	4"V	**$33**
41 Rem. Magnum	175	1250	1120	1030	605	490	410	0.8	3.4	4"V	**$14****
41 (Med. Vel.)	210	965	900	840	435	375	330	1.3	5.4	4"V	**$30**
41 Rem. Magnum	210	1300	1160	1060	790	630	535	0.7	3.2	4"V	**$33**
41 Rem. Magnum	240	1250	1151	1075	833	706	616	0.8	3.3	6.5V	**NA**
44											
44 S&W Russian	247	780	NA	NA	335	NA	NA	NA	NA	NA	**NA**
44 Special FTX	165	900	848	802	297	263	235	NA	NA	2.5"	**NA**
44 S&W Special	180	980	NA	NA	383	NA	NA	NA	NA	6.5"	**NA**

Notes: Blanks are available in 32 S&W, 38 S&W and 38 Special. "V" after barrel length indicates test barrel was vented to produce ballistics similar to a revolver with a normal barrel-to-cylinder gap. Ammo prices are per 50 rounds except when marked with an ** which signifies a 20 round box; *** signifies a 25-round box. Not all loads are available from all ammo manufacturers. Listed loads are those made by Remington, Winchester, Federal, and others. DISC. is a discontinued load. Prices are rounded to the nearest whole dollar and will vary with brand and retail outlet. † = new bullet weight this year; "c" indicates a change in data.

Cartridge	Bullet Wgt. Grs.	VELOCITY (fps)			ENERGY (ft. lbs.)			Mid-Range Traj. (in.)		Bbl. Lgth. (in).	Est. Price/ box
		Muzzle	50 yds.	100 yds.	Muzzle	50 yds.	100 yds.	50 yds.	100 yds.		
44 S&W Special	180	1000	935	882	400	350	311	NA	NA	7.5"V	**NA**
44 S&W Special	200†	875	825	780	340	302	270	1.2	6.0	6"	**$13****
44 S&W Special	200	1035	940	865	475	390	335	1.1	4.9	6.5"	**$13****
44 S&W Special	240/246	755	725	695	310	285	265	2.0	8.3	6.5"	**$26**
44-40 Win. Cowboy	225	750	723	695	281	261	242				**NA**
44 Rem. Magnum	180	1610	1365	1175	1035	745	550	0.5	2.3	4"V	**$18****
44 Rem. Magnum	200	1400	1192	1053	870	630	492	0.6	NA	6.5"	**$20**
44 Rem. Magnum	210	1495	1310	1165	1040	805	635	0.6	2.5	6.5"	**$18****
44 Rem. Mag. FlexTip	225	1410	1240	1111	993	768	617	NA	NA	NA	**NA**
44 (Med. Vel.)	240	1000	945	900	535	475	435	1.1	4.8	6.5"	**$17**
44 R.M. (Jacketed)	240	1180	1080	1010	740	625	545	0.9	3.7	4"V	**$18****
44 R.M. (Lead)	240	1350	1185	1070	970	750	610	0.7	3.1	4"V	**$29**
44 Rem. Magnum	250	1180	1100	1040	775	670	600	0.8	3.6	6.5"V	**$21**
44 Rem. Magnum	250	1250	1148	1070	867	732	635	0.8	3.3	6.5"V	**NA**
44 Rem. Magnum	275	1235	1142	1070	931	797	699	0.8	3.3	6.5"	**NA**
44 Rem. Magnum	300	1200	1100	1026	959	806	702	NA	NA	7.5"	**$17**
44 Rem. Magnum	330	1385	1297	1220	1406	1234	1090	1.83	0.00	NA	**NA**
440 CorBon	260	1700	1544	1403	1669	1377	1136	1.58	NA	10"	**NA**
45, 50											
450 Short Colt/450 Revolver	226	830	NA	NA	350	NA	NA	NA	NA	NA	**NEW**
45 S&W Schofield	180	730	NA	NA	213	NA	NA	NA	NA	NA	**NA**
45 S&W Schofield	230	730	NA	NA	272	NA	NA	NA	NA	NA	**NA**
45 G.A.P.	185	1090	970	890	490	385	320	1.0	4.7	5"	**NA**
45 G.A.P.	230	880	842	NA	396	363	NA	NA	NA	NA	**NA**
45 Automatic	165	1030	930	NA	385	315	NA	1.2	NA	5"	**NA**
45 Automatic Guard Dog	165	1140	1030	950	475	390	335	NA	NA	5"	**NA**
45 Automatic	185	1000	940	890	410	360	325	1.1	4.9	5"	**$28**
45 Auto. (Match)	185	770	705	650	245	204	175	2.0	8.7	5"	**$28**
45 Auto. (Match)	200	940	890	840	392	352	312	2.0	8.6	5"	**$20**
45 Automatic	200	975	917	860	421	372	328	1.4	5.0	5"	**$18**
45 Automatic	230	830	800	675	355	325	300	1.6	6.8	5"	**$27**
45 Automatic	230	880	846	816	396	366	340	1.5	6.1	5"	**NA**
45 Automatic +P	165	1250	NA	NA	573	NA	NA	NA	NA	NA	**NA**
45 Automatic +P	185	1140	1040	970	535	445	385	0.9	4.0	5"	**$31**
45 Automatic +P	200	1055	982	925	494	428	380	NA	NA	5"	**NA**
45 Super	185	1300	1190	1108	694	582	504	NA	NA	5"	**NA**
45 Win. Magnum	230	1400	1230	1105	1000	775	635	0.6	2.8	5"	**$14****
45 Win. Magnum	260	1250	1137	1053	902	746	640	0.8	3.3	5"	**$16****
45 Win. Mag. CorBon	320	1150	1080	1025	940	830	747	3.47			**NA**
455 Webley MKII	262	850	NA	NA	420	NA	NA	NA	NA	NA	**NA**
45 Colt FTX	185	920	870	826	348	311	280	NA	NA	3"V	**NA**
45 Colt	200	1000	938	889	444	391	351	1.3	4.8	5.5"	**$21**
45 Colt	225	960	890	830	460	395	345	1.3	5.5	5.5"	**$22**
45 Colt + P CorBon	265	1350	1225	1126	1073	884	746	2.65	0.0		**NA**
45 Colt + P CorBon	300	1300	1197	1114	1126	956	827	2.78	0.0		**NA**
45 Colt	250/255	860	820	780	410	375	340	1.6	6.6	5.5"	**$27**
454 Casull	250	1300	1151	1047	938	735	608	0.7	3.2	7.5"V	**NA**
454 Casull	260	1800	1577	1381	1871	1436	1101	0.4	1.8	7.5"V	**NA**
454 Casull	300	1625	1451	1308	1759	1413	1141	0.5	2.0	7.5"V	**NA**
454 Casull CorBon	360	1500	1387	1286	1800	1640	1323	2.01	0.0		**NA**
460 S&W	200	2300	2042	1801	2350	1851	1441	0	-1.60	NA	**NA**
460 S&W	260	2000	1788	1592	2309	1845	1464	NA	NA	7.5"V	**NA**
460 S&W	250	1450	1267	1127	1167	891	705	NA	NA	8.375-V	**NA**
460 S&W	250	1900	1640	1412	2004	1494	1106	0	-2.75	NA	**NA**
460 S&W	300	1750	1510	1300	2040	1510	1125	NA	NA	8.4-V	**NA**
460 S&W	395	1550	1389	1249	2108	1691	1369	0	-4.00	NA	**NA**
475 Linebaugh	400	1350	1217	1119	1618	1315	1112	NA	NA	NA	**NA**
480 Ruger	325	1350	1191	1076	1315	1023	835	2.6	0.0	7.5"	**NA**
50 Action Exp.	325	1400	1209	1075	1414	1055	835	0.2	2.3	6"	**$24****
500 S&W	275	1665	1392	1183	1693	1184	854	1.5	NA	8.375	**NA**
500 S&W	325	1800	1560	1350	2340	1755	1315	NA	NA	8.4-V	**NA**
500 S&W	350	1400	1231	1106	1523	1178	951	NA	NA	10"	**NA**
500 S&W	400	1675	1472	1299	2493	1926	1499	1.3	NA	8.375	**NA**
500 S&W	440	1625	1367	1169	2581	1825	1337	1.6	NA	8.375	**NA**
500 S&W	500	1425	1281	1164	2254	1823	1505	NA	NA	10"	**NA**

Note: The actual ballistics obtained with your firearm can vary considerably from the advertised ballistics.
Also, ballistics can vary from lot to lot with the same brand and type load.

Cartridge	Bullet Wt. Grs.	Velocity (fps) 22-1/2" Bbl.		Energy (ft. lbs.) 22-1/2" Bbl.		Mid-Range Traj. (in.)	Muzzle Velocity
		Muzzle	100 yds.	Muzzle	100 yds.	100 yds.	6" Bbl.
17 Aguila	20	1850	1267	NA	NA	NA	NA
CCI Quiet 22 LR	40	710	640	45	36	NA	NA
17 Hornady Mach 2	17	2100	1530	166	88	0.7	NA
17 HMR Lead Free	15.5	2550	1901	NA	NA	.90	NA
17 HMR TNT Green	16	2500	1642	222	96	NA	NA
17 HMR	17	2550	1902	245	136	NA	NA
17 HMR	20	2375	1776	250	140	NA	NA
5mm Rem. Rimfire Mag.	30	2300	1669	352	188	NA	24
22 Short Blank	—	—	—	—	—	—	—
22 Short CB	29	727	610	33	24	NA	706
22 Short Target	29	830	695	44	31	6.8	786
22 Short HP	27	1164	920	81	50	4.3	1077
22 Colibri	20	375	183	6	1	NA	NA
22 Super Colibri	20	500	441	11	9	NA	NA
22 Long CB	29	727	610	33	24	NA	706
22 Long HV	29	1180	946	90	57	4.1	1031
22 LR Pistol Match	40	1070	890	100	70	4.6	940
22 LR Shrt. Range Green	21	1650	912	127	NA	NA	NA
17 Hornady Mach 2	15.5	2525	1829	149	75	NA	NA
22 LR Sub Sonic HP	38	1050	901	93	69	4.7	NA
22 LR Segmented HP	40	1050	897	98	72	NA	NA
22 LR Standard Velocity	40	1070	890	100	70	4.6	940
22 LR AutoMatch	40	1200	990	130	85	NA	NA
22 LR HV	40	1255	1016	140	92	3.6	1060
22 LR Silhoutte	42	1220	1003	139	94	3.6	1025
22 SSS	60	950	802	120	86	NA	NA
22 LR HV HP	40	1280	1001	146	89	3.5	1085
22 Velocitor GDHP	40	1435	0	0	0	NA	NA
22 LR Segmented HP	37	1435	1080	169	96	2.9	NA
22 LR Hyper HP	32/33/34	1500	1075	165	85	2.8	NA
22 LR Expediter	32	1640	NA	191	NA	NA	NA
22 LR Stinger HP	32	1640	1132	191	91	2.6	1395
22 LR Lead Free	30	1650	NA	181	NA	NA	NA
22 LR Hyper Vel	30	1750	1191	204	93	NA	NA
22 LR Shot #12	31	950	NA	NA	NA	NA	NA
22 WRF LFN	45	1300	1015	169	103	3	NA
22 Win. Mag. Lead Free	28	2200	NA	301	NA	NA	NA
22 Win. Mag.	30	2200	1373	322	127	1.4	1610
22 Win. Mag. V-Max BT	33	2000	1495	293	164	0.60	NA
22 Win. Mag. JHP	34	2120	1435	338	155	1.4	NA
22 Win. Mag. JHP	40	1910	1326	324	156	1.7	1480
22 Win. Mag. FMJ	40	1910	1326	324	156	1.7	1480
22 Win. Mag. Dyna Point	45	1550	1147	240	131	2.60	NA
22 Win. Mag. JHP	50	1650	1280	300	180	1.3	NA
22 Win. Mag. Shot #11	52	1000	—	NA	—	—	NA

NOTES: * = 10 rounds per box. ** = 5 rounds per box. Pricing variations and number of rounds per box can occur with type and brand of ammunition. Listed pricing is the average nominal cost for load style and box quantity shown. Not every brand is available in all shot size variations. Some manufacturers do not provide suggested list prices. All prices rounded to nearest whole dollar. The price you pay will vary dependent upon outlet of purchase. # = new load spec this year; "C" indicates a change in data.

Dram Equiv.	Shot Ozs.	Load Style	Shot Sizes	Brands	Avg. Price/ box	Velocity (fps)
10 Gauge 3-1/2" Magnum						
Max	2-3/8	magnum blend	5, 6, 7	Hevi-shot	NA	1200
4-1/2	2-1/4	premium	BB, 2, 4, 5, 6	Win., Fed., Rem.	$33	1205
Max	2	premium	4, 5, 6	Fed., Win.	NA	1300
4-1/4	2	high velocity	BB, 2, 4	Rem.	$22	1210
Max	18 pellets	premium	00 buck	Fed., Win.	$7**	1100
Max	1-7/8	Bismuth	BB, 2, 4	Bis.	NA	1225
Max	1-3/4	high density	BB, 2	Rem.	NA	1300
4-1/4	1-3/4	steel	TT, T, BBB, BB, 1, 2, 3	Win., Rem.	$27	1260
Mag	1-5/8	steel	T, BBB, BB, 2	Win.	$27	1285
Max	1-5/8	Bismuth	BB, 2, 4	Bismuth	NA	1375
Max	1-1/2	hypersonic	BBB, BB, 2	Rem.	NA	1700
Max	1-1/2	heavy metal	BB, 2, 3, 4	Hevi-Shot	NA	1500
Max	1-1/2	steel	T, BBB, BB, 1, 2, 3	Fed.	NA	1450
Max	1-3/8	steel	T, BBB, BB, 1, 2, 3	Fed., Rem.	NA	1500
Max	1-3/8	steel	T, BBB, BB, 2	Fed., Win.	NA	1450
Max	1-3/4	slug, rifled	slug	Fed.	NA	1280
Max	24 pellets	Buckshot	1 Buck	Fed.	NA	1100
Max	54 pellets	Super-X	4 Buck	Win.	NA	1150
12 Gauge 3-1/2" Magnum						
Max	2-1/4	premium	4, 5, 6	Fed., Rem., Win.	$13*	1150
Max	2	Lead	4, 5, 6	Fed.	NA	1300
Max	2	Copper plated turkey	4, 5	Rem.	NA	1300
Max	18 pellets	premium	00 buck	Fed., Win., Rem.	$7**	1100
Max	1-7/8	Wingmaster HD	4, 6	Rem.	NA	1225
Max	1-7/8	heavyweight	5, 6	Fed.	NA	1300
Max	1-3/4	high density	BB, 2, 4, 6	Rem.		1300
Max	1-7/8	Bismuth	BB, 2, 4	Bis.	NA	1225
Max	1-5/8	blind side	Hex, 1, 3	Win.	NA	1400
Max	1-5/8	Hevi-shot	T	Hevi-shot	NA	1350
Max	1-5/8	Wingmaster HD	T	Rem.	NA	1350
Max	1-5/8	high density	BB, 2	Fed.	NA	1450
Max	1-5/8	Blind side	Hex, BB, 2	Win.	NA	1400
Max	1-3/8	Heavyweight	2, 4, 6	Fed.	NA	1450
Max	1-3/8	steel	T, BBB, BB, 2, 4	Fed., Win., Rem.	NA	1450
Max	1-1/2	FS steel	BBB, BB, 2	Fed.	NA	1500
Max	1-1/2	Supreme H-V	BBB, BB, 2, 3	Win.	NA	1475
Max	1-3/8	H-speed steel	BB, 2	Rem.	NA	1550
Max	1-1/4	Steel	BB, 2	Win.	NA	1625
Max	24 pellets	Premium	1 Buck	Fed.	NA	1100
Max	54 pellets	Super-X	4 Buck	Win.	NA	1050
12 Gauge 3" Magnum						
4	2	premium	BB, 2, 4, 5, 6	Win., Fed., Rem.	$9*	1175
4	1-7/8	premium	BB, 2, 4, 6	Win., Fed., Rem.	$19	1210
4	1-7/8	duplex	4x6	Rem.	$9*	1210

Dram Equiv.	Shot Ozs.	Load Style	Shot Sizes	Brands	Avg. Price/ box	Velocity (fps)
12 Gauge 3" Magnum *(cont.)*						
Max	1-3/4	turkey	4, 5, 6	Fed., Fio., Win., Rem.	NA	1300
Max	1-3/4	high density	BB, 2, 4	Rem.	NA	1450
Max	1-5/8	high density	BB, 2	Fed.	NA	1450
Max	1-5/8	Wingmaster HD	4, 6	Rem.	NA	1227
Max	1-5/8	high velocity	4, 5, 6	Fed.	NA	1350
4	1-5/8	premium	2, 4, 5, 6	Win., Fed., Rem.	$18	1290
Max	1-1/2	Wingmaster HD	T	Rem.	NA	1300
Max	1-1/2	Hevi-shot	T	Hevi-shot	NA	1300
Max	1-1/2	high density	BB, 2, 4	Rem.	NA	1300
Max	1-1/2	slug	slug	Bren.	NA	1604
Max	1-5/8	Bismuth	BB, 2, 4, 5, 6	Bis.	NA	1250
4	24 pellets	buffered	1 buck	Win., Fed., Rem.	$5**	1040
4	15 pellets	buffered	00 buck	Win., Fed., Rem.	$6**	1210
4	10 pellets	buffered	000 buck	Win., Fed., Rem.	$6**	1225
4	41 pellets	buffered	4 buck	Win., Fed., Rem.	$6**	1210
Max	1-3/8	heavyweight	5, 6	Fed.	NA	1300
Max	1-3/8	high density	B, 2, 4, 6	Rem. Win.	NA	1450
Max	1-3/8	slug	slug	Bren.	NA	1476
Max	1-3/8	blind side	Hex, 1, 3, 5	Win.	NA	1400
Max	1-1/4	slug, rifled	slug	Fed.	NA	1600
Max	1-3/16	saboted slug	copper slug	Rem.	NA	1500
Max	7/8	slug, rifled	slug	Rem.	NA	1875
Max	1-1/8	low recoil	BB	Fed.	NA	850
Max	1-1/8	steel	BB, 2, 3, 4	Fed., Win., Rem.	NA	1550
Max	1-1/16	high density	2, 4	Win.	NA	1400
Max	1	steel	4, 6	Fed.	NA	1330
Max	1-3/8	buckhammer	slug	Rem.	NA	1500
Max	1	slug, rifled	slug, magnum	Win., Rem.	$5**	1760
Max	1	saboted slug	slug	Rem., Win., Fed.	$10**	1550
Max	385 grs.	partition gold	slug	Win.	NA	2000
Max	1-1/8	Rackmaster	slug	Win.	NA	1700
Max	300 grs.	XP3	slug	Win.	NA	2100
3-5/8	1-3/8	steel	BBB, BB, 1, 2, 3, 4	Win., Fed., Rem.	$19	1275
Max	1-1/8	snow goose FS	BB, 2, 3, 4	Fed.	NA	1635
Max	1-1/8	steel	BB, 2, 4	Rem.	NA	1500
Max	1-1/8	steel	T, BBB, BB, 2, 4, 5, 6	Fed., Win.	NA	1450
Max	1-1/8	steel	BB, 2	Fed.	NA	1400
Max	1-1/8	FS lead	3, 4	Fed.	NA	1600
Max	1-3/8	Blind side	Hex, BB, 2	Win.	NA	1400
4	1-1/4	steel	T, BBB, BB, 1, 2, 3, 4, 6	Win., Fed., Rem.	$18	1400
Max	1-1/4	FS steel	BBB, BB, 2	Fed.	NA	1450

NOTES: * = 10 rounds per box. ** = 5 rounds per box. Pricing variations and number of rounds per box can occur with type and brand of ammunition. Listed pricing is the average nominal cost for load style and box quantity shown. Not every brand is available in all shot size variations. Some manufacturers do not provide suggested list prices. All prices rounded to nearest whole dollar. The price you pay will vary dependent upon outlet of purchase. # = new load spec this year; "C" indicates a change in data.

Dram Equiv.	Shot Ozs.	Load Style	Shot Sizes	Brands	Avg. Price/ box	Velocity (fps)
12 Gauge 2-3/4"						
Max	1-5/8	magnum	4, 5, 6	Win., Fed.	$8*	1250
Max	1-3/8	lead	4, 5, 6	Fiocchi	NA	1485
Max	1-3/8	turkey	4, 5, 6	Fio.	NA	1250
Max	1-3/8	steel	4, 5, 6	Fed.	NA	1400
Max	1-3/8	Bismuth	BB, 2, 4, 5, 6	Bis.	NA	1300
3-3/4	1-1/2	magnum	BB, 2, 4, 5, 6	Win., Fed., Rem.	$16	1260
Max	1-1/4	blind side	Hex, 2, 5	Win.	NA	1400
Max	1-1/4	Supreme H-V	4, 5, 6, 7-1/2	Win. Rem.	NA	1400
3-3/4	1-1/4	high velocity	BB, 2, 4, 5, 6, 7-1/2, 8, 9	Win., Fed., Rem., Fio.	$13	1330
Max	1-1/4	high density	B, 2, 4	Win.	NA	1450
Max	1-1/4	high density	4, 6	Rem.	NA	1325
3-1/4	1-1/4	standard velocity	6, 7-1/2, 8, 9	Win., Fed., Rem., Fio.	$11	1220
Max	1-1/8	Hevi-shot	5	Hevi-shot	NA	1350
3-1/4	1-1/8	standard velocity	4, 6, 7-1/2, 8, 9	Win., Fed., Rem., Fio.	$9	1255
Max	1-1/8	steel	2, 4	Rem.	NA	1390
Max	1	steel	BB, 2	Fed.	NA	1450
3-1/4	1	standard velocity	6, 7-1/2, 8	Rem., Fed., Fio., Win.	$6	1290
3-1/4	1-1/4	target	7-1/2, 8, 9	Win., Fed., Rem.	$10	1220
3	1-1/8	spreader	7-1/2, 8, 8-1/2, 9	Fio.	NA	1200
3	1-1/8	target	7-1/2, 8, 9, 7-1/2x8	Win., Fed., Rem., Fio.	$7	1200
2-3/4	1-1/8	target	7-1/2, 8, 8-1/2, 9, 7-1/2x8	Win., Fed., Rem., Fio.	$7	1145
2-3/4	1-1/8	low recoil	7-1/2, 8	Rem.	NA	1145
2-1/2	26 grams	low recoil	8	Win.	NA	980
2-1/4	1-1/8	target	7-1/2, 8, 8-1/2, 9	Rem., Fed.	$7	1080
Max	1	spreader	7-1/2, 8, 8-1/2, 9	Fio.	NA	1300
3-1/4	28 grams (1 oz)	target	7-1/2, 8, 9	Win., Fed., Rem., Fio.	$8	1290
3	1	target	7-1/2, 8, 8-1/2, 9	Win., Fio.	NA	1235
2-3/4	1	target	7-1/2, 8, 8-1/2, 9	Fed., Rem., Fio.	NA	1180
3-1/4	24 grams	target	7-1/2, 8, 9	Fed., Win., Fio.	NA	1325
3	7/8	light	8	Fio.	NA	1200
3-3/4	8 pellets	buffered	000 buck	Win., Fed., Rem.	$4**	1325
4	12 pellets	premium	00 buck	Win., Fed., Rem.	$5**	1290
3-3/4	9 pellets	buffered	00 buck	Win., Fed., Rem., Fio.	$19	1325
3-3/4	12 pellets	buffered	0 buck	Win., Fed., Rem.	$4**	1275
4	20 pellets	buffered	1 buck	Win., Fed., Rem.	$4**	1075
3-3/4	16 pellets	buffered	1 buck	Win., Fed., Rem.	$4**	1250
4	34 pellets	premium	4 buck	Fed., Rem.	$5**	1250
3-3/4	27 pellets	buffered	4 buck	Win., Fed., Rem., Fio.	$4**	1325

Dram Equiv.	Shot Ozs.	Load Style	Shot Sizes	Brands	Avg. Price/ box	Velocity (fps)
12 Gauge 2-3/4" *(cont.)*						
		PDX1	1 oz. slug, 3-00 buck	Win.	NA	1150
Max	1 oz	segmenting, slug	slug	Win.	NA	1600
Max	1	saboted slug	slug	Win., Fed., Rem.	$10**	1450
Max	1-1/4	slug, rifled	slug	Fed.	NA	1520
Max	1-1/4	slug	slug	Lightfield		1440
Max	1-1/4	saboted slug	attached sabot	Rem.	NA	1550
Max	1	slug, rifled	slug, magnum	Rem., Fio.	$5**	1680
Max	1	slug, rifled	slug	Win., Fed., Rem.	$4**	1610
Max	1	sabot slug	slug	Sauvestre		1640
Max	7/8	slug, rifled	slug	Rem.	NA	1800
Max	400	plat. tip	sabot slug	Win.	NA	1700
Max	385 grains	Partition Gold Slug	slug	Win.	NA	1900
Max	385 grains	Core-Lokt bonded	sabot slug	Rem.	NA	1900
Max	325 grains	Barnes Sabot	slug	Fed.	NA	1900
Max	300 grains	SST Slug	sabot slug	Hornady	NA	2050
Max	3/4	Tracer	#8 + tracer	Fio.	NA	1150
Max	130 grains	Less Lethal	.73 rubber slug	Lightfield	NA	600
Max	3/4	non-toxic	zinc slug	Win.	NA	NA
3	1-1/8	steel target	6-1/2, 7	Rem.	NA	1200
2-3/4	1-1/8	steel target	7	Rem.	NA	1145
3	1#	steel	7	Win.	$11	1235
3-1/2	1-1/4	steel	T, BBB, BB, 1, 2, 3, 4, 5, 6	Win., Fed., Rem.	$18	1275
3-3/4	1-1/8	steel	BB, 1, 2, 3, 4, 5, 6	Win., Fed., Rem., Fio.	$16	1365
3-3/4	1	steel	2, 3, 4, 5, 6, 7	Win., Fed., Rem., Fio.	$13	1390
Max	7/8	steel	7	Fio.	NA	1440
16 Gauge 2-3/4"						
3-1/4	1-1/4	magnum	2, 4, 6	Fed., Rem.	$16	1260
3-1/4	1-1/8	high velocity	4, 6, 7-1/2	Win., Fed., Rem., Fio.	$12	1295
Max	1-1/8	Bismuth	4, 5	Bis.	NA	1200
2-3/4	1-1/8	standard velocity	6, 7-1/2, 8	Fed., Rem., Fio.	$9	1185
2-1/2	1	dove	6, 7-1/2, 8, 9	Fio., Win.	NA	1165
2-3/4	1		6, 7-1/2, 8	Fio.	NA	1200
Max	15/16	steel	2, 4	Fed., Rem.	NA	1300
Max	7/8	steel	2, 4	Win.	$16	1300
3	12 pellets	buffered	1 buck	Win., Fed., Rem.	$4**	1225
Max	4/5	slug, rifled	slug	Win., Fed., Rem.	$4**	1570
Max	.92	sabot slug	slug	Sauvestre	NA	1560

NOTES: * = 10 rounds per box. ** = 5 rounds per box. Pricing variations and number of rounds per box can occur with type and brand of ammunition. Listed pricing is the average nominal cost for load style and box quantity shown. Not every brand is available in all shot size variations. Some manufacturers do not provide suggested list prices. All prices rounded to nearest whole dollar. The price you pay will vary dependent upon outlet of purchase. # = new load spec this year; "C" indicates a change in data.

Dram Equiv.	Shot Ozs.	Load Style	Shot Sizes	Brands	Avg. Price/ box	Velocity (fps)
20 Gauge 3" Magnum						
3	1-1/4	premium	2, 4, 5, 6, 7-1/2	Win., Fed., Rem.	$15	1185
Max	1-1/4	Wingmaster HD	4, 6	Rem.	NA	1185
3	1-1/4	turkey	4, 6	Fio.	NA	1200
Max	1-1/4	Hevi-shot	2, 4, 6	Hevi-shot	NA	1250
Max	1-1/8	high density	4, 6	Rem.	NA	1300
Max	18 pellets	buck shot	2 buck	Fed.	NA	1200
Max	24 pellets	buffered	3 buck	Win.	$5**	1150
2-3/4	20 pellets	buck	3 buck	Rem.	$4**	1200
Max	1	hypersonic	2, 3, 4	Rem.	NA	Rem.
3-1/4	1	steel	1, 2, 3, 4, 5, 6	Win., Fed., Rem.	$15	1330
Max	1	blind side	Hex, 2, 5	Win.	NA	1300
Max	7/8	steel	2, 4	Win.	NA	1300
Max	7/8	FS lead	3, 4	Fed.	NA	1500
Max	1-1/16	high density	2, 4	Win.	NA	1400
Max	1-1/16	Bismuth	2, 4, 5, 6	Bismuth	NA	1250
Mag	5/8	saboted slug	275 gr.	Fed.	NA	1900
20 Gauge 2-3/4"						
2-3/4	1-1/8	magnum	4, 6, 7-1/2	Win., Fed., Rem.	$14	1175
2-3/4	1	high velocity	4, 5, 6, 7-1/2, 8, 9	Win., Fed., Rem., Fio.	$12	1220
Max	1	Bismuth	4, 6	Bis.	NA	1200
Max	1	Hevi-shot	5	Hevi-shot	NA	1250
Max	1	Supreme H-V	4, 6, 7-1/2	Win. Rem.	NA	1300
Max	1	FS lead	4, 5, 6	Fed.	NA	1350
Max	7/8	Steel	2, 3, 4	Fio.	NA	1500
2-1/2	1	standard velocity	6, 7-1/2, 8	Win., Rem., Fed., Fio.	$6	1165
2-1/2	7/8	clays	8	Rem.	NA	1200
2-1/2	7/8	promotional	6, 7-1/2, 8	Win., Rem., Fio.	$6	1210
2-1/2	1	target	8, 9	Win., Rem.	$8	1165
Max	7/8	clays	7-1/2, 8	Win.	NA	1275
2-1/2	7/8	target	8, 9	Win., Fed., Rem.	$8	1200
Max	3/4	steel	2, 4	Rem.	NA	1425
2-1/2	7/8	steel - target	7	Rem.	NA	1200
1-1/2	7/8	low recoil	8	Win.	NA	980
Max	1	buckhammer	slug	Rem.	NA	1500
Max	5/8	Saboted Slug	Copper Slug	Rem.	NA	1500
Max	20 pellets	buffered	3 buck	Win., Fed.	$4	1200
Max	5/8	slug, saboted	slug	Win.,	$9**	1400
2-3/4	5/8	slug, rifled	slug	Rem.	$4**	1580
Max	3/4	saboted slug	copper slug	Fed., Rem.	NA	1450
Max	3/4	slug, rifled	slug	Win., Fed., Rem., Fio.	$4**	1570
Max	.9	sabot slug	slug	Sauvestre		1480
Max	260 grains	Partition Gold Slug	slug	Win.	NA	1900
Max	260 grains	Core-Lokt Ultra	slug	Rem.	NA	1900

Dram Equiv.	Shot Ozs.	Load Style	Shot Sizes	Brands	Avg. Price/ box	Velocity (fps)
20 Gauge 2-3/4" *(cont.)*						
Max	260 grains	saboted slug	platinum tip	Win.	NA	1700
Max	3/4	steel	2, 3, 4, 6	Win., Fed., Rem.	$14	1425
Max	250 grains	SST slug	slug	Hornady	NA	1800
Max	1/2	rifled, slug	slug	Rem.	NA	1800
Max	67 grains	Less lethal	2/.60 rubber balls	Lightfield	NA	900
28 Gauge 3"						
Max	7/8	tundra tungsten	4, 5, 6	Fiocchi	NA	TBD
28 Gauge 2-3/4"						
2	1	high velocity	6, 7-1/2, 8	Win.	$12	1125
2-1/4	3/4	high velocity	6, 7-1/2, 8, 9	Win., Fed., Rem., Fio.	$11	1295
2	3/4	target	8, 9	Win., Fed., Rem.	$9	1200
Max	3/4	sporting clays	7-1/2, 8-1/2	Win.	NA	1300
Max	5/8	Bismuth	4, 6	Bis.	NA	1250
Max	5/8	steel	6, 7	NA	NA	1300
Max	5/8	slug		Bren.	NA	1450
410 Bore 3"						
Max	11/16	high velocity	4, 5, 6, 7-1/2, 8, 9	Win., Fed., Rem., Fio.	$10	1135
Max	9/16	Bismuth	4	Bis.	NA	1175
Max	3/8	steel	6	NA	NA	1400
		judge	5 pellets 000 Buck	Fed.	NA	960
		judge	9 pellets #4 Buck	Fed.	NA	1100
Max	Mixed	Per. Defense	3DD/12BB	Win.	NA	750
410 Bore 2-1/2"						
Max	1/2	high velocity	4, 6, 7-1/2	Win., Fed., Rem.	$9	1245
Max	1/5	slug, rifled	slug	Win., Fed., Rem.	$4**	1815
1-1/2	1/2	target	8, 8-1/2, 9	Win., Fed., Rem., Fio.	$8	1200
Max	1/2	sporting clays	7-1/2, 8, 8-1/2	Win.	NA	1300
Max		Buckshot	5-000 Buck	Win.	NA	1135
		judge	12-bb's, 3 disks	Win.	NA	TBD
Max	Mixed	Per. Defense	4DD/16BB	Win.	NA	750
Max	42 grains	Less lethal	4/.41 rubber balls	Lightfield	NA	1150

ACCU-TEK AT-380 II 380 ACP PISTOL

Caliber: 380 ACP, 6-shot magazine. **Barrel:** 2.8". **Weight:** 23.5 oz. **Length:** 6.125" overall. **Grips:** Textured black composition. **Sights:** Blade front, rear adjustable for windage. **Features:** Made from 17-4 stainless steel, has an exposed hammer, manual firing-pin safety block and trigger disconnect. Magazine release located on the bottom of the grip. American made, lifetime warranty. Comes with two 6-round stainless steel magazines and a California-approved cable lock. Introduced 2006. Made in U.S.A. by Excel Industries.

Price: Satin stainless $262.00

AKDAL GHOST TR-01

Caliber: 9x19mm 15-round double stacked magazine. **Barrel:** 4.45". **Weight:** 29.10 oz. **Length:** 7.5" overall. **Grips:** Polymer black polycoat. **Sights:** Fixed, open type with notched rear sight dovetailed into the slide. Adjustable sight also available. **Features:** Compact single action pre-cocked, semiautomatic pistol with short recoil operation and locking breech. It uses modified Browning-type locking, in which barrel engages the slide with single lug, entering the ejection window. Pistol also has no manual safeties; instead, it has automatic trigger and firing pin safeties. The polymer frame features removable backstraps (of different sizes), and an integral accessory Picatinny rail below the barrel.

Price: $499.00

AKDAL GHOST TR-02

Caliber: 9x19mm 15-round double stacked magazine. **Barrel:** 4.45". **Weight:** 29.10 oz. **Length:** 7.5" overall. **Grips:** Polymer black polycoat. **Sights:** Fixed, open type with notched rear sight dovetailed into the slide. Adjustable sight also available. **Features:** Compact single action pre-cocked, semiautomatic pistol with short recoil operation and locking breech. It uses modified Browning-type locking, in which barrel engages the slide with single lug, entering the ejection window. Pistol also has no manual safeties; instead, it has automatic trigger and firing pin safeties. The polymer frame features removable backstraps (of different sizes), and an integral accessory Picatinny rail below the barrel.

Price: $499.00

AMERICAN CLASSIC 1911-A1

1911-style semiauto pistol chambered in .45 ACP. Features include 7+1 capacity, walnut grips, 5-inch barrel, blued or hard-chromed steel frame, checkered wood grips, drift adjustable sights. A .22 LR version is also available.

Price: $500.00

AMERICAN CLASSIC COMMANDER

1911-style semiauto pistol chambered in .45 ACP. Features include 7+1 capacity, checkered mahogany grips, 4.25-inch barrel, blued or hard-chromed steel frame, drift adjustable sights.

Price: $550.00

ARMALITE AR-24 PISTOL

Caliber: 9mm Para., 10- or 15-shot magazine. **Barrel:** 4.671", 6 groove, right-hand cut rifling. **Weight:** 34.9 oz. **Length:** 8.27" overall. **Grips:** Black polymer. **Sights:** Dovetail front, fixed rear, 3-dot luminous design. **Features:** Machined slide, frame and barrel. Serrations on forestrap and backstrap, external thumb safety and internal firing pin box, half cock. Two 15-round magazines, pistol case, pistol lock, manual and cleaning brushes. Manganese phosphate finish. Compact comes with two 13-round magazines, 3.89" barrel, weighs 33.4 oz. Made in U.S.A. by ArmaLite.

Price: AR-24 Full Size $550.00

Price: AR-24K Compact $550.00

ARMSCOR/ROCK ISLAND ARMORY 1911A1-45 FS GI

1911-style semiauto pistol chambered in .45 ACP (8 rounds), 9mm Parabellum, .38 Super (9 rounds). Features include checkered plastic or hardwood grips, 5-inch barrel, parkerized steel frame and slide, drift adjustable sights.

Price: $500.00

ARMSCOR/ROCK ISLAND ARMORY 1911A1-45 CS GI

1911-style Officer's-size semiauto pistol chambered in .45 ACP. Features plain hardwood grips, 3.5-inch barrel, parkerized steel frame and slide, drift adjustable sights.

Price: $500.00

ARMSCOR/ROCK ISLAND ARMORY MAP1 & MAPP1 PISTOLS

Caliber: 9mm, 16-round magazine. Browning short recoil action style pistols with: integrated front sight; Snag-free rear sight (police standard); Tanfoglio barrel; Single & double-action trigger; automatic safety on firing pin & manual on rear lever; standard hammer; side extractor; standard or Ambidextrous rear safety; combat slide stop; parkerized finish for nickel steel parts; polymer frame with accessory rail.

Price: $400.00

ARMSCOR/ROCK ISLAND ARMORY XT22 PISTOL

Caliber: .22 LR, 15-round magazine std. **Barrel:** 5" **Weight:** 38 oz. The XT-22 is a combat 1911 .22 pistol. Unlike most .22 1911 conversions, this pistol is built as a complete gun. Designed for durability, it is the only .22 1911 with a forged 4140 steel slide and the only .22 1911 with a one piece 4140 chrome moly barrel. Available soon.

Price: .... (pre-order) $473.99

AUTO-ORDNANCE TA5 SEMI-AUTO PISTOL

Caliber: 45 ACP, 30-round stick magazine (standard), 50- or 100-round drum magazine optional. **Barrel:** 10.5", finned. **Weight:** 6.5 lbs. **Length:** 25" overall. **Features:** Semi-auto pistol patterned after Thompson Model 1927 semi-auto carbine. Horizontal vertical foregrip, aluminum receiver, top cocking knob, grooved walnut pistolgrip.

Price: $1,143.00

AUTO-ORDNANCE 1911A1 AUTOMATIC PISTOL

Caliber: 45 ACP, 7-shot magazine. **Barrel:** 5". **Weight:** 39 oz. **Length:** 8.5" overall. **Grips:** Brown checkered plastic with medallion. **Sights:** Blade front, rear drift-adjustable for windage.

Features: Same specs as 1911A1 military guns-parts interchangeable. Frame and slide blued; each radius has non-glare finish. Introduced 2002. Made in U.S.A. by Kahr Arms.

Price: 1911PKZSE Parkerized, plastic grips **$627.00**
Price: 1911PKZSEW Parkerized........................**$662.00**
Price: 1911PKZMA Parkerized, Mass. Compliant (2008) **$627.00**

BAER H.C. 40 AUTO PISTOL

Caliber: 40 S&W, 18-shot magazine. **Barrel:** 5". **Weight:** 37 oz. **Length:** 8.5" overall. **Grips:** Wood. **Sights:** Low-mount adjustable rear sight with hidden rear leaf, dovetail front sight. **Features:** Double-stack Caspian frame, beavertail grip safety, ambidextrous thumb safety, 40 S&W match barrel with supported chamber, match stainless steel barrel bushing, lowered and flared ejection port, extended ejector, match trigger fitted, integral mag well, bead blast blue finish on lower, polished sides on slide. Introduced 2008. Made in U.S.A. by Les Baer Custom, Inc.
Price: **$2,960.00**

BAER 1911 BOSS .45

Caliber: .45 ACP, 8+1 capacity. **Barrel:** 5". **Weight:** 37 oz. **Length:** 8.5" overall. **Grips:** Premium Checkered Cocobolo Grips. **Sights:** Low-Mount LBC Adj Sight, Red Fiber Optic Front. **Features:** Speed Trgr, Beveled Mag Well, Rounded for Tactical. Rear cocking serrations on the slide, Baer fiber optic front sight (red), flat mainspring housing, checkered at 20 lpi, extended combat safety, Special tactical package, chromed complete lower, blued slide, (2) 8-round premium magazines.
Price: **$2,109.00**

BAER 1911 CUSTOM CARRY AUTO PISTOL

Caliber: 45 ACP, 7- or 10-shot magazine. **Barrel:** 5". **Weight:** 37 oz. **Length:** 8.5" overall. **Grips:** Checkered walnut. **Sights:** Baer improved ramp-style dovetailed front, Novak low-mount rear. **Features:** Baer forged NM frame, slide and barrel with stainless bushing. Baer speed trigger with 4-lb. pull. Partial listing shown. Made in U.S.A. by Les Baer Custom, Inc.
Price: Custom Carry 5", blued **$1,995.00**
Price: Custom Carry 5", stainless **$2,120.00**
Price: Custom Carry 4" Commanche length, blued **$1,995.00**
Price: Custom Carry 4" Commanche length, stainless **$2,120.00**

BAER 1911 ULTIMATE RECON PISTOL

Caliber: 45 ACP, 7- or 10-shot magazine. **Barrel:** 5". **Weight:** 37 oz. **Length:** 8.5" overall. **Grips:** Checkered cocobolo. **Sights:** Baer improved ramp-style dovetailed front, Novak low-mount rear. **Features:** NM Caspian frame, slide and barrel with stainless bushing. Baer speed trigger with 4-lb. pull. Includes integral Picatinny rail and Sure-Fire X-200 light. Made in U.S.A. by Les Baer Custom, Inc. Introduced 2006.
Price: Bead blast blued **$3,070.00**
Price: Bead blast chrome **$3,390.00**

BAER 1911 PREMIER II AUTO PISTOL

Caliber: 38 Super, 400 Cor-Bon, 45 ACP, 7- or 10-shot magazine. **Barrel:** 5". Weight: 37 oz. **Length:** 8.5" overall. **Grips:** Checkered rosewood, double diamond pattern. **Sights:** Baer dovetailed front, low-mount Bo-Mar rear with hidden leaf. **Features:** Baer NM forged steel frame and barrel with stainless bushing, deluxe Commander hammer and sear, beavertail grip safety with pad, extended ambidextrous safety; flat mainspring housing; 30 lpi checkered front strap. Made in U.S.A. by Les Baer Custom, Inc.
Price: 5" 45 ACP **$1,790.00**
Price: 5" 400 Cor-Bon **$1,890.00**
Price: 5" 38 Super **$2,070.00**
Price: 6" 45 ACP, 400 Cor-Bon, 38 Super, from **$1,990.00**
Price: Super-Tac, 45 ACP, 400 Cor-Bon, 38 Super, from ... **$2,280.00**

BAER 1911 S.R.P. PISTOL

Caliber: 45 ACP. **Barrel:** 5". **Weight:** 37 oz. **Length:** 8.5" overall. **Grips:** Checkered walnut. **Sights:** Trijicon night sights. **Features:** Similar to the F.B.I. contract gun except uses Baer forged steel frame. Has Baer match barrel with supported chamber, complete tactical action. Has Baer Ultra Coat finish. Introduced 1996. Made in U.S.A. by Les Baer Custom, Inc.
Price: Government or Commanche length **$2,590.00**

BAER 1911 STINGER PISTOL

Caliber: 45 ACP, 7-round magazine. **Barrel:** 5". **Weight:** 34 oz. **Length:** 8.5" overall. **Grips:** Checkered cocobolo. **Sights:** Baer dovetailed front, low-mount Bo-Mar rear with hidden leaf. **Features:** Baer NM frame. Baer Commanche slide, Officer's style grip frame, beveled mag well. Made in U.S.A. by Les Baer Custom, Inc.
Price: Blued **$1,890.00**
Price: Stainless **$1,970.00**

BAER 1911 PROWLER III PISTOL

Caliber: 45 ACP, 8-round magazine. **Barrel:** 5". **Weight:** 34 oz. **Length:** 8.5" overall. **Grips:** Checkered cocobolo. **Sights:** Baer dovetailed front, low-mount Bo-Mar rear with hidden leaf. **Features:** Similar to Premier II with tapered cone stub weight, rounded corners. Made in U.S.A. by Les Baer Custom, Inc.
Price: Blued **$2,580.00**

BERETTA 85FS CHEETAH

Caliber: 9x19 15-round double stack magazine. **Barrel:** 4.45". **Weight:** 29.10 oz. **Length:** 7.5" overall. **Grips:** Plastic and Wood. **Sights:** Standard 3-dot system. Notched rear sight is dovetailed to slide. Blade front sight is integral with slide. **Features:** An open slide design that increases the reliability of the firearm. The frame is made from an aluminum alloy that delivers the strength and durability of steel – but with 65% less weight. The automatic firing pin block (FS models) prevents the gun from firing in case of inadvertent drops or strikes against hard surfaces. Available in nickel finish.
Price: Standard (black) finish.......................... **$770.00**
Price: Nickel finish **$830.00**

BERETTA MODEL 92FS PISTOL

Caliber: 9mm Para., 10-shot magazine. **Barrel:** 4.9". **Weight:** 34 oz. **Length:** 8.5" overall. **Grips:** Checkered black plastic. **Sights:** Blade front, rear adjustable for windage. Tritium night sights available. **Features:** Double action. Extractor acts as chamber loaded indicator, squared trigger guard, grooved front and backstraps, inertia firing pin. Matte or blued finish. Introduced 1977. Made in U.S.A.
Price: With plastic grips **$650.00**

BERETTA MODEL 80 CHEETAH SERIES DA PISTOLS

Caliber: 380 ACP, 10-shot magazine (M84); 8-shot (M85); 22 LR, 7-shot (M87). **Barrel:** 3.82". **Weight:** About 23 oz. (M84/85); 20.8 oz. (M87). **Length:** 6.8" overall. **Grips:** Glossy black plastic (wood optional at extra cost). **Sights:** Fixed front, drift-adjustable rear. **Features:** Double action, quick takedown, convenient magazine release. Introduced 1977. Made in U.S.A.
Price: Model 84 Cheetah, plastic grips **$650.00**

BERETTA MODEL 21 BOBCAT PISTOL

Caliber: 22 LR or 25 ACP. Both double action. **Barrel:** 2.4". **Weight:** 11.5 oz.; 11.8 oz. **Length:** 4.9" overall. **Grips:** Plastic. **Features:** Available in nickel, matte, engraved or blue finish. Introduced in 1985.

Price: Bobcat, 22 or 25, blue **$335.00**
Price: Bobcat, 22, Inox **$420.00**
Price: Bobcat, 22 or 25, matte **$335.00**

BERETTA MODEL 3032 TOMCAT PISTOL

Caliber: 32 ACP, 7-shot magazine. **Barrel:** 2.45". **Weight:** 14.5 oz. **Length:** 5" overall. **Grips:** Checkered black plastic. **Sights:** Blade front, drift-adjustable rear. **Features:** Double action with exposed hammer; tip-up barrel for direct loading/unloading; thumb safety; polished or matte blue finish. Made in U.S.A. Introduced 1996.

Price: Matte **$435.00**
Price: Inox **$555.00**

BERETTA MODEL U22 NEOS

Caliber: 22 LR, 10-shot magazine. **Barrel:** 4.5"; 6". **Weight:** 32 oz.; 36 oz. **Length:** 8.8"; 10.3". **Sights:** Target.

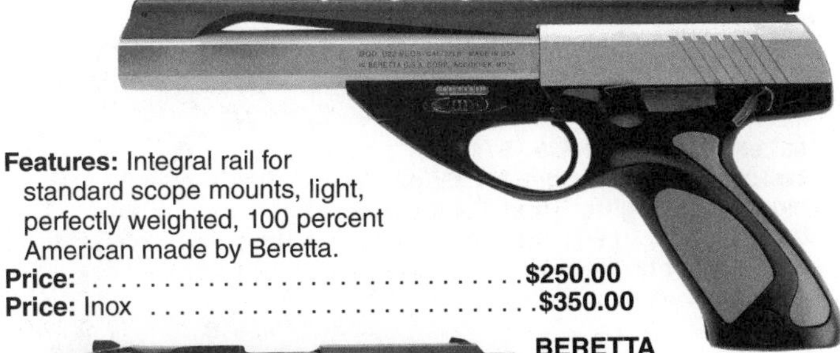

Features: Integral rail for standard scope mounts, light, perfectly weighted, 100 percent American made by Beretta.

Price: **$250.00**
Price: Inox **$350.00**

BERETTA MODEL PX4 STORM

Caliber: 9mm Para., 40 S&W. Capacity: 17 (9mm Para.); 14 (40 S&W). **Barrel:** 4". **Weight:** 27.5 oz. **Grips:** Black checkered w/3 interchangeable backstraps. **Sights:** 3-dot system coated in Superluminova; removable front and rear sights. **Features:** DA/SA, manual safety/hammer decocking lever (ambi) and automatic firing pin block safety. Picatinny rail. Comes with two magazines (17/10 in 9mm Para. and 14/10 in 40 S&W). Removable hammer unit. American made by Beretta. Introduced 2005.

Price: **$600.00**
Price: 45 ACP **$650.00**

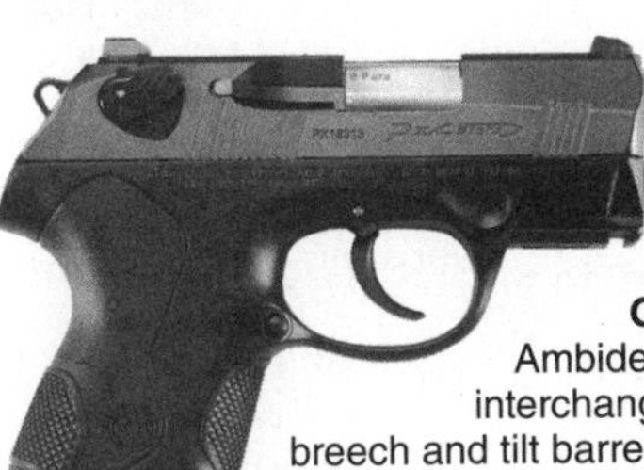

BERETTA MODEL PX4 STORM SUB-COMPACT

Caliber: 9mm, 40 S&W. Capacity: 13 (9mm); 10 (40 S&W). **Barrel:** 3". **Weight:** 26.1 oz. **Length:** 6.2" overall. **Grips:** NA. **Sights:** NA. **Features:** Ambidextrous manual safety lever, interchangeable backstraps included, lock breech and tilt barrel system, stainless steel barrel, Picatinny rail.

Price: **$600.00**

BERETTA MODEL M9

Caliber: 9mm Para. Capacity: 15. **Barrel:** 4.9". **Weight:** 32.2-35.3 oz. **Grips:** Plastic. **Sights:** Dot and post, low profile, windage adjustable rear. **Features:** DA/SA, forged aluminum alloy frame, delayed locking-bolt system, manual safety doubles as decocking lever, combat-style trigger guard, loaded chamber indicator. Comes with two magazines (15/10). American made by Beretta. Introduced 2005.

Price: **$650.00**

BERETTA MODEL M9A1

Caliber: 9mm Para. Capacity: 15. **Barrel:** 4.9". **Weight:** 32.2-35.3 oz. **Grips:** Plastic. **Sights:** Dot and post, low profile, windage adjustable rear. **Features:** Same as M9, but also includes integral Mil-Std-1913 Picatinny rail, has checkered frontstrap and backstrap. Comes with two magazines (15/10). American made by Beretta. Introduced 2005.

Price: **$750.00**

BERETTA NANO

Caliber: 9mm Para. Six-shot magazine. **Barrel:** 3.07". **Weight:** 17.7 oz. Length: 5.7" overall. **Grips:** Polymer. Sights: 3-dot low profile. **Features:** Double-action only, striker fired. Replaceable grip frames.

Price: **$475.00**

BERSA THUNDER 45 ULTRA COMPACT PISTOL

Caliber: 45 ACP. **Barrel:** 3.6". **Weight:** 27 oz. **Length:** 6.7" overall. **Grips:** Anatomically designed polymer. **Sights:** White outline rear. **Features:** Double action; firing pin safeties, integral locking system. Available in matte, satin nickel, gold, or duo-tone. Introduced 2003. Imported from Argentina by Eagle Imports, Inc.

Price: Thunder 45, matte blue **$402.00**
Price: Thunder 45, stainless **$480.00**
Price: Thunder 45, satin nickel **$445.00**

BERSA THUNDER 380 SERIES PISTOLS

Caliber: 380 ACP, 7 rounds **Barrel:** 3.5". **Weight:** 23 oz. **Length:** 6.6" overall. **Features:** Otherwise similar to Thunder 45 Ultra Compact. 380 DLX has 9-round capacity. 380 Concealed Carry has 8 round capacity. Imported from Argentina by Eagle Imports, Inc.

Price: Thunder 380 Matte **$310.00**
Price: Thunder 380 Satin Nickel **$336.00**
Price: Thunder 380 Blue DLX **$332.00**
Price: Thunder 380 Matte CC (2006) **$315.00**

BERSA THUNDER 9 ULTRA COMPACT/40 SERIES PISTOLS

Caliber: 9mm Para., 40 S&W. **Barrel:** 3.5". **Weight:** 24.5 oz. **Length:** 6.6" overall. **Features:** Otherwise similar to Thunder 45 Ultra Compact. 9mm Para. High Capacity model has 17-round capacity. 40 High Capacity model has 13-round capacity. Imported from Argentina by Eagle Imports, Inc.

Price: Thunder 9mm Para. Matte **$402.00**
Price: Thunder 40 High Capacity Satin Nickel . . **$419.00**

BROWNING 1911-22 COMPACT

Caliber: .22 L.R.,10-round magazine. **Barrel:** 3.625". **Weight:** 15 oz. **Length:** 6.5" overall. **Grips:** Brown composite. **Sights:** Fixed. **Features:** Slide is machined aluminum with alloy frame and matte blue finish. Blowback action and single action trigger with manual thumb and grip safetys. Works, feels and functions just like a full size 1911. It is simply scaled down and chambered in the best of all practice rounds: 22 LR. for focus on the fundamentals.

Price: **$600.00**

BROWNING 1911-22 A1

Caliber: .22 L.R.,10-round magazine. **Barrel:** 4.25". **Weight:** 16 oz. **Length:** 7.0625" overall. **Grips:** Brown

Prices given are believed to be accurate at time of publication however, many factors affect retail pricing so exact prices are not possible.

composite. **Sights:** Fixed. **Features:** Slide is machined aluminum with alloy frame and matte blue finish. Blowback action and single action trigger with manual thumb and grip safetys. Works, feels and functions just like a full size 1911. It is simply scaled down and chambered in the best of all practice rounds: 22 LR. for focus on the fundamentals

Price: **$600.00**

BROWNING HI POWER 9MM AUTOMATIC PISTOL

Caliber: 9mm Para., 13-round magazine; 40 S&W, 10-round magazine. **Barrel:** 4-5/8". **Weight:** 32 to 39 oz. **Length:** 7.75" overall. **Metal Finishes:** Blued (Standard); black-epoxy/silver-chrome (Practical); black-epoxy (Mark III). **Grips:** Molded (Mark III); wraparound Pachmayr (Practical); or walnut grips (Standard). **Sights:** Fixed (Practical, Mark III, Standard); low-mount adjustable rear (Standard). Cable lock supplied. **Features:** External hammer with half-cock and thumb safeties. Fixed rear sight model available. Commander-style (Practical) or spur-type hammer, single action. Includes gun lock. Imported from Belgium by Browning.

Price: Mark III **$979.00**

Price: Fixed Sights **$999.00**

Price: Standard, Adjustable sights **$1150.00**

BROWNING BUCK MARK PISTOLS

Currently offered in 15 different variations. **Caliber:** .22 LR with 10-shot magazine. Barrel: 4", 5.5" or 7.25". **Weight:** 28 to 39 oz. **LENGTH:** 8", 9.5" or 11.3" **Overall. Grips:** Laminate UDX (black or brown), Rosewood UDX, Composite URX, Cocobolo or Molded Comp, all ambidextrous. URX and UDX have finger grooves. **Sights:** Pro-Target adjustable rear, TRUGLO fiber-optic or ramp front. **Finish:** Matte blued, matte green or matte gray; matte stainless.

Price: .... **$380 to $560**

BUSHMASTER CARBON 15 .223 PISTOL

Caliber: 5.56/223, 30-round. **Barrel:** 7.25" stainless steel. **Weight:** 2.88 lbs. **Length:** 20" overall. **Grips:** Pistol grip, Hogue overmolded unit for ergonomic comfort. **Sights:** A2-type front with dual-aperture slip-up rear. **Features:** AR-style semi-auto pistol with carbon composite receiver, shortenend handguard, full-length optics rail.

Price: .... **N/A**

Price: Type 97 pistol, without handguard . . . **$1,055.00**

CHIAPPA 1911-22

A faithful replica of the famous John Browning 1911A1 pistol.

Caliber: .22 LR. Barrel: 5". **Weight:** 33.5 oz. Length: 8.5". **Grips:** Two-piece wood. **Sights:** Fixed. **Features:** Fixed barrel design, 10-shot magazine. Available in black, OD green or tan finish. Target and Tactical models have adjustable sights.

Price: .... **$300 to $419**

CHIAPPA M9-22 STANDARD

Caliber: .22 LR. **Barrel:** 5" **Weight:** 2.3 lbs. **Length:** 8.5". **Grips:** Black molded plastic or walnut. **Sights:** Fixed front sight and windage adjustable rear sight. **Features:** The M9-9mm has been a U.S. standard-issue service pistol since 1990. Chiappa's M9-22 is a replica of this pistol in 22 LR. The M9-22 has the same weight and feel as its 9mm counterpart but has an affordable 10 shot magazine for the 22 long rifle cartridge which makes it a true rimfire reproduction. Comes standard with steel trigger, hammer assembly and a 1/2-28 threaded barrel.

Price: .... **(available soon) $369.00**

CHIAPPA M9-22 TACTICAL

Caliber: .22 LR. **Barrel:** 5" **Weight:** 2.3 lbs. **Length:** 8.5". **Grips:** Black molded plastic. **Sights:** Fixed front sight and Novak style rear sites. **Features:** The M9-22 Tactical model has Novak style rear sites and comes with a fake suppressor (this ups the "cool factor" on the range and extends the barrel to make it even more accurate). It also has a 1/2 x 28 thread adaptor which can be used by those with a legal suppressor.

Price: .... **(available soon) $419.00**

CHRISTENSEN ARMS 1911 SERIES

Caliber: .45 ACP, .40 S&W, 9mm. **Barrel:** 3.7", 4.3", 5.5". **Features:** All models are built on a titanium frame with hand-fitted slide, match-grade barrel, tritium night sights, G10 Operator grip panels.

Price: **$3,195**

COBRA ENTERPRISES FS32, FS380 AUTO PISTOL

Caliber: 32 ACP, 380 ACP, 7-shot magazine. **Barrel:** 3.5". **Weight:** 2.1 lbs. **Length:** 6-3/8" overall. **Grips:** Black composition. **Sights:** Fixed. **Features:** Choice of bright chrome, satin nickel or black finish. Introduced 2002. Made in U.S.A. by Cobra Enterprises of Utah, Inc.

Price: **$165.00**

COBRA ENTERPRISES PATRIOT 45 PISTOL

Caliber: 45 ACP, 6, 7, or 10-shot magazine. **Barrel:** 3.3". **Weight:** 20 oz. **Length:** 6" overall. **Grips:** Black polymer. **Sights:** Rear adjustable. **Features:** Stainless steel or black melonite slide with load indicator; Semi-auto locked

breech, DAO. Made in U.S.A. by Cobra Enterprises of Utah, Inc.
Price: **$380.00**

COBRA ENTERPRISES CA32, CA380 PISTOL

Caliber: 32 ACP, 380 ACP. **Barrel:** 2.8". **Weight:** 22 oz. **Length:** 5.4". **Grips:** Black molded synthetic. **Sights:** Fixed. **Features:** Choice of black, satin nickel, or chrome finish. Made in U.S.A. by Cobra Enterprises of Utah, Inc.
Price: **$157.00**

COLT MODEL 1991 MODEL O AUTO PISTOL

Caliber: 45 ACP, 7-shot magazine. **Barrel:** 5". **Weight:** 38 oz. **Length:** 8.5" overall. **Grips:** Checkered black composition. **Sights:** Ramped blade front, fixed square notch rear, high profile. **Features:** Matte finish. Continuation of serial number range used on original G.I. 1911A1 guns. Comes with one magazine and molded carrying case. Introduced 1991.
Price: Blue **$900.00**
Price: Stainless **$960.00**

COLT XSE SERIES MODEL O AUTO PISTOLS

Caliber: 45 ACP, 8-shot magazine. **Barrel:** 5". **Grips:** Checkered, double diamond rosewood. **Sights:** Drift-adjustable 3-dot combat. **Features:** Brushed stainless finish; adjustable, two-cut aluminum trigger; extended ambidextrous thumb safety; upswept beavertail with palm swell; elongated slot hammer. Introduced 1999. From Colt's Mfg. Co., Inc.
Price: XSE Government (5" bbl.) **$1021.00**

COLT XSE LIGHTWEIGHT COMMANDER AUTO PISTOL

Caliber: 45 ACP, 8-shot. **Barrel:** 4.25". **Weight:** 26 oz. **Length:** 7.75" overall. **Grips:** Double diamond checkered rosewood. **Sights:** Fixed, glare-proofed blade front, square notch rear; 3-dot system. **Features:** Brushed stainless slide, nickeled aluminum frame; McCormick elongated slot enhanced hammer, McCormick two-cut adjustable aluminum hammer. Made in U.S.A. by Colt's Mfg. Co., Inc.
Price: **$1021.00**

COLT DEFENDER

Caliber: .45 ACP (7-round magazine), 9mm (8-round). **Barrel:** 3". **Weight:** 22-1/2 oz. **Length:** 6.75" overall. **Grips:** Pebble-finish rubber wraparound with finger grooves. **Sights:** White dot front, snag-free Colt competition rear. **Features:** Stainless finish; aluminum frame; combat-style hammer; Hi Ride grip safety, extended manual safety, disconnect safety. Introduced 1998. Made in U.S.A. by Colt's Mfg. Co., Inc.
Price: 07000D, stainless **$995.00**

COLT SERIES 70

Caliber: 45 ACP. **Barrel:** 5". **Weight:** 37.5 oz. **Length:** 8.5". **Grips:** Rosewood with double diamond checkering pattern. **Sights:** Fixed. **Features:** Custom replica of the Original Series 70 pistol with a Series 70 firing system, original rollmarks. Introduced 2002. Made in U.S.A. by Colt's Mfg. Co., Inc.
Price: Blued **$993.00**
Price: Stainless **$1027.00**

COLT 38 SUPER

Caliber: 38 Super. **Barrel:** 5". **Weight:** 36.5 oz. **Length:** 8.5" **Grips:** Checkered rubber (stainless and blue models); wood with double diamond checkering pattern (bright stainless model). **Sights:** 3-dot. **Features:** Beveled magazine well, standard thumb safety and service-style grip safety. Introduced 2003. Made in U.S.A. by Colt's Mfg. Co., Inc.
Price: Blued **$906.00**
Price: Stainless **$950.00**
Price: Bright Stainless **$1,248.00**

COLT MUSTANG POCKETLITE

Caliber: .380 ACP. Six-shot magazine. **Barrel:** 2.75". **Weight:** 12.5 oz. **Length:** 5.5". **Grips:** Black composite. **Finish:** Brushed stainless. **Features:** Thumb safety, firing-pin safety block.
Price: **$599**

COLT NEW AGENT

Caliber: 45 ACP (7+1), "9mm (8+1)". **Barrel:** 3". **Weight:** 25 oz. **Length:** 6.75" overall. **Grips:** Double diamond slim fit. **Sights:** Snag free trench style. **Features:** Semi-auto pistol with blued finish and enhanced black anodized aluminum receiver. Skeletonized aluminum trigger, series 80 firing system, front strap serrations, beveled magazine well. Also available in a double-action-only version (shown), in .45 ACP only.
Price: **$995.00**

COLT RAIL GUN

Caliber: 45 ACP (8+1). **Barrel:** NA. **Weight:** NA. **Length:** NA. **Grips:** Rosewood double diamond. **Sights:** White dot front and Novak rear. **Features:** 1911-style semi-auto. Stainless steel frame and slide, front and rear slide serrations, skeletonized trigger, integral; accessory rail, Smith & Alexander upswept beavertail grip palm swell safety, tactical thumb safety, National Match barrel.
Price: **$1087.00**

COLT SPECIAL COMBAT GOVERNMENT CARRY MODEL

Caliber: 45 ACP (8+1), 38 Super (9+1). **Barrel:** 5". **Weight:** NA. **Length:** NA. **Grips:** Black/silver synthetic. **Sights:** Novak front and rear night. **Features:** 1911-style semi-auto. Skeletonized three-hole trigger, slotted hammer, Smith & Alexander upswept beavertail grip palm swell safety and extended magazine well, Wilson tactical ambidextrous safety. Available in blued, hard chrome, or blue/satin nickel finish, depending on chambering.
Price: **$1,995.00**

CZ 75 B AUTO PISTOL

Caliber: 9mm Para., 40 S&W, 10-shot magazine. **Barrel:** 4.7". **Weight:** 34.3 oz. **Length:** 8.1" overall. **Grips:** High impact checkered plastic. **Sights:** Square post front, rear adjustable for windage; 3-dot system. **Features:** Single action/double action design; firing pin block safety; choice of black polymer, matte or high-polish blue finishes. All-steel frame. B-SA is a single action with a drop-free magazine. Imported from the Czech Republic by CZ-USA.

Price: 75 B, black polymer, 16-shot magazine **$597.00**
Price: 75 B, dual-tone or satin nickel **$617.00**
Price: 40 S&W, black polymer, 12-shot magazine **$615.00**
Price: 40 S&W, glossy blue, dual-tone, satin nickel **$669.00**
Price: 75 B-SA, 9mm Para./40 S&W, single action **$609.00**

CZ 75 BD DECOCKER
Similar to the CZ 75B except has a decocking lever in place of the safety lever. All other specifications are the same. Introduced 1999. Imported from the Czech Republic by CZ-USA.
Price: 9mm Para., black polymer . . . **$609.00**

CZ 75 B COMPACT AUTO PISTOL
Similar to the CZ 75 B except has 14-shot magazine in 9mm Para., 3.9" barrel and weighs 32 oz. Has removable front sight, non-glare ribbed slide top. Trigger guard is squared and serrated; combat hammer. Introduced 1993. Imported from the Czech Republic by CZ-USA.
Price: 9mm Para., black polymer **$631.00**
Price: 9mm Para., dual tone or satin nickel **$651.00**
Price: 9mm Para. D PCR Compact, alloy frame **$651.00**

CZ 75 P-07 DUTY
Caliber: 40 S&W, 9mm Luger (16+1). **Barrel:** 3.8". **Weight:** 27.2 oz. **Length:** 7.3" overall. **Grips:** Polymer black polycoat. **Sights:** Blade front, fixed groove rear. **Features:** The ergonomics and accuracy of the CZ 75 with a totally new trigger system. The new Omega trigger system simplifies the CZ 75 trigger system, uses fewer parts and improves the trigger pull. In addition, it allows users to choose between using the handgun with a decocking lever (installed) or a manual safety (included) by a simple parts change. The polymer frame design of the Duty and a new sleek slide profile (fully machined from bar stock) reduce weight, making the P-07 Duty a great choice for concealed carry.
Price: **$487.00**

CZ 75 TACTICAL SPORT
Similar to the CZ 75 B except the CZ 75 TS is a competition ready pistol designed for IPSC standard division (USPSA limited division). Fixed target sights, tuned single-action operation, lightweight polymer match trigger with adjustments for take-up and overtravel, competition hammer, extended magazine catch, ambidextrous manual safety, checkered walnut grips, polymer magazine well, two tone finish. Introduced 2005. Imported from the Czech Republic by CZ-USA.
Price: 9mm Para., 20-shot mag. **$1,338.00**
Price: 40 S&W, 16-shot mag. **$1,338.00**

CZ 75 SP-01 PISTOL
Similar to NATO-approved CZ 75 Compact P-01 model. Features an integral 1913 accessory rail on the dust cover, rubber grip panels, black polycoat finish, extended beavertail, new grip geometry with checkering on front and back straps, and double or single action operation. Introduced 2005. The Shadow variant designed as an IPSC "production" division competition firearm. Includes competition hammer, competition rear sight and fiber-optic front sight, modified slide release, lighter recoil and main spring for use with "minor power factor" competition ammunition. Includes polycoat finish and slim walnut grips. Finished by CZ Custom Shop. Imported from the Czech Republic by CZ-USA.
Price: SP-01 9mm Para., black polymer, 19+1 . . . . **$850.00**

CZ 75 SP-01 PHANTOM
Similar to the CZ 75 B. 9mm Luger, 19-round magazine, weighs 26 oz. and features a polymer frame with accessory rail, and a forged steel slide with a weight-saving scalloped profile. Two interchangeable grip inserts are included to accommodate users with different-sized hands.
Price: **$695.00**

CZ 85 B/85 COMBAT AUTO PISTOL
Same gun as the CZ 75 except has ambidextrous slide release and safety levers; non-glare, ribbed slide top; squared, serrated trigger guard; trigger stop to prevent overtravel. Introduced 1986. The CZ 85 Combat features a fully adjustable rear sight, extended magazine release, ambidextrous slide stop and safety catch, drop free magazine and overtravel adjustment. Imported from the Czech Republic by CZ-USA.
Price: 9mm Para., black polymer **$628.00**
Price: Combat, black polymer **$702.00**
Price: Combat, dual-tone, satin nickel **$732.00**

CZ 75 KADET AUTO PISTOL
Caliber: 22 LR, 10-shot magazine. **Barrel:** 4.88". **Weight:** 36 oz. **Grips:** High impact checkered plastic. **Sights:** Blade front, fully adjustable rear. **Features:** Single action/double action mechanism; all-steel construction. Introduced 1999. Kadet conversion kit consists of barrel, slide, adjustable sights, and magazine to convert the centerfire 75 to rimfire. Imported from the Czech Republic by CZ-USA.
Price: Black polymer **$689.00**
Price: Kadet conversion kit **$412.00**

CZ 83 DOUBLE-ACTION PISTOL
Caliber: 32 ACP, 380 ACP, 12-shot magazine. **Barrel:** 3.8". **Weight:** 26.2 oz. **Length:** 6.8" overall. **Grips:** High impact checkered plastic. **Sights:** Removable square post front, rear adjustable for windage; 3-dot system. **Features:** Single action/double action; ambidextrous magazine release and safety. Blue finish; non-glare ribbed slide top. Imported from the Czech Republic by CZ-USA.
Price: Glossy blue, 32 ACP or 380 ACP **$495.00**
Price: Satin Nickel **$522.00**

CZ 97 B AUTO PISTOL
Caliber: 45 ACP, 10-shot magazine. **Barrel:** 4.85". **Weight:** 40 oz. **Length:** 8.34" overall. **Grips:** Checkered walnut. **Sights:** Fixed. **Features:** Single action/double action; full-length slide rails; screw-in barrel bushing; linkless barrel; all-steel construction; chamber loaded indicator; dual transfer bars. Introduced 1999. Imported from the Czech Republic by CZ-USA.
Price: Black polymer **$779.00**
Price: Glossy blue **$799.00**

CZ 97 BD Decocker
Similar to the CZ 97 B except has a decocking lever in place of the safety lever. Tritium night sights. Rubber grips. All other specifications are the same. Introduced 1999. Imported from the Czech Republic by CZ-USA.
Price: 9mm Para., black polymer **$874.00**

CZ 2075 RAMI/RAMI P AUTO PISTOL
Caliber: 9mm Para., 40 S&W. **Barrel:** 3". **Weight:** 25 oz. **Length:** 6.5" overall. **Grips:** Rubber. **Sights:** Blade front with dot, white outline rear drift adjustable for windage. **Features:** Single-action/double-action; alloy or polymer frame, steel slide; has laser sight mount. Imported from the Czech Republic by CZ-USA.
Price: 9mm Para., alloy frame, 10 and 14-shot magazines . . . **$671.00**
Price: 40 S&W, alloy frame, 8-shot magazine **$671.00**
Price: RAMI P, polymer frame, 9mm Para., 40 S&W. **$612.00**

CZ P-01 AUTO PISTOL
Caliber: 9mm Para., 14-shot magazine. **Barrel:** 3.85". **Weight:** 27 oz. **Length:** 7.2" overall. **Grips:** Checkered rubber. **Sights:** Blade front

with dot, white outline rear drift adjustable for windage. **Features:** Based on the CZ 75, except with forged aircraft-grade aluminum alloy frame. Hammer forged barrel, decocker, firing-pin block, M3 rail, dual slide serrations, squared trigger guard, re-contoured trigger, lanyard loop on butt. Serrated front and back strap. Introduced 2006. Imported from the Czech Republic by CZ-USA.

Price: CZ P-01 . . . **$672.00**

DAN WESSON DW RZ-10 AUTO PISTOL

Caliber: 10mm, 9-shot. **Barrel:** 5". **Grips:** Diamond checkered cocobolo. **Sights:** Bo-Mar style adjustable target sight. **Weight:** 38.3 oz. **Length:** 8.8" overall. **Features:** Stainless-steel frame and serrated slide. Series 70-style 1911, stainless-steel frame, forged stainless-steel slide. Commander-style match hammer. Reintroduced 2005. Made in U.S.A. by Dan Wesson Firearms, distributed by CZ-USA.

Price: 10mm, 8+1 . . . . **$1,350.00**

DAN WESSON DW RZ-45 HERITAGE

Similar to the RZ-10 Auto except in 45 ACP with 7-shot magazine. Weighs 36 oz., length is 8.8" overall.

Price: 10mm, 8+1 . . . . **$1,298.00**

DAN WESSON VALOR 1911 PISTOL

Caliber: .45 ACP, 8-shot. **Barrel:** 5". **Grips:** Slim Line G10. **Sights:** Heinie ledge straight eight adjustable night sights. **Weight:** 2.4 lbs. **Length:** 8.8" overall. **Features:** The defensive style Valor, is a base stainless 1911 with our matte black "Duty" finish. This finish is a ceramic base coating that has set the standard for all coating tests. Other features include forged stainless frame and match barrel with 25 LPI checkering and undercut trigger guard, adjustable defensive night sites, and Slim line VZ grips. Made in U.S.A. by Dan Wesson Firearms, distributed by CZ-USA.

Price: **$2,012.00**

DAN WESSON V-BOB

Caliber: 45 ACP 8-shot magazine. **Barrel:** 4.25". **Weight:** 34 oz. **Length:** 8". **Grips:** Slim Line G10. **Sights:** Heinie Ledge Straight-Eight Night Sights. **Features:** Black matte or stainless finish. Bobtail forged grip frame with 25 lpi checkering front and rear.

Price: **$2077**

DESERT EAGLE MARK XIX PISTOL

Caliber: 357 Mag., 9-shot; 44 Mag., 8-shot; 50 AE, 7-shot. **Barrel:** 6", 10", interchangeable. **Weight:** 357 Mag.-62 oz.; 44 Mag.-69 oz.; 50 AE-72 oz. **Length:** 10.25" overall (6" bbl.). **Grips:** Polymer; rubber available. **Sights:** Blade on ramp front, combat-style rear. Adjustable available. **Features:** Interchangeable barrels; rotating three-lug bolt; ambidextrous safety; adjustable trigger. Military epoxy finish. Satin, bright nickel, chrome, brushed, matte or black-oxide finishes available. 10" barrel extra. Imported from Israel by Magnum Research, Inc.

Price: Black-6, 6" barrel **$1,594.00**
Price: Black-10, 10" barrel **$1,683.00**
Price: Component System Package, 3 barrels, carrying case, from **$2,910.00**

DESERT BABY MICRO DESERT EAGLE PISTOL

Caliber: 380 ACP, 6-rounds. **Barrel:** 2.22". **Weight:** 14 oz. **Length:** 4.52" overall. **Grips:** NA. **Sights:** Fixed low-profile. **Features:** Small-frame DAO pocket pistol. Steel slide, aluminum alloy frame, nickel-teflon finish.

Price: **$535.00**

DESERT BABY EAGLE PISTOLS

Caliber: 9mm Para., 40 S&W, 45 ACP, 10- or 15-round magazines. **Barrel:** 3.64", 3.93", 4.52". **Weight:** 26.8 to 39.8 oz. **Length:** 7.25" to 8.25" overall. **Grips:** Polymer. **Sights:** Drift-adjustable rear, blade front. **Features:** Steel frame and slide; slide safety; decocker. Reintroduced in 1999. Imported from Israel by Magnum Research, Inc.

Price: **$619.00**

DIAMONDBACK DB380 PISTOL

Caliber: .380, 6+1-shot capacity. **Barrel:** 2.8". **Weight:** 8.8 oz. **Features:** A micro-compact .380 automatic pistol made entirely in the USA. Designed with safety in mind, the DB380 features a "ZERO-Energy" striker firing system (patent pending) with a mechanical firing pin block, a steel magazine catch to secure a sheet metal magaine and real windage-adjustable sights, all in a lightweight pistol. A steel trigger with dual connecting bars allows for a crisp smooth, five-pound DAO trigger pull. The DB380 features a FEA (Finite Element Analysis) designed slide and barrel that is stronger than any comparable firearm, resulting in durability with less felt recoil, and the absence of removable pins or tools makes field stripping easier than ever. The slide, barrel, and internal parts are coated to resist corrosion.

Price: **290.00**

DIAMONDBACK DB9 PISTOL

Caliber: 9mm, 6+1-shot capacity. **Barrel:** 3". **Weight:** 11 oz. **Length:** 5.60". **Features:** A micro-compact 9mm automatic pistol made entirely in the USA. Designed with safety in mind, the DB9 features a "ZERO-Energy" striker firing system (patent pending) with a mechanical firing pin block, a steel magazine catch to secure a sheet metal magazine and real windage-adjustable sights, all in a lightweight pistol. A steel trigger with dual connecting bars allows for a crisp smooth, five-pound DAO trigger pull. The DB9 features a FEA (Finite Element Analysis) designed slide and barrel that is stronger than any comparable firearm, resulting in durability with less felt recoil, and the absence of removable pins or tools makes field stripping easier than ever. The slide, barrel, and internal parts are coated to resist corrosion.

Price: **$365.00**

EAA WITNESS FULL SIZE AUTO PISTOL

Caliber: 9mm Para., 38 Super, 18-shot magazine; 40 S&W, 10mm, 15-shot magazine; 45 ACP, 10-shot magazine. **Barrel:** 4.50". **Weight:** 35.33 oz. **Length:** 8.10" overall. **Grips:** Checkered rubber. **Sights:** Undercut blade front, open rear adjustable for windage. **Features:** Double-action/single-action trigger system; round trigger guard; frame-mounted safety. Introduced 1991. Polymer frame introduced 2005. Imported from Italy by European American Armory.

Price: 9mm Para., 38 Super, 10mm, 40 S&W, 45 ACP, full-size steel frame, Wonder finish **$514.00**
Price: 45/22 22 LR, full-size steel frame, blued **$472.00**
Price: 9mm Para., 40 S&W, 45 ACP, full-size polymer frame . . **$472.00**

Prices given are believed to be accurate at time of publication however, many factors affect retail pricing so exact prices are not possible.

EAA WITNESS COMPACT AUTO PISTOL

Caliber: 9mm Para., 40 S&W, 10mm, 12-shot magazine; 45 ACP, 8-shot magazine. **Barrel:** 3.6". **Weight:** 30 oz. **Length:** 7.3" overall. Otherwise similar to Full Size Witness. Polymer frame introduced 2005. Imported from Italy by European American Armory.

Price: 9mm Para., 10mm, 40 S&W, 45 ACP, steel frame, Wonder finish **$514.00**

Price: 9mm Para., 40 S&W, 45 ACP, polymer frame **$472.00**

EAA WITNESS-P CARRY AUTO PISTOL

Caliber: 10mm, 15-shot magazine; 45 ACP, 10-shot magazine. **Barrel:** 3.6". **Weight:** 27 oz. **Length:** 7.5" overall. Otherwise similar to Full Size Witness. Polymer frame introduced 2005. Imported from Italy by European American Armory.

Price: 10mm, 45 ACP, polymer frame, from **$598.00**

EAA ZASTAVA EZ PISTOL

Caliber: 9mm Para., 15-shot magazine; 40 S&W, 11-shot magazine; 45 ACP, 10-shot magazine. **Barrel:** 3.5" or 4." **Weight:** 30-33 oz. **Length:** 7.25" to 7.5" overall. **Features:** Ambidextrous decocker, slide release and magazine release; three dot sight system, aluminum frame, steel slide, accessory rail, full-length claw extractor, loaded chamber indicator. M88 compact has 3.6" barrel, weighs 28 oz. Introduced 2008. Imported by European American Armory.

Price: 9mm Para. or 40 S&W, blued **$547.00**
Price: 9mm Para. or 40 S&W, chromed **$587.00**
Price: 45 ACP, chromed **$587.00**
Price: M88, from **$292.00**

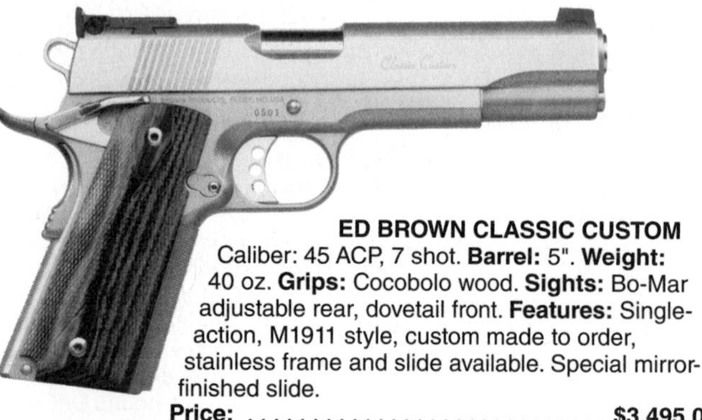

ED BROWN CLASSIC CUSTOM

Caliber: 45 ACP, 7 shot. **Barrel:** 5". **Weight:** 40 oz. **Grips:** Cocobolo wood. **Sights:** Bo-Mar adjustable rear, dovetail front. **Features:** Single-action, M1911 style, custom made to order, stainless frame and slide available. Special mirror-finished slide.

Price: **$3,495.00**

ED BROWN KOBRA AND KOBRA CARRY

Caliber: 45 ACP, 7-shot magazine. **Barrel:** 5" (Kobra); 4.25" (Kobra Carry). **Weight:** 39 oz. (Kobra); 34 oz. (Kobra Carry). **Grips:** Hogue exotic wood. **Sights:** Ramp, front; fixed Novak low-mount night sights, rear. **Features:** Has snakeskin pattern serrations on forestrap and mainspring housing, dehorned edges, beavertail grip safety.

Price: Kobra K-SS **$2,495.00**
Price: Kobra Carry **$2,745.00**

ED BROWN KOBRA CARRY LIGHTWEIGHT

Caliber: 45 ACP, 7-shot magazine. **Barrel:** 4.25" (Commander model slide). **Weight:** 27 oz. **Grips:** Hogue exotic wood. **Sights:** 10-8 Performance U-notch plain black rear sight with .156 notch, for fast aquisition of close targets. Fixed dovetail front night sight with high visibility white outlines. **Features:** Aluminium frame and Bobtail™ housing. Matte finished Gen III coated slide for low glare, with snakeskin on rear of slide only. Snakeskin pattern serrations on forestrap and mainspring housing, dehorned edges, beavertail grip safety. "LW" insignia on slide, which stands for "Lightweight".

Price: Kobra Carry Lightweight **$3,120.00**

Ed Brown Executive Pistols

Similar to other Ed Brown products, but with 25-lpi checkered frame and mainspring housing.

Price: . . . . **$2,695.00 - $2,945.00**

Ed Brown Special Forces Pistol

Similar to other Ed Brown products, but with ChainLink treatment on forestrap and mainspring housing. Entire gun coated with Gen III finish. "Square cut" serrations on rear of slide only. Dehorned. Introduced 2006.

Price: From **$2,495.00**

Ed Brown Special Forces Carry Pistol

Similar to the Special Forces basic models. Features a 4.25" Commander model slide, single stack commander Bobtail frame. Weighs approx. 35 oz. Fixed dovetail 3-dot night sights with high visibility white outlines.

Price: From **$2,745.00**

EXCEL ARMS ACCELERATOR MP-17/MP-22 PISTOLS

Caliber: 17 HMR, 22 WMR, 9-shot magazine. **Barrel:** 8.5" bull barrel. **Weight:** 54 oz. **Length:** 12.875" overall. **Grips:** Textured black composition. **Sights:** Fully adjustable target sights. **Features:** Made from 17-4 stainless steel, comes with aluminum rib, integral Weaver base, internal hammer, firing-pin block. American made, lifetime warranty. Comes with two 9-round stainless steel magazines and a California-approved cable lock. 22 WMR Introduced 2006. Made in U.S.A. by Excel Arms.

Price: **$433.00**
Price: Camo finishes (2008) **$520.00**

FIRESTORM AUTO PISTOLS

Caliber: 22 LR, 32 ACP, 10-shot magazine; 380 ACP, 7-shot magazine; 9mm Para., 40 S&W, 10-shot magazine; 45 ACP, 7-shot magazine. **Barrel:** 3.5". **Weight:** From 23 oz. **Length:** From 6.6" overall. **Grips:** Rubber. **Sights:** 3-dot. **Features:** Double action. Distributed by SGS Importers International.

Price: 22 LR, matte or duotone, from **$309.95**
Price: 380, matte or duotone, from. $311.95

Prices given are believed to be accurate at time of publication however, many factors affect retail pricing so exact prices are not possible.

Price: Mini Firestorm 9mm Para., matte, duotone, nickel, from **$395.00**
Price: Mini Firestorm 40 S&W, matte, duotone, nickel, from **$395.00**
Price: Mini Firestorm 45 ACP, matte, duotone, chrome, from **$402.00**

FN FNS SERIES

Caliber: 9mm, 17-shot magazine, .40 S&W (14-shot magazine). **Barrel:** 4". **Weight:** 25 oz. (9mm), 27.5 oz. (.40). **Length:** 7.25". **Grips:** Integral polymer with two interchangeable backstrap inserts. **Features:** Striker-fired, double action with manual safety, accessory rail, ambidextrous controls, 3-dot Night Sights.
Price: **$600**

FN FNX SERIES

Caliber: 9mm, 17-shot magazine, .40 S&W (14-shot), .45 ACP (10 or 14-shot). **Barrel:** 4" (9mm and .40), 4.5" .45. **Weight:** 22 to 32 oz (.45). **Length:** 7.4, 7.9" (.45). **Features:** Double-action/single-action operation with decocking/manual safety lever. Has external extractor with loaded-chamber indicator, front and rear cocking serrations, fixed 3-dot combat sights.
Price: **$650**

FN FNX .45 TACTICAL

Similar to standard FNX .45 except with 5.3" barrel with threaded muzzle, polished chamber and feed ramp, enhanced high-profile night sights, slide cut and threaded for red-dot sight (not included), MIL-STD 1913 accessory rail, ring-style hammer.
Price: **$1100**

GIRSAN MC27E PISTOL

Caliber: 9x19mm Parabellum. 15-shot magazine. **Barrel:** 98.5mm. **Weight:** 650 gr. (without magazine). **Length:** 184.5 mm overall. **Grips:** Black polymer. **Sights:** Fixed. **Features:** Cold forged barrel,polymer frame, short recoil operating system and locked breech. Semi-automatic, double action with a right and left safety sytem latch.
Price: . . . . **NA**

GLOCK 17/17C AUTO PISTOL

Caliber: 9mm Para., 17/19/33-shot magazines. **Barrel:** 4.49". **Weight:** 22.04 oz. (without magazine). **Length:** 7.32" overall. **Grips:** Black polymer. **Sights:** Dot on front blade, white outline rear adjustable for windage. **Features:** Polymer frame, steel slide; double-action trigger with "Safe Action" system; mechanical firing pin safety, drop safety; simple takedown without tools; locked breech, recoil operated action. ILS designation refers to Internal Locking System. Adopted by Austrian armed forces 1983. NATO approved 1984. Imported from Austria by Glock, Inc.
Price: Fixed sight **$690.00**

GLOCK GEN4 SERIES

In 2010 a new series of Generation Four pistols was introduced with several improved features. These included a multiple backstrap system offering three different size options, short, medium or large frame; reversible and enlarged magazine release; dual recoil springs; and RTF (Rough Textured Finish) surface. As of 2012, the following models were available in the Gen4 series: Models 17, 19, 21, 22, 23, 26, 27, 31, 32, 34, 35, 37. Price: Same as standard models
Price: . . . . **N/A**

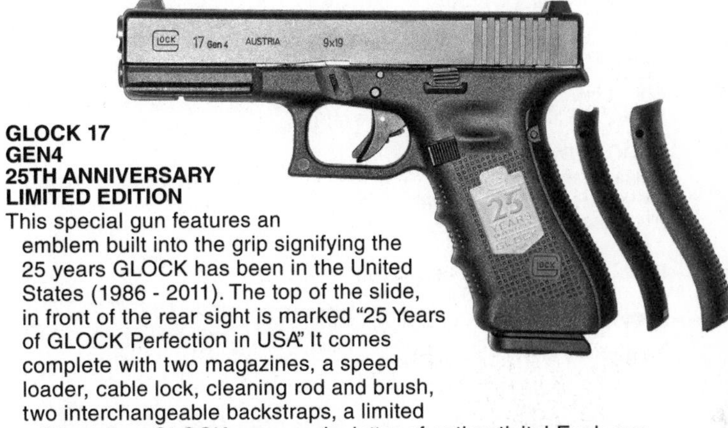

GLOCK 17 GEN4 25TH ANNIVERSARY LIMITED EDITION

This special gun features an emblem built into the grip signifying the 25 years GLOCK has been in the United States (1986 - 2011). The top of the slide, in front of the rear sight is marked "25 Years of GLOCK Perfection in USA." It comes complete with two magazines, a speed loader, cable lock, cleaning rod and brush, two interchangeable backstraps, a limited edition silver GLOCK case, and a letter of authenticity! Each gun is identified by the special prefix of 25YUSA. Similar to Model G17 but with multiple backstrap system allowing three options: a short frame version, medium frame or large frame; reversible, enlarged magazine release catch; dual recoil spring assembly; new Rough Textured Frame (RTF) surface designed to enhance grip traction.
Price: **$850.00**

GLOCK 19/19C AUTO PISTOL

Caliber: 9mm Para., 15/17/19/33-shot magazines. **Barrel:** 4.02". **Weight:** 20.99 oz. (without magazine). **Length:** 6.85" overall. Compact version of Glock 17. Pricing the same as Model 17. Imported from Austria by Glock, Inc.
Price: Fixed sight **$699.00**
Price: 19C Compensated (fixed sight) **$675.00**

GLOCK 20/20C 10MM AUTO PISTOL

Caliber: 10mm, 15-shot magazines. **Barrel:** 4.6". **Weight:** 27.68 oz. (without magazine). **Length:** 7.59" overall. **Features:** Otherwise similar to Model 17. Imported from Austria by Glock, Inc. Introduced 1990.
Price: Fixed sight, from **$700.00**

GLOCK MODEL 20 SF SHORT FRAME PISTOL

Caliber: 10mm. **Barrel:** 4.61" with hexagonal rifling. **Weight:** 27.51 oz. **Length:** 8.07" overall. **Sights:** Fixed. **Features:** Otherwise similar to Model 20 but with short-frame design, extended sight radius.
Price: **$664.00**

GLOCK 21/21C AUTO PISTOL

Caliber: 45 ACP, 13-shot magazines. **Barrel:** 4.6". **Weight:** 26.28 oz. (without magazine). **Length:** 7.59" overall. **Features:** Otherwise similar to Model 17. Imported from Austria by Glock, Inc. Introduced 1991. SF version has tactical rail, smaller diameter grip, 10-round magazine capacity. Introduced 2007.
Price: Fixed sight, from **$700.00**

GLOCK 22/22C AUTO PISTOL

Caliber: 40 S&W, 15/17-shot magazines. **Barrel:** 4.49". **Weight:** 22.92

oz. (without magazine). **Length:** 7.32" overall. **Features:** Otherwise similar to Model 17, including pricing. Imported from Austria by Glock, Inc. Introduced 1990.
Price: Fixed sight, from $641.00

GLOCK 23/23C AUTO PISTOL
Caliber: 40 S&W, 13/15/17-shot magazines. **Barrel:** 4.02". **Weight:** 21.16 oz. (without magazine). **Length:** 6.85" overall. **Features:** Otherwise similar to Model 22, including pricing. Compact version of Glock 22. Imported from Austria by Glock, Inc. Introduced 1990.
Price: Fixed sight $641.00
Price: 23C Compensated (fixed sight) $694.00

GLOCK 26 AUTO PISTOL
Caliber: 9mm Para. 10/12/15/17/19/33-shot magazines. **Barrel:** 3.46". **Weight:** 19.75 oz. **Length:** 6.29" overall. Subcompact version of Glock 17. Pricing the same as Model 17. Imported from Austria by Glock, Inc.
Price: Fixed sight $690.00

GLOCK 27 AUTO PISTOL
Caliber: 40 S&W, 9/11/13/15/17-shot magazines. **Barrel:** 3.46". **Weight:** 19.75 oz. (without magazine). **Length:** 6.29" overall. **Features:** Otherwise similar to Model 22, including pricing. Subcompact version of Glock 22. Imported from Austria by Glock, Inc. Introduced 1996.
Price: Fixed sight $750.00

GLOCK 29 AUTO PISTOL
Caliber: 10mm, 10/15-shot magazines. **Barrel:** 3.78". **Weight:** 24.69 oz. (without magazine). **Length:** 6.77" overall. **Features:** Otherwise similar to Model 20, including pricing. Subcompact version of Glock 20. Imported from Austria by Glock, Inc. Introduced 1997.
Price: Fixed sight $672.00

GLOCK MODEL 29 SF SHORT FRAME PISTOL
Caliber: 10mm. **Barrel:** 3.78" with hexagonal rifling. **Weight:** 24.52 oz. **Length:** 6.97" overall. **Sights:** Fixed. **Features:** Otherwise similar to Model 29 but with short-frame design, extended sight radius.
Price: $660.00

GLOCK 30 AUTO PISTOL
Caliber: 45 ACP, 9/10/13-shot magazines. **Barrel:** 3.78". **Weight:** 23.99 oz. (without magazine). **Length:** 6.77" overall. **Features:** Otherwise similar to Model 21, including pricing. Subcompact version of Glock 21. Imported from Austria by Glock, Inc. Introduced 1997. SF version has tactical rail, octagonal rifled barrel with a 1:15.75 rate of twist, smaller diameter grip, 10-round magazine capacity. Introduced 2008
Price: Fixed sight $700.00

GLOCK 31/31C AUTO PISTOL
Caliber: 357 Auto, 15/17-shot magazines. **Barrel:** 4.49". **Weight:** 23.28 oz. (without magazine). **Length:** 7.32" overall. **Features:** Otherwise similar to Model 17. Imported from Austria by Glock, Inc.
Price: Fixed sight, from $641.00

GLOCK 32/32C AUTO PISTOL
Caliber: 357 Auto, 13/15/17-shot magazines. **Barrel:** 4.02". **Weight:** 21.52 oz. (without magazine). **Length:** 6.85" overall. **Features:** Otherwise similar to Model 31. Compact. Imported from Austria by Glock, Inc.
Price: Fixed sight $669.00

GLOCK 33 AUTO PISTOL
Caliber: 357 Auto, 9/11/13/15/17-shot magazines. **Barrel:** 3.46". **Weight:** 19.75 oz. (without magazine). **Length:** 6.29" overall. **Features:** Otherwise similar to Model 31. Subcompact. Imported from Austria by Glock, Inc.
Price: Fixed sight, from $641.00

GLOCK 34 AUTO PISTOL
Caliber: 9mm Para. 17/19/33-shot magazines. **Barrel:** 5.32". **Weight:** 22.9 oz. **Length:** 8.15" overall. Competition version of Glock 17 with extended barrel, slide, and sight radius dimensions. Imported from Austria by Glock, Inc.
Price: Adjustable sight, from $648.00

GLOCK 35 AUTO PISTOL
Caliber: 40 S&W, 15/17-shot magazines. **Barrel:** 5.32". **Weight:** 24.52 oz. (without magazine). **Length:** 8.15" overall. **Features:** Otherwise similar to Model 22. Competition version of Glock 22 with extended barrel, slide, and sight radius dimensions. Imported from Austria by Glock, Inc. Introduced 1996.
Price: Adjustable sight.....................$648.00

GLOCK 36 AUTO PISTOL
Caliber: 45 ACP, 6-shot magazines. **Barrel:** 3.78". **Weight:** 20.11 oz. (without magazine). **Length:** 6.77" overall. **Features:** Single-stack magazine, slimmer grip than Glock 21/30. Subcompact. Imported from Austria by Glock, Inc. Introduced 1997.
Price: Adjustable sight $616.00

GLOCK 37 AUTO PISTOL
Caliber: 45 GAP, 10-shot magazines. **Barrel:** 4.49". **Weight:** 25.95 oz. (without magazine). **Length:** 7.32" overall. **Features:** Otherwise similar to Model 17. Imported from Austria by Glock, Inc. Introduced 2005.
Price: Fixed sight, from $562.00

GLOCK 38 AUTO PISTOL
Caliber: 45 GAP, 8/10-shot magazines. **Barrel:** 4.02". **Weight:** 24.16 oz. (without magazine). **Length:** 6.85" overall. **Features:** Otherwise similar to Model 37. Compact. Imported from Austria by Glock, Inc.
Price: Fixed sight $614.00

GLOCK 39 AUTO PISTOL
Caliber: 45 GAP, 6/8/10-shot magazines. **Barrel:** 3.46". **Weight:** 19.33 oz. (without magazine). **Length:** 6.3" overall. **Features:** Otherwise similar to Model 37. Subcompact. Imported from Austria by Glock, Inc.
Price: Fixed sight $614.00

GLOCK MODEL G17/G22/G19/G23 RTF
Similar to Models G17, G22, G19 and G23 but with rough textured frame.
Price: .... N/A

HECKLER & KOCH USP AUTO PISTOL

Caliber: 9mm Para., 15-shot magazine; 40 S&W, 13-shot magazine; 45 ACP, 12-shot magazine. **Barrel:** 4.25-4.41". **Weight:** 1.65 lbs. **Length:** 7.64-7.87" overall. **Grips:** Non-slip stippled black polymer. **Sights:** Blade front, rear adjustable for windage. **Features:** New HK design with polymer frame, modified Browning action with recoil reduction system, single control lever.

Prices given are believed to be accurate at time of publication however, many factors affect retail pricing so exact prices are not possible.

Special "hostile environment" finish on all metal parts. Available in SA/DA, DAO, left- and right-hand versions. Introduced 1993. 45 ACP Introduced 1995. Imported from Germany by Heckler & Koch, Inc.

Price: USP 45 . . . . $1,033.00
Price: USP 40 and USP 9mm 902.00

HECKLER & KOCH USP COMPACT AUTO PISTOL

Caliber: 9mm Para., 13-shot magazine; 40 S&W and .357 SIG, 12-shot magazine; 45 ACP, 8-shot magazine. Similar to the USP except the 9mm Para., 357 SIG, and 40 S&W have 3.58" barrels, measure 6.81" overall, and weigh 1.47 lbs. (9mm Para.). Introduced 1996. 45 ACP measures 7.09" overall. Introduced 1998. Imported from Germany by Heckler & Koch, Inc.

Price: USP Compact 45 . . . . $1,086.00
Price: USP Compact 9mm Para., 40 S&W $941.00

HECKLER & KOCH USP45 TACTICAL PISTOL

Caliber: 40 S&W, 13-shot magazine; 45 ACP, 12-shot magazine. **Barrel:** 4.90-5.09". **Weight:** 1.9 lbs. **Length:** 8.64" overall. **Grips:** Non-slip stippled polymer. **Sights:** Blade front, fully adjustable target rear. **Features:** Has extended threaded barrel with rubber O-ring; adjustable trigger; extended magazine floorplate; adjustable trigger stop; polymer frame. Introduced 1998. Imported from Germany by Heckler & Koch, Inc.

Price: USP Tactical 45 . . . . $1,325.00
Price: USP Tactical 40 . . . . $1,168.00

HECKLER & KOCH USP COMPACT TACTICAL PISTOL

Caliber: 45 ACP, 8-shot magazine. Similar to the USP Tactical except measures 7.72" overall, weighs 1.72 lbs. Introduced 2006. Imported from Germany by Heckler & Koch, Inc.

Price: USP Compact Tactical $1,288.00

HECKLER & KOCH MARK 23 SPECIAL OPERATIONS PISTOL

Caliber: 45 ACP, 12-shot magazine. **Barrel:** 5.87". **Weight:** 2.42 lbs. **Length:** 9.65" overall. **Grips:** Integral with frame; black polymer. **Sights:** Blade front, rear drift adjustable for windage; 3-dot. **Features:** Civilian version of the SOCOM pistol. Polymer frame; double action; exposed hammer; short recoil, modified Browning action. Introduced 1996. Imported from Germany by Heckler & Koch, Inc.

Price: $2,139.00

HECKLER & KOCH P30L AND P30LS AUTO PISTOLS

Caliber: 9mm x 19 and .40 S&W with 15-shot magazines. **Barrel:** 4.45". **Weight:** 27.52 oz. **Length:** 7.56" overall. **Grips:** Interchangeable panels. **Sights:** Open rectangular notch rear sight with contrast points (no radioactive). **Features:** Like the P30, the P30L was designed as a modern police and security pistol and combines optimal function and safety. Ergonomic features include a special grip frame with interchangeable backstraps inserts and lateral plates, allowing the pistol to be individually adapted to any user. Imported from Germany by Heckler & Koch, Inc. Browning type action with modified short recoil operation. Ambidextrous controls include dual slide releases, magazine release levers, and a serrated decocking button located on the rear of the frame (for applicable variants). A Picatinny rail molded into the front of the frame makes mounting lights, laser aimers, or other accessories easy and convenient. The extractor serves as a loaded chamber indicator providing a reminder of a loaded chamber that can be subtly seen and felt. The standard P30L is a 9 mm "Variant 3 (V3)" with a conventional double-action/single action trigger mode with a serrated decocking button on the rear of the slide.

Price: P30L $1,054.00
Price: P30L Variant 2 Law Enforcement Modification (LEM) enhanced DAO. $1,108.00
Price: P30L Variant 3 Double Action/Single Action (DA/SA) with Decocker $1,108.00
Price: P30LS. $1,054.00

HECKLER & KOCH P2000 AUTO PISTOL

Caliber: 9mm Para., 13-shot magazine; 40 S&W and .357 SIG, 12-shot magazine. **Barrel:** 3.62". **Weight:** 1.5 lbs. **Length:** 7" overall. **Grips:** Interchangeable panels. **Sights:** Fixed Patridge style, drift adjustable for windage, standard 3-dot. **Features:** Incorporates features of HK USP Compact pistol, including Law Enforcement Modification (LEM) trigger, double-action hammer system, ambidextrous magazine release, dual slide-release levers, accessory mounting rails, recurved, hook trigger guard, fiber-reinforced polymer frame, modular grip with exchangeable back straps, nitro-carburized finish, lock-out safety device. Introduced 2003. Imported from Germany by Heckler & Koch, Inc.

Price: $941.00
Price: P2000 LEM DAO, 357 SIG, intr. 2006 . . . . $941.00
Price: P2000 SA/DA, 357 SIG, intr. 2006 . . . . $941.00

HECKLER & KOCH P2000 SK AUTO PISTOL

Caliber: 9mm Para., 10-shot magazine; 40 S&W and .357 SIG, 9-shot magazine. **Barrel:** 3.27". **Weight:** 1.3 lbs. **Length:** 6.42" overall. **Sights:** Fixed Patridge style, drift adjustable. **Features:** Standard accessory rails, ambidextrous slide release, polymer frame, polygonal bore profile. Smaller version of P2000. Introduced 2005. Imported from Germany by Heckler & Koch, Inc.

Price: $983.00

HI-POINT FIREARMS MODEL 9MM COMPACT PISTOL

Caliber: 9mm Para., 8-shot magazine. **Barrel:** 3.5". **Weight:** 25 oz. **Length:** 6.75" overall. **Grips:** Textured plastic. **Sights:** Combat-style adjustable 3-dot system; low profile. **Features:** Single-action design; frame-mounted magazine release; polymer frame. Scratch-resistant matte finish. Introduced 1993. Comps are similar except they have a 4" barrel with muzzle brake/compensator. Compensator is slotted for laser or flashlight mounting. Introduced 1998. Made in U.S.A. by MKS Supply, Inc.

Price: C-9 9mm $155.00

HI-POINT FIREARMS MODEL 380 POLYMER PISTOL

Similar to the 9mm Compact model except chambered for 380 ACP, 8-shot magazine, adjustable 3-dot sights. Weighs 25 oz. Polymer frame. Action locks open after last shot. Includes 10-shot and 8-shot magazine; trigger lock. Introduced 1998. Comps are similar except they have a 4" barrel with muzzle compensator. Introduced 2001. Made in U.S.A. by MKS Supply, Inc.

Price: CF-380 . . . . $135.00

HI-POINT FIREARMS 40SW/POLY AND 45 AUTO PISTOLS

Caliber: 40 S&W, 8-shot magazine; 45 ACP (9-shot). **Barrel:** 4.5". **Weight:** 32 oz. **Length:** 7.72" overall. **Sights:** Adjustable 3-dot. **Features:** Polymer frames, last round lock-open, grip mounted magazine release, magazine disconnect safety, integrated accessory rail, trigger lock. Introduced 2002. Made in U.S.A. by MKS Supply, Inc.

Price: 40SW-B $186.00
Price: 45 ACP $186.00

HIGH STANDARD VICTOR 22 PISTOL
Caliber: 22 Long Rifle (10 rounds) or .22 Short (5 rounds). **Barrel:** 4.5"-5.5". **Weight:** 45 oz.-46 oz. **Length:** 8.5"-9.5" overall. **Grips:** Freestyle wood. **Sights:** Frame mounted, adjustable. **Features:** Semi-auto with drilled and tapped barrel, tu-tone or blued finish.
Price: **$845.00**

High Standard 10X Custom 22 Pistol
Similar to the Victor model but with precision fitting, black wood grips, 5.5" barrel only. High Standard Universal Mount, 10-shot magazine, barrel drilled and tapped, certificate of authenticity. Overall length is 9.5". Weighs 44 oz. to 46 oz. From High Standard Custom Shop.
Price: **$1,095.00**

HIGH STANDARD SUPERMATIC TROPHY 22 PISTOL
Caliber: 22 Long Rifle (10 rounds) or .22 Short (5 rounds/Citation version), not interchangable. **Barrel:** 5.5", 7.25". **Weight:** 44 oz., 46 oz. **Length:** 9.5", 11.25" overall. **Grips:** Wood. **Sights:** Adjustable. **Features:** Semi-auto with drilled and tapped barrel, tu-tone or blued finish with gold accents.
Price: 5.5" **$845.00**

High Standard Olympic Military 22 Pistol
Similar to the Supermatic Trophy model but in 22 Short only with 5.5" bull barrel, five-round magazine, aluminum alloy frame, adjustable sights. Overall length is 9.5", weighs 42 oz.
Price: **$875.00**

High Standard Supermatic Citation Series 22 Pistol
Similar to the Supermatic Trophy model but with heavier trigger pull, 10" barrel, and nickel accents. 22 Short conversion unit available. Overall length 14.5", weighs 52 oz.
Price: **$895.00**

HIGH STANDARD SUPERMATIC TOURNAMENT 22 PISTOL
Caliber: 22 LR. **Barrel:** 5.5" bull barrel. **Weight:** 44 oz. **Length:** 9.5" overall. **Features:** Limited edition; similar to High Standard Victor model but with rear sight mounted directly to slide.
Price: **$835.00**

HIGH STANDARD SPORT KING 22 PISTOL
Caliber: 22 LR. **Barrel:** 4.5" or 6.75" tapered barrel. **Weight:** 40 oz. to 42 oz. **Length:** 8.5" to 10.75". **Features:** Sport version of High Standard Supermatic. Two-tone finish, fixed sights.
Price: **$725.00**

HI-STANDARD SPACE GUN
Semiauto pistol chambered in .22 LR. Recreation of famed competition "Space Gun" from 1960s. Features include 6.75- 8- or 10-inch barrel; 10-round magazine; adjustable sights; barrel weight; adjustable muzzle brake; blue-black finish with gold highlights.
Price: **$1095.00**

KAHR CM SERIES
Caliber: 9mm (6+1), .40 S&W (6+1). **Barrel:** 3". **Weight:** 15.9 oz. **Length:** 5.42" overall. **Grips:** Textured polymer with integral steel rails molded into frame. **Sights:** CM9093 - Pinned in polymer sight; PM9093 - Drift adjustable, white bar-dot combat. **Features:** A conventional rifled barrel instead of the match grade polygonal barrel on Kahr's PM series; the CM slide stop lever is MIM (metal-injection-molded) instead of machined; the CM series slide has fewer machining operations and uses simple engraved markings instead of roll marking and finally the CM series are shipped with one magazine instead of two magazines.
The CM9 slide is only .90 inch wide and machined from solid 416 stainless slide with a matte finish, each gun is shipped with one 6 rd stainless steel magazine with a flush baseplate. Magazines are USA made, plasma welded, tumbled to remove burrs and feature Wolff Gunsprings. The magazine catch in the polymer frame is all metal and will not wear out on the stainless steel magazine after extended use.

Price: CM9093 . . . . **$565.00**
Price: PM9093 Match Grade **$786.00**

KAHR K SERIES AUTO PISTOLS
Caliber: K9: 9mm Para., 7-shot; K40: 40 S&W, 6-shot magazine. **Barrel:** 3.5". **Weight:** 25 oz. **Length:** 6" overall. **Grips:** Wraparound textured soft polymer. **Sights:** Blade front, rear drift adjustable for windage; bar-dot combat style. **Features:** Trigger-cocking double-action mechanism with passive firing pin block. Made of 4140 ordnance steel with matte black finish. Contact maker for complete price list. Introduced 1994. Made in U.S.A. by Kahr Arms.
Price: K9093C K9, matte stainless steel **$855.00**
Price: K9093NC K9, matte stainless steel w/tritium night sights **$985.00**
Price: K9094C K9 matte blackened stainless steel **$891.00**
Price: K9098 K9 Elite 2003, stainless steel **$932.00**
Price: K4043 K40, matte stainless steel **$855.00**
Price: K4043N K40, matte stainless steel w/tritium night sights **$985.00**
Price: K4044 K40, matte blackened stainless steel **$891.00**
Price: K4048 K40 Elite 2003, stainless steel **$932.00**

Kahr MK Series Micro Pistols
Similar to the K9/K40 except is 5.35" overall, 4" high, with a 3.08" barrel. Weighs 23.1 oz. Has snag-free bar-dot sights, polished feed ramp, dual recoil spring system, DA-only trigger. Comes with 5-round flush baseplate and 6-shot grip extension magazine. Introduced 1998. Made in U.S.A. by Kahr Arms.
Price: M9093 MK9, matte stainless steel **$855.00**
Price: M9093N MK9, matte stainless steel, tritium night sights **$958.00**
Price: M9098 MK9 Elite 2003, stainless steel **$932.00**
Price: M4043 MK40, matte stainless steel **$855.00**
Price: M4043N MK40, matte stainless steel, tritium night sights **$958.00**
Price: M4048 MK40 Elite 2003, stainless steel **$932.00**

KAHR P SERIES PISTOLS
Caliber: 380 ACP, 9x19, 40 S&W, 45 ACP. Similar to K9/K40 steel frame pistol except has polymer frame, matte stainless steel slide. Barrel length 3.5"; overall length 5.8"; weighs 17 oz. Includes two

7-shot magazines, hard polymer case, trigger lock. Introduced 2000. Made in U.S.A. by Kahr Arms.

Price: KP9093 9mm Para. **$739.00**
Price: KP4043 40 S&W **$739.00**
Price: KP4543 45 ACP **$805.00**
Price: KP3833 380 ACP (2008) **$649.00**

KAHR PM SERIES PISTOLS

Caliber: 9x19, 40 S&W, 45 ACP. Similar to P-Series pistols except has smaller polymer frame (Polymer Micro). Barrel length 3.08"; overall length 5.35"; weighs 17 oz. Includes two 7-shot magazines, hard polymer case, trigger lock. Introduced 2000. Made in U.S.A. by Kahr Arms.

Price: PM9093 PM9 . . . . **$786.00**
Price: PM4043 PM40 . . . . **$786.00**
Price: PM4543 (2007) **$855.00**

KAHR T SERIES PISTOLS

Caliber: T9: 9mm Para., 8-shot magazine; T40: 40 S&W, 7-shot magazine. **Barrel:** 4". **Weight:** 28.1-29.1 oz. **Length:** 6.5" overall. **Grips:** Checkered Hogue Pau Ferro wood grips. **Sights:** Rear: Novak low profile 2-dot tritium night sight, front tritium night sight. **Features:** Similar to other Kahr makes, but with longer slide and barrel upper, longer butt. Trigger cocking DAO; lock breech; "Browning-type" recoil lug; passive striker block; no magazine disconnect. Comes with two magazines. Introduced 2004. Made in U.S.A. by Kahr Arms.

Price: KT9093 T9 matte stainless steel **$831.00**
Price: KT9093-NOVAK T9, "Tactical 9," Novak night sight **$968.00**
Price: KT4043 40 S&W. **$831.00**

KAHR TP SERIES PISTOLS

Caliber: TP9: 9mm Para., 7-shot magazine; TP40: 40 S&W, 6-shot magazine. Barrel: 4". **Weight:** 19.1-20.1 oz. **Length:** 6.5-6.7" overall. **Grips:** Textured polymer. Similar to T-series guns, but with polymer frame, matte stainless slide. Comes with two magazines. TP40s introduced 2006. Made in U.S.A. by Kahr Arms.

Price: TP9093 TP9 . . . . **$697.00**
Price: TP9093-Novak TP9 (Novak night sights) **$838.00**
Price: TP4043 TP40 . . . . **$697.00**
Price: TP4043-Novak (Novak night sights) . . . **$838.00**
Price: TP4543 (2007) **$697.00**
Price: TP4543-Novak (4.04 barrel, Novak night sights) **$838.00**

KAHR CW SERIES PISTOL

Caliber: 9mm Para., 7-shot magazine; 40 S&W and 45 ACP, 6-shot magazine. **Barrel:** 3.5-3.64". **Weight:** 17.7-18.7 oz. **Length:** 5.9-6.36" overall. **Grips:** Textured polymer. Similar to P-Series, but CW Series have conventional rifling, metal-injection-molded slide stop lever, no front dovetail cut, one magazine. CW40 introduced 2006. Made in U.S.A. by Kahr Arms.

Price: CW9093 CW9 . . . . **$549.00**
Price: CW4043 CW40 . . . . **$549.00**
Price: CW4543 45 ACP (2008) **$606.00**

KAHR P380

Very small double action only semiauto pistol chambered in .380 ACP. Features include 2.5-inch Lothar Walther barrel; black polymer frame with stainless steel slide; drift adjustable white bar/dot combat/sights; optional tritium sights; two 6+1 magazines. Overall length 4.9 inches, weight 10 oz. without magazine.

Price: Standard sights **$649.00**

KEL-TEC P-11 AUTO PISTOL

Caliber: 9mm Para., 10-shot magazine. **Barrel:** 3.1". **Weight:** 14 oz. **Length:** 5.6" overall. **Grips:** Checkered black polymer. **Sights:** Blade front, rear adjustable for windage. **Features:** Ordnance steel slide, aluminum frame. Double-action-only trigger mechanism. Introduced 1995. Made in U.S.A. by Kel-Tec CNC Industries, Inc.

Price: From **$333.00**

KEL-TEC PF-9 PISTOL

Caliber: 9mm Para.; 7 rounds. **Weight:** 12.7 oz. **Sights:** Rear sight adjustable for windage and elevation. **Barrel Length:** 3.1". **Length:** 5.85". **Features:** Barrel, locking system, slide stop, assembly pin, front sight, recoil springs and guide rod adapted from P-11. Trigger system with integral hammer block and the extraction system adapted from P-3AT. MIL-STD-1913 Picatinny rail. Made in U.S.A. by Kel-Tec CNC Industries, Inc.

Price: From **$333.00**

KEL-TEC P-32 AUTO PISTOL

Caliber: 32 ACP, 7-shot magazine. **Barrel:** 2.68". **Weight:** 6.6 oz. **Length:** 5.07" overall. **Grips:** Checkered composite. **Sights:** Fixed. **Features:** Double-action-only mechanism with 6-lb. pull; internal slide stop. Textured composite grip/frame. Now available in 380 ACP. Made in U.S.A. by Kel-Tec CNC Industries, Inc.

Price: From **$318.00**

KEL-TEC P-3AT PISTOL

Caliber: 380 ACP; 7-rounds. **Weight:** 7.2 oz. **Length:** 5.2". **Features:** Lightest 380 ACP made; aluminum frame, steel barrel.

Price: From **$324.00**

KEL-TEC PLR-16 PISTOL

Caliber: 5.56mm NATO; 10-round magazine. **Weight:** 51 oz. **Sights:** Rear sight adjustable for windage, front sight is M-16 blade. **Barrel Length:** 9.2". **Length:** 18.5". **Features:** Muzzle is threaded 1/2"-28 to accept standard attachments such as a muzzle brake. Except for the barrel, bolt, sights, and mechanism, the PLR-16 pistol is made of high-impact glass fiber reinforced polymer. Gas-operated semi-auto. Conventional gas-piston operation with M-16 breech locking system. MIL-STD-1913 Picatinny rail. Made in U.S.A. by Kel-Tec CNC Industries, Inc.

Price: Blued **$665.00**

Kel-Tec PLR-22 Pistol
Semi-auto pistol chambered in 22 LR; based on centerfire PLR-16 by same maker. Blowback action, 26-round magazine. Open sights

and picatinny rail for mounting accessories; threaded muzzle. Overall length is 18.5", weighs 40 oz.
Price: $390.00

KEL-TEC PMR-30 Caliber: .22 Magnum (.22WMR) 30-rounds. **Barrel:** 4.3". **Weight:** 13.6 oz. **Length:** 7.9" overall. **Grips:** Glass reinforced Nylon (Zytel). **Sights:** Dovetailed aluminum with front & rear fiber optics. **Features:** Operates on a unique hybrid blowback/locked-breech system. It uses a double stack magazine of a new design that holds 30 rounds and fits completely in the grip of the pistol. Dual opposing extractors for reliability, heel magazine release to aid in magazine retention, Picatinny accessory rail under the barrel, Urethane recoil buffer, captive coaxial recoil springs. The barrel is fluted for light weight and effective heat dissipation. PMR30 disassembles for cleaning by removal of a single pin.
Price: $415.00

KIMBER MICRO CDP II .380
Caliber: .380 ACP (6-shot magazine). **Barrel:** 3". **Weight:** 17 oz. **Grips:** Double diamond rosewood. Mini 1911-style single action with no grip safety.
Price: $1100

KIMBER AEGIS II
Caliber: 9mm (9-shot magazine, 8-shot (Ultra model). **Barrel:** 3", 4" or 5". **Weight:** 25 to 38 oz. **Grips:** Scale-textured zebra wood. **Sights:** Tactical wedge 3-dot green night sights. **Features:** Made in the Kimber Custom Shop. Two-tone satin silver/matte black finish. Service Melt treatment that rounds and blends edges. **Available in three frame sizes:** Custom (shown), Pro and Ultra.
Price: $1299

KIMBER COVERT II
Caliber: .45 ACP (7-shot magazine). **Barrel:** 3", 4" or 5". **Weight:** 25 to 31 oz. **Grips:** Crimson Trace laser with camo finish. **Sights:** Tactical wedge 3-dot night sights. **Features:** Made in the Kimber Custom Shop. Desert tan frame and matte black slide finishes. Available in three frame sizes: Custom, Pro (shown) and Ultra.
Price: $1617

KIMBER CUSTOM II AUTO PISTOL
Caliber: 45 ACP. **Barrel:** 5". **Weight:** 38 oz. **Length:** 8.7" overall. **Grips:** Checkered black rubber, walnut, rosewood. **Sights:** Dovetailed front and rear, Kimber low profile adj. or fixed sights. **Features:** Slide, frame and barrel machined from steel or stainless steel. Match grade barrel, chamber and trigger group. Extended thumb safety, beveled magazine well, beveled front and rear slide serrations, high ride beavertail grip safety, checkered flat mainspring housing, kidney cut under trigger guard, high cut grip, match grade stainless steel barrel bushing, polished breech face, Commander-style hammer, lowered and flared ejection port, Wolff springs, bead blasted black oxide or matte stainless finish. Introduced in 1996. Made in U.S.A. by Kimber Mfg., Inc.
Price: Custom II $828.00
Price: Custom II Walnut (double-diamond walnut grips) $872.00

Kimber Stainless II Auto Pistols
Similar to Custom II except has stainless steel frame. 9mm Para. chambering and 45 ACP with night sights introduced 2008. Also chambered in 38 Super. Target version also chambered in 10mm.
Price: Stainless II 45 ACP $964.00
Price: Stainless II 9mm Para. (2008) $983.00
Price: Stainless II 45 ACP w/night sights (2008) $1,092.00
Price: Stainless II Target 45 ACP (stainless, adj. sight) $942.00

Kimber Pro Carry II Auto Pistol
Similar to Custom II, has aluminum frame, 4" bull barrel fitted directly to the slide without bushing. Introduced 1998. Made in U.S.A. by Kimber Mfg., Inc.
Price: Pro Carry II, 45 ACP $888.00
Price: Pro Carry II, 9mm $929.00
Price: Pro Carry II w/night sights $997.00

KIMBER RAPTOR II
Caliber: .45 ACP (8-shot magazine, 7-shot (Ultra and Pro models). **Barrel:** 3", 4" or 5". **Weight:** 25 to 31 oz. **Grips:** Thin milled rosewood. **Sights:** Tactical wedge 3-dot night sights. **Features:** Made in the Kimber Custom Shop. Matte black or satin silver finish. Available in three frame sizes: Custom (shown), Pro and Ultra.
Price: . . . .$1263 to $1530

KIMBER SOLO CARRY
Caliber: 9mm, 6-shot magazine. **Barrel:** 2.7". **Weight:** 17 oz. **Length:** 5.5" overall. **Grips:** Black synthetic, Checkered/smooth. **Sights:** Fixed low-profile dovetail-mounted 3-dot system. **Features:** Single action striker-fired trigger that sets a new standard for small pistols. A premium finish that is self-lubricating and resistant to salt and moisture. Ergonomics that ensure comfortable shooting. Ambidextrous thumb safety, slide release lever and magazine release button are pure 1911 – positive, intuitive and fast. The thumb safety provides additional security not found on most small pistols. Also available in stainless.
Price: $747.00

Kimber Compact Stainless II Auto Pistol
Similar to Pro Carry II except has stainless steel frame, 4-inch bbl., grip is .400" shorter than standard, no front serrations. Weighs 34 oz. 45 ACP only. Introduced in 1998. Made in U.S.A. by Kimber Mfg., Inc.
Price: $1,009.00

Kimber Ultra Carry II Auto Pistol
Lightweight aluminum frame, 3" match grade bull barrel fitted to slide without bushing. Grips .4" shorter. Low effort recoil. Weighs 25 oz. Introduced in 1999. Made in U.S.A. by Kimber Mfg., Inc.
Price: Stainless Ultra Carry II 45 ACP. $980.00
Price: Stainless Ultra Carry II 9mm Para. (2008) $1,021.00
Price: Stainless Ultra Carry II 45 ACP with night sights (2008) $1,089.00

Kimber Gold Match II Auto Pistol
Similar to Custom II models. Includes stainless steel barrel with match grade chamber and barrel bushing, ambidextrous thumb safety, adjustable sight, premium aluminum trigger, hand-checkered double diamond rosewood grips. Barrel hand-fitted for target accuracy. Made in U.S.A. by Kimber Mfg., Inc.

Prices given are believed to be accurate at time of publication however, many factors affect retail pricing so exact prices are not possible.

Price: Gold Match II **$1,345.00**
Price: Gold Match Stainless II 45 ACP **$1,519.00**
Price: Gold Match Stainless II 9mm Para. (2008) **$1,563.00**

Kimber Team Match II Auto Pistol
Similar to Gold Match II. Identical to pistol used by U.S.A. Shooting Rapid Fire Pistol Team, available in 45 ACP and 38 Super. Standard features include 30 lines-per-inch front strap extended and beveled magazine well, red, white and blue Team logo grips. Introduced 2008.
Price: 45 ACP **$1,539.00**
Price: 9mm **$1,546.00**

Kimber CDP II Series Auto Pistol
Similar to Custom II, but designed for concealed carry. Aluminum frame. Standard features include stainless steel slide, fixed Meprolight tritium 3-dot (green) dovetail-mounted night sights, match grade barrel and chamber, 30 LPI front strap checkering, two-tone finish, ambidextrous thumb safety, hand-checkered double diamond rosewood grips. Introduced in 2000. Made in U.S.A. by Kimber Mfg., Inc.
Price: Ultra CDP II 9mm Para. (2008) **$1,359.00**
Price: Ultra CDP II 45 ACP **$1,318.00**
Price: Compact CDP II 45 ACP **$1,318.00**
Price: Pro CDP II 45 ACP **$1,318.00**
Price: Custom CDP II (5" barrel, full length grip) **$1,318.00**

Kimber Eclipse II Series Auto Pistol
Similar to Custom II and other stainless Kimber pistols. Stainless slide and frame, black oxide, two-tone finish. Gray/black laminated grips. 30 lpi front strap checkering. All models have night sights; Target versions have Meprolight adjustable Bar/Dot version. Made in U.S.A. by Kimber Mfg., Inc.
Price: Eclipse Ultra II (3" barrel, short grip) **$1,236.00**
Price: Eclipse Pro II (4" barrel, full length grip) **$1,236.00**
Price: Eclipse Pro Target II (4" barrel, full length grip, adjustable sight) **$1,236.00**
Price: Eclipse Custom II 10mm **$1,291.00**
Price: Eclipse Target II (5" barrel, full length grip, adjustable sight) **$1,345.00**

KIMBER TACTICAL ENTRY II PISTOL
Caliber: 45 ACP, 7-round magazine. **Barrel:** 5". **Weight:** 40 oz. **Length:** 8.7" overall. **Features:** 1911-style semi auto with checkered frontstrap, extended magazine well, night sights, heavy steel frame, tactical rail.
Price: **$1,428.00**

KIMBER TACTICAL CUSTOM HD II PISTOL
Caliber: 45 ACP, 7-round magazine. **Barrel:** 5" match-grade. **Weight:** 39 oz. **Length:** 8.7" overall. **Features:** 1911-style semi auto with night sights, heavy steel frame.
Price: **$1,333.00**

KIMBER SUPER CARRY PRO
1911-syle semiauto pistol chambered in .45 ACP. Features include 8-round magazine; ambidextrous thumb safety; carry melt profiling; full length guide rod; aluminum frame with stainless slide; satin silver finish; super carry serrations; 4-inch barrel; micarta laminated grips; tritium night sights.
Price: **$1,530.00**

KIMBER SUPER CARRY HD SERIES
Designated as HD (Heavy Duty), each is chambered in .45 ACP and features a stainless steel slide and frame, premium KimPro II™ finish and night sights with cocking shoulder for one-hand operation. Like the original Super Carry pistols, HD models have directional serrations on slide, front strap and mainspring housing for unequaled control under recoil. A round heel frame and Carry Melt treatment make them comfortable to carry and easy to conceal.

SUPER CARRY ULTRA HD™
Caliber: .45 ACP, 7-shot magazine. **Barrel:** 3". **Weight:** 32 oz. **Length:** 6.8" overall. **Grips:** G-10, Checkered with border. **Sights:** Night sights with cocking shoulder radius (inches): 4.8. **Features:** Rugged stainless steel slide and frame with KimPro II finish. Aluminum match grade trigger with a factory setting of approximately 4-5 pounds.
Price: **$1,625.00**

SUPER CARRY PRO HD™
Caliber: .45 ACP, 8-shot magazine. **Barrel:** 4". **Weight:** 35 oz. **Length:** 7.7" overall. **Grips:** G-10, Checkered with border. **Sights:** Night sights with cocking shoulder radius (inches): 5.7. **Features:** Rugged stainless steel slide and frame with KimPro II finish. Aluminum match grade trigger with a factory setting of approximately 4-5 pounds.
Price: $1,625.00

SUPER CARRY CUSTOM HD™
Caliber: .45 ACP, 8-shot magazine. **Barrel:** 5". **Weight:** 38 oz. **Length:** 8.7" overall. **Grips:** G-10, Checkered with border. **Sights:** Night sights with cocking shoulder radius (inches): 4.8. **Features:** Rugged stainless steel slide and frame with KimPro II finish. Aluminum match grade trigger with a factory setting of approximately 4-5 pounds.
Price: **$1,625.00**

KIMBER ULTRA CDP II
Compact 1911-syle semiauto pistol chambered in .45 ACP. Features include 7-round magazine; ambidextrous thumb safety; carry melt profiling; full length guide rod; aluminum frame with stainless slide; satin silver finish; checkered frontstrap; 3-inch barrel; rosewood double diamond

Crimson Trace lasergrips grips; tritium 3-dot night sights.
Price: **$1,603.00**

KIMBER STAINLESS ULTRA TLE II
1911-syle semiauto pistol chambered in .45 ACP. Features include 7-round magazine; full length guide rod; aluminum frame with stainless slide; satin silver finish; checkered frontstrap; 3-inch barrel; tactical gray double diamond grips; tritium 3-dot night sights.
Price: **$1,210.00**

KIMBER ROYAL II
Caliber: .45 ACP, 7-shot magazine. **Barrel:** 5". **Weight:** 38 oz. **Length:** 8.7" overall. **Grips:** Solid bone-smooth. **Sights:** Fixed low profile radius (inches): 6.8. **Features:** A classic full-size pistol wearing a stunning charcoal blue finish complimented with solid bone grip panels. Frint and rear serations. Aluminum match grade trigger with a factory setting of approximately 4-5 pounds.
Price: **$1,938.00**

KORTH USA PISTOL SEMI-AUTO
Caliber: 9mm Para., 9x21. **Barrel:** 4", 4.5". **Weight:** 39.9 oz. **Grips:** Walnut, Palisander, Amboinia, Ivory. **Sights:** Fully adjustable. **Features:** DA/SA, 2 models available with either rounded or combat-style trigger guard, recoil-operated, locking block system, forged steel. Available finishes: High polish blue plasma, high polish or matted silver plasma, gray pickled finish, or high polish blue. "Schalldampfer Modell" has special threaded 4.5" barrel and thread protector for a suppressor, many deluxe options available, 10-shot mag. From Korth USA.
Price: From **$15,000.00**

MAGNUM RESEARCH MICRO DESERT EAGLE PISTOL
Double action only semiauto pistol chambered in .380. Features include steel slide, aluminum allow frame, black polymer grips, nickel silver or blue anodized frame, 6-round capacity, fixed sights, 2.2-inch barrel. Weight less than 14 oz.
Price: **$535.00**

MAGNUM RESEARCH DESERT EAGLE MAGNUM PISTOL
Enormous gas-operated semiauto pistol chambered in .50 AE, .44 Magnum, .357 Magnum. Features include 6- or 10-inch barrel, adjustable sights, variety of finishes. Now made in the USA.
Price: . . . . **$1,650.00 to $2,156.00.**

MPA380P PROTECTOR
Caliber: .380 ACP, 5+1 magazine capacity. **Barrel:** 2". **Weight:** 29 oz. **Length:** 6.7" overall. **Grips:** machined aluminum grips with a bead blasted finish. **Sights:** Fixed low-profile dovetail-mounted 3-dot system. **Features:** Dubbed the MPA380P (the "P" stands for "Premium"), the new model features bead blasted finish protected by a clear anodize coat, and an extended magazine pad for added shooting comfort. The Protector is a subcompact double-action-only semiauto. It features a fully machined 4140 steel upper slide, a fully machined 4140 steel lower receiver and advanced handle and grip designs. The pistol is American made and comes with a lifetime guarantee.
Price: **$345.90**

NORTH AMERICAN ARMS GUARDIAN DAO PISTOL
Caliber: 25 NAA, 32 ACP, 380 ACP, 32 NAA, 6-shot magazine. **Barrel:** 2.49". **Weight:** 20.8 oz. **Length:** 4.75" overall. **Grips:** Black polymer. **Sights:** Low profile fixed. **Features:** Double-action only mechanism. All stainless steel construction. Introduced 1998. Made in U.S.A. by North American Arms.
Price: From **$402.00**

OLYMPIC ARMS MATCHMASTER 5 1911 PISTOL
Caliber: 45 ACP, 7-shot magazine. **Barrel:** 5" stainless steel. **Weight:** 40 oz. **Length:** 8.75" overall. **Grips:** Smooth walnut with laser-etched scorpion icon. **Sights:** Ramped blade, LPA adjustable rear. **Features:** Matched frame and slide, fitted and head-spaced barrel, complete ramp and throat jobs, lowered and widened ejection port, beveled mag well, hand-stoned-to-match hammer and sear, lightweight long-shoe over-travel adjusted trigger, shaped and tensioned extractor, extended thumb safety, wide beavertail grip safety and full-length guide rod. Made in U.S.A. by Olympic Arms, Inc.
Price: **$903.00**

OLYMPIC ARMS MATCHMASTER 6 1911 PISTOL
Caliber: 45 ACP, 7-shot magazine. **Barrel:** 6" stainless steel. **Weight:** 44 oz. **Length:** 9.75" overall. **Grips:** Smooth walnut with laser-etched scorpion icon. **Sights:** Ramped blade, LPA adjustable rear. **Features:** Matched frame and slide, fitted and head-spaced barrel, complete ramp and throat jobs, lowered and widened ejection port, beveled mag well, hand-stoned-to-match hammer and sear, lightweight long-shoe over-travel adjusted trigger, shaped and tensioned extractor, extended thumb safety, wide beavertail grip safety and full length guide rod. Made in U.S.A. by Olympic Arms, Inc.
Price: **$973.00**

Prices given are believed to be accurate at time of publication however, many factors affect retail pricing so exact prices are not possible.

OLYMPIC ARMS ENFORCER 1911 PISTOL

Caliber: 45 ACP, 6-shot magazine. **Barrel:** 4" bull stainless steel. **Weight:** 35 oz. **Length:** 7.75" overall. **Grips:** Smooth walnut with etched black widow spider icon. **Sights:** Ramped blade front, LPA adjustable rear. **Features:** Compact Enforcer frame. Bushingless bull barrel with triplex counter-wound self-contained recoil system. Matched frame and slide, fitted and head-spaced barrel, complete ramp and throat jobs, lowered and widened ejection port, beveled mag well, hand-stoned-to-match hammer and sear, lightweight longshoe over-travel adjusted trigger, shaped and tensioned extractor, extended thumb safety, wide beavertail grip safety and full length guide rod. Made in U.S.A. by Olympic Arms.

Price: **$1,033.50**

OLYMPIC ARMS COHORT PISTOL

Caliber: 45 ACP, 7-shot magazine. **Barrel:** 4" bull stainless steel. **Weight:** 36 oz. **Length:** 7.75" overall. **Grips:** Fully checkered walnut. **Sights:** Ramped blade front, LPA adjustable rear. **Features:** Full size 1911 frame. Bushingless bull barrel with triplex counter-wound self-contained recoil system. Matched frame and slide, fitted and head-spaced barrel, complete ramp and throat jobs, lowered and widened ejection port, beveled mag well, hand-stoned-to-match hammer and sear, lightweight long-shoe over-travel adjusted trigger, shaped and tensioned extractor, extended thumb safety, wide beavertail grip safety and full length guide rod. Made in U.S.A. by Olympic Arms.

Price: **$973.70**

OLYMPIC ARMS BIG DEUCE PISTOL

Caliber: 45 ACP, 7-shot magazine. **Barrel:** 6" stainless steel. **Weight:** 44 oz. **Length:** 9.75" overall. **Grips:** Double diamond checkered exotic cocobolo wood. **Sights:** Ramped blade front, LPA adjustable rear. **Features:** Carbon steel parkerized slide with satin bead blast finish full size frame. Matched frame and slide, fitted and head-spaced barrel, complete ramp and throat jobs, lowered and widened ejection port, beveled mag well, hand-stoned-to-match hammer and sear, lightweight long-shoe over-travel adjusted trigger, shaped and tensioned extractor, extended thumb safety, wide beavertail grip safety and full length guide rod. Made in U.S.A. by Olympic Arms.

Price: **$1,033.50**

OLYMPIC ARMS WESTERNER SERIES 1911 PISTOLS

Caliber: 45 ACP, 7-shot magazine. **Barrel:** 4", 5", 6" stainless steel. **Weight:** 35-43 oz. **Length:** 7.75-9.75" overall. **Grips:** Smooth ivory laser-etched Westerner icon. **Sights:** Ramped blade, LPA adjustable rear. **Features:** Matched frame and slide, fitted and head-spaced barrel, complete ramp and throat jobs, lowered and widened ejection port, beveled mag well, hand-stoned-to-match hammer and sear, lightweight long-shoe over-travel adjusted trigger, shaped and tensioned extractor, extended thumb safety, wide beavertail grip safety and full length guide rod. Entire pistol is fitted and assembled, then disassembled and subjected to the color case hardening process. Made in U.S.A. by Olympic Arms, Inc.

Price: Constable, 4" barrel, 35 oz. . . .**$1,163.50**
Price: Westerner, 5" barrel, 39 oz. . . .**$1,033.50**
Price: Trail Boss, 6" barrel, 43 oz. . . .**$1,103.70**

OLYMPIC ARMS SCHUETZEN PISTOL WORKS 1911 PISTOLS

Caliber: 45 ACP, 7-shot magazine. **Barrel:** 4", 5.2", bull stainless steel. **Weight:** 35-38 oz. **Length:** 7.75-8.75" overall. **Grips:** Double diamond checkered exotic cocobolo wood. **Sights:** Ramped blade, LPA adjustable rear. **Features:** Carbon steel parkerized slide with satin bead blast finish full size frame. Matched frame and slide, fitted and head-spaced barrel, complete ramp and throat jobs, lowered and widened ejection port, beveled mag well, hand-stoned-to-match hammer and sear, lightweight long-shoe over-travel adjusted trigger, shaped and tensioned extractor, extended thumb safety, wide beavertail grip safety and full length guide rod. Custom made by Olympic Arms Schuetzen Pistol Works. Parts are hand selected and fitted by expert pistolsmiths. Several no-cost options to choose from. Made in U.S.A. by Olympic Arms Schuetzen Pistol Works.

Price: Journeyman, 4" bull barrel, 35 oz. **$1,293.50**
Price: Street Deuce, 5.2" bull barrel, 38 oz. **$1,293.50**

OLYMPIC ARMS OA-93 AR PISTOL

Caliber: 5.56 NATO. **Barrel:** 6.5" button-rifled stainless steel. **Weight:** 4.46 lbs. **Length:** 17" overall. **Sights:** None. **Features:** Olympic Arms integrated recoil system on the upper receiver eliminates the buttstock, flat top upper, free floating tubular match handguard,

threaded muzzle with flash suppressor. Made in U.S.A. by Olympic Arms, Inc.
Price: **$1,202.50**

OLYMPIC ARMS K23P AR PISTOL
Caliber: 5.56 NATO. **Barrel:** 6.5" button-rifled chrome-moly steel. **Length:** 22.25" overall. **Weight:** 5.12 lbs. **Sights:** Adjustable A2 rear, elevation adjustable front post. **Features:** A2 upper with rear sight, free floating tubular match handguard, threaded muzzle with flash suppressor, receiver extension tube with foam cover, no bayonet lug. Made in U.S.A. by Olympic Arms, Inc. Introduced 2007.
Price: **$973.70**

OLYMPIC ARMS K23P-A3-TC AR PISTOL
Caliber: 5.56 NATO. **Barrel:** 6.5" button-rifled chrome-moly steel. **Length:** 22.25" overall. **Weight:** 5.12 lbs. **Sights:** Adjustable A2 rear, elevation adjustable front post. **Features:** Flat-top upper with detachable carry handle, free floating FIRSH rail handguard, threaded muzzle with flash suppressor, receiver extension tube with foam cover, no bayonet lug. Made in U.S.A. by Olympic Arms, Inc. Introduced 2007.
Price: **$1,118.20**

OLYMPIC ARMS WHITNEY WOLVERINE PISTOL
Caliber: 22 LR, 10-shot magazine. **Barrel:** 4.625" stainless steel. **Weight:** 19.2 oz. **Length:** 9" overall. **Grips:** Black checkered with fire/safe markings. **Sights:** Ramped blade front, dovetail rear. **Features:** Polymer frame with natural ergonomics and ventilated rib. Barrel with 6-groove 1x16 twist rate. All metal magazine shell. Made in U.S.A. by Olympic Arms.
Price: **$291.00**

PARA USA BLACK OPS
Caliber: .45 ACP (8-shot magazine). **Barrel:** 5". **Weight:** 39 oz. **Grips:** G-10. **Sights:** Fixed night sights. Stainless receiver with IONBOND finish.
Price: **$1299**

PARA USA GI EXPERT PISTOLS
Caliber: .45 ACP, 7+1-round capacity. **Barrel:** 5" stainless. **Weight:** 39 oz. **Length:** 8.5" overall. **Grips:** Checkered Polymer. **Sights:** Dovetail Fixed, 3-White Dot. **Features:** The Para "GI Expert" is an entry level 1911 pistol that will allow new marksmen to own a pistol with features such as, Lowered and flared ejection port, beveled magazine well, flat mainspring housing, grip safety contoured for spur hammer.
Price: 1911 Wild Bunch (official SASS) **$789.00**
Price: 1911 LTC Single Action Single Stack Model (8+1) **$849.00**
Price: 1911 100th Anniversary w/cocobolo grips **$1079.00**

PARA USA PXT 1911 SINGLE-ACTION SINGLE-STACK AUTO PISTOLS
Caliber: 38 Super, 9mm Para., 45 ACP. **Barrel:** 3.5", 4.25", 5". **Weight:** 28-40 oz. **Length:** 7.1-8.5" overall. **Grips:** Checkered cocobolo, textured composition, Mother of Pearl synthetic. **Sights:** Blade front, low-profile Novak Extreme Duty adjustable rear. High visibility 3-dot system. **Features:** Available with alloy, steel or stainless steel frames. Skeletonized trigger, spurred hammer. Manual thumb, grip and firing pin lock safeties. Full-length guide rod. PXT designates new Para Power Extractor throughout the line. Introduced 2004. Made in U.S.A. by Para USA.
Price: 1911 SSP 9mm Para. (2008) **$959.00**
Price: 1911 SSP 45 ACP (2008) **$959.00**

PARA USA PXT 1911 SINGLE-ACTION HIGH-CAPACITY AUTO PISTOLS
Caliber: 9mm Para., 45 ACP, 10/14/18-shot magazines. **Barrel:** 3", 5". **Weight:** 34-40 oz. **Length:** 7.1-8.5" overall. **Grips:** Textured composition. **Sights:** Blade front, low-profile Novak Extreme Duty adjustable rear or fixed sights. High visibility 3-dot system. **Features:** Available with alloy, steel or stainless steel frames. Skeletonized match trigger, spurred hammer, flared ejection port. Manual thumb, grip and firing pin lock safeties. Full-length guide rod. Introduced 2004. Made in U.S.A. by Para USA.
Price: PXT P14-45 Gun Rights (2008), 14+1, 5" barrel **$1,149.00**
Price: P14-45 (2008), 14+1, 5" barrel **$919.00**

Para USA PXT Limited Pistols
Similar to the PXT-Series pistols except with full-length recoil guide system; fully adjustable rear sight; tuned trigger with over-travel stop; beavertail grip safety; competition hammer; front and rear slide serrations; ambidextrous safety; lowered ejection port; ramped match-grade barrel; dove-tailed front sight. Introduced 2004. Made in U.S.A. by Para USA.
Price: Todd Jarrett 40 S&W, 16+1, stainless **$1,729.00**

Para USA LDA Single-Stack Auto Pistols
Similar to LDA-series with double-action trigger mechanism. Cocobolo and polymer grips. Available in 45 ACP. Introduced 1999. Made in U.S.A. by Para USA.
Price: SSP, 8+1, 5" barrel **$899.00**

Para USA LDA Hi-Capacity Auto Pistols
Similar to LDA-series with double-action trigger mechanism. Polymer grips. Available in 9mm Para., 40 S&W, 45 ACP. Introduced 1999. Made in U.S.A. by Para USA.
Price: High-Cap 45, 14+1 ... **$1,279.00**

PARA USA STEALTH
Caliber: .45 ACP (6-shot magazine). **Barrel:** 3". **Weight:** 24 oz. **Grips:** G-10. **Sights:** Fixed night sights. Alloy receiver with IONBOND finish.
Price: **$1399**

PARA USA WARTHOG
Caliber: 9mm Para., 45 ACP, 6, 10, or 12-shot magazines. **Barrel:** 3". **Weight:** 24 to 31.5 oz. **Length:** 6.5". **Grips:** Varies by model. **Features:** Single action. Big Hawg (2008) is full-size .45 ACP on

lightweight alloy frame, 14+1, match grade ramped barrel, Power extractor, three white-dot fixed sights. Made in U.S.A. by Para USA.

Price: Slim Hawg (2006) single stack .45 ACP, stainless, 6+1 . . . . **$1,099.00**
Price: Nite Hawg .45 ACP, black finish, 10+1 . . **$1,099.00**
Price: Warthog .45 ACP, Regal finish, 10+1 . . . . . . **$959.00**
Price: Warthog Stainless **$1,069.00**
Price: Big Hawg (2008) **$959.00**
Price: PXT Hawg w/fiber optic sight,regal finish, 10+1 . . . . **$999.00**
Price: PXT Hawg 7 3.5" barrel, covert black finish, 7+1 . . . . . . **$919.00**

PARA USA PXT TACTICAL PISTOLS

Caliber: .45 ACP, 8+1 round capacity. **Barrel:** 4.25". **Weight:** 36 oz. **Length:** 8.5" overall. **Grips:** Checkered Polymer. **Sights:** Fiber-Optic Front/ Adj. Rear. **Features:** A compact tactical pistol equipped with a super strong integral light rail built into the dust shield. The front strap of the frame is checkered 30 lpi for improved gripping surface with or without gloves. The Match grade integral ramp 4.25-inch barrel is locked up at the muzzle with an Ed Brown National Match bushing. ylinder and Slide provides its Tactical II hammer, sear and disconnector for a clean crisp trigger. PARA's Power Extractor insures reliable extraction. A flat, checkered mainspring housing mates to the Ed Brown magazine well to funnel the 8-round PXT magazines with alloy base pads into the pistol.

Price: LTC Model **$1,599.00**
Price: 14•45 Model 14+1 high-capacity **$1,599.00**

PHOENIX ARMS HP22, HP25 AUTO PISTOLS

Caliber: 22 LR, 10-shot (HP22), 25 ACP, 10-shot (HP25). **Barrel:** 3". **Weight:** 20 oz. **Length:** 5.5" overall. **Grips:** Checkered composition. **Sights:** Blade front, adjustable rear. **Features:** Single action, exposed hammer; manual hold-open; button magazine release. Available in satin nickel, matte blue finish. Introduced 1993. Made in U.S.A. by Phoenix Arms.

Price: With gun lock **$130.00**
Price: HP Range kit with 5" bbl., locking case and accessories (1 Mag) **$171.00**
Price: HP Deluxe Range kit with 3" and 5" bbls., 2 mags, case **$210.00**

REMINGTON R1

Caliber: .45 (7-shot magazine). **Barrel:** 5". **Weight:** 38.5 oz. **Grips:** Double diamond walnut. **Sights:** Fixed, dovetail front and rear, 3-dot. **Features:** Flared and lowed ejection port. Comes with two magazines.

Price: **$729**

REMINGTON R1 ENHANCED

Same features as standard R1 except 8-shot magazine, stainless satin black oxide finish, wood laminate grips and adjustable rear sight.

Price: **$940**

ROCK RIVER ARMS LAR-15/LAR-9 PISTOLS

Caliber: .223/5.56mm NATO chamber 4-shot magazine. **Barrel:** 7", 10.5" Wilson chrome moly, 1:9 twist, A2 flash hider, 1/2-28 thread. **Weight:** 5.1 lbs. (7" barrel), 5.5 lbs. (10.5" barrel). **Length:** 23" overall. Stock: Hogue rubber grip. **Sights:** A2 front. **Features:** Forged A2 or A4 upper, single stage trigger, aluminum free-float tube, one magazine. Similar 9mm Para. LAR-9 also available. From Rock River Arms, Inc.

Price: LAR-15 7" A2 AR2115. . . . . **$955.00**
Price: LAR-15 10.5" A4 AR2120 . . . . **$945.00**
Price: LAR-9 7" A2 9MM2115 . . . . **$1,125.00**

ROHRBAUGH R9 SEMI-AUTO PISTOL

Caliber: 9mm Parabellum, 380 ACP. **Barrel:** 2.9". **Weight:** 12.8 oz. **Length:** 5.2" overall. **Features:** Very small double-action-only semi-auto pocket pistol. Stainless steel slide with matte black aluminum frame. Available with or without sights. Available with all-black (Stealth) and partial Diamond Black (Stealth Elite) finish.

Price: **$1,149.00**

RUGER SR9 AUTOLOADING PISTOL

Caliber: 9mm Para. **Barrel:** 4.14". **Weight:** 26.25, 26.5 oz. **Grips:** Glass-filled nylon in two color options—black or OD Green, w/flat or arched reversible backstrap. **Sights:** Adjustable 3-dot, built-in Picatinny-style rail. **Features:** Semi-DA, 6 configurations, striker-fired, through-hardened stainless steel slide, brushed or blackened stainless slide with black grip frame or blackened stainless slide with OD Green grip frame, ambi manual 1911-style safety, ambi mag release, mag disconnect, loaded chamber indicator, Ruger camblock design to absorb recoil, two 10 or 17-shot mags. Intr. 2008. Made in U.S.A. by Sturm, Ruger & Co.

Price: SR9 (17-Round), SR9-10 (SS) **$525.00**
Price: KBSR9 (17-Round), KBSR9-10 (Blackened SS). **$565.00**
Price: KODBSR9 (17-Round), KODBSR9-10 (OD Green Grip) **$565.00**

RUGER SR9C COMPACT PISTOL

Compact double action only semiauto pistol chambered in 9mm Parabellum. Features include 1911-style ambidextrous manual safety; internal trigger bar interlock and striker blocker; trigger safety; magazine disconnector; loaded chamber indicator; two magazines, one 10-round and the other 17-round; 3.5-inch barrel; 3-dot sights; accessory rail; brushed stainless or blackened allow finish. Weight 23.40 oz.

Price: **$525.00**

RUGER LC9

Caliber: 9mm luger, 7+1 capacity. **Barrel:** 3.12" **Weight:** 17.10 oz. **Grips:** Glass-filled nylon. **Sights:** Adjustable 3-dot. **Features:** double-action-only, hammer-fired, locked-breech pistol with a smooth trigger pull. Control and confident handling of the Ruger LC9 are accomplished through reduced recoil and aggressive frame checkering for a positive grip in all conditions. The Ruger LC9 features smooth "melted" edges for ease of holstering, carrying and drawing. Made in U.S.A. by Sturm, Ruger & Co.

Price: **$443.00**

RUGER LCP

Caliber: .380 (6-shot magazine). **Barrel:** 2.75" **Weight:** 9.4 oz. **Length:** 5.16" **Grips:** Glass-filled nylon. **Sights:** Fixed or LaserMax.

Price: **$379**
Price: . . . . **$443 (LaserMax)**

RUGER P95 AUTOLOADING PISTOL

Caliber: 9mm, 15-shot magazine. **Barrel:** 3.9". **Weight:** 30 oz. **Length:** 7.25" overall. **Grips:** Grooved; integral with frame. **Sights:** Blade front, rear drift adjustable for windage; 3-dot system. **Features:** Molded polymer grip frame, stainless steel or chrome-moly slide. Suitable for +P+ ammunition. Safety model, decocker. Introduced 1996. Made in U.S.A. by Sturm, Ruger & Co. Comes with lockable plastic case, spare magazine, loader and lock, Picatinny rails.

Price: KP95PR15 safety model, stainless steel. **$424.00**
Price: P95PR15 safety model, blued finish **$395.00**
Price: P95PR 10-round model, blued finish **$393.00**
Price: KP95PR 10-round model, stainless steel. **$424.00**

RUGER P345

Caliber: .45 ACP (8-shot magazine). **Barrel:** 4.2" **Weight:** 29 oz. **Length:** 7.5" **Sights:** Adjustable 3-dot. **Features:** Blued alloy/steel or stainless. Comes with two magazines, mag loader and hard plastic case.

Price: . . . . **$599, $639 (stainless)**

RUGER 22 CHARGER PISTOL

Caliber: .22 LR. **Barrel:** 10". **Weight:** 3.5 lbs (w/out bi-pod). Stock: Black Laminate. **Sights:** None. **Features:** Rimfire Autoloading, one configuration, 10/22 action, adjustable bi-pod, new mag release for easier removal, precision-rifled barrel, black matte finish, combination Weaver-style and tip-off scope mount, 10-shot mag. Intr. 2008. Made in U.S.A. by Sturm, Ruger & Co.

Price: CHR22-10. . . . . **$380.00**

RUGER MARK III STANDARD AUTOLOADING PISTOL

Caliber: 22 LR, 10-shot magazine. **Barrel:** 4.5", 4.75", 5.5", 6", or 6-7/8". **Weight:** 33 oz. (4.75" bbl.). **Length:** 9" (4.75" bbl.). **Grips:** Checkered composition grip panels. **Sights:** Fixed, fiber-optic front, fixed rear. **Features:** Updated design of original Standard Auto and Mark II series. Hunter models have lighter barrels. Target models have cocobolo grips; bull, target, competition, and hunter barrels; and adjustable sights. Introduced 2005.

Price: MKIII4, MKIII6 (blued) **$352.00**
Price: MKIII512 (blued bull barrel) **$417.00**
Price: KMKIII512 (stainless bull barrel) **$527.00**
Price: MKIII678 (blued) **$417.00**
Price: KMKIII678GC (stainless slabside barrel) **$606.00**
Price: KMKIII678H (stainless fluted barrel) **$620.00**
Price: KMKIII45HCL (Crimson Trace Laser Grips, intr. 2008) . **$787.00**
Price: KMKIII454 (2009) **$620.00**

Ruger 22/45 Mark III Pistol

Similar to other 22 Mark III autos except has Zytel grip frame that matches angle and magazine latch of Model 1911 45 ACP pistol. Available in 4" standard, 4.5", 5.5", 6-7/8" bull barrels. Comes with extra magazine, plastic case, lock. Introduced 1992. Hunter introduced 2006.

Price: P4MKIII, 4" bull barrel, adjustable sights **$380.00**
Price: P45GCMKIII, 4.5" bull barrel, fixed sights **$380.00**
Price: P512MKIII (5.5" bull blued barrel, adj. sights) **$380.00**
Price: KP512MKIII (5.5" stainless bull barrel, adj. sights **$475.00**
Price: Hunter KP45HMKIII 4.5" barrel (2007), KP678HMKIII, 6-7/8" stainless fluted bull barrel, adj. sights **$562.00**

RUGER SR22

Caliber: .22 LR (10-shot magazine). **Barrel:** 3.5". **Weight:** 17.5 oz. **Length:** 6.4". **Sights:** Adjustable 3-dot. **Features:** Ambidextrous manual safety/decocking lever and mag release. Comes with two interchangeable rubberized grips and two magazines.

Price: **$399**

RUGER SR1911

Caliber: .45 (8-shot magazine). **Barrel:** 5". **Weight:** 39 oz. **Length:** 8.6". **Grips:** Slim checkered hardwood. **Sights:** Novak LoMount Carry rear, standard front. **Features:** Based on Series 70 design. Flared and lowed ejection port. Extended mag release, thumb safety and slide-stop lever, oversized grip safety, checkered backstrap on the flat mainspring housing. Comes with one 7-shot and one 8-shot magazine.

Price: **$799**

SEECAMP LWS 32/380 STAINLESS DA AUTO

Caliber: 32 ACP, 380 ACP Win. Silvertip, 6-shot magazine. **Barrel:** 2", integral with frame. **Weight:** 10.5 oz. **Length:** 4-1/8" overall. **Grips:** Glass-filled nylon. **Sights:** Smooth, no-snag, contoured slide and barrel top. **Features:** Aircraft quality 17-4 PH stainless steel. Inertia-operated firing pin. Hammer fired double-action-only. Hammer automatically follows slide down to safety rest position after each shot, no manual safety needed. Magazine safety disconnector. Polished stainless. Introduced 1985. From L.W. Seecamp.

Price: 32 . . . . **$446.25**
Price: 380 . . . . **$795.00**

SIG SAUER 250 COMPACT AUTO PISTOL

Caliber: 9mm Para. (16-round magazine), 357 SIG, 40 S&W and 45 ACP. **Barrel:** NA. **Weight:** 24.6 oz. **Length:** 7.2" overall. **Grips:** Interchangeable polymer. **Sights:** Siglite night sights. **Features:** Modular design allows for immediate change in caliber and size; subcompact, compact and full. Six different grip combinations for each size. Introduced 2008. From Sig Sauer, Inc.

Price: P250 . . . . **$750.00**

SIG SAUER 1911 PISTOLS

Caliber: 45 ACP, 8-10 shot magazine. **Barrel:** 5". **Weight:** 40.3 oz. **Length:** 8.65" overall. **Grips:** Checkered wood grips. **Sights:** Novak night sights. Blade front, drift adjustable rear for windage. **Features:** Single-action 1911. Hand-fitted dehorned stainless-steel frame and slide; match-grade barrel, hammer/sear set and trigger; 25-lpi front strap checkering, 20-lpi mainspring housing checkering. Beavertail grip safety with speed bump, extended thumb safety, firing pin safety and hammer intercept notch. Introduced 2005. XO series has contrast sights, Ergo Grip XT textured polymer grips. Target line features adjustable target night sights, match barrel, custom wood grips, non-railed frame in stainless or Nitron finishes. TTT series is two-tone 1911 with Nitron slide and black controls on stainless frame. Includes burled maple grips, adjustable combat night sights. STX line available from Sig Sauer Custom Shop; two-tone 1911, non-railed, Nitron slide, stainless frame, burled maple grips. Polished cocking serrations, flat-top slide, magwell. Carry line has Novak night sights, lanyard attachment point, gray diamondwood or rosewood grips, 8+1 capacity. Compact series has 6+1 capacity, 7.7" OAL, 4.25" barrel, slim-profile wood grips, weighs 30.3 oz. RCS line (Compact SAS) is Customs Shop version with anti-snag dehorning. Stainless or Nitron finish, Novak night sights, slim-profile gray diamondwood or rosewood grips. 6+1 capacity. 1911 C3 (2008) is a 6+1 compact .45 ACP, rosewood custom wood grips, two-tone and Nitron finishes. **Weighs a**bout 30 ounces unloaded, lightweight alloy frame. **Length is** 7.7". Now offered in more than 30 different models with numerous options for frame size, grips, finishes, sight arrangements and other features. From SIG SAUER, Inc.

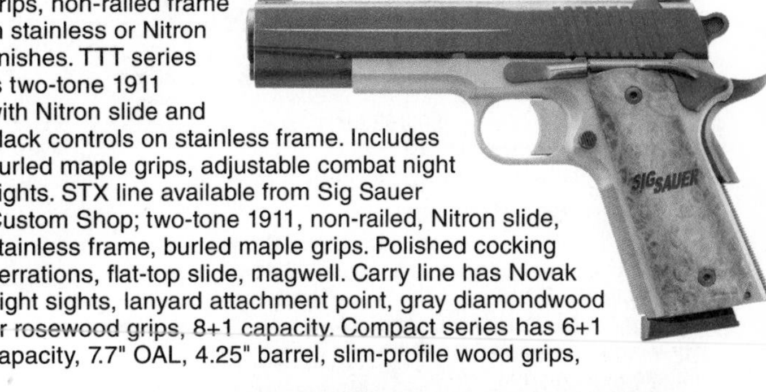

Price: Model 1911-22-B .22 LR w/custom wood grips **$399.99**
Price: Nitron **$1,200.00**
Price: Stainless **$1,170.00**
Price: XO Black **$1,005.00**
Price: Target Nitron (2006) **$1,230.00**
Price: TTT (2006) **$1,290.00**
Price: STX (2006) **$1,455.00**
Price: Carry Nitron (2006) **$1,200.00**
Price: Compact Nitron **$1,200.00**
Price: RCS Nitron **$1,305.00**
Price: C3 (2008) **$1,200.00**
Price: Platinum Elite **$1,275.00**
Price: Blackwater (2009) **$1,290.00**
Price: Scorpion **$1,128.00**

SIG SAUER P210 AUTO PISTOLS

Caliber: 9mm, 8-shot magazine. **Barrel:** 4.7". **Weight:** 37.4 oz. **Length:** 8.5" overall. **Grips:** Custom wood. **Sights:** Post and notch and adjustable target sights. **Features:** The carbon steel slide, machined from solid billet steel, now features a durable Nitron® coating, and the improved beavertail adorns the Nitron coated, heavy-style, carbon steel frame. The P210 Legend also offers an improved manual safety, internal drop safety, side magazine release, and

custom wood grips.
Price: P210-9-LEGEND....... **$2,199.00**
Price: P210-9-LEGEND-TGT w/adjustable target sights **$2,399.00**

SIG SAUER P220 AUTO PISTOLS

Caliber: 45 ACP, (7- or 8-shot magazine). **Barrel:** 4.4". **Weight:** 27.8 oz. **Length:** 7.8" overall. **Grips:** Checkered black plastic. **Sights:** Blade front, drift adjustable rear for windage. Optional Siglite night sights. **Features:** Double action. Stainless-steel slide, Nitron finish, alloy frame, M1913 Picatinny rail; safety system of decocking lever, automatic firing pin safety block, safety intercept notch, and trigger bar disconnector. Squared combat-type trigger guard. Slide stays open after last shot. Introduced 1976. P220 SAS Anti-Snag has dehorned stainless steel slide, front Siglite Night Sight, rounded trigger guard, dust cover, Custom Shop wood grips. Equinox line is Custom Shop product with Nitron stainless-steel slide with a black hard-anodized alloy frame, brush-polished flats and nickel accents. Truglo tritium fiber-optic front sight, rear Siglite night sight, gray laminated wood grips with checkering and stippling. From SIG SAUER, Inc.

Price: P220 Two-Tone, matte-stainless slide, black alloy frame **$1,110.00**
Price: P220 Elite Stainless (2008) **$1,350.00**
Price: P220 Two-Tone SAO, single action (2006), from **$1,086.00**
Price: P220 DAK (2006) **$853.00**
Price: P220 Equinox (2006) **$1,200.00**
Price: P220 Elite Dark (2009) **$1,200.00**
Price: P220 Elite Dark, threaded barrel (2009) **$1,305.00**

SIG SAUER P220 CARRY AUTO PISTOLS

Caliber: 45 ACP, 8-shot magazine. **Barrel:** 3.9". **Weight:** NA. **Length:** 7.1" overall. **Grips:** Checkered black plastic. **Sights:** Blade front, drift adjustable rear for windage. Optional Siglite night sights. **Features:** Similar to full-size P220, except is "Commander" size. Single stack, DA/SA operation, Nitron finish, Picatinny rail, and either post and dot contrast or 3-dot Siglite night sights. Introduced 2005. Many variations availble. From SIG SAUER, Inc.

Price: P220 Carry, from .... **$975.00; w/night sights $1,050.00**
Price: P220 Carry Elite Stainless (2008)................ **$1,350.00**

SIG SAUER P229 DA Auto Pistol

Similar to the P220 except chambered for 9mm Para. (10- or 15-round magazines), 40 S&W, 357 SIG (10- or 12-round magazines). Has 3.86" barrel, 7.1" overall length and 3.35" height. Weight is 32.4 oz. Introduced 1991. Snap-on modular grips. Frame made in Germany, stainless steel slide assembly made in U.S.; pistol assembled in U.S. Many variations available. From SIG SAUER, Inc.

Price: P229, from .... **$975.00; w/night sights** $1,050.00
Price: P229 Platinum Elite (2008)..................... **$1,275.00**
Price: P229 Enhanced Elite **$1,175.00**

SIG SAUER P226 Pistols

Similar to the P220 pistol except has 4.4" barrel, measures 7.7" overall, weighs 34 oz. Chambered in 9mm, 357 SIG, or 40 S&W. X-Five series has factory tuned single-action trigger, 5" slide and barrel, ergonomic wood grips with beavertail, ambidextrous thumb safety and stainless slide and frame with magwell, low-profile adjustable target sights, front cocking serrations and a 25-meter factory test target. Many variations available. Snap-on modular grips. From SIG SAUER, Inc.

Price: P226, from **$975.00**
Price: P226 Blackwater Tactical (2009) **$1,300.00**
Price: P226 Extreme **$1,146.00**

Price: P226 Enhanced Elite **$1,175.00**
Price: P226 Diamond Plate w/diamond plate detailed slide . **$1,100.00**

SIG SAUER SP2022 PISTOLS

Caliber: 9mm Para., 357 SIG, 40 S&W, 10-, 12-, or 15-shot magazines. **Barrel:** 3.9". **Weight:** 30.2 oz. **Length:** 7.4" overall. **Grips:** Composite and rubberized one-piece. **Sights:** Blade front, rear adjustable for windage. Optional Siglite night sights. **Features:** Polymer frame, stainless steel slide; integral frame accessory rail; replaceable steel frame rails; left- or right-handed magazine release, two interchangeable grips. From SIG SAUER, Inc.

Price: SP2009, Nitron finish **$613.00**

SIG SAUER P232 PERSONAL SIZE PISTOL

Caliber: 380 ACP, 7-shot. **Barrel:** 3.6". **Weight:** 17.6-22.4 oz. **Length:** 6.6" overall. **Grips:** Checkered black composite. **Sights:** Blade front, rear adjustable for windage. **Features:** Double action/ single action or DAO. Blow-back operation, stationary barrel. Introduced 1997. From SIG SAUER, Inc.

Price: P232, from **$660.00**

SIG SAUER P238 PISTOLS

Caliber: .380 ACP (9mm short), 6-7-shot magazine. **Barrel:** 2.7". **Weight:** 15.4 oz. **Length:** 5.5" overall. **Grips:** Hogue® G-10 and Rosewood grips. **Sights:** Contrast / SIGLITE night sights. **Features:** the P238 has redefined the role of a .380 ACP caliber pistol for concealed personal protection, ultimate firepower in an all metal beavertail-style frame.

Price: **$643.00**
Price: P238 Lady w/rosewood grips **$752.00**

Prices given are believed to be accurate at time of publication however, many factors affect retail pricing so exact prices are not possible.

Price: P238 Gambler w/rosewood grip **$752.00**
Price: P238 Extreme w/X-Grip extended magazine **$752.00**
Price: P238 Diamond Plate w/diamond plate detailed slide **$752.00**

SIG SAUER P290 PISTOLS
Caliber: 9mm, 6/8-shot magazine. **Barrel:** 2.9". **Weight:** 20.5 oz. **Length:** 5.5" overall. **Grips:** Polymer. **Sights:** Contrast / SIGLITE night sights. **Features:** Unlike many small pistols, the P290 features drift adjustable sights in the standard SIG SAUER dovetails. This gives shooters the option of either standard contrast sights or SIGLITE® night sights. The slide is machined from a solid billet of stainless steel and is available in a natural stainless or a durable Nitron® coating. A reversible magazine catch is left-hand adjustable. Interchangeable grip panels allow for personalization as well as a custom fit. In addition to the standard polymer inserts, optional panels will be available in aluminum, G10 and wood.
Price: Model 290-9-BSS **$758.00**
Price: Model 290-9-TSS **$786.00**
Price: Model 290-9-BSS-L with laser sights **$828.00**
Price: Model 290-9-TSS with laser sights **$856.00**

SIG SAUER P239 PISTOL
Caliber: 9mm Para., 8-shot, 357 SIG 40 S&W, 7-shot magazine. **Barrel:** 3.6". **Weight:** 25.2 oz. **Length:** 6.6" overall. **Grips:** Checkered black composite. **Sights:** Blade front, rear adjustable for windage. Optional Siglite night sights. **Features:** SA/DA or DAO; blackened stainless steel slide, aluminum alloy frame. Introduced 1996. Made in U.S.A. by SIG SAUER, Inc.
Price: P239, from **$840.00**

SIG SAUER MOSQUITO PISTOL
Caliber: 22 LR, 10-shot magazine. **Barrel:** 3.9". **Weight:** 24.6 oz. **Length:** 7.2" overall. **Grips:** Checkered black composite. **Sights:** Blade front, rear adjustable for windage. **Features:** Blowback operated, fixed barrel, polymer frame, slide-mounted ambidextrous safety. Introduced 2005. Made in U.S.A. by SIG SAUER, Inc.
Price: Mosquito, from **$375.00**

SIG SAUER P522 PISTOL
Semiauto blowback pistol chambered in .22 LR. Pistol version of SIG522 rifle. Features include a 10-inch barrel; lightweight polymer lower receiver with pistol grip; ambi mag catch; aluminum upper; faux gas valve; birdcage; 25-round magazine; quad rail or "clean" handguard; optics rail.
Price: . . . . **$572.00 to $643.00**

SIG SAUER P938
Caliber: 9mm (6-shot magazine). **Barrel:** 3.9". **Weight:** 16 oz. **Length:** 5.9". **Grips:** Rosewood, Blackwood, Hogue Extreme, Hogue Diamondwood. **Sights:** Siglite night sights or Siglite rear with Tru-Glo front. **Features:** Slightly larger version of P238 with 9mm chambering.
Price: . . . . **$809.00 to $823.00**

SPHINX PISTOLS
Caliber: 9mm Para., 45 ACP., 10-shot magazine. **Barrel:** 4.43". **Weight:** 39.15 oz. **Length:** 8.27" overall. **Grips:** Textured polymer. **Sights:** Fixed Trijicon Night Sights. **Features:** CNC engineered from stainless steel billet; grip frame in stainless steel, titanium or high-strength aluminum. Integrated accessory rail, high-cut beavertail, decocking lever. Made in Switzerland. Imported by Sabre Defence Industries.
Price: 45 ACP (2007) **$2,990.00**
Price: 9mm Para. Standard, titanium w/decocker **$2,700.00**

SPHINX SDP
Caliber: 9mm (15-shot magazine). **Barrel:** 3.7". **Weight:** 27.5 oz. **Length:** 7.4". **Sights:** Defiance Day & Night Green fiber/tritium front, tritium 2-dot red rear. **Features:** Double/single action with ambidextrous decocker, integrated slide postion safety, aluminum MIL-STD 1913 Picatinny rail, Blued alloy/steel or stainless. Aluminum and polymer frame, machined steel slide.
Price: . . . . **NA**

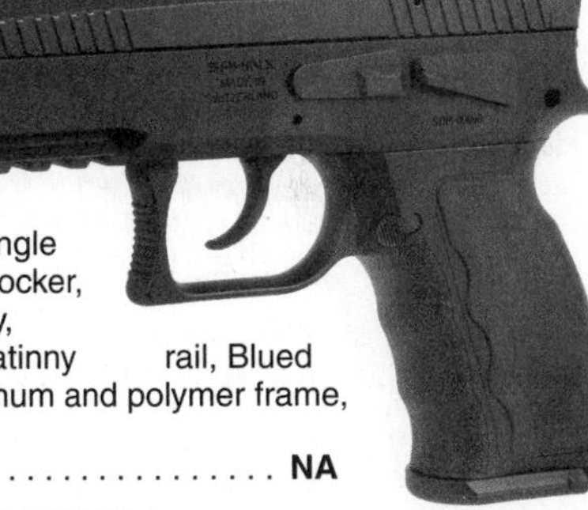

SMITH & WESSON M&P AUTO PISTOLS
Caliber: .22 LR, 9mm Para., 40 S&W, 357 Auto. **Barrel:** 4.25". **Weight:** 24.25 oz. **Length:** 7.5" overall. **Grips:** One-piece Xenoy, wraparound with straight backstrap. **Sights:** Ramp dovetail mount front; tritium sights optional; Novak Lo-mount Carry rear. **Features:** Zytel polymer frame, embedded stainless steel chassis; stainless steel slide and barrel, stainless steel structural components, black Melonite finish, reversible magazine catch, 3 interchangeable palmswell grip sizes, universal rail, sear deactivation lever, internal lock system, magazine disconnect. Ships with 2 magazines. Internal lock models available. Overall height: 5.5"; width: 1.2"; sight radius: 6.4". Introduced November 2005. 45 ACP version introduced 2007, 10+1 or 14+1 capacity. **Barrel:** 4.5". **Length:** 8.05". **Weight:** 29.6 ounces. **Features:** Picatinny-style equipment rail; black or bi-tone, dark-earth-brown frame. Bi-tone M&P45 includes ambidextrous, frame-mounted thumb safety, take down tool with lanyard attachment. Compact 9mm Para./357 SIG/40 S&W versions introduced 2007. Compacts have 3.5" barrel, OAL 6.7". 10+1 or 12+1 capacity. **Weight:** 21.7 ounces. **Features:** Picatinny-style equipment rail.

Made in U.S.A. by Smith & Wesson.
Price: M&P22 .22 LR model **$569.00 to $758.00**
Price: Crimson Trace Lasergrip models, from **$809.00**

SMITH & WESSON PRO SERIES MODEL M&P40
Striker-fired DAO semiauto pistol chambered in .40 S&W. Features include 4.25- or 5-inch barrel, matte black polymer frame and stainless steel slide, tactical rail, Novak front and rear sights or two-dot night sights, polymer grips, 15+1 capacity.

Price: **$830.00**
Price: VTAC® Viking Tactics **$779.00**

SMITH & WESSON PRO SERIES MODEL M&P9
Similar to M&P40 but chambered in 9mm Parabellum. Capacity 17+1, 4.25-inch barrel, two-dot night sights.
Price: **$830.00**

SMITH & WESSON MODEL SD9 PISTOLS
Caliber: .40 S&W and 9mm, 10+1, 14+1 and 16+1 round capacities. **Barrel:** 4". **Weight:** 39 oz. **Length:** 8.7". **Grips:** Wood or rubber. **Sights:** Front: Tritium Night Sight, Rear: Steel Fixed 2-Dot. **Features:** SDT™ - Self Defense Trigger for optimal, consistent pull first round to Last, standard picatinny-style rail, slim ergonomic textured grip, textured finger locator and aggressive front and back strap texturing with front and rear slide serrations.
Price: 9mm Std. Capacity **$459.00**
Price: 9mm Low Capacity **$459.00**
Price: .40 S&W Std. Capacity **$459.00**
Price: .40 S&W Low Capacity **$459.00**

SMITH & WESSON MODEL SW1911 PISTOLS
Caliber: 45 ACP, 8 rounds; 9mm, 11 rounds. **Barrel:** 5". **Weight:** 39 oz. **Length:** 8.7". **Grips:** Wood or rubber. **Sights:** Novak Lo-Mount Carry, white dot front. **Features:** Large stainless frame and slide with matte finish, single-side external safety. No. 108284 has adjustable target rear sight, ambidextrous safety levers, 20-lpi checkered front strap, comes with two 8-round magazines. DK model (Doug Koenig) also has oversized magazine well, Doug Koenig speed hammer, flat competition speed trigger with overtravel stop, rosewood grips with Smith & Wesson silver medallions, oversized magazine well, special serial number run. No. 108295 has olive drab Crimson Trace lasergrips. No. 108299 has carbon-steel frame and slide with polished flats on slide, standard GI recoil guide, laminated double-diamond walnut grips with silver Smith & Wesson medallions, adjustable target sights. Tactical Rail No. 108293 has a Picatinny rail, black Melonite finish, Novak Lo-Mount Carry Sights, scandium alloy frame. Tactical Rail Stainless introduced 2006. SW1911PD gun is Commander size, scandium-alloy frame, 4.25" barrel, 8" OAL, 28.0 oz., non-reflective black matte finish. Gunsite edition has scandium alloy frame, beveled edges, solid match aluminum trigger, Herrett's logoed tactical oval walnut stocks, special serial number run, brass bead Novak front sight. SC model has 4.25" barrel, scandium alloy frame, stainless-steel slide, non-reflective matte finish.
Price: From **$1,130.00**
Price: Crimson Trace Laser Grips **$1,493.00**
Price: SW1911 E Series .45 ACP **$919.00**
Price: SW1911 E Series Tactical Accessory Rail **$1,319.00**
Price: SW1911 E Series Round Butt, Scandium Frame **$1,369.00**
Price: SW1911 E Series Crimson Trace® Lasergrips **$1,089.00**

SMITH & WESSON MODEL 1911 SUB-COMPACT PRO SERIES
Caliber: 45 ACP, 7 + 1-shot magazine. **Barrel:** 3". **Weight:** 24 oz. **Length:** 6-7/8". **Grips:** Fully stippled synthetic. **Sights:** Dovetail white dot front, fixed white 2-dot rear. **Features:** Scandium frame with stainless steel slide, matte black finish throughout. Oversized external extractor, 3-hole curved trigger with overtravel stop, full-length guide rod, and cable lock. Introduced 2009.
Price: **$1,304.00**

SMITH & WESSON ENHANCED SIGMA SERIES DAO PISTOLS
Caliber: 9mm Para., 40 S&W; 10-, 16-shot magazine. **Barrel:** 4". **Weight:** 24.7 oz. **Length:** 7.25" overall. **Grips:** Integral. **Sights:** White dot front, fixed rear; 3-dot system. Tritium night sights available. **Features:** Ergonomic polymer frame; low barrel centerline; internal striker firing system; corrosion-resistant slide; Teflon-filled, electroless-nickel coated magazine, equipment rail. Introduced 1994. Made in U.S.A. by Smith & Wesson.
Price: From $482.00

SMITH & WESSON BODYGUARD® 380
Caliber: .380 Auto, 6+1 round capacity. **Barrel:** 2.75". **Weight:** 11.85 oz. **Length:** 5.25". **Grips:** Polymer. **Sights:** Integrated laser sights with front: stainless steel, rear: drift adjustable. **Features:** The frame of the Bodyguard is made of reinforced polymer, as is the magazine base plate and follower, magazine catch, and the trigger. The slide, sights, and guide rod are made of stainless steel, with the slide and sights having a Melonite hard coating.

Price: **$399.00**

SPRINGFIELD ARMORY EMP ENHANCED MICRO PISTOL
Caliber: 9mm Para., 40 S&W; 9-round magazine. **Barrel:** 3" stainless steel match grade, fully supported ramp, bull. **Weight:** 26 oz. **Length:**

Prices given are believed to be accurate at time of publication however, many factors affect retail pricing so exact prices are not possible.

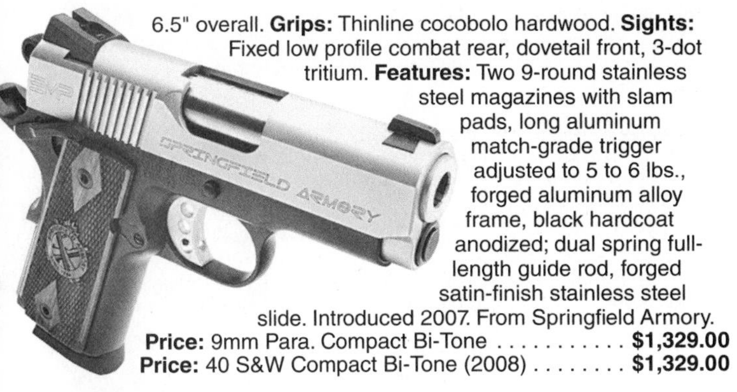

6.5" overall. **Grips:** Thinline cocobolo hardwood. **Sights:** Fixed low profile combat rear, dovetail front, 3-dot tritium. **Features:** Two 9-round stainless steel magazines with slam pads, long aluminum match-grade trigger adjusted to 5 to 6 lbs., forged aluminum alloy frame, black hardcoat anodized; dual spring full-length guide rod, forged satin-finish stainless steel slide. Introduced 2007. From Springfield Armory.

Price: 9mm Para. Compact Bi-Tone $1,329.00
Price: 40 S&W Compact Bi-Tone (2008) $1,329.00

SPRINGFIELD ARMORY XD POLYMER AUTO PISTOLS

Caliber: 9mm Para., 40 S&W, 45 ACP. **Barrel:** 3", 4", 5". **Weight:** 20.5-31 oz. **Length:** 6.26-8" overall. **Grips:** Textured polymer. **Sights:** Varies by model; Fixed sights are dovetail front and rear steel 3-dot units. **Features:** Three sizes in X-Treme Duty (XD) line: Sub-Compact (3" barrel), Service (4" barrel), Tactical (5" barrel). Three ported models available. Ergonomic polymer frame, hammer-forged barrel, no-tool disassembly, ambidextrous magazine release, visual/tactile loaded chamber indicator, visual/tactile striker status indicator, grip safety, XD gear system included. Introduced 2004. XD 45 introduced 2006. Compact line introduced 2007. Compacts ship with one extended magazine (13) and one compact magazine (10). From Springfield Armory.

Price: Sub-Compact OD Green 9mm Para./40 S&W, fixed sights $543.00
Price: Compact 45 ACP, 4" barrel, Bi-Tone finish (2008) $589.00
Price: Compact 45 ACP, 4" barrel, OD green frame, stainless slide (2008) $653.00
Price: Service Black 9mm Para./40 S&W, fixed sights $543.00
Price: Service Dark Earth 45 ACP, fixed sights $571.00
Price: Service Black 45 ACP, external thumb safety (2008) $571.00
Price: V-10 Ported Black 9mm Para./40 S&W $573.00
Price: Tactical Black 45 ACP, fixed sights $616.00
Price: Service Bi-Tone 40 S&W, Trijicon night sights (2008). . .$695.00

SPRINGFIELD ARMORY GI 45 1911A1 AUTO PISTOLS

Caliber: 45 ACP; 6-, 7-, 13-shot magazines. **Barrel:** 3", 4", 5". **Weight:** 28-36 oz. **Length:** 5.5-8.5" overall. **Grips:** Checkered double-diamond walnut, "U.S" logo. **Sights:** Fixed GI style. **Features:** Similar to WWII GI-issue 45s at hammer, beavertail, mainspring housing. From Springfield Armory.

Price: GI .45 4" Champion Lightweight, 7+1, 28 oz. $619.00
Price: GI .45 5" High Capacity, 13+1, 36 oz. $676.00
Price: GI .45 5" OD Green, 7+1, 36 oz. $619.00
Price: GI .45 3" Micro Compact, 6+1, 32 oz. $667.00

SPRINGFIELD ARMORY MIL-SPEC 1911A1 AUTO PISTOLS

Caliber: 38 Super, 9-shot magazines; 45 ACP, 7-shot magazines. **Barrel:** 5". **Weight:** 35.6-39 oz. **Length:** 8.5-8.625" overall. **Features:** Similar to GI 45s. From Springfield Armory.

Price: Mil-Spec Parkerized, 7+1, 35.6 oz. $715.00
Price: Mil-Spec Stainless Steel, 7+1, 36 oz. $784.00
Price: Mil-Spec 38 Super, 9+1, 39 oz. $775.00

Springfield Armory Custom Loaded Champion 1911A1 Pistol

Similar to standard 1911A1, slide and barrel are 4". 7.5" OAL. Available in 45 ACP only. Novak Night Sights. Delta hammer and cocobolo grips. Parkerized or stainless. Introduced 1989.

Price: Stainless, 34 oz.. . . . . $1,031.00
Price: Lightweight, 28 oz.. . . . .$989.00

Springfield Armory Custom Loaded Ultra Compact Pistol

Similar to 1911A1 Compact, shorter slide, 3.5" barrel, 6+1, 7" OAL. Beavertail grip safety, beveled magazine well, fixed sights. Videki speed trigger, flared ejection port, stainless steel frame, blued slide, match grade barrel, rubber grips. Introduced 1996. From Springfield Armory.

Price: Stainless Steel $1,031.00

SPRINGFIELD ARMORY CUSTOM LOADED MICRO-COMPACT 1911A1 PISTOL

Caliber: 45 ACP, 6+1 capacity. **Barrel:** 3" 1:16 LH. **Weight:** 24-32 oz. **Length:** 4.7". **Grips:** Slimline cocobolo. **Sights:** Novak LoMount tritium. Dovetail front. **Features:** Aluminum hard-coat anodized alloy frame, forged steel slide, forged barrel, ambi-thumb safety, Extreme Carry Bevel dehorning. Lockable plastic case, 2 magazines.

Price: Lightweight Bi-Tone $992.00

SPRINGFIELD ARMORY CUSTOM LOADED LONG SLIDE 1911A1 PISTOL

Caliber: 45 ACP, 7+1 capacity. **Barrel:** 6" 1:16 LH. **Weight:** 41 oz. **Length:** 9.5". **Grips:** Slimline cocobolo. **Sights:** Dovetail front; fully adjustable target rear. **Features:** Longer sight radius, 7.9".

Price: Bi-Tone Operator w/light rail $1,189.00

Springfield Armory Tactical Response Loaded Pistols

Similar to 1911A1 except 45 ACP only, checkered front strap and mainspring housing, Novak Night Sight combat rear sight and matching dove-tailed front sight, tuned, polished extractor, oversize barrel link; lightweight speed trigger and combat action job, match barrel and

bushing, extended ambidextrous thumb safety and fitted beavertail grip safety. Checkered cocobolo wood grips, comes with two Wilson 7-shot magazines. Frame is engraved "Tactical" both sides of frame with "TRP." Introduced 1998. TRP-Pro Model meets FBI specifications for SWAT Hostage Rescue Team. From Springfield Armory.
Price: 45 TRP Service Model, black Armory Kote finish, fixed Trijicon night sights $1,741.00

SPRINGFIELD ARMORY XDM SERIES
Calibers: 9mm, .40 S&W, .45 ACP. **Barrel:** 3.8 or 4.5". **Sights:** Fiber optic front with interchangeable red and green filaments, adjustable target rear. **Grips:** Integral polymer with three optional backstrap designs. **Features:** Variation of XD design with improved ergonomics, deeper and longer slide serrations, slightly modified grip contours and texturing. Black polymer frame, forged steel slide. Black and two-tone finish options.
Price: . . . . N/A

STOEGER COMPACT COUGAR PISTOL
Caliber: 9mm, 13+1 round capacity. **Barrel:** 3.6". **Weight:** 32 oz. **Length:** 7". **Grips:** Wood or rubber. **Sights:** Quick read 3-dot. **Features:** Double/single action with a Bruniton® Matte black finish. The ambidextrous safety and decocking lever is easily accessible to the thumb of a right-handed or left-handed shooter.
Price: $449.00

STI DUTY ONE PISTOL
1911-style semiauto pistol chambered in .45 ACP. Features include government size frame with integral tactical rail and 30 lpi checkered frontstrap; milled tactical rail on the dust cover of the frame; ambidextrous thumb safeties; high rise beavertail grip safety; lowered and flared ejection port; fixed rear sight; front and rear cocking serrations; 5-inch fully supported STI International ramped bull barrel.
Price: $1312.00

STI APEIRO PISTOL
1911-style semiauto pistol chambered in 9x19, .40 S&W, and .45 ACP. Features include Schuemann "Island" barrel; patented modular steel frame with polymer grip; high capacity double-stack magazine; stainless steel ambidextrous thumb safeties and knuckle relief high-rise beavertail grip safety; unique sabertooth rear cocking serrations; 5-inch fully ramped, fully supported "island" bull barrel, with the sight milled in to allow faster recovery to point of aim; custom engraving on the polished sides of the (blued) stainless steel slide; stainless steel magwell; STI adjustable rear sight and Dawson fiber optic front sight; blued frame.
Price: $2717.00

STI EAGLE PISTOL
1911-style semiauto pistol chambered in .45 ACP, 9mm, .40 S&W. Features include modular steel frame with polymer grip; high capacity doule-stack magazines; scalloped slide with front and rear cocking serrations; dovetail front sight and STI adjustable rear sight; stainless steel STI hi-ride grip safety and stainless steel STI ambi-thumb safety; 5- or 6-inch STI stainless steel fully supported, ramped bull barrel or the traditional bushing barrel; blued or stainless finish.
Price: $1964.00

STI ECLIPSE PISTOL
Compact 1911-tyle semiauto pistol chambered in 9x19, .40 S&W, and .45 ACP. Features include 3-inch slide with rear cocking serrations, oversized ejection port; 2-dot tritium night sights recessed into the slide; high-capacity polymer grip; single sided blued thumb safety; bobbed, high-rise, blued, knuckle relief beavertail grip safety; 3-inch barrel.
Price: $1843.00

STI ESCORT PISTOL
Similar to STI Eclipse but with aluminum allow frame and chambered in .45 ACP only.
Price: $1843.00

TAURUS MODEL 800 SERIES
Caliber: 9mm Para., 40 S&W, 45 ACP. **Barrel:** 4". **Weight:** 32 oz. **Length:** 8.25". **Grips:** Checkered. **Sights:** Novak. **Features:** DA/SA. Blue and Stainless Steel finish. Introduced in 2007. Imported from Brazil by Taurus International.
Price: 809B, 9mm Para., Blue, 17+1 . . . .$623.00

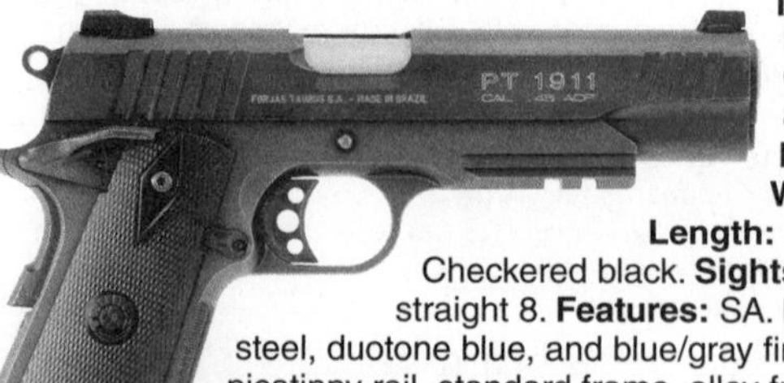

TAURUS MODEL 1911
Caliber: 45 ACP, 8+1 capacity. **Barrel:** 5". **Weight:** 33 oz. **Length:** 8.5". **Grips:** Checkered black. **Sights:** Heinie straight 8. **Features:** SA. Blue, stainless steel, duotone blue, and blue/gray finish. Standard/picatinny rail, standard frame, alloy frame, and alloy/picatinny rail. Introduced in 2007. Imported from Brazil by Taurus International.
Price: 1911B, Blue $719.00
Price: 1911SS, Stainless Steel $816.00
Price: 1911SS-1, Stainless Steel $847.00
Price: 1911 DT, Duotone Blue $795.00

TAURUS MODEL 917
Caliber: 9mm Para., 19+1 capacity. **Barrel:** 4.3". **Weight:** 32.2 oz. **Length:** 8.5". **Grips:** Checkered rubber. **Sights:** Fixed. **Features:** SA/DA. Blue and stainless steel finish. Medium frame. Introduced in 2007. Imported from Brazil by Taurus International.
Price: 917B-20, Blue $542.00
Price: 917SS-20, Stainless Steel $559.00

Prices given are believed to be accurate at time of publication however, many factors affect retail pricing so exact prices are not possible.

TAURUS MODEL PT-22/PT-25 AUTO PISTOLS

Caliber: 22 LR, 8-shot (PT-22); 25 ACP, 9-shot (PT-25). **Barrel:** 2.75". **Weight:** 12.3 oz. **Length:** 5.25" overall. **Grips:** Smooth rosewood or mother-of-pearl. **Sights:** Fixed. **Features:** Double action. Tip-up barrel for loading, cleaning. Blue, nickel, duo-tone or blue with gold accents. Introduced 1992. Made in U.S.A. by Taurus International.

Price: PT-22B or PT-25B, checkered wood grips **$248.00**

TAURUS PT2011 DT

Caliber: .380 (15-shot), 9mm (13-shot), .40 S&W(11-shot magazine). **Barrel:** 3.2". **Weight:** 21 oz. **Length:** 6.3". **Finish:** Blue or stainless. **Features:** Manual safety, removable polymer grip backstraps.

Price: . . . . . **$544 to $588**

TAURUS MODEL 22PLY SMALL POLYMER FRAME PISTOLS

Similar to Taurus Models PT-22 and PT-25 but with lightweight polymer frame. Features include 22 LR (9+1) or 25 ACP (8+1) chambering. 2.33" tip-up barrel, matte black finish, extended magazine with finger lip, manual safety. Overall length is 4.8". Weighs 10.8 oz.

Price: **$273.00**

TAURUS MODEL 24/7

Caliber: 9mm Para., 40 S&W, 45 ACP. **Barrel:** 4". **Weight:** 27.2 oz. **Length:** 7-1/8". **Grips:** "Ribber" rubber-finned overlay on polymer. **Sights:** Adjustable. **Features:** SA/DA; accessory rail, four safeties, blue or stainless finish. One-piece guide rod, flush-fit magazine, flared bushingless barrel, Picatinny accessory rail, manual safety, user changeable sights, loaded chamber indicator, tuned ejector and lowered port, one piece guide rod and flat wound captive spring. Introduced 2003. Long Slide models have 5" barrels, measure 8-1/8" overall, weigh 27.2 oz. Imported from Brazil by Taurus International.

Price: 40BP, 40 S&W, blued, 10+1 or 15+1 . . . . . **$452.00**
Price: 24/7-PRO Standard Series: 4" barrel; stainless, duotone or blued finish **$452.00**
Price: 24/7-PRO Compact Series; 3.2" barrel; stainless, titanium or blued finish **$467.00**
Price: 24/7-PRO Long Slide Series: 5.2" barrel; matte stainless, blued or stainless finish **$506.00**
Price: 24/7PLS, 5" barrel, chambered in 9mm Parabellum, 38 Super and 40 S&W **$506.00**

TAURUS 24/7 G2

Double/single action semiauto pistol chambered in 9mm Parabellum (15+1), .40 S&W (13+1), and .45 ACP (10+1). Features include blued or stainless finish; "Strike Two" capability; new trigger safety; low-profile adjustable rear sights for windage and elevation; ambidextrous magazine release; 4.2-inch barrel; Picatinny rail; polymer frame; polymer grip with metallic inserts and three interchangeable backstraps. Also offered in compact model with shorter grip frame and 3.5-inch barrel.

Price: **$523.00**

TAURUS MODEL 2045 LARGE FRAME PISTOL

Similar to Taurus Model 24/7 but chambered in 45 ACP only. Features include polymer frame, blued or matte stainless steel slide, 4.2" barrel, ambidextrous "memory pads" to promote safe finger position during loading, ambi three-position safety/decocker. Picatinny rail system, fixed sights. Overall length is 7.34". Weighs 31.5 oz.

Price: **$577.00**

TAURUS MODEL 58 PISTOL

Caliber: 380 ACP (19+1). **Barrel:** 3.25. **Weight:** 18.7 oz. **Length:** 6.125" overall. **Grips:** Polymer. **Sights:** Fixed. **Features:** SA/DA semi-auto. Scaled-down version of the full-size Model 92; steel slide, alloy frame, frame-mounted ambi safety, blued or stainless finish, and extended magazine.

Price: 58HCB **$602.00**
Price: 58HCSS **$617.00**

TAURUS MODEL 92 AUTO PISTOL

Caliber: 9mm Para., 10- or 17-shot mags. **Barrel:** 5". **Weight:** 34 oz. **Length:** 8.5" overall. **Grips:** Checkered rubber, rosewood, mother-of-pearl. **Sights:** Fixed notch rear. 3-dot sight system. Also offered with micrometer-click adjustable night sights. **Features:** Double action, ambidextrous 3-way hammer drop safety, allows cocked & locked carry. Blue, stainless steel, blue with gold highlights, stainless steel with gold highlights, forged aluminum frame, integral key-lock. .22 LR conversion kit available. Imported from Brazil by Taurus International.

Price: 92B **$542.00**
Price: 92SS **$559.00**

TAURUS MODEL 99 AUTO PISTOL

Similar to Model 92, fully adjustable rear sight.

Price: 99B $559.00

TAURUS MODEL 90-TWO SEMI-AUTO PISTOL

Similar to Model 92 but with one-piece wraparound grips, automatic disassembly latch, internal recoil buffer, addition slide serrations, picatinny rail with removable cover, 10- and 17-round magazine (9mm) or 10- and 12-round magazines (40 S&W). Overall length is 8.5". Weight is 32.5 oz.

Price: **$725.00**

TAURUS MODEL 100/101 AUTO PISTOL

Caliber: 40 S&W, 10- or 11-shot mags. **Barrel:** 5". **Weight:** 34 oz. **Length:** 8.5". **Grips:** Checkered rubber, rosewood, mother-of-pearl. **Sights:** 3-dot fixed or adjustable; night sights available. **Features:** Single/double action with three-position safety/decocker. Reintroduced in 2001. Imported by Taurus International.

Price: 100B **$542.00**

TAURUS MODEL 111 MILLENNIUM PRO AUTO PISTOL

Caliber: 9mm Para., 10- or 12-shot mags. **Barrel:** 3.25". **Weight:** 18.7 oz. **Length:** 6-1/8" overall. **Grips:** Checkered polymer. **Sights:** 3-dot fixed; night sights available. Low profile, 3-dot combat. **Features:** Double action only, polymer frame, matte stainless or blue steel slide, manual safety, integral key-lock. Deluxe models with wood grip inserts.

Price: 111BP, 111BP-12 . . . . . **$419.00**
Price: 111PTi titanium slide **$592.00**

TAURUS 132 MILLENNIUM PRO AUTO PISTOL

Caliber: 32 ACP, 10-shot mag. **Barrel:** 3.25". **Weight:** 18.7 oz. **Grips:** Polymer. **Sights:** 3-dot fixed; night sights available. **Features:** Double-action-only, polymer frame, matte stainless or blue steel slide, manual safety, integral key-lock action. Introduced 2001.

Price: 132BP **$419.00**

TAURUS 138 MILLENNIUM PRO SERIES

Caliber: 380 ACP, 10- or 12-shot mags. **Barrel:** 3.25". **Weight:** 18.7 oz. **Grips:** Polymer. **Sights:** Fixed 3-dot fixed. **Features:** Double-action-only, polymer frame, matte stainless or blue steel slide, manual safety, integral key-lock.

Price: 138BP **$419.00**

TAURUS 140 MILLENNIUM PRO AUTO PISTOL

Caliber: 40 S&W, 10-shot mag. **Barrel:** 3.25". **Weight:** 18.7 oz. **Grips:** Checkered polymer. **Sights:** 3-dot fixed; night sights available. **Features:** Double action only;

matte stainless or blue steel slide, black polymer frame, manual safety, integral key-lock action. From Taurus International.
Price: 140BP **$436.00**

TAURUS 145 MILLENNIUM PRO AUTO PISTOL
Caliber: 45 ACP, 10-shot mag. **Barrel:** 3.27". **Weight:** 23 oz. Stock: Checkered polymer. **Sights:** 3-dot fixed; night sights available. **Features:** Double-action only, matte stainless or blue steel slide, black polymer frame, manual safety, integral key-lock. Compact model is 6+1 with a 3.25" barrel, weighs 20.8 oz. From Taurus International.
Price: 145BP, blued **$436.00**
Price: 145SSP, stainless, ... **$453.00**

Taurus Model 609Ti-Pro
Similar to other Millennium Pro models but with titanium slide. Chambered in 9mm Parabellum. Weighs 19.7 oz. Overall length is 6.125". Features include 13+1 capacity, 3.25" barrel, checkered polymer grips, and Heinie Straight-8 sights.
Price: **$608.00**

TAURUS SLIM 700 SERIES
Compact double/single action semiauto pistol chambered in 9mm Parabellum (7+1), .40 S&W (6+1), and .380 ACP (7+1). Features include polymer frame; blue or stainless slide; single action/double action trigger pull; low-profile fixed sights. Weight 19 oz., length 6.24 inches, width less than an inch.
Price: . . . . **N/A**

TAURUS MODEL 709 G2 SLIM PISTOL
Caliber: 9mm., 9+1-shot magazine. **Barrel:** 3". **Weight:** 19 oz. **Length:** 6.24" overall. **Grips:** Black. **Sights:** Low profile. **Features:** The most heralded concealed carry semi-auto in company history is getting even better with the G2 Slim. Even under the lightest clothing the Slim design reveals nothing. Now with the best in features and performance from the elite G2 series. Also, with the G2 Slim, there are extra rounds with an extended magazine for added confidence.
Price: **$376.00**

TAURUS MODEL 738 TCP COMPACT PISTOL
Caliber: 380 ACP, 6+1 (standard magazine) or 8+1 (extended magazine). **Barrel:** 3.3". **Weight:** 9 oz. (titanium slide) to 10.2 oz. **Length:** 5.19". **Sights:** Low-profile fixed. **Features:** Lightweight DAO semi-auto with polymer frame; blued (738B), stainless (738SS) or titanium (738Ti) slide; concealed hammer; ambi safety; loaded chamber indicator.
Price: . . . . . **$623.00 to $686.00**

TAURUS SLIM 740 PISTOL
Caliber: .380 ACP and .40 cal., 6+1/8+1-shot magazines. **Barrel:** 4". **Weight:** 19 oz. **Length:** 6.24" overall. **Grips:** Polymer Grips. **Features:** Double action with stainless steel finish. Remarkably lean, lightweight design, but it still steps up with big firepower.
Price: **$483.00**

TAURUS 800 SERIES COMPACT
Compact double/single action semiauto pistol chambered in 9mm (12+1), .357 SIG (10+1) and .40 cal (10+1). Features include 3.5-inch barrel; external hammer; loaded chamber indicator; polymer frame; blued or stainless slide.
Price: . . . . **N/A**

TAURUS 809 COMPACT PISTOL
Caliber: 9mm, .357 SIG and .40 cal. 12+1 round capacity. **Barrel:** 3.5". **Grips:** Checkered Polymer. **Description:** Little brother of the 800 Series, these new pistols were born to perform. They give everything you could want in a 3.5" barrel semi-auto—the best in features, handling, speed and reliability.
Price: **$555.00**

THOMPSON CUSTOM 1911A1 AUTOMATIC PISTOL
Caliber: 45 ACP, 7-shot magazine. **Barrel:** 4.3". **Weight:** 34 oz. **Length:** 8" overall. **Grips:** Checkered laminate grips with a Thompson bullet logo inlay. **Sights:** Front and rear sights are black with serrations and are dovetailed into the slide. **Features:** Machined from 420 stainless steel, matte finish. Thompson bullet logo on slide. Flared ejection port, angled front and rear serrations on slide, 20-lpi checkered mainspring housing and frontstrap. Adjustable trigger, combat hammer, stainless steel full-length recoil guide rod, extended beavertail grip safety; extended magazine release; checkered slide-stop lever. Made in U.S.A. by Kahr Arms.
Price: 1911TC, 5", 39 oz., 8.5" overall, stainless frame **$813.00**

THOMPSON TA5 1927A-1 LIGHTWEIGHT DELUXE PISTOL
Caliber: 45 ACP, 50-round drum magazine. **Barrel:** 10.5" 1:16 right-hand twist. **Weight:** 94.5 oz. **Length:** 23.3" overall. **Grips:** Walnut, horizontal foregrip **Sights:** Blade front, open rear adjustable. **Features:** Based on Thompson machine gun design. Introduced 2008. Made in U.S.A. by Kahr Arms.
Price: TA5 (2008) **$1,237.00**

TURNBULL MFG. CO. 1911 CENTENIAL PISTOL
Features: Forged slide with appropriate shape and style. Proper size and shape of sights. Barrel of correct external contour. Safety lock is the thin style, with a knurled undercut thumb-piece. Short, wide spur hammer with standard checkering. Early style slide stop. Lanyard loop, punch and saw cut magazine, finished in two tone. Pistol is hand-polished in the same manner as an original early production vintage pistol. Period-correct Carbonia Charcoal Blueing on all parts. Stamped United States Property as original. Circled Turning Bull trademark on left of slide behind serrations. Early 1913 patent markings and Turnbull Mfg. Co. Bloomfield, NY slide address. Model(s) of 1911 U.S. Army, U.S. Navy and U.S. Marine Corps variations are all available. Inspector's marks are available from Doug Turnbull (TMC Owner, founder) and Keith VanOrman (TMC President).
Price: **$3895.00**

Prices given are believed to be accurate at time of publication however, many factors affect retail pricing so exact prices are not possible.

WALTHER PPS PISTOL

Caliber: 9mm Para., 40 S&W. 6-, 7-, 8-shot magazines for 9mm Para.; 5-, 6-, 7-shot magazines for 40 S&W. **Barrel:** 3.2". **Weight:** 19.4 oz. **Length:** 6.3" overall. Stocks: Stippled black polymer. **Sights:** Picatinny-style accessory rail, 3-dot low-profile contoured sight. **Features:** PPS-"Polizeipistole Schmal," or Police Pistol Slim. Measures 1.04 inches wide. Ships with 6- and 7-round magazines. Striker-fired action, flat slide stop lever, alternate backstrap sizes. QuickSafe feature decocks striker assembly when backstrap is removed. Loaded chamber indicator. First Edition model, limited to 1,000 units, has anthracite grey finish, aluminum gun case. Introduced 2008. Made in U.S.A. by Smith & Wesson.

Price: **$713.00**
Price: First Edition................................. **$665.00**

WALTHER PPK/S AMERICAN AUTO PISTOL

Caliber: 32 ACP, 380 ACP, 7-shot magazine. **Barrel:** 3.27". **Weight:** 23-1/2 oz. Length: 6.1" overall. Stocks: Checkered plastic. **Sights:** Fixed, white markings. **Features:** Double action; manual safety blocks firing pin and drops hammer; chamber loaded indicator on 32 and 380; extra finger rest magazine provided. Made in the United States. Introduced 1980. Made in U.S.A. by Smith & Wesson.

Price: **$605.00**

WALTHER MODEL PPK/S MACHINE ENGRAVED

Caliber: .380 ACP, 7 & 8-round capacity. **Barrel:** 3.3". **Weight:** 22.4 oz. **Length:** 6.1". **Grips:** Engraved wood. **Sights:** Fixed. **Features:** Traditional Double Action with Stainless frame, slide and barrel. Mahogany Presentation Case Included.

Price: $799.00

WALTHER P99 AUTO PISTOL

Caliber: 9mm Para., 9x21, 40 S&W, 10-shot magazine. **Barrel:** 4". **Weight:** 25 oz. Length: 7" overall. **Grips:** Textured polymer. **Sights:** Blade front (comes with three interchangeable blades for elevation adjustment), micrometer rear adjustable for windage. **Features:** Double-action mechanism with trigger safety, decock safety, internal striker safety; chamber loaded indicator; ambidextrous magazine release levers; polymer frame with interchangeable backstrap inserts. Comes with two magazines. Introduced 1997. Made in U.S.A. by Smith & Wesson.

Price: From . . . **$799.00**

WALTHER P99AS NIGHT SIGHT DEFENSE KIT

Striker-fired DAO semiauto pistol similar to Walther P99AS but with front and rear tritium sights. Chambered in .40 S&W (12 rounds) or 9mm Parabellum (15 rounds). Features include polymer frame and grip, decocker button, 4-inch (9mm) or 4.17-inch (.40) stainless steel barrel, integral weaver-style accessory rail, black Tenifer finish overall.

Price: .... **N/A**

WALTHER PK380

Caliber: .380 ACP (8-shot magazine). **Barrel:** 3.66". **Weight:** 19.4 oz. **Length:** 6.5". **Sights:** Three-dot system, drift adjustable rear. **Features:** Double action with external hammer, ambidextrous mag release and manual safety. Picatinny rail.

Price: **$389**

WALTHER PPQ

Caliber: 9mm, .40 S&W (12-shot magazine). **Barrel:** 4.2". **Weight:** 24.9 oz. **Length:** 7.2". **Sights:** Drift adjustable. **Features:** Quick Defense trigger, firing pin blck, ambidextrous slide lock and mag release, Picatinny rail. Comes with two extra magazines, two interchangeable frame backstraps and hard case.

Price: **$599**

WALTHER PPS NIGHT SIGHT DEFENSE KIT

Striker-fired compact DAO semiauto pistol similar to Walther PPS but with front and rear tritium sights. Chambered in .40 S&W (6 rounds) or 9mm Parabellum (7 rounds). Features include polymer frame and grip, decocker button, loaded chamber indicator, 3.2-inch stainless steel barrel, integral weaver-style accessory rail, black Tenifer finish overall.

Price: .... **N/A**

WALTHER P22 PISTOL

Caliber: 22 LR. **Barrel:** 3.4", 5". **Weight:** 19.6 oz. (3.4"), 20.3 oz. (5"). **Length:** 6.26", 7.83". **Grips:** NA. **Sights:** Interchangeable white dot, front, 2-dot adjustable, rear. **Features:** A rimfire version of the Walther P99 pistol, available in nickel slide with black frame, or green frame with black slide versions. Made in U.S.A. by Smith & Wesson.

Price: From **$362.00**

WILSON COMBAT ELITE PROFESSIONAL

Caliber: 9mm Para., 38 Super, 40 S&W; 45 ACP, 8-shot magazine. **Barrel:** Compensated 4.1" hand-fit, heavy flanged cone match grade. **Weight:** 36.2 oz. Length: 7.7" overall. **Grips:** Cocobolo. **Sights:** Combat Tactical yellow rear tritium inserts, brighter green tritium front insert. **Features:** High-cut front strap, 30-lpi checkering on front strap and flat mainspring housing, High-Ride Beavertail grip safety. Dehorned, ambidextrous thumb safety, extended ejector, skeletonized ultralight hammer, ultralight trigger, Armor-Tuff finish on frame and slide. Introduced 1997. Made in U.S.A. by Wilson Combat. This manufacturer offers more than 100 different 1911 models ranging in price from about $2800 to $5000.

Price: From **$3,650.00**

Prices given are believed to be accurate at time of publication however, many factors affect retail pricing so exact prices are not possible.

BAER 1911 ULTIMATE MASTER COMBAT PISTOL

Caliber: 38 Super, 400 Cor-Bon 45 ACP (others available), 10-shot magazine. **Barrel:** 5", 6"; Baer NM. **Weight:** 37 oz. **Length:** 8.5" overall. **Grips:** Checkered cocobolo. **Sights:** Baer dovetail front, low-mount Bo-Mar rear with hidden leaf. **Features:** Full-house competition gun. Baer forged NM blued steel frame and double serrated slide; Baer triple port, tapered cone compensator; fitted slide to frame; lowered, flared ejection port; Baer reverse recoil plug; full-length guide rod; recoil buff; beveled magazine well; Baer Commander hammer, sear; Baer extended ambidextrous safety, extended ejector, checkered slide stop, beavertail grip safety with pad, extended magazine release button; Baer speed trigger. Made in U.S.A. by Les Baer Custom, Inc.

Price: 45 ACP Compensated **$2,880.00**
Price: 38 Super Compensated **$3,140.00**

BAER 1911 NATIONAL MATCH HARDBALL PISTOL

Caliber: 45 ACP, 7-shot magazine. **Barrel:** 5". **Weight:** 37 oz. Length: 8.5" overall. **Grips:** Checkered walnut. **Sights:** Baer dovetail front with under-cut post, low-mount Bo-Mar rear with hidden leaf. **Features:** Baer NM forged steel frame, double serrated slide and barrel with stainless bushing; slide fitted to frame; Baer match trigger with 4-lb. pull; polished feed ramp, throated barrel; checkered front strap, arched mainspring housing; Baer beveled magazine well; lowered, flared ejection port; tuned extractor; Baer extended ejector, checkered slide stop; recoil buff. Made in U.S.A. by Les Baer Custom, Inc.

Price: **$1,960.00**

BAER 1911 BULLSEYE WADCUTTER PISTOL

Similar to National Match Hardball except designed for wadcutter loads only. Polished feed ramp and barrel throat; Bo-Mar rib on slide; full length recoil rod; Baer speed trigger with 3-1/2-lb. pull; Baer deluxe hammer and sear; Baer beavertail grip safety with pad; flat mainspring housing checkered 20 lpi. Blue finish; checkered walnut grips. Made in U.S.A. by Les Baer Custom, Inc.

Price: From **$2,140.00**

COLT GOLD CUP TROPHY PISTOL

Caliber: 45 ACP, 8-shot + 1 magazine. **Barrel:** 5". **Weight:** NA. **Length:** 8.5". **Grips:** Checkered rubber composite with silver-plated medallion. **Sights:** (O5070X) Dovetail front, Champion rear; (O5870CS) Patridge Target Style front, Champion rear. **Features:** Adjustable aluminum trigger, Beavertail grip safety, full length recoil spring and target recoil spring, available in blued finish and stainless steel.

Price: O5070X **$1,125.00**
Price: O5870CS **$1,175.00**

COLT SPECIAL COMBAT GOVERNMENT

Caliber: 45 ACP, 38 Super. **Barrel:** 5". **Weight:** 39 oz. Length: 8.5". **Grips:** Rosewood w/double diamond checkering pattern. **Sights:** Clark dovetail, front; Bo-Mar adjustable, rear. **Features:** A competition-ready pistol with enhancements such as skeletonized trigger, upswept grip safety, custom tuned action, polished feed ramp. Blue or satin nickel finish. Introduced 2003. Made in U.S.A. by Colt's Mfg. Co.

Price: **$1,995.00**

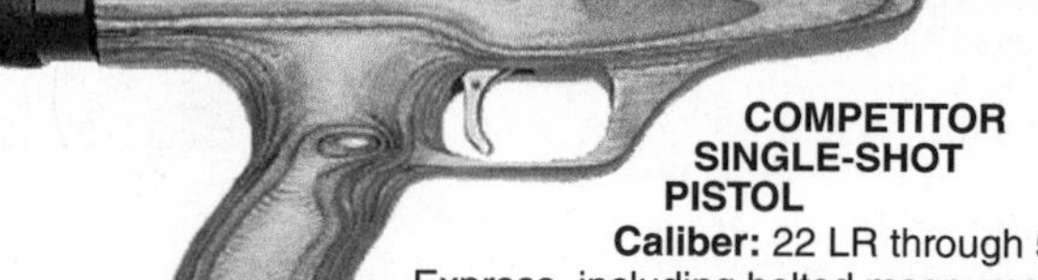

COMPETITOR SINGLE-SHOT PISTOL

Caliber: 22 LR through 50 Action Express, including belted magnums. **Barrel:** 14" standard; 10.5" silhouette; 16" optional. **Weight:** About 59 oz. (14" bbl.). **Length:** 15.12" overall. **Grips:** Ambidextrous; synthetic (standard) or laminated or natural wood. **Sights:** Ramp front, adjustable rear. **Features:** Rotary cannon-type action cocks on opening; cammed ejector; interchangeable barrels, ejectors. Adjustable single stage trigger, sliding thumb safety and trigger safety. Matte blue finish. Introduced 1988. From Competitor Corp., Inc.

Price: 14", standard calibers, synthetic grip **$660.00**

CZ 75 TS CZECHMATE

Caliber: 9mm Luger, 20-shot magazine. Barrel: 130mm. Weight: 1360 g Length: 266 mm overall. Features: The handgun is custom-built, therefore the quality of workmanship is fully comparable with race pistols built directly to IPSC shooters wishes. Individual parts and components are excellently match fitted, broke-in and tested. Every handgun is outfitted with a four-port compensator, nut for shooting without a compensator, the slide stop with an extended finger piece, the slide stop without a finger piece, ergonomic grip panels from aluminium with a new type pitting and side mounting provision with the C-More red dot sight. For the shooting without a red dot sight there is included a standard target rear sight of Tactical Sports type, package contains also the front sight.

Price: **$3,220.00**

CZ 75 TACTICAL SPORTS

Caliber: 9mm Luger and .40 S&W, 17-20-shot magazine capacity. **Barrel:** 114mm. **Weight:** 1270 g **Length:** 225 mm overall. **Features:** semi-automatic handgun with a locked breech. This pistol model is designed for competition shooting in accordance with world IPSC (International Practical Shooting Confederation) rules and regulations. The pistol allow rapid and accurate shooting within a very short time frame.The CZ 75 TS pistol model design stems from the standard CZ 75 model. However, this model feature number of special modifications, which are usually required for competitive handguns: - single-action trigger mechanism (SA) - match trigger made of plastic featuring option for trigger travel adjustments before discharge (using upper screw), and for overtravel (using bottom screw). The adjusting screws are set by the manufacturer - sporting hammer specially adapted for a reduced trigger pull weight - an extended magazine catch - grip panels made of walnut wood - guiding funnel made of plastic for quick inserting of the magazine into pistol's frame. Glossy blue slide, silver polycoat frame. Packaging includes 3 pcs of magazines.

Price: **$1,272.00**

CZ 85 COMBAT

Caliber: 9mm Luger, 16-shot magazine. **Barrel:** 114mm. **Weight:** 1000 g **Length:** 206 mm overall. **Features:** The CZ 85 Combat modification was created as an extension to the CZ 85 model in its standard configuration with some additional special elements. The rear sight is adjustable for elevation and windage, and the trigger for overtravel regulation. An extended magazine catch, elimination of the magazine brake and ambidextrous controlling elements directly predispose this model for sport shooting competitions. Characteristic features of all versions A universal handgun for both left-handers and right-handers,. The selective SA/DA firing mechanism, a large

capacity double-column magazine, a comfortable grip and balance in either hand lead to good results at instinctive shooting (without aiming). Low trigger pull weight and high accuracy of fire. A long service life and outstanding reliability - even when using various types of cartridges. The slide stays open after the last cartridge has been fired, suitable for COMBAT shooting. The sights are fitted with a three-dot illuminating system for better aiming in poor visibility conditions. The COMBAT version features an adjustable rear sight by means of micrometer screws.
Price: **$615.00**

DAN WESSON HAVOC

Caliber: 9mm Luger & .38 Super, 21-shot magazine capacity. **Barrel:** 4.25". **Weight:** 2.20 lbs. **Length:** 8" overall. **Features:** The HAVOC is based on an "All Steel" Hi-capacity version of the 1911 frame. It comes ready to dominate Open IPSC/USPSA division. The C-more mounting system offers the lowest possible mounting configuration possible, enabling extremely fast target acquisition. The barrel and compensator arrangement pairs the highest level of accuracy with the most effective compensator available. The combination of the all steel frame with industry leading parts delivers the most well balanced, softest shooting Open gun on the market.
Price: **$4,299.00**

DAN WESSON MAYHEM

Caliber: .40 S&W, 18-shot magazine capacity. **Barrel:** 6". **Weight:** 2.42 lbs. **Length:** 8.75" overall. **Features:** The MAYHEM is based on an "All Steel" Hi-capacity version of the 1911 frame. It comes ready to dominate Limited IPSC/USPSA division or fulfill the needs of anyone looking for a superbly accurate target grade 1911. Taking weight away from where you don't want it and adding it to where you do want it was the first priority in designing this handgun. The 6" bull barrel and the tactical rail add to the static weight "good weight". We wanted a 6" long slide for the added sight radius and the enhanced pointability, but that would add to the "bad weight" so the 6" slide has been lightened to equal the weight of a 5". The result is a 6" long slide that balances and feels like a 5" but shoots like a 6". The combination of the all steel frame with industry leading parts delivers the most well balanced, softest shooting 6" limited gun on the market.
Price: **$3,899.00**

DAN WESSON TITAN

Caliber: 10mm, 21-shot magazine capacity. **Barrel:** 4.25". **Weight:** 1.62 lbs. **Length:** 8" overall. **Features:** The TITAN is based on an "All Steel" Hi-capacity version of the 1911 frame. Turning the most well known defensive pistol "1911" into a true combat handgun was no easy task. The rugged HD night sights are moved forward and recessed deep in the slide yielding target accuracy and extreme durability. The Snake Scale serrations' aggressive 25 lpi checkering, and the custom competition G-10 grips ensure controllability even in the harshest of conditions. The combination of the all steel frame, bull barrel, and tactical rail enhance the balance and durability of the most formidable target grade Combat handgun on the market.
Price: **$3,829.00**

EAA WITNESS ELITE GOLD TEAM AUTO

Caliber: 9mm Para., 9x21, 38 Super, 40 S&W, 45 ACP. **Barrel:** 5.1". **Weight:** 44 oz. **Length:** 10.5" overall. **Grips:** Checkered walnut, competition-style. **Sights:** Square post front, fully adjustable rear. **Features:** Triple-chamber cone compensator; competition SA trigger; extended safety and magazine release; competition hammer; beveled magazine well; beavertail grip. Hand-fitted major components. Hard chrome finish. Match-grade barrel. From E.A.A. Custom Shop. Introduced 1992. Limited designed for IPSC Limited Class competition. Features include full-length dust-cover frame, funneled magazine well, interchangeable front sights. Stock (2005)

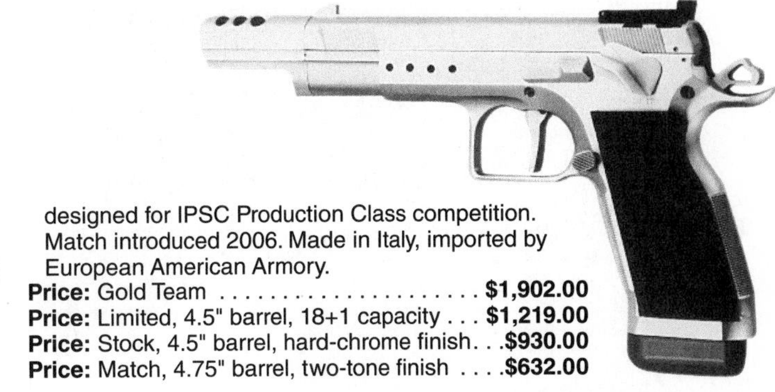

designed for IPSC Production Class competition. Match introduced 2006. Made in Italy, imported by European American Armory.
Price: Gold Team **$1,902.00**
Price: Limited, 4.5" barrel, 18+1 capacity . . . **$1,219.00**
Price: Stock, 4.5" barrel, hard-chrome finish. . .**$930.00**
Price: Match, 4.75" barrel, two-tone finish **$632.00**

FREEDOM ARMS MODEL 83 22 FIELD GRADE SILHOUETTE CLASS

Caliber: 22 LR, 5-shot cylinder. **Barrel:** 10". **Weight:** 63 oz. **Length:** 15.5" overall. **Grips:** Black micarta. **Sights:** Removable Patridge front blade; Iron Sight Gun Works silhouette rear, click adjustable for windage and elevation (optional adj. front sight and hood). **Features:** Stainless steel, matte finish, manual sliding-bar safety system; dual firing pins, lightened hammer for fast lock time, pre-set trigger stop. Introduced 1991. Made in U.S.A. by Freedom Arms.
Price: Silhouette Class **$2,237.00**

FREEDOM ARMS MODEL 83 CENTERFIRE SILHOUETTE MODELS

Caliber: 357 Mag., 41 Mag., 44 Mag.; 5-shot cylinder. **Barrel:** 10", 9" (357 Mag. only). **Weight:** 63 oz. (41 Mag.). **Length:** 15.5", 14.5" (357 only). **Grips:** Pachmayr Presentation. **Sights:** Iron Sight Gun Works silhouette rear sight, replaceable adjustable front sight blade with hood. **Features:** Stainless steel, matte finish, manual sliding-bar safety system. Made in U.S.A. by Freedom Arms.
Price: Silhouette Models, from **$1,970.00**

HIGH STANDARD SUPERMATIC TROPHY TARGET PISTOL

Caliber: 22 LR, 9-shot mag. **Barrel:** 5.5" bull or 7.25" fluted. **Weight:** 44-46 oz. **Length:** 9.5-11.25" overall. **Stock:** Checkered hardwood with thumbrest. **Sights:** Undercut ramp front, frame-mounted micro-click rear adjustable for windage and elevation; drilled and tapped for scope mounting. **Features:** Gold-plated trigger, slide lock, safety-lever and magazine release; stippled front grip and backstrap; adjustable trigger and sear. Barrel weights optional. From High Standard Manufacturing Co., Inc.
Price: 5.5" barrel, adjustable sights **$935.00**
Price: 7.25", adjustable sights **$985.00**

HIGH STANDARD VICTOR TARGET PISTOL

Caliber: 22 LR, 10-shot magazine. **Barrel:** 4.5" or 5.5" polished blue; push-button takedown. **Weight:** 46 oz. **Length:** 9.5" overall. **Stock:** Checkered walnut with thumbrest. **Sights:** Undercut ramp front, micro-click rear adjustable for windage and elevation. Also available with scope mount, rings, no sights. **Features:** Stainless steel frame. Full-length vent rib. Gold-plated trigger, slide lock, safety-lever and magazine release; stippled front grip and backstrap; polished blue slide; adjustable trigger and sear. Comes with barrel weight. From High Standard Manufacturing Co., Inc.

Price: 4.5" or 5.5" barrel, vented sight rib, universal scope base **$935.00**

KIMBER SUPER MATCH II

Caliber: 45 ACP, 8-shot magazine. **Barrel:** 5". **Weight:** 38 oz. **Length:** 8.7" overall. **Grips:** Rosewood double diamond. **Sights:** Blade front, Kimber fully adjustable rear. **Features:** Guaranteed shoot 1" group at 25 yards. Stainless steel frame, black KimPro slide; two-piece magazine well; premium aluminum match-grade trigger; 30 lpi front strap checkering; stainless match-grade barrel; ambidextrous safety; special Custom Shop markings. Introduced 1999. Made in U.S.A. by Kimber Mfg., Inc.

Price: **$2,225.00**

KIMBER RIMFIRE TARGET

Caliber: 22 LR, 10-shot magazine. **Barrel:** 5". **Weight:** 23 oz. **Length:** 8.7" overall. **Grips:** Rosewood, Kimber logo, double diamond checkering, or black synthetic double diamond. **Sights:** Blade front, Kimber fully adjustable rear. **Features:** Bumped beavertail grip safety, extended thumb safety, extended magazine release button. Serrated flat top slide with flutes, machined aluminum slide and frame, matte black or satin silver finishes, 30 lines-per-inch checkering on frontstrap and under trigger guard; aluminum trigger, test target, accuracy guarantee. No slide lock-open after firing the last round in the magazine. Introduced 1999. Made in U.S.A. by Kimber Mfg., Inc.

Price: **$833.00**

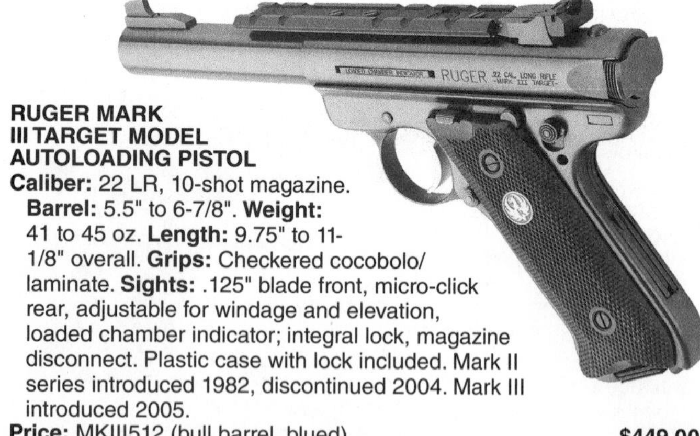

RUGER MARK III TARGET MODEL AUTOLOADING PISTOL

Caliber: 22 LR, 10-shot magazine. **Barrel:** 5.5" to 6-7/8". **Weight:** 41 to 45 oz. **Length:** 9.75" to 11-1/8" overall. **Grips:** Checkered cocobolo/laminate. **Sights:** .125" blade front, micro-click rear, adjustable for windage and elevation, loaded chamber indicator; integral lock, magazine disconnect. Plastic case with lock included. Mark II series introduced 1982, discontinued 2004. Mark III introduced 2005.

Price: MKIII512 (bull barrel, blued) **$449.00**
Price: KMKIII512 (bull barrel, stainless) **$559.00**
Price: MKIII678 (blued Target barrel, 6-7/8") **$449.00**
Price: KMKIII678GC (stainless slabside barrel) **$639.00**
Price: KMKIII678H (stainless fluted barrel) **$659.00**

SMITH & WESSON MODEL 41 TARGET

Caliber: 22 LR, 10-shot clip. **Barrel:** 5.5", 7". **Weight:** 41 oz. (5.5" barrel). **Length:** 10.5" overall (5.5" barrel). **Grips:** Checkered walnut with modified thumbrest, usable with either hand. **Sights:** 1/8" Patridge on ramp base; micro-click rear adjustable for windage and elevation. **Features:** 3/8" wide, grooved trigger; adjustable trigger stop drilled and tapped.

Price: S&W Bright Blue, either barrel **$1,288.00**

SMITH & WESSON MODEL 22A PISTOLS

Caliber: 22 LR, 10-shot magazine. **Barrel:** 4", 5.5" bull. **Weight:** 28-39

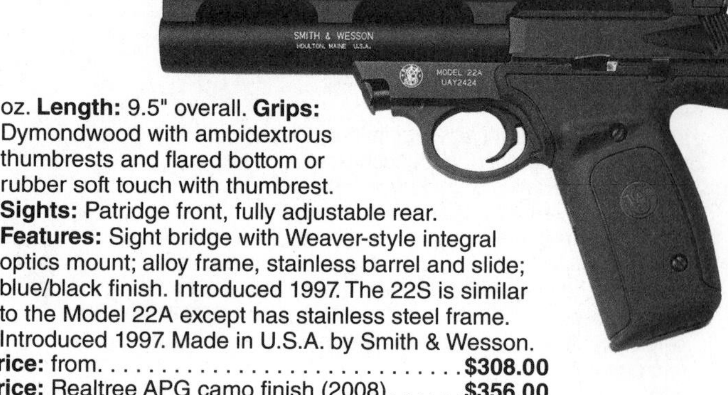

oz. **Length:** 9.5" overall. **Grips:** Dymondwood with ambidextrous thumbrests and flared bottom or rubber soft touch with thumbrest. **Sights:** Patridge front, fully adjustable rear. **Features:** Sight bridge with Weaver-style integral optics mount; alloy frame, stainless barrel and slide; blue/black finish. Introduced 1997. The 22S is similar to the Model 22A except has stainless steel frame. Introduced 1997. Made in U.S.A. by Smith & Wesson.

Price: from. **$308.00**
Price: Realtree APG camo finish (2008) **$356.00**

SPRINGFIELD ARMORY LEATHAM LEGEND TGO SERIES PISTOLS

Three models of 5" barrel, 45 ACP 1911 pistols built for serious competition. TGO 1 has deluxe low mount Bo-Mar rear sight, Dawson fiber optics front sight, 3.5 lb. trigger pull.

Price: TGO 1 . . . . **$3,095.00**

SPRINGFIELD ARMORY TROPHY MATCH PISTOL

Similar to Springfield Armory's Full Size model, but designed for bullseye and action shooting competition. Available with a Service Model 5" frame with matching slide and barrel in 5" and 6" lengths. Fully adjustable sights, checkered frame front strap, match barrel and bushing. In 45 ACP only. From Springfield Inc.

Price: **$1,573.00**

STI EAGLE 5.0, 6.0 PISTOL

Caliber: 9mm Para., 9x21, 38 & 40 Super, 40 S&W, 10mm, 45 ACP, 10-shot magazine. **Barrel:** 5", 6" bull. **Weight:** 34.5 oz. **Length:** 8.62" overall. **Grips:** Checkered polymer. **Sights:** STI front, Novak or Heinie rear. **Features:** Standard frames plus 7 others; adjustable match trigger; skeletonized hammer; extended grip safety with locator pad. Introduced 1994. Made in U.S.A. by STI International.

Price: (5.0 Eagle) **$1,940.12**
Price: (6.0 Eagle) **$1,049.98**

STI EXECUTIVE PISTOL

Caliber: 40 S&W. **Barrel:** 5" bull. **Weight:** 39 oz. **Length:** 8-5/8". **Grips:** Gray polymer. **Sights:** Dawson fiber optic, front; STI adjustable rear. **Features:** Stainless mag. well, front and rear serrations on slide. Made in U.S.A. by STI.

Price: **$2,464.00**

STI STEELMASTER

Caliber: 9mm minor, comes with one 126mm magazine. **Barrel:** 4.15". **Weight:** 38.9 oz. **Length:** 9.5" overall. **Features:** Based on the renowned STI race pistol design, the SteelMaster is a shorter and lighter pistol that allows for faster target acquisition with reduced muzzle flip and dip. Designed to shoot factory 9mm (minor) ammo, this gun delivers all the advantages of a full size race pistol in a smaller, lighter, faster reacting, and less violent package. The Steelmaster is built on the patented modular steel frame with polymer grip. It has a 4.15" classic slide which has been flat topped. Slide lightening cuts on the front and rear further reduce weight while "Sabertooth" serrations further enhance the aesthtics of this superior pistol. It also uses the innovative Trubor compensated barrel which has been designed

Prices given are believed to be accurate at time of publication however, many factors affect retail pricing so exact prices are not possible.

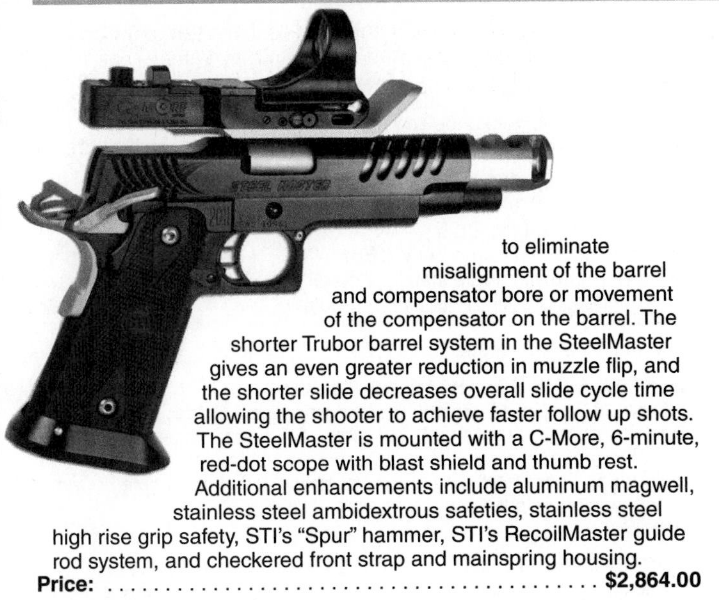

to eliminate misalignment of the barrel and compensator bore or movement of the compensator on the barrel. The shorter Trubor barrel system in the SteelMaster gives an even greater reduction in muzzle flip, and the shorter slide decreases overall slide cycle time allowing the shooter to achieve faster follow up shots. The SteelMaster is mounted with a C-More, 6-minute, red-dot scope with blast shield and thumb rest. Additional enhancements include aluminum magwell, stainless steel ambidextrous safeties, stainless steel high rise grip safety, STI's "Spur" hammer, STI's RecoilMaster guide rod system, and checkered front strap and mainspring housing.

Price: **$2,864.00**

STI TROJAN

Caliber: 9mm Para., 38 Super, 40 S&W, 45 ACP. **Barrel:** 5", 6". **Weight:** 36 oz. **Length:** 8.5". **Grips:** Rosewood. **Sights:** STI front with STI adjustable rear. **Features:** Stippled front strap, flat top slide, one-piece steel guide rod.

Price: (Trojan 5") **$1,110.00**

Price: (Trojan 6", not available in 38 Super) **$1,419.60**

STI TRUBOR

Caliber: 9mm 'Major', 9x23, .38 Super - USPSA, IPSC. **Barrel:** 5" with integrated compensator. **Weight:** 41.3 oz. (including scope and mount) **Length:** 10.5" overall. **Features:** Built on the patented modular steel frame with polymer grip, the STI Trubor utilizes the Trubor compensated barrel which is machined from ONE PIECE of 416, Rifle Grade, Stainless Steel. The Trubor is designed to eliminate misalignment of the barrel and compensator bore or movement of the compensator along the barrel threads, giving the shooter a more consistent performance and reduced muzzle flip. True to 1911 tradition, the Trubor has a classic scalloped slide with front and rear cocking serrations on a forged steel slide (blued) with polished sides, aluminum magwell, stainless steel ambidextrous safeties, stainless steel high rise grip safety, full length guide rod, checkered front strap, and checkered mainspring housing. With mountedC-More Railway sight included with the pistol.

Price: **$2,864.00**

CHARTER ARMS BULLDOG REVOLVER

Caliber: 44 Special. **Barrel:** 2.5". **Weight:** NA. **Sights:** Blade front, notch rear. **Features:** 6-round cylinder, soft-rubber pancake-style grips, shrouded ejector rod, wide trigger and hammer spur. American made by Charter Arms.

Price: Blued $414.00
Price: Stainless $426.00
Price: Target Bulldog, 4" barrel, 23 oz. $479.00
Price: Heller Commemortaive stainless 2.5" $1595.00

CHARTER ARMS CHIC LADY & CHIC LADY DAO REVOLVERS

Caliber: .38 special - 5-round cylinder. **Barrel:** 2". **Weight:** 12 oz. **Grip:** Combat. **Sights:** Fixed. **Features:** 2-tone pink & stainless with aluminum frame. American made by Charter Arms.

Price: Chic Lady $481.00
Price: Chic Lady DAO $492.00

CHARTER COUGAR UNDERCOVER LITE REVOLVER

Caliber: .38 special +P - 5-round cylinder. **Barrel:** 2". **Weight:** 12 oz. **Grip:** Full. **Sights:** Fixed. **Features:** 2-tone pink & stainless with aluminum frame. Constructed of tough aircraft-grade aluminum and steel, the Undercover Lite offers rugged reliability and comfort. This ultra-lightweight 5-shot .38 Special features a 2" barrel, fixed sights and traditional spurred hammer. American made by Charter Arms.

Price: $443.00

CHARTER ARMS CRIMSON UNDERCOVER REVOLVER

Caliber: .38 special +P - 5-round cylinder. **Barrel:** 2". **Weight:** 16 oz. **Grip:** Crimson Trace™. **Sights:** Fixed. **Features:** Stainless finish & frame. American made by Charter Arms.

Price: $525.00

CHARTER ARMS OFF DUTY REVOLVER

Caliber: 38 Spec. **Barrel:** 2". **Weight:** 12.5 oz. **Sights:** Blade front, notch rear. **Features:** 5-round cylinder, aluminum casting, DAO. American made by Charter Arms.

Price: Aluminum $410.00

CHARTER ARMS MAG PUG REVOLVER

Caliber: 357 Mag. **Barrel:** 2.2". **Weight:** 23 oz. **Sights:** Blade front, notch rear. **Features:** Five-round cylinder. American made by Charter Arms.

Price: Blued or stainless $400.00

CHARTER PANTHER BRONZE & BLACK CAMO STANDARD REVOLVER

Caliber: .22 Mag.- 5-round cylinder. **Barrel:** 1-1/8". **Weight:** 6 oz. **Grip:** Compact. **Sights:** Fixed. **Features:** 2-tone bronze & black with aluminum frame. Constructed of tough aircraft-grade aluminum and steel, the Undercover Lite offers rugged reliability and comfort. This ultra-lightweight 5-shot .38 Special features a 2" barrel, fixed sights and traditional spurred hammer. American made by Charter Arms.

Price: $443.00

CHARTER ARMS PINK LADY REVOLVER

Caliber: 32 H&R Magnum, 38 Special +P. **Barrel:** 2". **Weight:** 12 oz. **Grips:** Rubber Pachmayr-style. **Sights:** Fixed. **Features:** Snubnose, five-round cylinder. Pink anodized aluminum alloy frame.

Price: $422.00
Price: Lavender Lady, lavender frame $422.00
Price: Goldfinger, gold anodized frame, matte black barrel and cylinder assembly $422.00

CHARTER ARMS PIT BULL

Caliber: .40 S&W, 5-round cylinder. **Barrel:** 21.3". **Weight:** 20 oz. **Sights:** Fixed rear, ramp front. **Grips:** Rubber. **Features:** Matte stainless steel frame. Five-shot cylinder does not require moon clips.

Price: $465

CHARTER ARMS SOUTHPAW REVOLVER

Caliber: 38 Special +P. **Barrel:** 2". **Weight:** 12 oz. **Grips:** Rubber Pachmayr-style. **Sights:** NA. **Features:** Snubnose, five-round cylinder, matte black aluminum alloy frame with stainless steel cylinder. Cylinder latch and crane assembly are on right side of frame for convenience to left-hand shooters.

Price: $427.00

CHARTER ARMS TARGET PATHFINDER COMBO REVOLVER

Caliber: .22 LR / .22 Mag. - 6-round cylinder. **Barrel:** 4". **Weight:** 20 oz. **Grip:** Full. **Sights:** Fixed. **Features:** Stainless finish & frame. Charter's Target Pathfinder is a great introductory revolver for the novice shooter. It has the look, feel and weight of a higher-caliber revolver, allowing you to gain proficiency while using relatively inexpensive .22 ammo. Part of the fun of shooting is doing it well, and proficiency requires practice. That's why Charter makes target configurations, with 4" barrels and precision sights. American made by Charter Arms.

Price: $548.00

CHARTER ARMS UNDERCOVER REVOLVER

Caliber: Barrel: 2". **Weight:** 12 oz. **Sights:** Blade front, notch rear. **Features:** 6-round cylinder. American made by Charter Arms.

Price: Blued $352.00

CHARTER ARMS UNDERCOVER SOUTHPAW REVOLVER

Caliber: 38 Spec. +P. **Barrel:** 2". **Weight:** 12 oz. **Sights:** NA. **Features:** Cylinder release is on the right side and the cylinder opens to the right side. Exposed hammer for both single and double-action firing. 5-round cylinder. American made by Charter Arms.

Price: $428.00

CHARTER ARMS UNDERCOVER LITE, RED & BLACK STANDARD REVOLVER

Caliber: .38 special +P - 5-round cylinder. **Barrel:** 2". **Weight:** 12 oz. **Grip:** Standard. **Sights:** Fixed. **Features:** 2-tone red & black with aluminum frame. American made by Charter Arms.

Price: $422.00

CHIAPPA RHINO

Chambered in .357 Magnum. Features include 2-, 4-, 5- or 6-inch barrel; fixed or adjustable sights; visible hammer or hammerless design. Weight 24 to 33 oz. Walnut or synthetic grips with black frame; hexagonal-shaped cylinder. Unique design fires from bottom chamber of cylinder.

Price: $749.00

COMANCHE I, II, III DA REVOLVERS

Caliber: 22 LR, 9 shot. 38 Spec., 6 shot. 357 Mag, 6 shot. **Barrel:** 6", 22 LR; 2" and 4", 38 Spec.; 2" and 3", 357 Mag. **Weight:** 39 oz. **Length:** 10.8" overall. **Grips:** Rubber. **Sights:** Adjustable rear. **Features:** Blued or stainless. Distributed by SGS Importers.

Price: I Blue $236.95
Price: I Alloy $258.95
Price: II 38 Spec., 3" bbl., 6-shot, stainless, intr. 2006 . . . .$236.95

Price: II 38 Spec., 4" bbl., 6-shot, stainless **$219.95**
Price: III 357 Mag, 3" bbl., 6-shot, blue **$253.95**
Price: III 357 Mag. 4" bbl., 6-shot, blue **$274.95**

EAA WINDICATOR REVOLVERS
Caliber: 38 Spec., 6-shot; 357 Mag., 6-shot. **Barrel:** 2", 4". **Weight:** 30 oz. (4"). **Length:** 8.5" overall (4" bbl.). **Grips:** Rubber with finger grooves. **Sights:** Blade front, fixed or adjustable on rimfires; fixed only on 32, 38. **Features:** Swing-out cylinder; hammer block safety; blue finish. Introduced 1991. Imported from Germany by European American Armory.
Price: 38 Spec. 2" barrel, alloy frame **$308.00**
Price: 38 Spec. 4" barrel, alloy frame **$323.00**
Price: 357 Mag, 2" barrel, steel frame **$324.00**
Price: 357 Mag, 4" barrel, steel frame **$343.00**

KORTH USA REVOLVERS
Caliber: 22 LR, 22 WMR, 32 S&W Long, 38 Spec., 357 Mag., 9mm Para. **Barrel:** 3", 4", 5.25", 6". **Weight:** 36-52 oz. Grips, Combat, Sport: Walnut, Palisander, Amboinia, Ivory. Grips, Target: German Walnut, matte with oil finish, adjustable ergonomic competition style. **Sights:** Adjustable Patridge (Sport) or Baughman (Combat), interchangeable and adjustable rear w/Patridge front (Target) in blue and matte. **Features:** DA/SA, 3 models, over 50 configurations, externally adjustable trigger stop and weight, interchangeable cylinder, removable wide-milled trigger shoe on Target model. Deluxe models are highly engraved editions. Available finishes include high polish blue finish, plasma coated in high polish or matted silver, gold, blue, or charcoal. Many deluxe options available. 6-shot. From Korth USA.
Price: From **$8,000.00**
Price: Deluxe Editions, from **$12,000.00**

ROSSI R461/R462
Caliber: .357 Mag. **Barrel:** 2". **Weight:** 26-35 oz. **Grips:** Rubber. **Sights:** Fixed. **Features:** DA/SA, +P rated frame, blue carbon or high polish stainless steel, patented Taurus Security System, 6-shot.
Price: From **$389.00**

ROSSI MODEL R971/ R972 REVOLVERS
Caliber: 357 Mag. +P, 6-shot. **Barrel:** 4", 6". **Weight:** 32 oz. **Length:** 8.5" or 10.5" overall. **Grips:** Rubber. **Sights:** Blade front, adjustable rear. **Features:** Single/double action. Patented key-lock Taurus Security System; forged steel frame. Introduced 2001. Made in Brazil by Amadeo Rossi. Imported by BrazTech/Taurus.
Price: Model R971 (blued finish, 4" bbl.) **$452.00**
Price: Model R972 (stainless steel finish, 6" bbl.) **$508.00**

ROSSI MODEL 851
Similar to Model R971/R972, chambered for 38 Spec. +P. Blued finish, 4" barrel. Introduced 2001. Made in Brazil by Amadeo Rossi. From BrazTech/Taurus.
Price: **$389.00**

RUGER GP-100 REVOLVERS
Caliber: 327 Federal, 38 Spec. +P, 357 Mag., 6-shot, 327 Federal (7-shot cylinder). **Barrel:** 3" full shroud, 4" full shroud, 6" full shroud. **Weight:** 3" full shroud-36 oz., 4" full shroud-38 oz. **Sights:** Fixed; adjustable on 4" full shroud, all 6" barrels. **Grips:** Ruger Santoprene Cushioned Grip with Goncalo Alves inserts. **Features:** Uses action, frame features of both the Security-Six and Redhawk revolvers. Full length, short ejector shroud. Satin blue and stainless steel.

Price: .357 Mag., blued **$699.00**
Price: .357, satin stainless **$759.00**
Price: .357, Federal, stainless **$759.00**

RUGER LCR REVOLVER
Caliber: .22 LR (8-shot cylinder), .38 Special and .357 Mag., 5-shot cylinder. **Barrel:** 1-7/8". **Weight:** 13.5 oz.–17.10 oz. **Length:** 6-1/2" overall. **Grips:** Hogue® Tamer™ or Crimson Trace® Lasergrips® . **Sights:** Pinned ramp front, U-notch integral rear. **Features:** The Ruger Lightweight Compact Revolver (LCR), a 13.5 ounce, small frame revolver with a smooth, easy-to-control trigger and highly manageable recoil. Packed with the latest technological advances and features required by today's most demanding shooters.
Price: .22 LR, iron sights **$525.00**
Price: .38/.357, iron sights **$599.00**
Price: .22 LR, Crimson Trace Laser grip **$792.00**
Price: .38/.357, Crimson Trace Laser grip **$869.00**

RUGER SP-101 REVOLVERS
Caliber: 327 Federal, 6-shot; 38 Spec. +P, 357 Mag., 5-shot. **Barrel:** 2.25", 3-1/16". **Weight:** (38 & 357 mag models) 2.25"-25 oz.; 3-1/16"-27 oz. **Sights:** Adjustable on 327, fixed on others. **Grips:** Ruger Cushioned Grip with inserts. **Features:** Compact, small frame, double-action revolver. Full-length ejector shroud. Stainless steel only. Introduced 1988.
Price: Fixed sights **$639.00**
Price: Fiber optic sights **$689.00**

RUGER REDHAWK
Caliber: 44 Rem. Mag., 45 Colt, 6-shot. **Barrel:** 4", 5.5", 7.5". **Weight:** About 54 oz. (7.5" bbl.). **Length:** 13" overall (7.5" barrel). **Grips:** Square butt cushioned grip panels. **Sights:** Interchangeable Patridge-type front, rear adjustable for windage and elevation.

Features: Stainless steel, brushed satin finish, blued ordnance steel. 9.5" sight radius. Introduced 1979.
Price: KRH-44, stainless, 7.5" barrel **$989.00**
Price: KRH-44R, stainless 7.5" barrel w/scope mount **$989.00**
Price: KRH-445, stainless 5.5" barrel **$989.00**
Price: KRH-444, stainless 4" barrel (2007) . . . **$989.00**
Price: KRH-45-4, Hogue Monogrip, 45 Colt (2008) **$989.00**

RUGER SUPER REDHAWK REVOLVER

Caliber: 44 Rem. Mag., 45 Colt, 454 Casull, 480 Ruger, 5 or 6-shot. **Barrel:** 2.5", 5.5", 7.5", 9.5". **Weight:** About 54 oz. (7.5" bbl.). **Length:** 13" overall (7.5" barrel). **Grips:** Hogue Tamer Monogrip. **Features:** Similar to standard Redhawk except has heavy extended frame with Ruger Integral Scope Mounting System on wide topstrap. Wide hammer spur lowered for better scope clearance. Incorporates mechanical design features and improvements of GP-100. Ramp front sight base has Redhawk-style Interchangeable Insert sight blades, adjustable rear sight. Satin stainless steel and low-glare stainless finishes. Introduced 1987.
Price: .44 Magnum **$1049.00**
Price: .454 Casull **$1079.00**
Price: .454 Alaskan **$1079.00**
Price: .44 Mag. Alaskan **$1079.00**

SMITH & WESSON MODEL GOVENOR™ REVOLVER

Caliber: .410 2 1/2", .45 ACP, .45 Colt; 6 rounds. **Barrel:** 2.75". **Weight:** 35 oz. (2.5" barrel). **Length:** 7.5", (2.5" barrel). **Grip:** Synthetic. **Sights:** Front: Tritium Night Sight (Dovetailed), Rear: fixed. **Grips:** Synthetic. **Finish:** Matte Black. **Weight:** 29.6 oz. **Features:** Capable of chambering a mixture of .45 Colt, .45 ACP and .410 gauge 2 ½-inch shotshells, the Governor is suited for both close and distant encounters, allowing users to customize the load to their preference. The shooter's choice of ammunition is housed in the revolver's six-shot stainless PVD-coated cylinder, which adds an extra level of protection to this already rugged platform. On top of the revolver's compact 2-3/4" barrel, Smith & Wesson has added a dovetailed Tritium front night sight for enhanced accuracy in low-light conditions, while the Governor's fixed rear sight is aptly suited for this self-defense handgun. The Governor measures 8-1/2" inches in overall length along with a width of 1-3/4". Carry ability of this revolver has been further enhanced with the Governor's unloaded weight of 29.6 ounces and standard matte black finish designed to reduce unwanted glare while adding an all-business like demeanor to this self-defense handgun. On the lower portion of the frame, the revolver will be packaged with either shock absorbing synthetic grips or with factory-installed laser grips from Crimson Trace®. Accurate, rugged and reliable, the Governor is further enhanced by Smith & Wesson's renowned smooth double-action and crisp single-action trigger pull. The new revolver will also come standard with 2-round and 6-round moon clips. Made in U.S.A. by Smith & Wesson.
Price: **$679.00**
Price: with Crimson Trace® Laser Grip **$899.00**

SMITH & WESSON MODEL 14 CLASSIC

Caliber: 38 Spec. +P, 6-shot. Barrel: 6". Weight: 35 oz. Length: 11.5". Grips: Wood. Sights: Pinned Patridge front, micro adjustable rear. Features: Recreation of the vintage Model 14 revolver. Carbon steel frame and cylinder with blued finish.
Price: **$995.00**
Price: Model 14 150253, nickel finish **$1,074.00**

SMITH & WESSON NIGHT GUARD REVOLVERS

Caliber: 357 Mag., 38 Spec. +P, 5-, 6-, 7-, 8-shot. **Barrel:** 2.5 or 2.75" (45 ACP). **Weight:** 24.2 oz. (2.5" barrel). **Length:** 7.325" overall (2.5" barrel). **Grips:** Pachmayr Compac Custom. **Sights:** XS Sight 24/7 Standard Dot Tritium front, Cylinder & Slide Extreme Duty fixed rear. **Features:** Scandium alloy frame, stainless PVD cylinder, matte black finish. Introduced 2008. Made in U.S.A. by Smith & Wesson.
Price: Model 325, 45 ACP, 2.75" barrel, large-frame snubnose **$1,049.00**
Price: Model 327, 38/357, 2.5" barrel, large-frame snubnose **$1,049.00**
Price: Model 329, 44 Magnum/38 Special (interchangeable), 2.5" barrel, large-frame snubnose **$1,049.00**
Price: Model 386, 357 Magnum/44 Special +P (interchangeable), 2.5" barrel, medium-frame snubnose. **$979.00**

SMITH & WESSON J-FRAME REVOLVERS

The smallest S&W wheelguns come in a variety of chamberings, barrel lengths, and materials, as noted in the individual model listings.

SMITH & WESSON 60LS/642LS LADYSMITH REVOLVERS

Caliber: .38 Spec. +P, 357 Mag., 5-shot. **Barrel:** 1-7/8" (642LS); 2-1/8" (60LS) **Weight:** 14.5 oz. (642LS); 21.5 oz. (60LS); **Length:** 6.6" overall (60LS); . **Grips:** Wood. **Sights:** Black blade, serrated ramp front, fixed notch rear. **Features:** 60LS model has a Chiefs Special-style frame. 642LS has Centennial-style frame, frosted matte finish, smooth combat wood grips. Introduced 1996. Comes in a fitted carry/storage case. Introduced 1989. Made in U.S.A. by Smith & Wesson.
Price: From **$749.00**

SMITH & WESSON MODEL 63

Caliber: 22 LR, 8-shot. **Barrel:** 5". **Weight:** 28.8 oz. **Length:** 9.5" overall. **Grips:** Black rubber. **Sights:** Black ramp front sight, adjustable black blade rear sight. **Features:** Stainless steel construction throughout. Made in U.S.A. by Smith & Wesson.
Price: **$769.00**

SMITH & WESSON MODEL 442/637/638/642 AIRWEIGHT REVOLVERS

Caliber: 38 Spec. +P, 5-shot. **Barrel:** 1-7/8", 2-1/2". **Weight:** 15 oz. (37, 442); 20 oz. (3); 21.5 oz.; **Length:** 6-3/8" overall. **Grips:** Soft rubber. **Sights:** Fixed, serrated ramp front, square notch rear. **Features:** Aluminum-alloy frames. Models 37, 637; Chiefs Special-style frame with exposed hammer. Introduced 1996. Models 442, 642; Centennial-style frame, enclosed hammer. Model 638, Bodyguard style,

shrouded hammer. Comes in a fitted carry/storage case. Introduced 1989. Made in U.S.A. by Smith & Wesson.
Price: From $449.00

SMITH & WESSON MODELS 637 CT/638 CT/642 CT
Similar to Models 637, 638 and 642 but with Crimson Trace Laser Grips.
Price: $669.00

SMITH & WESSON MODEL 317 AIRLITE REVOLVERS
Caliber: 22 LR, 8-shot. **Barrel:** 1-7/8". **Weight:** 10.5 oz. **Length:** 6.25" overall (1-7/8" barrel). **Grips:** Rubber. **Sights:** Serrated ramp front, fixed notch rear. **Features:** Aluminum alloy, carbon and stainless steels, Chiefs Special-style frame with exposed hammer. Smooth combat trigger. Clear Cote finish. Introduced 1997. Made in U.S.A. by Smith & Wesson.
Price: Model 317, 1-7/8" barrel $699.00

SMITH & WESSON MODEL 340/340PD AIRLITE SC CENTENNIAL
Caliber: 357 Mag., 38 Spec. +P, 5-shot. **Barrel:** 1-7/8". **Weight:** 12 oz. **Length:** 6-3/8" overall (1-7/8" barrel). **Grips:** Rounded butt rubber. **Sights:** Black blade front, rear notch **Features:** Centennial-style frame, enclosed hammer. Internal lock. Matte silver finish. Scandium alloy frame, titanium cylinder, stainless steel barrel liner. Made in U.S.A. by Smith & Wesson.
Price: Model 340 .... $1,019.00

SMITH & WESSON MODEL 351PD REVOLVER
Caliber: 22 Mag., 7-shot. **Barrel:** 1-7/8". **Weight:** 10.6 oz. **Length:** 6.25" overall (1-7/8" barrel). **Sights:** HiViz front sight, rear notch. **Grips:** Wood. **Features:** Seven-shot, aluminum-alloy frame. Chiefs Special-style frame with exposed hammer. Nonreflective matte-black finish. Internal lock. Made in U.S.A. by Smith & Wesson.
Price: $759.00

SMITH & WESSON MODEL 360/360PD AIRLITE CHIEF'S SPECIAL
Caliber: 357 Mag., 38 Spec. +P, 5-shot. **Barrel:** 1-7/8". **Weight:** 12 oz. **Length:** 6-3/8" overall (1-7/8" barrel). **Grips:** Rounded butt rubber. **Sights:** Black blade front, fixed rear notch. **Features:** Chief's Special-style frame with exposed hammer. Internal lock. Scandium alloy frame, titanium cylinder, stainless steel barrel. Made in U.S.A. by Smith & Wesson.
Price: 360PD $988.00

SMITH & WESSON MODEL M&P360
Single/double-action J-frame revolver chambered in .357 Magnum. Features include 3-inch barrel, 5-round cylinder, fixed XS tritium sights, scandium frame, stainless steel cylinder, matte black finish, synthetic grips.
Price: $980.00

SMITH & WESSON BODYGUARD® 38 REVOLVER
Caliber: .38 S&W Special +P; 5 rounds. **Barrel:** 1.9". **Weight:** 14.3 oz. **Length:** 6.6". **Grip:** Synthetic. **Sights:** Front: Black ramp, Rear: integral. **Grips:** Synthetic. **Finish:** Matte Black. **Features:** The Smith & Wesson BODYGUARD® series is the first in personal protection with integrated lasers. The BODYGUARD® 38 and BODYGUARD® 380 are uniquely engineered as the most state-of-the-art, concealable and accurate personal protection possible. Lightweight, simple to use and featuring integrated laser sights – nothing protects like a BODYGUARD.
Price: $509.00

SMITH & WESSON MODEL 438
Caliber: 38 Spec. +P, 5-shot. **Barrel:** 1-7/8". **Weight:** 15.1 oz. **Length:** 6.31" overall. **Grips:** Synthetic. **Sights:** Fixed front and rear. **Features:** Aluminum alloy frame, stainless steel cylinder. Matte black finish throughout. Made in U.S.A. by Smith & Wesson.
Price: $449.00

SMITH & WESSON MODEL 640 CENTENNIAL DA ONLY
Caliber: 357 Mag., 38 Spec. +P, 5-shot. **Barrel:** 2-1/8". **Weight:** 23 oz. **Length:** 6.75" overall. **Grips:** Uncle Mike's Boot grip. **Sights:** Serrated ramp front, fixed notch rear. **Features:** Stainless steel. Fully concealed hammer, snag-proof smooth edges. Internal lock. Introduced 1995 in 357 Mag.
Price: $798.00

SMITH & WESSON MODEL 649 BODYGUARD REVOLVER
Caliber: 357 Mag., 38 Spec. +P, 5-shot. **Barrel:** 2-1/8". **Weight:** 23 oz. **Length:** 6-5/8" overall. **Grips:** Uncle Mike's Combat. **Sights:** Black pinned ramp front, fixed notch rear. **Features:** Stainless steel construction, satin finish. Internal lock. Bodyguard style, shrouded hammer. Made in U.S.A. by Smith & Wesson.
Price: $798.00

SMITH & WESSON K-FRAME/L-FRAME REVOLVERS
These mid-size S&W wheelguns come in a variety of chamberings, barrel lengths, and materials, as noted in individual model listings.

SMITH & WESSON MODEL 10 CLASSIC
Single/double action K frame revolver chambered in .38 Special. Features include bright blue steel frame and cylinder, checkered wood grips, 4-inch barrel, adjustable patridge-style sights.
Price: $719.00

SMITH & WESSON MODEL 48 CLASSIC
Single/double action K frame revolver chambered in .22 Magnum Rimfire (.22 WMR). Features include bright blue steel frame and cylinder, checkered wood grips, 4- or 6-inch barrel, adjustable patridge-style sights.
Price: .... $1,043.00 to $1,082.00

SMITH & WESSON MODEL 64/67 REVOLVERS

Caliber: 38 Spec. +P, 6-shot. **Barrel:** 3". **Weight:** 33 oz. **Length:** 8-7/8" overall. **Grips:** Soft rubber. **Sights:** Fixed, 1/8" serrated ramp front, square notch rear. Model 67 (**Weight:** 36 oz. **Length:** 8-7/8") similar to Model 64 except for adjustable sights. **Features:** Satin finished stainless steel, square butt.

Price: From . . . .**$689.00 to $749.00**

SMITH & WESSON MODEL 617 REVOLVERS

Caliber: 22 LR, 6- or 10-shot. **Barrel:** 4". **Weight:** 41 oz. (4" barrel). **Length:** 9-1/8" (4" barrel). **Grips:** Soft rubber. **Sights:** Patridge front, adjustable rear. Drilled and tapped for scope mount. **Features:** Stainless steel with satin finish; 4" has .312" smooth trigger, .375" semi-target hammer; 6" has either .312" combat or .400" serrated trigger, .375" semi-target or .500" target hammer; 8-3/8" with .400" serrated trigger, .500" target hammer. Introduced 1990.

Price: From **$829.00**

SMITH & WESSON MODELS 620 REVOLVERS

Caliber: 38 Spec. +P; 357 Mag., 7 rounds. **Barrel:** 4". **Weight:** 37.5 oz. **Length:** 9.5". **Grips:** Rubber. **Sights:** Integral front blade, fixed rear notch on the 619; adjustable white-outline target style rear, red ramp front on 620. **Features:** Replaces Models 65 and 66. Two-piece semi-lug barrel. Satin stainless frame and cylinder. Made in U.S.A. by Smith & Wesson.

Price: **$893.00**

SMITH & WESSON MODEL 386 XL HUNTER

Single/double action L-frame revolver chambered in .357 Magnum. Features include 6-inch full-lug barrel, 7-round cylinder, Hi-Viz fiber optic front sight, adjustable rear sight, scandium frame, stainless steel cylinder, black matte finish, synthetic grips.

Price: **$1,019.00**

SMITH & WESSON MODEL 686/686 PLUS REVOLVERS

Caliber: 357 Mag., 38 S&W Special; 6 rounds. **Barrel:** 2.5", 4", 6". **Weight:** 35 oz. (2.5" barrel). **Length:** 7.5", (2.5" barrel). **Grips:** Rubber. **Sights:** White outline adjustable rear, red ramp front. **Features:** Satin stainless frame and cylinder. Plus series guns have 7-shot cylinders. Introduced 1996. Powerport (PP) has Patridge front, adjustable rear sight. Introduced early 1980s. Stock Service Revolver (SSR) intr. 2007. **Capacity:** 6. **Barrel:** 4". **Sights:** Interchangeable front, adjustable rear. **Grips:** Wood. **Finish:** Satin stainless frame and cylinder. **Weight:** 38.3 oz. **Features:** Chamfered charge holes, custom barrel w/recessed crown, bossed mainspring. High-hold ergonomic grip. Made in U.S.A. by Smith & Wesson.

Price: 686 . . . .**$909.00**
Price: Plus, 7 rounds **$932.00**
Price: PP, 6" barrel, 6 rounds, 11-3/8" OAL **$877.00**
Price: SSR **$1,059.00**

SMITH & WESSON MODEL 686 PLUS PRO SERIES

Single/double-action L-frame revolver chambered in .357 Magnum. Features include 5-inch barrel with tapered underlug, 7-round cylinder, satin stainless steel frame and cylinder, synthetic grips, interchangeable and adjustable sights.

Price: **$1,059.00**

SMITH & WESSON N-FRAME REVOLVERS

These large-frame S&W wheelguns come in a variety of chamberings, barrel lengths, and materials, as noted in the individual model listings.

SMITH & WESSON MODEL 29 CLASSIC

Caliber: 44 Mag, 6-round. **Barrel:** 6.5". **Weight:** 48.5 oz. **Length:** 12". **Grips:** Altamont service walnut. **Sights:** Adjustable white-outline rear, red ramp front. **Features:** Carbon steel frame, polished-blued or nickel finish. Has integral key lock safety feature to prevent accidental discharges. Alo available with 3" barrel. Original Model 29 made famous by "Dirty Harry" character created in 1971 by Clint Eastwood.

Price: **$1240.00**

SMITH & WESSON MODEL 329PD AIRLITE REVOLVERS

Caliber: 44 Spec., 44 Mag., 6-round. **Barrel:** 4". **Weight:** 26 oz. **Length:** 9.5". **Grips:** Wood. **Sights:** Adj. rear, HiViz orange-dot front. **Features:** Scandium alloy frame, blue/black finish.

Price: From **$1,159.00**

SMITH & WESSON MODEL 625/625JM REVOLVERS

Caliber: 45 ACP, 6-shot. **Barrel:** 4", 5". **Weight:** 43 oz. (4" barrel). **Length:** 9-3/8" overall (4" barrel). **Grips:** Soft rubber; wood optional. **Sights:** Patridge front on ramp, S&W micrometer click rear adjustable for windage and elevation. **Features:** Stainless steel construction with .400" semi-target hammer, .312" smooth combat trigger; full lug barrel. Glass beaded finish. Introduced 1989. "Jerry Miculek" Professional (JM) Series has .265"-wide grooved trigger, special wooden Miculek Grip, five full moon clips, gold bead Patridge front sight on interchangeable front sight base, bead blast finish. Unique serial number run. Mountain Gun has 4" tapered barrel, drilled and tapped, Hogue Rubber Monogrip, pinned black ramp front sight, micrometer click-adjustable rear sight, satin stainless frame and barrel, weighs 39.5 oz.

Price: 625JM **$1,074.00**

SMITH & WESSON MODEL 629 REVOLVERS

Caliber: 44 Magnum, 44 S&W Special, 6-shot. **Barrel:** 4", 5", 6.5". **Weight:** 41.5 oz. (4" bbl.). **Length:** 9-5/8" overall (4" bbl.). **Grips:** Soft rubber; wood optional. **Sights:** 1/8" red ramp front, white outline rear, internal lock, adjustable for windage and elevation. Classic similar to standard Model 629, except Classic has full-lug 5" barrel, chamfered front of cylinder, interchangeable red ramp front sight with adjustable white outline rear, Hogue grips with S&W monogram, drilled and tapped for scope mounting. Factory accurizing and endurance packages. Introduced 1990. Classic Power Port has Patridge front sight and adjustable rear sight. Model 629CT has 5" barrel, Crimson Trace Hoghunter Lasergrips, 10.5" OAL, 45.5 oz. weight. Introduced 2006.

Price: From **$1,035.00**

SMITH & WESSON MODEL 329 XL HUNTER

Similar to Model 386 XL Hunter but built on large N-frame and chambered in .44 Magnum. Other features include 6-round cylinder and 6.5-barrel.

Price: **$1,138.00**

SMITH & WESSON X-FRAME REVOLVERS

These extra-large X-frame S&W wheelguns come in a variety of chamberings, barrel lengths, and materials, as noted in individual model listings.

SMITH & WESSON MODEL 500 REVOLVERS

Caliber: 500 S&W Mag., 5 rounds. **Barrel:** 4", 8-3/8". **Weight:** 72.5 oz. **Length:** 15" (8-3/8" barrel). **Grips:** Hogue Sorbothane Rubber. **Sights:** Interchangeable blade, front, adjustable rear. **Features:** Recoil compensator, ball detent cylinder latch, internal lock. 6.5"-barrel model has orange-ramp dovetail Millett front sight, adjustable black rear sight, Hogue Dual Density Monogrip, .312" chrome trigger with over-travel stop, chrome tear-drop hammer, glassbead finish. 10.5"-barrel model has red ramp front sight, adjustable rear sight, .312 chrome trigger with overtravel stop, chrome tear drop hammer with pinned sear, hunting sling. Compensated Hunter has .400 orange ramp dovetail front sight, adjustable black blade rear sight, Hogue Dual Density Monogrip, glassbead finish w/black clear coat. Made in U.S.A. by Smith & Wesson.

Price: From **$1,249.00**

SMITH & WESSON MODEL 460V REVOLVERS

Caliber: 460 S&W Mag., 5-shot. Also chambers 454 Casull, 45 Colt. **Barrel:** 8-3/8" gain-twist rifling. **Weight:** 62.5 oz. **Length:** 11.25". **Grips:** Rubber. **Sights:** Adj. rear, red ramp front. **Features:** Satin stainless steel frame and cylinder, interchangeable compensator. 460XVR (X-treme Velocity Revolver) has black blade front sight with interchangeable green Hi-Viz tubes, adjustable rear sight. 7.5"-barrel version has Lothar-Walther barrel, 360-degree recoil compensator, tuned Performance Center action, pinned sear, integral Weaver base, non-glare surfaces, scope mount accessory kit for mounting full-size scopes, flashed-chromed hammer and trigger, Performance Center gun rug and shoulder sling. Interchangeable Hi-Viz green dot front sight, adjustable black rear sight, Hogue Dual Density Monogrip, matte-black frame and shroud finish with glass-bead cylinder finish, 72 oz. Compensated Hunter has tear drop chrome hammer, .312 chrome trigger, Hogue Dual Density Monogrip, satin/matte stainless finish, HiViz interchangeable front sight, adjustable black rear sight. XVR introduced 2006.

Price: 460V **$1,519.00**
Price: 460XVR, from **$1,519.00**

SUPER SIX CLASSIC BISON BULL

Caliber: 45-80 Government, 6-shot. **Barrel:** 10" octagonal with 1:14 twist. **Weight:** 6 lbs. **Length:** 17.5"overall. **Grips:** NA. **Sights:** Ramp front sight with dovetailed blade, click-adjustable rear. **Features:** Manganese bronze frame. Integral scope mount, manual crossbolt safety.

Price: . . . . **Appx. $1,500.00**

TAURUS MODEL 17 "TRACKER"

Caliber: 17 HMR, 7-shot. **Barrel:** 6.5". **Weight:** 45.8 oz. **Grips:** Rubber. **Sights:** Adjustable. **Features:** Double action, matte stainless, integral key-lock.

Price: From **$453.00**

TAURUS MODEL 44 REVOLVER

Caliber: 44 Mag., 6-shot. **Barrel:** 4", 6.5", 8-3/8". **Weight:** 44-3/4 oz. **Grips:** Rubber. **Sights:** Adjustable. **Features:** Double-action. Integral key-lock. Introduced 1994. New Model 44S12 has 12" vent rib barrel. Imported from Brazil by Taurus International Manufacturing, Inc.

Price: From **$633.00**

TAURUS MODEL 65 REVOLVER

Caliber: 357 Mag., 6-shot. **Barrel:** 4". **Weight:** 38 oz. **Length:** 10.5" overall. **Grips:** Soft rubber. **Sights:** Fixed. **Features:** Double action, integral key-lock. Seven models for 2006 Imported by Taurus International.

Price: From **$419.00**

TAURUS MODEL 66 REVOLVER

Similar to Model 65, 4" or 6" barrel, 7-shot cylinder, adjustable rear sight. Integral key-lock action. Imported by Taurus International.

Price: From **$469.00**

TAURUS MODEL 82 HEAVY BARREL REVOLVER

Caliber: 38 Spec., 6-shot. **Barrel:** 4", heavy. **Weight:** 36.5 oz. **Length:** 9-1/4" overall (4" bbl.). **Grips:** Soft black rubber. **Sights:** Serrated ramp front, square notch rear. **Features:** Double action, solid rib, integral key-lock. Imported by Taurus International.

Price: From **$403.00**

TAURUS MODEL 85 REVOLVER

Caliber: 38 Spec., 5-shot. **Barrel:** 2". **Weight:** 17-24.5 oz., titanium 13.5-15.4 oz. **Grips:** Rubber, rosewood or mother-of-pearl. **Sights:** Ramp front, square notch rear. **Features:** Blue, matte stainless, blue with gold accents, stainless with gold accents; rated for +P ammo. Integral keylock. Some models have titantium frame. Introduced 1980. Imported by Taurus International.

Price: From **$403.00**

TAURUS 380 MINI REVOLVER

Caliber: .380 ACP (5-shot cylinder w/moon clip). **Barrel:** 1.75". Weight: 15.5 oz. **Length:** 5.95". **Grips:** Rubber. **Sights:** Adjustable rear, fixed front. **Features:** Double-action-only. Available in blued or stainless finish. Five Star (moon) clips included.

PRICE . . . . **$430 to $461**

TAURUS PROTECTOR POLYMER

Single/double action revolver chambered in .38 Special +P. Features include 5-round cylinder; polymer frame; faux wood rubber-feel grips; fixed sights; shrouded hammer with cocking spur; blued finish; 2.5-inch barrel. Weight 18.2 oz.

Price: . . . . **N/A**

TAURUS 851 & 651 REVOLVERS

Small frame SA/DA revolvers similar to Taurus Model 85 but with Centennial-style concealed-hammer frame. Chambered in 38 Special +P (Model 851) or 357 Magnum (Model 651). Features include five-shot cylinder; 2" barrel; fixed sights; blue, matte blue, titanium or stainless finish; Taurus security lock. Overall length is 6.5". Weighs 15.5 oz. (titanium) to 25 oz. (blued and stainless).

Price: From **$411.00**

TAURUS MODEL 94 REVOLVER

Caliber: 22 LR, 9-shot cylinder; 22 Mag, 8-shot cylinder **Barrel:** 2", 4", 5". **Weight:** 18.5-27.5 oz. **Grips:** Soft black rubber. **Sights:** Serrated ramp front, click-adjustable rear. **Features:** Double action, integral key-lock. Introduced 1989. Imported by Taurus International.

Price: From **$369.00**

TAURUS MODEL 4510 JUDGE

Caliber: 3" .410/45 LC, 2.5" .410/45 LC. **Barrel:** 3", 6.5" (blued finish). **Weight:** 35.2 oz., 22.4 oz. **Length:** 7.5". **Grips:** Ribber. **Sights:** Fiber Optic. **Features:** DA/SA. Matte Stainless and Ultra-Lite Stainless finish. Introduced in 2007. Imported from Brazil by Taurus International.

Price: 4510T TrackerSS Matte Stainless **$569.00**

Price: 4510TKR-3B Judge . **$558.00**
Price: 4510TKR-SSR, ported barrel, tactical rail **$608.00**

TAURUS JUDGE PUBLIC DEFENDER POLYMER

Single/double action revolver chambered in .45 Colt/.410 (2-1/2). Features include 5-round cylinder; polymer frame; Ribber rubber-feel grips; fiber-optic front sight; adjustable rear sight; blued or stainless cylinder; shrouded hammer with cocking spur; blued finish; 2.5-inch barrel. Weight 27 oz.
Price: . . . . **N/A**

TAURUS JUDGE PUBLIC DEFENDER ULTRA-LITE

Single/double action revolver chambered in .45 Colt/.410 (2-1/2). Features include 5-round cylinder; lightweight aluminum frame; Ribber rubber-feel grips; fiber-optic front sight; adjustable rear sight; blued or stainless cylinder; shrouded hammer with cocking spur; blued finish; 2.5-inch barrel. Weight 20.7 oz.
Price: . . . . **N/A**

TAURUS RAGING JUDGE MAGNUM

Single/double action revolver chambered for .454 Casull, .45 Colt, 2.5-inch and 3-inch .410. Features include 3- or 6-inch barrel; fixed sights with fiber-optic front; blued or stainless steel finish; vent rib for scope mounting (6-inch only); cushioned Raging Bull grips.
Price: . . . . **N/A**

TAURUS RAGING JUDGE MAGNUM ULTRA-LITE

Single/double action revolver chambered for .454 Casull, .45 Colt, 2.5-inch and 3-inch .410. Features include 3- or 6-inch barrel; aluminum alloy frame; fixed sights with fiber-optic front; blued or stainless steel finish; cushioned Raging Bull grips. Weight: 41.4 oz. (3-inch barrel).
Price: . . . . **N/A**

TAURUS RAGING BULL MODEL 416

Caliber: 41 Magnum, 6-shot. **Barrel:** 6.5". **Weight:** 61.9 oz. **Grips:** Rubber. **Sights:** Adjustable. **Features:** Double-action, ported, ventilated rib, matte stainless, integral key-lock.
Price: **$706.00**

TAURUS MODEL 425 TRACKER REVOLVERS

Caliber: 357 Mag., 7-shot; 41 Mag., 5-shot. **Barrel:** 4" and 6". **Weight:** 28.8-40 oz. (titanium) 24.3-28. (6"). **Grips:** Rubber. **Sights:** Fixed front, adjustable rear. **Features:** Double-action stainless steel, Shadow Gray or Total Titanium; vent rib (steel models only); integral key-lock action. Imported by Taurus International.
Price: From **$569.00**

TAURUS MODEL 444 ULTRA-LIGHT

Caliber: 44 Mag, 5-shot. **Barrel:** 4". **Weight:** 28.3 oz. **Length:** 9.8"overall. **Grips:** Cushioned inset rubber. **Sights:** Fixed red-fiber optic front, adjustable rear. **Features:** UltraLite titanium blue finish, titanium/alloy frame built on Raging Bull design. Smooth trigger shoe, 1.760" wide, 6.280" tall. Barrel rate of twist 1:16", 6 grooves. Introduced 2005. Imported by Taurus International.
Price: **$666.00**

TAURUS MODEL 416/444/454 RAGING BULL REVOLVERS

Caliber: 41 Mag., 44 Mag., 454 Casull. **Barrel:** 2.25" (454 Casull only), 5", 6.5", 8-3/8". **Weight:** 53-63 oz. **Length:** 12" overall (6.5" barrel). **Grips:** Soft black rubber. **Sights:** Patridge front, adjustable rear. **Features:** Double-action, ventilated rib, ported, integral key-lock. Introduced 1997. Imported by Taurus International.
Price: From **$641.00**

TAURUS MODEL 605 REVOLVER

Caliber: 357 Mag., 5-shot. **Barrel:** 2". **Weight:** 24 oz. **Grips:** Rubber. **Sights:** Fixed. **Features:** Double-action, blue or stainless or titanium, concealed hammer models DAO, porting optional, integral key-lock. Introduced 1995. Imported by Taurus International.
Price: From **$403.00**

TAURUS MODEL 608 REVOLVER

Caliber: 357 Mag. 38 Spec., 8-shot. **Barrel:** 4", 6.5", 8-3/8". **Weight:** 44-57 oz. **Length:** 9-3/8" overall. **Grips:** Soft black rubber. **Sights:** Adjustable. **Features:** Double-action, integral key-lock action. Available in blue or stainless. Introduced 1995. Imported by Taurus International.
Price: From **$584.00**

TAURUS MODEL 617 REVOLVER

Caliber: 357 Mag., 7-shot. **Barrel:** 2". **Weight:** 28.3 oz. **Length:** 6.75" overall. **Grips:** Soft black rubber. **Sights:** Fixed. **Features:** Double-action, blue, Shadow Gray, bright spectrum blue or matte stainless steel, integral key-lock. Available with porting, concealed hammer. Introduced 1998. Imported by Taurus International.
Price: **$436.00**

TAURUS MODEL 650 CIA REVOLVER

Caliber: 357 Mag., 5-shot. **Barrel:** 2". **Weight:** 24.5 oz. **Grips:** Rubber. **Sights:** Ramp front, square notch rear. **Features:** Double-action only, blue or matte stainless steel, integral key-lock, internal hammer. Introduced 2001. From Taurus International.
Price: From **$411.00**

TAURUS MODEL 651 PROTECTOR REVOLVER

Caliber: 357 Mag., 5-shot. **Barrel:** 2". **Weight:** 17-24.5 oz. **Grips:** Rubber. **Sights:** Fixed. **Features:** Concealed single-action/double-action design. Shrouded cockable hammer, blue, matte stainless, Shadow Gray, Total Titanium, integral key-lock. Made in Brazil. Imported by Taurus International Manufacturing, Inc.
Price: From **$411.00**

TAURUS MODEL 731 REVOLVER

Similar to the Taurus Model 605, except in .32 Magnum.
Price: **$469.00**

TAURUS MODEL 817 ULTRA-LITE REVOLVER

Caliber: 38 Spec., 7-shot. **Barrel:** 2". **Weight:** 21 oz. **Length:** 6.5" overall. **Grips:** Soft rubber. **Sights:** Fixed. **Features:** Double-action, integral key-lock. Rated for +P ammo. Introduced 1999. Imported from Brazil by Taurus International.
Price: From **$436.00**

TAURUS MODEL 850 CIA REVOLVER

Caliber: 38 Spec., 5-shot. **Barrel:** 2". **Weight:** 17-24.5 oz. **Grips:** Rubber, mother-of-pearl. **Sights:** Ramp front, square notch rear. **Features:** Double-action only, blue or matte stainless steel, rated for +P ammo, integral key-lock, internal hammer. Introduced 2001. From Taurus International.
Price: From **$411.00**

TAURUS MODEL 941 REVOLVER

Caliber: 22 LR (Mod. 94), 22 WMR (Mod. 941), 8-shot. **Barrel:** 2", 4", 5". **Weight:** 27.5 oz. (4" barrel). **Grips:** Soft black rubber. **Sights:** Serrated ramp front, rear adjustable. **Features:** Double-action, integral key-lock. Introduced 1992. Imported by Taurus International.
Price: From **$386.00**

TAURUS MODEL 970/971 TRACKER REVOLVERS

Caliber: 22 LR (Model 970), 22 Magnum (Model 971); 7-shot. **Barrel:** 6". **Weight:** 53.6 oz. **Grips:** Rubber. **Sights:** Adjustable. **Features:** Double barrel, heavy barrel with ventilated rib; matte stainless finish, integral key-lock. Introduced 2001. From Taurus International.
Price: **$453.00**
Price: Model 17SS6, chambered in 17 HMR **$453.00**

BERETTA STAMPEDE SINGLE-ACTION REVOLVER
Caliber: 357 Mag, 45 Colt, 6-shot. **Barrel:** 4.75", 5.5", 7.5", blued. **Weight:** 36.8 oz. (4.75" barrel). **Length:** 9.5" overall (4.75" barrel). **Grips:** Wood, walnut, black polymer. **Sights:** Blade front, notch rear. **Features:** Transfer-bar safety. Introduced 2003. Stampede Inox (2004) is stainless steel with black polymer grips. Compact Stampede Marshall (2004) has birdshead-style walnut grips, 3.5" barrel, color-case-hardened frame, blued barrel and cylinder. Manufactured for Beretta by Uberti.
Price: Nickel, 45 Colt **$630.00**
Price: Blued, 45 Colt, 357 Mag, 4.75", 5-1/2" **$575.00**
Price: Deluxe, 45 Colt, 357 Mag. 4.75", 5-1/2" **$675.00**
Price: Marshall, 45 Colt, 357 Mag. 3.5" **$575.00**
Price: Bisley nickel, 4.75", 5.5" **$775.00**
Price: Bisley, 4.75", 5.5" **$675.00**
Price: Stampede Deluxe, 45 Colt 7.5" **$775.00**
Price: Stampede Blued, 45 Colt 7.5" **$575.00**
Price: Marshall Old West, 45 Colt 3.5" **$650.00**

CHARTER DIXIE DERRINGER COMBO REVOLVER
Caliber: .38 special +P - 5-round cylinder. **Barrel:** 2". **Weight:** 12 oz. **Grip:** Compact. **Sights:** Fixed. **Features:** Stainless finish & frame. Chambered in .22 LR., .22 Magnum, or in Combo, the single action Dixie Derringer is a fun little pocket gun. It is also a lightweight revolver ideal for moderate-risk concealed carry applications. This quick-drawing pocket revolver is accurate at close range and features Charter's patent-pending hammer block safety. American made by Charter Arms.
Price: **$264.00**

CHARTER DIXIE DERRINGER REVOLVER
Caliber: .38 special +P - 5-round cylinder. **Barrel:** 2". **Weight:** 12 oz. **Grip:** Compact. **Sights:** Fixed. **Features:** Black & stainless finish & stainless frame. Chambered in .22 Magnum, the single action Dixie Derringer is a fun little pocket gun. It is also a lightweight revolver ideal for moderate-risk concealed carry applications. This quick-drawing pocket revolver is accurate at close range and features Charter's patent-pending hammer block safety. American made by Charter Arms.
Price: **$221.00**

CIMARRON 1872 OPEN TOP REVOLVER
Caliber: 38, 44 Special, 44 Colt, 44 Russian, 45 LC, 45 S&W Schofield. **Barrel:** 5.5" and 7.5". **Grips:** Walnut. **Sights:** Blade front, fixed rear. **Features:** Replica of first cartridge-firing revolver. Blue, charcoal blue, nickel or Original finish; Navy-style brass or steel Army-style frame. Introduced 2001 by Cimarron F.A. Co.
Price: **$467.31**

CIMARRON 1875 OUTLAW REVOLVER
Caliber: .357, .38 special, .44 W.C.F., .45 Colt, .45 ACP. **Barrel:** 5-1/2" and 7-1/2". **Weight:** 2.5-2.6 lbs. **Grip:** 1 piece walnut. **Features:** Standard blue finish with color case hardened frame.
Price: **$559.94**
Price: CA150 Dual Cyl. **$665.40**

CIMARRON MODEL 1890 REVOLVER
Caliber: .357, .38 special, .44 W.C.F., .45 Colt, .45 ACP. **Barrel:** 5-1/2". **Weight:** 2.4-2.5 lbs. **Grip:** 1 piece walnut. **Features:** Standard blue finish with standard blue frame.
Price: **$576.28**
Price: CA159 Dual Cyl. **$681.73**

CIMARRON BISLEY MODEL SINGLE-ACTION REVOLVERS
Similar to 1873 Model P, special grip frame and trigger guard, knurled wide-spur hammer, curved trigger. Available in 357 Mag., 44 WCF, 44 Spl., 45 Colt. Introduced 1999. Imported by Cimarron F.A. Co.
Price: From **$574.43**

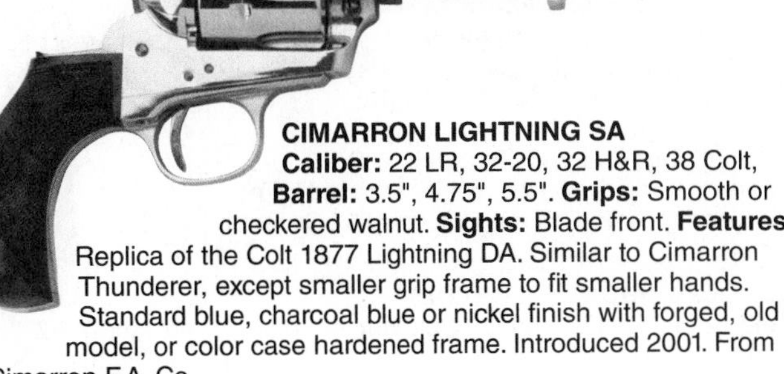

CIMARRON LIGHTNING SA
Caliber: 22 LR, 32-20, 32 H&R, 38 Colt, **Barrel:** 3.5", 4.75", 5.5". **Grips:** Smooth or checkered walnut. **Sights:** Blade front. **Features:** Replica of the Colt 1877 Lightning DA. Similar to Cimarron Thunderer, except smaller grip frame to fit smaller hands. Standard blue, charcoal blue or nickel finish with forged, old model, or color case hardened frame. Introduced 2001. From Cimarron F.A. Co.
Price: From **$480.70**

CIMARRON MAN WITH NO NAME REVOLVER
Caliber: .45 LC. **Barrel:** 4-3/4" and 5-1/2". **Weight:** 2.66-2.76 lbs. **Grip:** 1 piece walnut with silver rattle snake inlay in both sides. **Features:** Standard blue finish with case hardened pre-war frame. An accurate copy of the gun used by our nameless hero in the classic Western movies "Fist Full Of Dollars" & "For A Few Dollars More".
Price: **$889.71**

CIMARRON MODEL P
Caliber: 32 WCF, 38 WCF, 357 Mag., 44 WCF, 44 Spec., 45 Colt, 45 LC and 45 ACP. **Barrel:** 4.75", 5.5", 7.5". **Weight:** 39 oz. **Length:** 10" overall (4" barrel). **Grips:** Walnut. **Sights:** Blade front, fixed or adjustable rear. **Features:** Uses "old model" black powder frame with "Bullseye" ejector or New Model frame. Imported by Cimarron F.A. Co.
Price: From **$494.09**
Price: Laser Engraved, from **$879.00**
Price: New Sheriff, from **$494.09**

CIMARRON MODEL "P" JR.
Caliber: 32-20, 32 H&R, **Barrel:** 3.5", 4.75", 5.5". **Grips:** Checkered walnut. **Sights:** Blade front. **Features:** Styled after 1873 Colt Peacemaker, except 20 percent smaller. Blue finish with color case-hardened frame; Cowboy action. Introduced 2001. From Cimarron F.A. Co.
Price: **$400.36**

CIMARRON ROOSTER SHOOTER REVOLVER
Caliber: .357, .38 special, .45 Colt, and .44 W.C.F. **Barrel:** 4-3/4". **Weight:** 2.49-2.53 lbs. **Grip:** 1 piece orange finger grooved. **Features:** A replica of John Wayne's Colt® Single Action, used in many of his great Westerns, including his Oscar winning performance in "True Grit", where he brings thecolorful character Rooster Cogburn to life.
Price: **$845.11**

CIMARRON THUNDERER REVOLVER
Caliber: 357 Mag., 44 WCF, 45 Colt, 6-shot. **Barrel:** 3.5", 4.75", with ejector. **Weight:** 38 oz. (3.5" barrel). **Grips:** Smooth or checkered walnut. **Sights:** Blade front, notch rear. **Features:** Thunderer grip. Introduced 1993. Imported by Cimarron F.A. Co.
Price: Stainless **$534.26**

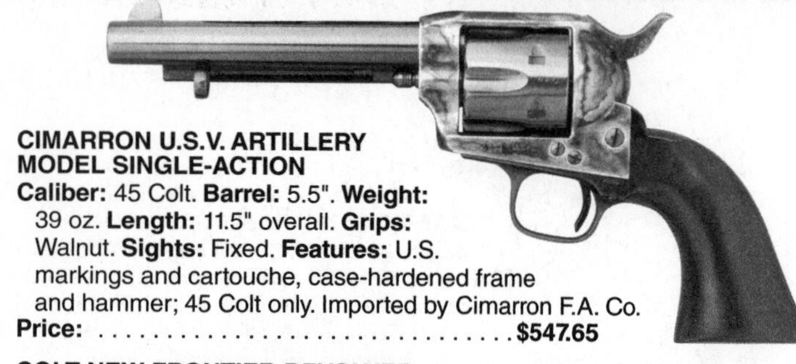

CIMARRON U.S.V. ARTILLERY MODEL SINGLE-ACTION

Caliber: 45 Colt. **Barrel:** 5.5". **Weight:** 39 oz. **Length:** 11.5" overall. **Grips:** Walnut. **Sights:** Fixed. **Features:** U.S. markings and cartouche, case-hardened frame and hammer; 45 Colt only. Imported by Cimarron F.A. Co.

Price: **$547.65**

COLT NEW FRONTIER REVOLVER

Caliber: .44 Special and .45 Colt. **Barrel:** 4-3/4", 5-1/2",and 7-1/2". **Grip:** Walnut. **Features:** The legend of Colt continues in the New Frontier®, Single Action Army. From 1890 to 1898, Colt manufactured a variation of the venerable Single Action Army with a uniquely different profile. The "Flattop Target Model" was fitted with an adjustable leaf rear sight and blade front sights. Colt has taken this concept several steps further to bring shooters a reintroduction of a Colt classic. The New Frontier has that sleek flattop design with an adjustable rear sight for windage and elevation and a target ready ramp style front sight. The guns are meticulously finished in Colt Royal Blue on both the barrel and cylinder, with a case colored frame.

Price: **$1455.00**

COLT SINGLE-ACTION ARMY REVOLVER

Caliber: 357 Mag., 45 Colt, 6-shot. **Barrel:** 4.75", 5.5", 7.5". **Weight:** 40 oz. (4.75" barrel). **Length:** 10.25" overall (4.75" barrel). **Grips:** Black Eagle composite. **Sights:** Blade front, notch rear. **Features:** Available in full nickel finish with nickel grip medallions, or Royal Blue with color case-hardened frame. Reintroduced 1992. Sheriff's Model and Frontier Six introduced 2008, available in nickel in 2010.

Price: P1540, 32-20, 4.75" barrel, color case-hardened/blued finish **$1,315.00**
Price: P1656, 357 Mag., 5.5" barrel, nickel finish **$1,518.00**
Price: P1876, 45 LC, 7.5" barrel, nickel finish **$1,518.00**
Price: P2830S SAA Sheriff's, 3" barrel, 45 LC (2008). **$1,315.00**
Price: P2950FSS Frontier Six Shooter, 5.5" barrel, 44-40 (2008) **$1,350.00**

EAA BOUNTY HUNTER SA REVOLVERS

Caliber: 22 LR/22 WMR, 357 Mag., 44 Mag., 45 Colt, 6-shot. **Barrel:** 4.5", 7.5". **Weight:** 2.5 lbs. Length: 11" overall (4-5/8" barrel). **Grips:** Smooth walnut. **Sights:** Blade front, grooved topstrap rear. **Features:** Transfer bar safety; 3-position hammer; hammer forged barrel. Introduced 1992. Imported by European American Armory.

Price: Blue or case-hardened, from **$392.00**
Price: Nickel **$432.00**
Price: 22 LR/22 WMR, blue **$292.00**
Price: As above, nickel **$325.00**

EMF MODEL 1873 FRONTIER MARSHAL

Caliber: 357 Mag., 45 Colt. **Barrel:** 4.75", 5-1/2", 7.5". **Weight:** 39 oz. **Length:** 10.5" overall. **Grips:** One-piece walnut. **Sights:** Blade front, notch rear. Features: Bright brass trigger guard and backstrap, color case-hardened frame, blued barrel and cylinder. Introduced 1998. Imported from Italy.

Price: **$485.00**

EMF HARTFORD SINGLE-ACTION REVOLVERS

Caliber: 357 Mag., 32-20, 38-40, 44-40, 44 Spec., 45 Colt. **Barrel:** 4.75", 5.5", 7.5". **Weight:** 45 oz. **Length:** 13" overall (7.5" barrel). **Grips:** Smooth walnut. **Sights:** Blade front, fixed rear. **Features:** Identical to the original Colts. All major parts serial numbered using original Colt-style lettering, numbering. Bullseye ejector head and color case-hardening on old model frame and hammer. Introduced 1990. Imported by E.M.F. Co.

Price: Old Model **$489.90**
Price: Case-hardened New Model frame **$489.90**

EMF GREAT WESTERN II EXPRESS SINGLE-ACTION REVOLVER

Same as the regular model except uses grip of the Colt Lightning revolver. Barrel lengths of 4.75". Introduced 2006. Imported by E.M.F. Co.

Price: Stainless, Ultra Ivory grips **$715.00**
Price: Walnut grips **$690.00**

EMF 1875 OUTLAW REVOLVER

Caliber: 357 Mag., 44-40, 45 Colt. **Barrel:** 7.5", 9.5". **Weight:** 46 oz. **Length:** 13.5" overall. **Grips:** Smooth walnut. **Sights:** Blade front, fixed groove rear. **Features:** Authentic copy of 1875 Remington with firing pin in hammer; color case-hardened frame, blue cylinder, barrel, steel backstrap and trigger guard. Also available in nickel, factory engraved. Imported by E.M.F. Co.

Price: All calibers **$479.90**
Price: Laser Engraved **$684.90**

EMF 1890 POLICE REVOLVER

Similar to the 1875 Outlaw except has 5.5" barrel, weighs 40 oz., with 12.5" overall length. Has lanyard ring in butt. No web under barrel. Calibers: 45 Colt. Imported by E.M.F. Co.

Price: **$489.90**

EMF 1873 GREAT WESTERN II

Caliber: .357, 45 LC, 44/40. **Barrel:** 4 3/4", 5.5", 7.5". **Weight:** 36 oz. **Length:** 11" (5.5"). **Grips:** Walnut. **Sights:** Blade front, notch rear. **Features:** Authentic reproduction of the original 2nd generation Colt single-action revolver. Standard and bone case hardening. Coil hammer spring. Hammer-forged barrel.

Price: 1873 Californian **$520.00**
Price: 1873 Custom series, bone or nickel, ivory-like grips . . **$689.90**
Price: 1873 Stainless steel, ivory-like grips **$589.90**

FREEDOM ARMS MODEL 83 PREMIER GRADE REVOLVER

Caliber: 357 Mag., 41 Mag., 44 Mag., 454 Casull, 475 Linebaugh, 500 Wyo. Exp., 5-shot. **Barrel:** 4.75", 6", 7.5", 9" (357 Mag. only), 10" (except 357 Mag. and 500 Wyo. Exp. **Weight:** 53 oz. (7.5" bbl. In 454 Casull). **Length:** 13" (7.5" bbl.). **Grips:** Impregnated hardwood. **Sights:** Adjustable rear with

Prices given are believed to be accurate at time of publication however, many factors affect retail pricing so exact prices are not possible.

replaceable front sight. Fixed rear notch and front blade. **Features:** Stainless steel construction with brushed finish; manual sliding safety bar. Micarta grips optional. 500 Wyo. Exp. Introduced 2006. Lifetime warranty. Made in U.S.A. by Freedom Arms, Inc.

Price: From **$1,870.00**

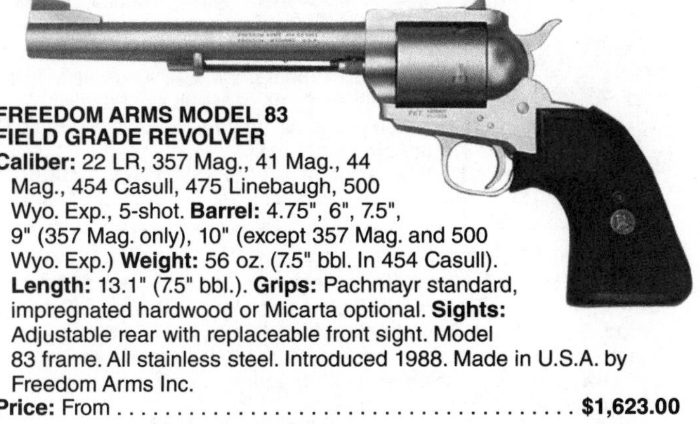

FREEDOM ARMS MODEL 83 FIELD GRADE REVOLVER

Caliber: 22 LR, 357 Mag., 41 Mag., 44 Mag., 454 Casull, 475 Linebaugh, 500 Wyo. Exp., 5-shot. **Barrel:** 4.75", 6", 7.5", 9" (357 Mag. only), 10" (except 357 Mag. and 500 Wyo. Exp.) **Weight:** 56 oz. (7.5" bbl. In 454 Casull). **Length:** 13.1" (7.5" bbl.). **Grips:** Pachmayr standard, impregnated hardwood or Micarta optional. **Sights:** Adjustable rear with replaceable front sight. Model 83 frame. All stainless steel. Introduced 1988. Made in U.S.A. by Freedom Arms Inc.

Price: From **$1,623.00**

FREEDOM ARMS MODEL 97 PREMIER GRADE REVOLVER

Caliber: 17 HMR, 22 LR, 32 H&R, 357 Mag., 6-shot; 41 Mag., 44 Special, 45 Colt, 5-shot. **Barrel:** 4.25", 5.5", 7.5", 10" (17 HMR, 22 LR & 32 H&R). **Weight:** 40 oz. (5.5" 357 Mag.). **Length:** 10.75" (5.5" bbl.). **Grips:** Impregnated hardwood; Micarta optional. **Sights:** Adjustable rear, replaceable blade front. Fixed rear notch and front blade. **Features:** Stainless steel construction, brushed finish, automatic transfer bar safety system. Introduced in 1997. Lifetime warranty. Made in U.S.A. by Freedom Arms.

Price: From **$1,891.00**

HERITAGE ROUGH RIDER REVOLVER

Caliber: 17 HMR, 17 LR, 32 H&R, 32 S&W, 32 S&W Long, 357 Mag, 44-40, 45 LC, 22 LR, 22 LR/22 WMR combo, 6-shot. **Barrel:** 2.75", 3.5", 4.75", 5.5", 6.5", 7.5", 9". **Weight:** 31 to 38 oz. **Length:** NA. **Grips:** Exotic cocobolo laminated wood or mother-of-pearl; bird's-head models offered. **Sights:** Blade front, fixed rear. Adjustable sight on 4", 6" and 9" models. **Features:** Hammer block safety. Transfer bar with Big Bores. High polish blue, black satin, silver satin, case-hardened and stainless finish. Introduced 1993. Made in U.S.A. by Heritage Mfg., Inc.

Price: From **$169.95**

LEGACY SPORTS PUMA M-1873 REVOLVER

Caliber: .22 LR / .22 Mag. **Barrel:** 4.75", 5.5", and 7.5". **Weight:** 2.2 lbs. - 2.4 lbs. **Grips:** Wood or plastic. **Features:** With the frame size and weight of a Single Action Army revolver, the M-1873 makes a great practice gun for Cowboy Action or an ideal carry gun for camping, hiking or fishing. The M-1873 loads from a side gate and at the half cock position just like a centerfire "Peacemaker," but is chambered for .22 LR or .22 magnum rounds. The hammer is made to traditional SAA appearance and feel. A key-operated, hammer block safety is standard on the left side of the recoil shield. The M-1873 is offered in matte black or antiqued finish. Construction is of alloy and steel.

Price: . . . . **$178.00 to $320.00**

MAGNUM RESEARCH BFR SINGLE ACTION REVOLVER

Caliber: .45/70, .480 Ruger/.475 Linebaugh, .450 Marlin, .500 S&W, .50AE, .444 Marlin, .30/30 Winchester, .45 Long Colt/.410 (not for sale in CA), and the new .460 S&W Magnum - as well as .454 Casull. **Barrel:** 6.5", 7.5", and 10". **Weight:** 3.6 lbs. - 5.3 lbs. **Grips:** Black rubber. **Sights:** Rear sights are the same configuration as the Ruger revolvers. Many after-market rear sights will fit the BFR. Front sights are machined by Magnum in four heights and anodized flat black. The four heights accommodate all shooting styles, barrel lengths and calibers. All sights are interchangeable with each BFR's. **Features:** Crafted in the U.S.A., the BFR single action 5-shot stainless steel revolver frames are CNC machined inside and out from a "pre-heat treated" investment casting. This is done to prevent warping and dimensional changes or shifting that occurs during the heat treat process. The result is a dimensionally perfect-machined frame. Magnum Research designed the frame with large calibers and large recoil in mind, built to close tolerances to handle the pressure of true big-bore calibers. The BFR is equiped with Transfer Bar. This is a safety feature that allows the gun to be carried safely with all five chambers loaded. The transfer bar allows the revolver to fire ONLY after the hammer has been fully cocked and trigger pulled. If the revolver is dropped or the hammer slips while in the process of cocking it the gun will not accidentally discharge.

Price: **$1050.00**

NAVY ARMS BISLEY MODEL SINGLE-ACTION REVOLVER

Caliber: 44-40 or 45 Colt, 6-shot cylinder. **Barrel:** 4.75", 5.5", 7.5". **Weight:** 40 oz. **Length:** 12.5" overall (7.5" barrel). **Grips:** Smooth walnut. **Sights:** Blade front, notch rear. **Features:** Replica of Colt's Bisley Model. Polished blue finish, color case-hardened frame. Introduced 1997. Imported by Navy Arms.

Price: **$503.00**

NAVY ARMS 1873 GUNFIGHTER SINGLE-ACTION REVOLVER

Caliber: 357 Mag., 44-40, 45 Colt, 6-shot cylinder. **Barrel:** 4.75", 5.5", 7.5". **Weight:** 37 oz. **Length:** 10.25" overall (4.75" barrel). **Grips:** Checkered black polymer. **Sights:** Blade front, notch rear. **Features:** Blued with color case-hardened receiver, trigger and hammer; German Silver backstrap and triggerguard. American made Wolff trigger and mainsprings installed. Introduced 2005. Imported by Navy Arms.

Price: **$545.00**

NAVY ARMS 1875 SCHOFIELD REVOLVER

Caliber: 44-40, 45 Colt, 6-shot cylinder. **Barrel:** 3.5", 5", 7". **Weight:** 39 oz. **Length:** 10.75" overall (5" barrel). **Grips:** Smooth walnut. **Sights:** Blade front, notch rear. **Features:** Replica of Smith &

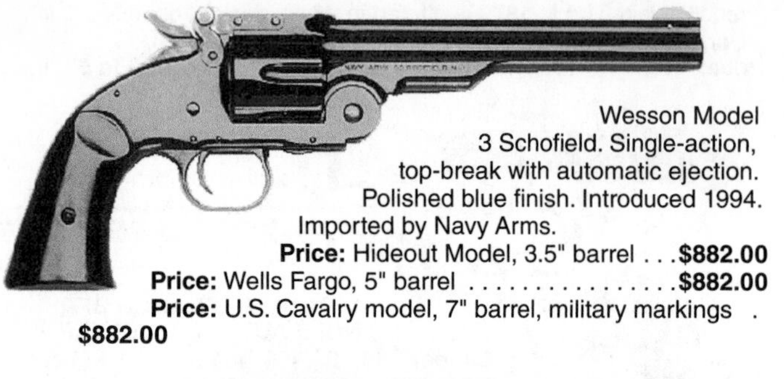

Wesson Model 3 Schofield. Single-action, top-break with automatic ejection. Polished blue finish. Introduced 1994. Imported by Navy Arms.
Price: Hideout Model, 3.5" barrel . . . **$882.00**
Price: Wells Fargo, 5" barrel **$882.00**
Price: U.S. Cavalry model, 7" barrel, military markings . **$882.00**

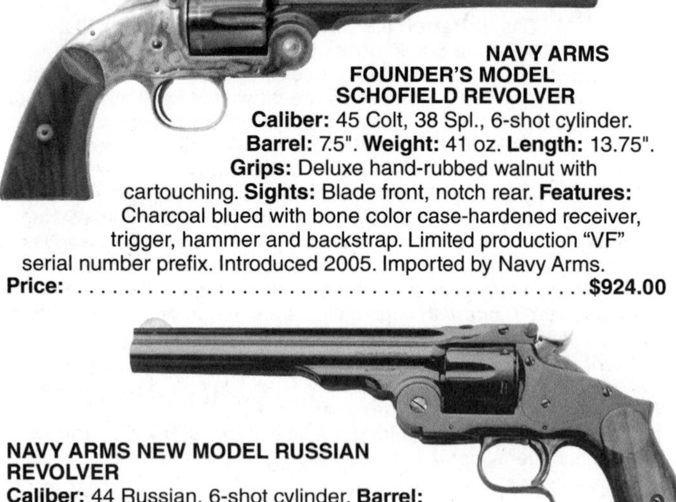

NAVY ARMS FOUNDER'S MODEL SCHOFIELD REVOLVER
Caliber: 45 Colt, 38 Spl., 6-shot cylinder. **Barrel:** 7.5". **Weight:** 41 oz. **Length:** 13.75". **Grips:** Deluxe hand-rubbed walnut with cartouching. **Sights:** Blade front, notch rear. **Features:** Charcoal blued with bone color case-hardened receiver, trigger, hammer and backstrap. Limited production "VF" serial number prefix. Introduced 2005. Imported by Navy Arms.
Price: **$924.00**

NAVY ARMS NEW MODEL RUSSIAN REVOLVER
Caliber: 44 Russian, 6-shot cylinder. **Barrel:** 6.5". **Weight:** 40 oz. **Length:** 12" overall. **Grips:** Smooth walnut. **Sights:** Blade front, notch rear. **Features:** Replica of the S&W Model 3 Russian Third Model revolver. Spur trigger guard, polished blue finish. Introduced 1999. Imported by Navy Arms.
Price: **$924.00**

NAVY ARMS SCOUT SMALL FRAME SINGLE-ACTION REVOLVER
Caliber: 38 Spec., 6-shot cylinder. **Barrel:** 4.75", 5.5". **Weight:** 37 oz. **Length:** 10.75" overall (5.5" barrel). **Grips:** Checkered black polymer. **Sights:** Blade front, notch rear. **Features:** Blued with color case-hardened receiver, trigger and hammer; German silver backstrap and triggerguard. Introduced 2005. Imported by Navy Arms.
Price: **$545.00**

NORTH AMERICAN ARMS MINI REVOLVERS
Caliber: 22 Short, 22 LR, 22 WMR, 5-shot. **Barrel:** 1-1/8", 1-5/8". **Weight:** 4 to 6.6 oz. **Length:** 3-5/8" to 6-1/8" overall. **Grips:** Laminated wood. **Sights:** Blade front, notch fixed rear. **Features:** All stainless steel construction. Polished satin and matte finish. Engraved models available. From North American Arms.
Price: 22 Short, 22 LR **$229.00**

NORTH AMERICAN ARMS MINI-MASTER
Caliber: 22 LR, 22 WMR, 5-shot cylinder. **Barrel:** 4". **Weight:** 10.7 oz. **Length:** 7.75" overall. **Grips:** Checkered hard black rubber. **Sights:** Blade front, white outline rear adjustable for elevation, or fixed. **Features:** Heavy vented barrel; full-size grips. Non-fluted cylinder. Introduced 1989.
Price: Fixed sight **$284.00**
Price: Adjustable sight **$314.00**

NORTH AMERICAN ARMS BLACK WIDOW REVOLVER
Similar to Mini-Master, 2" heavy vent barrel. Built on 22 WMR frame. Non-fluted cylinder, black rubber grips. Available with Millett Low Profile fixed sights or Millett sight adjustable for elevation only. Overall length 5-7/8", weighs 8.8 oz. From North American Arms.
Price: Adjustable sight, 22 LR or 22 WMR **$299.00**
Price: Fixed sight, 22 LR or 22 WMR **$269.00**

NORTH AMERICAN ARMS "THE EARL" SINGLE-ACTION REVOLVER
Caliber: 22 Magnum with 22 LR accessory cylinder, 5-shot cylinder. **Barrel:** 4" octagonal. **Weight:** 6.8 oz. **Length:** 7-3/4" overall. **Grips:** Wood. **Sights:** Barleycorn front and fixed notch rear. **Features:** Single-action mini-revolver patterned after 1858-style Remington percussion revolver. Includes a spur trigger and a faux loading lever that serves as cylinder pin release.
Price: . . . . **$289.00** (22 Magnum only); **$324.00** (convertible)

RUGER NEW MODEL SINGLE SIX & NEW MODEL .32 H&R SINGLE SIX REVOLVERS
Caliber: 17 HMR, 22 LR, 22 Mag. **Barrel:** 4-5/8", 5.5", 6.5", 7.5", 9.5". 6-shot. **Grips:** Rosewood, black laminate. **Sights:** Adjustable or fixed. **Features:** Blued or stainless metalwork, short grips available, convertible models available. Introduced 2003 in 17 HMR.
Price: 17 HMR (blued) **$519.00**
Price: 22 LR/22 Mag., from **$506.00**

RUGER SINGLE-TEN
Caliber: .22 LR, 10-shot cylinder. **Barrel:** 5.5". **Weight:** 38 oz. Length: 11". **Grips:** Hardwood Gunfighter. **Sights:** Williams adjustable fiber optic. **Finish:** Stainless steel.
Price: **$629**

RUGER NEW MODEL BLACKHAWK/BLACKHAWK CONVERTIBLE
Caliber: 30 Carbine, 327 Federal, 357 Mag./38 Spec., 41 Mag., 44 Special, 45 Colt, 6-shot. **Barrel:** 4-5/8", 5.5", 6.5", 7.5" (30 carbine and 45 Colt). **Weight:** 36 to 45 oz. Lengths: 10-3/8" to 13.5". **Grips:** Rosewood or black checkered. **Sights:** 1/8" ramp front, micro-click rear adjustable for windage and elevation. **Features:** Rosewood grips, Ruger transfer bar safety system, independent firing pin, hardened chrome-moly steel frame, music wire springs through-out. Case and lock included. Convertibles come with extra cylinder.
Price: 30 Carbine, 7.5" (BN31, blued) **$541.00**
Price: 357 Mag. (blued or satin stainless), from **$541.00**
Price: 41 Mag. (blued) **$541.00**
Price: 45 Colt (blued or satin stainless), from **$541.00**
Price: 357 Mag./9mm Para. Convertible (BN34XL, BN36XL) . **$617.00**
Price: 45 Colt/45 ACP Convertible (BN44X, BN455XL) **$617.00**

RUGER BISLEY SINGLE-ACTION REVOLVER
Similar to standard Blackhawk, hammer is lower with smoothly curved, deeply checkered wide spur. The trigger is strongly curved with wide smooth surface. Longer grip frame. Adjustable rear sight, ramp-style front. Unfluted cylinder and roll engraving, adjustable sights. Chambered for 44 Mag.

Prices given are believed to be accurate at time of publication however, many factors affect retail pricing so exact prices are not possible.

and 45 Colt; 7.5" barrel; overall length 13.5"; weighs 48-51 oz. Plastic lockable case. Orig. fluted cylinder introduced 1985; discontinued 1991. Unfluted cylinder introduced 1986.

Price: RB-44W (44 Mag), RB45W (45 Colt) **$683.00**

RUGER NEW MODEL SUPER BLACKHAWK

Caliber: 44 Mag., 6-shot. Also fires 44 Spec. **Barrel:** 4-5/8", 5.5", 7.5", 10.5" bull. **Weight:** 45-55 oz. **Length:** 10.5" to 16.5" overall. **Grips:** Rosewood. **Sights:** 1/8" ramp front, micro-click rear adjustable for windage and elevation. **Features:** Ruger transfer bar safety system, fluted or unfluted cylinder, steel grip and cylinder frame, round or square back trigger guard, wide serrated trigger, wide spur hammer. With case and lock.

Price: Blue, 4-5/8", 5.5", 7.5" (S-458N, S-45N, S-47N) **$650.00**

Price: Blue, 10.5" bull barrel (S-411N) **$667.00**

Price: Stainless, 4-5/8", 5.5", 7.5" (KS-458N, KS-45N, KS-47N) **$667.00**

Price: Stainless, 10.5" bull barrel (KS-411N) **$694.00**

Price: Super Blackhawk 50th Anniversary: Gold highlights, ornamentation; commemorates 50-year anniversary of Super Blackhawk **$729.00**

RUGER NEW MODEL SUPER BLACKHAWK HUNTER

Caliber: 44 Mag., 6-shot. **Barrel:** 7.5", full-length solid rib, unfluted cylinder. **Weight:** 52 oz. **Length:** 13-5/8". **Grips:** Black laminated wood. **Sights:** Adjustable rear, replaceable front blade. **Features:** Reintroduced Ultimate SA revolver. Includes instruction manual, high-impact case, set 1" medium scope rings, gun lock, ejector rod as standard.

Price: Hunter model, satin stainless, 7.5" (KS-47NHNN) **$781.00**

Price: Hunter model, Bisley frame, satin stainless 7.5" (KS-47NHB) **$781.00**

RUGER NEW VAQUERO SINGLE-ACTION REVOLVER

Caliber: 357 Mag., 45 Colt, 6-shot. **Barrel:** 4-5/8", 5.5", 7.5". **Weight:** 39-45 oz. **Length:** 10.5" overall (4-5/8" barrel). **Grips:** Rubber with Ruger medallion. **Sights:** Fixed blade front, fixed notch rear. **Features:** Transfer bar safety system and loading gate interlock. Blued model color case-hardened finish on frame, rest polished and blued. Engraved model available. Gloss stainless. Introduced 2005.

Price: 357 Mag., blued or stainless **$719.00**

Price: 45 Colt, blued or stainless **$719.00**

RUGER NEW MODEL BISLEY VAQUERO

Similar to New Vaquero but with Bisley-style hammer and grip frame. Chambered in 357 and 45 Colt. Features include a 5.5" barrel, simulated ivory grips, fixed sights, six-shot cylinder. Overall length is 11.12", weighs 45 oz.

Price: **$799.00**

RUGER NEW BEARCAT SINGLE-ACTION

Caliber: 22 LR, 6-shot. **Barrel:** 4". **Weight:** 24 oz. **Length:** 9" overall.

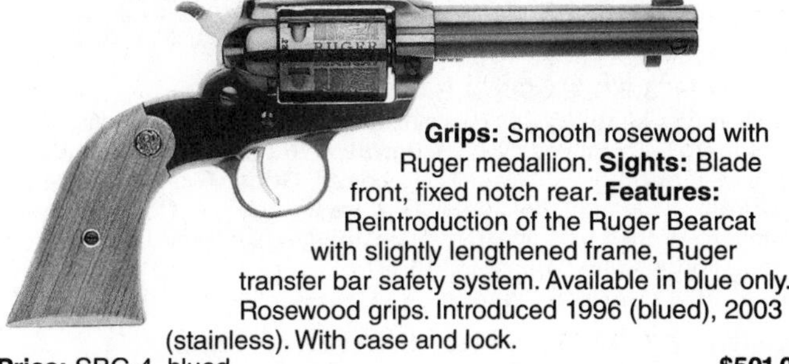

Grips: Smooth rosewood with Ruger medallion. **Sights:** Blade front, fixed notch rear. **Features:** Reintroduction of the Ruger Bearcat with slightly lengthened frame, Ruger transfer bar safety system. Available in blue only. Rosewood grips. Introduced 1996 (blued), 2003 (stainless). With case and lock.

Price: SBC-4, blued **$501.00**

Price: KSBC-4, satin stainless **$540.00**

STI TEXICAN SINGLE-ACTION REVOLVER

Caliber: 45 Colt, 6-shot. **Barrel:** 5.5", 4140 chrome-moly steel by Green Mountain Barrels. 1:16 twist, air gauged to .0002". Chamber to bore alignment less than .001". Forcing cone angle, 3 degrees. **Weight:** 36 oz. **Length:** 11". **Grips:** "No crack" polymer. **Sights:** Blade front, fixed notch rear. **Features:** Parts made by ultra-high speed or electron discharge machined processes from chrome-moly steel forgings or bar stock. Competition sights, springs, triggers and hammers. Frames, loading gates, and hammers are color case hardened by Turnbull Restoration. Frame, back strap, loading gate, trigger guard, cylinders made of 4140 re-sulphurized Maxell 3.5 steel. Hammer firing pin (no transfer bar). S.A.S.S. approved. Introduced 2008. Made in U.S.A. by STI International.

Price: 5.5" barrel **$1,299.99**

UBERTI 1851-1860 CONVERSION REVOLVERS

Caliber: 38 Spec., 45 Colt, 6-shot engraved cylinder. **Barrel:** 4.75", 5.5", 7.5", 8" **Weight:** 2.6 lbs. (5.5" bbl.). **Length:** 13" overall (5.5" bbl.). **Grips:** Walnut. **Features:** Brass backstrap, trigger guard; color case-hardened frame, blued barrel, cylinder. Introduced 2007. Imported from Italy by Stoeger Industries.

Price: 1851 Navy **$519.00**

Price: 1860 Army **$549.00**

UBERTI 1871-1872 OPEN TOP REVOLVERS

Caliber: 38 Spec., 45 Colt, 6-shot engraved cylinder. **Barrel:** 4.75", 5.5", 7.5". **Weight:** 2.6 lbs. (5.5" bbl.). **Length:** 13" overall (5.5" bbl.). **Grips:** Walnut. **Features:** Blued backstrap, trigger guard; color case-hardened frame, blued barrel, cylinder. Introduced 2007. Imported from Italy by Stoeger Industries.

Price: **$499.00**

UBERTI 1873 CATTLEMAN SINGLE-ACTION

Caliber: 45 Colt; 6-shot fluted cylinder. **Barrel:** 4.75", 5.5", 7.5". **Weight:** 2.3 lbs. (5.5" bbl.). **Length:** 11" overall (5.5" bbl.). **Grips:** Styles: Frisco (pearl styled); Desperado (buffalo horn styled); Chisholm (checkered walnut); Gunfighter (black checkered), Cody (ivory styled), one-piece walnut. **Sights:** Blade front, groove rear. **Features:** Steel or brass backstrap, trigger guard; color case-hardened frame, blued barrel, cylinder. NM designates New Model plunger style frame; OM designates Old Model screw cylinder pin retainer. Imported from Italy by Stoeger Industries.

Price: 1873 Cattleman Frisco **$789.00**

Price: 1873 Cattleman Desperado (2006) **$789.00**

Price: 1873 Cattleman Chisholm (2006) **$539.00**

Price: 1873 Cattleman NM, blued 4.75" barrel **$479.00**

Price: 1873 Cattleman NM, Nickel finish, 7.5" barrel **$609.00**

Price: 1873 Cattleman Cody **$789.00**

UBERTI 1873 CATTLEMAN BIRD'S HEAD SINGLE ACTION

Caliber: 357 Mag., 45 Colt; 6-shot fluted cylinder **Barrel:** 3.5", 4", 4.75", 5.5". **Weight:** 2.3 lbs. (5.5" bbl.). **Length:** 10.9" overall (5.5" bbl.). **Grips:** One-piece walnut. **Sights:** Blade front, groove rear. **Features:** Steel or brass backstrap, trigger guard; color case-

hardened frame, blued barrel, cylinder. Imported from Italy by Stoeger Industries.
Price: 1873 Cattleman Bird's Head OM 3.5" barrel **$539.00**

UBERTI 1873 BISLEY SINGLE-ACTION REVOLVER
Caliber: 357 Mag., 45 Colt (Bisley); 22 LR and 38 Spec. (Stallion), both with 6-shot fluted cylinder. **Barrel:** 4.75", 5.5", 7.5". **Weight:** 2 to 2.5 lbs. **Length:** 12.7" overall (7.5" barrel). **Grips:** Two-piece walnut. **Sights:** Blade front, notch rear. **Features:** Replica of Colt's Bisley Model. Polished blue finish, color case-hardened frame. Introduced 1997. Imported by Stoeger Industries.
Price: 1873 Bisley, 7.5" barrel **$569.00**

UBERTI 1873 BUNTLINE AND REVOLVER CARBINE SINGLE-ACTION
Caliber: 357 Mag., 44-40, 45 Colt; 6-shot fluted cylinder **Barrel:** 18". **Length:** 22.9" to 34". **Grips:** Walnut pistol grip or rifle stock. **Sights:** Fixed or adjustable. **Features:** Imported from Italy by Stoeger Industries.
Price: 1873 Revolver Carbine, 18" barrel, 34" OAL **$729.00**
Price: 1873 Catttleman Buntline Target, 18" barrel, 22.9" OAL **$639.00**

UBERTI OUTLAW, FRONTIER, AND POLICE REVOLVERS
Caliber: 45 Colt, 6-shot fluted cylinder. **Barrel:** 5.5", 7.5". **Weight:** 2.5 to 2.8 lbs. **Length:** 10.8" to 13.6" overall. **Grips:** Two-piece smooth walnut. **Sights:** Blade front, notch rear. **Features:** Cartridge version of 1858 Remington percussion revolver. Nickel and blued finishes. Imported by Stoeger Industries.
Price: 1875 Outlaw nickel finish **$629.00**
Price: 1875 Frontier, blued finish **$539.00**
Price: 1890 Police, blued finish **$549.00**

UBERTI 1870 SCHOFIELD-STYLE TOP BREAK REVOLVER
Caliber: 38, 44 Russian, 44-40, 45 Colt, 6-shot cylinder. **Barrel:** 3.5", 5", 7". **Weight:** 2.4 lbs. (5" barrel) **Length:** 10.8" overall (5" barrel). **Grips:** Two-piece smooth walnut or pearl. **Sights:** Blade front, notch rear. **Features:** Replica of Smith & Wesson Model 3 Schofield. Single-action, top break with automatic ejection. Polished blue finish (first model). Introduced 1994. Imported by Stoeger Industries.
Price: No. 3-2nd Model, nickel finish **$1,369.00**

U.S. FIRE ARMS SINGLE-ACTION REVOLVER
Caliber: 45 Colt (standard); 32 WCF, 38 WCF, 38 Spec., 44 WCF, 44 Special, 6-shot cylinder. **Barrel:** 4.75", 5.5", 7.5". **Weight:** 37 oz. **Length:** NA. **Grips:** Hard rubber. **Sights:** Blade front, notch rear. **Features:** Recreation of original guns; 3" and 4" have no ejector. Available with all-blue, blue with color case-hardening, or full nickel-plate finish. Other models include Custer Battlefield Gun ($1,625, 7.5" barrel), Flattop Target ($1,625), Sheriff's Model ($875, with barrel lengths starting at 2"), Snubnose ($1,475, barrel lengths 2", 3", 4"), Omni-Potent Six-Shooter and Omni-Target Six-Shooter (from $1,625), Bisley ($1,350, introduced 2006). Made in U.S.A. by United States Fire Arms Mfg. Co.
Price: Blue/cased-colors **$1,150.00**
Price: Nickel **$1,220.00**

U.S. FIRE ARMS U.S. PRE-WAR
Caliber: 45 Colt (standard); 32 WCF, 38 WCF, 38 Spec., 44 WCF, 44 Special. **Barrel:** 4.75", 5.5", 7.5". **Grips:** Hard rubber. **Features:** Armory bone case/Armory blue finish standard, cross-pin or black powder frame. Introduced 2002. Made in U.S.A. by United States Firearms Mfg. Co.
Price: **$1,495.00**

BOND ARMS TEXAS DEFENDER DERRINGER
Caliber: From 22 LR to 45 LC/410 shotshells. **Barrel:** 3". **Weight:** 20 oz. **Length:** 5". **Grips:** Rosewood. **Sights:** Blade front, fixed rear. **Features:** Interchangeable barrels, stainless steel firing pins, cross-bolt safety, automatic extractor for rimmed calibers. Stainless steel construction, brushed finish. Right or left hand.
Price: **$399.00**
Price: Interchangeable barrels, 22 LR thru 45 LC, 3" **$139.00**
Price: Interchangeable barrels, 45 LC, 3.5" . . . . . **$159.00 to $189.00**

BOND ARMS RANGER
Caliber: 45 LC/.410 shotshells. **Barrel:** 4.25". **Weight:** 23.5 oz. **Length:** 6.25". **Features:** Similar to Snake Slayer except no trigger guard. Intr. 2008. From Bond Arms.
Price: **$649.00**

BOND ARMS CENTURY 2000 DEFENDER
Caliber: 45 LC/.410 shotshells. **Barrel:** 3.5". **Weight:** 21 oz. **Length:** 5.5". **Features:** Similar to Defender series.
Price: **$420.00**

BOND ARMS COWBOY DEFENDER
Caliber: From 22 LR to 45 LC/.410 shotshells. **Barrel:** 3". **Weight:** 19 oz. **Length:** 5.5". **Features:** Similar to Defender series. No trigger guard.
Price: **$399.00**

BOND ARMS SNAKE SLAYER
Caliber: 45 LC/.410 shotshell (2.5" or 3"). **Barrel:** 3.5". **Weight:** 21 oz. **Length:** 5.5". **Grips:** Extended rosewood. **Sights:** Blade front, fixed rear. **Features:** Single-action; interchangeable barrels; stainless steel firing pin. Introduced 2005.
Price: **$469.00**

BOND ARMS SNAKE SLAYER IV
Caliber: 45 LC/410 shotshell (2.5" or 3"). **Barrel:** 4.25". **Weight:** 22 oz. **Length:** 6.25". **Grips:** Extended rosewood. **Sights:** Blade front, fixed rear. **Features:** Single-action; interchangeable barrels; stainless steel firing pin. Introduced 2006.
Price: **$499.00**

CHARTER ARMS DIXIE DERRINGERS
Caliber: 22 LR, 22 WMR. **Barrel:** 1.125". **Weight:** 6 oz. **Length:** 4" overall. **Grips:** Black polymer **Sights:** Blade front, fixed notch rear. **Features:** Stainless finish. Introduced 2006. Made in U.S.A. by Charter Arms.
Price: **$215.00**

COBRA BIG BORE DERRINGERS
Caliber: 22 WMR, 32 H&R Mag., 38 Spec., 9mm Para., 380 ACP. **Barrel:** 2.75". **Weight:** 14 oz. **Length:** 4.65" overall. **Grips:** Textured black or white synthetic or laminated rosewood. **Sights:** Blade front, fixed notch rear. **Features:** Alloy frame, steel-lined barrels, steel breech block. Plunger-type safety with integral hammer block. Black, chrome or satin finish. Introduced 2002. Made in U.S.A. by Cobra Enterprises of Utah, Inc.
Price: **$165.00**

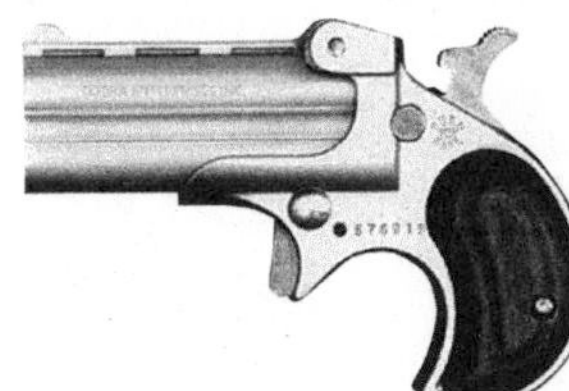

COBRA STANDARD SERIES DERRINGERS
Caliber: 22 LR, 22 WMR, 25 ACP, 32 ACP. **Barrel:** 2.4". **Weight:** 9.5 oz. Length: 4" overall. **Grips:** Laminated wood or pearl. **Sights:** Blade front, fixed notch rear. **Features:** Choice of black powder coat, satin nickel or chrome finish. Introduced 2002. Made in U.S.A. by Cobra Enterprises of Utah, Inc.
Price: **$145.00**

COBRA LONG-BORE DERRINGERS
Caliber: 22 WMR, 38 Spec., 9mm Para. **Barrel:** 3.5". **Weight:** 16 oz. **Length:** 5.4" overall. **Grips:** Black or white synthetic or rosewood. **Sights:** Fixed. **Features:** Chrome, satin nickel, or black Teflon finish. Introduced 2002. Made in U.S.A. by Cobra Enterprises of Utah, Inc.
Price: **$165.00**

COBRA TITAN .45 LC/.410 DERRINGER
Caliber: .45 LC, .410 or 9mm, 2 round capacity. **Barrel:** 3-1/2". **Weight:** 16.4 oz. **Grip:** Rosewood. **Features:** The Titan is a powerhouse derringer designed to shoot a .45 Long Colt or the wide range of personal protection .410 shells with additional calibers to follow soon. Standard finshes include: satin stainless, black stainless, and brushed stainless. Made in U.S.A. by Cobra Enterprises of Utah, Inc.
Price: **$419.00**

COMANCHE SUPER SINGLE-SHOT PISTOL
Caliber: 45 LC, .410 **Barrel:** 10". **Sights:** Adjustable. **Features:** Blue finish, not available for sale in CA, MA. Distributed by SGS Importers International, Inc.
Price: **$200.00**

MAXIMUM SINGLE-SHOT PISTOL
Caliber: 22 LR, 22 Hornet, 22 BR, 22 PPC, 223 Rem., 22-250, 6mm BR, 6mm PPC, 243, 250 Savage, 6.5mm-35M, 270 MAX, 270 Win., 7mm TCU, 7mm BR, 7mm-35, 7mm INT-R, 7mm-08, 7mm Rocket, 7mm Super-Mag., 30 Herrett, 30 Carbine, 30-30, 308 Win., 30x39, 32-20, 350 Rem. Mag., 357 Mag., 357 Maximum, 358 Win., 375 H&H, 44 Mag., 454 Casull. **Barrel:** 8.75", 10.5", 14". **Weight:** 61 oz. (10.5" bbl.); 78 oz. (14" bbl.). **Length:** 15", 18.5" overall (with 10.5" and 14" bbl.,

respectively). **Grips:** Smooth walnut stocks and forend. Also available with 17" finger groove grip. **Sights:** Ramp front, fully adjustable open rear. **Features:** Falling block action; drilled and tapped for M.O.A. scope mounts; integral grip frame/receiver; adjustable trigger; Douglas barrel (interchangeable). Introduced 1983. Made in U.S.A. by M.O.A. Corp.

Price: Stainless receiver, blue barrel **$839.00**
Price: Stainless receiver, stainless barrel **$937.00**

PUMA BOUNTY HUNTER RIFLE

Caliber: .44/40, .44 Mag. and .45 Colt, 6-shot magazine capacity. **Barrel:** 12". **Weight:** 4.5 lbs. **Length:** 24". **Stock:** Walnut. **Sights:** Fixed sights. **Features:** A piece of 1950's TV nostalgia, the Bounty Hunter is a reproduction of the gun carried by Western character Josh Randall in the series "Wanted: Dead or Alive". The Bounty Hunter is based on a Model 92 rifle, but is considered by Federal Law as a pistol, because it is built from the ground up as a handgun. Manufactured in the U.S.A. by Chiappa Firearms of Dayton, OH, the Bounty Hunter features a 12" barrel and 6 round tubular magazine. At just 24" OAL, the Bounty Hunter makes an ideal pack gun or camp defense pistol. The Bounty Hunter has a teardrop shaped loop lever and is built with the same fit, finish and high grade Italian walnut stocks as our Puma M-92 and M-86 rifles.

Price: .45LC, Case Hardened/Blued **$1,372.00**
Price: .44/40, Case Hardened/Blued. **$1,372.00**
Price: .44MAG, Case Hardened/Blued **$1,372.00**

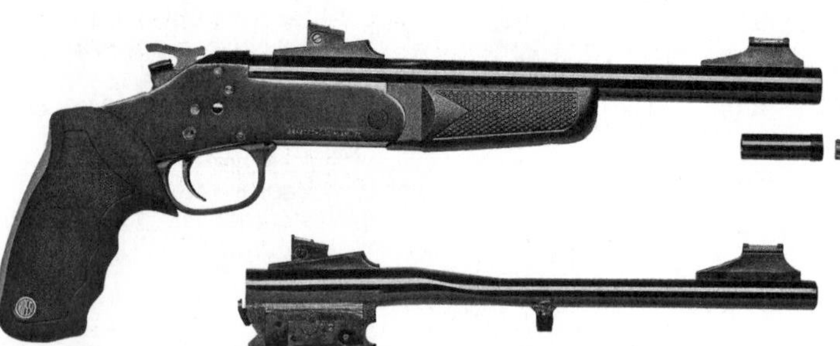

ROSSI MATCHED PAIR PISTOL, "DUAL THREAT PERFORMER"

Caliber: .22LR, .45 Colt and .410 GA. 2.5" shotshells, single shot. **Sights:** Fiber optic front sights, adjustable rear. **Features:** Two-in-one pistol system with sinle-shot simplicity. Removable choke and cushioned grip with a Taurus Security System.

Price: **$336.00**

ROSSI RANCH HAND PISTOL

Caliber: .38/.357, .45 Colt or .44 magnum, 6-shot. **eight:** 4 lbs. **Length:** 24" overall. **Stock:** Brazilian hardwood. **Sights:** Adjustable buckhorn. **Features:** Matte blue or case hardened finish with oversized lever loop to accomodate gloved hands. Equipped with classic buckhorn sights for fast target aquisition and a Taurus Security Sytem.

Price: **$615.00**

ROSSI WIZARD PISTOL

Caliber: .243 Win. or .22-.250 Rem with other calibers coming soon, single shot. **Barrel:** 11" **Length:** 20.4" **Features:** Offered in blue finish, additional features include pistol grip with custom grooves for fast handling and comfort, manual safety with "S" mark for visual confirmation, hammer extension, scope rail and the unique onboard Taurus Security System. Pistol offers outstanding and reliable performance in a versatile package. Its ingenious break-open barrel system changes quickly by unscrewing the front swivel with no tools needed.

Price: . . . . **N/A**

THOMPSON/CENTER ENCORE PISTOL

Caliber: 22-250, 223, 204 Ruger, 6.8 Rem., 260 Rem., 7mm-08, 243, 308, 270, 30-06, 375 JDJ, 204 Ruger, 44 Mag., 454 Casull, 480 Ruger, 444 Marlin single shot, 450 Marlin with muzzle tamer, no sights. **Barrel:** 12", 15", tapered round. **Weight:** NA. **Length:** 21" overall with 12" barrel. **Grips:** American walnut with finger grooves, walnut forend. **Sights:** Blade on ramp front, adjustable rear, or none. **Features:** Interchangeable barrels; action opens by squeezing the trigger guard; drilled and tapped for scope mounting; blue finish. Announced 1996. Made in U.S.A. by Thompson/Center Arms.

Price: **$761.00**

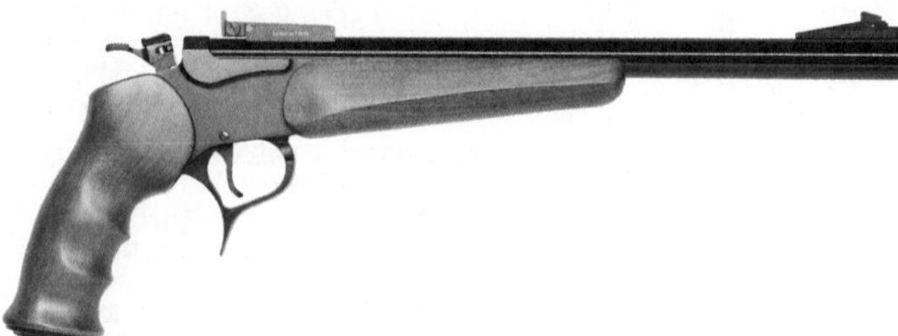

THOMPSON/CENTER G2 CONTENDER PISTOL

A second generation Contender pistol maintaining the same barrel interchangeability with older Contender barrels and their corresponding forends (except Herrett forend). The G2 frame will not accept old-style grips due to the change in grip angle. Incorporates an automatic hammer block safety with built-in interlock. Features include trigger adjustable for overtravel, adjustable rear sight; ramp front sight blade, blued steel finish.

Price: **$809.00**

Prices given are believed to be accurate at time of publication however, many factors affect retail pricing so exact prices are not possible.

ARMALITE M15A2 CARBINE
Caliber: 223 Rem., 30-round magazine. **Barrel:** 16" heavy chrome lined; 1:9" twist. **Weight:** 7 lbs. **Length:** 35-11/16" overall. **Stock:** Green or black composition. **Sights:** Standard A2. **Features:** Upper and lower receivers have push-type pivot pin; hard coat anodized; A2-style forward assist; M16A2-type raised fence around magazine release button. Made in U.S.A. by ArmaLite, Inc.
Price: Green **$1,150.00**
Price: Black **$1,150.00**

ARMALITE AR-10A4 SPECIAL PURPOSE RIFLE
Caliber: 308 Win., 10- and 20-round magazine. **Barrel:** 20" chrome-lined, 1:11.25" twist. **Weight:** 9.6 lbs. **Length:** 41" overall. **Stock:** Green or black composition. **Sights:** Detachable handle, front sight, or scope mount available; comes with international style flattop receiver with Picatinny rail. **Features:** Forged upper receiver with case deflector. Receivers are hard-coat anodized. Introduced 1995. Made in U.S.A. by ArmaLite, Inc.
Price: Green **$1,557.00**
Price: Black **$1,557.00**

ARMALITE AR-10A2
Utilizing the same 20" double-lapped, heavy barrel as the ArmaLite AR10A4 Special Purpose Rifle. Offered in 308 Win. only. Made in U.S.A. by ArmaLite, Inc.
Price: AR-10A2 rifle or carbine **$1,561.00**

ARMALITE AR-10B RIFLE
Caliber: 308 Win. **Barrel:** 20" chrome lined. **Weight:** 9.5 lbs. **Length:** 41". **Stock:** Synthetic. **Sights:** Rear sight adjustable for windage, small and large apertures. **Features:** Early-style AR-10. Lower and upper receivers made of forged aircraft alloy. Brown Sudanese-style furniture, elevation scale window. Charging handle in carry handle. Made in U.S.A. by Armalite.
Price: **$1,699.00**

ARSENAL, INC. SLR-107F
Caliber: 7.62x39mm. **Barrel:** 16.25". **Weight:** 7.3 lbs. **Stock:** Left-side folding polymer stock. **Sights:** Adjustable rear. **Features:** Stamped receiver, 24mm flash hider, bayonet lug, accessory lug, stainless steel heat shield, two-stage trigger. Introduced 2008. Made in U.S.A. by Arsenal, Inc.
Price: SLR-107FR, includes scope rail **$1,035.00**

ARSENAL, INC. SLR-107CR
Caliber: 7.62x39mm. **Barrel:** 16.25". **Weight:** 6.9 lbs. **Stock:** Left-side folding polymer stock. **Sights:** Adjustable rear. **Features:** Stamped receiver, front sight block/gas block combination, 500-meter rear sight, cleaning rod, stainless steel heat shield, scope rail, and removable muzzle attachment. Introduced 2007. Made in U.S.A. by Arsenal, Inc.
Price: SLR-107CR **$1,200.00**

ARSENAL, INC. SLR-106CR
Caliber: 5.56 NATO. **Barrel:** 16.25", Steyr chrome-lined barrel, 1:7 twist rate. **Weight:** 6.9 lbs. **Stock:** Black polymer folding stock with cutout for scope rail. Stainless-steel heatshield handguard. **Sights:** 500-meter rear sight and rear sight block calibrated for 5.56 NATO. Warsaw Pact scope rail. **Features:** Uses Arsenal, Bulgaria, Mil-Spec receiver, two-stage trigger, hammer and disconnector. Polymer magazines in 5- and 10-round capacity in black and green, with Arsenal logo. Others are 30-round black waffles, 20- and 30-round versions in clear/smoke waffle, featuring the "10" in a double-circle logo of Arsenal, Bulgaria. Ships with 5-round magazine, sling, cleaning kit in a tube, 16" cleaning rod, oil bottle. Introduced 2007. Made in U.S.A. by Arsenal, Inc.
Price: SLR-106CR **$1,200.00**

AUTO-ORDNANCE 1927A-1 THOMPSON
Caliber: 45 ACP. **Barrel:** 16.5". **Weight:** 13 lbs. **Length:** About 41" overall (Deluxe). **Stock:** Walnut stock and vertical forend. **Sights:** Blade front, open rear adjustable for windage. **Features:** Recreation of Thompson Model 1927. Semi-auto only. Deluxe model has finned barrel, adjustable rear sight and compensator; Standard model has plain barrel and military sight. From Auto-Ordnance Corp.
Price: Deluxe **$1,420.00**
Price: Lightweight model (9.5 lbs.) **$1,145.00**

AUTO-ORDNANCE THOMPSON M1/M1-C
Similar to the 1927 A-1 except is in the M-1 configuration with side cocking knob, horizontal forend, smooth unfinned barrel, sling swivels on butt and forend. Matte-black finish. Introduced 1985.
Price: M1 semi-auto carbine **$1,334.00**
Price: M1-C lightweight semi-auto **$1,065.00**

AUTO-ORDNANCE 1927 A-1 COMMANDO
Similar to the 1927 A-1 except has Parkerized finish, black-finish wood butt, pistol grip, horizontal forend. Comes with black nylon sling. Introduced 1998. Made in U.S.A. by Auto-Ordnance Corp.
Price: T1-C **$1,393.00**

AUTO ORDNANCE M1 CARBINE
Caliber: .30 Carbine (15-shot magazine). **Barrel:** 18". **Weight:** 5.4 to 5.8 lbs. **Length:** 36.5". **Stock:** Wood or polymer. **Sights:** Blade front, flip style rear. A faithful recreation of the military carbine.
Price: **$816.00**

BARRETT MODEL 82A-1 SEMI-AUTOMATIC RIFLE

Caliber: 50 BMG, 10-shot detachable box magazine. **Barrel:** 29". **Weight:** 28.5 lbs. **Length:** 57" overall. **Stock:** Composition with energy-absorbing recoil pad. **Sights:** Scope optional. **Features:** Semi-automatic, recoil operated with recoiling barrel. Three-lug locking bolt; muzzle brake. Adjustable bipod. Introduced 1985. Made in U.S.A. by Barrett Firearms.
Price: From **$8,900.00**

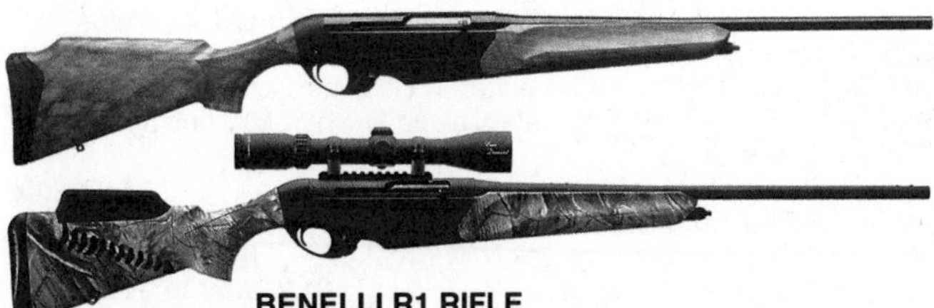

BENELLI R1 RIFLE
Caliber: .30-06 (4+1), .300 Win Mag (3+1), .338 Win Mag (3+1). **Weight:** 7.1 lbs. **Length:** 43.75" to 45.75". **Stock:** Select satin walnut or synthetic. **Sights:** None. **Features:** Auto-regulating gas-

operated system, three-lug rotary bolt, interchangeable barrels, optional recoil pads. Introduced 2003. Imported from Italy by Benelli USA.
Price: .... $1,019.00 to $1,249.00

BENELLI MR1 RIFLE
Gas-operated semiauto rifle chambered in 5.56 NATO. Features include 16-inch 1:9 hard chrome-lined barrel, synthetic stock with pistol grip, rotating bolt, military-style aperture sights with picatinny rail. Comes equipped with 5-round detachable magazine but accepts M16 magazines.
Price: $1299.00

BERETTA CX4/PX4 STORM CARBINE
Caliber: 9mm Para., 40 S&W, 45 ACP. **Weight:** 5.75 lbs. **Barrel Length:** 16.6", chrome lined, rate of twist 1:16 (40 S&W) or 1:10 (9mm Para.). **Length:** NA. **Stock:** Black synthetic. **Sights:** NA. **Features:** Introduced 2005. Imported from Italy by Beretta USA.
Price: $900.00

BROWNING BAR SAFARI AND SAFARI W/BOSS SEMI-AUTO RIFLES
Caliber: Safari: 243 Win., 25-06 Rem., 270 Win., 7mm Rem. Mag.., 30-06 Spfl., 308 Win., 300 Win. Mag., 338 Win. Mag. Safari w/ BOSS: 270 Win., 7mm Rem. Mag., 30-06 Spfl., 300 Win. Mag., 338 Win. Mag., plus 270 WSM, 7mm WSM, 300 WSM. **Barrel:** 22-24" round tapered. **Weight:** 7.4-8.2 lbs. **Length:** 43-45" overall. **Stock:** French walnut pistol grip stock and forend, hand checkered. **Sights:** No sights. **Features:** Has new bolt release lever; removable trigger assembly with larger trigger guard; redesigned gas and buffer systems. Detachable 4-round box magazine. Scroll-engraved receiver is tapped for scope mounting. BOSS barrel vibration modulator and muzzle brake system available. Mark II Safari introduced 1993. Imported from Belgium by Browning.
Price: BAR MK II Safari, from $1,300.00
Price: BAR Safari w/BOSS, from $1,500.00

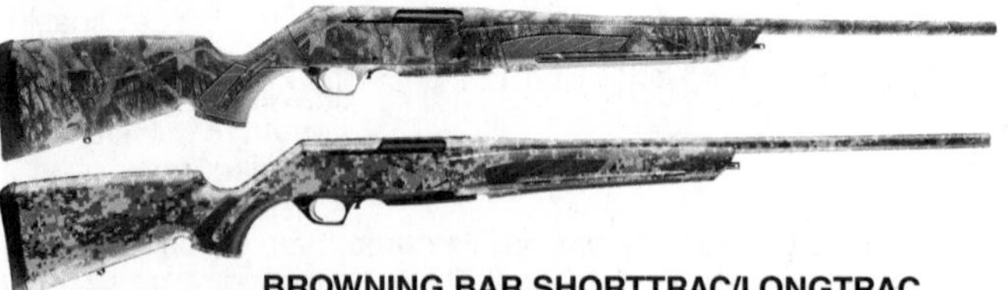

BROWNING BAR SHORTTRAC/LONGTRAC AUTO RIFLES
Caliber: (ShortTrac models) 270 WSM, 7mm WSM, 300 WSM, 243 Win., 308 Win., 325 WSM; (LongTrac models) 270 Win., 30-06 Spfl., 7mm Rem. Mag., 300 Win. Mag. **Barrel:** 23". **Weight:** 6 lbs. 10 oz. to 7 lbs. 4 oz. **Length:** 41.5" to 44". **Stock:** Satin-finish walnut, pistol-grip, fluted forend. **Sights:** Adj. rear, bead front standard, no sights on BOSS models (optional). **Features:** Designed to handle new WSM chamberings. Gas-operated, blued finish, rotary bolt design (LongTrac models).
Price: BAR ShortTrac, 243 Win., 308 Win. from $1,079.00
Price: BAR ShortTrac Left-Hand, intr. 2007, from $1,129.00
Price: BAR ShortTrac Mossy Oak New Break-up .... $1,249.00 to $1,349.00
Price: BAR LongTrac Left Hand, 270 Win., 30-06 Spfl., from $1,129.00
Price: BAR LongTrac, from $1,079.00
Price: BAR LongTrac Mossy Oak Break Up, intr. 2007, from $1,249.00
Price: Bar LongTrac, Digital Green camo (2009) .... $1,247.00 to $1,347.00

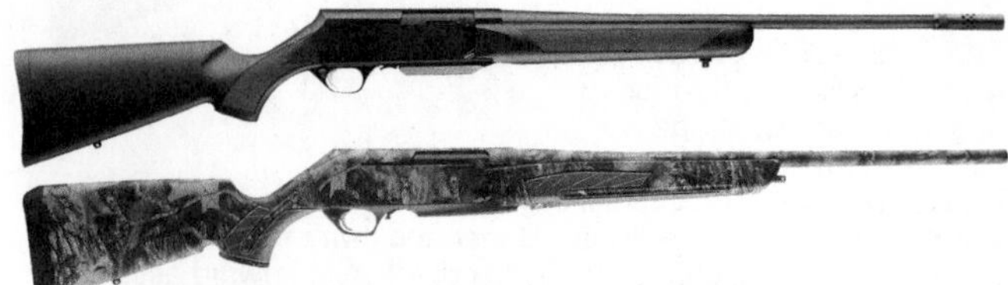

BROWNING BAR STALKER AUTO RIFLES
Caliber: 243 Win., 308 Win., 270 Win., 30-06 Spfl., 270 WSM, 7mm WSM, 300 WSM, 300 Win. Mag., 338 Win. Mag. **Barrel:** 20-24". **Weight:** 7.1-7.75 LBS. **Length:** 41-45" overall. **Stock:** Black composite stock and forearm. **Sights:** Hooded front and adjustable rear. **Features:** Gas-operated action with seven-lug rotary bolt; dual action bars; 2-, 3- or 4-shot magazine (depending on cartridge). Introduced 2001. Imported by Browning.
Price: BAR ShortTrac or LongTrac Stalker, from.......... $1,340.00
Price: BAR Lightweight Stalker, from $1,230.00

BUSHMASTER 300 AAC BLACKOUT
Caliber: .300 AAC. New cartridge for AR platform that matches 7.62x39 ballistics. **Features:** Utilizes regular AR magazines at full capacity. Muzzle brake. Magpul stock and grip.
Price: $1471

BUSHMASTER 308 HUNTER RIFLES
Caliber: .308 Win / 7.62 NATO., 5-round magazine. **Barrel:** 20". **Weight:** 8-1/2 lbs. **Length:** 38-1/4" overall. **Stock:** Standard A2 stock with Hogue® rubberized pistol grip. **Sights:** Two ¾" mini-risers for optics mounting. **Features:** These top quality Bushmaster .308 Rifles were developed for the Hunter who intends to immediately add optics (scope, red dot or holographic sight) to the rifle. The premium 20" heavy fluted profile barrel is chrome lined in both bore and chamber to provide Bushmaster accuracy, durability and maintenance ease.
Price: 308 Hunter.................................. $1518.00
Price: 308 Vista Hunter.. .... $1,618.00

BUSHMASTER ACR RIFLES
Caliber: 5.56mm, 6.5mm, 6.8mm., 30-round polymer magazine. **Barrel:** All three calibers are availaible with 10-1/2", 14-1/2", 16-1/2" and 18" barrels. **Weight:** 14-1/2" bbl 7 lbs.. **Length:** 14-1/5" bbl with stock folded: 25-3/4", with stock deployed (mid) 32-5/8", 10.5" bbl with stock folded: 21-5/16", with stock deployed (mid): 27-7/8", with stock deployed and extended: 31-3/4". Folding Stock Length of Pull - 3". **Stock:** Fixed high-impact composite A-frame stock with rubber butt pad and sling mounts (ORC & A-TACS®) **Features:** Cold hammer-forged barrels with melonite coating for extreme long life. A2 birdcage-type hider to control muzzle flash and adjustable, two-position, gas piston-driven system for firing suppressed or unsuppressed, supported by hardened internal bearing rails. Tool-less, quick-change barrel system available in 10.5", 14.5" and 16.5" and in multiple calibers. Multi-caliber bolt carrier assembly quickly and easily changes from 223/5.56mm NATO to 6.8mm Rem SPC (spec II chamber) Free-floating MIL-STD 1913 monolithic top rail for optic mounting. Fully ambidextrous controls including magazine release, bolt catch and release, fire selector and non reciprocating charging handle. High-impact composite hand guard with heat shield – accepts rail inserts. High-impact composite lower receiver with textured magazine well and modular grip storage. Fire Control – Semi and Full Auto two-stage standard AR capable of accepting drop-in upgrade. Magazine – Optimized for MagPul PMAG Accepts standard NATO/M-16 magazines.
Price: Basic ORC Configuration $2,343.00
Price: A-TACS Basic Configuration $2,540.00

Prices given are believed to be accurate at time of publication however, many factors affect retail pricing so exact prices are not possible.

Price: Basic Folder Configuration **$2,490.00**
Price: Basic State Compliant Configuration **$2,343.00**

BUSHMASTER SUPERLIGHT CARBINES
Caliber: 223 Rem., 30-shot magazine. **Barrel:** 16", heavy; 1:9" twist. **Weight:** 6.25 lbs. **Length:** 31.25-34.5" overall. **Stock:** 6-position telestock or Stubby (7.25" length). **Sights:** Fully adjustable M16A2 sight system. **Features:** Adapted from original G.I. pencil-barrel profile. Chrome-lined barrel with manganese phosphate finish. "Shorty" handguards. Has forged aluminum receivers with pushpin. Made in U.S.A. by Bushmaster Firearms, Inc.
Price: From **$1, 250.00**

BUSHMASTER XM15 E2S DISSIPATOR CARBINE
Similar to the XM15 E2S Shorty carbine except has full-length "Dissipator" handguards. Weighs 7.6 lbs.; 34.75" overall; forged aluminum receivers with push-pin style takedown. Made in U.S.A. by Bushmaster Firearms, Inc.
Price: From **$1,240.00**

BUSHMASTER XM15 E25 AK SHORTY CARBINE
Similar to the XM15 E2S Shorty except has 14.5" barrel with an AK muzzle brake permanently attached giving 16" barrel length. Weighs 7.3 lbs. Introduced 1999. Made in U.S.A. by Bushmaster Firearms, Inc.
Price: From **$1,215.00**

BUSHMASTER M4 POST-BAN CARBINE
Similar to the XM15 E2S except has 14.5" barrel with Mini Y compensator, and fixed telestock. MR configuration has fixed carry handle.
Price: **$1,190.00**

BUSHMASTER VARMINTER RIFLE
Caliber: 223 Rem., 5-shot. **Barrel:** 24", 1:9" twist, fluted, heavy, stainless. **Weight:** 8.75 lbs. **Length:** 42.25". **Stock:** Rubberized pistol grip. **Sights:** 1/2" scope risers. **Features:** Gas-operated, semi-auto, two-stage trigger, slotted free floater forend, lockable hard case.
Price: **$1,360.00**
Price: Bushmaster Predator: 20" 1:8 barrel, 223 Rem. **$1,245.00**
Price: Bushmaster Stainless Varmint Special: Same as Varminter but with 24" stainless barrel **$1,277.00**

BUSHMASTER 6.8 SPC CARBINE
Caliber: 6.8 SPC, 26-shot mag. **Barrel:** 16" M4 profile. **Weight:** 6.57 lbs. **Length:** 32.75" overall. **Features:** Semi-auto AR-style with Izzy muzzle brake, six-position telestock. Available in A2 (fixed carry handle) or A3 (removable carry handle) configuration.
Price: **$1,500.00**

BUSHMASTER ORC CARBINE
Caliber: 5.56/223. **Barrel:** 16" M4 profile. **Weight:** 6 lbs. **Length:** 32.5" overall. **Features:** AR-style carbine with chrome-lined barrel, fixed carry handle, receiver-length picatinny optics rail, heavy oval M4-style handguards.
Price: **$1,085.00**

BUSHMASTER 11.5" BARREL CARBINE
Caliber: 5.56/223, 30-shot mag. **Barrel:** 11.5". **Weight:** 6.46 lbs. or 6.81 lbs. **Length:** 31.625" overall. **Features:** AR-style carbine with chrome-lined barrel with permanently attached BATF-approved 5.5" flash suppressor, fixed or removable carry handle, optional optics rail.
Price: **$1,215.00**

BUSHMASTER HEAVY-BARRELED CARBINE
Caliber: 5.56/223. **Barrel:** 16". **Weight:** 6.93 lbs. to 7.28 lbs. **Length:** 32.5" overall. **Features:** AR-style carbine with chrome-lined heavy profile vanadium steel barrel, fixed or removable carry handle, six-position telestock.
Price: **$1,215.00**

BUSHMASTER MODULAR CARBINE
Caliber: 5.56/223, 30-shot mag. **Barrel:** 16". **Weight:** 7.3 lbs. **Length:** 36.25" overall. **Features:** AR-style carbine with chrome-lined chrome-moly vanadium steel barrel, skeleton stock or six-position telestock, clamp-on front sight and detachable flip-up dual aperature rear.
Price: **$1,745.00**

BUSHMASTER CARBON 15 TOP LOADER RIFLE
Caliber: 5.56/223, internal 10-shot mag. **Barrel:** 16" chrome-lined M4 profile. **Weight:** 5.8 lbs. **Length:** 32.75" overall. **Features:** AR-style carbine with standard A2 front sight, dual aperture rear sight, receiver-length optics rail, lightweight carbon fiber receiver, six-position telestock. Will not accept detachable box magazines.
Price: **$1,070.00**

BUSHMASTER CARBON 15 FLAT-TOP CARBINE
Caliber: 5.56/223, 30-shot mag. **Barrel:** 16" M4 profile. **Weight:** 5.77 lbs. **Length:** 32.75" overall. **Features:** AR-style carbine Izzy flash suppressor, AR-type front sight, dual aperture flip, lightweight carbon composite receiver with receiver-length optics rail.
Price: **$1,155.00**
Price: Carbon 15 9mm, chambered in 9mm Parabellum . . . **$1,025.00**

BUSHMASTER 450 RIFLE AND CARBINE
Caliber: 450 Bushmaster. **Barrel:** 20" (rifle), 16" (carbine), five-round mag. **Weight:** 8.3 lbs. (rifle), 8.1 lbs. (carbine). **Length:** 39.5" overall (rifle), 35.25" overall (carbine). **Features:** AR-style with chrome-lined chrome-moly barrel, synthetic stock, Izzy muzzle brake.
Price: **$1,350.00**

BUSHMASTER GAS PISTON RIFLE
Caliber: 223, 30-shot mag. **Barrel:** 16". **Weight:** 7.46 lbs. **Length:** 32.5" overall. **Features:** Semi-auto AR-style with telescoping stock, carry handle, piston assembly rather than direct gas impingement.
Price: **$1,795.00**

BUSHMASTER TARGET RIFLE
Caliber: 5.56/223, 30-shot mag. **Barrel:** 20" or 24» heavy or standard. **Weight:** 8.43 lbs. to 9.29 lbs. **Length:** 39.5" or 43.5" overall. **Features:** Semi-auto AR-style with chrome-lined or stainless steel 1:9 barrel, fixed or removable carry handle, manganese phosphate finish.
Price: **$1,195.00**

BUSHMASTER M4A3 TYPE CARBINE
Caliber: 5.56/223, 30-shot mag. **Barrel:** 16". **Weight:** 6.22 to 6.7 lbs. **Length:** 31" to 32.5» overall. **Features:** AR-style carbine with chrome-moly vanadium steel barrel, Izzy-type flash-hider, six-position telestock, various sight options, standard or multi-rail handguard, fixed or removable carry handle.
Price: **$1,270.00**
Price: Patrolman's Carbine: Standard mil-style sights **$1,270.00**
Price: State Compliance Carbine: Compliant with various state regulations **$1,270.00**

CENTURY INTERNATIONAL AES-10 HI-CAP RIFLE
Caliber: 7.62x39mm. 30-shot magazine. **Barrel:** 23.2". **Weight:** NA. **Length:** 41.5" overall. **Stock:** Wood grip, forend. **Sights:** Fixed-notch rear, windage-adjustable post front. **Features:** RPK-style, accepts standard double-stack AK-type mags. Side-mounted scope mount, integral carry handle, bipod. Imported by Century Arms Int'l.
Price: AES-10, from. **$450.00**

CENTURY INTERNATIONAL GP WASR-10 HI-CAP RIFLE
Caliber: 7.62x39mm. 30-shot magazine. **Barrel:** 16.25", 1:10 right-hand twist. **Weight:** 7.2 lbs. **Length:** 34.25" overall. **Stock:** Wood laminate or composite, grip, forend. **Sights:** Fixed-notch rear, windage-adjustable post front. **Features:** Two 30-rd. detachable

box magazines, cleaning kit, bayonet. Version of AKM rifle; U.S.-parts added for BATFE compliance. Threaded muzzle, folding stock, bayonet lug, compensator, Dragunov stock available. Made in Romania by Cugir Arsenal. Imported by Century Arms Int'l.

Price: GP WASR-10, from **$350.00**

CENTURY INTERNATIONAL WASR-2 HI-CAP RIFLE

Caliber: 5.45x39mm. 30-shot magazine. **Barrel:** 16.25". **Weight:** 7.5 lbs. **Length:** 34.25" overall. Stocks: Wood laminate. **Sights:** Fixed-notch rear, windage-adjustable post front. **Features:** 1 30-rd. detachable box magazine, cleaning kit, sling. WASR-3 HI-CAP chambered in 223 Rem. Imported by Century Arms Int'l.

Price: GP WASR-2/3, from **$250.00**

CENTURY INTERNATIONAL M70AB2 SPORTER RIFLE

Caliber: 7.62x39mm. 30-shot magazine. **Barrel:** 16.25". **Weight:** 7.5 lbs. **Length:** 34.25" overall. Stocks: Metal grip, wood forend. **Sights:** Fixed-notch rear, windage-adjustable post front. **Features:** 2 30-rd. double-stack magazine, cleaning kit, compensator, bayonet lug and bayonet. Paratrooper-style Kalashnikov with under-folding stock. Imported by Century Arms Int'l.

Price: M70AB2, from **$480.00**

COLT MATCH TARGET MODEL RIFLE

Caliber: 223 Rem., 5-shot magazine. **Barrel:** 16.1" or 20". **Weight:** 7.1 to 8.5 lbs. **Length:** 34.5" to 39" overall. **Stock:** Composition stock, grip, forend. **Sights:** Post front, rear adjustable for windage and elevation. **Features:** 5-round detachable box magazine, flash suppressor, sling swivels. Forward bolt assist included. Introduced 1991. Made in U.S.A. by Colt's Mfg. Co., Inc.

Price: Match Target HBAR MT6601 . . . . **$1,182.00**

DPMS PANTHER ARMS AR-15 RIFLES

Caliber: .204 Ruger, 6.8x43mm SPC. **Barrel:** 16" to 24". **Weight:** 7.75 to 11.75 lbs. **Length:** 34.5" to 42.25" overall. **Stock:** Black Zytel composite. **Sights:** Square front post, adjustable A2 rear. **Features:** Steel or stainless steel heavy or bull barrel; hardcoat anodized receiver; aluminum free-float tube handguard; many options. From DPMS Panther Arms.

Price: . . . . **$939.00 to $1,269.00**

DPMS PANTHER ARMS PRAIRIE PANTHER

Semiauto AR-style rifle chambered in 5.56 NATO. Features include 20-inch 416 stainless fluted heavy 1:8 barrel; phosphated steel bolt; free-floated carbon fiber handguard; flattop upper with Picatinny rail; aluminum lower; two 30-round magazines; skeletonized Zytel stock; finished in King's Desert Shadow camo overall.

Price: **$1,249.00**

DPMS PANTHER ARMS PANTHER REPR

Semiauto AR-style rifle chambered in .308 Win./7.62 NATO. Features include 18-inch 416 stainless steel 1:10 barrel; phosphated steel bolt; 4-rail free-floated handguard; no sights; aluminum lower; two 19-round magazines; Coyote Brown camo finish overall.

Price: **$2,549.00**

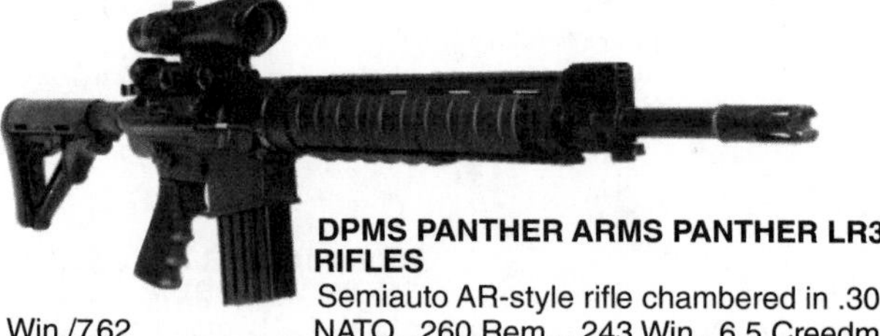

DPMS PANTHER ARMS PANTHER LR308 RIFLES

Semiauto AR-style rifle chambered in .308 Win./7.62 NATO, .260 Rem., .243 Win., 6.5 Creedmoor, .338 Federal. Features include 16-inch 4140 chrome-moly heavy 1:10 barrel; phosphated steel bolt; 4-rail free-floated handguard; flip-up front and rear sights; aluminum lower; two 19-round magazines; matte black finish overall; Magpul CTR adjustable stock.

Price: **$2,549.00**

DSA Z4 GTC CARBINE WITH C.R.O.S.

Caliber: 5.56 NATO **Barrel:** 16" 1:9 twist M4 profile fluted chrome lined heavy barrel with threaded Vortec flash hider. **Weight:** 7.6 lbs. **Stock:** 6 position collapsible M4 stock, Predator P4X free float tactical rail. **Sights:** Chrome lined Picatinny gas block w/removable front sight. **Features:** The Corrosion Resistant Operating System incorporates the new P.O.F. Gas Trap System with removable gas plug eliminates problematic features of standard AR gas system, Forged 7075T6 DSA lower receiver. Introduced 2006. Made in U.S.A. by DSA, Inc.

Price: **$1,800.00**

DSA CQB MRP, STANDARD MRP

Caliber: 5.56 NATO **Barrel:** 16" or 18" 1:7 twist chrome-lined or stainless steel barrel with A2 flash hider **Stock:** 6 position collapsible M4 stock. **Features:** LMT 1/2" MRP upper receiver with 20.5" Standard quad rail or 16.5" CQB quad rail, LMT-enhanced bolt with dual extractor springs, free float barrel, quick change barrel system, forged 7075T6 DSA lower receiver. EOTech and vertical grip additional. Introduced 2006. Made in U.S.A. by DSA, Inc.

Price: CQB MRP w/16" chrome-lined barrel **$2,420.00**
Price: CQB MRP w/16" stainless steel barrel **$2,540.00**
Price: Standard MRP w/16" chrome-lined barrel. **$2,620.00**
Price: Standard MRP w/16" or 18" stainless steel barrel. . . . **$2,740.00**

DSA STD CARBINE

Caliber: 5.56 NATO. **Barrel:** 16" 1:9 twist D4 w/A2 flash hider. **Weight:** 6.25 lbs. **Length:** 31". **Stock:** A2 buttstock, D4 handguard w/ heatshield. **Sights:** Forged A2 front sight with lug. **Features:** Forged 7075T6 DSA lower receiver, forged A2 or flattop upper receiver. Introduced 2006. Made in U.S.A. by DSA, Inc.

Price: A2 or Flattop STD Carbine **$1,025.00**
Price: With LMT SOPMOD stock **$1,267.00**

DSA 1R CARBINE

Caliber: 5.56 NATO. **Barrel:** 16" 1:9 twist D4 w/A2 flash hider. **Weight:** 6.25 lbs. **Length:** Variable. **Stock:** 6 position collapsible M4 stock, D4 handguard w/heatshield. **Sights:** Forged A2 front sight with lug. **Features:** Forged 7075T6 DSA lower receiver, forged A2 or flattop upper receiver. Introduced 2006. Made in U.S.A. by DSA, Inc.

Price: A2 or Flattop 1R Carbine **$1,055.00**
Price: With VLTOR ModStock **$1,175.00**

DSA XM CARBINE

Caliber: 5.56 NATO. **Barrel:** 11.5" 1:9 twist D4 with 5.5" permanently

Prices given are believed to be accurate at time of publication however, many factors affect retail pricing so exact prices are not possible.

attached flash hider. **Weight:** 6.25 lbs. **Length:** Variable. **Stock:** Collapsible, Handguard w/heatshield. **Sights:** Forged A2 front sight with lug. **Features:** Forged 7075T6 DSA lower receiver, forged A2 upper receiver. Introduced 2006. Made in U.S.A. by DSA, Inc.

Price: $1,055.00

DSA STANDARD

Caliber: 5.56 NATO. **Barrel:** 20" 1:9 twist heavy barrel w/A2 flash hider. **Weight:** 6.25 lbs. **Length:** 38-7/16". **Stock:** A2 buttstock, A2 handguard w/heatshield. **Sights:** Forged A2 front sight with lug. **Features:** Forged 7075T6 DSA lower receiver, forged A2 or flattop upper receiver. Introduced 2006. Made in U.S.A. by DSA, Inc.

Price: A2 or Flattop Standard $1,025.00

DSA DCM RIFLE

Caliber: 223 Wylde Chamber. **Barrel:** 20" 1:8 twist chrome moly match grade Badger Barrel. **Weight:** 10 lbs. **Length:** 39.5". **Stock:** DCM freefloat handguard system, A2 buttstock. **Sights:** Forged A2 front sight with lug. **Features:** NM two stage trigger, NM rear sight, forged 7075T6 DSA lower receiver, forged A2 upper receiver. Introduced 2006. Made in U.S.A. by DSA, Inc.

Price: $1,520.00

DSA S1

Caliber: 223 Rem. Match Chamber. **Barrel:** 16", 20" or 24" 1:8 twist stainless steel bull barrel. **Weight:** 8.0, 9.5 and 10 lbs. **Length:** 34.25", 38.25" and 42.25". **Stock:** A2 buttstock with free float aluminum handguard. **Sights:** Picatinny gas block sight base. **Features:** Forged 7075T6 DSA lower receiver, Match two stage trigger, forged flattop upper receiver, fluted barrel optional. Introduced 2006. Made in U.S.A. by DSA, Inc.

Price: $1,155.00

DSA SA58 CONGO, PARA CONGO

Caliber: 308 Win. **Barrel:** 18" w/ short Belgian short flash hider. **Weight:** 8.6 lbs. (Congo); 9.85 lbs. (Para Congo). **Length:** 39.75" **Stock:** Synthetic w/military grade furniture (Congo); Synthetic with non-folding steel para stock (Para Congo). **Sights:** Elevation adjustable protected post front sight, windage adjustable rear peep (Congo); Belgian type Para Flip Rear (Para Congo). **Features:** Fully-adjustable gas system, high-grade steel upper receiver with carry handle. Made in U.S.A. by DSA, Inc.

Price: Congo $1,850.00
Price: Para Congo $2,095.00

DSA SA58 GRAY WOLF

Caliber: 308 Win. **Barrel:** 21" match-grade bull w/target crown. **Weight:** 13 lbs. **Length:** 41.75". **Stock:** Synthetic. **Sights:** Elevation-adjustable post front sight, windage-adjustable match rear peep. **Features:** Fully-adjustable gas system, high-grade steel upper receiver, Picatinny scope mount, DuraCoat finish. Made in U.S.A. by DSA, Inc.

Price: $2,120.00

DSA SA58 PREDATOR

Caliber: 243 Win., 260 Rem., 308 Win. **Barrel:** 16" and 19" w/target crown. **Weight:** 9 to 9.3 lbs. **Length:** 36.25" to 39.25". **Stock:** Green synthetic. **Sights:** Elevation-adjustable post front; windage-adjustable match rear peep. **Features:** Fully-adjustable gas system, high-grade steel upper receiver, Picatinny scope mount, DuraCoat solid and camo finishes. Made in U.S.A. by DSA, Inc.

Price: 243 Win., 260 Rem. $1,695.00
Price: 308 Win. $1,640.00

DSA SA58 T48

Caliber: 308 Win. **Barrel:** 21" with Browning long flash hider. **Weight:** 9.3 lbs. **Length:** 44.5". **Stock:** European walnut. **Sights:** Elevation-adjustable post front, windage adjustable rear peep. **Features:** Gas-operated semi-auto with fully adjustable gas system, high grade steel upper receiver with carry handle. DuraCoat finishes. Made in U.S.A. by DSA, Inc.

Price: $1,995.00

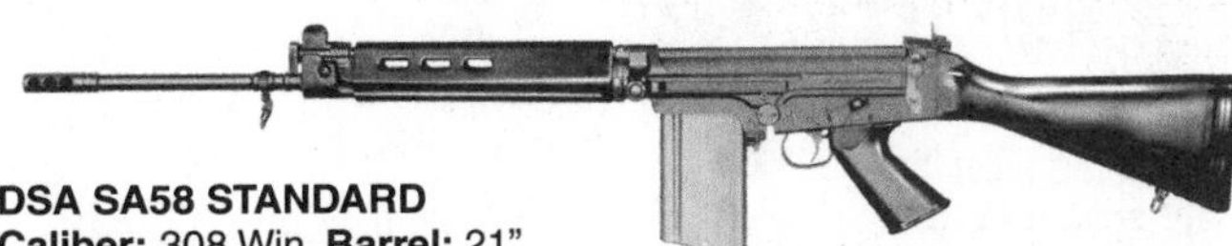

DSA SA58 G1

Caliber: 308 Win. **Barrel:** 21" with quick-detach flash hider. **Weight:** 10.65 lbs. **Length:** 44". **Stock:** Steel bipod cut handguard with hardwood stock and synthetic pistol grip. **Sights:** Elevation-adjustable post front, windage adjustable rear peep. **Features:** Gas-operated semi-auto with fully adjustable gas system, high grade steel upper receiver with carry handle, original GI steel lower receiver with GI bipod. DuraCoat finishes. Made in U.S.A. by DSA, Inc.

Price: $1,850.00

DSA SA58 STANDARD

Caliber: 308 Win. **Barrel:** 21" bipod cut w/threaded flash hider. **Weight:** 8.75 lbs. **Length:** 43". **Stock:** Synthetic, X-Series or optional folding para stock. **Sights:** Elevation-adjustable post front, windage-adjustable rear peep. **Features:** Fully adjustable short gas system, high grade steel or 416 stainless upper receiver. Made in U.S.A. by DSA, Inc.

Price: High-grade steel $1,595.00
Price: Folding para stock $1,845.00

DSA SA58 CARBINE

Caliber: 308 Win. **Barrel:** 16.25" bipod cut w/threaded flash hider. **Weight:** 8.35 lbs. **Length:** 37.5". **Stock:** Synthetic, X-Series or optional folding para stock. **Sights:** Elevation-adjustable post front, windage-adjustable rear peep. **Features:** Fully adjustable short gas system, high grade steel or 416 stainless upper receiver. Made in U.S.A. by DSA, Inc.

Price: High-grade steel $1,595.00
Price: Stainless steel $1,850.00

DSA SA58 TACTICAL CARBINE

Caliber: 308 Win. **Barrel:** 16.25" fluted with A2 flash hider. **Weight:** 8.25 lbs. **Length:** 36.5". **Stock:** Synthetic, X-Series or optional folding para stock. **Sights:** Elevation-adjustable post front, windage-adjustable match rear peep. **Features:** Shortened fully adjustable short gas system, high grade steel or 416 stainless upper receiver. Made in U.S.A. by DSA, Inc.

Price: High-grade steel **$1,595.00**
Price: Stainless steel **$1,850.00**

DSA SA58 MEDIUM CONTOUR

Caliber: 308 Win. **Barrel:** 21" w/ threaded flash hider. **Weight:** 9.75 lbs. **Length:** 43". **Stock:** Synthetic military grade. **Sights:** Elevation-adjustable post front, windage-adjustable match rear peep. **Features:** Gas-operated semi-auto with fully adjustable gas system, high grade steel receiver. Made in U.S.A. by DSA, Inc.

Price: **$1,595.00**

DSA SA58 BULL BARREL RIFLE

Caliber: 308 Win. **Barrel:** 21". **Weight:** 11.1 lbs. **Length:** 41.5". **Stock:** Synthetic, free floating handguard. **Sights:** Elevation-adjustable windage-adjustable post front, match rear peep. **Features:** Gas-operated semi-auto with fully adjustable gas system, high grade steel or stainless upper receiver. Made in U.S.A. by DSA, Inc.

Price: **$1,745.00**
Price: Stainless steel **$1,995.00**

DSA SA58 MINI OSW

Caliber: 308 Win. **Barrel:** 11" or 13" w/A2 flash hider. **Weight:** 9 to 9.35 lbs. **Length:** 32.75" to 35". **Stock:** Fiberglass reinforced short synthetic handguard, para folding stock and synthetic pistol grip. **Sights:** Adjustable post front, para rear sight. **Features:** Semi-auto or select fire with fully adjustable short gas system, optional FAL rail handguard, SureFire Vertical Foregrip System, EOTech HOLOgraphic Sight and ITC cheekrest. Made in U.S.A. by DSA, Inc.

Price: **$1,845.00**

EXCEL ARMS ACCELERATOR RIFLES

Caliber: 17 HMR, 22 WMR, 17M2, 22 LR, 9-shot magazine. **Barrel:** 18" fluted stainless steel bull barrel. **Weight:** 8 lbs. **Length:** 32.5" overall. Grips: Textured black polymer. **Sights:** Fully adjustable target sights. **Features:** Made from 17-4 stainless steel, aluminum shroud w/Weaver rail, manual safety, firing-pin block, last-round bolt-hold-open feature. Four packages with various equipment available. American made, lifetime warranty. Comes with one 9-round stainless steel magazine and a California-approved cable lock. Introduced 2006. Made in U.S.A. by Excel Arms.

Price: MR-17 17 HMR. **$488.00**
Price: MR-22 22 WMR **$523.00**

EXCEL ARMS X-5.7R/X-30R RIFLE

Caliber: 5.57x28mm (10 or 25-round), .30 Carbine (10 or 20-round magazine). **Barrel:** 18". Weight: 6.25 lbs. Length: 34 to 38". Available with or without adjustable iron sights. Blow-back action (5.57x28) or delayed blow-back (.30 Carbine.)

PRICE: . . . . **$795.00 to $916.00**

HECKLER & KOCH MODEL MR556A1 RIFLE

Caliber: .223 Remington/5.56 NATO, 10+1 capacity. **Barrel:** 16.5". **Weight:** 8.9 lbs. **Length:** 33.9"-37.68". **Stock:** Black Synthetic Adjustable. **Features:** Uses the gas piston system found on the HK 416 and G26, which does not introduce propellant gases and carbon fouling into the rifle's interior.

Price: **$2,995.00**

HECKLER & KOCH MODEL MR762A1

Caliber: Similar to Model MR556A1 except chambered for 7.62x51mm/.308 Win. cartridge. **Weight:** 10 lbs. w/empty magazine. **Length:** 36 to 39.5". Variety of optional sights are available. Stock has five adjustable positions.

Price: **$3995**

HECKLER & KOCH USC CARBINE

Caliber: 45 ACP, 10-shot magazine. **Barrel:** 16". **Weight:** 8.6 lb. **Length:** 35.4" overall. **Stock:** Skeletonized polymer thumbhole. **Sights:** Blade front with integral hood, fully adjustable diopter. **Features:** Based on German UMP submachine gun. Blowback operation; almost entirely constructed of carbon fiber-reinforced polymer. Free-floating heavy target barrel. Introduced 2000. From H&K.

Price: **$1,249.00**

HI-POINT 9MM CARBINE

Caliber: 9mm Para., 40 S&W, 10-shot magazine. **Barrel:** 16.5" (17.5" for 40 S&W). **Weight:** 4.5 lbs. **Length:** 31.5" overall. **Stock:** Black polymer, camouflage. **Sights:** Protected post front, aperture rear. Integral scope mount. **Features:** Grip-mounted magazine release. Black or chrome finish. Sling swivels. Available with laser or red dot sights. Introduced 1996. Made in U.S.A. by MKS Supply, Inc.

Price: 995-B (black) **$220.00**
Price: 995-CMO (camo) **$235.00**

LES BAER CUSTOM ULTIMATE AR 223 RIFLES

Caliber: 223. **Barrel:** 18", 20", 22", 24". **Weight:** 7.75 to 9.75 lb. **Length:** NA. **Stock:** Black synthetic. **Sights:** None furnished; Picatinny-style flattop rail for scope mounting. **Features:** Forged receiver; Ultra single-stage trigger (Jewell two-stage trigger optional); titanium firing pin; Versa-Pod bipod; chromed National Match carrier; stainless steel, hand-lapped and cryo-treated barrel; guaranteed to shoot

Prices given are believed to be accurate at time of publication however, many factors affect retail pricing so exact prices are not possible.

1/2 or 3/4 MOA, depending on model. Made in U.S.A. by Les Baer Custom Inc.

Price: Super Varmint Model **$2,390.00**
Price: Super Match Model (introduced 2006) **$2,490.00**
Price: M4 Flattop model **$2,360.00**
Price: Police Special 16" (2008) **$1,690.00**
Price: IPSC Action Model **$2,640.00**

LR 300 RIFLES

Caliber: 5.56 NATO, 30-shot magazine. **Barrel:** 16.5"; 1:9" twist. **Weight:** 7.4-7.8 lbs. **Length:** NA. **Stock:** Folding. **Sights:** YHM flip front and rear. **Features:** Flattop receive, full length top picatinny rail. Phantom flash hider, multi sling mount points, field strips with no tools. Made in U.S.A. from Z-M Weapons.

Price: AXL, AXLT. **$2,139.00**
Price: NXL **$2,208.00**

MERKEL MODEL SR1 SEMI-AUTOMATIC RIFLE

Caliber: 308 Win., 300 Win Mag. **Features:** Streamlined profile, checkered walnut stock and forend, 19.7- (308) or 20-8" (300 SM) barrel, two- or five-shot detachable box magazine. Adjustable front and rear iron sights with Weaver-style optics rail included. Imported from Germany by Merkel USA.

Price: **$1,595.00**

OLYMPIC ARMS K9, K10, K40, K45 PISTOL-CALIBER AR15 CARBINES

Caliber: 9mm Para., 10mm, 40 S&W, 45 ACP; 32/10-shot modified magazines. **Barrel:** 16" button rifled stainless steel, 1x16 twist rate. **Weight:** 6.73 lbs. **Length:** 31.625" overall. **Stock:** A2 grip, M4 6-point collapsible stock. **Features:** A2 upper with adjustable rear sight, elevation adjustable front post, bayonet lug, sling swivel, threaded muzzle, flash suppressor, carbine length handguards. Made in U.S.A. by Olympic Arms, Inc.

Price: K9GL, 9mm Para., Glock lower **$1,092.00**
Price: K10, 10mm, modified 10-round Uzi magazine **$1,006.20**
Price: K40, 40 S&W, modified 10-round Uzi magazine. **$1,006.20**
Price: K45, 45 ACP, modified 10-round Uzi magazine **$1,006.20**

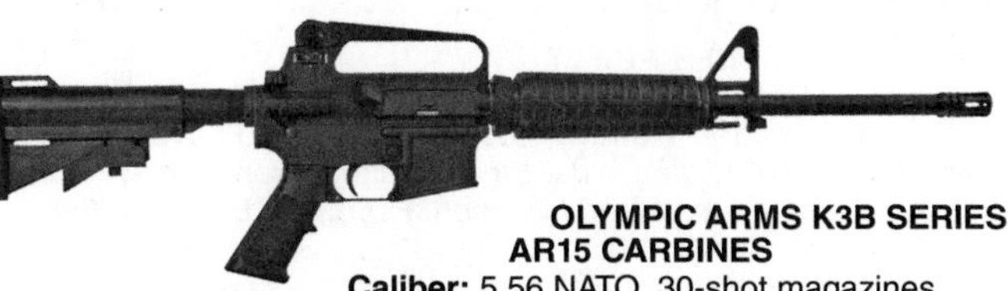

OLYMPIC ARMS K3B SERIES AR15 CARBINES

Caliber: 5.56 NATO, 30-shot magazines. **Barrel:** 16" button rifled chrome-moly steel, 1x9 twist rate. **Weight:** 5-7 lbs. **Length:** 31.75" overall. **Stock:** A2 grip, M4 6-point collapsible buttstock. **Features:** A2 upper with adjustable rear sight, elevation adjustable front post, bayonet lug, sling swivel, threaded muzzle, flash suppressor, carbine length handguards. Made in U.S.A. by Olympic Arms, Inc.

Price: K3B base model, A2 upper. **$815.00**
Price: K3B-M4 M4 contoured barrel & handguards **$1,038.70**
Price: K3B-M4-A3-TC A3 upper, M4 barrel, FIRSH rail handguard. **$1,246.70**
Price: K3B-CAR 11.5" barrel with 5.5" permanent flash suppressor **$968.50**
Price: K3B-FAR 16" featherweight contoured barrel **$1,006.20**

OLYMPIC ARMS PLINKER PLUS AR15 MODELS

Caliber: 5.56 NATO, 30-shot magazine. Barrel 16" or 20" button-rifled chrome-moly steel, 1x9 twist. **Weight:** 7.5-8.5 lbs. **Length:** 35.5"-39.5" overall. **Stock:** A2 grip, A2 buttstock with trapdoor. **Sights:** A1 windage rear, elevation-adjustable front post. **Features:** A1 upper, fiberlite handguards, bayonet lug, threaded muzzle and flash suppressor. Made in U.S.A. by Olympic Arms, Inc.

Price: Plinker Plus. **$713.70**
Price: Plinker Plus 20 . . . . **$843.70**

OLYMPIC ARMS GAMESTALKER

Sporting AR-style rifle chambered in .223, .243 and .25 WSSM and .300 OSSM. Features include forged aluminum upper and lower; flat top receiver with Picatinny rail; gas block front sight; 22-inch stainless steel fluted barrel; free-floating slotted tube handguard; camo finish overall; ACE FX skeleton stock.

Price: **$1,359.00**

REMINGTON MODEL R-15 MODULAR REPEATING RIFLE

Caliber: 223, 450 Bushmaster **and 30 Rem. AR, five-shot magazine. Barrel:** 18" (carbine), 22", 24". **Weight:** 6.75 to 7.75 lbs. **Length:** 36.25" to 42.25". **Stock:** Camo. **Features:** AR-style with optics rail, aluminum alloy upper and lower.

Price: R-15 Hunter: 30 Rem. AR, 22" barrel, Realtree AP HD camo **$1,225.00**
Price: R-15 VTR Byron South Edition: 223, 18" barrel, Advantage MAX-1 HD camo **$1,772.00**
Price: R-15 VTR SS Varmint: Same as Byron South Edition but with 24" stainless steel barrel **$1,412.00**
Price: R-15 VTR Thumbhole: Similar to R-15 Hunter but with thumbhole stock **$1,412.00**
Price: R-15 VYR Predator: 204 Ruger or .223, 22" barrel . . **$1,225.00**
Price: R-15 Predator Carbine: Similar to above but with 18" barrel **$1,225.00**

REMINGTON MODEL R-25 MODULAR REPEATING RIFLE

Caliber: 243, 7mm-08, 308 Win., four-shot magazine. **Barrel:** 20" chrome-moly. **Weight:** 7.75 lbs. **Length:** 38.25" overall. **Features:** AR-style semi-auto with single-stage trigger, aluminum alloy upper and lower, Mossy Oak Treestand camo finish overall.

Price: **$1,567.00**

REMINGTON MODEL 750 WOODSMASTER

Caliber: 243 Win., 270 Win., 308 Win., 30-06 Spfl., 35 Whelen. 4-shot magazine. **Barrel:** 22" round tapered. **Weight:** 7.5 lbs. **Length:** 42.6" overall. **Stock:** Restyled American walnut forend and stock with machine-cut checkering. Satin finish. **Sights:** Gold bead front sight on ramp; step rear sight with windage adjustable. **Features:** Replaced wood-stocked Model 7400 line introduced 1981. Gas action, SuperCell recoil pad. Positive cross-bolt safety. Carbine chambered in 308 Win., 30-06 Spfl., 35 Whelen. Receiver tapped for scope mount. Introduced 2006. Made in U.S.A. by Remington Arms Co.

Price: 750 Woodsmaster. **$1,004.00**

Price: 750 Woodsmaster Carbine (18.5" bbl.) **$1,004.00**
Price: 750 Synthetic stock (2007) **$884.00**

ROCK RIVER ARMS STANDARD A2 RIFLE

Caliber: 45 ACP. **Barrel:** NA. **Weight:** 8.2 lbs. **Length:** NA. **Stock:** Thermoplastic. **Sights:** Standard AR-15 style sights. **Features:** Two-stage, national match trigger; optional muzzle brake. Pro-Series Government package includes side-mount sling swivel, chrome-lined 1:9 twist barrel, mil-spec forged lower receiver, Hogue rubber grip, NM two-stage trigger, 6-position tactical CAR stock, Surefire M73 quad rail handguard, other features. Made in U.S.A. From Rock River Arms.

Price: Standard A2 AR1280 . . . . **$945.00**
Price: Pro-Series Government Package GOVT1001 (2008) **$2,290.00**
Price: Elite Comp AR1270 (2008) **$1,145.00**

RUGER SR-556

AR-style semiauto rifle chambered in 5.56 NATO. Feature include two-stage piston; quad rail handguard; Troy Industries sights; black synthetic fixed or telescoping buttstock; 16.12-inch 1:9 steel barrel with birdcage; 10- or 30-round detachable box magazine; black matte finish overall.

Price: **$1,995.00**

RUGER MINI-14 RANCH RIFLE AUTOLOADING RIFLE

Caliber: 223 Rem., 5-shot detachable box magazine. **Barrel:** 18.5". Rifling twist 1:9". **Weight:** 6.75 to 7 lbs. **Length:** 37.25" overall. **Stock:** American hardwood, steel reinforced, or synthetic. **Sights:** Protected blade front, fully adjustable Ghost Ring rear. **Features:** Fixed piston gas-operated, positive primary extraction. New buffer system, redesigned ejector system. Ruger S100RM scope rings included on Ranch Rifle. Heavier barrels added in 2008, 20-round magazine added in 1009.

Price: Mini-14/5, Ranch Rifle, blued, scope rings **$855.00**
Price: K-Mini-14/5, Ranch Rifle, stainless, scope rings **$921.00**
Price: K-Mini-6.8/5P, All-Weather Ranch Rifle, stainless, synthetic stock (2008) **$921.00**
Price: Mini-14 Target Rifle: laminated thumbhole stock, heavy crowned 22" stainless steel barrel, other refinements **$1,066.00**
Price: Mini-14 ATI Stock: Tactical version of Mini-14 but with six-position collapsible stock or folding stock, grooved pistol grip. multiple picatinny optics/accessory rails . . . **$872.00**
Price: Mini-14 Tactical Rifle: Similar to Mini-14 but with 16-21" barrel with flash hider, black synthetic stock, adjustable sights **$894.00**

RUGER MINI THIRTY RIFLE

Similar to the Mini-14 Ranch Rifle except modified to chamber the 7.62x39 Russian service round. **Weight:** 6.75 lbs. Has 6-groove barrel with 1:10" twist, Ruger Integral Scope Mount bases and protected blade front, fully adjustable Ghost Ring rear. Detachable 5-shot staggered box magazine. Available 2010 with two 30-round magazines. Stainless w/synthetic stock. Introduced 1987.

Price: Stainless, scope rings **$921.00**

SABRE DEFENCE SABRE RIFLES

Caliber: 5.56 NATO, 6.5 Grendel, 30-shot magazines. **Barrel:** 20" 410 stainless steel, 1x8 twist rate; or 18" vanadium alloy, chrome-lined barrel with Sabre Gill-Brake. **Weight:** 6.77 lbs. **Length:** 31.75" overall. **Stock:** SOCOM 3-position stock with Samson M-EX handguards. **Sights:** Flip-up front and rear sights. **Features:** Fluted barrel, Harris bipod, and two-stage match trigger, Ergo Grips; upper and matched lower CNC machined from 7075-T6 forgings. SOCOM adjustable stock, Samson tactical handguards, M4 contour barrels available in 14.5" and 16" are made of MIL-B-11595 vanadium alloy and chrome lined. Introduced 2002. From Sabre Defence Industries.

Price: 6.5 Grendel, from **$1,409.00**
Price: Competition Extreme, 20" barrel, from **$2,189.00**
Price: Competition Deluxe, from **$2,299.00**
Price: Competition Special, 5.56mm, 18" barrel, from. **$1,899.00**
Price: SPR Carbine, from **$2,499.00**
Price: M4 Tactical, from **$1,969.00**
Price: M4 Carbine, 14.5" barrel, from **$1,399.00**
Price: M4 Flat-top Carbine, 16" barrel, from **$1,349.00**
Price: M5 Flat-top, 16" barrel, from **$1,399.00**
Price: M5 Tactical, 14.5" barrel, from **$2,099.00**
Price: M5 Carbine, from **$1,309.00**
Price: Precision Marksman, 20" barrel, from **$2,499.00**
Price: A4 Rifle, 20" barrel, from **$1,349.00**
Price: A3 National Match, 20" barrel **$1,699.00**
Price: Heavy Bench Target, 24" barrel, from **$1,889.00**
Price: Varmint, 20" barrel **$1,709.00**

SIG 556 AUTOLOADING RIFLE

Caliber: 223 Rem., 30-shot detachable box magazine. **Barrel:** 16". Rifling twist 1:9". **Weight:** 6.8 lbs. **Length:** 36.5" overall. **Stock:** Polymer, folding style. **Sights:** Flip-up front combat sight, adjustable for windage and elevation. **Features:** Based on SG

Prices given are believed to be accurate at time of publication however, many factors affect retail pricing so exact prices are not possible.

550 series rifle. Two-position adjustable gas piston operating rod system, accepts standard AR magazines. Polymer forearm, three integrated Picatinny rails, forward mount for right- or left-side sling attachment. Aircraft-grade aluminum alloy trigger housing, hard-coat anodized finish; two-stage trigger, ambidextrous safety, 30-round polymer magazine, battery compartments, pistol-grip rubber-padded watertight adjustable butt stock with sling-attachment points. SIG 556 SWAT model has flat-top Picatinny railed receiver, tactical quad rail. SIG 556 HOLO sight options include front combat sight, flip-up rear sight, and red-dot style holographic sighting system with four illuminated reticle patterns. DMR features a 24" military grade cold hammer-forged heavy contour barrel, 5.56mm NATO, target crown. Imported by Sig Sauer, Inc.

Price: From **$1,667.00**

SIG-SAUER SIG516 GAS PISTON RIFLE

AR-style rifle chambered in 5.56 NATO. Features include 14.5-, 16-, 18- or 20-inch chrome-lined barrel; free-floating, aluminum quad rail fore-end with four M1913 Picatinny rails; threaded muzzle with a standard (0.5x28TPI) pattern; aluminum upper and lower receiver is machined; black anodized finish; 30-round magazine; flattop upper; various configurations available.

Price: . . . . **$1,262.00 to $1,734.00**

SIG-SAUER SIG716 TACTICAL PATROL RIFLE

AR-10 type rifle chambered in 7.62 NATO/.308 Winchester. Features include gas-piston operation with 3 round-position (4-position optional) gas valve; 16-, 18- or 20-inch chrome-lined barrel with threaded muzzle and nitride finish; free-floating aluminum quad rail fore-end with four M1913 Picatinny rails; telescroping buttstock; lower receiver is machined from a 7075-T6 Aircraft grade aluminum forging; upper receiver, machined from 7075-T6 aircraft grade aluminum with integral M1913 Picatinny rail.

Price: . . . . **$1,866.00 to $2,200.00**

SMITH & WESSON M&P15 RIFLES

Caliber: 5.56mm NATO/223, 30-shot steel magazine. **Barrel:** 16", 1:9 **Weight:** 6.74 lbs., w/o magazine. **Length:** 32-35" overall. **Stock:** Black synthetic. **Sights:** Adjustable post front sight, adjustable dual aperture rear sight. **Features:** 6-position telescopic stock, thermo-set M4 handguard. 14.75" sight radius. 7-lbs. (approx.) trigger pull. 7075 T6 aluminum upper, 4140 steel barrel. Chromed barrel bore, gas key, bolt carrier. Hard-coat black-anodized receiver and barrel finish. Introduced 2006. Made in U.S.A. by Smith & Wesson.

Price: From . . . . **$1,039.00 to $1,700.00**
Price: Sport Model **$739.00**

SMITH & WESSON M&P15-22

Caliber: .22 LR. (10-round magazine). **Barrel:** 16". Weight: 5.5 lbs. **Length:** 30.5 to 33.75". **Stock:** 6-position adjustable. **Sights:** Adjustable. Offered in several variations.

Price: . . . . **$549 to $769**

SMITH & WESSON M&P15-300

Caliber: .300 Whisper/.300 AAC Blackout. Other specifications the same of 5.56 models.

Price: **$1119**

SMITH & WESSON MODEL M&P15VTAC VIKING TACTICS MODEL

Caliber: 223 Remington/5.56 NATO, 30-round magazine. **Barrel:** 16". **Weight:** 6.5 lbs. **Length:** 35" extended, 32" collapsed, overall. **Features:** Six-position CAR stock. Surefire flash-hider and G2 light with VTAC light mount; VTAC/JP handguard; JP single-stage match trigger and speed hammer; three adjustable picatinny rails; VTAC padded two-point adjustable sling.

Price: **$2,196.00**

SMITH & WESSON M&P15PC CAMO

Caliber: 223 Rem/5.56 NATO, A2 configuration, 10-round mag. **Barrel:** 20" stainless with 1:8 twist. **Weight:** 8.2 lbs. **Length:** 38.5" overall. **Features:** AR-style, no sights but integral front and rear optics rails. Two-stage trigger, aluminum lower. Finished in Realtree Advantage Max-1 camo.

Price: **$2,046.00**

SMITH & WESSON M&P15 PISTON RIFLE

Similar to AR-derived M&P15 but with gas piston. Chambered in 5.56 NATO. Features include adjustable gas port, optional Troy quad mount handguard, chromed bore/gas key/bolt carrier/chamber, 6-position telescoping or MagPul MOE stock, flattop or folding MBUS sights, aluminum receiver, alloy upper and lower, black anodized finish, 30-round magazine, 16-inch barrel with birdcage.

Price Standard handguard. **$1,531.00**
Price: Troy quad mount handguard **$1,692.00**

SPRINGFIELD ARMORY M1A RIFLE

Caliber: 7.62mm NATO (308), 5- or 10-shot box magazine. **Barrel:** 25-1/16" with flash suppressor, 22" without suppressor. **Weight:** 9.75 lbs. **Length:** 44.25" overall. **Stock:** American walnut with walnut-colored heat-resistant fiberglass handguard. Matching walnut handguard available. Also available with fiberglass stock. **Sights:** Military, square blade front, full click-adjustable aperture rear. **Features:** Commercial equivalent of the U.S. M-14 service rifle with no provision for automatic firing. From Springfield Armory

Price: SOCOM 16 . . . . **$1,855.00**
Price: SOCOM II, from **$2,090.00**
Price: Scout Squad, from **$1,726.00**
Price: Standard M1A, from **$1,608.00**
Price: Loaded Standard, from **$1,759.00**
Price: National Match, from **$2,249.00**
Price: Super Match (heavy premium barrel) about **$2,818.00**
Price: Tactical, from. **$3,780.00**

STAG ARMS MODEL 3 RIFLE

Caliber: 5.56 NATO., 30-shot magazine capacity. **Barrel:** 16". **Stock:** Six position collapsible stock. **Sights:** N/A. **Features:** A short barrel with a chrome lined bore and a 6 position collapsible stock. It uses a gas-operated firing system, so the recoil is delayed until the

round exits the barrel. Although it doesn't have any sights, it does have a Diamondhead Versa Rail System, which allows users to add Picatinny rails to the top, bottom and sides. The Picatinny rail allows for easy mounting of optics and accessories. Features the Diamondhead Versa Rail System; and right and left handed models are available. Perfect for modification, the Stag Arms Model 3 AR 15 is made to mil-spec requirements to give you the most authentic experience possible.
Price: **$895.00**

STONER SR-15 M-5 RIFLE
Caliber: 223. **Barrel:** 20". **Weight:** 7.6 lbs. **Length:** 38" overall. **Stock:** Black synthetic. **Sights:** Post front, fully adjustable rear (300-meter sight). **Features:** Modular weapon system; two-stage trigger. Black finish. Introduced 1998. Made in U.S.A. by Knight's Mfg.
Price: **$1,695.00**

STONER SR-25 CARBINE
Caliber: 7.62 NATO, 10-shot steel magazine. **Barrel:** 16" free-floating **Weight:** 7.75 lbs. **Length:** 35.75" overall. **Stock:** Black synthetic. **Sights:** Integral Weaver-style rail. Scope rings, iron sights optional. **Features:** Shortened, non-slip handguard; removable carrying handle. Matte black finish. Introduced 1995. Made in U.S.A. by Knight's Mfg. Co.
Price: **$3,345.00**

TAURUS CT G2 CARBINE
Caliber: .40 S&W, 9 mm and .45 ACP, Capacity is 34+1 for 9mm, 15+1 for .40 S&W and 10+1 for .45 ACP. **Barrel:** 16". **Weight:** 134-148 ozs. **Length:** 35.75" overall. **Stock:** Aluminum & Polymer. **Sights:** Adjustable rear sight and fixed front sight. **Features:** Full length Picatinny rail, ambidextrous slide catch, two-position safety/fire selector (semi-auto only...) Made in U.S.A. by Knight's Mfg. Co.
Price: **$639.00**

WILSON COMBAT TACTICAL RIFLES
Caliber: 5.56mm NATO, accepts all M-16/AR-15 Style Magazines, includes one 20-round magazine. **Barrel:** 16.25", 1:9 twist, match-grade fluted. **Weight:** 6.9 lbs. **Length:** 36.25" overall. **Stock:** Fixed or collapsible. **Features:** Free-float ventilated aluminum quad-rail handguard, Mil-Spec parkerized barrel and steel components, anodized receiver, precision CNC-machined upper and lower receivers, 7075 T6 aluminum forgings. Single stage JP Trigger/Hammer Group, Wilson Combat Tactical Muzzle Brake, nylon tactical rifle case. M-4T version has flat-top receiver for mounting optics, OD green furniture, 16.25" match-grade M-4 style barrel. SS-15 Super Sniper Tactical Rifle has 1-in-8 twist, heavy 20" match-grade fluted stainless steel barrel. Made in U.S.A by Wilson Combat.
Price: .... **$2,225.00 to $2,450.00**

Prices given are believed to be accurate at time of publication however, many factors affect retail pricing so exact prices are not possible.

BERETTA 1873 RENEGADE SHORT LEVER-ACTION RIFLE
Caliber: 45 Colt, 357 Magnum. **Barrel:** 20" round or 24-1/2" octagonal. **Features:** Blued finish, checkered walnut buttstock and forend, adjustable rear sight and fixed blade front, ten-round tubular magazine.
Price: **$1,350.00**

BERETTA GOLD RUSH SLIDE-ACTION RIFLE AND CARBINE
Caliber: 357 Magnum, 45 Colt. **Barrel:** 20" round or 24-1/2"octagonal. **Features:** External replica of old Colt Lightning Magazine Rifle. Case-hardened receiver, walnut buttstock and forend, crescent buttplate, 13-round (rifle) or 10-round (carbine) magazine. Available as Standard Carbine, Standard Rifle, or Deluxe Rifle.
Price: Standard Carbine **$1,375.00**
Price: Standard Rifle **$1,425.00**
Price: Deluxe Rifle **$11,950.00**

BIG HORN ARMORY MODEL 89 RIFLE AND CARBINE
Lever action rifle or carbine chambered for .500 S&W Magnum. Features include 22-or 18-inch barrel; walnut or maple stocks with pistol grip; aperture rear and blade front sights; recoil pad; sling swivels; enlarged lever loop; magazine capacity 5 (rifle) or 7 (carbine) rounds.
Price: **$1,889.00**

BROWNING BLR RIFLES
Action: Lever action with rotating bolt head, multiple-lug breech bolt with recessed bolt face, side ejection. Rack-and-pinion lever. Flush-mounted detachable magazines, with 4+1 capacity for magnum cartridges, 5+1 for standard rounds. **Barrel:** Button-rifled chrome-moly steel with crowned muzzle. **Stock:** Buttstocks and forends are American walnut with grip and forend checkering. Recoil pad installed. Trigger: Wide-groove design, trigger travels with lever. Half-cock hammer safety; fold-down hammer. **Sights:** Gold bead on ramp front; low-profile square-notch adjustable rear. **Features:** Blued barrel and receiver, high-gloss wood finish. Receivers are drilled and tapped for scope mounts, swivel studs included. Action lock provided. Introduced 1996. Imported from Japan by Browning.

BROWNING BLR LIGHTWEIGHT W/PISTOL GRIP, SHORT AND LONG ACTION; LIGHTWEIGHT '81, SHORT AND LONG ACTION
Calibers: Short Action, 20" Barrel: 22-250 Rem., 243 Win., 7mm-08 Rem., 308 Win., 358, 450 Marlin. Calibers: Short Action, 22" Barrel: 270 WSM, 7mm WSM, 300 WSM, 325 WSM. Calibers: Long Action 22" Barrel: 270 Win., 30-06. Calibers: Long Action 24" Barrel: 7mm Rem. Mag., 300 Win. Mag. **Weight:** 6.5-7.75 lbs. **Length:** 40-45" overall. **Stock:** New checkered pistol grip and Schnabel forearm. Lightweight '81 differs from Pistol Grip models with a Western-style straight grip stock and banded forearm. Lightweight w/Pistol Grip Short Action and Long Action introduced 2005. Model '81 Lightning Long Action introduced 1996.
Price: Lightweight w/Pistol Grip Short Action, from. **$1,020.00**
Price: Lightweight w/Pistol Grip Long Action **$1,100.00**
Price: Lightweight '81 Short Action **$960.00**
Price: Lightweight '81 Long Action **$1,040.00**
Price: Lightweight '81 Takedown Short Action, intr. 2007, from **$1,040.00**
Price: Lightweight '81 Takedown Long Action, intr. 2007, from **$1,120.00**

CHARLES DALY MODEL 1892 LEVER-ACTION RIFLES
Caliber: 45 Colt; 5-shot magazine with removable plug. **Barrel:** 24.25" octagonal. **Weight:** 6.8 lbs. **Length:** 42" overall. **Stock:** Two-piece American walnut, oil finish. **Sights:** Post front, adjustable open rear. **Features:** Color case-hardened receiver, lever, buttplate, forend cap. Introduced 2007. Discontinued.
Price: 1892 Rifle . . . . **N/A**
Price: Take Down Rifle . . . . **N/A**

CIMARRON 1860 HENRY RIFLE CIVIL WAR MODEL
Caliber: 44 WCF, 45 LC; 12-shot magazine. **Barrel:** 24" (rifle). **Weight:** 9.5 lbs. **Length:** 43" overall (rifle). **Stock:** European walnut. **Sights:** Bead front, open adjustable rear. **Features:** Brass receiver and buttplate. Uses original Henry loading system. Copy of the original rifle. Charcoal blue finish optional. Introduced 1991. Imported by Cimarron F.A. Co.
Price: From **$1,444.78**

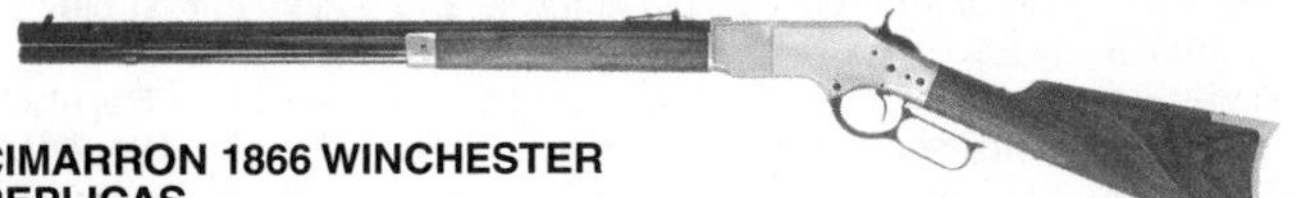

CIMARRON 1866 WINCHESTER REPLICAS
Caliber: 38 Spec., 357, 45 LC, 32 WCF, 38 WCF, 44 WCF. **Barrel:** 24" (rifle), 20" (short rifle), 19" (carbine), 16" (trapper). **Weight:** 9 lbs. **Length:** 43" overall (rifle). **Stock:** European walnut. **Sights:** Bead front, open adjustable rear. **Features:** Solid brass receiver, buttplate, forend cap. Octagonal barrel. Copy of the original Winchester '66 rifle. Introduced 1991. Imported by Cimarron F.A. Co.
Price: 1866 Sporting Rifle, 24" barrel, from. **$1,096.64**
Price: 1866 Short Rifle, 20" barrel, from **$1,096.64**
Price: 1866 Carbine, 19" barrel, from **$1,123.42**
Price: 1866 Trapper, 16" barrel, from **$1,069.86**

CIMARRON 1873 SHORT RIFLE
Caliber: 357 Mag., 38 Spec., 32 WCF, 38 WCF, 44 Spec., 44 WCF, 45 Colt. **Barrel:** 20" tapered octagon. **Weight:** 7.5 lbs. **Length:** 39" overall. **Stock:** Walnut. **Sights:** Bead front, adjustable semi-buckhorn rear. **Features:** Has half "button" magazine. Original-type markings, including caliber, on barrel and elevator and "Kings" patent. From Cimarron F.A. Co.
Price: **$1,203.76**

CIMARRON 1873 DELUXE SPORTING RIFLE
Similar to the 1873 Short Rifle except has 24" barrel with half-magazine.
Price: **$1,324.70**

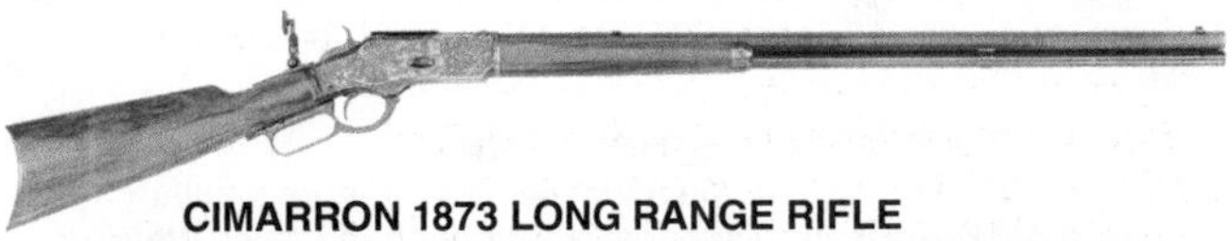

CIMARRON 1873 LONG RANGE RIFLE
Caliber: 44 WCF, 45 Colt. **Barrel:** 30", octagonal. **Weight:** 8.5 lbs. **Length:** 48" overall. **Stock:** Walnut. **Sights:** Blade front, semi-buckhorn ramp rear. Tang sight optional. **Features:** Color case-hardened frame; choice of modern blue-black or charcoal blue for other parts. Barrel marked "Kings Improvement." From Cimarron F.A. Co.
Price: **$1,284.10**

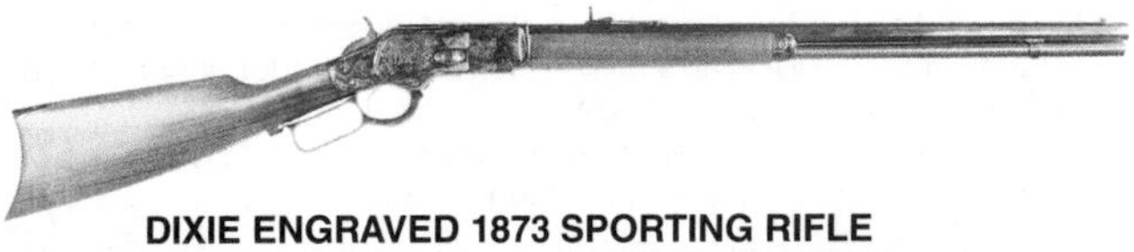

DIXIE ENGRAVED 1873 SPORTING RIFLE
Caliber: 44-40, 13-shot magazine. **Barrel:** 24.25", tapered octagon. **Weight:** 8.25 lbs. **Length:** 43.25" overall. **Stock:** Walnut. **Sights:** Blade front, adjustable rear. **Features:** Engraved frame polished bright (casehardened on plain). Replica of Winchester 1873. Made in Italy. From Dixie Gun Works.
Price: Plain, blued rifle in .44/40, .45 LC, .32/20, .38/40. . . . **$ 1,050.00**

DIXIE 1873 DELUXE SPORTING RIFLE
Caliber: .44-40, .45 LC, .32-20 and .38-40, 13-shot magazine. **Barrel:** 24.25", tapered octagon. **Weight:** 8.25 lbs. **Length:** 43.25" overall. **Stock:** Walnut. Checkered pistol grip buttstock and forearm. **Sights:** Blade front, adjustable rear. **Features:** Color casehardened frame. Engraved frame polished bright. Replica of Winchester 1873. Made in Italy. From Dixie Gun Works.
Price: . . . . **$ 1,050.00 to $ 1,100.00**

DIXIE LIGHTNING RIFLE AND CARBINE
Caliber: .44-40 or .45 LC, 10-shot magazine. **Barrel:** 26" round or octagon, 1:16" or 1:36" twist. **Weight:** 7.25 lbs. **Length:** 43" overall. **Stock:** Walnut. **Sights:** Blade front, open adjustable rear. **Features:** Checkered forearm, blued steel furniture. Made by Pedersoli in Italy. Imported by Dixie Gun Works.
Price: **$1,095.00**
Price: Carbine **$1,225.00**

EMF 1860 HENRY RIFLE
Caliber: 44-40 or 45 Colt. **Barrel:** 24". **Weight:** About 9 lbs. **Length:** About 43.75" overall. **Stock:** Oil-stained American walnut. **Sights:** Blade front, rear adjustable for elevation. **Features:** Reproduction of the original Henry rifle with brass frame and buttplate, rest blued. Imported by EMF.
Price: Brass frame **$1,149.90**
Price: Casehardened frame **$1,229.90**

EMF 1866 YELLOWBOY LEVER ACTIONS
Caliber: 38 Spec., 44-40, 45 LC. **Barrel:** 19" (carbine), 24" (rifle). **Weight:** 9 lbs. **Length:** 43" overall (rifle). **Stock:** European walnut. **Sights:** Bead front, open adjustable rear. **Features:** Solid brass frame, blued barrel, lever, hammer, buttplate. Imported from Italy by EMF.
Price: Rifle. **$1,044.90**
Price: Border Rifle, Short **$969.90**

EMF MODEL 1873 LEVER-ACTION RIFLE
Caliber: 32/20, 357 Mag., 38/40, 44-40, 45 Colt. **Barrel:** 18", 20", 24", 30". **Weight:** 8 lbs. **Length:** 43.25" overall. **Stock:** European walnut. **Sights:** Bead front, rear adjustable for windage and elevation. **Features:** Color case-hardened frame (blue on carbine). Imported by EMF.
Price: **$1,099.90**

EMF MODEL 1873 REVOLVER CARBINE
Caliber: 357 Mag., 45 Colt. **Barrel:** 18". **Weight:** 4 lbs., 8 oz. **Length:** 43-3/4" overall. **Stock:** One-piece walnut. **Sights:** Blade front, notch rear. **Features:** Color case-hardened frame, blue barrel, backstrap and trigger guard. Introduced 1998. Imported from Italy by EMF.
Price: Standard . . . . **$979.90 to $1,040.00**

HENRY .45-70
Caliber: .45-70 (4-shot magazine). **Barrel:** 18.5". Weight: 7 lbs. **Stock:** Pistol grip walnut. **Sights:** XS Ghost Rings with blade front.
PRICE: **$800**

HENRY BIG BOY LEVER-ACTION CARBINE
Caliber: 357 Magnum, 44 Magnum, 45 Colt, 10-shot tubular magazine. **Barrel:** 20" octagonal, 1:38 right-hand twist. **Weight:** 8.68 lbs. **Length:** 38.5" overall. **Stock:** Straight-grip American walnut, brass buttplate. **Sights:** Marbles full adjustable semi-buckhorn rear, brass bead front. **Features:** Brasslite receiver not tapped for scope mount. Made in U.S.A. by Henry Repeating Arms.
Price: H006 44 Magnum, walnut, blued barrel **$899.95**
Price: H006DD Deluxe 44 Magnum, engraved receiver **$1,995.95**

HENRY .30/30 LEVER-ACTION CARBINE
Same as the Big Boy except has straight grip American walnut, 30-30 only, 6-shot. Receivers are drilled and tapped for scope mount. Made in U.S.A. by Henry Repeating Arms.
Price: H009 Blued receiver, round barrel **$749.95**
Price: H009B Brass receiver, octagonal barrel **$969.95**

MARLIN MODEL 336C LEVER-ACTION CARBINE
Caliber: 30-30 or 35 Rem., 6-shot tubular magazine. **Barrel:** 20" Micro-Groove. **Weight:** 7 lbs. **Length:** 38.5" overall. **Stock:** Checkered American black walnut, capped pistol grip. Mar-Shield finish; rubber buttpad; swivel studs. **Sights:** Ramp front with Wide-Scan hood, semi-buckhorn folding rear adjustable for windage and elevation. **Features:** Hammer-block safety. Receiver tapped for scope mount, offset hammer spur; top of receiver sandblasted to prevent glare. Includes safety lock.
Price: **$530.00**

MARLIN MODEL 336SS LEVER-ACTION CARBINE
Same as the 336C except receiver, barrel and other major parts are machined from stainless steel. 30-30 only, 6-shot; receiver tapped for scope. Includes safety lock.
Price: **$650.00**

MARLIN MODEL 336W LEVER-ACTION RIFLE
Similar to the Model 336C except has walnut-finished, cut-checkered Maine birch stock; blued steel barrel band has integral sling swivel; no front sight hood; comes with padded nylon sling; hard rubber buttplate. Introduced 1998. Includes safety lock. Made in U.S.A. by Marlin.
Price: **$452.00**
Price: With 4x scope and mount **$495.00**

MARLIN 336BL
Lever action rifle chambered for .30-30. Features include 6-shot full length tubular magazine; 18-inch blued barrel with Micro-Groove rifling (12 grooves); big-loop finger lever; side ejection; blued steel receiver; hammer block safety; brown laminated hardwood pistol-grip stock with fluted comb; cut checkering; deluxe recoil pad; blued swivel studs.
Price: . . . . **N/A**

MARLIN 336 DELUXE
Lever action rifle chambered in .30-30. Features include 6-shot tubular magazine; side ejection; solid top receiver; highly polished deep blue finish; hammer block safety; #1 grade full fancy American black walnut stock and forend; 20-inch barrel with Micro-Groove rifling (12 grooves); adjustable semi-buckhorn folding rear, ramp front sight with brass bead and Wide-Scan™ hood. Solid top receiver tapped for scope mount; offset hammer spur (right or left hand) for scope use.
Price: . . . . **N/A**

MARLIN MODEL XLR LEVER-ACTION RIFLES
Similar to Model 336C except has an 24" stainless barrel with Ballard-type cut rifling, stainless steel receiver and other parts, laminated hardwood stock with pistol grip, nickel-plated swivel studs. Chambered for 30-30 Win. with Hornady spire-pointed Flex-Tip cartridges. Includes safety lock. Introduced 2006. Similar models chambered for 308 Marlin Express introduced in 2007
Price: Model 336XLR **$816.00**

MARLIN MODEL 308/338 MXLR
Caliber: 338 Marlin Express. **Barrel:** 24" stainless steel. **Weight:** 7.5 lbs. **Length:** 42.5" overall. **Features:** Stainless steel receiver, lever and magazine tube. Black/gray laminated checkered stock and forend. Hooded ramp front sight and adjustable semi-buckhorn rear; drilled and tapped for scope mounts. Receiver-mounted crossbolt safety.
Price: Model 338MXLR **$806.00**
Price: Model 308MXLR: 308 Marlin Express **$806.00**
Price: Model 338MX: Similar to Model 338MXLR but with blued metal and walnut stock and forend **$611.00**
Price: Model 308MX: 308 Marlin Express **$611.00**

MARLIN MODEL 444 LEVER-ACTION SPORTER
Caliber: 444 Marlin, 5-shot tubular magazine. **Barrel:** 22" deep cut Ballard rifling. **Weight:** 7.5 lbs. **Length:** 40.5" overall. **Stock:** Checkered American black walnut, capped pistol grip, rubber rifle buttpad. Mar-Shield finish; swivel studs. **Sights:** Hooded ramp front, folding semi-buckhorn rear adjustable for windage and elevation. **Features:** Hammer-block safety. Receiver tapped for scope mount; offset hammer spur. Includes safety lock.
Price: **$619.00**

MARLIN MODEL 444XLR LEVER-ACTION RIFLE
Similar to Model 444 except has an 24" stainless barrel with Ballard-

type cut rifling, stainless steel receiver and other parts, laminated hardwood stock with pistol grip, nickel-plated swivel studs. Chambered for 444 Marlin with Hornady Evolution spire-pointed Flex-Tip cartridges. Includes safety lock. Introduced 2006.
Price: (Model 444XLR) **$816.00**

MARLIN MODEL 1894 LEVER-ACTION CARBINE
Caliber: 44 Spec./44 Mag., 10-shot tubular magazine. **Barrel:** 20" Ballard-type rifling. **Weight:** 6 lbs. **Length:** 37.5" overall. **Stock:** Checkered American black walnut, straight grip and forend. Mar-Shield finish. Rubber rifle buttpad; swivel studs. **Sights:** Wide-Scan hooded ramp front, semi-buckhorn folding rear adjustable for windage and elevation. **Features:** Hammer-block safety. Receiver tapped for scope mount, offset hammer spur, solid top receiver sand blasted to prevent glare. Includes safety lock.
Price: **$576.00**

MARLIN MODEL 1894C CARBINE
Similar to the standard Model 1894 except chambered for 38 Spec./357 Mag. with full-length 9-shot magazine, 18.5" barrel, hammer-block safety, hooded front sight. Introduced 1983. Includes safety lock.
Price: **$576.00**

MARLIN MODEL 1894 COWBOY
Caliber: 357 Mag., 44 Mag., 45 Colt, 10-shot magazine. **Barrel:** 20" tapered octagon, deep cut rifling. **Weight:** 7.5 lbs. **Length:** 41.5" overall. **Stock:** Straight grip American black walnut, hard rubber buttplate, Mar-Shield finish. **Sights:** Marble carbine front, adjustable Marble semi-buckhorn rear. **Features:** Squared finger lever; straight grip stock; blued steel forend tip. Designed for Cowboy Shooting events. Introduced 1996. Includes safety lock. Made in U.S.A. by Marlin.
Price: **$822.00**

MARLIN MODEL 1894SS
Similar to Model 1894 except has stainless steel barrel, receiver, lever, guard plate, magazine tube and loading plate. Nickel-plated swivel studs.
Price: **$704.00**

MARLIN 1894 DELUXE
Lever action rifle chambered in .44 Magnum/.44 Special. Features include 10-shot tubular magazine; squared finger lever; side ejection; richly polished deep blued metal surfaces; solid top receiver; hammer block safety; #1 grade fancy American black walnut straight-grip stock and forend; cut checkering; rubber rifle butt pad; Mar-Shield finish; blued steel fore-end cap: swivel studs; deep-cut Ballard-type rifling (6 grooves).
Price: .... **N/A**

MARLIN 1894CSS
Lever action rifle chambered in .357 Magnum/.38 Special. Features include 9-shot tubular magazine; stainless steel receiver, barrel, lever, trigger and hammer; squared finger lever; side ejection; solid top receiver; hammer block safety; American black walnut straight-grip stock and forend; cut checkering; rubber rifle butt pad; Mar-Shield finish.
Price: .... **N/A**

MARLIN MODEL 1895 LEVER-ACTION RIFLE
Caliber: 45-70 Govt., 4-shot tubular magazine. **Barrel:** 22" round. **Weight:** 7.5 lbs. **Length:** 40.5" overall. **Stock:** Checkered American black walnut, full pistol grip. Mar-Shield finish; rubber buttpad; quick detachable swivel studs. **Sights:** Bead front with Wide-Scan hood, semi-buckhorn folding rear adjustable for windage and elevation. **Features:** Hammer-block safety. Solid receiver tapped for scope mounts or receiver sights; offset hammer spur. Includes safety lock.
Price: **$619.00**

MARLIN MODEL 1895G GUIDE GUN LEVER-ACTION RIFLE
Similar to Model 1895 with deep-cut Ballard-type rifling; straight-grip walnut stock. Overall length is 37", weighs 7 lbs. Introduced 1998. Includes safety lock. Made in U.S.A. by Marlin.
Price: **$630.00**

MARLIN MODEL 1895GS GUIDE GUN
Similar to Model 1895G except receiver, barrel and most metal parts are machined from stainless steel. Chambered for 45-70 Govt., 4-shot, 18.5" barrel. Overall length is 37", weighs 7 lbs. Introduced 2001. Includes safety lock. Made in U.S.A. by Marlin.
Price: **$752.00**

MARLIN MODEL 1895 SBLR
Similar to Model 1895GS Guide Gun but with stainless steel barrel (18.5"), receiver, large loop lever and magazine tube. Black/gray laminated buttstock and forend, XS ghost ring rear sight, hooded ramp front sight, receiver/barrel-mounted top rail for mounting accessory optics. Chambered in 45-70 Government. Overall length is 42.5", weighs 7.5 lbs.
Price: **$979.00**

MARLIN MODEL 1895 COWBOY LEVER-ACTION RIFLE
Similar to Model 1895 except has 26" tapered octagon barrel with Ballard-type rifling, Marble carbine front sight and Marble adjustable semi-buckhorn rear sight. Receiver tapped for scope or receiver sight. Overall length is 44.5", weighs about 8 lbs. Introduced 2001. Includes safety lock. Made in U.S.A. by Marlin.
Price: **$785.00**

MARLIN MODEL 1895XLR LEVER-ACTION RIFLE
Similar to Model 1895 except has an 24" stainless barrel with Ballard-type cut rifling, stainless steel receiver and other parts, laminated hardwood stock with pistol grip, nickel-plated swivel studs. Chambered for 45-70 Govt. Government with Hornady Evolution spire-pointed Flex-Tip cartridges. Includes safety lock. Introduced 2006.
Price: (Model 1895MXLR)........................... **$816.00**

MARLIN 1895GBL
Lever action rifle chambered in .45-70 Government. Features include 6-shot, full-length tubular magazine; 18-1/2-inch barrel with deep-cut Ballard-type rifling (6 grooves); big-loop finger lever; side ejection; solid-top receiver; deeply blued metal surfaces; hammer block safety; pistol-grip two tone brown laminate stock with cut checkering; ventilated recoil pad; Mar-Shield finish, swivel studs.
Price: .... **N/A**

MOSSBERG 464 LEVER ACTION RIFLE
Caliber: 30-30 Win., 6-shot tubular magazine. **Barrel:** 20" round. **Weight:** 6.7 lbs. **Length:** 38.5" overall. **Stock:** Hardwood with straight or pistol grip, quick detachable swivel studs. **Sights:** Folding rear sight, adjustable for windage and elevation. **Features:** Blued receiver and barrel, receiver drilled and tapped, two-position top-tang safety. Available with straight grip or semi-pistol grip. Introduced 2008. From O.F. Mossberg & Sons, Inc.
Price: **$497.00**

NAVY ARMS 1874 SHARPS #2 CREEDMORE RIFLE
Caliber: .45-70 Govt. **Barrel:** 30" octagon. **Weight:** 10 lbs. **Length:** 48" overall. **Sights:** Soule target grade rear tang sight, front globe with 12 inserts. **Features:** Highly polished nickel receiver and action, double-set triggers. From Navy Arms.
Price: Model SCR072 (2008) **$1,816.00**

NAVY ARMS MILITARY HENRY RIFLE
Caliber: 44-40 or 45 Colt, 12-shot magazine. **Barrel:** 24.25". **Weight:** 9 lbs., 4 oz. **Stock:** European walnut. **Sights:** Blade front, adjustable

ladder-type rear. **Features:** Brass frame, buttplate, rest blued. Replica of the model used by cavalry units in the Civil War. Has full-length magazine tube, sling swivels; no forend. Imported from Italy by Navy Arms.

Price: **$1,199.00**

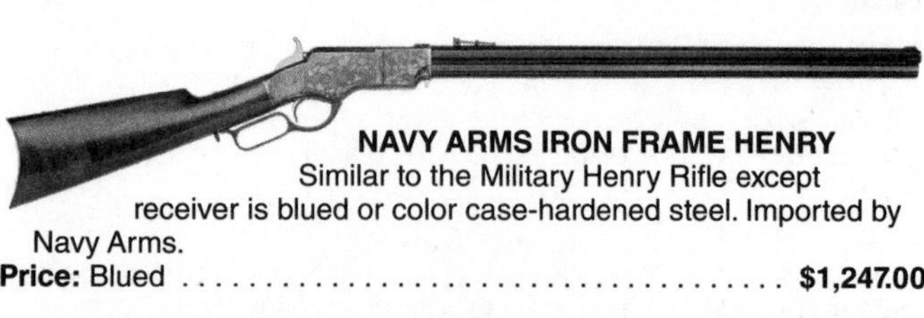

NAVY ARMS IRON FRAME HENRY

Similar to the Military Henry Rifle except receiver is blued or color case-hardened steel. Imported by Navy Arms.

Price: Blued **$1,247.00**

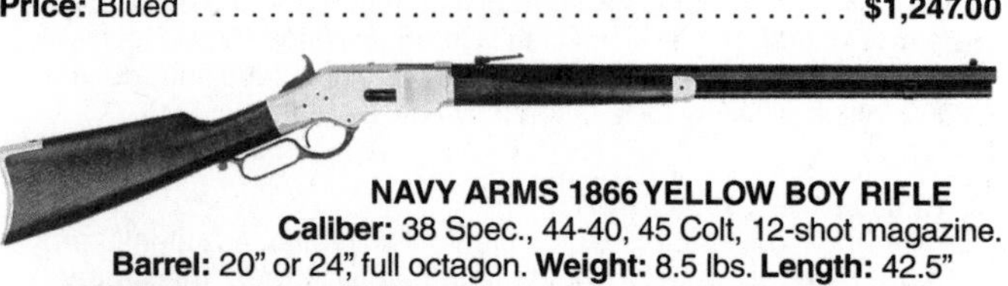

NAVY ARMS 1866 YELLOW BOY RIFLE

Caliber: 38 Spec., 44-40, 45 Colt, 12-shot magazine. **Barrel:** 20" or 24", full octagon. **Weight:** 8.5 lbs. **Length:** 42.5" overall. **Stock:** Walnut. **Sights:** Blade front, adjustable ladder-type rear. **Features:** Brass frame, forend tip, buttplate, blued barrel, lever, hammer. Introduced 1991. Imported from Italy by Navy Arms.

Price: Yellow Boy Rifle, 24.25" barrel. **$915.00**
Price: Yellow Boy Carbine, 19" barrel **$882.00**

NAVY ARMS 1873 WINCHESTER-STYLE RIFLE

Caliber: 357 Mag., 44-40, 45 Colt, 12-shot magazine. **Barrel:** 24.25". **Weight:** 8.25 lbs. **Length:** 43" overall. **Stock:** European walnut. **Sights:** Blade front, buckhorn rear. **Features:** Color case-hardened frame, rest blued. Full-octagon barrel. Imported by Navy Arms.

Price: **$1,047.00**
Price: 1873 Carbine, 19" barrel **$1,024.00**
Price: 1873 Sporting Rifle (octagonal bbl., checkered walnut stock and forend) **$1,183.00**
Price: 1873 Border Model, 20" octagon barrel **$1,047.00**
Price: 1873 Deluxe Border Model **$1,183.00**

PUMA BOUNTY HUNTER RIFLE

Caliber: .44/40, .44 Mag. and .45 Colt, 6-shot magazine capacity. **Barrel:** 12". **Weight:** 4.5 lbs. **Length:** 24". **Stock:** Walnut. **Sights:** Fixed sights. **Features:** A piece of 1950's TV nostalgia, the Bounty Hunter is a reproduction of the gun carried by Western character Josh Randall in the series "Wanted: Dead or Alive". The Bounty Hunter is based on a Model 92 rifle, but is considered by Federal Law as a pistol, because it is built from the ground up as a handgun. Manufactured in the U.S.A. by Chiappa Firearms of Dayton, OH, the Bounty Hunter features a 12" barrel and 6 round tubular magazine. At just 24" OAL, the Bounty Hunter makes an ideal pack gun or camp defense pistol. The Bounty Hunter has a teardrop shaped loop lever and is built with the same fit, finish and high grade Italian walnut stocks as our Puma M-92 and M-86 rifles.

Price: .45LC, Case Hardened/Blued **$1,372.00**
Price: .44/40, Case Hardened/Blued. **$1,372.00**
Price: .44MAG, Case Hardened/Blued **$1,372.00**

PUMA MODEL 92 RIFLES AND CARBINES

Caliber: 17 HMR (XP and Scout models, only; intr. 2008), 38 Spec./357 Mag., 44 Mag., 45 Colt, 454 Casull, 480 Ruger (.44-40 in 20" octagonal barrel). **Barrel:** 16" and 20" round; 20" and 24" octagonal. 1:30" rate of twist (exc. 17 HMR is 1:9"). **Weight:** 7.7 lbs. **Stock:** Walnut stained hardwood. **Sights:** Blade front, V rear, buckhorn sights sold separately. **Features:** Finishes available in blue/blue, blue/case colored and stainless/stainless with matching crescent butt plates. .454 and .480 calibers have rubber recoil pads. Full-length magazines, thumb safety. Large lever loop or HiViz sights available on select models. Magazine capacity is 12 rounds with 24" bbl.; 10 rounds with 20" barrel; 8 rounds in 16" barrel. Introduced in 2002. Scout includes long-eye-relief scope, rail, elevated cheekpiece, intr. 2008. XP chambered in 17 HMR, 38 Spec./357 Mag. and 44 Mag., loads through magazine tube or loading gate, intr. 2008. Imported from Brazil by Legacy Sports International.

Price: From **$959.00**
Price: Scout Model, w/2.5x32 Nikko-Stirling Nighteater scope, intr. 2008, from **$739.00**
Price: XP Model, tube feed magazine, intr. 2008, from. **$613.00**

REMINGTON MODEL 7600/7615 PUMP ACTION

Caliber: 243 Win., 270 Win., 30-06 Spfl., 308; 223 Rem. (7615 only). **Barrel:** 22" round tapered. **Weight:** 7.5 lbs. **Length:** 42.6" overall. **Stock:** Cut-checkered walnut pistol grip and forend, Monte Carlo with full cheekpiece. Satin or high-gloss finish. Also, black synthetic. **Sights:** Gold bead front sight on matted ramp, open step adjustable sporting rear. **Features:** Redesigned and improved version of the Model 760. Detachable 4-shot clip. Cross-bolt safety. Receiver tapped for scope mount. Introduced 1981. Model 7615 Tactical chambered in 223 Rem. **Features:** Knoxx SpecOps NRS (Non Recoil Suppressing) adjustable stock, parkerized finish, 10-round detachable magazine box, sling swivel studs. Introduced 2007.

Price:7600 Wood. **$792.00**
Price:7600 Synthetic. **$665.00**
Price: 7615 Ranch Carbine **$955.00**
Price: 7615 Camo Hunter **$1,009.00**
Price: 7615 Tactical 223 Rem., 16.5" barrel, 10-rd. magazine (2008). **$932.00**

ROSSI R92 LEVER-ACTION CARBINE

Caliber: 38 Special/357 Mag, 44 Mag., 44-40 Win., 45 Colt, 454 Casull. **Barrel:** 16" or 20" with round barrel, 20" or 24" with octagon barrel. **Weight:** 4.8 lbs. to 7 lbs. **Length:** 34» to 41.5». **Features:** Blued or stainless finish. Various options available in selected chamberings (large lever loop, fiber optic sights, cheekpiece, etc.).

Price: From **$559.00**

ROSSI RIO GRANDE

Caliber: .30-30 or .45-70. **Barrel:** 20". Weight. 7 lbs. **Sights:** Adjustable rear, post front. **Stock:** Hardwood or camo.

PRICE: . . . . **$545, $559 (.45-70)**

TRISTAR SHARPS 1874 SPORTING RIFLE

Caliber: 45-70 Govt. **Barrel:** 28", 32", 34" octagonal. **Weight:** 9.75 lbs. **Length:** 44.5" overall. **Stock:** Walnut. **Sights:** Dovetail front, adjustable rear. **Features:** Cut checkering, case colored frame finish.

Price: **$1,099.00**

UBERTI 1873 SPORTING RIFLE

Caliber: 357 Mag., 44-40, 45 Colt. **Barrel:** 19" to 24.25". **Weight:** Up to 8.2 lbs. **Length:** Up to 43.3" overall. **Stock:** Walnut, straight grip and pistol grip. **Sights:** Blade front adjustable for windage, open rear adjustable for elevation. **Features:** Color case-hardened frame, blued barrel, hammer, lever, buttplate, brass elevator. Imported by Stoeger Industries.

Price: 1873 Carbine, 19" round barrel **$1,199.00**
Price: 1873 Short Rifle, 20" octagonal barrel **$1,249.00**
Price: 1873 Special Sporting Rifle, 24.25" octagonal barrel . **$1,379.00**

UBERTI 1866 YELLOWBOY CARBINE, SHORT RIFLE, RIFLE

Caliber: 38 Spec., 44-40, 45 Colt. **Barrel:** 24.25", octagonal. **Weight:** 8.2 lbs. **Length:** 43.25" overall. **Stock:** Walnut.

Prices given are believed to be accurate at time of publication however, many factors affect retail pricing so exact prices are not possible.

Sights: Blade front adjustable for windage, rear adjustable for elevation. **Features:** Frame, buttplate, forend cap of polished brass, balance charcoal blued. Imported by Stoeger Industries.
Price: 1866 Yellowboy Carbine, 19" round barrel. **$1,079.00**
Price: 1866 Yellowboy Short Rifle, 20" octagonal barrel **$1,129.00**
Price: 1866 Yellowboy Rifle, 24.25" octagonal barrel **$1,129.00**

UBERTI 1860 HENRY RIFLE
Caliber: 44-40, 45 Colt. **Barrel:** 24.25", half-octagon. **Weight:** 9.2 lbs. **Length:** 43.75" overall. **Stock:** American walnut. **Sights:** Blade front, rear adjustable for elevation. Imported by Stoeger Industries.
Price: 1860 Henry Trapper, 18.5" barrel, brass frame **$1,329.00**
Price: 1860 Henry Rifle Iron Frame, 24.25" barrel **$1,419.00**

UBERTI LIGHTNING RIFLE
Caliber: 357 Mag., 45 Colt, 10+1. **Barrel:** 20" to 24.25". **Stock:** Walnut. Finish: Blue or case-hardened. Introduced 2006. Imported by Stoeger Industries.
Price: 1875 Lightning Rifle, 24.25" barrel **$1,259.00**
Price: 1875 Lightning Short Rifle, 20" barrel **$1,259.00**
Price: 1875 Lightning Carbine, 20" barrel **$1,179.00**

UBERTI SPRINGFIELD TRAPDOOR RIFLE
Caliber: 4-70, single shot. **Barrel:** 22" or 32.5". **Stock:** Walnut. Finish: Blue and case-hardened. Introduced 2006. Imported by Stoeger Industries.
Price: Springfield Trapdoor Carbine, 22" barrel. **$1,429.00**
Price: Springfield Trapdoor Army, 32.5" barrel **$1,669.00**

WINCHESTER MODEL 94 SHORT RIFLE
Caliber: .30-30, .38-55. Barrel: 20". Weight: 6.75 lbs. Sights: Semi-buckhorn rear, gold bead front. Stock: Walnut with straight grip. Fore-end has black grip cap. Also available in takedown design in .450 Marlin or .30-30.
Price: . . . . **$1230 to $1460** (Takedown)

WINCHESTER MODEL 94 SPORTER
Caliber: .30-30, .38-55. Barrel: 24". Weight: 7.5 lbs. Same features of Model 94 Short Rifle except for crescent butt and steel buttplate, 24" half-round, half-octagon barrel, checkered stock.
Price: **$1400**

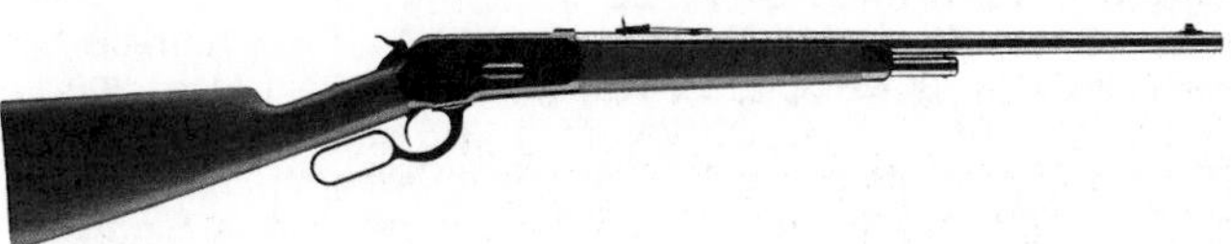

WINCHESTER MODEL 1886 EXTRA LIGHT RIFLE
Caliber: .45-70. Barrel: 22". Weight: 7.25 lbs. Sights: Adjustable buckhorn rear, blade front. Also offered in Short Rifle model in .45-70 or .45-90 with crescent butt.
Price . . . . **$1269 to $1340 (Short Rifle)**

BARRETT MODEL 95 BOLT-ACTION RIFLE

Caliber: 50 BMG, 5-shot magazine. **Barrel:** 29". **Weight:** 23.5 lbs. **Length:** 45" overall. **Stock:** Energy-absorbing recoil pad. **Sights:** Scope optional. **Features:** Bolt-action, bullpup design. Disassembles without tools; extendable bipod legs; match-grade barrel; muzzle brake. Introduced 1995. Made in U.S.A. by Barrett Firearms Mfg., Inc.

Price: From **$6,500.00**

BARRETT MODEL 98B

Caliber: .338 Lapua Magnum (10-shot magazine). **Barrel:** 27" fluted or 20". **Weight:** 13.5 lbs. **Length:** 49.8". Comes with two magazines, bipod, monopod, side accessory rail, hard case.

PRICE: **$4850**

BLASER R93 BOLT-ACTION RIFLE

Caliber: 22-250 Rem., 243 Win., 6.5x55, 270 Win., 7x57, 7mm-08 Rem., 308 Win., 30-06 Spfl., 257 Wby. Mag., 7mm Rem. Mag., 300 Win. Mag., 300 Wby. Mag., 338 Win. Mag., 375 H&H, 416 Rem. Mag. **Barrel:** 22" (standard calibers), 26" (magnum). **Weight:** 7 lbs. **Length:** 40" overall (22" barrel). **Stock:** Two-piece European walnut. **Sights:** None furnished; drilled and tapped for scope mounting. **Features:** Straight pull-back bolt action with thumb-activated safety slide/cocking mechanism; interchangeable barrels and bolt heads. Introduced 1994. Imported from Germany by Blaser USA.

Price: R93 Prestige, wood grade 3 . . . . **$3,275.00**
Price: R93 Luxus **$4,460.00**
Price: R93 Professional **$2,950.00**
Price: R93 Grand Luxe **$8,163.00**
Price: R93 Attache **$6,175.00**

BROWNING A-BOLT RIFLES

Common Features: Short-throw (60") fluted bolt, three locking lugs, plunger-type ejector; adjustable trigger is grooved. Chrome-plated trigger sear. Hinged floorplate, detachable box magazine. Slide tang safety. Receivers are drilled and tapped for scope mounts, swivel studs included. Barrel is free-floating and glass-bedded, recessed muzzle. Safety is top-tang sliding button. Engraving available for bolt sleeve or rifle body. Introduced 1985. Imported from Japan by Browning.

BROWNING A-BOLT HUNTER

Calibers: 22" Barrel: 223 Rem., 22-250 Rem., 243 Win., 270 Win., 30-06 Spfl., 7mm-08 Rem., 308 Win. **Barrel:** 270 WSM, 7mm WSM, 300 WSM, 325 WSM (intr. 2005). **Calibers:** 24" Barrel: 25-06 Rem. **Calibers:** 26" Barrel: 7mm Rem. Mag., 300 Win. Mag., 338 Win. Mag. **Weight:** 6.25-7.2 lbs. **Length:** 41.25-46.5" overall. **Stock:** Sporter-style walnut; checkered grip and forend. **Metal Finish:** Low-luster blueing.

Price: Hunter, left-hand, from **$819.00**

BROWNING A-BOLT HUNTER FLD

Caliber: 23" Barrel: 270 WSM, 7mm WSM, 300 WSM, 325 WSM (intr. 2005). **Weight:** 6.6 lbs. **Length:** 42.75" overall. **Features:** FLD has low-luster blueing and select Monte Carlo stock with right-hand palm swell, double-border checkering. Otherwise similar to A-Bolt Hunter.

Price: FLD **$899.00**

BROWNING A-BOLT TARGET

Similar to A-Bolt Hunter but with 28" heavy bull blued barrel, blued receiver, satin finish gray laminated stock with adjustable comb and

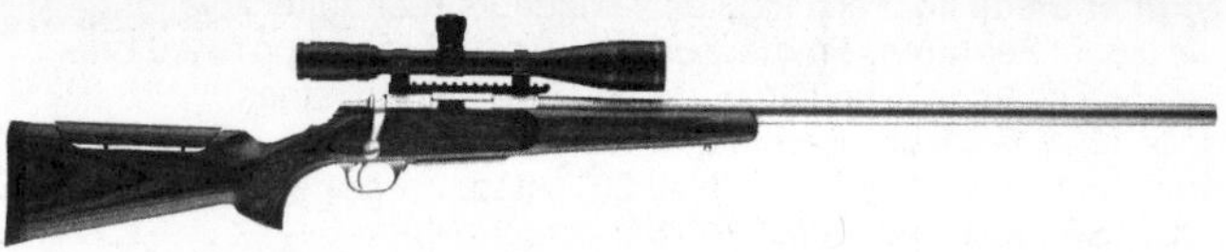

semi-beavertail forend. Chambered in 223, 308 Winchester and 300 WSM. Available also with stainless receiver and barrel.

Price: From **$1,269.00**
Price: Stainless, from **$1,489.00**

BROWNING A-BOLT MICRO HUNTER AND MICRO HUNTER LEFT-HAND

Calibers: .22 Hornet **Barrel:** 20" Barrel: 22-250 Rem., 243 Win., 308 Win., 7mm-08. 22" **Weight:** 6.25-6.4 lbs. **Length:** 39.5-41.5" overall. **Features:** Classic walnut stock with 13.3" LOP. Otherwise similar to A-Bolt Hunter.

Price: Micro Hunter, from **$759.00**
Price: Micro Hunter left-hand, from **$799.00**

BROWNING A-BOLT MEDALLION

Calibers: 22" Barrel: 223 Rem., 22-250 Rem., 243 Win., 308 Win., 270 Win., 280 Rem., 30-06.; 23" Barrel: 270 WSM, 7mm WSM, 300 WSM, 325 WSM (intr. 2005); 24" Barrel: 25-06 Rem.; 26" Barrel: 7mm Rem. Mag., 300 Win. Mag., 338 Win. Mag., 375 H&H. **Weight:** 6.25-7.1 lbs. **Length:** 41.25-46.5" overall. **Stock:** Select walnut stock, glossy finish, rosewood grip and forend caps, checkered grip and forend. Metal Finish: Engraved high-polish blued receiver.

Price: **$1,120.00**

BROWNING A-BOLT STAINLESS STALKER, STAINLESS STALKER LEFT-HAND

Calibers: 22" Barrel: 223 Rem., 243 Win., 270 Win., 280 Rem., 7mm-08 Rem., 30-06 Spfl., 308 Win. Calibers: 23" Barrel: 270 WSM, 7mm WSM, 300 WSM, 325 WSM (intr. 2005). Calibers: 24" Barrel: 25-06 Rem. Calibers: 26" Barrel: 7mm Rem. Mag., 300 Win. Mag., 338 Win. Mag., 375 H&H. **Weight:** 6.1-7.2 lbs. **Length:** 40.9-46.5" overall. **Features:** Similar to the A-Bolt Hunter model except receiver and barrel are made of stainless steel; other exposed metal surfaces are finished silver-gray matte. Graphite-fiberglass composite textured stock. No sights are furnished, except on 375 H&H, which comes with open sights. Introduced 1987.

Price: Stainless Stalker left-hand, from **$1,029.00**
Price: Stainless Stalker w/Boss, from **$1,119.00**

BROWNING A-BOLT COMPOSITE STALKER

Calibers: 22 Barrel: 270 Win., 30-06 Sprg.; 23» Barrel: 270 WSM, 7mm WSM, 300 WSM, 325 WSM; 24» Barrel: 25-06 Rem.; 26» Barrel: 7mm Rem. Mag., 300 Win. Mag., 338 Win. Mag. **Weight:** 6.6-7.3 lbs. **Length:** 42.5-46.5» overall. **Features:** Similar to the A-Bolt Stainless Stalker except has black composite stock with textured finish and matte-blued finish on all exposed metal surfaces except bolt sleeve. No sights are furnished.

Price: Composite Stalker w/BOSS, from **$869.00**
Price: Stainless Stalker **$1,009.00**
Price: Stainless Stalker w/Boss, from **$1,079.00**

BROWNING A-BOLT ECLIPSE HUNTER W/BOSS, M-1000 ECLIPSE W/BOSS, M-1000 ECLIPSE WSM, STAINLESS M-1000 ECLIPSE WSM

Calibers: 22" Barrel: 270 Win., 30-06. Calibers: 26" Barrel: 7mm Rem. Mag., 300 Win. Mag., 270 WSM, 7mm WSM, 300 WSM. **Weight:** 7.5-9.9 lbs. **Length:** 42.75-46.5" overall. **Features:** All models have gray/black laminated thumbhole stock. Introduced 1996.

Two versions have BOSS barrel vibration modulator and muzzle brake. Hunter has sporter-weight barrel. M-1000 Eclipses have long actions and heavy target barrels, adjustable triggers, bench-style forends, 3-shot magazines. Introduced 1997.

Price: Eclipse Hunter w/BOSS, from **$1,430.00**
Price: M-1000 Eclipse, from **$1,340.00**
Price: M-1000 Eclipse w/BOSS, from **$1,440.00**
Price: Stainless M-1000 Eclipse WSM, from **$1,640.00**
Price: Stainless M-1000 Eclipse w/BOSS, from **$1,740.00**

BROWNING X-BOLT HUNTER

Calibers: 223, 22-250, 243 Win., 25-06 Rem., 270 Win., 270 WSM, 280 Rem., 30-06 Spfl., 300 Win. Mag., 300 WSM, 308 Win., 325 WSM, 338 Win. Mag., 375 H&H Mag., 7mm Rem. Mag., 7mm WSM, 7mm-08 Rem. **Barrels:** 22", 23", 24", 26", varies by model. Matte blued or stainless free-floated barrel, recessed muzzle crown. **Weight:** 6.3-7 lbs. **Stock:** Hunter and Medallion models have wood stocks; Composite Stalker and Stainless Stalker models have composite stocks. Inflex Technology recoil pad. **Sights:** None, drilled and tapped receiver, X-Lock scope mounts. **Features:** Adjustable three-lever Feather Trigger system, polished hard-chromed steel components, factory pre-set at 3.5 lbs., alloy trigger housing. Bolt unlock button, detachable rotary magazine, 60-degree bolt lift, three locking lugs, top-tang safety, sling swivel studs. Medallion has metal engraving, gloss finish walnut stock, rosewood fore-end grip and pistol grip cap. Introduced 2008. From Browning.

BROWNING X-BOLT MICRO HUNTER

Similar to Browning X-Bolt Hunter but with compact dimensions (13-15/16 length of pull, 41-1/4 overall length).

Price: Standard chamberings **$839.00**
Price: Magnum **$869.00**

BROWNING X-BOLT MICRO MIDAS RIFLES

Caliber: 243 Win., 7mm-08 Rem., 308 Win., 22-250 Rem. **Barrel:** 20". **Weight:** 6 lbs.1 oz. **Length:** 37-5/8" to 38-1/8" overall. **Stock:** Satin finish checkered walnut stock. **Sights:** Hooded front and adjustable rear. **Features:** Steel receiver with low-luster blued finish. Glass bedded, drilled and tapped for scope mounts. Barrel is free-floating and hand chambered with target crown. Bolt-action with adjustable Feather Trigger™ and detachable rotary magazine. Compact 12-1/2" length of pull for smaller shooters, designed to fit smaller-framed shooters like youth and women. This model has all the same features as the full-size model with sling swivel studs installed and Inflex Technology recoil pad. (Scope and mounts not included).

Price: 243 Win. **$800**
Price: 7mm-08 Rem. **$800**
Price: 308 Win. **$800**
Price: 22-250 Rem. **$800**

BROWNING X-BOLT VARMINT STALKER

Similar to Browning X-Bolt Stalker but with medium-heavy free-floated barrel, target crown, composite stock. Chamberings available: 223, 22-250, 243 Winchester and 308 Winchester only.

Price: **$1,019.00**

BROWNING X-BOLT RMEF WHITE GOLD

Similar to X-Bolt Medallion but with gold-engraved matte stainless finish and Rocky Mountain Elk Foundation grip cap. Chambered in 325 WSM only.

Price: **$1,399.00**

BROWNING X-BOLT RMEF SPECIAL HUNTER

Similar to above but with matte blued finish without gold highlights.

Price: **$919.00**

BUSHMASTER BA50 BOLT-ACTION RIFLE

Caliber: 50 Browning BMG. **Barrel:** 30" (rifle), 22" (carbine), 10-round mag. **Weight:** 30 lbs. (rifle), 27 lbs. (carbine). **Length:** 58" overall (rifle), 50" overall (carbine). **Features:** Free-floated Lother Walther barrel with muzzle brake, Magpul PRS adjustable stock.

Price: **$5,300.00**

CARBON ONE BOLT-ACTION RIFLE

Caliber: 22-250 to 375 H&H. **Barrel:** Up to 28". **Weight:** 5.5 to 7.25 lbs. **Length:** Varies. **Stock:** Synthetic or wood. **Sights:** None furnished. **Features:** Choice of Remington, Browning or Winchester action with free-floated Christensen graphite/epoxy/steel barrel, trigger pull tuned to 3 to 3.5 lbs. Made in U.S.A. by Christensen Arms.

Price: Carbon One Hunter Rifle, 6.5 to 7 lbs. **$1,775.00**
Price: Carbon One Custom, 5.5 to 6.5 lbs., Shilen trigger . . **$3,900.00**
Price: Carbon Extreme **$2,450.00**

CENTURY INTERNATIONAL M70 SPORTER DOUBLE-TRIGGER BOLT ACTION RIFLE

Caliber: 22-250 Rem., 270 Win., 300 Win. Mag, 308 Win., 24" barrel. **Weight:** 7.95 lbs. **Length:** 44.5". **Sights:** Flip-up U-notch rear sight, hooded blade front sight. **Features:** Mauser M98-type action; 5-rd fixed box magazine. 22-250 has hinged floorplate. Monte Carlo stock, oil finish. Adjustable trigger on double-trigger models. 300 Win. Mag. Has 3-rd. fixed box magazine. 308 Win. holds 5 rounds. 300 and 308 have buttpads. Manufactured by Zastava in Yugoslavia, imported by Century International.

Price: M70 Sporter Double-Trigger **$500.00**
Price: M70 Sporter Double-Trigger 22-250 . . . . **$475.00**
Price: M70 Sporter Single-Trigger .300 Win. Mag. **$475.00**
Price: M70 Sporter Single/Double Trigger 308 Win. **$500.00**

CHEYTAC M-200

Caliber: 408 CheyTac, 7-round magazine. **Barrel:** 30". **Length:** 55", stock extended. **Weight:** 27 lbs. (steel barrel); 24 lbs. (carbon fiber barrel). **Stock:** Retractable. **Sights:** None, scope rail provided. **Features:** CNC-machined receiver, attachable Picatinny rail M-1913, detachable barrel, integral bipod, 3.5-lb. trigger pull, muzzle brake. Made in U.S. by CheyTac, LLC.

Price: **$13,795.00**

COOPER MODEL 21 BOLT-ACTION RIFLE

Caliber: 17 Rem., 19-223, Tactical 20, .204 Ruger, 222 Rem, 222 Rem. Mag., 223 Rem, 223 Rem A.I., 6x45, 6x47. **Barrel:** 22" or 24" in Classic configurations, 24"-26" in Varminter configurations. **Weight:** 6.5-8.0 lbs., depending on type. **Stock:** AA-AAA select claro walnut, 20 lpi checkering. **Sights:** None furnished. **Features:** Three front locking-lug bolt-action single shot. Action: 7.75" long, Sako extractor. Button ejector. Fully adjustable single-stage trigger. Options include wood upgrades, case-color metalwork, barrel fluting, custom LOP, and many others.

Price: From **$1,695.00**

COOPER MODEL 22 BOLT-ACTION RIFLE

Caliber: 22-250 Rem., 22-250 Rem. AI, 25-06 Rem., 25-06 Rem. AI, 243 Win., 243 Win. AI, 220 Swift, 250/3000 AI, 257 Roberts, 257 Roberts AI, 7mm-08 Rem., 6mm Rem., 260 Rem., 6 x 284, 6.5 x 284, 22 BR, 6mm BR, 308 Win. **Barrel:** 24" or 26" stainless match in Classic configurations. 24" or 26" in Varminter configurations. **Weight:** 7.5 to 8.0 lbs. depending on type. **Stock:** AA-AAA select claro walnut, 20 lpi checkering. **Sights:** None furnished. **Features:** Three front locking-lug bolt-action single shot. Action: 8.25" long, Sako style extractor. Button ejector. Fully adjustable single-stage trigger. Options include wood upgrades, case-color metalwork, barrel fluting, custom LOP, and many others.

Price: From **$1,695.00**

COOPER MODEL 38 BOLT-ACTION RIFLE

Caliber: 17 Squirrel, 17 He Bee, 17 Ackley Hornet, 17 Mach IV, 19 Calhoon, 20 VarTarg, 221 Fireball, 22 Hornet, 22 K-Hornet, 22 Squirrel, 218 Bee, 218 Mashburn Bee. **Barrel:** 22" or 24" in Classic configurations, 24" or 26" in Varminter configurations. **Weight:** 6.5-8.0 lbs. depending on type. **Stock:** AA-AAA select claro walnut, 20 lpi checkering. **Sights:** None furnished. **Features:** Three front locking-lug bolt-action single shot. Action: 7" long, Sako style extractor. Button ejector. Fully adjustable single-stage trigger. Options include wood upgrades, case-color metalwork, barrel fluting, custom LOP, and many others.

Price: From **$1,695.00**

COOPER MODEL 56 BOLT-ACTION RIFLE

Caliber: .257 Weatherby Mag., .264 Win. Mag., .270 Weatherby Mag., 7mm Remington Mag., 7mm Weatherby Mag., 7mm Shooting Times Westerner, .300 Holland & Holland, .300 Winchester Mag., .300 Weatherby Mag., .308 Norma Mag., 8mm Rem. Mag., .338 Win. Mag., .340 Weatherby V. **Barrel:** 22" or 24" in Classic configurations, 24" or 26" in Varminter configurations. **Weight:** 7.75 - 8 lbs. depending on type. **Stock:** AA-AAA select claro walnut, 20 lpi checkering. **Sights:** None furnished. **Features:** Three front locking-lug bolt-action single shot. Action: 7" long, Sako style extractor. Button ejector. Fully adjustable single-stage trigger. Options include wood upgrades, case-color metalwork, barrel fluting, custom LOP, and many others.

Price: Classic. **$1518.00**
Price: Custom Classic. **$1,618.00**
Price: Western Classic. **$1518.00**
Price: Jackson Game. **$1,618.00**
Price: Jackson Hunter. **$1518.00**
Price: Excalibur. **$1,618.00**

CZ 527 LUX BOLT-ACTION RIFLE

Caliber: 204 Ruger, 22 Hornet, 222 Rem., 223 Rem., detachable 5-shot magazine. **Barrel:** 23.5"; standard or heavy barrel. **Weight:** 6 lbs., 1 oz. **Length:** 42.5" overall. **Stock:** European walnut with Monte Carlo. **Sights:** Hooded front, open adjustable rear. **Features:** Improved mini-Mauser action with non-rotating claw extractor; single set trigger; grooved receiver. Imported from the Czech Republic by CZ-USA.

Price: Brown laminate stock **$718.00**
Price: Model FS, full-length stock, cheekpiece **$827.00**

CZ 527 AMERICAN BOLT-ACTION RIFLE

Similar to the CZ 527 Lux except has classic-style stock with 18 lpi checkering; free-floating barrel; recessed target crown on barrel. No

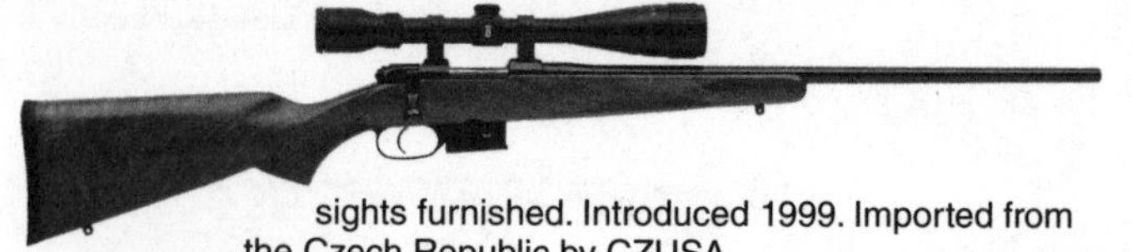

sights furnished. Introduced 1999. Imported from the Czech Republic by CZUSA.

Price: From **$751.00**

CZ 550 AMERICAN CLASSIC BOLT-ACTION RIFLE

Caliber: 22-250 Rem., 243 Win., 6.5x55, 7x57, 7x64, 308 Win., 9.3x62, 270 Win., 30-06. **Barrel:** free-floating barrel; recessed target crown. **Weight:** 7.48 lbs. **Length:** 44.68" overall. **Stock:** American classic-style stock with 18 lpi checkering or FS (Mannlicher). **Sights:** No sights furnished. **Features:** Improved Mauser-style action with claw extractor, fixed ejector, square bridge dovetailed receiver; single set trigger. Introduced 1999. Imported from the Czech Republic by CZ-USA.

Price: FS (full stock) **$894.00**
Price: American, from **$827.00**

CZ 550 SAFARI MAGNUM/AMERICAN SAFARI MAGNUM BOLT-ACTION RIFLES

Similar to CZ 550 American Classic. Chambered for 375 H&H Mag., 416 Rigby, 458 Win. Mag., 458 Lott. Overall length is 46.5"; barrel length 25"; weighs 9.4 lbs., 9.9 lbs (American). Hooded front sight, express rear with one standing, two folding leaves. Imported from the Czech Republic by CZ-USA.

Price: $1,179.00
Price: American **$1,261.00**
Price: American Kevlar **$1,714.00**

CZ 550 VARMINT BOLT-ACTION RIFLE

Similar to CZ 550 American Classic. Chambered for 308 Win. and 22-250. Kevlar, laminated stocks. Overall length is 46.7"; barrel length 25.6"; weighs 9.1 lbs. Imported from the Czech Republic by CZ-USA.

Price: **$841.00**
Price: Kevlar **$1,037.00**
Price: Laminated **$966.00**

CZ 550 MAGNUM H.E.T. BOLT-ACTION RIFLE

Similar to CZ 550 American Classic. Chambered for 338 Lapua, 300 Win. Mag., 300 RUM. Overall length is 52"; barrel length 28"; weighs 14 lbs. Adjustable sights, satin blued barrel. Imported from the Czech Republic by CZ-USA.

Price: **$3,673.00**

CZ 550 ULTIMATE HUNTING BOLT-ACTION RIFLE

Similar to CZ 550 American Classic. Chambered for 300 Win Mag. Overall length is 44.7"; barrel length 23.6"; weighs 7.7 lbs. Imported from the Czech Republic by CZ-USA.

Price: $4,242.00

CZ 750 SNIPER RIFLE

Caliber: 308 Winchester, 10-shot magazine. **Barrel:** 26". **Weight:** 11.9 lbs. **Length:** 48" overall. **Stock:** Polymer thumbhole. **Sights:** None furnished; permanently attached Weaver rail for scope mounting. **Features:** 60-degree bolt throw; oversized trigger guard and bolt handle for use with gloves; full-length equipment rail on forend; fully adjustable trigger. Introduced 2001. Imported from the Czech Republic by CZ-USA.

Price: **$2,404.00**

DAKOTA 76 TRAVELER TAKEDOWN RIFLE

Caliber: 257 Roberts, 25-06 Rem., 7x57, 270 Win., 280 Rem., 30-06 Spfl., 338-06, 35 Whelen (standard length); 7mm Rem. Mag., 300 Win. Mag., 338 Win. Mag., 416 Taylor, 458 Win. Mag. (short magnums); 7mm, 300, 330, 375 Dakota Magnums. **Barrel:** 23". **Weight:** 7.5 lbs. **Length:** 43.5" overall. **Stock:** Medium fancy-grade walnut in classic style. Checkered grip and forend; solid buttpad. **Sights:** None furnished; drilled and tapped for scope mounts. **Features:** Threadless disassembly. Uses modified Model 76 design with many features of the Model 70 Winchester. Left-hand model also

Prices given are believed to be accurate at time of publication however, many factors affect retail pricing so exact prices are not possible.

available. Introduced 1989. African chambered for 338 Lapua Mag., 404 Jeffery, 416 Rigby, 416 Dakota, 450 Dakota, 4-round magazine, select wood, two stock cross-bolts. 24" barrel, weighs 9-10 lbs. Ramp front sight, standing leaf rear. Introduced 1989.Made in U.S.A. by Dakota Arms, Inc.

Price: Classic **$6,495.00**
Price: Safari **$8,395.00**
Price: African **$9,495.00**

DAKOTA 76 CLASSIC BOLT-ACTION RIFLE

Caliber: 257 Roberts, 270 Win., 280 Rem., 30-06 Spfl., 7mm Rem. Mag., 338 Win. Mag., 300 Win. Mag., 375 H&H, 458 Win. Mag. **Barrel:** 23". **Weight:** 7.5 lbs. **Length:** 43.5" overall. **Stock:** Medium fancy grade walnut in classic style. Checkered pistol grip and forend; solid buttpad. **Sights:** None furnished; drilled and tapped for scope mounts. **Features:** Has many features of the original Winchester Model 70. One-piece rail trigger guard assembly; steel gripcap. Model 70-style trigger. Many options available. Left-hand rifle available at same price. Introduced 1988. From Dakota Arms, Inc.

Price: From **$5,395.00**

DAKOTA MODEL 97 BOLT-ACTION RIFLE

Caliber: 22-250 to 330. **Barrel:** 22" to 24". **Weight:** 6.1 to 6.5 lbs. **Length:** 43" overall. **Stock:** Fiberglass. **Sights:** Optional. **Features:** Matte blue finish, black stock. Right-hand action only. Introduced 1998. Made in U.S.A. by Dakota Arms, Inc.

Price: From **$3,395.00**

DSA DS-MP1

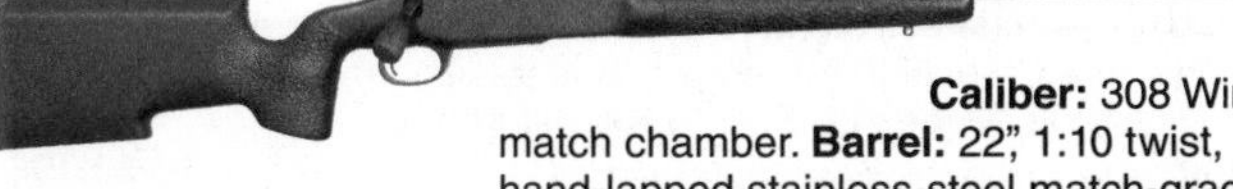

Caliber: 308 Win. match chamber. **Barrel:** 22", 1:10 twist, hand-lapped stainless-steel match-grade Badger Barrel with recessed target crown. **Weight:** 11.5 lbs. **Length:** 41.75". **Stock:** Black McMillan A5 pillar bedded in Marine-Tex with 13.5" length of pull. **Sights:** Tactical Picatinny rail. **Features:** Action, action threads and action bolt locking shoulder completely trued, Badger Ordnance precision ground heavy recoil lug, machined steel Picatinny rail sight mount, trued action threads, action bolt locking shoulder, bolt face and lugs, 2.5-lb. trigger pull, barrel and action finished in Black DuraCoat, guaranteed to shoot 1/2 MOA at 100 yards with match-grade ammo. Introduced 2006. Made in U.S.A. by DSA, Inc.

Price: **$2,800.00**

EAA/ZASTAVA M-93 BLACK ARROW RIFLE

Caliber: 50 BMG. **Barrel:** 36". **Weight:** 7 to 8.5 lbs. **Length:** 60". **Stock:** Synthetic. **Sights:** Scope rail and iron sights. **Features: Features:** Mauser action, developed in early 1990s by Zastava Arms Factory. Fluted heavy barrel with recoil reducing muzzle brake, self-leveling and adjustable folding integral bipod, back up iron sights, heavy duty carry handle, detachable 5 round box magazine, and quick detachable scope mount. Imported by EAA. Imported from Russia by EAA Corp.

Price: **$6,986.25**

HOWA M-1500 RANCHLAND COMPACT

Caliber: 223 Rem., 22-250 Rem., 243 Win., 308 Win. and 7mm-08. **Barrel:** 20" #1 contour, blued finish. **Weight:** 7 lbs. **Stock:** Hogue Overmolded in black, OD green, Coyote Sand colors. 13.87" LOP. **Sights:** None furnished; drilled and tapped for scope mounting. **Features:** Three-position safety, hinged floor plate, adjustable trigger, forged one-piece bolt, M-16 style extractor, forged flat-bottom receiver. Also available with Nikko-Stirling Nighteater 3-9x42 riflescope. Introduced in 2008. Imported from Japan by Legacy Sports International.

Price: Rifle Only, (2008) **$479.00**
Price: Rifle with 3-9x42 Nighteater scope (2008) **$599.00**

HOWA M-1500 THUMBHOLE SPORTER

Caliber: 204, 223 Rem., 22-250 Rem., 243 Win., 6.5x55 (2008) 25-06 Rem., 270 Win., 7mm Rem. Mag., 308 Win., 30-06 Spfl., 300 Win. Mag., 338 Win. Mag., 375 Ruger. Similar to Camo Lightning except stock. **Weight:** 7.6 to 7.7 lbs. **Stock:** S&K laminated wood in nutmeg (brown/black) or pepper (grey/black) colors, raised comb with forward taper, flared pistol grip and scalloped thumbhole. **Sights:** None furnished; drilled and tapped for scope mounting. **Features:** Three-position safety, hinged floor plate, adjustable trigger, forged one-piece bolt, M-16 style extractor, forged flat-bottom receiver. Introduced in 2001. Imported from Japan by Legacy Sports International.

Price: Blue/Nutmeg, standard calibers . . . . **$649.00 to $669.00**
Price: Stainless/Pepper, standard calibers . . . . **$749.00 to $769.00**

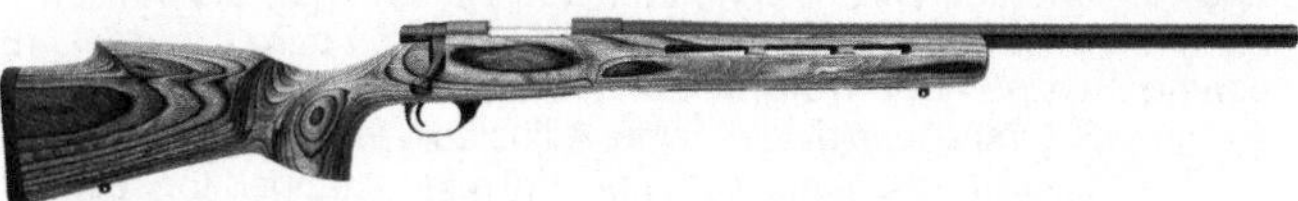

HOWA M-1500 VARMINTER SUPREME AND THUMBHOLE VARMINTER SUPREME

Caliber: 204, 223 Rem., 22-250 Rem., 243 Win., 308 Win. **Stock:** Varminter Supreme: Laminated wood in nutmeg (brown), pepper (grey) colors, raised comb and rollover cheekpiece, full pistol grip with palm-filling swell and broad beavertail forend with six vents for barrel cooling. Thumbhole Varminter Supreme similar, adds a high, straight comb, more vertical pistol grip. **Sights:** None furnished; drilled and tapped for scope mounting. **Features:** Three-position safety, hinged floor plate, adjustable trigger, forged one-piece bolt, M-16 style extractor, forged flat-bottom receiver, hammer forged bull barrel and recessed muzzle crown; overall length, 43.75", 9.7 lbs. Introduced 2001. Barreled actions imported by Legacy Sports International; stocks by S&K Gunstocks.

Price: Varminter Supreme, Blue/Nutmeg **$679.00**
Price: Varminter Supreme, Stainless/Pepper **$779.00**
Price: Thumbhole Varminter Supreme, Blue/Nutmeg **$679.00**
Price: Thumbhole Varminter Supreme, Stainless/Pepper **$779.00**

HOWA CAMO LIGHTNING M-1500

Caliber: 204, 223 Rem., 22-250 Rem., 243 Win., 25-06 Rem., 270 Win., 308 Win., 30-06 Spfl., 300 Win. Mag., 338 Win. Mag., 7mm Rem. Mag. **Barrel:** 22" standard calibers; 24" magnum calibers; #2 and #6 contour; blue and stainless. **Weight:** 7.6 to 9.3 lbs. **Length:** 42" to 44.5" overall. **Stock:** Synthetic with molded cheek piece, checkered grip and forend. **Sights:** None furnished; drilled and tapped for scope mounting. **Features:** Three-position safety, hinged floor plate, adjustable trigger, forged one-piece bolt, M-16 style extractor, forged flat bottom receiver. Introduced in 1993. Barreled actions imported by Legacy Sports International.

Price: Blue, #2 barrel, standard calibers **$377.00**
Price: Stainless, #2 barrel, standard calibers **$479.00**
Price: Blue, #2 barrel, magnum calibers **$390.00**
Price: Stainless, #2 barrel, magnum calibers **$498.00**
Price: Blue, #6 barrel, standard calibers **$425.00**
Price: Stainless, #6 barrel, standard calibers **$498.00**

HOWA/HOGUE M-1500

Caliber: 204, 223 Rem., 22-250 Rem., 243 Win., 6.5x5 (2008), 25-06 Rem., 270 Win., 308 Win., 30-06 Spfl., 300 Win. Mag., 338 Win. Mag., 7mm Rem. Mag., 375 Ruger (2008). **Barrel:** Howa barreled action; stainless or blued, 22" #2 contour. **Weight:** 7.4 to 7.6 lbs. **Stock:** Hogue Overmolded, black, or OD green; ambidextrous palm swells. **Sights:** None furnished; drilled and tapped for scope mounting. **Length:** 42" to 44.5" overall. **Features:** Three-position safety, hinged floor plate, adjustable trigger, forged one-piece bolt, M-16 style extractor, forged flat bottom receiver, aluminum pillar bedding and free-floated barrels. Introduced in 2006. Available w/3-10x42 Nikko-Stirling Nighteater scope, rings, bases (2008). from Imported from Japan by Legacy Sports International.

Price: Blued, rifle only . . . . **$479.00 to $499.00**
Price: Blue, rifle with scope package (2008) . . . . . **$599.00 to $619.00**
Price: Stainless, rifle only . . . . **$625.00 to $675.00**

HOWA/HOGUE M-1500 COMPACT HEAVY BARREL VARMINTER

Chambered in 223 Rem., 308 Win., has 20" #6 contour heavy barrel, recessed muzzle crown. **Stock:** Hogue Overmolded, black, or OD green; ambidextrous palm swells. **Sights:** None furnished; drilled and tapped for scope mounting. **Length:** 44.0" overall. **Features:** Three-position safety, hinged floor plate, adjustable trigger, forged one-piece bolt, M-16 style extractor, forged flat bottom receiver, aluminum pillar bedding and free-floated barrels. **Weight:** 9.3 lbs. Introduced 2008. Imported from Japan by Legacy Sports International.

Price: From **$559.00**

HOWA/AXIOM M-1500

Caliber: 204, 223 Rem., 22-250 Rem., 243 Win., 6.5x55 (2008), 25-06 Rem. (2008), 270 Win., 308 Win., 30-06 Spfl., 7mm Rem, 300 Win. Mag., 338 Win. Mag., 375 Ruger standard barrel; 204, 223 Rem., 243 Win. and 308 Win. heavy barrel. **Barrel:** Howa barreled action, 22" contour standard barrel, 20" #6 contour heavy barrel, and 24" #6 contour heavy barrel. **Weight:** 8.6-10 lbs. **Stock:** Knoxx Industries Axiom V/S synthetic, black or camo. Adjustable length of pull from 11.5" to 15.5". **Sights:** None furnished; drilled and tapped for scope mounting. **Features:** Three-position safety, adjustable trigger, hinged floor plate, forged receiver with large recoil lug, forged one-piece bolt with dual locking lugs Introduced in 2007. Standard-barrel scope packages come with 3-10x42 Nikko-Stirling Nighteater scope, rings, bases (2008). Heavy barrels come with 4-16x44 Nikko-Stirling scope. Imported from Japan by Legacy Sports International.

Price: Axiom Standard Barrel, black stock, from **$699.00**
Price: Axiom 20" and 24" Varminter, black or camo stock, from **$799.00**
Price: Axiom 20" and 24" Varminter, camo stock w/scope (2008), from **$819.00**

HOWA M-1500 ULTRALIGHT 2-N-1 YOUTH

Caliber: 223 Rem., 22-250 Rem., 243 Win., 308 Win., 7mm-08. **Barrel:** 20" #1 contour, blued. **Weight:** 6.8 lbs. **Length:** 39.25" overall. **Stock:** Hogue Overmolded in black, 12.5" LOP. Also includes adult-size Hogue Overmolded in OD green. **Sights:** None furnished; drilled and tapped for scope mounting. **Features:** Bolt and receiver milled to reduce weight, three-position safety, hinged floor plate, adjustable trigger, forged one-piece bolt, M-16 style extractor, forged flat-bottom receiver. Scope package includes 3-9x42 Nikko-Stirling riflescope with bases and rings. Imported from Japan by Legacy Sports International.

Price: Blue, Youth Rifle **$539.00**
Price: w/Scope package (2008) **$589.00**

H-S PRECISION PRO-SERIES BOLT-ACTION RIFLES

Caliber: 30 chamberings, 3- or 4-round magazine. **Barrel:** 20", 22", 24" or 26", sporter contour Pro-Series 10X match-grade stainless steel barrel. Optional muzzle brake on 30 cal. or smaller. **Weight:** 7.5 lbs. **Length:** NA. **Stock:** Pro-Series synthetic stock with full-length bedding block chassis system, sporter style. **Sights:** None; drilled and tapped for bases. **Features:** Accuracy guarantee: up to 30 caliber, 1/2 minute of angle (3 shots at 100 yards), test target supplied. Stainless steel action, stainless steel floorplate with detachable magazine, matte black Teflon finish. Made in U.S.A. by H-S Precision, Inc.

Price: SPR **$2,680.00**
Price: SPL Lightweight (2008) **$2,825.00**

KEL-TEC RFB

Caliber: 7.62 NATO (308 Win.). **Barrels:** 18" to 32". **Weight:** 11.3 lbs. (unloaded). **Length:** 40» overall. **Features:** Gas-operated semi-auto bullpup-style, forward-ejecting. Fully ambidextrous controls, adjustable trigger mechanism, no open sights, four-sided picatinny forend. Accepts standard FAL-type magazines. Production of the RFB has been delayed due to redesign but was expected to begin first quarter 2009.

Price: **$1,800.00**

KENNY JARRETT BOLT-ACTION RIFLE

Caliber: 223 Rem., 243 Improved, 243 Catbird, 7mm-08 Improved, 280 Remington, .280 Ackley Improved, 7mm Rem. Mag., 284 Jarrett, 30-06 Springfield, 300 Win. Mag., .300 Jarrett, 323 Jarrett, 338 Jarrett, 375 H&H, 416 Rem., 450 Rigby., other modern cartridges. **Barrel:** NA. **Weight:** NA. **Length:** NA. **Stock:** NA. **Features:** Tri-Lock receiver. Talley rings and bases. Accuracy guarantees and custom loaded ammunition.

Price: Signature Series. **$7,640.00**
Price: Wind Walker **$7,380.00**

Price: Original Beanfield (customer's receiver) **$5,380.00**
Price: Professional Hunter **$10,400.00**
Price: SA/Custom **$6,630.00**

KIMBER MODEL 8400 BOLT-ACTION RIFLE

Caliber: 25-06 Rem., 270 Win., 7mm, 30-06 Spfl., 300 Win. Mag., 338 Win. Mag., or 325 WSM, 4 shot. **Barrel:** 24". **Weight:** 6 lbs. 3 oz. to 6 lbs 10 oz. **Length:** 43.25". **Stock:** Claro walnut or Kevlar-reinforced fiberglass. **Sights:** None; drilled and tapped for bases. **Features:** Mauser claw extractor, two-position wing safety, action bedded on aluminum pillars and fiberglass, free-floated barrel, match grade adjustable trigger set at 4 lbs., matte or polished blue or matte stainless finish. Introduced 2003. Sonora model (2008) has brown laminated stock, hand-rubbed oil finish, chambered in 25-06 Rem., 30-06 Spfl., and 300 Win. Mag. Weighs 8.5 lbs., measures 44.50" overall length. Front swivel stud only for bipod. Stainless steel bull barrel, 24" satin stainless steel finish. Made in U.S.A. by Kimber Mfg. Inc.

Price: Classic **$1,172.00**
Price: Classic Select Grade, French walnut stock (2008) . . . **$1,359.00**
Price: SuperAmerica, AAA walnut stock **$2,240.00**
Price: Sonora **$1,359.00**
Price: Police Tactical, synthetic stock, fluted barrel (300 Win. Mag only) **$2,575.00**

KIMBER MODEL 8400 CAPRIVI BOLT-ACTION RIFLE

Similar to 8400 bolt rifle, but chambered for .375 H&H and 458 Lott, 4-shot magazine. Stock is Claro walnut or Kevlar-reinforced fiberglass. Features twin steel crossbolts in stock, AA French walnut, pancake cheekpiece, 24 lines-per-inch wrap-around checkering, ebony forend tip, hand-rubbed oil finish, barrel-mounted sling swivel stud, 3-leaf express sights, Howell-type rear sling swivel stud and a Pachmayr Decelerator recoil pad in traditional orange color. Introduced 2008. Made in U.S.A. by Kimber Mfg. Inc.

Price: **$3,196.00**

KIMBER MODEL 8400 TALKEETNA BOLT-ACTION RIFLE

Similar to 8400 bolt rifle, but chambered for .375 H&H, 4-shot magazine. Weighs 8 lbs, overall length is 44.5". Stock is synthetic. Features free-floating match grade barrel with tapered match grade chamber and target crown, three-position wing safety acts directly on the cocking piece for greatest security, and Pacmayr Decelerator. Made in U.S.A. by Kimber Mfg. Inc.

Price: **$2,108.00**

KIMBER MODEL 84M BOLT-ACTION RIFLE

Caliber: 22-250 Rem., 204 Ruger, 223 Rem., 243 Win., 260 Rem., 7mm-08 Rem., 308 Win., 5-shot. **Barrel:** 22", 24", 26". **Weight:** 5 lbs., 10 oz. to 10 lbs. **Length:** 41" to 45". **Stock:** Claro walnut, checkered with steel gripcap; synthetic or gray laminate. **Sights:** None; drilled and tapped for bases. **Features:** Mauser claw extractor, three-position wing safety, action bedded on aluminum pillars, free-floated barrel, match-grade trigger set at 4 lbs., matte blue finish. Includes cable lock. Introduced 2001. Montana (2008) has synthetic stock, Pachmayr Decelerator recoil pad, stainless steel 22" sporter barrel. Made in U.S.A. by Kimber Mfg. Inc.

Price: Classic (243 Win., 260, 7mm-08 Rem., 308) **$1,114.00**
Price: Varmint (22-250) **$1,224.00**
Price: Montana **$1,276.00**
Price: Classic Stainless, matte stainless steel receiver and barrel (243 Win., 7mm-08, 308 Win.) **$1,156.00**

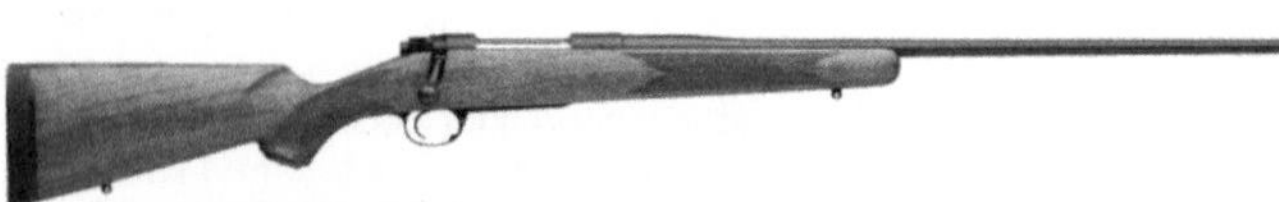

KIMBER MODEL 84L CLASSIC RIFLE

Bolt action rifle chambered in .270 Win. and .30-06. Features include 24-inch sightless matte blue sporter barrel; hand-rubbed A-grade walnut stock with 20 lpi panel checkering; pillar and glass bedding; Mauser claw extractor; 3-position M70-style safety; 5-round magazine; adjustable trigger.

Price: **$1,172.00**

Prices given are believed to be accurate at time of publication however, many factors affect retail pricing so exact prices are not possible.

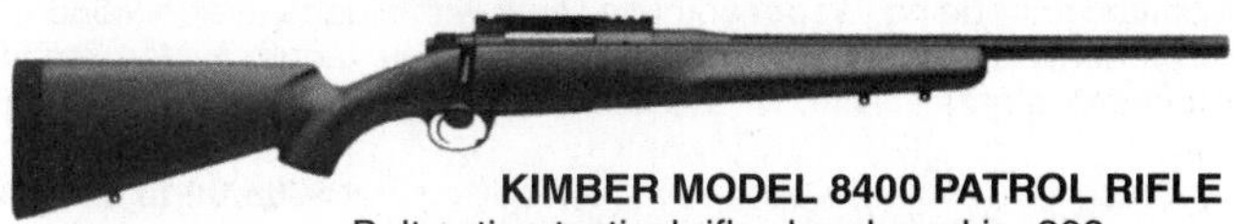

KIMBER MODEL 8400 PATROL RIFLE

Bolt action tactical rifle chambered in .308 Win. Features include 20-inch 1:12 fluted sightless matte blue heavy barrel; black epoxy-coated laminated wood stock with 20 lpi panel checkering; pillar and glass bedding; Mauser claw extractor; 3-position M70-style safety; 5-round magazine; adjustable trigger.

Price: **$1,476.00**

L.A.R. GRIZZLY 50 BIG BOAR RIFLE

Caliber: 50 BMG, single shot. **Barrel:** 36". **Weight:** 30.4 lbs. **Length:** 45.5" overall. **Stock:** Integral. Ventilated rubber recoil pad. **Sights:** None furnished; scope mount. **Features:** Bolt-action bullpup design, thumb and bolt stop safety. All-steel construction. Introduced 1994. Made in U.S.A. by L.A.R. Mfg., Inc.

Price: From **$2,350.00**

MAGNUM RESEARCH MOUNTAIN EAGLE MAGNUMLITE RIFLES

Caliber: .22-250, .223, .224, .243, .257, 7mm Rem. Mag., 7mm WSM, .280, .300 Win. Mag., .300 WSM, .30-06, 3-shot magazine. **Barrel:** 24" sport taper graphite; 26" bull barrel graphite. **Weight:** 7.1-9.2 lbs. **Length:** 44.5-48.25" overall (adjustable on Tactical model). **Stock:** Hogue OverMolded synthetic, H-S Precision Tactical synthetic, H-S Precision Varmint synthetic. **Sights:** None. **Features:** Remington Model 700 receiver. Introduced in 2001. From Magnum Research, Inc.

Price: MLR3006ST24 Hogue stock. **$2,295.00**
Price: MLR7MMBST24 Hogue stock **$2,295.00**
Price: MLRT22250 H-S Tactical stock, 26" bull barrel. **$2,400.00**
Price: MLRT300WI Tactical **$2,400.00**

MARLIN XL7 BOLT ACTION RIFLE

Caliber: 25-06 Rem. 270 Win., 30-06 Spfl., 4-shot magazine. **Barrel:** 22" 1:10" right-hand twist, recessed barrel crown. **Weight:** 6.5 lbs. **Length:** 42.5" overall. **Stock:** Black synthetic or Realtree APG-HD camo, Soft-Tech recoil pad, pillar bedded. **Sights:** None. **Features:** Pro-Fire trigger is user adjustable down to 2.5 lbs. Fluted bolt, steel sling swivel studs, high polished blued steel, checkered bolt handle, molded checkering, one-piece scope base. Introduced in 2008. From Marlin Firearms, Inc.

Price: Black Synthetic. **$391.00**
Price: Camouflaged **$426.00**

MARLIN XS7 SHORT-ACTION BOLT-ACTION RIFLE

Similar to Model XL7 but chambered in 7mm-08, 243 Winchester and 308 Winchester.

Price: **$391.00**
Price: XS7Y Youth **$391.00**
Price: XS7C Camo, Realtree APG HD camo stock **$426.00**
Price: XS7S Stainless. **$500.00**

MERKEL KR1 BOLT-ACTION RIFLE

Caliber: 223 Rem., 243 Rem., 6.5x55, 7mm-08, 308 Win., 270 Win., 30-06, 9.3x62, 7mm Rem. Mag., 300 Win. Mag., 270 WSM, 300 WSM, 338 Win. Mag. **Features:** Short lock, short bolt movement, take-down design with interchangeable barrel assemblies, three-position safety, detachable box magazine, fine trigger with set feature, checkered walnut pistol-grip semi-schnable stock. Adjustable iron sights with quick release mounts. Imported from Germany by Merkel USA.

Price: **$1,995.00**
Price: Model KR1 Stutzen Antique: 20.8" barrel, case-colored receiver, Mannlicher-style stock **$3,395.00**

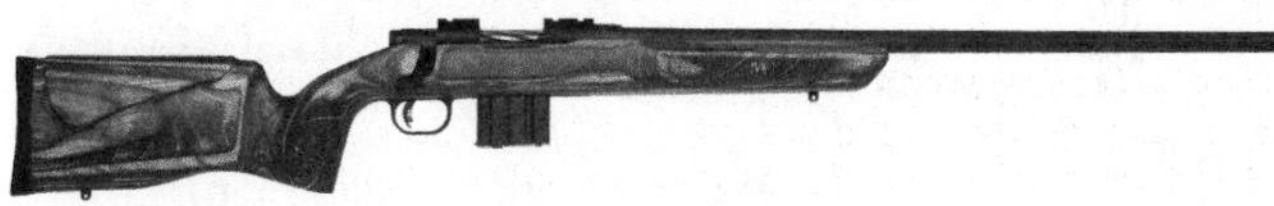

MOSSBERG 100 ATR BOLT-ACTION RIFLE

Caliber: 243 Win. (2006), 270 Win., 308 Win. (2006), 30-06 Spfl., 4-round magazine. **Barrel:** 22", 1:10 twist, free-floating, button-rifled, recessed muzzle crown. **Weight:** 6.7 to 7.75 lbs. **Length:** 42"-42.75" overall. **Stock:** Black synthetic, walnut, Mossy Oak New Break Up camo, Realtree AP camo. **Sights:** Factory-installed Weaver-style scope bases; scoped combos include 3x9 factory-mounted, bore-sighted scopes. **Features:** Marinecote and matte blue metal finishes, free gun lock, side lever safety. Introduced 2005. Night Train (2008)comes with Picatinny rail and factory-mounted 4-16x50mm variable scope. From O.F. Mossberg & Sons, Inc.

Price: Short-Action 243 Win., wood stock, matte blue, from . . .**$424.00**
Price: Long-Action 270 Win., Mossy Oak New Break Up camo, matte blue, from **$424.00**
Price: Scoped Combo 30-06 Spfl., Walnut-Dura-Wood stock, Marinecote finish, from **$481.00**
Price: Bantam Short Action 308 Win., 20" barrel. **$471.00**
Price: Night Train Short-Action Scoped Combo (2008). **$567.00**

MOSSBERG MVP

Caliber: .223 Rem. (10-shot magazine). **Barrel:** 24". Stock: Laminated benchrest. **Features:** Adjustable trigger. Accepts AR-style magazines.

Price: **$649**

MOSSBERG 4X4

Caliber: Most popular calibers from .22-250 to .338 Win. Mag. **Barrel:** 24" free floating with muzzle brake. **Stock:** Gray laminate or American black walnut, with Monte Carlo cheek piece, fore-end vents, recoil pad. Matte blue finish, adjustable trigger.

Price: . . . . **From $456**

NOSLER MODEL 48 LEGACY AND TROPHY

Caliber: Offered in most popular calibers including .280 Ackley Improved wildcat. **Barrel:** 24". Weight: 7.25 to 8 lbs. **Stock:** Walnut or composite.

Price: Legacy **$2495**
Price: Trophy. **$1995**

NOSLER MODEL 48 VARMINT RIFLE

Caliber: 204 Ruger, .223 Rem., 22-250 Rem., Heavy barrel, 4-shot capacity. **Barrel:** 24". **Weight:** 7.25 lbs. **Stock:** Coyote tan or Onyx black Kevlar® and carbon fiber. **Sights:** Fixed sights. **Features:** The NoslerCustom® Model 48 is built on the same action as our Custom rifles. Nosler's proprietary push-feed action features a 2-position safety and an adjustable trigger set to a crisp, 3 lb. let-off. The action features a classic one-piece bottom metal and trigger guard. To achieve the highest level of accuracy, the Model 48 integrates the unique MicroSlick™ Coating on interior metal surfaces, including inside the bolt body, and on the firing pin and firing pin spring, for maximum corrosion and wear-resistance, even with extensive dry firing.

Price: 204 Ruger **$2,995.00**
Price: .223 Rem., (Black) **$2,995.00**
Price: 22-250, (Black) **$2,995.00**
Price: 22-250, (Grey) **$2,995.00**

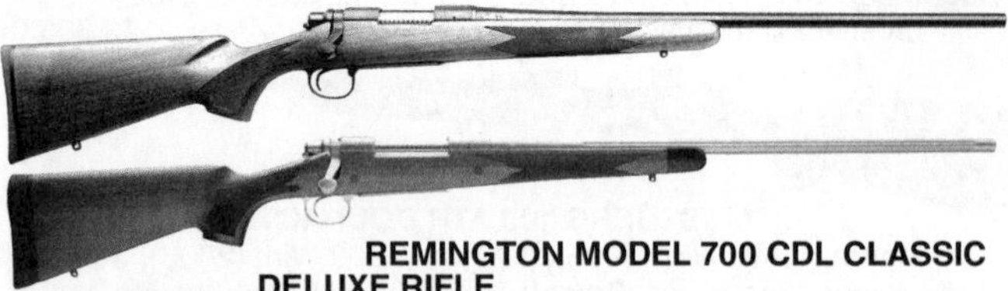

REMINGTON MODEL 700 CDL CLASSIC DELUXE RIFLE

Caliber: 223 Rem., 243 Win., 25-06 Rem., 270 Win., 7mm-08 Rem., 280 Remington, 7mm Rem. Mag., 7mm Rem. Ultra Mag., 30-06 Spfl., 300 Rem. Ultra Mag., 300 Win. Mag., 35 Whelen. **Barrel:** 24" or 26" round tapered. **Weight:** 7.4 to 7.6 lbs. **Length:** 43.6" to 46.5" overall. **Stock:** Straight-comb American walnut stock, satin finish, checkering, right-handed cheek piece, black fore-end tip and grip cap, sling swivel studs. **Sights:** None. **Features:** Satin blued finish, jeweled bolt body, drilled and tapped for scope mounts. Hinged-floorplate magazine capacity: 4, standard calibers; 3, magnum calibers. SuperCell recoil pad, cylindrical receiver, integral extractor. Introduced 2004. CDL SF (stainless fluted) chambered for 260 Rem., 257 Wby. Mag., 270 Win., 270 WSM, 7mm-08 Rem., 7mm Rem. Mag., 30-06 Spfl., 300 WSM. Left-hand versions introduced 2008 in six calibers. Made in U.S. by Remington Arms Co., Inc.

Price: Standard Calibers from .... **$1,019.00 to $1,077.00**
Price: CDL SF from .... **$1,197.00 to $1,259.00**

REMINGTON MODEL 700 BDL RIFLE

Caliber: 243 Win., 270 Win., 7mm Rem. Mag. 30-06 Spfl., 300 Rem Ultra Mag. **Barrel:** 22, 24, 26" round tapered. **Weight:** 7.25-7.4 lbs. **Length:** 41.6-46.5" overall. **Stock:** Walnut. Gloss-finish pistol grip stock with skip-line checkering, black forend tip and gripcap with white line spacers. Quick-release floorplate. **Sights:** Gold bead ramp front; hooded ramp, removable step-adjustable rear with windage screw. **Features:** Side safety, receiver tapped for scope mounts, matte receiver top, quick detachable swivels.

Price: Standard Calibers **$985.00**
Price: Magnum Calibers **$1,014.00**

REMINGTON MODEL 700 SPS RIFLES

Caliber: 17 Rem. Fireball, 204 Ruger, 22-250 Rem., 6.8 Rem SPC, 223 Rem., 243 Win., 270 Win. 270 WSM, 7mm-08 Rem., 7mm Rem. Mag., 7mm Rem. Ultra Mag., 30-06 Spfl., 308 Win., 300 WSM, 300 Win. Mag., 300 Rem. Ultra Mag. **Barrel:** 20", 24" or 26" carbon steel. **Weight:** 7 to 7.6 lbs. **Length:** 39.6" to 46.5" overall. **Stock:** Black synthetic, sling swivel studs, SuperCell recoil pad. **Sights:** None. Introduced 2005. SPS Stainless replaces Model 700 BDL Stainless Synthetic. **Barrel:** Bead-blasted 416 stainless steel. **Features:** Plated internal fire control component. SPS DM features detachable box magazine. Buckmaster Edition versions feature Realtree Hardwoods HD camouflage and Buckmasters logo engraved on floorplate. SPS Varmint includes X-Mark Pro trigger, 26" heavy contour barrel, vented beavertail forend, dual front sling swivel studs. Made in U.S. by Remington Arms Co., Inc.

Price: From .... **$709.00 to $813.00**

REMINGTON 700 SPS TACTICAL

Bolt action rifle chambered in .223 and .308 Win. Features include 20-inch heavy-contour tactical-style barrel; dual-point pillar bedding; black synthetic stock with Hogue overmoldings; semi-beavertail fore-end; X-Mark Pro adjustable trigger system; satin black oxide metal finish; hinged floorplate magazine; SuperCell recoil pad.

Price: From .... **$765.00 to $817.00**

REMINGTON 700 VTR A-TACS CAMO

Bolt action rifle chambered in .223 and .308 Win. Features include ATACS camo finish overall; triangular contour 22-inch barrel has an integral muzzle brake; black overmold grips; 1:9 (.223 caliber) 0r 1:12 (.308) twist.

Price: **$959.00**

REMINGTON MODEL 700 VLS RIFLES

Caliber: 204 Ruger, 223 Rem., 22-250 Rem., 243 Win., 308 Win. **Barrel:** 26" heavy contour barrel (0.820" muzzle O.D.), concave target-style barrel crown **Weight:** 9.4 lbs. **Length:** 45.75" overall. **Stock:** Brown laminated stock, satin finish, with beavertail forend, gripcap, rubber buttpad. **Sights:** None. **Features:** Introduced 1995. VLSS TH (varmint laminate stock stainless) thumbhole model introduced 2007. Made in U.S. by Remington Arms Co., Inc.

Price: **$1,045.00**

REMINGTON MODEL 700 VSSF-II/SENDERO SF II RIFLES

Caliber: 17 Rem. Fireball, 204 Ruger, 220 Swift, 223 Rem., 22-250 Rem., 308 Win. **Barrel:** satin blued 26" heavy contour (0.820" muzzle O.D.). VSSF has satin-finish stainless barreled action with 26" fluted barrel. **Weight:** 8.5 lbs. **Length:** 45.75" overall. **Stock:** H.S. Precision composite reinforced with aramid fibers, black (VSSF-II) Contoured beavertail fore-end with ambidextrous finger grooves, palm swell, and twin front tactical-style swivel studs. **Sights:** None. **Features:** Aluminum bedding block, drilled and tapped for scope mounts, hinged floorplate magazines. Introduced 1994. Sendero model is similar to VSSF-II except chambered for 264 Win. Mag, 7mm Rem. Mag., 7mm Rem. Ultra Mag., 300 Win. Mag., 300 Rem. Ultra Mag. Polished stainless barrel. Introduced 1996. Made in U.S. by Remington Arms Co., Inc.

Price: VSSF-II **$1,450.00**
Price: Sendero SF II **$1,450.00**

REMINGTON MODEL 700 XCR CAMO RMEF

Similar to Model 700 XCR but with stainless barrel and receiver, AP HD camo stock, TriNyte coating overall, 7mm Remington Ultra Mag chambering.

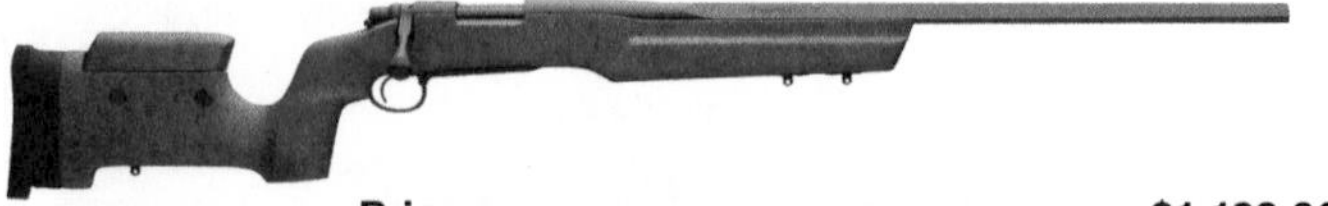

Price: **$1,199.00**

REMINGTON MODEL 700 TARGET TACTICAL RIFLE

Caliber: 308 Win. Barrel: 26" triangular counterbored, 1:11-1/2 rifling. **Weight:** 11.75 lbs. **Length:** 45-3/4" overall. **Features:** Textured green Bell & Carlson varmint/tactical stock with adjustable comb and length of pull, adjustable trigger, satin black oxide finish on exposed metal surfaces, hinged floorplate, SuperCell recoil pad, matte blue on exposed metal surfaces.

Price: **$2,117.00**

REMINGTON MODEL 700 VTR VARMINT/TACTICAL RIFLE

Caliber: .22-250, 223 Rem., 243 Win., 308 Win. **Barrel:** 22" triangular counterbored. **Weight:** 7.5 lbs. **Length:** 41-5/8" overall. **Features:** Olive drab overmolded or Digital Tiger TSP Desert Camo stock with vented semi-beavertail forend, tactical-style dual swivel mounts for bipod, matte blue on exposed metal surfaces.

Price: From .... **$908.00 to $959.00**

Prices given are believed to be accurate at time of publication however, many factors affect retail pricing so exact prices are not possible.

REMINGTON MODEL 700 VARMINT SF RIFLE

Caliber: 17 Rem. Fireball, 204 Ruger, 22-250, 223, 220 Swift. **Barrel:** 26" stainless steel fluted. **Weight:** 8.5 lbs. **Length:** 45.75». **Features:** Synthetic stock with ventilated forend, stainless steel/ triggerguard/floorplate, dual tactical swivels for bipod attachment.

Price: **$981.00**

REMINGTON MODEL 700 MOUNTAIN SS

Calibers: .25-06, .270 Win., .280 Rem., 7mm-08, .308 Win., .30-06. **Barrel:** 22". **Length:** 40.6". **Weight:** 6.5 lbs. Satin stainless finish, Bell & Carlson Aramid Fiber stock.

Price: **$1123**

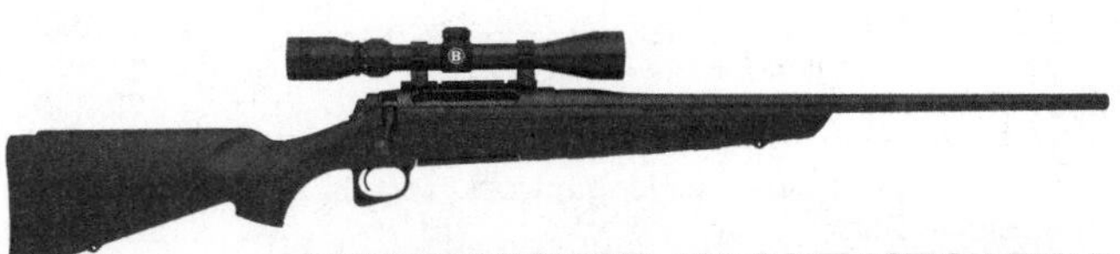

REMINGTON MODEL 770 BOLT-ACTION RIFLE

Caliber: 243 Win., 270 Win., 7mm Rem. Mag., 7mm-08 Rem., 308 Win., 30-06 Spfl., 300 Win. Mag. **Barrel:** 22" or 24", button rifled. **Weight:** 8.5 lbs. **Length:** 42.5" to 44.5" overall. **Stock:** Black synthetic. **Sights:** Bushnell Sharpshooter 3-9x scope mounted and bore-sighted. **Features:** Upgrade of Model 710 introduced 2001. Unique action locks bolt directly into barrel; 60-degree bolt throw; 4-shot dual-stack magazine; all-steel receiver. Introduced 2007. Made in U.S.A. by Remington Arms Co.

Price: **$375.00**
Price: Youth, 243 Win. **$375.00**
Price: Stainless Camo (2008), stainless barrel, nickel-plated bolt, Realtree camo stock **$458.00**

REMINGTON MODEL SEVEN CDL

Calibers: .243, .260 Rem., 7mm-08, .308 Win. **Barrel:** 20". **Weight:** 6.5 lbs. **Length:** 39.25". **Stock:** Walnut with black fore-end tip, satin finish. Predator model in .223, .22-250 and .243 has Mossy Oak Brush camo stock, 22" barrel.

Price: **$1,029.00**
Price: Predator **$886.00**

REMINGTON 40-XB TACTICAL

Bolt action rifle chambered in .308 Winchester. Features include stainless steel bolt with Teflon coating; hinged floorplate; adjustable trigger; 27-1/4-inch tri-fluted 1:14 barrel; H-S precision pro series tactical stock, black color with dark green spiderweb; two front swivel studs; one rear swivel stud; vertical pistol grip.

Price: From the Remington Custom Shop. .... **POR**

REMINGTON 40-XS TACTICAL - 338LM SYSTEM

Bolt action rifle chambered in .338 Lapua Magnum. Features include 416 stainless steel Model 40-X 24-inch 1:12 barreled action; black polymer coating; McMillan A3 series stock with adjustable length of pull and adjustable comb; adjustable trigger and Sunny Hill heavy duty, all-steel trigger guard; Harris bi-pod with quick adjust swivel lock Leupold Mark IV 3.5-10x40mm long range M1 scope with Mil Dot reticle; Badger Ordnance all-steel Picatinny scope rail and rings.

Price: .... **NA**

RUGER AMERICAN RIFLE

Caliber: .243, .308, .270 Win., .30-06 (4-shot rotary magazine). **Barrel:** 22". **Length:** 42.5". **Weight:** 6.25 lbs. **Stock:** Black composite. **Finish:** Matte black. **Features:** Tang safety, hammer-forged free floating barrel.

Price: **$449**

RUGER COMPACT MAGNUMS

Caliber: .338 RCM, .300 RCM; 3-shot magazine. **Barrel:** 20". **Weight:** 6.75 lbs. **Length:** 39.5-40" overall. **Stock:** American walnut and black synthetic; stainless steel and Hawkeye Matte blued finishes. **Sights:** Adjustable Williams "U" notch rear sight and brass bead front sight. **Features:** Based on a shortened .375 Ruger case, the .300 and .338 RCMs match the .300 and .338 Win. Mag. in performance; RCM stock is 1/2 inch shorter than standard M77 Hawkeye stock; LC6 trigger; steel floor plate engraved with Ruger logo and "Ruger Compact Magnum"; Red Eagle recoil pad; Mauser-type controlled feeding; claw extractor; 3-position safety; hammer-forged steel barrels; Ruger scope rings. Walnut stock includes extensive cut-checkering and rounded profiles. Intr. 2008. Made in U.S.A. by Sturm, Ruger & Co.

Price: **$929.00**

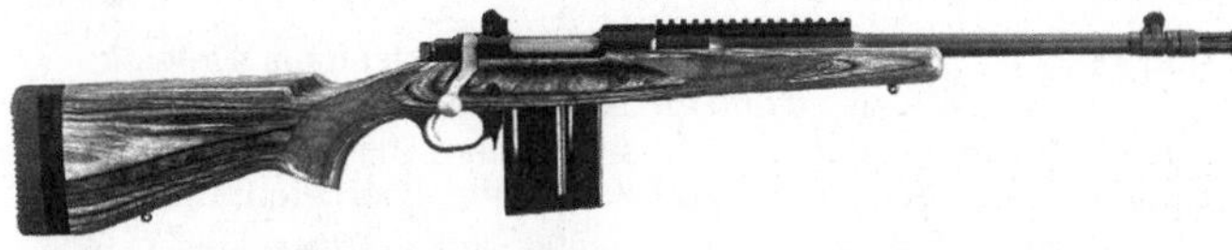

RUGER GUNSITE SCOUT RIFLE

Caliber: .308 WIN., 10-shot magazine capacity. **Barrel:** 16.5". **Weight:** 7 lbs. **Length:** 38-39.5". **Stock:** Black laminate. **Sights:** Front post sight and rear adjustable. **Features:** Gunsite Scout Rifle is a credible rendition of Col. Jeff Cooper's "fighting carbine" Scout Rifle. The Ruger Gunsite Scout Rifle is a new platform in the Ruger M77 family. While the Scout Rifle has M77 features such as controlled round feed and integral scope mounts (scope rings included), the 10-round detachable box magazine is the first clue this isn't your grandfather's Ruger rifle. The Ruger Gunsite Scout Rifle has a 16.5 medium contour, cold hammer-forged, alloy steel barrel with a Mini-14 protected non-glare post front sight and receiver mounted, adjustable ghost ring rear sight for out-of-the-box usability. A forward mounted Picatinny rail offers options in mounting an assortment of optics – including Scout Scopes available from Burris and Leupold, for "both eyes open" sighting and super-fast target acquisition.

Price: **$995.00**

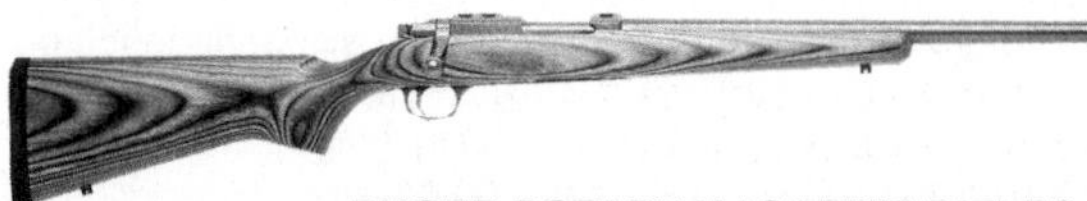

RUGER ROTARY MAGAZINE RIFLES

Caliber: .22 Hornet, .357 Magnum, . 44 Magnum (capacity 4 to 6 rounds). **Barrel:** 20", .22 Hornet, 18.5" .357 & .44 Magnums). **Weight:** 5.5 to 7.5 lbs. **Stock:** American walnut, black synthetic or camo.

Price: From **$829**

RUGER M77 HAWKEYE RIFLES

Caliber: 204 Ruger, 223 Rem., 22-250 Rem., 243 Win., 257 Roberts, 25-06 Rem., 270 Win., 280 Rem., 6.5 Creedmoor, 7mm/08, 7mm Rem. Mag., 308 Win., 30-06 Spfl., 300 Win. Mag., 338 Win. Mag., 338 Federal, 358 Win. Mag., 416 Ruger, 375 Ruger, 300 Ruger Compact Magnum, 338 Ruger Compact Magnum; 4-shot magazine, except 3-shot magazine for magnums; 5-shot magazine for 204 Ruger and 223 Rem. **Barrel:** 22", 24". **Weight:** 6.75 to 8.25 lbs. **Length:** 42-44.4" overall. **Stock:** American walnut. **Sights:** None furnished. Receiver has Ruger integral scope mount base, Ruger 1" rings. **Features:** Includes Ruger LC6 trigger, new red rubber recoil pad, Mauser-type controlled feeding, claw extractor, 3-position safety, hammer-forged steel barrels, Ruger scope rings. Walnut stock includes wrap-around cut checkering on the forearm and, more rounded contours on stock

and top of pistol grips. Matte stainless version features synthetic stock. Hawkeye Alaskan and African chambered in 375 Ruger. Alaskan features matte-black finish, 20" barrel, Hogue OverMolded synthetic stock. African has 23" blued barrel, checkered walnut stock, left-handed model. 375's have windage-adjustable shallow "V" notch rear sight, white bead front sights. Introduced 2007. Left-hand models available 2008.

Price: Standard, right- and left-hand **$859.00**
Price: All-Weather **$859.00**
Price: Compact **$859.00**
Price: Laminate Compact **$929.00**
Price: Compact Magnum **$929.00**
Price: African **$1,099.00**
Price: Alaskan **$1,099.00**
Price: Sporter **$929.00**
Price: Tactical **$1,199.00**
Price: Predator **$999.00**

RUGER M77VT TARGET RIFLE

Caliber: 22-250 Rem., 223 Rem., 204 Ruger, 243 Win., 25-06 Rem., 308 Win., 6.5 Creedmoor **Barrel:** 26" heavy stainless steel with target grey finish. **Weight:** 9 to 9.75 lbs. **Length:** Approx. 45.75" to 46.75" overall. **Stock:** Laminated American hardwood with beavertail forend, steel swivel studs; no checkering or gripcap. **Sights:** Integral scope mount bases in receiver. **Features:** Ruger diagonal bedding system. Ruger steel 1" scope rings supplied. Fully adjustable trigger. Steel floorplate and trigger guard. New version introduced 1992.

Price: KM77VT MKII **$935.00**

SAKO A7 AMERICAN BOLT-ACTION RIFLE

Caliber: 270 Win., 300 WSM. **Barrel:** 22-7/16" standard, 24-3/8" magnum. **Weight:** 6 lbs. 3 oz. to 6 lbs. 13 oz. **Length:** 42-5/16" to 44-5/16" overall. **Features:** Blued or stainless barrel and receiver, black composite stock with sling swivels and recoil pad, two-position safety, adjustable trigger, detachable 3+1 box magazine.

Price: From **$1,375.00**

SAKO TRG-22 TACTICAL RIFLE

Bolt action rifles chambered in .308 Winchester (TRG-22). Features include target grade Cr-Mo or stainless barrels with muzzle brake; three locking lugs; 60° bolt throw; adjustable two-stage target trigger; adjustable or folding synthetic stock; receiver-mounted integral 17mm axial optics rails with recoil stop-slots; tactical scope mount for modern three turret tactical scopes (30 and 34 mm tube diameter); optional bipod.

Price: **$3,450.00**

SAKO MODEL 85 BOLT-ACTION RIFLES

Caliber: 22-250 Rem., 243 Win., 25-06 Rem., 260, 6.5x55mm, 270 Win., 270 WSM, 7mm-08 Rem., 308 Win., 30-06; 7mm WSM, 300 WSM, 338 Federal. **Barrel:** 22.4", 22.9", 24.4". **Weight:** 7.75 lbs. **Length:** NA. **Stock:** Polymer, laminated or high-grade walnut, straight comb, shadow-line cheekpiece. **Sights:** None furnished. **Features:** Controlled-round feeding, adjustable trigger, matte stainless or nonreflective satin blue. Offered in a wide range of variations and models. Introduced 2006. Imported from Finland by Beretta USA.

Price: Grey Wolf **$1,600.00**
Price: Black Bear **$1,850.00**
Price: Kodiak **$1,925.00**
Price: Varmint Laminated **$2,000.00**
Price: Classic **$2,200.00**
Price: Bavarian . . . . **$2,200.00 - $2,300.00**
Price: Bavarian carbine, Full-length stock **$925.00**
Price: Brown Bear **$2,175.00**

SAKO 85 FINNLIGHT

Similar to Model 85 but chambered in 243 Win., 25-06, 260 Rem., 270 Win., 270 WSM, 300 WSM, 30-06, 300 WM, 308 Win., 6.5x55mm, 7mm Rem Mag., 7mm-08. Weighs 6 lbs., 3 oz. to 6 lbs. 13 oz. Stainless steel barrel and receiver, black synthetic stock.

Price: **$1,600.00**

SAVAGE AXIS SERIES BOLT ACTION RIFLES

Caliber: .243 WIN., 7mm-08 REM., .308 WIN., .25-06 REM., .270 WIN, .30-06 SPFLD., .223 REM., .22-250 REM. **Barrel:** 22". **Weight:** 6.5 lbs. **Length:** 43.875". **Stock:** Black synthetic. **Sights:** Drilled and tapped for scope mounts. **Features:** The AXIS Stainless has a very sleek and modern design plus a silky-smooth operation. It benefits from a very handy detachable box magazine and is available only as a rifle and in a scoped package. It sports a stainless steel barrel with a high luster finish. The stock is synthetic and has a black matte finish. It is one of the most affordable rifles in the 2011 Savage lineup of hunting guns.

Price: From . . . . **$363.00 to $485.00**

SAVAGE MODEL 25 BOLT ACTION RIFLES

Caliber: .17 Hornet, .22 Hornet, .222 Rem., 204 Ruger, 223 Rem., 4-shot magazine. **Barrel:** 24", medium-contour fluted barrel with recessed target crown, free-floating sleeved barrel, dual pillar bedding. **Weight:** 8.25 lbs. **Length:** 43.75" overall. **Stock:** Brown laminate with beavertail-style forend. **Sights:** Weaver-style bases installed. **Features:** Diameter-specific action built around the 223 Rem. bolthead dimension. Three locking lugs, 60-degree bolt lift, AccuTrigger adjustable from 2.5 to 3.25 lbs. Model 25 Classic Sporter has satin lacquer American walnut with contrasting forend tip, wraparound checkering, 22" blued barrel. **Weight:** 7.15 lbs. **Length:** 41.75". Introduced 2008. Made in U.S.A. by Savage Arms, Inc.

Price: From . . . . **$707.00 to $754.00**

SAVAGE CLASSIC SERIES MODEL 14/114 RIFLES

Caliber: 204 Ruger, 223 Rem., 22-250 Rem., 243 Win., .250 Savage, 7mm-08 Rem., 308 Win., 2- or 4-shot magazine; 270 Win., 7mm Rem. Mag., 30-06 Spfl., 300 Win. Mag. (long action Model 114), 3- or 4-shot magazine. **Barrel:** 22" or 24". **Weight:** 7 to 7.5 lbs. **Length:** 41.75" to 43.75" overall (Model 14); 43.25" to 45.25" overall (Model 114). **Stock:** Satin lacquer American walnut with ebony forend, wraparound checkering, Monte Carlo Comb and cheekpiece. **Sights:** None furnished. Receiver drilled and tapped for scope mounting. **Features:** AccuTrigger, high luster blued barreled action, hinged floorplate. From Savage Arms, Inc.

Price: **$850.00**
Price: Stainless **$995.00**

SAVAGE MODEL 12 SERIES VARMINT RIFLES

Caliber: 204 Ruger, 223 Rem., 22-250 Rem. 4-shot magazine. **Barrel:** 26" stainless barreled action, heavy fluted, free-floating and button-rifled barrel. **Weight:** 10 lbs. **Length:** 46.25" overall. **Stock:** Dual pillar bedded, low profile, laminated stock with extra-wide beavertail forend. **Sights:** None furnished; drilled and tapped for scope mounting. **Features:** Recessed target-style muzzle. AccuTrigger, oversized bolt handle, detachable box magazine, swivel studs. Model 112BVSS has heavy target-style prone laminated stock with high comb, Wundhammer palm swell, internal box magazine. Model 12FVSS has black synthetic stock, additional chamberings in 308 Win., 270 WSM, 300 WSM. Model 12FV has blued receiver. Model 12BTCSS has brown laminate vented thumbhole stock. Made in U.S.A. by Savage Arms, Inc.

Price: From . . . . **$698.00 to $1,355.00**

SAVAGE MODEL 16/116 WEATHER WARRIORS

Caliber: 204 Ruger, 223 Rem., 22-250 Rem., 243 Win., 7mm-08 Rem., 308 Win., 270 WSM, 7mm WSM, 300 WSM (short action Model 16), 2- or 4-shot magazine; 270 Win., 7mm Rem. Mag., 30-06 Spfl., 300 Win. Mag., 338 Win. Mag. (long action Model 114), 3- or 4-shot magazine. **Barrel:** 22", 24"; stainless steel with matte finish, free-floated barrel. **Weight:** 6.5 to 6.75 lbs. **Length:** 41.75" to 43.75" overall (Model 16); 42.5" to 44.5" overall (Model 116). **Stock:** Graphite/fiberglass filled composite. **Sights:** None furnished; drilled and tapped for scope mounting. **Features:** Quick-detachable swivel studs; laser-etched bolt. Left-hand models available. Model 116FSS introduced 1991; 116FSAK introduced 1994. Made in U.S.A. by Savage Arms, Inc.

Price: From . . . . **$825.00 to $966.00**

SAVAGE MODEL 11/111 HUNTER SERIES BOLT ACTIONS

Caliber: 223 Rem., 22-250 Rem., 243 Win., 6.5 Creedmoor, .260 Rem., 6.5x284 Norma, .338 Lapua, 7mm-08 Rem., 308 Win., 2- or 4-shot magazine; 25-06 Rem., 270 Win., 7mm Rem. Mag., 30-06 Spfl., 300 Win. Mag., (long action Model 111), 3- or 4-shot magazine. **Barrel:** 22" or 24"; blued free-floated barrel. **Weight:** 6.5 to 6.75 lbs. **Length:** 41.75" to 43.75" overall (Model 11); 42.5" to 44.5" overall (Model 111). **Stock:** Graphite/fiberglass filled composite or hardwood. **Sights:** Ramp front, open fully adjustable rear; drilled and tapped for scope mounting. **Features:** Three-position top tang safety, double front locking lugs. Introduced 1994. Made in U.S.A. by Savage Arms, Inc.

Price: From . . . . **$899.00 to $1,029.00**
Price: .338 Lapua **$1,239.00**

SAVAGE MODEL 10 BAS LAW ENFORCEMENT BOLT-ACTION RIFLE

Caliber: .308 Win., .300 Win., .338 Lapua. **Barrel:** 24" fluted heavy with muzzle brake. **Weight:** 13.4 lbs. **Length:** NA. **Features:** Bolt-action repeater based on Model 10 action but with M4-style collapsible buttstock, pistolgrip with palm swell, all-aluminum Accustock, picatinny rail for mounting optics.

Price: . . . . **$2,218.00 to $2,394.00**

SAVAGE MODEL 10FP/110FP LAW ENFORCEMENT SERIES RIFLES

Caliber: 223 Rem., 308 Win. (Model 10), 4-shot magazine; 25-06 Rem., 300 Win. Mag., (Model 110), 3- or 4-shot magazine. **Barrel:** 24"; matte blued free-floated heavy barrel and action. **Weight:** 6.5 to 6.75 lbs. **Length:** 41.75" to 43.75" overall (Model 10); 42.5" to

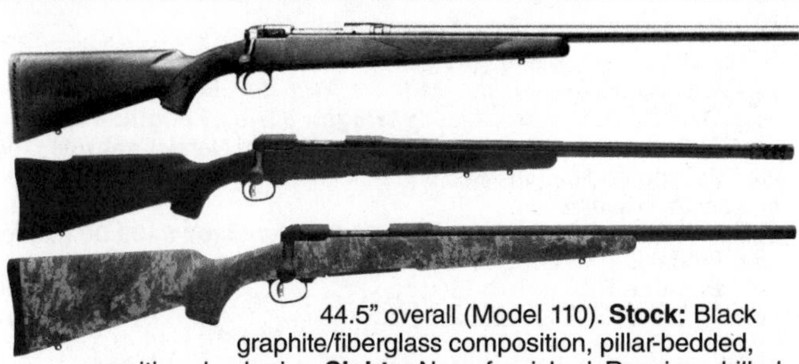

44.5" overall (Model 110). **Stock:** Black graphite/fiberglass composition, pillar-bedded, positive checkering. **Sights:** None furnished. Receiver drilled and tapped for scope mounting. **Features:** Black matte finish on all metal parts. Double swivel studs on the forend for sling and/or bipod mount. Right- or left-hand. Model 110FP introduced 1990. Model 10FP introduced 1998. Model 10FCPXP has HS Precision black synthetic tactical stock with molded alloy bedding system, Leupold 3.5-10x40mm black matte scope with Mil Dot reticle, Farrell Picatinny Rail Base, flip-open lens covers, 1.25" sling with QD swivels, Harris bipod, Storm heavy duty case. Made in U.S.A. by Savage Arms, Inc.

Price: Model 10FP, 10FLP (left hand), 110FP **$649.00**
Price: Model 10FP folding Choate stock **$896.00**
Price: Model 10FCP McMillan, McMillan fiberglass tactical stock **$1,178.00**
Price: Model 10FCP-HS HS Precision, HS Precision tactical stock **$984.00**
Price: Model 10FPXP-HS Precision **$2,715.00**
Price: Model 10FCP **$866.00**
Price: Model 10FLCP, left-hand model, standard stock or Accu-Stock **$866.00**
Price: Model 110FCP **$866.00**
Price: Model 10 Precision Carbine, 20" medium contour barrel, synthetic camo Accu-Stock, 223/308 . . . . **$829.00**
Price: Model 10 FCM Scout **$646.00**

SAVAGE MODEL 10 PREDATOR SERIES

Caliber: 223, 22-250, 243, 204 Ruger, 6.5 Creedmoor, 6.5x284 Norma. **Barrel:** 22", medium-contour. **Weight:** 7.25 lbs. **Length:** 43"overall. **Stock:** Synthetic with rounded forend and oversized bolt handle. **Features:** Entirely covered in either Mossy Oak Brush or Realtree Hardwoods Snow pattern camo. Also features AccuTrigger, AccuStock, detachable box magazine.

Price: . . . . **$880.00 to $915.00**

SAVAGE MODEL 12 PRECISION TARGET SERIES BENCHREST RIFLE

Caliber: 308 Win, 6.5x284 Norma, 6mm Norma BR. **Barrel:** 29" ultra-heavy. **Weight:** 12.75 lbs. **Length:** 50" overall. **Stock:** Gray laminate. Features: New Left-Load, Right-Eject target action, Target AccuTrigger adjustable from approx 6 oz to 2.5 lbs, oversized bolt handle, stainless extra-heavy free-floating and button-rifled barrel.

Price: **$1,505.00**

SAVAGE MODEL 12 PRECISION TARGET PALMA RIFLE

Similar to Model 12 Benchrest but in .308 Win. only, 30" barrel, multi-adjustable stock, weighs 13.3 lbs.

Price: **$1,927.00**

SAVAGE MODEL 12 F CLASS TARGET RIFLE

Similar to Model 12 Benchrest but in 6.5x284 Norma, 6 Norma BR, 30" barrel, weighs 11.5 lbs.

Price: **$1,480.00**

SAVAGE MODEL 12 F/TR TARGET RIFLE

Similar to Model 12 Benchrest but in 308 Win. only, 30" barrel, weighs 12.65 lbs.

Price: **$1,381.00**

STEVENS MODEL 200 BOLT-ACTION RIFLES

Caliber: 223, 22-250, 243, 7mm-08, 308 Win. (short action) or 25-06, 270 Win., 30-06, 7mm Rem. Mag., 300 Win Mag. Barrel: 22" (short action) or 24" (long action blued). **Weight:** 6.5 lbs. **Length:** 41.75" overall. **Stock:** Black synthetic or camo. **Sights:** None. **Features:** Free-floating and button-rifled barrel, top loading internal box magazine, swivel studs.

Price: . . . . **$399.00** (standard); **$439.00** (camo)

Price: Model 200XP Long or Short Action Package Rifle with 4x12 scope **$449.00**

Price: Model 200XP Camo, camo stock **$499.00**

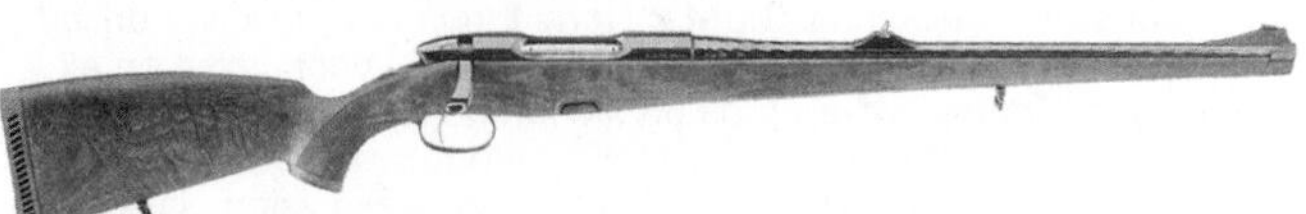

STEYR MANNLICHER CLASSIC RIFLE

Caliber: 222 Rem., 223 Rem., 243 Win., 25-06 Rem., 308 Win., 6.5x55, 6.5x57, 270 Win., 270 WSM, 7x64 Brenneke, 7mm-08 Rem., 7.5x55, 30-06 Spfl., 9.3x62, 6.5x68, 7mm Rem. Mag., 300 WSM, 300 Win. Mag., 8x68S, 4-shot magazine. **Barrel:** 23.6" standard; 26" magnum; 20" full stock standard calibers. **Weight:** 7 lbs. **Length:** 40.1" overall. **Stock:** Hand-checkered fancy European oiled walnut with standard forend. **Sights:** Ramp front adjustable for elevation, V-notch rear adjustable for windage. **Features:** Single adjustable trigger; 3-position roller safety with "safe-bolt" setting; drilled and tapped for Steyr factory scope mounts. Introduced 1997. Imported from Austria by Steyr Arms, Inc.

Price: Half stock, standard calibers. **$3,799.00**

Price: Full stock, standard calibers **$4,199.00**

STEYR PRO HUNTER RIFLE

Similar to the Classic Rifle except has ABS synthetic stock with adjustable butt spacers, straight comb without cheekpiece, palm swell, Pachmayr 1" swivels. Special 10-round magazine conversion kit available. Introduced 1997. Imported from Austria by Steyr Arms, Inc.

Price: From **$1,500.00**

STEYR SCOUT BOLT-ACTION RIFLE

Caliber: 308 Win., 5-shot magazine. **Barrel:** 19", fluted. **Weight:** NA. **Length:** NA. **Stock:** Gray Zytel. **Sights:** Pop-up front & rear, Leupold M8 2.5x28 IER scope on Picatinny optic rail with Steyr mounts. **Features:** luggage case, scout sling, two stock spacers, two magazines. Introduced 1998. Imported from Austria by Steyr Arms, Inc.

Price: From **$2,199.00**

STEYR SSG08 BOLT-ACTION RIFLE

Caliber: 7.62x51mmNATO (.308Win) or 7.62x63B (.300 Win Mag)., 10-shot magazine capacity. **Barrel:** 508mm or 600mm. **Weight:** 5.5 kg - 5.7 kg. **Length:** 1090mm - 1182mm. **Stock:** Dural aluminium foldingstock black with 280 mm long UIT-rail and various Picatinny-rails. **Sights:** Front post sight and rear adjustable. **Features:** The STEYR SSG 08 features high grade alumnium folding stock, adjustable cheek piece and butt plate with height marking, and an ergonomical exchangeable pistol grip. The STEYR SSG 08 also features a Versa-Pod, a muzzle brake, a Picatinny rail, a UIT rail on stock and various Picatinny rails on fore end, and a 10-round HC-magazine. SBSrotary bolt action with four frontal locking lugs, arranged in pairs.Coldhammer-forged barrels are available in standard or compact lengths.

Price: **$4,915.00**

STEYR SSG 69 PII BOLT-ACTION RIFLE

Caliber: 22-250 Rem., 243 Win., 308 Win., detachable 5-shot rotary magazine. **Barrel:** 26". **Weight:** 8.5 lbs. **Length:** 44.5" overall. **Stock:** Black ABS Cycolac with spacers for length of pull adjustment. **Sights:** Hooded ramp front adjustable for elevation, V-notch rear adjustable for windage. **Features:** Sliding safety; NATO rail for bipod; 1" swivels; Parkerized finish; single or double-set triggers. Imported from Austria by Steyr Arms, Inc.

Price: **$1,889.00**

THOMPSON/CENTER ICON BOLT-ACTION RIFLE

Caliber: 22-250 Rem., 243 Win., 308 Win., 6.5 Creedmoor, 30TC, 3-round box magazine. **Barrel:** 24", button rifled. **Weight:** 7.5 lbs. **Length:** 44.5" overall. **Stock:** Walnut, 20-lpi grip and forend cut checkering with ribbon detail. **Sights:** None; integral Weaver style scope mounts. **Features:** Interchangeable bolt handle, 60-degree bolt lift, Interlok Bedding System, 3-lug bolt with T-Slot extractor, cocking indicator, adjustable trigger, preset to 3 to 3.5 lbs of pull. Introduced 2007. From Thompson/Center Arms.

Price: **$1,200.00**

THOMPSON/CENTER ICON PRECISION HUNTER RIFLE

Similar to the basic ICON model. Available in 204 Ruger, 223 Rem., 22-250 Rem., 243 Win. and 308 Win., 6.5 Creedmoor, 22" heavy barrel, blued finish, varminter-style stock. Introduced 2009.

Price: **$1,370.00**

THOMPSON/CENTER VENTURE BOLT-ACTION RIFLE

Caliber: 270 Win., 7mm Rem. Mag., 30-06 Springfield, 300 Win. Mag., 3-round magazine. **Barrel:** 24". **Weight:** NA. **Length:** NA. **Stock:** Composite. **Sights:** NA. **Features:** Nitride fat bolt design, externally adjustable trigger, two-position safety, textured grip. Introduced 2009.

Price: **$489.00**

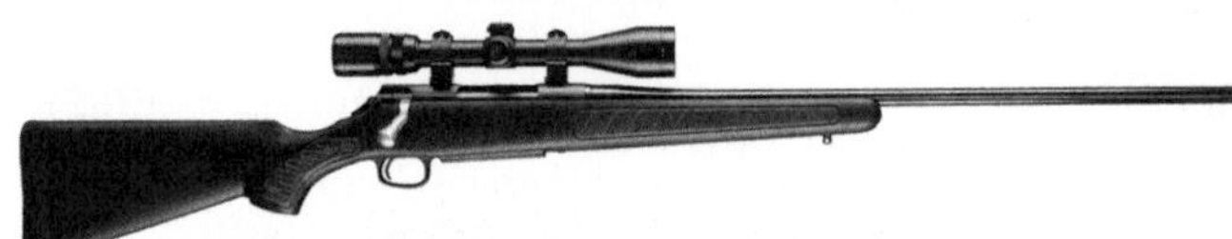

THOMPSON/CENTER VENTURE MEDIUM ACTION RIFLE

Bolt action rifle chambered in .204, .22-250, .223, .243, 7mm-08, .308 and 30TC. Features include a 24-inch crowned medium weight barrel, classic styled composite stock with inlaid traction grip panels, adjustable 3.5 to 5 pound trigger along with a drilled and tapped receiver (bases included). 3+1 detachable nylon box magazine. **Weight:** 7 lbs. **Length**: 43.5 inches.

Price: **$499.00**

THOMPSON/CENTER VENTURE PREDATOR PDX RIFLE

Bolt action rifle chambered in .204, .22-250, .223, .243, .308. Similar to Venture Medium action but with heavy, deep-fluted 22-inch barrel and Max-1 camo finish overall. **Weight:** 8 lbs. **Length:** 41.5 inches.

Price: . . . . **$549.00 to $599.00**

TIKKA T3 HUNTER

Caliber: 223 Rem., 22-250 Rem., 243 Win., 308 Win., 25-06 Rem., 270 Win., 30-06 Spfl., 300 Win. Mag., 338 Win. Mag., 270 WSM, 300 WSM, 6.5x55 Swedish Mauser, 7mm Rem. Mag. **Stock:** Walnut. **Sights:** None furnished. **Barrel:** 22-7/16", 24-3/8". **Features:** Detachable magazine, aluminum scope rings. Introduced 2005. Imported from Finland by Beretta USA.

Price: **$675.00**

TIKKA T3 STAINLESS SYNTHETIC

Similar to the T3 Hunter except stainless steel, synthetic stock. Available in 243 Win., 2506, 270 Win., 308 Win., 30-06 Spfl., 270 WSM,

300 WSM, 7mm Rem. Mag., 300 Win. Mag., 338 Win. Mag. Introduced 2005. Imported from Finland by Beretta USA.

Price: **$700.00**

TIKKA T3 LITE BOLT-ACTION RIFLE

Similar to the T3 Hunter, available in 223 Rem., 22-250 Rem., 308 Win., 243 Win., 25-06 Rem., 270 Win., 270 WSM, 30-06 Sprg., 300 Win Mag., 300 WSM, 338 Federal, 338 Win Mag., 7mm Rem. Mag., 7mm-08 Rem. Barrel lengths vary from 22-7/16" to 24-3/8". Made in Finland by Sako. Imported by Beretta USA.

Price: **$695.00**
Price: Stainless steel synthetic **$600.00**
Price: Stainless steel synthetic, left-hand **$700.00**

TIKKA T3 VARMINT/SUPER VARMINT RIFLE

Similar to the T3 Hunter, available in 223 Rem., 22-250 Rem., 308 Win. Length is 23-3/8" (Super Varmint). Made in Finland by Sako. Imported by Beretta USA.

Price: **$900.00**
Price: Super Varmint **$1,425.00**

ULTRA LIGHT ARMS BOLT-ACTION RIFLES

Caliber: 17 Rem. to 416 Rigby. **Barrel:** Douglas, length to order. **Weight:** 4.75 to 7.5 lbs. **Length:** Varies. **Stock:** Kevlar graphite composite, variety of finishes. **Sights:** None furnished; drilled and tapped for scope mounts. **Features:** Timney trigger, hand-lapped action, button-rifled barrel, hand-bedded action, recoil pad, sling-swivel studs, optional Jewell trigger. Made in U.S.A. by New Ultra Light Arms.

Price: Model 20 (short action) **$3,000.00**
Price: Model 24 (long action) **$3,100.00**
Price: Model 28 (magnum action) **$3,400.00**
Price: Model 40 (300 Wby. Mag., 416 Rigby) **$3,400.00**
Price: Left-hand models, add **$100.00**

WEATHERBY MARK V BOLT-ACTION RIFLES

Caliber: Deluxe version comes in all Weatherby calibers plus 243 Win., 270 Win., 7mm-08 Rem., 30-06 Spfl., 308 Win. **Barrel:** 24", 26", 28". **Weight:** 6.75 to 10 lbs. **Length:** 44" to 48.75" overall. **Stock:** Walnut, Monte Carlo with cheekpiece; high luster finish; checkered pistol grip and forend; recoil pad. **Sights:** None furnished. **Features:** 4 models with Mark V action and wood stocks; other common elements include cocking indicator; adjustable trigger; hinged floorplate, thumb safety; quick detachable sling swivels. Ultramark has hand-selected exhibition-grade walnut stock, maplewood/ebony spacers, 20-lpi checkering. Chambered for 257 and 300 Wby Mags. Lazermark same as Mark V Deluxe except stock has extensive oak leaf pattern laser carving on pistol grip and forend; chambered in Wby. Magnums—257, 270 Win., 7mm., 300, 340, with 26" barrel. Introduced 1981. Sporter is same as the Mark V Deluxe without the embellishments. Metal has low-luster blue, stock is Claro walnut with matte finish, Monte Carlo comb, recoil pad. Chambered for these Wby. Mags: 257, 270 Win., 7mm, 300, 340. Other chamberings: 7mm Rem. Mag., 300 Win. Introduced 1993. Six Mark V models come with synthetic stocks. Ultra Lightweight rifles weigh 5.75 to 6.75 lbs.; 24", 26" fluted stainless barrels with recessed target crown; Bell & Carlson stock with CNC-machined aluminum bedding plate and tan "spider web" finish, skeletonized handle and sleeve. Available in 243 Win., Wby. Mag., 25-06 Rem., 270 Win., 7mm-08 Rem., 7mm Rem. Mag., 280 Rem, 308 Win., 30-06 Spfl., 300 Win. Mag. Wby. Mag chamberings: 240, 257, 270 Win., 7mm, 300. Introduced 1998. Accumark uses Mark V action with heavy-contour 26" and 28" stainless barrels with black oxidized flutes, muzzle diameter of .705". No sights, drilled and tapped for scope mounting. Stock is composite with matte gel-coat finish, full length aluminum bedding Hasblock. Weighs 8.5 lbs. Chambered for these Wby. Mags: 240 (2007), 257, 270, 7mm, 300, 340, 338-378, 30-378. Other chamberings: 22-250 (2007), 243 Win. (2007), 25-06 Rem. (2007), 270 Win. (2007), 308 Win. (2007), 7mm Rem. Mag., 300 Win. Mag. Introduced 1996. SVM (Super VarmintMaster) has 26" fluted stainless barrel, spiderweb-pattern tan laminated synthetic stock, fully adjustable trigger. Chambered for 223 Rem., 22-250 Rem., 243. Mark V Synthetic has lightweight injection-molded synthetic stock with raised Monte Carlo comb, checkered grip and forend, custom floorplate release. Weighs 6.5-8.5 lbs., 24-28" barrels. Available in 22-250 Rem., 243 Win., 25-06 Rem., 270 Win., 7mm-08 Rem., 7mm Rem., Mag, 280 Rem., 308 Win., 30-06 Spfl., 308 Win., 300 Win. Mag., 375 H&H Mag, and these Wby. Magnums: 240, 257, 270 Win., 7mm, 300, 30-378, 338-378, 340. Introduced 1997. Fibermark composites are similar to other Mark V models except has black Kevlar and fiberglass composite stock and bead-bead-blast blue or stainless finish. Chambered for 9 standard and magnum calibers. Introduced 1983; reintroduced 2001. SVR comes with 22" button-rifled chrome-moly barrel, .739 muzzle diameter. Composite stock w/bedding block, gray spiderweb pattern. Made in U.S.A. From Weatherby.

Price: Mark V Deluxe **$2,300.00**
Price: Mark V Ultramark **$3,100.00**
Price: Mark V Lazermark **$2,600.00**
Price: Mark V Sporter **$1,600.00**
Price: Mark V Ultra Lightweight **$1,900.00 to $2,100.00**
Price: Mark V Accumark **$2,300.00**
Price: Mark V Synthetic **$1,300.00 to $1,600.00**

WEATHERBY VANGUARD BOLT-ACTION RIFLES

Caliber: 257, 300 Wby Mags; 223 Rem., 22-250 Rem., 243 Win., 25-06 Rem. (2007), 270 Win., 270 WSM, 7mm Rem. Mag., 308 Win., 30-06 Spfl., 300 Win. Mag., 300 WSM, 338 Win. Mag. **Barrel:** 24" barreled action, matte black. **Weight:** 7.5 to 8.75 lbs. **Length:** 44" to 46-3/4" overall. **Stock:** Raised comb, Monte Carlo, injection-molded composite stock. **Sights:** None furnished. **Features:** One-piece forged, fluted bolt body with three gas ports, forged and machined receiver, adjustable trigger, factory accuracy guarantee. Vanguard Stainless has 410-Series stainless steel barrel and action, bead blasted matte metal finish. Vanguard Deluxe has raised comb, semi-fancy grade Monte Carlo walnut stock with maplewood spacers, rosewood forend and grip cap, polished action with high-gloss-blued metalwork. Vanguard Synthetic Package includes Vanguard Synthetic rifle with Bushnell Banner 3-9x40mm scope mounted and boresighted, Leupold Rifleman rings and bases, Uncle Mikes nylon sling, and Plano PRO-MAX injection-molded case. Sporter has Monte Carlo walnut stock with satin urethane finish, fineline diamond point checkering, contrasting rosewood forend tip, matte-blued metalwork. Sporter SS metalwork is 410 Series bead-blasted stainless steel. Vanguard Youth/Compact has 20" No. 1 contour barrel, short action, scaled-down non-reflective matte black hardwood stock with 12.5" length of pull and full-size, injection-molded composite stock. Chambered for 223 Rem., 22-250 Rem., 243 Win., 7mm-08 Rem., 308 Win. Weighs 6.75 lbs.; OAL 38.9". Sub-MOA Matte and Sub-MOA Stainless models have pillar-bedded Fiberguard composite stock (Aramid, graphite unidirectional fibers and fiberglass) with 24" barreled action; matte black metalwork, Pachmayr Decelerator recoil pad. Sub-MOA Stainless metalwork is 410 Series bead-blasted stainless steel. Sub-MOA Varmint guaranteed to shoot 3-shot group of .99" or less when used with specified Weatherby factory or premium (non-Weatherby calibers) ammunition. Hand-laminated, tan Monte Carlo composite stock with black spiderwebbing; CNC-machined aluminum bedding block, 22" No. 3 contour barrel, recessed target crown. Varmint Special has tan injection-molded Monte Carlo composite stock, pebble grain finish, black spiderwebbing. 22" No. 3 contour barrel (.740 muzzle dia.), bead blasted matte black finish, recessed target crown. Made in U.S.A. From Weatherby.

Price: Vanguard Synthetic **$599.00**
Price: Vanguard Stainless **$749.00**
Price: Vanguard Deluxe, 7mm Rem. Mag., 300 Win. Mag. (2007) **$1,049.00**
Price: Vanguard Synthetic Package, 25-06 Rem. (2007) **$799.00**
Price: Vanguard Sporter **$749.00**
Price: Vanguard Youth/Compact **$549.00**

WINCHESTER MODEL 70 BOLT-ACTION RIFLES

Caliber: Varies by model. **Barrel:** Blued, or free-floating, fluted stainless hammer-forged barrel, 22", 24", 26". Recessed target crown. **Weight:** 6.75 to 7.25 lbs. **Length:** 41 to 45.75 " overall. **Stock:** Walnut (three models) or Bell and Carlson composite; textured charcoal-grey matte finish, Pachmayr Decelerator recoil pad. **Sights:** None. **Features:** Claw extractor, three-position safety, M.O.A. three-lever trigger system, factory-set at 3.75 lbs. Super Grade features fancy grade walnut stock, contrasting black fore-end tip and pistol grip cap, and sculpted shadowline cheekpiece. Featherweight Deluxe has angled-comb walnut stock, Schnabel fore-end, satin finish, cut checkering. Sporter Deluxe has satin-finished walnut stock, cut checkering, sculpted cheekpiece. Extreme Weather SS has composite stock, drop @ comb, 0.5"; drop @ heel, 0.5". Introduced 2008. Made in U.SA. from Winchester Repeating Arms.

Price: Extreme Weather SS, 270 Win., 270 WSM, 30-06 Spfl., 300 Win. Mag., 300 WSM, 308 Win., 325 WSM, 243 Winchester, 7mm WSM, from **$1,200.00**

Price: Super Grade, 30-06 Sprg., 300 Win. Mag., 270 WSM, 300 WSM, 270 Winchester, from **$1,300.00**

WINCHESTER MODEL 70 COYOTE LIGHT

Caliber: 22-250, 243 Winchester, 308 Winchester, 270 WSM, 300 WSM and 325 WSM, five-shot magazine (3-shot in 270 WSM, 300 WSM and 325 WSM). **Barrel:** 22" fluted stainless barrel (24" in 270 WSM, 300 WSM and 325 WSM). **Weight:** 7.5 lbs. **Length:** NA. **Features:** Composite Bell and Carlson stock, Pachmayr Decelerator pad. Controlled round feeding. No sights but drilled and tapped for mounts.

Price: **$1,099.00**

WINCHESTER MODEL 70 FEATHERWEIGHT

Caliber: 22-250, 243, 7mm-08, 308, 270 WSM, 7mm WSM, 300 WSM, 325 WSM, 25-06, 270, 30-06, 7mm Rem. Mag., 300 Win. Mag., 338 Win. Mag. Capacity 5 rounds (short action) or 3 rounds (long action). **Barrel:** 22" blued barrel (24" in magnum chamberings). **Weight:** 6-1/2 to 7-1/4 lbs. **Length:** NA. **Features:** Satin-finished checkered Grade I walnut stock, controlled round feeding. Pachmayr Decelerator pad. No sights but drilled and tapped for scope mounts.

Price: **$880.00**

WINCHESTER MODEL 70 SPORTER

Caliber: 270 WSM, 7mm WSM, 300 WSM, 325 WSM, 25-06, 270, 30-06, 7mm Rem. Mag., 300 Win. Mag., 338 Win. Mag. Capacity 5 rounds (short action) or 3 rounds (long action). Barrel: 22", 24" or 26" blued. Weight: 6-1/2 to 7-1/4 lbs. Length: NA. Features: Satin-finished checkered Grade I walnut stock with sculpted cheekpiece, controlled round feeding. Pachmayr Decelerator pad. No sights but drilled and tapped for scope mounts.

Price: **$920.00**

WINCHESTER MODEL 70 ULTIMATE SHADOW

Caliber: 243, 308, 270 WSM, 7mm WSM, 300 WSM, 325 WSM, 270, 30-06, 7mm Rem. Mag., 300 Win. Mag. Capacity 5 rounds (short action) or 3 rounds (long action). **Barrel:** 22" matte stainless (24" or 26" in magnum chamberings). **Weight:** 6-1/2 to 7-1/4 lbs. **Length:** NA. **Features:** Synthetic stock with WinSorb recoil pad, controlled round feeding. Pachmayr Decelerator pad. No sights but drilled and tapped for scope mounts.

Price: . . . . **$760.00 to $970.00**

ARMALITE AR-50 RIFLE

Caliber: 50 BMG **Barrel:** 31". **Weight:** 33.2 lbs. **Length:** 59.5" **Stock:** Synthetic. **Sights:** None furnished. **Features:** A single-shot bolt-action rifle designed for long-range shooting. Available in left-hand model. Made in U.S.A. by Armalite.

Price: **$3,359.00**

BALLARD 1875 1 1/2 HUNTER RIFLE

Caliber: NA. **Barrel:** 26-30". **Weight:** NA **Length:** NA. **Stock:** Hand-selected classic American walnut. **Sights:** Blade front, Rocky Mountain rear. **Features:** Color case-hardened receiver, breechblock and lever. Many options available. Made in U.S.A. by Ballard Rifle & Cartridge Co.

Price: **$3,250.00**

BALLARD 1875 #3 GALLERY SINGLE SHOT RIFLE

Caliber: NA. **Barrel:** 24-28" octagonal with tulip. **Weight:** NA. **Length:** NA. **Stock:** Hand-selected classic American walnut. **Sights:** Blade front, Rocky Mountain rear. **Features:** Color case-hardened receiver, breechblock and lever. Many options available. Made in U.S.A. by Ballard Rifle & Cartridge Co.

Price: **$3,300.00**

BALLARD 1875 #4 PERFECTION RIFLE

Caliber: 22 LR, 32-40, 38-55, 40-65, 40-70, 45-70 Govt., 45-90, 45-110, 50-70, 50-90. **Barrel:** 30" or 32" octagon, standard or heavyweight. **Weight:** 10.5 lbs. (standard) or 11.75 lbs. (heavyweight bbl.). **Length:** NA. **Stock:** Smooth walnut. **Sights:** Blade front, Rocky Mountain rear. **Features:** Rifle or shotgun-style buttstock, straight grip action, single or double-set trigger, "S" or right lever, hand polished and lapped Badger barrel. Made in U.S.A. by Ballard Rifle & Cartridge Co.

Price: **$3,950.00**

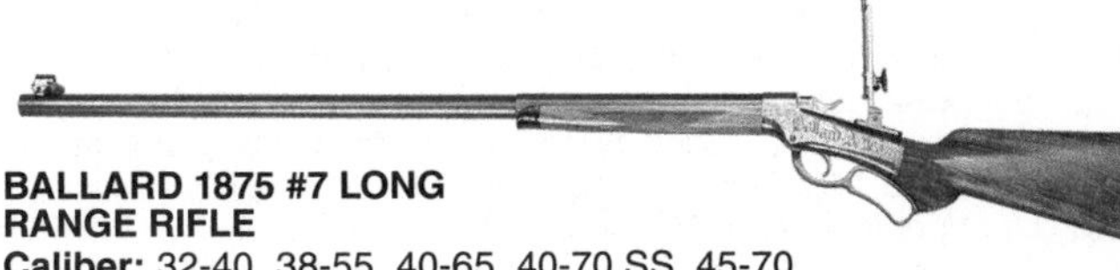

BALLARD 1875 #7 LONG RANGE RIFLE

Caliber: 32-40, 38-55, 40-65, 40-70 SS, 45-70 Govt., 45-90, 45-110. **Barrel:** 32", 34" half-octagon. **Weight:** 11.75 lbs. **Length:** NA. **Stock:** Walnut; checkered pistol grip shotgun butt, ebony forend cap. **Sights:** Globe front. **Features:** Designed for shooting up to 1000 yards. Standard or heavy barrel; single or double-set trigger; hard rubber or steel buttplate. Introduced 1999. Made in U.S.A. by Ballard Rifle & Cartridge Co.

Price: From **$3,600.00**

BALLARD 1875 #8 UNION HILL RIFLE

Caliber: 22 LR, 32-40, 38-55, 40-65 Win., 40-70 SS. **Barrel:** 30" half-octagon. **Weight:** About 10.5 lbs. **Length:** NA. **Stock:** Walnut; pistol grip butt with cheekpiece. **Sights:** Globe front. **Features:** Designed for 200-yard offhand shooting. Standard or heavy barrel; double-set triggers; full loop lever; hook Schuetzen buttplate. Introduced 1999. Made in U.S.A. by Ballard Rifle & Cartridge Co.

Price: From **$4,175.00**

BALLARD MODEL 1885 LOW WALL SINGLE SHOT RIFLE

Caliber: NA. **Barrel:** 24-28". **Weight:** NA. **Length:** NA. **Stock:** Hand-selected classic American walnut. **Sights:** Blade front, sporting rear. **Features:** Color case hardened receiver, breech block and lever. Many options available. Made in U.S.A. by Ballard Rifle & Cartridge Co.

Price: **$3,300.00**

BALLARD MODEL 1885 HIGH WALL STANDARD SPORTING SINGLE SHOT RIFLE

Caliber: 17 Bee, 22 Hornet, 218 Bee, 219 Don Wasp, 219 Zipper, 22 Hi-Power, 225 Win., 25-20 WCF, 25-35 WCF, 25 Krag, 7mmx57R, 30-30, 30-40 Krag, 303 British, 33 WCF, 348 WCF, 35 WCF, 35-30/30, 9.3x74R, 405 WCF, 50-110 WCF, 500 Express, 577 Express. **Barrel:** Lengths to 34". **Weight:** NA. **Length:** NA. **Stock:** Straight-grain American walnut. **Sights:** Buckhorn or flattop rear, blade front. **Features:** Faithful copy of original Model 1885 High Wall; parts interchange with original rifles; variety of options available. Introduced 2000. Made in U.S.A. by Ballard Rifle & Cartridge Co.

Price: **$3,300.00**

BALLARD MODEL 1885 HIGH WALL SPECIAL SPORTING SINGLE SHOT RIFLE

Caliber: NA. **Barrel:** 28-30" octagonal. **Weight:** NA. **Length:** NA. **Stock:** Hand-selected classic American walnut. **Sights:** Blade front, sporting rear. **Features:** Color case hardened receiver, breech block and lever. Many options available. Made in U.S.A. by Ballard Rifle & Cartridge Co.

Price: **$3,600.00**

BARRETT MODEL 99 SINGLE SHOT RIFLE

Caliber: 50 BMG. **Barrel:** 33". **Weight:** 25 lbs. **Length:** 50.4" overall. **Stock:** Anodized aluminum with energy-absorbing recoil pad. **Sights:** None furnished; integral M1913 scope rail. **Features:** Bolt action; detachable bipod; match-grade barrel with high-efficiency muzzle brake. Introduced 1999. Made in U.S.A. by Barrett Firearms.

Price: From **$4,000.00**

BROWN MODEL 97D SINGLE SHOT RIFLE

Caliber: 17 Ackley Hornet through 45-70 Govt. **Barrel:** Up to 26", air gauged match grade. **Weight:** About 5 lbs., 11 oz. **Stock:** Sporter style with pistol grip, cheekpiece and Schnabel forend. **Sights:** None furnished; drilled and tapped for scope mounting. **Features:** Falling block action gives rigid barrel-receiver matting; polished blue/black finish. Hand-fitted action. Many options. Made in U.S.A. by E. Arthur Brown Co., Inc.

Price: From **$999.00**

C. SHARPS ARMS MODEL 1875 TARGET & SPORTING RIFLE

Caliber: 38-55, 40-65, 40-70 Straight or Bottlenecks, 45-70, 45-90. Barrel: 30" heavy taperred round. Weight: 11 lbs. Length: NA. Stock: American walnut. Sights: Globe with post front sight. Features: Long Range Vernier tang sight with windage adjustments. Pistol grip stock with cheek rest; checkered steel buttplate. Introduced 1991. From C. Sharps Arms Co.

Price: Without sights **$1,325.00**
Price: With blade front & Buckhorn rear barrel sights **$1,420.00**
Price: With standard Tang & Globe w/post & ball front sights **$1,615.00**
Price: With deluxe vernier Tang & Globe w/spirit level & aperture sights **$1,730.00**
Price: With single set trigger, add **$125.00**

C. SHARPS ARMS 1875 CLASSIC SHARPS

Similar to New Model 1875 Sporting Rifle except 26", 28" or 30" full octagon barrel, crescent buttplate with toe plate, Hartford-style forend with cast German silver nose cap. Blade front sight, Rocky Mountain buckhorn rear. Weighs 10 lbs. Introduced 1987. From C. Sharps Arms Co.

Price: **$1,670.00**

C. SHARPS ARMS 1874 BRIDGEPORT SPORTING RIFLE

Caliber: 38-55 TO 50-3.25. **Barrel:** 26", 28", 30" tapered octagon. **Weight:** 10.5 lbs. **Length:** 47". **Stock:** American black walnut; shotgun butt with checkered steel buttplate; straight grip, heavy forend with Schnabel tip. **Sights:** Blade front, buckhorn rear. Drilled and tapped for tang sight. **Features:** Double-set triggers. Made in U.S.A. by C. Sharps Arms.

Price: **$1,895.00**

C. SHARPS ARMS NEW MODEL 1885 HIGHWALL RIFLE

Caliber: 22 LR, 22 Hornet, 219 Zipper, 25-35 WCF, 32-40 WCF, 38-55 WCF, 40-65, 30-40 Krag, 40-50 ST or BN, 40-70 ST or BN, 40-90 ST or BN, 45-70 Govt. 2-1/10" ST, 45-90 2-4/10" ST, 45-100 2-6/10" ST, 45-110 2-7/8" ST, 45-120 3-1/4" ST. **Barrel:** 26", 28", 30", tapered full octagon. **Weight:** About 9 lbs., 4 oz. **Length:** 47" overall. **Stock:** Oil-finished American walnut; Schnabel-style forend. **Sights:** Blade front, buckhorn rear. Drilled and tapped for optional tang sight. **Features:** Single trigger; octagonal receiver top; checkered steel buttplate; color case-hardened receiver and buttplate, blued barrel. Many options available. Made in U.S.A. by C. Sharps Arms Co.

Price: From **$1,750.00**

C. SHARPS ARMS CUSTOM NEW MODEL 1877 LONG RANGE TARGET RIFLE

Caliber: 44-90 Sharps/Rem., 45-70 Govt., 45-90, 45-100 Sharps. **Barrel:** 32", 34" tapered round with Rigby flat. **Weight:** About 10 lbs. **Stock:** Walnut checkered. Pistol grip/forend. **Sights:** Classic long range with windage. **Features:** Custom production only.

Price: From **$7,250.00**

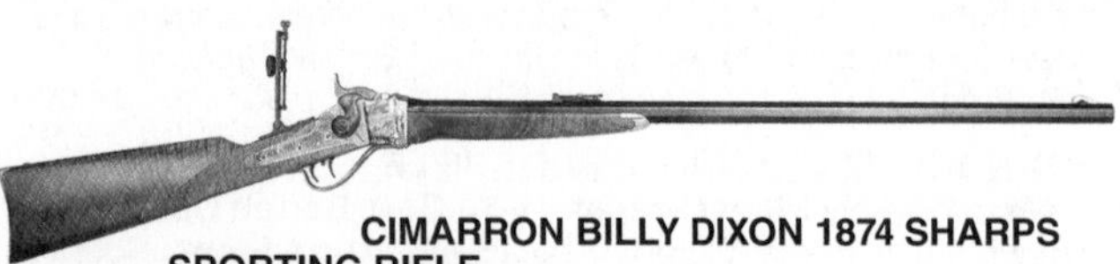

CABELA'S 1874 SHARPS SPORTING RIFLE

Caliber: 45-70. **Barrel:** 32", tapered octabon. **Weight:** 10.5 lbs. **Length:** 49.25" overall. **Stock:** Checkered walnut. **Sights:** Blade front, open adjustable rear. **Features:** Color case-hardened receiver and hammer, rest blued. Introduced 1995. Imported by Cabela's.

Price: 45-70 . . . . **$1,399.99**
Price: Quigley Sharps, 45-70 Govt., 45-120, 45-110 . . . . . . **$1,699.99**

CIMARRON BILLY DIXON 1874 SHARPS SPORTING RIFLE

Caliber: 40-40, 50-90, 50-70, 45-70 Govt. **Barrel:** 32" tapered octagonal. **Weight:** NA. **Length:** NA. **Stock:** European walnut. **Sights:** Blade front, Creedmoor rear. **Features:** Color case-hardened frame, blued barrel. Hand-checkered grip and forend; hand-rubbed oil finish. Introduced 1999. Imported by Cimarron F.A. Co.

Price: From **$1,987.70**

CIMARRON QUIGLEY MODEL 1874 SHARPS SPORTING RIFLE

Caliber: 45-110, 50-70, 50-40, 45-70 Govt., 45-90, 45-120. **Barrel:** 34" octagonal. **Weight:** NA. **Length:** NA. **Stock:** Checkered walnut. **Sights:** Blade front, adjustable rear. **Features:** Blued finish; double-set triggers. From Cimarron F.A. Co.

Price: From **$2,156.70**

CIMARRON SILHOUETTE MODEL 1874 SHARPS SPORTING RIFLE

Caliber: 45-70 Govt. **Barrel:** 32" octagonal. **Weight:** NA. **Length:** NA. **Stock:** Walnut. **Sights:** Blade front, adjustable rear. **Features:** Pistol-grip stock with shotgun-style buttplate; cut-rifled barrel. From Cimarron F.A. Co.

Price: **$1,597.70**

CIMARRON MODEL 1885 HIGH WALL RIFLE

Caliber: 38-55, 40-65, 45-70 Govt., 45-90, 45-120, 30-40 Krag, 348 Winchester. **Barrel:** 30" octagonal. **Weight:** NA. **Length:** NA. **Stock:** European walnut. **Sights:** Bead front, semi-buckhorn rear. **Features:** Replica of the Winchester 1885 High Wall rifle. Color case-hardened receiver and lever, blued barrel. Curved buttplate. Optional double-set triggers. Introduced 1999. Imported by Cimarron F.A. Co.

Price: From **$1,002.91**
Price: With pistol grip, from **$1,136.81**

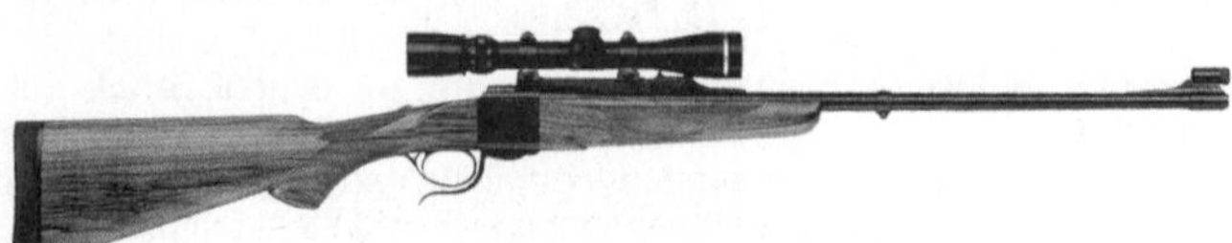

DAKOTA MODEL 10 SINGLE SHOT RIFLE

Caliber: Most rimmed and rimless commercial calibers. **Barrel:** 23". **Weight:** 6 lbs. **Length:** 39.5" overall. **Stock:** Medium fancy grade walnut in classic style. Checkered grip and forend. **Sights:** None furnished. Drilled and tapped for scope mounting. **Features:** Falling block action with underlever. Top tang safety. Removable trigger plate for conversion to single set trigger. Introduced 1990. Made in U.S.A. by Dakota Arms.

Price: From **$4,695.00**
Price: Action only **$1,875.00**
Price: Magnum action only **$1,875.00**

DAKOTA SHARPS

Calibers: Virtually any caliber from .17 Ackley Hornet to .30-40 Krag. Features include a 26" octagon barrel, XX-grade walnut stock with straight grip and tang sight. Many options and upgrades are available.

Price: From **$3995**

EMF PREMIER 1874 SHARPS RIFLE

Caliber: 45/70, 45/110, 45/120. **Barrel:** 32", 34". **Weight:** 11-13 lbs. **Length:** 49", 51" overall. **Stock:** Pistol grip, European walnut. **Sights:** Blade front, adjustable rear. **Features:** Superb quality reproductions of the 1874 Sharps Sporting Rifles; casehardened locks; double-set triggers; blue barrels. Imported from Pedersoli by EMF.

Price: Business Rifle **$1,199.90**
Price: "Quigley", Patchbox, heavy barrel **$1,799.90**
Price: Silhouette, pistol-grip **$1,499.90**
Price: Super Deluxe Hand Engraved **$3,500.00**

HARRINGTON & RICHARDSON ULTRA VARMINT/ULTRA HUNTER RIFLES

Caliber: 204 Ruger, 22 WMR, 22-250 Rem., 223 Rem., 243 Win., 25-06 Rem., 30-06. **Barrel:** 22" to 26" heavy taper. **Weight:** About 7.5 lbs. **Stock:** Laminated birch with Monte Carlo comb or skeletonized polymer. **Sights:** None furnished. Drilled and tapped for scope mounting. **Features:** Break-open action with side-lever release, positive ejection. Scope mount. Blued receiver and barrel. Swivel studs. Introduced 1993. Ultra Hunter introduced 1995. From H&R 1871, Inc.

Price: Ultra Varmint Fluted, 24" bull barrel, polymer stock **$406.00**
Price: Ultra Hunter Rifle, 26" bull barrel in 25-06 Rem., laminated stock **$357.00**
Price: Ultra Varmint Rifle, 22" bull barrel in 223 Rem., laminated stock **$357.00**

HARRINGTON & RICHARDSON/NEW ENGLAND FIREARMS STAINLESS ULTRA HUNTER WITH THUMBHOLE STOCK

Caliber: 45-70 Govt. **Barrel:** 24". **Weight:** 8 lbs. **Length:** 40". **Features:** Stainless steel barrel and receiver with scope mount rail, hammer extension, cinnamon laminate thumbhole stock.

Price: **$439.00**

HARRINGTON & RICHARDSON/NEW ENGLAND FIREARMS HANDI-RIFLE/SLUG GUN COMBOS

Chamber: 44 Mag./12-ga. rifled slug and 357 Mag./20-ga. rifled slug. **Barrel:** Rifle barrel 22" for both calibers; shotgun barrels 28" (12 ga.) and 40" (20 ga.) fully rifled. **Weight:** 7-8 lbs. **Length:** 38" overall (both rifle chamberings). **Features:** Single-shot break-open rifle/shotgun combos (one rifle barrel, one shotgun barrel per combo). Rifle barrels are not interchangeable; shotgun barrels are interchangeable. Stock is black matte high-density polymer with sling swivel studs, molded checkering and recoil pad. No iron sights; scope rail included.

Price: **$362.00**

HARRINGTON & RICHARDSON CR-45LC

Caliber: 45 Colt. Barrel: 20». Weight: 6.25 lbs. Length: 34»overall. Features: Single-shot break-open carbine. Cut-checkered American black walnut with case-colored crescent steel buttplate, open sights, case-colored receiver.

Price: **$407.00**

HARRINGTON & RICHARDSON BUFFALO CLASSIC RIFLE

Caliber: 45-70 Govt. **Barrel:** 32" heavy. **Weight:** 8 lbs. **Length:** 46" overall. **Stock:** Cut-checkered American black walnut. **Sights:**

Prices given are believed to be accurate at time of publication however, many factors affect retail pricing so exact prices are not possible.

Williams receiver sight; Lyman target front sight with 8 aperture inserts. **Features:** Color case-hardened Handi-Rifle action with exposed hammer; color case-hardened crescent buttplate; 19th century checkering pattern. Introduced 1995. Made in U.S.A. by H&R 1871, Inc.

Price: Buffalo Classic Rifle **$449.00**

KRIEGHOFF HUBERTUS SINGLE-SHOT RIFLE

Caliber: 222, 243 Win., 270 Win., 308 Win., 30-06 Spfl., 5.6x50R Mag., 5.6x52R, 6x62R Freres, 6.5x57R, 6.5x65R, 7x57R, 7x65R, 8x57JRS, 8x75RS, 9.3x74R, 7mm Rem. Mag., 300 Win. Mag. **Barrel:** 23.5". **Weight:** 6.5 lbs. **Length:** 40.5. **Stock:** High-grade walnut. **Sights:** Blade front, open rear. **Features:** Break-open loading with manual cocking lever on top tang; takedown; extractor; Schnabel forearm; many options. Imported from Germany by Krieghoff International Inc.

Price: Hubertus single shot, from **$5,995.00**
Price: Hubertus, magnum calibers **$6,995.00**

MEACHAM HIGHWALL SILHOUETTE OR SCHUETZEN RIFLE

Caliber: any rimmed cartridge. **Barrel:** 26-34". **Weight:** 8-15 lbs. **Sights:** none. Tang drilled for Win. base, 3/8 dovetail slot front. **Stock:** Fancy eastern walnut with cheekpiece; ebony insert in forearm tip. **Features:** Exact copy of 1885 Winchester. With most Winchester factory options available, including double set triggers. Introduced 1994. Made in U.S.A. by Meacham T&H Inc.

Price: From **$4,999.00**

MERKEL K1 MODEL LIGHTWEIGHT STALKING RIFLE

Caliber: 243 Win., 270 Win., 7x57R, 308 Win., 30-06 Spfl., 7mm Rem. Mag., 300 Win. Mag., 9.3x74R. **Barrel:** 23.6". **Weight:** 5.6 lbs. unscoped. **Stock:** Satin-finished walnut, fluted and checkered; sling-swivel studs. **Sights:** None (scope base furnished). **Features:** Franz Jager single-shot break-open action, cocking/uncocking slide-type safety, matte silver receiver, selectable trigger pull weights, integrated, quick detach 1" or 30mm optic mounts (optic not included). Imported from Germany by Merkel USA.

Price: Jagd Stutzen Carbine **$3,795.00**

MERKEL K-2 CUSTOM SINGLE-SHOT "WEIMAR" STALKING RIFLE

Caliber: 308 Win., 30-06 Spfl., 7mm Rem. Mag., 300 Win. Mag. **Features:** Franz Jager single-shot break-open action, cocking. uncocking slide safety, deep relief engraved hunting scenes on silvered receiver, octagin barrel, deluxe walnut stock. Includes front and reare adjustable iron sights, scope rings. Imported from Germany by Merkel USA.

Price: Jagd Stutzen Carbine **$15,595.00**

MILLER ARMS

Calibers: Virtually any caliber from .17 Ackley Hornet to .416 Remington. Falling block design with 24" premium match-grade barrel, express sights, XXX-grade walnut stock and fore-end with 24 lpi checkering. Made in several styles including Classic, Target and Varmint. Many options and upgrades are available. From Dakota Arms.

Price: From **$4995**

NAVY ARMS 1874 SHARPS "QUIGLEY" RIFLE

Caliber: .45-70 Govt. **Barrel:** 34" octagon. **Weight:** 10 lbs. **Length:** 50" overall. Grips: Walnut checkered at wrist and forend. **Sights:** High blade front, full buckhorn rear. **Features:** Color case-hardened receiver, trigger, military patchbox, hammer and lever. Double-set triggers, German silver gripcap. Reproduction of rifle from "Quigley Down Under" movie.

Price: Model SQR045 (20087) **$2,026.00**

NAVY ARMS 1874 SHARPS #2 CREEDMOOR RIFLE

Caliber: 45/70. **Barrel:** 30" tapered round. **Stock:** Walnut. **Sights:** Front globe, "soule" tang rear. **Features:** Nickel receiver and action. Lightweight sporting rifle.

Price: **$1,816.00**

NAVY ARMS SHARPS SPORTING RIFLE

Same as the Navy Arms Sharps Plains Rifle except has pistol grip stock. Introduced 1997. Imported by Navy Arms.

Price: 45-70 Govt. only **$1,711.00**
Price: #2 Sporting with case-hardened receiver **$1,739.00**
Price: #2 Silhouette with full octagonal barrel **$1,739.00**

NAVY ARMS 1885 HIGH WALL RIFLE

Caliber: 45-70 Govt.; others available on special order. **Barrel:** 28" round, 30" octagonal. **Weight:** 9.5 lbs. **Length:** 45.5" overall (30" barrel). **Stock:** Walnut. **Sights:** Blade front, vernier tang-mounted peep rear. **Features:** Replica of Winchester's High Wall designed by Browning. Color case-hardened receiver, blued barrel. Introduced 1998. Imported by Navy Arms.

Price: 28", round barrel, target sights. **$1,120.00**
Price: 30" octagonal barrel, target sights **$1,212.00**

NAVY ARMS 1873 SPRINGFIELD CAVALRY CARBINE

Caliber: 45-70 Govt. **Barrel:** 22". **Weight:** 7 lbs. **Length:** 40.5" overall. **Stock:** Walnut. **Sights:** Blade front, military ladder rear. **Features:** Blued lockplate and barrel; color case-hardened breechblock; saddle ring with bar. Replica of 7th Cavalry gun. Officer's Model Trapdoor has single-set trigger, bone case-hardened buttplate, trigger guard and breechblock. Deluxe walnut stock hand-checkered at the wrist and forend. German silver forend cap and rod tip. Adjustable rear peep target sight. Authentic flip-up 'Beech' front target sight. Imported by Navy Arms.

Price: Model STC073 . . . . **$1,261.00**
Price: Officer's Model Trapdoor (2008) **$1,648.00**

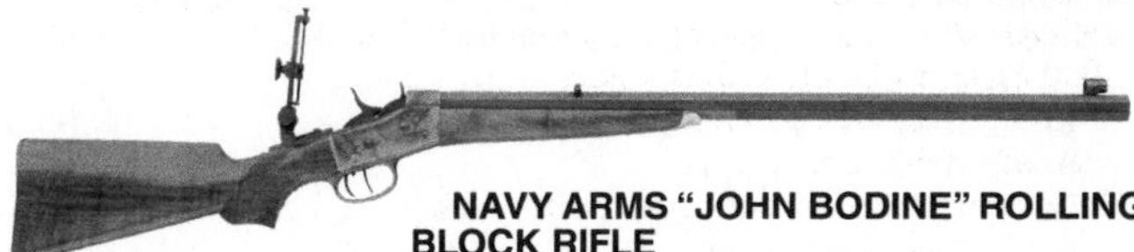

NAVY ARMS "JOHN BODINE" ROLLING BLOCK RIFLE

Caliber: 45-70 Govt. **Barrel:** 30" heavy octagonal. **Stock:** Walnut. **Sights:** Globe front, "soule" tang rear. **Features:** Double-set triggers.

Price: **$1,928.00**
Price: (#2 with deluxe nickel finished receiver) **$1,928.00**

NAVY ARMS 1874 SHARPS NO. 3 LONG RANGE RIFLE

Caliber: 45-70 Govt. **Barrel:** 34" octagon. **Weight:** 10 lbs., 14 oz. **Length:** 51.2". **Stock:** Deluxe walnut. **Sights:** Globe target front and match grade rear tang. **Features:** Shotgun buttplate, German silver forend cap, color case hardened receiver. Imported by Navy Arms.

Price: **$2,432.00**

NEW ENGLAND FIREARMS HANDI-RIFLE

Caliber: 204 Ruger, 22 Hornet, 223 Rem., 243 Win., 30-30, 270 Win., 280 Rem., 7mm-08 Rem., 308 Win., 7.62x39 Russian, 30-06 Spfl., 357 Mag., 35 Whelen, 44 Mag., 45-70 Govt., 500 S&W. **Barrel:** From 20" to 26", blued or stainless. **Weight:** 5.5 to 7 lbs. **Stock:** Walnut-finished hardwood or synthetic. **Sights:** Vary by model, but most have ramp front, folding rear, or are drilled and tapped for scope mount. **Features:** Break-open action with side-lever release. Swivel studs on all models. Blue finish. Introduced 1989. From H&R 1871, Inc.

Price: Various cartridges **$292.00**
Price: 7.62x39 Russian, 35 Whelen, intr. 2006 . . . .**$292.00**
Price: Youth, 37" OAL, 11.75" LOP, 6.75 lbs. **$292.00**
Price: Handi-Rifle/Pardner combo, 20 ga. synthetic, intr. 2006 . . . .**$325.00**
Price: Handi-Rifle/Pardner Superlight, 20 ga., 5.5 lbs., intr. 2006 . . . .**$325.00**
Price: Synthetic **$302.00**
Price: Stainless **$364.00**
Price: Superlight, 20" barrel, 35.25" OAL, 5.5 lbs. **$302.00**

NEW ENGLAND FIREARMS SURVIVOR RIFLE

Caliber: 223 Rem., 308 Win., .410 shotgun, 45 Colt, single shot. **Barrel:** 20" to 22". **Weight:** 6 lbs. **Length:** 34.5" to 36" overall. **Stock:** Black polymer, thumbhole design. **Sights:** None furnished; scope mount provided. **Features:** Receiver drilled and tapped for scope mounting. Stock and forend have storage compartments for ammo, etc.; comes with integral swivels and black nylon sling. Introduced 1996. Made in U.S.A. by H&R 1871, Inc.

Price: Blue or nickel finish **$304.00**

NEW ENGLAND FIREARMS SPORTSTER/VERSA PACK RIFLE

Caliber: 17M2, 17 HMR, 22 LR, 22 WMR, .410 bore single shot. **Barrel:** 20" to 22". **Weight:** 5.4 to 7 lbs. **Length:** 33" to 38.25" overall. **Stock:** Black polymer. **Sights:** Adjustable rear, ramp front. **Features:** Receiver drilled and tapped for scope mounting. Made in U.S.A. by H&R 1871, Inc.

Price: Sportster 17M2, 17 HMR **$193.00**
Price: Sportster **$161.00**
Price: Sportster Youth **$161.00**

REMINGTON MODEL SPR18 SINGLE SHOT RIFLES

Caliber: 223 Rem., 243 Win., 270 Win., .30-06 Spfl., 308 Win., 7.62x39mm. **Barrel:** 23.5" chrome-lined hammer forged, all steel receiver, spiral-cut fluting. **Weight:** 6.75 lbs. **Stock:** Walnut stock and fore-end, swivel studs. **Sights:** adjustable, with 11mm scope rail. **Length:** 39.75" overall. **Features:** Made in U.S. by Remington Arms Co., Inc.

Price: Blued/walnut (2008) **$277.00**
Price: Nickel/walnut (2008) **$326.00**

REMINGTON NO. 1 ROLLING BLOCK MID-RANGE SPORTER

Caliber: 45-70 Govt. **Barrel:** 30" round. **Weight:** 8.75 lbs. **Length:** 46.5" overall. **Stock:** American walnut with checkered pistol grip and forend. **Sights:** Beaded blade front, adjustable center-notch buckhorn rear. **Features:** Recreation of the original. Polished blue metal finish. Many options available. Introduced 1998. Made in U.S.A. by Remington.

Price: **$2,927.00**
Price: Silhouette model with single-set trigger, heavy barrel **$3,366.00**

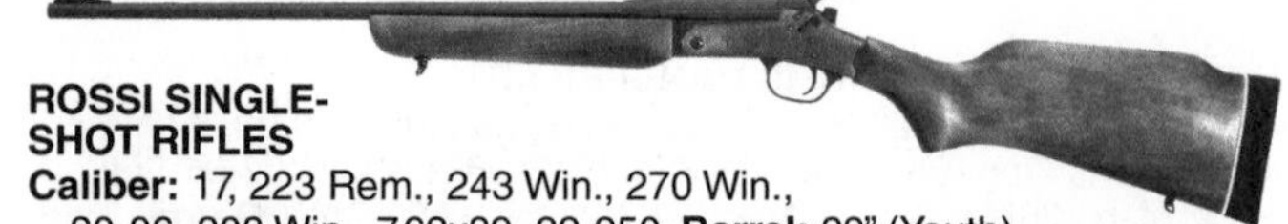

ROSSI SINGLE-SHOT RIFLES

Caliber: 17, 223 Rem., 243 Win., 270 Win., .30-06, 308 Win., 7.62x39, 22-250. **Barrel:** 22" (Youth), 23". **Weight:** 6.25-7 lbs. Stocks: Wood, Black Synthetic (Youth). **Sights:** Adjustable sights, drilled and tapped for scope. **Features:** Single-shot break open, 13 models available, positive ejection, internal transfer bar mechanism, manual external safety, trigger block system, Taurus Security System, Matte blue finish, youth models available.

Price: **$238.00**

ROSSI MATCHED PAIRS

Gauge/Caliber: 12, 20, .410, 22 Mag, 22 LR, 17 HMR, 223 Rem, 243 Win., 270 Win., .30-06, 308Win., .50 (black powder). **Barrel:** 23", 28". **Weight:** 5-6.3 lbs. Stocks: Wood or black synthetic. **Sights:** Bead front on shotgun barrel, fully adjustable front and rear on rifle barrel, drilled and tapped for scope, fully adjustable fiber optic sights (black powder). **Features:** Single-shot break open, 27 models available, internal transfer bar mechanism, manual external safety, blue finish, trigger block system, Taurus Security System, youth models available.

Price: Rimfire/Shotgun, from **$178.00**
Price: Centerfire/Shotgun **$299.00**
Price: Black Powder Matched Pair, from **$262.00**

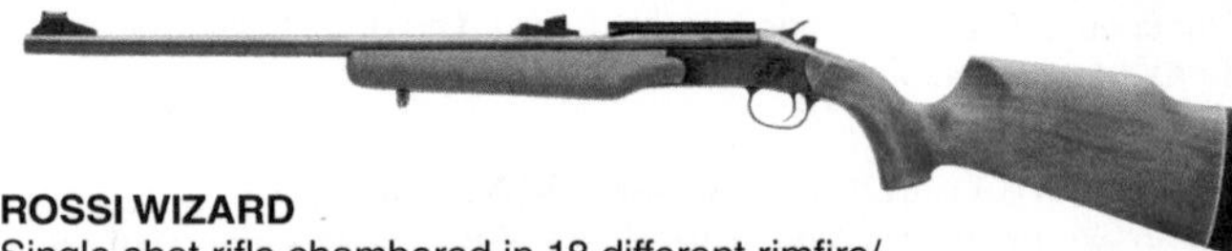

ROSSI WIZARD

Single shot rifle chambered in 18 different rimfire/centerfire/shotshell/muzzleloading configurations. Featured include drop-barrel action; quick, toolless barrel interchangeability; fiber optic front sight; adjustable rear sight with barrel-mounted optics rail; hardwood or camo Monte Carlo stock.

Price: . . . .**$369.00 to $410.00**

RUGER NO. 1-A LIGHT SPORTER

Caliber: .243, 6.5 Creedmoor, .270 Win., .303 British, .308 Win., .300 RCM, .30-06. Barrel: 22". **Weight:** 7.25 lbs. **Length:** 38.5". **Stock:** Two-piece American walnut. **Sights:** Adjustable rear, bead front. **Features:** Under-lever falling-block design with automatic ejector, top tang safety.

Price: **$1299**

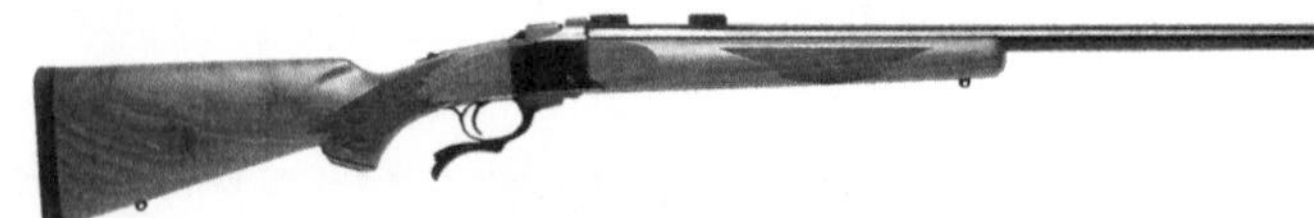

RUGER NO. 1-V VARMINTER

Similar to the No. 1-B Standard Rifle except has 24" heavy barrel. Semi-beavertail forend, barrel ribbed for target scope block, with 1" Ruger scope rings. Calibers 204 Ruger (26" barrel), 22-250 Rem., 223 Rem., 25-06 Rem., 6.5 Creedmoor. Weight about 9 lbs.

Price: No. 1-V **$1,147.00**

Prices given are believed to be accurate at time of publication however, many factors affect retail pricing so exact prices are not possible.

RUGER NO. 1 INTERNATIONAL

Similar to the No. 1-B Standard Rifle except has lightweight 20" barrel, full-length International-style forend with loop sling swivel, adjustable folding leaf rear sight on quarter-rib, ramp front with gold bead. Calibers 30-06 Spfl., 270 and 7x57. Weight is about 7.25 lbs.

Price: No. 1 RSI **$1,349.00**

RUGER NO. 1-H TROPICAL RIFLE

Similar to the No. 1-B Standard Rifle except has Alexander Henry forend, adjustable folding leaf rear sight on quarter-rib, ramp front with dovetail gold bead, 24" heavy barrel. Calibers .375 H&H, .450/400 Nitro Express, .458 Lott., 3" (weighs about 9 lbs.).

Price: No. 1H **$1,299.00**

RUGER NO. 1-S MEDIUM SPORTER

Similar to the No. 1-B Standard Rifle except has Alexander Henry-style forend, adjustable folding leaf rear sight on quarter-rib, ramp front sight base and dovetail-type gold bead front sight. Calibers include 9.3x74R, 45-70 Govt. with 22" barrel, .300 H&H, .300 Mag., .45-70 Gov't., .460 S&W Mag., .475 Linebaugh, .480 Ruger. Weighs about 7.25 lbs.

Price: **$1,299.00**

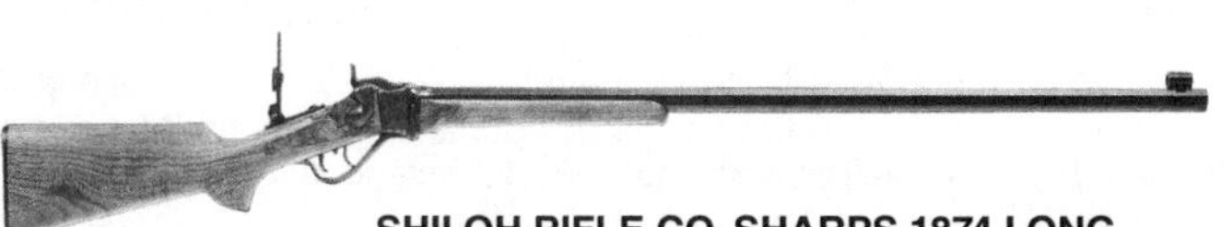

SHILOH RIFLE CO. SHARPS 1874 LONG RANGE EXPRESS

Caliber: 40-50 BN, 40-70 BN, 40-90 BN, 45-70 Govt. ST, 45-90 ST, 45-110 ST, 50-70 ST, 50-90 ST, 38-55, 40-70 ST, 40-90 ST. **Barrel:** 34" tapered octagon. **Weight:** 10.5 lbs. **Length:** 51" overall. **Stock:** Oil-finished walnut (upgrades available) with pistol grip, shotgun-style butt, traditional cheek rest, Schnabel forend. **Sights:** Customer's choice. **Features:** Re-creation of the Model 1874 Sharps rifle. Double-set triggers. Made in U.S.A. by Shiloh Rifle Mfg. Co.

Price: **$1,902.00**

Price: Sporter Rifle No. 1 (similar to above except with 30" barrel, blade front, buckhorn rear sight) **$1,902.00**

Price: Sporter Rifle No. 3 (similar to No. 1 except straight-grip stock, standard wood) **$1,800.00**

SHILOH RIFLE CO. SHARPS 1874 QUIGLEY

Caliber: 45-70 Govt., 45-110. **Barrel:** 34" heavy octagon. **Stock:** Military-style with patch box, standard grade American walnut. **Sights:** Semi buckhorn, interchangeable front and midrange vernier tang sight with windage. **Features:** Gold inlay initials, pewter tip, Hartford collar, case color or antique finish. Double-set triggers.

Price: **$3,298.00**

SHILOH RIFLE CO. SHARPS 1874 SADDLE RIFLE

Caliber: 38-55, 40-50 BN, 40-65 Win., 40-70 BN, 40-70 ST, 40-90 BN, 40-90 ST, 44-77 BN, 44-90 BN, 45-70 Govt. ST, 45-90 ST, 45-100 ST, 45-110 ST, 45-120 ST, 50-70 ST, 50-90 ST. **Barrel:** 26" full or half octagon. **Stock:** Semi fancy American walnut. Shotgun style with cheekrest. **Sights:** Buckhorn and blade. **Features:** Double-set trigger, numerous custom features can be added.

Price: **$1,852.00**

SHILOH RIFLE CO. SHARPS 1874 MONTANA ROUGHRIDER

Caliber: 38-55, 40-50 BN, 40-65 Win., 40-70 BN, 40-70 ST, 40-90 BN, 40-90 ST, 44-77 BN, 44-90 BN, 45-70 Govt. ST, 45-90 ST, 45-100 ST, 45-110 ST, 45-120 ST, 50-70 ST, 50-90 ST. **Barrel:** 30" full or half octagon. **Stock:** American walnut in shotgun or military style. **Sights:** Buckhorn and blade. **Features:** Double-set triggers, numerous custom features can be added.

Price: **$1,902.00**

SHILOH RIFLE CO. SHARPS CREEDMOOR TARGET

Caliber: 38-55, 40-50 BN, 40-65 Win., 40-70 BN, 40-70 ST, 40-90 BN, 40-90 ST, 44-77 BN, 44-90 BN, 45-70 Govt. ST, 45-90 ST, 45-100 ST, 45-110 ST, 45-120 ST, 50-70 ST, 50-90 ST. **Barrel:** 32", half round-half octagon. **Stock:** Extra fancy American walnut. Shotgun style with pistol grip. **Sights:** Customer's choice. **Features:** Single trigger, AA finish on stock, polished barrel and screws, pewter tip.

Price: **$2,743.00**

THOMPSON/CENTER ENCORE RIFLE

Caliber: 22-250 Rem., 223 Rem., 243 Win., 204 Ruger, 6.8 Rem. Spec., 25-06 Rem., 270 Win., 7mm-08 Rem., 308 Win., 30-06 Spfl., 7mm Rem. Mag., 300 Win. Mag. **Barrel:** 24", 26". **Weight:** 6 lbs., 12 oz. (24" barrel). **Length:** 38.5" (24" barrel). **Stock:** American walnut. Monte Carlo style; Schnabel forend or black composite. **Sights:** Ramp-style white bead front, fully adjustable leaf-type rear. **Features:** Interchangeable barrels; action opens by squeezing trigger guard; drilled and tapped for T/C scope mounts; polished blue finish. Introduced 1996. Made in U.S.A. by Thompson/Center Arms.

Price: **$817.00**

Price: Extra barrels **$328.00**

THOMPSON/CENTER STAINLESS ENCORE RIFLE

Similar to blued Encore except stainless steel with blued sights, black composite stock and forend. Available in 22-250 Rem., 223 Rem., 7mm-08 Rem., 30-06 Spfl., 308 Win. Introduced 1999. Made in U.S.A. by Thompson/Center Arms.

Price: . . . . **$680.00 to $738.00**

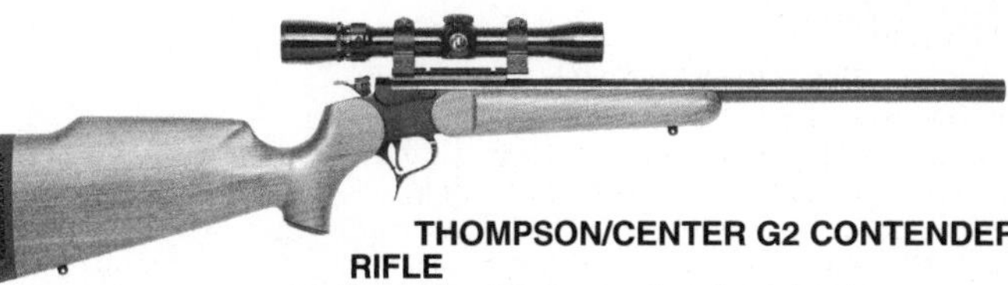

THOMPSON/CENTER G2 CONTENDER RIFLE

Similar to the G2 Contender pistol, but in a compact rifle format. Weighs 5.5 lbs. Features interchangeable 23" barrels, chambered for 17 HMR, 22 LR, 223 Rem., 30/30 Win. and 45/70 Govt.; plus a 45 cal. muzzleloading barrel. All of the 16.25" and 21" barrels made for the old-style Contender will fit. Introduced 2003. Made in U.S.A. by Thompson/Center Arms.

Price: . . . . **$840.00 to $872.00**

THOMPSON/CENTER ENCORE PROHUNTER PREDATOR RIFLE

Contender-style break-action single shot rifle chambered in .204 Ruger, .223 Remington, .22-250 and .308 Winchester. Features include 28-inch deep-fluted interchangeable barrel, composite

buttstock and forend with non-slip inserts in cheekpiece, pistol grip and forend. Max 1 camo finish overall. Overall length: 42.5 inches. Weight: 7-3/4 lbs.

Price: $965.00

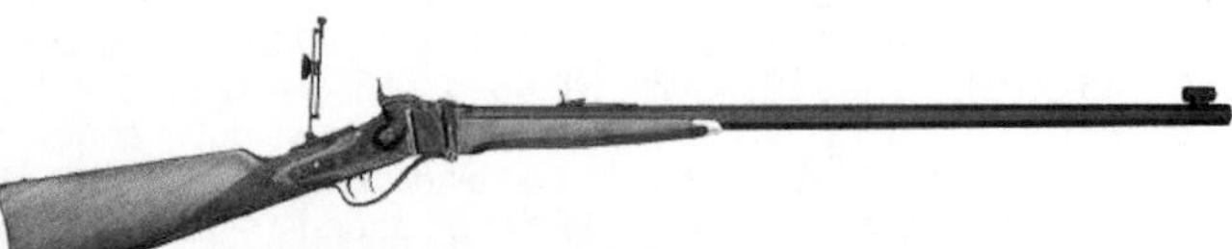

TRADITIONS 1874 SHARPS DELUXE RIFLE

Caliber: 45-70 Govt. **Barrel:** 32" octagonal; 1:18" twist. **Weight:** 11.67 lbs. **Length:** 48.8" overall. **Stock:** Checkered walnut with German silver nose cap and steel buttplate. **Sights:** Globe front, adjustable Creedmore rear with 12 inserts. **Features:** Color case-hardened receiver; double-set triggers. Introduced 2001. Imported from Pedersoli by Traditions.

Price: $1,545.00

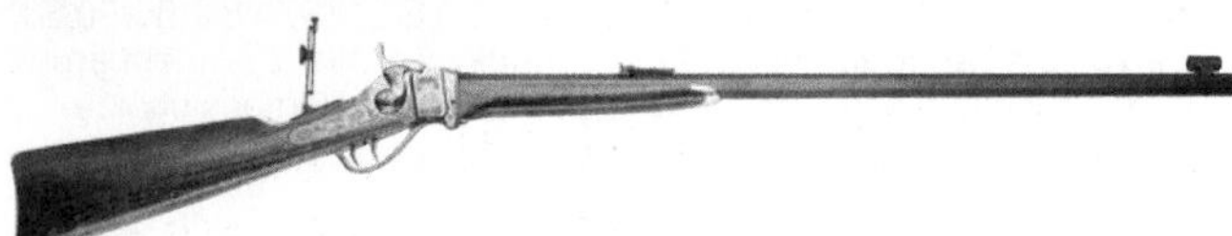

TRADITIONS 1874 SHARPS SPORTING DELUXE RIFLE

Similar to Sharps Deluxe but custom silver engraved receiver, European walnut stock and forend, satin finish, set trigger, fully adjustable.

Price: $2,796.00

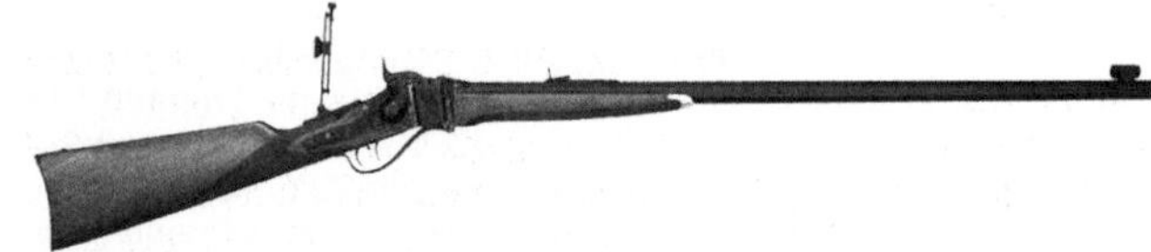

TRADITIONS 1874 SHARPS STANDARD RIFLE

Similar to 1874 Sharps Deluxe except has blade front and adjustable buckhorn-style rear sight. Weighs 10.67 pounds. Introduced 2001. Imported from Pedersoli by Traditions.

Price: $1,324.00

TRADITIONS ROLLING BLOCK SPORTING RIFLE

Caliber: 45-70 Govt. **Barrel:** 30" octagonal; 1:18" twist. **Weight:** 11.67 lbs. **Length:** 46.7" overall. **Stock:** Walnut. **Sights:** Blade front, adjustable rear. **Features:** Antique silver, color case-hardened receiver, drilled and tapped for tang/globe sights; brass buttplate and trigger guard. Introduced 2001. Imported from Pedersoli by Traditions.

Price: $1,029.00

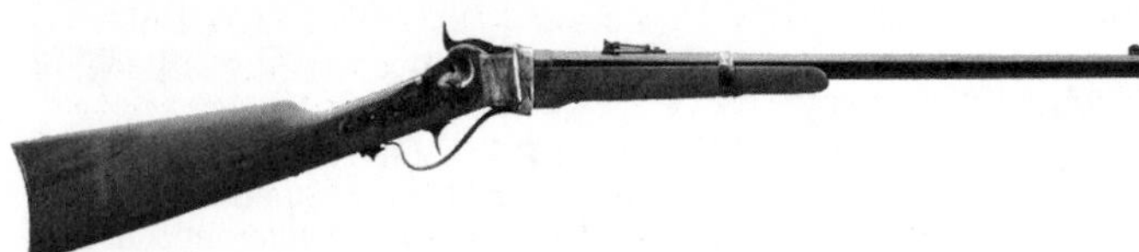

UBERTI 1874 SHARPS SPORTING RIFLE

Caliber: 45-70 Govt. **Barrel:** 30", 32", 34" octagonal. **Weight:** 10.57 lbs. with 32" barrel. **Length:** 48.9" with 32" barrel. **Stock:** Walnut. **Sights:** Dovetail front, Vernier tang rear. **Features:** Cut checkering, case-colored finish on frame, buttplate, and lever. Imported by Stoeger Industries.

Price: Standard Sharps (2006), 30" barrel **$1,459.00**
Price: Special Sharps (2006) 32" barrel **$1,729.00**
Price: Deluxe Sharps (2006) 34" barrel **$2,749.00**
Price: Down Under Sharps (2006) 34" barrel **$2,249.00**
Price: Long Range Sharps (2006) 34" barrel **$2,279.00**
Price: Buffalo Hunters Sharps, 32" barrel **$2,219.00**
Price: Calvary Carbine Sharps, 22" barrel **$1,569.00**
Price: Sharps Extra Deluxe, 32" barrel (2009) **$4,199.00**
Price: Sharps Hunter, 28" barrel **$1,459.00**

UBERTI 1885 HIGH-WALL SINGLE-SHOT RIFLES

Caliber: 45-70 Govt., 45-90, 45-120 single shot. **Barrel:** 28" to 23". **Weight:** 9.3 to 9.9 lbs. **Length:** 44.5" to 47" overall. **Stock:** Walnut stock and forend. **Sights:** Blade front, fully adjustable open rear. **Features:** Based on Winchester High-Wall design by John Browning. Color case-hardened frame and lever, blued barrel and buttplate. Imported by Stoeger Industries.

Price: 1885 High-Wall, 28" round barrel **$969.00**
Price: 1885 High-Wall Sporting, 30" octagonal barrel **$1,029.00**
Price: 1885 High-Wall Special Sporting, 32" octagonal barrel **$1,179.00**

Prices given are believed to be accurate at time of publication however, many factors affect retail pricing so exact prices are not possible.

BERETTA EXPRESS SSO O/U DOUBLE RIFLES

Caliber: 375 H&H, 458 Win. Mag., 9.3x74R. **Barrel:** 25.5". **Weight:** 11 lbs. **Stock:** European walnut with hand-checkered grip and forend. **Sights:** Blade front on ramp, open V-notch rear. **Features:** Sidelock action with color case-hardened receiver (gold inlays on SSO6 Gold). Ejectors, double triggers, recoil pad. Introduced 1990. Imported from Italy by Beretta U.S.A.

Price: SSO6 . . . . **$21,000.00**
Price: SSO6 Gold **$23,500.00**

BERETTA MODEL 455 SXS EXPRESS RIFLE

Caliber: 375 H&H, 458 Win. Mag., 470 NE, 500 NE 3", 416 Rigby. **Barrel:** 23.5" or 25.5". **Weight:** 11 lbs. **Stock:** European walnut with hand-checkered grip and forend. **Sights:** Blade front, folding leaf V-notch rear. **Features:** Sidelock action with easily removable sideplates; color case-hardened finish (455), custom big game or floral motif engraving (455EELL). Double triggers, recoil pad. Introduced 1990. Imported from Italy by Beretta U.S.A.

Price: Model 455. . . . . **$36,000.00**
Price: Model 455EELL **$47,000.00**

BRNO MODEL 802 COMBO GUN

Caliber/Gauge: .243 Win./12 ga. Over/under. **Barrels:** 23.6". **Weight:** 7.5 lbs. **Length:** 41". **Stock:** Walnut. **Features:** Double trigger, shotgun barrel is improved-modified chokes. Imported by CZ USA.

Price: **$2181**

CZ 584 SOLO COMBINATION GUN

Caliber/Gauge: 7x57R; 12, 2-3/4" chamber. **Barrel:** 24.4". **Weight:** 7.37 lbs. **Length:** 45.25" overall. **Stock:** Circassian walnut. **Sights:** Blade front, open rear adjustable for windage. **Features:** Kersten-style double lump locking system; double-trigger Blitz-type mechanism with drop safety and adjustable set trigger for the rifle barrel; auto safety, dual extractors; receiver dovetailed for scope mounting. Imported from the Czech Republic by CZ-USA.

Price: **$851.00**

CZ 589 STOPPER OVER/UNDER GUN

Caliber: 458 Win. Magnum. Barrels: 21.7". **Weight:** 9.3 lbs. **Length:** 37.7" overall. **Stock:** Turkish walnut with sling swivels. **Sights:** Blade front, fixed rear. **Features:** Kersten-style action; Blitz-type double trigger; hammer-forged, blued barrels; satin-nickel, engraved receiver. Introduced 2001. Imported from the Czech Republic by CZ USA.

Price: **$2,999.00**
Price: Fully engraved model **$3,999.00**

GARBI EXPRESS DOUBLE RIFLE

Caliber: 7x65R, 9.3x74R, 375 H&H. **Barrel:** 24.75". **Weight:** 7.75 to 8.5 lbs. **Length:** 41.5" overall. **Stock:** Turkish walnut. **Sights:** Quarter-rib with express sight. **Features:** Side-by-side double; H&H-pattern sidelock ejector with reinforced action, chopper lump barrels of Boehler steel; double triggers; fine scroll and rosette engraving, or full coverage ornamental; coin-finished action. Introduced 1997. Imported from Spain by Wm. Larkin Moore.

Price: **$25,000.00**

HOENIG ROTARY ROUND ACTION DOUBLE RIFLE

Caliber: Most popular calibers from 225 Win. to 9.3x74R. **Barrel:** 22" to 26". **Stock:** English Walnut; to customer specs. **Sights:** Swivel hood front with button release (extra bead stored in trap door gripcap), express-style rear on quarter-rib adjustable for windage and elevation; scope mount. **Features:** Round action opens by rotating barrels, pulling forward. Inertia extractor system, rotary safety blocks strikers. Single lever quick-detachable scope mount. Simple takedown without removing forend. Introduced 1997. Made in U.S.A. by George Hoenig.

Price: **$19,980.00**

HOENIG ROTARY ROUND ACTION COMBINATION

Caliber: 28 ga. **Barrel:** 26". **Weight:** 7 lbs. **Stock:** English Walnut to customer specs. **Sights:** Front ramp with button release blades. Foldable aperture tang sight windage and elevation adjustable. Quarter-rib with scope mount. **Features:** Round action opens by rotating barrels, pulling forward. Inertia extractor; rotary safety blocks strikers. Simple takedown without removing forend. Made in U.S.A. by George Hoenig.

Price: **$25,000.00**

KRIEGHOFF CLASSIC DOUBLE RIFLE

Caliber: 7x57R, 7x65R, 308 Win., 30-06 Spfl., 8x57 JRS, 8x75RS, 9.3x74R, 375NE, 500/416NE, 470NE, 500NE. **Barrel:** 23.5". **Weight:** 7.3 to 8 lbs; 10-11 lbs. Big 5. **Stock:** High grade European walnut. Standard model has conventional rounded cheekpiece, Bavaria model has Bavarian-style cheekpiece. **Sights:** Bead front with removable, adjustable wedge (375 H&H and below), standing leaf rear on quarter-rib. **Features:** Boxlock action; double triggers; short opening angle for fast loading; quiet extractors; sliding, self-adjusting wedge for secure bolting; Purdey-style barrel extension; horizontal firing pin placement. Many options available. Introduced 1997. Imported from Germany by Krieghoff International.

Price: With small Arabesque engraving **$8,950.00**
Price: With engraved sideplates **$12,300.00**
Price: For extra barrels **$5,450.00**
Price: Extra 20-ga., 28" shotshell barrels **$3,950.00**

KRIEGHOFF CLASSIC BIG FIVE DOUBLE RIFLE

Similar to the standard Classic except available in 375 Flanged Mag. N.E., 500/416 NE, 470 NE, 500 NE. Has hinged front trigger, non-removable muzzle wedge (models larger than 375 caliber), Universal Trigger System, Combi Cocking Device, steel trigger guard, specially weighted stock bolt for weight and balance. Many options available. Introduced 1997. Imported from Germany by Krieghoff International. Imperial Model introduced 2006.

Price: **$11,450.00**
Price: With engraved sideplates **$14,800.00**

LEBEAU-COURALLY EXPRESS RIFLE SXS

Caliber: 7x65R, 8x57JRS, 9.3x74R, 375 H&H, 470 N.E. **Barrel:** 24" to 26". **Weight:** 7.75 to 10.5 lbs. **Stock:** Fancy French walnut with cheekpiece. **Sights:** Bead on ramp front, standing left express rear on quarter-rib. **Features:** Holland & Holland-type sidelock with automatic ejectors; double triggers. Built to order only. Imported from Belgium by Wm. Larkin Moore.

Price: **$50,000.00**

MERKEL DRILLINGS

Caliber/Gauge: 12, 20, 3" chambers, 16, 2-3/4" chambers; 22 Hornet, 5.6x50R Mag., 5.6x52R, 222 Rem., 243 Win., 6.5x55, 6.5x57R, 7x57R, 7x65R, 308 Win., 30-06 Spfl., 8x57JRS, 9.3x74R, 375 H&H. **Barrel:** 25.6". **Weight:** 7.9 to 8.4 lbs. depending upon caliber. **Stock:** Oil-finished walnut with pistol grip; cheekpiece on 12-, 16-gauge. **Sights:** Blade front, fixed rear. **Features:** Double barrel locking lug with Greener cross bolt; scroll-engraved, case-hardened receiver; automatic trigger safety; Blitz action; double triggers. Imported from Germany by Merkel USA.

Price: Model 96K (manually cocked rifle system), from. **$8,495.00**
Price: Model 96K engraved (hunting series on receiver) **$9,795.00**

MERKEL BOXLOCK DOUBLE RIFLES

Caliber: 5.6x52R, 243 Winchester, 6.5x55, 6.5x57R, 7x57R, 7x65R, 308 Win., 30-06 Springfield, 8x57 IRS, 9.3x74R. **Barrel:** 23.6". **Weight:** 7.7 oz. **Length:** NA. **Stock:** Walnut, oil finished, pistol grip. **Sights:** Fixed 100 meter. **Features:** Anson & Deely boxlock action with cocking indicators, double triggers, engraved color case-hardened receiver. Introduced 1995. Imported from Germany by Merkel USA.

Price: Model 140-2, from. **$11,995.00**
Price: Model 141 Small Frame SXS Rifle; built on smaller frame, chambered for 7mm Mauser, 30-06, or 9.3x74R **$8,195.00**
Price: Model 141 Engraved; fine hand-engraved hunting scenes on silvered receiver **$9,495.00**

RIZZINI EXPRESS 90L DOUBLE RIFLE

Caliber: 30-06 Spfl., 7x65R, 9.3x74R. **Barrel:** 24". **Weight:** 7.5 lbs. **Length:** 40" overall. **Stock:** Select European walnut with satin oil finish; English-style cheekpiece. **Sights:** Ramp front, quarter-rib with express sight. **Features:** Color case-hardened boxlock action; automatic ejectors; single selective trigger; polished blue barrels. Extra 20 gauge shotgun barrels available. Imported from Italy by Connecticut Shotgun Co.

Price: With case **$5,355.00**

AMERICAN TACTICAL IMPORTS GSG-522

Semiauto tactical rifle chambered in .22 LR. Features include 16.25-inch barrel; black finish overall; polymer forend and buttstock; backup iron sights; receiver-mounted Picaatinny rail; 10-round magazine. Several other rifle and carbine versions available.

Price: **$475.00**

BROWNING BUCK MARK SEMI-AUTO RIFLES

Caliber: 22 LR, 10+1. Action: A rifle version of the Buck Mark Pistol; straight blowback action; machined aluminum receiver with integral rail scope mount; manual thumb safety. **Barrel:** Recessed crowns. **Stock:** Stock and forearm with full pistol grip. **Features:** Action lock provided. Introduced 2001. Four model name variations for 2006, as noted below. **Sights:** FLD Target, FLD Carbon, and Target models have integrated scope rails. Sporter has Truglo/Marble fiber optic sights. Imported from Japan by Browning.

Price: FLD Target, 5.5 lbs., bull barrel, laminated stock **$659.00**
Price: Target, 5.4 lbs., blued bull barrel, wood stock **$639.00**
Price: Sporter, 4.4 lbs., blued sporter barrel w/sights **$639.00**

BROWNING SA-22 SEMI-AUTO 22 RIFLES

Caliber: 22 LR, 11+1. **Barrel:** 16.25". **Weight:** 5.2 lbs. **Length:** 37" overall. **Stock:** Checkered select walnut with pistol grip and semi-beavertail forend. **Sights:** Gold bead front, folding leaf rear. **Features:** Engraved receiver with polished blue finish; cross-bolt safety; tubular magazine in buttstock; easy takedown for carrying or storage. The Grade VI is available with either grayed or blued receiver with extensive engraving with gold-plated animals: right side pictures a fox and squirrel in a woodland scene; left side shows a beagle chasing a rabbit. On top is a portrait of the beagle. Stock and forend are of high-grade walnut with a double-bordered cut checkering design. Introduced 1987. Imported from Japan by Browning.

Price: Grade I, scroll-engraved blued receiver **$700.00**
Price: Grade VI BL, gold-plated engraved blued receiver . . **$1,580.00**

CITADEL M-1 CARBINE

Caliber: .22LR., 10-round magazines. **Barrel:** 18". **Weight:** 4.8 lbs. **Length:** 35". **Features:** Straight from the pages of history ... the greatest conflict of modern times, World War II ... comes the new Citadel M-1 carbine. Built to the exacting specifications of the G.I. model used by U.S. infantrymen in both WWII theaters of battle and in Korea, this reproduction rifle comes to you chambered in the fun and economical .22 LR cartridge. Used by officers as well as tankers, drivers, artillery crews, mortar crews, and other personnel in lieu of the larger, heavier M1 Garand rifle, the M-1 carbine weighed only 4.5 to 4.75 pounds. The Citadel M-1, made by Chiappa in Italy, weighs in at 4.8 lbs. – nearly the exact weight of the original. Barrel length and OAL are also the same as the "United States Carbine, Caliber .30, M1", its official military designation.

Price: synthetic stock. **$399.00**
Price: wood stock.. . . . . **$399.00**

CZ MODEL 512 RIFLE

Caliber: .22 LR/.22 WMR, 5-round magazines. **Barrel:** 20.6". **Weight:** 5.9 lbs. **Length:** 39.3". **Stock:** Beech. **Sights:** Fixed adjustable. **Features:** The CZ 512 is an entirely new semi-auto rimfire rifle from CZ. The modular design is easily maintained, requiring only a coin as a tool for field stripping. The action of the 512 is composed of an aluminum alloy upper receiver that secures the barrel and bolt assembly and a fiberglass reinforced polymer lower half that houses the trigger mechanism and detachable magazine. The 512 shares the same magazines and scope rings with the CZ 455 making it the perfect companion to your bolt-action rifle.

Price: **$449.00**

HENRY U.S. SURVIVAL RIFLE AR-7 22

Caliber: 22 LR, 8-shot magazine. **Barrel:** 16" steel lined. **Weight:** 2.25 lbs. **Stock:** ABS plastic. **Sights:** Blade front on ramp, aperture rear. **Features:** Takedown design stores barrel and action in hollow stock. Light enough to float. Silver, black or camo finish. Comes with two magazines. Introduced 1998. From Henry Repeating Arms Co.

Price: H002S Silver finish **$245.00**
Price: H002B Black finish **$245.00**
Price: H002C Camo finish. **$310.00**

KEL-TEC SU-22CA

Caliber: 22 LR. **Features:** Blowback action, cross bolt safety, adjustable front and rear sights with integral picatinny rail. Threaded muzzle, 26-round magazine.

Price: . . . . **Appx. $400.00**

MAGNUM RESEARCH MAGNUMLITE RIFLES

Caliber: 22 WMR, 17 HMR, 22 LR 17M2, 10-shot magazine. **Barrel:** 17" graphite. **Weight:** 4.45 lbs. **Length:** 35.5" overall. **Stock:** Hogue OverMolded synthetic or walnut. **Sights:** Integral scope base. **Features:** Magnum Lite graphite barrel, French grey anodizing, match bolt, target trigger. 22 LR/17M2 rifles use factory Ruger 10/22 magazines. 4-5 lbs. average trigger pull. Graphite carbon-fiber barrel weighs approx. 13.04 ounces in 22 LR, 1:16 twist. Introduced: 2007. From Magnum Research, Inc.

Price: MLR22H 22 LR. **$640.00**

MARLIN MODEL 60 AUTO RIFLE

Caliber: 22 LR, 14-shot tubular magazine. **Barrel:** 19" round tapered. **Weight:** About 5.5 lbs. **Length:** 37.5" overall. **Stock:** Press-checkered, walnut-finished Maine birch with Monte Carlo, full pistol grip; Mar-Shield finish. **Sights:** Ramp front, open adjustable rear. **Features:** Matted receiver is grooved for scope mount. Manual bolt hold-open; automatic last-shot bolt hold-open. Model 60C is similar except has hardwood Monte Carlo stock with Mossy Oak Break-Up camouflage pattern. From Marlin.

Price: **$179.00**
Price: With 4x scope **$186.00**
Price: Model 60C camo **$211.00**

MARLIN MODEL 60SS SELF-LOADING RIFLE

Same as the Model 60 except breech bolt, barrel and outer magazine tube are made of stainless steel; most other parts are either nickel-plated or coated to match the stainless finish. Monte Carlo stock is of black/gray Maine birch laminate, and has nickel-plated swivel studs, rubber buttpad. Introduced 1993. From Marlin.

Price: **$283.00**

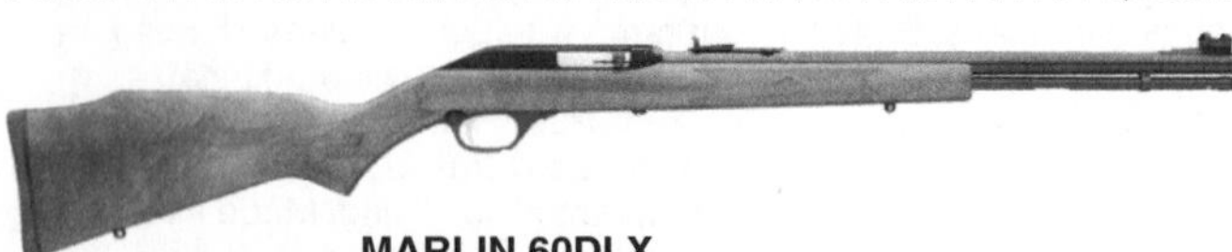

MARLIN 60DLX

Semiauto rifle chambered for .22 LR. Features include 14-shot tubular magazine; side ejection; manual and automatic last-shot bolt hold-opens; receiver top with serrrated, non-glare finish; cross-bolt

safety; steel charging handle; Monte Carlo American walnut-finished hardwood; full pistol grip; tough Mar-Shield finish; 19-inch barrel with Micro-Groove® rifling. Limited availability.
Price: **$248.00**

MARLIN 70PSS PAPOOSE STAINLESS RIFLE
Caliber: 22 LR, 7-shot magazine. **Barrel:** 16.25" stainless steel, Micro-Groove rifling. **Weight:** 3.25 lbs. **Length:** 35.25" overall. **Stock:** Black fiberglass-filled synthetic with abbreviated forend, nickel-plated swivel studs, molded-in checkering. **Sights:** Ramp front with orange post, cut-away Wide Scan hood; adjustable open rear. Receiver grooved for scope mounting. **Features:** Takedown barrel; cross-bolt safety; manual bolt hold-open; last shot bolt hold-open; comes with padded carrying case. Introduced 1986. Made in U.S.A. by Marlin.
Price: **$284.00**

MARLIN MODEL 795 AUTO RIFLE
Caliber: 22. **Barrel:** 18" with 16-groove Micro-Groove rifling. Ramp front sight, adjustable rear. Receiver grooved for scope mount. **Stock:** Black synthetic, hardwood, synthetic thumbhole, solid pink, pink camo, or Mossy Oak New Break-up camo finish. **Features:** 10-round magazine, last shot hold-open feature. Introduced 1997. SS is similar to Model 795 except stainless steel barrel. Most other parts nickel-plated. Adjustable folding semi-buckhorn rear sights, ramp front high-visibility post and removable cutaway wide scan hood. Made in U.S.A. by Marlin Firearms Co.
Price: 795 . . . . **$157.00**
Price: 795SS **$227.00**

MOSSBERG MODEL 702 PLINKSTER AUTO RIFLE
Caliber: 22 LR, 10-round detachable magazine. **Barrel:** 18" free-floating. **Weight:** 4.1 to 4.6 lbs. **Sights:** Adjustable rifle. Receiver grooved for scope mount. **Stock:** Solid pink or pink marble finish synthetic. **Features:** Ergonomically placed magazine release and safety buttons, crossbolt safety, free gun lock. Made in U.S.A. by O.F. Mossberg & Sons, Inc.
Price: Pink Plinkster (2008). **$199.00**

MOSSBERG MODEL 702 PLINKSTER AUTOLOADING RIFLE WITH MUZZLE BRAKE
Semiauto rifle chambered in .22 LR. Features include a black synthetic stock with Schnabel, 10-round detachable box magazine, 21-inch matte blue barrel with muzzle brake, receiver grooved for scope mount.
Price: **$271.00**

REMINGTON MODEL 552 BDL DELUXE SPEEDMASTER RIFLE
Caliber: 22 S (20), L (17) or LR (15) tubular magazine. **Barrel:** 21" round tapered. **Weight:** 5.75 lbs. **Length:** 40" overall. **Stock:** Walnut. Checkered grip and forend. **Sights:** Big game. **Features:** Positive cross-bolt safety, receiver grooved for tip-off mount.
Price: **$667.00**

REMINGTON 597 AUTO RIFLE
Caliber: 22 LR, 10-shot clip; 22 WMR, 8-shot clip. **Barrel:** 20". **Weight:** 5.5 lbs. **Length:** 40" overall. **Stock:** Black synthetic. **Sights:** Big game. **Features:** Matte black finish, nickel-plated bolt. Receiver is grooved and drilled and tapped for scope mounts. Introduced 1997. Made in U.S.A. by Remington.
Price: Synthetic Scope Combo (2007) **$239.00**
Price: Model 597 Magnum **$492.00**
Price: Model 597 w/Mossy Oak Blaze Pink or Orange, 22 LR (2008) **$260.00**
Price: Model 597 Stainless TVP, 22 LR (2008). **$552.00**
Price: Model 597 TVP: Skeletonized laminated stock with undercut forend, optics rail **$552.00**
Price: Model 597 FLX: Similar to Model 597, Blaze/Pink camo but with FLX Digital Camo stock **$260.00**
Price: Model 597 AAC-SD. **$231.00**

REMINGTON 597 VTR - QUAD RAIL
Semiauto rifle chambered in .22 LR, styled to resemble AR. Features include matte blued finished and black synthetic stock; 16-inch barrel; Pardus A2-style collapsible pistol-grip stock; quad-rail free-floated tube; 10-round magazine.
Price: **$618.00**

REMINGTON 597 VTR A-2 FIXED STOCK
Similar to Remington 597 VTR - Quad Rail but with fixed A2-style stock and standard handguard with quad rail.
Price: **$618.00**

REMINGTON 597 VTR COLLAPSIBLE STOCK
Similar to 597 VTR A-2 Fixed Stock but with Pardus A2-style collapsible pistol-grip stock.
Price: **$618.00**

REMINGTON 597 VTR A-TACS CAMO
Semiauto rifle chambered in .22 LR, styled to resemble AR. Features include ATACS camo finish overall; 16-inch barrel; Pardus A2-style collapsible pistol-grip stock; round handguard without rails; receiver-mounted optics rail; 10-round magazine.
Price: **$618.00**

RUGER 10/22 AUTOLOADING CARBINE
Caliber: 22 LR, 10-shot rotary magazine. **Barrel:** 18.5" round tapered. **Weight:** 5 lbs. **Length:** 37.25" overall. **Stock:** American hardwood with pistol grip and barrel band or synthetic. **Sights:** Brass bead front, folding leaf rear adjustable for elevation. **Features:** Detachable rotary magazine fits flush into stock, cross-bolt safety, receiver tapped and grooved for scope blocks or tip-off mount. Scope base adaptor furnished with each rifle.
Price: Model 10/22-RB (black matte) **$269.00**
Price: Model 10/22-CRR Compact RB (black matte), 2006 . . . **$307.00**

RUGER 10/22 DELUXE SPORTER
Same as 10/22 Carbine except walnut stock with hand checkered pistol grip and forend; straight buttplate, no barrel band, has sling swivels.
Price: Model 10/22-DSP **$355.00**

RUGER 10/22-T TARGET RIFLE
Similar to the 10/22 except has 20" heavy, hammer-forged barrel with tight chamber dimensions, improved trigger pull, laminated hardwood stock dimensioned for optical sights. No iron sights supplied. Introduced 1996. Made in U.S.A. by Sturm, Ruger & Co.
Price: 10/22-T **$485.00**
Price: K10/22-T, stainless steel **$533.00**

RUGER K10/22-RPF ALL-WEATHER RIFLE
Similar to the stainless K10/22/RB except has black composite stock of thermoplastic polyester resin reinforced with fiberglass; checkered grip and forend. Brushed satin, natural metal finish with clear hardcoat finish. Weighs 5 lbs., measures 37" overall. Introduced 1997. From Sturm, Ruger & Co.
Price: **$318.00**

RUGER 10/22VLEH TARGET TACTICAL RIFLE
Semiauto rimfire rifle chambered in .22 LR. Features include precision-rifled, cold hammer-forged, spiral-finished 16-1/8-inch crowned match

barrel; Hogue® OverMolded® stock; 10/22T target trigger; precision-adjustable bipod for steady shooting from the bench; 10-round rotary magazine. Weight: 6-7/8 lbs.

Price: **$555.00**

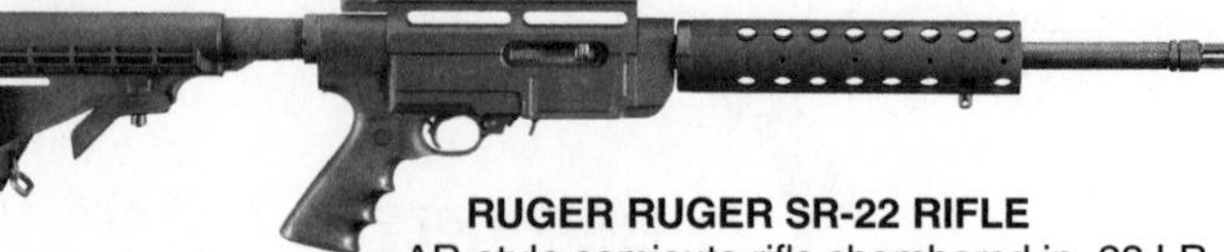

RUGER RUGER SR-22 RIFLE

AR-style semiauto rifle chambered in .22 LR, based on 0/22 action. Features include all-aluminum chassis replicating the AR-platform dimensions between the sighting plane, buttstock height, and grip; Picatinny rail optic mount includes a six-position, telescoping M4-style buttstock (on a Mil-Spec diameter tube); Hogue Monogrip pistol grip; buttstocks and grips interchangeable with any AR-style compatible option; round, mid-length handguard mounted on a standard-thread AR-style barrel nut; precision-rifled, cold hammer forged 16-1/8-inch alloy steel barrel capped with an SR-556/Mini-14 flash suppressor.

Price: .... **NA**

SAVAGE MODEL 64G AUTO RIFLE

Caliber: 22 LR, 10-shot magazine. **Barrel:** 20", 21". **Weight:** 5.5 lbs. **Length:** 40", 41". **Stock:** Walnut-finished hardwood with Monte Carlo-type comb, checkered grip and forend. **Sights:** Bead front, open adjustable rear. Receiver grooved for scope mounting. **Features:** Thumb-operated rotating safety. Blue finish. Side ejection, bolt hold-open device. Introduced 1990. Made in Canada, from Savage Arms.

Price: .... **From $187.00**

SAVAGE BRJ SERIES SEMIAUTO RIMFIRE RIFLES

Similar to Mark II, Model 93 and Model 93R17 semiauto rifles but feature spiral fluting pattern on a heavy barrel, blued finish and Royal Jacaranda wood laminate stock.

Price: Mark II BRJ – .22 LR) **$456.00**
Price: Model 93 BRJ – .22 Mag. **$464.00**
Price: Model 93 R17 BRJ – .17 HMR $464 .... **$464.00**

SAVAGE TACTICAL SEMIAUTO RIMFIRE RIFLES

Similar to Savage Model BRJ series semiauto rifles but feature heavy barrel, matte finish and a tactical-style wood stock.

Price: Mark II TR – .22 LR) **$469.00**
Price: Mark II TRR – .22 LR with three-way accessory rail) . **$539.00**
Price: Model 93R17 TR – .17 HMR. **$477.00**
Price: Model 93R17 TRR – .17 HMR with three-way accessory rail) **$536.00**

SMITH & WESSON M&P15-22

.22 LR rimfire verson of AR-derived M&P tactical autoloader. Features include blowback action, 15.5- or 16-inch barrel, 6-position telescoping or fixed stock, quad mount picatinny rails, plain barrel or compensator, alloy upper and lower, matte black finish, 10- or 25-round magazine.

Price: **$589.00**

THOMPSON/CENTER 22 LR CLASSIC RIFLE

Caliber: 22 LR, 8-shot magazine. **Barrel:** 22" match-grade. **Weight:** 5.5 pounds. **Length:** 39.5" overall. **Stock:** Satin-finished American walnut with Monte Carlo-type comb and pistol gripcap, swivel studs. **Sights:** Ramp-style front and fully adjustable rear, both with fiber optics. **Features:** All-steel receiver drilled and tapped for scope mounting; barrel threaded to receiver; thumb-operated safety; trigger guard safety lock included. New 22 Classic Benchmark TGT target rifle variant has 18" heavy barrel, brown laminated target stock, blued with matte finish, 10-shot magazine and no sights; drilled and tapped.

Price: T/C 22 LR Classic (blue). **$396.00**
Price: T/C 22 LR Classic Benchmark **$505.00**

UMAREX COLT TACTICAL RIMFIRE M4 OPS CARBINE

Blowback semiauto rife chambered in .22 LR, styled to resemble Colt M16. Features include 16.2.2-inch barrel; front sight adjustable for elevation; adjustable rear sight; alloy lower; adjustable telestock; flattop receiver with removable carry handle; 10- or 30-round detachable magazine.

Price: **$599.00**

UMAREX COLT TACTICAL RIMFIRE M4 CARBINE

Blowback semiauto rifle chambered in .22 LR, styled to resemble Colt M4. Features include 16.2-inch barrel; front sight adjustable for elevation; adjustable rear sight; alloy lower; adjustable telestock; flattop receiver with optics rail; 10- or 30-round detachable magazine.

Price: **$640.00**

UMAREX COLT TACTICAL RIMFIRE M16 RIFLE

Blowback semiauto rifle chambered in .22 LR, styled to resemble Colt M16. Features include 21.2-inch barrel; front sight adjustable for elevation; adjustable rear sight; alloy lower; fixed stock; flattop receiver; removable carry handle; 10- or 30-round detachable magazine.

Price: **$599.00**

UMAREX COLT TACTICAL RIMFIRE M16 SPR RIFLE

Blowback semiauto rifle chambered in .22 LR, styled to resemble Colt M16 SPR. Features include 21.2-inch barrel; front sight adjustable for elevation; adjustable rear sight; alloy lower; fixed stock; flattop receiver with optics rail; removable carry handle; 10- or 30-round detachable magazine.

Price: **$670.00**

UMAREX H&K 416-22

Blowback semiauto rife chambered in .22 LR, styled to resemble H&K 416. Features include metal upper and lower receivers; RIS – rail interface system; retractable stock; pistol grip with storage compartment; on-rail sights; rear sight adjustable for wind and elevation; 16.1-inch barrel; 10- or 20-round magazine. Also available in pistol version with 9-inch barrel.

Price: **$675.00**

UMAREX H&K MP5 A5

Blowback semiauto rifle chambered in .22 LR, styled to resemble H&K MP5. Features include metal receiver; compensator; bolt catch; NAVY pistol grip; on-rail sights; rear sight adjustable for wind and elevation; 16.1-inch barrel; 10- or 25-round magazine. Also available in pistol version with 9-inch barrel. Also available with SD-type forend.

Price: **$525.00**

BROWNING BL-22 RIFLES

Action: Short-throw lever action, side ejection. Rack-and-pinion lever. Tubular magazines, with 15+1 capacity for 22 LR. **Barrel:** Recessed muzzle. **Stock:** Walnut, two-piece straight grip Western style. Trigger: Half-cock hammer safety; fold-down hammer. **Sights:** Bead post front, folding-leaf rear. Steel receiver grooved for scope mount. **Weight:** 5-5.4 lbs. **Length:** 36.75-40.75" overall. **Features:** Action lock provided. Introduced 1996. FLD Grade II Octagon has octagonal 24" barrel, silver nitride receiver with scroll engraving, gold-colored trigger. FLD Grade I has satin-nickel receiver, blued trigger, no stock checkering. FLD Grade II has satin-nickel receivers with scroll engraving; gold-colored trigger, cut checkering. Both introduced 2005. Grade I has blued receiver and trigger, no stock checkering. Grade II has gold-colored trigger, cut checkering, blued receiver with scroll engraving. Imported from Japan by Browning.

Price: BL-22 Grade I/II, from **$529.00**
Price: BL-22 FLD Grade I/II, from **$569.00**
Price: BL-22 FLD, Grade II Octagon **$839.00**

HENRY LEVER-ACTION RIFLES

Caliber: 22 Long Rifle (15 shot), 22 Magnum (11 shots), 17 HMR (11 shots). **Barrel:** 18.25" round. **Weight:** 5.5 to 5.75 lbs. **Length:** 34" overall (22 LR). **Stock:** Walnut. **Sights:** Hooded blade front, open adjustable rear. **Features:** Polished blue finish; full-length tubular magazine; side ejection; receiver grooved for scope mounting. Introduced 1997. Made in U.S.A. by Henry Repeating Arms Co.

Price: H001 Carbine 22 LR **$325.00**
Price: H001L Carbine 22 LR, Large Loop Lever **$340.00**
Price: H001Y Youth model (33" overall, 11-round 22 LR) **$325.00**
Price: H001M 22 Magnum, 19.25" octagonal barrel, deluxe walnut stock **$475.00**
Price: H001V 17 HMR, 20" octagonal barrel, Williams Fire Sights **$549.95**

HENRY LEVER OCTAGON FRONTIER MODEL

Same as Lever rifles except chambered in 17 HMR, 22 Short/22 Long/22 LR, 22 Magnum; 20" octagonal barrel **Sights:** Marbles full adjustable semi-buckhorn rear, brass bead front. Weighs 6.25 lbs. Made in U.S.A. by Henry Repeating Arms Co.

Price: H001T Lever Octagon. **$425.00**
Price: H001TM Lever Octagon 22 Magnum **$539.95**

HENRY GOLDEN BOY 22 LEVER-ACTION RIFLE

Caliber: 17 HMR, 22 LR (16-shot), 22 Magnum. **Barrel:** 20" octagonal. **Weight:** 6.25 lbs. **Length:** 38" overall. **Stock:** American walnut. **Sights:** Blade front, open rear. **Features:** Brasslite receiver, brass buttplate, blued barrel and lever. Introduced 1998. Made in U.S.A. from Henry Repeating Arms Co.

Price: H004 22 LR **$515.00**
Price: H004M 22 Magnum **$595.00**
Price: H004V 17 HMR **$615.00**
Price: H004DD 22 LR Deluxe, engraved receiver. **$1,200.00**

HENRY PUMP-ACTION 22 PUMP RIFLE

Caliber: 22 LR, 15-shot. **Barrel:** 18.25". **Weight:** 5.5 lbs. **Length:** NA. **Stock:** American walnut. **Sights:** Bead on ramp front, open adjustable rear. **Features:** Polished blue finish; receiver grooved for scope mount; grooved slide handle; two barrel bands. Introduced 1998. Made in U.S.A. from Henry Repeating Arms Co.

Price: H003T 22 LR **$515.00**
Price: H003TM 22 Magnum **$595.00**

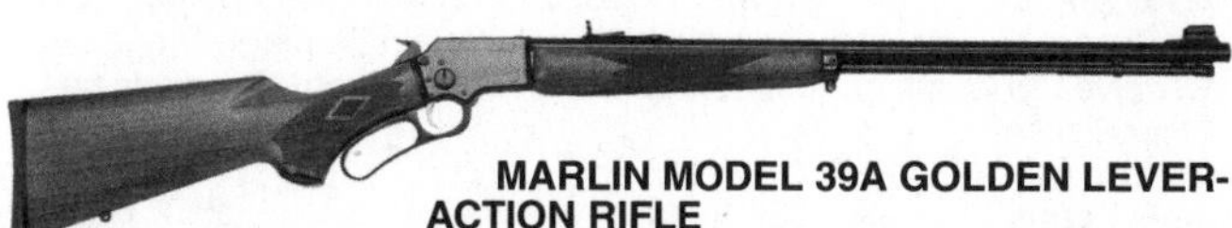

MARLIN MODEL 39A GOLDEN LEVER-ACTION RIFLE

Caliber: 22, S (26), L (21), LR (19), tubular magazine. **Barrel:** 24" Micro-Groove. **Weight:** 6.5 lbs. **Length:** 40" overall. **Stock:** Checkered American black walnut; Mar-Shield finish. Swivel studs; rubber buttpad. **Sights:** Bead ramp front with detachable Wide-Scan hood, folding rear semi-buckhorn adjustable for windage and elevation. **Features:** Hammer block safety; rebounding hammer. Takedown action, receiver tapped for scope mount (supplied), offset hammer spur, gold-colored steel trigger. From Marlin Firearms.

Price: **$593.00**

MOSSBERG MODEL 464 RIMFIRE LEVER-ACTION RIFLE

Caliber: 22 LR. **Barrel:** 20" round blued. **Weight:** 5.6 lbs. **Length:** 35-3/4" overall. **Features:** Adjustable sights, straight grip stock, 124-shot tubular magazine, plain hardwood straight stock and forend.

Price: . . . . **NA; apparently not yet in production**

REMINGTON 572 BDL DELUXE FIELDMASTER PUMP RIFLE

Caliber: 22 S (20), L (17) or LR (15), tubular magazine. **Barrel:** 21" round tapered. **Weight:** 5.5 lbs. **Length:** 40" overall. **Stock:** Walnut with checkered pistol grip and slide handle. **Sights:** Big game. **Features:** Cross-bolt safety; removing inner magazine tube converts rifle to single shot; receiver grooved for tip-off scope mount.

Price: **$607.00**

RUGER MODEL 96 LEVER-ACTION RIFLE

Caliber: 22 WMR, 9 rounds; 17 HMR, 9 rounds. **Barrel:** 18.5". **Weight:** 5.25 lbs. **Length:** 37-3/8" overall. **Stock:** Hardwood. **Sights:** Gold bead front, folding leaf rear. **Features:** Sliding cross button safety, visible cocking indicator; short-throw lever action. Introduced 1996. Made in U.S.A. by Sturm, Ruger & Co.

Price: 96/22M, 22 WMR or 17 HMR **$451.00**

ANSCHUTZ 1416D/1516D CLASSIC RIFLES

Caliber: 22 LR (1416D888), 22 WMR (1516D), 5-shot clip. **Barrel:** 22.5". **Weight:** 6 lbs. **Length:** 41" overall. **Stock:** European hardwood with walnut finish; classic style with straight comb, checkered pistol grip and forend. **Sights:** Hooded ramp front, folding leaf rear. **Features:** Uses Match 64 action. Adjustable single-stage trigger. Receiver grooved for scope mounting. Imported from Germany by Merkel USA.

Price: 1416D KL, 22 LR **$899.00**
Price: 1416D KL Classic left-hand **$949.00**
Price: 1516D KL, 22 WMR **$919.00**

ANSCHUTZ 1710D CUSTOM RIFLE

Caliber: 22 LR, 5-shot clip. **Barrel:** 24.25". **Weight:** 7-3/8 lbs. **Length:** 42.5" overall. **Stock:** Select European walnut. **Sights:** Hooded ramp front, folding leaf rear; drilled and tapped for scope mounting. **Features:** Match 54 action with adjustable single-stage trigger; roll-over Monte Carlo cheekpiece, slim forend with Schnabel tip, Wundhammer palm swell on pistol grip, rosewood gripcap with white diamond insert; skip-line checkering on grip and forend. Introduced 1988. Imported from Germany by Merkel USA.

Price: **$1,649.00**

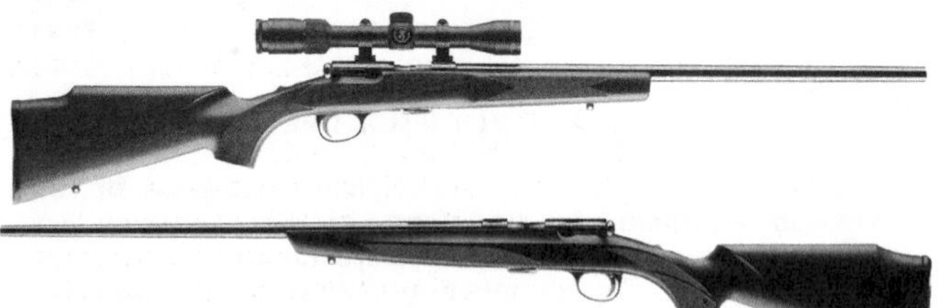

BROWNING T-BOLT RIMFIRE RIFLE

Caliber: 22 LR, 17 HMR, .22 WMR, 10-round rotary box Double Helix magazine. **Barrel:** 22", free-floating, semi-match chamber, target muzzle crown. **Weight:** 4.8 lbs. **Length:** 40.1" overall. **Stock:** Walnut, satin finish, cut checkering, synthetic buttplate. **Sights:** None. **Features:** Straight-pull bolt-action, three-lever trigger adjustable for pull weight, dual action screws, sling swivel studs. Crossbolt lockup, enlarged bolt handle, one-piece dual extractor with integral spring and red cocking indicator band, gold-tone trigger. Top-tang, thumb-operated two-position safety, drilled and tapped for scope mounts. Varmint model has raised Monte Carlo comb, heavy barrel, wide forearm. Introduced 2006. Imported from Japan by Browning. Left-hand models added in 2009.

Price: .22 LR, from .... **$750.00 to $780.00**
Price: .17 HMR/.22 WMR, from .... **$790.00 to $830.00**

BUSHMASTER DCM-XR COMPETITION RIFLE

Caliber: 223 Rem, 10-shot mag. (2). **Barrel:** Heavy 1"-diameter free-floating match. **Weight:** 13.5 lbs. **Length:** 38.5" overall. **Features:** Fitted bolt, aperture rear sight that accepts four different inserts, choice of two front sight blades, two-stage competition trigger, weighted buttstock. Available in pre-and post-ban configurations.

Price: From .... **NA**

BUSHMASTER PIT VIPER 3-GUN COMPETITION RIFLE

Caliber: 5.56/223 Rem, 20-shot mag. (2). **Barrel:** Lapped/crowned 18" A2-profile 1:8. **Weight:** 7.5 lbs. **Length:** 38" overall. **Features:** AR-style semi-auto rifle designed for three-gun competition. Hybrid chambering to accept mil-spec ammunition, titanium nitride-coated bolt, free-floating handguard with two 3" rails and two 4" rails, JR tactical sight.

Price: From .... **NA**

COOPER MODEL 57-M BOLT-ACTION RIFLE

Caliber: 22 LR, 22 WMR, 17 HMR, 17 Mach 2. **Barrel:** 22" or 24" stainless steel or 4140 match grade. **Weight:** 6.5-7.5 lbs. **Stock:** AA-AAA select Claro walnut, 22 lpi hand checkering. **Sights:** None furnished. **Features:** Three rear locking lug, repeating bolt-action with 5-shot magazine. for 22 LR and 17M2; 4-shot magazine for 22 WMR and 17 HMR. Fully adjustable trigger. Left-hand models add

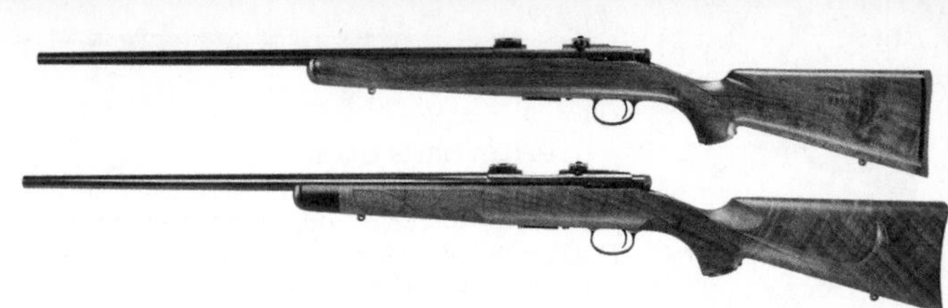

$150 to base rifle price. 1/4"-group rimfire accuracy guarantee at 50 yards; 0.5"-group centerfire accuracy guarantee at 100 yards. Options include wood upgrades, case-color metalwork, barrel fluting, custom LOP, and many others.

Price: Classic **$1,400.00**
Price: LVT **$1,595.00**
Price: Custom Classic **$2,395.00**
Price: Western Classic **$3,295.00**
Price: TRP-3 (22 LR only, benchrest style) **$1,395.00**
Price: Jackson Squirrel Rifle **$1,595.00**
Price: Jackson Hunter (synthetic) **$1,495.00**

CZ 452 LUX BOLT-ACTION RIFLE

Caliber: 22 LR, 22 WMR, 5-shot detachable magazine. **Barrel:** 24.8". **Weight:** 6.6 lbs. **Length:** 42.63" overall. **Stock:** Walnut with checkered pistol grip. **Sights:** Hooded front, fully adjustable tangent rear. **Features:** All-steel construction, adjustable trigger, polished blue finish. Imported from the Czech Republic by CZ-USA.

Price: 22 LR, 22 WMR **$427.00**

CZ 452 VARMINT RIFLE

Similar to the Lux model except has heavy 20.8" barrel; stock has beavertail forend; weighs 7 lbs.; no sights furnished. Available in 22 LR, 22 WMR, 17HMR, 17M2. Imported from the Czech Republic by CZ-USA.

Price: From **$497.00**

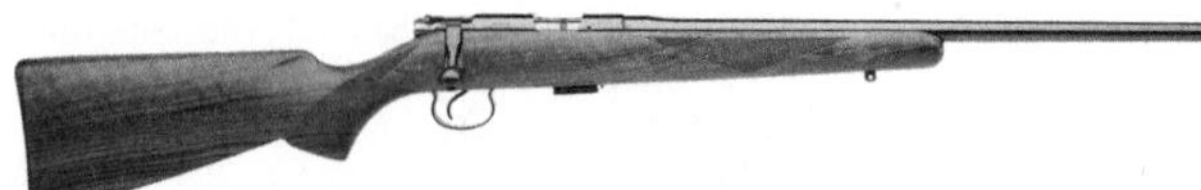

CZ 452 AMERICAN BOLT-ACTION RIFLE

Similar to the CZ 452 M 2E Lux except has classic-style stock of Circassian walnut; 22.5" free-floating barrel with recessed target crown; receiver dovetail for scope mounting. No open sights furnished. Introduced 1999. Imported from the Czech Republic by CZ-USA.

Price: 22 LR, 22 WMR **$463.00**

CZ 455 AMERICAN

Caliber: .17 HMR, .22 LR, .22 WMR (5-round magazine). **Barrel:** 20.5". **Weight:** 6.1 lbs. **Length:** 38.2". **Stock:** walnut. **Sights:** None. Intergral 11mm dovetail scope base. **Features:** Adjustable trigger. Six versions available including blue laminate with thumbhole stock, Varmint model with .866" heavy barrel, full-length Mannlicher walnut stock, and others. American Combo Package includes interchangeable barrel to switch calibers.

Price: from .... **$424 to $524**

DAVEY CRICKETT SINGLE SHOT RIFLE

Caliber: 22 LR, 22 WMR, single shot. **Barrel:** 16-1/8". **Weight:** About 2.5 lbs. **Length:** 30" overall. **Stock:** American walnut. **Sights:** Post on ramp front, peep rear adjustable for windage and elevation. **Features:** Drilled and tapped for scope mounting using special Chipmunk base ($13.95). Engraved model also available. Made in U.S.A. Introduced 1982. Formerly Chipmunk model. From Keystone Sporting Arms.

Price: From **$220.00**

HENRY ACU-BOLT RIFLE

Caliber: 22, 22 Mag., 17 HMR; single shot. **Barrel:** 20". **Weight:** 4.15 lbs. **Length:** 36". **Stock:** One-piece fiberglass synthetic. **Sights:** Scope mount and 4x scope included. **Features:** Stainless barrel and receiver, bolt-action.

Price: H007 22 LR **$399.95**

HENRY "MINI" BOLT ACTION 22 RIFLE

Caliber: 22 LR, single shot youth gun. **Barrel:** 16" stainless, 8-groove rifling. **Weight:** 3.25 lbs. **Length:** 30", LOP 11.5". **Stock:** Synthetic, pistol grip, wraparound checkering and beavertail forearm. **Sights:** William Fire sights. **Features:** One-piece bolt configuration manually operated safety.

Price: H005 22 LR, black fiberglass stock. **$249.95**
Price: H005S 22 LR, orange fiberglass stock **$249.95**

MARLIN MODEL XT-17 SERIES BOLT ACTION RIFLES

Features: The XT Pro-Fire™ Adjustable Trigger produces an extremely consistent trigger pull with an ultra-clean break. Included are 4 and 7-shot clip magazines. The rugged walnut-finished hardwood Monte Carlo stock comes with sling swivel studs. The receiver is drilled, tapped and grooved for your choice of convenient scope mounting options. Also available with a factory-mounted and boresighted 3-9x32mm scope.

Price: . . . . **N/A**

MARLIN MODEL XT-22 SERIES BOLT ACTION RIFLES

Features: This is the new line of 22 caliber rimfire rifles from Marlin. Perfect for target practice and small game, these bolt-action 22s are reliable, accurate and fun to shoot. They come in several different models, with 4 or 7-shot clip magazines or 12-shot tube magazines; synthetic, hardwood or laminated stocks; ramp sights, hood sights or fiber-optic sights. All of them have Marlin innovations such as the Pro-Fire™ Adjustable Trigger and Micro-Groove® rifling. The XT-22 series comes chambered in 22 Short, 22 Long, 22 Long Rifle or 22 Winchester Magnum Rifle (WMR). Made in U.S.A. by Marlin Firearms Co.

Price: . . . . **N/A**

MARLIN MODEL XT-22 YOUTH SERIES BOLT ACTION RIFLES

Features: the first series of rifles designed exclusively for young shooters. It features a shorter stock, shorter trigger reach, smaller grip and a raised comb; making it easier for a youth to acquire and hold the proper sight picture. These guns also feature a reduced bolt release force, for smoother loading and to prevent jams. Our Pro-Fire™ Adjustable Trigger adjusts the trigger pull, too.

Price: . . . . **N/A**

MEACHAM LOW-WALL RIFLE

Caliber: Any rimfire cartridge. **Barrel:** 26-34". **Weight:** 7-15 lbs. **Sights:** none. Tang drilled for Win. base, 3/8" dovetail slot front. **Stock:** Fancy eastern walnut with cheekpiece; ebony insert in forearm tip. Features; Exact copy of 1885 Winchester. With most Winchester factory options available including double set triggers. Introduced 1994. Made in U.S.A. by Meacham T&H Inc.

Price: From **$4,999.00**

MOSSBERG MODEL 817 VARMINT BOLT-ACTION RIFLE

Caliber: 17 HMR, 5-round magazine. **Barrel:** 21"; free-floating bull barrel, recessed muzzle crown. **Weight:** 4.9 lbs. (black synthetic), 5.2 lbs. (wood). **Stock:** Black synthetic or wood; length of pull, 14.25". **Sights:** Factory-installed Weaver-style scope bases. **Features:** Blued or brushed chrome metal finishes, crossbolt safety, gun lock. Introduced 2008. Made in U.S.A. by O.F. Mossberg & Sons, Inc.

Price: Black synthetic stock, chrome finish (2008) **$279.00**

MOSSBERG MODEL 801/802 BOLT RIFLES

Caliber: 22 LR, 10-round detachable magazine. **Barrel:** 18" free-floating. **Weight:** 4.1 to 4.6 lbs. **Sights:** Adjustable rifle. Receiver grooved for scope mount. **Stock:** Solid pink or pink marble finish synthetic. **Features:** Ergonomically placed magazine release and safety buttons, crossbolt safety, free gun lock. 801 Half Pint has 12.25" length of pull, 16" barrel, and weighs 4 lbs. Hardwood stock; removable magazine plug. Made in U.S.A. by O.F. Mossberg & Sons, Inc.

Price: Pink Plinkster (2008). **$199.00**
Price: Half Pint (2008). **$199.00**

NEW ENGLAND FIREARMS SPORTSTER SINGLE-SHOT RIFLES

Caliber: 22 LR, 22 WMR, 17 HMR, single-shot. **Barrel:** 20". **Weight:** 5.5 lbs. **Length:** 36.25" overall. **Stock:** Black polymer. **Sights:** None furnished; scope mount included. **Features:** Break open, side-lever release; automatic ejection; recoil pad; sling swivel studs; trigger locking system. Introduced 2001. Made in U.S.A. by New England Firearms.

Price: **$149.00**
Price: Youth model (20" barrel, 33" overall, weighs 5-1/3 lbs.) . **$149.00**
Price: Sportster 17 HMR **$180.00**

NEW ULTRA LIGHT ARMS 20RF BOLT-ACTION RIFLE

Caliber: 22 LR, single shot or repeater. **Barrel:** Douglas, length to order. **Weight:** 5.25 lbs. **Length:** Varies. **Stock:** Kevlar/graphite composite, variety of finishes. **Sights:** None furnished; drilled and tapped for scope mount. **Features:** Timney trigger, hand-lapped action, button-rifled barrel, hand-bedded action, recoil pad, sling-swivel studs, optional Jewell trigger. Made in U.S.A. by New Ultra Light Arms.

Price: 20 RF single shot **$1,300.00**
Price: 20 RF repeater **$1,350.00**

ROSSI MATCHED PAIR SINGLE-SHOT RIFLE/SHOTGUN

Caliber: 17 HMR, 22 LR, 22 Mag. **Barrel:** 18.5" or 23". **Weight:** 6 lbs. **Stock:** Hardwood (brown or black finish). **Sights:** Fully adjustable front and rear. **Features:** Break-open breech, transfer-bar manual safety, includes matched 410-, 20 or 12 gauge shotgun barrel with bead front sight. Introduced 2001. Imported by BrazTech/Taurus.

Price: S121280RS. **$160.00**
Price: S121780RS **$200.00**
Price: S122280RS **$160.00**
Price: S201780RS **$200.00**

RUGER 77/22 RIMFIRE BOLT-ACTION RIFLE

Caliber: 22 LR, 10-shot rotary magazine; 22 WMR, 9-shot rotary magazine. **Barrel:** 20". **Weight:** About 6 lbs. **Length:** 39.25" overall. **Stock:** Checkered American walnut, laminated hardwood, or synthetic stocks, stainless sling swivels. **Sights:** Plain barrel with 1" Ruger rings. **Features:** Mauser-type action uses Ruger's rotary magazine. Three-position safety, simplified bolt stop, patented bolt locking system. Uses the dual-screw barrel attachment system of the 10/22 rifle. Integral scope mounting system with 1" Ruger rings. Blued model introduced 1983. Stainless steel and blued with synthetic stock introduced 1989.

Price: walnut stock **$829.00**
Price: laminated stock **$929.00**

RUGER 77/17 RIMFIRE BOLT-ACTION RIFLE

Caliber: 17 HMR (9-shot rotary magazine. **Barrel:** 22" to 24". **Weight:**

6.5-7.5 lbs. **Length:** 41.25-43.25" overall. **Stock:** Checkered American walnut, laminated hardwood; stainless sling swivels. **Sights:** Plain barrel with 1" Ruger rings. **Features:** Mauser-type action uses Ruger's rotary magazine. Three-position safety, simplified bolt stop, patented bolt locking system. Uses the dual-screw barrel attachment system of the 10/22 rifle. Integral scope mounting system with 1" Ruger rings. Introduced 2002.

Price: walnut stock $829.00
Price: laminated stock $929.00

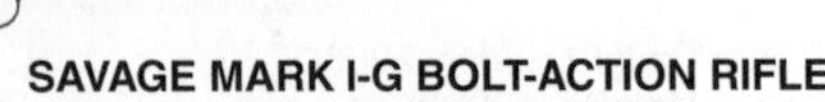

SAVAGE MARK I-G BOLT-ACTION RIFLE

Caliber: 22 LR, single shot. **Barrel:** 20.75". **Weight:** 5.5 lbs. **Length:** 39.5" overall. **Stock:** Walnut-finished hardwood with Monte Carlo-type comb, checkered grip and forend. **Sights:** Bead front, open adjustable rear. Receiver grooved for scope mounting. **Features:** Thumb-operated rotating safety. Blue finish. Rifled or smooth bore. Introduced 1990. Made in Canada, from Savage Arms Inc.

Price: $246.00

SAVAGE MARK II BOLT-ACTION RIFLE

Caliber: 22 LR, .17 HMR, 10-shot magazine. **Barrel:** 20.5". **Weight:** 5.5 lbs. **Length:** 39.5" overall. **Stock:** Walnut-finished hardwood with Monte Carlo-type comb, checkered grip and forend. **Sights:** Bead front, open adjustable rear. Receiver grooved for scope mounting. **Features:** Thumb-operated rotating safety. Blue finish. Introduced 1990. Made in Canada, from Savage Arms, Inc.

Price: . . . .$214.00 to $374.00

SAVAGE MARK II-FSS STAINLESS RIFLE

Similar to the Mark II except has stainless steel barreled action and black synthetic stock with positive checkering, swivel studs, and 20.75" free-floating and button-rifled barrel with detachable magazine. Weighs 5.5 lbs. Introduced 1997. Imported from Canada by Savage Arms, Inc.

Price: $273.00

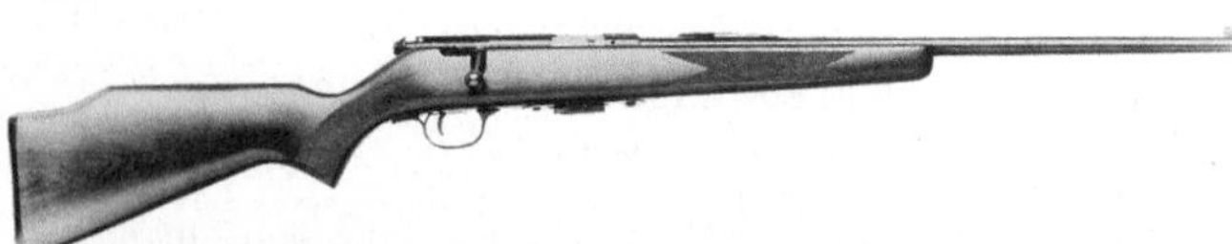

SAVAGE MODEL 93G MAGNUM BOLT-ACTION RIFLE

Caliber: 22 WMR, 5-shot magazine. **Barrel:** 20.75". **Weight:** 5.75 lbs. **Length:** 39.5" overall. **Stock:** Walnut-finished hardwood with Monte Carlo-type comb, checkered grip and forend. **Sights:** Bead front, adjustable open rear. Receiver grooved for scope mount. **Features:** Thumb-operated rotary safety. Blue finish. Introduced 1994. Made in Canada, from Savage Arms.

Price: Model 93G $260.00
Price: Model 93F (as above with black graphite/fiberglass stock) $241.00
Price: Model 93 Classic, American walnut stock (2008) $566.00
Price: Model 93 Classic T, American walnut thumbhole stock (2008) $604.00

SAVAGE MODEL 93FSS MAGNUM RIFLE

Similar to Model 93G except stainless steel barreled action and black synthetic stock with positive checkering. Weighs 5.5 lbs. Introduced 1997. Imported from Canada by Savage Arms, Inc.

Price: $306.00

SAVAGE MODEL 93FVSS MAGNUM RIFLE

Similar to Model 93FSS Magnum except 21" heavy barrel with recessed target-style crown, satin-finished stainless barreled action, black graphite/fiberglass stock. Drilled and tapped for scope mounting; comes with Weaver-style bases. Introduced 1998. Imported from Canada by Savage Arms, Inc.

Price: $347.00

SAVAGE MODEL 30G STEVENS "FAVORITE"

Caliber: 22 LR, 22 WMR Model 30GM, 17 HMR Model 30R17. **Barrel:** 21". **Weight:** 4.25 lbs. **Length:** 36.75". **Stock:** Walnut, straight grip, Schnabel forend. **Sights:** Adjustable rear, bead post front. **Features:** Lever action falling block, inertia firing pin system, Model 30G half octagonal barrel, Model 30GM full octagonal barrel.

Price: Model 30G $344.00
Price: Model 30 Takedown $360.00

SAVAGE CUB T MINI YOUTH

Caliber: 22 S, L, LR; 17 Mach 2. **Barrel:** 16". **Weight:** 3.5 lbs. **Length:** 33". **Stock:** Walnut finished hardwood thumbhole stock. **Sights:** Bead post, front; peep, rear. **Features:** Mini single-shot bolt action, free-floating button-rifled barrel, blued finish. From Savage Arms.

Price: Cub T Thumbhole, walnut stained laminated $266.00
Price: Cub T Pink Thumbhole (2008) $280.00

THOMPSON/CENTER HOTSHOT YOUTH RIFLE

Single-shot dropping-barrel rifle chambered in .22 Long Rifle. Features include a crowned 19-inch steel barrel, exposed hammer, synthetic forend and buttstock, peep sight (receiver drilled and tapped for optics), three stock pattern options (black, Realtree AP and pink AP). Overall weight 3 lbs., 11.5-inch length of pull.

Price: . . . . $229.00 to $249.00

Prices given are believed to be accurate at time of publication however, many factors affect retail pricing so exact prices are not possible

ANSCHUTZ 1903 MATCH RIFLE
Caliber: 22 LR, single shot. **Barrel:** 21.25". **Weight:** 8 lbs. **Length:** 43.75" overall. **Stock:** Walnut-finished hardwood with adjustable cheekpiece; stippled grip and forend. **Sights:** None furnished. **Features:** Uses Anschutz Match 64 action. A medium weight rifle for intermediate and advanced Junior Match competition. Available from Champion's Choice.
Price: Right-hand **$965.00**

ANSCHUTZ 64-MP R SILHOUETTE RIFLE
Caliber: 22 LR, 5-shot magazine. **Barrel:** 21.5", medium heavy; 7/8" diameter. **Weight:** 8 lbs. **Length:** 39.5" overall. **Stock:** Walnut-finished hardwood, silhouette-type. **Sights:** None furnished. **Features:** Uses Match 64 action. Designed for metallic silhouette competition. Stock has stippled checkering, contoured thumb groove with Wundhammer swell. Two-stage #5098 trigger. Slide safety locks sear and bolt. Introduced 1980. Available from Champion's Choice.
Price: 64-MP R **$950.00**
Price: 64-S BR Benchrest (2008) **$1,175.00**

ANSCHUTZ 2007 MATCH RIFLE
Uses same action as the Model 2013, but has a lighter barrel. European walnut stock in right-hand, true left-hand or extra-short models. Sights optional. Available with 19.6" barrel with extension tube, or 26", both in stainless or blue. Introduced 1998. Available from Champion's Choice.
Price: Right-hand, blue, no sights **$2,410.90**

ANSCHUTZ 1827BT FORTNER BIATHLON RIFLE
Caliber: 22 LR, 5-shot magazine. **Barrel:** 21.7". **Weight:** 8.8 lbs. with sights. **Length:** 40.9" overall. **Stock:** European walnut with cheekpiece, stippled pistol grip and forend. **Sights:** Optional globe front specially designed for Biathlon shooting, micrometer rear with hinged snow cap. **Features:** Uses Super Match 54 action and nine-way adjustable trigger; adjustable wooden buttplate, biathlon butthook, adjustable hand-stop rail. Uses Anschutz/Fortner system straight-pull bolt action, blued or stainless steel barrel. Introduced 1982. Available from Champion's Choice.
Price: Nitride finish with sights, about **$2,895.00**

ANSCHUTZ SUPER MATCH SPECIAL MODEL 2013 RIFLE
Caliber: 22 LR, single shot. **Barrel:** 25.9". **Weight:** 13 lbs. **Length:** 41.7" to 42.9". **Stock:** Adjustable aluminum. **Sights:** None furnished. **Features:** 2313 aluminum-silver/blue stock, 500mm barrel, fast lock time, adjustable cheek piece, heavy action and muzzle tube, w/ handstop and standing riser block. Introduced in 1997. Available from Champion's Choice.
Price: Right-hand **$3,195.00**

ANSCHUTZ 1912 SPORT RIFLE
Caliber: 22 LR. **Barrel:** 26" match. **Weight:** 11.4 lbs. **Length:** 41.7" overall. **Stock:** Non-stained thumbhole stock adjustable in length with adjustable butt plate and cheek piece adjustment. Flat forend raiser block 4856 adjustable in height. Hook butt plate. **Sights:** None furnished. **Features:** "Free rifle" for women. Smallbore model 1907 with 1912 **stock:** Match 54 action. Delivered with: Hand stop 6226, forend raiser block 4856, screw driver, instruction leaflet with test target. Available from Champion's Choice.
Price: **$2,595.00**

ANSCHUTZ 1913 SUPER MATCH RIFLE
Same as the Model 1911 except European walnut International-type stock with adjustable cheekpiece, or color laminate, both available with straight or lowered forend, adjustable aluminum hook buttplate, adjustable hand stop, weighs 13 lbs., 46" overall. Stainless or blue barrel. Available from Champion's Choice.
Price: Right-hand, blue, no sights, walnut stock **$2,695.00**

ANSCHUTZ 1907 STANDARD MATCH RIFLE
Same action as Model 1913 but with 7/8" diameter 26" barrel (stain-

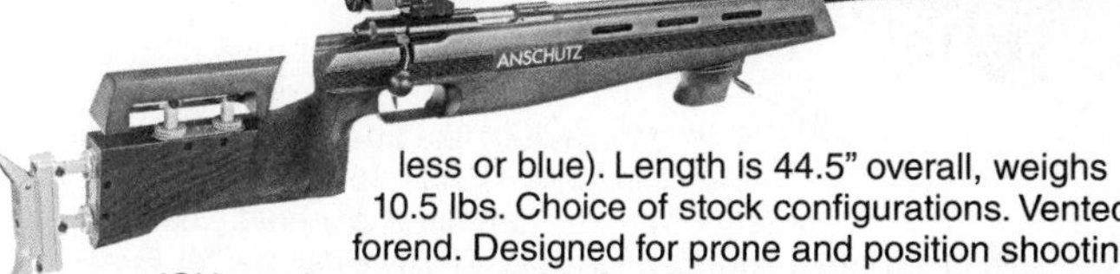

less or blue). Length is 44.5" overall, weighs 10.5 lbs. Choice of stock configurations. Vented forend. Designed for prone and position shooting ISU requirements; suitable for NRA matches. Also available with walnut flat-forend stock for benchrest shooting. Available from Champion's Choice.
Price: Right-hand, blue, no sights **$1,655.00**

ARMALITE AR-10(T) RIFLE
Caliber: 308 Win., 10-shot magazine. **Barrel:** 24" target-weight Rock 5R custom. **Weight:** 10.4 lbs. **Length:** 43.5" overall. **Stock:** Green or black composition; N.M. fiberglass handguard tube. **Sights:** Detachable handle, front sight, or scope mount available. Comes with international-style flattop receiver with Picatinny rail. **Features:** National Match two-stage trigger. Forged upper receiver. Receivers hard-coat anodized. Introduced 1995. Made in U.S.A. by ArmaLite, Inc.
Price: Black **$1,912.00**
Price: AR-10, 338 Federal **$1,912.00**

ARMALITE AR-10 NATIONAL MATCH
Caliber: .308/7.62 NATO. **Barrel:** 20", triple lapped Match barrel, 1:10" twist rifling. **Weight:** 11.5 lbs. **Length:** 41". **Features:** Stainless steel flash suppressor, two-stage National Match trigger. Forged flat top receiver with Picatinny rail and forward assist.
Price: **$2,365.00**

ARMALITE M15A4(T) EAGLE EYE RIFLE
Caliber: 223 Rem., 10-round magazine. **Barrel:** 24" heavy stainless; 1:8" twist. **Weight:** 9.2 lbs. **Length:** 42-3/8" overall. **Stock:** Green or black butt, N.M. fiberglass handguard tube. **Sights:** One-piece international-style flattop receiver with Weaver-type rail, including case deflector. **Features:** Detachable carry handle, front sight and scope mount (30mm or 1") available. Upper and lower receivers have push-type pivot pin, hard coat anodized. Made in U.S.A. by ArmaLite, Inc.
Price: Green or black furniture **$1,296.00**

ARMALITE M15 A4 CARBINE 6.8 & 7.62X39
Caliber: 6.8 Rem, 7.62x39. **Barrel:** 16" chrome-lined with flash suppressor. **Weight:** 7 lbs. **Length:** 26.6". **Features:** Front and rear picatinny rails for mounting optics, two-stage tactical trigger, anodized aluminum/phosphate finish.
Price: **$1,107.00**

BLASER R93 LONG RANGE SPORTER 2 RIFLE
Caliber: 308 Win., 10-shot detachable box magazine. **Barrel:** 24". **Weight:** 10.4 lbs. **Length:** 44" overall. **Stock:** Aluminum with synthetic lining. **Sights:** None furnished; accepts detachable scope mount. **Features:** Straight-pull bolt action with adjustable trigger; fully adjustable stock; quick takedown; corrosion resistant finish. Introduced 1998. Imported from Germany by Blaser USA.
Price: **$3,848.00**

BUSHMASTER A2/A3 TARGET RIFLE
Caliber: 5.56mm, 223 Rem., 30-round magazine **Barrel:** 20", 24". **Weight:** 8.43 lbs. (A2); 8.78 lbs. (A3). **Length:** 39.5" overall (20" barrel). **Stock:** Black composition; A2 type. **Sights:** Adjustable post

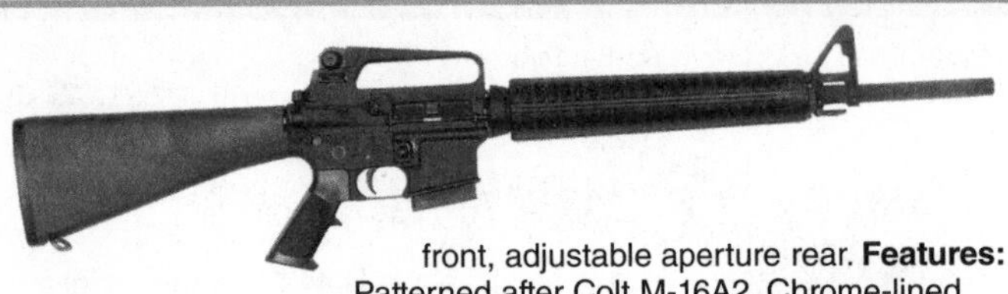

front, adjustable aperture rear. **Features:** Patterned after Colt M-16A2. Chrome-lined barrel with manganese phosphate exterior. Available in stainless barrel. Made in U.S.A. by Bushmaster Firearms Co.

Price: (A3 type) **$1,135.00**

BUSHMASTER DCM-XR COMPETITION RIFLE

Caliber: 5.56mm, 223 Rem., 10-round magazine. **Barrel:** 20" extra-heavy (1" diameter) barrel with 1.8" twist for heavier competition bullets. **Weight:** About 12 lbs. with balance weights. **Length:** 38.5". **Stock:** NA. **Sights:** A2 rear sight. **Features:** Has special competition rear sight with interchangeable apertures, extra-fine 1/2- or 1/4-MOA windage and elevation adjustments; specially ground front sight post in choice of three widths. Full-length handguards over free-floater barrel tube. Introduced 1998. Made in U.S.A. by Bushmaster Firearms, Inc.

Price: A2 . . . . **$1,150.00**
Price: A3 . . . . **$1,250.00**

BUSHMASTER VARMINTER RIFLE

Caliber: 5.56mm. **Barrel:** 24", fluted. **Weight:** 8.4 lbs. **Length:** 42.25" overall. **Stock:** Black composition, A2 type. **Sights:** None furnished; upper receiver has integral scope mount base. **Features:** Chrome-lined .950" extra heavy barrel with counter-bored crown, manganese phosphate finish, free-floating aluminum handguard, forged aluminum receivers with push-pin takedown, hard anodized mil-spec finish. Competition trigger optional. Made in U.S.A. by Bushmaster Firearms, Inc.

Price: **$1,360.00**

COLT MATCH TARGET COMPETITION HBAR RIFLE

Similar to the Match Target except has removable carry handle for scope mounting, 1:9" rifling twist, 9-round magazine. Weighs 8.5 lbs. Introduced 1991.

Price: Model MT6700C **$1,250.00**

COLT MATCH TARGET COMPETITION HBAR II RIFLE

Similar to the Match Target Competition HBAR except has 16:1" barrel, overall length 34.5", and weighs 7.1 lbs. Introduced 1995.

Price: Model MT6731 . . . . **$1,172.00**

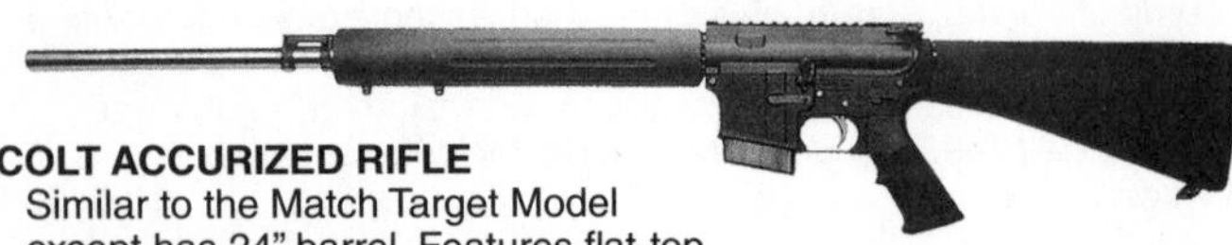

COLT ACCURIZED RIFLE

Similar to the Match Target Model except has 24" barrel. Features flat-top receiver for scope mounting, stainless steel heavy barrel, tubular handguard, and free-floating barrel. Matte black finish. Weighs 9.25 lbs. Made in U.S.A. by Colt's Mfg. Co., Inc.

Price: Model CR6724 . . . . **$1,334.00**

EAA/HW 660 MATCH RIFLE

Caliber: 22 LR. **Barrel:** 26". **Weight:** 10.7 lbs. **Length:** 45.3" overall. **Stock:** Match-type walnut with adjustable cheekpiece and buttplate. **Sights:** Globe front, match aperture rear. **Features:** Adjustable match trigger; stippled pistol grip and forend; forend accessory rail. Introduced 1991. Imported from Germany by European American Armory.

Price: About **$999.00**
Price: With laminate stock **$1,159.00**

OLYMPIC ARMS SM SERVICEMATCH AR15 RIFLES

Caliber: 223 Rem. minimum SAAMI spec, 30-shot magazine. **Barrel:** 20" broach-cut Ultramatch stainless steel 1x8 twist rate. **Weight:** 10 lbs. **Length:** 39.5" overall. **Stock:** A2 grip, A2 buttstock with trapdoor. **Sights:** A2 NM rear, elevation adjustable front post. **Features:** DCM-ready AR15, free-floating handguard looks standard, A2 upper, threaded muzzle, flash suppressor. Premium model adds pneumatic recoil buffer, Bob Jones interchangeable sights, two-stage trigger and Turner Saddlery sling. Made in U.S.A. by Olympic Arms, Inc.

Price: SM-1, 20" DCM ready. **$1,272.70**
Price: SM-1P, Premium 20" DCM ready **$1,727.70**

OLYMPIC ARMS UM ULTRAMATCH AR15 RIFLES

Caliber: 223 Rem. minimum SAAMI spec, 30-shot magazine. **Barrel:** 20" or 24" bull broach-cut Ultramatch stainless steel 1x10 twist rate. **Weight:** 8-10 lbs. **Length:** 38.25" overall. **Stock:** A2 grip, A2 buttstock with trapdoor. **Sights:** None, flat-top upper and gas block with rails. **Features:** Flat top upper, free floating tubular match handguard, Picatinny gas block, crowned muzzle, factory trigger job and "Ultramatch" pantograph. Premium model adds pneumatic recoil buffer, Harris S-series bipod, hand selected premium receivers and William Set Trigger. Made in U.S.A. by Olympic Arms, Inc.

Price: UM-1, 20" Ultramatch **$1,332.50**
Price: UM-1P **$1,805.70**

OLYMPIC ARMS ML-1/ML-2 MULTIMATCH AR15 CARBINES

Caliber: 223 Rem. minimum SAAMI spec, 30-shot magazine. **Barrel:** 16" broach-cut Ultramatch stainless steel 1x10 twist rate. **Weight:** 7-8 lbs. **Length:** 34-36" overall. **Stock:** A2 grip and varying buttstock. **Sights:** None. **Features:** The ML-1 includes A2 upper with adjustable rear sight, elevation adjustable front post, free floating tubular match handguard, bayonet lug, threaded muzzle, flash suppressor and M4 6-point collapsible buttstock. The ML-2 includes bull diameter barrel, flat top upper, free floating tubular match handguard, Picatinny gas block, crowned muzzle and A2 buttstock with trapdoor. Made in U.S.A. by Olympic Arms, Inc.

Price: ML-1 or ML-2. . . . . **$1,188.20**

OLYMPIC ARMS K8 TARGETMATCH AR15 RIFLES

Caliber: 5.56 NATO, 223 WSSM, 243 WSSM, .25 WSSM 30/7-shot magazine. **Barrel:** 20", 24" bull button-rifled stainless/chrome-moly steel 1x9/1x10 twist rate. **Weight:** 8-10 lbs. **Length:** 38"-42" overall. **Stock:** A2 grip, A2 buttstock with trapdoor. **Sights:** None. **Features:** Barrel has satin bead-blast finish; flat-top upper, free-floating tubular match handguard, Picatinny gas block, crowned muzzle and "Targetmatch" pantograph on lower receiver. K8-MAG model uses Winchester Super Short Magnum cartridges. Includes 24" bull chrome-moly barrel, flat-top upper, free-floating tubular match handguard, Picatinny gas block, crowned muzzle and 7-shot magazine. Made in U.S.A. by Olympic Arms, Inc.

Price: K8 . . . . **$908.70**
Price: K8-MAG **$1,363.70**

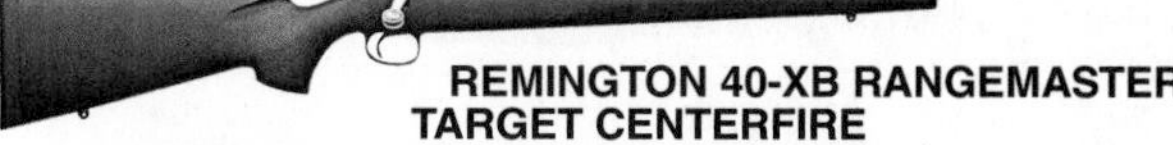

REMINGTON 40-XB RANGEMASTER TARGET CENTERFIRE

Caliber: 15 calibers from 220 Swift to 300 Win. Mag. **Barrel:** 27.25". **Weight:** 11.25 lbs. **Length:** 47" overall. **Stock:** American walnut, laminated thumbhole or Kevlar with high comb and beavertail forend stop. Rubber non-slip buttplate. **Sights:** None. Scope blocks installed. **Features:** Adjustable trigger. Stainless barrel and action. Receiver drilled and tapped for sights. Model 40-XB Tactical (2008) chambered in 308 Win., comes with guarantee of 0.75-inch maximum 5-shot groups at 100 yards. **Weight:** 10.25 lbs. Includes Teflon-coated stainless button-rifled barrel, 1:14 twist, 27.25 inch long, three longitudinal flutes. Bolt-action repeater, adjustable 40-X trigger and precision machined aluminum bedding block. Stock is H-S Precision Pro Series synthetic tactical stock, black with green web finish, vertical pistol grip. From Remington Custom Shop.

Price: 40-XB KS, aramid fiber stock, single shot **$2,780.00**
Price: 40-XB KS, aramid fiber stock, repeater **$2,634.00**
Price: 40-XB Tactical 308 Win. (2008). **$2,927.00**
Price: 40-XB Thumbhole Repeater. **$2,927.00**

REMINGTON 40-XBBR KS

Caliber: Five calibers from 22 BR to 308 Win. **Barrel:** 20" (light varmint class), 24" (heavy varmint class). **Weight:** 7.25 lbs. (light varmint class); 12 lbs. (heavy varmint class). **Length:** 38" (20" bbl.), 42" (24"bbl.). **Stock:** Aramid fiber. **Sights:** None. Supplied with scope blocks. **Features:** Unblued benchrest with stainless steel barrel, trigger adjustable from 1-1/2 lbs. to 3.5 lbs. Special two-oz. trigger extra cost. Scope and mounts extra.

Price: Single shot **$3,806.00**

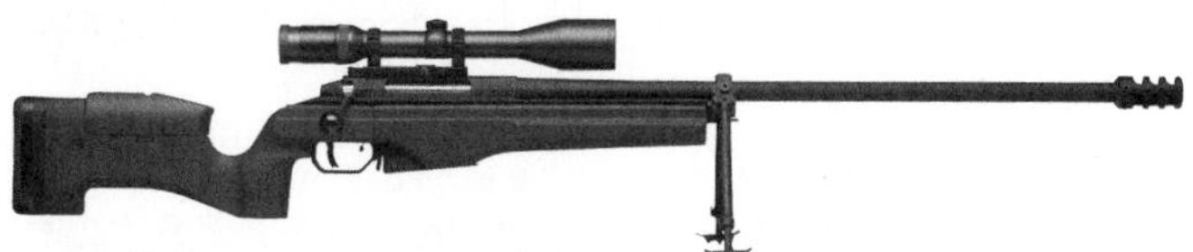

REMINGTON 40-XC KS TARGET RIFLE

Caliber: 7.62 NATO, 5-shot. **Barrel:** 24", stainless steel. **Weight:** 11 lbs. without sights. **Length:** 43.5" overall. **Stock:** Aramid fiber. **Sights:** None furnished. **Features:** Designed to meet the needs of competitive shooters. Stainless steel barrel and action.

Price: **$3,000.00**

REMINGTON 40-XR CUSTOM SPORTER

Caliber: 22 LR, 22 WM. **Barrel:** 24" stainless steel, no sights. **Weight:** 9.75 lbs. **Length:** 40". **Features:** Model XR-40 Target rifle action. Many options available in stock, decoration or finish.

Price: Single shot **$4,391.00**
Price: 40-XRBR KS, bench rest 22 LR **$2,927.00**

SAKO TRG-22 BOLT-ACTION RIFLE

Caliber: 308 Win., 10-shot magazine. **Barrel:** 26". **Weight:** 10.25 lbs. **Length:** 45.25" overall. **Stock:** Reinforced polyurethane with fully adjustable cheekpiece and buttplate. **Sights:** None furnished. Optional quick-detachable, one-piece scope mount base, 1" or 30mm rings. **Features:** Resistance-free bolt, free-floating heavy stainless barrel, 60-degree bolt lift. Two-stage trigger is adjustable for length, pull, horizontal or vertical pitch. Introduced 2000. Imported from Finland by Beretta USA.

Price: TRG-22 folding stock **$3,540.00**

SPRINGFIELD ARMORY M1A SUPER MATCH

Caliber: 308 Win. **Barrel:** 22", heavy Douglas Premium. **Weight:** About 11 lbs. **Length:** 44.31" overall. **Stock:** Heavy walnut competition stock with longer pistol grip, contoured area behind the rear sight, thicker butt and forend, glass bedded. **Sights:** National Match front and rear. **Features:** Has figure-eight-style operating rod guide. Introduced 1987. From Springfield Armory.

Price: About **$2,479.00**

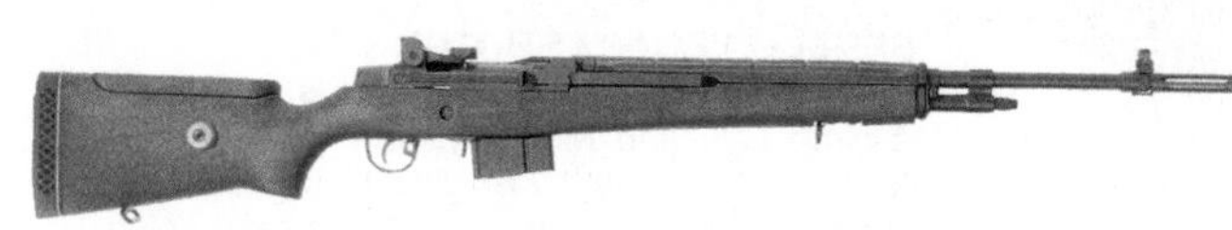

SPRINGFIELD ARMORY M1A/M-21 TACTICAL MODEL RIFLE

Similar to M1A Super Match except special sniper stock with adjustable cheekpiece and rubber recoil pad. Weighs 11.6 lbs. From Springfield Armory.

Price: **$2,975.00**

SPRINGFIELD ARMORY M-1 GARAND AMERICAN COMBAT RIFLES

Caliber: 30-06 Spfl., 308 Win., 8-shot. **Barrel:** 24". **Weight:** 9.5 lbs. **Length:** 43.6". **Stock:** American walnut. **Sights:** Military square post front, military aperture, MOA adjustable rear. **Features:** Limited production, certificate of authenticity, all new receiver, barrel and stock with remaining parts USGI mil-spec. Two-stage military trigger.

Price: About **$2,479.00**

STI SPORTING COMPETITION RIFLE

AR-style semiauto rifle chambered in 5.56 NATO. Features include 16-inch 410 stainless 1:8 barrel; mid-length gas system; Nordic Tactical Compensator and JP Trigger group; custom STI Valkyrie hand guard and gas block; flat-top design with picatinny rail; anodized finish with black Teflon coating. Also available in Tactical configuration.

Price: **$1328.53**

STONER SR-15 MATCH RIFLE

Caliber: 223. **Barrel:** 20". **Weight:** 7.9 lbs. **Length:** 38" overall. **Stock:** Black synthetic. **Sights:** None furnished; flattop upper receiver for scope mounting. **Features:** Short Picatinny rail, two-stage match trigger. Introduced 1998. Made in U.S.A. by Knight's Mfg. Co.

Price: **$1,650.00**

STONER SR-25 MATCH RIFLE

Caliber: 7.62 NATO, 10-shot steel magazine, 5-shot optional. **Barrel:** 24" heavy match; 1:11.25" twist. **Weight:** 10.75 lbs. **Length:** 44" overall. **Stock:** Black synthetic AR-15A2 design. Full floating forend of mil-spec synthetic attaches to upper receiver at a single point. **Sights:** None furnished. Has integral Weaver-style rail. Rings and iron sights optional. **Features:** Improved AR-15 trigger, AR-15-style seven-lug rotating bolt. Introduced 1993. Made in U.S.A. by Knight's Mfg. Co.

Price: **$3,345.00**
Price: SR-25 Lightweight Match (20" medium match target contour barrel, 9.5 lbs., 40" overall) **$3,345.00**

TIME PRECISION 22 RF BENCH REST RIFLE

Caliber: 22 LR, single shot. **Barrel:** Shilen match-grade stainless. **Weight:** 10 lbs. with scope. **Length:** NA. **Stock:** Fiberglass. Pillar bedded. **Sights:** None furnished. **Features:** Shilen match trigger removable trigger bracket, full-length steel sleeve, aluminum receiver. Introduced 2008. Made in U.S.A. by Time Precision.

Price: **$2,200.00**

BENELLI LEGACY SHOTGUN

Gauge: 12, 20, 2-3/4" and 3" chamber. **Barrel:** 24", 26", 28" (Full, Mod., Imp. Cyl., Imp. Mod., cylinder choke tubes). Mid-bead sight. **Weight:** 5.8 to 7.4 lbs. **Length:** 49-5/8" overall (28" barrel). **Stock:** Select AA European walnut with satin finish. **Features:** Uses the rotating bolt inertia recoil operating system with a two-piece steel/aluminum etched receiver (bright on lower, blue upper). Drop adjustment kit allows the stock to be custom fitted without modifying the stock. Introduced 1998. Ultralight model has gloss-blued finish receiver. Weight is 6.0 lbs., 24" barrel, 45.5" overall length. WeatherCoat walnut stock. Introduced 2006. Imported from Italy by Benelli USA, Corp.

Price: Legacy **$1,689.00**
Price: Sport (2008) **$2,269.00**

BENELLI ULTRA LIGHT SHOTGUN

Gauge: 28,12, 20, 3" chamber. **Barrel:** 24", 26". Mid-bead sight. **Weight:** 5.2 to 6 lbs. **Features:** Similar to Legacy line. Drop adjustment kit allows the stock to be custom fitted without modifying the stock. WeatherCoat walnut stock. Lightened receiver, shortened magazine tube, carbon-fiber rib and grip cap. Introduced 2008. Imported from Italy by Benelli USA, Corp.

Price: 12 and 20 gauge. **$1,649.00**
Price: 28 gauge. **$1,799.00**

BENELLI M2 FIELD SHOTGUNS

Gauge: 20 ga., 12 ga., 3" chamber. **Barrel:** 21", 24", 26", 28". **Weight:** 5.4 to 7.2 lbs. **Length:** 42.5 to 49.5" overall. **Stock:** Synthetic, Advantage Max-4 HD, Advantage Timber HD, APG HD. **Sights:** Red bar. **Features:** Uses the Inertia Driven bolt mechanism. Vent rib. Comes with set of five choke tubes. Imported from Italy by Benelli USA.

Price: Synthetic ComforTech gel recoil pad **$1,319.00**
Price: Camo ComforTech gel recoil pad **$1,335.00**
Price: Satin walnut **$1,229.00**
Price: Rifled slug synthetic **$1,380.00**
Price: Camo turkey model w/SteadyGrip stock. **$1,429.00**
Price: Realtree APG HD ComforTech stock (2007). **$1,429.00**
Price: Realtree APG HD ComforTech 20 ga. (2007) **$1,429.00**
Price: Realtree APG HD LH ComforTech (2007) **$1,429.00**
Price: Realtree APG HD ComforTech Slug (2007) **$1,429.00**
Price: Realtree APG HD w/SteadyGrip stock (2007) **$1,429.00**
Price: Black Synthetic Grip Tight 20 ga. (2007). **$1,319.00**

BENELLI MONTEFELTRO SHOTGUNS

Gauge: 12 and 20 ga. Full, Imp. Mod, Mod., Imp. Cyl., Cyl. choke tubes. **Barrel:** 24", 26", 28". **Weight:** 5.3 to 7.1 lbs. **Stock:** Checkered walnut with satin finish. **Length:** 43.6 to 49.5" overall. **Features:** Uses the Inertia Driven rotating bolt system with a simple inertia recoil design. Finish is blue. Introduced 1987.

Price: 24", 26", 28" **$1,219.00**
Price: Left hand. **$1,229.00**
Price: 20 ga. **$1,219.00**
Price: 20 ga. short stock (LOP: 12.5") **$1,120.00**
Price: Silver (AA walnut; nickel-blue receiver). **$1,649.00**
Price: Silver 20 ga. **$1,649.00**

BENELLI SUPER BLACK EAGLE II SHOTGUNS

Gauge: 12, 3-1/2" chamber. **Barrel:** 24", 26", 28" (Cyl. Imp. Cyl., Mod., Imp. Mod., Full choke tubes). **Weight:** 7.1 to 7.3 lbs. **Length:** 45.6 to 49.6" overall. **Stock:** European walnut with satin finish, polymer, or camo. Adjustable for drop. **Sights:** Red bar front. **Features:** Uses Benelli inertia recoil bolt system. Vent rib. Advantage Max-4 HD, Advantage Timber HD camo patterns. Features ComforTech stock.

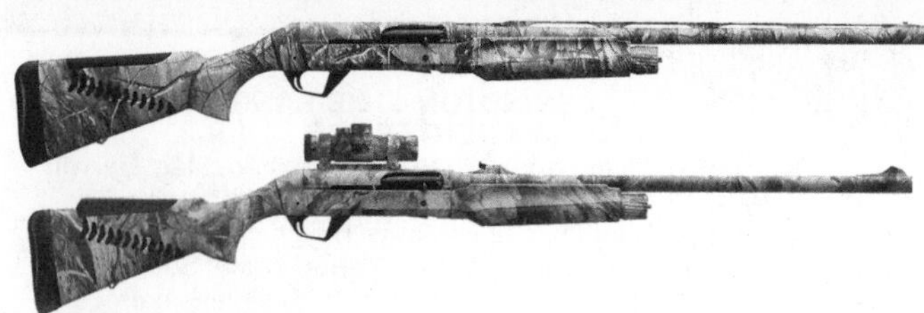

Introduced 1991. Left-hand models available. Imported from Italy by Benelli USA.

Price: Satin walnut, non-ComforTech **$1,549.00**
Price: Camo stock, ComforTech gel recoil pad **$1,759.00**
Price: Black Synthetic stock **$1,649.00**
Price: Max-4 HD Camo stock **$1,759.00**
Price: Timber HD turkey model w/SteadyGrip stock **$1,680.00**
Price: Realtree APG HD w/ComforTech stock (2007) **$1,759.00**
Price: Realtree APG HD LH ComforTech stock (2007) **$1,759.00**
Price: Realtree APG HD Slug Gun (2007) **$1,730.00**

BENELLI SUPER BLACK EAGLE II WATERFOWL EDITION

Gauge: 12, (3+1 capacity), chambered for 2 ¾", 3" and 3 ¼" ammunition. **Barrel:** 28". **Weight:** 7.3 lbs. **Length:** 49.6". **Features:** Lengthened and polished forcing cone, Rob Roberts Custom choke tubes, Realtree Max-4 camo finish, Hi Viz front sight, metal middle bead.

Price: **$2899**

BENELLI CORDOBA SHOTGUN

Gauge: 20; 12; 3" chamber. **Barrel:** 28" and 30", ported, 10mm sporting rib. **Weight:** 7.2 to 7.3 lbs. **Length:** 49.6 to 51.6". **Features:** Designed for high-volume sporting clays and Argentina dove shooting. Inertia-driven action, Extended Sport CrioChokes, 4+1 capacity. Ported. Imported from Italy by Benelli USA.

Price: Black synthetic GripTight ComforTech stock. **$1,869.00**
Price: Black synthetic GripTight ComforTech stock, 20 ga., (2007) **$1,869.00**
Price: Max-4 HD ComforTech stock (2007). **$2,039.00**

BENELLI SUPERSPORT & SPORT II SHOTGUNS

Gauge: 20; 12; 3" chamber. **Barrel:** 28" and 30", ported, 10mm sporting rib. **Weight:** 7.2 to 7.3 lbs. **Length:** 49.6 to 51.6". **Stock:** Carbon fiber, ComforTech (Supersport) or walnut (Sport II). **Sights:** Red bar front, metal midbead. Sport II is similar to the Legacy model except has nonengraved dual tone blue/silver receiver, ported wide-rib barrel, adjustable buttstock, and functions with all loads. Walnut stock with satin finish. Introduced 1997. **Features:** Designed for high-volume sporting clays. Inertia-driven action, Extended CrioChokes, 4+1 capacity. Ported. Imported from Italy by Benelli USA.

Price: Carbon fiber ComforTech stock. **$1,979.00**
Price: Carbon fiber ComforTech stock, 20 ga. (2007) **$1,979.00**
Price: Sport II 20 ga. (2007) **$1,699.00**

BENELLI VINCI

Gas-operated semiauto shotgun chambered for 2-3/4- and 3-inch 12-gauge. Features include modular disassembly; interchangeable choke tubes; 24- to 28-inch ribbed barrel; black, MAX-4HD or APG HD finish; synthetic contoured stocks; optional Steady-Grip model;. Weight 6.7 to 6.9 lbs.

Price: . . . . **$1379.00 to $1599.00**

BENELLI SUPER VINCI

Gauge: 12 - 2-3/4", 3" and 3-1/2" chamber. **Barrel:** 26" and 28" barrels. **Weight:** 6.9-7 lbs.. **Length:** 48.5"-50.5". **Stock:** Black synthetic, Realtree Max4® and Realtree APG®. **Features:** 3+1 capacity, Crio® Chokes: C,IC,M,IM,F. Length of Pull: 14-3/8". Drop at Heel: 2". Drop at

Prices given are believed to be accurate at time of publication however, many factors affect retail pricing so exact prices are not possible.

Comb: 1-3/8". Type of Sights: Red bar front sight and metal bead mid-sight. Minimum recommended load: 3-dram, 1-1/8 oz. loads (12-ga.). Receiver drilled and tapped for scope mounting. Imported from Italy by Benelli USA., Corp.

Price: 28" Black synthetic **$1,649.00**
Price: 28" Black synthetic. **$1,649.00**
Price: 28" Realtree Max4®. **$1,759.00**
Price: 28" Realtree APG® **$1,759.00**
Price: 28" Realtree Max4®. **$1,759.00**

BENELLI LEGACY SPORT

Gas-operated semiauto shotgun chambered for 12, 20 (2-3/4- and 3-inch) gauge. Features include Inertia Driven system; sculptured lower receiver with classic game scene etchings; highly polished blued upper receiver; AA-Grade walnut stock; gel recoil pad; ported 24- or 26-inch barrel, Crio chokes. Weight 7.4 to 7.5 lbs.

Price: **$2,369.00**

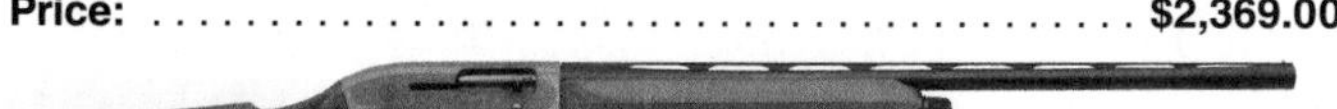

BERETTA 3901 SHOTGUNS

Gauge: 12, 3-inch chamber. **Barrel:** 28". Weight: 7.2 lbs. **Stock:** Synthetic. **Features:** Gas operating system, Mobilchokes, removable trigger group.

Price: **$645.00**

BERETTA A400 XPLOR UNICO SEMIAUTO SHOTGUN

Self-regulation gas-operated shotgun chambered to shoot all 12-ga, loads from 2-3/4 to 3.5 inches. Features include Kick-Off3 hydraulic damper; 26- or 28-inch "Steelium" barrel with interchangeable choke tubes; anodized aluminum receiver; sculpted, checkered walnut buttstock and forend.

Price: **$1,755.00**

BERETTA A400 XPLOR LIGHT SEMIAUTO SHOTGUN

Gauge: 12-gas operated - 2-3/4" & 3" chamber. **Barrel:** 18" barrel. **Weight:** 6.4 lbs.. **Length:** 39.2". **Stock:** Walnut & polymer. **Features:** The A400 Light combines Beretta's exclusive Blink operating system, self compensating exhaust valve and self cleaning piston, steelium barrel design with 1/4" x 1/4" ventilated rib and Optima-Choke HP, also fitted with the Micro-Core recoil pad. The stock is a wood-oil finish with a mix of walnut and polymer to maximize performance from the forend insert to the trigger guard. Continuing the A400 proprietary family design, the A400 Light is also available with Beretta's improved Kick-Off damper system. Imported from Italy by Benelli USA., Corp.

Price: **$1,620.00**

BERETTA AL391 URIKA 2 AUTO SHOTGUN

Gauge: 12, 20 gauge; 3" chamber. **Barrel:** 22", 24", 26", 28", 30"; five Mobilchoke choke tubes. **Weight:** 5.95 to 7.28 lbs. **Length:** Varies by model. **Stock:** Walnut, black or camo synthetic; shims, spacers and interchangeable recoil pads allow custom fit. **Features:** Self-compensating gas operation handles full range of loads; recoil reducer in receiver; enlarged trigger guard; reduced-weight receiver, barrel and forend; hard-chromed bore. Introduced 2000. AL391 Urika 2 (2007) has self-cleaning action, X-Tra Grain stock finish. AL391 Urika 2 Gold has higher-grade select oil-finished wood stock, upgraded engraving (gold-filled gamebirds on field models, gold-filled laurel leaf on competition version). Kick-Off recoil reduction system

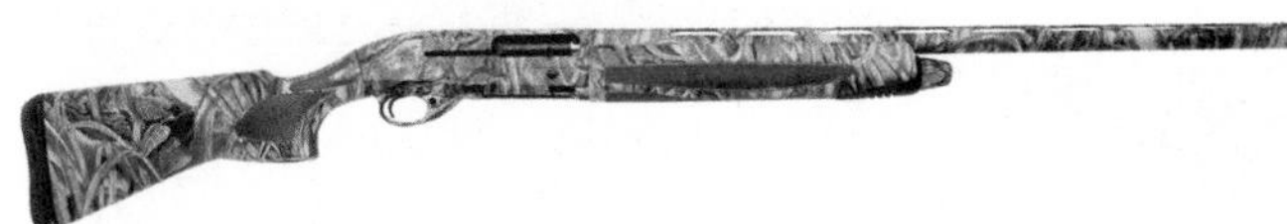

available in Synthetic, Realtree Advantage Max-4 and AP models. Imported from Italy by Beretta USA.

Price: from. . . . . **$1,105.00 to $1,620.00**

BERETTA A391 XTREMA 2 SEMIAUTO SHOTGUN

Gauge: 12 ga. 3.5" chamber. **Barrel:** 24", 26", 28". **Weight:** 7.8 lbs. **Stock:** Synthetic. **Features:** Gas operation system with exhaust valve and self-cleaning gas cylinder and piston that automatically vents the excess gases of the most powerful cartridges.The result is that the shotgun, without any adjustment, fires everything from the weakest 28g (1 ounce, 3 ¾ dram equivalent) game load to the heaviest 64g (2 ¼ ounce) Super Magnum cartridge. The exhaust valve remains attached to the barrel, ensuring easy and quick assembly and disassembly of the shotgun. Semiauto goes with two-lug rotating bolt, extended tang, cross bolt safety, self-cleaning, with case. Also, all steel par ts are now manufactured from stainless steel or are plated with either: nickel, Bruniton, PVD, Aqua Film (receiver & barrel) or chrome (barrel, bore and bolt), making the Xtrema2 a match for even the most extreme environments.

Price: From . . . . **$1,350.00 - $1,700.00**

BREDA GRIZZLY

Gauge: 12, 3.5" chamber. **Barrel:** 28". **Weight:** 7.2 lbs. **Stock:** Black synthetic or Advantage Timber with matching metal parts. **Features:** Chokes tubes are Mod., IC, Full; inertia-type action, four-round magazine. Imported from Italy by Legacy Sports International.

Price: Blued/black (2008) **$1,826.00**
Price: Advantage Timber Camo (2008). **$2,121.00**

BREDA XANTHOS

Gauge: 12, 3" chamber. **Barrel:** 28". **Weight:** 6.5 lbs. **Stock:** High grade walnut. **Features:** Chokes tubes are Mod., IC, Full; inertia-type action, four-round magazine, spark engraving with hand-engraved details and hand-gilding figures on receiver. Blued, Grey or Chrome finishes. Imported from Italy by Legacy Sports International.

Price: Blued (2007). **$2,309.00**
Price: Grey (2007). **$2,451.00**
Price: Chrome (2007) **$3,406.00**

BREDA ECHO

Gauge: 12, 20. 3" chamber. **Barrel:** 28". **Weight:** 6.0-6.5 lbs. **Stock:** Walnut. **Features:** Chokes tubes are Mod., IC, Full; inertia-type action, four-round magazine, blue, grey or nickel finishes, modern engraving, fully checkered pistol grip. Imported from Italy by Legacy Sports International.

Price: Blued, 12 ga. (2008) **$1,897.00**
Price: Grey, 12 ga. (2008) **$1,969.00**
Price: Nickel, 12 ga. (2008). **$2,214.00**
Price: Nickel, 20 ga. (2008). **$2,214.00**

BREDA ALTAIR

Gauge: 12, 20. 3" chamber. **Barrel:** 28". **Weight:** 5.7-6.1 lbs. **Stock:** Oil-rubbed walnut. **Features:** Chokes tubes are Mod., IC, Full; gas-actuated action, four-round magazine, blued finish, lightweight frame. Imported from Italy by Legacy Sports International.

Price: Blued, 12 ga. (2008) **$1,320.00**
Price: Grey, 20 ga. (2008) **$1,320.00**

BROWNING A5

Gauge: 12, 3" chamber. **Barrel:** 26, 28 or 30". **Weight:** 6.6 to 7 lbs. **Length:** 47.25 to 51.5". **Stock:** Gloss finish walnut with 22 lpi checkering, black synthetic or camo. Adjustable for cast and drop. **Features:** Operates on Kinematic short-recoil system. Lengthened forcing cone, three choke tubes (IC, M, F), flat ventilated rib, brass bead front sight, ivory middle bead. Available in Mossy Oak Duck Blind or Break-up Infinity camo.

Price: . . . . **$1,400 to $1,600**

BROWING MAXUS HUNTER SEMIAUTO SHOTGUN

Gauge: 12 ga., 3" & 3-1/2" chamber. **Barrel:** 26", 28" & 30" flat ventilated rib with fixed cylinder choke; stainless Steel; Matte finish. **Weight:** 7 lbs. 2 ozs. **Length:** 40.75". **Stock:** Gloss finish walnut stock with close radius pistol grip, sharp 22 lines-per-inch checkering, speed Lock Forearm, shim adjustable for length of pull, cast and drop. **Features:** Vector Pro™ lengthened forcing cone, three Invector-Plus™ choke tubes, Inflex Technology recoil pad, ivory front bead sight, One 1/4" stock spacer. Strong, lightweight aluminum alloy receiver with durable satin nickel finish & laser engraving (pheasant on the right, mallard on the left).

Price: 3" chamber **$1,500.00**
Price: 3-1/2" chamber **$1,640.00**

BROWING MAXUS MOSSY OAK BOTTOMLAND SEMIAUTO SHOTGUN

Gauge: 12 ga., 3-1/2" chamber. **Barrel:** 28" flat ventilated rib. **Weight:** 6 lbs. 15 ozs. **Length:** 49.25". **Stock:** Composite stock with close radius pistol grip; Speed Lock forearm; textured gripping surfaces; shim adjustable for length of pull, cast and drop; Mossy Oak® Bottomland™ camo finish; Dura-Touch® Armor Coating. **Features:** Vector ProTM lengthened forcing cone; three Invector Plus™ choke tubes (F,M,IC); Inflex Technology recoil pad; ivory front bead sight; one 1/4" stock spacer.

Price: **$1,539.00**

BROWING MAXUS MOSSY OAK DUCK BLIND SEMIAUTO SHOTGUN

Gauge: 12 ga., 3" & 3-1/2" chamber. **Barrel:** 26"& 28" flat ventilated rib with fixed cylinder choke; stainless Steel; Matte finish. **Weight:** 6 lbs. 14 ozs.-6 lbs. 15 ozs. **Length:** 47.25"-49.25". **Stock:** Composite stock with close radius pistol grip, Speed Lock forearm, textured gripping surfaces, Mossy Oak® Duck Blind® camo finish, Dura-Touch® Armor Coating. **Features:** Vector Pro™ lengthened forcing cone, three Invector-Plus™ choke tubes, Inflex Technology recoil pad, ivory front bead sight, One 1/4" stock spacer. Strong, lightweight aluminum alloy receiver. Gas-operated autoloader, new Power Drive Gas System reduces recoil and cycles a wide range of loads.

Price: 3" chamber **$1,470.00**
Price: 3-1/2" chamber **$1,600.00**

BROWING MAXUS SPORTING SEMIAUTO SHOTGUN

Gauge: 12 ga., 3" chamber. **Barrel:** 28" & 30" flat ventilated rib. **Weight:** 7 lbs. 2 ozs. **Length:** 49.25"-51.25". **Stock:** Gloss finish high grade walnut stock with close radius pistol grip , Speed Lock forearm, shim adjustable for length of pull, cast and drop. **Features:** This new model is sure to catch the eye, with its laser engraving of game birds transforming into clay birdson the lightweight alloy receiver. Quail are on the right side, and a mallard duck on the left. The Power Drive Gas System reduces recoil and cycles a wide array of loads. It's available in a 28" or 30" barrel length. The high grade walnut stock and forearm are generously checkered, finished with a deep, high gloss. The stock is adjustable and one 1/4" stock spacer is included. For picking up either clay or live birds quickly, the HiViz Tri-Comp fiber-optic front sight with mid-bead ivory sight does a great job, gathering light on the most overcast days. Vector Pro™ lengthened forcing cone, five Invector-Plus™ choke tubes, Inflex Technology recoil pad ,HiViz® Tri-Comp fiber-optic front sight, ivory mid-bead sight, one ¼" stock spacer.

Price: **$1,700.00**

BROWING MAXUS SPORTING CARBON FIBER SEMIAUTO SHOTGUN

Gauge: 12 ga., 3" chamber. **Barrel:** 28" & 30" flat ventilated rib. **Weight:** 6 lbs. 15 ozs. - 7 lbs. **Length:** 49.25"-51.25". **Stock:** Composite stock with close radius pistol grip, Speed Lock forearm, textured gripping surfaces, shim adjustable for length of pull, cast and drop, carbon fiber finish, Dura-Touch® Armor Coating. **Features:** Strong, lightweight aluminum alloy, carbon fiber finish on top and bottom The stock is finished with Dura-Touch Armor Coating for a secure, non-slip grip when the gun is wet. It has the Browning exclusive Magazine Cut-Off, a patented Turn-Key Magazine Plug and Speed Load Plus. It will be an impossible task to locate an autoloading shotgun for the field with such shooter-friendly features as the Browning Maxus, especially with this deeply finished look of carbon fiber and the Dura-Touch Armor Coating feel. Vector Pro™ lengthened forcing cone, five Invector-Plus™ choke tubes, Inflex Technology recoil pad, HiViz® Tri-Comp fiber-optic front sight, ivory mid-bead sight, one 1/4" stock spacer.

Price: **$1,500.00**

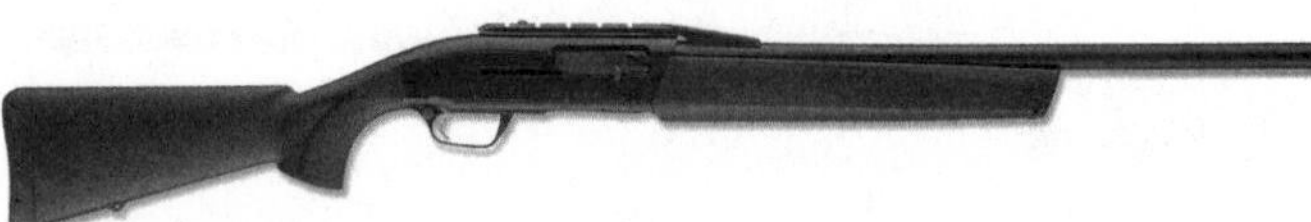

BROWING RIFLED DEER STALKER SEMIAUTO SHOTGUN

Gauge: 12 ga., 3" chamber. **Barrel:** 22" thick-walled, fully rifled for slug ammunition only. **Weight:** 7 lbs. 3 ozs. **Length:** 43.25". **Stock:** Composite stock with close radius pistol grip, Speed Lock forearm, textured gripping surfaces, shim adjustable for length of pull, cast and drop, matte black finish Dura-Touch® Armor Coating. **Features:** Stock is adjustable for length of pull, cast and drop. Cantilever scope mount, one 1/4" stock spacer.

Price: **$1,400.00**

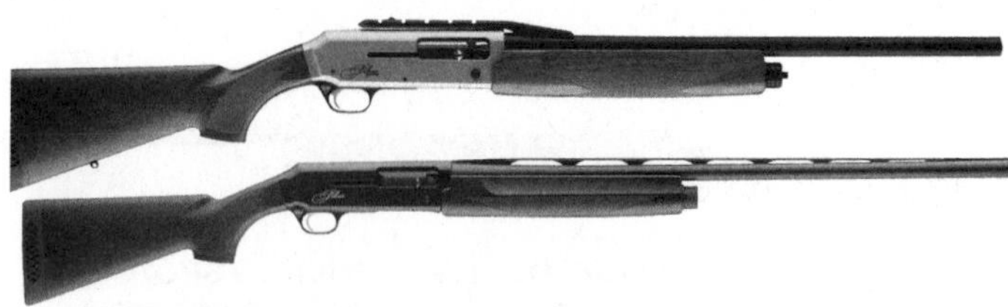

BROWNING SILVER AUTO SHOTGUNS

Gauge: 12, 3" or 3-1/2" chamber; 20, 3" chamber. Barrel: 12 ga.-26", 28", 30", Invector Plus choke tubes. Weight: 7 lbs., 9 oz. (12 ga.), 6 lbs., 7 oz. (20 ga.). Stock: Satin finish walnut. Features: Active Valve gas system, semi-humpback receiver. Invector Plus tube system, three choke tubes. Imported by Browning.

Price: Silver Hunter, 12 ga., 3.5" chamber **$1,340.00**
Price: Silver Hunter, 20 ga., 3" chamber, intr. 2008 . . . . **$1,180.00**
Price: Silver Sporting, 12 ga., 2-3/4" chamber, intr. 2009 . . . . **$1,300.00**
Price: Silver Sporting Micro, 12 ga., 2-3/4" chamber, intr. 2008 . . . . **$1,300.00**
Price: Silver Rifled Deer, Mossy Oak New Break-Up, 12 ga., 3" chamber, intr. 2008 . . . . **$1,419.00**
Price: Silver Rifled Deer Stalker, 12 ga., 3" chamber, intr. 2008 . . . . **$1,280.00**
Price: Silver Rifled Deer Satin, satin-finished aluminum alloy receiver and satin-finished walnut buttstock and forend **$1,340.00**
Price: Silver Stalker, black composite buttstock and forend **$1,179.00**

CZ MODEL 712/720

Gauge: 12, 20 (4+1 capacity). **Barrel:** 26". **Weight:** 6.3 lbs. **Stock:** Turkish walnut with 14.5" length of pull. **Features:** Chrome-lined

barrel with 3-inch chamber, ventilated rib, five choke tubes. Matte black finish.

Price: $499

ESCORT AVERY WATERFOWL EXTREME SEMIAUTO SHOTGUN

Gauge: 12 & 20 ga., 2-3/4" through 3-1/2" chamber, multi 5+1 capacity. **Barrel:** 28". **Weight:** 7.4 lbs. **Length:** 48". **Stock:** Composite stock with close radius pistol grip; Speed Lock forearm; textured gripping surfaces; shim adjustable for length of pull, cast and drop; Mossy Oak® Bottomland™ camo finish; Dura-Touch® Armor Coating. **Features:** The addition of non-slip grip pads on the forend and pistol grip that give you a superior hold in all weather conditions. These grip panels look great and are strategically placed to give you the wet weather grip you need to control your shot. Escort shotguns also have SMART™ Valve gas pistons that regulate gas blowback to cycle every round – from 2.75 inch range loads through 3.5 inch heavy magnums. Escorts also have FAST™ loading systems that allow one-handed round changes without changing aiming position. Next, we've added Avery Outdoors' KW1™ or Buck Brush™ camo patterns to make these shotguns invisible in the field. We are also offering a HiVis MagniSight™ fiber optic, magnetic sight to enhance sight acquisition in low light conditions. Finally, we went to Hevi•Shot and got their mid-range choke tube for waterfowl to round out the perfect hunting machine.

Price: Black/Synthetic **$623.00**
Price: Avery BuckBrush Camo **$790.00**
Price: Avery KW1 Camo **$790.00**
Price: 3.5" Black/Synthetic **$748.00**
Price: 3.5" Avery KW1 Camo **$873.00**
Price: Left Black/Synthetic **$623.00**
Price: Left Avery KW1 Camo **$790.00**
Price: Left 3.5" Black Synthetic **$748.00**
Price: Left 3.5" Avery KW1 Camo **$873.00**
Price: Black/Synthetic 20 gauge **$623.00**

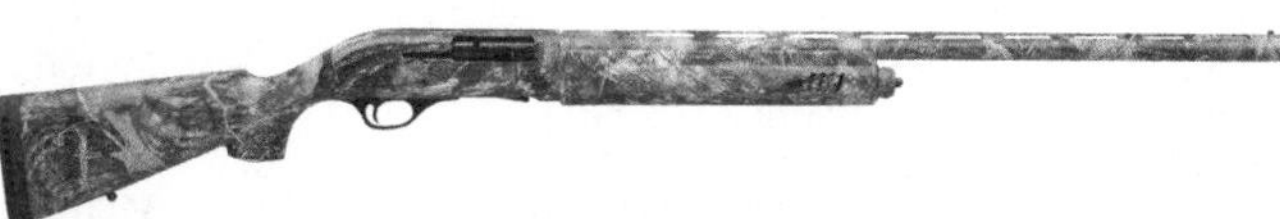

ESCORT SEMIAUTO SHOTGUNS

Gauge: 12, 20; 3" or 3.5" chambers. **Barrel:** 22" (Youth), 26" and 28". **Weight:** 6.7-7.8 lbs. **Stock:** Polymer in black, Shadow Grass® or Obsession® camo finish, Turkish walnut, select walnut. **Sights:** Optional HiViz Spark front. **Features:** Black-chrome or dipped-camo metal parts, top of receiver dovetailed for sight mounts, gold plated trigger, trigger guard safety, magazine cut-off. Three choke tubes (IC, M, F) except the Waterfowl/Turkey Combo, which adds a .665 turkey choke to the standard three. Waterfowl/Turkey combo is two-barrel set, 24"/26" and 26"/28". Several models have Trio recoil pad. Models are: AS, AS Select, AS Youth, AS Youth Select, PS, PS Spark and Waterfowl/Turkey. Introduced 2002. Camo introduced 2003. Youth, Slug and Obsession camo introduced 2005. Imported from Turkey by Legacy Sports International.

Price: .... **$425.00 to $589.00**

FABARM XLR5 VELOCITY

Gauge: 12. **Barrel:** 30 or 32". **Weight:** 8.4 to 9.9 lbs. Gas-operated model designed for competition shooting. Features include a unique adjustable rib that allows a more upright shooting position. There is also an adjustable trigger shoe, magazine cap adjustable weight system. Five interchangeable choke tubes. Field grade verstions available.

Price: **$2885**
Price: Field grade **$2200**

FRANCHI INERTIA I-12 SHOTGUN

Gauge: 12, 3" chamber. **Barrel:** 24", 26", 28" (Cyl., IC, Mod., IM, F choke tubes). **Weight:** 7.5 to 7.7. lbs. **Length:** 45" to 49". **Stock:** 14-3.8" LOP, satin walnut with checkered grip and forend, synthetic, Advantage Timber HD or Max-4 camo patterns. **Features:** Inertia-Driven action. AA walnut stock. Red bar front sight, metal mid sight. Imported from Italy by Benelli USA.

Price: Synthetic **$839.00**
Price: Camo **$949.00**
Price: Satin walnut **$949.00**

FRANCHI MODEL 720 SHOTGUNS

Gauge: 20, 3" chamber. **Barrel:** 24", 26", 28" w/(IC, Mod., F choke tubes). **Weight:** 5.9 to 6.1 lbs. **Length:** 43.25" to 49". **Stock:** WeatherCoat finish walnut, Max-4 and Timber HD camo. **Sights:** Front bead. **Features:** Made in Italy and imported by Benelli USA.

Price: **$1,049.00**
Price: Walnut, 12.5" LOP, 43.25" OAL **$999.00**

FRANCHI 48AL FIELD AND DELUXE SHOTGUNS

Gauge: 20 or 28, 2-3/4" chamber. **Barrel:** 24", 26", 28" (Full, Cyl., Mod., choke tubes). **Weight:** 5.4 to 5.7 lbs. **Length:** 42.25" to 48". **Stock:** Walnut with checkered grip and forend. **Features:** Long recoil-operated action. Chrome-lined bore; cross-bolt safety. Imported from Italy by Benelli USA.

Price: AL Field 20 ga. **$839.00**
Price: AL Deluxe 20 ga., A grade walnut **$1,099.00**
Price: AL Field 28 ga. **$999.00**

FRANCHI 720 COMPETITION SHOTGUN

Gauge: 20; 4+1. **Barrel:** 28" ported; tapered target rib and bead front sight. **Weight:** 6.2 lbs. **Stock:** Walnut with WeatherCoat. **Features:** Gas-operated, satin nickel receiver.

Price: **$1,149.00**

HARRINGTON & RICHARDSON EXCELL AUTO 5 SHOTGUNS

Gauge: 12, 3" chamber. **Barrel:** 22", 24", 28", four screw-in choke tubes (IC, M, IM, F). **Weight:** About 7 lbs. **Length:** 42.5" to 48.5" overall, depending on barrel length. **Stock:** American walnut with satin finish; cut checkering; ventilated buttpad. Synthetic stock or camo-finish. **Sights:** Metal bead front or fiber-optic front and rear. **Features:** Ventilated rib on all models except slug gun. Imported by H&R 1871, Inc.

Price: Synthetic, black, 28" barrel, 48.5" OAL **$415.00**
Price: Walnut, checkered grip/forend, 28" barrel, 48.5" OAL ... **$461.00**
Price: Waterfowl, camo finish **$521.00**
Price: Turkey, camo finish, 22" barrel, fiber optic sights **$521.00**
Price: Combo, synthetic black stock, with slug barrel **$583.00**

LANBER SEMIAUTOMATIC SHOTGUNS

Gauge: 12, 3". **Barrel:** 26", 28", chrome-moly alloy steel, welded, ventilated top and side ribs. **Weight:** 6.8 lbs. **Length:** 48-3/8". **Stock:** Walnut, oiled finish, laser checkering, rubber buttplate. **Sights:** Fiber-optic front. **Features:** Extractors or automatic ejectors, control and unblocking button. Rated for steel shot. Lanber Polichokes. Imported by Lanber USA.

Price: Model 2533 .... **$635.00**

MOSSBERG 930 AUTOLOADER

Gauge: 12, 3" chamber, 4-shot magazine. **Barrel:** 24", 26", 28", over-bored to 10-gauge bore dimensions; factory ported, Accu-Choke tubes. **Weight:** 7.5 lbs. **Length:** 44.5" overall (28" barrel). **Stock:** Walnut or synthetic. Adjustable stock drop and cast spacer system. **Sights:** "Turkey Taker" fiber-optic, adjustable windage and elevation. Front bead fiber-optic front on waterfowl models. **Features:** Self-regulating gas system, dual gas-vent system and piston, EZ-Empty magazine button, cocking indicator. Interchangeable Accu-Choke tube set (IC, Mod, Full) for waterfowl and field models. XX-Full turkey Accu-Choke tube included with turkey models. Ambidextrous thumb-operated safety, Uni-line stock and receiver. Receiver drilled and tapped for scope base attachment, free gun lock. Introduced 2008. From O.F. Mossberg & Sons, Inc.

Price: Turkey, from **$545.00**
Price: Waterfowl, from **$545.00**
Price: Combo, from **$604.00**
Price: Field, from **$568.00**
Price: Slugster, from **$539.00**
Price: Turkey Pistolgrip; full pistolgrip stock, matte black or Mossy Oak Obsession camo finish overall **$628.00**
Price: Tactical; 18.5" tactical barrel, black synthetic stock

and matte black finish **$653.00**
Price: Road Blocker; includes muzzle brake **$697.00**
Price: SPX; no muzzle brake, M16-style front sight, ghost ring rear sight, full pistolgrip stock, eight-round extended magazine **$667.00**
Price: SPX; conventional synthetic stock **$700.00**
Price: Home Security/Field Combo; 18.5" Cylinder bore barrel and 28" ported Field barrel; black synthetic stock and matte black finish **$604.00**

MOSSBERG MODEL 935 MAGNUM AUTOLOADING SHOTGUNS
Gauge: 12; 3" and 3.5» chamber, interchangeable. **Barrel:** 22", 24», 26», 28». **Weight:** 7.25 to 7.75 lbs. **Length:** 45" to 49" overall. **Stock:** Synthetic. **Features:** Gas-operated semiauto models in blued or camo finish. Fiber optics sights, drilled and tapped receiver, interchangeable Accu-Mag choke tubes.
Price: 935 Magnum Turkey: Realtree Hardwoods, Mossy Oak New Break-up or Mossy Oak Obsession camo overall, 24" barrel. **$732.00**
Price: 935 Magnum Turkey Pistolgrip; full pistolgrip stock . . . **$831.00**
Price: 935 Magnum Grand Slam: 22" barrel, Realtree Hardwoods or Mossy Oak New Break-up camo overall . **$747.00**
Price: 935 Magnum Flyway: 28" barrel and Advantage Max-4 camo overall **$781.00**
Price: 935 Magnum Waterfowl: 26"or 28" barrel, matte black, Mossy Oak New Break-up, Advantage Max-4 or Mossy Oak Duck Blind cam overall . . . . **$613.00 to $725.00**
Price: 935 Magnum Slugster: 24" fully rifled barrel, rifle sights, Realtree AP camo overall **$747.00**
Price: 935 Magnum Turkey/Deer Combo: interchangeable 24" Turkey barrel, Mossy Oak New Break-up camo overall **$807.00**
Price: 935 Magnum Waterfowl/Turkey Combo: 24" Turkey and 28" Waterfowl barrels, Mossy Oak New Break-up finish overall **$807.00**

MOSSBERG SA-20
Gauge: 20. 20 (Tactical), 26 or 28". **Weight:** 5.5 to 6 lbs. **Stock:** Black synthetic. Gas operated action, matte blue finish. Tactical model has ghost-ring sight, accessory rail.
Price: **$500**

REMINGTON MODEL 11-87 SPORTSMAN SHOTGUNS
Gauge: 12, 20, 3" chamber. **Barrel:** 26", 28", RemChoke tubes. Standard contour, vent rib. **Weight:** About 7.75 to 8.25 lbs. **Length:** 46" to 48" overall. **Stock:** Black synthetic or Mossy Oak Break Up Mossy Oak Duck Blind, and Realtree Hardwoods HD and AP Green HD camo finishes. **Sights:** Single bead front. **Features:** Matte-black metal finish, magazine cap swivel studs. Sportsman Deer gun has 21-inch fully rifled barrel, cantilever scope mount.
Price: . . . . **$804.00 to $929.00**

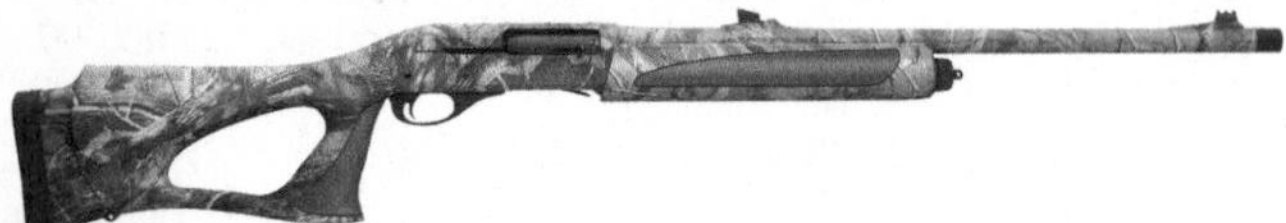

REMINGTON 11-87 SPORTSMAN SUPER MAG SYNTHETIC
Semiauto shotgun chambered in 12-ga. 3-1/2-inch. Features include black matte synthetic stock and forend; rubber overmolded grip panels on the stock and forend; black padded sling; HiViz sights featuring interchangeable light pipe; 28-inch vent rib barrel; SuperCell recoil pad; RemChoke.
Price: **$859.00**

REMINGTON 11-87 SPORTSMAN SUPER MAG SHURSHOT TURKEY
Similar to 11-87 Sportsman Super Mag Synthetic but with ambidextrous ShurShot pistol-grip stock; full Realtree APG HD coverage; 23-inch barrel with fully adjustable TruGlo rifle sights. Wingmaster HD Turkey Choke included.
Price: **$972.00**

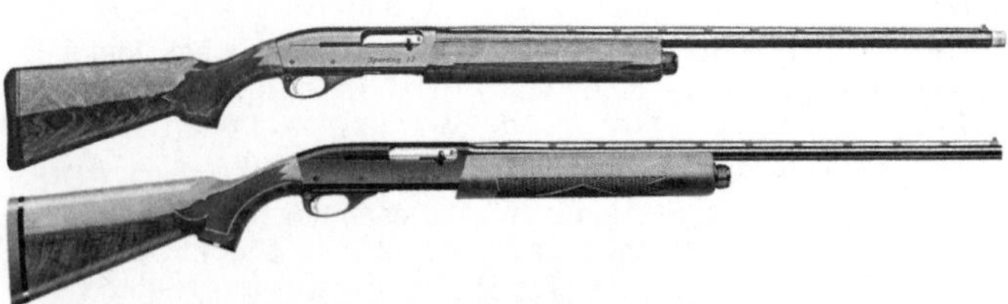

REMINGTON MODEL 1100 TARGET SHOTGUNS
Gauge: .410 bore, 28, 20, 12. **Barrel:** 26", 27", 28", 30" light target contoured vent rib barrel with twin bead target sights. **Stock:** Semi-fancy American walnut stock and forend, cut checkering, high gloss finish. **Features:** Gold-plated trigger. Four extended choke tubes: Skeet, Improved Cylinder, Light Modified and Modified. 1100 Tournament Skeet (20 and 12 gauge) receiver is roll-marked with "Tournament Skeet." 26" light contour, vent rib barrel has twin bead sights, Extended Target Choke Tubes (Skeet and Improved Cylinder). Model 1100 Premier Sporting (2008) has polished nickel receiver, gold accents, light target contoured vent rib Rem Choke barrels. Wood is semi-fancy American walnut stock and forend, high-gloss finish, cut checkering, sporting clays-style recoil pad. Gold trigger, available in 12, 20, 28 and .410 bore options, Briley extended choke tubes, Premier Sporting hard case. Competition model (12 gauge) has overbored (0.735" bore diameter) 30" barrel. **Weight:** 8 lbs. 10mm target-style rib with twin beads. Extended ProBore choke tubes in Skeet, Improved Cylinder, Light-Modified, Modified and Full. Semi-fancy American walnut stock and forend. Classic Trap model has polished blue receiver with scroll engraving, gold accents, 30" low-profile, light-target contoured vent rib barrel with standard .727" dimensions. Comes with specialized Rem Choke trap tubes: Singles (.027"), Mid Handicap (.034"), and Long Handicap (.041"). Monte Carlo stock of semi-fancy American walnut, deep-cut checkering, high-gloss finish.
Price: Sporting 12, 28" barrel, 8 lbs. **$1,105.00**
Price: Sporting 20, 28" barrel, 7 lbs. **$1,105.00**
Price: Sporting 28, 27" barrel, 6.75 lbs.. . . . . **$1,159.00**
Price: Sporting 410, 27" barrel, 6.75 lbs. **$1,159.00**
Price: Classic Trap, 12 ga. 30" barrel **$1,159.00**
Price: Premier Sporting (2008), from. **$1,359.00**
Price: Competition, standard stock, 12 ga. 30" barrel **$1,692.00**
Price: Competition, adjustable comb **$1,692.00**
Price: Competition Synthetic **$1242.00**

REMINGTON MODEL 1100 TAC-4
Similar to Model 1100 but with 18" or 22" barrel with ventilated rib; 12 gauge 2-3/4"only; standard black synthetic stock or Knoxx SpecOps SpeedFeed IV pistolgrip stock; RemChoke tactical choke tube; matte black finish overall. Length is 42-1/2" and weighs 7-3/4 lbs.
Price: **$945.00**

REMINGTON MODEL SP-10 MAGNUM SHOTGUN
Gauge: 10, 3-1/2" chamber, 2-shot magazine. **Barrel:** 23", 26", 30" (full and mod. RemChokes). **Weight:** 10.75 to 11 lbs. **Length:** 47.5" overall (26" barrel). **Stock:** Walnut with satin finish (30" barrel) or camo synthetic (26" barrel). Checkered grip and forend. **Sights:** Twin bead. **Features:** Stainless steel gas system with moving cylinder; 3/8" vent rib. Receiver and barrel have matte finish. Brown recoil pad. Comes with padded Cordura nylon sling. Introduced 1989. SP-10 Magnum Camo has buttstock, forend, receiver, barrel and magazine cap covered with Mossy Oak Duck Blind Obsession camo finish; bolt body and trigger guard have matte black finish. RemChoke tube, 26" vent rib barrel with mid-rib bead and Bradley-style front sight, swivel studs and quick-detachable swivels, non-slip Cordura carrying sling. Introduced 1993.
Price: SP-10 Magnum, satin finish walnut stock **$1,772.00**

Prices given are believed to be accurate at time of publication however, many factors affect retail pricing so exact prices are not possible.

Price: SP-10 Magnum Full Camo **$1,932.00**
Price: SP-10 Magnum Waterfowl..................... **$1,945.00**

REMINGTON VERSA MAX™ SERIES SEMIAUTO SHOTGUN

Gauge: 12 ga., 2 3/4", 3", 3 1/2" chamber. **Barrel:** 26" and 28" flat ventilated rib. **Weight:** 7.5 lbs.-7.7 lbs. **Length:** 40.25". **Stock:** Synthetic. **Features:** Reliably cycles 12-gauge rounds from 2 3/4" to 3 1/2" magnum. Versaport™ gas system regulates cycling pressure based on shell length. Reduces recoil to that of a 20-gauge. Self-cleaning - Continuously cycled thousands of rounds in torture test. Synthetic stock and fore-end with grey overmolded grips. Drilled and tapped receiver. Enlarged trigger guard opening and larger safety for easier use with gloves. TriNyte® Barrel and Nickel Teflon plated internal components offer extreme corrosion resistance. Includes 5 Flush Mount Pro Bore™ Chokes (Full, Mod, Imp Mod Light Mod, IC)
Price: 26" barrel **$1399.00**
Price: 28" barrel **$1399.00**

STOEGER MODEL 2000 SHOTGUNS

Gauge: 12, 3" chamber, set of five choke tubes (C, IC, M, F, XFT). **Barrel:** 24", 26", 28", 30". **Stock:** Walnut, synthetic, Timber HD, Max-4. **Sights:** Red bar front. **Features:** Inertia-recoil. Minimum recommended load: 3 dram, 1-1/8 oz. Imported by Benelli USA.
Price: Walnut...................................... **$499.00**
Price: Synthetic................................... **$499.00**
Price: Max-4 .... **$549.00**
Price: Black synthetic pistol grip (2007) **$499.00**
Price: APG HD camo pistol grip (2007), 18.5" barrel......... **$549.00**

TRISTAR VIPER SEMIAUTOMATIC SHOTGUNS

Gauge: 12, 20; shoots 2-3/4" or 3" interchangeably. **Barrel:** 26", 28" barrels (carbon fiber only offered in 12-ga. 28" and 20-ga. 26"). **Stock:** Wood, black synthetic, Mossy Oak Duck Blind camouflage, faux carbon fiber finish (2008) with the new Comfort Touch technology. **Features:** Magazine cut-off, vent rib with matted sight plane, brass front bead (camo models have fiber-optic front sight), five round magazine-shot plug included, and 3 Beretta-style choke tubes (IC, M, F). Viper synthetic, Viper camo have swivel studs. Five-year warranty. Viper Youth models have shortened length of pull and 24" barrel. Imported by Tristar Sporting Arms Ltd.
Price: From **$469.00**
Price: Camo models (2008), from...................... **$569.00**

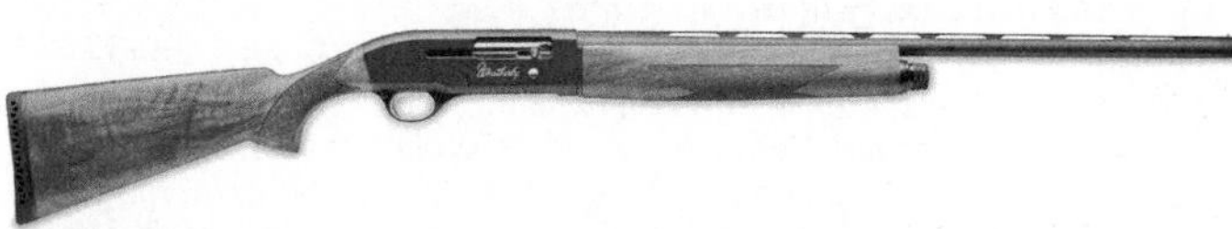

WEATHERBY SA-08 SERIES SEMIAUTO SHOTGUN

Gauge: 12 ga. & 20 ga., 3" chamber. **Barrel:** 26" and 28" flat ventilated rib. **Weight:** 6.5 lbs. **Stock:** Wood and synthetic. **Features:** The SA-08 is a reliable workhorse that lets you move from early season dove loads to late fall's heaviest waterfowl loads in no time. Available with wood and synthetic stock options in 12 and 20 gauge models, including a scaled-down youth model to fit 28 ga. Comes with 3 application-specific choke tubes (SK/IC/M). Made in Turkey.
Price: SA-08 Upland **$733.00**
Price: SA-08 Synthetic (New 2011) **$509.00**
Price: SA-08 Waterfowler 3.0 .... **$710.00**
Price: SA-08 Synthetic Youth........................... **$565.00**
Price: SA-08 Deluxe **$754.00**
Price: SA-08 Entre Rios **$749.00**

WINCHESTER SUPER X3 SHOTGUNS

Gauge: 12, 3" and 3.5" chambers. **Barrel:** 26", 28", .742" back-bored; Invector Plus choke tubes. **Weight:** 7 to 7.25 lbs. **Stock:** Composite, 14.25"x1.75"x2". Mossy Oak New Break-Up camo with Dura-Touch Armor Coating. Pachmayr Decelerator buttpad with hard heel insert, customizable length of pull. **Features:** Alloy magazine tube, gunmetal grey Perma-Cote UT finish, self-adjusting Active Valve gas action, lightweight recoil spring system. Electroless nickel-plated bolt, three choke tubes, two length-of-pull stock spacers, drop and cast adjustment spacers, sling swivel studs. Introduced 2006. Made in Belgium, assembled in Portugal by U.S. Repeating Arms Co.
Price: Composite...................... **$1,119.00 to $1.239.00**
Price: Cantilever Deer............................. **$1,179.00**
Price: Waterfowl w/Mossy Oak Brush camo, intr. 2007..... **$1,439.00**
Price: Field model, walnut stock, intr. 2007............. **$1,439.00**
Price: Gray Shadow **$1,299.00**
Price: All-Purpose Field **$1,439.00**
Price: Classic Field **$1,159.00**
Price: NWTF Cantiliever Extreme Turkey **$1,499.00**

BENELLI SUPERNOVA PUMP SHOTGUNS

Gauge: 12; 3.5" chamber. **Barrel:** 24", 26", 28". **Length:** 45.5-49.5". **Stock:** Synthetic; Max-4 , Timber, APG HD (2007). **Sights:** Red bar front, metal midbead. **Features:** 2-3/4", 3" chamber (3-1/2" 12 ga. only). Montefeltro rotating bolt design with dual action bars, magazine cut-off, synthetic trigger assembly, adjustable combs, shim kit, choice of buttstocks. 4-shot magazine. Introduced 2006. Imported from Italy by Benelli USA.

Price: .... **$549.00 to $669.00**
Price: Rifle slug model .... **$829.00 to $929.00**

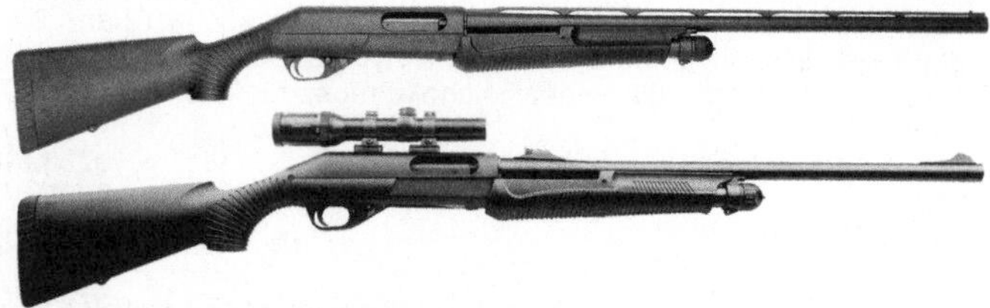

BENELLI NOVA PUMP SHOTGUNS

Gauge: 12, 20. **Barrel:** 24", 26", 28". **Stock:** Black synthetic, Max-4, Timber and APG HD. **Sights:** Red bar. **Features:** 2-3/ 4", 3" chamber (3-1/2" 12 ga. only). Montefeltro rotating bolt design with dual action bars, magazine cut-off, synthetic trigger assembly, 4-shot magazine. Introduced 1999. Field & Slug Combo has 24" barrel and rifled bore; open rifle sights; synthetic stock; weighs 8.1 lbs. Imported from Italy by Benelli USA.

PrPrice: Max-4 HD camo stock **$499.00**
Price: H_20 model, black synthetic, matte nickel finish **$599.00**
Price: APG HD stock , 20 ga. (2007) **$529.00**
Price: Tactical, 18.5" barrel, Ghost Ring sight **$429.00**
Price: Black synthetic youth stock, 20 ga. **$429.00**
Price: APG HD stock (2007), 20 ga... .... **$529.00**

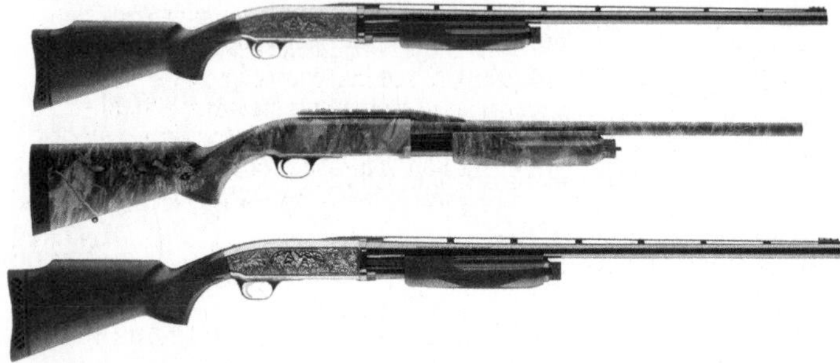

BROWNING BPS PUMP SHOTGUNS

Gauge: 10, 12, 3-1/2" chamber; 12, 16, or 20, 3" chamber (2-3/4" in target guns), 28, 2-3/4" chamber, 5-shot magazine, .410, 3" chamber. **Barrel:** 10 ga.-24" Buck Special, 28", 30", 32" Invector; 12, 20 ga.-22", 24", 26", 28", 30", 32" (Imp. Cyl., Mod. or Full), .410-26" barrel. (Imp. Cyl., Mod. and Full choke tubes.) Also available with Invector choke tubes, 12 or 20 ga.; Upland Special has 22" barrel with Invector tubes. BPS 3" and 3-1/2" have back-bored barrel. **Weight:** 7 lbs., 8 oz. (28" barrel). **Length:** 48.75" overall (28" barrel). **Stock:** 14.25"x1.5"x2.5". Select walnut, semi-beavertail forend, full pistol grip stock. **Features:** All 12 gauge 3" guns except Buck Special and game guns have back-bored barrels with Invector Plus choke tubes. Bottom feeding and ejection, receiver top safety, high post vent rib. Double action bars eliminate binding. Vent rib barrels only. All 12 and 20 gauge guns with 3" chamber available with fully engraved receiver flats at no extra cost. Each gauge has its own unique game scene. Introduced 1977. Stalker is same gun as the standard BPS except all exposed metal parts have a matte blued finish and the stock has a black finish with a black recoil pad. Available in 10 ga. (3-1/2") and 12 ga. with 3" or 3-1/2" chamber, 22", 28", 30" barrel with Invector choke system. Introduced 1987. Rifled Deer Hunter is similar to the standard BPS except has newly designed receiver/magazine tube/barrel mounting system to eliminate play, heavy 20.5" barrel with rifle-type sights with adjustable rear, solid receiver scope mount, "rifle" stock dimensions for scope or open sights, sling swivel studs. Gloss or matte finished wood with checkering, polished blue metal. Introduced 1992. Imported from Japan by Browning.

Price: Stalker, from .... **$660.00 to $760.00**
Price: Rifled Deer Hunter **$790.00**
Price: Trap **$800.00**
Price: Hunter, 12, 20 ga. **$660.00**
Price: Hunter, 16, 28 ga., .410 .... **$700.00**
Price: Mossy Oak camo finishes, 3" chamber **$780.00**
Price: Mossy Oak camo finishes, 3-1/2" chamber .... **$900.00 to $980.00**
Price: Rifled Deer, Mossy Oak .... **$830.00 to $940.00**

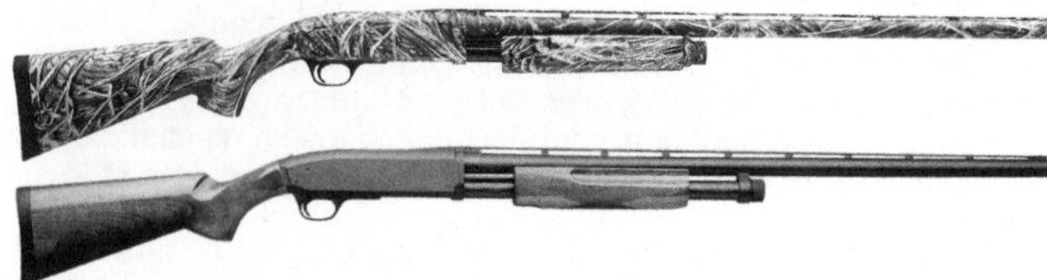

BROWNING BPS 10 GAUGE SERIES

Similar to the standard BPS except completely covered with Mossy Oak Shadow Grass camouflage. Available with 26" and 28" barrel. Introduced 1999. Imported by Browning

Price: Mossy Oak camo .... **$900.00 to $980.00**
Price: Synthetic stock, Stalker **$760.00**

BROWNING BPS NWTF TURKEY SERIES PUMP SHOTGUN

Similar to the standard BPS except has full coverage Mossy Oak Break-Up camo finish on synthetic stock, forearm and exposed metal parts. Offered in 12 gauge, 3" or 3-1/2" chamber; 24" bbl. has extra-full choke tube and HiViz fiber-optic sights. Introduced 2001. From Browning.

Price: 12 ga., 3-1/2" chamber **$859.00**
Price: 12 ga., 3" chamber **$709.00**

BROWNING BPS MICRO PUMP SHOTGUN

Similar to the BPS Stalker except 20 ga. only, 22" Invector barrel, stock has pistol grip with recoil pad. Length of pull is 13.25"; weighs 6 lbs., 12 oz. Introduced 1986.

Price: **$569.00**

BROWING BPS ALL WEATHER HIGH CAPACITY PUMP SHOTGUN

Gauge: 12 ga. 3" chamber. **Barrel:** 20" fixed Cylinder choke; stainless Steel; Matte finish. **Weight:** 7 lbs. 2 ozs. **Length:** 40.75". **Stock:** Black composite on All Weather with matte finish. **Features:** Forged and machined steel; satin nickel finish. Bottom ejection; dual steel action bars; top tang safety. HiViz Tactical fiber-optic front sight; stainless internal mechanism; swivel studs installed. 5 total magazine capacity.

Price: From **$689.00**

CHARLES DALY FIELD PUMP SHOTGUNS

Gauge: 12, 20. **Barrel:** Interchangeable 18.5", 24", 26", 28", 30" multi-choked. **Weight:** NA. **Stock:** Synthetic, various finishes, recoil pad. Receiver: Machined aluminum. **Features:** Field Tactical and Slug models come with adustable sights; Youth models may be upgraded to full size. Discontinued.

Price: Field Tactical .... **N/A**
Price: Field Hunter .... **N/A**
Price: Field Hunter, Realtree Hardwood .... **N/A**
Price: Field Hunter Advantage .... **N/A**

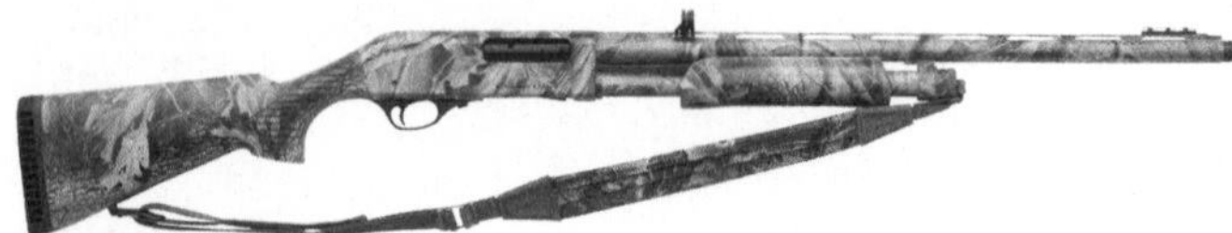

CHARLES DALY
MAXI-MAG PUMP SHOTGUNS

Gauge: 12 gauge, 3-1/2". **Barrel:** 24", 26", 28"; multi-choke system. **Weight:** NA. **Stock:** Synthetic black, Realtree Hardwoods, or Advantage Timber receiver, aluminum alloy. **Features:** Handles 2-3/4", 3" and 3-1/2" loads. Interchangeable ported barrels; Turkey package includes sling, HiViz sights, XX Full choke. Discontinued.

Price: Field Hunter .... **N/A**
Price: Field Hunter Advantage .... **N/A**
Price: Field Hunter Hardwoods .... **N/A**
Price: Field Hunter Turkey .... **N/A**

Prices given are believed to be accurate at time of publication however, many factors affect retail pricing so exact prices are not possible.

EMF OLD WEST PUMP (SLIDE ACTION) SHOTGUN
Gauge: 12. **Barrel:** 20". **Weight:** 7 lbs. **Length:** 39-1/2" overall. **Stock:** Smooth walnut with cushioned pad. **Sights:** Front bead. **Features:** Authentic reproduction of Winchester 1897 pump shotgun; blue receiver and barrel; standard modified choke. Introduced 2006. Imported from China for EMF by TTN.
Price: **$449.90**

ESCORT PUMP SHOTGUNS
Gauge: 12, 20; 3" chamber. **Barrel:** 18" (AimGuard and MarineGuard), 22" (Youth Pump), 26", and 28" lengths. **Weight:** 6.7-7.0 lbs. **Stock:** Polymer in black, Shadow Grass® camo or Obsession® camo finish. Two adjusting spacers included. Youth model has Trio recoil pad. **Sights:** Bead or Spark front sights, depending on model. AimGuard and MarineGuard models have blade front sights. **Features:** Black-chrome or dipped camo metal parts, top of receiver dovetailed for sight mounts, gold plated trigger, trigger guard safety, magazine cut-off. Three choke tubes (IC, M, F) except AimGuard/MarineGuard which are cylinder bore. Models include: FH, FH Youth, AimGuard and Marine Guard. Introduced in 2003. Imported from Turkey by Legacy Sports International.
Price: . . . . **$389.00 to $469.00**

HARRINGTON & RICHARDSON PARDNER PUMP FIELD GUN FULL-DIP CAMO
Gauge: 12, 20; 3" chamber. **Barrel:** 28" fully rifled. **Weight:** 7.5 lbs. **Length:** 48-1/8" overall. **Stock:** Synthetic or hardwood. **Sights:** NA. **Features:** Steel receiver, double action bars, cross-bolt safety, easy takedown, vent rib, screw-in Modified choke tube. Ventilated recoil pad and grooved forend with Realtree APG-HDTM full camo dip finish.
Price: Full camo version **$278.00**

IAC MODEL 87W-1 LEVER-ACTION SHOTGUN
Gauge: 12; 2-3/4" chamber only. **Barrel:** 20" with fixed Cylinder choke. **Weight:** NA. **Length:** NA. **Stock:** American walnut. **Sights:** Bead front. **Features:** Modern replica of Winchester Model 1887 lever-action shotgun. Includes five-shot tubular magazine, pivoting split-lever design to meet modern safety requirements. Imported by Interstate Arms Corporation.
Price: **$429.95**

ITHACA MODEL 37 FEATHERWEIGHT
Gauge: 12, 20, 16, 28 (4+1 capacity). Barrel: 26, 28 or 30" with 3" chambers (12 and 20 ga.), plain or ventiltate rib. Weight: 6.1 to 7.6 lbs. Stock: Fancy grade black walnut with Pachmayr Decelerator recoil pad. Checkered fore-end made of matching walnut. Features: Receiver machined from a single block of steel or aluminum. Barrel is steel shot compatible. Three Briley choke tubes provided. Available in several variations including turkey, home defense, tactical and high-grade.
Price: 12, 16 or 20 ga. from. . **$759.00** (plain barrel) **$859.00** (vent rib)
Price: 28 ga. from **$999.00**

ITHACA DEERSLAYER III SLUG SHOTGUN
Gauge: 12, 20; 3» chamber. **Barrel:** 26" fully rifled, heavy fluted with 1:28 twist for 12 ga.; 1:24 for 20 ga. **Weight:** 8.14 lbs. to 9.5 lbs. with scope mounted. **Length:** 45.625" overall. **Stock:** Fancy black walnut stock and forend. **Sights:** NA. **Features:** Updated, slug-only version of the classic Model 37. Bottom ejection, blued barrel and receiver.
Price: **$1,189.00**

MOSSBERG MODEL 835 ULTI-MAG PUMP SHOTGUNS
Gauge: 12, 3-1/2" chamber. **Barrel:** Ported 24" rifled bore, 24", 28", Accu-Mag choke tubes for steel or lead shot. **Weight:** 7.75

lbs. **Length:** 48.5" overall. **Stock:** 14"x1.5"x2.5". Dual Comb. Cut-checkered hardwood or camo synthetic; both have recoil pad. **Sights:** White bead front, brass mid-bead; fiber-optic rear. **Features:** Shoots 2-3/4", 3" or 3-1/2" shells. Back-bored and ported barrel to reduce recoil, improve patterns. Ambidextrous thumb safety, twin extractors, dual slide bars. Mossberg Cablelock included. Introduced 1988.
Price: Thumbhole Turkey. **$674.00**
Price: Tactical Turkey. **$636.00**
Price: Synthetic Thumbhole Turkey, from **$493.00**
Price: Turkey, from. **$487.00**
Price: Waterfowl, from **$437.00**
Price: Combo, from **$559.00**

MOSSBERG 835 ULTI-MAG SPECIAL PURPOSE SERIES PUMP SHOTGUN
Gauge: 12 ga., 2 3/4", 3", 3 1/2" chamber. **Barrel:** 20", 24", 26" and 28" flat ventilated rib. **Weight:** 7.25 lbs. **Length:** 40.25". **Stock:** Large selection of wood, synthetic and camo pattern models available. **Features:** Each and every component of the 835® was designed and tested around the demanding requirements of high-power 3 1/2" 12 gauge magnum ammo. Unlike other new-comers to this specialized market, who just modified their existing 2 3/4" - 3" shotguns, the 835® was designed to stay the course. The robust bolt, receiver, and other components are specifically sized for the longer shells and the downrange punishment they dish out. In addition, all 835® Ulti-Mag® smooth bore barrels are overbored to 10 gauge bore dimensions, reducing recoil and producing exceptionally uniform patterns from both light and heavy shot charges. Working in tandem with the performance-enhancing overbored barrels, strategic placement of eight ports on each side of the 835® barrel direct gasses upward and outward to not only reduce felt recoil, but to minimize muzzle jump for quick second shot recovery.
Price: Turkey THUG Series **$642.00**
Price: Thumbhole Turkey Series **$674.00**
Price: Tactical Turkey™ Series **$674.00**
Price: Synthetic Thumbhole Turkey Series . . . . **$522.00 - $603.00**

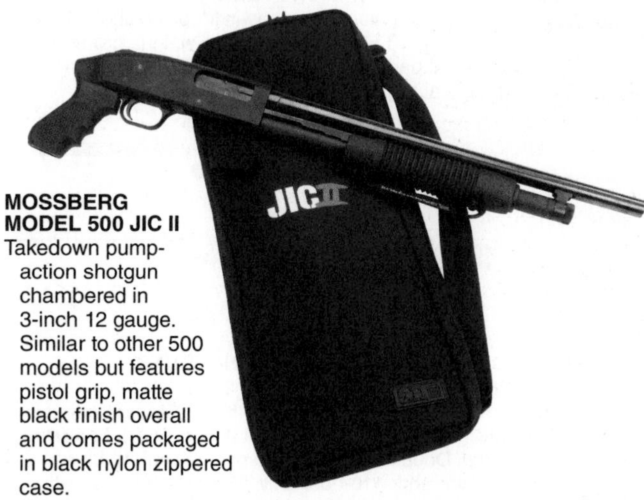

MOSSBERG MODEL 500 JIC II
Takedown pump-action shotgun chambered in 3-inch 12 gauge. Similar to other 500 models but features pistol grip, matte black finish overall and comes packaged in black nylon zippered case.
Price: **$435.00**

MOSSBERG MODEL 500 SPORTING PUMP SHOTGUNS
Gauge: 12, 20, .410, 3" chamber. **Barrel:** 18.5" to 28" with fixed or Accu-Choke, plain or vent rib. **Weight:** 6-1/4 lbs. (.410), 7-1/4 lbs. (12). **Length:** 48" overall (28" barrel). **Stock:** 14"x1.5"x2.5". Walnut-stained hardwood, black synthetic, Mossy Oak Advantage

camouflage. Cut-checkered grip and forend. **Sights:** White bead front, brass mid-bead; fiber-optic. **Features:** Ambidextrous thumb safety, twin extractors, disconnecting safety, dual action bars. Quiet Carry forend. Many barrels are ported. From Mossberg.
Price: Turkey **$435.00**
Price: Waterfowl, from **$435.00**
Price: Combo, from **$414.00**
Price: Field, from **$375.00**
Price: Slugster, from **$375.00**

MOSSBERG 510 MINI BANTAM PUMP SHOTGUN
Gauge: 20 & .410 ga., 3" chamber. **Barrel:** 18 1/2 " vent-rib. **Weight:** 5 lbs. **Length:** 34 3/4". **Stock:** Synthetic withoption Mossy Oak Break-Up Infinity **Features:** Available in either 20 gauge or .410 bore, the Mini features an 18 1/2 " vent-rib barrel with dual-bead sights. Parents don't have to worry about their young shooter growing out of this gun too quick, the adjustable classic stock can be adjusted from 10 1/2" to 11 1/2" length of pull so the Mini can grow with your child. This adjustability also helps provide a proper fit for young shooters and allowing for a more safe and enjoyable shooting experience. Weighing in at 5 pounds and only 34 3/4" long, the 510 Mini proves that big things do come in small packages.
Price: Standard Stock **$389.00**

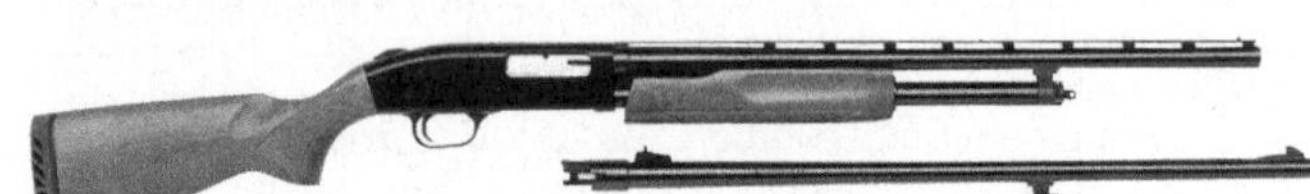

MOSSBERG MODEL 500 BANTAM PUMP SHOTGUN
Same as the Model 500 Sporting Pump except 12 or 20 gauge, 22" vent rib Accu-Choke barrel with choke tube set; has 1" shorter stock, reduced length from pistol grip to trigger, reduced forend reach. Introduced 1992.
Price: **$375.00**
Price: Super Bantam (2008), from **$484.00**

NEW ENGLAND PARDNER PUMP SHOTGUN
Gauge: 12 ga., 3". **Barrel:** 28" vent rib, screw-in Modified choke tube. **Weight:** 7.5 lbs. **Length:** 48.5". **Stock:** American walnut, grooved forend, ventilated recoil pad. **Sights:** Bead front. **Features:** Machined steel receiver, double action bars, five-shot magazine.
Price: **$265.00**

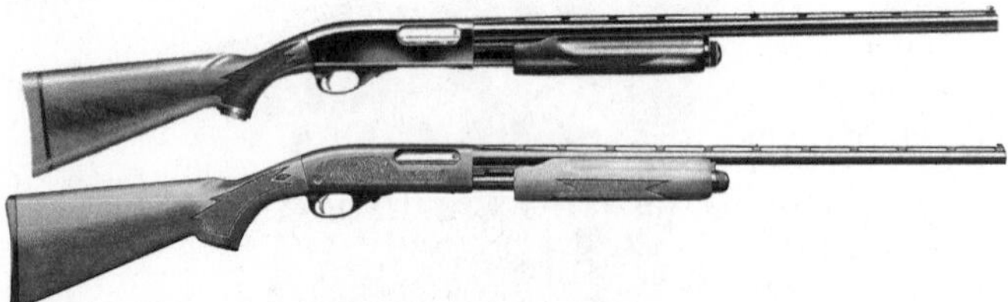

REMINGTON MODEL 870 WINGMASTER SHOTGUNS
Gauge: 12, 20, 28 ga., .410 bore. **Barrel:** 25", 26", 28", 30" (RemChokes). **Weight:** 7-1/4 lbs. **Length:** 46", 48". **Stock:** Walnut, hardwood. **Sights:** Single bead (Twin bead Wingmaster). **Features:** Light contour barrel. Double action bars, cross-bolt safety, blue finish. LW is 28 gauge and .410-bore only, 25" vent rib barrel with RemChoke tubes, high-gloss wood finish. Gold-plated trigger, American B Grade walnut stock and forend, high-gloss finish, fleur-de-lis checkering.
Price: .... **$818.00 to $929.00**

REMINGTON MODEL 870 MARINE MAGNUM SHOTGUN
Similar to 870 Wingmaster except all metal plated with electroless

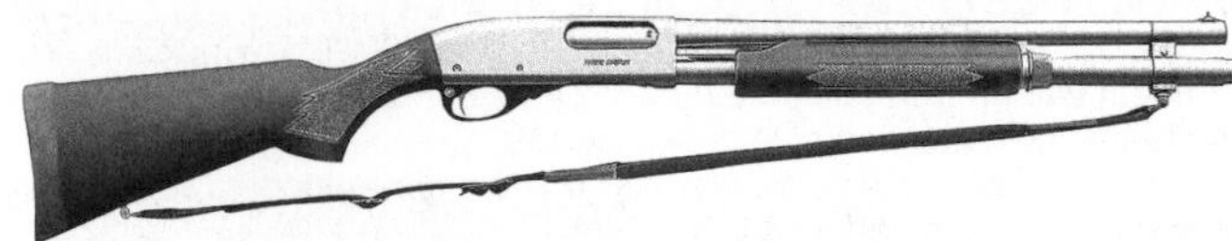

nickel, black synthetic stock and forend. Has 18" plain barrel (cyl.), bead front sight, 7-shot magazine. Introduced 1992. XCS version with TriNyte corrosion control introduced 2007.
Price: **$829.00**

REMINGTON MODEL 870 CLASSIC TRAP SHOTGUN
Similar to Model 870 Wingmaster except has 30" vent rib, light contour barrel, singles, mid- and long-handicap choke tubes, semi-fancy American walnut stock, high-polish blued receiver with engraving. Chamber 2.75". From Remington Arms Co.
Price: **$1,039.00**

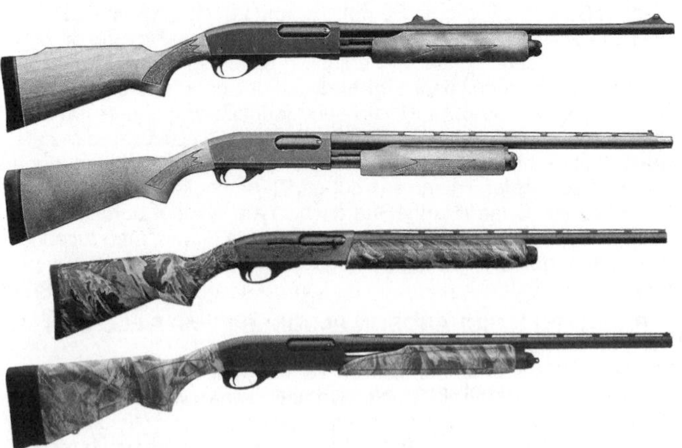

REMINGTON MODEL 870 EXPRESS SHOTGUNS
Similar to Model 870 Wingmaster except laminate, synthetic black, or camo stock with solid, black recoil pad and pressed checkering on grip and forend. Outside metal surfaces have black oxide finish. Comes with 26" or 28" vent rib barrel with mod. RemChoke tube. ShurShot Turkey (2008) has ShurShot synthetic pistol-grip thumbhole design, extended forend, Mossy Oak Obsession camouflage, matte black metal finish, 21" vent rib barrel, twin beads, Turkey Extra Full Rem Choke tube. Receiver drilled and tapped for mounting optics. ShurShot FR CL (Fully Rifled Cantilever, 2008) includes compact 23" fully-rifled barrel with integrated cantilever scope mount.
Price: .... **$411.00 to $571.00**

REMINGTON MODEL 870 EXPRESS SUPER MAGNUM SHOTGUN
Similar to Model 870 Express except 28" vent rib barrel with 3-1/2" chamber, vented recoil pad. Introduced 1998. Model 870 Express Super Magnum Waterfowl (2008) is fully camouflaged with Mossy Oak Duck Blind pattern, 28-inch vent rib Rem Choke barrel, "Over Decoys" Choke tube (.007") fiber-optic HiViz single bead front sight; front and rear sling swivel studs, padded black sling.
Price: .... **$462.00 to $620.00**

REMINGTON MODEL 870 SPECIAL PURPOSE SHOTGUNS (SPS)
Similar to the Model 870 Express synthetic, chambered for 12 ga. 3" and 3-1/2" shells, has Realtree Hardwoods HD or APG HD camo-synthetic stock and metal treatment, TruGlo fiber-optic sights. Introduced 2001. SPS Max Gobbler introduced 2007. Knoxx SpecOps adjustable stock, Williams Fire Sights fiber-optic sights, R3 recoil pad, Realtree APG HD camo. Drilled and tapped for Weaver-style rail
Price: SPS 12 ga. 3" **$671.00**
Price: SPS Super Mag Max Gobbler (2007) **$819.00**
Price: SPS Super Mag Max Turkey ShurShot 3-1/2" (2008) ... **$644.00**
Price: SPS Synthetic ShurShot FR Cantilever 3" (2008) **$671.00**

Prices given are believed to be accurate at time of publication however, many factors affect retail pricing so exact prices are not possible.

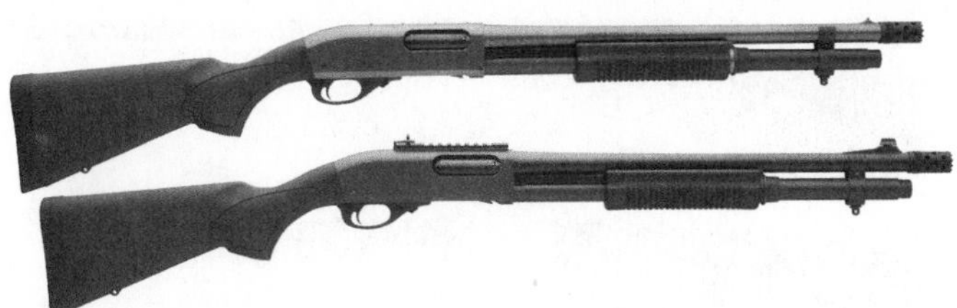

REMINGTON MODEL 870 EXPRESS TACTICAL

Similar to Model 870 but in 12 gauge only (2-2/4" and 3" interchangeably) with 18.5" barrel, Tactical RemChoke extended/ported choke tube, black synthetic buttstock and forend, extended magazine tube, gray powdercoat finish overall. 38.5" overall length, weighs 7.5 lbs.

Price: **$372.00**
Price: Model 870 TAC Desert Recon; desert camo stock and sand-toned metal surfaces **$692.00**
Price: Model 870 Express Tactical with Ghost Ring Sights; Top-mounted accessories rail and XS ghost ring rear sight **$505.00**

REMINGTON MODEL 870 SPS SHURSHOT SYNTHETIC SUPER SLUG

Gauge: 12; 2-3/4" and 3" chamber, interchangeable. **Barrel:** 25.5" extra-heavy, fully rifled pinned to receiver. **Weight:** 7-7/8 lbs. **Length:** 47" overall. **Features:** Pump-action model based on 870 platform. SuperCell recoil pad. Drilled and tapped for scope mounts with Weaver rail included. Matte black metal surfaces, Mossy Oak Treestand Shurshot buttstock and forend.

Price: **$829.00**
Price: 870 SPS ShurShot Synthetic Cantilever; cantilever scope mount and Realtree Hardwoods camo buttstock and forend . **$532.00**
Price: 870 SPS ShurShot Synthetic Turkey; adjustable sights and APG HD camo buttstock and forend **$532.00**

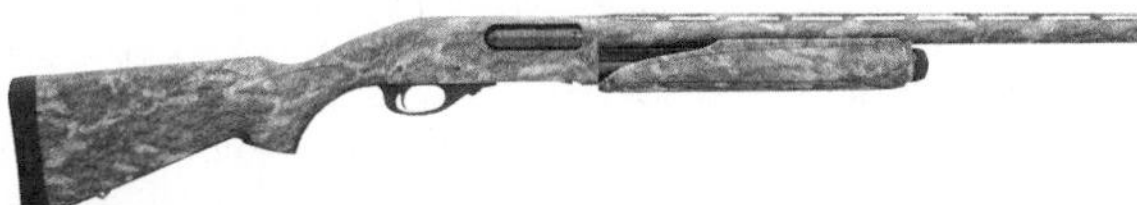

REMINGTON 870 EXPRESS SYNTHETIC SUPER MAG TURKEY-WATERFOWL CAMO

Pump action shotgun chambered in 12-ga., 2-3/4 to 3-1/2 inch. Features include full Mossy Oak Bottomland camo coverage; 26-inch barrel with HiViz fiber-optics sights; Wingmaster HD Waterfowl and Turkey Extra Full RemChokes; SuperCell recoil pad; drilled and tapped receiver.

Price: **$601.00**

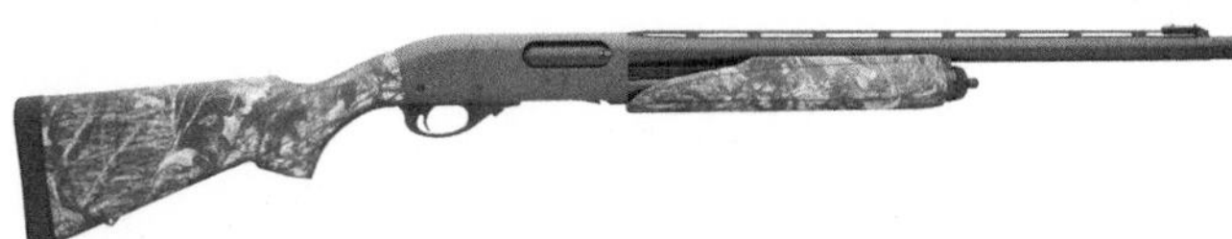

REMINGTON 870 EXPRESS SYNTHETIC TURKEY CAMO

Pump action shotgun chambered for 2-3/4 and 3-inch 12-ga. Features include 21-inch vent rib bead-sighted barrel; standard Express finish on barrel and receiver; Turkey Extra Full RemChoke; synthetic stock with integrated sling swivel attachment.

Price: **$445.00**

REMINGTON 870 SUPER MAG TURKEY-PREDATOR CAMO WITH SCOPE

Pump action shotgun chambered in 12-ga., 2-3/4 to 3-1/2 inch. Features include 20-inch barrel; TruGlo red/green selectable illuminated sight mounted on pre-installed Weaver-style rail; black padded sling; Wingmaster HD™ Turkey/Predator RemChoke; full Mossy Oak Obsession camo coverage; ShurShot pistol grip stock with black overmolded grip panels; TruGlo 30mm Red/Green Dot Scope pre-mounted.

Price: **$679.00**

REMINGTON MODEL 887 NITRO MAG PUMP SHOTGUN

Gauge: 12; 3.5", 3", and 2-3/4" chambers. **Barrel:** 28". **Features:** Pump-action model based on the Model 870. Interchangeable shells, black matte ArmoLokt rustproof coating throughout. SuperCell recoil pad. Solid rib and Hi-Viz front sight with interchangeable light tubes. Black synthetic stock with contoured grip panels.

Price: **$399.00**
Price: Model 887 Nitro Mag Waterfowl, Advantage Max-4 camo overall **$532.00**

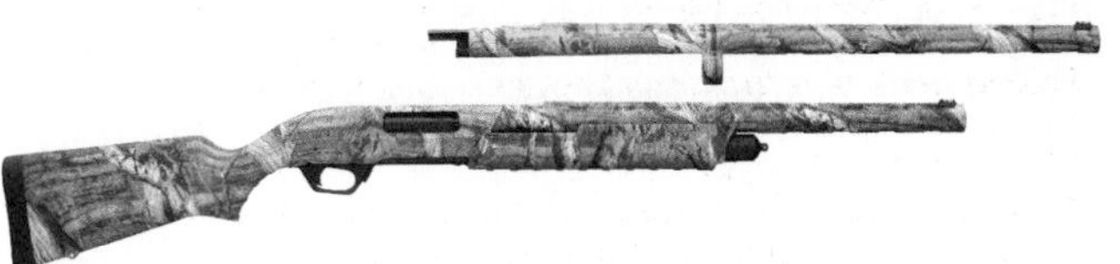

REMINGTON 887 NITRO MAG CAMO COMBO

Pump action shotgun chambered in 12-ga., 2-3/4 to 3-1/2 inch. Features include 22-inch turkey barrel with HiViz fiber-optic rifle sights and 28-inch waterfowl with a HiViz sight; extended Waterfowl and Super Full Turkey RemChokes are included; SuperCell recoil pad; synthetic stock and forend with specially contoured grip panels; full camo coverage.

Price: **$728.00**

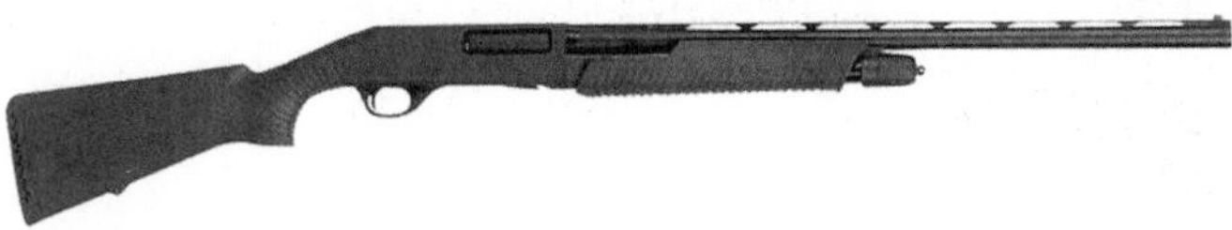

STEVENS MODEL 350 PUMP SHOTGUN

Pump-action shotgun chambered for 2.5- and 3-inch 12-ga. Features include all-steel barrel and receiver; bottom-load and -eject design; black synthetic stock; 5+1 capacity.

Price: Field Model with 28-inch barrel, screw-in choke **$267.00**
Price: Security Model with 18-inch barrel, fixed choke **$241.00**
Price: Combo Model with Field and Security barrels **$307.00**
Price: Security Model with 18.25-inch barrel w/ghost ring rear sight. **$254.00**

STOEGER MODEL P350 SHOTGUNS

Gauge: 12, 3.5" chamber, set of five choke tubes (C, IC, M, IM, XF). **Barrel:** 18.5",24", 26", 28". **Stock:** Black synthetic, Timber HD, Max-4 HD, APG HD camos. **Sights:** Red bar front. **Features:** Inertia-recoil, mercury recoil reducer, pistol grip stocks. Imported by Benelli USA.

Price: Synthetic. **$329.00**
Price: Max-4, Timber HD. **$429.00**
Price: Black synthetic pistol grip (2007) **$329.00**
Price: APG HD camo pistol grip (2007). **$429.00**

WEATHERBY PA-08 SERIES PUMP SHOTGUN

Gauge: 12 ga. chamber. **Barrel:** 26" and 28" flat ventilated rib. **Weight:** 6.5 lbs. -7 lbs. **Stock:** Walnut. **Features:** The PA-08 # Walnut stock

Prices given are believed to be accurate at time of publication however, many factors affect retail pricing so exact prices are not possible.

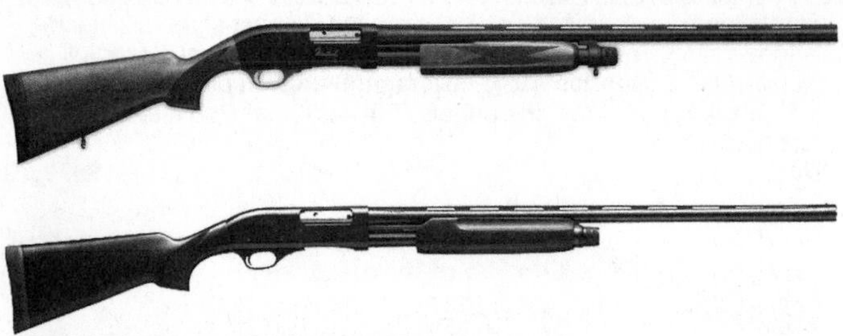

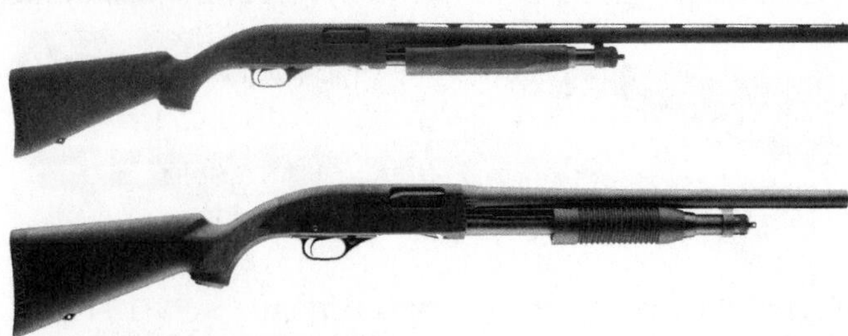

with gloss finish, all metalwork is gloss black for a distinctive look, vented top rib dissipates heat and aids in target acquisition. Comes with 3 application-specific choke tubes (IC/M/F). Made in Turkey.

Price: PA-08 Upland **$449.00**
Price: PA-08 Synthetic (New 2011) **$399.00**

WINCHESTER SUPER X PUMP SHOTGUNS

Gauge: 12, 3" or 3.5" chambers. **Barrel:** 18"; 26" and 28" barrels are .742" back-bored, chrome plated; Invector Plus choke tubes. **Weight:** 7 lbs. **Stock:** Walnut or composite. **Features:** Rotary bolt, four lugs, dual steel action bars. Walnut Field has gloss-finished walnut stock and forearm, cut checkering. Black Shadow Field has composite stock and forearm, non-glare matte finish barrel and receiver. Speed Pump Defender has composite stock and forearm, chromed plated, 18" cylinder choked barrel, non-glare metal surfaces, five-shot magazine, grooved forearm. Weight, 6.5 lbs. Reintroduced 2008. Made in U.S.A. from Winchester Repeating Arms Co.

Price: Black Shadow Field, 3" **$470.00**
Price: Black Shadow Field, 3.5" **$500.00**
Price: Defender **$400.00**
Price: Waterfowl Hunter, 3" **$530.00**
Price: Waterfowl Hunter, 3.5". **$580.00**
Price: Turkey Hunter, 3.5" **$600.00**

BERETTA DT10 TRIDENT SHOTGUNS

Gauge: 12, 2-3/4", 3" chambers. **Barrel:** 28", 30", 32", 34"; competition-style vent rib; fixed or Optima choke tubes. **Weight:** 7.9 to 9 lbs. **Stock:** High-grade walnut stock with oil finish; hand-checkered grip and forend, adjustable stocks available. **Features:** Detachable, adjustable trigger group, raised and thickened receiver, forend iron has adjustment nut to guarantee wood-to-metal fit. Introduced 2000. Imported from Italy by Beretta USA.

Price: DT10 Trident Trap, adjustable stock. **$8,650.00**
Price: DT10 Trident Skeet **$8,050.00**
Price: DT10 Trident Sporting, from **$7,650.00**

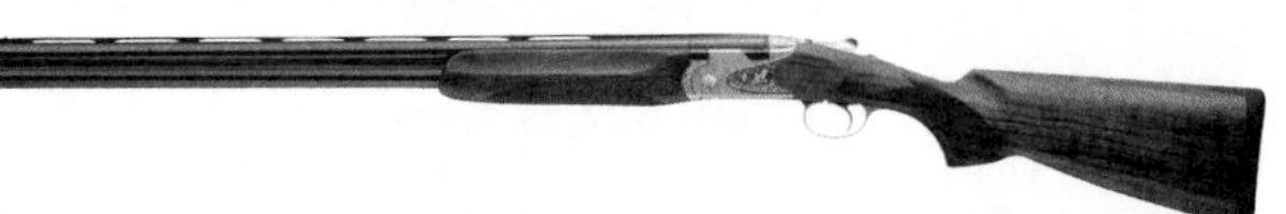

BERETTA SV10 PERENNIA O/U SHOTGUN

Gauge: 12, 3" chambers. **Barrel:** 26", 28", 30". Optima-Bore profile, polished blue. Bore diameter 18.6mm (0.73 in.) Self-adjusting dual conical longitudinal locking lugs, oversized monobloc bearing shoulders, replaceable hinge pins. Ventilated top rib, 6x6mm. Long guided extractors, automatic ejection or mechanical extraction. Optimachoke tubes. **Weight:** 7.3 lbs. **Stock:** Quick take-down stock with pistol grip or English straight stock. Kick-off recoil reduction system available on request on Q-Stock. **Length of pull:** 14.7", drop at comb, 1.5", drop at heel, 2.36" or 1.38"/2.17". Semibeavertail forend with elongated forend lever. New checkering pattern, matte oil finish, rubber pad. **Features:** Floral motifs and game scenes on side panels; nickel-based protective finish, arrowhead-shaped sideplates, solid steel alloy billet. Kick-Off recoil reduction mechanism available on select models. Fixed chokes on request, removable trigger group, titanium single selective trigger. Manual or automatic safety, newly designed safety and selector lever. Gel-Tek recoil pad available on request. Polypropylene case, 5 chokes with spanner, sling swivels, plastic pad, Beretta gun oil. Introduced 2008. Imported from Italy by Beretta USA.

Price: From . . . . **$2,890.00 to $3,295.00**

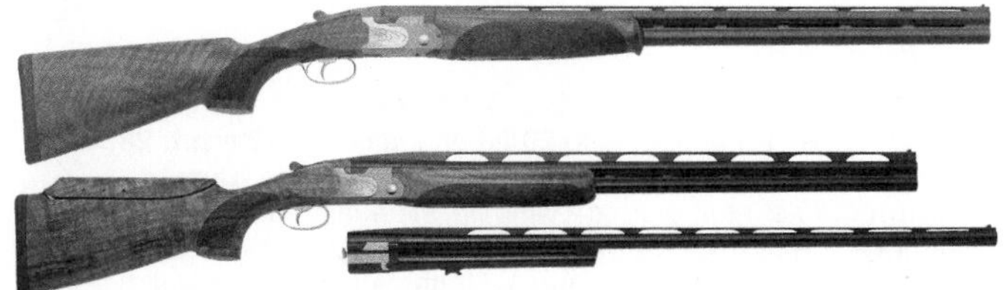

BERETTA SERIES 682 GOLD E SKEET, TRAP, SPORTING O/U SHOTGUNS

Gauge: 12, 2-3/4" chambers. **Barrel:** skeet-28"; trap-30" and 32", Imp. Mod. & Full and Mobilchoke; trap mono shotguns-32" and 34" Mobilchoke; trap top single guns-32" and 34" Full and Mobilchoke; trap combo sets-from 30" O/U, to 32" O/U, 34" top single. **Stock:** Close-grained walnut, hand checkered. **Sights:** White Bradley bead front sight and center bead. **Features:** Receiver has Greystone gunmetal gray finish with gold accents. Trap Monte Carlo stock has deluxe trap recoil pad. Various grades available. Imported from Italy by Beretta USA.

Price: 682 Gold E Trap with adjustable stock **$4,800.00**
Price: 682 Gold E Sporting. **$4,600.00**
Price: 682 Gold E Skeet, adjustable stock **$4,800.00**

BERETTA 686 ONYX O/U SHOTGUNS

Gauge: 12, 20, 28; 3", 3.5" chambers. **Barrel:** 26", 28" (Mobilchoke tubes). **Weight:** 6.8-6.9 lbs. **Stock:** Checkered American walnut. **Features:** Intended for the beginning sporting clays shooter. Has wide, vented target rib, radiused recoil pad. Polished black finish on receiver and barrels. Introduced 1993. Imported from Italy by Beretta U.S.A.

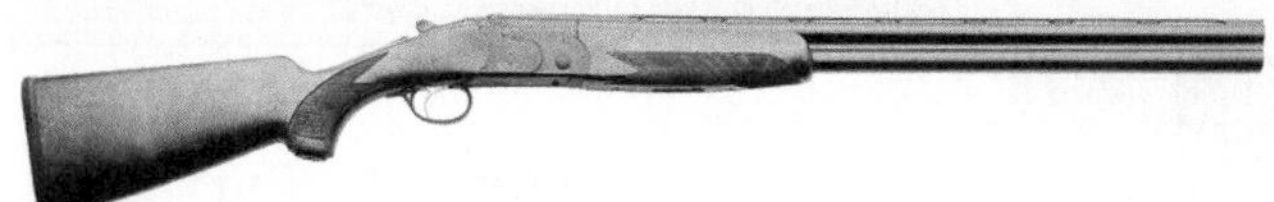

Price: White Onyx **$2,240.00**
PPrice: White Onyx Sporting **$2,460.00**

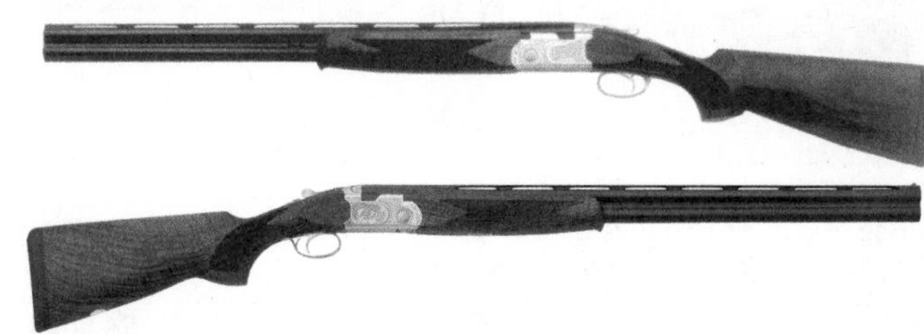

BERETTA SILVER PIGEON O/U SHOTGUNS

Gauge: 12, 20, 28, 3" chambers (2-3/4" 28 ga.). .410 bore, 3" chamber. **Barrel:** 26", 28". **Weight:** 6.8 lbs. **Stock:** Checkered walnut. **Features:** Interchangeable barrels (20 and 28 ga.), single selective gold-plated trigger, boxlock action, auto safety, Schnabel forend.

Price: . . . . **$2,240.00 to $4075.00**

BERETTA ULTRALIGHT O/U SHOTGUNS

Gauge: 12, 2-3/4" chambers. **Barrel:** 26", 28", Mobilchoke tubes. **Weight:** About 5 lbs., 13 oz. **Stock:** Select American walnut with checkered grip and forend. **Features:** Low-profile aluminum alloy receiver with titanium breech face insert. Electroless nickel receiver with game scene engraving. Single selective trigger; automatic safety. Introduced 1992. Ultralight Deluxe except has matte electroless nickel finish receiver with gold game scene engraving; matte oil-finished, select walnut stock and forend. Imported from Italy by Beretta U.S.A.

Price: **$2,075.00**
Price: Ultralight Deluxe **$2,450.00**

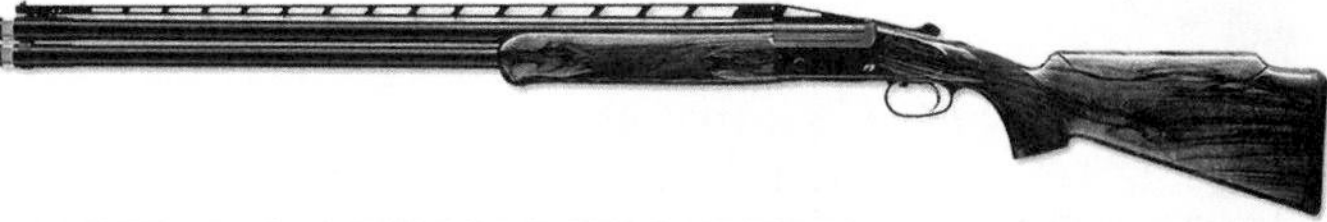

BLASER F3 SUPERSPORT O/U SHOTGUN

Gauge: 12 ga., 3" chamber. **Barrel:** 32". **Weight:** 9 lbs. **Stock:** Adustable semi-custom, turkish walnut wood grade: 4. **Features:** The latest addition to the F3 family is the F3 SuperSport. The perfect blend of overall weight, balance and weight distribution make the F3 SuperSport the ideal competitor. Briley Spectrum-5 chokes, free floating barrels, adjustable barrel hanger system on o/u, chrome plated barrels full length, revolutionary ejector ball system, barrels finished in a powder coated nitride, selectable competition trigger.

Price: From **$7,250.00**

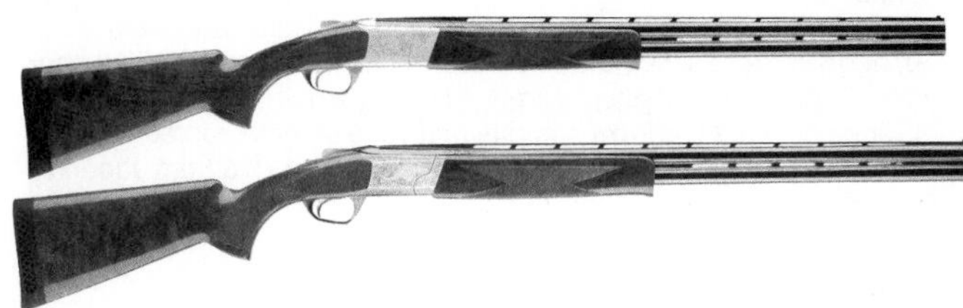

BROWNING CYNERGY O/U SHOTGUNS

Gauge: .410, 12, 20, 28. **Barrel:** 26", 28", 30", 32". **Stock:** Walnut or composite. **Sights:** White bead front most models; HiViz Pro-Comp sight on some models; mid bead. **Features:** Mono-Lock hinge, recoil-reducing interchangeable Inflex recoil pad, silver nitride receiver; striker-based trigger, ported barrel option. Models include: Cynergy Sporting, Adjustable Comb; Cynergy Sporting Composite CF; Cynergy Field, Composite; Cynergy Classic Sporting; Cynergy Classic Field; Cynergy Camo Mossy Oak New Shadow Grass; Cynergy Camo Mossy Oak New Break-Up; and Cynergy Camo Mossy Oak Brush. Imported from Japan by Browning.

Price: Field Grade Model, 12 ga.. . . . . **$2,800.00**

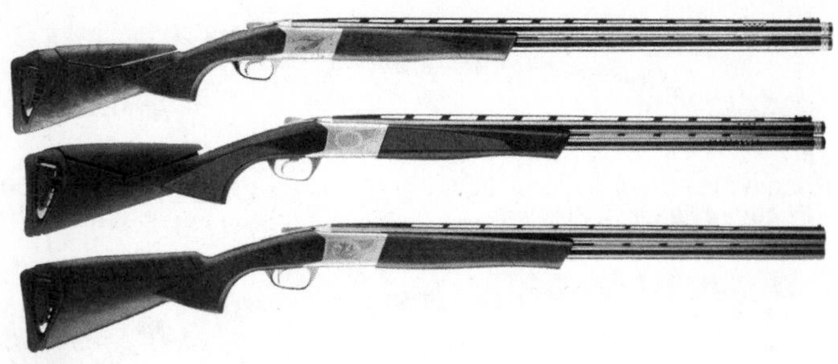

Price: Field, small gauges. **$2,860.00**
Price: Feather model, from **$2,900.00**
Price: Sporting, from **$4,020.00**
Price: Sporting w/adjustable comb **$4,500.00**
Price: Sporting composite w/adjustable comb **$3,870.00**
Price: Classic Field, Sporting from . . . . **$2,540.00 to $3,640.00**
Price: Classic Field Grade III, from **$4,000.00**
Price: Classic Field Grade VI, from **$6,100.00**

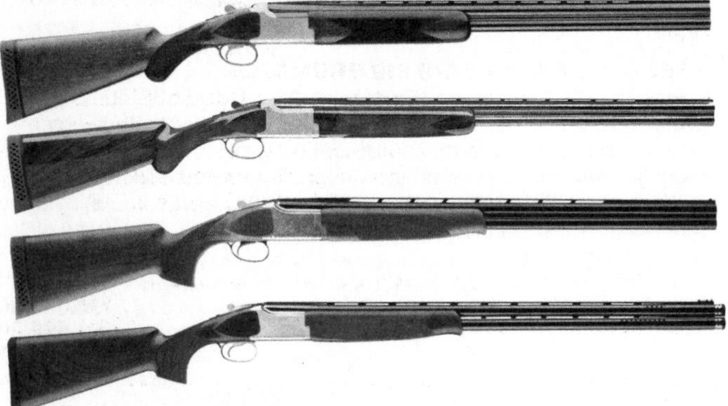

BROWNING CITORI O/U SHOTGUNS
Gauge: 12, 20, 28 and .410. **Barrel:** 26", 28" in 28 and .410. Offered with Invector choke tubes. All 12 and 20 gauge models have back-bored barrels and Invector Plus choke system. **Weight:** 6 lbs., 8 oz. (26" .410) to 7 lbs., 13 oz. (30" 12 ga.). **Length:** 43" overall (26" bbl.). **Stock:** Dense walnut, hand checkered, full pistol grip, beavertail forend. Field-type recoil pad on 12 ga. field guns and trap and skeet models. **Sights:** Medium raised beads, German nickel silver. **Features:** Barrel selector integral with safety, automatic ejectors, three-piece takedown. Citori 625 Field (intr. 2008) includes Vector Pro extended forcing cones, new wood checkering patterns, silver-nitride finish with high-relief engraving, gloss oil finish with Grade II/III walnut with radius pistol grip, Schnabel forearm, 12 gauge, three Invector Plus choke tubes. Citori 625 Sporting (intr. 2008) includes standard and adjustable combs, 32", 30", and 28" barrels, five Diamond Grade extended Invector Plus choke tubes. Triple Trigger System allows adjusting length of pull and choice of wide checkered, narrow smooth, and wide smooth canted trigger shoe. HiViz Pro-Comp fiber-optic front sights. Imported from Japan by Browning.

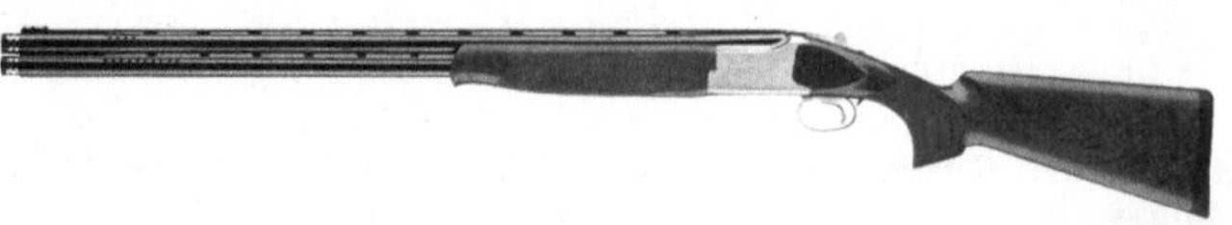

Price: Lightning, from **$1,990.00**
Price: White Lightning, from **$2,070.00**
Price: Superlight Feather **$2,390.00**
Price: Lightning Feather, combo 20 and 28 ga. **$3,580.00**
Price: 625 Field, 12, 20 or 28 ga. and 410. Weighs 6 lbs. 12 oz. to 7 lbs. 14 oz. **$2,630.00**
Price: 625 Sporting, 12, 20 or 28 ga. and 410, standard comb, intr. 2008 . . . . **$3,550.00**

BROWNING 725 CITORI
Gauge: 12, 3" chambers. **Barrel:** 26, 28, 30". **Weight:** 7.25 to 7.6 lbs. **Length:** 43.75 to 50". **Stock:** Gloss oil finish grade II/III walnut. Features include a new receiver that is significantly lower in profile than other 12-gauge Citori models. Other features include a mechanical trigger, Vector Pro lengthened forcing cones, three Invector-DS choke tubes, silver nitride finish with high relief engraving.
Price: 725 Field **$2,470.00**
Price: 725 Sporting **$3,140.00**

BROWNING CITORI HIGH GRADE SHOTGUNS
Similar to standard Citori except has engraved hunting scenes and gold inlays, high-grade, hand-oiled walnut stock and forearm. Introduced 2000. From Browning.
Price: Grade IV Lightning, engraved gray receiver, introduced 2005, from **$3,500.00**
Price: Grade VII Lightning, engraved gray or blue receiver, introduced 2005, from **$5,560.00**

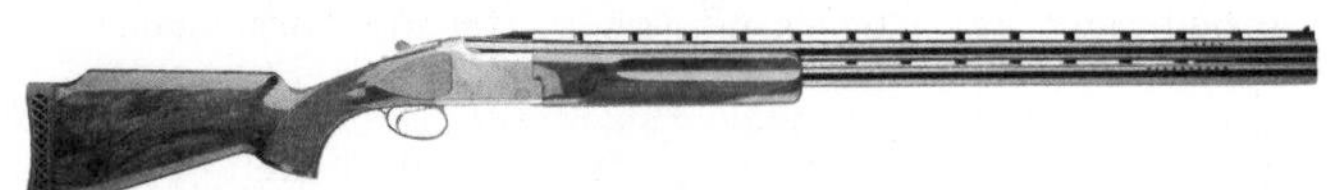

BROWNING CITORI XT TRAP O/U SHOTGUN
Similar to the Citori XS Special except has engraved silver nitride receiver with gold highlights, vented side barrel rib. Available in 12 gauge with 30" or 32" barrels, Invector-Plus choke tubes, adjustable comb and buttplate. Introduced 1999. Imported by Browning.
Price: XT Trap **$2,960.00**
Price: XT Trap w/adjustable comb. **$3,390.00**

CAESAR GUERINI ELLIPSE O/U SHOTGUN
Gauge: 12, 20, 28 gauge, also 20/28 gauge combo. **Barrel:** 28". **Weight:** 6.5 lbs. **Length:** 49.25". **Stock:** High grade walnut. **Features:** Fast as a grouse's wing tip, sleek as a pheasant's tail feather - The new Caesar Guerini Ellipse EVO represents the next generation of upland game gun. With graceful rounded action and streamlined stock it handles, feels and looks like the world's best handmade round body shotguns. We obsessed over every detail from the engraving created to accentuate the curve of the action to something as obscure as the shape of the trigger. This is not a quick makeover of our existing models; the barrels, action and stock are all different. The Ellipse is simply the evolution of the fine over-and-under hunting gun. The Ellipse comes in a fitted case with five choke tube. The EVO is the more expensive of the two Ellipse models and as such boasts more elaborate engraving, a higher grade of walnut in the stock, and a few other aesthetic touches. Otherwise, the two are identical. $205 Additional Charge for Left Hand Stock.
Price: Limited . . . . **$3,995.00 - $5,605.00**
Price: EVO . . . . **$5,495.00 - $7,365.00**

CZ SPORTING OVER/UNDER
Gauge: 12, 3" chambers. **Barrel:** 30", 32" chrome-lined, back-bored with extended forcing cones. **Weight:** 9 lbs. **Length:** NA. **Stock:** Neutral cast stock with an adjustable comb, trap style forend, pistol grip and ambidextrous palm swells. #3 grade Circassian walnut. At lowest position, drop at comb: 1-5/8"; drop at heel: 2-3/8"; length of pull: 14-1/2". **Features:** Designed for Sporting Clays and FITASC competition. Hand engraving, satin black-finished receiver. Tapered

Prices given are believed to be accurate at time of publication however, many factors affect retail pricing so exact prices are not possible.

rib with center bead and a red fiber-optic front bead, 10 choke tubes with wrench, single selective trigger, automatic ejectors, thin rubber pad with slick plastic top. Introduced 2008. From CZ-USA.
Price: **$2,509.00**

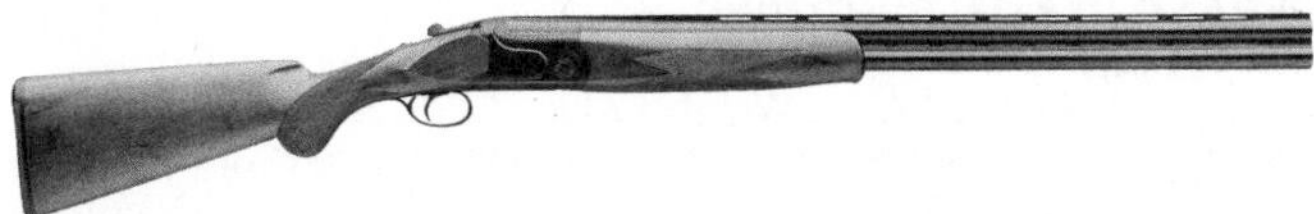

CZ CANVASBACK
Gauge: 12, 20, 3" chambers. **Barrel:** 26", 28". **Weight:** 7.3 lbs. **Length:** NA. **Stock:** Round-knob pistol grip, Schnabel forend, Turkish walnut. **Features:** Single selective trigger, set of 5 screw-in chokes, black chrome finished receiver. From CZ-USA.
Price: **$819.00**

CZ MALLARD
Gauge: 12, 20, 28, .410, 3" chambers. **Barrel:** 26". **Weight:** 7.7 lbs. **Length:** NA. **Stock:** Round-knob pistol grip, Schnabel forend, Turkish walnut. **Features:** Double triggers and extractors, coin finished receiver, multi chokes. From CZ-USA.
Price: **$562.00**

CZ REDHEAD
Gauge: 12, 20, 3" chambers. **Barrel:** 28". **Weight:** 7.4 lbs. **Length:** NA. **Stock:** Round-knob pistol grip, Schnabel forend, Turkish walnut. **Features:** Single selective triggers and extractors (12 & 20 ga.), screw-in chokes (12, 20, 28 ga.) choked IC and Mod (.410), coin finished receiver, multi chokes. From CZ-USA.
Price: **$965.00**

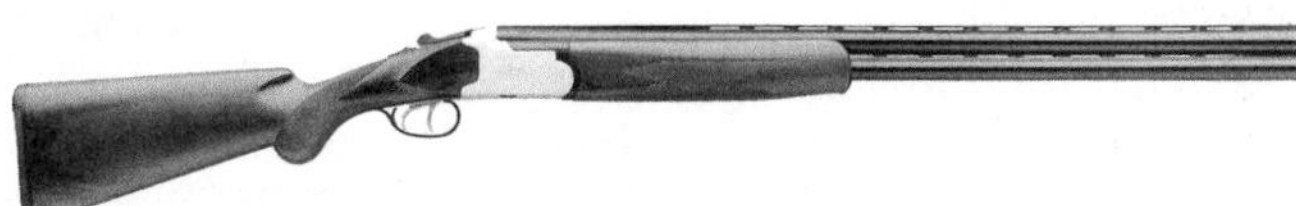

CZ WINGSHOOTER O/U SHOTGUN
Gauge: 12, 20, 28 & .410 ga., 2-3/4" chamber. **Barrel:** 28" flat ventilated rib. **Weight:** 6.3 lbs. **Length:** 45.5". **Stock:** Turkish walnut. **Features:** This colorful Over and Under shotgun has the same old world craftsmanship as all of our shotguns but with a new stylish look. This elegant hand engraved work of art is available in four gauges and its eye-catching engraving will stand alone in the field or range. 12 and 20 gauge models have auto ejectors, while the 28 gauge and .410 have extractors only. Heavily engraved scroll work with special side plate design, mechanical selective triggers, box Lock frame design, 18 LPI checkering, coil spring operated hammers, chrome lined, 5 interchangeable choke tubes and special engraved skeleton butt plate.
Price: **$1,040.00**

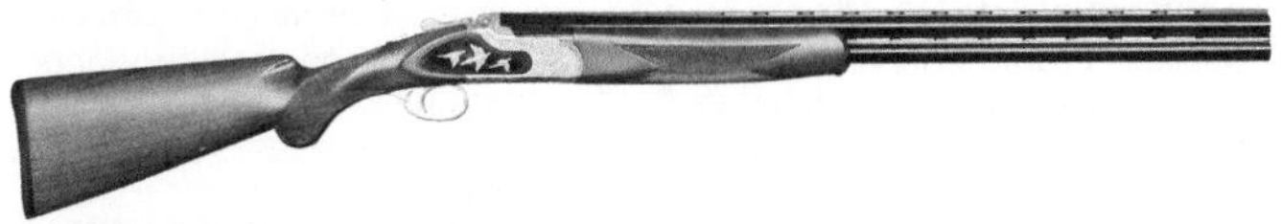

CZ WOODCOCK
Gauge: 12, 20, 28, .410, 3" chambers. **Barrel:** 26". **Weight:** 7.7 lbs. **Length:** NA. **Stock:** Round-knob pistol grip, Schnabel forend, Turkish walnut. **Features:** Single selective triggers and extractors (auto ejectors on 12 & 20 ga.), screw-in chokes (12, 20, 28 ga.) choked IC and Mod (.410), coin finished receiver, multi chokes. The sculptured frame incorporates a side plate, resembling a true side lock, embellished with hand engraving and finished with color casehardening. From CZ-USA.
Price: **$1,246.00**

ESCORT OVER/UNDER SHOTGUNS
Gauge: 12, 3" chamber. **Barrel:** 28". **Weight:** 7.4 lbs. **Stock:** Walnut or select walnut with Trio recoil pad; synthetic stock with adjustable comb. Three adjustment spacers. **Sights:** Bronze front bead. **Features:** Blued barrels, blued or nickel receiver. Trio recoil pad. Five interchangeable chokes (SK, IC, M, IM, F); extractors or ejectors (new, 2008), barrel selector. Hard case available. Introduced 2007. Imported from Turkey by Legacy Sports International.
Price: **$599.00**

FAUSTI CLASSIC ROUND BODY
Gauge: 16, 20, 28. **Barrels:** 28 or 30". **Weight:** 5.8 to 6.3 lbs. **Length:** 45.5 to 47.5". **Stock:** Turkish walnut Prince of Wales style with oil finish. Features include automatic ejectors, single selective trigger, laser-engraved receiver.
Price: 20 gauge. **$4,199.00**
Price: 16 gauge. **$4,299.00**
Price: 28 gauge. **$4,599.00**

FRANCHI INSTINCT SERIES
Gauge: 12, 20 with 3" chambers. **Barrels:** 26 or 28". **Weight:** 5.3 to 6.4 lbs. **Length:** 42.5 to 44.5". **Stock:** AA-grade satin walnut (LS), A-grade (L) with rounded pistol grip and recoil pad. Single trigger, automatic ejectors, tang safety, choke tubes. LS model has aluminum alloy receiver, L model has steel receiver.
Price: (Instinct L). **$1149**
Price: (Instinct LS) **$1349**

KOLAR SPORTING CLAYS O/U SHOTGUNS
Gauge: 12, 2-3/4" chambers. **Barrel:** 30", 32", 34"; extended choke tubes. **Stock:** 14-5/8"x2.5"x1-7/8"x1-3/8". French walnut. Four stock versions available. **Features:** Single selective trigger, detachable, adjustable for length; overbored barrels with long forcing cones; flat tramline rib; matte blue finish. Made in U.S. by Kolar.
Price: Standard **$9,595.00**
Price: Prestige. **$14,190.00**
Price: Elite Gold **$16,590.00**
Price: Legend **$17,090.00**
Price: Select **$22,590.00**
Price: Custom . . . . **Price on request**

KOLAR AAA COMPETITION TRAP O/U SHOTGUN
Similar to the Sporting Clays gun except has 32" O/U /34" Unsingle or 30" O/U /34" Unsingle barrels as an over/under, unsingle, or combination set. Stock dimensions are 14.5"x2.5"x1.5"; American or French walnut; step parallel rib standard. Contact maker for full listings. Made in U.S.A. by Kolar.
Price: from. **$10,995.00**

KOLAR AAA COMPETITION SKEET O/U SHOTGUN
Similar to the Sporting Clays gun except has 28" or 30" barrels with Kolarite AAA sub gauge tubes; stock of American or French walnut with matte finish; flat tramline rib; under barrel adjustable for point of impact. Many options available. Contact maker for complete listing. Made in U.S.A. by Kolar.
Price: **$12,395.00**

KRIEGHOFF K-80 SPORTING CLAYS O/U SHOTGUN
Gauge: 12. **Barrel:** 28", 30", 32", 34" with choke tubes. **Weight:** About 8 lbs. **Stock:** #3 Sporting stock designed for gun-down shooting. **Features:** Standard receiver with satin nickel finish and classic scroll engraving. Selective mechanical trigger adjustable for position. Choice of tapered flat or 8mm parallel flat barrel rib. Free-floating barrels. Aluminum case. Imported from Germany by Krieghoff International, Inc.
Price: Standard grade with five choke tubes, from **$9,395.00**

KRIEGHOFF K-80 SKEET O/U SHOTGUNS
Gauge: 12, 2-3/4" chambers. **Barrel:** 28", 30", 32", (skeet & skeet), optional choke tubes). **Weight:** About 7.75 lbs. **Stock:** American skeet or straight skeet stocks, with palm-swell grips. Walnut. **Features:** Satin gray receiver finish. Selective mechanical trigger adjustable for position. Choice of ventilated 8mm parallel flat rib or ventilated 8-12mm tapered flat rib. Introduced 1980. Imported from Germany by Krieghoff International, Inc.

Price: Standard, skeet chokes **$8,375.00**
Price: Skeet Special (28", 30", 32" tapered flat rib, skeet & skeet choke tubes) **$9,100.00**

KRIEGHOFF K-80 TRAP O/U SHOTGUNS
Gauge: 12, 2-3/4" chambers. **Barrel:** 30", 32" (Imp. Mod. & Full or choke tubes). **Weight:** About 8.5 lbs. **Stock:** Four stock dimensions or adjustable stock available; all have palm-swell grips. Checkered European walnut. **Features:** Satin nickel receiver. Selective mechanical trigger, adjustable for position. Ventilated step rib. Introduced 1980. Imported from Germany by Krieghoff International, Inc.
Price: K-80 O/U (30", 32", Imp. Mod. & Full), from **$8,850.00**
Price: K-80 Unsingle (32", 34", Full), standard, from **$10,080.00**
Price: K-80 Combo (two-barrel set), standard, from **$13,275.00**

KRIEGHOFF K-20 O/U SHOTGUN
Similar to the K-80 except built on a 20-gauge frame. Designed for skeet, sporting clays and field use. Offered in 20, 28 and .410; 28", 30" and 32" barrels. Imported from Germany by Krieghoff International Inc.
Price: K-20, 20 gauge, from **$9,575.00**
Price: K-20, 28 gauge, from **$9,725.00**
Price: K-20, .410, from **$9,725.00**

LEBEAU-COURALLY BOSS-VEREES O/U SHOTGUN
Gauge: 12, 20, 2-3/4" chambers. **Barrel:** 25" to 32". **Weight:** To customer specifications. **Stock:** Exhibition-quality French walnut. **Features:** Boss-type sidelock with automatic ejectors; single or double triggers; chopper lump barrels. A custom gun built to customer specifications. Imported from Belgium by Wm. Larkin Moore.
Price: From **$96,000.00**

LJUTIC LM-6 SUPER DELUXE O/U SHOTGUNS
Gauge: 12. **Barrel:** 28" to 34", choked to customer specs for live birds, trap, international trap. **Weight:** To customer specs. **Stock:** To customer specs. Oil finish, hand checkered. **Features:** Custom-made gun. Hollow-milled rib, pull or release trigger, push-button opener in front of trigger guard. From Ljutic Industries.
Price: Super Deluxe LM-6 O/U **$19,995.00**
Price: Over/Under combo (interchangeable single barrel, two trigger guards, one for single trigger, one for doubles) **$27,995.00**
Price: Extra over/under barrel sets, 29"-32" **$6,995.00**

MERKEL MODEL 2001EL O/U SHOTGUN
Gauge: 12, 20, 3" chambers, 28, 2-3/4" chambers. **Barrel:** 12-28"; 20, 28 ga.-26.75". **Weight:** About 7 lbs. (12 ga.). **Stock:** Oil-finished walnut; English or pistol grip. **Features:** Self-cocking Blitz boxlock action with cocking indicators; Kersten double cross-bolt lock; silver-grayed receiver with engraved hunting scenes; coil spring ejectors; single selective or double triggers. Imported from Germany by Merkel USA.
Price: **$9,995.00**
Price: Model 2001EL Sporter; full pistol grip stock **$9,995.00**

MERKEL MODEL 2000CL O/U SHOTGUN
Similar to Model 2001EL except scroll-engraved case-hardened receiver; 12, 20, 28 gauge. Imported from Germany by Merkel USA.
Price: **$8,495.00**
Price: Model 2016 CL; 16 gauge **$8,495.00**

PERAZZI MX8/MX8 SPECIAL TRAP, SKEET O/U SHOTGUNS
Gauge: 12, 2-3/4" chambers. **Barrel:** Trap: 29.5" (Imp. Mod. & Extra Full), 31.5" (Full & Extra Full). Choke tubes optional. Skeet: 27-5/8" (skeet & skeet). **Weight:** About 8.5 lbs. (trap); 7 lbs., 15 oz. (skeet). **Stock:** Interchangeable and custom made to customer specs. **Features:** Has detachable and interchangeable trigger group with flat V springs. Flat 7/16" vent rib. Many options available. Imported from Italy by Perazzi U.S.A., Inc.
Price: MX Trap Single **$10,934.00**

PERAZZI MX8 SPECIAL SKEET O/U SHOTGUN
Similar to the MX8 Skeet except has adjustable four-position trigger, skeet stock dimensions. Imported from Italy by Perazzi U.S.A., Inc.
Price: From **$11,166.00**

PERAZZI MX8 O/U SHOTGUNS
Gauge: 12, 2-3/4" chambers. **Barrel:** 28-3/8" (Imp. Mod. & Extra Full), 29.5" (choke tubes). **Weight:** 7 lbs., 12 oz. **Stock:** Special specifications. **Features:** Has single selective trigger; flat 7/16" x 5/16" vent rib. Many options available. Imported from Italy by Perazzi U.S.A., Inc.
Price: Standard **$12,532.00**
Price: Sporting **$11,166.00**
Price: Trap Double Trap (removable trigger group) **$15,581.00**
Price: Skeet **$12,756.00**
Price: SC3 grade (variety of engraving patterns) . . . . **$23,000.00+**
Price: SCO grade (more intricate engraving, gold inlays) . **$39,199.00+**

PERAZZI MX8/20 O/U SHOTGUN
Similar to the MX8 except has smaller frame and has a removable trigger mechanism. Available in trap, skeet, sporting or game models with fixed chokes or choke tubes. Stock is made to customer specifications. Introduced 1993. Imported from Italy by Perazzi U.S.A., Inc.
Price: From **$11,731.00**

PERAZZI MX12 HUNTING O/U SHOTGUNS
Gauge: 12, 2-3/4" chambers. **Barrel:** 26.75", 27.5", 28-3/8", 29.5" (Mod. & Full); choke tubes available in 27-5/8", 29.5" only (MX12C). **Weight:** 7 lbs., 4 oz. **Stock:** To customer specs; interchangeable. **Features:** Single selective trigger; coil springs used in action; Schnabel forend tip. Imported from Italy by Perazzi U.S.A., Inc.
Price: From **$11,166.00**
Price: MX12C (with choke tubes). From **$11,960.00**

PERAZZI MX20 HUNTING O/U SHOTGUNS
Similar to the MX12 except 20 ga. frame size. Non-removable trigger group. Available in 20, 28, .410 with 2-3/4" or 3" chambers. 26" standard, and choked Mod. & Full. Weight is 6 lbs., 6 oz. Imported from Italy by Perazzi U.S.A., Inc.
Price: From **$11,166.00**
Price: MX20C (as above, 20 ga. only, choke tubes). From . **$11,960.00**

PERAZZI MX10 O/U SHOTGUN
Gauge: 12, 2-3/4" chambers. **Barrel:** 29.5", 31.5" (fixed chokes). **Weight:** NA. **Stock:** Walnut; cheekpiece adjustable for elevation and cast. **Features:** Adjustable rib; vent side rib. Externally selective trigger. Available in single barrel, combo, over/under trap, skeet, pigeon and sporting models. Introduced 1993. Imported from Italy by Perazzi U.S.A., Inc.
Price: MX200410 . . . . **$18,007.00**

PERAZZI MX28, MX410 GAME O/U SHOTGUN
Gauge: 28, 2-3/4" chambers, .410, 3" chambers. **Barrel:** 26" (Imp. Cyl. & Full). **Weight:** NA. **Stock:** To customer specifications. **Features:** Made on scaled-down frames proportioned to the gauge. Introduced 1993. Imported from Italy by Perazzi U.S.A., Inc.
Price: From **$22,332.00**

PIOTTI BOSS O/U SHOTGUN
Gauge: 12, 20. **Barrel:** 26" to 32", chokes as specified. **Weight:** 6.5 to 8 lbs. **Stock:** Dimensions to customer specs. Best quality figured walnut. **Features:** Essentially a custom-made gun with many options. Introduced 1993. Imported from Italy by Wm. Larkin Moore.
Price: From **$69,000.00**

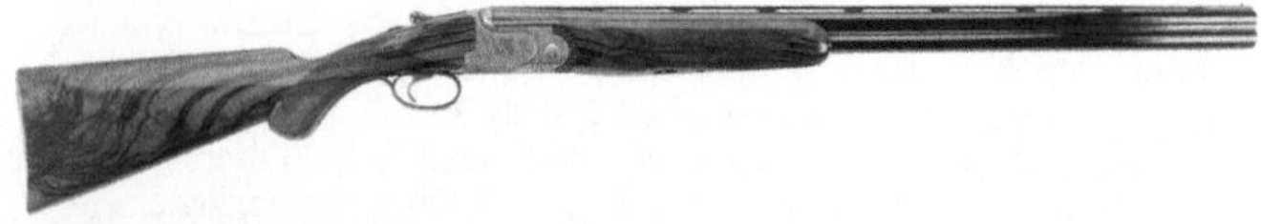

RIZZINI S790 EMEL O/U SHOTGUN
Gauge: 20, 28, .410. **Barrel:** 26", 27.5" (Imp. Cyl. & Imp. Mod.).

Weight: About 6 lbs. **Stock:** 14"x1.5"x2-1/8". Extra fancy select walnut. **Features:** Boxlock action with profuse engraving; automatic ejectors; single selective trigger; silvered receiver. Comes with Nizzoli leather case. Introduced 1996. Imported from Italy by Wm. Larkin Moore & Co.
Price: From **$14,600.00**

RIZZINI S792 EMEL O/U SHOTGUN
Similar to S790 EMEL except dummy sideplates with extensive engraving coverage. Nizzoli leather case. Introduced 1996. Imported from Italy by Wm. Larkin Moore & Co.
Price: From **$15,500.00**

RIZZINI UPLAND EL O/U SHOTGUN
Gauge: 12, 16, 20, 28, .410. **Barrel:** 26", 27.5", Mod. & Full, Imp. Cyl. & Imp. Mod. choke tubes. **Weight:** About 6.6 lbs. **Stock:** 14.5"x1-1/2"x2.25". **Features:** Boxlock action; single selective trigger; ejectors; profuse engraving on silvered receiver. Comes with fitted case. Introduced 1996. Imported from Italy by Wm. Larkin Moore & Co.
Price: From **$5,200.00**

RIZZINI ARTEMIS O/U SHOTGUN
Same as Upland EL model except dummy sideplates with extensive game scene engraving. Fancy European walnut stock. Fitted case. Introduced 1996. Imported from Italy by Wm. Larkin Moore & Co.
Price: From **$3.260.00**

RIZZINI S782 EMEL O/U SHOTGUN
Gauge: 12, 2-3/4" chambers. **Barrel:** 26", 27.5" (Imp. Cyl. & Imp. Mod.). **Weight:** About 6.75 lbs. **Stock:** 14.5"x1.5"x2.25". Extra fancy select walnut. **Features:** Boxlock action with dummy sideplates, extensive engraving with gold inlaid game birds, silvered receiver, automatic ejectors, single selective trigger. Nizzoli leather case. Introduced 1996. Imported from Italy by Wm. Larkin Moore & Co.
Price: From **$18,800.00**

SAVAGE MILANO O/U SHOTGUNS
Gauge: 12, 20, 28, and 410, 2-3/4" (28 ga.) and 3" chambers. **Barrel:** 28"; chrome lined, elongated forcing cones, automatic ejectors. 12, 20, and 28 come with 3 Interchokes (F-M-IC); 410 has fixed chokes (M-IC). **Weight:** 12 ga., 7.5 lbs; 20, 28 gauge, .410, 6.25 lbs. **Length:** NA. **Stock:** Satin finish Turkish walnut stock with laser-engraved checkering, solid rubber recoil pad, Schnabel forend. **Features:** Single selective, mechanical set trigger, fiber-optic front sight with brass mid-rib bead. Introduced 2006. Imported from Italy by Savage Arms, Inc.
Price: **$1,714.00**

STEVENS MODEL 512 GOLD WING SHOTGUNS
Gauge: 12, 20, 28, .410; 2-3/4" and 3" chambers. **Barrel:** 26", 28". **Weight:** 6 to 8 lbs. **Sights:** NA. **Features:** Five screw-in choke tubes with 12, 20, and 28 gauge; .410 has fixed M/IC chokes. Black chrome, sculpted receiver with a raised gold pheasant, laser engraved trigger guard and forend latch. Turkish walnut stock finished in satin lacquer and beautifully laser engraved with fleur-de-lis checkering on the side panels, wrist and Schnabel forearm.
Price: **$649.00**

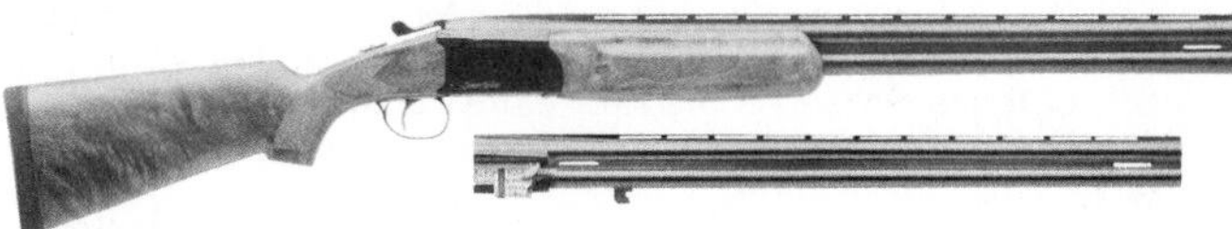

STOEGER CONDOR O/U SHOTGUNS
Gauge: 12, 20, 2-3/4" 3" chambers; 16, .410. Barrel: 22", 24", 26", 28", 30". Weight: 5.5 to 7.8 lbs. Sights: Brass bead. Features: IC, M, or F screw-in choke tubes with each gun. Oil finished hardwood with pistol grip and forend. Auto safety, single trigger, automatic extractors.
Price: from. . . . . **$449.00 to $789.00**

TRISTAR HUNTER EX O/U SHOTGUN
Gauge: 12, 20, 28, .410. **Barrel:** 26", 28". **Weight:** 5.7 lbs. (.410); 6.0 lbs. (20, 28), 7.2-7.4 lbs. (12). Chrome-lined steel mono-block barrel, five Beretta-style choke tubes (SK, IC, M, IM, F). **Length:** NA. **Stock:** Walnut, cut checkering. 14.25"x1.5"x2-3/8". **Sights:** Brass front sight. **Features:** All have extractors, engraved receiver, sealed actions, self-adjusting locking bolts, single selective trigger, ventilated rib. 28 ga. and .410 built on true frames. Five-year warranty. Imported from Italy by Tristar Sporting Arms Ltd.
Price: From **$619.00**

WEATHERBY ATHENA GRADE V AND GRADE III CLASSIC FIELD O/U SHOTGUNS
Gauge: Grade III and Grade IV: 12, 20, 3" chambers; 28, 2-3/4" chambers. Grade V: 12, 20, 3» chambers. **Barrel:** 26", 28" monobloc, IMC multi-choke tubes. Modified Greener crossbolt action. Matte ventilated top rib with brilliant front bead. **Weight:** 12 ga., 7.25 to 8 lbs.; 20 ga. 6.5 to 7.25 lbs. **Length:** 43" to 45". **Stock:** Rounded pistol grip, slender forend, Old English recoil pad. Grade V has oil-finished AAA American Claro walnut with 20-lpi checkering. Grade III has AA Claro walnut with oil finish, fine-line checkering. **Features:** Silver nitride/gray receivers; Grade III has hunting scene engraving. Grade IV has chrome-plated false sideplates featuring single game scene gold plate overlay. Grade V has rose and scroll engraving with gold-overlay upland game scenes. Top levers engraved with gold Weatherby flying "W". Introduced 1999. Imported from Japan by Weatherby.
Price: Grade III **$2,599.00**
Price: Grade IV **$2,799.00**
Price: Grade V **$3,999.00**

WEATHERBY ORION D'ITALIA O/U SHOTGUNS
Gauge: 12, 20, 3" chambers; 28, 2-3/4" chamber. **Barrel:** 26", 28", IMC multi-choke tubes. Matte ventilated top rib with brilliant bead front sight. **Weight:** 6-1/2 to 8 lbs. **Stock:** 14.25"x1.5"x2.5". American walnut, checkered grip and forend. Old English recoil pad. **Features:** All models have a triggerguard that features Weatherby's "Flying W" engraved with gold fill. D'Italia I available in 12 and 20 gauge, 26» and 28» barrels. Walnut stock with high lustre urethane finish. Metalwork is blued to high lustre finishand has a gold-plated trigger for corrosion protection. D'Italia II available in 12, 20 and 28 gauge with 26" and 28" barrels. Fancy grade walnut stock, hard chrome receiver with sculpted frameheads, elaborate game and floral engraving pattern, and matte vent mid & top rib with brilliant front bead sight. D'Italia III available in 12 and 20 gauge with 26" and 28" barrels. Hand-selected, oil-finished walnut stock wtih 20 LPI checkering, intricate engraving and gold plate game scene overlay, and damascened monobloc barrel and sculpted frameheads. D'Italia SC available in 12 gauge only with barrel lengths of 28", 30", and 32", weighs 8 lbs. Features satin, oil-finished walnut stock that is adjustable for cheek height with target-style pistol grip and Schnaubel forend, shallow receiver aligns hands for improved balance and pointability, ported barrels reduce muzzle jump, and fiber optic front sight for quick targer acquisition. Introduced 1998. Imported from Japan by Weatherby.
Price: D'Italia I **$1,699.00**
Price: D'Italia II **$1,899.00**
Price: D'Italia III **$2,199.00**
Price: D'Italia SC. **$2,599.00**

WINCHESTER MODEL 101 O/U SHOTGUNS
Gauge: 12, 2-3/4", 3" chambers. **Barrel:** 28", 30", 32", ported, Invector Plus choke system. **Weight:** 7 lbs. 6 oz. to 7 lbs. 12. oz. **Stock:** Checkered high-gloss grade II/III walnut stock, Pachmayr Decelerator sporting pad. **Features:** Chrome-plated chambers; back-bored barrels; tang barrel selector/safety; Signature extended choke tubes. Model 101 Field comes with solid brass bead front sight, three tubes, engraved receiver. Model 101 Sporting has adjustable trigger, 10mm runway rib, white mid-bead, Tru-Glo front sight, 30" and 32" barrels. Camo version of Model 101 Field comes with full-coverage Mossy Oak Duck Blind pattern. Model 101 Pigeon Grade Trap has 10mm steel runway rib, mid-bead sight, interchangeable fiber-optic front sight, porting and vented side ribs, adjustable trigger shoe, fixed raised comb or adjustable comb, Grade III/IV walnut, 30" or 32" barrels, molded ABS hard case. Reintroduced 2008. From Winchester Repeating Arms. Co.
Price: Field **$1,870.00**
Price: Sporting **$2,320.00**
Price: Pigeon Grade Trap, intr. 2008 . . . . **$2,470.00**
Price: Pigeon Grade Trap w/adj. comb, intr. 2008 . . . . **$2,630.00**

ARRIETA SIDELOCK DOUBLE SHOTGUNS

Gauge: 12, 16, 20, 28, .410. **Barrel:** Length and chokes to customer specs. **Weight:** To customer specs. **Stock:** To customer specs. Straight English with checkered butt (standard), or pistol grip. Select European walnut with oil finish. **Features:** Essentially custom gun with myriad options. H&H pattern hand-detachable sidelocks, selective automatic ejectors, double triggers (hinged front) standard. Some have selfopening action. Finish and engraving to customer specs. Imported from Spain by Quality Arms, Inc.

Price: Model 557. . . . . **$4,500.00**
Price: Model 570. . . . . **$5,350.00**
Price: Model 578. . . . . **$5,880.00**
Price: Model 600 Imperial. **$7,995.00**
Price: Model 601 Imperial Tiro **$9,160.00**
Price: Model 801. . . . . **$14,275.00**
Price: Model 802. . . . . **$14,275.00**
Price: Model 803. . . . . **$9,550.00**
Price: Model 871. . . . . **$6,670.00**
Price: Model 872. . . . . **$17,850.00**
Price: Model 873. . . . . **$16,275.00**
Price: Model 874. . . . . **$13,125.00**
Price: Model 875. . . . . **$19,850.00**
Price: Model 931. . . . . **$20,895.00**

AYA MODEL 4/53 SHOTGUNS

Gauge: 12, 16, 20, 28, 410. **Barrel:** 26", 27", 28", 30". **Weight:** To customer specifications. **Length:** To customer specifications. **Features:** Hammerless boxlock action; double triggers; light scroll engraving; automatic safety; straight grip oil finish walnut stock; checkered butt. Made in Spain. Imported by New England Custom Gun Service, Lt.

Price: **$2,999.00**
Price: No. 2. . . . . **$4,799.00**
Price: No. 2 Rounded Action. **$5,199.00**

BERETTA 471 SIDE-BY-SIDE SHOTGUNS

Gauge: 12, 20; 3" chamber. **Barrel:** 24", 26", 28"; 6mm rib. **Weight:** 6.5 lbs. **Stock:** English or pistol stock, straight butt for various types of recoil pads. Beavertail forend. English stock with recoil pad in red or black rubber, or in walnut and splinter forend. Select European walnut, checkered, oil finish. **Features:** Optima-Choke Extended Choke Tubes. Automatic ejection or mechanical extraction. Firing-pin block safety, manual or automatic, open top-lever safety. Introduced 2007. Imported from Italy by Beretta U.S.A.

Price: Silver Hawk. **$3,750.00**

CONNECTICUT SHOTGUN MANUFACTURING COMPANY RBL SIDE-BY-SIDE SHOTGUN

Gauge: 12, 16, 20, 28. **Barrel:** 26", 28", 30", 32". **Weight:** NA. **Length:** NA. **Stock:** NA. **Features:** Round-action SXS shotguns made in the USA. Scaled frames, five TruLock choke tubes. Deluxe fancy grade walnut buttstock and forend. Quick Change recoil pad in two lengths. Various dimensions and options available depending on gauge.

Price: 12 gauge **$2,850.00**
Price: 16 gauge . . . . **POR**
Price: 20 gauge **$3,995.00**
Price: 28 gauge **$5,450.00**

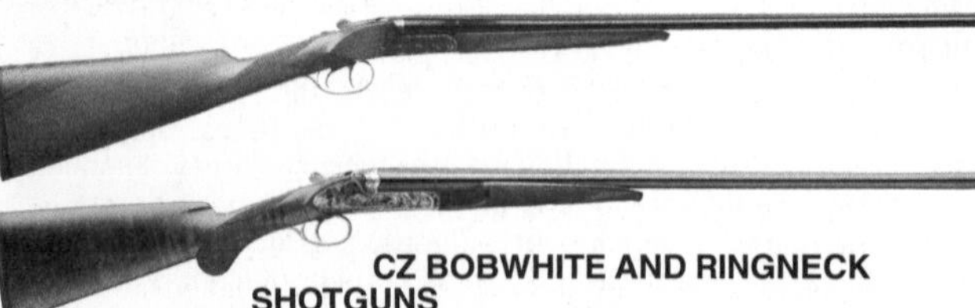

CZ BOBWHITE AND RINGNECK SHOTGUNS

Gauge: 12, 20, 28, .410. (5 screw-in chokes in 12 and 20 ga. and fixed chokes in IC and Mod in .410). **Barrel:** 20". **Weight:** 6.5 lbs. **Length:** NA. **Stock:** Sculptured Turkish walnut with straight English-style grip and double triggers (Bobwhite) or conventional American pistol grip with a single trigger (Ringneck). Both are hand checkered 20 lpi. **Features:** Both color case-hardened shotguns are hand engraved.

Price: Bobwhite. **$789.00**
Price: Ringneck. **$1,036.00**

CZ HAMMER COACH SHOTGUNS

Gauge: 12, 3" chambers. **Barrel:** 20". **Weight:** 6.7 lbs. **Length:** NA. **Stock:** NA. **Features:** Following in the tradition of the guns used by the stagecoach guards of the 1880's, this cowboy gun features double triggers, 19th century color case-hardening and fully functional external hammers.

Price: **$904.00**

EMF OLD WEST HAMMER SHOTGUN

Gauge: 12. **Barrel:** 20". **Weight:** 8 lbs. **Length:** 37" overall. **Stock:** Smooth walnut with steel butt place. **Sights:** Large brass bead. **Features:** Colt-style exposed hammers rebounding type; blued receiver and barrels; cylinder bore. Introduced 2006. Imported from China for EMF by TTN.

Price: **$474.90**

FOX, A.H., SIDE-BY-SIDE SHOTGUNS

Gauge: 16, 20, 28, .410. **Barrel:** Length and chokes to customer specifications. Rust-blued Chromox or Krupp steel. **Weight:** 5-1/2 to 6.75 lbs. **Stock:** Dimensions to customer specifications. Hand-checkered Turkish Circassian walnut with hand-rubbed oil finish. Straight, semi or full pistol grip; splinter, Schnabel or beavertail forend; traditional pad, hard rubber buttplate or skeleton butt. **Features:** Boxlock action with automatic ejectors; double or Fox single selective trigger. Scalloped, rebated and color case-hardened receiver; hand finished and handengraved. Grades differ in engraving, inlays, grade of wood, amount of hand finishing. Introduced 1993. Made in U.S. by Connecticut Shotgun Mfg.

Price: CE Grade **$14,500.00**
Price: XE Grade **$16,000.00**
Price: DE Grade **$19,000.00**
Price: FE Grade **$24,000.00**
Price: 28/.410 CE Grade. **$16,500.00**
Price: 28/.410 XE Grade. **$18,000.00**
Price: 28/.410 DE Grade. **$21,000.00**
Price: 28/.410 FE Grade **$26,000.00**

GARBI MODEL 100 DOUBLE SHOTGUN

Gauge: 12, 16, 20, 28. **Barrel:** 26", 28", choked to customer specs. **Weight:** 5-1/2 to 7.5 lbs. **Stock:** 14.5"x2.25"x1.5". European walnut. Straight grip, checkered butt, classic forend. **Features:** Sidelock action, automatic ejectors, double triggers standard. Color case-hardened action, coin finish optional. Single trigger; beavertail forend, etc. optional. Five additional models available. Imported from Spain by Wm. Larkin Moore.

Price: From **$4,850.00**

GARBI MODEL 101 SIDE-BY-SIDE SHOTGUN

Similar to the Garbi Model 100 except hand engraved with scroll engraving; select walnut stock; better overall quality than the Model 100. Imported from Spain by Wm. Larkin Moore.

Price: From **$6,250.00**

GARBI MODEL 103 A & B SIDE-BY-SIDE SHOTGUNS

Similar to the Garbi Model 100 except has Purdey-type fine scroll and rosette engraving. Better overall quality than the Model 101. Model 103B has nickel-chrome steel barrels, H&H-type easy opening mechanism; other mechanical details remain the same. Imported from Spain by Wm. Larkin Moore.

Price: Model 103A. From. **$14,100.00**
Price: Model 103B. From. **$21,600.00**

GARBI MODEL 200 SIDE-BY-SIDE SHOTGUN

Similar to the Garbi Model 100 except has heavy-duty locks, magnum proofed. Very fine Continental-style floral and scroll engraving, well figured walnut stock. Other mechanical features remain the same. Imported from Spain by Wm. Larkin Moore.

Price: **$17,100.00**

LEBEAU-COURALLY BOXLOCK SIDE-BY-SIDE SHOTGUN

Gauge: 12, 16, 20, 28, .410-bore. **Barrel:** 25" to 32". **Weight:** To customer specifications. **Stock:** French walnut. **Features:** Anson & Deely-type action with automatic ejectors; single or double triggers. Custom gun built to customer specifications. Imported from Belgium by Wm. Larkin Moore.

Price: From **$25,500.00**

LEBEAU-COURALLY SIDELOCK SIDE-BY-SIDE SHOTGUN
Gauge: 12, 16, 20, 28, .410-bore. **Barrel:** 25" to 32". **Weight:** To customer specifications. **Stock:** Fancy French walnut. **Features:** Holland & Holland-type action with automatic ejectors; single or double triggers. Custom gun built to customer specifications. Imported from Belgium by Wm. Larkin Moore.
Price: From **$56,000.00**

MERKEL MODEL 47E, 147E SIDE-BY-SIDE SHOTGUNS
Gauge: 12, 3" chambers, 16, 2.75" chambers, 20, 3" chambers. **Barrel:** 12, 16 ga.-28"; 20 ga.-26.75" (Imp. Cyl. & Mod., Mod. & Full). **Weight:** About 6.75 lbs. (12 ga.). **Stock:** Oil-finished walnut; straight English or pistol grip. **Features:** Anson & Deeley-type boxlock action with single selective or double triggers, automatic safety, cocking indicators. Color case-hardened receiver with standard arabesque engraving. Imported from Germany by Merkel USA.
Price: Model 47E (H&H ejectors) **$4,595.00**
Price: Model 147E (as above with ejectors) **$5,795.00**

MERKEL MODEL 47EL, 147EL SIDE-BY-SIDE SHOTGUNS
Similar to Model 47E except H&H style sidelock action with cocking indicators, ejectors. Silver-grayed receiver and sideplates have arabesque engraving, engraved border and screws (Model 47E), or fine hunting scene engraving (Model 147E). Limited edition. Imported from Germany by Merkel USA.
Price: Model 47EL **$7,195.00**
Price: Model 147EL. **$7,695.00**

MERKEL MODEL 280EL, 360EL SHOTGUNS
Similar to Model 47E except smaller frame. Greener cross bolt with double under-barrel locking lugs, fine engraved hunting scenes on silver-grayed receiver, luxury-grade wood, Anson and Deely boxlock action. H&H ejectors, single-selective or double triggers. Introduced 2000. Imported from Germany by Merkel USA.
Price: Model 280EL (28 gauge, 28" barrel, Imp. Cyl. and Mod. chokes) **$7,695.00**
Price: Model 360EL (.410, 28" barrel, Mod. and Full chokes). **$7,695.00**
Price: Model 280EL Combo **$11,195.00**

MERKEL MODEL 280SL AND 360SL SHOTGUNS
Similar to Model 280EL and 360EL except has sidelock action, double triggers, English-style arabesque engraving. Introduced 2000. Imported from Germany by Merkel USA.
Price: Model 280SL (28 gauge, 28" barrel, Imp. Cyl. and Mod. chokes) **$10,995.00**
Price: Model 360SL (.410, 28" barrel, Mod. and Full chokes). **$10,995.00**

MERKEL MODEL 1620 SIDE-BY-SIDE SHOTGUN
Gauge: 16. Features: Greener crossbolt with double under-barrel locking lugs, scroll-engraved case-hardened receiver, Anson and Deely boxlock aciton, Holland & Holland ejectors, English-style stock, single selective or double triggers, or pistol grip stock with single selective trgger. Imported from Germany by Merkel USA.
Price: **$4,995.00**
Price: Model 1620E; silvered, engraved receiver **$5,995.00**
Price: Model 1620 Combo; 16- and 20-gauge two-barrel set **$7,695.00**
Price: Model 1620EL; upgraded wood **$7,695.00**
Price: Model 1620EL Combo; 16- and 20-gauge two-barrel set **$11,195.00**

PIOTTI KING NO. 1 SIDE-BY-SIDE SHOTGUN
Gauge: 12, 16, 20, 28, .410. **Barrel:** 25" to 30" (12 ga.), 25" to 28" (16, 20, 28, .410). To customer specs. Chokes as specified. **Weight:** 6.5 lbs. to 8 lbs. (12 ga. to customer specs.). **Stock:** Dimensions to customer specs. Finely figured walnut; straight grip with checkered butt with classic splinter forend and hand-rubbed oil finish standard. Pistol grip, beavertail forend. **Features:** Holland & Holland pattern sidelock action, automatic ejectors. Double trigger; non-selective single trigger optional. Coin finish standard; color case-hardened optional. Top rib; level, file-cut; concave, ventilated optional. Very fine, full coverage scroll engraving with small floral bouquets. Imported from Italy by Wm. Larkin Moore.
Price: From **$38,300.00**

PIOTTI LUNIK SIDE-BY-SIDE SHOTGUN
Similar to the Piotti King No. 1 in overall quality. Has Renaissance-style large scroll engraving in relief. Best quality Holland & Holland-pattern sidelock ejector double with chopper lump (demi-bloc) barrels. Other mechanical specifications remain the same. Imported from Italy by Wm. Larkin Moore.
Price: From **$39,900.00**

PIOTTI PIUMA SIDE-BY-SIDE SHOTGUN
Gauge: 12, 16, 20, 28, .410. **Barrel:** 25" to 30" (12 ga.), 25" to 28" (16, 20, 28, .410). **Weight:** 5-1/2 to 6-1/4 lbs. (20 ga.). **Stock:** Dimensions to customer specs. Straight grip stock with walnut checkered butt, classic splinter forend, hand-rubbed oil finish are standard; pistol grip, beavertail forend, satin luster finish optional. **Features:** Anson & Deeley boxlock ejector double with chopper lump barrels. Level, file-cut rib, light scroll and rosette engraving, scalloped frame. Double triggers; single non-selective optional. Coin finish standard, color case-hardened optional. Imported from Italy by Wm. Larkin Moore.
Price: From **$19,200.00**

RIZZINI SIDELOCK SIDE-BY-SIDE SHOTGUN
Gauge: 12, 16, 20, 28, .410. **Barrel:** 25" to 30" (12, 16, 20 ga.), 25" to 28" (28, .410). To customer specs. Chokes as specified. **Weight:** 6.5 lbs. to 8 lbs. (12 ga. to customer specs). **Stock:** Dimensions to customer specs. Finely figured walnut; straight grip with checkered butt with classic splinter forend and hand-rubbed oil finish standard. Pistol grip, beavertail forend. **Features:** Sidelock action, auto ejectors. Double triggers or non-selective single trigger standard. Coin finish standard. Imported from Italy by Wm. Larkin Moore.
Price: 12, 20 ga. From. **$106,000.00**
Price: 28, .410 bore. From. **$95,000.00**

STOEGER UPLANDER SIDE-BY-SIDE SHOTGUNS
Gauge: 16, 28, 2-3/4 chambers. 12, 20, .410, 3" chambers. **Barrel:** 22", 24", 26", 28". **Weight:** 7.3 lbs. **Sights:** Brass bead. **Features:** Double trigger, IC & M fixed choke tubes with gun.
Price: With fixed or screw-in chokes **$369.00**
Price: Supreme, screw-in chokes, 12 or 20 ga.. . . . .**$489.00**
Price: Youth, 20 ga. or .410, 22" barrel, double trigger **$369.00**
Price: Combo, 20/28 ga. or 12/20 ga. **$649.00**

STOEGER COACH GUN SIDE-BY-SIDE SHOTGUNS
Gauge: 12, 20, 2-3/4", 3" chambers. **Barrel:** 20". **Weight:** 6.5 lbs. **Stock:** Brown hardwood, classic beavertail forend. **Sights:** Brass bead. **Features:** IC & M fixed chokes, tang auto safety, auto extractors, black plastic buttplate. Imported by Benelli USA.
Price: Supreme blued finish **$469.00**
Price: Supreme blued barrel, stainless receiver **$469.00**
Price: Silverado Coach Gun with English synthetic stock **$469.00**

TRISTAR BRITTANY CLASSIC SIDE-BY-SIDE SHOTGUN
Gauge: 12, 16, 20, 28, .410, 3" chambers. **Barrel:** 27", chrome lined, three Beretta-style choke tubes (IC, M, F). **Weight:** 6.3 to 6.7 lbs. **Stock:** Rounded pistol grip, satin oil finish. **Features:** Engraved case-colored one-piece frame, auto selective ejectors, single selective trigger, solid raised barrel rib, top tang safety. Imported from Spain by Tristar Sporting Arms Ltd.
Price: From **$1,419.00**

WEATHERBY SBS ATHENA D'ITALIA SIDE-BY-SIDE SHOTGUNS
Gauge: D'Italia: 12, 20, 2-3/4" or 3" chambers, 28, 2-3/4" chambers. **Barrel:** 26" on 20 and 28 gauges; 28" on 12 ga. Chrome-lined, lengthened forcing cones, backbored. **Weight:** 6.75 to 7.25 lbs. **Length:** 42.5" to 44.5". **Stock:** Walnut, 20-lpi laser cut checkering, "New Scottish" pattern. **Features:** All come with foam-lined take-down case. Machined steel receiver, hardened and chromed with coin finish, engraved triggerguard with roll-formed border. D'Italia has double triggers, brass front bead. PG is identical to D'Italia, except for rounded pistol grip and semi-beavertail forearm. Deluxe features sculpted frameheads, Bolino-style engraved game scene with floral engraving. AAA Fancy Turkish walnut, straight grip, 24-lpi hand checkering, hand-rubbed oil finish. Single mechanical trigger; right barrel fires first. Imported from Italy by Weatherby.
Price: SBS Athena D'Italia SBS **$3,129.00**
Price: SBS Athena D'Italia PG SBS **$3,799.00**

BERETTA DT10 TRIDENT TRAP TOP SINGLE SHOTGUN

Gauge: 12, 3" chamber. **Barrel:** 34"; five Optima Choke tubes (Full, Full, Imp. Modified, Mod. and Imp. Cyl.). **Weight:** 8.8 lbs. **Stock:** High-grade walnut; adjustable. **Features:** Detachable, adjustable trigger group; Optima Bore for improved shot pattern and reduced recoil; slim Optima Choke tubes; raised and thickened receiver for long life. Introduced 2000. Imported from Italy by Beretta USA.

Price: **$8,650.00**

BROWNING BT-99 TRAP O/U SHOTGUNS

Gauge: 12. **Barrel:** 30", 32", 34". **Stock:** Walnut; standard or adjustable. **Weight:** 7 lbs. 11 oz. to 9 lbs. **Features:** Back-bored single barrel; interchangeable chokes; beavertail forearm; extractor only; high rib.

Price: BT-99 w/conventional comb, 32" or 34" barrels **$1,529.00**

Price: BT-99 w/adjustable comb, 32" or 34" barrels **$1,839.00**

Price: BT-99 Golden Clays w/adjustable comb, 32" or 34" barrels **$3,989.00**

Price: BT-99 Grade III, 32" or 34" barrels, intr. 2008 . . . . **$2,369.00**

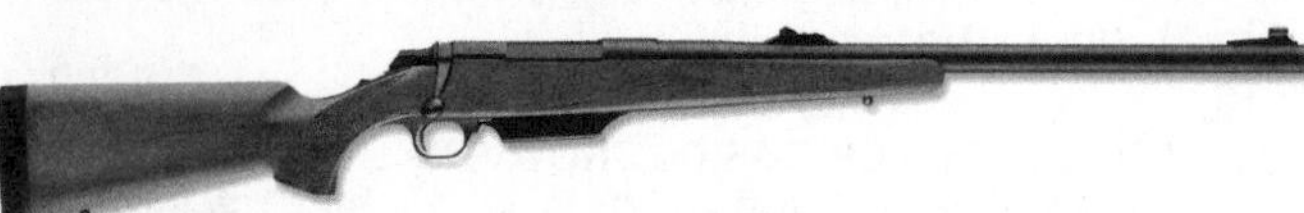

BROWNING A-BOLT SHOTGUN HUNTER BOLT ACTION SHOTGUN

Gauge: 12 ga. 3" chamber. **Barrel:** 22". **Weight:** 7 lbs. 2 ozs. **Length:** 43.75". **Stock:** Satin finish walnut stock and forearm – checkered. **Features:** Drilled and tapped for scope mounts, 60° bolt action lift, detachable two-round magazine, and top-tang safety. Sling swivel studs installed, rrecoil pad, TRUGLO®/Marble's® fiber-optic front sight with rear sight adjustable for windage and elevation.

Price: From **$1,200.00**

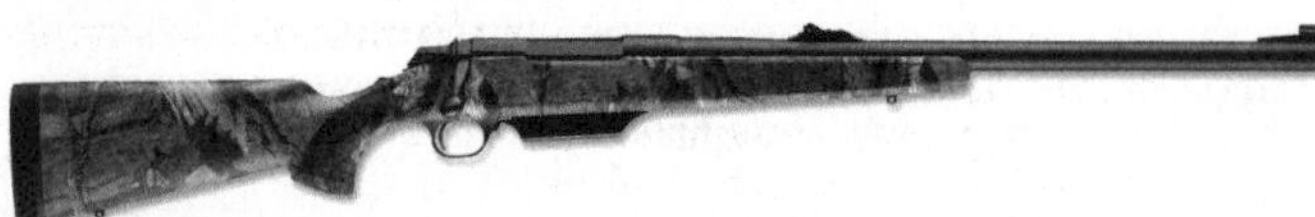

BROWNING A-BOLT SHOTGUN, MOSSY OAK BREAK-UP INFINITY BOLT ACTION SHOTGUN

Gauge: 12 ga. 3" chamber. **Barrel:** 22". **Weight:** 7 lbs. 2 ozs. **Length:** 43.75". **Stock:** Composite stock and forearm, textured gripping surfaces, Mossy Oak® Break-Up® Infinity™ camo finish • Dura-Touch® Armor Coating. **Features:** Drilled and tapped for scope mounts, 60° bolt action lift, detachable two-round magazine, and top-tang safety. Sling swivel studs installed, rrecoil pad, TRUGLO®/Marble's® fiber-optic front sight with rear sight adjustable for windage and elevation.

Price: From **$1,240.00**

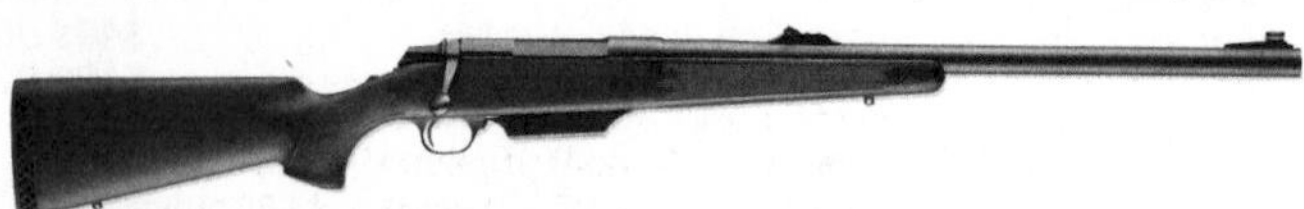

BROWNING A-BOLT SHOTGUN STALKER BOLT ACTION SHOTGUN

Gauge: 12 ga. 3" chamber. **Barrel:** 22". **Weight:** 7 lbs. **Length:** 43.75". **Stock:** Composite stock and forearm, textured gripping surfaces, Dura-Touch® Armor Coating. **Features:** Drilled and tapped for scope mounts, 60° bolt action lift, detachable two-round magazine, and top-tang safety. Sling swivel studs installed, rrecoil pad, TRUGLO®/Marble's® fiber-optic front sight with rear sight adjustable for windage and elevation.

Price: From **$1,100.00**

HARRINGTON & RICHARDSON ULTRA SLUG HUNTER/TAMER SHOTGUNS

Gauge: 12, 20 ga., 3" chamber, .410. **Barrel:** 20" to 24" rifled. **Weight:** 6 to 9 lbs. **Length:** 34.5" to 40". **Stock:** Hardwood, laminate, or polymer with full pistol grip; semi-beavertail forend. **Sights:** Gold bead front. **Features:** Break-open action with side-lever release, automatic ejector. Introduced 1994. From H&R 1871, LLC.

Price: Ultra Slug Hunter, blued, hardwood **$273.00**

Price: Ultra Slug Hunter Youth, blued, hardwood, 13-1/8" LOP **$273.00**

Price: Ultra Slug Hunter Deluxe, blued, laminated **$273.00**

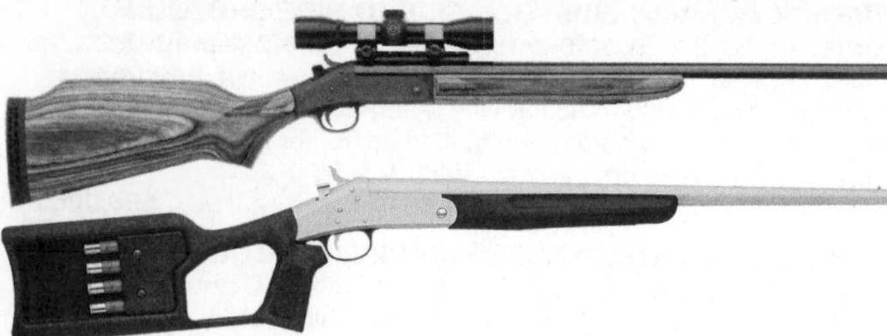

Price: Tamer .410 bore, stainless barrel, black polymer stock **$173.00**

HARRINGTON & RICHARDSON ULTRA LITE SLUG HUNTER

Gauge: 12, 20 ga., 3" chamber. **Barrel:** 24" rifled. **Weight:** 5.25 lbs. **Length:** 40". **Stock:** Hardwood with walnut finish, full pistol grip, recoil pad, sling swivel studs. **Sights:** None; base included. **Features:** Youth Model, available in 20 ga. has 20" rifled barrel. Deluxe Model has checkered laminated stock and forend. From H&R 1871, LLC.

Price: **$194.00**

HARRINGTON & RICHARDSON ULTRA SLUG HUNTER THUMBHOLE STOCK

Similar to the Ultra Lite Slug Hunter but with laminated thumbhole stock and weighs 8.5 lbs.

Price: . . . . **NA**

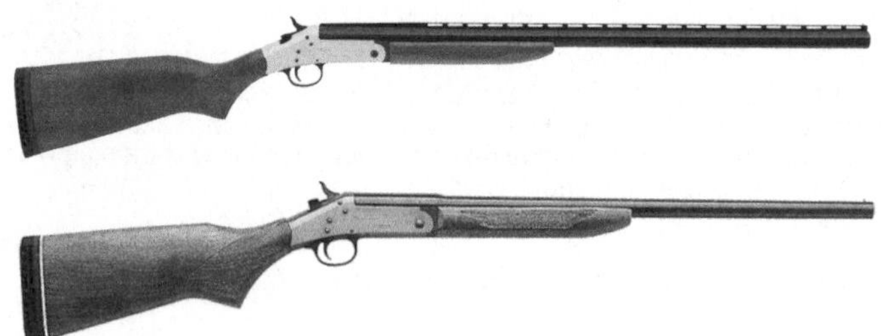

HARRINGTON & RICHARDSON TOPPER MODELS

Gauge: 12, 16, 20, .410, up to 3.5" chamber. **Barrel:** 22 to 28". **Weight:** 5-7 lbs. **Stock:** Polymer, hardwood, or black walnut. **Features:** Satin nickel frame, blued barrel. Reintroduced 1992. From H&R 1871, LLC.

Price: Deluxe Classic, 12/20 ga., 28" barrel w/vent rib **$225.00**

Price: Topper Deluxe 12 ga., 28" barrel, black hardwood **$179.00**

Price: Topper 12, 16, 20 ga., .410, 26" to 28", black hardwood **$153.00**

Price: Topper Junior 20 ga., .410, 22" barrel, hardwood **$160.00**

Price: Topper Junior Classic, 20 ga., .410, checkered hardwood **$160.00**

HARRINGTON & RICHARDSON TOPPER TRAP GUN

Similar to other Topper Models but with select checkered walnut stock and forend wtih fluted comb and full pistol grip; 30" barrel with two white beads and screw-in chokes (Improved Modified Extended included); deluxe Pachmayr trap recoil pad.

Price: **$360.00**

KRIEGHOFF K-80 SINGLE BARREL TRAP GUN

Gauge: 12, 2-3/4" chamber. **Barrel:** 32" or 34" Unsingle. Fixed Full or choke tubes. **Weight:** About 8-3/4 lbs. **Stock:** Four stock dimensions or adjustable stock available. All hand-checkered European walnut. **Features:** Satin nickel finish. Selective mechanical trigger adjustable for finger position. Tapered step vent rib. Adjustable point of impact.

Price: Standard grade Full Unsingle, from **$10,080.00**

KRIEGHOFF KX-5 TRAP GUN

Gauge: 12, 2-3/4" chamber. **Barrel:** 32", 34"; choke tubes. **Weight:**

Prices given are believed to be accurate at time of publication however, many factors affect retail pricing so exact prices are not possible.

About 8.5 lbs. **Stock:** Factory adjustable stock. European walnut. **Features:** Ventilated tapered step rib. Adjustable position trigger, optional release trigger. Fully adjustable rib. Satin gray electroless nickel receiver. Fitted aluminum case. Imported from Germany by Krieghoff International, Inc.
Price: **$5,395.00**

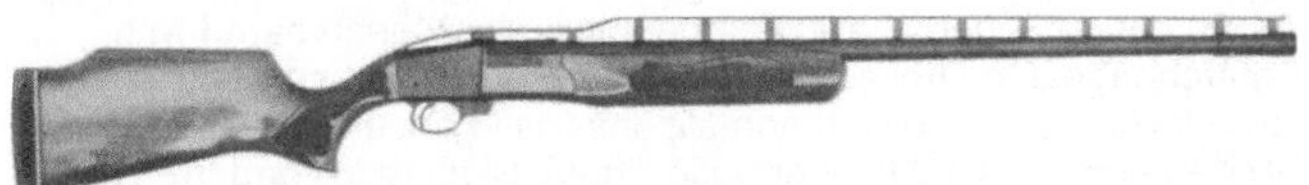

LJUTIC MONO GUN SINGLE BARREL SHOTGUN
Gauge: 12 only. **Barrel:** 34", choked to customer specs; hollow-milled rib, 35.5" sight plane. **Weight:** Approx. 9 lbs. **Stock:** To customer specs. Oil finish, hand checkered. **Features:** Custom gun. Pull or release trigger; removable trigger guard contains trigger and hammer mechanism; Ljutic pushbutton opener on front of trigger guard. From Ljutic Industries.
Price: Std., med. or Olympic rib, custom bbls., fixed choke. . **$7,495.00**
Price: Stainless steel mono gun **$8,495.00**

LJUTIC LTX PRO 3 DELUXE MONO GUN
Deluxe, lightweight version of the Mono gun with high quality wood, upgrade checkering, special rib height, screw-in chokes, ported and cased.
Price: **$8,995.00**
Price: Stainless steel model **$9,995.00**

NEW ENGLAND FIREARMS PARDNER AND TRACKER II SHOTGUNS
Gauge: 10, 12, 16, 20, 28, .410, up to 3.5" chamber for 10 and 12 ga. 16, 28, 2-3/4" chamber. **Barrel:** 24" to 30". **Weight:** Varies from 5 to 9.5 lbs. **Length:** Varies from 36" to 48". **Stock:** Walnut-finished hardwood with full pistol grip, synthetic, or camo finish. **Sights:** Bead front on most. **Features:** Transfer bar ignition; break-open action with side-lever release. Introduced 1987. From New England Firearms.
Price: Pardner, all gauges, hardwood stock, 26" to 32" blued barrel, Mod. or Full choke **$140.00**
Price: Pardner Youth, hardwood stock, straight grip, 22" blued barrel. **$149.00**
Price: Pardner Screw-In Choke model, intr. 2006 . . . . **$164.00**
Price: Turkey model, 10/12 ga., camo finish or black. . . . . **$192.00 to $259.00**
Price: Youth Turkey, 20 ga., camo finish or black. **$192.00**
Price: Waterfowl, 10 ga., camo finish or hardwood **$227.00**
Price: Tracker II slug gun, 12/20 ga., hardwood **$196.00**

ROSSI CIRCUIT JUDGE
Revolving shotgun chambered in .410 (2-1/2- or 3-inch/.45 Colt. Based on Taurus Judge handgun. Features include 18.5-inch barrel; fiber optic front sight; 5-round cylinder; hardwood Monte Carlo stock.
Price: **$475.00**
Price: Tactical Black Synthetic **$633.00**
Price: 44Mag. **$633.00**
Price: 28Ga. **$633.00**
Price: Stainless Bl Hardwood Monte Carlo Stk. **$680.00**

ROSSI SINGLE-SHOT SHOTGUNS
Gauge: 12, 20, .410. **Barrel:** 22" (Youth), 28". **Weight:** 3.75-5.25 lbs. **Stocks:** Wood. **Sights:** Bead front sight, fully adjustable fiber optic sight on Slug and Turkey. **Features:** Single-shot break open, 8 models available, positive ejection, internal transfer bar mechanism, trigger block system, Taurus Security System, blued finish, Rifle Slug has ported barrel.
Price: From **$117.00**

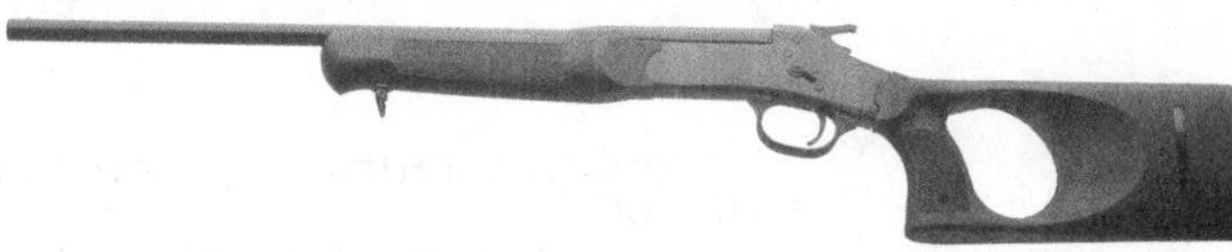

ROSSI TUFFY SHOTGUN
Gauge: .410. **Barrel:** 18-1/2". **Weight:** 3 lbs. **Length:** 29.5" overall. **Features:** Single-shot break-open model with black synthetic thumbhole stock in blued or stainless finish.
Price: . . . . **$164.00-$172.00**

ROSSI MATCHED PAIRS
Gauge/Caliber: 12, 20, .410, .22 Mag, .22LR, .17HMR, .223 Rem, .243 Win, .270 Win, .30-06, .308 Win, .50 (black powder). **Barrel:** 23", 28". **Weight:** 5-6.3 lbs. **Stocks:** Wood or black synthetic. **Sights:** Bead front on shotgun barrel, fully adjustable front and rear on rifle barrel, drilled and tapped for scope, fully adjustable fiber optic sights (black powder). **Features:** Single-shot break open, 27 models available, internal transfer bar mechanism, manual external safety, blue finish, trigger block system, Taurus Security System, youth models available.
Price: Rimfire/Shotgun, from. **$160.00**
Price: Centerfire/Shotgun **$271.95**
Price: Black Powder Matched Pair, from **$262.00**

ROSSI MATCHED SET
Gauge/Caliber: 12, 20, .22 LR, .17 HMR, .243 Win, .270 Win, .50 (black powder). **Barrel:** 33.5". **Weight:** 6.25-6.3 lbs. **Stocks:** Wood. **Sights:** Bead front on shotgun barrel, fully adjustable front and rear on rifle barrel, drilled and tapped for scope, fully adjustable fiber optic sights (black powder). **Features:** Single-shot break open, 4 models available, internal transfer bar mechanism, manual external safety, blue finish, trigger block system, Taurus Security System, youth models available.
Price: From **$374.00**

TAR-HUNT RSG-12 PROFESSIONAL RIFLED SLUG GUN
Gauge: 12, 2-3/4" or 3" chamber, 1-shot magazine. **Barrel:** 23", fully rifled with muzzle brake. **Weight:** 7.75 lbs. **Length:** 41.5" overall. **Stock:** Matte black McMillan fiberglass with Pachmayr Decelerator pad. **Sights:** None furnished; comes with Leupold windage or Weaver bases. **Features:** Uses rifle-style action with two locking lugs; two-position safety; Shaw barrel; single-stage, trigger; muzzle brake. Many options available. All models have area-controlled feed action. Introduced 1991. Made in U.S. by Tar-Hunt Custom Rifles, Inc.
Price: 12 ga. Professional model. **$2,585.00**
Price: Left-hand model add. **$110.00**

TAR-HUNT RSG-16 ELITE SHOTGUN
Similar to RSG-12 Professional except 16 gauge; right- or left-hand versions.
Price: **$2,585.00**

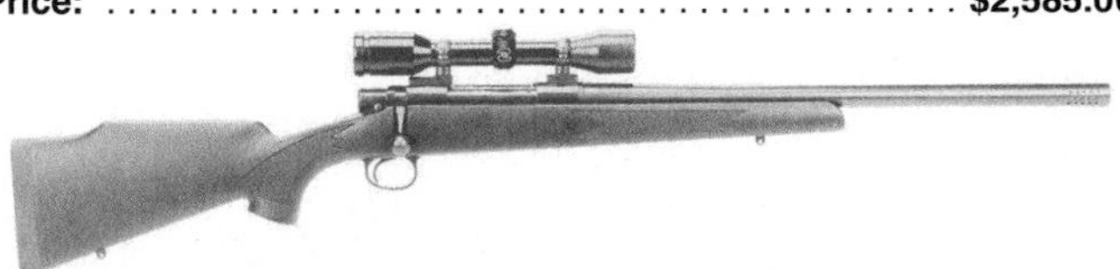

TAR-HUNT RSG-20 MOUNTAINEER SLUG GUN
Similar to the RSG-12 Professional except chambered for 20 gauge (2-3/4" and 3" shells); 23" Shaw rifled barrel, with muzzle brake; two-lug

Prices given are believed to be accurate at time of publication however, many factors affect retail pricing so exact prices are not possible.

bolt; one-shot blind magazine; matte black finish; McMillan fiberglass stock with Pachmayr Decelerator pad; receiver drilled and tapped for Rem. 700 bases. Right- or left-hand versions. Weighs 6.5 lbs. Introduced 1997. Made in U.S. by Tar-Hunt Custom Rifles, Inc.
Price: **$2,585.00**

THOMPSON/CENTER ENCORE RIFLED SLUG GUN
Gauge: 20, 3" chamber. **Barrel:** 26", fully rifled. **Weight:** About 7 lbs. **Length:** 40.5" overall. **Stock:** Walnut with walnut forearm. **Sights:** Steel; click-adjustable rear and ramp-style front, both with fiber optics. **Features:** Encore system features a variety of rifle, shotgun and muzzle-loading rifle barrels interchangeable with the same frame. Break-open design operates by pulling up and back on trigger guard spur. Composite stock and forearm available. Introduced 2000.
Price: **$684.00**

THOMPSON/CENTER ENCORE TURKEY GUN
Gauge: 12 ga. **Barrel:** 24". **Features:** All-camo finish, high definition Realtree Hardwoods HD camo.
Price: **$763.00**

THOMPSON/CENTER ENCORE PROHUNTER TURKEY GUN
Contender-style break-action single shot shotgun chambered in 12 or 20 gauge 3-inch shells. Features include 24-inch barrel with interchangeable choke tubes (Extra Full supplied), composite buttstock and forend with non-slip inserts in cheekpiece, pistol grip and forend. Adjustable fiber optic sights, Sims recoil pad, AP camo finish overall. Overall length: 40.5 inches. Weight: 6-1/2 lbs.
Price: **$799.00**

BENELLI M3 CONVERTIBLE SHOTGUN

Gauge: 12, 2-3/4", 3" chambers, 5-shot magazine. **Barrel:** 19.75" (Cyl.). **Weight:** 7 lbs., 4oz. **Length:** 41" overall. **Stock:** High-impact polymer with sling loop in side of butt; rubberized pistol grip on stock. **Sights:** Open rifle, fully adjustable. Ghost ring and rifle type. **Features:** Combination pump/auto action. Alloy receiver with inertia recoil rotating locking lug bolt; matte finish; automatic shell release lever. Introduced 1989. Imported by Benelli USA. Price with pistol grip, open rifle sights.

Price: With ghost ring sights, pistol grip stock. **$1,589.00**

BENELLI M2 TACTICAL SHOTGUN

Gauge: 12, 2-3/4", 3" chambers, 5-shot magazine. **Barrel:** 18.5" IC, M, F choke tubes. **Weight:** 6.7 lbs. **Length:** 39.75" overall. **Stock:** Black polymer. **Sights:** Rifle type ghost ring system, tritium night sights optional. **Features:** Semiauto intertia recoil action. Cross-bolt safety; bolt release button; matte-finish metal. Introduced 1993. Imported from Italy by Benelli USA.

Price: from. . . . . **$1,239.00 to $1,359.00**

BENELLI M4 TACTICAL SHOTGUN

Gauge: 12 ga., 3" chamber. **Barrel:** 18.5". **Weight:** 7.8 lbs. **Length:** 40" overall. **Stock:** Synthetic. **Sights:** Ghost Ring rear, fixed blade front. **Features:** Auto-regulating gas-operated (ARGO) action, choke tube, Picatinny rail, standard and collapsible stocks available, optional LE tactical gun case. Introduced 2006. Imported from Italy by Benelli USA.

Price: Pistol grip stock, black synthetic **$1,699.00**
Price: Desert camo pistol grip (2007) **$1,829.00**

BERETTA TX4 STORM SEMIAUTO SHOTGUN

Gauge: 12-gas operated - 3" chamber. **Barrel:** 18" barrel. **Weight:** 6.4 lbs.. **Length:** 39.2". **Stock:** Fixed in synthetic material with black ruber overlays. **Features:** The reduced felt recoil is complemented by the infallible reliability Beretta shotguns are known for. Weighing under 6 ½ pounds, the compact Tx4 with its 18" barrel is very maneuverable, while maintaining a 5+1 round capacity. Like the Cx4, the shotgun's length of pull may be adjusted with ½" spacers (one included), while the soft rubber grip inlays on the stock and fore-end ensure a firm grip in all situations. A metal Picatinny rail is mounted to the receiver to accept your optics or the included rugged and fully adjustable ghost ring sight. Adopting Beretta's new Optimabore HP choke tube system, the included choke may be replaced with several optional accessories. Imported from Italy by Benelli USA., Corp.

Price: **$1,450.00**

CITADEL LE TACTICAL PUMP SHOTGUN

Gauge: 12 ga., 3" chamber. **Barrel:** 22". **Weight:** 5.8 lbs -7.15 lbs. **Length:** 49". **Stock:** Composite stock with close radius pistol grip; Speed Lock forearm; textured gripping surfaces; shim adjustable for length of pull, cast and drop; Mossy Oak® Bottomland™ camo finish; Dura-Touch® Armor Coating. **Features:** These shotguns are built in the U.S.A., insuring exacting parts match and a superior fit/finish. Using a common receiver and trigger group, the Citadel LE comes in four models: Spec-Ops, Talon, Pistol Grip with Heat Shield and Standard. All models feature a lightweight receiver, 7 +1 magazine capacity, 20 inch barrel, ergonomic forend, quick feed short stroke pump and rifle style sights. The Spec-Ops model features the BLACKHAWK!® Spec-Ops stock, which is adjustable for 4 inches of LOP, and estimated at absorbing up to 70% of felt recoil. The Spec-Ops gets you on target quickly – and keeps you there shot after shot. The Talon model also offers 70% felt recoil reduction with a skeletonized thumbhole stock from BLACKHAWK! that permits free hand movement with even the heaviest of gloves, and a short, 13.5 inch LOP. Finally, the Pistol Grip and Standard models offer a traditional, synthetic stock with a fixed, 13.5 inch LOP.

Price: Standard Stock **$466.00**
Price: Spec-Ops **$632.00**
Price: Talon **$632.00**
Price: Pistol grip with heat shield **$495.00**

KEL-TEC KSG BULL-PUP TWIN-TUBE SHOTGUN

The shotgun bears a stunning resemblance to the South African designed Neostead pump action scattergun. The operator is able to move a switch located near the top of the grip to select the right or left tube, or move the switch to the center to eject a shell without chambering another round. The bull-pup design results in an overall length of only 26" with an 18.5" barrel while the bottom eject design makes the firearm truly ambidextrous. The incredibly short overall length makes it more nimble than a sawed off shotgun, and with a 14+1 capacity with 2 3/4" you don't sacrifice ammunition capacity to get a shotty in a small package. Optional accessories include a factory installed picatinny rail with flip-up sights and a pistol grip.

Price: **$800.00**

MOSSBERG MODEL 500 SPECIAL PURPOSE SHOTGUNS

Gauge: 12, 20, .410, 3" chamber. **Barrel:** 18.5", 20" (Cyl.). **Weight:** 7 lbs. **Stock:** Walnut-finished hardwood or black synthetic. **Sights:** Metal bead front. **Features:** Available in 6- or 8-shot models. Top-mounted safety, double action slide bars, swivel studs, rubber recoil pad. Blue, Parkerized, Marinecote finishes. Mossberg Cablelock included. From Mossberg. The HS410 Home Security model chambered for .410 with 3" chamber; has pistol grip forend, thick recoil pad, muzzle brake and has special spreader choke on the 18.5" barrel. Overall length is 37.5", weight is 6.25 lbs. Blue finish; synthetic field stock. Mossberg Cablelock and video included. Mariner model has Marinecote metal finish to resist rust and corrosion. Synthetic field stock; pistol grip kit included. 500 Tactical 6-shot has black synthetic tactical stock. Introduced 1990.

Price: Rolling Thunder, 6-shot. **$471.00**
Price: Tactical Cruiser, 18.5" barrel **$434.00**
Price: Persuader/Cruiser, 6 shot, from **$394.00**
Price: Persuader/Cruiser, 8 shot, from **$394.00**
Price: HS410 Home Security **$404.00**
Price: Mariner 6 or 9 shot, from **$538.00**
Price: Tactical 6 shot, from **$509.00**
Price: 500 Blackwater SPX **$447.00**
Price: 500 Chainsaw pistol grip only; removable top handle . . . **$491.00**
Price: 500 Tactical Tri-Rail Adjustable 6-shot **$553.00-789.00**

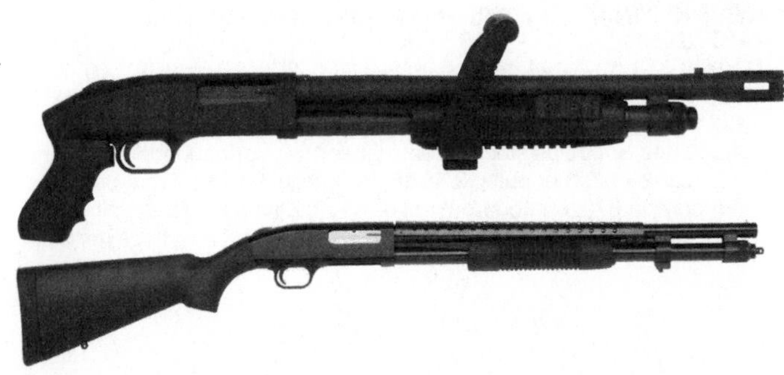

MOSSBERG MODEL 590 SPECIAL PURPOSE SHOTGUN

Gauge: 12, 3" chamber, 9 shot magazine. **Barrel:** 20" (Cyl.). **Weight:** 7.25 lbs. **Stock:** Synthetic field or Speedfeed. **Sights:** Metal bead front or Ghost Ring. **Features:** Top-mounted safety, double slide action bars. Comes with heat shield, bayonet lug, swivel studs,

rubber recoil pad. Blue, Parkerized or Marinecote finish. Mossberg Cablelock included. From Mossberg.
Price: Synthetic stock, from. **$471.00**
Price: Speedfeed stock, from **$552.00**

MOSSBERG 930 TACTICAL AUTOLOADER WITH HEAT SHIELD
Similar to Model 930 Tactical but with ventilated heat shield handguard.
Price: **$626.00**

MOSSBERG 930 SPECIAL PURPOSE SERIES SEMIAUTO SHOTGUN
Gauge: 12 ga., 3" chamber. **Barrel:** 28" flat ventilated rib. **Weight:** 7.3 lbs. **Length:** 49". **Stock:** Composite stock with close radius pistol grip; Speed Lock forearm; textured gripping surfaces; shim adjustable for length of pull, cast and drop; Mossy Oak® Bottomland™ camo finish; Dura-Touch® Armor Coating. **Features:** 930 Special Purpose shotguns feature a self-regulating gas system that vents excess gas to aid in recoil reduction and eliminate stress on critical components. All 930 autoloaders chamber both 2 3/4 inch and 3-inch 12-gauge shotshells with ease—from target loads, to non-toxic magnum loads, to the latest sabot slug ammo. Magazine capacity is 7+1 on models with extended magazine tube, 4+1 on models without. To complete the package, each Mossberg 930 includes a set of specially designed spacers for quick adjustment of the horizontal and vertical angle of the stock, bringing a custom-feel fit to every shooter. All 930 Special Purpose models feature a drilled and tapped receiver, factory-ready for Picatinny rail, scope base or optics installation. 930 SPX models conveniently come with a factory-mounted Picatinny rail and LPA/M16-Style Ghost Ring combination sight right out of the box. Other sighting options include a basic front bead, or white-dot front sights. Mossberg 930 Special Purpose shotguns are available in a variety of configurations; 5-shot tactical barrel, 5-shot with muzzle brake, 8-shot pistol-grip, and even a 5-shot security / field combo.
Price: 930 Blackwater Series **$807.00**
Price: 930 Roadblocker. **$650.00**
Price: 930 Spx Pistol Grip. **$824.00**
Price: 930 Home Security. **$572.00**
Price: 930 Special Purpose. **$634.00**
Price: 930 Special Purpose Tactical **$617.00**
Price: 930 Tactical Lpa M-16 . . . .**$734.00**
Price: 930 Tactical Barrel With Heat Shield. **$638.00**

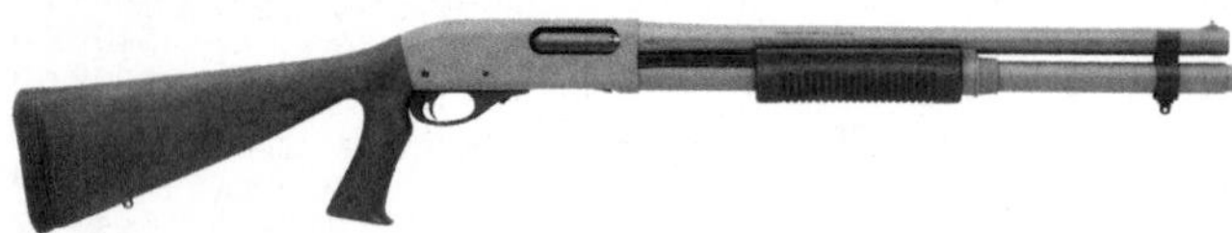

REMINGTON MODEL 870 AND MODEL 1100 TACTICAL SHOTGUNS
Gauge: 870: 12, 2-3/4 or 3" chamber; 1100: 2-3/4". **Barrel:** 18", 20", 22" (Cyl or IC). **Weight:** 7.5-7.75 lbs. **Length:** 38.5-42.5" overall. **Stock:** Black synthetic, synthetic Speedfeed IV full pistol-grip stock, or Knoxx Industries SpecOps stock w/recoil-absorbing spring-loaded cam and adjustable length of pull (12" to 16", 870 only). **Sights:** Front post w/ dot only on 870; rib and front dot on 1100. **Features:** R3 recoil pads, LimbSaver technology to reduce felt recoil, 2-, 3- or 4-shot extensions based on barrel length; matte-olive-drab barrels and receivers. Model 1100 Tactical is available with Speedfeed IV pistol grip stock or standard black synthetic stock and forend. Speedfeed IV model has an 18" barrel with two-shot extension. Standard synthetic-stocked version is equipped with 22" barrel and four-shot extension. Introduced 2006. From Remington Arms Co.
Price: 870, Speedfeed IV stock, 3" chamber, 38.5" overall, from. **$587.00**
Price: 870, SpecOps stock, 3" chamber, 38.5" overall, from . . . **$587.00**
Price: 1100, synthetic stock, 2-3/4" chamber, 42.5" overall **$945.00**
Price: 870 TAC Desert Recon (2008), 18" barrel, 2-shot. **$692.00**

REMINGTON 870 EXPRESS TACTICAL A-TACS CAMO
Pump action shotgun chambered for 2-3/4- and 3-inch 12-ga. Features include full A-TACS digitized camo; 18-1/2-inch barrel; extended ported Tactical RemChoke; SpeedFeed IV pistol-grip stock with SuperCell recoil pad; fully adjustable XS® Ghost Ring Sight rail with removable white bead front sight; 7-round capacity with factory-installed 2-shot extension; drilled and tapped receiver; sling swivel stud.
Price: **$665.00**

REMINGTON 887 NITRO MAG TACTICAL
Pump action shotgun chambered in 12-ga., 2-3/4 to 3-1/2 inch. Features include 18-1/2-inch barrel with ported, extended tactical RemChoke; 2-shot magazine extension; barrel clamp with integral Picatinny rails; ArmorLokt coating; synthetic stock and forend with specially contour grip panels.
Price: **$498.00**

TACTICAL RESPONSE TR-870 STANDARD MODEL SHOTGUNS
Gauge: 12, 3" chamber, 7-shot magazine. **Barrel:** 18" (Cyl.). **Weight:** 9 lbs. **Length:** 38" overall. **Stock:** Fiberglass-filled polypropolene with non-snag recoil absorbing butt pad. Nylon tactical forend houses flashlight. **Sights:** Trak-Lock ghost ring sight system. Front sight has Tritium insert. **Features:** Highly modified Remington 870P with Parkerized finish. Comes with nylon three-way adjustable sling, high visibility non-binding follower, high performance magazine spring, Jumbo Head safety, and Side Saddle extended 6-shot shell carrier on left side of receiver. Introduced 1991. From Scattergun Technologies, Inc.
Price: Standard model **$1,050.00**
Price: Border Patrol model, from **$1,050.00**
Price: Professional model, from **$1,070.00**

TRISTAR COBRA PUMP
Gauge: 12, 3". **Barrel:** 28". **Weight:** 6.7 lbs. Three Beretta-style choke tubes (IC, M, F). **Length:** NA. **Stock:** Matte black synthetic stock and forearm. **Sights:** Vent rib with matted sight plane. **Features:** Five-year warranty. Cobra Tactical Pump Shotgun magazine holds 7, return spring in forearm, 20" barrel, Cylinder choke. Introduced 2008. Imported by Tristar Sporting Arms Ltd.
Price: Tactical **$349.00**

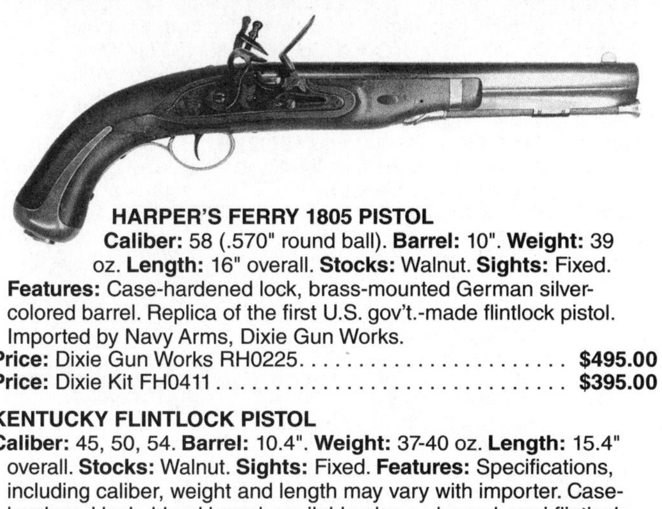

HARPER'S FERRY 1805 PISTOL

Caliber: 58 (.570" round ball). **Barrel:** 10". **Weight:** 39 oz. **Length:** 16" overall. **Stocks:** Walnut. **Sights:** Fixed. **Features:** Case-hardened lock, brass-mounted German silver-colored barrel. Replica of the first U.S. gov't.-made flintlock pistol. Imported by Navy Arms, Dixie Gun Works.

Price: Dixie Gun Works RH0225. . . . . **$495.00**
Price: Dixie Kit FH0411 . . . . **$395.00**

KENTUCKY FLINTLOCK PISTOL

Caliber: 45, 50, 54. **Barrel:** 10.4". **Weight:** 37-40 oz. **Length:** 15.4" overall. **Stocks:** Walnut. **Sights:** Fixed. **Features:** Specifications, including caliber, weight and length may vary with importer. Case-hardened lock, blued barrel; available also as brass barrel flintlock Model 1821. Imported by The Armoury.

Price: Single cased set (Navy Arms) **$375.00**

KENTUCKY PERCUSSION PISTOL

Similar to Flint version but percussion lock. Imported by The Armoury, Navy Arms, CVA (50-cal.).

Price: . . . . **$129.95 to $225.00**
Price: Steel barrel (Armoury) **$179.00**
Price: Single cased set (Navy Arms) **$355.00**
Price: Double cased set (Navy Arms) **$600.00**

LE PAGE PERCUSSION DUELING PISTOL

Caliber: .45. **Barrel:** 10.25" octagon, rifled. **Weight:** 36-41 oz. **Length:** 16.9" overall. **Stocks:** Walnut, fluted butt. **Sights:** Blade front, open style rear. **Features:** Double set trigger. Bright barrel, brass furniture (silver plated). Imported by Dixie Gun Works

Price: PH0310. . . . .**$525.00**

LYMAN PLAINS PISTOL

Caliber: 50 or 54. **Barrel:** 8"; 1:30" twist, both calibers. **Weight:** 50 oz. **Length:** 15" overall. **Stocks:** Walnut half-stock. **Sights:** Blade front, square notch rear adjustable for windage. **Features:** Polished brass trigger guard and ramrod tip, color case-hardened coil spring lock, springloaded trigger, stainless steel nipple, blackened iron furniture. Hooked patent breech, detachable belt hook. Introduced 1981. From Lyman Products.

Price: Finished **$370.00**
Price: Kit **$310.00**

PEDERSOLI MANG TARGET PISTOL

Caliber: 38. **Barrel:** 10.5", octagonal; 1:15" twist, **Weight:** 2.5 lbs. **Length:** 17.25" overall. **Stocks:** Walnut with fluted grip. **Sights:** Blade front, open rear adjustable for windage. **Features:** Browned barrel, polished breech plug, remainder color case-hardened. Imported from Italy by Dixie Gun Works.

Price: PH0503. . . . . **$1,500.00**

QUEEN ANNE FLINTLOCK PISTOL

Caliber: 50 (.490" round ball). **Barrel:** 7.5", smoothbore. **Stocks:** Walnut. **Sights:** None. **Features:** German silver-colored steel barrel, fluted brass trigger guard, brass mask on butt. Lockplate left in the white. Made by Pedersoli in Italy. Introduced 1983. Imported by Dixie Gun Works.

Price: RH0211 . . . . **$425.00**

TRADITIONS KENTUCKY PISTOL

Caliber: 50. **Barrel:** 10"; octagon with 7/8" flats; 1:20" twist. **Weight:** 40 oz. **Length:** 15" overall. **Stocks:** Stained beech. **Sights:** Blade front, fixed rear. **Features:** Bird's-head grip; brass thimbles; color case-hardened lock. Percussion only. Introduced 1995. From Traditions.

Price: Finished **$209.00**
Price: Kit **$174.00**

TRADITIONS TRAPPER PISTOL

Caliber: 50. **Barrel:** 9.75"; 7/8" flats; 1:20" twist. **Weight:** 2.75 lbs. **Length:** 16" overall. **Stocks:** Beech. **Sights:** Blade front, adjustable rear. **Features:** Double-set triggers; brass buttcap, trigger guard, wedge plate, forend tip, thimble. From Traditions.

Price: Percussion **$286.00**
Price: Flintlock **$312.00**
Price: Kit **$149.00**

TRADITIONS VEST-POCKET DERRINGER

Caliber: 31. **Barrel:** 2.25"; brass. **Weight:** 8 oz. **Length:** 4.75" overall. **Stocks:** Simulated ivory. **Sights:** Bead front. **Features:** Replica of riverboat gamblers' derringer; authentic spur trigger. From Traditions.

Price: **$165.00**

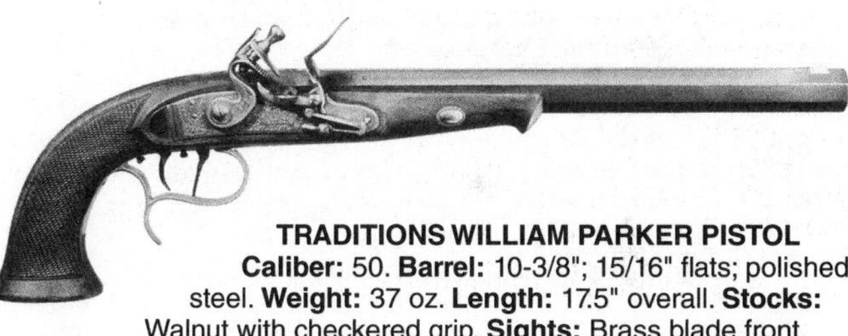

TRADITIONS WILLIAM PARKER PISTOL

Caliber: 50. **Barrel:** 10-3/8"; 15/16" flats; polished steel. **Weight:** 37 oz. **Length:** 17.5" overall. **Stocks:** Walnut with checkered grip. **Sights:** Brass blade front, fixed rear. **Features:** Replica dueling pistol with 1:20" twist, hooked breech. Brass wedge plate, trigger guard, cap guard; separate ramrod. Double-set triggers. Polished steel barrel, lock. Imported by Traditions.

Price: **$381.00**

ARMY 1860 PERCUSSION REVOLVER

Caliber: 44, 6-shot. **Barrel:** 8". **Weight:** 40 oz. **Length:** 13-5/8" overall. **Stocks:** Walnut. **Sights:** Fixed. **Features:** Engraved Navy scene on cylinder; brass trigger guard; case-hardened frame, loading lever and hammer. Some importers supply pistol cut for detachable shoulder stock, have accessory stock available. Imported by Cabela's (1860 Lawman), EMF, Navy Arms, The Armoury, Cimarron, Dixie Gun Works (half-fluted cylinder, not roll engraved), Euroarms of America (brass or steel model), Armsport, Traditions (brass or steel), Uberti U.S.A. Inc., United States Patent Fire-Arms.

Price: from. . . . . **$350.00 to $400.00**

BABY DRAGOON 1848, 1849 POCKET, WELLS FARGO

Caliber: 31. **Barrel:** 3", 4", 5", 6"; seven-groove; RH twist. **Weight:** About 21 oz. **Stocks:** Varnished walnut. **Sights:** Brass pin front, hammer notch rear. **Features:** No loading lever on Baby Dragoon or Wells Fargo models. Unfluted cylinder with stagecoach holdup scene; cupped cylinder pin; no grease grooves; one safety pin on cylinder and slot in hammer face; straight (flat) mainspring. From Armsport, Cimarron F.A. Co., Dixie Gun Works, EMF, Uberti U.S.A. Inc.

Price: from. . . . . **$300.00 to $375.00**

DIXIE WYATT EARP REVOLVER

Caliber: 44. **Barrel:** 12", octagon. **Weight:** 46 oz. **Length:** 18" overall. **Stocks:** One-piece hardwood. **Sights:** Fixed. **Features:** Highly polished brass frame, backstrap and trigger guard; blued barrel and cylinder; case-hardened hammer, trigger and loading lever. Navy-size shoulder stock requires minor fitting. From Dixie Gun Works.

Price: RH0130. . . . . **$187.50**

LE MAT REVOLVER

Caliber: 44/20 ga. **Barrel:** 6.75" (revolver); 4-7/8" (single shot). **Weight:** 3 lbs., 7 oz. **Length:** 14" overall. **Stocks:** Hand-checkered walnut. **Sights:** Post front, hammer notch rear. **Features:** Exact reproduction with all-steel construction; 44-cal. 9-shot cylinder, 20-gauge single barrel; color case-hardened hammer with selector; spur trigger guard; ring at butt; lever-type barrel release. From Navy Arms.

Price: Cavalry model (lanyard ring, spur trigger guard) **$750.00**
Price: Army model (round trigger guard, pin-type barrel release). **$750.00**
Price: Naval-style (thumb selector on hammer) **$750.00**

NAVY MODEL 1851 PERCUSSION REVOLVER

Caliber: 36, 44, 6-shot. **Barrel:** 7.5". **Weight:** 44 oz. **Length:** 13" overall. **Stocks:** Walnut finish. **Sights:** Post front, hammer notch rear. **Features:** Brass backstrap and trigger guard; some have 1st Model squareback trigger guard, engraved cylinder with navy battle scene; case-hardened frame, hammer, loading lever. Imported by The Armoury, Cabela's, Cimarron F.A. Co., Navy Arms, EMF, Dixie Gun Works, Euroarms of America, Armsport, CVA (44-cal. only), Traditions (44 only), Uberti U.S.A. Inc., United States Patent Fire-Arms.

Price: Brass frame (Dixie Gun Works RH0100) **$275.00**
Price: Steel frame (Dixie Gun Works RH0210). **$200.00**
Price: Engraved model (Dixie Gun Works RH0110) **$275.00**
Price: Confederate Navy (Cabela's) **$139.99**
Price: Hartford model, steel frame, German silver trim, cartouche (EMF) **$190.00**
Price: Man With No Name Conversion (Cimarron, 2006) . . . **$480.00**

NEW MODEL 1858 ARMY PERCUSSION REVOLVER

Caliber: 36 or 44, 6-shot. **Barrel:** 6.5" or 8". **Weight:** 38 oz. **Length:** 13.5" overall. **Stocks:** Walnut. **Sights:** Blade front, groove-in-frame rear. **Features:** Replica of Remington Model 1858. Also available from some importers as Army Model Belt Revolver in 36-cal., a shortened and lightened version of the 44. Target Model (Uberti U.S.A. Inc., Navy Arms) has fully adjustable target rear sight, target front, 36 or 44. Imported by Cimarron F.A. Co., CVA (as 1858 Army, brass frame, 44 only), Navy Arms, The Armoury, EMF, Euroarms of America (engraved, stainless and plain), Armsport, Traditions (44 only), Uberti U.S.A. Inc.

Price: Steel frame, Dixie RH0220 . . . . **$315.00**
Price: Steel frame kit (Euroarms) . . . . **$115.95 to $150.00**
Price: Stainless steel Model 1858 (Euroarms, Uberti U.S.A. Inc., Navy Arms, Armsport, Traditions) . . . . **$169.95 to $380.00**
Price: Target Model, adjustable rear sight (Cabela's, Euroarms, Uberti U.S.A. Inc., Stone Mountain Arms) . . . . **$95.95 to $399.00**
Price: Brass frame (CVA, Cabela's, Traditions, Navy Arms) . . . . **$79.95 to $199.99**
Price: Buffalo model, 44-cal. (Cabela's) **$119.99**
Price: Hartford model, steel frame, cartouche (EMF) **$225.00**
Price: Improved Conversion (Cimarron) **$492.00**

NORTH AMERICAN COMPANION PERCUSSION REVOLVER

Caliber: 22. **Barrel:** 1-1/8". **Weight:** 5.1 oz. **Length:** 4.5" overall. **Stocks:** Laminated wood. **Sights:** Blade front, notch fixed rear. **Features:** All stainless steel construction. Uses standard #11 percussion caps. Comes with bullets, powder measure, bullet seater, leather clip holster, gun rag. Long Rifle or Magnum frame size. Introduced 1996. Made in U.S. by North American Arms.

Price: Long Rifle frame **$215.00**

North American Super Companion Percussion Revolver

Similar to the Companion except has larger frame. Weighs 7.2 oz., has 1-5/8" barrel, measures 5-7/16" overall. Comes with bullets, powder measure, bullet seater, leather clip holster, gun rag. Introduced 1996. Made in U.S. by North American Arms.

Price: **$230.00**

Prices given are believed to be accurate at time of publication however, many factors affect retail pricing so exact prices are not possible.

POCKET POLICE 1862 PERCUSSION REVOLVER
Caliber: 36, 5-shot. **Barrel:** 4.5", 5.5", 6.5", 7.5". **Weight:** 26 oz. **Length:** 12" overall (6.5" bbl.). **Stocks:** Walnut. **Sights:** Fixed. **Features:** Round tapered barrel; half-fluted and rebated cylinder; case-hardened frame, loading lever and hammer; silver or brass trigger guard and backstrap. Imported by Dixie Gun Works, Navy Arms (5.5" only), Uberti U.S.A. Inc. (5.5", 6.5" only), United States Patent Fire-Arms and Cimarron F.A. Co.
Price: Dixie Gun Works RH0422 . . . . **$315.00**
Price: Hartford model, steel frame, cartouche (EMF) **$300.00**

ROGERS & SPENCER PERCUSSION REVOLVER
Caliber: 44. **Barrel:** 7.5". **Weight:** 47 oz. **Length:** 13.75" overall. **Stocks:** Walnut. **Sights:** Cone front, integral groove in frame for rear. **Features:** Accurate reproduction of a Civil War design. Solid frame; extra large nipple cut-out on rear of cylinder; loading lever and cylinder easily removed for cleaning. From Dixie Gun Works, Euroarms of America (standard blue, engraved, burnished, target models), Navy Arms.
Price: Dixie Gun Works RH1320 . . . . **$425.00**
Price: Nickel-plated **$215.00**
Price: Engraved (Euroarms) **$430.00**
Price: Target version (Euroarms) . . . . **$239.00 to $270.00**
Price: Burnished London Gray (Euroarms) . . . . . **$245.00 to $370.00**

SHERIFF MODEL 1851 PERCUSSION REVOLVER
Caliber: 36, 44, 6-shot. **Barrel:** 5". **Weight:** 40 oz. **Length:** 10.5" overall. **Stocks:** Walnut. **Sights:** Fixed. **Features:** Brass backstrap and trigger guard; engraved navy scene; case-hardened frame, hammer, loading lever. Imported by EMF.
Price: Steel frame **$169.95**
Price: Brass frame **$140.00**

SPILLER & BURR REVOLVER
Caliber: 36 (.375" round ball). **Barrel:** 7", octagon. **Weight:** 2.5 lbs. **Length:** 12.5" overall. **Stocks:** Two-piece walnut. **Sights:** Fixed. **Features:** Reproduction of the C.S.A. revolver. Brass frame and trigger guard. Also available as a kit. From Dixie Gun Works, Navy Arms.
Price: **$232.50**

UBERTI 1847 WALKER REVOLVERS
Caliber: 44 6-shot engraved cylinder. **Barrel:** 9" 7 grooves. **Weight:** 4.5 lbs. **Length:** 15.7" overall. **Stocks:** One-piece hardwood. **Sights:** Fixed. **Features:** Copy of Sam Colt's first commercially-made revolving pistol, loading lever available, no trigger guard. Case-hardened hammer. Blued finish. Made in Italy by Uberti, imported by Benelli USA.
Price: **$429.00**

UBERTI 1848 DRAGOON AND POCKET REVOLVERS
Caliber: 44 6-shot engraved cylinder. **Barrel:** 7.5" 7 grooves. **Weight:** 4.1 lbs. **Stocks:** One-piece walnut. **Sights:** Fixed. **Features:** Copy of Eli Whitney's design for Colt using Walker parts. Blued barrel, backstrap, and trigger guard. Made in Italy by Uberti, imported by Benelli USA.
Price: 1848 Whitneyville Dragoon, 7.5" barrel **$429.00**
Price: 1848 Dragoon, 1st-3rd models, 7.5" barrel . . **$409.00**
Price: 1848 Baby Dragoon, 4" barrel **$339.00**

UBERTI 1858 NEW ARMY REVOLVERS
Caliber: 44 6-shot engraved cylinder. **Barrel:** 8" 7 grooves. **Weight:** 2.7 lbs. **Length:** 13.6". **Stocks:** Two-piece walnut. **Sights:** Fixed. **Features:** Blued or stainless barrel, backstrap; brass trigger guard. Made in Italy by Uberti, imported by Benelli USA.
Price: 1858 New Army Stainless 8" barrel **$429.00**
Price: 1858 New Army 8" barrel **$349.00**
Price: 1858 Target Carbine 18" barrel **$549.00**
Price: 1862 Pocket Navy 5.5" barrel, 36 caliber **$349.00**
Price: 1862 Police 5.5" barrel, 36 caliber **$349.00**

UBERTI 1861 NAVY PERCUSSION REVOLVER
Caliber: 36, 6-shot. **Barrel:** 7.5", 7-groove, round. **Weight:** 2 lbs., 6 oz. **Length:** 13". **Stocks:** One-piece walnut. **Sights:** German silver blade front sight. **Features:** Rounded trigger guard, "creeping" loading lever, fluted or round cylinder, steel backstrap, trigger guard, cut for stock. Imported by Cimarron F.A. Co., Uberti U.S.A. Inc., Dixie Gun Works.
Price: Dixie RH0420 . . . . **$295.00**

1862 POCKET NAVY PERCUSSION REVOLVER
Caliber: 36, 5-shot. **Barrel:** 5.5", 6.5", octagonal, 7-groove, LH twist. **Weight:** 27 oz. (5.5" barrel). **Length:** 10.5" overall (5.5" bbl.). **Stocks:** One-piece varnished walnut. **Sights:** Brass pin front, hammer notch rear. **Features:** Rebated cylinder, hinged loading lever, brass or silver-plated backstrap and trigger guard, color-cased frame, hammer, loading lever, plunger and latch, rest blued. Has original-type markings. From Cimarron F.A. Co., Uberti U.S.A. Inc., Dixie Gun Works.
Price: With brass backstrap, trigger guard **$250.00**

WALKER 1847 PERCUSSION REVOLVER
Caliber: 44, 6-shot. **Barrel:** 9". **Weight:** 84 oz. **Length:** 15.5" overall. **Stocks:** Walnut. **Sights:** Fixed. **Features:** Case-hardened frame, loading lever and hammer; iron backstrap; brass trigger guard; engraved cylinder. Imported by Cabela's, Cimarron F.A. Co., Navy Arms, Uberti U.S.A. Inc., EMF, Cimarron, Traditions, United States Patent Fire-Arms.
Price: Dixie RH0200 . . . . **$385.00**
Price: Dixie Kit RH0400 . . . . **$300.00**
Price: Hartford model, steel frame, cartouche (EMF) **$350.00**

ARMOURY R140 HAWKEN RIFLE
Caliber: 45, 50 or 54. **Barrel:** 29". **Weight:** 8.75 to 9 lbs. **Length:** 45.75" overall. **Stock:** Walnut, with cheekpiece. **Sights:** Dovetailed front, fully adjustable rear. **Features:** Octagon barrel, removable breech plug; double set triggers; blued barrel, brass stock fittings, color case-hardened percussion lock. From Armsport, The Armoury.
Price: .... **$225.00 to $245.00**

BOSTONIAN PERCUSSION RIFLE
Caliber: 45. **Barrel:** 30", octagonal. **Weight:** 7.25 lbs. **Length:** 46" overall. **Stock:** Walnut. **Sights:** Blade front, fixed notch rear. **Features:** Color case-hardened lock, brass trigger guard, buttplate, patchbox. Imported from Italy by EMF.
Price: **$285.00**

CABELA'S BLUE RIDGE RIFLE
Caliber: 32, 36, 45, 50, .54. **Barrel:** 39", octagonal. **Weight:** About 7.75 lbs. **Length:** 55" overall. **Stock:** American black walnut. **Sights:** Blade front, rear drift adjustable for windage. **Features:** Color case-hardened lockplate and cock/hammer, brass trigger guard and buttplate, double set, double-phased triggers. From Cabela's.
Price: Percussion **$569.99**
Price: Flintlock **$599.99**

CABELA'S TRADITIONAL HAWKEN
Caliber: 50, 54. **Barrel:** 29". **Weight:** About 9 lbs. **Stock:** Walnut. **Sights:** Blade front, open adjustable rear. **Features:** Flintlock or percussion. Adjustable double-set triggers. Polished brass furniture, color case-hardened lock. Imported by Cabela's.
Price: Percussion, right-hand or left-hand................ **$339.99**
Price: Flintlock, right-hand **$399.99**

CABELA'S KODIAK EXPRESS DOUBLE RIFLE
Caliber: 50, 54, 58, 72. **Barrel:** Length NA; 1:48" twist. **Weight:** 9.3 lbs. **Length:** 45.25" overall. **Stock:** European walnut, oil finish. **Sights:** Fully adjustable double folding-leaf rear, ramp front. **Features:** Percussion. Barrels regulated to point of aim at 75 yards; polished and engraved lock, top tang and trigger guard. From Cabela's.
Price: 50, 54, 58 calibers **$929.99**
Price: 72 caliber **$959.99**

COOK & BROTHER CONFEDERATE CARBINE
Caliber: 58. **Barrel:** 24". **Weight:** 7.5 lbs. **Length:** 40.5" overall. **Stock:** Select walnut. **Features:** Re-creation of the 1861 New Orleans-made artillery carbine. Color case-hardened lock, browned barrel. Buttplate, trigger guard, barrel bands, sling swivels and nosecap of polished brass. From Euroarms of America.
Price: **$563.00**
Price: Cook & Brother rifle (33" barrel) **$606.00**

CVA OPTIMA ELITE BREAK-ACTION RIFLE
Caliber: 45, 50. **Barrel:** 28" fluted. **Weight:** 8.8 lbs. **Stock:** Ambidextrous solid composite in standard or thumbhole. **Sights:** Adj. fiber-optic. **Features:** Break-action, stainless No. 209 breech plug, aluminum loading rod, cocking spur, lifetime warranty.
Price: CR4002 (50-cal., blued/Realtree HD) **$398.95**
Price: CR4002X (50-cal., stainless/Realtree HD) **$456.95**
Price: CR4003X (45-cal., stainless/Realtree HD)......... **$456.95**
Price: CR4000T (50-cal), blued/black fiber grip thumbhole) . **$366.95**
Price: CR4000 (50-cal., blued/black fiber grip **$345.95**
Price: CR4002T (50-cal., blued/Realtree HD thumbhole) ... **$432.95**
Price: CR4002S (50-cal., stainless/Realtree HD thumbhole) **$422.95**
Price: CR4000X (50-cal., stainless/black fiber grip thumbhole) **$451.95**
Price: CR4000S (50-cal., stainless steel/black fiber grip) ... **$400.95**

CVA Optima 209 Magnum Break-Action Rifle
Similar to Optima Elite but with 26" bbl., nickel or blue finish, 50 cal.
Price: PR2008N (nickel/Realtree HD thumbhole) **$345.95**
Price: PR2004N (nickel/Realtree) **$322.95**
Price: PR2000 (blued/black) **$229.95**
Price: PR2006N (nickel/black) **$273.95**

CVA Wolf 209 Magnum Break-Action Rifle
Similar to Optima 209 Mag but with 24 barrel, weighs 7 lbs, and in 50-cal. only.
Price: PR2101N (nickel/camo) **$253.95**
Price: PR2102 (blued/camo)......................... **$231.95**
Price: PR2100 (blued/black) **$180.95**
Price: PR2100N (nickel/black) **$202.95**
Price: PR2100NS (nickel/black scoped package) **$277.95**
Price: PR2100S (blued/black scoped package) **$255.95**

CVA APEX
Caliber: 45, 50. **Barrel:** 27", 1:28 twist. **Weight:** 8 lbs. **Length:** 42". **Stock:** Synthetic. **Features:** Ambi stock with rubber grip panels in black or Realtree APG camo, crush-zone recoil pad, reversible hammer spur, quake claw sling, lifetime warranty.
Price: CR4010S (50-cal., stainless/black) **$738.00**

CVA ACCURA
Similar to Apex but weighs 7.3 lbs., in stainless steel or matte blue finish, cocking spur.
Price: PR3106S (50-cal, stainless steel/Realtree APG thumbhole) **$495.95**
Price: PR3107S (45-cal., stainless steel/Realtree APG thumbhole) **$495.95**
Price: PR 3104S (50-cal., stainless steel/black fibergrip thumbhole) **$438.95**
Price: PR3100 (50-cal., blued/black fibergrip **$345.95**
Price: PR3100S (50-cal., stainless steel/black fibergrip **$403.95**
Price: PR3102S (50-cal., stainless steel/Realtree APG) **$460.95**

CVA BUCKHORN 209 MAGNUM
Caliber: 50. **Barrel:** 24". **Weight:** 6.3 lbs. **Sights:** Illuminator fiber-optic. **Features:** Grip-dot stock, thumb-actuated safety; drilled and tapped for scope mounts.
Price: Black stock, blue barrel **$177.00**

DIXIE EARLY AMERICAN JAEGER RIFLE
Caliber: 54. **Barrel:** 27.5" octagonal; 1:24" twist. **Weight:** 8.25 lbs. **Length:** 43.5" overall. **Stock:** American walnut; sliding wooden patchbox on butt. **Sights:** Notch rear, blade front. **Features:** Flintlock or percussion. Browned steel furniture. Imported from Italy by Dixie Gun Works.
Price: Flintlock FR0838............................. **$695.00**
Price: Percussion PR0835, case-hardened **$695.00**
Price: Kit **$775.00**

DIXIE DELUXE CUB RIFLE
Caliber: 32, 36, 40, 45. **Barrel:** 28" octagon. **Weight:** 6.25 lbs. **Length:** 44" overall. **Stock:** Walnut. **Sights:** Fixed. **Features:** Short rifle for small game and beginning shooters. Brass patchbox and furniture. Flint or percussion, finished or kit. From Dixie Gun Works
Price: Deluxe Cub (45-cal.) **$525.00**
Price: Deluxe Cub (flint) **$530.00**
Price: Super Cub (50-cal) **$530.00**
Price: Deluxe Cub (32-cal. flint) **$725.00**
Price: Deluxe Cub (36-cal. flint) **$725.00**
Price: Deluxe Cub kit (32-cal. percussion) **$550.00**
Price: Deluxe Cub kit (36-cal. percussion) **$550.00**
Price: Deluxe Cub (45-cal. percussion) **$675.00**
Price: Super Cub (percussion) **$450.00**
Price: Deluxe Cub (32-cal. percussion) **$675.00**
Price: Deluxe Cub (36-cal. percussion) **$675.00**

DIXIE PEDERSOLI 1857 MAUSER RIFLE
Caliber: 54. **Barrel:** 39-3/8". **Weight:** 9.5 lbs. **Length:** 54.75" overall. **Stock:** European walnut with oil finish, sling swivels. **Sights:** Fully adjustable rear, lug front. **Features:** Percussion (musket caps). Armory bright finish with color case-hardened lock and barrel tang, engraved lockplate, steel ramrod. Introduced 2000. Imported from Italy by Dixie Gun Works.
Price: PR1330.. **$995.00**

DIXIE SHARPS NEW MODEL 1859 MILITARY RIFLE
Caliber: 54. **Barrel:** 30", 6-groove; 1:48" twist. **Weight:** 9 lbs. **Length:** 45.5" overall. **Stock:** Oiled walnut. **Sights:** Blade front, ladder-style rear. **Features:** Blued barrel, color case-hardened barrel bands, receiver, hammer, nosecap, lever, patchbox cover and buttplate. Introduced 1995. Imported from Italy by Dixie Gun Works.

Prices given are believed to be accurate at time of publication however, many factors affect retail pricing so exact prices are not possible.

Price: PR0862 . . . . **$1,100.00**
Price: Carbine (22 barrel, 7-groove, 39-1/4" overall, weighs 8 lbs.) **$925.00**

DIXIE U.S. MODEL 1816 FLINTLOCK MUSKET
Caliber: .69. **Barrel:** 42", smoothbore. **Weight:** 9.75 lbs. **Length:** 56 7/8" overall. **Stock:** Walnut w/oil finish. **Sights:** Blade front. **Features:** All metal finished "National Armory Bright," three barrel bands w/ springs, steel ramrod w/button-shaped head. Imported by Dixie Gun Works.
Price: FR0305 . . . . **$1,200.00**
Price: PR0257, Percussion conversion **$995.00**

EMF 1863 SHARPS MILITARY CARBINE
Caliber: 54. **Barrel:** 22", round. **Weight:** 8 lbs. **Length:** 39" overall. **Stock:** Oiled walnut. **Sights:** Blade front, military ladder-type rear. **Features:** Color case-hardened lock, rest blued. Imported by EMF.
Price: **$759.90**

EUROARMS VOLUNTEER TARGET RIFLE
Caliber: 451. **Barrel:** 33" (two-band), 36" (three-band). **Weight:** 11 lbs. (two-band). **Length:** 48.75" overall (two-band). **Stock:** European walnut with checkered wrist and forend. **Sights:** Hooded bead front, adjustable rear with interchangeable leaves. **Features:** Alexander Henry-type rifling with 1:20" twist. Color case-hardened hammer and lockplate, brass trigger guard and nosecap, remainder blued. Imported by Euroarms of America, Dixie Gun Works.
Price: PR1031 . . . . **$925.00**

EUROARMS 1861 SPRINGFIELD RIFLE
Caliber: 58. **Barrel:** 40". **Weight:** About 10 lbs. **Length:** 55.5" overall. **Stock:** European walnut. **Sights:** Blade front, three-leaf military rear. **Features:** Reproduction of the original three-band rifle. Lockplate marked "1861" with eagle and "U.S. Springfield." White metal. Imported by Euroarms of America.
Price: **$730.00**

EUROARMS ZOUAVE RIFLE
Caliber: 54, 58 percussion. **Barrel:** 33". **Weight:** 9.5 lbs. Overall **length:** 49". **Features:** One-piece solid barrel and bolster. For 54 caliber, .535 R.B., .540 minnie. For 58 caliber, .575 R.B., .577 minnie. 1863 issue. Made in Italy. Imported by Euroarms of America.
Price: **$469.00**

EUROARMS HARPERS FERRY RIFLE
Caliber: 58 flintlock. **Barrel:** 35". **Weight:** 9 lbs. Overall **length:** 59.5". **Features:** Antique browned barrel. Barrel .575 RB. .577 minnie. 1803 issue. Made in Italy. Imported by Euroarms of America.
Price: **$735.00**

GONIC MODEL 93 M/L RIFLE
Caliber: 45, 50. **Barrel:** 26"; 1:24" twist. **Weight:** 6.5 to 7 lbs. **Length:** 43" overall. **Stock:** American hardwood with black finish. **Sights:** Adjustable or aperture rear, hooded post front. **Features:** Adjustable trigger with side safety; unbreakable ramrod; comes with A. Z. scope bases installed. Introduced 1993. Made in U.S. by Gonic Arms, Inc.
Price: Model 93 Standard (blued barrel) **$720.00**
Price: Model 93 Standard (stainless brl., 50 cal. only) **$782.00**

Gonic Model 93 Deluxe M/L Rifle
Similar to the Model 93 except has classic-style walnut or gray laminated wood stock. Introduced 1998. Made in U.S. by Gonic Arms, Inc.
Price: Blue barrel, sights, scope base, choice of stock **$902.00**
Price: Stainless barrel, sights, scope base, choice of stock (50 cal. only) **$964.00**

Gonic Model 93 Mountain Thumbhole M/L Rifles
Similar to the Model 93 except has high-grade walnut or gray laminate stock with extensive hand-checkered panels, Monte Carlo cheekpiece and beavertail forend; integral muzzle brake. Introduced 1998. Made in U.S. by Gonic Arms, Inc.
Price: Blued or stainless **$2,700.00**

HARPER'S FERRY 1803 FLINTLOCK RIFLE
Caliber: 54 or 58. **Barrel:** 35". **Weight:** 9 lbs. **Length:** 59.5" overall.

Stock: Walnut with cheekpiece. **Sights:** Brass blade front, fixed steel rear. **Features:** Brass trigger guard, sideplate, buttplate; steel patchbox. Imported by Euroarms of America, Navy Arms (54-cal. only), and Dixie Gun Works.
Price: 54-cal. (Navy Arms) **$625.00**
Price: 54-cal. (Dixie Gun Works), FR0171 . . . . **$995.00**
Price: 54-cal. (Euroarms) **$809.00**

HAWKEN RIFLE
Caliber: 45, 50, 54 or 58. **Barrel:** 28", blued, 6-groove rifling. **Weight:** 8.75 lbs. **Length:** 44" overall. **Stock:** Walnut with cheekpiece. **Sights:** Blade front, fully adjustable rear. **Features:** Coil mainspring, double-set triggers, polished brass furniture. From Armsport and EMF.
Price: . . . . **$220.00 to $345.00**

J.P. HENRY TRADE RIFLE
Caliber: 54. **Barrel:** 34"; 1" flats. **Weight:** 8.5 lbs. **Length:** 45" overall. **Stock:** Premium curly maple. **Sights:** Silver blade front, fixed buckhorn rear. **Features:** Brass buttplate, side plate, trigger guard and nosecap; browned barrel and lock; L&R Large English percussion lock; single trigger. Made in U.S. by J.P. Gunstocks, Inc.
Price: **$965.50**

J.P. MURRAY 1862-1864 CAVALRY CARBINE
Caliber: 58 (.577" Minie). **Barrel:** 23". **Weight:** 7 lbs., 9 oz. **Length:** 39" overall. **Stock:** Walnut. **Sights:** Blade front, rear drift adjustable for windage. **Features:** Blued barrel, color case-hardened lock, blued swivel and band springs, polished brass buttplate, trigger guard, barrel bands. From Dixie Gun Works.
Price: Dixie Gun Works PR0173 . . . . **$750.00**

KENTUCKY FLINTLOCK RIFLE
Caliber: 44, 45, or 50. **Barrel:** 35". **Weight:** 7 lbs. **Length:** 50" overall. **Stock:** Walnut stained, brass fittings. **Sights:** Fixed. **Features:** Available in carbine model also, 28" bbl. Some variations in detail, finish. Kits also available from some importers. Imported by The Armoury.
Price: About . . . . **$217.95 to $345.00**

Kentucky Percussion Rifle
Similar to Flintlock except percussion lock. Finish and features vary with importer. Imported by The Armoury and CVA.
Price: About **$259.95**
Price: 45 or 50 cal. (Navy Arms) **$425.00**
Price: Kit, 50 cal. (CVA) **$189.95**

KNIGHT MOUNTAINEER FOREST GREEN
Caliber: .50, .52. **Barrel:** 27" fluted stainless steel, free floated. **Weight:** 8 lbs. (thumbhole stock), 8.3 lbs., (straight stock). **Length:** 45.5". **Sights:** Fully adjustable metallic fiber optic. **Features:** Adjustable match-grade trigger, aluminum ramrod with carbon core.
Price: **$810**

KNIGHT LONG RANGE HUNTER
Caliber: 50. **Barrel:** 27" custom fluted; 1:28" twist. **Weight:** 8 lbs. 6 oz. **Length:** 45.5" overall. **Stock:** Cast-off design thumbhole, checkered, recoil pad, sling swivel studs, in Forest

Green or Sandstone. **Sights:** Fully-adjustable, metallic fiber-optic. **Features:** Full plastic jacket ignition system. Made in U.S. by Knight Rifles (Modern Muzzleloading).

Price: SS Forest Green **$769.99**
Price: SS Forest Green Thumbhole **$799.99**

KNIGHT EXTREME

Caliber: 50, 52. **Barrel:** 26", fluted staincss, 1:28" twist. **Weight:** 7 lbs. 14 oz to 8 lbs. **Length:** 45" overall. **Stock:** Stainless steel laminate, blued walnut, black composite thumbhole with blued or SS, Realtree Hardwoods Green HD with thumbhole. **Sights:** Fully adjustable metallic fiber-optics. **Features:** Full plastic jacket ignition system. Made in U.S. by Knight Rifles (Modern Muzzleloading).

Price: 50 SS/Realtree (2009) **$529.99**
Price: 52 SS/black (2009) **$229.94**
Price: 50 SS/black **$459.99**
Price: 50 SS/black w/thumbhole **$489.99**
Price: 50 SS/brown **$569.99**

KNIGHT BIGHORN

Caliber: 50. **Barrel:** 26"; 1:28" twist. **Weight:** 7 lbs. 3 oz. **Length:** 44.5" overall. **Stock:** Realtree Advantage MAX-1 HD or black composite thumbhole, checkered with recoil pad, sling swivel studs. **Sights:** Fully adjustable metallic fiber-optic. **Features:** Uses 4 different ignition systems (included): #11 nipple, musket nipple, bare 208 shotgun primer and 209 Extreme shotgun primer system (Extreme weatherproof full plastic jacket system); one-piece removable hammer assembly. Made in U.S. by Knight Rifles (Modern Muzzleloading).

Price: Stainless/Realtree w/thumbhole (2009) **$459.99**
Price: Stainless/black **$419.99**
Price: Stainless/black w/thumbhole **$439.99**

LONDON ARMORY 1861 ENFIELD MUSKETOON

Caliber: 58, Minie ball. **Barrel:** 24", round. **Weight:** 7 to 7.5 lbs. **Length:** 40.5" overall. **Stock:** Walnut, with sling swivels. **Sights:** Blade front, graduated military-leaf rear. **Features:** Brass trigger guard, nosecap, buttplate; blued barrel, bands, lockplate, swivels. Imported by Euroarms of America, Navy Arms.

Price: . . . . **$300.00 to $521.00**
Price: Kit . . . . **$365.00 to $402.00**

LONDON ARMORY 2-BAND 1858 ENFIELD

Caliber: .577" Minie, .575" round ball. **Barrel:** 33". **Weight:** 10 lbs. **Length:** 49" overall. **Stock:** Walnut. **Sights:** Folding leaf rear adjustable for elevation. **Features:** Blued barrel, color case-hardened lock and hammer, polished brass buttplate, trigger guard, nosecap. From Navy Arms, Euroarms of America, Dixie Gun Works.

Price: PR0330 . . . . **$650.00**

LONDON ARMORY 3-BAND 1853 ENFIELD

Caliber: 58 (.577" Minie, .575" round ball, .580" maxi ball). **Barrel:** 39". **Weight:** 9.5 lbs. **Length:** 54" overall. **Stock:** European walnut. **Sights:** Inverted "V" front, traditional Enfield folding ladder rear. **Features:** Re-creation of the famed London Armory Company Pattern 1853 Enfield Musket. One-piece walnut stock, brass buttplate, trigger guard and nosecap. Lockplate marked "London Armoury Co." and with a British crown. Blued Baddeley barrel bands. From Euroarms of America, Navy Arms.

Price: About . . . . **$350.00 to $606.00**

LYMAN TRADE RIFLE

Caliber: 50, 54. **Barrel:** 28" octagon;1:48" twist. **Weight:** 10.8 lbs. **Length:** 45" overall. **Stock:** European walnut. **Sights:** Blade front, open rear adjustable for windage or optional fixed sights. **Features:** Fast twist rifling for conical bullets. Polished brass furniture with blue steel parts, stainless steel nipple. Hook breech, single trigger, coil spring percussion lock. Steel barrel rib and ramrod ferrules. Introduced 1980. From Lyman.

Price: 50-cal. percussion **$474.95**
Price: 50-cal. flintlock **$499.95**
Price: 54-cal. percussion **$474.95**
Price: 54-cal. flintlock **$499.95**

LYMAN DEERSTALKER RIFLE

Caliber: 50, 54. **Barrel:** 24", octagonal; 1:48" rifling. **Weight:** 10.4 lbs. **Stock:** Walnut with black rubber buttpad. **Sights:** Lyman #37MA beaded front, fully adjustable fold-down Lyman #16A rear. **Features:** Stock has less drop for quick sighting. All metal parts are blackened, with color case-hardened lock; single trigger. Comes with sling and swivels. Available in flint or percussion. Introduced 1990. From Lyman.

Price: 50-cal. flintlock **$529.95**
Price: 50-, 54-cal., flintlock, left-hand **$569.95**
Price: 54 cal. flintlock **$529.95**
Price: 50-, 54 cal. percussion **$487.95**
Price: 50-, 54-cal. stainless steel **$609.95**

LYMAN GREAT PLAINS RIFLE

Caliber: 50, 54. **Barrel:** 32"; 1:60" twist. **Weight:** 11.6 lbs. **Stock:** Walnut. **Sights:** Steel blade front, buckhorn rear adjustable for windage and elevation and fixed notch primitive sight included. **Features:** Blued steel furniture. Stainless steel nipple. Coil spring lock, Hawken-style trigger guard and double-set triggers. Round thimbles recessed and sweated into rib. Steel wedge plates and toe plate. Introduced 1979. From Lyman.

Price: Percussion **$654.95**
Price: Flintlock **$699.95**
Price: Percussion kit **$519.95**
Price: Flintlock kit **$574.95**
Price: Left-hand percussion **$669.95**
Price: Left-hand flintlock **$709.95**

LYMAN GREAT PLAINS HUNTER MODEL

Similar to Great Plains model except 1:32" twist shallow-groove barrel and comes drilled and tapped for Lyman 57GPR peep sight.

Price: Percussion **$654.95**
Price: Flintlock **$699.95**
Price: Left-hand percussion **$669.95**

MISSISSIPPI 1841 PERCUSSION RIFLE

Caliber: 54, 58. **Barrel:** 33". **Weight:** 9.5 lbs. **Length:** 48-5/8" overall. **Stock:** One-piece European walnut full stock with satin finish. **Sights:** Brass blade front, fixed steel rear. **Features:** Case-hardened lockplate marked "U.S." surmounted by American eagle. Two barrel bands, sling swivels. Steel ramrod with brass end, browned barrel. From Navy Arms, Dixie Gun Works, Euroarms of America.

Price: Dixie Gun Works PR0870 . . . . **$825.00**

NAVY ARMS 1861 MUSKETOON

Caliber: 58. **Barrel:** 39". **Weight:** NA. **Length:** NA. **Stock:** NA. **Sights:** Front is blued steel base and blade, blued steel lip-up rear adjustable for elevation. **Features:** Brass nosecap, triggerguard, buttplate, blued steel barrel bands, color case-hardened lock with engraved lockplate marked "1861 Enfield" ahead of hammer & crown over "PH" on tail. Barrel is marked "Parker Hale LTD Birmingham England." Imported by Navy Arms.

Price: **$900.00**

NAVY ARMS PARKER-HALE 1853 THREE-BAND ENFIELD

Caliber: 58. **Barrel:** 39", tapered, round, blued. **Weight:** NA. **Length:** 55-1/4" overall. **Stock:** Walnut. **Sights:** Front is blued steel base and blade, blued steel lip-up rear adjustable for

Prices given are believed to be accurate at time of publication however, many factors affect retail pricing so exact prices are not possible.

elevation. **Features:** Meticulously reproduced based on original gauges and patterns. Features brass nosecap, triggerguard, buttplate, blued steel barrel bands, color case-hardened lock with engraved lockplate marked "Parker-Hale" ahead of hammer & crown over "PH" on tail. Barrel is marked "Parker Hale LTD Birmingham England." From Navy Arms.
Price: Finished rifle **$1,050.00**

NAVY ARMS PARKER-HALE 1858 TWO-BAND ENFIELD
Similar to the Three-band Enfield with 33" barrel, 49" overall length. Engraved lockplate marked "1858 Enfield" ahead of hammer & crown over "PH" on tail. Barrel is marked "Parker Hale LTD Birmingham England."
Price: **$1,050.00**

NAVY ARMS PARKER-HALE VOLUNTEER RIFLE
Caliber: 451. **Barrel:** 32", 1:20" twist. **Weight:** 9.5 lbs. **Length:** 49" overall. **Stock:** Walnut, checkered wrist and forend. **Sights:** Globe front, adjustable ladder-type rear. **Features:** Recreation of the type of gun issued to volunteer regiments during the 1860s. Rigby-pattern rifling, patent breech, detented lock. Stock is glass beaded for accuracy. Engfaved lockplate marked "Alex Henry" & crown on tail, barrel marked "Parker Hale LTD Birmingham England" and "Alexander Henry Rifling .451" Imported by Navy Arms.
Price: **$1,400.00**

NAVY ARMS PARKER-HALE WHITWORTH MILITARY TARGET RIFLE
Caliber: 45. **Barrel:** 36". **Weight:** 9.25 lbs. **Length:** 52.5" overall. **Stock:** Walnut. Checkered at wrist and forend. **Sights:** Hooded post front, open step-adjustable rear. **Features:** Faithful reproduction of Whitworth rifle. Trigger has detented lock, capable of fine adjustments without risk of the sear nose catching on the half-cock notch and damaging both parts. Engraved lockplate marked "Whitworth" ahead of hammer & crown on tail. Barrel marked "Parker Hale LTD Birmingham England" in one line on front of sight and "Sir Joseph Whitworth's Rifling .451" on left side. Introduced 1978. Imported by Navy Arms.
Price: **$1,550.00**

NAVY ARMS BROWN BESS MUSKET
Caliber: 75, smoothbore. **Barrel:** 41.8". **Weight:** 9 lbs., 5 oz. **Length:** 41.8" overall. **Features:** Brightly polished steel and brass, one-piece walnut stock. Signature of gunsmith William Grice and the date 1762, the crown and alphabetical letters GR (Georgius Rex). Barrel is made of steel, satin finish; the walnut stock is oil finished. From Navy Arms.
Price: **$1,100.00**

NAVY ARMS COUNTRY HUNTER
Caliber: 50. **Barrel:** 28.4", 6-groove, 1:34 twist. **Weight:** 6 lbs. **Length:** 44" overall. **Features:** Matte finished barrel. From Navy Arms.
Price: **$450.00**

NAVY ARMS PENNSYLVANIA RIFLE
Caliber: 32, 45. **Barrel:** 41.6". **Weight:** 7 lbs. 12 oz. to 8 lbs. 6 oz. **Length:** 56.1" overall. **Features:** Extra long rifle finished wtih rust brown color barrel and one-piece oil finished walnut stock. Adjustable double-set trigger. Vertically adjustable steel front and rear sights. From Navy Arms.
Price: **$675.00**

NEW ENGLAND FIREARMS SIDEKICK
Caliber: 50, 209 primer ignition. **Barrel:** 26" (magnum). **Weight:** 6.5 lbs. **Length:** 41.25". **Stock:** Black matte polymer or hardwood. **Sights:** Adjustable fiber-optic open, tapped for scope mounts. **Features:** Single-shot based on H&R break-open action. Uses No. 209 shotgun primer held in place by special primer carrier. Telescoping brass ramrod. Introduced 2004.
Price: Wood stock, blued frame, black-oxide barrel) **$216.00**
Price: Stainless barrel and frame, synthetic stock) **$310.00**

NEW ENGLAND FIREARMS HUNTSMAN
Caliber: 50, 209 primer ignition. **Barrel:** 22" to 26". **Weight:** 5.25 to 6.5 lbs. **Length:** 40" to 43". **Stock:** Black matte polymer or hardwood. **Sights:** Fiber-optic open sights, tapped for scope mounts. **Features:** Break-open action, transfer-bar safety system, breech plug removable for cleaning. Introduced 2004.

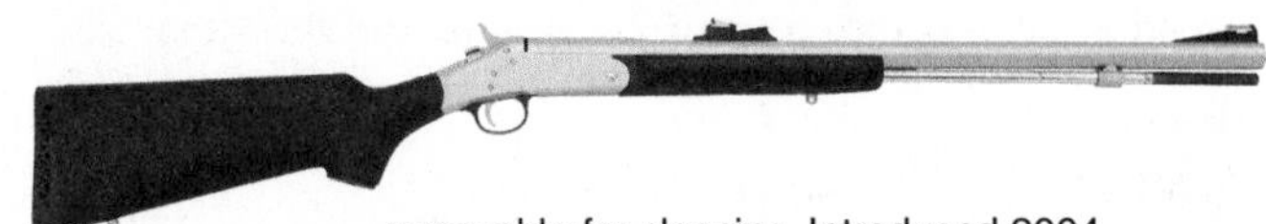

Price: Stainless Huntsman **$306.00**
Price: Huntsman **$212.00**
Price: Pardner Combo 12 ga./50 cal muzzleloader **$259.00**
Price: Tracker II Combo 12 ga. rifled slug barrel /50 cal. **$288.00**
Price: Handi-Rifle Combo 243/50 cal. **$405.00**

NEW ENGLAND FIREARMS STAINLESS HUNTSMAN
Similar to Huntsman, but with matte nickel finish receiver and stainless bbl. Introduced 2003. From New England Firearms.
Price: **$381.00**

PACIFIC RIFLE MODEL 1837 ZEPHYR
Caliber: 62. **Barrel:** 30", tapered octagon. **Weight:** 7.75 lbs. **Length:** NA. **Stock:** Oil-finished fancy walnut. **Sights:** German silver blade front, semi-buckhorn rear. Options available. **Features:** Improved underhammer action. First production rifle to offer Forsyth rifle, with narrow lands and shallow rifling with 1:14" pitch for high-velocity round balls. Metal finish is slow rust brown with nitre blue accents. Optional sights, finishes and integral muzzle brake available. Introduced 1995. Made in U.S. by Pacific Rifle Co.
Price: From **$995.00**

PACIFIC RIFLE BIG BORE AFRICAN RIFLES
Similar to the 1837 Zephyr except in 72-caliber and 8-bore. The 72-caliber is available in standard form with 28" barrel, or as the African with flat buttplate, checkered upgraded wood; weight is 9 lbs. The 8-bore African has dual-cap ignition, 24" barrel, weighs 12 lbs., checkered English walnut, engraving, gold inlays. Introduced 1998. Made in U.S. by Pacific Rifle Co.
Price: 72-caliber, from **$1,150.00**
Price: 8-bore, from **$2,500.00**

RICHMOND, C.S., 1863 MUSKET
Caliber: 58. **Barrel:** 40". **Weight:** 11 lbs. **Length:** 56.25" overall. **Stock:** European walnut with oil finish. **Sights:** Blade front, adjustable folding leaf rear. **Features:** Reproduction of the three-band Civil War musket. Sling swivels attached to trigger guard and middle barrel band. Lockplate marked "1863" and "C.S. Richmond." All white metal. Brass buttplate and forend cap. Imported by Euroarms of America, Navy Arms, and Dixie Gun Works.
Price: Euroarms **$730.00**
Price: Dixie Gun Works PR0846 . . . . **$1,050.00**
Price: Navy Arms **$1,005.00**

ROCKY MOUNTAIN HAWKEN
Caliber: NA. **Barrel:** 34-11/16". **Weight:** 10 lbs. **Length:** 52" overall. **Stock:** Walnut or maple. **Sights:** Blade front, drift adjustable rear. Fea-tures: Percussion, double set trigger, casehard-ened furniture, hook breech, brown barrel. Made by Pedersoli in Italy. Imported by Dixie Gun Works.
Price: Maple Stock PR3430 . . . . **$925.00**
Price: Walnut Stock PR3435. . . . . **$875.00**

SECOND MODEL BROWN BESS MUSKET
Caliber: 75, uses .735" round ball. **Barrel:** 42", smoothbore. **Weight:** 9.5 lbs. **Length:** 59" overall. **Stock:** Walnut (Navy); walnut-stained hardwood (Dixie). **Sights:** Fixed. **Features:** Polished barrel and lock with brass trigger guard and buttplate. Bayonet and scabbard available. From Navy Arms, Dixie Gun Works.
Price: Finished . . . . **$475.00 to $950.00**
Price: Kit, Dixie Gun Works, FR0825 . . . . **$875.00**
Price: Carbine (Navy Arms) **$835.00**
Price: Dixie Gun Works FR0810 . . . . **$995.00**

THOMPSON/CENTER TRIUMPH MAGNUM MUZZLELOADER
Caliber: 50. **Barrel:** 28" Weather Shield coated. **Weight:** NA. **Length:** NA. **Stock:** Black composite or Realtree AP HD Camo. **Sights:** NA.

Features: QLA 209 shotshell primer ignition. Introduced 2007. Made in U.S. by Thompson/Center Arms.
Price: **$457.00**

THOMPSON/CENTER BONE COLLECTOR
Similar to the Triumph Magnum but with added Flex Tech technology and Energy Burners to a shorter stock. Also added is Thompson/Center's premium fluted barrel with Weather Shield and their patented Power Rod.
Price: **$708.00**

THOMPSON/CENTER ENCORE 209X50 MAGNUM
Caliber: 50. **Barrel:** 26"; interchangeable with centerfire calibers. **Weight:** 7 lbs. **Length:** 40.5" overall. **Stock:** American walnut butt and forend, or black composite. **Sights:** TruGlo fiber-optic front and rear. **Features:** Blue or stainless steel. Uses the stock, frame and forend of the Encore centerfire pistol; break-open design using trigger guard spur; stainless steel universal breech plug; uses #209 shotshell primers. Introduced 1998. Made in U.S. by Thompson/Center Arms.
Price: Stainless with camo stock. **$772.00**
Price: Blue, walnut stock and forend **$678.00**
Price: Blue, composite stock and forend **$637.00**
Price: Stainless, composite stock and forend **$713.00**
Price: All camo Realtree Hardwoods **$729.00**

THOMPSON/CENTER FIRE STORM RIFLE
Caliber: 50. **Barrel:** 26"; 1:28" twist. **Weight:** 7 lbs. **Length:** 41.75" overall. **Stock:** Black synthetic with rubber recoil pad, swivel studs. **Sights:** Click-adjustable steel rear and ramp-style front, both with fiber-optic inserts. **Features:** Side hammer lock is the first designed for up to three 50-grain Pyrodex pellets; patented Pyrodex Pyramid breech directs ignition fire 360 degrees around base of pellet. Quick Load Accurizor Muzzle System; aluminum ramrod. Flintlock only. Introduced 2000. Made in U.S. by Thompson/Center Arms.
Price: Blue finish, flintlock model with 1:48" twist for round balls, conicals **$436.00**
Price: SST, flintlock **$488.00**

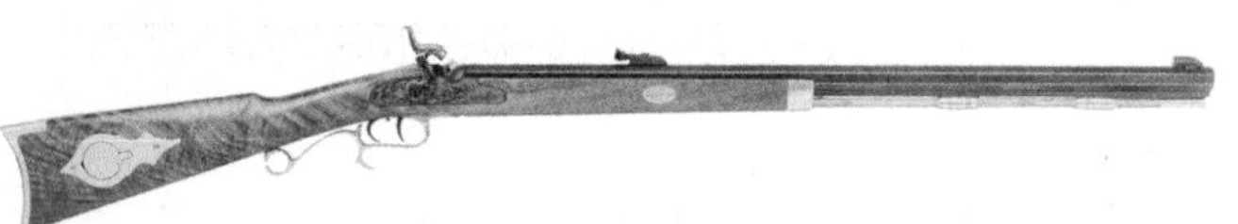

THOMPSON/CENTER HAWKEN RIFLE
Caliber: 50. **Barrel:** 28" octagon, hooked breech. **Stock:** American walnut. **Sights:** Blade front, rear adjustable for windage and elevation. **Features:** Solid brass furniture, double-set triggers, button rifled barrel, coil-type mainspring. From Thompson/Center Arms.
Price: Percussion model **$590.00**
Price: Flintlock model **$615.00**

THOMPSON/CENTER OMEGA
Caliber: 50". **Barrel:** 28", fluted. **Weight:** 7 lbs. **Length:** 42" overall. **Stock:** Composite or laminated. **Sights:** Adjustable metal rear sight with fiber-optics; metal ramp front sight with fiber-optics. **Features:** Drilled and tapped for scope mounts. Thumbhole stock, sling swivel studs. From T/C..
Price: **$777.00**

THOMPSON/CENTER IMPACT MUZZLELOADING RIFLE
50-caliber single shot rifle. Features include 209 primer ignition, sliding hood to expose removable breechplug, synthetic stock adjustable from 12.5 to 13.5 inches, 26-inch blued 1:28 rifled barrel, adjustable fiber optic sights, aluminum ramrod, camo composite stock, QLA muzzle system. Weight 6.5 lbs.

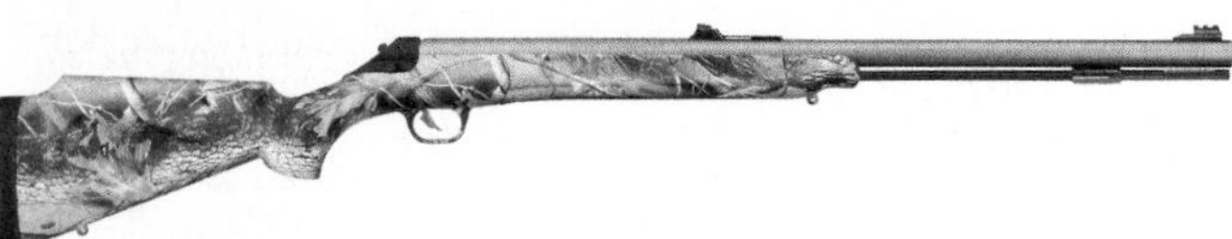

Price: Impact Camo, Impact Camo / WS Camo, Impact Composite, Impact Weather Shield Black, Impact Weather Shield Camo . . . . **$249.00 to $269.00**

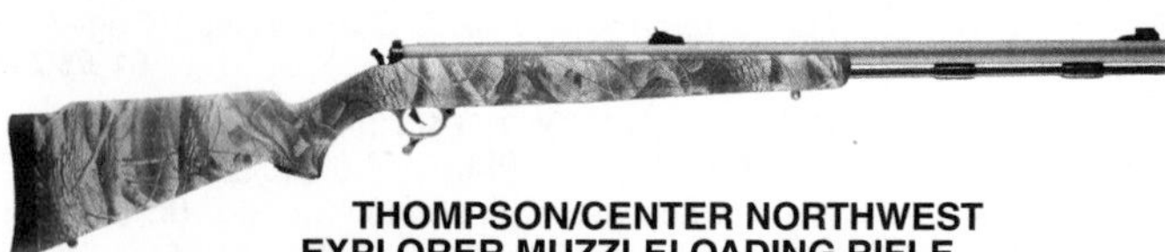

THOMPSON/CENTER NORTHWEST EXPLORER MUZZLELOADING RIFLE
50-caliber single shot rifle. Features include dropping block action, #11 percussion cap ignition, 28-inch blued or Weathershield 1:48 rifled barrel, adjustable fiber optic sights, aluminum ramrod, black or camo composite stock with recoil pad, QLA muzzle system. Weight 7 lbs.
Price: . . . . **$329.00 to $399.00**

TRADITIONS BUCKSKINNER CARBINE
Caliber: 50. **Barrel:** 21"; 15/16" flats, half octagon, half round; 1:20" or 1:66" twist. **Weight:** 6 lbs. **Length:** 37" overall. **Stock:** Beech or black laminated. **Sights:** Beaded blade front, fiber-optic open rear click adjustable for windage and elevation or fiber-optics. **Features:** Uses V-type mainspring, single trigger. Non-glare hardware; sling swivels. From Traditions.
Price: Flintlock. **$249.00**
Price: Flintlock, laminated stock **$303.00**

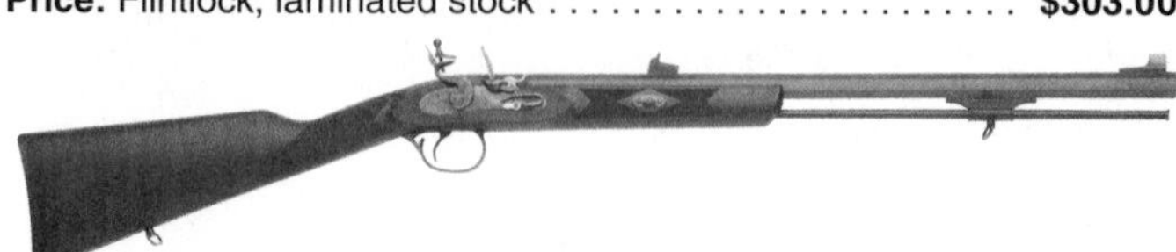

TRADITIONS DEERHUNTER RIFLE SERIES
Caliber: 32, 50 or 54. **Barrel:** 24", octagonal; 15/16" flats; 1:48" or 1:66" twist. **Weight:** 6 lbs. **Length:** 40" overall. **Stock:** Stained hardwood or All-Weather composite with rubber buttpad, sling swivels. **Sights:** Lite Optic blade front, adjustable rear fiber-optics. **Features:** Flint or percussion with color case-hardened lock. Hooked breech, oversized trigger guard, blackened furniture, PVC ramrod. All-Weather has composite stock and C-nickel barrel. Drilled and tapped for scope mounting. Imported by Traditions, Inc.
Price: Percussion, 50-cal.; blued barrel; 1:48" twist **$228.00**
Price: Flintlock, 50 caliber only; 1:48" twist **$278.00**
Price: 50-cal., synthetic/blued **$224.00**
Price: Flintlock, 50-cal., synthetic/blued **$256.00**
Price: Redi-Pak, 50 cal. flintlock **$308.00**
Price: Flintlock, left-handed hardwood, 50 cal. **$337.00**
Price: 50-cal., hardwood/blued **$264.00**

TRADITIONS PURSUIT ULTRALIGHT MUZZLELOADER
Caliber: .50. **Barrel:** 26", Chromoly Tapered, Fluted Barrel with Premium CeraKote Finish. **Weight:** 5.5 lbs. **Length:** 44" overall. **Stock:** Soft Touch camouflage stocks with thumbhole stocks available. **Sights:** 3-9x40 scope with medium rings and bases mounted and bore sighted by a factory trained technician. **Features:** Williams™ fiber optic metal sights provide a clear sight picture even in low light conditions. The Pursuit™ Ultralight comes equipped with our Accelerator Breech Plug™. This patented and award winning breech plug removes in three full rotations and requires no tools! This full featured gun is rounded out with a corrosion resistant lightweight frame that improves overall handling.
Price: **$435.00**

TRADITIONS PURSUIT BREAK-OPEN MUZZLELOADER
Caliber: 45, 54 and 12 gauge. **Barrel:** 28", tapered, fluted; blued, stainless or Hardwoods Green camo. **Weight:** 8.25 lbs. **Length:** 44" overall. **Stock:** Synthetic black or Hardwoods Green. **Sights:** Steel fiber-optic rear, bead front. Introduced 2004 by Traditions, Inc.
Price: Steel, blued, 45 or 50 cal., synthetic stock **$279.00**

Prices given are believed to be accurate at time of publication however, many factors affect retail pricing so exact prices are not possible.

Price: Steel, nickel, 45 or 50 cal., synthetic stock **$309.00**
Price: Steel, nickel w/Hardwoods Green stock **$359.00**
Price: Matte blued; 12 ga., synthetic stock **$369.00**
Price: Matte blued; 12 ga. w/Hardwoods Green stock **$439.00**
Price: Lightweight model, blued, synthetic stock **$199.00**
Price: Lightweight model, blued, Mossy Oak® Break-Up™ Camo stock **$239.00**
Price: Lightweight model, nickel, Mossy Oak® Break-Up™ Camo stock **$279.00**

TRADITIONS EVOLUTION LONG DISTANCE BOLT-ACTION BLACKPOWDER RIFLE

Caliber: 45, 50 percussion. **Barrel:** 26", fluted with porting. **Sights:** Steel fiber-optic. **Weight:** 7 to 7.25 lbs. **Length:** 45" overall. **Features:** Bolt-action, cocking indicator, thumb safety, aluminum ramrod, sling studs. Wide variety of stocks and metal finishes. Introduced 2004 by Traditions, Inc.

Price: 50-cal. synthetic stock. **$314.00**
Price: 45-cal, synthetic stock **$259.00**
Price: 50-cal. AW/Adv. Timber HD **$370.00**
Price: 50-cal. synthetic black/blued **$293.00**

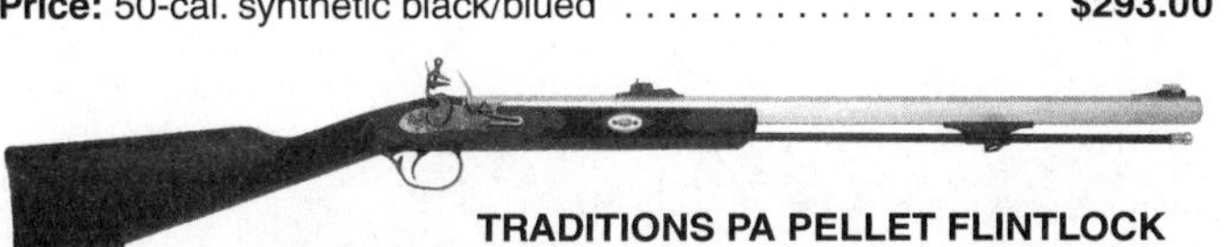

TRADITIONS PA PELLET FLINTLOCK

Caliber: 50. **Barrel:** 26", blued, nickel. **Weight:** 7 lbs. **Stock:** Hardwood, synthetic and synthetic break-up. **Sights:** Fiber-optic. **Features:** Removeable breech plug, left-hand model with hardwood stock. 1:48" twist.

Price: Hardwood, blued. **$379.00**
Price: Hardwood left, blued **$469.00**

TRADITIONS HAWKEN WOODSMAN RIFLE

Caliber: 50. **Barrel:** 28"; 15/16" flats. **Weight:** 7 lbs., 11 oz. **Length:** 44.5" overall. **Stock:** Walnut-stained hardwood. **Sights:** Beaded blade front, hunting-style open rear adjustable for windage and elevation. **Features:** Percussion only. Brass patchbox and furniture. Double triggers. From Traditions.

Price: percussion **$429.00**
Price: flintlock **$469.00**

TRADITIONS KENTUCKY RIFLE

Caliber: 50. **Barrel:** 33.5"; 7/8" flats; 1:66" twist. **Weight:** 7 lbs. **Length:** 49" overall. **Stock:** Beech; inletted toe plate. **Sights:** Blade front, fixed rear. **Features:** Full-length, two-piece stock; brass furniture; color case-hardened lock. From Traditions.

Price: percussion **$389.00**
Price: flintlock **$439.00**

TRADITIONS PENNSYLVANIA RIFLE

Caliber: 50. **Barrel:** 40.25"; 7/8" flats; 1:66" twist, octagon. **Weight:** 9 lbs. **Length:** 57.5" overall. **Stock:** Walnut. **Sights:** Blade front, adjustable rear. **Features:** Brass patchbox and ornamentation. Double-set triggers. From Traditions.

Price: percussion **$719.00**
Price: flintlock **$789.00**

TRADITIONS SHENANDOAH RIFLE

Caliber: 36, 50. **Barrel:** 33.5" octagon; 1:66" twist. **Weight:** 7 lbs., 3 oz. **Length:** 49.5" overall. **Stock:** Walnut. **Sights:** Blade front, buckhorn rear. **Features:** V-type mainspring; double-set trigger; solid brass buttplate, patchbox, nosecap, thimbles, trigger guard. Introduced 1996. From Traditions.

Price: percussion **$599.00**
Price: flintlock **$629.00**

TRADITIONS TENNESSEE RIFLE

Caliber: 50. **Barrel:** 24", octagon; 15/16" flats; 1:66" twist. **Weight:** 6 lbs. **Length:** 40.5" overall. **Stock:** Stained beech. **Sights:** Blade front, fixed rear. **Features:** One-piece stock has inletted brass furniture, cheekpiece; double-set trigger; V-type mainspring. Flint or percussion. From Traditions.

Price: percussion **$459.00**
Price: flintlock **$519.00**

TRADITIONS TRACKER 209 IN-LINE RIFLES

Caliber: 45, 50. **Barrel:** 22" blued or C-nickel finish; 1:28" twist, 50 cal. 1:20" 45 cal. **Weight:** 6 lbs., 4 oz. **Length:** 41" overall. **Stock:** Black, Advantage Timber® composite, synthetic. **Sights:** Lite Optic blade front, adjustable rear. **Features:** Thumb safety; adjustable trigger; rubber butt pad and sling swivel studs; takes 150 grains of Pyrodex pellets; one-piece breech system takes 209 shotshell primers. Drilled and tapped for scope. From Traditions.

Price: (Black composite or synthetic stock, 22" blued barrel) . **$161.00**
Price: (Black composite or synthetic stock, 22" C-nickel barrel) **$184.00**
Price: (Advantage Timber® stock, 22" C-nickel barrel) **$249.00**
Price: (Redi-Pak, black stock and blued barrel, powder flask, capper, ball starter, other accessories) **$219.00**
Price: (Redi-Pak, synthetic stock and blued barrel, with scope) **$265.00**

ULTRA LIGHT ARMS MODEL 209 MUZZLELOADER

Caliber: 45 or 50. **Barrel:** 24" button rifled; 1:32 twist. **Weight:** Under 5 lbs. **Stock:** Kevlar/Graphite. **Features:** Recoil pad, sling swivels included. Some color options available. Adj. Timney trigger, positive primer extraction.

Price: **$1,800.00**

ZOUAVE PERCUSSION RIFLE

Caliber: 58, 59. **Barrel:** 32.5". **Weight:** 9.5 lbs. **Length:** 48.5" overall. **Stock:** Walnut finish, brass patchbox and buttplate. **Sights:** Fixed front, rear adjustable for elevation. **Features:** Color case-hardened lockplate, blued barrel. From Navy Arms, Dixie Gun Works, EMF, Euroarms of America.

Price: Dixie Gun Works PR0853 (58) **$525.00**

CABELA'S BLACKPOWDER SHOTGUNS
Gauge: 10, 12, 20. **Barrel:** 10-ga., 30"; 12-ga., 28.5" (Extra-Full, Mod., Imp. Cyl. choke tubes); 20-ga., 27.5" (Imp. Cyl. & Mod. fixed chokes). **Weight:** 6.5 to 7 lbs. **Length:** 45" overall (28.5" barrel). **Stock:** American walnut with checkered grip; 12- and 20-gauge have straight stock, 10-gauge has pistol grip. **Features:** Blued barrels, engraved, color case-hardened locks and hammers, brass ramrod tip. From Cabela's.
Price: 10-gauge. **$849.99**
Price: 12-gauge **$719.99**
Price: 20-gauge **$659.99**

DIXIE MAGNUM PERCUSSION SHOTGUN
Gauge: 10, 12, 20. **Barrel:** 30" (Imp. Cyl. & Mod.) in 10-gauge; 28" in 12-gauge. **Weight:** 6.25 lbs. **Length:** 45" overall. **Stock:** Hand-checkered walnut, 14" pull. **Features:** Double triggers; light hand engraving; case-hardened locks in 12-gauge, polished steel in 10-gauge; sling swivels. From Dixie Gun Works.
Price: 12 ga. PS0930 . . . . **$825.00**
Price: 12-ga. Kit PS0940 . . . . **$725.00**
Price: 20-ga. PS0334 . . . . **$825.00**
Price: 10-ga. PS1030 . . . . **$900.00**
Price: 10-ga. kit PS1040 . . . . **$725.00**
Price: Coach Gun, 12 ga. 20" bbl PS0914 . . . . **$800.00**

KNIGHT TK2000 NEXT G-1 CAMO MUZZLELOADING SHOTGUN
Gauge: 12. **Barrel:** 26", extra-full choke tube. **Weight:** 7 lbs., 7 oz. **Length:** 45" overall. **Stock:** Synthetic black or Realtree Hardwoods; recoil pad; swivel studs. **Sights:** Fully adjustable rear, blade front with fiber-optics. **Features:** Receiver drilled and tapped for scope mount; in-line ignition; adjustable trigger; removable breech plug; double safety system; Imp. Cyl. choke tube available. Made in U.S. by Knight Rifles (Modern Muzzleloading)
Price: **$379.99**

SMOKELESS MUZZLELOADERS

BAD BULL X-SERIES MUZZLELOADER RIFLES
Caliber: 45. **Barrel:** 28". **Stock:** Laminated thumbhole stock. **Weight:** 9 lbs., 10 oz. **Length:** 50" overall. **Features:** Remington bolt action, Shilen select stainless steel barrel, Harrell's custom muzzle brake, laminated thumbhole stock, adjustable trigger, pillar bedded, glass bedded, free floated barrel, 1" decelerator pad, Warne rings/weaver, mag-prime 2 stage breech plug.
Price: **$3950.00**

BAD BULL FB SERIES MUZZLELOADER RIFLES
Caliber: 45. **Barrel:** 26". **Stock:** Laminated thumbhole stock. **Weight:** 8 lbs., 1 oz. **Length:** 44" overall. **Features:** Ruger falling block action, Shilen select stainless steel barrel, Harrell's custom muzzle brake, black and gray laminated stock and forearm, mag-prime 2 stage breech plug, 1" decelerator pad, Warne rings, open sights (optional).
Price: **$3950.00**

BAD BULL G SERIES MUZZLELOADER RIFLES
Caliber: 45. **Barrel:** 26". **Stock:** Laminated thumbhole stock. **Weight:** 7 lbs., 14 oz. **Length:** 46.75" overall. **Features:** Remington bolt action, Shilen stainless steel barrel, Harrell's custom muzzle brake, classic laminated stock, trigger adjusted to 2 ½ lbs., Double pillar bedded, 1" recoil pad, mag prime 2 stage breech plug, Warne rings & grand slam bases. The Bad Bull G Series has the short length and lightweight of the FB Series and the extreme accuracy of the X Series. It is a great hunting muzzleloader. The 275 grain Parker/BB Bullet is used with IMR 4350 Powder. With this combination, we are producing MOA or less. If you are a hunter who likes a shorter, lighter muzzleloader with great accuracy capability all the way to 500 yards, this is your muzzleloader.
Price: **$3950.00**

AIRFORCE TALON P
Caliber: .25, single shot. **Barrel:** 12". **Weight:** 3.5 lbs. **Length:** 24.2". Quick-detachable air tank with adjustable power. Air tank volume 231 cc.
Price: **$421.00**

ARS HUNTING MASTER AR6 AIR PISTOL
Caliber: .22 (.177 + 20 special order). **Barrel:** 12" rifled. **Weight:** 3 lbs. **Length:** 18.25 overall. **Power:** NA. **Grips:** Indonesian walnut with checkered grip. **Sights:** Adjustable rear, blade front. **Features:** 6 shot repeater with rotary magazine, single or double action, receiver grooved for scope, hammer block and trigger block safeties.
Price: **$659.00**

BEEMAN P1 MAGNUM AIR PISTOL
Caliber: .177, 20. **Barrel:** 8.4". **Weight:** 2.5 lbs. **Length:** 11" overall. **Power:** Top lever cocking; spring-piston. **Grips:** Checkered walnut. **Sights:** Blade front, square notch rear with click micrometer adjustments for windage and elevation. Grooved for scope mounting. **Features:** Dual power for .177 and 20 cal.; low setting gives 350-400 fps; high setting 500-600 fps. All Colt 45 auto grips fit gun. Dry-firing feature for practice. Optional wood shoulder stock. Imported by Beeman.
Price: .... **$499.95 to $525.95**

BEEMAN P3 PNEUMATIC AIR PISTOL
Caliber: .177. **Barrel:** NA. **Weight:** 1.7 lbs. **Length:** 9.6" overall. **Power:** Single-stroke pneumatic; overlever barrel cocking. **Grips:** Reinforced polymer. **Sights:** Front and rear fiber-optic sights. **Features:** Velocity 410 fps. Polymer frame; automatic safety; two-stage trigger; built-in muzzle brake.
Price: **$245.95**
Price: With scope **$335.95**

BEEMAN/FEINWERKBAU P44
Caliber: .177, single shot. **Barrel:** 9.17". **Weight:** 2.10 lbs. **Length:** 16.54" overall. **Power:** Pre-charged pneumatic. **Grips:** Walnut grip. **Sights:** front and rear sights. **Features:** 500 fps, sighting line adjustable from 360 to 395mm, adjustable 3-d grip in 3 sizes, adjustable match trigger, delivered in special transport case.
Price: **$2,575.95**
Price: Left-hand model **$2,655.95**

BEEMAN/FEINWERKBAU P56
Caliber: .177, 5-shot magazine. **Barrel:** 8.81". **Weight:** 2.43 lbs. **Length:** 16.54" overall. **Power:** Pre-charged pneumatic. **Grips:** Walnut Morini grip. **Sights:** front and rear sights. **Features:** 500 fps, match-adjustable trigger, adjustable rear sight, front sight accepts interchangeable inserts, delivered in special transport case.
Price: **$2,654.00**

BEEMAN/FWB 103 AIR PISTOL
Caliber: .177. **Barrel:** 10.1", 12-groove rifling. **Weight:** 2.5 lbs. **Length:** 16.5" overall. **Power:** Single-stroke pneumatic, underlever cocking. **Grips:** Stippled walnut with adjustable palm shelf. **Sights:** Blade front, open rear adjustable for windage and elevation. Notch size adjustable for width. Interchangeable front blades. **Features:** Velocity 510 fps. Fully adjustable trigger. Cocking effort 2 lbs. Imported by Beeman.
Price: Right-hand **$2,110.00**
Price: Left-hand **$2,350.00**

BEEMAN HW70A AIR PISTOL
Caliber: .177. **Barrel:** 6-1/4", rifled. **Weight:** 38 oz. **Length:** 12-3/4" overall. **Power:** Spring, barrel cocking. **Grips:** Plastic, with thumbrest. **Sights:** Hooded post front, square notch rear adjustable for windage and elevation. Comes with scope base. **Features:** Adjustable trigger, 31-lb. cocking effort, 440 fps MV; automatic barrel safety. Imported by Beeman.
Price: **$289.95**

BENJAMIN & SHERIDAN CO2 PISTOLS
Caliber: .22, single shot. **Barrel:** 6-3/8", brass. **Weight:** 1 lb. 12 oz. **Length:** 9" overall. **Power:** 12-gram CO2 cylinder. **Grips:** American Hardwood. **Sights:** High ramp front, fully adjustable notched rear. **Features:** Velocity to 500 fps. Turnbolt action with cross-bolt safety. Gives about 40 shots per CO2 cylinder. Black or nickel finish. Made in U.S. by Crosman Corp.
Price: EB22 (.22) **$118.59**

BENJAMIN & SHERIDAN PNEUMATIC PELLET PISTOLS
Caliber: .177, .22, single shot. **Barrel:** 9-3/8", rifled brass. **Weight:** 2 lbs., 8 oz. **Length:**12.25" overall. **Power:** Underlever pnuematic, hand pumped. **Grips:** American Hardwood. **Sights:** High ramp front, fully adjustable notch rear. **Features:** Velocity to 525 fps (variable). Bolt action with cross-bolt safety. Choice of black or nickel finish. Made in U.S. by Crosman Corp.
Price: Black finish, HB17 (.177), HB22 (.22) **$133.59**

CROSMAN C-TT
Caliber: BB, 18-shot magazine. **Length:** 8". Semi-auto CO2-powered repeater styled after Russian Tarev TT-30. Metal frame and polymer grip.
Price: **$100.00**

CROSMAN C11
Caliber: .177, 18-shot BB or pellet. **Weight:** 1.4 lbs. **Length:** 8.5". **Power:** 12g CO2. **Sights:** Fixed. **Features:** Compact semi-automatic BB pistol. Velocity up to 480 fps. Under barrel weaver style rail.
Price: **$50.00**
Price: (Tactical) **$50.00**

CROSMAN 2240
Caliber: .22. **Barrel:** Rifled steel. **Weight:** 1 lb. 13 oz. **Length:** 11.125".

Power: CO2. **Grips:** NA. **Sights:** Blade front, rear adjustable. **Features:** Ergonomically designed ambidextrous grip fits the hand for perfect balance and comfort with checkering and a thumbrest on both grip panels. From Crosman.
Price: **$69.00**

CROSMAN 3576 REVOLVER
Caliber: .177, pellets. **Barrel:** Rifled steel. **Weight:** 2 lbs. **Length:** 11.38". **Power:** CO2. **Grips:** NA. **Sights:** Blade front, rear adjustable. **Features:** Semi-auto 10-shot with revolver styling and finger-molded grip design, 6" barrel for increased accuracy. From Crosman.
Price: **$60.00**

CROSMAN MODEL 1088 REPEAT AIR PISTOL
Caliber: .177, 8-shot pellet clip. **Barrel:** Rifled steel. **Weight:** 17 oz. **Length:** 7.75" overall. **Power:** CO2 Powerlet. **Grips:** Checkered black plastic. **Sights:** Fixed blade front, adjustable rear. **Features:** Velocity about 430 fps. Single or double semi-automatic action. From Crosman.
Price: **$75.00**

CROSMAN PRO77
Caliber: .177, 17-shot BB. **Weight:** 1.31 lbs. **Length:** 6.75". **Power:** 12g CO2. **Sights:** Fixed. **Features:** Compact pistol with realistic recoil. Under the barrel weaver style rail. Velocity up to 325 fps.
Price: Pro77CS **$90.00**

CROSMAN T4
Caliber: .177, 8-shot BB or pellet. **Weight:** 1.32 lbs. **Length:** 8.63". **Power:** 12g CO2. **Sights:** Fixed front, windage adjustable rear. **Features:** Shoots BBs or pellets. Easy patent-pending CO2 piercing mechanism. Under the barrel weaver style rail.
Price: T4CS **$85.00**
Price: T4OPS, includes adjustable Red Dot sight, barrel compensator, and pressure operated tactical flashlight. Comes in foam padeed, hard sided protective case **$167.99**

DAISY POWERLINE® MODEL 15XT AIR PISTOL
Caliber: .177 BB, 15-shot built-in magazine. **Barrel:** NA. **Weight:** NA. **Length:** 7.21". **Power:** CO2. **Grips:** NA. **Sights:** NA. **Features:** Velocity 425 fps. Made in the U.S.A. by Daisy Mfg. Co.
Price: **$70.00**
Price: With electronic point sight **$84.00**

DAISY MODEL 717 AIR PISTOL
Caliber: .177, single shot. **Weight:** 2.25 lbs. **Length:** 13-1/2" overall. **Grips:** Molded checkered woodgrain with contoured thumbrest. **Sights:** Blade and ramp front, open rear with windage and elevation adjustments. **Features:** Single pump pneumatic pistol. Rifled steel barrel. Crossbolt trigger block. Muzzle velocity 360 fps. From Daisy Mfg. Co.
Price: **$255.00**

DAISY MODEL 747 TRIUMPH AIR PISTOL
Caliber: .177, single shot. **Weight:** 2.35 lbs. **Length:** 13-1/2" overall. **Grips:** Molded checkered woodgrain with contoured thumbrest. **Sights:** Blade and ramp front, open rear with windage and elevation adjustments. **Features:** Single pump pneumatic pistol. Lothar Walther rifled high-grade steel barrel; crowned 12 lands and grooves, right-hand twist. Precision bore sized for match pellets. Muzzle velocity 360 fps. From Daisy Mfg. Co.
Price: **$264.99**

DAISY POWERLINE® 201
Caliber: .177 BB or pellet. **Weight:** 1 lb. **Length:** 9.25" overall. **Sights:** Blade and ramp front, fixed open rear. **Features:** Spring-air action, trigger-block safety and smooth-bore steel barrel. Muzzle velocity 230 fps. From Daisy Mfg. Co.
Price: **$29.99**

DAISY POWERLINE® 693 AIR PISTOL
Caliber: .177, single shot. **Weight:** 1.10 lbs. **Length:** 7.9" overall. **Grips:** Molded checkered. **Sights:** Blade and ramp front, fixed open rear. **Features:** Semi-automoatic BB pistol with a nickel finish and smooth bore steel barrel. Muzzle veocity 400 fps. From Daisy Mfg. Co.
Price: **$76.99**

DAISY POWERLINE® 5170 CO2 PISTOL
Caliber: .177 BB. **Weight:** 1 lb. **Length:** 9.5" overall. **Sights:** Blade and ramp front, open rear. **Features:** CO2 semi-automatic action, manual trigger-block safety, upper and lower rails for mounting sights and other accessories and a smooth-bore steel barrel. Muzzle velocity 520 fps. From Daisy Mfg. Co.
Price: **$59.99**

DAISY POWERLINE® 5501 CO2 BLOWBACK PISTOL
Caliber: .177 BB. **Weight:** 1 lb. **Length:** 9.5" overall. **Sights:** Blade and ramp front, open rear. **Features:** CO2 semi-automatic blow-back action, manual trigger-block safety, and a smooth-bore steel barrel. Muzzle velocity 430 fps. From Daisy Mfg. Co.
Price: **$99.99**

EAA/BAIKAL IZH-M46 TARGET AIR PISTOL
Caliber: .177, single shot. **Barrel:** 10". **Weight:** 2.4 lbs. **Length:** 16.8" overall. **Power:** Underlever single-stroke pneumatic. **Grips:** Adjustable wooden target. **Sights:** Micrometer fully adjustable rear, blade front. **Features:** Velocity about 440 fps. Hammer-forged, rifled barrel. Imported from Russia by European American Armory.
Price: **$430.00**

GAMO P-23, P-23 LASER PISTOL
Caliber: .177, 12-shot. **Barrel:** 4.25". **Weight:** 1 lb. **Length:** 7.5". **Power:** CO2 cartridge, semi-automatic, 410 fps. **Grips:** Plastic. **Sights:** NA. **Features:** Walther PPK cartridge pistol copy, optional laser sight. Imported from Spain by Gamo.
Price: . . . . **$89.95**, (with laser) **$139.95**

GAMO PT-80, PT-80 LASER PISTOL
Caliber: .177, 8-shot. **Barrel:** 4.25". **Weight:** 1.2 lbs. **Length:** 7.2". **Power:** CO2 cartridge, semi-automatic, 410 fps. **Grips:** Plastic. **Sights:** 3-dot. **Features:** Optional laser sight and walnut grips available. Imported from Spain by Gamo.
Price: . . . . **$108.95**, (with laser) **$159.95**
Price: (with walnut grip) **$119.95**

HAMMERLI AP-40 AIR PISTOL
Caliber: .177. **Barrel:** 10". **Weight:** 2.2 lbs. **Length:** 15.5". **Power:** NA. **Grips:** Adjustable orthopedic. **Sights:** Fully adjustable micrometer. **Features:** Sleek, light, well balanced and accurate.
Price: **$1,400.00**

MAGNUM RESEARCH DESERT EAGLE
Caliber: .177, 8-shot pellet. 5.7" rifled. **Weight:** 2.5 lbs. 11" overall. **Power:** 12g CO2. **Sights:** Fixed front, adjustable rear. Velocity of 425 fps. 8-shot rotary clip. Double or single action. The first .177 caliber air pistol with BLOWBACK action. Big and weighty, designed in the likeness of the real Desert Eagle.
Price: **$172.31**

MAGNUM BABY DESERT
Caliber: .177, 15-shot BB. 4" **Weight:** 1.0 lbs. 8-1/4" overall. **Power:** 12g CO2. **Sights:** Fixed front and rear. Velocity of 420 fps. Double action BB repeater. Comes with bonus Picatinny top rail and built-in bottom rail.
Price: **$41.54**

MORINI CM 162 EL MATCH AIR PISTOLS
Caliber: .177, single shot. **Barrel:** 9.4". **Weight:** 32 oz. **Length:** 16.1" overall. **Power:** Scuba air. **Grips:** Adjustable match type. **Sights:** Interchangeable blade front, fully adjustable match-type rear. **Features:** Power mechanism shuts down when pressure drops to a

Prices given are believed to be accurate at time of publication however, many factors affect retail pricing so exact prices are not possible.

preset level. Adjustable electronic trigger.
Price: **$1,075.00**

PARDINI K58 MATCH AIR PISTOLS
Caliber: .177, single shot. **Barrel:** 9". **Weight:** 37.7 oz. **Length:** 15.5" overall. **Power:** Precharged compressed air; single-stroke cocking. **Grips:** Adjustable match type; stippled walnut. **Sights:** Interchangeable post front, fully adjustable match rear. **Features:** Fully adjustable trigger. Short version K-2 available. Imported from Italy by Larry's Guns.
Price: **$819.00**

RUGER MARK I
Caliber: .177. **Barrel:** 6.5". **Weight:** 48 oz. **Sights:** Fiber optic front, open rear. Spring-piston operated pellet pistol up to 500 fps velocity with lead pellets, 600 fps with alloy.
Price: **$75.00**

RWS 9B/9N AIR PISTOLS
Caliber: .177, single shot. **Barrel:** 8". **Weight:** 2.38 lbs. **Length:** 10.4". **Power:** 550 fps. **Grips:** Right hand with thumbrest. **Sights:** Adjustable. **Features:** Spring-piston powered. Black or nickel finish.
Price: 9B/9N **$150.00**

SMITH & WESSON 586
Caliber: .177, 10-shot pellet. Rifled. **Power:** 12g CO2. **Sights:** Fixed front, adjustable rear. 10-shot rotary clip. Double or single action. Replica revolvers that duplicate both weight and handling.
Price: 4" barrel, 2.5 lbs, 400 fps **$215.34**
Price: 6" barrel, 2.8 lbs, 425 fps **$231.49**
Price: 8" barrel, 3.0 lbs, 460 fps **$247.65**
Price: S&W 686 Nickel, 6" barrel, 2.8 lbs, 425 fps **$253.03**

STEYR LP10P MATCH AIR PISTOL
Caliber: .177, single shot. **Barrel:** 9". **Weight:** 38.7 oz. **Length:** 15.3" overall. **Power:** Scuba air. **Grips:** Adjustable Morini match, palm shelf, stippled walnut. **Sights:** Interchangeable blade in 4mm, 4.5mm or 5mm widths, adjustable open rear, interchangeable 3.5mm or 4mm leaves. **Features:** Velocity about 500 fps. Adjustable trigger, adjustable sight radius from 12.4" to 13.2". With compensator. Recoil elimination.
Price: **$1,400.00**

TECH FORCE SS2 OLYMPIC COMPETITION AIR PISTOL
Caliber: .177 pellet, single shot. **Barrel:** 7.4". **Weight:** 2.8 lbs. **Length:** 16.5" overall. **Power:** Spring piston, sidelever. **Grips:** Hardwood. **Sights:** Extended adjustable rear, blade front accepts inserts. **Features:** Velocity 520 fps. Recoilless design; adjustments allow duplication of a firearm's feel. Match-grade, adjustable trigger; includes carrying case. Imported from China by Compasseco, Inc.
Price: **$295.00**

TECH FORCE 35 AIR PISTOL
Caliber: .177 pellet, single shot. **Weight:** 2.86 lbs. **Length:** 14.9" overall. **Power:** Spring-piston, underlever. **Grips:** Hardwood. **Sights:** Micrometer adjustable rear, blade front. **Features:** Velocity 400 fps. Grooved for scope mount; trigger safety. Imported from China by Compasseco, Inc.
Price: **$39.95**

Tech Force S2-1 Air Pistol
Similar to Tech Force 8 except basic grips and sights for plinking.
Price: **$29.95**

WALTHER LP300 MATCH PISTOL
Caliber: .177. **Barrel:** 236mm. **Weight:** 1.018g. **Length:** NA. **Power:** NA. **Grips:** NA. **Sights:** Integrated front with three different widths, adjustable rear. **Features:** Adjustable grip and trigger.
Price: **$1,800.00**

WALTHER PPK/S
Caliber: .177, 15-shot steel BB. 3-1/2". **Weight:** 1.2 lbs. 6-1/4" overall. **Power:** 12g CO2. **Sights:** Fixed front and rear. Velocity of 295 fps. Lookalike of one of the world's most famous pistols. Realistic recoil. Heavyweight steel construction.
Price: **$71.92**
Price: With laser sight **$94.23**
Price: With BiColor pistol, targets, shooting glasses, BBs **$84.62**

WALTHER CP99 COMPACT
Caliber: .177, 17-shot steel BB semi-auto. 3". **Weight:** 1.7 lbs. 6-1/2" overall. **Power:** 12g CO2. **Sights:** Fixed front and rear. Velocity of 345 fps. Realistic recoil, blowback action. Heavyweight steel construction. Built-in Picatinny mount.
Price: **$83.08**

WINCHESTER MODEL 11
Caliber: BB. CO2-powered pistol with 16-round removable magazine. **Weight:** 30 ozs. Can be fired double or single action. Slide stays open after last shot. Dimensions and operating controls the same as 1911 pistol.
Price: **$110.00**

AIRFORCE CONDOR RIFLE

Caliber: .177, .22 single shot. **Barrel:** 24" rifled. **Weight:** 6.5 lbs. **Length:** 38.75" overall. **Power:** Pre-charged pneumatic. **Stock:** NA. **Sights:** Intended for scope use, fiber-optic open sights optional. **Features:** Lothar Walther match barrel, adjustable power levels from 600-1,300 fps. 3,000 psi fill pressure. Automatic safety. Air tank volume: 490cc. An integral extended scope rail allows easy mounting of the largest air-gun scopes. Operates on high-pressure air from scuba tank or hand pump. Manufactured in the U.S.A by AirForce Airguns.

Price: Gun only (.22 or .177) **$631.00**

AIRFORCE TALON AIR RIFLE

Caliber: .177, .22, single shot. **Barrel:** 18" rifled. **Weight:** 5.5 lbs. **Length:** 32.6". **Power:** Pre-charged pneumatic. **Stock:** NA. **Sights:** Intended for scope use, fiber-optic open sights optional. **Features:** Lothar Walther match barrel, adjustable power levels from 400-1,000 fps, 3,000 psi fill pressure. Automatic safety. Air tank volume: 490cc. Operates on high-pressure air from scuba tank or hand pump. Manufactured in the U.S.A. by AirForce Airguns.

Price: Gun only (.22 or .177). **$514.25**

AIRFORCE TALON SS AIR RIFLE

Caliber: .177, .22, single shot. **Barrel:** 12" rifled. **Weight:** 5.25 lbs. **Length:** 32.75". **Power:** Pre-charged pneumatic. **Stock:** NA. **Sights:** Intended for scope use, fiber-optic open sights optional. **Features:** Lothar Walther match barrel, adjustable power levels from 400-1,000 fps. 3,000 psi fill pressure. Automatic safety. Chamber in front of barrel strips away air turbulence, protects muzzle and reduces firing report. Air tank volume: 490cc. Operates on high-pressure air from scuba tank or hand pump. Manufactured in the U.S.A. by AirForce Airguns.

Price: Gun only (.22 or .177). **$535.50**

AIRROW MODEL A-8SRB STEALTH AIR RIFLE

Caliber: .177, .22, .25, 9-shot. **Barrel:** 20"; rifled. **Weight:** 6 lbs. **Length:** 34" overall. **Power:** CO2 or compressed air; variable power. **Stock:** Telescoping CAR-15-type. **Sights:** Variable 3.5-10x scope. **Features:** Velocity 1100 fps in all calibers. Pneumatic air trigger. All aircraft aluminum and stainless steel construction. Mil-spec materials and finishes. From Swivel Machine Works, Inc.

Price: About **$2,299.00**

AIRROW MODEL A-8S1P STEALTH AIR RIFLE

Caliber: #2512 16" arrow. **Barrel:** 16". **Weight:** 4.4 lbs. **Length:** 30.1" overall. **Power:** CO2 or compressed air; variable power. **Stock:** Telescoping CAR-15-type. **Sights:** Scope rings only. 7 oz. rechargeable cylinder and valve. **Features:** Velocity to 650 fps with 260-grain arrow. Pneumatic air trigger. Broadhead guard. All aircraft aluminum and stainless steel construction. Mil-spec materials and finishes. A-8S Models perform to 2,000 PSIG above or below water levels. Waterproof case. From Swivel Machine Works, Inc.

Price: **$1,699.00**

ARS HUNTING MASTER AR6 AIR RIFLE

Caliber: .22, 6-shot repeater. **Barrel:** 25-1/2". **Weight:** 7 lbs. **Length:** 41-1/4" overall. **Power:** Precompressed air from 3000 psi diving tank. **Stock:** Indonesian walnut with checkered grip; rubber buttpad. **Sights:** Blade front, adjustable peep rear. **Features:** Velocity over 1000 fps with 32-grain pellet. Receiver grooved for scope mounting. Has 6-shot rotary magazine. Imported by Air Rifle Specialists.

Price: **$1,500.00**

BEEMAN HW100

Caliber: .177 or .22, 14-shot magazine. **Barrel:** 21-1/2". **Weight:** 9 lbs. **Length:** 42.13" overall. **Power:** Pre-charged. **Stock:** Walnut Sporter checkering on the pistol grip & forend; walnut thumbhose with lateral finger grooves on the forend & stippling on the pistol grip. **Sights:** None. Grooved for scope mounting. **Features:** 1140 fps .177 caliber; 945 fps .22 caliber. 14-shot magazine, quick-fill cylinder. Two-stage adjustable match trigger and manual safety.

Price: .177 or .22 caliber Sport Stock **$1,649.95**
Price: .177 or .22 caliber Thumbhole Stock **$1,649.95**

BEEMAN R1 AIR RIFLE

Caliber: .177, .20 or .22, single shot. **Barrel:** 19.6", 12-groove rifling. **Weight:** 8.5 lbs. **Length:** 45.2" overall. **Power:** Spring-piston, barrel cocking. **Stock:** Walnut-stained beech; cut-checkered pistol grip; Monte Carlo comb and cheekpiece; rubber buttpad. **Sights:** Tunnel front with interchangeable inserts, open rear click-adjustable for windage and elevation. Grooved for scope mounting. **Features:** Velocity 940-1000 fps (.177), 860 fps (20), 800 fps (.22). Non-drying nylon piston and breech seals. Adjustable metal trigger. Milled steel safety. Right- or left-hand stock. Adjustable cheekpiece and buttplate at extra cost. Custom and Super Laser versions available. Imported by Beeman.

Price: Right-hand **$729.95**
Price: Left-hand **$789.95**

BEEMAN R7 AIR RIFLE

Caliber: .177, .20, single shot. **Barrel:** 17". **Weight:** 6.1 lbs. **Length:** 40.2" overall. **Power:** Spring-piston. **Stock:** Stained beech. **Sights:** Hooded front, fully adjustable micrometer click open rear. **Features:** Velocity to 700 fps (.177), 620 fps (20). Receiver grooved for scope mounting; double-jointed cocking lever; fully adjustable trigger; checkered grip. Imported by Beeman.

Price: .177. . . . . **$409.95**
Price: .20 . . . . **$429.95**

BEEMAN R9 AIR RIFLE

Caliber: .177, .20, single shot. **Barrel:** NA. **Weight:** 7.3 lbs. **Length:** 43" overall. **Power:** Spring-piston, barrel cocking. **Stock:** Stained hardwood. **Sights:** Tunnel post front, fully adjustable open rear. **Features:** Velocity to 1000 fps (.177), 800 fps (20). Adjustable Rekord trigger; automatic safety; receiver dovetailed for scope mounting. Imported from Germany by Beeman Precision Airguns.

Price: .177. . . . . **$499.95**
Price: .20 . . . . **$524.95**

BEEMAN R11 MKII AIR RIFLE

Caliber: .177, single shot. **Barrel:** 19.6". **Weight:** 8.6 lbs. **Length:** 43.5" overall. **Power:** Spring-piston, barrel cocking. **Stock:** Walnut-stained beech; adjustable buttplate and cheekpiece. **Sights:** None furnished. Has dovetail for scope mounting. **Features:** Velocity 910-940 fps. All-steel barrel sleeve. Imported by Beeman.

Price: **$679.95**

BEEMAN RX-2 GAS-SPRING MAGNUM AIR RIFLE

Caliber: .177, .20, .22, .25, single shot. **Barrel:** 19.6", 12-groove rifling. **Weight:** 8.8 lbs. **Power:** Gas-spring piston air; single stroke barrel cocking. **Stock:** Laminated wood stock. **Sights:** Tunnel front, click-adjustable rear. **Features:** Velocity adjustable to about 1200 fps. Imported by Beeman.

Price: .177, right-hand **$889.95**
Price: .20, right-hand **$909.95**
Price: .22, right-hand **$889.95**
Price: .25, right-hand **$909.95**

BEEMAN R1 CARBINE

Caliber: .177,. 20, .22 single shot. **Barrel:** 16.1". **Weight:** 8.6 lbs. **Length:** 41.7" overall. **Power:** Spring-piston, barrel cocking. **Stock:** Stained beech; Monte Carlo comb and checkpiece; cut checkered pistol grip; rubber buttpad. **Sights:** Tunnel front with interchangeable inserts, open adjustable rear; receiver grooved for scope mounting. **Features:** Velocity up to 1000 fps (.177). Non-drying nylon piston and breech seals. Adjustable metal trigger. Machined steel receiver end cap and safety. Right- or left-hand stock. Imported by Beeman.

Price: .177, 20, .22, right-hand **$749.95**

BEEMAN/FEINWERKBAU 700 P ALUMINUM OR WOOD STOCK

Caliber: .177, single shot. **Barrel:** 16.6". **Weight:** 10.8 lbs. Aluminum; 9.9 lbs. Wood. **Length:** 43.3-46.25" Aluminum; 43.7" Wood. **Power:** Pre-charged pneumatic. **Stock:** Aluminum stock P laminated hardwood. **Sights:** Tunnel front sight with interchangeable inserts, click micrometer match aperture rear sight. **Features:** Velocity 570 fps. Recoilless action. Anatomical grips can be tilted and pivoted to

the barrel axis. Adjustable buttplate and cheekpiece.
Price: Aluminum 700, right, blue or silver **$3,934.95**
Price: Aluminum 700, universal. **$3,069.95**

BEEMAN/FEINWERKBAU P70 FIELD TARGET
Caliber: .177, single shot. **Barrel:** 24.6". **Weight:** 10.6 lbs. **Length:** 43.3" overall. **Power:** Pre-charged pneumatic. **Stock:** Aluminum stock (red or blue) anatomical grips, buttplate & cheekpiece. **Sights:** None, receiver grooved for scope mounting. **Features:** 870 fps velocity. At 50 yards, this air rifle is capable of achieving 1/2-inch groups. Match adjustable trigger. 2001 US Field Target National Champion.
Price: P70FT, precharged, right (red or blue) **$3,819.95**
Price: P70FT, precharged, left (red or blue) **$3,964.95**

BEEMAN/HW 97 AIR RIFLE
Caliber: .177, .20, .22, single shot. **Barrel:** 17.75". **Weight:** 9.2 lbs. **Length:** 44.1" overall. **Power:** Spring-piston, underlever cocking. **Stock:** Walnut-stained beech; rubber buttpad. **Sights:** None. Receiver grooved for scope mounting. **Features:** Velocity 830 fps (.177). Fixed barrel with fully opening, direct loading breech. Adjustable trigger. Imported by Beeman Precision Airguns.
Price: .177. . . . . **$779.95**
Price: .20, .22 . . . . **$799.95**

BENJAMIN & SHERIDAN PNEUMATIC (PUMP-UP) AIR RIFLE
Caliber: .177 or .22, single shot. **Barrel:** 19-3/8", rifled brass. **Weight:** 5-1/2 lbs. **Length:** 36-1/4" overall. **Power:** Underlever pneumatic, hand pumped. **Stock:** American walnut stock and forend. **Sights:** High ramp front, fully adjustable notched rear. **Features:** Variable velocity to 800 fps. Bolt action with ambidextrous push-pull safety. Black or nickel finish. Made in the U.S. by Benjamin Sheridan Co.
Price: 392 or 397 . . . . **$249.40**

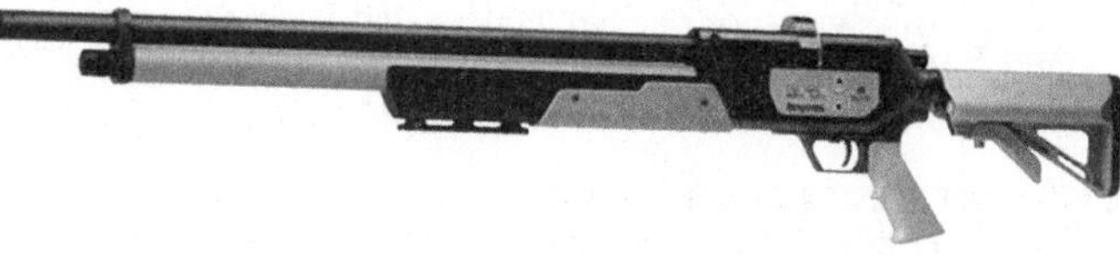

BENJAMIN ROGUE .357 CALIBER MULTI-SHOT AIR RIFLE
Caliber: .357, 6-shot mag (optional single-shot tray). **Features:** Electronic precharged pneumatic (ePCP), Bolt-action, 2-stage adjustable electronic trigger with dual electronic switches, Ambidextrous synthetic stock w/adjustable buttstock & sling swivel studs, 11mm, Adjustable power, Up to 900 fps (250 ft-lbs. max), 3000 psi (206 bar) max fill pressure (delivers full-power shots with as little as 1000 psi), Shrouded for stealthy hunting, Up to 20 shots at 100 ft-lbs. when filled to 3000 psi, Built-in manometer (air pressure gauge), Weaver bipod rail, LCD screen for EPiC controls on left side of gun, includes fill adapter. Made in the U.S. by Benjamin Sheridan Co.
Price: **$1,500.00**

BERETTA CX4 STORM
Caliber: .177, 30-shot semi-auto. 17-1/2", rifled. **Weight:** 5.25 lbs. **Length:** 30.75" overall. **Power:** 88g CO2. **Stock:** Replica style. **Sights:** Adjustable front and rear. Blowback action. Velocity of 600 fps. Accessory rails.
Price: **$276.92**

BSA SUPERTEN MK3 AIR RIFLE
Caliber: .177, .22 10-shot repeater. **Barrel:** 17-1/2". **Weight:** 7 lbs., 8 oz. **Length:** 37" overall. **Power:** Precharged pneumatic via buddy bottle. **Stock:** Oil-finished hardwood; Monte Carlo with cheekpiece, cut checkered grip; adjustable recoil pad. **Sights:** No sights; intended for scope use. **Features:** Velocity 1000+ fps (.177), 1000+ fps (.22). Patented 10-shot indexing magazine, bolt-action loading. Left-hand version also available. Imported from U.K.
Price: **$599.95**

BSA SUPERTEN MK3 BULLBARREL
Caliber: .177, .22, .25, single shot. **Barrel:** 18-1/2". **Weight:** 8 lbs., 8 oz. **Length:** 43" overall. **Power:** Spring-air, underlever cocking. **Stock:** Oil-finished hardwood; Monte Carlo with cheekpiece, checkered at grip; recoil pad. **Sights:** Ramp front, micrometer adjustable rear. Maxi-Grip scope rail. **Features:** Velocity 950 fps (.177), 750 fps (.22), 600 fps (25). Patented rotating breech design. Maxi-Grip scope rail protects optics from recoil; automatic anti-beartrap plus manual safety. Imported from U.K.
Price: Rifle, MKII Carbine (14" barrel, 39-1/2" overall) **$349.95**

BSA MAGNUM SUPERSPORT AIR RIFLE, CARBINE
Caliber: .177, .22, .25, single shot. **Barrel:** 18-1/2". **Weight:** 6 lbs., 8 oz. **Length:** 41" overall. **Power:** Spring-air, barrel cocking. **Stock:** Oil-finished hardwood; Monte Carlo with cheekpiece, recoil pad. **Sights:** Ramp front, micrometer adjustable rear. Maxi-Grip scope rail. **Features:** Velocity 950 fps (.177), 750 fps (.22), 600 fps (25). Patented Maxi-Grip scope rail protects optics from recoil; automatic anti-beartrap plus manual tang safety. Muzzle brake standard. Imported for U.K.
Price: **$194.95**
Price: Carbine, 14" barrel, muzzle brake **$214.95**

BSA METEOR AIR RIFLE
Caliber: .177, .22, single shot. **Barrel:** 18-1/2". **Weight:** 6 lbs. **Length:** 41" overall. **Power:** Spring-air, barrel cocking. **Stock:** Oil-finished hardwood. **Sights:** Ramp front, micrometer adjustable rear. **Features:** Velocity 650 fps (.177), 500 fps (.22). Automatic anti-beartrap; manual tang safety. Receiver grooved for scope mounting. Imported from U.K.
Price: Rifle **$144.95**
Price: Carbine **$164.95**

CROSMAN M4-177
Caliber: .177 pellet or BB. Removable 5-shot magazine. **Weight:** 3.5 lbs. **Length:** 34". **Sights:** Windage-adjustable flip-up rear, elevation-adjustable front. **Features:** Rifled barrel, adjustable stock, pneumatic multi-pump operation gives up to 660 fps muzzle velocity. Bolt-action variation of AR-style rifle. Also available in kit form.
Price: **$94.00**

CROSMAN MODEL POWERMASTER 664SB AIR RIFLES
Caliber: .177 (single shot pellet) or BB, 200-shot reservoir. **Barrel:** 20", rifled steel. **Weight:** 2 lbs. 15 oz. **Length:** 38-1/2" overall. **Power:** Pneumatic; hand-pumped. **Stock:** Wood-grained ABS plastic; checkered pistol grip and forend. **Sights:** Fiber-optic front, fully adjustable open rear. **Features:** Velocity about 645 fps. Bolt action, cross-bolt safety. From Crosman.
Price: **$105.50**

CROSMAN MODEL PUMPMASTER 760 AIR RIFLES
Caliber: .177 pellets (single shot) or BB (200-shot reservoir). **Barrel:** 19-1/2", rifled steel. **Weight:** 2 lbs., 12 oz. **Length:** 33.5" overall. **Power:** Pneumatic, hand-pump. **Stock:** Walnut-finished ABS plastic stock and forend. **Features:** Velocity to 590 fps (BBs, 10 pumps). Short stroke, power determined by number of strokes. Fiber-optic front sight and adjustable rear sight. Cross-bolt safety. From Crosman.
Price: Model 760 . . . . **$40.59**

CROSMAN MODEL REPEATAIR 1077 RIFLES
Caliber: .177 pellets, 12-shot clip. **Barrel:** 20.3", rifled steel. **Weight:** 3 lbs., 11 oz. **Length:** 38.8" overall. **Power:** CO2 Powerlet. **Stock:** Textured synthetic or hardwood. **Sights:** Blade front, fully adjustable rear. **Features:** Velocity 590 fps. Removable 12-shot clip. True semi-automatic action. From Crosman.
Price: **$73.99**

CROSMAN MODEL .2260 AIR RIFLE

Caliber: .22, single shot. **Barrel:** 24". **Weight:** 4 lbs., 12 oz. **Length:** 39.75" overall. **Power:** CO2 Powerlet. **Stock:** Hardwood. **Sights:** Blade front, adjustable rear open or peep. **Features:** Variable pump power; three pumps give 395 fps, six pumps 530 fps, 10 pumps 600 fps (average). Full-size adult air rifle. From Crosman.

Price: **$83.84**

CROSMAN MODEL CLASSIC 2100 AIR RIFLE

Caliber: .177 pellets (single shot), or BB (200-shot BB reservoir). **Barrel:** 21", rifled. **Weight:** 4 lbs., 13 oz. **Length:** 39-3/4" overall. **Power:** Pump-up, pneumatic. **Stock:** Wood-grained checkered ABS plastic. **Features:** Three pumps give about 450 fps, 10 pumps about 755 fps (BBs). Cross-bolt safety; concealed reservoir holds over 200 BBs. From Crosman.

Price: Model 2100B **$62.99**

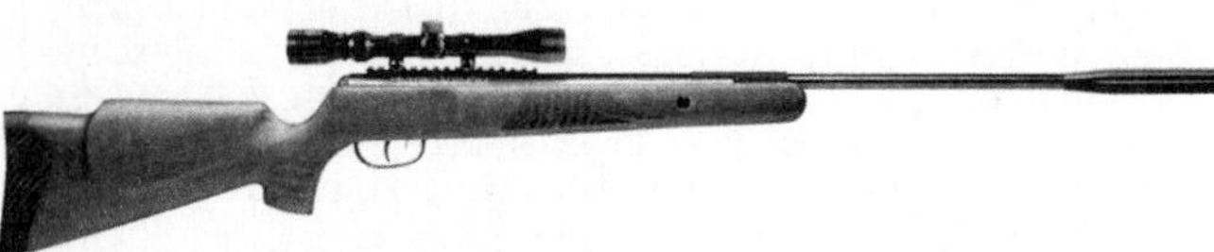

CROSMAN MODEL NITRO VENOM AIR RIFLE

Caliber: .177 & .22. **Features:** Nitro Venom air rifle feature precision, rifled barrel with fluted muzzle brake and sculpted rubber recoil pad. The rifle is equipped with a CenterPoint 3-9x32mm precision scope and a quick-lock mounting system for quick and easy optic mounting. The ambidextrous hardwood stock with raised cheek piece and modified, beavertail forearm. Crosman Nitro Venom air rifle delivers serious hunting power with muzzle energy up to 21 fpe and up to 1200 fps. Take one on a hunt to experience the power, stability and stealth of Nitro Piston® technology.

Price: .177. . . . . **$209.99**
Price: .22 . . . . **N/A**

CROSMAN MODEL NITRO VENOM DUSK AIR RIFLE

Caliber: .177 & .22. **Features:** Nitro Venom air rifle feature precision, rifled barrel with fluted muzzle brake and sculpted rubber recoil pad. The rifle is equipped with a CenterPoint 3-9x32mm precision scope and a quick-lock mounting system for quick and easy optic mounting. The ambidextrous hardwood stock with raised cheek piece and modified, beavertail forearm. Crosman Nitro Venom air rifle delivers serious hunting power with muzzle energy up to 21 fpe and up to 1200 fps. Take one on a hunt to experience the power, stability and stealth of Nitro Piston® technology.

Price: .177 . . . . **$209.99**
Price: .22 . . . . **N/A**

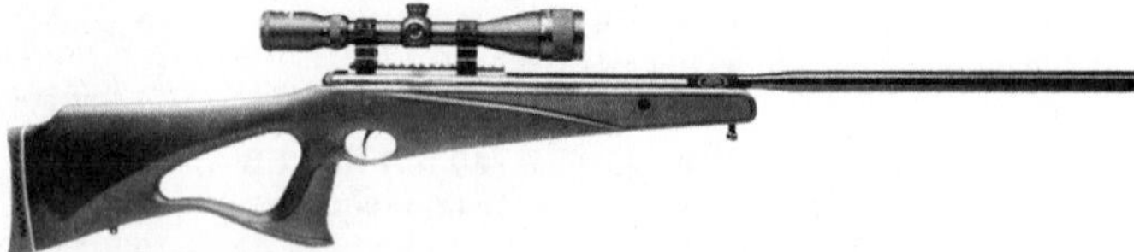

CROSMAN MODEL TRAIL NP ALL WEATHER & LAMINATED HARDWOOD AIR RIFLES

Caliber: .177, .22 & .25, up to 1200 fps (.177), 950 fps (.22) & 900 fps (.25). **Weight:** 6.65 lbs. - 8 lbs. **Length:** 43" overall. **Features:** The Nitro Venom Dusk air rifle features a precision, rifled barrel with fluted muzzle break and sculpted rubber recoil pad. The rifle is equipped with a CenterPoint 3-9x32mm precision scope and a quick-lock mounting system for quick and easy optic mounting. The ambidextrous synthetic stock has a raised cheek piece and modified, beavertail forearm. Crosman Nitro Venom air rifles delivers serious hunting power with muzzle energy up to 18 fpe and up to 1200 fps.. Take one on a hunt to experience the power, stability and stealth of Nitro Piston® technology. The .22 caliber series is equiped with various harwood and laminated thumbhole and standard stocks and also models with bull barrels, imposing 23 ft-lbs of muzzle energy provides 16% more downrange energy than .177 cal. The new XL725 provides 24% more downrange energy than a .177 caliber offers. This is the most powerful Nitro Piston® break barrel available.

Price: .177 Trail NP **$247.00**
Price: .177 Trail NP XL 1500 . . . . **$247.00**
Price: .22 Trail NP All Weather **$247.00**
Price: .22 Trail NP Hardwood **$299.00**
Price: .22 Trail NP All Weather with Realtree APG **$279.95**
Price: .22 Trail NP All Weather 495fps **$299.00**
Price: .22 Trail NP Laminated Hardwood . . . . **N/A**
Price: .22 Trail NP XL 1100 . . . . **$359.00**
Price: .25 Trail NP XL 725. . . . . **$329.00**

DAISY 1938 RED RYDER AIR RIFLE

Caliber: BB, 650-shot repeating action. **Barrel:** Smoothbore steel with shroud. **Weight:** 2.2 lbs. **Length:** 35.4" overall. **Stock:** Wood stock burned with Red Ryder lariat signature. **Sights:** Post front, adjustable open rear. **Features:** Walnut forend. Saddle ring with leather thong. Lever cocking. Gravity feed. Controlled velocity. From Daisy Mfg. Co.

Price: **$55.99**

DAISY MODEL 840B GRIZZLY AIR RIFLE

Caliber: .177 pellet single shot; or BB 350-shot. **Barrel:** 19", smoothbore, steel. **Weight:** 2.25 lbs. **Length:** 36.8" overall. **Power:** Single pump pneumatic. **Stock:** Molded wood-grain stock and forend. **Sights:** Ramp front, open, adjustable rear. **Features:** Muzzle velocity 320 fps (BB), 300 fps (pellet). Steel buttplate; straight pull bolt action; cross-bolt safety. Forend forms pump lever. From Daisy Mfg. Co.

Price: **$60.99**
Price: (840C in Mossy Oak Breakup Camo) **$64.99**

DAISY MODEL 4841 GRIZZLY

Caliber: .177 pellet single shot. **Barrel:** NA. **Weight:** NA. **Length:** 36.8" overall. **Power:** Single pump pneumatic. **Stock:** Composite camo. **Sights:** Blade and ramp front. **Features:** Muzzle velocity 350 fps. Fixed Daisy Model 808 scope. From Daisy Mfg. Co.

Price: **$69.99**

DAISY MODEL 105 BUCK AIR RIFLE

Caliber: .177 or BB. **Barrel:** Smoothbore steel. **Weight:** 1.6 lbs. **Length:** 29.8" overall. **Power:** Lever cocking, spring air. **Stock:** Stained solid wood. **Sights:** TruGlo fiber-optic, open fixed rear. **Features:** Velocity to 275. Crossbolt trigger block safety. From Daisy Mfg. Co.

Price: **$39.99**

DAISY AVANTI MODEL 888 MEDALIST

Caliber: .177, pellet. **Barrel:** Lothar Walther rifled high-grade steel, crowned, 12 lands and grooves, right-hand twist. Precision bore sized for match pellets. **Weight:** 6.9 lbs. **Length:** 38.5" overall. **Power:** CO2 single shot bolt. **Stock:** Sporter-style multicolored laminated hardwood. **Sights:** Hooded front with interchangeable aperture inserts; micrometer adjustable rear peep sight. **Features:** Velocity to 500. Crossbolt trigger block safety. From Daisy Mfg. Co.

Price: **$525.99**

DAISY AVANTI MODEL 887 GOLD MEDALIST

Caliber: 177, pellet. **Barrel:** Lothar Walther rifled high-grade steel, crowned, 12 lands and grooves, right hand twist. Precision bore sized for match pellets. **Weight:** 7.3 lbs. **Length:** 39.5" overall. **Power:** CO2 power single shot bolt. **Stock:** Laminated hardwood. **Sights:** Front globe sight with changeable aperture inserts: rear diopter sight with micrometer click adjustment for windage and elevation. **Features:** Velocity to 500. Crossbolt trigger block safety. Includes rail adapter. From Daisy Mfg. Co.

Price: **$599.99**

DAISY MODEL 853 LEGEND

Caliber: .177, pellet. **Barrel:** Lothar Walther rifled high-grade steel barrel, crowned, 12 lands and grooves, right-hand twist. Precision bore sized for match pellets. **Weight:** 5.5 lbs. **Length:** 38.5" overall. **Power:** Single-pump pneumatic, straight pull-bolt. **Stock:** Full-length, sporter-style hardwood with adjustable length. **Sights:** Hooded front with interchangeable aperture inserts; micrometer adjustable rear. **Features:** Velocity to 510. Crossbolt trigger block safety with red indicator. From Daisy Mfg. Co.

Price: **$432.00**
Price: Model 835 Legend EX; velocity to 490 . . . . **$432.00**

Prices given are believed to be accurate at time of publication however, many factors affect retail pricing so exact prices are not possible.

DAISY MODEL 753 ELITE
Caliber: .177, pellet. **Barrel:** Lothar Walther rifled high-grade steel barrel, crowned, 12 lands and grooves, right-hand twist. Precision bore sized for match pellets. **Weight:** 6.4 lbs. **Length:** 39.75" overall. **Power:** Recoilless single pump pneumatic, straight pull bolt. **Stock:** Full length match-style hardwood stock with raised cheek piece and adjustable length. **Sights:** Front globe sight with changeable aperture inserts, diopter rear sight with micrometer adjustable rear. **Features:** Velocity to 510. Crossbolt trigger block safety with red indicator. From Daisy Mfg. Co.
Price: **$558.99**

DAISY MODEL 105 BUCK AIR RIFLE
Caliber: .177 or BB. **Barrel:** Smoothbore steel. **Weight:** 1.6 lbs. **Length:** 29.8" overall. **Power:** Lever cocking, spring air. **Stock:** Stained solid wood. **Sights:** TruGlo fiber-optic, open fixed rear. **Features:** Velocity to 275. Cross-bolt trigger block safety. From Daisy Mfg. Co.
Price: **$39.99**

DAISY POWERLINE® TARGETPRO 953 AIR RIFLE
Caliber: .177 pellets, single shot. **Weight:** 6.40 lbs. **Length:** 39.75" overall. **Power:** Pneumatic single-pump cocking lever; straight-pull bolt. **Stock:** Full-length, match-style black composite. **Sights:** Front and rear fiber optic. **Features:** Rifled high-grade steel barrel with 1:15 twist. Max. Muzzle Velocity of 560 fps. From Daisy Mfg. Co.
Price: **$29.99**

DAISY POWERLINE® 500 BREAK BARREL
Caliber: .177 pellet, single shot. **Barrel:** Rifled steel. **Weight:** 6.6 lbs. **Length:** 45.7" overall. **Stock:** Stained solid wood. **Sights:** Truglo® fiber-optic front, micro-adjustable open rear, adjustable 4x32 riflescope. **Features:** Auto rear-button safety. Velocity to 490 fps. Made in U.S.A. by Daisy Mfg. Co.
Price: **$120.99**

DAISY POWERLINE® 800 BREAK BARREL
Caliber: .177 pellet, single shot. **Barrel:** Rifled steel. **Weight:** 6.6 lbs. **Length:** 46.7" overall. **Stock:** Black composite. **Sights:** Truglo fiber-optic front, micro-adjustable open rear, adjustable 4x32 riflescope. **Features:** Auto rear-button safety. Velocity to 800 fps. Made in U.S.A. by Daisy Mfg. Co.
Price: **$120.99**

DAISY POWERLINE® 880 AIR RIFLE
Caliber: .177 pellet or BB, 50-shot BB magazine, single shot for pellets. **Barrel:** Rifled steel. **Weight:** 3.7 lbs. **Length:** 37.6" overall. **Power:** Multi-pump pneumatic. **Stock:** Molded wood grain; Monte Carlo comb. **Sights:** Hooded front, adjustable rear. **Features:** Velocity to 685 fps. (BB). Variable power (velocity, range) increase with pump strokes; resin receiver with dovetailed scope mount. Made in U.S.A. by Daisy Mfg. Co.
Price: **$71.99**

DAISY POWERLINE® 901 AIR RIFLE
Caliber: .177. **Barrel:** Rifled steel. **Weight:** 3.7 lbs. **Length:** 37.5" overall. **Power:** Multi-pump pneumatic. **Stock:** Advanced composite. **Sights:** Fiber-optic front, adjustable rear. **Features:** Velocity to 750 fps. (BB); advanced composite receiver with dovetailed mounts for optics. Made in U.S.A. by Daisy Mfg. Co.
Price: **$83.99**

DAISY POWERLINE® 1000 BREAK BARREL
Caliber: .177 pellet, single shot. **Barrel:** Rifled steel. **Weight:** 6.6 lbs. **Length:** 46.7" overall. **Stock:** Black composite. **Sights:** Truglo® fiber-optic front, micro-adjustable open rear, adjustable 4x32 riflescope. **Features:** Auto rear-button safety. Velocity to 750 fps (BB). Made in U.S.A. by Daisy Mfg. Co.
Price: **$231.99**

EAA/BAIKAL IZH61 AIR RIFLE
Caliber: .177 pellet, 5-shot magazine. **Barrel:** 17.8". **Weight:** 6.4 lbs. **Length:** 31" overall. **Power:** Spring-piston, side-cocking lever. **Stock:** Black plastic. **Sights:** Adjustable rear, fully hooded front. **Features:** Velocity 490 fps. Futuristic design with adjustable stock. Imported from Russia by European American Armory.
Price: **$122.65**

GAMO SHADOW AIR RIFLES
Caliber: .177. **Barrel:** 18", fluted polymer bull. **Weight:** 6.1 to 7.15 lbs. **Length:** 43" to 43.3". **Power:** Single-stroke pneumatic, 850-1,000 fps. **Stock:** Tough all-weather molded synthetic. **Sights:** NA. **Features:** Single shot, manual safety,
Price: Sport. **$219.95**
Price: Hunter **$219.95**
Price: Big Cat 1200 . . . . **$169.95**
Price: Fox **$279.95**

GAMO HUNTER AIR RIFLES
Caliber: .177. **Barrel:** NA. **Weight:** 6.5 to 10.5 lbs. **Length:** 43.5-48.5". **Power:** Single-stroke pneumatic, 850-1,000 fps. **Stock:** Wood. **Sights:** Varies by model **Features:** Adjustable two-stage trigger, rifled barrel, raised scope ramp on receiver. Realtree camo model available.
Price: Sport. **$219.95**
Price: Pro **$279.95**
Price: Extreme (.177), Extreme .22. . . . . **$529.95**

GAMO SILENT STALKER WHISPER
Caliber: 177. Single shot, break-barrel cocking system. **Weight:** 7.15 lbs. **Length:** 43". Stock: Molded synthetic with cheekpiece, non-slip texture design on grip and fore-end. Adjustable trigger. Manual safety. 3-9x40 scope included.
Price: **$300.00**

GAMO WHISPER AIR RIFLES
Caliber: .177, .22. **Barrel:** 18", fluted polymer bull. **Weight:** 5.28 to 7.4 lbs. **Length:** 45.7" to 46". **Stock:** Tough all-weather molded synthetic. **Sights:** Fiber-optic front with sight guard, adjustable rear. **Features:** Single shot, manual trigger safety. Non-removable noise dampener (with up to 52 percent reduction).
Price: Whisper. **$279.95**
Price: Whisper Deluxe **$319.95**
Price: Whisper VH (Varmint Hunter/Whisper in one rifle) **$329.95**
Price: Whisper .22 . . . . **$299.95**
Price: CSI Camo (.177) **$329.95**
Price: CSI Camo (.22) **$329.95**

HAMMERLI 850 AIR MAGNUM
Caliber: .177, .22, 8-shot repeater. 23-1/2", rifled. **Weight:** 5.8 lbs. 41" overall. **Power:** 88g CO2. **Stock:** All-weather polymer, Monte Carlo, textured grip and forearm. **Sights:** Hooded fiber optic front, fiber optic adjustable rear. Velocity of 760 fps (.177), 655 (22). Blue finish. Rubber buttpad. Bolt-action. Scope compatible.
Price: .177, .22 . . . . **$349.00**

RWS 460 MAGNUM
Caliber: .177, .22, single shot. 18-7/16", rifled. **Weight:** 8.3 lbs. 45" overall. **Power:** Spring-air, underlever cocking. **Stock:** American Sporter, checkered grip and forearm. **Sights:** Ramp front, adjustable rear. Velocity of 1350 fps (.177), 1150 (.22). 36 lbs. cocking effort. Blue finish. Rubber buttpad. Top-side loading port. Scope compatible.
Price: .177, .22 . . . . **$630.99**

RWS MODEL 34
Caliber: .177, .22, single shot. **Barrel:** 19-1/2", rifled. **Weight:** 7.3 lbs. **Length:** 45" overall. **Power:** Spring-air, break-barrel cocking. **Stock:** Wood. **Sights:** Hooded front, adjustable rear. **Features:** Velocity of

Prices given are believed to be accurate at time of publication however, many factors affect retail pricing so exact prices are not possible.

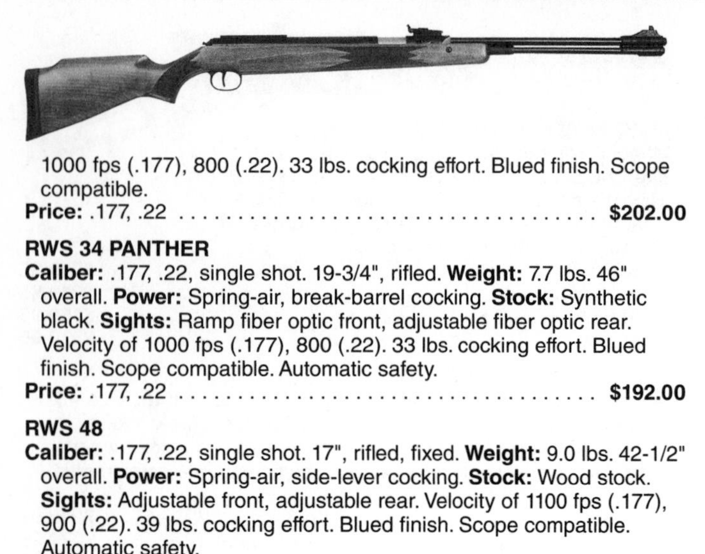

1000 fps (.177), 800 (.22). 33 lbs. cocking effort. Blued finish. Scope compatible.
Price: .177, .22 .... **$202.00**

RWS 34 PANTHER
Caliber: .177, .22, single shot. 19-3/4", rifled. **Weight:** 7.7 lbs. 46" overall. **Power:** Spring-air, break-barrel cocking. **Stock:** Synthetic black. **Sights:** Ramp fiber optic front, adjustable fiber optic rear. Velocity of 1000 fps (.177), 800 (.22). 33 lbs. cocking effort. Blued finish. Scope compatible. Automatic safety.
Price: .177, .22 .... **$192.00**

RWS 48
Caliber: .177, .22, single shot. 17", rifled, fixed. **Weight:** 9.0 lbs. 42-1/2" overall. **Power:** Spring-air, side-lever cocking. **Stock:** Wood stock. **Sights:** Adjustable front, adjustable rear. Velocity of 1100 fps (.177), 900 (.22). 39 lbs. cocking effort. Blued finish. Scope compatible. Automatic safety.
Price: .177, .22 .... **$330.00**

TECH FORCE 6 AIR RIFLE
Caliber: .177 pellet, single shot. **Barrel:** 14". **Weight:** 6 lbs. **Length:** 35.5" overall. **Power:** Spring-piston, sidelever action. **Stock:** Paratrooper-style folding, full pistol grip. **Sights:** Adjustable rear, hooded front. **Features:** Velocity 800 fps. All-metal construction; grooved for scope mounting. Imported from China by Compasseco, Inc.
Price: **$69.95**

TECH FORCE 99 AIR RIFLE
Caliber: .177, .22, single shot. **Barrel:** 18", rifled. **Weight:** 8 lbs. **Length:** 44.5" overall. **Power:** Spring piston. **Stock:** Beech wood; raised cheek piece and checkering on pistol grip and forearm, plus soft rubber recoil pad. **Sights:** Insert type front. **Features:** Velocity 1,100 fps (.177; 900 fps: .22); fixed barrel design has an underlever cocking mechanism with an anti-beartrap lock and automatic safety. Imported from China by Compasseco, Inc.
Price:177 or .22 caliber **$152.96**

WALTHER LEVER ACTION
Caliber: .177, 8-shot lever action. **Barrel:** 19", rifled. **Weight:** 7.5 lbs. **Length:** 38" overall. **Power:** Two 12g CO2. **Stock:** Wood. **Sights:** Fixed front, adjustable rear. **Features:** Classic design. Velocity of 630 fps. Scope compatible.
Price: **$475.50**

WINCHESTER MODEL 1029S
Caliber: .177 pellet. Single shot. **Weight:** 6.6 lbs. **Length:** 46.7". Rifled steel barrel. Composite stock with thumbhole grip. Thumb safety. Comes with 3-9x32 scope. Distributed by Daisy.
Price: **$250.00**

THE 2013 GUN DIGEST web directory

BY HOLT BODINSON

The *Gun Digest* Web Directory is now in its fourteenth year of publication and grows with every edition. The firearms industry has done a remarkably good job of adapting to e-commerce; most of the major sites now include Facebook and Twitter options as wellfor the informed consumer.

The world has become a mobile internet culture, and that's why web directories like our own have become such essential references. The focus of our directory is on companies that have a proven track record of product success and have been in business for several years.

The following index of web addresses is offered to our readers as a convenient jumping-off point. Half the fun is just exploring what's out there. Considering that most of the web pages have hot links to other firearm-related web pages, the Internet trail just goes on and on.

Here are a few pointers to using this directly most efficiently:

If the web site you desire is not listed, try using the full name of the company or product, typed without spaces, between "www." and ".com", for example, www.krause.com. Probably 95 percent of current websites are based on this simple, self-explanatory format.

The other option is to go directly to the dominant search engines, www.google.com or www.bing.com, and enter the name of the company or product for which you are searching. This is also an excellent method of finding companies that have recently changed their web addresses. If you're conducting a general subject search, try using a variety of key words such as "gun," "firearm," "rifle," "pistol," "blackpowder," "shooting," "hunting"—frankly, any word that relates to the sport.

Finally don't forget to access www.YouTube.com for short videos on the subjects you are pursuing. Firearms enthusiasts and companies have posted thousands of subject-related videos, some good, some bad, but always interesting.

—Holt Bodinson

AMMUNITION AND COMPONENTS

A-Square Co. **www.asquarecompany.com**
3-D Ammunition **www.3dammo.com**
Accurate Arms Co. Inc **www.accuratepowder.com**
ADCO/Nobel Sport Powder **www.adcosales.com**
Advanced Armament Corp. **www.300aacblackout.com**
Aguila Ammunition **www.aguilaammo.com**
Alexander Arms **www.alexanderarms.com**
Alliant Powder **www.alliantpowder.com**
American Ammunition **www.a-merc.com**
American Derringer Co. **www.amderringer.com**
American Pioneer Powder **www.americanpioneerpowder.com**
Ammo Depot **www.ammodepot.com**
Arizona Ammunition, Inc. **www.arizonaammunition.com**
Ballistic Products,Inc. **www.ballisticproducts.com**
Barnaul Cartridge Plant **www.ab.ru/~stanok**
Barnes Bullets **www.barnesbullets.com**
Baschieri & Pellagri **www.baschieri-pellagri.com**
Beartooth Bullets **www.beartoothbullets.com**
Bell Brass **www.bellbrass.com**
Berger Bullets, Ltd. **www.bergerbullets.com**
Berry's Mfg., Inc. **www.berrysmfg.com**
Big Bore Bullets of Alaska **www.awloo.com/bbb/index.htm**
Big Bore Express **www.powerbeltbullets.com**
Bismuth Cartridge Co. **www.bismuth-notox.com**
Black Dawge Cartridge **www.blackdawgecartridge.com**
Black Hills Ammunition, Inc. **www.black-hills.com**
Black Hills Shooters Supply **www.bhshooters.com**
BlackHorn209 **www.blackhorn209.com**
Brenneke of America Ltd. **www.brennekeusa.com**
Buffalo Arms **www.buffaloarms.com**
Buffalo Bore Ammunition **www.buffalobore.com**
Calhoon, James, Bullets **www.jamescalhoon.com**
Cartuchos Saga **www.saga.es**
Cast Performance Bullet **www.castperformance.com**
CBC **www.cbc.com.br**
CCI **www.cci-ammunition.com**
Centurion Ordnance **www.aguilaammo.com**
Century International Arms **www.centuryarms.com**
Cheaper Than Dirt **www.cheaperthandirt.com**
Cheddite France **www.cheddite.com**
Claybuster Wads **www.claybusterwads.com**
Clean Shot Powder **www.cleanshot.com**

Cole Distributing **www.cole-distributing.com**
Combined Tactical Systems **www.less-lethal.com**
Cor-Bon/Glaser **www.cor-bon.com**
Cowboy Bullets **www.cowboybullets.com**
D. Dupleks, Ltd. **www.ddupleks.lv**
Defense Technology Corp. **www.defense-technology.com**
Denver Bullet Co. **denbullets@aol.com**
Dillon Precision **www.dillonprecision.com**
Dionisi Cartridge **www.dionisi.com**
DKT, Inc. **www.dktinc.com**
D.L. Unmussig Bullets .14,.17 &.20 cal (804)320-1165
Double Tap Ammunition **www.doubletapammo.com**
Down Range Mfg. **www.downrangemfg.com**
Dynamic Research Technologies **www.drtammo.com**
Dynamit Nobel RWS Inc. **www.dnrws.com**
Elephant/Swiss Black Powder **www.elephantblackpowder.com**
Eley Ammunition **www.eleyusa.com**
Eley Hawk Ltd. **www.eleyhawk.com**
Environ-Metal **www.hevishot.com**
Estate Cartridge **www.estatecartridge.com**
Extreme Shock Munitions **www.extremeshockusa.com**
Federal Cartridge Co. **www.federalpremium.com**
Fiocchi of America **www.fiocchiusa.com**
Fowler Bullets **www.benchrest.com/fowler**
Gamebore Cartridge **www.gamebore.com**
Garrett Cartridges **www.garrettcartridges.com**
Gentner Bullets **www.benchrest.com/gentner/**
Glaser Safety Slug, Inc. **www.corbon.com**
GOEX Inc. **www.goexpowder.com**
GPA **www.cartouchegpa.com**
Graf & Sons **www.grafs.com**
Grizzly Cartridge Co. **www.grizzlycartridge.com**
Haendler & Natermann **www.hn-sport.de**
Hawk Bullets **www.hawkbullets.com**
Herter's Ammuniition **www.cabelas.com**
Hevi.Shot **www.hevishot.com**
Hi-Tech Ammunition **www.iidbs.com/hitech**
Hodgdon Powder **www.hodgdon.com**
Hornady **www.hornady.com**
HSM Ammunition **www.thehuntingshack.com**
Hull Cartridge **www.hullcartridge.com**
Huntington Reloading Products **www.huntingtons.com**
Impact Bullets **www.impactbullets.com**
IMR Smokeless Powders **www.imrpowder.com**
International Cartridge Corp **www.iccammo.com**
Israel Military Industries **www.imisammo.co.il**
ITD Enterprise **www.itdenterpriseinc.com**
Jagemann Technologies **www.jagemanntech.com**
James Calhoon **www.jamescalhoon.com**
Kent Cartridge America **www.kentgamebore.com**
Knight Bullets **www.benchrest.com/knight/**
Kynoch Ammunition **www.kynochammunition.com**
Lapua **www.lapua.com**
Lawrence Brand Shot **www.metalico.com**
Lazzeroni Arms Co. **www.lazzeroni.com**
Leadheads Bullets **www.proshootpro.com**
Lightfield Ammunition Corp **www.lightfieldslugs.com**
Lomont Precision Bullets **www.klomont.com/kent**
Lost River Ballistic Technologies,Inc. **www.lostriverballistic.com**
Lyman **www.lymanproducts.com**
Magkor Industries **www.magkor.com**
Magnum Muzzleloading Products **www.mmpsabots.com**
Magnus Bullets **www.magnusbullets.com**
MagSafe Ammunition **www.realpages.com/magsafeammo**
Magtech **www.magtechammunition.com**
Masterclass Bullet Co. **www.mastercast.com**
Maxam **www.maxam-outdoors.com**
Meister Bullets **www.meisterbullets.com**
MEN **www.men-defencetec.de**
Midway USA **www.midwayusa.com**
Miltex,Inc. **www.miltexusa.com**
Mitchell Mfg. Co. **www.mitchellsales.com**
MK Ballistic Systems **www.mkballistics.com**
Mullins Ammunition **www.mullinsammunition.com**
National Bullet Co. **www.nationalbullet.com**
Navy Arms **www.navyarms.com**
Nobel Sport **www.nobelsportammo.com**
Norma **www.norma.cc**
North Fork Technologies **www.northforkbullets.com**
Nosler Bullets,Inc. **www.nosler.com**
Old Western Scrounger **www.ows-ammunition.com**
One Shot, Inc. **www.oneshotmunitions.com**
Oregon Trail/Trueshot Bullets **www.trueshotbullets.com**
Pattern Control **www.patterncontrol.com**
PCP Ammunition **www.pcpammo.com**
Pierce Munitions **www.piercemunitions.com**
Piney Mountain Ammunition
www.pineymountainammunitionco.com
PMC **www.pmcammo.com**
Polywad **www.polywad.com**
PowerBelt Bullets **www.powerbeltbullets.com**
PPU Ammunition **www.prvipartizan.com**
PR Bullets **www.prbullet.com**
Precision Ammunition **www.precisionammo.com**
Precision Reloading **www.precisionreloading.com**
Pro Load Ammunition **www.proload.com**
Prvi Partizan Ammunition **www.prvipartizan.com**
Quality Cartridge **www.qual-cart.com**
Rainier Ballistics **www.rainierballistics.com**
Ram Shot Powder **www.ramshot.com**

Rare Ammunition **www.rareammo.com**
Reloading Specialties Inc. **www.reloadingspecialties.com**
Remington **www.remington.com**
Rio Ammunition **www.rioammo.com**
Rocky Mountain Cartridge **www.rockymountaincartride.com**
RUAG Ammotec **www.ruag.com**
RWS **www.ruag-usa.com**
Samco Global Arms **www.samcoglobal.com**
Sauvestre Ammunition **www.centuryarms.com**
SBR Ammunition **www.sbrammunition.com**
Scharch Mfg. **www.scharch.com**
Schuetzen Powder **www.schuetzenpowder.com**
Sellier & Bellot **www.sellier-bellot.cz**
Shilen **www.shilen.com**
Sierra **www.sierrabullets.com**
Silver State Armory **www.ssarmory.com**
Simunition **www.simunition.com**
SinterFire, Inc. **www.sinterfire.com**
Spectra Shot **www.spectrashot.com**
Speer Ammunition **www.speer-ammo.com**
Speer Bullets **www.speer-bullets.com**
Sporting Supplies Int'l Inc. **www.ssiintl.com**
Starline **www.starlinebrass.com**
Superior Ballistics **www.superiorballistics.com**
Swift Bullets Co. **www.swiftbullet.com**
Ted Nugent Ammunition **www.americantactical.us**
Ten-X Ammunition **www.tenxammo.com**
Top Brass **www.topbrass.com**
Triton Cartridge **www.a-merc.com**
Trueshot Bullets **www.trueshotbullets.com**
Tru-Tracer **www.trutracer.com**
TulAmmo **www.tulammousa.com**
Ultramax Ammunition **www.ultramaxammunition.com**
Vihtavuori Lapua **www.vihtavuori-lapua.com**
Weatherby **www.weatherby.com**
West Coast Bullets **www.westcoastbullet.com**
Western Powders Inc. **www.westernpowders.com**
Widener's Reloading & Shooters Supply **www.wideners.com**
Winchester Ammunition **www.winchester.com**
Windjammer Tournament Wads. **www.windjammer-wads.com**
Wolf Ammunition **www.wolfammo.com**
Woodleigh Bullets **www.woodleighbullets.com.au**
Zanders Sporting Goods **www.gzanders.com**

CASES, SAFES, GUN LOCKS, AND CABINETS

Ace Case Co. **www.acecase.com**
AG English Sales Co. **www.agenglish.com**
All Americas' Outdoors **www.innernet.net/gunsafe**
Alpine Cases **www.alpinecases.com**
Aluma Sport by Dee Zee **www.deezee.com**
American Security Products **www.amsecusa.com**
Americase **www.americase.com**
Assault Systems **www.elitesurvival.com**
Avery Outdoors, Inc. **www.averyoutdoors.com**
Bear Track Cases **www.beartrackcases.com**
Bore-Stores **www.borestores.com**
Boyt Harness Co. **www.boytharness.com**
Bulldog Gun Safe Co. **www.gardall.com**
Cannon Safe Co. **www.cannonsafe.com**
CCL Security Products **www.cclsecurity.com**
Concept Development Corp. **www.saf-t-blok.com**
Doskocil Mfg. Co. **www.doskocilmfg.com**
Fort Knox Safes **www.ftknox.com**
Franzen Security Products **www.securecase.com**
Frontier Safe Co. **www.frontiersafe.com**
Goldenrod Dehumidifiers **www.goldenroddehumidifiers.com**
Granite Security Products **www.granitesafe.com**
Gunlocker Phoenix USA Inc. **www.gunlocker.com**
Gun Storage Solutions **www.storemoreguns.com**
GunVault **www.gunvault.com**
Hakuba USA Inc. **www.hakubausa.com**
Heritage Safe Co. **www.heritagesafecompany.com**
Hide-A-Gun **www.hide-a-gun.com**
Homak Safes **www.homak.com**
Hunter Company **www.huntercompany.com**
Integrity Gunbags **www.integrity-gunbags.com**
Kalispel Case Line **www.kalispelcaseline.com**
Knouff & Knouff, Inc. **www.kkair.com**
Knoxx Industries **www.knoxx,com**
Kolpin Mfg. Co. **www.kolpin.com**
Liberty Safe & Security **www.libertysafe.com**
LockSfa **www.locksfa.com**
Morton Enterprises **www.uniquecases.com**
New Innovative Products **www.starlightcases**
Noble Security Systems Inc. **www.noble.co.Il**
Phoenix USA Inc. **www.gunlocker.com**
Plano Molding Co. **www.planomolding.com**
Plasticase, Inc. **www.nanuk.com**
Rhino Gun Cases **www.rhinoguns.com**
Rhino Safe **www.rhinosafe.com**
Rotary Gun Racks **www.gun-racks.com**
Sack-Ups **www.sackups.com**
Safe Tech, Inc. **www.safrgun.com**
Saf-T-Hammer **www.saf-t-hammer.com**
Saf-T-Lok Corp. **www.saf-t-lok.com**
San Angelo All-Aluminum Products Inc. **sasptuld@x.netcom.com**
Secure Firearm Products **www.securefirearmproducts.com**
Securecase **www.securecase.com**

Shot Lock Corp. **www.shotlock.com**
SKB Cases **www.skbcases.com**
Smart Lock Technology Inc. **www.smartlock.com**
Sportsmans Steel Safe Co. **www.sportsmansteelsafes.com**
Stack-On Products Co. **www.stack-on.com**
Starlight Cases **www.starlightcases.com**
Strong Case **www.strongcasebytnb.com**
Sun Welding **www.sunwelding.com**
Technoframes **www.technoframes.com**
T.Z. Case Int'l **www.tzcase.com**
U.S. Explosive Storage **www.usexplosivestorage.com**
Versatile Rack Co. **www.versatilegunrack.com**
V-Line Industries **www.vlineind.com**
Winchester Safes **www.winchestersafes.com**
Ziegel Engineering **www.ziegeleng.com**
Zonetti Armor **www.zonettiarmor.com**

CHOKE DEVICES, RECOIL REDUCERS, SUPPRESSORS AND ACCURACY DEVICES

100 Straight Products **www.100straight.com**
Advanced Armament Corp. **www.advanced-armament.com**
Answer Products Co. **www.answerrifles.com**
AWC Systems Technology **www.awcsystech.com**
Briley Mfg **www.briley.com**
Carlson's **www.choketube.com**
Colonial Arms **www.colonialarms.com**
Comp-N-Choke **www.comp-n-choke.com**
Elite Iron **www.eliteiron.net**
Gemtech **www.gem-tech.com**
KDF, Inc. **www.kdfguns.com**
Kick's Industries **www.kicks-ind.com**
LimbSaver **www.limbsaver.com**
Mag-Na-Port Int'l Inc. **www.magnaport.com**
Metro Gun **www.metrogun.com**
Patternmaster Chokes **www.patternmaster.com**
Poly-Choke **www.poly-choke.com**
SilencerCo **www.silencerco.com**
Sims Vibration Laboratory **www.limbsaver.com**
SRT Arms **www.srtarms.com**
SureFire **www.surefire.com**
SWR Mfg. **www.swrmfg.com**
Teague Precision Chokes **www.teague.ca**
Truglo **www.truglo.com**
Trulock Tool **www.trulockchokes.com**
Vais Arms,Inc. **www.muzzlebrakes.com**

CHRONOGRAPHS AND BALLISTIC SOFTWARE

Barnes Ballistic Program **www.barnesbullets.com**
Ballisticard Systems **www.ballisticards.com**
Competition Electronics **www.competitionelectronics.com**
Competitive Edge Dynamics **www.cedhk.com**
Hodgdon Shotshell Program **www.hodgdon.com**
Lee Shooter Program **www.leeprecision.com**
Load From A Disk **www.loadammo.com**
NECO **www.neconos.com**
Oehler Research Inc. **www.oehler-research.com**
PACT **www.pact.com**
Pjsa Ballistics **Pejsa@sprintmail.com**
ProChrony **www.competitionelectronics.com**
Quickload **www.neconos.com**
RCBS Load **www.rcbs.com**
Shooting Chrony Inc **www.shootingchrony.com**
Sierra Infinity Ballistics Program **www.sierrabullets.com**
Winchester Ballistics Calculator **www.winchester.com**

CLEANING PRODUCTS

Accupro **www.accupro.com**
Ballistol USA **www.ballistol.com**
Battenfeld Technologies **www.battenfeldtechnologies.com**
Birchwood Casey **www.birchwoodcasey.com**
Blue Wonder **www.bluewonder.com**
Bore Tech **www.boretech.com**
Break-Free, Inc. **www.break-free.com**
Bruno Shooters Supply **www.brunoshooters.com**
Butch's Bore Shine **www.lymanproducts.com**
C.J. Weapons Accessories **www.cjweapons.com**
Clenzoil **www.clenzoil.com**
Corrosion Technologies **www.corrosionx.com**
Dewey Mfg. **www.deweyrods.com**
DuraCoat **www.lauerweaponry.com**
Eezox Inc. **www.xmission.com**
Emby Enterprises **www.alltemptacticallube.com**
Extreme Gun Care **www.extremeguncare.com**
G96 **www.g96.com**
Gun Cleaners **www.guncleaners.com**
Gunslick Gun Care **www.gunslick.com**
Gunzilla **www.topduckproducts.com**
Hollands Shooters Supply **www.hollandgun.com**
Hoppes **www.hoppes.com**
Hydrosorbent Products **www.dehumidify.com**
Inhibitor VCI Products **www.theinhibitor.com**
Iosso Products **www.iosso.com**
KG Industries **www.kgcoatings.com**
Kleen-Bore Inc. **www.kleen-bore.com**
L&R Ultrasoncics **www.lrultrasonics.com**
Lyman **www.lymanproducts.com**
Mil-Comm Products **www.mil-comm.com**

Militec-1 **www.militec-1.com**
Montana X-Treme **www.montanaxtreme.com**
MPT Industries **www.mptindustries.com**
Mpro7 Gun Care **www.mp7.com**
Old West Snake Oil **www.oldwestsnakeoil.com**
Otis Technology, Inc. **www.otisgun.com**
Outers **www.outers-guncare.com**
Ox-Yoke Originals Inc. **www.oxyoke.com**
Parker-Hale Ltd. **www.parker-hale.com**
Prolix Lubricant **www.prolixlubricant.com**
ProShot Products **www.proshotproducts.com**
ProTec Lubricants **www.proteclubricants.com**
Rigel Products **www.rigelproducts.com**
Rusteprufe Labs **www.rusteprufe.com**
Sagebrush Products **www.sagebrushproducts.com**
Sentry Solutions Ltd. **www.sentrysolutions.com**
Shooters Choice Gun Care **www.shooters-choice.com**
Silencio **www.silencio.com**
Slip 2000 **www.slip2000.com**
Southern Bloomer Mfg. **www.southernbloomer.com**
Stony Point Products **www.uncle-mikes.com**
Tetra Gun **www.tetraproducts.com**
The TM Solution **thetmsolution@comsast.net**
Top Duck Products **www.topduckproducts.com**
Triangle Patch **www.trianglepatch.com**
Ultra Bore Coat **www.ultracoatingsinc.com**
Wipe-Out **www.sharpshootr.com**
World's Fastest Gun Bore Cleaner **www.michaels-oregon.com**

FIREARM AUCTION SITES

A&S Auction Co. **www.asauction.com**
Alderfer Austion **www.alderferauction.com**
Amoskeag Auction Co. **www.amoskeagauction.com**
Antique Guns **www.antiqueguns.com**
Auction Arms **www.auctionarms.com**
Batterman's Auctions **www.battermans.com**
Bonhams & Butterfields **www.bonhams.com/usarms**
Cowan's **www.cowans.com**
Fontaine's Auction Gallery **www.fontainesauction.net**
Greg Martin Auctions **www.gregmartinauctions.com**
Guns America **www.gunsamerica.com**
Gun Broker **www.gunbroker.com**
Guns International **www.gunsinternational.com**
Heritage Auction Gallaries **www.ha.com**
James D. Julia, Inc. **www.jamesdjulia.com**
J.C. Devine, Inc. **www.jcdevine.com**
Little John's Auction Service **www.littlejohnsauctionservice.com**
Morphy Auctions **www.morphyauctions.com**
Poulin Auction Co. **www.poulinantiques.com**
Rock Island Auction Co. **www.rockislandauction.com**
Wallis & Wallis **www.wallisandwallis.org**

FIREARM MANUFACTURERS AND IMPORTERS

AAR, Inc. **www.iar-arms.com**
A-Square **www.asquarecompany.com**
Accuracy Int'l North America **www.accuracyinternational.com**
Accuracy Rifle Systems **www.mini-14.net**
Ace Custom 45's **www.acecustom45.com**
Advanced Weapons Technology **www.AWT-Zastava.com**
AIM **www.aimsurplus.com**
AirForce Airguns **www.airforceairguns.com**
Air Gun, Inc. **www.airrifle-china.com**
Airguns of Arizona **www.airgunsofarizona.com**
Airgun Express **www.airgunexpress.com**
Akkar Sporting Arms **www.akkar-usa.com**
Alchemy Arms **www.alchemyltd.com**
Alexander Arms **www.alexanderarms.com**
American Classic **www.americanclassic1911.com**
American Derringer Corp. **www.amderringer.com**
American Rifle Co. **www.americanrifleco.com**
American Spirit Arms Corp. **www.gunkits.com**
American Tactical Imports **www.americantactical.us**
American Western Arms **www.awaguns.com**
Anics Corp. **www.anics.com**
Anschutz **www.anschutz-sporters.com**
Answer Products Co. **www.answerrifles.com**
AR-7 Industries,LLC **www.ar-7.com**
Ares Defense Systems **www.aresdefense.com**
Armalite **www.armalite.com**
Armi Sport **www.armisport.com**
Armory USA **www.globaltraders.com**
Armsco **www.armsco.net**
Armscorp USA Inc. **www.armscorpusa.com**
Arnold Arms **www.arnoldarms.com**
Arrieta **www.arrietashotguns.com**
Arsenal Inc. **www.arsenalinc.com**
Arthur Brown Co. **www.eabco.com**
Atlanta Cutlery Corp. **www.atlantacutlery.com**
ATA Arms **www.ataarms.com**
Auction Arms **www.auctionarms.com**
Autauga Arms,Inc. **www.autaugaarms.com**
Auto-Ordnance Corp. **www.tommygun.com**
AWA Int'l **www.awaguns.com**
Axtell Rifle Co. **www.riflesmith.com**
Aya **www.aya-fineguns.com**
Baikal **www.baikalinc.ru/eng/**
Badger Ordnance **www.badgerordnance.com**
Ballard Rifles,LLC **www.ballardrifles.com**
Barrett Firearms Mfg. **www.barrettrifles.com**
Bat Machine Co. **www.batmachine.com**

Beeman Precision Airguns **www.beeman.com**
Benelli USA Corp. **www.benelliusa.com**
Benjamin Sheridan **www.crosman.com**
Beretta U.S.A. Corp. **www.berettausa.com**
Bernardelli **www.bernardelli.com**
Bersa **www.bersa.com**
Bighorn Arms **www.bighornarms.com**
Bill Hanus Birdguns **www.billhanusbirdguns.com**
Blaser Jagdwaffen Gmbh **www.blaser.de**
Bleiker **www.bleiker.ch**
Bluegrass Armory **www.bluegrassarmory.com**
Bond Arms **www.bondarms.com**
Borden's Rifles, Inc. **www.bordensrifles.com**
Boss & Co. **www.bossguns.co.uk**
Bowen Classic Arms **www.bowenclassicarms.com**
Briley Mfg **www.briley.com**
BRNO Arms **www.zbrojovka.com**
Brown, David McKay **www.mckaybrown.com**
Brown, Ed Products **www.edbrown.com**
Browning **www.browning.com**
BRP Corp. **www.brpguns.com**
BSA Guns **www.bsagunusa.com**
BUL Ltd. **www.bultransmark.com**
Bushmaster Firearms/Quality Parts **www.bushmaster.com**
BWE Firearms **www.bwefirearms.com**
Cabot Guns **www.cabotguns.com**
Caesar Guerini USA **www.gueriniusa.com**
Carbon 15 **www.professional-ordnance.com**
Caspian Arms, Ltd. **www.caspianarmsltd.8m.com**
Casull Arms Corp. **www.casullarms.com**
Calvary Arms **www.calvaryarms.com**
CDNN Investments, Inc. **www.cdnninvestments.com**
Century Arms **www.centuryarms.com**
Chadick's Ltd. **www.chadicks-ltd.com**
Champlin Firearms **www.champlinarms.com**
Chapuis Arms **www.doubleguns.com/chapuis.htm**
Charles Daly **www.charlesdaly.com**
Charter Arms **www.charterfirearms.com**
CheyTac USA **www.cheytac.com**
Chiappa Firearms **www.chiappafirearms.com**
Christensen Arms **www.christensenarms.com**
Cimarron Firearms Co. **www.cimarron-firearms.com**
Clark Custom Guns **www.clarkcustomguns.com**
Cobra Enterprises **www.cobrapistols.com**
Cogswell & Harrison **www.cogswell.co.uk/home.htm**
Collector's Armory, Ltd. **www.collectorsarmory.com**
Colt's Mfg Co. **www.colt.com**
Compasseco, Inc. **www.compasseco.com**
Connecticut Shotgun Mfg. Co. **www.connecticutshotgun.com**
Connecticut Valley Arms **www.cva.com**
Coonan, Inc. **www.coonaninc.com**
Cooper Firearms **www.cooperfirearms.com**
Core 15 Rifle Systems **www.core15.com**
Corner Shot **www.cornershot.com**
CPA Rifles **www.singleshotrifles.com**
Crosman **www.crosman.com**
C.Sharp Arms Co. **www.csharparms.com**
CVA **www.cva.com**
Cylinder & Slide Shop **www.cylinder-slide.com**
Czechp Int'l **www.czechpoint-usa.com**
CZ USA **www.cz-usa.com**
Daisy Mfg Co. **www.daisy.com**
Dakota Arms Inc. **www.dakotaarms.com**
Dan Wesson Firearms **www.danwessonfirearms.com**
Daniel Defense, Inc. **www.danieldefense.com**
Davis Industries **www.davisindguns.com**
Detonics USA **www.detonicsusa.com**
Diana **www.diana-airguns.de**
Dixie Gun Works **www.dixiegunworks.com**
Dlask Arms Corp. **www.dlask.com**
DoubleTap **www.heizerdefense.com**
D.P.M.S., Inc. **www.dpmsinc.com**
D.S.Arms,Inc. **www.dsarms.com**
Dumoulin **www.dumoulin-herstal.com**
Dynamit Noble **www.dnrws.com**
EAA Corp. **www.eaacorp.com**
Eagle Imports,Inc. **www.bersa-llama.com**
Ed Brown Products **www.edbrown.com**
EDM Arms **www.edmarms.com**
E.M.F. Co. **www.emf-company.com**
Enterprise Arms **www.enterprise.com**
E R Shaw **www.ershawbarrels.com**
European American Armory Corp. **www.eaacorp.com**
Evans, William **www.williamevans.com**
Excel Arms **www.excelarms.com**
Fabarm **www.fabarm.com**
FAC-Guns-N-Stuff **www.gunsnstuff.com**
Falcon Pneumatic Systems **www.falcon-airguns.com**
Fausti Stefano **www.faustistefanoarms.com**
Firestorm **www.firestorm-sgs.com**
Flodman Guns **www.flodman.com**
FN Herstal **www.fnherstal.com**
FNH USA **www.fnhusa.com**
Franchi **www.franchiusa.com**
Freedom Arms **www.freedomarms.com**
Freedom Group, Inc. **www.freedom-group.com**
Galazan **www.connecticutshotgun.com**
Gambo Renato **www.renatogamba.it**
Gamo **www.gamo.com**
Gary Reeder Custom Guns **www.reeder-customguns.com**
Gazelle Arms **www.gazellearms.com**
German Sport Guns **www.germansportguns.com**
Gibbs Rifle Company **www.gibbsrifle.com**
Glock **www.glock.com**

Griffin & Howe **www.griffinhowe.com**
Grizzly Big Boar Rifle **www.largrizzly.com**
GSI Inc. **www.gsifirearms.com**
Guerini **www.gueriniusa.com**
Gunbroker.Com **www.gunbroker.com**
Gun Room Co. **www.onlylongrange.com**
Hammerli **www.carl-walther.com**
Hatfield Gun Co. **www.hatfield-usa.com**
Hatsan Arms Co. **www.hatsan.com.tr**
Heckler and Koch **www.hk-usa.com**
Henry Repeating Arms Co. **www.henryrepeating.com**
Heritage Mfg. **www.heritagemfg.com**
Heym **www.heym-waffenfabrik.de**
High Standard Mfg. **www.highstandard.com**
Hi-Point Firearms **www.hi-pointfirearms.com**
Holland & Holland **www.hollandandholland.com**
H&R 1871 Firearms **www.hr1871.com**
H-S Precision **www.hsprecision.com**
Hunters Lodge Corp. **www.hunterslodge.com**
IAR Inc. **www.iar-arms.com**
Imperial Miniature Armory **www.1800miniature.com**
Interarms **www.interarms.com**
International Military Antiques, Inc. **www.ima-usa.com**
Inter Ordnance **www.interordnance.com**
Intrac Arms International LLC **www.hsarms.com**
Israel Arms **www.israelarms.com**
ISSC, LLC **www.issc-austria.com**
Iver Johnson Arms **www.iverjohnsonarms.com**
Izhevsky Mekhanichesky Zavod **www.baikalinc.ru**
James River Mfg. **www.jamesriverarmory.com**
Jarrett Rifles,Inc. **www.jarrettrifles.com**
J&G Sales, Ltd. **www.jgsales.com**
Johannsen Express Rifle **www.johannsen-jagd.de**
Jonathan Arthur Ciener **www.22lrconversions.com**
JP Enterprises, Inc. **www.jprifles.com**
Kahr Arms/Auto-Ordnance **www.kahr.com**
K.B.I. **www.kbi-inc.com**
KDF, Inc. **www.kdfguns.com**
Kelby's **www.kelby.com**
Kel-Tec CNC Ind., Inc. **www.kel-tec.com**
Keystone Sporting Arms **www.keystonesportingarmsllc.com**
Kifaru **www.kifaru.net**
Kimber **www.kimberamerica.com**
Knight's Armament Co. **www.knightsarmco.com**
Knight Rifles **www.knightrifles.com**
Korth **www.korthwaffen.de**
Krebs Custom Guns **www.krebscustom.com**
Kriss **www.kriss-usa.com**
Krieghoff Int'l **www.krieghoff.com**
KY Imports, Inc. **www.kyimports.com**
K-VAR **www.k-var.com**
Lanber **www.lanber.net**
L.A.R Mfg. **www.largrizzly.com**
Lazzeroni Arms Co. **www.lazzeroni.com**
Legacy Sports International **www.legacysports.com**
Les Baer Custom, Inc. **www.lesbaer.com**
Lewis Machine & Tool Co. **www.lewismachine.net**
Linebaugh Custom Sixguns **www.sixgunner.com/linebaugh**
Ljutic **www.ljuticgun.com**
Llama **www.bersa-llama.com**
Lone Star Rifle Co. **www.lonestarrifle.com**
LRB Arms **www.lrbarms.com**
Lyman **www.lymanproducts.com**
LWRC Int'l **www.lwrifles.com**
Magnum Research **www.magnumresearch.com**
Majestic Arms **www.majesticarms.com**
Markesbery Muzzleloaders **www.markesbery.com**
Marksman Products **www.marksman.com**
Marlin **www.marlinfirearms.com**
MasterPiece Arms **www.masterpiecearms.com**
Mauser **www.mauser.com**
McMillan Bros Rifle Co. **www.mcfamily.com**
MDM **www.mdm-muzzleloaders.com**
Meacham Rifles **www.meachamrifles.com**
Merkel **www.hk-usa.com**
Milkor USA **www.milkorusainc.com**
Miller Arms **www.millerarms.com**
Miltech **www.miltecharms.com**
Miltex, Inc. **www.miltexusa.com**
Mitchell's Mausers **www.mausers.net**
MK Ballistic Systems **www.mkballistics.com**
M-Mag **www.mmag.com**
Montana Rifle Co. **www.montanarifleman.com**
Mossberg **www.mossberg.com**
Navy Arms **www.navyarms.com**
Nesika **www.nesika.com**
New England Arms Corp. **www.newenglandarms.com**
New England Custom Gun Svc, Ltd. **www.newenglandcustomgun.com**
New England Firearms **www.hr1871.com**
New Ultra Light Arms **www.newultralight.com**
Nighthawk Custom **www.nighthawkcustom.com**
North American Arms **www.northamericanarms.com**
Nosler Bullets,Inc. **www.nosler.com**
Nowlin Mfg. Inc. **www.nowlinguns.com**
O.F. Mossberg & Sons **www.mossberg.com**
Ohio Ordnance Works **www.ohioordnanceworks.com**
Olympic Arms **www.olyarms.com**
Osprey Defense **www.gaspiston.com**
Panther Arms **www.dpmsinc.com**
Para-USA **www.para-usa.com**
Pedersoli Davide & Co. **www.davide-pedersoli.com**
Perazzi **www.perazzi.com**
Pietta **www.pietta.it**

Pistol Dynamics **www.pistoldynamics.com**
PKP Knife-Pistol **www.sanjuanenterprise.com**
Power Custom **www.powercustom.com**
Precision Small Arm Inc. **www.precisionsmallarms.com**
Primary Weapons Systems **www.primaryweapons.com**
Professional Arms **www.professional-arms.com**
PTR 91,Inc. **www.ptr91.com**
Purdey & Sons **www.purdey.com**
Pyramid Air **www.pyramidair.com**
RAAC **www.raacfirearms.com**
Red Jacket Firearms **www.redjacketfirearms.com**
Remington **www.remington.com**
Republic Arms Inc. **www.republicarmsinc.com**
Rhineland Arms, Inc. **www.rhinelandarms.com**
Rigby **www.johnrigbyandco.com**
Rizzini USA **www.rizziniusa.com**
RM Equipment, Inc. **www.40mm.com**
Robar Companies, Inc. **www.robarguns.com**
Robinson Armament Co. **www.robarm.com**
Rock River Arms, Inc. **www.rockriverarms.com**
Rogue Rifle Co. Inc. **www.chipmunkrifle.com**
Rohrbaugh Firearms **www.rohrbaughfirearms.com**
Rossi Arms **www.rossiusa.com**
RPM **www.rpmxlpistols.com**
Russian American Armory **www.raacfirearms.com**
RUAG Ammotec **www.ruag.com**
Sabatti SPA **www.sabatti.com**
Saco Defense **www.sacoinc.com**
Safari Arms **www.olyarms.com**
Sako **www.berettausa.com**
Samco Global Arms Inc. **www.samcoglobal.com**
Sarco **www.sarcoinc.com**
Sarsilmaz Silah San **www.sarsilmaz.com**
Sauer & Sohn **www.sauer.de**
Savage Arms Inc. **www.savagearms.com**
Scattergun Technologies Inc. **www.wilsoncombat.com**
Schmeisser Gmbh **www.schmeisser-germany.de**
Searcy Enterprises **www.searcyent.com**
Sharps Rifle Companies **www.asquareco.com**
Shaw **www.ershawbarrels.com**
Shiloh Rifle Mfg. **www.shilohrifle.com**
Sig Sauer, Inc. **www.sigsauer.com**
Simpson Ltd. **www.simpsonltd.com**
SKB Shotguns **www.skbshotguns.com**
Smith & Wesson **www.smith-wesson.com**
SOG International, Inc. **soginc@go-concepts.com**
Sphinx System **www.sphinxarms.com**
Springfield Armory **www.springfield-armory.com**
SSK Industries **www.sskindustries.com**
Stag Arms **www.stagarms.com**
Steyr Arms, Inc. **www.steyrarms.com**
STI International **www.stiguns.com**
Stoeger Industries **www.stoegerindustries.com**
Strayer-Voigt Inc. **www.sviguns.com**
Sturm, Ruger & Company **www.ruger-firearms.com**
Super Six Classic **www.bisonbull.com**
Surgeon Rifles **www.surgeonrifles.com**
Tactical Rifles **www.tacticalrifles.com**
Tactical Solutions **www.tacticalsol.com**
Tar-Hunt Slug Guns, Inc. **www.tar-hunt.com**
Taser Int'l **www.taser.com**
Taurus **www.taurususa.com**
Taylor's & Co., Inc. **www.taylorsfirearms.com**
Tempco Mfg. Co. **www.tempcomfg.com**
Tennessee Guns **www.tennesseeguns.com**
TG Int'l **www.tnguns.com**
The 1877 Sharps Co. **www.1877sharps.com**
Thompson Center Arms **www.tcarms.com**
Tikka **www.berettausa.com**
TNW, Inc. **www.tnwfirearms.com**
Traditions **www.traditionsfirearms.com**
Tristar Sporting Arms **www.tristarsportingarms.com**
Turnbull Mfg. Co. **www.turnbullmfg.com**
Uberti **www.ubertireplicas.com**
Ultralite 50 **www.ultralite50.com**
Ultra Light Arms **www.newultralight.com**
Umarex **www.umarex.com**
U.S. Armament Corp. **www.usarmamentcorp.com**
U.S. Firearms Mfg. Co. **www.usfirearms.com**
Uselton Arms, Inc. **www.useltonarmsinc.com**
Valkyrie Arms **www.valkyriearms.com**
Vektor Arms **www.vektorarms.com**
Verney-Carron **www.verney-carron.com**
Volquartsen Custom Ltd. **www.volquartsen.com**
Vulcan Armament **www.vulcanarmament.com**
Walther USA **www.waltheramerica.com**
Weatherby **www.weatherby.com**
Webley and Scott Ltd. **www.webley.co.uk**
Westley Richards **www.westleyrichards.com**
Widley **www.widleyguns.com**
Wild West Guns **www.wildwestguns.com**
William Larkin Moore & Co. **www.doublegun.com**
Wilson Combat **www.wilsoncombat.com**
Winchester Rifles and Shotguns
www.winchesterguns.com

GUN PARTS, BARRELS, AFTER-MARKET ACCESSORIES

100 Straight Products **www.100straight.com**
300 Below **www.300below.com**
Accuracy International of North America
www.accuracyinternational.org
Accuracy Speaks, Inc. **www.accuracyspeaks.com**

Accurary Systems **www.accuracysystemsinc.com**
Adam Arms **www.adamarms.net**
Advanced Barrel Systems **www.carbonbarrels.com**
Advantage Arms **www.advantagearms.com**
Aim Surplus **www.aimsurplus.com**
AK-USA **www.ak-103.com**
American Spirit Arms Corp. **www.gunkits.com**
Amhurst-Depot **www.amherst-depot.com**
AMT Gun Parts **www.amt-gunparts.com**
Armatac Industries **www.armatac.com**
Asia Sourcing Corp. **www.asiasourcing.com**
Badger Barrels, Inc. **www.badgerbarrels.com**
Barnes Precision Machine **www.barnesprecision.com**
Bar-Sto Precision Machine **www.barsto.com**
Battenfeld Technologies **www.battenfeldtechnologies.com**
Bellm TC's **www.bellmtcs.com**
Belt Mountain Enterprises **www.beltmountain.com**
Bergara Barrels **www.bergarabarrels.com**
Beyer Barrels **www.beyerbarrels.com**
Bill Wiseman & Co. **www.wisemanballistics.com**
Briley **www.briley.com**
Brownells **www.brownells.com**
B-Square **www.b-square.com**
Buffer Technologies **www.buffertech.com**
Bullberry Barrel Works **www.bullberry.com**
Bulldog Barrels **www.bulldogbarrels.com**
Bushmaster Firearms/Quality Parts **www.bushmaster.com**
Butler Creek Corp **www.butler-creek.com**
Cape Outfitters Inc. **www.capeoutfitters.com**
Caspian Arms Ltd. **www.caspianarms.com**
Cheaper Than Dirt **www.cheaperthandirt.com**
Chesnut Ridge **www.chestnutridge.com/**
Chip McCormick Corp **www.chipmccormickcorp.com**
Choate Machine & Tool Co. **www.riflestock.com**
Christie's Products **www.1022cental.com**
Cierner, Jonathan Arthur **www.22lrconversions.com**
CJ Weapons Accessories **www.cjweapons.com**
Colonial Arms **www.colonialarms.com**
Comp-N-Choke **www.comp-n-choke.com**
Cylinder & Slide Shop **www.cylinder-slide.com**
Daniel Defense **www.danieldefense.com**
Dave Manson Precision Reamers. **www.mansonreamers.com**
Digi-Twist **www.fmtcorp.com**
Dixie Gun Works **www.dixiegun.com**
Douglas Barrels **www.benchrest.com/douglas/**
DPMS **www.dpmsinc.com**
D.S.Arms,Inc. **www.dsarms.com**
eBay **www.ebay.com**
Ed Brown Products **www.edbrown.com**
EFK Marketing/Fire Dragon Pistol Accessories **www.flmfire.com**
E.R. Shaw **www.ershawbarrels.com**
FJ Fedderson Rifle Barrels **www.gunbarrels.net**
Forrest Inc. **www.gunmags.com**
Fulton Armory **www.fulton-armory.com**
Galazan **www.connecticutshotgun.com**
Gemtech **www.gem-tech.com**
Gentry, David **www.gentrycustom.com**
GG&G **www.gggaz.com**
Green Mountain Rifle Barrels **www.gmriflebarrel.com**
Gun Parts Corp. **www.e-gunparts.com**
Guntec USA **www.guntecusa.com**
Harris Engineering **www.harrisbipods.com**
Hart Rifle Barrels **www.hartbarrels.com**
Hastings Barrels **www.hastingsbarrels.com**
Heinie Specialty Products **www.heinie.com**
HKS Products, Inc. **www.hksspeedloaders.com**
Holland Shooters Supply **www.hollandgun.com**
H-S Precision **www.hsprecision.com**
I.M.A. **www.ima-usa.com**
Jack First Gun Shop **www.jackfirstgun.com**
Jarvis, Inc. **www.jarvis-custom.com**
J&T Distributing **www.jtdistributing.com**
John's Guns **www.johnsguns.com**
John Masen Co. **www.johnmasen.com**
Jonathan Arthur Ciener, Inc. **www.22lrconversions.com**
JP Enterprises **www.jpar15.com**
Keng's Firearms Specialities **www.versapod.com**
KG Industries **www.kgcoatings.com**
Kick Eez **www.kickeez.com**
Kidd Triggers **www.coolguyguns.com**
King's Gunworks **www.kingsgunworks.com**
Knoxx Industries **www.knoxx.com**
Krieger Barrels **www.kriegerbarrels.com**
K-VAR Corp. **www.k-var.com**
LaRue Tactical **www.laruetactical.com**
Les Baer Custom, Inc. **www.lesbaer.com**
Lilja Barrels **www.riflebarrels.com**
Lone Star Rifle Co. **www.lonestarrifles.com**
Lone Wolf Dist. **www.lonewolfdist.com**
Lothar Walther Precision Tools Inc. **www.lothar-walther.de**
M&A Parts, Inc. **www.m-aparts.com**
MAB Barrels **www.mab.com.au**
Magpul Industries Corp. **www.magpul.com**
Majestic Arms **www.majesticarms.com**
Marvel Products, Inc. **www.marvelprod.com**
MEC-GAR USA **www.mec-gar.com**
Mesa Tactical **www.mesatactical.com**
Michaels of Oregon Co. **www.michaels-oregon.com**
Midway USA **www.midwayusa.com**
New England Custom Gun Service
www.newenglandcustomgun.com
NIC Industries **www.nicindustries.com**
North Mfg. Co. **www.rifle-barrels.com**
Numrich Gun Parts Corp. **www.e-gunparts.com**

Osprey Defense LLC **www.gaspiston.com**
Pachmayr **www.pachmayr.com**
Pac-Nor Barrels **www.pac-nor.com**
Power Custom, Inc. **www.powercustom.com**
Para Ordinance Pro Shop **www.ltms.com**
Point Tech Inc. **pointec@ibm.net**
Precision Reflex **www.pri-mounts.com**
Promag Industries **www.promagindustries.com**
RCI-XRAIL **www.xrailbyrci.com**
Red Star Arms **www.redstararms.com**
Rock Creek Barrels **www.rockcreekbarrels.com**
Rocky Mountain Arms **www.rockymountainarms.com**
Royal Arms Int'l **www.royalarms.com**
R.W. Hart **www.rwhart.com**
Sage Control Ordnance **www.sageinternationalltd.com**
Sarco Inc. **www.sarcoinc.com**
Scattergun Technologies Inc. **www.wilsoncombat.com**
Schuemann Barrels **www.schuemann.com**
Score High Gunsmithing **www.scorehi.com**
Seminole Gunworks Chamber Mates **www.chambermates.com**
Shaw Barrels **www.ershawbarrels.com**
Shilen **www.shilen.com**
Sims Vibration Laboratory **www.limbsaver.com**
Smith & Alexander Inc. **www.smithandalexander.com**
Speed Shooters Int'l **www.shooternet.com/ssi**
Sprinco USA Inc. **sprinco@primenet.com**
Springfield Sporters, Inc. **www.ssporters.com**
STI Int'l **www.stiguns.com**
S&S Firearms **www.ssfirearms.com**
SSK Industries **www.sskindustries.com**
Sun Devil Mfg. **www.sundevilmfg.com**
Sunny Hill Enterprises **www.sunny-hill.com**
Tac Star **www.lymanproducts.com**
Tactical Innovations **www.tacticalinc.com**
Tactical Solutions **www.tacticalsol.com**
Tactilite **www.tactilite.com**
Tapco **www.tapco.com**
Trapdoors Galore **www.trapdoors.com**
Triple K Manufacturing Co. Inc. **www.triplek.com**
U.S.A. Magazines Inc. **www.usa-magazines.com**
Verney-Carron SA **www.verney-carron.com**
Vintage Ordnance **www.vintageordnance.com**
Vltor Weapon Systems **www.vltor.com**
Volquartsen Custom Ltd. **www.volquartsen.com**
W.C. Wolff Co. **www.gunsprings.com**
Waller & Son **www.wallerandson.com**
Weigand Combat Handguns **www.weigandcombat.com**
Western Gun Parts **www.westerngunparts.com**
Wilson Arms **www.wilsonarms.com**
Wilson Combat **www.wilsoncombat.com**
Wisner's Inc. **www.wisnerinc.com**
Z-M Weapons **www.zmweapons.com/**home.htm

GUNSMITHING SUPPLIES AND INSTRUCTION

American Gunsmithing Institute **www.americangunsmith.com**
Baron Technology **www.baronengraving.com**
Battenfeld Technologies **www.battenfeldtechnologies.com**
Bellm TC's **www.bellmtcs.com**
Blue Ridge Machinery & Tools **www.blueridgemachinery.com**
Brownells, Inc. **www.brownells.com**
B-Square Co. **www.b-square.com**
Cerakote Firearm Coatings **www.nciindustries.com**
Clymer Mfg. Co. **www.clymertool.com**
Craftguard Metal Finishing **crftgrd@aol.com**
Dem-Bart **www.dembartco.com**
Doug Turnbull Restoration **www.turnbullrestoration.com**
Du-Lite Corp. **www.dulite.com**
DuraCoat Firearm Finishes **www.lauerweaponry.com**
Dvorak Instruments **www.dvorakinstruments.com**
Gradiant Lens Corp. **www.gradientlens.com**
Grizzly Industrial **www.grizzly.com**
Gunline Tools **www.gunline.com**
Harbor Freight **www.harborfreight.com**
JGS Precision Tool Mfg. LLC **www.jgstools.com**
Mag-Na-Port International **www.magnaport.com**
Manson Precision Reamers **www.mansonreamers.com**
Midway USA **www.midwayusa.com**
Murray State College **www.mscok.edu**
New England Custom Gun Service
www.newenglandcustomgun.com
Olympus America Inc. **www.olympus.com**
Pacific Tool & Gauge **www.pacifictoolandgauge.com**
Precision Metalsmiths, Inc. **www.precisionmetalsmiths.com**
Rail Vise Technologies **www.railvise.com**
Trinidad State Junior College **www.trinidadstate.edu**

HANDGUN GRIPS

A&G Supply Co. **www.gripextender.com**
Ajax Custom Grips, Inc. **www.ajaxgrips.com**
Altamont Co. **www.altamontco.com**
Aluma Grips **www.alumagrips.com**
Badger Grips **www.pistolgrips.com**
Barami Corp. **www.hipgrip.com**
Blu Magnum Grips **www.blumagnum.com**
Buffalo Brothers **www.buffalobrothers.com**
Crimson Trace Corp. **www.crimsontrace.com**
Decal Grip **www.decalgrip.com**
Eagle Grips **www.eaglegrips.com**
Falcon Industries **www.ergogrips.net**
Herrett's Stocks **www.herrettstocks.com**
Hogue Grips **www.getgrip.com**
Kirk Ratajesak **www.kgratajesak.com**
Lett Custom Grips **www.lettgrips.com**

N.C. Ordnance **www.gungrip.com**
Nill-Grips USA **www.nill-grips.com**
Pachmayr **www.pachmayr.com**
Pearce Grips **www.pearcegrip.com**
Rio Grande Custom Grips **www.riograndecustomgrips.com**
Trausch Grips Int.Co. **www.trausch.com**
Tyler-T Grips **www.t-grips.com**
Uncle Mike's: **www.uncle-mikes.com**

HOLSTERS AND LEATHER PRODUCTS

Active Pro Gear **www.activeprogear.com**
Akah **www.akah.de**
Aker Leather Products **www.akerleather.com**
Alessi Distributor R&F Inc. **www.alessiholsters.com**
Alfonso's of Hollywood **www.alfonsogunleather.com**
Armor Holdings **www.holsters.com**
Bagmaster **www.bagmaster.com**
Bianchi International **www.bianchi-intl.com**
Black Dog Machine **www.blackdogmachinellc.net**
Blackhawk Outdoors **www.blackhawk.com**
Blackhills Leather **www.blackhillsleather.com**
BodyHugger Holsters **www.nikolais.com**
Boyt Harness Co. **www.boytharness.com**
Brigade Gun Leather **www.brigadegunleather.com**
Center of Mass **www.comholsters.com**
Chimere **www.chimere.com**
Clipdraw **www.clipdraw.com**
Conceal It **www.conceal-it.com**
Concealment Shop Inc. **www.theconcealmentshop.com**
Coronado Leather Co. **www.coronadoleather.com**
Covert Carry **www.covertcarry.com**
Creedmoor Sports, Inc. **www.creedmoorsports.com**
Cross Breed Holsters **www.crossbreedholsters.com**
Custom Leather Wear **www.customleatherwear.com**
Defense Security Products **www.thunderwear.com**
Dennis Yoder **www.yodercustomleather.com**
DeSantis Holster **www.desantisholster.com**
Dillon Precision **www.dillonprecision.com**
Don Hume Leathergoods, Inc. **www.donhume.com**
Elite Survival **www.elitesurvival.com**
Ernie Hill International **www.erniehill.com**
Fist **www.fist-inc.com**
Fobus USA **www.fobusholster.com**
Front Line Ltd. **frontlin@internet-zahav.net**
Galco **www.usgalco.com**
Gilmore's Sports Concepts **www.gilmoresports.com**
Gould & Goodrich **www.gouldusa.com**
Gunmate Products **www.gun-mate.com**
Hellweg Ltd. **www.hellwegltd.com**
Hide-A-Gun **www.hide-a-gun.com**
High Noon Holsters **www.highnoonholsters.com**
Holsters.Com **www.holsters.com**
Horseshoe Leather Products **www.horseshoe.co.uk**
Hunter Co. **www.huntercompany.com**
JBP/Master's Holsters **www.jbpholsters.com**
Kirkpatrick Leather Company **www.kirkpatrickleather.com**
KNJ **www.knjmfg.com**
Kramer Leather **www.kramerleather.com**
Law Concealment Systems **www.handgunconcealment.com**
Levy's Leathers Ltd. **www.levysleathers.com**
Mernickle Holsters **www.mernickleholsters.com**
Michaels of Oregon Co. **www.michaels-oregon.com**
Milt Sparks Leather **www.miltsparks.com**
Mitch Rosen Extraordinary Gunleather **www.mitchrosen.com**
Old World Leather **www.gun-mate.com**
Pacific Canvas & Leather Co. **paccanadleather@directway.com**
Pager Pal **www.pagerpal.com**
Phalanx Corp. **www.smartholster.com**
Purdy Gear **www.purdygear.com**
PWL **www.pwlusa.com**
Rumanya Inc. **www.rumanya.com**
S.A. Gunleather **www.elpasoleather.com**
Safariland Ltd. Inc. **www.safariland.com**
Shooting Systems Group Inc. **www.shootingsystems.com**
Skyline Tool Works **www.clipdraw.com**
Strictly Anything Inc. **www.strictlyanything.com**
Strong Holster Co. **www.strong-holster.com**
Tex Shoemaker & Sons **www.texshoemaker.com**
The Belt Co. **www.conceal-it.com**
The Leather Factory Inc. **lflandry@flash.net**
The Outdoor Connection **www.outdoorconnection.com**
Top-Line USA inc. **www.toplineusa.com**
Tuff Products **www.tuffproducts.com**
Triple K Manufacturing Co. **www.triplek.com**
Wilson Combat **www.wilsoncombat.com**

MISCELLANEOUS SHOOTING PRODUCTS

10X Products Group **www.10Xwear.com**
Aero Peltor **www.aearo.com**
American Body Armor **www.americanbodyarmor.com**
American Tactical Imports **www.americantactical.com**
Ammo-Up **www.ammoupusa.com**
Armor Holdings Products **www.armorholdings.com**
AutoGun Tracker **www.autoguntracker.com**
Battenfeld Technologies **www.battenfeldtechnologies.com**
Beamhit **www.beamhit.com**
Beartooth **www.beartoothproducts.com**
Bodyguard by S&W **www.yourbodyguard.com**
Burnham Brothers **www.burnhambrothers.com**
Collectors Armory **www.collectorsarmory.com**

Dalloz Safety **www.cdalloz.com**
Deben Group Industries Inc. **www.deben.com**
Decot Hy-Wyd Sport Glasses **www.sportyglasses.com**
Defense Technology **www.safariland.com/lesslethal**
E.A.R., Inc. **www.earinc.com**
First Choice Armor **www.firstchoicearmor.com**
Gunstands **www.gunstands.com**
Howard Leight Hearing Protectors **www.howardleight.com**
Hunters Specialities **www.hunterspec.com**
Johnny Stewart Wildlife Calls **www.hunterspec.com**
Joseph Chiarello Gun Insurance **www.guninsurance.com**
Mec-Gar USA **www.mec-gar.com**
Merit Corporation **www.meritcorporation.com**
Michaels of Oregon **www.michaels-oregon.com**
MPI Outdoors **www.mpioutdoors.com**
MT2, LLC **www.mt2.com**
MTM Case-Gard **www.mtmcase-gard.com**
North Safety Products **www.northsafety-brea.com**
Oakley, Inc. **www.usstandardissue.com**
Plano Molding **www.planomolding.com**
Practical Air Rifle Training Systems **www.smallarms.com**
Pro-Ears **www.pro-ears.com**
Second Chance Body Armor Inc. **www.secondchance.com**
Silencio **www.silencio.com**
Smart Lock Technologies **www.smartlock.com**
SportEAR **www.sportear.com**
STRAC, Inc. **www.stractech.com**
Surefire **www.surefire.com**
Taser Int'l **www.taser.com**
Vyse-Gelatin Innovations **www.gelatininnovations.com**
Walker's Game Ear Inc. **www.walkersgameear.com**

MUZZLELOADING FIREARMS AND PRODUCTS

American Pioneer Powder **www.americanpioneerpowder.com**
Armi Sport **www.armisport.com**
Barnes Bullets **www.barnesbullets,com**
Black Powder Products **www.bpiguns.com**
Buckeye Barrels **www.buckeyebarrels.com**
Cabin Creek Muzzleloading **www.cabincreek.net**
CVA **www.cva.com**
Caywood Gunmakers **www.caywoodguns.com**
Davide Perdsoli & co. **www.davide-pedersoli.com**
Dixie Gun Works, Inc. **www.dixiegun.com**
Elephant/Swiss Black Powder **www.elephantblackpowder.com**
Goex Black Powder **www.goexpowder.com**
Green Mountain Rifle Barrel Co. **www.gmriflebarrel.com**
Gunstocks Plus **www.gunstocksplus.com**
Harvester Muzzleloading **www.harvestermuuzzleloading.com**
Honorable Company of Horners **www.hornguild.org**
Hornady **www.hornady.com**
Jedediah Starr Trading Co. **www.jedediah-starr.com**
Jim Chambers Flintlocks **www.flintlocks.com**
Kahnke Gunworks **www.powderandbow.com/kahnke/**
Knight Rifles **www.knightrifles.com**
Knob Mountain Muzzleloading
www.knobmountainmuzzleloading.com
The leatherman **www.blackpowderbags.com**
Log Cabin Shop **www.logcabinshop.com**
L&R Lock Co. **www.lr-rpl.com**
Lyman **www.lymanproducts.com**
Magkor Industries **www.magkor.com**
MDM Muzzleloaders **www.mdm-muzzleloaders.com**
Middlesex Village Trading **www.middlesexvillagetrading.com**
Millennium Designed Muzzleloaders
www.mdm-muzzleloaders.com
MSM, Inc. **www.msmfg.com**
Muzzleloader Builders Supply
www.muzzleloadersbuilderssupply.com
Muzzleload Magnum Products **www.mmpsabots.com**
Muzzleloading Shotguns **www.muzzleloadingshotguns.com**
Muzzleloading Technologies, Inc.
www.mtimuzzleloading.com
Navy Arms **www.navyarms.com**
Northwest Trade Guns **www.northstarwest.com**
Nosler, Inc. **www.nosler.com**
October Country Muzzleloading **www.oct-country.com**
Ox-Yoke Originals Inc. **www.rmcoxyoke.com**
Pacific Rifle Co. **pacificrifle@aol.com**
Palmetto Arms **www.palmetto.it**
Pietta **www.pietta.it**
Powerbelt Bullets **www.powerbeltbullets.com**
PR Bullets **www.prbullets.com**
Precision Rifle Dead Center Bullets **www.prbullet.com**
R.E. Davis Co. **www.redaviscompany.com**
Rightnour Mfg. Co. Inc. **www.rmcsports.com**
The Rifle Shop **trshoppe@aol.com**
Savage Arms, Inc. **www.savagearms.com**
Schuetzen Powder **www.schuetzenpowder.com**
TDC **www.tdcmfg.com**
Tennessee Valley Muzzleloading **www.avsia.com/tvm**
Thompson Center Arms **www.tcarms.com**
Tiger Hunt Stocks **www.gunstockwood.com**
Track of the Wolf **www.trackofthewolf.com**
Traditions Performance Muzzleloading
www.traditionsfirearms.com
Vernon C. Davis & Co.
www.stonewallcreekoutfitters.com

PUBLICATIONS, VIDEOS, AND CD'S

Arms and Military Press **www.skennerton.com**

A&J Arms Booksellers **www.ajarmsbooksellers.com**
American Cop **www.americancopmagazine.com**
American Firearms Industry **www.amfire.com**
American Gunsmiting Institute **www.americangunsmith.com**
American Handgunner **www.americanhandgunner.com**
American Hunter **www.nrapublications.org**
American Pioneer Video **www.americanpioneervideo.com**
American Rifleman **www.nrapublications.org**
American Shooting Magazine **www.americanshooting.com**
Backwoodsman **www.backwoodsmanmag.com**
Black Powder Cartridge News **www.blackpowderspg.com**
Blue Book Publications **www.bluebookinc.com**
Combat Handguns **www.combathandguns.com**
Concealed Carry **www.uscca.us**
Cornell Publications **www.cornellpubs.com**
Countrywide Press **www.countrysport.com**
DBI Books/Krause Publications **www.krause.com**
Fouling Shot **www.castbulletassoc.org**
George Shumway Publisher **www.shumwaypublisher.com**
Gun List **www.gunlist.com**
Gun Video **www.gunvideo.com**
GUNS Magazine **www.gunsmagazine.com**
Guns & Ammo **www.gunsandammomag.com**
Gun Week **www.gunweek.com**
Gun World **www.gunworld.com**
Harris Publications **www.harrispublications.com**
Hendon Publishing Co. **www.hendonpub.com**
Heritage Gun Books **www.gunbooks.com**
Krause Publications **www.krause.com**
Law and Order **www.hendonpub.com**
Man at Arms **www.manatarmsbooks.com**
Muzzleloader **www.muzzleloadermag.com**
On-Target Productions **www.ontargetdvds.com**
Outdoor Channel **www.outdoorchannel.com**
Paladin Press **www.paladin-press.com**
Police and Security News **www.policeandsecuritynews.com**
Police Magazine **www.policemag.com**
Precision Shooting **www.precisionshooting.com**
Pursuit Channel **www.pursuitchannel.com**
Rifle and Handloader Magazines **www.riflemagazine.com**
Safari Press Inc. **www.safaripress.com**
Schiffer Publishing **www.schifferbooks.com**
Scurlock Publishing **www.muzzleloadingmag.com**
Shoot! Magazine **www.shootmagazine.com**
Shooting Illustrated **www.nrapublications.org**
Shooting Industry **www.shootingindustry.com**
Shooting Sports Retailer **www.shootingsportsretailer.com**
Shooting Sports USA **www.nrapublications.org**
Shotgun News **www.shotgunnews.com**
Shotgun Report **www.shotgunreport.com**
Shotgun Sports Magazine **www.shotgun-sports.com**
Single Shot Rifle Journal **www.assra.com**
Small Arms Review **www.smallarmsreview.com**
Small Caliber News **www.smallcaliber.com**
Sporting Clays Web Edition **www.sportingclays.net**
Sports Afield **www.sportsafield.comm**
Sportsmen on Film **www.sportsmenonfilm.com**
SWAT Magazine **www.swatmag.com**
The Single Shot Exchange Magazine **singleshot@earthlink.net**
The Sixgunner **www.sskindustries.com**
Varmint Hunter **www.varminthunter.org**
VSP Publications **www.gunbooks.com**

RELOADING TOOLS

Antimony Man **www.theantimonyman.com**
Ballisti-Cast Mfg. **www.ballisti-cast.com**
Battenfeld Technologies **www.battenfeldtechnologies.com**
Bruno Shooters Supply **www.brunoshooters.com**
Buffalo Arms **www.buffaloarms.com**
CabineTree **www.castingstuff.com**
Camdex, Inc. **www.camdexloader.com**
CH/4D Custom Die **www.ch4d.com**
Colorado Shooters Supply **www.hochmoulds.com**
Corbin Mfg & Supply Co. **www.corbins.com**
Dillon Precision **www.dillonprecision.com**
Forster Precision Products **www.forsterproducts.com**
Gracey Trimmer **www.matchprep.com**
GSI International, Inc. **www.gsiinternational.com**
Hanned Line **www.hanned.com**
Harrell's Precision **www.harrellsprec.com**
Holland's Shooting Supplies **www.hollandgun.com**
Hornady **www.hornady.com**
Hunter's Supply, Inc. **wwwhunters-supply.com**
Huntington Reloading Products **www.huntingtons.com**
J & J Products Co. **www.jandjproducts.com**
Lead Bullet Technology **www.lbtmoulds.com**
Lee Precision, Inc. **www.leeprecision.com**
Littleton Shotmaker **www.leadshotmaker.com**
Load Data **www.loaddata.com**
Lyman **www.lymanproducts.com**
Magma Engineering **www.magmaengr.com**
Mayville Engineering Co. (MEC) **www.mecreloaders.com**
Midway **www.midwayusa.com**
Moly-Bore **www.molybore.com**
Montana Bullet Works **www.montanabulletworks.com**
MTM Case-Guard **www.mtmcase-guard.com**
NECO **www.neconos.com**
NEI **www.neihandtools.com**
Neil Jones Custom Products **www.neiljones.com**
New Lachaussee SA **www.lachaussee.com**
Ponsness/Warren **www.reloaders.com**
Precision Reloading **www.precisionreloading.com**

Quinetics Corp. **www.quineticscorp.com**
Ranger Products **www.pages.prodigy.com**
Rapine Bullet Mold Mfg Co. **www.bulletmoulds.com**
RCBS **www.rcbs.com**
Redding Reloading Equipment **www.redding-reloading.com**
Russ Haydon's Shooting Supplies **www.shooters-supply.com**
Sinclair Int'l Inc. **www.sinclairintl.com**
Stoney Point Products Inc **www.stoneypoint.com**
Thompson Bullet Lube Co. **www.thompsonbulletlube.com**
Vickerman Seating Die **www.castingstuff.com**
Wilson (L.E. Wilson) **www.lewilson.com**

RESTS— BENCH, PORTABLE, ATTACHABLE

Accu-Shot **www.accu-shot.com**
Battenfeld Technolgies **www.battenfeldtechnologies.com**
Bench Master **www.bench-master.com**
B-Square **www.b-square.com**
Bullshooter **www.bullshooterssightingin.com**
Center Mass, Inc. **www.centermassinc.com**
Desert Mountain Mfg. **www.benchmasterusa.com**
DOA Tactical **www.doatactical.com**
Harris Engineering Inc. **www.harrisbipods**
KFS Industries **www.versapod.com**
Kramer Designs **www.snipepod.com**
L Thomas Rifle Support **www.ltsupport.com**
Level-Lok **www.levellok.com**
Midway **www.midwayusa.com**
Predator Sniper Styx **www.predatorsniperstyx.com**
Ransom International **www.ransom-intl.com**
Rotary Gun Racks **www.gun-racks.com**
R.W. Hart **www.rwhart.com**
Sinclair Intl, Inc. **www.sinclairintl.com**
Shooters Ridge **www.shooterridge.com**
Shooting Bench USA **www.shootingbenchusa.com**
Stoney Point Products **www.stoneypoint.com**
Target Shooting **www.targetshooting.com**
Varmint Masters **www.varmintmasters.com**
Versa-Pod **www.versa-pod.com**

SCOPES, SIGHTS, MOUNTS AND ACCESSORIES

Accumount **www.accumounts.com**
Accusight **www.accusight.com**
ADCO **www.shooters.com/adco/index/htm**
Adirondack Opitcs **www.adkoptics.com**
Advantage Tactical Sight **www.advantagetactical.com**
Aimpoint **www.aimpoint.com**
Aim Shot, Inc. **www.aimshot.com**
Aimtech Mount Systems **www.aimtech-mounts.com**
Alpec Team, Inc. **www.alpec.com**
Alpen Outdoor Corp. **www.alpenoutdoor.com**
American Technologies Net**work, Corp. www.atncorp.com**
AmeriGlo, LLC **www.ameriglo.net**
ArmaLaser **www.armalaser.com**
Armament Technology, Inc. **www.armament.com**
ARMS **www.armsmounts.com**
Aro-Tek, Ltd. **www.arotek.com**
ATN **www.atncorp.com**
Badger Ordnance **www.badgerordnance.com**
Barrett **www.barrettrifles.com**
Beamshot-Quarton **www.beamshot.com**
BKL Technologies, Inc. **www.bkltech.com**
BSA Optics **www.bsaoptics.com**
B-Square Company, Inc. **www.b-square.com**
Burris **www.burrisoptics.com**
Bushnell Performance Optics **www.bushnell.com**
Carl Zeiss Optical Inc. **www.zeiss.com**
Carson Optical **www.carson-optical.com**
CenterPoint Precision Optics **www.centerpointoptics.com**
Centurion Arms **www.centurionarms.com**
C-More Systems **www.cmore.com**
Conetrol Scope Mounts **www.conetrol.com**
Crimson Trace Corp. **www.crimsontrace.com**
Crossfire L.L.C. **www.amfire.com/hesco/html**
Cylinder & Slide, Inc. **www.cylinderslide.com**
DCG Supply Inc. **www.dcgsupply.com**
D&L Sports **www.dlsports.com**
DuraSight Scope Mounting Systems **www.durasight.com**
EasyHit, Inc. **www.easyhit.com**
EAW **www.eaw.de**
Elcan Optical Technologies **www.armament.com, www.elcan.com**
Electro-Optics Technologies **www.eotechmdc.com/holosight**
EoTech **www.eotech-inc.com**
Europtik Ltd. **www.europtik.com**
Fujinon, Inc. **www.fujinon.com**
GG&G **www.w.gggaz.com**
Gilmore Sports **www.gilmoresports.com**
Gradient Lens Corp. **www.gradientlens.com**
Hakko Co. Ltd. **www.hakko-japan.co.jp**
Hahn Precision **www.hahn-precision.com**
Hesco **www.hescosights.com**
Hi-Lux Optics **www.hi-luxoptics.com**
Hitek Industries **www.nightsight.com**
HIVIZ **www.hivizsights.com**
Hollands Shooters Supply **www.hollandguns.com**
Horus Vision **www.horusvision.com**
Hunter Co. **www.huntercompany.com**
Huskemaw Optics **www.huskemawoptics.com**
Innovative Weaponry,Inc. **www.ptnightsights.com**
Insight **www.insighttechnology.com**
Ironsighter Co. **www.ironsighter.com**

ITT Night Vision **www.ittnightvision.com**
Kahles **www.kahlesoptik.com**
KenSight **www.kensight.com**
Knight's Armament **www.knightarmco.com**
Kowa Optimed Inc. **www.kowascope.com**
Kwik-Site Co. **www.kwiksitecorp.com**
L-3 Communications-Eotech **www.l-3com.com**
LaRue Tactical **www.laruetactical.com**
Laser Bore Sight **www.laserboresight.com**
Laser Devices Inc. **www.laserdevices.com**
Lasergrips **www.crimsontrace.com**
LaserLyte **www.laserlytesights.com**
LaserMax Inc. **www.lasermax.com**
Laser Products **www.surefire.com**
Leapers, Inc. **www.leapers.com**
Leatherwood **www.hi-luxoptics.com**
Legacy Sports **www.legacysports.com**
Leica Camera Inc. **www.leica-camera.com/usa**
Leupold **www.leupold.com**
Lewis Machine & Tool **www.lewismachine.net**
LightForce/NightForce USA **www.nightforcescopes.com**
Lyman **www.lymanproducts.com**
Lynx **www.b-square.com**
MaTech **www.adcofirearms.com**
Marble's Gunsights **www.marblearms.com**
MDS,Inc. **www.mdsincorporated.com**
Meopta **www.meopta.com**
Meprolight **www.kimberamerica.com**
Micro Sight Co. **www.microsight.com**
Millett **www.millettsights.com**
Miniature Machine Corp. **www.mmcsight.com**
Mini-Scout-Mount **www.amegaranges.com**
Minox USA **www.minox.com**
Montana Vintage Arms **www.montanavintagearms.com**
Moro Vision **www.morovision.com**
Mounting Solutions Plus **www.mountsplus.com**
NAIT **www.nait.com**
Newcon International Ltd. **www.newcon-optik.com**
Night Force Optics **www.nightforcescopes.com**
Night Optics USA, Inc. **www.nightoptics.com**
Night Owl Optics **www.nightowloptics.com**
Night Vision Systems **www.nightvisionsystems.com**
Nikon Inc. **www.nikonhunting.com**
North American Integrated Technologies **www.nait.com**
O.K. Weber, Inc. **www.okweber.com**
Optolyth-Optic **www.optolyth.de**
Osprey Optics **www.osprey-optics.com**
Pentax Corp. **www.pentaxlightseeker.com**
Precision Reflex **www.pri-mounts.com**
Pride Fowler, Inc. **www.rapidreticle.com**
Premier Reticles **www.premierreticles.com**
Redfield **www.redfieldoptics.com**
Rifle Electronics **www.theriflecam.com**
R&R Int'l Trade **www.nightoptic.com**
Schmidt & Bender **www.schmidt-bender.com**
Scopecoat **www.scopecoat.com**
Scopelevel **www.scopelevel.com**
Segway Industries **www.segway-industries.com**
Shepherd Scope Ltd. **www.shepherdscopes.com**
Sig Sauer **www.sigsauer.com**
Sightmark **www.sightmark.com**
Sightron **www.sightron.com**
Simmons **www.simmonsoptics.com**
S&K **www.scopemounts.com**
Springfield Armory **www.springfield-armory.com**
Sun Optics USA **www.sunopticsusa.com**
Sure-Fire **www.surefire.com**
Swarovski/Kahles **www.swarovskioptik.com**
SWATSCOPE **www.swatscope.com**
Swift Optics **www.swiftoptics.com**
Talley Mfg. Co. **www.talleyrings.com**
Target Scope Blocks-Steve Earl Products
Steven.m.earle@comcast.net
Tasco **www.tascosales.com**
Tech Sights **www.tech-sights.com**
Trijicon Inc. **www.trijicon.com**
Troy Industries **www.troyind.com**
Truglo Inc. **www.truglo.com**
Ultimak **www.ultimak.com**
UltraDot **www.ultradotusa.com**
Unertl Optical Co. **www.unertlopics.com**
US Night Vision **www.usnightvision.com**
U.S. Optics Technologies Inc. **www.usoptics.com**
Valdada-IOR Optics **www.valdada.com**
Viridian Green Laser Sights **www.viridiangreenlaser.com**
Vortex Optics **www.vortexoptics.com**
Warne **www.warnescopemounts.com**
Weaver Mounts **www.weaver-mounts.com**
Weaver Scopes **www.weaveroptics.com**
Wilcox Industries Corp **www.wilcoxind.com**
Williams Gun Sight Co. **www.williamsgunsight.com**
Wilson Combat **www.wilsoncombat.com**
XS Sight Systems **www.xssights.com**
Zeiss **www.zeiss.com**

SHOOTING ORGANIZATIONS, SCHOOLS AND RANGES

Amateur Trapshooting Assoc. **www.shootata.com**
American Custom Gunmakers Guild **www.acgg.org**
American Gunsmithing Institute **www.americangunsmith.com**
American Pistolsmiths Guild **www.americanpistol.com**
American Shooting Sports Council **www.assc.com**

American Single Shot Rifle Assoc. **www.assra.com**
American Snipers **www.americansnipers.org**
Antique Shooting Tool Collector's Assoc. **www.oldshootingtools.org**
Assoc. of Firearm & Tool Mark Examiners **www.afte.org**
BATF **www.atf.ustreas.gov**
Blackwater Lodge and Training Center
www.blackwaterlodge.com
Boone and Crockett Club **www.boone-crockett.org**
Buckmasters, Ltd. **www.buckmasters.com**
Cast Bullet Assoc. **www.castbulletassoc.org**
Citizens Committee for the Right to Keep & Bear Arms
www.ccrkba.org
Civilian Marksmanship Program **www.odcmp.com**
Colorado School of Trades **www.gunsmith-school.com**
Cylinder & Slide Pistolsmithing Schools **www.cylinder-slide.com**
Ducks Unlimited **www.ducks.org**
4-H Shooting Sports Program **www.4-hshootingsports.org**
Fifty Caliber Institute **www.fiftycal.org**
Fifty Caliber Shooters Assoc. **www.fcsa.org**
Firearms Coalition **www.nealknox.com**
Front Sight Firearms Training Institute **www.frontsight.com**
German Gun Collectors Assoc. **www.germanguns.com**
Gun Clubs **www.associatedgunclubs.org**
Gun Owners' Action League **www.goal.org**
Gun Owners of America **www.gunowners.org**
Gun Trade Asssoc. Ltd. **www.brucepub.com/**gta
Gunsite Training Center, Inc. **www.gunsite.com**
Handgun Hunters International **www.sskindustries.com**
Hunting and Shooting Sports Heritage Fund **www.huntandshoot.org**
I.C.E. Traing **www.icetraining.com**
IWA **www.iwa.info**
International Defense Pistol Assoc. **www.idpa.com**
International Handgun Metallic Silhouette Assoc. **www.ihmsa.org**
International Hunter Education Assoc. **www.ihea.com**
Int'l Law Enforcement Educators and Trainers Assoc.
www.ileeta.com
International Single Shot Assoc. **www.issa-schuetzen.org**
Jews for the Preservation of Firearms Ownership **www.jpfo.org**
Mule Deer Foundation **www.muledeer.org**
Muzzle Loaders Assoc. of Great Britain **www.mlagb.com**
National 4-H Shooting Sports **www.4-hshootingsports.org**
National Association of Sporting Goods Wholesalers **www.nasgw.org**
National Benchrest Shooters Assoc. **www.benchrest.com**
National Defense Industrial Assoc. **www.ndia.org**
National Firearms Act Trade & Collectors Assoc. **www.nfatca.org**
National Muzzle Loading Rifle Assoc. **www.nmlra.org**
National Reloading Manufacturers Assoc **www.reload-nrma.com**
National Rifle Assoc. **www.nra.org**
National Rifle Assoc. ILA **www.nraila.org**
National Shooting Sports Foundation **www.nssf.org**
National Skeet Shooters Association **www.nssa-nsca.com**
National Sporting Clays Assoc. **www.nssa-nsca.com**
National Tactial Officers Assoc. **www.ntoa.org**
National Wild Turkey Federation **www.nwtf.com**
NICS/FBI **www.fbi.gov**
North American Hunting Club **www.huntingclub.com**
Order of Edwardian Gunners (Vintagers)
www.vintagers.org
Outdoor Industry Foundation
www.outdoorindustryfoundation.org
Pennsylvania Gunsmith School **www.pagunsmith.com**
Piedmont Community College **www.piedmontcc.edu**
Quail Unlimited **www.qu.org**
Remington Society of America **www.remingtonsociety.com**
Right To Keep and Bear Arms **www.rkba.org**
Rocky Mountain Elk Foundation **www.rmef.org**
SAAMI **www.saami.org**
Safari Club International **www.scifirstforhunters.org**
Scholastic Clay Target Program **www.nssf.org/sctp**
Scholastic Shooting Sports Foundation **www.shootsctp.com**
Second Amendment Foundation **www.saf.org**
Second Amendment Sisters **www.2asisters.org**
Shooting for Women Alliance
www.shootingforwomenalliance.com
Shooting Ranges Int'l **www.shootingranges.com**
Sig Sauer Academy **www.sigsauer.com**
Single Action Shooting Society **www.sassnet.com**
Steel Challenge Pistol Tournament **www.steelchallenge.com**
Students for Second Amendment **www.sf2a.org**
Sturgis Economic Developemtn Corp.
www.sturgisdevelopment.com
Suarez Training **www.warriortalk.com**
S&W Academy and Nat'l Firearms Trng. Center
www.sw-academy.com
Tactical Defense Institute **www.tdiohio.com**
Tactical Life **www.tactical-life.com**
Ted Nugent United Sportsmen of America **www.tnugent.com**
Thunder Ranch **www.thunderranchinc.com**
Trapshooters Homepage **www.trapshooters.com**
Trinidad State Junior College **www.trinidadstate.edu**
United Sportsmen's Youth Foundation **www.usyf.com**
Universal Shooting Academy
www.universalshootingacademy.com
U.S. Concealed Carry Association **www.uscca.us**
U.S. Int'l Clay Target Assoc. **www.usicta.com**
U.S. Fish and Wildlife Service **www.fws.gov**
U.S. Practical Shooting Assoc. **www.uspsa.org**
U.S. Sportsmen's Alliance **www.ussportsmen.org**
USA Shooting **www.usashooting.com**
Varmint Hunter's Assoc. **www.varminthunter.org**
Winchester Arms Collectors Assoc.
www.winchestercollector.com
Women Hunters **www.womanhunters.com**
Women's Shooting Sports Foundation **www.wssf.org**

STOCKS, GRIPS, FOREARMS

Ace, Ltd. **www.aceltdusa.com**
Advanced Technology **www.atigunstocks.com**
Battenfeld Technologies **www.battenfeldtechnologies.com**
Bell & Carlson, Inc. **www.bellandcarlson.com**
Boyd's Gunstock Industries, Inc. **www.boydgunstocks.com**
Butler Creek Corp **www.butler-creek.com**
Cadex **www.vikingtactics.com**
Calico Hardwoods, Inc. **www.calicohardwoods.com**
Choate Machine **www.riflestock.com**
Command Arms **www.commandarms.com**
C-More Systems **www.cmore.com**
D&L Sports **www.dlsports.com**
Duo Stock **www.duostock.com**
Elk Ridge Stocks **www.reamerrentals.com/elk_ridge.htm**
FAB Tactical **www.botachtactical.com**
Fajen **www.battenfeldtechnologies.com**
Falcon Ergo Grip **www.ergogrips.com**
Great American Gunstocks **www.gunstocks.com**
Grip Pod **www.grippod.com**
Gun Stock Blanks **www.gunstockblanks.com**
Herrett's Stocks **www.herrettstocks.com**
High Tech Specialties **www.bansnersrifle.com/hightech**
Hogue Grips **www.getgrip.com**
Holland's Shooting Supplies **www.hollandgun.com**
Knight's Mfg. Co. **wwwknightarmco.com**
Knoxx Industries **www.blackhawk.com**
KZ Tactical **www.kleyzion.com**
LaRue Tactical **www.laruetactical.com**
Laser Stock **www.laserstock.com**
Lewis Machine & Tool **www.lewismachine.net**
Lone Wolf **www.lonewolfriflestocks.com**
Magpul **www.magpul.com**
Manners Compostie Stocks **www.mannerstocks.com**
McMillan Fiberglass Stocks **www.mcmfamily.com**
MPI Stocks **www.mpistocks.com**
Precision Gun Works **www.precisiongunstocks.com**
Ram-Line **www.outers-guncare.com**
Richards Microfit Stocks **www.rifle-stocks.com**
Rimrock Rifle Stock **www.rimrockstocks.com**
Royal Arms Gunstocks **www.imt.net/~royalarms**
S&K Industries **www.sandkgunstocks.com**
Speedfeed **www.safariland.com**
TacStar/Pachmayr **www.tacstar.com**
Tango Down **www.tangodown.com**
TAPCO **www.tapco.com**
Stocky's **www.newriflestocks.com**
Surefire **www.surefire.com**
Tiger-Hunt Curly Maple Gunstocks **www.gunstockwood.com**
Vltor **www.vltor.com**
Wenig Custom Gunstocks Inc. **www.wenig.com**
Wilcox Industries **www.wilcoxind.com**
Yankee Hill **www.yhm.net**

TARGETS AND RANGE EQUIPMENT

Action Target Co. **www.actiontarget.com**
Advanced Interactive Systems **www.ais-sim.com**
Advanced Training Systems **www.atsusa.biz**
Arntzen Targets **www.arntzentargets.com**
Birchwood Casey **www.birchwoodcasey.com**
Bullet Proof Electronics **www.thesnipertarget.com**
Caswell Meggitt Defense Systems
www.mds-caswell.com
Champion Traps & Targets **www.championtarget.com**
Handloader/Victory Targets **www.targetshandloader.com**
Just Shoot Me Products **www.ballistictec.com**
Laser Shot **www.lasershot.com**
MGM Targets **www.mgmtargets.com**
Mountain Plains Industries **www.targetshandloader.com**
MTM Products **www.mtmcase-gard.com**
National Muzzleloading Rifle Assoc. **www.nmlra.org**
National Target Co. **www.nationaltarget.com**
Newbold Target Systems **www.newboldtargets.com**
PJL Targets **www.pjltargets.com**
Porta Target,Inc. **www.portatarget.com**
Range Management Services Inc. **www.casewellintl.com**
Range Systems **www.shootingrangeproducts.com**
Reactive Target Systems Inc. **chrts@primenet.com**
Rolling Steel Targets **www.rollingsteeltargets.com**
Savage Range Systems **www.savagerangesystems.com**
ShatterBlast Targets **www.daisy.com**
Super Trap Bullet Containment Systems
www.supertrap.com
Thompson Target Technology **www.thompsontarget.com**
Tombstone Tactical Targets **www.tttargets.com**
Visible Impact Targets **www.crosman.com**
White Flyer **www.whiteflyer.com**

TRAP AND SKEET SHOOTING EQUIPMENT AND ACCESSORIES

10X Products Group **www.10Xwear.com**
Atlas Trap Co **www.atlastraps.com**
Auto-Sporter Industries **www.auto-sporter.com**
Claymaster Traps **www.claymaster.com**
Do-All Traps, Inc. **www.doalloutdoors.com**
Laporte USA **www.laporte-shooting.com**
Outers **www.blount.com**
Promatic, Inc. **www.promatic.biz**
Trius Products Inc. **www.triustraps.com**
White Flyer **www.whiteflyer.com**

TRIGGERS

American Trigger Corp. **www.americantrigger.com**
Brownells **www.brownells.com**
Chip McCormick Corp. **www.chipmccormickcorp.com**
E-Z Pull Triggers **www.ezpulltriggerassist.com**
Geissele Automatics, LLC **www.ar15triggers.com**
Huber Concepts **www.huberconcepts.com**
Jard, Inc. **www.jardinc.com**
Jewell Triggers **(512)353-2999**
Kidd Triggers. **www.coolguyguns.com**
Shilen **www.shilen.com**
Spec-Tech Industries, Inc. **www.spec-tech-industries.com**
Timney Triggers **www.timneytrigger.com**
Williams Trigger Specialties **www.williamstriggers.com**

MAJOR SHOOTING WEB SITES AND LINKS

24 Hour Campfire **www.24hourcampfire.com**
Alphabetic Index of Links **www.gunsgunsguns.com**
Auction Arms **www.auctionarms.com**
Benchrest Central **www.benchrest.com**
Big Game Hunt **www.biggamehunt.net**
Bullseye Pistol **www.bullseyepistol.com**
Firearms History **www.researchpress.co.uk/firearms**
Glock Talk **www.glocktalk.com**
Gun Broker Auctions **www.gunbroker.com**
Gun Industry **www.gunindustry.com**
Gun Blast **www.gunblast.com**
Gun Boards **www.gunboards.com**
GunsAmerica.com **www.gunsamerica.com**
Guns Unified Nationally Endorsing Dignity **www.guned.com**
Gun Shop Finder **www.gunshopfinder.com**
GUNS and Hunting **www.gunsandhunting.com**
Hunt and Shoot (NSSF) **www.huntandshoot.org**
Keep and Bear Arms **www.keepandbeararms.com**
Leverguns **www.leverguns.com**
Load Swap **www.loadswap.com**
Outdoor Press Room **www.outdoorpressroom.com**
Real Guns **www.realguns.com**
Ruger Forum **www.rugerforum.com**
SavageShooters **www.savageshooters.com**
Shooters Forum **www.shootersforum.com**
Shotgun Sports Resource Guide **www.shotgunsports.com**
Shotgun World **www.shotgunworld.com**
Sixgunner **www.sixgunner.com**
Sniper's Hide **www.snipershide.com**
Sportsman's Web **www.sportsmansweb.com**
Surplus Rifles **www.surplusrifle.com**
Tactical-Life **www.tactical-life.com**
The Gun Room **www.doublegun.com**
Wing Shoooting USA **www.wingshootingusa.org**

Gun Digest® Books

An imprint of F+W Media, Inc.
www.gundigeststore.com

We Know Guns So You Know Guns

Your passion and appreciation for firearms be it for recreation, protection, or historical interest and collectability is something we share; and work to support. From firearms-related references and resources to tools and accessories and instruction and advice, at www.GunDigestStore.com you'll find what you're after, at affordable prices.

All of the products in our store have been handpicked and curated here for you by our staff of firearms experts. These are the products our team uses and the brands we trust to get the best results and performance every time. Shop with us anytime, day or night, we're here for you.

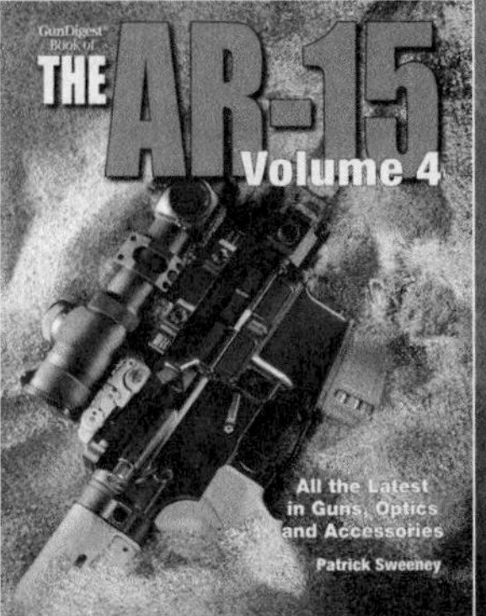

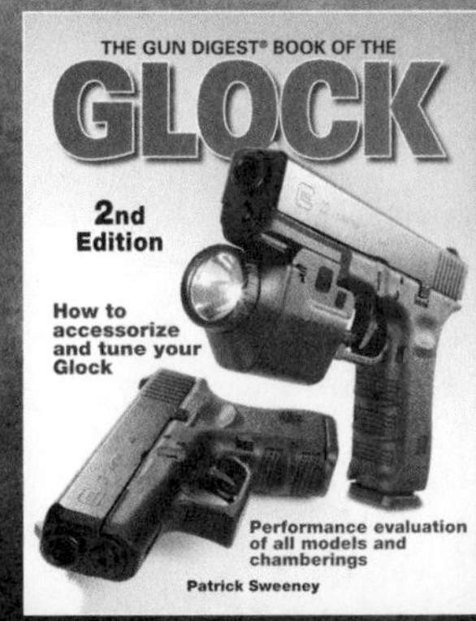

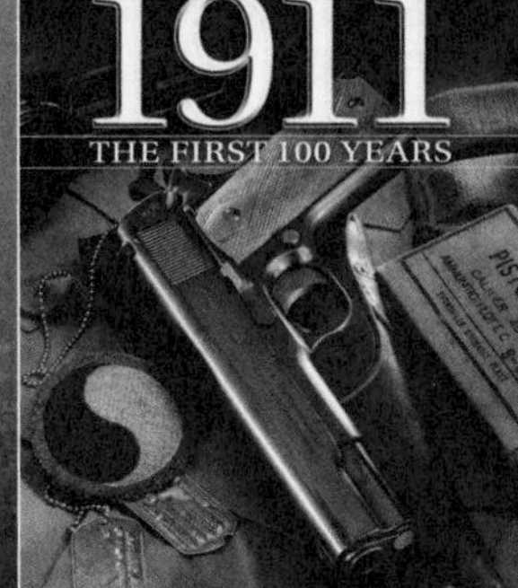

www.GunDigestStore.com

ebooks.gundigest.com

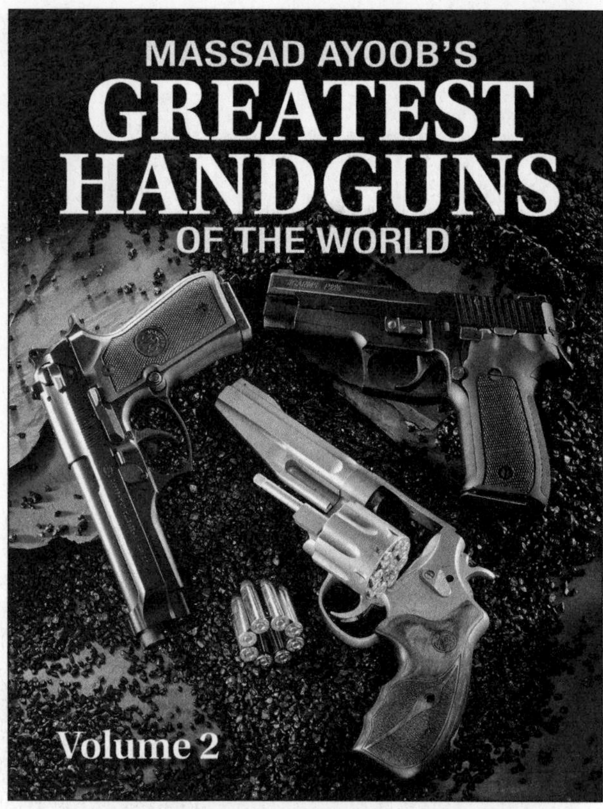

MASSAD AYOOB'S GREATEST HANDGUNS OF THE WORLD, V2
W6538 • $27.99

ASSORTED TOPICS

GUN DIGEST BOOK OF THE .22 RIFLE
Z8581 • $19.99

GUN DIGEST BUYER'S GUIDE TO CONCEALED CARRY HANDGUNS
Z8905 • $24.99

ARMED FOR PERSONAL DEFENSE
Z9404 • $19.99

GREATEST GUNS OF THE GUN DIGEST
Z9830 • $24.99

GUNSMITHING

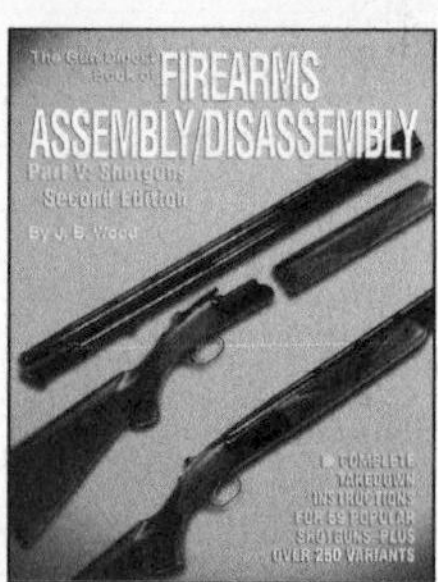

GUN DIGEST BOOK OF FIREARMS ASSEMBLY/ DISASSEMBLY PART V
AS5R2 • $24.99

GUN DIGEST BOOK OF THE AR-15
GDAR • $27.99

GUNSMITHING RIFLES
GRIF • $26.99

CUSTOMIZE THE RUGER 10/22
NGRTT • $29.99

GUN DIGEST BOOK OF RIMFIRE RIFLES ASSEMBLY/DISASSEMBLY
W1577 • $34.99

GUN DIGEST BOOK OF EXPLODED GUN DRAWINGS
Y0047 • $36.99

GUN DIGEST BOOK OF REVOLVERS ASSEMBLY/DISASSEMBLY
Y0773 • $34.99

GUN DIGEST BOOK OF AUTOMATIC PISTOL ASSEMBLY / DISSASEMBLY
W7933 • $39.99

To order, go to www.GunDigestStore.com.

MAPPING TROPHY BUCKS
TRTT • $24.99

DEER & DEER HUNTING'S GUIDE TO BETTER BOW HUNTING
V6706 • $9.99

WE KILL IT WE GRILL IT
V6707 • $9.99

301 VENISON RECIPES
VR01 • $10.95

HUNTING MATURE WHITETAILS THE LAKOSKY WAY
W4542 • $29.99

WHITETAIL LEGENDS
(July 2012)
W7618 • $29.99

STRATEGIES FOR WHITETAILS
WTLDD • $24.99

PREDATOR CALLING WITH GERRY BLAIR
Z0740 • $19.99

TROPHY BUCKS IN ANY WEATHER
Z1781 • $21.99

BIG BUCKS THE BENOIT WAY
Z2193 • $29.99

TOM DOKKEN'S RETRIEVER TRAINING
Z3235 • $19.99

THE COMPLETE PREDATOR HUNTER
Z3652 • $22.99

GUT IT. CUT IT. COOK IT.
Z5014 • $24.99

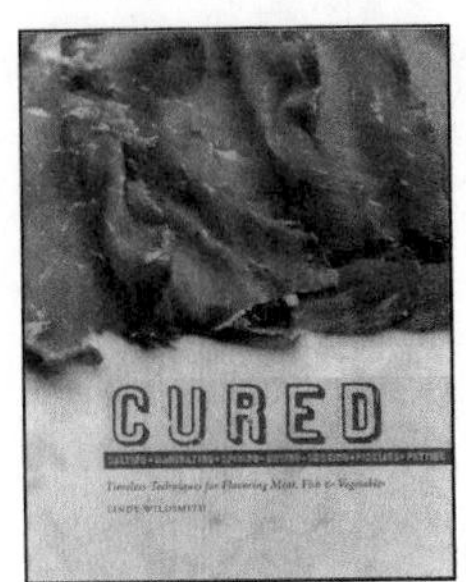

CURED
Z6078 • $30.00

WHITETAIL RACKS
Z7239 • $29.99

WHITETAILS
Z8906 • $32.00

To order, go to www.GunDigestStore.com.

GunDigest
THE WORLD'S FOREMOST GUN AUTHORITY